March 13–17, 2016
Carrboro, NC, USA

I0047463

**Association for
Computing Machinery**

Advancing Computing as a Science & Profession

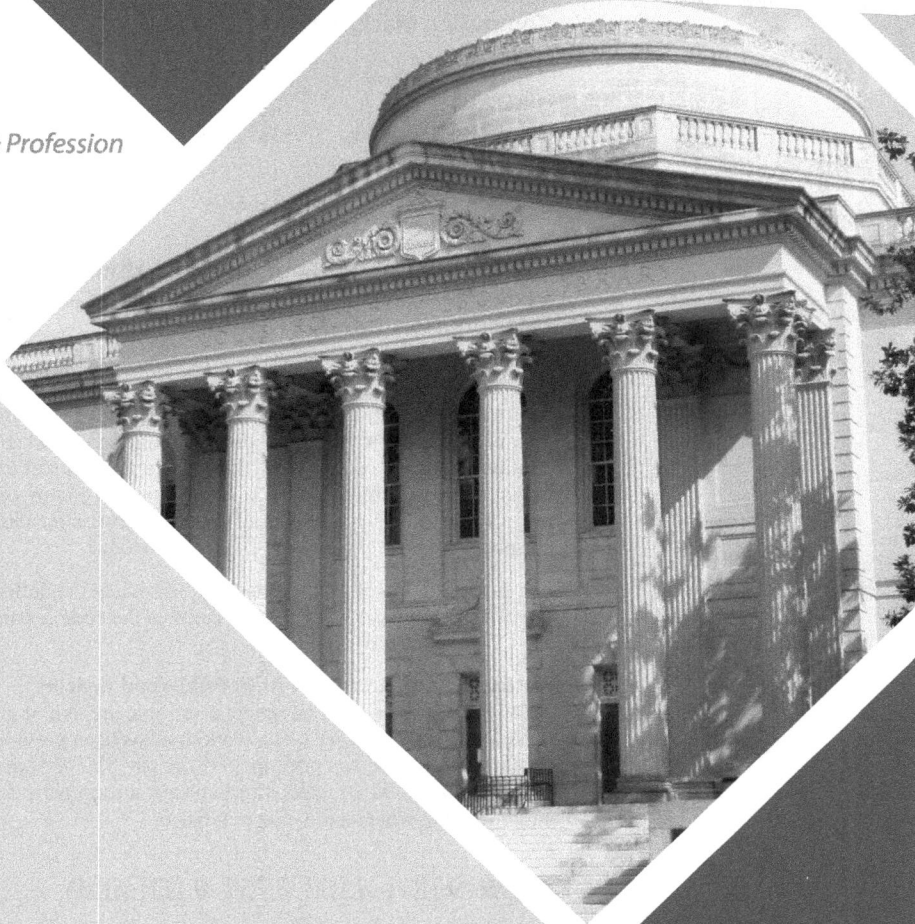

CHIIR'16

Proceedings of the 2016 ACM
Conference on Human Information Interaction and Retrieval

Sponsored by:
ACM SIGIR

In cooperation with:
ACM SIGCHI

Supported by:
**Google, Microsoft Research, Lucidworks,
and University of North Carolina at Chapel Hill**

Association for
Computing Machinery

Advancing Computing as a Science & Profession

The Association for Computing Machinery
2 Penn Plaza, Suite 701
New York, New York 10121-0701

Notice to Past Authors of ACM-Published Articles
ACM intends to create a complete electronic archive of all articles and/or other material previously published by ACM. If you have written a work that has been previously published by ACM in any journal or conference proceedings prior to 1978, or any SIG Newsletter at any time, and you do NOT want this work to appear in the ACM Digital Library, please inform permissions@acm.org, stating the title of the work, the author(s), and where and when published.

ISBN: 978-1-4503-3751-9 (Digital)

ISBN: 978-1-4503-4472-2 (Print)

Additional copies may be ordered prepaid from:

ACM Order Department
PO Box 30777
New York, NY 10087-0777, USA

Phone: 1-800-342-6626 (USA and Canada)
+1-212-626-0500 (Global)
Fax: +1-212-944-1318
E-mail: acmhelp@acm.org
Hours of Operation: 8:30 am – 4:30 pm ET

Printed in the USA

Welcome from the General Chairs

It is our great pleasure to welcome you to the *2016 ACM SIGIR Conference on Information Interaction and Retrieval (CHIIR'16)*. *CHIIR'16* (pronounced "cheer") is the first installment of what we hope will be a strong and prolific conference series that focuses on the user-centered aspects of information interaction and information retrieval. The formation of *CHIIR*, and its sponsorship by *SIGIR*, reflects the growing recognition of the importance of understanding the human in the context of information retrieval and follows a steady stream of research since the early 1960s, which has focused on information retrieval, human computer interaction and the user experience. We are grateful to the committee of people from the *Information Interaction in Context* and *Human Computer Information Retrieval* groups that came together to create the charter for *CHIIR*, and to *ACM SIGIR* for agreeing to fully sponsor this conference.

We would like to recognize the people who helped make *CHIIR'16* a success. We thank the Program Chairs, Nicholas J. Belkin, Jaime Teevan and Pertti Vakarri, the sixteen meta-reviewers and the many reviewers, who worked together to select the papers for the Full Paper program. We also thank the authors who contributed their work and allowed us to review it. Of special note is our new category of full paper, New Perspectives, which seeks to provide a venue for researchers to argue systematically for a new approach, methodology or larger theory, rather than report empirical research. We hope the inclusion of such papers will stimulate new ideas and discussion, and help move the field forward. We thank Jacek Gwizdka and Paul Thomas, who co-chaired the Short Papers program and all the people who reviewed and submitted papers. We also thank Luanne Freund for chairing the Workshops program, and Pia Borlund and Mark Smucker for co-chairing the Doctoral Consortium, which attracted students from all over the world. Finally, we thank our keynote speakers, Mark Ackerman and Pia Borlund, for agreeing to share their insights with us on this inaugural occasion, and Barbara Wildemuth, Charlie Clark, Mark Smucker and Emine Yilmaz for providing free tutorials to attendees.

Our local organizing team deserves special recognition: Jaime Arguello, who served as Treasurer; Ryan Shaw, Amelia Gibson, Sandeep Avula and Yinglong Zhang, who served as local organizing co-chairs; Emily Vardell, Proceedings Chair; Kathy Brennan, Melanie Feinberg, and Barbara Wildemuth, co-chairs of the Student Volunteers program; Anita Crescenzi and Brad Hemminger, who served as Registration Co-Chairs; Gary Marchchionini, who served as Sponsorship Chair; and finally, Kathy Brennan and Patrick Golden, who served as Social Media Chair and Webmaster, respectively. We also thank Susan Sylvester from SILS for her advice and guidance.

CHIIR'16 would not have taken place without our sponsors and supporters, for whom we are grateful: *ACM SIGIR*, the School of Information and Library Science at the University of North Carolina at Chapel Hill, Google, Microsoft Research and Lucidworks. We also acknowledge *ACM SIGCHI* with whom this conference is held in-cooperation.

We hope you enjoy the conference and take the opportunity to catch-up with old friends and make new ones in the fun and relaxed surroundings of Chapel Hill-Carrboro, North Carolina.

Diane Kelly
CHIIR'16 General Co-Chair
University of North Carolina at
Chapel Hill, USA

Rob Capra
CHIIR'16 General Co-Chair
University of North Carolina at
Chapel Hill, USA

CHIIR 2016 Program Overview

We are delighted to welcome you to the first ACM SIGIR Conference on Human Information Interaction and Retrieval (CHIIR, pronounced "cheer"), held in Chapel Hill, North Carolina, USA from March 13 to March 17, 2016. CHIIR provides a forum for the dissemination and discussion of research on the user-centered aspects of information interaction and information retrieval. CHIIR focuses on elements such as human involvement in search activities, and information seeking and use in context. The conference represents a merger of two successful past events: the Information Interaction in Context conference (IIiX) and the Human Computer Information Retrieval symposium (HCIR), which have run since 2006 and 2007 respectively. We are pleased to present here the proceedings of their successor, CHIIR 2016.

The CHIIR 2016 program consists of Full (ten page) papers and Short (four page) papers. We received a total of 58 Full paper submissions, of which 23 were accepted for publication in the proceedings, resulting in an acceptance rate of 39.7%. One of these Full papers is a New Perspectives paper, which is intended to argue systematically for a new approach, methodology, or theory in the field. We also received a total of 54 Short paper submissions, out of which 26 were accepted for publication, for an acceptance rate of 48.1%. Full papers are allocated a 30-minute presentation slot in the program. Short papers are presented as posters during a special evening session, with a short boaster presentation earlier in the day.

In addition to contributed papers, the CHIIR program features two keynotes by prominent academic researchers, Mark Ackerman (University of Michigan, Ann Arbor, USA) and Pia Borlund (Royal School of Library and Information Science, Aalborg, Denmark). We thank the keynote speakers for their illuminating talks and for sharing their insights and wisdom with the conference attendees. It also features three Workshops, two Tutorials, and a Doctoral Consortium.

We would like to acknowledge the tremendous work of the Organizing Committee, including the Short Papers Co-Chairs, Paul Thomas (Microsoft, Australia) and Jacek Gwizdka (University of Texas at Austin, USA), the Doctoral Consortium Co-Chairs, Pia Borlund (Royal School of Library and Information Science, Aalborg, Denmark) and Mark Smucker (University of Waterloo, Canada), and the Workshops Chair, Luanne Freund (University of British Columbia, Canada), as well as the 16 Senior Program Committee members and 145 Program Committee members who reviewed submissions. The credit for creating a high quality technical program goes to them.

We would also like to thank the general chairs, Diane Kelly (University of North Carolina at Chapel Hill, USA) and Rob Capra (University of North Carolina at Chapel Hill, USA), who were wonderful partners in putting the conference program together, and provided us with insightful guidance and advice all along the way. Finally, we are grateful to the authors and attendees, whose support and enthusiasm are what make this emerging conference a success in its first year.

We hope that you find the CHIIR 2016 program interesting and thought-provoking. Our goal was not only to create the opportunity for researchers and practitioners from around the world to share their research, but also to foster new research and innovation related to the user-centered aspects of information interaction and information retrieval.

Nicholas Belkin
CHIIR'16 Program Co-Chair
Rutgers University, USA

Jaime Teevan
CHIIR'16 Program Co-Chair
Microsoft Research, USA

Pertti Vakkari
CHIIR'16 Program Co-Chair
University of Tampere, Finland

Table of Contents

PAPER SESSION 4: Assisting People during Search

Session Chair: Max Wilson *(University of Nottingham)*

PAPER SESSION 5: Interaction in Contexts

Session Chair: Jaime Teevan *(Microsoft Research)*

Keynote Address

Session Chair: Diane Kelly *(University of North Carolina at Chapel Hill)*

PAPER SESSION 6: Usefulness, Learning and Relevance

Session Chair: Charlie L.A. Clarke *(University of Waterloo)*

PAPER SESSION 7: Reading, Writing and Searching

Session Chair: Dan Russell *(Google)*

PAPER SESSION 8: Modeling Connections
Session Chair: Leif Azzopardi *(University of Glasgow)*

SHORT PAPERS
Session Chair: Jacek Gwidza *(University of Texas at Austin)*

Workshops
Session Chair: Luanne Freund *(University of British Columbia)*

Doctoral Consortium
Session Chairs: Pia Borlund *(University of Copenhagen)*, Mark Smucker *(University of Waterloo)*

CHIIR 2016 Conference Organization

General Co-Chairs: Diane Kelly *(University of North Carolina at Chapel Hill, USA)*
Rob Capra *(University of North Carolina at Chapel Hill, USA)*

Program Co-Chairs: Nick Belkin *(Rutgers University, USA)*
Jaime Teevan *(Microsoft Research, USA)*
Pertti Vakkari *(University of Tampere, Finland)*

Short Papers Co-Chairs: Jacek Gwizdka *(University of Texas at Austin, USA)*
Paul Thomas *(CSIRO, Australia)*

Doctoral Consortium Co-Chairs: Pia Borlund *(Royal School of Library and Information Science, Aalborg, Denmark)*
Mark Smucker *(University of Waterloo, Canada)*

Workshops Chair: Luanne Freund *(University of British Columbia, Canada)*

Proceedings Chair: Emily Vardell *(University of North Carolina at Chapel Hill, USA)*

Best Paper Committee Chair: Peter Ingwersen *(University of Copenhagen, Denmark)*

Treasurer: Jaime Arguello *(University of North Carolina at Chapel Hill, USA)*

Local Arrangements Co-Chairs Amelia Gibson *(University of North Carolina at Chapel Hill, USA)*
Ryan Shaw *(University of North Carolina at Chapel Hill, USA)*
Sandeep Avula *(University of North Carolina at Chapel Hill, USA)*
Yinglong Zhang *(University of North Carolina at Chapel Hill, USA)*

Student Volunteer Co-Chairs: Kathy Brennan *(University of North Carolina at Chapel Hill, USA)*
Melanie Feinberg *(University of North Carolina at Chapel Hill, USA)*
Barbara Wildemuth *(University of North Carolina at Chapel Hill, USA)*

Registration Co-Chairs: Brad Hemminger *(University of North Carolina at Chapel Hill, USA)*
Anita Crescenzi *(University of North Carolina at Chapel Hill, USA)*

Sponsorship Chair: Gary Marchionini *(University of North Carolina at Chapel Hill, USA)*

Social Media Chair: Kathy Brennan *(University of North Carolina at Chapel Hill, USA)*

Webmaster: Patrick Golden *(University of North Carolina at Chapel Hill, USA)*

CHIIR 2016 Sponsor & Supporters

Sponsor: **SIGIR**
Special Interest Group
on Information Retrieval

In cooperation with: SIGCHI

Supporters: Google   Microsoft Research

Lucidworks   UNC
SCHOOL OF INFORMATION
AND LIBRARY SCIENCE

Information (Re)Use in Context

Mark S. Ackerman
School of Information and Department of EECS
University of Michigan, Ann Arbor

Abstract

Over the last 25-30 years, an enormous amount has been learned about how people seek, use, maintain, and reuse information *and* expertise in groups and other collectivities. We have also seen major changes in the kinds of information available and in how it is available.

I believe we're on the cusp of the next generation of computational environments and user experiences. It goes under many names - pervasive environments, Internet of Things, Big Data, ubicomp, and on and on - but what is clear is that things are about to change for information - and for users.

This talk considers some of the changes that might occur, grounding them in current work - then and tries to find the new roles and characteristics that search and information seeking will have. (Spoiler Alert: search and seeking will more tightly intertwine.).

Keywords

Information access; information seeking; pervasive environments; ubicomp; Computer-Supported Cooperative Work; CSCW.

Short Bio

Mark Ackerman is is the George Herbert Mead Collegiate Professor of Human-Computer Interaction and a Professor in the School of Information and in the Department of Electrical Engineering and Computer Science at the University of Michigan, Ann Arbor. His major research area is Human-Computer Interaction (HCI), primarily Computer-Supported Cooperative Work (CSCW). He has published widely in HCI and CSCW, investigating collaborative information access in online knowledge communities, medical and health settings, expertise sharing, and pervasive environments. Mark is a member of the CHI Academy (HCI Fellow) and an ACM Fellow.

Previously, Mark was a faculty member at the University of California, Irvine, and a research scientist at MIT's Laboratory for Computer Science (now CSAIL). Before becoming an academic, Mark led the development of the first home banking system, had three Billboard Top-10 games for the Atari 2600, and worked on the X Window System's first user-interface widget set. Mark has degrees from the University of Chicago, Ohio State, and MIT.

CHIIR'16, March 13–17, 2016, Carrboro, North Carolina, USA
ACM ISBN: 978-1-4503-3751-9/16/03.
DOI: http://dx.doi.org/10.1145/2854946.2855007

Active and Passive Utility of Search Interface Features in Different Information Seeking Task Stages

Hugo C. Huurdeman
University of Amsterdam
The Netherlands
huurdeman@uva.nl

Max L. Wilson
University of Nottingham
United Kingdom
max.wilson@nottingham.ac.uk

Jaap Kamps
University of Amsterdam
The Netherlands
kamps@uva.nl

ABSTRACT

Models of information seeking, including Kuhlthau's Information Search Process model, describe fundamentally different macro-level *stages*. Current search systems usually do not provide support for these stages, but provide a static set of features predominantly focused on supporting micro-level search interactions. This paper investigates the utility of search user interface (SUI) features at different macro-level *stages* of complex tasks. A user study was designed, using simulated work tasks, to explicitly place users within different stages of a complex task: pre-focus, focus, and post-focus. Active use, passive use and perceived usefulness of features were analysed in order to derive *when* search features are most useful. Our results identify significant differences in the utility of SUI features between each stage. Specifically, we have observed that *informational* features are naturally useful in every stage, while *input, control* features decline in usefulness after the pre-focus stage, and *personalisable* features become more useful after the pre-focus stage. From these findings, we conclude that features less commonly found in web search interfaces can provide value for users, without cluttering simple searches, when provided at the right times.

Keywords

information seeking, stages, user interfaces, information retrieval

1. INTRODUCTION

Research into Search User Interfaces (SUIs) [10, 24, 38] has proposed many different interactive features, from search suggestions [22] to facets [29] to personal spaces to collect useful results [6]. Although their usefulness has been proven in micro-level studies of complex and exploratory tasks, many of these features have not been adopted by search engines, perhaps because they can impede search during simple lookup tasks [5]. In contrast, information seeking theory [16, 30] often highlights the existence of *stages* of search *within tasks* involving learning and construction, suggesting that we should consider *when* SUI features might be useful within tasks, rather than whether they are useful for tasks. Different categories of features, such as *input, control, informational* and *personalisable*

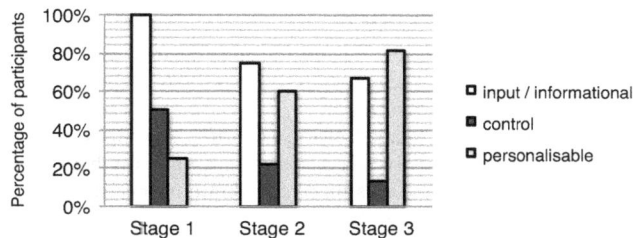

Figure 1: SUI feature categories perceived most useful by stage

features [38], might support users in different ways, both actively and passively. An understanding of the utility of features at different stages may help to overcome the apparent divide between the dynamic stages documented in macro-level information seeking models and the more static SUIs currently available online.

This work aims to directly examine how different SUI features can support distinct macro-level task stages, through a user study using a custom search system called SearchAssist (see §3.2). Tasks were designed to take users through pre-focus, focus, and post-focus task stages [30] in order to gather active, passive, and subjective measures of when SUI features provide most value and support. More specifically, we have three research questions.

RQ1 *How does the user's search stage influence active behaviour at the interface level?*

For RQ1, we looked at *active* behaviour, the behaviour which can be directly and indirectly determined from logged interaction, such as clicks and submitted queries. Our main finding is that some features such as *informational* features (providing information about results) are used frequently throughout, while *input* and *control* features (for refinement of results) are used less frequently after the first stage.

RQ2 *How does the user's search stage influence passive behaviour at the interface level?*

For RQ2, we looked at *passive* behaviour, i.e. behaviour not typically caught in interaction logs, such as eye fixations and mouse movements. Our main finding is the difference with the active results: evidently, users look often at actively used features, but other features that are less actively used (such as the recent queries feature) are more used in a passive way, suggesting a different type of support offered by these features.

RQ3 *How is active and passive behaviour reflected in the perceived usefulness of features?*

For RQ3, we were interested in the subjective opinions of users about the usefulness of features; this data also formed a reference point for interpreting other observed data from the previous research questions. Our main finding is that the perceived usefulness of features differs radically per search stage, as summarised in Figure 1. First, the most familiar *input* and *informational* features (the search box and results list) were perceived as very relevant overall, but declined after the initial stage. Similarly, a set of assistive *control* features (search filters, tags and query suggestions), less commonly included in SUIs were also perceived as most useful in the beginning, but less useful in consecutive stages. Third, *personalisable* features (query history and a feature to save results), are considered as less useful in the beginning, but their usefulness significantly increases over time, even surpassing the value of common SUI features. Hence, our results indicate that the macro-level process has a large influence on the usefulness of SUI features.

2. RELATED WORK

This section discusses related work in the context of task-based information seeking and searching, search user interfaces, and the utility of SUI features over time.

As Toms [28] has indicated, the *"raison-d'être of information retrieval systems is to deliver task-specific information that leads to problem resolution."* Tasks may have different levels: a *work task* may be composed of several *search tasks*, set in a particular *environment* [28]. Categorizations of tasks may include complexity and specificity [35, 36]. For instance, tasks can range from simple lookup tasks, to exploratory and open-ended tasks [21]. Past research has shown that search behaviour varies significantly by task type [20]. Complex tasks may involve learning, and "understanding, sense-making and problem formulation are essential" [3]. In this paper, we use the often-used paper writing task, as employed by [30] and [16], to study information seeking and information searching.

2.1 Information Seeking & Searching

Wilson [40] has differentiated between information behaviour, information seeking and information searching. Information behaviour, encompasses the "totality of human behavior in relation to sources and channels of information" [40]. Information seeking is related to "searching or seeking information using information sources and (interactive) information retrieval systems" [12]. Finally, information searching, as a subset of information seeking, looks at the *interaction* between information users and the information system.

At the level of information *seeking*, various models exist which describe the information seeking process from a macro perspective. These models include for instance Wilson's problem-solving model [40] and Foster's non-linear model [8]. Ellis [7]'s model includes behavioural patterns of information seeking, which are not necessarily linear. Carol Kuhlthau, in her Information Search Process (ISP) model [16], describes a more sequential and temporally-based set of stages. Based on a number of longitudinal studies, Kuhlthau found "common patterns" in tasks involving learning and construction, going through six phases: *Initiation*, *Selection*, *Exploration*, *Formulation*, *Collection* and *Presentation*. The thoughts, feelings, uncertainty, and actions of a user rise, fall, and evolve as the users pass through different stages. Vakkari [30] later refined Kuhlthau's model and summarized its stages into *pre-focus*, *focus formulation* and *post-focus* stages. By studying students at three stages during a semester-long project, Vakkari found changes in relevance judgements, search tactics, terms and operators across stages.

Whilst information seeking models may inform the general design of IR systems, information *search* models (or information retrieval interaction models) often times focus on the *means* to improve design, specifically the interaction between users and information systems. This includes Spink's model of the IR interaction process [27], which describes cycles of interaction with IR systems,

including user judgements, search strategies, tactics and moves. Saracevic' Stratified model of Information Retrieval Interaction [25] views IR interaction as a dialogue between user and computer, and includes different levels (strata) of interactions. Finally, Marchionini's Information-seeking Process Model consists of various sub-processes and their relationships (e.g. 'define problem', 'select source' and 'formulate query'). These are *micro*-level models, which can help us to *design* novel SUI features.

2.2 Search User Interfaces

Search user interfaces (SUIs) serve as an intermediary between the user and the underlying data in an information retrieval system. As Hearst [10] indicates, SUIs aid "users in the expression of their information needs, in the formulation of their queries, in the understanding of their search results, and in keeping track of the progress of their information seeking efforts." SUIs may be designed in vastly different ways, though designing effective SUIs with a high usability is a complex process, as Shneiderman and Pleasant [26] argue, and it often involves finding trade-offs in simplicity and functionality. This difficulty in designing effective SUIs has led to a growing number of guidelines and theories [26].

Research into Search User Interfaces (SUIs) [10, 24, 38] has suggested many different interactive features, from search suggestions [22] to facets [29] to personal spaces to collect useful results [6]. Though their usefulness has been proved in various studies, most of these features have not been adapted in common search engines. Hearst suggests some underlying reasons for the lack of adoption of advanced features: searching is used as a means to achieve a broader aim, search is mentally intensive and search systems should be understandable for people with different knowledge and experience [10]. Hence, overly complex search engines may distract from a user's core task. Furthermore, the usefulness of features may depend on the task type and complexity. Some work ties the need for advanced features to different types of tasks, such as Exploratory Search tasks [33]. Although Diriye [5] argued that in the context of known-item search tasks, excessive search features may impede people's information searching, most tasks involve at least some exploratory elements [32].

Given the multitude of features which could potentially be integrated in SUIs, it may be useful to divide the types of features in different groups, based on their functions. Wilson [38] proposed a taxonomy, which distinguishes four groups of interface features. *Input* features aid users in expressing their needs, *control* features allow users to restrict or modify their input, *informational* features provide results or information about results, and *personalisable* features are tailored to the search experience of a user. In this paper, we use this categorization to analyze the usefulness of features in different stages of search.

2.3 Utility of SUI Features Over Time

A number of user studies have looked at the utility of search system features across stages, but most authors consider 'stage' a temporal segment of a singular session, and have retrospectively identified stages in people's search. Very few authors, however, have used an explicit multistage task design. Liu and Belkin [19], for example, used one motivating work task but performed during three distinct sessions. They looked at the influence of task stage, type and topic knowledge on the interpretation of dwell time over multiple task sessions. While not directly looking at the use of SUI features, they found that task stage and topic knowledge could help to interpret time as an indicator of usefulness. Similarly, Wilson and Schraefel [39] conducted a longitudinal study of keyword and faceted search, finding that the latter only occurred after the second visit of an online video archive (likely due to confidence and interface understanding).

Other authors did not perform longitudinal studies, but used various simulated work tasks, performed during one session. Kules and Capra [17] looked at searchers' interactions with a faceted library catalog. Using a number of assigned exploratory search tasks, they examined differences in gaze behaviour on four SUI features (query box, results, facets, and breadcrumbs). Users were asked to retrospectively assign stages to segments of their search sessions, using a customly defined set of stages (most similar to the micro-analysis of search discussed before). Kules and Capra found differences in the use of Facets, which were used more in 'decision making stages.' Similarly, White et al. [34] have looked at implicit and explicit Relevance Feedback (RF), and divided search sessions into equal parts ('beginning', 'middle' and 'end') to look at stage differences. Their results indicate that implicit RF is used more in the middle stages, while explicit RF is used more towards the latter stages, and there is also an influence of task complexity.

In their user study, Niu and Kelly [22] also divided search sessions into temporal segments, rather than explicit stages, and found that query suggestions were frequently used for difficult topics and during later task stages. They suggest that participants, in the latter parts of a task, "may be exploring the various facets of the topic and/or looking for specific information". In addition, they may have exhausted their original ideas and "need alternative queries." Similarly, Diriye et al. [5] performed a user study using a rich experimental search interface. By looking at the temporal distribution of the use of four interface features during a task, they found that certain features (starter pages and search box) were search stage sensitive and other features search stage agnostic (facets and filters).

Finally, Huurdeman and Kamps [11] looked at conceptual ways to bridge macro and micro-level information seeking models, and based on changes in gaze behaviour of a small-scale user study involving book search, found evidence for differences in the use of *input* and *personalisable* features over time, such as the query box and book basket, while other features were used throughout the task.

As opposed to previous literature, mainly studying singular tasks, we use an explicit multistage approach to look at the passive and active utility of a different SUI features across macro-level stages, to provide richer insights into exactly when different types of features become more useful.

3. USER STUDY SETUP

This section details the experimental setup of the user study. To study the active and passive use of interface features in different search stages, we conducted a within-participants user study with task stage as the independent variable. For dependent variables, active system interactions were logged, passive mouse and eye movements were tracked, and questionnaires were used to collect data on perceived usefulness. Participants made use of *SearchAssist*[1], an experimental search system similar to a regular Web search engine, with different categories of SUI features potentially useful for each stage.

3.1 Task Design and Participants

While some prior work has inferred task stage, we constructed 3 task descriptions to explicitly represent three key *stages*, inspired by previous literature on tasks involving learning and construction [16, 30]. Stage 1 was modeled after the initial stages of Kuhlthau's ISP model (initiation, topic selection, exploration), summarized by Vakkari [30] as the pre-focus stage. Stage 2 was aimed to make users formulate their specific topic (focus formulation), and a question about this topic. Finally, Stage 3 was based on the final stages

---

[1] The source code of SearchAssist and eye tracking software used in this study is available via: https://github.com/timelessfuture/SearchAssist

Table 1: Assigned multistage tasks

Introduction: For a class called "Computers in Society", the professor has given you the assignment to write a 5-page essay on some aspect of [topic]. Having a good grade for this essay is critical for passing the course. The essay is due in a week, but you have yet to decide on an exact topic. In a deliverable due tomorrow, you have to define your topic, a specific question about the topic and a list of sources.

Stage 1: Prepare a list of at least 3 ideas for a topic to write about in the context of [topic]. They should cover many different aspects of the topic, and unusual or provocative ideas are good. Search the web using the SearchAssist system to find out what information is available. Write down your ideas for topics in the text field below. Save any webpages you encounter via the SearchAssist system which are useful for writing on these topics (utilizing the "save result" feature).

Stage 2: Select one of the topics which you defined in the previous task. Choose the topic which interests you most, about which you are able to find enough information, and which you think you are able to finish in the allotted time. Use the SearchAssist system to find information to help you to decide on the topic, and save sources if needed using "save result". Write down the topic in the text box below. After having selected a topic you ask yourself the question "what is it that I want to find out about this topic?" Search the web using the SearchAssist system and formulate a specific question you would like to ask about this topic. You can save any pages you encounter which are useful for answering this question.

Stage 3: To be able to start writing your essay, take the specific question you have formulated in the previous step, and gather as much useful information as you can by searching the internet using SearchAssist. Find around 20 additional pages. Select the 5-10 pages that you could cite in your essay, and which are most relevant for answering the question you formulated in the previous step. If you have time left, formulate a draft answer to your question based on the information you have encountered (max. 300 words) and write it in the text box below.

---

of Kuhlthau's model (collection and presenting), summarized by Vakkari as the *post-focus* stage. In this stage, users had to collect sources relevant to their focused topic, and to provide a draft answer to the formulated question about their topic.

Written as simulated work tasks [1] (see Table 1), the stage descriptions used elements of exploratory work tasks from previous studies [18, 19], focused on the often used 'essay writing' task. Following Borlund's guidance [1], the simulated work tasks were designed so that participants could relate to them, that they were topically interesting, and would add 'enough imaginative context'. After pilot tests and discussions with staff, two topics were selected: 'virtual reality', and 'autonomous vehicles'. The participants were undergraduate students of the School of Computer Science of the University of Nottingham (UK campus). The participants were recruited via posters, the Facebook page of Mixed Reality Lab, e-mails, and via *callforparticipants.com*. Upon completing the experiment, participants received a £10 Amazon voucher, and an additional £25 Amazon voucher was awarded to the participant with the best task outcome. In total, 26 participants joined the experiment. Two participants, however, were excluded from our analysis, where one was unable to complete all three stages, and the eye tracking data was not sufficiently accurate for the other. Of the remaining 24 participants, 18 were male and 6 were female; 22 participants were aged 18-25 and 2 were between 26-35.

3.2 Data and Interface

For this study we designed *SearchAssist*, an experimental search system based on PHP, Javascript and MySQL, depicted in Figure 2. Search results, query corrections and query suggestions were retrieved in the JSON format via the Bing Search API and displayed as a familiar Web interface, similar to common Web search engines. The use of the Search API allowed participants to access a variety of sources, including scholarly, encyclopedic and news sources.

Figure 2: Screenshot SearchAssist. *Left column (1, 2, 3): control features. Middle (4): input and informational features. Right Column (5, 6): personalisable features. (7): task bar*

The SearchAssist interface consisted of the following elements: *1. Category filters.* Using the category filters, searchers could filter the set of results. The categories were derived from the top-level categories of the Open Directory Project (DMOZ). Retrieved results were matched against all DMOZ categories using the hostname of each result, and the top-level categories could be used to filter the result set. *2. Tag cloud.* Using the tag cloud, it was possible to add one or more keywords to a query. The tag cloud was generated based on the most frequently occurring words in the snippets of the first 50 retrieved results. *3. Query suggestions.* Query suggestions were retrieved from the Bing Query Suggestions API, and they could be clicked to perform a new search. *4. Search box and results.* The SearchAssist interface featured a standard search box and results were retrieved from the Bing Web Search API; the Bing Spelling Suggestions API was also used. Each resultset item contained the title of the page, a URL, the DMOZ category, the snippet and a button to save a result. To better facilitate eye tracking, 8 search results were displayed at a time, similar to e.g. [13]. *5. Recent queries.* The recent queries feature showed the last 15 queries performed across all tasks of the experiment, and allowed them to be resubmitted to the search engine. *6. Saved results.* The saved results feature allowed users to view (and remove) saved webpages, to reorder collected webpages by dragging and dropping, and to add (or remove) category labels to the gathered results. *7. Task bar.* The task bar contained task-related material, including a link to open the task instructions and a link to finish the current task, after which a user was prompted to fill out the corresponding questionnaire. The task instructions were shown in a Google Doc, which was also used to collect their responses.

3.3 Protocol

The experiment started with signing the consent forms and a pre-questionnaire, asking for demographics and ratings for knowledge about the potential task topics. As domain experts would behave differently than domain novices, participants were assigned the topic that they knew least about. Participants were then introduced to the features of the experimental system via a structured Powerpoint presentation, and given a training task (approx. 5 min.), which was used to mitigate the familiarity affects in the study, and to check the calibration of the eye tracker. The task stages were performed in sequence; the stage order could not be counter-balanced without

losing the cumulative learning required from stage to stage. Participants were given 15 minutes for each stage, including a one minute warning, however participants were allowed to continue after this final minute passed. After each stage, users filled out a questionnaire about the perceived usefulness of features. After the final stage, participants also completed the post-questionnaire and a short debriefing interview (taking 5-10 minutes), focused on their experiences with the system. The total time to participate in the experiment varied between 55 and 90 minutes.

3.4 Logging and Eye Tracking

The system logged the active and passive interactions in three ways: via system logging, browser history and eye tracking, and the experiment was carried out using the Chromium browser. After each experiment, the browser history was exported in JSON format using the "Export history" browser extension, and the local browser history was deleted. All user actions were saved in a database via MySQL, and as plain text files using Log4Javascript. The logged data included all clicked interface features, all entered text (in the query box), and which page was active in the browser (the search interface, a webpage or the task page). In addition, all results items, query suggestions and query corrections retrieved via the Bing API were saved in their original JSON format.

For passive behaviour, the system logged the position of the mouse cursor, and for context, took a screenshot of the user's screen four times per second. Eye tracking was performed using the EyeTribe eye tracker, calibrated using the included software. The Python-based PyGaze framework [4], and the PyTribe toolbox (a Python wrapper for the EyeTribe eye tracker) were customized to our needs and tightly integrated with the experimental interface. For the eye tracking data, the fixation counts and durations were calculated. Fixations were considered as sequences of eye tracking measurements within a 25 pixel radius; within a timeframe of at least 80ms (similar to e.g. [2]). We defined bounding boxes for each SUI element of the *SearchAssist* interface to detect the Area of Interest (AoI) of the fixation. In addition, to derive the depth of results list items inspected, we defined a bounding box for each results list item. The same methods were used to calculate the counts and duration of mouse movements in each AoI.

3.5 Data and Task Validation

First, we sought to confirm that the two topics, 'virtual reality' (VR) and 'autonomous vehicles' (AV), were comparable. No significant differences were found between overall task time, number of queries, results viewed, nor in the majority of usefulness ratings.

Only one significant difference was found, using the Mann-Whitney test, in the post-stage usefulness ratings for the 'saved results' feature for the first (U=30, p=0.01) and second stage (U=34, p=0.02), although logged usage of this feature was not significantly different. Informal observations indicate that there may have been a higher number of *relevant* results that *could* be found in the AV topic, but that these have not affected the majority of behaviour. Overall, however, we conclude that the topics invoked comparable behaviours and continue to analyse the data from both topics as a single set.

Second, we examined the validity of our task descriptions in terms of invoking correct stages. In post-stage questionnaires users selected the activities they had conducted from a randomized list derived from Kuhlthau's model[2]. For the first stage, the most commonly selected activity was 'exploring' (N=17), followed by 'gathering' (16); corresponding to the initiation and exploration activities associated with the initial stages of Kuhlthau's model. After the

---

[2]Specifically: *exploring, focusing, formulating, collecting, gathering, becoming informed, choosing,* and *getting an overview*

second stage (focus formulation) users most often chose 'focusing' (16) and 'collecting' (12) as words representing their activities. The common use of focusing corresponds to the focus formulation activity, while collecting may refer to the collected documents in that stage. Finally, for the third task also 'focusing' (17) and 'collecting' (14) were the most common words. We conclude that even though the separations between stages are not always dichotomous, our experiment correctly invoked the main activities in each stage.

4. RESULTS

This section examines the results of the study, and whether the participants showed distinct behaviour in the different stages of their overall task. Together, the 24 participants issued 502 queries and clicked on 684 results. Participants spent an average of 32:56 minutes to complete the 3 task stages. Of this time, 36.8% was spent in the SUI, 33.0% on the task screen, and 30.2% on the webpages. Participants spent, on average, 11:32 minutes on the first stage, 8:24 minutes on the second stage, and 12:59 minutes on the third stage.

4.1 Search Stage & Active Behaviour

This section focused on our first research question (**RQ1**): How does the user's search stage influence active behaviour at the interface level? We define active behaviour as the behaviour that can be directly and indirectly derived from the logged interactions, such as clicks, queries, and pages visited.

SUI features Table 2 summarizes the main interaction with each available SUI feature. The use of the *Query Box* (counted as the clicks on the 'search' button) is most frequent in the first stage, and decreases in the second and third stage. Using the within-participants, repeated measures ANOVA, we found a significant difference in the use of the search button ($p < 0.01$, $F(2) = 13.6$). Post hoc tests, using the Bonferroni correction, showed that there is a significant difference between the first and second ($p < 0.01$), and the first and third stage ($p < 0.01$). Hence, users use the search button more in the first stage, most likely to explore the assigned topic [37].

The clicks on retrieved results items, via the *Results List* feature, remain more or less stable without significant differences per stage. The number of times a result is saved using the adjacent 'save result' link, however, is decreasing after the first stage. Users also appear to examine the results beyond the first page more frequently in the third stage (by clicking 'next page') but these differences, like the differences in result clicks and result saves, are not significant.

The *Category Filters* feature is used significantly less frequently after the first stage, and thus seem to be most useful in the initial task stage ($p < 0.01$, $F(1.2) = 8.6$, Greenhouse-Geisser correction). The differences, with Bonferroni correction, are most prominent between the first and third stage ($p < 0.01$), but also occur between the other stages (1->2: $p = 0.03$, 2->3: $p = 0.03$). Similarly, the clicks on the *Tag Cloud* feature are significantly different ($p < 0.01$, $F(1.4) = 8.5$, Greenhouse-Geisser correction). Again, the first stage features the highest number of clicks, and using a pairwise comparison, with Bonferroni correction, we found significant changes in clicks between the first and second stage ($p = 0.02$), and between the first and third stage ($p = 0.01$).

Compared to the other features, the *Query Suggestions* and *Recent Queries* features are not frequently used, and a slight decrease in use of the Query Suggestions and a slight increase in the use of the Recent Queries feature is visible in the data, but are not significant.

Although the differences in the use of the 'Save result' link in the Results List were not significant, the statistics for the *Saved Results* feature indicate that users add categories to these items mostly in the first stage ($p < 0.01$, $F(2) = 8.1$). Pairwise comparisons, with Bonferroni correction, show that the significant differences

Table 2: SUI active interaction (clicks), from system logs

mean	stage1	%	stage2	%	stage3	%
Query Box						
search clicks**	8.4	*24.3*	4.5	*19.8*	4.6	*14.9*
Results List						
result clicks	7.3	*20.9*	5.5	*24.2*	7.8	*25.2*
result saves	6.1	*17.5*	4.3	*19*	3.7	*11.8*
next page clicks	0.8	*2.4*	1.2	*5.1*	1.7	*5.5*
Category Filters						
clicks**	2.9	*8.3*	1.1	*4.7*	0.6	*2*
Tag Cloud						
clicks**	1.6	*4.7*	0.7	*3.1*	0.5	*1.7*
Query Suggestions						
clicks	0.8	*2.3*	0.4	*1.7*	0.5	*1.7*
Recent Queries						
clicks	0.3	*1*	0.6	*2.5*	0.8	*2.4*
Saved Results						
clicks**	0.7	*2*	0.9	*3.9*	6.3	*20.4*
add category**	2.2	*6.4*	0.9	*3.9*	0.6	*1.9*
move item	3.5	*10*	2	*8.8*	2.4	*7.7*
remove category	<0.1	*<0.1*	0.3	*1.1*	0.3	*0.9*
remove item	<0.1	*<0.1*	0.5	*2.2*	1.2	*3.8*
Total	34.7	*100*	22.8	*100*	31.1	*100*

*Within-subjects ANOVA: * significant ($p < 0.05$); ** significant ($p < 0.01$)*

occur between the first and second ($p = 0.02$), and the first and third ($p < 0.01$) stage. Hence, participants save and categorize items in the saved results list most frequently in the first stage. The clicks on the saved results (bookmarks), on the other hand, are clearly most frequent in the last stage ($p < 0.01$, $F(1.1) = 18.8$, Greenhouse Geisser correction). A pairwise comparison shows significant differences between the first and third stage ($p < 0.01$), and the second and third stage ($p < 0.01$). Finally, the last stages show a slight increase in the removal of categories and saved items, as opposed to the additions in the first stage, but no significant differences were found.

Queries & Page Visits As we observed in Table 2, participants used the Query Box feature most often in the first stage. Now, we look at the queries in more detail, summarized in Table 3. The total number of queries submitted, including tag cloud suggestions and use of the Recent Queries feature, is significantly different per stage ($p < 0.01$, $F(2) = 8.9$). A pairwise comparison, with Bonferroni correction, indicates that the differences are significant between the first and second ($p < 0.01$), and between the first and third stage ($p < 0.01$). Likewise, the unique queries are significantly different ($p < 0.01$, $F(2) = 7.9$), again with a significant difference between the first and second ($p < 0.01$) or third stage ($p < 0.01$). Most queries performed were unique, though there is some overlap in the queries between the first, second and third stage, meaning that participants reuse queries in latter parts of the experiment (i.e. by re-entering the same query or using the Recent Queries feature). In the first stage, the majority of queries are initiated from the Query Box. However, subsequent stages show an increase of the relative use of the Recent Queries feature, and a stable share of the Query Suggestions.

While the number of queries decreases after the first stage, the number of *words per query* increases. The highest mean number of query words occurs in the second stage (4.5), and an almost equally high value during the third stage (4.4). The higher number of queries may be related to exploration activities in the first stage, which require various queries to explore various topics. The increasing number of query words, on the other hand, may occur because a person is searching for a more specific topic, and may have built a conceptual representation of a topic [30]. For example, one user (P.02) started with the query "virtual reality" in the first stage, but queried for "the impact of virtual reality on society art and gaming

Table 3: SUI active interaction (queries and page visits)

mean	stage1	stage2	stage3
Queries**	9.5	5.5	5.9
*via Query Box**	88%	81%	78%
via Recent Queries	3%	11%	13%
via Query Suggestions	8%	7%	8%
Unique queries**	8.1	5.1	5.3
Overlap queries prev. stages	0	1.4	1.8
Mean num. query words**	3.2	4.5	4.4
Levenshtein distance (query diversity)	13.2	13.9	17.0
Visited pages**	8.0	6.4	14.2
via Results List	91%	86%	56%
*via Saved Results**	9%	14%	44%
Unique visited pages**	7.3	5.9	10.8
Overlap visited pages prev. stages	0	0.8	2.8
Mean rank visited pages	3.1	5.1	6.4

*Within-subjects ANOVA: * significant (p<0.05); ** significant (p<0.01)*

Table 4: Passive use: mouse hovers *not* leading to a click

mean	stage1	%	stage2	%	stage3	%
Query Box**	344.7	16.6	250.2	19.5	210.2	14.6
Results List**	1226.8	59.1	701.9	54.7	872.9	60.7
Category Filters**	124.6	6.0	57	4.4	67.7	4.7
Tag Cloud*	165.9	8.0	73.1	5.7	47.2	3.3
Query Suggestions	91.3	4.4	58.5	4.6	56.6	3.9
Recent Queries	17.6	0.8	18.3	1.4	21.3	1.5
Saved Results	103.7	5.0	123.5	9.6	163.3	11.3
Total	2074.6	100	1282.5	100	1439	100

*Within-subjects ANOVA: * significant (p<0.05); ** significant (p<0.01)*

culture" in the third stage. Or, the queries from another participant (P.06) evolved from short queries such as "autonomous vehicles" to longer queries like "autonomous vehicles costs insurance industry". The differences in the number of query words are significant (p<0.01, F(2)=5.3), specifically between the first and second stage (p<0.01, Bonferroni correction). Finally, we calculated the query diversity, based on the Levenshtein distance between all pairs of unique queries of a user in a certain stage. The query diversity is similar during the first and second stage, but is highest in the third stage, meaning that the edit distance between users' queries is greater; although these differences are not significant.

Participants in our experiment visited the highest number of pages in the third stage (p<0.01, F(1.3)=11.6, Greenhouse-Geisser correction), when collecting materials. The differences are significant between the first and third stage (p=0.02) and between the second and third stage (p<0.01). This variance seems to be explained primarily by the revisiting of pages from the Saved Results feature (p<0.01, see previous section), as page visits from the Results List were not significantly different. This finding is reflected in the uniquely visited pages (p<0.01, F(1.5)=8.1, Greenhouse-Geisser correction), but here the only significant changes occur between the second and third stage (p<0.01). Further, the result is also reflected in the mean dwell times on the webpages, which are highest in the first (12.9 sec.) and second stage (14.4 sec.), but lower in the third stage (8.9 sec.). The dwell times are significantly different (p<0.01, F(2)=7.8), between the first and second (p<0.01), and between the second and third stage (p<0.01). Participants also explored further down the result set in the later task stages, with the mean visited rank increasing from 3.1 to 5.1 and 6.4 respectively, but this was not significant within our current sample.

Summarizing, this section has focused on the active interaction with the system during the experiment. Utilizing the categorizations of Wilson's framework for SUI features [38], the results show various tendencies: *input* features (the Query Box) and *control* features (Category Filters, Tag Cloud and Query Suggestions) are clearly used less often in subsequent stages, while the use of the *informational* (Results list) features remains stable. The results for the *personalisable* features (Recent Queries and Saved Results) differ. The Recent Queries feature is scarcely used, but an increasing tendency can be observed across stages. Similarly, users mostly click on their saved results in the last stage, but save the actual results and add categories most frequently in the first stages. Hence, the Saved Results feature is initially used to store and categorize important results, but later to revisit previous results. Also, users start out with a significantly higher number of queries, as compared to later stages,

while the number of page revisits substantially increases in the last stage. Evidence for the learning aspects of the used tasks are found in the increase of the number of query words and query diversity [16, 30], as users seem more able to express their needs in queries.

Finally, another contrast can be observed, namely between commonly used features and scarcely used features. Together, the Query Box, Results List and Saved Results features take up over 80% of all clicks, while the remaining set of features takes up less than 20% of all clicks (see Table 2). The infrequent *active* use of certain features, in particular the Query Suggestions and Recent Queries features, lead to the question whether some features are perhaps used in a *passive* way, which we will further examine in the next section.

4.2 Search Stage & Passive Behaviour

In this section, we focus on the following research question (**RQ2**): How does the user's search stage influence passive behaviour at the interface level? We examine the user's mouse position and eye fixation data to look at the passive behaviour in each search stage.

Mouse hovers Participants' mouse movements can shed more light on the use and utility of SUI features in different stages. Mouse moves in a particular area can be simply movements to reach or click a SUI feature, but may also indicate different types of usage, i.e. mouse moves aiding users in processing the contents of results pages [23]. In our analysis, we look at the *passive* mouse movements: the mouse hovers in a SUI feature area that did *not* lead to a click.

Table 4 shows the mean count of mouse movements over time. We counted mouse hovers (defined as a change in the coordinates of the mouse pointer) within each SUI feature's Area of Interest. There are significant differences for the following features: the Query Box (p<0.01, F(2)=6.4), the Results List (p<0.01, F(2)=6.9), the Category Filters (p<0.01, F(2)=7.0) and the Tag Cloud feature (p=0.03, F(1.5)=4.5, Greenhouse-Geisser correction). Mouse hovers in these SUI areas are most common in the first stage, and significantly decrease in the second or third stage. The other features do not show significant changes over time. The results for this measure show overlap with the active interaction measure of the previous section, with the exception of a "dip" in mouse hovers on the Results List in the second stage, and a higher relative amount of hovers over the Query Suggestions, especially in the second and third stage. The higher and more stable degree of mouse hovers around the Query Suggestions may indicate that users use this feature passively in all three stages, as opposed to the decreasing use tendency visible in the active use measure. To gain further insights, we next look at passive use, not even involving the mouse, using eye tracking.

Eye tracking fixations To gain an initial overview of eye movements within the SearchAssist interface, we generated heatmaps for each stage across all participants. These heatmaps (Figure 3) show the spatial distribution of the fixations. A visual inspection reveals a consistent focus on the Query Box and Results List SUI features in each stage (middle pane). The Category Filters, Tag Cloud and Query Suggestions features (left pane) are most intensively used in

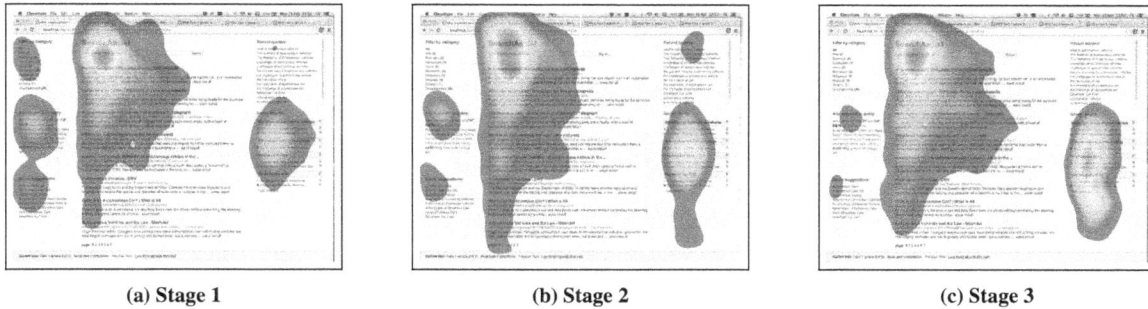

| (a) Stage 1 | (b) Stage 2 | (c) Stage 3 |

Figure 3: Eye tracking heatmaps, based on fixations (over 80ms)

the first stage, while the Saved Results feature (lower right panel) appears to be most intensely used in the last stage.

These differences can be inspected in more detail using the absolute and relative fixation counts (with a minimum duration of 80 ms), summarized in Table 5. For the most part, the results for the passive use of SUI features confirm the results regarding active use. The number of fixations on the Query Box is significantly decreasing after the first stage (p=0.01, F(2)=4.9), which is comparable with the lower number of unique queries performed in the second and third stage observed in the active interactions. In particular, the difference is significant between the first and second stage (p=0.02). In addition, the less frequent active use of the Tag Cloud and Category Filters is reflected in a decrease in the number of fixations in the second and third stage, and this difference is significant for both Category Filters (p=0.01) and Tag Cloud (p<0.01). A pairwise comparison reveals significant differences between the first and second stage for the Category Filters (p=0.03), and between the first and second (p=0.01) or third stage (p=0.02) for the Tag Cloud.

The fixations on the results list decrease significantly after the first stage (p=0.02, F(2)=4.4). A significant difference for the fixations on the Results List feature exists between the first and second stage (p<0.01, Bonferroni correction), though the relative degree of fixations changes less. Table 2 in the previous section, however, did not show a significant difference for the number of clicks on resultset items in any stage. Similarly, the decreasing number of clicks on the Query Suggestions features are coupled with a lower number of fixations on this feature. These differences are significant (p=0.04, F(2)=3.5) between the first and second stage (p=0.01). As in the case of the active interactions, the Recent Queries feature does not show a significant difference, but the relative values for the fixations increase in the second stage. Finally, the fixations on the Saved Results feature rise during the stages, which is similar to the measured increase in the previous section, but the difference for the fixations is not significant (p=0.09).

The previous section showed some features which were used frequently, in particular the Query Box, Results List and Saved Results feature, and other features which were used infrequently, such as the Query Suggestions and Recent Queries. We would expect that the often-used SUI features also have a high degree of fixations. The results confirm this: the Results List takes up more than half of the fixations, and also the relative degree of the fixations on the Query Box and Saved Results is high. There is a difference, however, for features that were little used in an active way, such as the Query Suggestions and Recent Queries features. The percentage of fixations on the Query Suggestions over all three stages is 3.6% instead of 1.9% of clicks, and the fixation percentage for the Recent Queries is 3.01% instead of 1.97%. While the difference is relatively small, it does provide evidence that participants may use these features more passively than actively. Another difference can be observed for the Category Filters and Tag Cloud: participants look

Table 5: Passive SUI use: mean eye tracking fixation count

mean	stage1	%	stage2	%	stage3	%
Query Box*	58.08	14	35	13.1	41.42	11.8
Results List*	224.88	54.3	139.83	52.5	187.17	53.5
Category Filters*	17.63	4.3	10.46	3.9	11.42	3.3
Tag Cloud**	31.71	7.7	14.58	5.5	15.5	4.4
Query Suggestions*	16.88	4.1	9.71	3.6	10.83	3.1
Recent Queries	10.92	2.6	9.79	3.7	10.13	2.9
Saved Results	54.38	13.1	47.17	17.7	73.63	21
Total	414.48	100	266.54	100	350.1	100

*Within-subjects ANOVA: * significant (p<0.05); ** significant (p<0.01)*

more at the Tag Cloud (5.8%), than they click on it (3.1%), while a contrary situation exist for the Category Filters (5% of all clicks, but 3.8% of all fixations).

Summarizing, on the one hand, the fixations and mouse movements by users validate the active behaviour, showing similar tendencies. The significant differences in the use of the Query Box, Category Filters and Tag Cloud confirm the findings from the previous section, while the eye tracking data also suggests significant changes in the use of Query Suggestions. On the other hand, subtle differences exists in the passive use of less often used features, such as the Query Suggestions and Recent Queries features. This suggests that some features may not be used often in an active way, but that they are still used passively. In Section 4.3, we validate and contextualize these findings with subjective ratings of usefulness and qualitative feedback from participants.

4.3 Search Stage & Perceived Usefulness

Our final research question looks at the potential influence of search stages on the *perceived* usefulness of SUI features: (**RQ3**): How is active and passive behaviour reflected in the perceived usefulness of features? Findings from questionnaires after each stage, after finishing the whole experiment, and brief post-experiment interviews are used to contextualize the findings so far.

Usefulness ratings After each task stage, participants were asked to rate the usefulness of each SUI feature of SearchAssist on a Likert scale of 1 to 7, as shown in Table 6. Somewhat expectedly, the most highly rated features are the Search Box and Results List features. As it turns out, however, this is closely followed by the Saved Results feature, which was also deemed to be very useful by most of the participants. Conversely, the least popular features among the participants were the Tag Cloud and Category Filter features. The most useful features were also rated most consistently among participants: the standard deviation values for the Search Box, Results List and Saved Results are substantially lower than for the other SUI features. Conversely, the most "controversial" feature was the Tag Cloud, with a standard deviation of 1.71, suggesting a relatively high variability of user ratings: some participants found it useful, and others did not perceive it as useful.

9

Table 6: Mean usefulness ratings, gathered after each stage (s.dev.). Bold: stage with highest rating for feature.

mean	stage 1	stage 2	stage 3	total
Search Box/Results*	**6.67 (0.7)**	6.33 (0.9)	6.08 (1.1)	6.36 (0.9)
Category Filters	**4.08 (1.5)**	3.79 (1.6)	3.46 (1.7)	3.78 (1.6)
Tag Cloud	**3.92 (1.7)**	3.54 (1.5)	3.63 (1.9)	3.70 (1.7)
Query Suggestions	**4.80 (1.4)**	4.00 (1.7)	4.00 (1.6)	4.26 (1.6)
Recent Queries*	3.46 (1.6)	4.13 (1.7)	**4.71 (1.6)**	4.10 (1.6)
Saved Results	5.83 (1.2)	6.17 (1.1)	**6.30 (0.9)**	6.08 (1.0)

*Non-parametric Friedman test: * significant (p<0.05)*

Table 7: Mean post-experiment usefulness ratings – at which moment were the SUI features most useful (% of participants).

perc	stage1	stage2	stage3
Query Box/Results List**	**100.00%**	75.00%	66.67%
Category Filters**	**54.17%**	20.83%	12.50%
Tag Cloud**	**41.67%**	16.67%	8.33%
Query Suggestions*	**54.17%**	29.17%	20.83%
Recent Queries*	12.50%	54.17%	**70.83%**
Saved Results **	37.50%	66.67%	**91.67%**

*Chi-square test: * significant (p<0.05); ** significant (p<0.01)*

Comparing the stages, the Search Box and Results, Category Filters, Tag Cloud and Query Suggestions are all rated most highly in the first stage, which generally corresponds with the results for the active and passive interaction in the previous sections. The inter-stage differences for the Search Box and Results List (non-parametric Friedman test, p<0.01, $\chi^2(2)=13.3$) are significant. The Query Suggestions feature has significance ratings close to 0.05 (Friedman, p=0.07, $\chi^2(2)=5.4$); and is deemed most useful in the first stage. While the previous features are rated slightly lower in successive stages, the opposite holds true for the Recent Queries and Saved Results features, which both have their highest rating in the third stage. In the case of the Recent Queries feature, the differences are significant (Friedman, p<0.01, $\chi^2(2)=15.2$). Here, we note that the Recent Queries feature did not show any significant differences using the previous active and passive interaction measures, though a general increase of use could be observed.

Table 7 summarizes the users' ratings after the *whole* experiment, which are also visualised in Figure 1. Participants were asked to indicate in which stage or stages a feature was *most* useful, and were allowed zero to multiple answers for each feature. This table shows similar tendencies as Table 6, but the differences are more pronounced. Hence, participants judged the usefulness of interface features slightly more explicit after completing the full experiment, perhaps at that moment having an overview of the stages involved in it. A chi-square test indicates that the differences are significant for all SUI features (p<0.01, $\chi^2(10)=33.5$). The feature ratings show a clear division: the Search Box/Results List, Category Filters, Query Suggestions and Tag Cloud were most useful in the first and second stage. The opposite is true for the Recent Queries and Saved Results, which were deemed more useful in the latter stages.

Questionnaire and interview data The data from the questionnaires and interviews were collected to provide insight into the utility of features at different moments of the task, and to contextualize our measurements. Here, we focus mainly on the *control* and *personalisable* features, which may support a user, but are not commonly included in regular search engines.

The general tendency for the *control* features (the Category Filters, Tag Cloud and Query Suggestions), as visualized in Table 7, is that their usefulness decreases over time. In particular, the Tag Cloud feature is deemed less useful in the second and third stage, and is a 'controversial' feature with a considerable variation in user ratings. In the post-stage questionnaires, some participants emphasize the usefulness: *"the tag cloud really aids exploring the topic"* (P.6), and *"the tag cloud came up with words that I hadn't thought of using that were very useful"*. However, especially after the second and third stage, a number of participants (P.05, P.16, P.18, P.21, P.27) indicated that the tag cloud is not so useful, saying that it *"contributed little during this task"* (P.05), that *"the tag system doesn't help to narrow the search much"* (P.18) and that it *"in the end seemed to be too general"* (P.07). P.12 summarizes this in the interview after the experiment: *"The Tag Cloud, I think, was good at the beginning, because when you are not exactly sure what you are looking for,*

it can give inspiration" [14]. This can explain the fluctuations in use and perceived usefulness: the Tag Cloud is mainly useful in the beginning of the task, when users are exploring the topic, since provides basic vocabulary to the user (using frequent words in the retrieved snippets), and it may provide inspiration. In another interview, P.15 emphasizes the support of the Tag Cloud feature in generating ideas: *"it was nice to look at what other kinds of ideas [exist] that maybe you didn't think of. Then one word might spark your interest"*. However, once a user had built up a certain level of background knowledge about the topic, the value of the Tag Cloud seemed to diminish, because the user may already be familiar with the words that it displays. A similar situation exists for the Category Filters, as P.11 suggests: *"Category Filters, [those were] good at the start (...) but later I wanted something more specific"*. Hence, the refining of search results using general categories may be useful in the initial stages, but later users have more specific ideas of what they want to search for, and wish for more specific categories. For example, P.16 indicated in the questionnaire after the second stage that *"Category Filters could be more specific in its categories"*, and P.26 ideally wanted to choose a custom set of categories.

The Query Suggestions also have a similar variation in perceived value. While deemed more useful than both the Category Filters and Tag Cloud in the initial stage, the usefulness ratings for the Query Suggestions decrease in the subsequent stages. As in the case of the Category Filters, users ask after the second and third stage for improved precision, and quality (P.2, P.19), and indicate that the suggestions were *"not relevant"* for the current task (P.6, P.8). Again, this can be further contextualized using the interview data: P.11 suggested that the Query Suggestions feature *"was good at the start, but as soon as I got more specific into my topic, that went down"*. P.23 provided a suggestion for design improvement of such a feature, and indicates that over time, the Query Suggestions should take into account previous searches and *"tailor to the kinds results"* he was visiting. Still, some users mentioned, similar to the Tag Cloud, that the Query Suggestions may provide inspiration, but also serendipity: *"I clicked the query suggestions a few times. They gave me sort of serendipitous results, which are useful."* (P.24)

As opposed to the previously discussed *control* features, the *personalisable* features, the Recent Queries and Saved Results features, were increasingly highly rated. Except for some small usability issues (e.g. indicated by P.03 and P.17), users were enthusiastic about the Saved Results feature, and 13 participants wrote down positive comments in the questionnaires (P.04,P.07,P.13-16,P.18,P.21,P.23-27). P.15 remarked: *"I really found the save results feature useful, very easy to use, I wish my search engine had this!"*. The ability to categorize results was also seen as useful: *"The way that I can categorize all the pages I get is useful"* (P.27), and *"I just felt I was organizing my research a little bit."* (P.18). One participant (P.07) also indicated that the Saved Results feature helped to lay out the plans for his search. It also encouraged participants that normally do not use bookmarks to save results. Regarding the usefulness over time, various participants (for example P.12) indicate that the Saved

Results *"are most useful in the end"*. One of the participants also provided feedback in the interview that can explain the previous findings that the highest number of links were saved in the first stage (P.20): *"at the start [I was] saving a lot of a general things about different topics. Later on I went back to the saved ones for the topic I chose and then sort of went on from that and see what else I should search."* Hence, users may search and save many items in the beginning, but, if they formulated a focus, will save more specific sources later. Similarly, P.26 said *"I guess in the end I was looking for a more specific search, while my search in the beginning was just simple – [I] just searched virtual reality [and] didn't do anything on top of that"*.

Some participants indicated that the Recent Queries feature, like the Saved Results feature, was more useful later in the experiment: *"Recent queries were more useful in the end because I had more searches from before"* (P.26). The fixation data analyzed in the previous section has shown some evidence that users look more at this feature than that they actually click on it, or hover over it with the mouse. P.23 provides insight into this finding: *"the previous searches became more useful 'as I made' them, because they were there and I could see what I searched before. I was sucking myself in and could work by looking at those."* Thus, the continuous display of recent queries may aid users in their process by providing feedback about the previous paths followed; this may be the case especially in the context of complex tasks.

Summarizing, this section has looked at the perceived usefulness of features. The user ratings of different SUI features largely confirmed the findings from the previous sections, in that certain *input* and *control* features were deemed highly useful in most stages (Query Box and Results), while *personalisable* features become increasingly useful (Recent Queries, Saved Results) and *control* features decreasingly useful (Category Filters, Tag Cloud and Query Suggestions). The changes in ratings after each stage are significant for the Recent Queries and Search Box/Results feature. The increasing use of the Recent Queries feature could be observed in both active and passive interactions, but the significant difference in the usefulness ratings provides more substantial evidence for when this feature provides most value. Finally, the questionnaires and interviews provided contextualization to the active and passive interactions: the variations in the use of certain features, like the Tag Cloud and Query Suggestion feature, are caused by a user's increasing domain knowledge. As the participants indicated in the questionnaires and interviews, the features useful at the start do not provide the specific information needed in later stages, hence do not take into account a user's growing understanding of a topic.

5. DISCUSSION AND CONCLUSIONS

This section discusses the results of the study, the answers to our research questions, and broader implications for search systems. The main aim of this study was to directly examine how different SUI features can support distinct macro-level stages. By looking at active, passive and perceived utility of SUI features during different stages of a complex task, we have observed that *informational* features are naturally useful in every stage, while *input*, *control* and *personalisable* features varied by stage.

At a user's initial pre-focus stage, as Vakkari and Hakala [31] have indicated, thoughts of users are "general, fragmented and vague." Searchers are unable to express "specifically what information is needed," and their "relevance criteria are vague." At this stage, the uniqueness of encountered information is high, while the redundancy of found information is low [16]. The first stage of our experiment represented pre-focus user activities, and at this stage the *input*, *informational* and *control* features are most useful. Naturally,

input features, are needed at this stage to express users' needs in terms of queries, while users retrieve results via the *informational* features. The user's vague understanding, the trouble in expressing her need, limited domain knowledge, but also the large amount of new information can explain the prominent role of *control* features in this initial stage: users may utilize them to explore different kinds of information, and to control their result set.

As Vakkari and Kuhlthau [16, 31] suggest, the subsequent focus formulation stage is crucial in the process. During this stage, "the search for information becomes more directed", and a better understanding drives persons to seek relevant information, using differentiated criteria. This stage was represented by the second task of our experiment. Our experimental results show that the *control* features become less essential at this point, likely caused by user's improved understanding and emerging focus. This even causes provided categories, suggested tags and searches to be "not specific enough" anymore. The *personalisable* features, on the other hand, become more important during the focus formulation stage and beyond. Contrary to control features, personalisable features may continously support users in their process, providing feedback on the paths followed in their information journey. These features "grow" with the emerging understanding of a user. For example, users in our experiment repeatedly updated their categorizations and saved results along the way, and one participant even indicated that these features helped him to lay out the plans of his research.

Finally, the third, post-focus stage features specific searches for information, and re-checks for additional information [31]. Searchers may collect information pertinent to their focused topic [16]. At this stage, users are able to "express precisely what information is needed", and encounter low uniqueness, and high redundancy of information [16]. In our experiment, participants performed long, specific queries at this stage, and frequently reopened previous URLs and queries (via the personalisable features). The importance of the *control*, and to a lesser extent, *input* features further declined in the post-focus stage. *Personalisable* features on the other hand, were used relatively often. These features allowed users to keep track of their previous searches and captured material.

Besides insights into *when* SUI features may be useful, our findings have shown that some features were frequently used in an active way, while others were used more passively, but still received a high user rating. Hence, some features, like the Query Box and Result List, directly support users in performing their task, while other features, such as the Recent Queries feature, provide more indirect support, for example by providing context or help them manage their task progress.

Most web search systems have converged over fairly static and familiar designs, where some trialled features, such as the *personalisable* SearchPad [6] feature and Google's Wonder Wheel *control* feature, have struggled to provide value for searchers. This is perhaps because, at the wrong times, SUI features can actually impede search [5]. Conversely, these more novel control and personalisable features appear consistently in systems like online retail stores, where users are more likely to perform more complex tasks. The results of our work help to provide the insights needed to consider *when* SUI features might be useful during evolving search episodes, such that we could design responsive SUIs that introduce features at the times when they provide value, even on web search. This pleads for UIs that adapt to the needs of the task and task stage at hand.

Our results provide characteristics of behaviour observed as users transfer between different stages of a complex essay-writing task, and thus could be used to detect when live users are in pre-focus, focus, and post-focus stages. In future work, this may be extended to other types of complex tasks. Furthermore, this study has focused on one user population (undergraduate students in Computer Science), therefore future work could expand towards other user groups. Future work may also consider turning the analysis around, and try to train a classifier to accurately detect which stage a user is in. Our results, however, indicate that *control* features also need to evolve with the maturity of the the users knowledge level. Similarly, our results suggest that *personalisable* features provide more support after users move on from initial querying stages. These results support, for example, the premise behind Golovchinsky's work on Querium [9], which personalised control features with metadata about a users search history, to give users filters that develop with their task over time. This naturally leads to further research into task-aware search systems [15] and into additional features which could be useful at different stages (such as co-author visualizations, or user hints and assistance), as well as research into functions which could support interruptions and reinitiating complex search tasks. Thus, future work should directly test how dynamic provision of SUI features does support searchers when exhibiting behaviour indicative of different stages, without being impeded when features are not needed. This complex tension between support and impedence, however, is challenging to study.

Concluding, our findings suggest that the active, passive and perceived utility of SUI features across stages, especially in the context of complex and learning tasks, is inherently *dynamic* with different types of features being useful in different task stages. This is in line with macro-level information seeking models, describing broad changes in information behaviour across stages, and sheds light on the type of support needed in each stage. This provides new handles to overcome the largely *static* support for information seeking in current search systems, and facilitate a move towards more dynamic and responsive SUIs, providing tailored support to different information seeking stages.

Acknowledgments

This research is supported by EPSRC Platform Grant EP/M000877/1 and the Netherlands Organization for Scientific Research (WebART, # 640.005.001).
Data access statement: consent was not gained from participants to release their study data online, and so a dataset is not openly available.

REFERENCES

[1] P. Borlund. The IIR evaluation model: a framework for evaluation of interactive information retrieval systems. *Inf. Res.*, 8(3), 2003.

[2] G. Buscher, A. Dengel, and L. van Elst. Eye movements as implicit relevance feedback. In *CHI'08 extended abstracts on Human factors in computing systems*, pages 2991–2996. ACM, 2008.

[3] K. Byström and K. Järvelin. Task complexity affects information seeking and use. *IP&M*, 31(2):191–213, 1995.

[4] E. S. Dalmaijer, S. Mathôt, and S. Van der Stigchel. PyGaze: An open-source, cross-platform toolbox for minimal-effort programming of eyetracking experiments. *Behav. Res. Meth.*, 46(4):913–921, 2013.

[5] A. Diriye, A. Blandford, and A. Tombros. When is system support effective? In *Proc. IIiX*, pages 55–64. ACM, 2010.

[6] D. Donato, F. Bonchi, T. Chi, and Y. Maarek. Do You Want to Take Notes?: Identifying Research Missions in Yahoo! Search Pad. In *Proc. WWW'10*, pages 321–330, 2010. ACM.

[7] D. Ellis. A behavioural approach to information retrieval system design. *J. Doc.*, 45:171–212, 1989.

[8] A. Foster. Nonlinear information seeking. In *Theories of information behavior*. Information Today, 2005.

[9] G. Golovchinsky, A. Diriye, and T. Dunnigan. The future is in the past: Designing for exploratory search. In *IIiX*, pages 52–61. ACM, 2012.

[10] M. A. Hearst. *Search user interfaces*. Cambridge University Press, 2009.

[11] H. C. Huurdeman and J. Kamps. From Multistage Information-seeking Models to Multistage Search Systems. In *Proc. IIiX'14*, pages 145–154, 2014. ACM.

[12] P. Ingwersen and K. Järvelin. *The turn: Integration of information seeking and retrieval in context*. Springer, 2005.

[13] J. Jiang, D. He, and J. Allan. Searching, Browsing, and Clicking in a Search Session: Changes in User Behavior by Task and over Time. In *Proc. SIGIR'14*, pages 607–616, 2014. ACM.

[14] D. Kelly. Query suggestions as idea tactics for information search. In *Proc. HCIR'09*, pages 9–12, 2009.

[15] D. Kelly, J. Arguello, and R. Capra. NSF workshop on task-based information search systems. *SIGIR Forum*, 47(2):116–127, Jan. 2013.

[16] C. C. Kuhlthau. *Seeking Meaning: A Process Approach to Library and Information Services*. Libraries Unlimited, 2004.

[17] B. Kules and R. Capra. Influence of training and stage of search on gaze behavior in a library catalog faceted search interface. *JASIST*, 63: 114–138, 2012.

[18] B. Kules and B. Shneiderman. Users can change their web search tactics: Design guidelines for categorized overviews. *IP&M*, 44(2): 463–484, 2008.

[19] J. Liu and N. J. Belkin. Personalizing information retrieval for multi-session tasks. *JASIST*, 66(1):58–81, Jan. 2015.

[20] J. Liu, M. J. Cole, C. Liu, R. Bierig, J. Gwizdka, N. J. Belkin, J. Zhang, and X. Zhang. Search behaviors in different task types. In *JCDL*, pages 69–78. ACM, 2010.

[21] G. Marchionini. Exploratory search: from finding to understanding. *CACM*, 49(4):41–46, 2006.

[22] X. Niu and D. Kelly. The use of query suggestions during information search. *IPM*, 50:218–234, 2014.

[23] K. Rodden, X. Fu, A. Aula, and I. Spiro. Eye-mouse coordination patterns on web search results pages. In *CHI'08 Extended Abstracts*, pages 2997–3002. ACM, 2008.

[24] T. Russell-Rose and T. Tate. *Designing the search experience: The information architecture of discovery*. Newnes, 2012.

[25] T. Saracevic. The stratified model of information retrieval interaction: Extension and applications. In *Proc. of the ASIS Annual Meeting*, volume 34, pages 313–327. Learned Information (Europe) Ltd, 1997.

[26] B. Shneiderman and C. Pleasant. *Designing the user interface: strategies for effective human-computer interaction*. Pearson Education, 2005.

[27] A. Spink. Study of interactive feedback during mediated information retrieval. *JASIS*, 48(5):382–394, 1997.

[28] E. G. Toms. Task-based information searching and retrieval. In *Interactive Information Seeking, Behaviour and Retrieval*. Facet, 2011.

[29] D. Tunkelang. Faceted search. *Synthesis lectures on information concepts, retrieval, and services*, 1(1):1–80, 2009.

[30] P. Vakkari. A theory of the task-based information retrieval process: a summary and generalisation of a longitudinal study. *J. Doc.*, 57:44–60, 2001.

[31] P. Vakkari and N. Hakala. Changes in relevance criteria and problem stages in task performance. *J. Doc.*, 56:540–562, 2000.

[32] R. W. White and S. M. Drucker. Investigating Behavioral Variability in Web Search. In *Proc. WWW'07*, pages 21–30, 2007. ACM.

[33] R. W. White and R. A. Roth. Exploratory search: Beyond the query-response paradigm. *Synthesis Lectures on Information Concepts, Retrieval, and Services*, 1:1–98, 2009.

[34] R. W. White, I. Ruthven, and J. M. Jose. A study of factors affecting the utility of implicit relevance feedback. In *Proc. SIGIR*, pages 35–42. ACM, 2005.

[35] B. Wildemuth, L. Freund, and E. G. Toms. Untangling search task complexity and difficulty in the context of interactive information retrieval studies. *J. Doc.*, 70(6):1118–1140, 2014.

[36] B. M. Wildemuth and L. Freund. Search tasks and their role in studies of search behaviors. In *Proc. HCIR'09*, pages 17–2, 2009.

[37] M. L. Wilson. Keyword search: Quite exploratory actually. In *Proc. HCIR'09*, pages 106–108, 2009.

[38] M. L. Wilson. Search user interface design. *Synthesis Lectures on Information Concepts, Retrieval, and Services*, 3(3):1–143, 2011.

[39] M. L. Wilson and m. c. schraefel. A longitudinal study of exploratory and keyword search. In *In Proc. JCDL'08*, pages 52–56. ACM, 2008.

[40] T. D. Wilson. Models in information behaviour research. *J. Doc.*, 55: 249–270, 1999.

The Forgotten Needle in My Collections: Task-Aware Ranking of Documents in Semantic Information Space

Tuan Tran[1], Sven Schwarz[2], Claudia Niederée[1], Heiko Maus[2], Nattiya Kanhabua[1,3]

[1]L3S Research Center / Leibniz Universität Hannover, Germany
[2]German Research Center for Artificial Intelligence (DFKI) / Kaiserslautern, Germany
[3]Department of Computer Science, Aalborg University, Denmark
[1]{ttran, niederee}@l3s.de, [2]{heiko.maus, sven.schwarz}@dfki.de, [3]nattiya@cs.aau.dk

ABSTRACT

With the growing amount of content stored in personal and organizational information spaces, finding and re-finding documents becomes both more crucial and challenging. In this work, we propose an approach to reduce information overload in navigation by automatically focusing on important documents, adaptively to the tasks at hand. Based on the idea of managed forgetting, we present a ranking method, which unifies activity logs and semantic information about documents into a common framework to identify important documents to the user's current tasks. Our experiments on two real-world datasets, both collected from knowledge work activities in professional scenarios, show that our ranking approach outperforms the baseline methods for both subsequent access prediction and the effectiveness in ranking important documents. Furthermore, we implemented and demonstrated a system for decluttering information spaces as a proof of concept of our managed forgetting approach.

Categories and Subject Descriptors [Information Systems]: Desktop Search, Retrieval Models and Ranking

General Terms Algorithms, Experimentation

Keywords Desktop Search, Temporal Ranking, Propagation

1. INTRODUCTION

The advance of technologies has supported the idea of massive digital content creation and sharing, as well as the reluctance of content removal. This leads to a growing number of data, making finding and re-finding a particular resource increasingly difficult. In non-public sources such as the personal and organizational information spaces, navigation is a preferred mechanism to find a document for a task at hand, due to its lower cognitive load, its consistency and the strength of the location metaphor [6]. However, with the huge amount of digital content generated every day, access via navigation becomes challenging. The mission is more frustrating in large heterogenous information

CHIIR '16, March 13-17, 2016, Carrboro, NC, USA

© 2016 ACM. ISBN 978-1-4503-3751-9/16/03... $15.00

DOI: http://dx.doi.org/10.1145/2854946.2854971

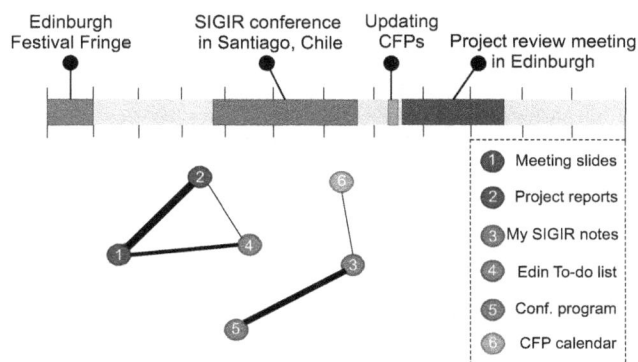

Figure 1: Recommended documents in a personal information management system: The upper bar corresponds to the timeline of tasks. Bottom right is the recommended documents. User accessed the documents when conducting the tasks (displayed with the same color). Graph on bottom left represents the document relations. Width of lines indicates the strength of the connections. The forgotten document 4 resurges due to its relevance to the current task.

ecosystems such as in different devices, or in systems that get cluttered after long-time working on different tasks.

For decluttering such information spaces and supporting the finding or re-finding of resources according to the user's short-term interest, we propose a *ranking* approach to ease the navigation, based on the idea of *managed forgetting*. The idea is inspired by science of forgetting and remembering [21, 23]: The human brain is very effective in focusing on important things, while forgetting irrelevant details. This trait is reflected in human practices of organizing their collections, i.e., they often create shortcuts to easily navigate to relevant resources in the desktop environment or mobile home screens, or bookmark important Web pages. Managed forgetting aims to relieve such manual efforts by automatically computing the *short-term* importance of a document with respect to the user attention. It replaces the binary decision on importance by a gradually changing value: Information sinks away from the user with a decreasing value, which we call *memory buoyancy*. This value can be used for ranking important resources for a task at hand, thereby decluttering the information spaces adaptively.

As in human forgetting, memory buoyancy is driven by resource usage, importance decay, and semantic associations [2]. In Information Retrieval, different algorithms and systems have been proposed to identify important documents in an information space [11, 24]. Many existing approaches rely on activity logs and assumes that recently accessed documents are also more likely to be accessed in the future [34]. As a result, many proposed algorithms assess documents based on recency and frequency evidences of access. They ignore a wide variety of other factors, which equally influence the importance of a document for a task at hand. For instance, according to the associative character of the brain, a document might be important because of its relatedness to the current task, even if the document has not been touched for a long time [2, 27]. In the example shown in Figure 1, while preparing for a business trip to Edinburgh, the user might recall or might have forgotten useful notes from her private holiday in Edinburgh some years ago. Ideally, a system should bring this information up again, but it is infeasible when only relying on the activity history alone. This example demonstrates the need for a more comprehensive ranking method, taking into account the intrinsic relatedness of documents to current tasks.

Our method combines evidences from activity logs with semantic associations between documents to devise a unified document ranking framework. The idea is that a document is important to the user's current task, if it either has been frequently accessed by the user, or is highly related to other important documents. This is illustrated in Figure 1 for six documents. The user's intensive accesses to "Meeting slides" and "Project reports" during the preparation for the project meeting in Edinburgh (dark-blue part of the upper horizontal bar) give the documents higher ranks. Meanwhile, the connections between these documents and the "To-do list" from a past trip to Edinburgh endorses this list to the current task, bringing it back to the user's attention.

The importance of considering document relationships to rank documents, e.g, in personal information management (PIM) systems, has been shown in [30, 8]. The common idea is to propagate the "importance score" of a document to other related documents in a graph of different document relationship. However, most of existing work studies the document relations in isolation, assumes they are equally important, or puts arbitrary weights to the relations in an ad-hoc manner [30]. In contrast, we propose a unified framework based on machine-learning methods. We conduct studies in different settings, and systematically evaluate the effectiveness of our framework from the quantitative to qualitative perspectives. In summary, our contributions are:

1. A novel framework for realizing managed forgetting based on a machine-learning method. It unifies activity log information and semantic relationships to rank documents based on user's current tasks.

2. Experiments on two real-world data sets acquired from daily usages in professional scenarios, which show the effectiveness of our proposed method.

3. Implementation of the managed forgetting into a real-world Semantic Desktop system for decluttering professional information spaces.

2. RELATED WORK

In the area of personal information management (PIM) systems, there has been a rich body of work studying how to organize and find information effectively [17, 11, 15, 7].

Based on findings about user preferences in information navigation [17, 7, 31], different methods have been proposed to improve the finding and re-finding process [11, 15]. Existing work relies on structural signals of documents, which do not reflect the user preferences in finding, but rather in organizing the file systems [17]. Other work, such as studies by Teevan et al. [31] and by Bergman et al. [5], address the retrieval needs (findding and re-finding of documents); but they lack the deep understanding of user intents when interacting with documents of different semantics. The limitation comes from the fact that such semantics of document attributes and associations are not easily observed in traditional PIM systems. The advances of annotation and information extraction technologies have enabled this with the emerging of Semantic Desktop systems [28]. The NEPO-MUK Semantic Desktop [1] has built an infrastructure providing a semantic layer over conventional documents (e.g., emails, Web pages, documents, pictures, etc.) with a personalized vocabulary resembling the mental model of the user [29]. A similar approach was also employed in other systems, including Haystack [26], MyLifeBits [16], etc. This trend opens a new line of research in document finding and re-finding, exploiting the semantic information. To the best of our knowledge, our study is the first in this direction.

In the context of document ranking, many solutions have been proposed for PIM systems, which can be classified in two categories: activity logs-based and relation-based. The former involves analysing user behaviour from the past activities, ranking documents based on their recency and frequency testimony. This can be estimated by different decay functions, each has a different cognitive plausibility and encodings [25, 14, 10, 2]. It can also be modeled via Markovian processes [14], or balanced with short- and long-term aspects [34]. The relation-based method, on the other hand, exploits the relationships between documents to propagate their importance scores along the relation graph. Such "propagation" technique has been proven to be useful in a wide variety of domains and retrieval scenarios, from personal file search [30, 33] to collaboration spaces [13]. The document relations can come from different evidences. Most established methods attempt to identify related documents by their correlation in access behaviour (e.g., Web pages that are often visited together, files that are opened in the same session, etc.). These methods then employ techniques such as approximating sessions and file operation timelines [33], or use session signals in some applications such as web browser [24]. Recently, there are attempts to combine these two categories into one framework, using one-step propagation to actitivy-based ranking in a layered approach, or linearly combine in a hybrid model [3]. In contrast to existing work, we propose a new unified framework that leverages both activity logs and document relationships in principled manner, based on machine-learning models with no manual-defined training data. Our model also works for any heterogenous relation networks, and to that extent, generalizes existing work, which focuses on individual relations [24].

There has been extensive work in the area of *desktop search*. The common approach is to combine content-based techniques from traditional ad-hoc text retrieval with contextual information learnt from user's activities. For instance, the system can complement search with document metadata such as attributes and types [9, 7, 12], or exploit additional information from environments (related tasks, directory structures) to adjust the document relevance. Typical ranking approach includes graph-based propagation methods such as random walks [8, 30, 33]. From the perspective of search interface, Bergman et al. [6] suggested that navigation is a better way to interactively explore the search results due to its cognitive advantages. The idea is also realized in systems such as Stuff I've Seen [11], Search Directed Navigation [15]. While these systems study conventional desktop, we are the first to study in a Semantic Desktop setting.

3. APPROACH

In this section, we describe our approach to managed forgetting, which exploits document's access information, and subsequently applies different forgetting (or decay) functions as well as propagates the importance of related documents via semantic relationships.

3.1 Preliminaries

A semantic information space in a PIM system is a collection of documents or resources, which is denoted as D. A document or a resource d can be of different types (e.g., photo, office document, folder, web page, etc.) and has different attributes (e.g., title, authors, and creation time). Between any two documents d_1 and d_2 can exist multiple relations with different semantics. For instance, d_1 and d_2 are both created by the same author, or d_1 is the containing folder of the file d_2. Relations can be associated with some scores indicating the strength of their relation, for instance, the cosine score for content similarities. Let R denote a set of all semantic relations. For each pair (d_i, d_j), we have an $|R|$-dimensional vector $X_{ij} = (x_{ij1}, x_{ij2}, \ldots, x_{ij|R|})^T$, where $x_{ijk} \geq 0$ represents the score of the k-th relation between d_i and d_j, $x_{ijk} = 0$ if the d_i and d_j are not connected by the relation. Usually, the number of relations is small compared to the number of all documents in the information space. The collection of relation scores $X = \{X_{ij}\}$ forms the weights of edges in a multigraph, where nodes are all documents in D, and each edge corresponds to a semantic relation.

In our work, we model time as the sequence of equal time intervals and denote by $T = (t_1, t_2, \ldots, t_m)$, where the time point t_i is the index of i-th interval from the beginning of the PIM system. In one interval, a document can be accessed and used by one or multiple users. Each access is represented by a triple $a = (d, u, t)$, indicating that the user u performed an action on the document d at time t. Given a user u (or a group of users $U = \{u_i\}$), a document d and a time point of interest t, the sequence of actions on all documents of D, performed by u (or in the case of U, by at least one user u_i), happened before t and in chronological order, forms an activity history of u (or U) in the information space, and is denoted by $L_t = (a_1, a_2, \ldots, a_n)$. Given a document d and time t, we refer to as a document access history, denoted by $L_{d,t}$, as those actions performed on d. A sequence of time points t_i for actions in $L_{d,t}$ (can be repeated because of multiple accesses to d within one interval) constitutes the access times of d, denoted by $T_{d,t}$. The most recent access time to d before t (last time point in $T_{d,t}$) is denoted by t_d.

Problem. Given a collection of documents D, a set of relation scores X, time of interest t, and an activity history L_t corresponding to a user u, or to a group of users U, identify documents with highest importance with respect to u's or U's tasks at time t, as inferred from L_t.

Method name	Function	Parameters
Most Recently Used	$MRU(d,t) = \frac{1}{t - t_d + 1}$	None
Polynomial Decay	$PD(d,t) = \frac{1}{(t - t_d)^\alpha + 1}$	α: Decay rate
Ebbinghaus Curve	$Ebb(d,t) = e^{\frac{(t_d - t)}{S}}$	S: Relative memory strength
Weibull Distribution	$Wei(d,t) = e^{-\frac{\alpha(t - t_d)^s}{s}}$	s: Forgetting steepness, α: Volume of what can be remembered

Table 1: List of Activity-based ranking functions

We tackle the aforementioned problem in two steps. In the first step, we mine the activity history and devise a memory buoyancy scoring function based on the recency and frequency (see Section 3.2), so that more recently and frequently accessed documents get higher memory buoyancy scores. In the second step, we employ a *propagation* method that identifies highly connected documents, to transfer the activity-based scores of documents along the connection. This is similar to the layered approach by Kawase et al. [18]. However, while the authors merely identify connections from sessions of the activity history, we devise a generalized framework that works with different heterogenous relations.

3.2 Activity-based Memory Buoyancy

In order to compute the memory buoyancy scores, we use the access times of the document from the access history. We estimate the score of a document through the distances of previous access time points and the time of interest. The scoring function is formally defined as follows:

DEFINITION 1. *An activity-based memory buoyancy scoring function is a function that takes as input the time t and document d, and outputs a value $v(d, t) \in [0, 1]$ (memory buoyancy score) such that:*
1. *$v(d, t) = 0$ if $T_{d,t} = \emptyset$*
2. *$v(d, t_{i+1}) < v(d, t_i)\ \forall t_i, t_{i+1} \in T_{d,t}$*
3. *$v(d_1, t) < v(d_2, t)$ if $|T_{d_1,t}| < |T_{d_2,t}|$ or $t_{d_1} < t_{d_2}$*

The above conditions ensure that the memory buoyancy scores, if no other evidences present, is driven by the decay effect. In Table 1, we present different activity-based scoring functions studied in this work, each corresponds to one decay function. Each of these functions only considers the most recent time t_d, and can be considered as a basic **recency-based** method.

Frequency. In [2], Anderson et al. suggest that the frequency of interactions also play an important role in the human's recalling process of a resource, as by the re-learning effect. Hence, for each of the functions in Table 1, we introduce a "frequency"-based variant, which aggregates the effect of decays in different time points:

$$v_f(d, t) = \sum_{t_i \in W} v_r(d, t_i) \qquad (1)$$

where $v_r(d, t_i)$ can be any of recency-based functions in Table 1. The sequence $W \subseteq T_{d,t}$ represents the time window in which all time points are taken into consideration for the ranking. For instance, if $W = T_{d,t}$ and $v_r = MRU$, we have the well-established *most frequently used* method in cache replacement policies. If $W = T_{d,t}$ and $v_r = PD$, we have the decay ranking model in [24]. The *Frequency* algorithm used in Mozilla Firefox [10], on the other hand, constructs W from only the last ten items of $T_{d,t}$, in order to avoid the convolution of too old accesses into the current rank. In this work, we follow this idea, and only aggregate from the last ten time points of accesses for each document.

3.3 Propagation Methods

The drawback of recency-based and frequency-based scoring functions is that they consider each document in isolation. In practice, however, humans tend to recall and find documents together within some contexts, e.g., they can follow some cues and associate a document with other related documents which are easier to recall and navigate. This exploitation of document relations is inspired by the cognitive science of associative memory [8], and is studied in a rich body of work [30, 8, 33, 18]. Most of the related work employs a propagation method in the document relations graph, which "transfer" the ranking score of each individual document to other related documents along the edges of the graph. However, these methods are non-learning and largely based on heuristics to combine relations weight, which requires extensive tuning, as mentioned in [30].

In our work, we develop a propagation method that combines different relations into a unified framework, and learns the weighting for the combination automatically. We model the process that the user finds an important document as a Markov process, where she recalls and searches for important documents via the related resources. For each pair of connected documents (d_i, d_j), we define the transition probability from document d_i to document d_j as:

$$p_{ij}(w) = \begin{cases} \frac{\sum_{k=1}^{|R|} w_k x_{ijk}}{\sum_{l=1}^{|D|} \sum_{k=1}^{|R|} w_k x_{ilk}} & \text{if } X_{ij} \neq \emptyset \text{ and } L_{d_j,t} \neq \emptyset \\ 0 & \text{otherwise} \end{cases}$$
(2)

where w is the weighting vector for the semantic relations in R. The condition $L_{d_j,t} \neq \emptyset$ ensures that the propagation has no effect on the documents that have not been created before the time t, i.e., no propagation to the future. Similarly, the indices l's run only over the documents d_l with $L_{d_l,t} \neq \emptyset$. Consequently, we have $\sum_j p_{ij} = 1$ for all documents d_i. In practice, to avoid rank sink when performing the propagation process, if a document has no relations at all, we assume a dummy edge from it to all other documents with zero probability.

Next, we describe our propagation framework. Let P denote the transition matrix of documents in D, we follow PageRank model and define the propagation as the iterative process, where in each iteration, the memory buoyancy values of documents are updated by the following equation,

$$\mathbf{s}^{(n+1)} = \lambda P^T \mathbf{s}^{(n)} + (1 - \lambda)\mathbf{v}$$
(3)

where $\mathbf{s}^{(n)} = (s(d_1, t), s(d_2, t), ..., s(d_m, t))$ is the vector of documents' memory buoyancy values at iteration n, (m is the number of documents appearing in L_t), $\mathbf{v}$ is the vector of values obtained by an activity-based scoring method, and λ is the damping factor. In Equation 3, we need to learn the model of weighting parameters w in order to complete the transition matrix P, described in the following.

3.4 Learning to Propagate

The aim of the learning is to identify the weights $w_1, .., w_{|R|}$ of the semantic relations with which we obtain the best pre-diction of document rankings. In this work, we propose to exploit the activity history to learn the optimal w. In particular, we simulate the navigation of the user at each time points t' in the past, and compare the computed ranks of the documents with the ranks based on the frequency of access in the time point $t' + 1$. The idea is to learn w so as to minimize the number of mis-ranked pairs, e.g., a pair (d_1, d_2) with $s(d_1, t') > s(d_2, t')$ but d_1 has been accessed less frequently than d_2 until $t' + 1$.

Formally, we define the label $y_{ij} = s(d_i, t') - s(d_j, t')$ and the groundtruth $\hat{y}$; $\hat{y}_{ij} = -1$ if d_i has less access than d_j at $t' + 1$ and $\hat{y}_{ij} = 1$ otherwise. We learn w by the following optimization problem:

$$\min_w F(w) = \|w\|^2 + \theta \sum_{(d_i, d_j) \in A} h(y_{ij})$$
(4)

where A is the training data, θ is the regularization parameter that controls the complexity of the model (i.e., $\|w\|^2$) while minimizes the mis-ranked pairs in A via the loss function h. In this work, we apply the simple hinge loss function: $h(y) = \max(0, 1 - \hat{y}.y)$. Next, we explain how to solve Equation 4 and how we collected the training data A.

Optimization Solution. Following [4], we solve Equation 4 by a gradient descent method. The partial derivative of $F(w)$ with respect to each relation weight w_k is:

$$\frac{\partial F}{\partial w_k} = 2w_k + \theta \sum_{(d_i, d_j) \in A} \frac{\partial h(y_{ij})}{\partial y_{ij}} \left(\frac{\partial s(d_i, t')}{\partial w_k} - \frac{\partial s(d_j, t')}{\partial w_k} \right)$$
(5)

The derivative of the hinge function is trivial. For $s(d, t)$, we have from Equation 3:

$$\frac{\partial s(d_i, t')}{\partial w_k} = \lambda \sum_j \left(p_{ji} \frac{\partial s(d_j, t')}{\partial w_k} + s(d_j, t') \frac{\partial p_{ji}}{\partial w_k} \right)$$
(6)

and:

$$\frac{\partial p_{ji}}{\partial w_k} = \frac{x_{jik} \sum_i \sum_k w_k x_{jik} - (\sum_k w_k x_{jik})(\sum_i x_{jik})}{(\sum_i \sum_k w_k x_{jik})^2}$$
(7)

From Equations 6 and 7, we can calculate the gradients $\frac{\partial s}{\partial w_k}$ by a power-iteration algorithm such as in [4], and then apply a gradient descent-based learning method, for instance L-BFGS method [20], into Equation 5 to learn w.

Soft Labeling. We start with identifying the training time points t' to observe the subsequent accesses. In principle, any time point before the time of interest t can be chosen. In practice, however, we observe that time points during the burst periods, i.e., the period where there is a significantly higher number of access than usual, are more "interesting" to observe both correctly and falsely ranked pairs. The burst can also indicate an implicit event or task happening [32]. To this extent, we apply the Kleinberg algorithm [19] to identify the burst periods from the times series of the document accesses. Then, for each period, we pick up the time point with highest number of access for the training.

Next, we build a balanced set of positive and negative pairs for the training data as follows (Figure 2). For each training time point t', we extract the set of all documents accessed by the user at $t' + 1$, denoted $D_{t'+1}$. Then, we apply a baseline activity-based scoring method with respect to t for documents in D, and sort them in descending order of the memory buoyancy values. From this sorted list, we get

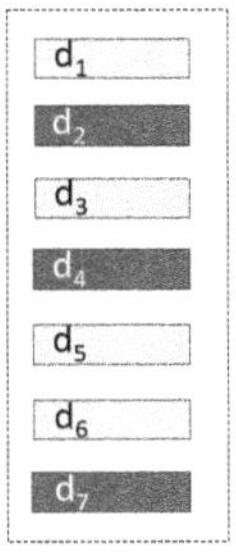

(d_1, d_2)	-1	(d_3, d_4)	-1
(d_1, d_4)	-1	(d_3, d_7)	-1
(d_1, d_7)	-1	(d_4, d_5)	1
(d_2, d_3)	1	(d_4, d_6)	1
(d_2, d_5)	1	(d_5, d_7)	-1
(d_2, d_6)	1	(d_6, d_7)	-1

Figure 2: Example training data: Left-hand side is a baseline document ranks. Documents in dark blue are accessed in the next time point. All documents from the first rank to the lowest rank of the accessed documents (d_7) are used for the training. Table in the right-hand side consists of training pairs, together with the labels.

the top-scored documents until all documents in $D_{t'+1}$ are included. We call this set S. The set $E = S \setminus D_{t'+1}$ consists of documents with high memory buoyancy scores but not accessed in the next time points, i.e., the false positives. Finally, we construct the training pairs (d_i, d_j) by picking d_i from the sets $D_{t'+1}$ or E, such that d_i, d_j are not in the same set, and that the estimated memory buoyancy score of d_i is higher than of d_j. As an example from Figure 2, we have (d_1, d_2) is a training pair, but (d_2, d_1) is not, because the estimated score of the document d_2 is smaller than d_1's. Similarly, $(d_1, d_3) \notin A$ because both d_1 and d_3 are in E.

To assign the training labels, if $d_i \in D_{t'+1}$ and $d_j \in E$, then we assign $\hat{y}_{ij} = 1$. Otherwise, if $d_i \in E$ and $d_j \in D_{t'+1}$, we set $\hat{y}_{ij} = -1$ (see Figure 2).

3.5 Semantic Graphs

The semantic relations R play an important role in the propagation method. Depending on specific domains of applications and scenarios, we can have different types of semantic relations, which can be classified in two categories:

Explicit Relations. This category consists of relations that are observable from the structures of the documents and the information space, e.g., references or hyperlinks from one document to others, the containment relations between folders and files, etc. The relations can be specified by users with the help of some software components and interfaces, such as aforementioned NEPOMUK Semantic Desktop. Recently, with the proliferation of Semantic Web and RDF technologies, some semantic relations are standardized as predicates between documents, such as hasPartOf, hasAttachment, etc.

Implicit Relations. This category includes relations that are inferred from the contents of documents, or from user activity patterns; for instance, content similarities, the correlation of two documents being accessed frequently in the same or close sessions or time. The advantage of this type of relations as compared to the explicit ones is that it can be constructed automatically without much human effort. In the following, we will focus on this type of relations. Note that while many explicit relations are asymmetric, the implicit relations discussed below are symmetric. To unify them in the same relation space R, for each implicit relation between documents d_i and d_j, we fill the score into the corresponding dimension in both X_{ij} and X_{ji}. In this work, we consider the following types of implicit relations.

Text-based Relation: This type of relation relies on the similarity of document contents. More specifically, for each document, we build the bag of words from its main content body, and calculate the Cosine similarity of the two documents to measure the strength of their relation.

Atribute-based Relation: The text-based relation is only applicable for rich-text types such as e-mails, web pages, office documents, etc. For other types of documents, we assume the Cosine similarity is zero, as no textual content can be extracted. For these documents, we rely on metadata specified by the users or software components. These attributes are often represented in form of <attribute, set of values>. For instance, tags of a photo, list recipients of an email, etc. We define one relation for each specific attribute, and measure the relation strength by calculating the Jaccard similarity over the two corresponding sets of values.

Time-based Relation: This relation is derived from the activity history. It is based on the assumption that two documents are highly related with respect some latent tasks, if the user accessed to both of them in many sessions. To identify the "good" sessions for two documents d_1 and d_2, we apply the same heuristic as for building the training data: We extract all time points from the burst time periods of $T_{d_1,t}$ and $T_{d_2,t}$ to create the two sub-sequences for d_1, d_2 respectively. We then calculate Jaccard similarity between these sequences and use t as the time-based relation strength.

4. EXPERIMENTS

4.1 Datasets

In this work, we conduct experiments on two real-world datasets with different characteristics. Table 2 summarizes the statistics of these datasets. In the following, we give more detailed information for each dataset.

4.1.1 Semantic Desktop

The first dataset (named Person) consists of personal collections obtained via a Semantic Desktop infrastructure described in [22] and deployed at the DFKI. The resulting knowledge base consists of resources, their semantic representations and relations with concepts spanning a semantic graph based on the PIMO (Personal Information Model), a state-of-the-art ontology for PIM [29]. At the time of evaluation, the Semantic Desktop infrastructure has been used for over 3 years in the Knowledge Management team at DFKI on a daily basis by 17 users, who are employees and students in DFKI. Among these users, 7 are active with usage of 4 to 8 hours per day, others are occasional users such as interns or assistant students. The PIMO data is stored in a knowledge base on a central server and is related to professional or research activities, e.g., business meetings, project proposals, tasks, and notes, etc. The knowledge base is accessed via the Semantic Desktop infrastructure consisting of components such as a plug-in embedded into the Windows file explorer, a Firefox add-on, a plug-in to an email client, and a web-based stand-alone application.[1] These are installed on each individual's computer at work, and are used on a daily basis. It enables the user to easily annotate documents when they conduct their regular tasks: Browsing the Web, reading emails, managing files on hard disks or creating calendar events. The user is also enable to create and use semantic

---

[1]For a detailed explanation and videos see our ForgetIT Pilot documentation at https://pimo.opendfki.de/wp9-pilot/

Figures	Person	Collaboration
No. of documents	20363	1437
Time span	Sep 2011 - Sep 2014	Oct 2008 - Sep 2014
Users	17	268
Relations	155539	126326
Activity log entries	337528	217588

Table 2: Statistics of the datasets

concepts, such as topics, locations, persons, tasks, events, or documents. To this extent, a semantic layer is built over the "physical" information objects, e.g., in the file system, mapping each document or concept to a *resource*. In our experiments, we apply our methods to provide ranks for these semantic PIMO concepts instead of the actual documents.

As for the activity history, a monitoring tool[2] was used to capture each event on the user's computer in a centralized database (only the owner can explore the log in raw format). To guarantee the privacy of personal data, real data resides in the knowledge base, only encoded information of document metadata and action logs (no content and physical files) are sent to our system for the experiments.

Relationship. All explicit semantic relations are represented in the form of RDF predicates (Table 3). Some explicit relations are symmetric, while others have inverse relations (displayed in Table 3 in parentheses). Concerning the implicit relations, as we could not obtain the contents due to privacy, we only construct a number of attribute-based and time-based relations (Table 3).

4.1.2 Collaborative Wiki

The second dataset (named **Collaboration**) is a intranet portal used within L3S Research Center or communicating daily research activities. The portal has been continuously used in the course of 6 years and includes research information such as collaboration projects with external partners, internal research activities, as well as administration information of the lab. Documents are mostly in hypertext format, but also include digital files uploaded to the portal. In contrast to the **Person** dataset, the **Collaboration** dataset has no full-fledged ontologies, and the documents are not associated with abstract concepts. Nevertheless, the portal runs on top of the Dokuwiki platform[3], and supports annotation via different plug-in: Tagging with words, showing document author and contributors, etc. For the activity history, it uses Squid cache[4] to log HTTP access requests to the portal resources. In addition, an archiving tool is developed to log all revisions of the portal documents, together with their edit activities. The dataset are obtained in the form of an archive with all raw data content.

Relationship. Compared with the dataset **Person**, the documents in this dataset have much less explicit semantic relations, and all come from the structure of the portal (Table 3). However, as we have access to contents of the documents, we can build more implicit relations, listed in Table 3. The tagged-token-based (TTB) relations are constructed as follows. First, we extracted the content of all documents from the portal developing a Dokuwiki parser and using a MIME paser. Next, we sample the documents related to 4 different collaborative research projects, tokenize the corresponding texts, and remove highly frequent words and stop words. An

experienced colleague working in numerous projects is asked to annotate the tokens with respect to 6 different classes: 1) Person or Person role, 2) Location, 3) Organisation, 4 Technical word (e.g., middleware), 5) Professional domain (e.g., meeting), and 6) Project-specific terms. Each class is then treated as one attribute of the documents, with their tagged tokens treated as values, for calculating the corresponding attribute-based relation.

4.2 Experiment Setup

4.2.1 Baselines

We evaluate our system against the following baselines.

Recency-Frequency: This set of baselines use values of the activity-based scoring functions to provide the final ranking, without using propagation. This includes the two recency-based methods MRU and Ebb, and their frequency-based variants, denoted by FMRU and FEbb (Table 1). For polynomial and Weibull functions, we evaluate only the frequency-based methods, denoted by FPD and FWei, as they are shown to outperform the recency versions [25].

PageRank: This baseline ranks the documents by their authority scores, estimated in a graph of documents relations. The scores of documents are initialized equally. It can be thought of as the propagation method without the activity-based rankings and the semantics of relation. PageRank is shown to be effective in file retrieval tasks in non-semantic systems [30]. In our case, we adapt the PageRank algorithm by aggregating all relations between two documents into one single relation, with the weighting score obtained by averaging out all the individual relation weights.

SUPRA: Papadakis et al. [24] proposed combining the activity-based ranking results with a one-step propagation in a layered framework. The relations are constructed simply by identifying documents accessed in the same sessions. In our scenarios, we define the "sessions" to be one unit time step, which is one hour. We only study the MRU decay prior and simple connectivity transition matrix for this baseline, as it is among the best performing variants and requires no parameter tuning. We use the implementation provided by the authors[5].

4.2.2 Parameter Tuning

In all experiments, we set the granularity of the time intervals to be one day. We use MRU as the baseline scoring method for building the trading data. The parameters of the activity-based scoring functions are chosen empirically via grid search with respect to the success rate at 1 for the access prediction task (see Section 4.3). The best performing for each function is as follows. For FEbb, $S = 90$; for FPD, $\alpha = 1.5$; for FWei, $s = 0.9, \alpha = 0.3$. The damping factor is set to $\lambda = 0.25$, as for the standard PageRank as well as for our propagation method. As for the regularization parameter θ, we experiment with a few number of different values and see no significant changes in the performance, possibly due to the small number of dimensions of our relation weight vectors X. We empirically set $\theta = 1$.

4.3 Experiments on Revisit Prediction

The first experiment aims to evaluate how well the system performs in the revisit prediction task, i.e., predicting the likelihood that a document will be accessed by the user in the

---

[2]http://usercontext.opendfki.de/
[3]https://www.dokuwiki.org/dokuwiki
[4]http://www.squid-cache.org

[5]http://sourceforge.net/projects/supraproject

Dataset Person		Dataset Collaboration	
Relation(s)	*Description*	*Relation(s)*	*Description*
hasPart (isPartOf)	Relations between a container document (folder, albums, etc.) and individual files	page_namespace	Relations between a page and a dokuwiki namespace
hasNewerVersion (isNewerVersionOf)	Two revisions of a document	hyperlink	A webpage is linked to other page
hasLocation (isLocationOf)	A document is tagged with a location	attachement	A webpage is attached with a file
hasRecipient (isRecipientOf)	Relations between emails and the recipient		
hasSender (isSenderOf)	Relations between emails and the recipient		
creates (isCreatedBy)	Relations between documents and owners		
isRelatedTo	Two document contents are related		
hasTopic (isTopicOf)	A resource has a topic, which is another resource		
Attribute(s)	*Description*	*Attribute(s)*	*Description*
member	Relations based on shared number of members annotated with the documents	contributors	Relations between shared number of contributors to the page
containedThing	Relations based on related Thing instances	TTB	Tagged token-based relations
task	Relations based on tasks tagged to the documents	tag	Relations between tags of each dokuwiki page

Table 3: Selected semantic relations used in two datasets **Person** and **Collaboration**. The upper part corresponds to the explicit relations, the lower-part corresponds to the attribute-based implicit relations.

subsequent time point. This is the well-established task in research on web recommendation [10], personal file retrieval [14], etc. We evaluate the correlation between the predicted rank of a document at a time point t and the real document accesses at the time point $t+1$. Inspired by [18], we employ the following evaluation metrics.

1. *Success at 1* (**S@1**): It quantifies the fraction of time points t (from all time points of study) at which the first-ranked documents according to a ranking method is truly accessed at $t+1$. This resembles the Precision at 1 (P@1) metric in traditional retrieval tasks.

2. *Success at 10* (**S@10**): It quantifies the fraction of documents truly accessed in the next time point, from all documents ranked at top 10, averaging over all time points of study in the micro-average manner (i.e., per-document average).

3. *Average Ranking Position* (**ARP**): This metric starts from the subsequent document access backwards. It computes the average ranking position of accessed documents as produced by a ranking method. The lower the value is, the better the performance of the corresponding ranking system.

For each dataset, we run the burst detection algorithm to identify the "interesting" time points (Section 3.4), resulting in 122 points in the dataset Person and 203 points in Collaboration. We partition each set of time points into the training and testing sets using 5-fold cross validation.

Results. The average results over the two datasets are summarized in Table 4. Among the ranking methods, PageRank has the worst predictive performance. This is because it ignores the recency and frequency signals of the documents. Other interesting observation is that for activity-based ranking methods, adding frequency into the ranking function did not really help in revisit prediction: FMRU performs worse than MRU and FEbb performs worse than Ebb in all metrics, although the differences are not significant. At the first look, this contradicts somewhat to previous findings on the influence of frequency in document ranking [25]. However, by performing a deeper analysis, we believe that the cause stems from the fact that a revisiting action typically involves very recent documents, as also argued in [18]. Aggregating

recency scores over a time span (10 day-window as in our case) can introduce some documents belonging to different tasks and thus bring more noise to the ranking results. One possible way to solve this is to design a more flexible time window size which adapt to the user's task. We leave this direction to be explored in the future.

Method	S@1	S@10	ARP
MRU	0.162	0.310	76
FMRU	0.131	0.291	87
Ebb	0.213	0.357	65
FEbb	0.193	0.328	70
FPD	0.195	0.331	68
FWei	0.220	0.378	60
PageRank	0.120	0.231	112
SUPRA	0.320$^\triangle$	0.671$^\triangle$	39
MRU+Prop	0.353$^\triangle$	0.710$^\blacktriangle$	34
FMRU+Prop	0.402$^\triangle$	0.762$^\blacktriangle$	30
Ebb+Prop	0.416$^\triangle$	0.733$^\triangle$	42
FEbb+Prop	0.452$^\blacktriangle$	0.780$^\blacktriangle$	25
FPD+Prop	**0.512**$^\blacktriangle$	**0.818**$^\blacktriangle$	**20**
FWei+Prop	0.430$^\triangle$	0.750$^\blacktriangle$	40

Table 4: **Results on the revisit prediction task. The upper part reports baseline results, the lower part reports results of the proposed system. Symbol $\triangle$ confirms significance against the baseline MRU. Symbol $\blacktriangle$ confirms both significance against the baselines MRU and SUPRA.**

Compared to the sole activity-based ranking methods, adding propagation shows clear improvements in prediction, starting from the baseline SUPRA. Bringing semantic relations into the propagation improves even further, producing significantly higher performance for all case of temporal priors. The best performing method, propagation with polynomial decay prior, improves the results by 60% as compared to SUPRA. In contrast to the observed trend in the activity-based ranking, here the combination of frequency and recency with the propagation actually produces better results than the only combination between recency and the propagation. This is because using frequency makes the scores of all documents higher (Equation 3.2), thus enhance the contribution in the propagation point, as there will be more documents with non-zero scores than in the case of

	Dataset Person				Dataset Collaboration			
Method	P@1	P@10	NDCG@10	MAP	P@1	P@10	NDCG@10	MAP
MRU	0.365	0.283	0.219	0.207	0.461	0.375	0.285	0.267
FMRU	0.329	0.307	0.221	0.213	0.457	0.346	0.271	0.258
Ebb	0.407	0.350	0.258	0.218	0.507	0.392	0.287	0.256
FEbb	0.391	0.292	0.217	0.213	0.493	0.357	0.275	0.260
FPD	0.382	0.290	0.214	0.220	0.480	0.400	0.301	0.288
FWei	0.443	0.402	0.324	0.293	0.552	0.424	0.319	0.290
PageRank	0.318	0.251	0.195	0.164	0.388	0.325	0.195	0.204
SUPRA$^\triangle$	0.547	0.502	0.426	0.389	0.590	0.469	0.345	0.333
MRU+Prop$^\triangle$	0.518	0.456	0.358	0.333	0.561	0.448	0.334	0.340
FMRU+Prop$^\triangle$	0.592	0.511	0.431	0.366	0.630	0.493	0.400	0.361
Ebb+Prop$^\triangle$	0.615	0.529	0.503	0.481	0.752	0.642	0.501	0.476
FEbb+Prop$^\blacktriangle$	**0.728**	0.621	**0.556**	**0.540**	**0.821**	**0.679**	**0.528**	**0.519**
FPD+Prop$^\blacktriangle$	0.710	**0.635**	0.523	0.510	0.780	0.667	0.500	0.482
FWei+Prop	0.678	0.575	0.521	0.478	0.715	0.634	0.479	0.460

Table 5: Performances of ranking methods in the user study. Symbols $^\triangle$,$^\blacktriangle$ indicate the significance test in all scores of the method against MRU and SUPRA respectively.

using recency only. This effect is similar to smoothing in standard information retrieval.

4.4 User-perceived Evaluation

We next evaluate the effectiveness of our proposed system with respect to the user perception and appreciation. We do this by simulating the way users re-access and re-assess the documents in their collections. The experiment is set up as follows. We first ask the user to pick up different time periods of one week length from the past, such that each week covers some prominent events or tasks, and thus manifests considerable amount of user activities on many documents. For example, the user can choose the week when she conducts intensive work on a scientific publication, or on a project review. Within each week of study, we extract the set of documents that draw high attention from the user back in the time. These documents can be chosen manually from the user (e.g., dataset Person), or from the set of highest-frequently accessed document (e.g., dataset Collaboration). Then, the user is presented with the document information and contents[6], and is asked the question "What do you prefer to do with this document as for now ?". The options are:

1. *Pin*: The document is needed for now, I would keep it as short-cut or highlight.
2. *Show*: I would keep the document, but not in the highlight.
3. *Fade*: I would not keep the document.
4. *Trash*: I would delete the document *now*.

Each option corresponds to the user's perception of the current importance of the document, from the highest score (*Pin*) to the lowest one (*Trash*). From the perspective of information retrieval, these can be treated as the relevance feedback, and to that extent, we can use standard IR metrics to evaluate the ranking system.

In the dataset Person, each assessor chose 4 weeks to evaluate. For the dataset Collaboration, 2 assessors are asked to choose 3 weeks per each, all are related to joint events they participated in. The activity history is constructed accord-

---

[6]For the Person dataset, the user study is conducted in each computer of the assessor, thereby all information and contents are accessible.

ing to this pair of users. The ranking methods are configured to provide the ranks of documents with respect to the same time step of the user's evaluations. For the Person, we cannot calculate the inter-agreement as the documents to be ranked are usually private. For the Collaboration, the inter-agreement under the Cohen's Kappa is 0.6, suggesting the shared perception of the raters on the evaluated documents.

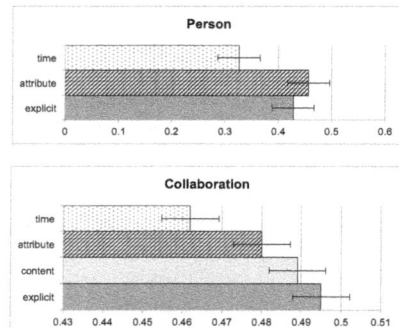

Figure 3: Performance of propagation framework (measured in MAP) with ablated relation sets

Result. The results are summarized in Table 5 for each dataset, as measured as precision, NDCG and MAP scores. The same trend as the prediction task can be observed here: The activity-based ranking methods perform better than PageRank but worse than SUPRA and our propagation variants. Similarly, the frequency-based functions perform worse than the recency ones as isolated methods, but improve the results when combining with the propagation. All propagation methods except the MRU prior-based give higher results than SUPRA. In addition, compared to the prediction task, the performance of all methods in the user-perceived study are slightly higher. This suggests that many documents, although not accessed subsequently, are still deemed "important" to the user. Of the two datasets, methods produce higher performance in the Collaboration than in Person. This can be explained in two ways. Firstly, data in Collaboration is more homogenous, and the model is learnt with respect to the group of users. In contrast, in Person, the

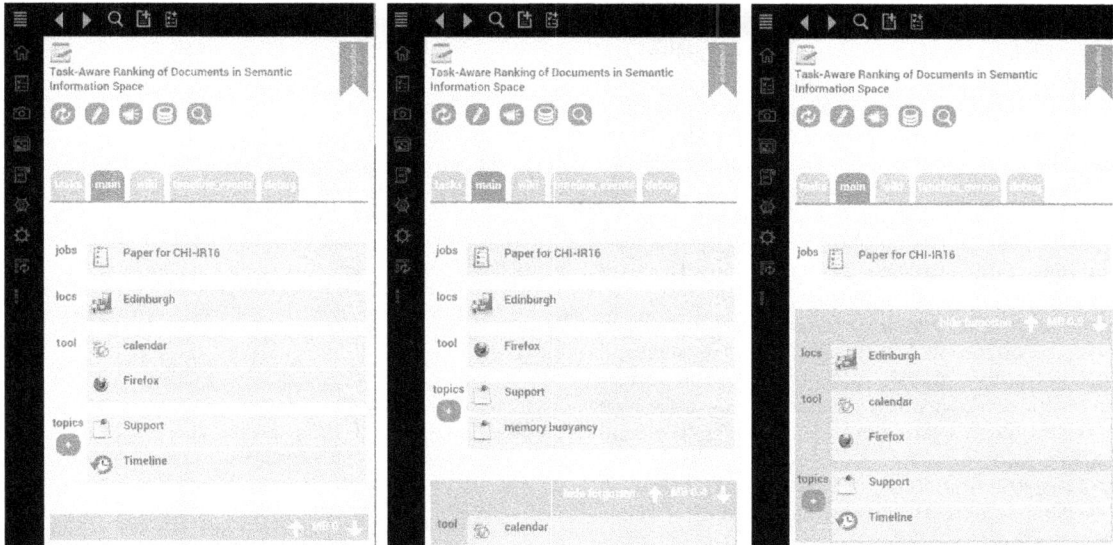

Figure 4: Illustration of decluttering functionality in the Semantic Desktop. From left to right: The list of recommended documents at different cut-off (MB) thresholds, 0 (left), 0.4 (middle), 0.9 (right)

data are highly diverse and the model is learnt over each user, resulting in higher variance level. Secondly, when assessing documents in the collaboration environment, users tend to be more skeptical, and will not likely to assess one document as "Trash" unless completely certain. This results in a higher number of relevant documents than in the case of the dataset Person.

Influence of Semantic Relations.

Next, we study the influence of different types of semantic relations. We use *FEbb+Prop* method as it performs the best in the user study. The evaluation is done via an ablation study: We repeatedly remove from the semantic graph the relations of a certain group (see Section 3.5), then re-execute the framework and re-evaluate using the user study. Finally, we observe the reduction in the performance of the system measured by MAP score (Figure 3). In both datasets, removing time-based relations cause the biggest loss in the performance, suggesting the highest influence of this relation type. This also agrees with the existing findings [18, 33]. In the dataset Person, removal of the explicit relations affects more than removal of attribute-based relations[7]. This suggests the higher contributions of human-defined relations in the dataset. On the other hand, in Collaboration, the attribute-based relations has higher influence than the explicit one. This reflects the characteristics of the dataset, as the tagged tokens are Dokuwiki tags are more representative than the other evidences.

4.5 Application: Reducing Information Overload in PIM

In addition to the empirical experiments, we also demonstrate the effectiveness of our system in real-world usage. We integrated memory buoyancy into the Semantic Desktop infrastructure (Section 4.1.1) used for *decluttering* information in the HTML5 UI of the Semantic Desktop designed to be used on desktop and mobile devices (see Figure 4).

For instance, after days of working in the Semantic Desktop accomplishing various tasks, many things were created in the knowledge base such as new tasks and sub-tasks, notes, new topics, persons, events, annotated web-pages, documents in different versions or only temporary relevant. That means, the user's desktop as well the UI's of the Semantic Desktop start to clutter. Imagine this over several years, lots of once relevant and now irrelevant materials are still shown and pile up, i.e., the PIM application is on the verge to build an information overload to its users.

Therefore, we apply the approach presented in this paper to enable the user to focus on the main concepts and resources such as documents of the current attention, thereby to "declutter" the PIM application without manual re-organisation efforts.[8] Figure 4 illustrates this functionality: a note is shown containing a text of this paper which was used to prepare the writing. Now choosing the "Main" tab, the related things are shown categorised according to their supertype such as Location (e.g., City, Building, Room) or Job (e.g., Process, Task). Now to focus on the currently most relevant things, only those things are shown above a certain threshold (displayed in the interface as MB or "Memory Buoyancy" in the gray bar; per default this bar is closed, but can be expanded to show "forgotten" things). The user is able to change the cut-off thresholds to show more forgotten things or to focus on most relevant from user interaction. The default threshold is set differently on the desktop (equal to 0.5) vs. being on a mobile (equal to 0.8) to account for a more focused information provision on a mobile (to reduce cognitive load and data consumption). A second functionality is to propose files to be forgotten (e.g., removing from the desktop and keeping them just in the Semantic Desktop cloud) if they drop below a certain threshold, thus also decluttering the user's desktop. All these things are associated in the semantic graph and the activity history logs. This shows the generalizability of our method: It does not only work with digital files, but can also be applied to any concepts, given the availability of their activity history logs.

---

[7]Recall that we could not construct the content-based relations in this dataset

[8]see also: https://pimo.opendfki.de/wp9-pilot/#9

5. CONCLUSIONS AND FUTURE WORK

In this paper, we have presented an adaptive ranking approach for identifying documents that are important to the current focus and task of the user. This contributes to helping the user in navigating and decluttering the growing information spaces. Based on the idea of managed forgetting, our framework unifies evidences from activity logs and semantic relations in a principled way for computing the memory buoyancy of resources. In our method we employ machine learning techniques that automatically learn from the user access history without manual supervision efforts.

Our experiments with two real-world datasets have shown that incorporating the importance propagation via semantic relations between resource significantly improves the performance of the method. As a proof of concept, we have also developed a prototypical system for decluttering personal information space using an existing Semantic Desktop.

This work is just the first step towards realizing managed forgetting. We plan to extend our approach to better tailor to particular scenarios (.e.g navigation on desktop is different from on mobile phones). We also plan a more in-depth user study in order to better understand the user expectation in several dimensions such as interactions and injecting human preferences (For instance, in which scenarios or domains the activity-based system works better than the activation, etc.) Other direction is the consideration of more complex user tasks in the learning model, for instance, investigating cross-device tasks or recurrent tasks.

Acknowledgements. This work was funded by the EU FP7 project ForgetIT (Grant No. 600826)[9].

6. REFERENCES

[1] B. Adrian, M. Klinkigt, H. Maus, and A. Dengel. Using iDocument for document categorization in Nepomuk Social Semantic Desktop. In *I-SEMANTICS*, pages 638–643, 2009.

[2] J. R. Anderson and L. J. Schooler. Reflections of the environment in memory. *Psychological Science*, 6(2):396–408, 1991.

[3] M. Awad, L. Khan, and B. Thuraisingham. Predicting www surfing using multiple evidence combination. *The VLDB Journal*, 17(3):401–417, 2008.

[4] L. Backstrom and J. Leskovec. Supervised random walks: Predicting and recommending links in social networks. In *WSDM*, pages 635–644, 2011.

[5] O. Bergman, R. Beyth-Marom, and R. Nachmias. The user-subjective approach to personal information management systems. *JASIST*, 54(9):872–878, 2003.

[6] O. Bergman, R. Beyth-Marom, R. Nachmias, N. Gradovitch, and S. Whittaker. Improved search engines and navigation preference in personal information management. *ACM TOIS*, 26(4):20, 2008.

[7] T. Blanc-Brude and D. L. Scapin. What do people recall about their documents?: Implications for desktop search tools. In *IUI*, pages 102–111, 2007.

[8] J. Chen, H. Guo, W. Wu, and W. Wang. iMecho: An Associative Memory Based Desktop Search System. In *CIKM*, pages 731–740, 2009.

[9] P.-A. Chirita, S. Costache, W. Nejdl, and R. Paiu. Beagle^{++}: Semantically enhanced searching and ranking on the desktop. In *ESWC*, pages 348–362, 2006.

[10] M. Connor and S. Spitzer. The places frecency algorithm. https://developer.mozilla.org/en-US/docs/Mozilla/Tech/Places/Frecency_algorithm, (Accessed Aug 31, 2015).

[11] S. Dumais, E. Cutrell, J. Cadiz, G. Jancke, R. Sarin, and D. C. Robbins. Stuff I've seen: A system for personal information retrieval and re-use. In *SIGIR*, pages 72–79, 2003.

[12] D. Elsweiler, M. Baillie, and I. Ruthven. Exploring memory in email refinding. *ACM TOIS*, 26(4):21, 2008.

[13] D. Fisher and P. Dourish. Social and temporal structures in everyday collaboration. In *SIGCHI*, pages 551–558, 2004.

[14] S. Fitchett and A. Cockburn. AccessRank: Predicting what users will do next. In *SIGCHI*, pages 2239–2242, 2012.

[15] S. Fitchett, A. Cockburn, and C. Gutwin. Improving navigation-based file retrieval. In *SIGCHI*, pages 2329–2338, 2013.

[16] J. Gemmell, G. Bell, and R. Lueder. Mylifebits: a personal database for everything. *CACM*, 49(1):88–95, 2006.

[17] W. Jones. *Keeping Found Things Found: The Study and Practice of Personal Information Management*. Morgan Kaufmann Publishers Inc., San Francisco, CA, USA, 2008.

[18] R. Kawase, G. Papadakis, E. Herder, and W. Nejdl. Beyond the usual suspects: Context-aware revisitation support. In *ACM Hypertext*, pages 27–36, 2011.

[19] J. Kleinberg. Bursty and hierarchical structure in streams. *KDD*, 7(4):373–397, 2003.

[20] D. C. Liu and J. Nocedal. On the limited memory BFG-S method for large scale optimization. *Mathematical programming*, 45(1-3):503–528, 1989.

[21] R. H. Logie. The functional organization and capacity limits of working memory. *Current Directions in Psychological Science*, 20(4):240–245, 2011.

[22] H. Maus, S. Schwarz, and A. Dengel. Weaving personal knowledge spaces into office applications. In *Integration of Practice-Oriented Knowledge Technology: Trends and Prospectives*, pages 71–82. Springer, 2013.

[23] C. Niederée, N. Kanhabua, F. Gallo, and R. H. Logie. Forgetful digital memory: Towards brain-inspired long-term data and information management. *ACM SIGMOD Record*, 44(2):41–46, 2015.

[24] G. Papadakis, R. Kawase, E. Herder, and C. Niederée. A layered approach to revisitation prediction. In *ICWE*, volume 6757, pages 258–273. 2011.

[25] M.-H. Peetz and M. De Rijke. Cognitive temporal document priors. In *ECIR*, pages 318–330. Springer, 2013.

[26] D. Quan, D. Huynh, and D. R. Karger. Haystack: A platform for authoring end user semantic web applications. In *ISWC*, pages 738–753. 2003.

[27] M. Ringel, E. Cutrell, S. Dumais, and E. Horvitz. Milestones in Time: The value of landmarks in retrieving information from personal stores. In *INTERACT*, volume 2003, pages 184–191, 2003.

[28] L. Sauermann, A. Bernardi, and A. Dengel. Overview and Outlook on the Semantic Desktop. In *Proceedings of the First Semantic Desktop Workshop at ISWC'05*, 2005.

[29] L. Sauermann, L. van Elst, and A. Dengel. PIMO – A Framework for Representing Personal Information Models. In *I-SEMANTICS*, J.UCS, pages 270–277, 2007.

[30] C. Soules and G. Ganger. Connections: Using context to enhance file search. In *SOSP*, pages 119–132, 2005.

[31] J. Teevan. How people recall search result lists. In *CHI (Extended Abstract)*, pages 1415–1420, 2006.

[32] T. Tran, A. Ceroni, M. Georgescu, K. D. Naini, and M. Fisichella. Wikipevent: Leveraging wikipedia edit history for event detection. In *Web Information Systems Engineering–WISE*, pages 90–108, 2014.

[33] T. Watanabe, T. Kobayashi, and H. Yokota. Fridal: A desktop search system based on latent interfile relationships. In *Software and Data Technologies*, pages 220–234. 2013.

[34] R. W. White, P. N. Bennett, and S. T. Dumais. Predicting short-term interests using activity-based search context. In *CIKM*, pages 1009–1018, 2010.

[9]http://www.forgetit-project.eu/

Behaviour Mining for Automatic Task-Keeping and Visualisations for Task-Refinding

Charlie Abela
Department of Intelligent Computer Systems
University of Malta
charlie.abela@um.edu.mt

Chris Staff
Department of Intelligent Computer Systems
University of Malta
chris.staff@um.edu.mt

ABSTRACT

When people perform some tasks on their desktop, they tend to spend a considerable amount of time looking back, establishing past references and remembering. A task contains an evolving collection of documents to which the user is referring and that are relevant to the task. In the case of Web documents people tend to rely on their organisational skills and use a variety of "keeping" and "re-finding" tools which traditionally include bookmarks, history and search, amongst others. This paper reports the results of surveys conducted to investigate the way that people keep and re-find Web based tasks. As tasks can be interrupted or conducted over different sessions a user needs to keep, re-find, and resume them. A prototype called *PiMxT* is also presented, which uses an incremental density-based clustering approach to automatically generate and keep task-clusters by considering the user's window and tab switching, and re-visitation behaviour. The algorithm attempts to identify those documents that pertain to the same task-cluster, and also when a switch between two documents is effectively a task-switch. *PiMxT* allows for searching and filtering across the task-clusters as well as task-resumption through different visualisations. This tool was evaluated through a usability study and a questionnaire, and it was found that the time taken by the 15 participants to re-find and resume tasks was on average 44% less in 77% of the cases. Furthermore, although the participants expected *PiMxT* to be more complete and accurate they all recognised its usefulness.

1. INTRODUCTION

When an individual performs some tasks on their desktops, whether it's searching for information on the Web, replying to emails or resuming writing some document which they've worked on the day before, they spend a considerable amount of time looking back, establishing past references and remembering [19]. To ease this chore individuals tend to keep information that they deem important so that they are able to re-find it at some later stage [15]. To do this, they

rely on their organisational skills and use an array of techniques and supporting tools [5, 16]. Yet most of these tools are application-specific and consider the user's information-seeking activities as unrelated events, unlike the way they actually organise the things that they want to keep for future reference [20, 27]. More specifically [27] refers to the concept of a task which we define as *"an evolving collection of documents to which the user is referring and that are relevant to the task"*.

Research studies conducted to investigate how individuals tend to keep and re-find documents found that a myriad of personal concocted methods are used and that no one specific tool was available that completely satisfied a user's keeping and re-finding needs [15, 5]. On the other hand, [20] conducts a survey where they investigate re-finding of a task context and suggests that browsers should provide support for task re-finding.

In this paper Morris et al's work [20] is leveraged to investigate whether there have been any changes in the way that people keep and re-find information related to their Web-based tasks. Two surveys were conducted over a period of two years where the emphasis was on methods for keeping and re-finding tasks rather than single documents. The findings from the surveys indicate that the *status-quo* persists. People still use different keeping and re-finding methods, and they adapt these methods depending on the tools made available to them and whether the documents are related to short-term or long-term standing tasks. Based on these findings an innovative solution that addresses both keeping and re-finding of tasks is being proposed.

This research presents an automatic task-keeping approach that exploits automatic task-identification [22, 4] to relieve the user from having to resort to different keeping methods, irrespective of whether the user is working on short-term or long-term standing tasks. This approach uses an extended version of the *iDeTaCt* algorithm [1], called *X-iDeTaCt* to automatically generate and keep task-clusters.

The interesting aspect behind *iDeTaCt* is that it generates task-clusters by only considering the user's switching and re-visitation behaviour while she is performing some task. *X-iDeTaCt* also takes into consideration the type of switching performed by the user, that is, whether she clicked on a hyperlink or whether she used the back and forward buttons, as well as particular search patterns. The algorithm was evaluated using the tasks dataset collected during a controlled experiment described in [1], which consists of a set of pre-defined tasks performed by 20 participants. The average recall for *X-iDeTaCt* was found to be 80% in certain

CHIIR '16, March 13-17, 2016, Carrboro, NC, USA

© 2016 ACM. ISBN 978-1-4503-3751-9/16/03. . . $15.00

DOI: http://dx.doi.org/10.1145/2854946.2854966

cases and this is a considerable improvement over the recall obtained for *iDeTaCt* which was closer to 50% [1] using the same dataset.

A prototype called *PiMxT* (Personal information Management for Tasks) is also presented, which uses the keeping method based on *X-iDeTaCt* and further allows the user to re-find and resume tasks. *PiMxT* combines keyword search and time-window filtering with different exploratory visualisations. This prototype was evaluated through a 5-day usability study to gain both quantitative and qualitative feedback. 15 individuals participated in this evaluation during which system-usage was logged. At the end of the 5-day period a one-to-one interview was conducted during which each participant was asked to re-find some of the tasks that they had worked on during the evaluation period, without and with *PiMxT*. This was followed by a questionnaire through which qualitative feedback was collected about the participants' experience using the tool. Although a longer usability study would have been preferred, when it comes to evaluating PIM systems through field studies one has to find a compromise between the time-commitment required from the participants, the potential disruption of the participants' usual working habits, and more importantly the kind of personal information that the participants are required to expose [16]. Due to this time limitation and potential disruptions the generalisability of the results is somewhat restricted, nevertheless these are still considered to be interesting and potentially very promising.

In the rest of the paper the authors first present research that is closely related to their own. Section 3 discusses the findings from two investigative surveys, which is followed by Section 4 that presents the automatic task-keeping method based on the extended algorithm *X-iDeTaCt*. This is then followed by Section 5 which introduces the prototype *PiMxT* and describes the concepts behind the various visualisations. The evaluation methodology used for *PiMxT* and the relevant findings are discussed in Section 6 which is then followed by the conclusion.

2. RELATED WORK

2.1 Keeping and Re-Finding

There is a substantial amount of research on how individuals tend to keep and re-find information. In their seminal paper [15] Jones et al highlighted the problem of "keeping" and "re-finding" information and the need to address this through the development of suitable tools. In line with this work, research conducted by [9] presented *Stuff I've Seen* which addresses desktop search by indexing all the information that an individual sees on her computer and uses context cues such as time, author, thumbnails and previews to enhance the way information is presented to the user. Later on [8] presented *Phlat*, which combined keyword and property-value search with an intuitive interface and exploited content tagging.

Web browsers provide various tools, such as bookmarks, history and the back button to allow people to get back at the pages that they have visited. The average probability that a page is effectively re-visited was recently found to be close to 45% by [24]. In [17] the focus was on exploiting re-visitation to re-find already visited Web pages. They presented a dynamic browser toolbar that provided suggestions based on the pages the user had visited. The prototype that

is presented in Section 5.1 uses the browser's window and tab switching activity and exploits re-visitation to keep and re-find tasks.

2.2 Task-Keeping and Re-Finding

When it comes to "keeping" information related to Web-based tasks, tools such as bookmarks and history have various limitations that affect their usability. Bruce [6] refers to an "intelligent automated helper" that "magically" solves people's challenges associated with the management of collections or tasks.

In his thesis [19], Mayer presents an integrative history and visualization tool entitled *SessionGraphs*. The tool allowed a user to view her browsing activity as an animated, interactive graph and to organise the visualisations around sessions and tasks. Similarly in *PiMxT*, different visualisations are used to support task re-finding, however differently from [19], the task-keeping method is automated.

The search bar presented in [20] persistently maintains a hierarchical Web history organised around search topics and queries. It assists users in organising complex searches and re-acquiring the context of a suspended search, based mainly on topic and query-driven groupings. The multitasking bar presented by [27] copes with both multiple tasks as well as multiple session tasks. They considered a task as having different states and it was up to the user to maintain and organise a task. The approach adopted in this paper however aims at transparently automating the task-cluster generation without requiring any user intervention. Furthermore, in the case of a task that is performed over multiple sessions the *X-iDeTaCt* algorithm attempts to maintain the same task-cluster.

The task-keeping problem was considered from a task-identification perspective by [22]. The developed prototype, called *SWISH*, identified the documents that pertained to a task by first computing document content similarity and then applying a maximal clique-finding algorithm over the user's switching activities. Unlike *SWISH*, the authors currently do not exploit the content of the accessed documents, however they consider the incremental characteristics underlying the information-finding process.

In [4] a PageRank-like association heuristic was used to compute the association between windows opened on the desktop. The application was called *Taskposé* and presented a visualisation through which windows that were frequently clicked in sequence, were displayed closer together. Although documents were grouped together there was no re-finding mechanism in place. In this paper however, task-clusters are kept and tool-support is furthermore provided to aid re-finding.

A semi-automated approach that addresses the problem of task identification was adopted by [7] that used activity-log analysis to group the accessed resources based on cues generated by an individual while performing some task. The research reported in this paper also uses a dedicated application plug-in to collect information about the user's activity. A global Web history that includes information about all the accessed Web documents and queries, is maintained and exploited.

Table 1: Methods for Keeping

Methods	S1	S2
Leave windows/tabs open	56.5%	83.01%
Bookmark only important pages	38.2%	54.9%
Take notes about important pages	11%	22.88%
Bookmark all pages	22%	14.9%
Important URLs saved to document	22.7%	13.73%
All URLs saved in another document	20.4%	9.8%
Print out important pages	11.4%	8.5%
Close all windows/tabs	6.2%	3.27%

Table 2: Methods for Re-Finding

Methods	S1	S2
Search through open windows/tabs	52.3%	80.1%
Search through bookmarks	48.5%	64.71%
Search the browser's history	30.4%	64.1%
Use a search engine	79.6%	60.13%
Use browser's auto-complete	21.3%	44.4%
Check written/digital notes	29.1%	33.3%

3. INVESTIGATING KEEPING AND RE-FINDING

In [15] and [5] the focus was on the methods that individuals use for keeping and re-finding documents. The conclusion was that people tend to use a variety of keeping and re-finding methods and that their choice of methods is very flexible and creative. In this research the authors are interested in methods for keeping and re-finding of tasks, where a task is defined as *"an evolving collection of documents to which the user is referring and that are relevant to the task"*.

In this regards, over the past two years, two surveys were conducted intended to investigate the status of "keeping" and "re-finding" methods, with an emphasis on tasks. The first survey labelled *S1* was available for 15 days and 438 participants (47% were males and 53% were females) fully completed the survey. In the second survey *S2* the number of participants that fully completed the questionnaire was 153 (51.3% were males and 48.7% were females). In both surveys the participants were mainly undergraduate and postgraduate students and their age ranged between 18 and 60 years.

S1 first investigated how individuals tend to keep and refind different kinds of collections such as files, photographs, music playlists, emails and Web documents. Then it investigated how the participants tend to keep and re-find task-related documents on their desktop. In *S2* the focus was primarily on Web-related tasks and the participants were asked the same set of questions that were had asked in *S1*. In particular participants were asked about (i.) the methods that they adopt to keep Web pages related to a task when they have to switch to some other task and (ii.) the methods that they adopt when they need to re-find Web pages that pertain to a previous task-context.

The results from both *S1* and *S2* are presented in Table 1 and Table 2. Leaving windows and tabs open to keep pages available and then sifting through them to re-find the pages is increasingly becoming the predominant way of keeping and re-finding. Browsers nowadays are able to support this method by providing the ability to restore sessions and to re-open recently closed windows. Furthermore, a host of different browser plug-ins are available that provide similar facilities.

When it comes to traditional tools provided by (or through) the browser, bookmarks are still considered to be an important keeping tool, however people still forget about their bookmarks when they need to re-find stuff. Almost equally popular is the browser's history, which nowadays includes improved search and filtering facilities. Trailing slightly behind in popularity as a re-finding method is the use of a search engine and facilities such as auto-completion.

Furthermore, it is evident from both *S1* and *S2* that the participants use more than one tool for keeping and re-finding. To understand better how these participants utilise and combine the various keeping and re-finding tools, the participants of *S2* were asked whether they would like to be interviewed about the matter and 15 accepted. Table 3 provides highlights from this interview of five representative participants.

The findings from *S1* and *S2* validate the research results found by [15, 5], more specifically that, as yet there isn't one single tool that completely satisfies the individual for both keeping and re-finding. Furthermore, from the interviews it transpired that people use a mix of tools and techniques to address the short and long term task keeping and re-finding needs. The findings from these surveys were taken into consideration in the realisation of an automatic task-keeping solution, discussed in the following sections, that also provides also for task-refinding and resumption.

4. BEHAVIOUR MINING FOR TASK-KEEPING

The research work described in [1] describes the incremental density-based clustering algorithm *iDeTaCt* and its evaluation using a tasks dataset collected during a controlled experiment. The 20 participants in this experiment performed three predefined information-seeking tasks using three different execution strategies: sequential-with no interruptions, interrupted-single session, interrupted-multiple sessions. The average recall for the interrupted-single session was found to be close to 50%, however a number of the accessed documents were not being clustered at all. To address these issues an extended version of the algorithm, referred to as *X-iDeTaCt* was implemented and this was used to keep task-clusters for future use.

4.1 iDeTaCt: incremental density-based clustering

iDeTaCt considers accessed documents as nodes and the switching between any two such documents is used to compute a weighted edge. The algorithm was inspired from [11] and relies on the idea that the neighbourhood of a node up to some given radius ϵ defines the *"importance"* of that node. Nodes that have a minimum number, η, of other nodes at a distance less than ϵ are termed as *core nodes*. On the other hand, a node that has no such neighbourhood is given the status of *weak node*, unless it is contained within the neighbourhood of a core node, in which case it is assigned the status of a *border node*. Thus ϵ and η ensure that node neighbourhoods are dense areas.

The clustering of documents that pertain to the same task can be represented by a graph and *iDeTaCt* allows for the following graph updates:

i. the *creation* of a new cluster: when the association between two nodes exceeds the ϵ threshold;

ii. *merging* of two clusters: when either a core or bor-

Table 3: Statements about Keeping and Re-finding

User	Keeping and Re-finding
User 1	*Predominantly uses opened windows and tabs, and organises them regularly. She keeps "collections" of tabs in the same window for e.g. social network profile, email and news portal to the left while the other navigated tabs related to her tasks to the right. She rarely uses bookmarks. Re-finding pages related to specific tasks is at times difficult, especially if tasks were worked upon weeks or months ago.*
User 2	*Uses opened windows and tabs for the short to medium term tasks and bookmarks for long term tasks. He does not use any particular method for opening/keeping tabs. He irregularly organises bookmarks (mainly when starting a new important task) and finds it at times difficult to re-find long-term tasks using bookmarks.*
User 3	*She tends to start a task and finishes it so that she is productive. She tries to limit multi-tasking by compartmentalising activities related to the current task. She is very organised and leaves windows and tabs open (never shuts down). In case that she needs to restart or the machine crashes, she restores the session using a session manager plug-in in her browser. She also uses third party applications, in particular one that allows for colour coding and labelling of different tasks. She states that for her re-finding is rather efficient.*
User 4	*In between tasks and on a regular basis he switches between his social network page and email. He mainly uses the browser's history for re-finding, however he uses also bookmarks. The downside is that he rarely re-finds stuff by browsing his bookmarks. At times he clears parts of the history to remove sensitive browsed information. Re-finding in his case is not that straight forward, especially when pages are accessed weeks or months before. In which case he uses the search engine and re-queries.*
User 5	*He tends to leave windows and tabs opened and organised by topic. A new window is opened whenever a new topic/theme/task is started. He also uses bookmarks for storing documents in the long-term, which he organises on a regular basis. He uses a third party application to save an interesting article that he wants to get back to later on (e.g. an article related to research which is not currently in focus).*

der node in one cluster gets strongly associated with another core or border node in another cluster;

iii. *absorption* (a growing cluster): when the association between a core or a border node and a new node exceeds the threshold ϵ.

The algorithm uses an association edge-weighting function $W : \mathbf{R} \to \mathbf{R}$ that maps the number of window-switches between two documents to an edge weight $w(u, v)$. This edge weight is inversely proportional to the number of window-switches. Thus a higher number of switches will result in a lower edge weighting. This is similar to the *proximity* and *influence* functions used in [11, 13] respectively, whereby two nodes are considered to be closer together if the edge weight between them is less. The edge-weighting function $W(\frac{n}{h})$ is based on the Epanechnikov kernel since this is a smooth function and is defined in Equation 1.

$$W(x) = \begin{cases} \frac{3}{4}(1 - x^2) & |x| \leq 1 \\ 0 & \text{else} \end{cases} \quad (1)$$

The basic idea behind kernel density estimations is to estimate the density function at a point x using neighbouring observations. In our case $x = \frac{n}{h}$, where n is the number of edges between any two nodes and h is a defined constant. We do this to scale the weights.

4.2 Extending iDeTaCt with Event types

The *iDeTaCt* algorithm suffers from a rather low recall (approximately 50%) and the edge-weights linking a number of acccessed documents that were labelled as *weak nodes* never exceeded the ϵ threshold with the consequence that these were not being clustered. The extended version, called *X-iDeTaCt* addresses these issues in two ways: (i) by considering the type of switch and (ii) by queueing those nodes that did not cluster immediately and definitely resolve them to a cluster after some decay threshold is exceeded (unless they had already been resolved).

4.2.1 *Computing Semantic Proximity*

In *X-iDeTaCt* "semantic" information related to three different switches is captured and exploited to determine the strength of the relation between the accessed pages. When an individual clicks on a hyperlink within a page, the explicit linking of the two pages is taken up by the algorithm as has been done by other link-based algorithms like PageRank [23]. Similarly the use of the back and forward buttons to revisit pages, although their popularity is on the decline as highlighted by [24], also indicates a possible relation between the visited pages since these are also seen within the same window. Nevertheless this kind of switch is considered to be indicative of a slightly weaker relation than the previous one, since the user might be switching between two, totally unrelated pages. Furthermore, *X-iDeTaCt* also considers search queries due to the ensuing hub-and-spoke navigation.

Table 4: Switch-type Valuation

Switch-type	Value
Search followed by Hyperlink	+2
Hyperlink	+1.5
Back and Forward buttons	+1

X-iDeTaCt is complimented with a valuation mechanism (see Table 4) through which different types of switches are assigned a value in a similar way that ObjectRank [3] assigns different weightings to different relationships. A switch is by default assigned a value of 1, however in the case of the three switches mentioned previously, this is increased by some relative amount, to emphasise the importance of that switch. The algorithm uses these accumulated values to compute what is referred to as the *"semantic proximity"* (semprox), defined in Equation 2, which is a modified version of the *proximity* defined earlier in Section 4.1.

$$W(x) = \begin{cases} \frac{3}{4}(1 - semprox^2) & |semprox| \leq 1 \\ 0 & \text{else} \end{cases} \quad (2)$$

4.2.2 *Resolving Weak Nodes*

To resolve those pages (nodes) that keep falling through the clustering process the concept of *late clustering* is introduced. Whenever a node cannot be immediately clustered, this is not only labelled as *weak*, but it is also queued. This happens because the algorithm does not have enough information to decide whether to cluster such nodes with an existing cluster or whether to create a new cluster. It could be the case however, that over time, new information is received that allows *X-iDeTaCt* to cluster them appropriately.

Nonetheless, there are situations whereby after a span of time from the last access, a definite clustering decision about a node could not be made. To address this, the algorithm keeps track of the number of switches made between all the nodes and uses a polynomial decay-based mechanism similar to the one adopted in [25], together with a threshold. When this threshold is exceeded, *X-iDeTaCt* classifies the document into the nearest cluster. This cluster will the one from which the *weak node* has the smallest *semantic proximity* (even though this does not exceed ϵ).

With the introduction of the *semantic proximity* and *late clustering* the average recall of *X-iDeTaCt* was found to be approximately 80% when the dataset from [1] was used and in particular when using the tasks that were performed in sequence and without interruptions. The recall dropped to approximately 75% when the tasks with interruptions were considered.

4.2.3 *Keeping Task-Clusters*

The *X-iDeTaCt* algorithm can be used either online as well as offline. In either case the generated clusters are persisted as *turtle*[1] files, which is essentially a compact and natural form of RDF.

The structure of each cluster file was partially inspired from GraphML[2] and includes general information about the cluster, such as a unique cluster ID, a timestamp of the last update made to that cluster, as well as references to all the switches (edges) made between accessed pages (nodes).

Each of the switch descriptions links a parent node with a child node and includes also the weight from the computed *semantic proximity*. For each node in the cluster there is a unique ID based on the URL, a set of keywords from the window caption (captured when the page was accessed), as well as a weight that is a combination of the number of incident edges and the type of node (whether its a core, border or weak node). This weight is used to compute a ranking for all the nodes in the cluster. In this way it is possible to identify what is referred to as the *"Most Significant Document"* in the cluster.

The algorithm automatically updates the relevant cluster or clusters depending on whether new ones are created and/or whether a number of clusters are merged together.

5. TASK RE-FINDING AND RESUMPTION

Section 4 described the success obtained by *X-iDeTaCt* when using the data from the aforementioned controlled experiment. However, the authors wanted to verify how accurate and useful the algorithm was when used in a "normal" user environment where users are expected to perform different task-based activities such as searching for a task or within a task, interacting with automatically separated tasks that contain the same keyword, and effectively resuming a task. To do this a prototype was built for the users so they could perform these task-based activities after *X-iDeTaCt* has automatically clustered their tasks.

The implemented *PiMxT* prototype uses *X-iDeTaCt* and addresses task re-finding and resumption through different

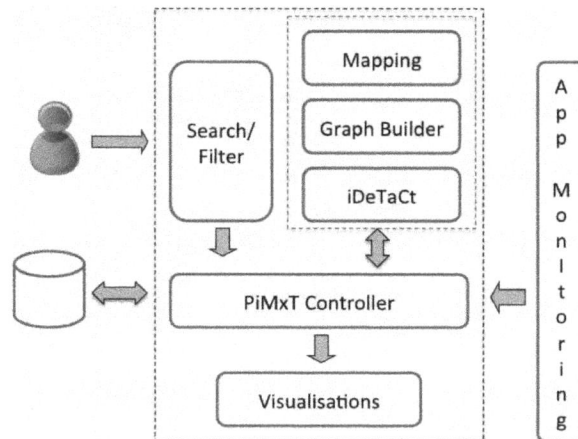

Figure 1: PiMxT Architecture

visualisations. In this case the authors leverage on existing work [9, 19] and experiment with different visualisations whose design is based on Shneiderman's visual information-seeking mantra "Overview first, zoom and filter, then details-on-demand" [26].

PiMxT's UI is still reasonably rudimentary and would ideally be more deeply embedded within the operating system's user interface. Recognising that participating users were most likely to use a variety of operating systems, the prototype was constructed as a Java application instead.

5.1 PiMxT: Personal Task Management

The architecture of *PiMxT* is shown in Figure 1 and includes both the keeping, and the re-finding and resuming components. The keeping component uses an application-monitoring layer whereby it is possible for different plug-ins to be used to track the events that a user generates when interacting with particular applications such as browsers, email clients and other OS-specific applications. In this paper, only a Firefox[3] plug-in is used, which is an adapted version of the Dragontalk plug-in[4]. The plug-in maps each of the user's switches to an event model as explained in [2].

The stream of captured browsing events are mapped onto unique event objects and passed on to a graph builder component that verifies whether the URL (which the user switches to) has already been indexed or not and updates the *activity graph* accordingly. This graph is undirected and can easily grow to several hundreds of nodes and considerably more edges over a short period of time. For instance, in the graphs we collected from the controlled experiment, which lasted on average 1.5 hours, the average number of pages visited was of approximately 92 pages while the number of switches was approximately 204 (with an average re-visitation of 53%).

The *X-iDeTaCt* algorithm takes the new event and decides whether to create a new cluster, merge two clusters or whether to add the node to an existing cluster, depending on the computed edge weight and the status of the node (based on η). Clusters are automatically maintained as explained in Section 4.2.3.

On the other hand the re-finding component includes a

---

[1] http://www.w3.org/TeamSubmission/turtle/
[2] http://graphml.graphdrawing.org/

[3] https://www.mozilla.org/firefox/
[4] http://dragontalk.opendfki.de/

27

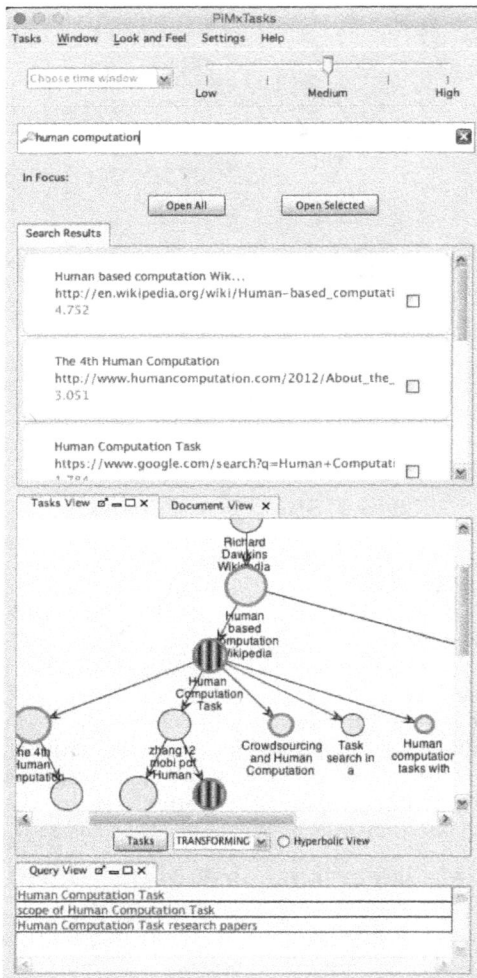

Figure 2: PiMxT Interface

text search and a time-window filtering facility as can be seen in Figure 2. The former is based on Jena's text-search[5] and uses a Lucene[6] index over all triples. The search is performed across all clusters and since each cluster is essentially a set of RDF triples, it considers all URIs, certain properties and their related string objects (limited to the text in the window captions). The time-window filtering facility allows a user to filter the clusters by particular time-windows which range from "1 hour ago" up to "4 hours ago", "Today", "Yesterday" and up to "7 days ago" (we limited this to 7 days since the evaluation was planned to be done over 5 days).

The result from a search or time-window filter is rendered in the different visualisations. There are four such visualisations: (i) the *tasks view* renders the tasks as a set of minimum spanning trees, (ii) the *document view* renders the tasks as undirected graphs using a force-directed layout, (iii) the *search results view* displays single document results returned by the search facility as a ranked list and (iv) the *query view* lists those queries that have been submitted to third-party search engines and are related to re-found or re-

---

[5]https://jena.apache.org/documentation/query/text-query.html
[6]http://lucene.apache.org/core/

sumed tasks. Both the *tasks view* and the *document view* are based on the Jung[7] graph API. Nodes are labelled with a minimal set of keywords (to avoid clutter) based on the text from window caption, captured when the page was accessed.

Although the *tasks view* and the *document view* both abide to Shneiderman's top-down visualisation design [26], the detail of the overview phase is different. While in the former all nodes pertaining to a task are displayed, the latter only shows the graph generated by computing the shortest path between all the nodes returned by the search keywords. Both views however, provide different visual interactive dynamics such as those highlighted by [14]. These include zooming in and out, click-and-drag a whole graph, and selecting and dragging single nodes. The visualisation also provides for a movable and modifiable, magnification facility that transforms areas of the displayed region such that a contextual region is magnified.

Furthermore, in both visualisations, different colours are used to indicate the pertinence of nodes to a task-cluster. Red-coloured borders are introduced to highlight those nodes that either match the page currently being seen by a user or nodes whose details match the search keywords. Nodes that represent query result pages (performed through a search engine) are displayed using transitioned colours. Furthermore, the size of the nodes is varied based on the ranking computed for each node by $X\text{-}iDeTaCt$, as briefly explained in Section 4.2.3. The user can glean insight into the tasks displayed in the *tasks view* by using the right-click context menu that allows her to display subtrees (parts of a task) and show only particular tasks while hiding others. It is also possible to cache different tasks, possibly found through different searches or different time-window filters, and display them next to each other.

In the *document view* the user can expand the somewhat reduced graph by double-clicking each node. If a node has a neighbourhood, this is displayed. In this way the user has some control over the amount of detail that she wants to explore. Currently however, there is no indication as to the size of the neighbourhood that will be displayed as a result of such expansion. Although the right-click context menu is also available for this view, the actions are limited to displaying or hiding specific tasks and to collapsing the expanded neighbourhoods. This was done intentionally so that through the evaluation process the users' preferences are better understood.

The *search results view* is tightly bound to the keyword search and displays the set of documents that satisfy the query as labelled, clickable, coloured items. The label includes different excerpts of information such as the URL, related window caption and the computed ranking. The colour of each result item is the same as that of the task-cluster to which the document pertains.

The *tasks* and *document* views allow for task-resumption through the context menu, which makes it possible to resume single documents, documents pertaining to some task context (a subgraph) or whole tasks, by reopening them in the browser as separate tabs. With regards to the *search results view* users can resume either single documents or all the documents returned by a search query.

Whenever the user interacts with *PiMxT* to re-find some task, the *query view* automatically displays a list of queries

---

[7]http://jung.sourceforge.net/

that the user had submitted to third-party search engines while performing that task. Each query item can be clicked and the relevant results page is displayed in a new tab in the browser.

The prototype just presented introduces an automatic task-keeping approach and allows for different visualisations intended to provide different task re-finding and resumption experiences. In the next section this prototype is evaluated through a usability study, during which the participants were interviewed, and a follow up questionnaire.

6. EVALUATION

At the end of survey *S2* the authors took the opportunity to invite the participants to take part in an evaluation exercise which included a 5-day long usability study. During this period the participants had to use *PiMxT* in their "normal" daily activities, and then participate in a follow up interview and questionnaire. Out of the 153 participants that contributed to *S2*, 22 agreed to participate. However, in the end only 15 actually did, and each one was paid € 20 for their participation.

When performing PIM-related evaluations one has to always keep in mind that potential participants are busy people and that they hate disruptions which effect their working habits [16]. Furthermore, people are keen on privacy issues and are not readily willing to share personal information. For this reason it was made clear *a priori* to potential participants that the primary focus of the experiment will be their experience using *PiMxT* and that their browser's history will not be collected. Still, only 10% of the initial number of participants accepted to continue the experiment, 10 were males while 5 were females. The participants were mostly undergraduate and postgraduate students, while two of them were lecturing staff members from our faculty[8]. Although 15 is not a large number, previous experiments by [10] concluded that between 5 and 12 participants is an acceptable number for a system usability study. Furthermore, [21] reports that 5 users are enough to find 75% of any existing problems.

Prior to starting the 5-day long usability study, one of the authors met with each participant and explained how *PiMxT* can be installed and configured, and how they can use it to re-find and resume tasks. A short manual was also packaged with the software for future reference and a help guide accessible through *PiMxT*'s user interface provided information about each of the available features and how they can be accessed.

Through the evaluation process the authors wanted to address a number of questions in line with [12], such as (a) "How good is it?", which was concerned with the usability of the system, (b) "Which one is better?", which compares *PiMxT* with an alternative and (c) "Why is it bad?", where the goal was to find out the weaknesses of the system in order to improve it.

6.1 PiMxT: the Usability Study

During the 5-day period each participant had to use *PiMxT* in conjunction with Firefox, within their "normal" working environment. However, for 6% of our participants, this caused some disruption, since Firefox was not their preferred browser (as stated by them in *S2*). For the rest, this was

not an issue since they used multiple browsers, including Firefox. At the end of the 5-day period each participant was interviewed separately and presented with a questionnaire. The methodology and the results from the interview are described and discussed below.

For this interview timesheets were used to keep the data collected during the evaluation task. Each participant had to perform certain activities, with and without *PiMxT* and these activities were timed. A specific set of questions were asked by a researcher after each activity. Furthermore, the participant's behaviour as well as any comments and problems encountered were annotated. This evaluation process took an average of one hour per participant and included four parts.

In the first part each participant was asked to choose an ID from an available batch. This ID was used also in the questionnaire that followed and was intended to anonymise the participant. Each participant was then asked to identify a number of tasks (at least four) that were worked upon during the last five days. The concept of a task is subjective and some of the participants asked whether each search query can be considered as a task or whether checking one's social network or the weather channel can be considered to be tasks. The concept of a task was clarified by the researcher in line with the definition that was provided earlier in Section 1.

Each of the identified tasks had to be labelled so that during the rest of the interview it was clear which task was being referred to. Furthermore the task labels were listed in the order that the tasks were worked-upon during the 5-day evaluation period.

In the second part of the interview each participant was asked to re-find any two of the listed tasks, one being more recent than the other. Participants were instructed to re-find documents related to each task using the tool or tools that each one of them normally used. Each re-finding process was timed. The timer was stopped whenever a participant was confident that they had found the useful documents that they were working on while performing that task. The researcher then asked a number of questions intended to establish the effectiveness of the adopted re-finding process. The questions inquired about the number of documents pertaining to a task that were found and whether the participant thought that they had found all the documents. If not, they were asked to explain why they thought this was the case.

In the next part of the evaluation task, each participant was asked to re-find another two (different from those found in part two) of the enlisted labelled tasks (again one more recent than the other), this time however using *PiMxT*. The process was again timed and a set of questions were asked. In particular participants were asked about the number of documents that the tool managed to find, the number of documents that were considered to be useful, whether important documents were missed and how many of the found documents were not considered to be useful. During the process the researcher took note of the participant's behaviour, whether she used the search or time-window filtering, the views that she used and how she used them and whether any problems were encountered.

The final part of the interview consisted in each participant again using *PiMxT*, but this time to re-find the same tasks that were chosen in part two. The process was again timed and the participants were asked the same set of ques-

---

[8]Faculty of ICT, at the University of Malta

tions asked in part three of the experiment. The researcher again took note of the *PiMxT* features that were used and how.

6.1.1 Results

The two tasks chosen by the participants for the second and the final part of the evaluation were classified along the categories identified by [18]: fact-finding (10%), information-gathering (47%), browsing (17%), transaction (13%) and other (13%). A summary of the duration of the re-finding task process without and with *PiMxT* can be seen in Table 5. What is interesting from this table is that in 73% of the time taken to re-find Task 1 (T1), the more recent task, and in 80% of the time taken to re-find Task 2 (T2), the less recent task, *PiMxT*'s re-finding time was less in both.

In the particular case of participant 12, the tool's re-finding time was more in both T1 and T2. More specifically this participant took 32% and 7% respectively, more time to re-find his tasks using *PiMxT* than when using his "normal" method. From the researcher's notes it was observed that this participant relies on keeping windows and tabs open as a way to keep and re-find documents related to his tasks. He is also very organised and tends to compartmentalise his tasks, only switching to another task once the current one is finished. Furthermore, he maintains his tabs quite organised, with "those related to long-lived tasks on the left and I use different browser instances to differentiate between types of tasks (personal/work related)". Although the timings are against *PiMxT* in this case, it was reported that the tool still managed to find the useful and important documents for both tasks. Furthermore, in the case of this participant, *PiMxT* might have been considered to be more of a disruption, since over the years he has managed to adapt to an efficient keeping and re-finding methodology and possibly this affected the outcome.

The worst re-finding time was clocked by user 19 when re-finding T1. To perform this task she mainly used the search and the task view. However, the search did not return any documents. This result is attributed to some limitations of the search facility. *PiMxT* only indexes the text from the window caption and this at times does not reflect the content of the document. Furthermore, the search is based on exact keyword matching and although it is possible to use wild cards, it is not something that everyone is accustomed to. This same participant then used the time-window filter and switched to the task view and managed to locate the documents which were attached to a subtree (thus they were not correctly separated). She then opened the documents using *PiMxT*'s open by context facility from the context menu. Although the re-finding process took relatively more time in this case, the tool still managed to re-find all the important documents and very few of the returned documents were considered not to be useful.

When considering *PiMxT*'s overall re-finding times these are found to be quite positive. Furthermore, although the performed tasks are different from one user to the other, it is still useful to consider the average improvement, which is approximately 47% and 41%, for T1 and T2 respectively. The overall improvement is approximately 44%. In some cases, for example, re-finding with *PiMxT* of T1 by user 4 and of T2 by user 1 took approximately 80% less time when compared to the time taken by the same users to re-find these task using their "normal" methods.

Table 5: Timed Re-finding with/without PiMxT

	Normal Tools		Using PiMxT	
User	T1 (sec)	T2 (sec)	T1 (sec)	T2 (sec)
1	25	150	22	30
4	230	76	48	27
6	53	97	31	86
7	36	25	12	13
8	80	69	72	70
9	51	54	21	26
10	70	29	24	23
11	35	65	25	54
12	47	22	51	56
13	25	21	6	8
14	34	45	32	78
15	22	31	33	25
16	27	65	37	23
18	100	129	24	89
19	17	135	214	81

From the observations and comments made during the interview, the users mainly started the re-finding process using the search facility and rarely started-off with the time-window filtering. The view which was most popular was the *search results view*, which is tightly coupled with the search facility. Users then either used the *tasks* or the *document views* to find more documents. The *tasks view*'s tree structure and layout were more appreciated than the undirected graph structure and force-directed layout in the *document view* by the majority of the participants. However, some participants said that the *document view*'s approach to keep the neighbourhoods of nodes hidden until expanded, had its advantages, since it resulted in less clutter. This is possibly because the exploratory design behind this view is more in line with the visualisation design referred to by [26]. The *query view* on the other hand, was never used during the re-finding process. Participants found quite useful the various features accessible through the different views that allowed them to open single or multiple documents in the browser, effectively resuming tasks.

In conclusion, when using *PiMxT*, individuals did not need to waste time thinking about how to keep documents related to a task. Furthermore, re-finding of tasks took on average approximately 44% less time in 77% of the re-finding cases, even though one has to keep in mind that the tasks performed by each participant were different.

6.2 PiMxT: the Questionnaire

At the end of the interview the researcher presented the participants with a questionnaire which was available online and intended to collect further qualitative feedback about how they (the participants) valued their experience with *PiMxT*. The average time spent by the participants to answer this questionnaire was on average 15 minutes.

The questionnaire was based on a 5-point Likert scale and allowed for 2 positive and 2 negative ratings together with a neutral opinion. The first set of questions was related to the usage frequency of the tool. These were followed by a set of questions intended to measure the usability of *PiMxT* in terms of the evaluation criteria expressed in [16]. More specifically these included, *effectiveness, efficiency, completeness, accuracy, usefulness, satisfaction, ease of use* and *ease of learning*. The next part of the questionnaire was intended to measure the usefulness of the different *PiMxT* features.

The subsequent questions inquired about the intuitiveness of the visualisations and the layouts used, as well as whether

Table 6: Usability Criteria

	Strongly Agree	Agree	Neutral	Disagree	Strongly Disagree
Effective	3	7	5	0	0
Efficient	2	11	2	0	0
Complete	3	3	5	4	0
Accurate	1	5	7	2	0
Useful	6	8	1	0	0
Satisfying	0	10	5	0	0
Easy to use	2	9	4	0	0
Easy to learn	4	6	4	1	0

the level of information presented by the tool was suitable or not. These were followed by questions through which the participants could express their opinion about the features they would like to see improved, those that they think could be removed and other new ones that they would like to see included. An explanation in each case was required. At the end of the questionnaire the researcher asked the summative question, "Would you be interested in continuing to use PiMxT?".

6.2.1 Results

When asked about the use of *PiMxT* during the 5-day period prior to the interview, 46.7% of the participants said that they used *PiMxT* every day, 27% said that they used it regularly (for example, user 9 said during working hours and user 6 said whenever there was the need to re-find a task), while 26% said that they used it irregularly (for example, user 1 said that she used it 3 to 4 times, while user 13 said that he used it 2 to 3 times).

With regards to the evaluation criteria expressed in [16], the participants were asked to express their level of agreement with the supplied statements. The results are summarised in Table 6.

The participants, strongly-agreed (40%) and agreed (53.3%) that *PiMxT* is useful. They also mostly agreed about its efficiency, effectiveness, satisfaction, ease of use and ease to learning. However, 26.7% and 13.3% of the participants tended to disagree with *PiMxT*'s completeness and accuracy, respectively. Being a prototype it is far from complete, so to some extent this was to be expected, however with regards to accuracy, this is attributed to the keeping and/or re-finding mechanisms. Thus although the overall result is very encouraging it is important to keep in mind that for such a tool to be accepted by a broad user base, it will need to provide benefits that outweigh those provided by long-established tools such as bookmarks and history.

With regards to the results related to the usefulness of the various *PiMxT* features, all the participants confirmed the popularity of the search facility and the *search results view* (as stated in Section 6.1.1). In fact 66.7% and 33.3%, strongly agreed and agreed respectively with the usefulness of this feature. Although participants rarely used the time-window filter during the interview, through the questionnaire it was found that 46.7% strongly agreed and another 46.7% agreed with the usefulness of this feature.

In relation to the other visualisations, the participants' agreement about the usefulness of the *tasks view* and the *document view* was 60% and 53.3% respectively. On the other hand only 20% agreed that the *query view* was useful (this view was not used by the participants during the experiment).

Other features that were rated high include those that al-

lowed the found documents to be opened in a browser. More specifically *open document in browser* (73.3%) and *open selected document* (66.6%) were found to be more useful than *open document in context* (46.7%) and *open task in browser* (46.7%). There were however some features that were considered to be less useful by a small portion of the participants (13.3%). These included *hide tasks, collapse all documents, double-click and expand* and *open all documents in browser.*

Overall the participants found that the use of nodes to represent documents was intuitive (86.6%) and that the layout in the *tasks view* was effective (93%). However, only 53.3% of the participants thought that the force-directed layout in the *document view* was effective. The level of information provided was found to be: at the right level by 53.3%, too little by 20% and too much by 26.7% of our participants. In this regards it is important to reconsider certain visualisation decisions as well as improve the labelling associated with each node.

A number of improvements were also suggested by the participants, most notably: improve the accuracy of the tool, to embed the tool within the browser and develop a similar tool for other browsers (like Chrome and Safari), to turn the tool into a system tray (in Windows) application, add auto-completion to the search, use more representative keywords to label the nodes, improve the layout for the *document view* and the possibility for the user to effect manual pruning of the tasks. Participants also suggested the removal of certain features which they did not find interesting such as the magnification feature and the *query view.*

Finally when asked whether they would continue using *PiMxT* if the prototype is improved along the lines of their feedback, 66.7% said that they would use it, 26.6% said that they would use unconditionally and 6.7% said that they would use if bugs are resolved.

7. CONCLUSION

This paper first presents investigative research that shows that individuals are still using a mix of tools and techniques to address keeping and re-finding, since as yet there isn't a tool that completely satisfies their needs. The paper then focuses on *PiMxT*'s automatic task-keeping mechanism that is based on the *X-iDeTaCt* algorithm which has a recall of approximately 75% (an improvement over that of 50% obtained for its predecessor *iDeTaCt*) when using data previously collected during a controlled experiment. *PiMxT*'s task re-finding and resumption mechanisms together with the different visualisations were described next. An evaluation of *PiMxT* was performed using a usability study and a questionnaire. The time taken by the 15 participants to re-find tasks was on average 44% less in 77% of the cases. Although the participants expected *PiMxT* to be more complete and accurate they all recognised the usefulness of tool. These results, although on a small scale, are still considered to be very encouraging. Furthermore, *PiMxT* is still a prototype and therefore there is still scope for further improvement which is even more challenging and exciting.

8. REFERENCES

[1] C. Abela, C. Staff, and S. Handschuh. Automatic task-cluster generation based on document switching and revisitation. In *Proceedings of the 1st Workshop on Deep Content Analytics Technqiues for*

Personalized and Intelligent Services, DECAT'15, UMAP'15, 2015.

[2] C. Abela, C. Staff, and S. Handschuh. Collecting and analysing personal information management data. In *Proceedings of the First DIACHRON Workshop on Managing the Evolution and Preservation of the Data Web co-located with 12th European Semantic Web Conference, ESWC'15*, pages 22–27, 2015.

[3] A. Balmin, V. Hristidis, and Y. Papakonstantinou. Objectrank: Authority-based keyword search in databases. In *Proceedings of the Thirtieth International Conference on Very Large Data Bases - Volume 30*, VLDB '04, pages 564–575. VLDB Endowment, 2004.

[4] M. Bernstein, J. Shrager, and T. Winograd. Taskpose: Exploring fluid boundaries in an associative window visualization. In S. Cousins and M. Beaudouin-Lafon, editors, *UIST '08: Proceedings of the 21st annual ACM symposium on User Interface Software and Technology*, pages 231–234, New York, NY, USA, 2008. ACM Press.

[5] H. Bruce, W. Jones, and S. Dumais. Keeping and re-finding information on the web: What do people do and what do they need? *Proceedings of the American Society for Information Science and Technology*, 41(1):129–137, 2004.

[6] H. Bruce, A. Wenning, E. Jones, J. Vinson, and W. Jones. Seeking an ideal solution to the management of personal information collections. In *ISIC '10: Proceedings of the 8th Annual Information Seeking in Context Conference*, Murcia, Spain, 2010.

[7] S. Costache, J. Gaugaz, E. Ioannou, C. Niederee, and W. Nejdl. Detecting contexts on the desktop using bayesian networks. In *DESKTOP Search Workshop co-located with SIGIR*, 2010.

[8] E. Cutrell, D. Robbins, S. Dumais, and R. Sarin. Fast, flexible filtering with phlat. In *Proceedings of the SIGCHI Conference on Human Factors in Computing Systems*, CHI '06, pages 261–270, New York, NY, USA, 2006. ACM.

[9] S. Dumais, E. Cutrell, J. Cadiz, G. Jancke, R. Sarin, and D. Robbins. Stuff i've seen: a system for personal information retrieval and re-use. In *Proceedings of the 26th annual international ACM SIGIR conference on Research and development in informaion retrieval*, SIGIR '03, pages 72–79, New York, NY, USA, 2003. ACM.

[10] J. Dumas and J. Redish. *A Practical Guide to Usability Testing*. Greenwood Publishing Group Inc., Westport, CT, USA, 1993.

[11] T. Falkowski, A. Barth, and M. Spiliopoulou. Dengraph: A density-based community detection algorithm. In *Proceedings of the IEEE/WIC/ACM International Conference on Web Intelligence*, WI '07, pages 112–115, Washington, DC, USA, 2007. IEEE Computer Society.

[12] G. Gediga and K. Hamborg. Evaluation of software systems. *Encyclopedia of Computer Science and Technology*, 45, 2001.

[13] S. Gunnemann and T. Seidl. Subgraph mining on directed and weighted graphs. In *Proc. 14th Pacific-Asia Conference on Knowledge Discovery and Data Mining (PAKDD 2010), 21-24 June, 2010 - Hyderabad, India. Lecture Notes in Artificial Intelligence (LNAI)*, pages 133–146. Springer, 2010.

[14] J. Heer and B. Shneiderman. Interactive dynamics for visual analysis. *Commun. ACM*, 55(4):45–54, 2012.

[15] W. Jones, H. Bruce, and S. Dumais. Keeping found things found on the web. In *Proceedings of the tenth international conference on Information and knowledge management*, CIKM '01, pages 119–126, New York, NY, USA, 2001. ACM.

[16] W. Jones and J. Teevan. *Personal Information Management*. University of Washington Press, 2007.

[17] R. Kawase, G. Papadakis, and E. Herder. Supporting revisitation with contextual suggestions. In *Proceedings of the 11th annual international ACM/IEEE joint conference on Digital libraries*, JCDL '11, pages 227–230, New York, NY, USA, 2011. ACM.

[18] M. Kellar, C. Watters, and M. Shepherd. A goal-based classification of web information tasks. *Proceedings of the American Society for Information Science and Technology*, 43(1):1–22, 2006.

[19] M. Mayer. *Visualizing web sessions: improving web browser history by a better understanding of web page revisitation and a new session- and task-based, visual web history approach*. PhD thesis, University of Hamburg, 2008.

[20] D. Morris, M. R. Morris, and G. Venolia. Searchbar: a search-centric web history for task resumption and information re-finding. In *Proceedings of the twenty-sixth annual SIGCHI conference on Human factors in computing systems*, CHI '08, pages 1207–1216, New York, NY, USA, 2008. ACM.

[21] J. Nielsen. Why you only need to test with 5 users, 2000.

[22] N. Oliver, G. Smith, C. Thakkar, and A. Surendran. Swish: semantic analysis of window titles and switching history. In *Proceedings of the 11th international conference on Intelligent user interfaces*, pages 194–201, New York, NY, USA, 2006. ACM.

[23] L. Page, S. Brin, R. Motwani, and T. Winograd. The pagerank citation ranking: Bringing order to the web. Technical Report 1999-66, Stanford InfoLab, November 1999.

[24] G. Papadakis, R. Kawase, E. Herder, and W. Nejdl. Methods for web revisitation prediction: survey and experimentation. *User Modeling and User-Adapted Interaction*, pages 1–39, 2015.

[25] G. Papadakis, C. Niederée, and W. Nejdl. Decay-based ranking for social application content. In *WEBIST (1)*, pages 276–281, 2010.

[26] B. Shneiderman. The eyes have it: A task by data type taxonomy for information visualizations. In *Proceedings of the 1996 IEEE Symposium on Visual Languages*, VL '96, Washington, DC, USA, 1996. IEEE Computer Society.

[27] Q. Wang and H. Chang. Multitasking bar: prototype and evaluation of introducing the task concept into a browser. In *Proceedings of the 28th International Conference on Human Factors in Computing Systems, CHI 2010*, pages 103–112, New York, NY, USA, 2010. ACM.

Contextual Support for Collaborative Information Retrieval

Shuguang Han[1], Daqing He[1], Zhen Yue[2] and Jiepu Jiang[3]
[1] University of Pittsburgh, 135 N Bellefield Ave., Pittsburgh, PA, USA
[2] Yahoo! Labs, 701 First Ave., Sunnyvale, CA, USA
[3] Center for Intelligent Information Retrieval, University of Massachusetts Amherst
{shh69,dah44}@pitt.edu, zhenyue@yahoo-inc.com, jpjiang@cs.umass.edu

ABSTRACT

Recent research shows that Collaborative Information Retrieval (CIR), in which two or more users collaborate on the same search task, has become increasingly popular. The presence of both search and collaboration behaviors makes CIR a complex search format, which further drives a critical need to understand CIR's search context. The contextual support for CIR should consider search contexts derived from both team members' search histories (including users' own search histories and partners' search histories) and their explicit collaboration (e.g., chatting). As it stands, existing studies on contextual search support only focus on Individual Information Retrieval (IIR) and only utilize individuals' own search histories. In this paper, we examine the unique search contexts (e.g., partners' search histories and team collaboration histories) in CIR. Based on a user study data collection with 54 participants, we find that compared to the use of individuals' own search histories, CIR contextual support is more effective when utilizing partners' search histories and teams' collaboration behaviors. More interestingly, though the explicit communication information (i.e., chat content) often involves massive noisy information, involving such noise does not affect the ranking of relevant documents since it also does not appear in relevant documents.

Keywords

Collaborative information retrieval, context-sensitive information retrieval, relevance feedback

1. INTRODUCTION

Despite the fact that information retrieval is often viewed as an individual behavior, recent studies [14, 15] report that collaborative information retrieval (CIR), in which two or more users collaborate and coordinate on the same search task, has increased from 0.9% in 2006 to 11% in 2012. A typical example of CIR is: two friends communicate over Facebook and search for nearby restaurants to go for dinner. In this task scenario, they may search and communicate

CHIIR '16, March 13-17, 2016, Carrboro, NC, USA
© 2016 ACM. ISBN 978-1-4503-3751-9/16/03. . . $15.00
DOI: http://dx.doi.org/10.1145/2854946.2854963

in multiple rounds until reaching a final agreement. Therefore, unlike Individual Information Retrieval (IIR), CIR not only includes search activities, but also involves a significant amount of team collaboration such as sharing visited information and communicating with partners (i.e., chat) [19, 28]. In addition to these differences, researchers observe that users in CIR often develop new search tactics and strategies, compared to that in IIR [28].

Compared with IIR, CIR tasks are usually more complex and require more user exploration [15, 28]. This makes the inference of users' search contexts and the contextual support of CIR more difficult, and it is unclear whether or not the previously proposed IIR-based contextual support approach [23] is still useful. To handle these challenges, we investigate the contextual support for CIR in this paper.

The most common approach for inferring users' search context is to utilize users' search histories, which often include query history and click-through history [23]. Both have been demonstrated to be effective in improving search performance in IIR [1, 3, 23], whereas the contextual support for CIR is not well studied [17]. A straightforward CIR contextual support method is to ignore user collaboration and consider each team member as an individual user. In this way, the contextual support algorithms developed in IIR can be directly employed. However, the current literature has not yet provided a clear conclusion for the validity of this approach, and this is the focus of our first research question. In addition, considering that this approach does not take advantage of the unique contextual information only available in CIR, our further research questions examine how the new contextual information will support CIR search.

CIR involves more than one user so that the search histories can either come from the given user him/herself or from his/her partners. Although existing studies already explore the ways of incorporating search histories from other users [6, 26], the involved users are not designated as the given users' search partners. This is critically different from CIR because users in the above two studies have no direct or indirect collaborations, whereas collaboration has its unique importance in CIR. Consequently, an effective contextual support for CIR should be studied further, with particular focus on analyzing the utility of users' own and partners' search histories. This is a relatively new research topic; existing literature has examined it as algorithm-mediated CIR [17, 22, 24], where search results are customized based on users' search roles. The roles are either predefined or mined from their search histories. These studies have demonstrated the overall effectiveness of algorithm-mediated CIR, but it is unclear whether the boost of search performance comes from utilizing users' own or partners' search histories or if it comes from users' role-based result customization. Therefore, we will examine the approach that purely utilizes users' own and partners' search histories and not consider user roles.

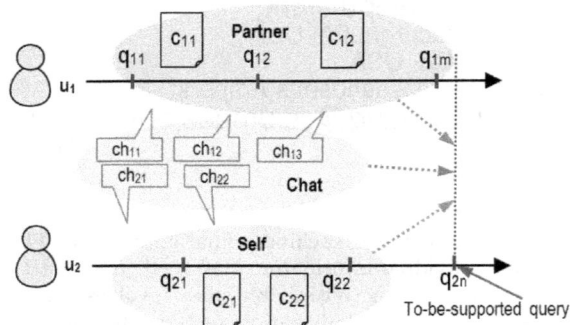

Figure 1: Context-sensitive retrieval framework for IIR and CIR. IIR only employs users' own search history whereas CIR can utilize self-history, partner-history and also chat messages.

CIR also contains considerable user collaboration behaviors (i.e., chat). Chat was found to have significant impact on the formation of CIR search strategies and their query reformulations [29]. However, modeling search context with chat information remains an open research topic with numerous challenges. The first challenge is that chats usually contain a massive amount of noise [27], some of which is not even task-related. It is also unclear that what effective methods can be applied to remove the noise and whether such noise will exert significant negative impacts on supporting usersâĂŹ search queries. The second challenge is that users may chat for different purposes - some may discuss a specific subtopic for the search task, some may coordinate different sub-tasks, while still others may be chatting for social purposes. It is unclear which type(s) of chat could be useful for contextual supports.

In this paper, we are interested in understanding the effectiveness of two unique types of contextual information (i.e., a partner's search history and a team's chat history) in CIR. Following the context-sensitive retrieval algorithm [23] developed in IIR, we refer to the contextual support for CIR as Context-sensitive Collaborative Information Retrieval (CCIR). Figure 1 illustrates CCIR in a collaborative search with two users u_1 and u_2. The search contexts for supporting the new query q_{2n} of u_2 can be inferred from the historical search queries - q_{11}, q_{12} ... for u_1, and q_{21}, q_{22} ... for u_2; the clicked documents - c_{11}, c_{12} ... for u_1, and c_{21}, c_{22} ... for u_2; and the chat between u_1 and u_2 - c_{11}, c_{12} ... for u_1, and c_{21}, c_{22} ... for u_2. In IIR, context-sensitive IR will aim to provide a better document ranking using u_2's search histories, whereas CCIR can employ three types of histories to infer users' search contexts: u_2's own search history, u_2's partner search history (i.e., u_1's search history) and their chat histories.

However, our research goal in this paper does not aim to propose an optimal contextual-based CIR ranking model; instead, we are more concerned with exploring the utilities of different types of search contexts. Thus, this paper repre-

sents an exploratory work for demonstrating the necessity of utilizing the contextual factors in CIR. Consequently, we are interested in the following three research questions (RQs):

- RQ1: Can the context-sensitive retrieval algorithms developed in IIR [23] be directly applied in CIR without handling complex CIR user interactions?

- RQ2: Can partners' search histories in CIR be employed for better modeling of users' search contexts and to further improve the search performance?

- RQ3: Can team members' chat histories in CIR be employed for modeling users' search contexts and further improve the search performance?

2. RELATED WORK

The related work of our paper occupies three areas. The first one involves studying users' CIR search behaviors. Many CIR studies [20, 21, 28] observe that team members do collaborate very frequently, and the collaboration does indeed bring in diverse expertise [28]. However, users' collaboration also intervenes with and complicates an individual user's normal search process. Therefore, users in CIR also exhibit several new search patterns. For example, through the exploration of Kuhlthau's ISP model [13] for IIR, Hyldegard [10] suggests that the ISP model in CIR should incorporate social and contextual factors. Similarly, through mapping Kuhlthau's ISP model to CIR, Shah and Gonzalez-Ibanez [20] declare that social elements are missing. Yue et al. [28] compare the search tactic/strategy differences between IIR and CIR, to find that CIR involves more sense-making related search tactics. These above-mentioned studies all indicate the high complexity of CIR search processes.

The second related area is concerned with search supports in CIR. Pickens et al. [17] mention two types of supports in a CIR system: user-mediated support and system-mediated support. The user-mediated search support provides simple and user-transparent functions, often at the interface level, to assist users in completing their search tasks [19]. Most of the existing CIR-support systems, including SearchTogether [16], Coagmento [18], and CollabSearch [28], fall into this category. System-mediated support focuses on merging relevant documents by integrating inputs from partners. Then, the relevant documents are redistributed to different users based on certain strategies. CIR systems, such as Cerchiamo [17] and Querium [5], belong to this category. Current studies on system-mediated CIR support only explore the strategy of regrouping search results based on user roles [17, 22, 24], which are either manually predefined [17, 22] or automatically learned from users' behavior logs [24]. However, these studies restrict user roles into predefined categories (e.g., Prospector or Miner, and Gatherer or Surveyor [24]), while the collaboration styles of real users may vary significantly. Thus, to provide a more flexible CIR support, either a robust role-mining algorithm or a new result differentiation method is needed.

The last related area involves search context modeling in CIR. Previous researchers have identified that users' search histories can provide effective feedback to improve retrieval performance [3, 11, 23]. However, this effectiveness was only tested in IIR. There are indeed several studies that take into account the search histories from other users. For example, White et al. [26] found that it is beneficial to include the search history information from other users who performed similar search tasks to support the given users' queries. Similar ideas have also been explored as social navigation [2, 6, 9, 8], where social cues (e.g. the highlighted content) generated from other users are utilized to assist current users' information-seeking processes. However, unlike the users in CIR, these users are not explicit search partners. Therefore, the effectiveness of utilizing other users' search histories needs to be reexamined. In addition, because chat information is unique contextual information in CIR, its effectiveness as a CIR search context should also be properly studied. These are also our research focuses in this paper.

3. OBTAINING EXPERIMENTAL DATASET

3.1 User Study Design

To examine the above-mentioned research questions, we need to build a collaborative web search data collection. In this paper, the data collection was obtained through a laboratory-controlled user study. We do acknowledge that lab study may introduce certain artificial factors since search tasks are not originated from the users themselves but are instead preassigned. However, this approach with simulated tasks is an effective way to evaluate interactive information retrieval systems [4] and is commonly used in CIR studies too [22, 19, 28].

Our study employed CollabSearch[1], a collaborative web search system developed by Yue et al. [28]. The two exploratory web search tasks were also borrowed from [28] - one was an academic task (T1) that asked participants to collect information about a social networking service and the other was a leisure task (T2) that asked participants to collect information for planning a trip. We chose these two tasks because they are representative collaborative web search tasks that are commonly adopted in many other CIR studies [20, 22, 24, 28].

To simulate a real collaborative web search scenario, we recruited participants as pairs so that two of them could work together on the same task. The pairs were asked to have past collaboration experience (e.g., past course collaboration experience) before attending our studies. Following the majority of CIR studies [17, 19, 28], we only worked on the CIR teams with two persons. Previous literature also showed that pairs are the most common team format involved in collaborative web searches [15].

Our study also included an IIR scenario for comparison. We took a between-subject design for this comparison so that the participants for IIR were recruited separately instead of asking the collaborative teams to continue working on IIR tasks. The first motivation for this design is to use the same tasks for both IIR and CIR to eliminate task effect. Here, we cannot adopt within-subject design because CIR participants cannot further work on IIR since they already completed the tasks in the CIR condition. Secondly, each team usually spent about two hours on CIR tasks. They would be exhausted and generate low quality results if we followed the within-subject design and continued asking them to perform IIR search tasks.

We do acknowledge that the current design of the study (i.e., using only two search tasks and a relatively small number of participants) may cause the conclusion of insufficient generalizablility. It is still useful for this exploratory work

[1]http://crystal.exp.sis.pitt.edu:8080/CollaborativeSearch/

to point out insights for further research directions. More importantly, this current design helps to significantly reduce the complexity and time span of the user study, which enables researchers to avoid the limitation that users in a larger and longer study may see diverse search results at different time periods since CollabSearch depends on Google to return real-time search results that can change over time.

3.2 User Study Procedure

After being introduced to the study and completing an entry questionnaire to establish their search experience background, the participants then worked on a training task for 15 minutes to get familiar with the system. Then, each team worked for 30 minutes on each of the two assigned tasks. The task order was rotated and preassigned to each team to avoid learning and fatigue effects. During the search for each task, the participants were instructed to save as many relevant web pages as possible. At the end of each task, the participants were asked to rate the relevance (at the task level) of each saved web page on a 5-point Likert scale, with 1 denoting non-relevant and 5 being highly relevant. These scores will be used for building the ground-truth.

3.3 User Study Data

Our study recruited 36 collaborative participants (i.e., 18 pairs) and 18 individuals. These 54 participants are comprised of 26 females and 28 males. Twenty-four participants are undergraduate students and 30 are graduates, all from University of Pittsburgh or Carnegie Mellon University. They have strong computer experience and conduct web search on a daily basis. In response to a question regarding their search experience, where 1 denotes the least experience and 7 the most experience, all of the participants rated their experience from 4 to 7.

In total, the participants issued 970 search queries (537 for T1 and 433 for T2), clicked 1,384 web pages and saved 909 pages. We downloaded the HTML sources of the top 100 Google search results for all 970 queries to build a data collection. In total, the collection includes 54,364 unique web pages. Additionally, we applied a state-of-the-art content extraction algorithm [12] to extract the full text of each web page and to remove the advertisements and copyright information for each web page.

4. CONTEXT-SENSITIVE CIR

4.1 Experiment Setup

To answer the research questions raised in the Introduction, we design the following simulation experiment. After obtaining users' search logs from CollabSearch system, we extract each of an individual's search queries q, its issuing time t and the user u in a temporal order. The goal of the simulation experiment is to provide a better document ranking for q by combining the content of q and different types of contextual information inferred from users' search and chat histories (before time t). In this manner, we simulate the contextual support for all user-issued search queries in a sequential order.

As shown in the CCIR framework (Figure 1), it is possible to utilize different types of contextual information in CIR. Depending on the sources and types of users' histories that are used to infer contextual information, we can obtain six types of search contexts, as shown in Figure 2. We

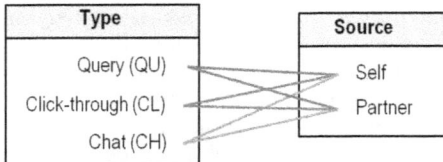

Figure 2: Different types of contextual information available in CIR

denote the query, click-through, and chat histories as H_{QU}, H_{CL} and H_{CH}, respectively. They can be further differentiated by their sources - H_{XS} for self and H_{XP} for partner, where $X \in \{QU,CL,CH\}$. Since chat usually requires extensive involvement from both users, we do not further differentiate the users' own and partners' chats in our experiments. Therefore, in total, there are five types of contextual information. Following the context-sensitive retrieval algorithm in [23], users' behavior histories are converted to contextual language models and then used for search result re-ranking.

4.2 Estimating Contextual Language Models

After obtaining users' search histories, the next step is to estimate their corresponding contextual language models (θ_{HX}) [11, 23]. In this paper, we estimate a unigram language model for each type of contextual information, which can be formalized as Formula (1) and (2). H_X can be any type of user history (i.e., H_{QU}, H_{CL} and H_{CH}). Note that H_X can either come from the given user or his/her partners. $c(w, X_i)$ denotes the count of word w in the search history element X_i, $|X_i|$ is the word count of X_i and k is the total number of user histories (i.e., the number of historical queries, chat messages or clicked documents) of type X.

$$p(w|H_X) = \frac{1}{K} \sum_{i=1}^{K} p(w|X_i) \qquad (1)$$

$$p(w|X_i) = \frac{c(w, X_i)}{|X_i|} \qquad (2)$$

4.3 Document Re-ranking

We apply the following procedure to re-rank relevant documents for each to-be-supported query. For each candidate document, we estimate its document language model using Dirchilet smoothing [31], where we set the smoothing parameter $\mu = 100$. The similarity between each candidate document and the contextual model is measured by the KL divergence between their estimated language models [30]. The matching between a candidate document and the query is determined by Google rank position of the given candidate document. This is because our experimental system uses Google results as the default.

Instead of using linear interpolation proposed by Shen et al. [23], we employ LambaMART in RankLib[2] to build a pairwise learning-to-rank approach for combining different features. To be specific, for each query-document pair, we employ two features: (1) Google rank position (G) of the candidate document for the given query, and (2) KL divergence between a contextual language model (i.e., θ_{HX}) and

---

[2]http://sourceforge.net/p/lemur/wiki/RankLib/

the candidate document language model. The parameters of LambaMART are set as default in RankLib, except the number of leaves is set to 10. We use 10% of our training samples as validation data, and the features are normalized using the sum of all feature values to make different features in a same scale. Our parameter settings are set as the same to a previous study [9], which tries to handle a similar re-ranking problem.

4.4 Ground-truth and Evaluation

4.4.1 Building Ground-truth

To evaluate the effectiveness of the above-mentioned contextual information, we need the ground-truth data. The ground-truth is built at the task level, in which we aggregate the relevant documents saved by all participants. Furthermore, we assume that the goal for each user is to find the new relevant documents for the whole team (not including the already-explored documents from all team members). Therefore, the ground-truth removed all of the already-saved documents from both team members. Figure 3 illustrates the ground-truth building procedure. To support the search query q of user u at time t, we aggregate the saved documents from all participants except u and v. We also remove the already-saved documents from u and v (u's search partner) up to time t.

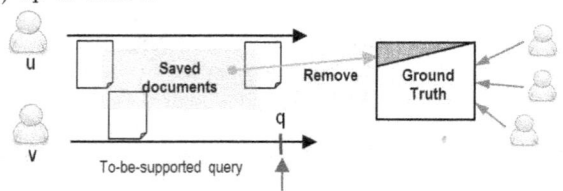

Figure 3: CCIR ground-truth building procedure

After obtaining the ground-truth pool, we compute the relevance of each document in the pool. Note that the participants are asked to rate the relevance of their saved documents on a 5-point Likert scale at the end of each task (see Section 3.1). These relevance scores are used to generate the final aggregated relevance. The simplest way to aggregate multiple scores from different users is to compute the average of these scores. However, the average can be biased when only a small number of participants rate the web page. A Bayesian smoothing approach [9] is adopted to remove this bias. Specifically, the smoothed average relevance score $\hat{r}'(d_i)$ for document d_i is computed based on the interpolation between its average score $\hat{r}(d_i)$ and the group average, as shown in Formula (3). C is the average rating for all documents, and v denotes the number of participants who saved the document d_i.

$$\hat{r}'(d_i) = \frac{\hat{r}(d_i)v + C}{v + 1} \qquad (3)$$

4.4.2 Evaluation Setup

In the evaluation, we randomly split the data collection into training and testing datasets using a five-fold cross-validation. The random division is repeated 10 times to remove biases. Our model parameters are learned from the training dataset, and then these parameters are applied to the learning-to-rank model in the testing dataset for evaluation. In our evaluation, the effectiveness of the learned models based on different contextual information was measured by MAP (Note that MAP only cares about the binary relevance of a document, i.e., relevant and non-reelvant. In our study, a document is defined as a relevant document if the score computed using Equation 3 is bigger than 3.0) and nDCG@N (N was set to be 1, 2,..., 20 in this paper). The reported MAP and nDCG values were the averages across five folds and over all 10 runs.

5. RESULT ANALYSIS

5.1 Experiment Overview

Our result analysis includes extensive statistical tests using non-parametric Wilcoxon signed-rank test (with Bonferroni correction) since the data is not normally distributed. Because we will consider two tasks and two evaluation metrics and compare multiple systems in result analysis at the same time, we do not provide Z-scores and P-values in this paper since there are too many values to report. Particularly, there are 20 different cutoffs for nDCG evaluation metric. Therefore. we set the statistical significance at 0.05 level and only report significant results. We design the following three experiments to answer our research questions mentioned in the Introduction.

- Although query and click-through search histories have been proved to be useful in supporting complex IIR tasks [9, 11, 25], they have not been extensively studied in the context of CIR. Therefore, our first experiment explores the effectiveness of applying IIR-based contextual support in CIR. This experiment targets RQ1. The details are provided in Section 5.2.

- The second experiment addresses RQ2, which is to better understand the utility of applying partners' search histories for CIR contextual support. The details of this experiment are presented in Section 5.3.

- The third experiment answers RQ3, and we focus on studying the effectiveness of utilizing chat information to support CIR search processes. Since not all chat messages contain useful task-related information, we further categorize chat information into different groups and compare each group's effectiveness. The details of this experiment are presented in Section 5.4.

5.2 Utilizing Users' Own Search Histories

5.2.1 Overall Results

The goal of our first experiment is to understand whether the IIR-based contextual support still works in CIR. We develop two search contexts based on users' own query histories and click-through histories, as shown below.

- H_QUS: query history for user u;
- H_CLS: click-through history for the given user u.

These two search contexts are then combined with the baseline Google ranking feature (G) to produce two contextual models (i.e., the search result re-ranking models), which are noted as G+H_QUS and G+H_CLS. The MAP and nDCG evaluations on these two models are provided in Figure 4, where we find that both models perform significantly better than the Google baseline on MAP. For nDCG, we also

observe statistically significant results at almost all cutoffs (we do not provide Z-scores here since there are too many values to report), which reveals that the context-sensitive retrieval model developed in IIR [23] also works well in CIR tasks. Although users' collaborations may potentially disrupt their individual search processes, users' search histories are still useful contextual information and should be properly considered for better contextual support.

Second, the statistical test shows that G+H_QUS is significantly better than G+H_CLS. That is, the search context inferred from query history is more effective than that from click-through history. This result is different from several previous studies about IIR [9, 11, 23], in which click-through is found to be more effective than query history. We think that there are two possible reasons. The first one is that the tasks involved in our study are different from the tasks included in previous IIR studies; our study's tasks are more complex and contain diverse sub-tasks. If task difference is the reason, the query history will also be more effective in IIR. The other potential reason is that users' normal search processes might be interrupted by the involvement of collaborative activities. This may drive people to issue different types of search queries and click different kinds of web pages. If this is true, the performance difference may be more related to the synergy effect between search and collaboration. We will examine them in the next section.

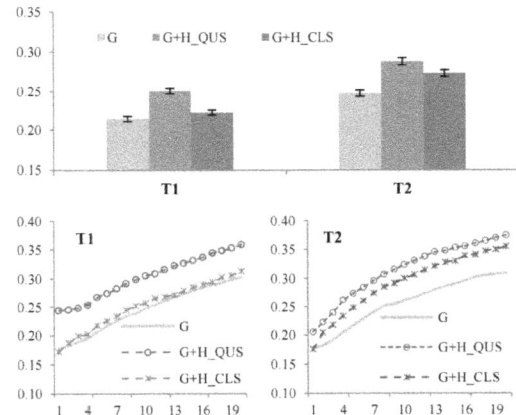

Figure 4: MAP (top) and nDCG (bottom) evaluation on the effectiveness of different CIR search contexts. X: task/cutoff. Y: MAP/nDCG values.

5.2.2 Comparing with IIR

Our user study also includes an IIR search condition, where the participants search individually for the same tasks as those in CIR. Using such data, we can compare the effectiveness of IIR-based search contexts with the CIR search contexts. The support for IIR search queries follows the same procedure used for CIR, except that we cannot access partners' search histories. Like in CIR, we also consider three ranking models, including the Google baseline (G) and two contextual models: G+H_QUS and G+H_CLS.

According to the MAP and nDCG evaluations for IIR in Figure 5, we find that the search history-based contextual information also helps in IIR - G+H_QUS (H_CLS) has significant performance boosts over the Google baseline (G). However, the improvement greatly depends on the

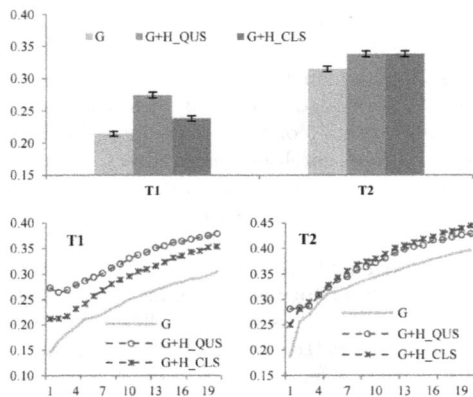

Figure 5: MAP (top) and nDCG (bottom) evaluation on the effectiveness of different IIR search contexts. X: task/cutoff. Y: MAP/nDCG values.

task. Wilcoxon signed-rank tests on T1 show that the query history significantly boosts performance more than the click-through history on both MAP and nDCG. This is consistent with the CIR results for T1. However, the results for T2 show that utilizing the click-through history is equivalent or even better than query history, particularly for nDCG at high cutoffs (bigger than 10). This is inconsistent with the results for CIR shown in Figure 4. One possible explanation for this is that the synergy between search and collaboration in CIR affects users' query and click behaviors, and further causes inconsistency. Since the inconsistency only happens in T2, if our hypothesis is correct, there might be a stronger synergy effect in T2 than in T1.

Table 1: Mean (S.D.) for different measures in CIR

	T1	T2	Sig.
#chat messages	21.56 (20.98)	38.86 (27.24)	$p < 0.001$
#queries	12.97 (6.98)	9.25 (5.30)	$p < 0.001$
#click-through	24.00 (13.23)	14.44 (7.25)	$p < 0.001$

To test this hypothesis, we compute additional measures (including number of queries, number of click-through documents and number of chat messages) for each task and compare their differences. Table I shows that within the same amount of time (30 minutes for each task), users in T1 issued more queries and clicked more documents, but composed fewer chat messages than the users in T2. Thus, T1 can be viewed as a search-intensive task where people spend more time searching and reading search results, whereas T2 is a collaboration-intensive task, since users spend more time on communication and collaboration. Consequently, it makes sense that CIR for T1 is more similar to the patterns observed in IIR, because users spend less time on collaboration and behave more like they are searching individually. Linking back to the hypothesis in the last paragraph of Section 5.2.1, we find that both task nature and synergy effect between collaboration and search can affect the search performance. The synergy effect may have a greater impact when there are more collaborations.

5.3 Involving Partners' Search Histories

To answer RQ2, we develop two search contexts extracted from partners' search histories, including:

- H_QU: query histories for u and u's search partner v;
- H_CL: click-through histories from both u and v.

We also include the search contexts from the above sections for comparison. In total, five ranking models are used, including the Google baseline (G) and four contextual models (G+H_QUS, G+H_CLS, G+H_QU and G+H_CL). Partners' search histories are not used separately, but instead are integrated with users' own histories. This is because different team members may have different search traces. Solely applying partners' search histories could distort users' own search traces, which is a risky approach to apply in a real search system. In contrast, aggregating search histories from all team members can highlight the relevant information without losing content diversity.

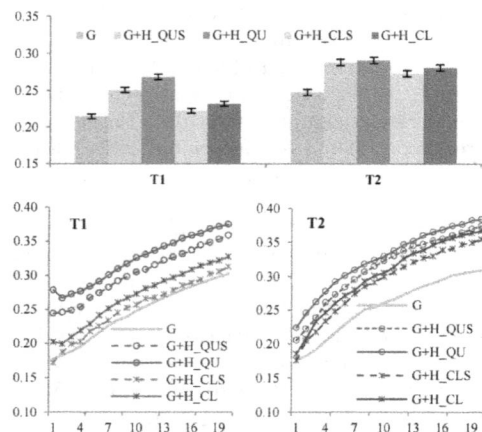

Figure 6: MAP (top) and nDCG (bottom) evaluation on the effectiveness of different search contexts in IIR. X: task/cutoff. Y: MAP/nDCG values.

The MAP and nDCG evaluations on these five ranking models are provided in Figure 6. Compared with users' own search histories, aggregating partners' search histories provides a better contextual support. This is based on the significant MAP and nDCG improvements on G+H_X over G+H_XS, where X∈{QU,CL}. The nDCG improvement may come from the fact that utilizing both users' own and their partners' histories can help identify the most relevant information. However, combining information from both users may potentially reduce information diversity. This means that the MAP of our exploratory web search tasks may be reduced because they usually cover multiple relevant or partially relevant subtopics. However, the significant MAP increases instead of decreases in Figure 6 further eliminates our concerns.

5.4 Utilizing Chat Histories

5.4.1 Overall Results

Another important distinction between CIR and IIR is that CIR involves explicit communication (i.e., chat) among users. To better understand the utility of applying chat content in supporting CIR queries, we conduct the following experiments. Firstly, we compare four different ranking models, including the Google baseline (G) and three contextual models (G+H_QU, G+H_CL and G+H_CH). H_CH refers to the search context inferred from chat messages. H_QU and H_CL are two additional baselines because of their superior performances in the above experiments. Stemming and stop-word removal are adopted when utilizing H_CH.

According to Yue et al. [27], around 30% chat messages are not directly related to the task content in CIR. We initially anticipated a poor result by applying the chat-based contextual support. However, as shown in Figure 7, G+H_CH surprisingly outperforms G+H_CL on MAP and nDCG in both tasks. Furthermore, it even significantly outperforms G+H_QU on T2 for MAP and nDCG. This implies that chat-based search context is highly effective in CIR support. In addition, we also observe the joint influence between task and chat-based search context. Chat-based search context achieves the best performance in T2, whereas it is only the second-best in T1. We think that the collaboration-intensive task (T2) may have more chat messages on discussing task content, and thus can provide better support than search intensive task (T1). To further understand the reasons, our next experiment attempts to separate different types of chat messages and compares their impact on search effectiveness.

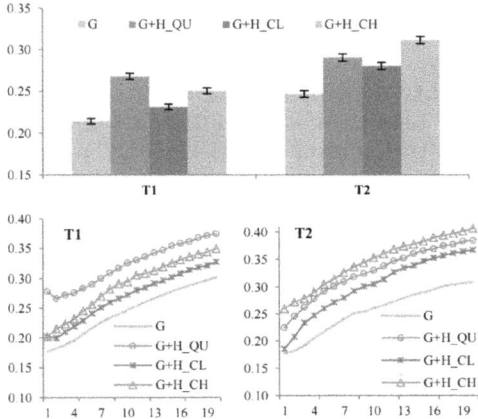

Figure 7: MAP (top) and nDCG (bottom) evaluation on the effectiveness of different search contexts in CIR. X: task/cutoff. Y: MAP/nDCG values

5.4.2 Chat Functionality Analysis

We categorize chat into four groups based on its functionality, which includes task content (TT), task coordination (TC), task social (TS) and non-task (NT). This schema (Table II) is directly adopted from a previous study on CIR [7] with only slight modifications. Task social chat messages usually attempt to provide social support between team members. Typical examples are greetings, encouragement between team members and opinions on the obtained information (e.g., *"well, hello there"*, *" yeah! we are going to Helsinki!"*, *"everything looks great so far!"*). Labor division and task progress checking are two major types of task coordination chat messages (e.g., *"you do stats and I'll do impacts on students and professionals"*, *"have you done impact yet?"*). Chat messages about task requirements and assessments of the obtained information belong to task content (e.g., *"ok so outdoor activities will be hard"*, *"in December they set up tons of markets and stuff in the streets"*). And, there are also several non-task chat messages that are not

related to the task itself (e.g., *"Can we eat after this?"*, *"I wish there was a notification every time we saved a page"*).

Table 2: Categorization schema for chat

Category	Description
Task social	Chat messages concerning group effort or attitude to the obtained information
Task coordination	Chat messages regarding the coordination of the search task, including division of labor and checking task status
Task content	Chat messages related to the content of the search task, including task requirement and information resource assessment
Non-task	Chat messages that are not related to the search task or the user study

To ensure data quality, we manually labeled the category for each chat message. Two coders went through all chat messages and manually assigned a category for each. The first round of coding was performed by each coder independently, with an agreement of 86.1% for T1 and 83.3% for T2. Then, a second round of coding was performed to resolve the disagreements. Based on the labeled data, we computed the percentages of different chat types. As shown in Table 3, T2 had a relatively large number of chat messages that discuss task content, whereas T1 has more chat messages focusing on task coordination. We also observe that there is a large number of chat messages that are irrelevant to the current task (22% for T1 and 13% for T2).

Table 3: Percentages (S.D.) of chat messages in different categories.

	T1	T2	Sig.
Task social	16.46 (16.24)	12.93 (9.16)	p=0.293
Task content	25.43 (21.66)	58.77 (22.00)	p<0.001
Task coordination	36.51 (24.27)	15.42 (8.49)	p<0.001
Non-task related	21.60 (24.48)	12.88 (17.10)	p=0.060

We think different chat types may have different impact, which motivates us to compare the difference among different chat types. We consider the following five types of chat messages, each inferred from one chat type. Combining each of these search contexts with the Google ranking feature, we propose five contextual models, represented as G+H_CH, G+H_TT, G+H_TC, G+H_TS and G+H_NT, where:

- H_CH: using all chat messages;
- H_TT: using the chat messages of task content;
- H_TC: using the chat messages of task coordination;
- H_TS: using the chat messages of task social;
- H_NT: using the chat messages of non-task.

MAP and nDCG evaluations of the five contextual models, along with the Google baseline (G), are provided in Figure 8. We have several interesting observations based on the results. Firstly, utilizing any type of chat message, even the non-task chat, can help improve search performance over the Google baseline (for both MAP and nDCG). Secondly, the involvement of all chat messages achieves the best performance. This implies that different types of chat messages all contain useful information. Wilcoxon signed-rank tests show that, at most cutoffs, MAP and nDCG of G+H_CH have significant performance improvement over the use of other types of chat messages. However, different types of chat messages may help with different aspects. For example, task coordination (TC) and task content (TT) are the two most effective search contexts. TC has better search performance in T1, whereas TT performs better in T2. We think this is related to the amount of messages for each type of chat in each task (see Table III) - TT occurs the most in T2, whereas TC occurs the most in T1. Note that the contextual feature used in our re-ranking model is already normalized by the number of chat messages (see Formula 2), a better search performance of a contextual model means that the amount of useful information contains in one unit of chat message is richer than that in other models.

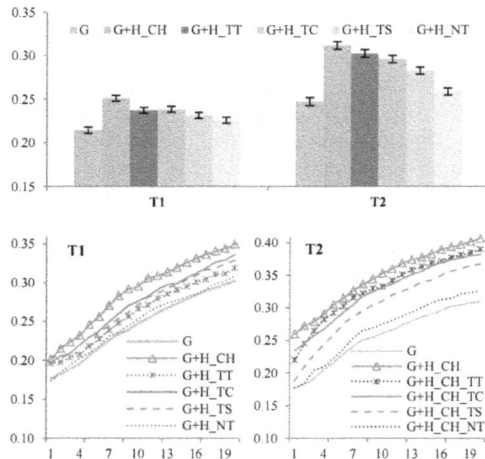

Figure 8: MAP (top) and nDCG (bottom) evaluation on the effectiveness of different search contexts in CIR. X: task/cutoff. Y: MAP/nDCG values.

Since non-task (NT) chat contains a large amount of noise information, unsurprisingly, G+H_NT is the least effective chat-based contextual model. Despite this, we still observe a significant MAP and nDCG (at most of the cutoffs) increase when utilizing the NT chat, which may due to the following two reasons. First, one chat message in our study refers to all content typed into the chat box before a user hits the submit button. Therefore, one chat message may contain more than one type of chat information. However, in our manually-labeled dataset, one chat message is forced to be put into one of the four chat types. It is possible that the effectiveness of the NT chat comes from these chat messages that contain multiple chat types. Second, the noise information in the NT chat messages probably does not hurt the search result ranking either. We hypothesize that the noisy information from NT chat messages (e.g., *lol*, *hah*) is so different that it has little chance to be included in both relevant and non-relevant documents. Therefore, the noise has no impact on the result re-ranking. We will test this in the next section.

5.4.3 Analyzing Non-task Chat Messages

This section tries to answer the following two questions: (1) whether the involvement or removal of non-task chat messages will influence the effectiveness of chat-based contextual support; and (2) why the noise information involved in non-task chat messages does not hurt search performance.

In the first experiment, we introduce an additional search context, which includes all chat messages except NT chat messages. We name it H_NT_R. Combining this search context with the Google ranking feature (G), we can obtain a new contextual model, G+H_NT_R. Then, we compare its performance with two baselines - G and G+H_CH. As shown in Figure 9, the MAP and nDCG evaluations of G+H_NT_R are almost identical to that of G+H_CH except for a slightly better performance over G+H_CH on nDCG (though no statistical significance is detected). This implies that despite providing useful contextual information (see Figure 8), NT chat is already covered by the chat messages of other types.

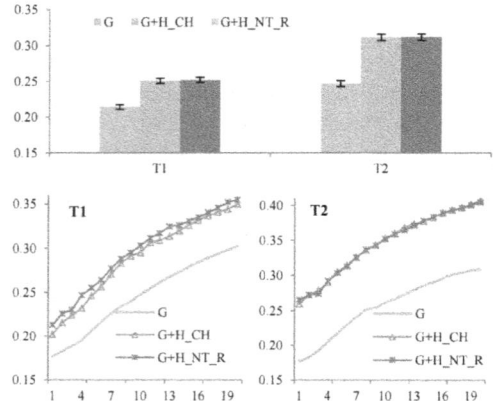

Figure 9: MAP (top) and nDCG (bottom) evaluation on the effectiveness of different search contexts in CIR. X: task/cutoff. Y: MAP/nDCG values

Next, we examine the impact of noisy information in the NT chat messages. Specifically, we want to know whether non-chat information is equally likely to occur in relevant documents and in the whole data corpus, which can be seen as a representation of non-relevant documents (for each query, the relevant document is usually only a small proportion of the whole data corpus). If NT chat messages are equally likely to occur in relevant and non-relevant documents, we can think that the NT chat messages have no impact on retrieving relevant documents. We use the term occurrence probability to measure this likelihood. $p(t|R)$ is the term occurrence probability in the relevant document pool, and $p(t|C)$ is the term occurrence probability in the whole data corpus, where t is a single term, R denotes the relevant document pool, and C denotes the whole data corpus. The relevant documents are decided based on the ground-truth relevance, which is calculated using Formula (3). A document with a ground-truth relevance score of more than 3.0 is used to form R.

We compute both the term occurrence probability for NT chat messages and for task-related chat messages (TT, TS and TC). As shown in Table IV, the NT chat has almost the same term occurrence probability in the relevant document pool and in the whole data corpus. However, the chat term occurrence probability of task-related chats in the relevant document pool is almost 1.5 times of the whole data corpus. This explains why including noise information from the NT chat does not influence the search performance.

5.5 Discussions and Insights

Our current evaluation procedure prefers the models that produce more relevant documents. However, not all CIR tasks are concerned on saving relevant documents. User

Table 4: Term occurrence probabilities for NT and non-NT chat (TT+TS+TC) for both two tasks.

Task		NT (10^{-3})	TT+TS+TC (10^{-3})
T1	p$(t\|C)$	0.520	1.936
T1	p$(t\|R)$	0.509	2.422
T2	p$(t\|C)$	0.333	2.120
T2	p$(t\|R)$	0.346	3.139

communication and collaboration may play more important roles in defining task success. So far, a robust evaluation metric to quantify all of these effects is still missing, and this remains an open issue in the CIR research community [19]. In CIR, existing evaluation metrics and the methods for ground-truth construction are mostly derived from IIR. Therefore, it is unsurprising to observe that the pure Google search performance for IIR is higher than CIR in T2 (see Figure 4 and Figure 5, for both the MAP and nDCG), which means that the ground-truth data may be more biased towards the individuals' search queries. Once the new CIR-based evaluation metrics are defined, we can further re-examine the effectiveness of different search contexts. This is one of our current limitations.

Another limitation is about the task generalizability. So far, this study only considers two types of tasks - an academic task and a leisure task. Although they are commonly adopted in CIR studies [20, 22, 24, 28], these tasks cannot cover the wide variety of the tasks employed in CIR. We plan to develop more search tasks and recruit more users to test the generalizability of our conclusions.

Our experimental results demonstrate that the contextual supports developed in IIR can be directly applied in CIR. However, their effectiveness highly depends on task types. In our study, the contextual support for CIR is consistent with that for IIR in search-intensive tasks, while differing in collaboration-intensive tasks. The result difference between two task types is due to the degree of user collaboration. Having more collaboration from team members may potentially change users' own search traces so that he/she may issue different types of search queries and click different types of web pages. This suggests that researchers should be more careful when applying IIR models in CIR, particularly when the search tasks require significant user collaborations.

We also find that the unique contextual information in CIR, including both partners' search histories and team members' chat histories, can significantly boost performance. However, the chat-based contextual support in CIR is also easily affected by task types. The utilities of chat-based search contexts may be related to the quality and quantity of chat messages that are available in CIR. For example, we found that chat-based contextual support can produce better search performance in chat-intensive tasks than in search-intensive tasks. When both search and chat histories are not enough, a proper leverage (e.g., combining) of both is needed.

6. CONCLUSIONS AND FUTURE WORK

Observing the increasing popularity of Collaborative Information Retrieval (CIR) in modern search systems [15], our study in this paper targets the support of CIR using contextual information. To be specific, we study: (1) whether the contextual supports developed in IIR can also be ap-

plied in CIR; and (2) if the unique information available in CIR, including chat information and partners' search histories, can be applied for better modeling of users' search contexts. These two questions are answered based on a list of our properly designed contextual support experiments, which are built on the data obtained through a user study with 54 participants working on two CIR search tasks.

Using the collected dataset, we set up a Context-sensitive Collaborative Information Retrieval (CCIR) framework to examine the effectiveness of different types of contextual information. Based on our experimental results, we find that the contextual support developed in IIR can be directly applied into CIR without significant adjustments. Specifically, the contextual search support for CIR is similar to IIR in search-intensive tasks, while it differs in collaboration-intensive tasks. We also find that the CIR contextual support can benefit from the unique information that is only available in CIR - i.e., partners' search behaviors and explicit collaboration among team members through chat. Particularly, although the chat often includes a massive amount of noisy information, such noise does not affect the document re-ranking because they do not occur in relevant documents.

We will explore several new topics in the future. First, chat is demonstrated to be an effective contextual resource, particularly in the chat-intensive search tasks. However, as we mentioned in Section 5.4.2, there is no clear definition for the unit of a chat message. For now, one chat message is defined as *all of the content a user types in the chat box before he/she hits the submit button*. Under this definition, however, it is very commonly observed that multiple messages focus on the same topic and/or subtopic or one message talks about multiple topics and subtopics. Segmenting chat messages into multiple semantic units may provide a better understanding of the chat-based search contexts.

Second, we want to develop an innovative contextual support algorithm to accommodate different search strategies for different users. CIR is usually associated with complex information needs, where both an individual user and a whole team usually develop various search strategies. For example, some teams may start their searches with general topics for two users, and then discuss and narrow down the search scopes. Other teams may prefer to divide the search tasks into several small subtopics and assign these subtopics for different team members at the very beginning. Identifying different search strategies and providing proper support for each one is an important future consideration.

Third, we have thus so far explored several search contexts and observed that most of them can provide positive contributions for supporting CIR search processes. However, we have not taken advantage of combining multiple search contexts into one unified model. This is another potential research topic for the future.

7. REFERENCES

[1] R. Baeza-Yates, B. Ribeiro-Neto, et al. *Modern information retrieval*, volume 463. ACM press, 1999.

[2] S. Bateman, C. Gutwin, and G. McCalla. Social navigation for loosely-coupled information seeking in tightly-knit groups using webwear. In *Proceedings of the 2013 conference on Computer supported cooperative work*, pages 955–966. ACM, 2013.

[3] P. Bennett, R. White, W. Chu, S. Dumais, P. Bailey, F. Borisyuk, and X. Cui. Modeling the impact of

short-and long-term behavior on search personalization. In *Proceedings of the 35th ACM SIGIR conference on Research and development in information retrieval*, pages 185–194, 2012.

[4] P. Borlund. Experimental components for the evaluation of interactive information retrieval systems. *Journal of documentation*, 56(1):71–90, 2000.

[5] A. Diriye and G. Golovchinsky. Querium: a session-based collaborative search system. In *Advances in Information Retrieval*, pages 583–584. 2012.

[6] R. Farzan. *A study of social navigation support under different situational and personal factors*. PhD thesis, University of Pittsburgh, 2009.

[7] R. González-Ibáñez, M. Haseki, and C. Shah. Let's search together, but not too close! an analysis of communication and performance in collaborative information seeking. *Information Processing & Management*, 49(5):1165–1179, 2013.

[8] S. Han, D. He, Z. Yue, and P. Brusilovsky. Supporting cross-device web search with social navigation-based mobile touch interactions. In *User Modeling, Adaptation and Personalization - 23rd International Conference, UMAP 2015, Dublin, Ireland, June 29 - July 3, 2015. Proceedings*, pages 143–155, 2015.

[9] S. Han, Z. Yue, and D. He. Understanding and supporting cross-device web search for exploratory tasks with mobile touch interactions. *ACM Transactions on Information Systems (TOIS)*, 33(4):16, 2015.

[10] J. Hyldegård. Collaborative information behaviour - exploring kuhlthau's information search process model in a group-based educational setting. *Information Processing & Management*, 42(1):276–298, 2006.

[11] J. Jiang, S. Han, J. Wu, and D. He. Pitt at trec 2011 session track. In *TREC*, 2011.

[12] C. Kohlschütter, P. Fankhauser, and W. Nejdl. Boilerplate detection using shallow text features. In *Proceedings of the third ACM international conference on Web search and data mining*, pages 441–450, 2010.

[13] C. C. Kuhlthau. Inside the search process: Information seeking from the user's perspective. *JASIS*, 42(5):361–371, 1991.

[14] M. Morris. A survey of collaborative web search practices. In *Proceedings of the SIGCHI Conference on Human Factors in Computing Systems*, pages 1657–1660, 2008.

[15] M. Morris. Collaborative search revisited. In *Proceedings of the 2013 conference on Computer supported cooperative work*, pages 1181–1192, 2013.

[16] M. R. Morris and E. Horvitz. Searchtogether: an interface for collaborative web search. In *Proceedings of the 20th annual ACM symposium on User interface software and technology*, pages 3–12, 2007.

[17] J. Pickens, G. Golovchinsky, C. Shah, P. Qvarfordt, and M. Back. Algorithmic mediation for collaborative exploratory search. In *Proceedings of the 31st ACM SIGIR conference on Research and development in information retrieval*, pages 315–322, 2008.

[18] C. Shah. Coagmento-a collaborative information seeking, synthesis and sense-making framework. *Integrated demo at CSCW*, pages 6–11, 2010.

[19] C. Shah. Collaborative information seeking. *Journal of the Association for Information Science and Technology*, 65(2):215–236, 2014.

[20] C. Shah and R. González-Ibáñez. Exploring information seeking processes in collaborative search tasks. *Proceedings of the American Society for Information Science and Technology*, 47(1):1–7, 2010.

[21] C. Shah and G. Marchionini. Awareness in collaborative information seeking. *Journal of the American Society for Information Science and Technology*, 61(10):1970–1986, 2010.

[22] C. Shah, J. Pickens, and G. Golovchinsky. Role-based results redistribution for collaborative information retrieval. *Information processing & management*, 46(6):773–781, 2010.

[23] X. Shen, B. Tan, and C. Zhai. Context-sensitive information retrieval using implicit feedback. In *Proceedings of the 28th annual international ACM SIGIR conference on Research and development in information retrieval*, pages 43–50, 2005.

[24] L. Soulier, C. Shah, and L. Tamine. User-driven system-mediated collaborative information retrieval. In *Proceedings of the 37th international ACM SIGIR conference on Research & development in information retrieval*, pages 485–494, 2014.

[25] B. Tan, X. Shen, and C. Zhai. Mining long-term search history to improve search accuracy. In *Proceedings of the 12th ACM SIGKDD international conference on Knowledge discovery and data mining*, pages 718–723, 2006.

[26] R. W. White, W. Chu, A. Hassan, X. He, Y. Song, and H. Wang. Enhancing personalized search by mining and modeling task behavior. In *Proceedings of the 22nd international conference on World Wide Web*, pages 1411–1420, 2013.

[27] Z. Yue, S. Han, and D. He. An investigation of search processes in collaborative exploratory web search. *Proceedings of the American Society for Information Science and Technology*, 49(1):1–4, 2012.

[28] Z. Yue, S. Han, and D. He. Modeling search processes using hidden states in collaborative exploratory web search. In *Proceedings of the 17th ACM conference on Computer supported cooperative work & social computing*, pages 820–830, 2014.

[29] Z. Yue, S. Han, D. He, and J. Jiang. Influences on query reformulation in collaborative web search. *Computer, IEEE*, (3):46–53, 2014.

[30] C. Zhai and J. Lafferty. Model-based feedback in the language modeling approach to information retrieval. In *Proceedings of the tenth international conference on Information and knowledge management*, pages 403–410, 2001.

[31] C. Zhai and J. Lafferty. A study of smoothing methods for language models applied to ad hoc information retrieval. In *Proceedings of the 24th annual international ACM SIGIR conference on Research and development in information retrieval*, pages 334–342, 2001.

(The Lack of) Privacy Concerns with Sharing Web Activity at Work and the Implications for Collaborative Search

Scott Bateman
Faculty of Computer Science
University of New Brunswick
Fredericton, New Brunswick, Canada
+1 (506) 453-4566
scottb@unb.ca

Carl Gutwin
Department of Computer Science
University of Saskatchewan
Saskatoon, Saskatchewan, Canada
+1 (306) 966-4886
gutwin@cs.usask.ca

ABSTRACT

Collaborative information seeking frequently occurs in an opportunistic and loosely-coupled fashion that is supported by awareness of others' activities on the web. Automatically sharing traces of information about web activity could substantially improve these collaborative information tasks, but conventional wisdom suggests that people are very reluctant to share information about web usage. Because work settings have different rules and practices about privacy, we carried out the first systematic study of people's privacy concerns about sharing web activity within workgroups. To provide a better understanding of privacy concerns about sharing web activity at work, we conducted a two-week diary study with 18 participants. Our study system asked participants to report on their search tasks and privacy concerns. Surprisingly, our results showed that people have little concern about sharing the majority of their activities with their work colleagues, and had even fewer concerns with sharing work-related activities. Our results provide new insights into the possibilities of sharing web activities within workgroups, and provide evidence that tools based on automatic sharing of awareness information can be feasible.

Categories and Subject Descriptors

H.5.3 Group and Organization Interfaces: *Computer-supported cooperative work*

General Terms

Measurement, Human Factors.

Keywords

privacy, collaborative search, loosely-coupled collaboration

1. INTRODUCTION

People often collaborate on information tasks in a loosely-coupled fashion – that is, they do not work together on explicit and immediate activities, but rather work independently towards a shared goal. Loosely-coupled tasks are often set in a social context, where we use our knowledge about other peoples' actions, experience and knowledge to guide our information seeking activities. For example, we might trust and use the information in an article because an expert we know cited it, or

CHIIR '16, March 13 - 17, 2016, Carrboro, NC, USA
Copyright is held by the owner/author(s). Publication rights licensed to ACM.
ACM 978-1-4503-3751-9/16/03...$15.00
DOI: http://dx.doi.org/10.1145/2854946.2854977

we might hunt for a recipe because our officemates have raved about it. In such situations, the awareness information needed to support this type of loose, informal collaboration is gathered opportunistically; e.g., having a chance conversation with colleagues, seeing what they are doing, what they have on their desks, or with whom they are speaking [10][14]. Loosely-coupled collaborative information tasks are a important part of group work, and actually occur more frequently than explicit, heavyweight forms of collaboration [14].

Previous work on collaborative search has almost exclusively focused on tightly-coupled forms of collaboration (e.g., [16][17][24]). In tightly-coupled collaboration, people work together closely and deliberately, with explicitly-shared information needs. Because of the style of collaboration, tightly-coupled collaboration typically requires more time to setup, and more time and effort to conduct.

Less is known about how to support loosely-coupled information tasks where people work together in an opportunistic and lightweight way. However, it is likely that loosely-coupled information seeking is at least as common more tightly-coupled information seeking. Because loosely-coupled tasks are often more fleeting, and require less explicit thought or effort, they are not often thought of as collaborations. For example, we might search for an online video because a friend mentioned it, or we might search for a hotel recommended by a neighbor. As in tightly-coupled collaborations [19], loosely-coupled collaboration is concerned with how people can maintain the group awareness that allows them to work in a coordinated fashion, to efficiently divide labor, and to avoid duplication of effort. People could explicitly tell others about their activities (e.g., regularly reporting to others in the group about what sources of information they have looked at), but people often use the most convenient source of information possible, and often want to end their information seeking tasks as soon as they have minimally satisfied their information need [6]. This means that explicit communication can often be too time-consuming and laborious for the opportunistic and immediate needs of loosely-coupled web search tasks.

One simple alternative is to automatically share traces of information about each person's activity within a trusted group. This way, if and when awareness information is needed, it can be made available. In particular, since the WWW and web search are central to many information-based tasks, it is likely that sharing Web activities (such as the title and URL of a visited page, and the time and duration of the visit) with a workgroup could provide valuable awareness information that would support coordination and loosely-coupled collaboration. Recent research has demonstrated that there can be several benefits to sharing web activities at work – that automatically sharing simple details about web browsing and search activities can provide the awareness needed to support loosely-coupled collaborative search [2].

However, many people are reluctant to let others see their web activities because of privacy concerns [5]. Researchers have typically assumed that this reluctance rules out systems that depend on this type of sharing, but there may still be a route forward for sharing-based systems that focus specifically on work settings. Work environments are something of a special case for privacy, because in many workplaces (e.g., open-plan offices), people have relatively little control over who sees the contents of their computer monitors [3], and because the organization may frown on activities that are not related to work. If people's attitudes towards sharing web activity are different for work environments, then it is possible that sharing-based awareness systems can succeed.

There is very little information available, however, about whether people are willing to share work-related web activities with their colleagues. People naturally conduct activities on the Web that are work-related when at the office, and in many cases these do not need to be kept private. Further, personal information activities might be seen as shareable as well, because people have a lower expectation of privacy at work and typically only carry out "safe for work" activities in the that environment. It could also be that people are mainly concerned about certain types of web-based tasks: for example, people might be more willing to share fact-finding activities as compared to details relating transaction-type tasks (including banking, shopping or communications). Such contextual factors may be important for providing a better understanding of what and when people might be willing to share with others in a work environment.

To provide a basic understanding of people's actual privacy concerns about sharing web activities in the workplace, we carried out a two-week diary study of 18 students who work in office environments. Participants carried out their normal web-based activities, and our system periodically asked them to report on how concerned they would be if details about the page and activity they were working on at that time was shared with their colleagues. Our survey also collected details about the contextual factors around the web activity to provide detail about differences in people's willingness to share.

There are five main results from our study:

- People were surprisingly willing to share work-related web activity with colleagues – overall, participants were open to sharing over 76% of their web activity.

- When at work, people evenly split their web-based activities between work related and non-work (i.e., personal) related tasks. However, people felt less concern about sharing their work related activities than their non-work activities – participants were open to sharing over 90% of the work-related web activity.

- People rated task types differently, and expressed more concern about transaction and browsing tasks than about fact-finding and information gathering tasks. Transaction and browsing tasks were more frequently non-work tasks, whereas fact-finding and information gathering tasks were most often work tasks.

- Although information-seeking tasks frequently involved some form of collaboration (58% of the time), people were no more concerned about sharing with their colleagues when tasks were or were not collaborative.

- Of three specific privacy concerns raised, people were most concerned in non-work situations that their colleagues might feel they are wasting their time or that they should be working rather than conducting personal tasks. However, overall ratings of specific concerns were low (below neutral).

Our study is the first to systematically explore privacy concerns about sharing web activities in workgroups. Although more work needs to be done to replicate and generalize these findings, our results show that sharing web activity in work environments can be a feasible way to enable group awareness for loosely-coupled information seeking tasks. The results point to a new direction for collaborative search research, where ways to provide awareness about group information seeking activities are explored, in order to support lightweight, opportunistic forms of collaboration.

2. RELATED WORK

2.1 Loosely-Coupled Collaboration

The majority of information sharing in most workplaces occurs in a lightweight and informal way. Most workplace interactions (81%) occur in an informal, unplanned, and opportunistic fashion [1]. This is also true for collaborative search. Observations of collocated collaborative information-seeking tasks found that the majority of instances also occurs in an unplanned manner; e.g., in one study, 62% of collaborations occurred without pre-planning [1]. These kinds of collaborations often involve *loosely-coupled* work [14] – coupling describes the amount of work that people can do individually before they require communication or actions from another person [10].

In loosely-coupled work, people often work independently towards a shared goal, and communication with collaborators must be low-cost, because the collaboration is often secondary to the underlying task; if the cost of communication is too high, people will simply not engage in it [1][10][14].

Recognizing how collaborative work and search situations arise in real world workgroups has important implications for research into collaborative search. In particular, collaborative tools must be lightweight, easy to use and fast to access, because if they are not people will likely not use them and find other solutions [15][18].

2.2 Collaborative Search and Information Seeking

Collaborative search has been defined as a situation where users have "explicitly shared information needs" [9] and work together to fulfill those needs. The area of collaborative search has been active over the past decade and has produced many sophisticated, well-designed and free tools to allow people to collaborate in search tasks in a wide variety of collaborative scenarios (e.g., [16][17][24]; see [19] for a review). Recent findings suggest that collaborative search systems have not been adopted because people opt for lighter-weight alternatives (e.g., emailing links) [15].

Recently, Bateman, et al. [2] showed that automatic sharing of web activity can provide a lightweight approach for supporting loosely-coupled information seeking. They created the WebWear system that shares and presents identifiable web activity of people within a small, trusted group of colleagues. WebWear was a browser extension designed to require less effort: people are able to continue using the familiar support tools that are built into the webpages and search engines that people already use; and people can control sharing with the group using a simple On/Off switch. Through a lab study and field trial, WebWear was shown to successfully support both simulated and real instances of unplanned collaboration on the Web [2].

2.3 Awareness Systems and Privacy

Many collaborative search systems can be considered as awareness systems; they provide information that facilitates different forms of collaboration through being aware of other people's actions. Research into awareness systems has noted that too much awareness can be a bad thing because it raises privacy concerns [12]. In the physical world it is often immediately clear to people what is private and what is public, and people are able to adjust their behavior accordingly to protect their own privacy and to respect the privacy of others [12]. However, in the digital world we often lack the cues that are needed to distinguish between public and private spaces. This means there is often a tradeoff between providing awareness information and protecting privacy. On the one hand, providing a little awareness information preserves privacy, but will likely not facilitate collaboration. On the other hand, providing a lot of awareness information can compromise privacy, but can improve collaboration [4][12].

For a person to feel that their privacy has been protected requires that they are comfortable with the information that a system has about them. In particular, people must feel they have control over the flow of information [4]. Managing and controlling privacy can be difficult because it is a dynamic process that is under continuous refinement, with the boundaries between public and private changing based on contextual factors [21] (e.g., who might see the information, what am I currently doing, etc.). Because of this complexity there are still few good lightweight mechanisms that allow finely-grained control over the distribution of awareness information. Most solutions require too much user effort and only allow coarse-grained schemes for distributing information [4]. Because the cost of effort for users to maintain their privacy is too high, it can prevent people from sharing awareness information (in order to avoid privacy concerns). The tension between user effort and the need for fine-grained contextual control has led to the investigation of different factors that mediate privacy concerns.

2.4 Privacy Concerns with Sharing Web and Search Activity

There is some research that has investigated the use of web activity in awareness systems and what privacy concerns this might raise. It is known that most search engine users believe that having their search history tracked by search engines is an undesirable thing [22]; the existence and success of search engines like DuckDuckGo (which does not collect or employ usage data) provide evidence for this. One survey of information sharing preferences within a large company has suggested that people may not want to broadcast the pages they are visiting to their entire company, and would prefer to share their web activity with smaller groups of close colleagues [5]. However, people are generally much more willing to share activity about the work-related websites they have visited than the non-work related websites. People treat the sharing of their work-related web activity similarly to other work related activities (e.g., sharing information about the work-related documents they have accessed, their availability, or their workplace calendar entries). Further, people have a high willingness to share their work-related website activity with trusted colleagues and managers [20]. Other research has shown that people are willing to make a large portion of their activity (42% on average) completely viewable to people who may incidentally see their screen, but people vary widely on exactly what details of web activity they are willing to share [11].

Perceived risks (such as those associated with privacy) can be a powerful influence on the decisions we make, and often outweigh perceived benefits (called negativity bias) [23]. This means that awareness systems must minimize perceived privacy risks as much as possible, in order for people to willingly share their web activity. However, little is still known about the contextual factors within workplace information seeking that lead people to have higher or lower levels of concern for their privacy.

In the previously described field trial of the WebWear system [2], which automatically shared and presented web activity with a group of trusted colleagues, participants expressed the general view that the workplace was an appropriate context for this type of sharing. However, a few still expressed concerns about privacy, despite the fact that WebWear had actually been used in the context of workplace activities. This suggests that, even though people feel that sharing web activity can be appropriate and helpful, there are still contexts in which privacy concerns occur during workplace information seeking.

Overall, past research has shown that people are willing to share awareness information for a large portion of their web activity. Further, it seems people are more willing to share work-related web activity with work colleagues, but little is known about what other contextual factors may play a role in these situations, what the specific reasons for privacy concern might be.

3. DIARY STUDY

To better understand people's overall privacy concerns with sharing web activities within workgroups, we designed a diary study that asked people to describe and make judgments about their visits to different webpages. We also identified three previously unexplored (or minimally explored) contextual factors that can provide important insights into situational factors that may contribute to privacy concerns:

1) *work relatedness*: whether the task is a work or non-work task,

2) *task type*: the type of information-seeking task that is being conducted, and

3) *collaboration*: whether the task is part of an established collaboration or not.

Work Relatedness: First, the Web allows us to easily perform many different tasks regardless of where we are. Therefore, it could be that many people carry out personal tasks while at work. In information-seeking tasks that are not related to work activities (or non-work tasks), people may prefer to keep the details of the task private from their colleagues. To explore if work relatedness may be connected to people's privacy concerns we asked people to classify the task they were currently working on as being either a work task (part of their primary employment) or a non-work task. Previous work has suggested that people believe they would be willing to share their work-related web browsing with close colleagues [5], but these judgments have not been made within the context of real information-seeking tasks.

Task Type: Second, the type of information-seeking task being conducted can vary greatly, and might present very different privacy concerns (e.g., a transaction task, like online banking, is more likely to be kept private than a fact-finding task, such as looking up a weather forecast). To investigate if task type may be a good predictor of privacy concerns in workplace information seeking, participants classified their current task as being one of five different task types (based on Kellar et al.'s information-seeking task types [13]):

- *Fact-finding* involves the seeker looking for a specific piece of information like the weather, a recipe, or a piece of software;

- *Information Gathering* involves collecting information from multiple sources over a period of time, and unlike fact-finding, there may be no set finish point;

- *Browsing* involves reviewing information and web sites with no specific goal in mind, although, a broad goal such as "what's new" may be set;

- *Transactions* involve online actions such as sending an email or banking; and,

- *Other* tasks include all tasks that do not fit into the previous four categories.

Collaboration: Third, previous work suggests that collaboration in information seeking is common [1][7][8]. In collaborative situations one might expect that since the information being sought will be shared at some point, people will have fewer concerns if their activities are public. However, there is little information on whether sharing details about collaborative tasks is less of a privacy concern than details of personal tasks.

3.1 Research Questions

The diary study was designed to provide insight into privacy concerns as they relate to six main research questions, which summarize the factors described above (location of the related results section is listed in brackets):

- How often are people concerned with the idea of sharing their workplace web activities with their colleagues? (Section 4.1)

- Do people differ in the amount and types of situations they identify as being a concern? (Section 4.1)

- Do people frequently conduct non-work related tasks during their workdays, and if so, how do people's privacy concerns differ between work tasks and non-work tasks? (Section 4.2)

- What are people's specific concerns with sharing web activities, and do they differ in work and non-work tasks? (Section 4.2.1)

- Does the type of information-seeking task result in different levels of concern about sharing web activities? (Section 4.3)

- Are information-seeking tasks that involve collaboration less of a privacy concern than individual tasks? (Section 4.4)

3.2 Participants

Eighteen people participated in the study (12 male); the average age was 27.6 years (sd. 5.0), and all participants were either graduate students or research assistants. All spent most of their working time in large, open workspaces with individual workstations. 15 people reported using a computer at least 7 hours/day on typical workdays, and the remaining four at least 3 hours/day. All participants used their main work computer to complete the study, of which five were laptops that were used both at home and work. Participants were given a $20 honorarium. Fourteen of the participants were members of the same research lab; four others were individuals from other labs.

3.3 Procedure

Participants were solicited through an email invitation that explained the details of the study, provided a link to a walkthrough video, and a link to download the diary study system (a Chrome browser extension). The video demonstrated all stages of the study, including the installation of the study system and an introduction to the surveys. Upon installation in a participant's

browser, the study system presented a consent form and demographics survey, and would then start periodically making requests to the participant for diary entries to be completed.

Figure 2. A request to complete a survey made by the diary study system (indicated by the red arrow).

Participants were asked to complete a total of 30 surveys over two weeks. Each survey required 3-5 minutes to complete. The system would display a request popup to ask participants to fill out a survey every 15 minutes, but would only make a request if the Chrome browser was currently the active application and a webpage was being displayed (see Figure 1). The request popup displayed the current number of surveys completed and optionally allowed the participant to mark the page as a "do not ask" page (preventing the system from asking about that URL in future). To encourage a wider range of responses and tasks, the system would also not make a request on URLs for which a participant had already completed a survey.

If participants opted not to complete a survey at the time of a request, another request would not be made for at least 15 minutes. If participants agreed to complete a survey, a form was embedded in the page they were currently viewing, to allow participants to consider their responses within the context of the page and their current task (see Figure 2). Once a survey was completed, the system would wait 30 minutes before making another request.

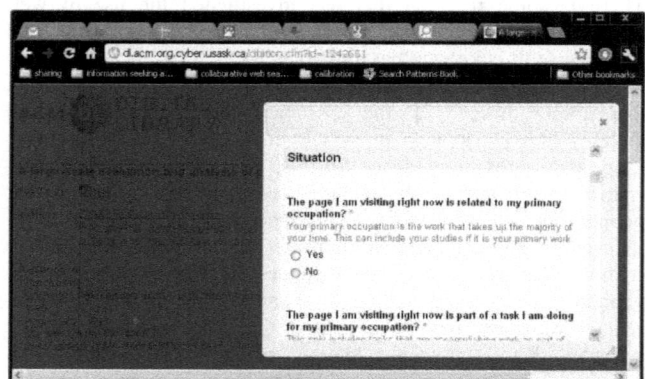

Figure 2. A survey from the diary system embedded in the current webpage being visited by a participant.

3.4 Questions and Data

The data collected in the diary study consisted of the survey responses only – as was clearly explained to participants, no other information was collected[1] (e.g., the name of the page or any content). This was done to reduce privacy concerns about participating and to encourage participants to make honest reports about their activities during workdays. The study system did not collect any identifiable data. Upon installation of the diary system, a random unique ID was generated, and allowed survey responses from the same individual to be connected together.

Surveys consisted of 11 questions, which fell into two broad categories: *situation questions,* which asked about the situation and task surrounding the participant's visit to the current page; and, *sharing questions,* which asked about participant feeling towards having their web activity made visible to their colleagues for the page they were currently visiting, and their interest in seeing the web activities of their colleagues for the same page.

The six situation questions were forced-choice questions, which in some cases allowed participants to select "Other" and provide a textual description of the situation. Situation questions allowed participants to describe the three situational factors: work relatedness, task type, and collaboration (described above).

The five questions about participants' views towards sharing were Likert-scale questions on either a 5-point or 7-point scale. These questions asked participants to rate how concerned they would be if their colleagues could see the web activities describing their visit to the particular page and what those concerns might be. Colleagues were defined of the other "members of your primary workgroup." A free-text space also allowed participants to further describe their concerns about having their web activities shared for the page they were currently visiting.

The main criteria used to judge participants' level of privacy concern, were agreement ratings to the statement: "*I would be concerned if the people in my primary workgroup saw details about my visit to this page. The details would include that I visited the page, when I visited and for how long.*" Participants rated their agreement with this statement on a seven-point scale (*strongly disagree, disagree, slightly disagree, neutral, slightly agree, agree, strongly agree*). Other Likert-scale questions were used in analysis to reveal further details about privacy concerns. These are described with the results where appropriate.

Our specific phrasing for the question was based upon previous work that looked at privacy concerns when sharing activities in the workplace [20]. We also piloted several alternatives of the question on paper with several study participants before the study began.

3.4.1 Data Analysis
Responses to Likert-scale questions were initially converted to numeric values to facilitate comparison, for both 7-point scales (0=strongly disagree to 6=strongly agree) and 5-point scales (0=strongly disagree to 4=strongly agree). All questions were phrased in the same way relating to 'concern', so that the mean values could be directly compared for the overall question, and for each of the three contextual factors (work relatedness, task type, and collaboration). In this way, higher mean values meant that there were higher levels of concern about privacy, and lower mean values that there were lower levels of concerns. In the analysis, participants were considered to be concerned about sharing if they responded at neutral or on the agreement side of the scale, and to be not overly concerned if they rated a question below neutral (on the disagreement side of the scale).

---

[1] One-way hashes of the URLs were captured to ensure that no single page was reported on twice by any individual.

The three contextual factors had the following levels:

- *Work relatedness*: work task or non-work task.
- *Task type*: fact-finding, information gathering, browsing, transaction, or other.
- *Collaboration*: collaborative or non-collaborative.

The surveys contained two questions relating to whether or not the task was part of a collaboration. The first asked whether or not the participant had communicated with someone about the task before or during their visit to the current page. The second asked if participants planned on sharing any of the information on the page with anyone, either directly (through some form of communication) or indirectly (i.e., it would be used to inform future communications). In our analysis, we combined these two questions to indicate whether or not a task was collaborative.

The two-week sample of 30 survey responses provided a limited scope to collect individual information-seeking behavior. This means that an individual participant's information seeking might be dominated by a particular set of contextual factors during the diary period (e.g., the participant conducted more information gathering tasks than normal because they were working on a literature review during the study). To avoid the bias that this may cause in overall results, the values for Likert-scale responses are first averaged over an individual for a particular contextual factor, and then averaged over all participants.

Where appropriate we conducted statistical tests to compare the levels of privacy concern. Non-parametric Friedman and Wilcoxon tests were used to test for differences between privacy concerns between multiple and two groups, respectively. Privacy concerned ratings in all situations were converted to numeric values and averaged over each participant for a group of interest.

4. RESULTS
All eighteen participants completed the study by answering at least 30 surveys within the two-week period. Seven surveys were discarded due to system errors; in total, we analysed 533 surveys.

For questions relating to task type and whether the task was collaborative, participants could select "Other" and describe the situation they were in as it related to the contextual factor. These descriptions were used to recode the response to the best value based on their description, if possible; otherwise, the response was left as "Other". Recoding occurred for a total of 37 questions. For example, one participant described the type of task they were conducting as "Searching for a specific resource", which was recoded as a "Fact-Finding" task.

4.1 Overall Privacy Concerns
Overall, participants were not overly concerned with their web activities being shared with colleagues (mean agreement = 1.58, std. dev.=0.95). Figure 3 shows mean ratings by participant. Only two participants expressed overall concern, and 13 of the 18 participants rated their level of concern below 2 ("disagree").

Examining the individual ratings revealed that participants were not overly concerned about privacy for 76% of the pages visited. However, two individuals did express concern with workgroup sharing and accounted for roughly one third of all incidents where concerns were expressed (participant 5 and 12). These two individuals expressed concerns in over half of the tasks they reported on. In contrast, three other participants had extremely low concern on average, with average ratings between 0 and 1. These results suggest that in general peoples' overall level of concern is quite low with regards to sharing web activities in the context of workplace information seeking. However, certain individuals may have important concerns much more frequently.

4.1.1 Anonymous Sharing

Participants also rated their agreement with the statement *"I would be concerned if the people in my primary workgroup saw anonymous details about my visit to this page (the fact that someone in the group visited the page, when, and for how long)."* Participants' level of concern about anonymous sharing was less than that about identifiable sharing (mean agreement = 1.03, s.d.=1.1). However, this did not reduce the level of concern for participants 5 and 12.

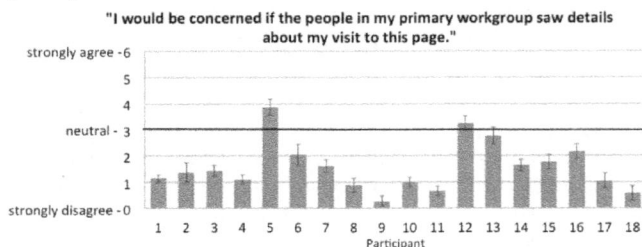

Figure 3. Mean concern level about sharing. Higher values indicate greater concern.

4.2 Relationship between Work Tasks and Privacy Concerns

In the diary study, work tasks were defined as only including *"tasks that are accomplishing work as part of your primary occupation or studies."* Overall, participants' information-seeking tasks completed during the workday were evenly split between work and non-work tasks – 268 were deemed as work tasks and 265 as non-work tasks. However, between participants there was variation in the proportion of work and non-work tasks (see Figure 4). These findings show that people commonly mix work and non-work information-seeking tasks throughout their day.

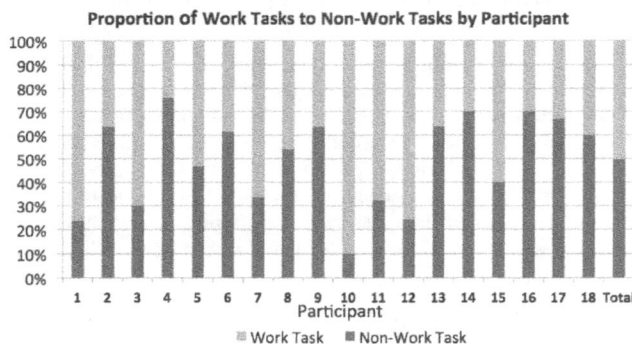

Figure 4. Proportion of work tasks, by participant.

There was a clear relationship between ratings of concern about sharing and whether a task is a work task. Figure 5 splits the data from Figure 3 by work relatedness (work task or non-work task). Overall, participants reported significantly lower level of concern for work tasks (mean agreement=1.10, sd=1.19) than for non-work tasks (mean agreement=2.16, sd=1.02); z=-3.157, $p < .005$.

It should be noted that overall participants' were not overly concerned about either work tasks or non-work tasks. However, concern was reduced for work tasks (people were unconcerned about 86% of work tasks). Further, only 6 of the 18 participants reported specific instances where they had any concerns about work tasks (rating of neutral or above).

The large majority of work tasks where there were concerns came from participants 5 and 12, who accounted for 22 of the 28 instances where concerns were reported during work tasks. When not considering the responses of participant 5 and 12, the remainder of participants reported not being overly concerned in 94% of the work tasks reported.

Overall, participants had a lower level of concern for work tasks. However, for a few individuals the level of concern remained the same or increased slightly for work tasks. Participant 13's mean rating went up slightly from non-work to work tasks. Participant 5 also expressed a much higher level of concern for work tasks than non-work tasks. The exact reasons behind why there was inconsistency between individuals in not entirely clear (although see participant comments below about specific concerns).

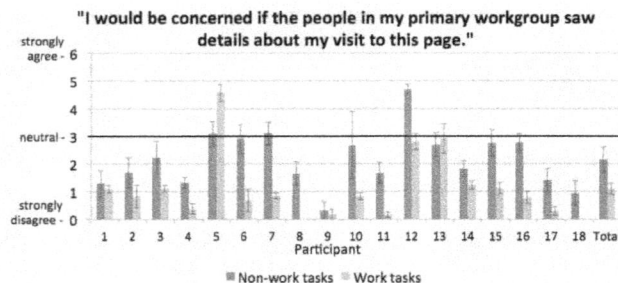

Figure 5. Mean concern level, by work relatedness. (Missing bars indicate a mean ratings of 0).

4.2.1 Specific Privacy Concerns

4.2.1.1 Free-text Comments

In general, participants had less concern in work related tasks, and more concern in non-work tasks. Free-text comments from participants provide some insight into this general trend related to non-work tasks. These comments suggested that participants conducted personal tasks that were outside of the context of their professional relationships and work related duties. For example, participant 3 described a personal task in which they had more privacy concern: *"although the page I'm visiting right now is about a 'good cause', it's not exactly work-related so it might have been better for me to look at this web page at home instead of at work"*. Participant 2 provided another example of having more privacy concern in a non-work task: *"This is a torrent page [where I can download unlicensed software and media that] I am collaboratively browsing with someone in my office and my employer would certainly not like it."*

There were several entries where participants described situations that were contrary to the general trend (of more privacy concern in non-work tasks, less in work tasks). Participant 12, provided an example of having privacy concerns in a work related task:

> As I use the web to find out common information, such as converting centimetres to feet & inches, I would feel like my peers would belittle me for the fact I used google to make these conversions for me, rather than doing these things in my head. So I would rather that this info wasn't shared with others and that others did not see the details of these pages specifically for calculations and conversions.

This comment raises an important consequence of workplace sharing; that is, even if tasks are related to work, there can be a preference to keep them private because of how they might be judged by others.

4.2.1.2 Ratings of Specific Concerns

We also collected ratings about several privacy concerns. For each survey, participants rated their agreement with three specific concerns (on a five-point Likert scale). The three specific worries had been identified in previous work [2]:

* *Misinterpretation of the activity*: "Someone might misinterpret what I am doing";
* *Perception of time-wasting*: "Someone might think I should be doing something else"; and,
* *Negative judgment of activity*: "Someone might not like or might not respect what I am doing."

Again, ratings for specific worries were split into work and non-work tasks in order to explore how participants' level of concern may change in work and non-work situations. Consistent with previous findings, participants were not overly concerned about any of the three specific worries, and levels of concern were again higher in non-work tasks (see Figure 6).

All of the concerns were rated significantly higher in non-work tasks than in work tasks, for: misinterpretation of the activity (Z=-2.947, p<.005), perception of time-wasting (Z=-3.549, p<.001), and negative judgment of activity (Z=-3.258 p≤.001).

While these differences were reliable, the differences in ratings were not large for 'misinterpretation of the task' or 'negative judgment of the activity'. There was a larger difference for 'perception of time-wasting', which indicated that participants were particularly sensitive to others feeling they should be working in the work place rather than conducting a non-work task. Given the prevalence of non-work tasks in the workplace (see Figure 4), it is likely that this specific concern would contribute substantially to the more frequent concerns reported in non-work tasks.

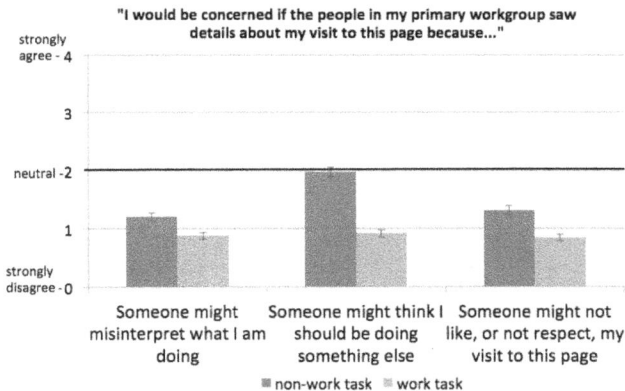

Figure 6. Participant ratings of agreement with specific concerns for sharing web activities with colleagues.

4.3 The Relationship between Task Type and Privacy Concerns

In each survey, participants categorized the type of task that led them to the current page they were visiting as being one of fact-finding, information gathering, browsing, transactions, or other (see above). Because of the privacy differences observed in work and non-work tasks, we first present the frequency of each task type in work and non-work situations (see Figure 7).

All four task types (browsing, fact-finding, info. gathering and transaction) occurred frequently. All participants reported at least one of the four task types in their surveys, with the exception of browsing, which was not reported by two participants. Tasks classified as "other" and that did not fit into the other four categories were only reported in 11 instances, making it difficult to report on observable patterns for this category. Browsing tasks were roughly six times more likely to be conducted in non-work than in work situations. This may indicate that browsing tasks are most often conducted as a leisure activity, which people may prefer to keep to themselves. Transactions were also more frequently non-work tasks, whereas information gathering and fact-finding tasks were mostly completed in work situations. Again, concern levels were still rated as being below neutral for all tasks. Overall, people were more concerned with task types that tend towards personal activity and away from work.

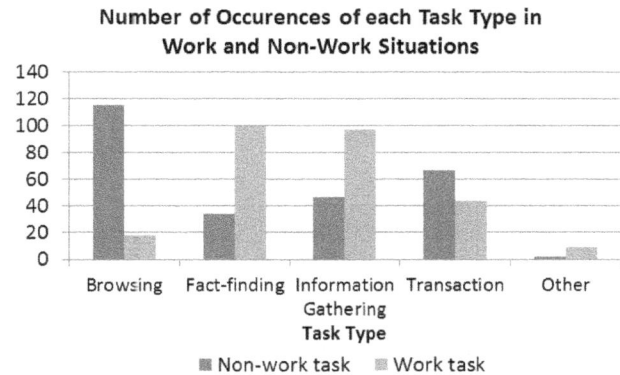

Figure 7. The number of occurrences of each task type reported in the diary study in work and non-work situations.

Regardless of task type, participants were not overly concerned about their colleagues seeing their web activities (see Figure 8). We performed a Friedman test to look for differences between tasks types, but we omitted the 'other' category from this task because of the sparse reporting. There was an effect of task type on concern about sharing with colleagues $\chi^2(3, n=16)=14.006$, p<.005. Pairwise comparisons revealed (with an adjusted alpha of .0083 for multiple comparisons) found that concern was significantly higher for transactions than for fact-finding (Z=-2.657, p<.008) and information gathering (Z=-2.940, p< .005).

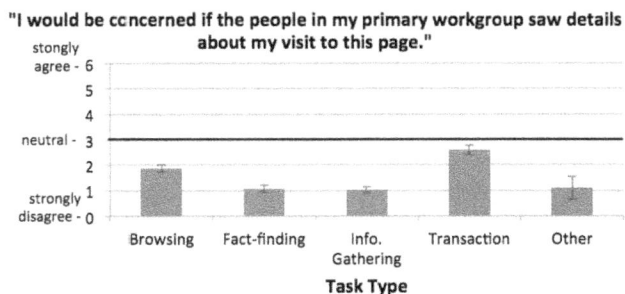

Figure 8. The mean agreement of being concerned with web activities by task type.

Examination of the individual reports, 51 of the 129 tasks (40%) where there were concerns occurred in transaction tasks. Participants' higher concerns during transaction tasks might be explained by the fact that transactions include the use of an online system such as email or online banking. It could be such tasks are part of a secure system where task details are more sensitive.

4.4 Relationship between Collaboration and Privacy Concerns

Collaboration was frequent among participants' information-seeking tasks, with some form of collaboration reported in 58% of surveys. Collaboration was more common in work scenarios, with over two-thirds of tasks involving collaboration. Non-work tasks, in contrast, were more frequently individual (see Figure 9).

Count of Collaboration in Work and Non-Work Tasks

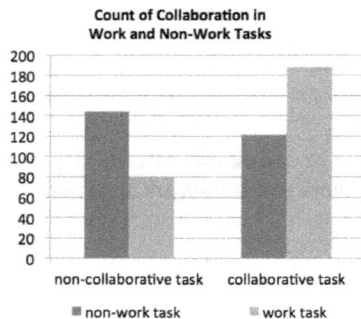

Figure 9. The total number of information-seeking tasks that involved some form of collaboration, split by work and non-work situations.

We expected that people would have a lower level of concern when collaboration had already been established, because there is already information being shared with others. However, this was not the case: there was no significant difference between privacy concerns when collaboration was already established; Z=-1.612, p=.107 (see Figure 10).

"I would be concerned if the people in my primary workgroup saw details about my visit to this page."

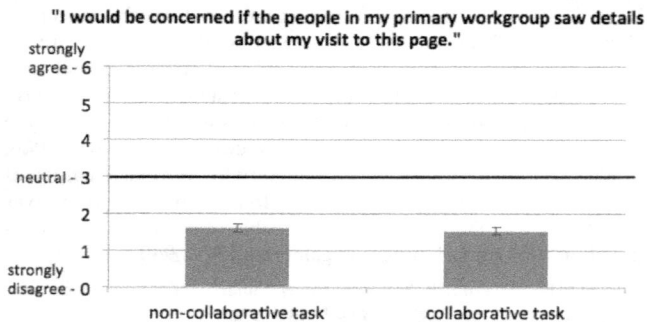

Figure 10. Mean concern level, comparing non-collaborative and collaborative tasks.

4.5 Summary of Results

The diary study of people's privacy concerns with sharing web activities in the workplace provides six results:

1. Overall, people are not overly concerned with sharing the majority of their web activities from workplace information seeking with colleagues. Showing that the workplace can be an appropriate place for sharing web activities.

2. People felt less concern about sharing work-related web activity than non-work activity. Overall, people were open to sharing more than 90% of their work related web activity.

3. People rated task types differently. People expressed more concerns in transaction than in fact-finding and information gathering tasks. Transaction and browsing tasks were more frequently non-work tasks, whereas fact-finding and information gathering tasks were most often work tasks.

4. Although information-seeking tasks frequently involve collaboration (58% of tasks), people had equally low concerns about collaborative and individual tasks.

5. Some individuals expressed privacy concerns much more frequently than others. Two of the eighteen participants expressed concerns at much higher rate.

6. For non-work tasks, people were most concerned that colleagues would feel they were wasting their time or that they should be working. However, overall ratings of specific concerns remained low (below neutral).

The diary study focused on uncovering the potential contextual factors that may exist in workplace sharing, which could be used to understand when privacy concerns may arise. Overall, the diary study showed that people's level of concern about sharing web activities in the workplace was low, that they are willing to share 75% of their overall information seeking activity. Further, simply identifying a task as a work task consistently identified situations where participants had even lower levels of concern.

5. DISCUSSION

In the following paragraphs we consider why people's levels of concern were low in the study, whether the overall lack of concern would actually lead people to share information in a real system, how our participants and study setting generalize to other kinds of organizations, and the implications of our findings for future studies of collaborative search.

Why were levels of privacy concerns low in the diary study, and particularly low for work tasks?

Given people's general wariness about being tracked by computer systems [22], we expected that the overall level of privacy concern seen in the study would have been higher, and that incidents where there were concerns would have been more frequent. However, when people actually made judgments about their concerns relating to privacy, they were not overly concerned most of the time. Privacy concerns are likely subject to negativity bias [23] (where negative experiences are much more memorable and meaningful than positive ones), and people may feel that the negative incidents that they do experience or hear about are more common and widespread than they actually are. While the majority of concerns that were expressed came from a few individuals, all participants expressed having at least one incident in the diary study where they had concerns with sharing. This means that privacy concerns are not an uncommon experience in general, but for the most part, concern remains low overall – possibly because people have an established relationship with their workplace colleagues. Because of the trust that exists with colleagues, most people appear to have few concerns about sharing their web activities in the context of work.

Levels of concern were also lower when participants were actually performing a work task – although the study showed that roughly half the tasks conducted at work were non-work tasks. Participants were more worried that others would feel they were wasting time or that they should be doing something else during these personal tasks. It is clear that participants tended to have more concern about personal tasks: this increase may have been because these tasks are outside their relationships with colleagues, may contain confidential details, and are more likely to be misunderstood (colleagues lack the contextual knowledge to accurately interpret the activities). Further, sharing information about work activities was less of a concern, possibly because colleagues often know about these activities already, or because sharing may be seen as beneficial for colleagues to know about.

Would the low levels of concern seen in the study lead people to share their web and search history with their workgroup?

Whether people would share or not with a real system in a real work setting is likely a function of several factors, including the perceived risks of unwanted viewing and the cost of effort in managing the collection of information. Previous work suggests that the feeling of having control [5] is also an important factor when considering sharing personal history traces. People are likely to feel in control if they are sharing within a trusted group, they are guaranteed that unwanted history in the system could be permanently removed, and that no collection can happen when a collection systems is disabled.

Further, if the effort of managing how and when data is shared can be kept to a minimum, people will be more apt to share. Sharing web activity in practice might be managed in a number of ways. For example, the WebWear system described earlier provided a simple on/off switch for sharing – this trivial approach could be sufficient because of the natural temporal clustering of work and personal activities (i.e., people tend to carry out work tasks in a block, and then personal tasks). Another simple mechanism might include white and/or black lists for allowing or preventing sharing. Yet another approach might be to have different profiles set up for workplace web browsers. One profile would be used to share web history automatically, and could be colored red to make its role obvious ("the work browser"). Another browser could be colored gray and used for personal or private web tasks, and where no web activity is shared ("the private browser"). Future work will explore the different mechanisms and schemes that people prefer, and that provide them with the desired level of control with the minimal effort.

Two of 18 participants in the diary study were much less willing to share information – they expressed higher levels of concern much more frequently that the other participants. While these participants might not be easily convinced to share their web activity, it is important to note that the diary study did not provide a strong context or reason for sharing. It could be that these participants did not see value in sharing, and so their ratings reflect their preference to keep things private when a need for sharing was not evident. Many commonly used systems that do a lot of usage tracking (including Facebook, Twitter, Google, etc.) are careful to provide clear utility back to their users. These examples show that people might be more willing to share, if there was clear value from doing so. Future work will also include exploring new systems that appropriately support loosely-coupled collaborations through shared web activities.

Can the insights from the study generalize to other workgroups?

We consider three main aspects of our study in terms of generalizability: our participant population, the activities that people undertook during the study, and the physical setting. First, our participants were graduate students and research assistants, who work in an environment that is different from some organizations, and who may have different attitudes towards privacy than other people. Some of these differences may help to strengthen our results, and others will need to be considered further in future studies. For example, students are likely to visit a wider range of sites on the web (since organizational culture in a research lab may allow more freedom and flexibility), and so our participants may have encountered more content on the web that could be considered inappropriate. It could also be (for this reason or other reasons) that the type of web activity people do in the research lab does not correlate well to the type of activity people do outside of academia. While we have no reason to believe that

the research lab is vastly different from other work environments, it is likely that there are certainly some work groups where the culture would dictate a strong unwillingness towards sharing. The fact that our participants had few concerns about sharing suggests that people in a less-flexible organizational culture, where a larger proportion of web content needs to be "safe for work," may be similarly willing to share. The freer nature of the research lab, however, also raises an issue that will need to be studied further – our participants were considerably less likely to be punished or penalized for being on an inappropriate website, and people in more restrictive settings may be more reluctant to share any information that could be used against them in future.

Second, the tasks that our participants carried out were less explicitly collaborative than clearly-defined project groups; participants were part of a larger lab (20-30 people) and project groups were not often well-defined, and participants most often work individually. In an organization where small-group project work is the norm, we believe that people will likely be even more willing to share work-related activity with their colleagues – for the simple reason that people in these settings understand the value that can come from awareness of the activities of a workgroup (as seen in previous research [3]). This willingness is highly dependent on the organizational culture, but equal-peer teams are now a common way for projects to be carried out in many settings.

Third, our study was carried out in a large open-plan lab that shares many physical characteristics with other organizational settings. In particular, the open plan creates certain expectations about baseline privacy levels – that is, that most activities carried out in the lab can be seen by others [3] – that may contribute to a greater willingness to share. This effect of the physical setting is likely to be similar across many organizations with open-plan layouts, but further work is needed to consider settings that have greater privacy by default (e.g., individual offices).

How can the results inform collaborative search research?

Research in the area of collaborative information seeking addresses situations where users have "explicitly-shared information needs" [9], and where people actively work together to fulfill those needs. The focus on explicitly shared information needs means that research has been oriented towards pre-planned work and tightly-coupled collaborations. As described in the related work section, however, most collaboration occurs in an unplanned, loosely-coupled way, and may be better supported by lighter-weight solutions that fit into existing, individual tools and practices (such as conventional browsers and search engines). It is likely that many opportunities for supporting collaborative search are being missed by the current focus on formal, more explicit types of collaboration.

Our main finding (that people most often have little-to-no concern about sharing their web activities at work) is surprising given a widely held view that people would not want others to see what they do on the Web. Further, the fact that this is true for over 90% of work related tasks in our study means that research into web activity for collaboration and awareness is an important direction for future work. We believe that our results open up the possibility of an additional focus of collaborative search. Rather than focus solely on systems that support tightly-coupled forms of collaboration in search tasks, we should also investigates systems that support more loosely-coupled forms of collaboration.

For example, recent work on the previously described WebWear system [2] has shown that automatically sharing web activity within work groups can be an effective way to support loosely-coupled search collaborations. The results of our study provides further evidence that lightweight forms of collaboration are viable through the sharing of web activity in small groups.

6. CONCLUSION

Collaborative information seeking frequently occurs in an opportunistic and loosely-coupled fashion that is supported by awareness of others' activities on the Web. Automatically sharing traces of information about web activity could substantially improve these collaborative information tasks, but conventional wisdom suggests that people are very reluctant to share information about web usage with other people. Because work settings have different rules and practices about privacy, we carried out the first systematic study of people's privacy concerns about sharing web activity within workgroups.

In the first study to investigate the factors affecting peoples' views on sharing their web activity in the workplace, we conducted a diary study and collected over 530 entries from 18 people during a two-week period. Surprisingly, our results showed that people have little concern about sharing the majority of their activities with their work colleagues, and had even fewer concerns with sharing work-related activities. While the results do not suggest that people's concerns about privacy can be ignored completely, they shed important new light onto the possibility of sharing web activities within workgroups, and provide evidence that tools based on automatic sharing of awareness information can be feasible. We believe our findings will be valuable to a future work in web search, collaborative work and at their intersection in collaborative search.

While previous work in collaborative search has focused on systems that support tightly-coupled collaborative search (where information-seeking work is planned and well defined), our study opens up the possibility of sharing web activities within small trusted groups as a means to support loosely-coupled forms of collaboration, where collaborative search occurs in unplanned and opportunistic ways.

7. ACKNOWLEDGEMENTS

We thank the study participants for openness and time. This work was supported by NSERC through the Discovery Grant Program and the GRAND NCE.

8. REFERENCES

[1] Amershi, S. & Morris, M.R. Co-located Collaborative Web Search: Understanding Status Quo Practices. Proc. *CHI*, 2009, 3937-3640.

[2] Bateman, S., Gutwin, C., & McCalla, G. Social Navigation for Loosely-Coupled Information Seeking in Tightly-Knit Groups using WebWear. In *Proc. CSCW*, 2013. 955-966.

[3] Birnholtz, J., Gutwin, C., Hawkey, K. Privacy in the Open: How Attention Mediates Awareness and Privacy in Open-Plan Offices. In *Proc. of ACM Group*, 2007, 51-60.

[4] Boyle, M. & Greenberg, S. The language of privacy: Learning from video media space analysis and design. *ACM TOCHI*. 12, 2, June 2005, 328-370.

[5] Brush, A.J.B., Meyers, B., Scott, J., & Venolia, G. Exploring awareness needs and information display preferences between coworkers. In *Proc. CHI*, 2009, 2091-2094.

[6] Case, D.O. Principle of least effort. In K. E. Fisher, S. Erdelez & L. McKechnie. *Theories of Information Behaviour*. ASIST Monograph Series, Medford, New Jersey. Information Today, Inc, 2005.

[7] Chi, E.H. Information Seeking Can Be Social. *IEEE Computer*, 42, 3, March 2009, 42-46.

[8] Evans, B.M., and Chi, E.H. An elaborated model of social search. Information Processing and Management,46, 6, November 2010, 656-678.

[9] Golovchinsky, G., Qvarfordt, P., and Pickens, J. Collaborative information seeking. *IEEE Computer*, 42,3, 2009, 47-51.

[10] Gutwin, C., Greenberg, S., Blum, R., Dyck, J., Tee, K., & McEwan, G. Supporting Informal Collaboration in Shared-Workspace Groupware. *JUCS*, 14(9), 2008, 1411-34.

[11] Hawkey, K. & Inkpen, K.M. Privacy Gradients: Exploring Ways to Manage Incidental Information During Co-Located Collaboration. In *Proc. CHI EA*, 2005, 1431-1434.

[12] Hudson, S E., & Smith, I. Techniques for Addressing Fundamental Privacy and Disruption Tradeoffs in Awareness Support Systems. In the *Proc. CSCW*, 1996, 248-257.

[13] Kellar, M., Watters, C., & Sheppard, M. A field study characterizing Web-based information-seeking tasks. *JASIST*, 58, 7, May 2007, 999-1018.

[14] Kraut, R., Fish, R., Root, R., & Chalfonte, B., Informal Communication in Organizations: Form, Function, and Technology, in R. Baecker, *Readings in Groupware and Computer Supported Cooperative Work*, 1993.

[15] Morris, M.R. Collaborative search revisited. In *Proc*. CSCW, 2013. 1181-1192.

[16] Morris, MR. & Horvitz, E. SearchTogether: an interface for collaborative web search. Proc. *UIST*, 2007, 3-12.

[17] Morris, M.R. and Horvitz, E. S3: Storable, Shareable Search. Proc. *Interact*, 2007, 120-123.

[18] Morris, M.R. A survey of collaborative web search practices. *In Proc. CHI*, 2008, 1657-1660.

[19] Morris, M. R., and Teevan, J. *Collaborative Web Search: Who, What, Where, When, and Why*. Morgan and Claypool Publishers, San Rafael, CA, USA, 2010.

[20] Olson, J., Grudin, J., & Horvitz, E. Toward Understanding Preferences for Sharing and Privacy. *Microsoft Technical Report (MSR-TR-2004-138)*, 2004, 10 pages. Available at: http://research.microsoft.com/pubs/70123/tr-2004-138.pdf

[21] Palen, L., and Dourish, P. Unpacking "Privacy" for a Networked World, In *Proc. CHI*, 2003, 129-136.

[22] Purcell, K., Brenner, J., & Rainie, L. *Search Engine Use 2012*. Tech. Report, Pew Internet and American Life Project. March, 2012. Available at http://www.pewinternet.org/Reports/2012/Search-Engine-Use-2012.aspx

[23] Rozin, P., Royzman, E.B. Negativity Bias, Negativity Dominance, and Contagion. *Personality and Social Psychology Review*, 5, 296–320.

[24] Shah, C. & Marchionini, G. Awareness in collaborative information seeking. *JASIS*, 61, 2010, 1970–86.

An AID for Avoiding Inadvertent Disclosure: Supporting Interactive Review for Privilege in E-Discovery

Jyothi K. Vinjumur
College of Information Studies
University of Maryland
College Park, MD USA
jyothikv@umd.edu

Douglas W. Oard
College of Information Studies
& UMIACS
University of Maryland
College Park, MD USA
oard@umd.edu

Amittai Axelrod
UMIACS
University of Maryland
College Park, MD USA
amittai@umiacs.umd.edu

ABSTRACT

When searching for evidence in civil litigation, parties to a lawsuit have the right to withhold some content on grounds of specific privileges that serve to foster socially desirable outcomes such as open communication between attorneys and their clients. As inadvertent disclosure of privileged content can adversely impact a client's interests, review for privilege is a high-stakes process that is most often performed manually. Because the circumstances in which privilege can be claimed are generally well defined, review for privilege is amenable to some degree of automation. This paper describes the design of an interactive system to support privilege review in which the goals are to improve the speed and accuracy of privilege review. Results are reported for a within-subjects study in which six reviewers with different levels of expertise examined email for attorney-client privilege or any other valid basis for withholding the content from release. Quantitative results indicate that substantial and statistically significant improvements in recall can be achieved, but no significant differences in average review speed were detected. Participants self-reported that the identity features exposed by the system were most useful to them, and that the present implementation of features based on content or date added no discernible additional value.

Keywords

Experimentation; Human Factors; Privilege Review; Email Classification

1. INTRODUCTION

In 1989, a court in Washington, DC granted a temporary restraining order to preserve a collection of electronic messages that had been shared between members of the National Security Council in the Executive Office of the President of the United States [1]. The basis for this order was a claim that electronic messages can constitute records of the activity of an organization. In 2006, the Federal Rules of Civil Procedure were amended to make it clear that all forms of electronically stored information, including email, were within the scope of evidence that could be requested from a counterparty incident to civil litigation in the United States. Thus was born the multi-billion dollar industry that has come to be called "e-discovery."[1] The high cost of e-discovery results from two factors: (1) because the standard for relevance is expansive, large numbers of relevant documents could be found, and (2) parties can assert privilege on some relevant documents to withhold some content. Hence each of the relevant documents must typically be reviewed for privilege.

The cost of review for relevance can be controlled using text classification techniques (e.g., based on supervised machine learning), but attorneys are naturally reluctant to trust fully automated techniques for privilege review so long as the scale of the privilege review (i.e., the number of relevant documents) is not so great as to preclude manual review. For this reason, our work in this paper is focused on enhancing the performance of human reviewers. Several types of privilege might be asserted, but in this paper we focus principally on attorney-client privilege. The rationale behind attorney-client privilege is that justice will be best served when attorneys can communicate freely with their clients (e.g., on matters of fact, intent, or legal strategy), and open communication can be fostered by prospectively protecting such communication from disclosure.

Our basic approach to supporting privilege review is to train automated annotators[2] to label specific components of a message with information that we expect might help a reviewer to rapidly make a correct decision. We use a total of five annotators to enrich three types of components: people (or, more specifically, the email addresses for senders and recipients of a message), terms (words found in the message or in attachments to the message), and the date (on which the message was sent). In each case, we compute a numerical score for which higher values indicate a greater likelihood of privilege [18]; for people we also annotate job responsibilities (when known) or organization type (when known, if the job responsibilities are not known).

CHIIR '16, March 13-17, 2016, Carrboro, NC, USA
© 2016 ACM. ISBN 978-1-4503-3751-9/16/03...$15.00
DOI: http://dx.doi.org/10.1145/2854946.2854964

---

[1]"Discovery" in this context refers to a stage in civil litigation in which parties are entitled to request from each other evidence that they believe may be relevant to the case.

[2]We use the word "annotator" to refer to an automated system that generates the assistance.

We have studied the usefulness of these features to human reviewers using a within-subjects user study in which six lawyers each reviewed two sets of documents (email messages, together with their attachments), one set using a baseline system with no annotations, and the second set using our AID system (named for our goal of Avoiding Inadvertent Disclosures) in which annotations were shown for people, terms, and dates. Quantitative measures of review accuracy (e.g., precision and recall) and of review speed are augmented with analysis of self-reported response to questionnaires and interviews. We seek to answer three research questions:

- Do the accuracy of the user's privilege review judgments improve when system-generated annotations are presented during privilege review?

- Does the user's review speed improve when system-generated annotations are presented during privilege review?

- Which system-generated annotations do users believe are most helpful?

Our results indicate that recall can be enhanced by displaying annotations. Although the improvements in recall come at some cost in precision, given the nature of this application, that cost may be acceptable. Participants in the study principally attribute the beneficial effects to annotations of people (rather than of terms or of dates). These formative evaluation results have implications for annotator and interface design.

The remainder of this paper is organized as follows. In Section 2 we begin by reviewing the nature of attorney-client privilege and then we introduce the document collection that we used in our study. Section 3 describes the design of our AID system. We follow this with a description of our user study design in Section 4. Section 5 presents and discusses our results, and in Section 6 we conclude with some remarks on future work.

2. BACKGROUND

2.1 Privilege Review

Privilege in legal context is a right given to the parties in a lawsuit to provide protection against the involuntary disclosure of information. Attorney-client privilege in particular exists to protect the information exchange between "privileged persons" for the purpose of obtaining legal advice. Privileged persons include [8]: (1) the client (an individual or an organization), (2) the client's attorney, (3) communicating representatives of either the client or the attorney, and (4) other representatives of the attorney who may assist the attorney in providing legal advice to the client. However, privilege does not arise simply because privileged persons communicate; it can only be claimed when the content of the communication merits the claim. For example, an email from Jeff Skilling (Enron's president) sent only to James Derick (Enron's general counsel) about pending litigation would be privileged; an email with the same content sent to both James Derrick and a personal friend of Skilling's who was not involved in Enron's business operations would not be, and an email from James Derrick to Skilling that indicated (only) his intent to resign in order to spend more time with his family also would not be privileged.

In e-discovery, documents that are initially marked as responsive to a production request (i.e., a specific request for evidence by the counterparty) are then typically subjected to a linear manual review for privilege in order to be sure that content that could properly be withheld is not inadvertently revealed. Failure to identify a privileged document could jeopardize the interests of the party performing the review, so it is common practice to have highly qualified (and thus expensive) lawyers perform the privilege review. Of course, even experts make mistakes, as the related literature on judging topical relevance clearly indicates. One way of characterizing accuracy is by measuring inter-assessor agreement, which has consistently proven to be lower than one might expect [21, 20]. When searches are done by different users, disagreement might reflect different notions of relevance or, in our application, different ways of reaching decisions regarding privilege. In e-discovery, however, there is a single senior attorney who ultimately certifies the correctness and completeness of the review process, and their interpretation of privilege is thus taken to be authoritative [15].[3]

Carterette and Soboroff have found that when judgments from one person are used to predict system preferences that would be obtained by computing evaluation measures using the judgments of another person, the quality of the prediction can be enhanced by selecting a relatively conservative assessor (i.e., one that has a lower tendency to make a false positive error) as the source of judgments that are the basis for the prediction [5]. This is an intriguing result for our application because in privilege review it is the risk of false negative errors that would generate the greatest concern on the part of the party performing the review.

Recent work has shown that automated techniques that are trained on limited number of human judgments can approach human performance for some review tasks, and in particular on the first-stage relevance review [10]. While there has also been some work on the design and evaluation of automated classifiers to actually perform the privilege review task [7, 9, 19], there is a widely held belief among attorneys that (absent compelling reasons to the contrary such as a need for privilege review at a scale that would otherwise be impractical), reliance on a fully automated classifier for privilege review would incur an undesirable level of as-yet uncharacterized risk. Thus automated classifiers are more often used for consistency checking on the results of a manual privilege review process than as the principal basis for that review. In this paper, we explore a second possible use of the technology. That is, use of automated annotations to (hopefully) improve the accuracy or the cost of a manual review process.

2.2 Document Collection

For our study, we needed a set of documents that we know to be relevant to some request that we might typically see in e-discovery. To train our annotators, we also need a set of similar documents that we know to be privileged. We thus need a test collection that contains some relevance and some privilege judgments. One such collection, which we used in this paper, was produced during the TREC Legal Track in 2010.

In the 2010 TREC Legal Track's "Interactive task",[4] one

---

[3]This certification can itself be litigated; in such cases the court would make the authoritative determination.

[4]A task in which participants design both a system and an

Table 1: TREC 2010 privilege judgments for the training-set and the two review sets of families.

	Training	D_1	D_2
Privileged	932	2	3
Not Privileged	5,799	1	1

task (Topic 303) was to find *"all documents or communications that describe, discuss, refer to, report on, or relate to activities, plans or efforts (whether past, present or future) aimed, intended or directed at lobbying public or other officials regarding any actual, pending, anticipated, possible or potential legislation, including but not limited to, activities aimed, intended or directed at influencing or affecting any actual, pending, anticipated, possible or potential rule, regulation, standard, policy, law or amendment thereto."* [7] The collection to be searched was version 2 of the EDRM Enron Email Collection, which includes both messages and attachments. The items to be retrieved were "document families," where (following typical practice in e-discovery) a family was defined as an email message together with all of its attachments. Five teams contributed a total of six interactive runs for Topic 303, with each run being a binary assignment of all families as relevant or not relevant. A stratified sample of families was drawn from submitted runs, and 1,090 of those families were judged to be relevant [7]. We have drawn a random sample of 200 of those relevant families for use in our study. Our automated annotation pipeline failed on 12 of those 200 families which lacked a critical field (From, To, or Date), so we removed those 12 families from consideration and randomly split the remaining families into two disjoint sets of 94 families each, which we refer to as D_1 and D_2. We consistently use set D_2 with our Baseline system and set D_1 with our AID system.

In the 2010 TREC Legal Track's Interactive task, a second task (called "Topic 304") was to find *"all documents or communications that are subject to a claim of attorney-client privilege, work-product, or any other applicable privilege or protection"* [7]. Two teams submitted a total of five runs, with each run being a binary assignment of every family as Privileged or Not Privileged. A stratified sample of 6,736 families were marked as privileged or not privileged by experienced reviewers,[5] and prior work has shown that these annotations can be used to train a privilege classifier with reasonable levels of accuracy [19]. A total of seven families from this random sample were, by chance, also present in either D_1 or D_2, and we removed the five that had been judged as Privileged from the set that we used for training our numerical annotators.[6] As Table 1 indicates, this resulted in a total of 932 families annotated as Privileged and 5,799 families annotated as Not Privileged that could be used for training our automated annotators.

3. THE AID SYSTEM

Our AID system is a research prototype that is designed to help explore the design space for providing automated

interactive process for using that system

[5] 13 of these 6,736 had actually been marked as Unjudged, but during our experiments those 13 were treated as Not Privileged. The effect of this is negligible.
[6] Because of presentation order neither of those Not Privileged documents was seen by any participant in the user study that we describe in this paper.

assistance to users during privilege review. In this section, we first describe the design of the five types of automated annotators that we have built. We next explain the interface and interaction design of our AID system. A total of 61 of the 94 families in D_1 were reviewed using the AID system by at least one participant during the user study. We characterize the coverage of each of our automated annotators as the fraction of the unique items (people, terms or dates) in those 61 families for which annotations are available.

3.1 Propensity Annotation

Given the central responsibility of people in the definition of attorney-client privilege, a natural choice for an annotator is one that can determine which people have the greatest propensity to engage in privileged communication. As a simplifying assumption, we treat each email address[7] as being associated with a different person. We automatically compute privilege propensity estimates for people using both power iteration and heuristic expansion through egocentric networks [18]. The intuition behind the method is that an initial privilege propensity can be estimated from the annotated training data, and that a fixed point algorithm (similar to PageRank) can then be used to arrive at a somewhat better informed propensity estimate. This approach implicitly assumes that people who communicate with others who have higher propensity should themselves have somewhat higher propensity). One-hop spreading activation is then used to estimate the privilege propensity for email addresses that were not seen in training. We arbitrarily threshold these (non-negative) propensity values at 0.3 and 0.5 to form three categories that indicate weak, moderate, or strong propensity to engage in privileged communication. Of the 345 unique email addresses that appear as a sender or recipient in at least one of the 61 families viewed using the AID system, 19 were annotated with strong propensity, 34 with moderate propensity, and the remaining 292 with low propensity.

3.2 Person Role Annotation

Propensity annotation is intended to help call a user's attention to a specific person, but actually knowing how to interpret the importance of that person requires additional information. Professional reviewers would typically have information about the roles of specific people (e.g., they might know who the attorneys and the senior executives are), and in complex cases such lists could be quite extensive. The speed, and perhaps the accuracy, of the review process might be enhanced if we could embed that information in the review system. For this purpose, we need a role annotator that can associate each email address with some (generic or specific) version of their job title. For our experiments we therefore built a simple role annotator using table lookup. We manually populated this table for 160 of the 1,611 unique email addresses that appear in at least one of the 188 families in either of our two test-sets. We obtained these roles from the MySQL database released by Shetty and Abidi [16], from ground truth produced for evaluating the Author-Recipient-Topic model of McCallum et al

[7] In Enron's email system, person names were sometimes present in the From, To, Cc or Bcc field in lieu of an email address; we treat such cases as if the person name actually was an email address.

55

agreement

termination

credit provision **master** counterparty

ENA changes tax draft issue

payment **comments** terms

form seller **legal** court without

mark litigation provided

collateral agreements

trading upon language respect

event agree transactions

delivery amounts use otherwise claim

swap gtc **obligations** third could claims

kay notice guaranty date damages non

sara **transaction** law price

memo documents **letter** whether

pursuant paragraph defaulting amount

provisions counsel support subject

parties contract ISDA case

buyer arbitration

entities

section

Figure 1: Indicative terms; Terms with larger font size indicate higher Negative Entropy Difference

[12], from other lists found on the Web,[8] from manual examination of automatically inserted signature blocks in email messages throughout the collection, from public profiles such as LinkedIn, and through manual Web searches. The roles were manually edited for consistency and conciseness. A total of 57 of the 345 unique email addresses that appear as a sender or recipient in at least one of the 61 reviewed families were annotated for person role.

3.3 Organization Type Annotation

When the role of a specific person is sometimes not known, reviewers might benefit in such cases from knowing the type of the organization for which that person works. We therefore used the same lookup table to annotate the organization in such cases. We did this by manually examining the domain name of an email address and then using a current domain name registry, a Web search, or our personal knowledge to label the organization's type, when possible. For example, some messages in the Enron collection are from addresses with the domain 'brobeck.com', and Wikipedia indicates that (at the time) Brobeck, Phleger & Harrison was a law firm. We were able to find what we believe to be reasonable organization types for a total of 21 of the 288 unique email addresses that appear as a sender or recipient in at least one of the 61 reviewed families but that have no person role annotation.

3.4 Indicative Terms

Term unigrams have been reported to be a useful feature set for privilege classification [17], so it is natural to also consider annotating terms. The families in our collection

---

[8]http://cis.jhu.edu/~parky/Enron/employees, http://www.desdemonadespair.net/2010/09/bushenron-chronology.html

contain many more terms than the email addresses. Hence some approach to feature selection is needed if we are to avoid the display clutter that would result from annotating every term. We perform this feature selection by obtaining the entropy difference for each term. The entropy difference score identifies words that are like words in the Privileged set and also unlike words in the Not Privileged set [13]. To do this, we first tokenize the email message subject field, email message body and extracted text from each attachment for each family in the training set and in the test-set. We then build two unigram language models on these terms (i.e., the unstemmed tokens), one for the 932 families in the training set that were labeled as Privileged, and the other for the 5,799 families in the training set that were labeled as Not Privileged. We then rank each term w present in either of the test-set families using the entropy difference:

$$score(w) = H_p(w) - H_{np}(w)$$

where $H_p(w)$ and $H_{np}(w)$ respectively represent the entropy of the token w in the Privileged and the Not Privileged language models. We then ranked the terms based on the entropy difference score [4]. Negative Entropy difference scores indicate terms that are indicative of privilege. We used the top 350 of 3389 (roughly 10%) unique terms with a high negative entropy difference value. Out the the top 350 terms, we annotate 117 terms with the highest negative entropy difference as strongly indicative of privilege, the middle set of 117 terms as moderately indicative of privilege, and the remaining 116 terms as somewhat indicative of privilege.

3.5 Temporal Likelihood

Email communications that focus on the lawsuits often occur during specific time intervals, so it seems reasonable to expect that privileged communication regarding those events might exhibit some predictable temporal variation. We therefore also built an annotator for dates that estimates the likelihood of privileged communication on (or near) that date. To do that, we parse the date field of the email that heads each family in the training set. We then use maximum likelihood estimation with Laplace smoothing to estimate the probability that a family sampled from the set of training families sent on a specific date would be privileged. We calculate that probability estimate as:

$$P(d_i|n_d^x) = \frac{n_{d_i}^p + 1}{n_{d_i}^p + n_{d_i}^{np} + 2}$$

where d_i is the date of the message, $n_{d_i}^p$ and $n_{d_i}^{np}$ are the total number of Privileged and Not-Privileged families sent on d_i respectively. Because TREC performed stratified sampling, designed to oversample potentially privileged families, we expect this to be a substantial overestimate of the actual probability. Nonetheless, we would expect relative values of the estimate to be informative. Of the 55 unique dates on which at least one of the 61 families viewed using the AID system was sent, we are able to annotate temporal likelihood in this way for 36 of those dates.

3.6 Interface and Interaction Design

Figure 2 shows a screenshot for our AID system. Documents are presented to every user in the same order, and the user must record a judgment (Privileged, Not Privileged, or No Decision) before being shown the next document. They could return to any previously judged document to change

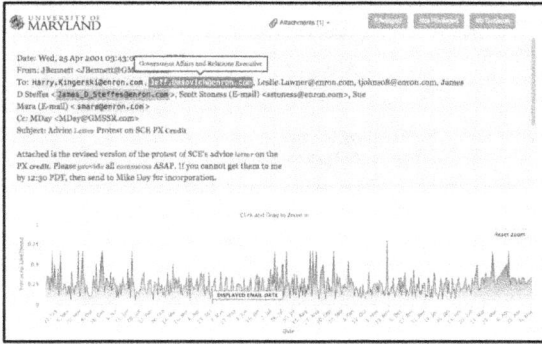

Figure 2: The AID system.

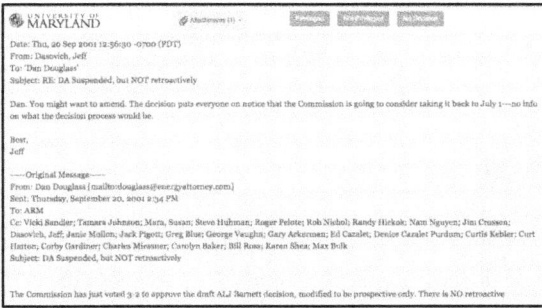

Figure 3: The Baseline system.

their judgment if they chose to do so. Annotations are provided as visual scaffolds during the privilege review process. Whenever a person role or organization type annotation is available, the associated email address is displayed with a red background, and the role or type annotation can be displayed in a manner similar to a "tool tip" (using a graphical control element that is activated when the user hovers the mouse over the shaded area). We shade the background with variations of the color red to indicate the propensity category (darker red for strong propensity, lighter red for moderate propensity, very light red for all other cases in which role or type information is available).[9] On average (across the 61 viewed families), 58% of the email addresses appearing as senders or recipients had a role or a type annotation available (55% for person role, 3% for organization type). About two-thirds of those cases in which role or type annotation were available, were displayed with shading indicating strong or moderate propensity.

The display of terms that are indicative of privilege in the subject line, email message body, or attachments follows a similar pattern, but by altering the color of the typeface rather than the background. For example, the term "credit" is rendered in the darkest shade of red[10] in Figure 2, thus indicating it was strongly indicative of privilege. On average (across the 61 viewed families), 2% of all term occurrences are highlighted.

---

[9]Low propensity addresses for which no role or organization type information is available have no background shading.

[10]We chose to use the same color gradations for terms and email addresses to simplify training, but the question of optimal color choices merits further investigation.

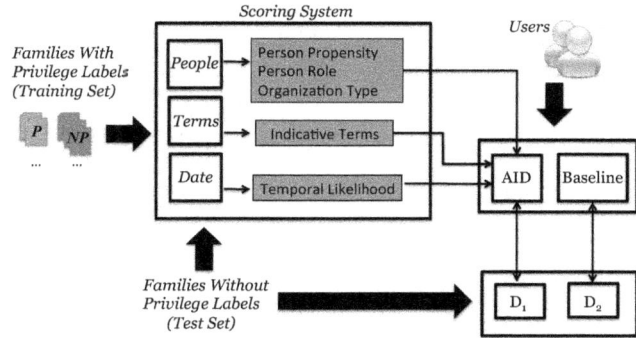

Figure 4: User study overview

Temporal likelihood is plotted as a connected line plot, with date as the horizontal axis and temporal likelihood as the vertical axis. This has the effect of visually performing linear interpolation of temporal likelihood for dates on which that likelihood can not be computed directly. The displayed date range can be reduced (by a click and drag zoom-in functionality) by the user for finer-grained display.

Figure 3 shows the user interface of our Baseline system. As can be seen, the only differences from the AID system are that none of the annotations are present, and the omission of the temporal likelihood plot permits more of the content to be displayed. Both the systems log the time, family ID, user ID and judgment (Privileged, Not Privileged, or No Decision) for each reviewed family.

4. USER STUDY DESIGN

The principal goal of our user study was to determine whether any of our system-generated annotators could help the users to perform the review task more quickly, more accurately, or both. A secondary goal was to determine whether there were usability issues with our current interface design that might adversely affect our ability to determine the effects of specific annotators. A third goal was to use our current AID system design as an artifact around which we could discuss specific as-yet unimplemented capabilities that experts might believe would provide useful support for the task. In this section we describe the design of the study, including a brief description of a pilot study that we performed to finalize our procedures, a description of the participants in our study, and a description of the procedures that we ultimately used with each of those participants.

4.1 Pilot Study

We chose to save our limited pool of qualified participants for our actual study. Thus, for the pilot study in which our only goal was to wring out our system design and study procedures, we recruited two participants, neither of whom had a law degree nor previous privilege review experience. Each pilot study participant completed the full study as depicted in Figure 5, including completing questionnaires and participating in a semi-structured interview. As in our actual study, we counterbalanced the presentation order, with one pilot study participant using the AID system first and then the Baseline system; the other participant used the two systems in the other order. We made three consequential changes as a result of our pilot study: (1) The organiza-

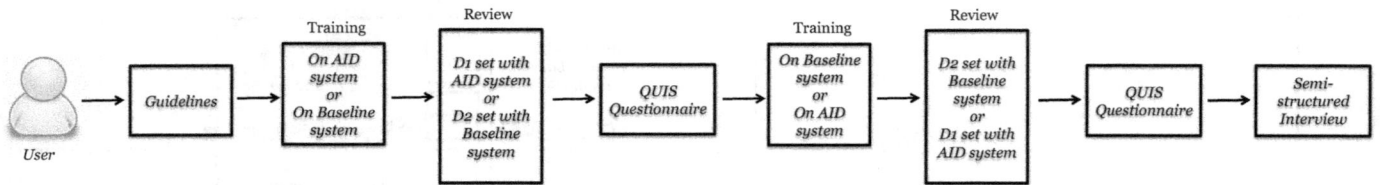

Figure 5: User study procedure.

tion type annotator was built, based on a suggestion from one pilot study participant, (2) some aspects of the brief written summary of the study procedure that we presented to participants during training were clarified, and (3) the semi-structured interview questions were improved.

4.2 Participants

In recruiting participants for our study, we initially sought people who were (in preference order) (1) a practicing attorney, (2) a law school graduate, (3) a law school student (preferably in their 3rd year), or (4) a law librarian. As it happened, we were able to recruit a total of six participants from the first two groups, which we judged to be adequate for the comparisons we wished to make, so we limited our study to those six participants.[11]

Two of the six were senior attorneys employed by law firms with a current e-discovery practice. These senior attorneys are experienced litigators who have extensive experience conducting both relevance and privilege review for email using commercial Technology Assisted Review (TAR) tools.[12] We refer to these senior attorneys as S_1 and S_2.

The remaining four participants were law school graduates. Two of the four had prior experience conducting relevance and privilege review using commercial TAR tools, but neither was currently working in an e-discovery practice; one of the two is a graduate student in another discipline, the other is an intellectual property attorney. We refer to this pair of experienced reviewers as E_1 and E_2. By coincidence, E_2 had experience working as a reviewer during the original Enron litigation.

The remaining two participants had experience conducting e-discovery reviews some time ago, principally on paper, but neither had experience using current TAR tools. One was a retired attorney, the other was currently a faculty member in another discipline. We refer to these (TAR) inexperienced reviewers as I_1 and I_2. I_2 had little direct experience using computers.

4.3 Procedure

Participants were given the opportunity to choose the time and the location of their session; 4 came to our lab, and for the other 2 we went to their office. As both the AID and Baseline systems are Web applications, participants were free to use their own computer if they wished; S_1 and S_2 did so.

---

[11] One of our goals was to identify usability issues, and Nielsen claims that most usability problems can be identified with a maximum of five users [14]. More users would have resulted in greater statistical power for our quantitative comparisons, but at this point our system design is not yet sufficiently mature to merit looking for small effect sizes.

[12] Tools like Recommind, Nuix, kCura, etc.

Table 2: Task Order

Participant	Task Order
S_1	Baseline — AID
S_2	AID — Baseline
E_2	Baseline — AID
E_1	AID — Baseline
I_2	Baseline — AID
I_1	AID — Baseline

Because we chose a within-subjects design, we needed to present different families in the two conditions in order to avoid memory effects. We did not have a sufficient number of participants to counterbalance document-system interactions or presentation order effects, so we elected to present the same documents, in the same order, to every participant who used the same system. The presentation order for each of the two collections (D_1 and D_2) was thus randomized once and then frozen. Thus what we refer to as a "system" in our study (i.e., AID or Baseline) is actually an invariant combination of the system, the collection assigned to that system, and the presentation order assigned to that collection.

The participants were randomly assigned to one of the two conditions, either AID first or Baseline first, as shown in Table 2.[13] This counterbalancing was intended to control (to some degree) for learning and fatigue effects. Thus we have two independent variables; user type (S, E, or I) and system.

Figure 5 summarizes the study procedure for one of the six single-participant sessions. Each participant completed the study in about two hours, with a 10 minute break at the end of the first hour. Participants were given an overview of the review task and were asked to read a written description of the study that we provided before signing a consent form. Each participant then received a 5 minute tutorial on the first system they would use, presented by the investigator (the first author of this paper), in which the different parts of the system were demonstrated using a few example families drawn from outside either test collection. Participants were then offered an opportunity to practice using those example families until they felt ready. The participant then logged in to the review system (with an anonymized user-ID that we provided) and perform the review task for 30 minutes without interruption. The review task required each participant to sequentially read and mark each family in the test set associated with their system (D_1 for AID, D_2 Base-

---

[13] The E and I participants were assigned randomly without regard to the pairings that we made because prior to the study we did not have enough insight on the background of our participants to recognize the optimal pairings. We are thus fortunate that our post-hoc assignment of participants to comparable pairs turned out to be counterbalanced.

Table 3: Contingency table for annotations of the same families by S_1 and S_2)

	S_1: Privileged	S_1 Not Privileged	S_1: No Decision	S_1: Not Seen
S_2: Privileged	15	7	0	5
S_2: Not Privileged	5	62	0	16
S_2: No Decision	6	12	1	3
S_2: Not Seen	0	1	0	75

†There was one family that was skipped in sequence by chance by S_2; but was not skipped by S_1.

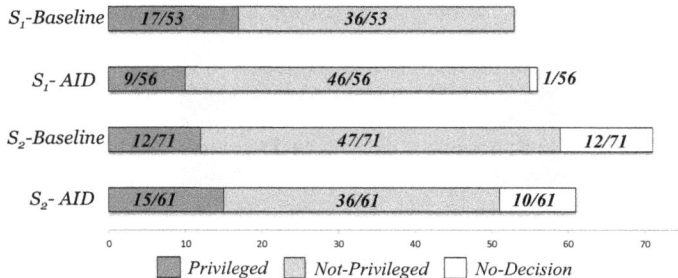

Figure 6: S_1 and S_2 Judgments by type

line) as either Privileged, Not Privileged or No Decision. Participants were able to refer to their copy of the written task description as they performed the task. At the end of 30 minutes (which always occurred before the users had recorded decisions for every family in a test set), participants were presented with a short usability questionnaire for that system that we created by tailoring the Questionnaire for User Interaction Satisfaction (QUIS) [6] to use 9-level scales for each question. After a 10-minute break, they were then trained on the second system (using the same procedure as before) and asked to log in to that system using their anonymized user-ID and complete a second 30-minute review of the families in the test collection associated with that system. After a second QUIS questionnaire for that system, participants were asked a set of semi-structured interview questions, some of which called for subjective judgments. The goal of the semi-structured interview was to obtain the participant's perspectives on the degree to which they found specific types of annotations to be useful, and to characterize the extent to which they found aspects of the task design to be mentally demanding or frustrating. With the participant's permission, this brief (5 minute) semi-structured interview was recorded to facilitate later analysis. At the conclusion of the session, each participant received US$25.

5. RESULTS

In this section we first focus on quantitative results for accuracy and speed. Following that we contextualize these results from qualitative results from our interview and from our usability questionnaire. We then draw insights from each of these analyses to discuss what we see as the most important conclusions that can be drawn from this study.

5.1 Selecting a Benchmark for Evaluation

If we are to make any useful statements about the accuracy of a privilege review, we must first select an informative set of judgments as benchmark against which accuracy can be measured. This benchmark judgments need not be per-

fect for the resulting measures to be informative, but we will have the greatest confidence in our results if we select the best available benchmark judgments. Thus it is natural to begin by characterizing the results from the two senior attorneys, since we would expect their judgments to be natural candidates as a benchmark.

Figure 6 shows the number of judgments of each type made by S_1 and S_2 for each of the two conditions. As can be seen, S_2 is somewhat faster than S_1 (making 33% more judgments in the same 30 minutes in the Baseline condition, and 9% more in the AID condition). S_2 records many more No Decision judgments (22 for S_2 vs. 1 for S_1).[14] As Table 3 shows, senior attorney S_1 marked a total 15+5+6=26 families as Privileged while S_2 marked a total of 15+7+5=27 families as Privileged. Among the families seen by both senior attorneys (using either system), 15 families were marked as Privileged by both. Computing chance corrected inter-annotator agreement between S_1 and S_2 using Cohen's Kappa (κ) yields 0.68, a value that Landis and Koch [11] characterize as "substantial." Indeed, given the class prevalence in our test sets, chance agreement would be 0.57, making very high levels of κ difficult to achieve [3].

As Table 1 showed, TREC 2010 Interactive Task Topic 304 privilege judgments are available for seven of the families in our test set. Of those seven, 5 were Privileged and 2 were Not Privileged. Of the 5, three families were adjudicated by the Topic Authority (a senior attorney whose judgments were authoritative) who was responsible for providing guidance and adjudicating disputes. Out of the three Privileged families adjudicated by the TREC Topic Authority, two were reviewed by both S_1 and S_2. S_1 agreed with the Topic Authority on one of the two families by marking one of the two families as Privileged while the other as Not-Privileged. S_2 never agreed with the Topic Authority. S_2 marked one of the two families as Not Privileged (the same family marked as Not Privileged by S_1) and the other was marked as No Decision. Comparisons on two judgments is not sufficient to determine whether the two senior attorneys in our user study are (1) generally more inclined to judge documents as Not Privileged than the TREC Topic Authority would have been (2) generally inclined to agree with each other, but we can say that there is no evidence to refute such a claim.

From this analysis, either senior attorney could reasonably be chosen as a benchmark against which the other participant's judgments could be measured for accuracy. However, because S_2 left 19 families unjudged and skipped reviewing 1 family throughout the review sequence and all 24 of the families that were not seen by S_1 were late in the review sequence, a larger number of useful judgments are available

---

[14]Participants mark a family as No Decision when a clear distinction between Privileged and Not Privileged could not be made on the email message or any of its attachments.

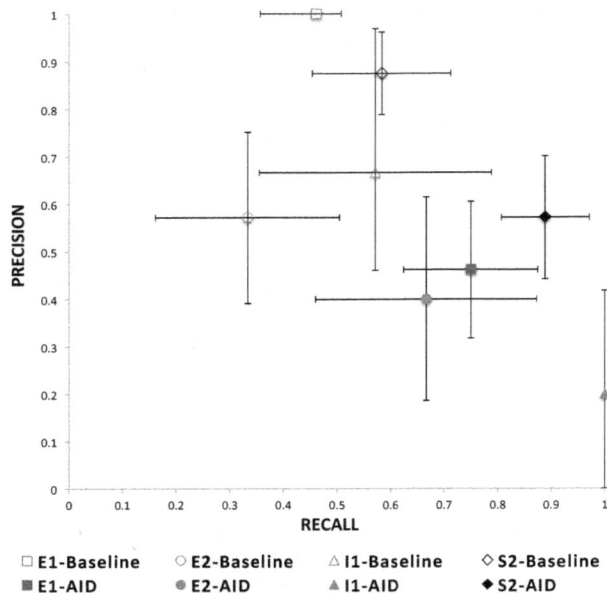

Figure 7: Evaluation - S_1 judgments as Benchmark.

from S_1. We therefore use judgments from S_1 as a benchmark for evaluation. We evaluate participants on the basis of precision and recall estimates that we report in Figure 7.

5.2 Accuracy

Figure 7 shows the privilege review effectiveness of S_1, E_1, E_2, and I_1 for the Baseline and AID conditions, evaluated as if the judgments by S_1 were the ground truth. We calculate point estimates for precision and recall using only the cases judged as Privileged or Not Privileged by both S_1 and by the participant whose decisions are being evaluated (i.e., we omit No Decision and Not Seen cases from both). Because we are comparing estimates for different sets of documents, we also show the 95% confidence intervals for recall and for precision, computed using the standard approximation method described by Agresti et al. [2]. Results for I_2 are not shown because after removal of the 21 No Decision judgments recorded by I_2 there were only 7 families judged by I_2 (3 in the AID condition, 4 in the Baseline condition), a number insufficient for useful estimation of intervals.[15]

From Figure 7 we can conclude that there is a consistent and statistically significant improvement in recall when the review task is performed using our AID system for all four participants (S_2, E_1, E_2, I_1).[16] This improvement is, however, accompanied by a statistically significant reduction in precision for three of the four participants. Using S_2 as a reference to evaluate S_1, E_1, E_2, and I_1 (not shown) yields results, with statistically significant improvements in recall in 1 of 4 cases and statistically significant decreases in precision in 2 of 4 cases. Since the principal goal of our AID

[15] All 7 were judged as Privileged, suggesting that participant I_2 may have intended to record judgments of Not Privileged and instead incorrectly selected No Decision. It was participant I_2 who had only limited personal experience using computers.

[16] We consider a difference to be statistically significant if each point estimate lies outside the 95% confidence interval for the other condition.

system is to avoid inadvertent disclosures, this consistent bias in favor of recall (i.e., in avoiding false negatives), regardless of which senior attorney we select as a reference, is well in line with that goal.

5.3 Speed

To characterize the effect of the choice of system on review speed, we computed the number of families reviewed by each participant in 30 minutes using the Baseline and the AID systems, observing little difference in the means (averaging 40.1 families for the AID condition and 43.6 families for the Baseline condition).[17] A paired t-test found no detectable difference in average review speed across the two conditions ($p > 0.38$). From these results we conclude that there is no indication that our AID system results in faster review, and indeed it is possible that our AID system might result in marginally slower review.

5.4 Usability

Table 4 summarizes participant responses to six of the seven QUIS questions (a seventh question, about layout, evoked no useful differences in the responses). Five of the six participants assigned a higher rating to the overall experience with the AID system than with the Baseline system (and the sixth participant noted no difference). All six participants gave more positive scores to the AID system than to the Baseline system in response to the question about adequacy of the displayed information. Person highlighting was reported to be useful (to at least some degree) by five of the six participants, whereas term highlighting and the date graph were each reported to be useful to some degree by only two of the six participants.

5.5 Usefulness

During the semi-structured interview session, we asked each participant which type of system-generated annotation they found to be most useful; five of the six named person annotation. The following excerpts are representative of responses that participants gave to our open-ended questions.

"I think having the role or type information in-line on the user interface was very helpful. All I had to do was to hover over the name instead of looking it up on a sheet of paper as we normally do." — S_1

"I would honestly like the people highlighting concept much more if it would give me more information about the metadata. Having information about the domain addresses of people who are not Enron employees is one such information." — S_2

"The presence of highlighted people made me look into the documents more carefully in non obvious cases for the presence of potentially privilege content. It help me to make a filtering decision about which document need more attention. The highlighting helped me to be quicker." — E_1

"I think the trickiest part was to review the document when the information about a sub-set of the people was missing. For example, if there were 6 people and we have information about 3 of them but not the other 3, it is hard to predict who the other players are." — E_2

"I think the highlighting of the people was useful to do the review; the highlighting of the terms were less useful because almost all emails contain the same boilerplate language and the term highlights did not provide much information; and

[17] Data from participant I_2 is omitted from this analysis.

Table 4: QUIS Summary(SA=Strongly Agree, A=Agree, MA=Moderately Agree, SD=Strongly Disagree, D=Disagree, MD=Moderately Disagree; NF=Neutral Feedback, blank indicates not applicable; BL=Baseline).

	S_1 BL	S_1 AID	S_2 BL	S_2 AID	E_1 BL	E_1 AID	E_2 BL	E_2 AID	I_1 BL	I_1 AID	I_2 BL	I_2 AID
Overall review experience	NF	Good	Bad	Good	Good	Great	Good	Good	Bad	Good	Fair	Good
Information provided was adequate	D	A	SD	MD	A	SA	A	SA	SD	MD	SD	A
People highlighting was useful		SA		A		A		SA		SA		NF
Term highlighting was useful		SA		NF		MA		NF		NF		SD
Date graph was useful		NF		D		D		MA		D		A
Use of colors was logical		A		A		SA		NF		A		A

about the dates, I did not feel the need to use the date information displayed on the graph." — I_1

"The ideas presented in the AID system are good, however the information provided was sometimes confusing to me. The role and type information provided was useful but the term highlighting was distracting; mainly because the highlighted terms did not make sense to determine privilege and I lost my faith on the terms." — I_2

5.6 Discussion

Our quantitative results clearly indicate that our AID system resulted in a greater ability to detect privileged documents, and that that improvement is more than would be expected from chance variations resulting from the presence of different families in the test collections for each condition. The QUIS and our semi-structured interviews provide consistent and well triangulated support to our belief that our annotation of people (or, more specifically, of email addresses) is principally responsible for this improvement. Of the three ways we annotate people (for propensity, for person role, or for organization type) we have the strongest evidence for a claim that role and organization type annotation was believed by our participants to be useful; we do not have sufficient evidence to separately identify the effect of propensity annotation. Neither our present implementations of term highlighting nor the date graph were often commented on favorably by the participants. From these observations, we conclude that our current AID system achieves its principal objective of helping to avoid inadvertant disclosure, that further study is needed to separately analyze the value of propensity annotation, that the value of term annotation has not yet been shown, and that further refinement of our approach to date annotation will not be among our highest near-term priorities. We base this last conclusion in part on the following comment by S_1, who said *"Date information could be helpful during responsiveness review. But for privilege review, it is less likely to be useful"*.

We were somewhat surprised by the magnitude and consistency of the drop in precision that accompanied the increases in recall that we observed from the use of our AID system. In privilege review, low precision could result in incorrectly withholding some families that should properly have been turned over to the requesting party. Perhaps such cases might be discovered and corrected in a second stage of privilege review, but a two-stage review process would naturally lead to higher costs. Future work aimed at understanding the reason for the reduction in precision will thus be a high priority. Moreover, trade-offs between recall and precision are natural, so it may be that similar results might be obtained in other ways (e.g., by providing

financial incentives based on the number of privileged documents found). In future work it will therefore be important to develop task-tuned utility measures that account for the relative importance of recall and precision for the privilege review task and to develop study designs in which recall at comparable levels of precision can be studied.

Our participants made some suggestions for improvements that might be made to our AID system. One useful suggestion was to consider highlighting multi-word expressions that are indicative of privilege, rather than only single-terms as our present system does. Another useful suggestion was to consider augmenting our role annotations with an opportunity to drill down to learn more (e.g., date assigned to that role, previous roles, or supervisory relationships). In future work we are interested in exploring the potential for viewing privilege review as a structured collaboration task, and when we asked about this several of our participants (three of the five who we asked) indicated that system support for collaboration might be of interest for privilege review.

6. CONCLUSIONS & FUTURE WORK

In recent years, system support for relevance review has been the center of the action. As the technology-assisted review tools are deployed and adopted, it is natural to expect larger cases to be tackled, with a concomitant increase in the number of relevant documents that require privilege review being one predictable consequence. It therefore seems timely to begin to think seriously about how the tools that are ultimately built to support privilege review will differ from those that support relevance review. Our design thinking for that problem began with the idea that modeling attributes of people such as their roles and their propensity to engage in privileged communication might be particularly important for the privilege review task, and our results provide support for that belief. Our results also indicate that dates, while unquestionably important for relevance review, may be of less value for privilege review (at least in the way we are doing things now). We have noted that the increases in recall that we observed were often accompanied by substantial declines in precision, and further study will be needed to better characterize this effect and to control for it in future experiments. Contrary to our expectations, we also noted no evidence of improvements in review speed, although of course even our most expert participants were novice users of the particular interface that we presented them with. In future work we may therefore consider longitudinal studies that would allow us to see how the same users behave at different points in their personal learning curve.

One obvious next step will be to run small-scale studies to tune specific components (e.g., what types of multi-word expressions should be considered for highlighting? how many terms or multi-word expressions should be highlighted? how many categories of term highlighting are useful?). Studies along those lines might ultimately lead to test collections that could be used as a basis for tuning and evaluating specific system components; for that we will also need to give thought to intrinsic measures for evaluating the performance of individual components. Another productive research direction would be to explore whether we might productively use surrogates for attorneys in some early studies. Would law students be suitable? Law librarians? Crowd-sourcing services such as Mechanical Turk? Surely we can go some distance in this direction; the key question is how far can we productively go. Another important direction for future research will be to unpack the human decision process a bit to study how it is that attorneys actually make privilege judgments in specific cases; that could be a productive source for design inspiration. Further study is also needed on the question of the degree to which use of such a system over time could (or should!) engender trust on the part of reviewers who themselves bring expert knowledge to the task. Yet another direction we might go is to consider what happens when things change. Manually constructing lists of person roles and organization types was a useful expedient for this study, but actual cases evolve dynamically, and they do so within organizations that are themselves often dynamically restructuring. There is, therefore, great scope for integrating techniques that can learn to make useful inferences from raw content.

Finally, we should note that this work could be extended in other settings where search amidst sensitive content is inevitable. On December 8, 2009, President Barack Obama of the United States wrote *"Information maintained by the Federal Government is a national asset. My Administration will take appropriate action, consistent with law and policy, to disclose information rapidly in forms that the public can readily find and use. Executive departments and agencies should harness new technologies to put information about their operations and decisions online and readily available to the public."* Perhaps paradoxically, the caveat "consistent with law and policy" means that before his nation can reap the full benefits of the information that can and should be disclosed, his government will need the ability to affordably separate that vast trove of immediately useful information from that which – at least for now – can not and must not be disclosed. That problem bears an uncanny resemblance to the challenge of privilege review in e-discovery, and indeed progress on one could well lead to progress on the other.

7. ACKNOWLEDGMENTS

This work has been supported in part by NSF award 1065250. Opinions, findings and conclusions are those of the authors only and does not reflect NSF views.

8. REFERENCES

[1] Armstrong v. Bush, 1989.

[2] A. Agresti and B. A. Coull. Approximate is better than "exact" for interval estimation of binomial proportions. *The American Statistician*, 1998.

[3] R. Artstein and M. Poesio. Inter-coder agreement for computational linguistics. *Computational Linguistics*, 2008.

[4] A. Axelrod, X. He, and J. Gao. Domain adaptation via pseudo in-domain data selection. In *Proceedings of the Conference on Empirical Methods in Natural Language Processing*, 2011.

[5] B. Carterette and I. Soboroff. The effect of assessor error on IR system evaluation. In *Proceedings of the ACM SIGIR conference*, 2010.

[6] J. P. Chin, V. A. Diehl, and K. L. Norman. Development of an instrument measuring user satisfaction of the human-computer interface. In *Proceedings of the SIGCHI conference on Human factors in computing systems*, 1988.

[7] G. V. Cormack, M. R. Grossman, B. Hedin, and D. W. Oard. Overview of the TREC 2010 legal track. In *TREC*, 2010.

[8] E. S. Epstein. The Attorney-Client Privilege and the Work-product Doctrine. American Bar Association, 2001.

[9] M. Gabriel, C. Paskach, and D. Sharpe. The challenge and promise of predictive coding for privilege. In *ICAIL, DESI V Workshop*, 2013.

[10] M. R. Grossman and G. V. Cormack. Technology-assisted review in e-discovery can be more effective and more efficient than exhaustive manual review. *Rich. JL & Tech.*, 2011.

[11] J. R. Landis and G. G. Koch. An application of hierarchical kappa-type statistics in the assessment of majority agreement among multiple observers. *Biometrics*, pages 363–374, 1977.

[12] A. McCallum, A. Corrada-Emmanuel, and X. Wang. The author-recipient-topic model for topic and role discovery in social networks: Experiments with enron and academic email. 2005.

[13] R. C. Moore and W. Lewis. Intelligent selection of language model training data. In *ACL*, 2010.

[14] J. Nielsen. *Usability engineering*. Elsevier, 1994.

[15] D. W. Oard and W. Webber. Information retrieval for e-discovery. *Foundations and Trends in Information Retrieval*, 2013.

[16] J. Shetty and J. Adibi. The Enron email Dataset; Database schema and brief statistical report. *Information Sciences Institite technical report, University of Southern California*, 2004.

[17] J. K. Vinjumur. Evaluating expertise and sample bias effects for privilege classification in e-discovery. In *Proceedings of the 15th International Conference on Artificial Intelligence and Law*. ACM, 2015.

[18] J. K. Vinjumur and D. W. Oard. Finding the privileged few: Supporting privilege review for e-discovery. *ASIS&T*, 2015.

[19] J. K. Vinjumur, D. W. Oard, and J. H. Paik. Assessing the reliability and reusability of an e-discovery privilege test collection. In *Proceedings of the ACM SIGIR conference on Research & Development in Information Retrieval*, 2014.

[20] E. M. Voorhees. Variations in relevance judgments and the measurement of retrieval effectiveness. *Information processing & management*, 2000.

[21] W. Webber. Re-examining the effectiveness of manual review. In *Proceedings of the SIGIR Information Retrieval for E-Discovery Workshop*, 2011.

Deepening the Role of the User: Neuro-Physiological Evidence as a Basis for Studying and Improving Search

Javed Mostafa
Info. Science & BRIC
UNC at Chapel Hill, NC, USA
jm@unc.edu

Jacek Gwizdka
School of Information
University of Texas at Austin, TX, USA
chiir2016@gwizdka.com

ABSTRACT

In this paper, the potential for expanding the set of scientific evidence and insights associated with the users' role during the search process is explored. As it is intended to be a position paper and not a systematic survey, a comprehensive review of literature is not presented here. However, the authors draw on some early stage research, in this emerging area, to describe and explain the generation of neuro-physiological evidence using three types of modalities. The modalities and the associated methods described here, presented in order of increasing complexity, include Eye-tracking, EEG, and fMRI. The paper concludes with a few critical observations regarding the promises and perils of using neuro-physiological approaches in studying search and search behavior.

General Terms

Experimentation, Human Factors, Measurement.

Author Keywords

Neuro-physiological methods; Eye-tracking; EEG; fMRI.

1. INTRODUCTION

With the emergence of the CHIIR as a new venue and an important milestone in the continued development of the IR field, it is appropriate to take a reflective view and investigate new potential avenues of research and scholarship that the CHIIR may catalyze and help advance. We argue that the CHIIR marks a deepening of interest in understanding the role and the influence of humans in the search process and therefore it behooves us to bring up some additional areas or topics that have not thus far found appropriate outlets in the mainline IR venues or even in the well-established HCI-oriented forums. One such area is neuro-physiological (NP) methods in explicating the search process, particularly interpreting human-responses to search tasks and the influence of search complexity on search outcomes. In this paper, we begin by broadening the conceptualization of the search process by using humans' psycho-physiological condition as a frame for understanding search. We then use three particular modalities, namely Eye-tracking, EEG, and fMRI, as examples of NP methods to discuss the utility of such methods in elucidating the search process. Then we present an example of application of NP methods. Following this, critical advantages and disadvantages of NP methods are described. Finally, the paper ends with a set of

CHIIR '16, March 13-17, 2016, Carrboro, NC, USA
© 2016 ACM. ISBN 978-1-4503-3751-9/16/03...$15.00
DOI: http://dx.doi.org/10.1145/2854946.2854979

aims for advancing the area of HII&R by integrating NP methods into the field of IR.

2. BACKGROUND

Search has largely been examined and studied in a manner which is agnostic to the human's psycho-physiological condition. That is in most IR studies that engage humans, the particular psychological or physiological condition of the humans are not directly measured and it is not the central focus of those studies. Yet, we must recognize that search is no longer an occasional activity that humans engage in. Humans no longer rely on search only to address specialized or complex information needs. Humans now conduct search frequently, under a variety of circumstances, and often as the first response when faced with an information need. It is therefore not a stretch to claim that search activity is now routine, highly personal, and interweaved with everyday activities of millions of users. A number of factors could be the cause for this change, but it is highly likely that wide-scale availability of computers and relatively affordable mobile devices promote more searching. It is well known that humans go through a wide variety of psycho-physiological conditions as they experience their world in the course of a single day, an hour, or even a few minutes. Hence, the psycho-physiological conditions of users are highly likely to trigger, shape, and influence humans' search behavior and performance. Imagine how a muted response from an otherwise jolly friend can quickly reveal something is off and can become a powerful signal indicating that the friend is experiencing a "down period". Now imagine how the same type of a psychological response, expressed in abnormal typing behavior or uncommon errors, detected by software could become a signal for tracking and understanding the human's condition. There is strong likelihood that specific NP conditions and tracking them may open up a new window to understand humans' behavior as they engage in searching. Given the fact that search has now become a significant activity of everyday behavior, it potentially is an untapped and underleverage source of insights and observation for humans' psycho-physiological condition.

2.1 NP Responses as a Two-way Street

It should be apparent from the discussion above that the psycho-physiological conditions of users both shape and in turn is shaped by their human-computer interaction (HCI) experience. To amplify our understanding of the role of the user in the interaction process, it is important that *the identification of specific NP responses is conducted in isolation from efforts that focus on shaping or changing the NP responses by manipulating the interaction.*

In other words to establish the actual roots and the patterns of NP responses, research on NP methods, must begin by establishing reliable "healthy" or "normal" baseline responses to common search tasks. It is important to start with baseline responses and a carefully selected set of search tasks so that the corresponding NP responses can be predicted accurately and consistently from the search tasks users perform (or typically perform). Such an investigation with the goal of establishing NP baselines may identify common regions in the brain that display neuronal activities as a response to fact-oriented searches (e.g., What is the capital of Colombia?). Or, in order to establish response to higher levels of cognitive load, such a line of NP research may purposefully and systematically increase the search task complexity and derive baseline EEG alpha wave forms and dynamics of pupil dilation from healthy and capable users that indicate the level of user engagement and deliberations necessary to execute complex search tasks.

At this point, we feel it is necessary to introduce a critical concept for explaining the importance of baseline NP patterns. The concept is known as "markers" in biological and clinical research. The concept refers to concrete and robust physiological human characteristics that indicate a specific disease or abnormality. For example, the existence of a mutated form of BRCA1 gene is considered a strong indicator of the likelihood of eventually leading to cancer and hence it is a now a well-established "bio" marker. Similarly, we believe it is possible, upon careful observation and analysis of NP data to establish behavioral correlates or markers that indicate normal or abnormal psycho-physiological conditions. For example, through careful scrutiny of neuronal activation patterns associated with simple fact- oriented searches we could establish a stronger basis for typical behavior and interaction responses of healthy and capable users. The baseline NP patterns would in other words assist in establishing the behavioral correlates (e.g., time to conduct such searches and error rates) as robust and consistent indicators or markers for a specific type of user group and a specific type of search tasks. Such behavioral markers in turn could be used to categorize search behavior more accurately, efficiently, perhaps even dynamically as search is taking place, without the need to rely on NP evidence. Hence, the larger goal of applying NP methods to establish baseline HCI patterns is to gain predictive accuracy and confidence in utilizing behavioral markers (**Figure 1**).

The opposite side of the road in NP research is the potential for shaping and improving HCI as it takes place in searching. For example, as a derivative research, based on a good understanding of NP responses and behavioral markers (from the line of research described above), the interface and the interaction could be designed to be more intelligent and adaptive. If the behavioral markers indicate that the user is significantly off from "normal" responses, the response from the search software could be appropriately attenuated to gently "move" the user to more "normal" behavior or response. For example, the elements of the interface could be adjusted to facilitate improved interaction (e.g., font size or placement of content on the screen). The line of research involving generation of adaptive responses to robust behavioral markers requires a highly precise way to classify interaction signals and detect subtle changes dynamically. Studying such dynamic adaption of interaction and their influence on search performance could be driven by both prior and parallel research on NP patterns, which would increase the confidence in adjustments to be made to particular interface components and their influence on the user's response and performance.

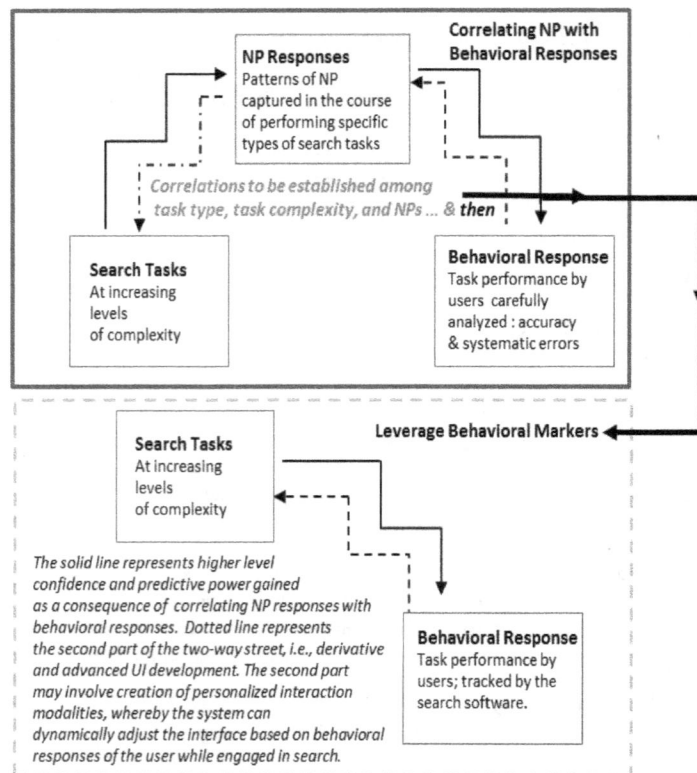

Figure 1. Two-way street of NP evidence: 1) First, correlating NP responses with specific behavioral responses in the context of search, and 2) Second, based on increased confidence in behavioral responses, leveraging them in adapting and improving interactions.

3. NP METHODS FOR STUDYING SEARCH

In this section, we discuss three NP modalities and methods. We chose Eye-tracking, EEG, and fMRI particularly as they have been used more often than other modalities and they represent a gradual increase in the level of complexity of NP methods. It is our intention to only offer an overview of these modalities in this section. We recommend the following [5, 10, 20, 27, 31, 35, 38–40, 47, 52] as relevant resources that scholars in the HII&R community may find useful.

Based on the overviews presented in this section, our goal is to point out and motivate the potential applications of the three modalities in the context of human-information interaction tasks and to deepen our knowledge of NPs and to discuss some of the critical limitations or the pitfalls.

3.1 Eye-tracking

Eye-tracking (ET) is the oldest (dating back to late XIX c., [10, 27]) and one of the most widely used NP modalities in IR research. The essential functioning of ET is based on eye-mind link hypothesis [29] which states that our attention is where our eyes are looking. While this statement needs to be qualified by considering covert attention, that is cases when our attention moves without our eyes moving, for the purpose of this paper, however, we will ignore this phenomenon, since, as explained below, it has little effect on textual IR.

At any point in time human eye can see with full acuity an area spanning less than 2° of visual field (roughly the size of a thumb at arm's length). Therefore to see surrounding environment sharply, we need to move our eyes constantly. To perceive an object (e.g., a word) our eyes remain focused on the object for a short period of time (between tens of milliseconds to seconds) – this is called a *fixation*. Our eyes then move very fast to the next fixation (e.g., the next word) – this rapid eye movement is called a *saccade*. Saccades are very short (30-80ms) and are the fastest movement human body is capable of (30-500° per second).

Eye-tracking hardware and software typically detects fixation events, while faster and more expensive eye-trackers are also able to detect saccade events. Fixations provide us with information where a user's attention is focused on screen, or, more generally, in the environment. This link to attention has been used in HCI and IR research for over two decades [17, 28]. In the context of search eye-tracking informs us about user interaction with a search environment at different stages of the search process (Figure 2).

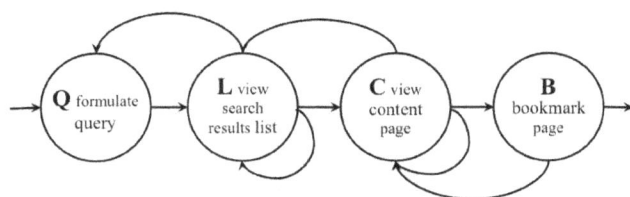

Figure 2. A simplified four-stage search process [21].

At the query formulation and re-formulation stage (Q), we can learn from eye-tracking, for example, whether users pay attention to query suggestions or auto-completion [25, 37]. We can also learn the likely sources of user entered query terms [12]. We can do this by considering whether the entered words were fixated on in query suggestions or in documents. At the search results list review stage (L), we learn which search result surrogates users pay attention to, in which order, and how much time they spend on each of them [9, 17, 19]. At the document viewing stage (C), we learn which elements of a document are being paid attention to and which are not, how carefully a document is read and how much it is just skimmed.

Eye-tracking can also help in understanding the search process complexity. In particular, in reading, which is relatively well understood in traditional settings [46], several indicators of cognitive effort were identified. The effort indicators include: fixation duration, the existence and number of regression fixations in the reading sequence (moving back in the sequence), the spacing of fixations in the sequence, the reading speed. Plausibly higher cognitive effort is taking place when users are acquiring new information, or are integrating that information with existing concepts. In this way, the eye-tracking based cognitive effort indicators may also identify when and how much learning is taking place during the search process.

While examination of areas of visual attention based on fixation duration and their timing provides useful information, it is only one type of information eye-tracking delivers. More advanced uses of eye-tracking data include considering eye movement patterns and pupil dilation.

In basic and applied psychology research, eye movements were used, for example, as a diagnostic tool in detecting dyslexia [16, 43], mental workload [18] and even in biometric identification of a person [26, 32]. More interestingly for research in IR, distinct eye movements were found to be associated with memory recall [6],

thus indicating a possibility of distinguishing internal (memory) and external (query suggestions, document text) sources of query terms.

In interactive information retrieval, eye movement patterns have been used in investigating reading patterns on relevant vs. irrelevant documents/web pages [1, 2, 7, 20, 49]. We learn that different patterns are associated with different levels of document relevance (Figure 3). One should note that these patterns may depend on the text layout, which could limit their use as NP responses. More generally, investigation into reading eye movement patterns in the search process has a potential to move beyond the settings traditionally studied by psychology and to bring new knowledge not only to IR but also to cognitive and educational psychology.

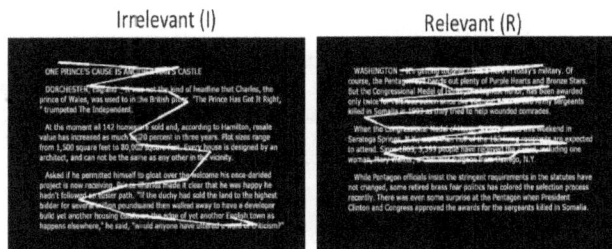

Figure 3. Eye movement reading patterns on irrelevant and relevant document [20].

Pupil dilation is arguably the most intriguing and most under-utilized aspect of the eye-tracking method in application to IR. Pupil diameter is controlled by the Autonomic Nervous System [42]. Under constant illumination, it has been associated with a number of cognitive functions, including mental effort [30], interest [34] surprise [45], and making a decision. The sources of variation in pupil's size are related to attention [24, 53] and, thus, plausibly, it should reflect some aspects of cognitive processing of documents. Indeed, recent results obtained in two experiments (N=24 and N=32) by one of the paper authors demonstrated pupil dilation on relevant and pupil contraction on irrelevant text documents and web pages [20, 23]. This effect is particularly apparent for changes in pupil size in the last couple of seconds before a participant's relevance judgment. Other research have shown similar differences on image stimuli [41]. Pupil dilation on visits to relevant stimuli indicates, in part, a higher mental effort and an increased level of attention paid to relevant information. Pupil dilation analysis is independent of the layout, and thus it presents a good candidate for an NP response signal.

3.2 EEG

Electroencephalography gained popularity in clinical use, particularly to detect abnormal electrical signals that are highly correlated with brain disorders, drug effects, and lesions or brain damages. It is well-known that the brain is an extremely dense structure, consisting of billions of neurons, which interchanges signals at the rate of once every 5 milliseconds (thousandth of a sec). Generally, in order to map the physiological responses of a brain the objective is to pinpoint the location of the signal as well as the strength of the signal. EEG is temporally precise in detecting signal instantiations, and based on modern signal converters the signals can be quickly characterized (or "filtered") into specific wave patterns. The patterns are dependent on number of waves per second and the amplitude or height of each wave. The amplitudes correspond to the strengths of the electric signals and modern

EEGs can detect signals in the range of 1/1 millionth of volt (or micro volt). On the other hand, EEG is far less precise in terms of establishing specific brain locations where signals originate from, as it is placed on the surface of the brain and can detect signals close to the skull level and only in the range of centimeters[1].

The standard or common EEG wave patterns include alpha, beta, theta, and gamma waves. The common wave patterns represent specific frequency and amplitude patterns. There are now several relatively inexpensive EEG tools in the market, specifically aimed at usability and human factors researchers that come with built-in hardware and software capabilities to capture, amplify, and represent all the common EEG wave patterns. The relatively inexpensive EEG systems are wired and have few electrodes. While at the higher end are those that have numerous electrodes (thus offering better spatial resolution), have built-in amplifiers in each electrode, are wireless, and have customized classifiers and visualization software to support easier interpretation of data. Based on the alpha, beta, theta, and gamma waves it is possible to capture and determine brain signals that are un-induced (i.e., no special stimuli or tasks are used) and by comparing these wave patterns to well-known "normative" or "abnormal" patterns one can draw general conclusions regarding the status of the subject's functioning brain.

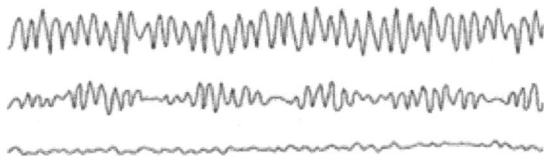

Figure 4. Variations observed in Alpha waves: 1) Top-most pattern representing the characteristic, typical wave form during relaxation, 2) The pattern in the middle is an intermediate stage when the subject is beginning to concentrate, and 3) The last wave, with the almost flat pattern, represents full attenuation while the subject is completely engaged in an activity with open eyes [11].

In contrast to understanding the current status of a functioning brain, a researcher may wish to investigate the response of the brain to specific stimuli or tasks. When a specific NP response is elicited as a consequence of presenting a stimuli or a task, such an NP is called an induced or evoked response. It is possible to rely on the standard alpha, beta, theta, and gamma waves to discern and clarify their association with certain characteristic NP responses and what these responses imply. For example, it is well-known that when a subject is in a relaxed mood and/or has their eyes closed alpha waves are particularly prominent and have high amplitudes, and in contrast when the same subject opens her eyes and concentrates on a demanding task there is attenuation (i.e., flattening) of the alpha waves (see Figure 4). Similarly, it has been shown that numerous occurrences of beta waves in diverse frequencies and with low amplitudes indicate active concentration and anxious states.

There are more precise characteristic response waves that have been demonstrated to strongly correlate with the onset of certain specific stimuli and these characteristic NP responses have been utilized in a wide variety of psycho-social studies. These responses are termed event-related potentials (ERPs) [36]. For example, the

occurrence of P300 wave patterns[2] has been linked to categorization and evaluation tasks, and particularly strongly associated in execution of odd-ball tasks involving detection of low-probability occurrences of stimuli. Similarly, the N400 wave patterns have shown to be prominently associated with analysis and processing of meaningful stimuli such as words, icons, faces, etc. Given the potential for generating human-responses such as concentration, categorization, and processing of symbolic and semantic stimuli such as words, it should be apparent to the reader by now that there are obvious opportunities to apply the EEG modality exclusively or complementarily in establishing a clearer understanding of the search process. We find examples of early applications of the EEG modality in IR in recently published papers [3, 13]. However, there remain certain critical limitations associated with the EEG modality that the human-information interaction researcher must be aware of and we will discuss some of these limitations in our concluding section.

3.3 fMRI

During brain's engagement in support of executing tasks, blood flow to neurons in the specialized areas of the brain relevant to those tasks increases and correspondingly the oxygenation level in those specialized areas also increases. The powerful magnets in the MR machines are capable of detecting the subtle changes in the blood oxygenation levels. Thus, the measurement of neurological response based on the differentiated oxygenation levels is called blood-oxygenation level dependent measure or BOLD. A synonymous term also used to refer to changes in the blood oxygenation levels is known as the hemodynamic response (HR). In contrast to the EEG, the mapping of active sites or locations based on BOLD is highly precise, and it is typically captured as voxels (volumetric pixels) at the range of millimeter (one tenth of a centimeter). In contrast, however, the temporal resolution measured using BOLD is rather coarse – typically in the range of few seconds.

Similar to the process of measuring the impact of evoked responses in EEG, while inside an MR machine a subject is presented with a stimuli or asked to conduct a simple task. In order to enhance the effect of the task and gain clear evidence of the impact, subjects are typically requested to conduct the same task or the same type of task repeatedly while inside the MR machine. The tasks are usually interspersed with short durations of "non-activities" or "resting" periods. An experimental session which utilizes repeated exposure to similar tasks with boundaries defined by resting periods is called an event-based session (or event-based design). To avoid the potential impact of the subject gradually learning from the repeated exposure to the same tasks, the session usually involves conducting a fixed of set of different types of tasks that are randomly interspersed in the even-based design.

In a recent pilot experimental session, conducted by one of the authors of this paper, an event-based design was employed which involved two types of search result presentations: high precision (i.e., relevant search results were placed in high rank order) and low-precision. Subjects, while inside the MR machine, were shown a search question, for example, What is the capital of Japan? It was followed by a display one of two types of result-screens. Subjects were then requested to identify one relevant result from the screen by pressing a button representing the rank order of the relevant

---

[1] For a comparison, consider the fact that a square millimeter (one tenth of a centimeter) contains approximately 100,000 neurons.

[2] The numeric designator 300 represents a latency factor in milliseconds, post introduction of stimuli.

item in the result-screen, where each result item was labeled with the corresponding rank order e.g., 1, 2, 3. Each subject was requested to perform 80 scan tasks, divided into blocks of 16, with 5 resting boundary intervals separating each block of tasks. During the resting intervals subjects were presented with a screen containing only a "+" sign. Every task took about half a minute and the intervals were about 1 second long. To minimize the impact of the learning-effect, the scan tasks were randomly interspersed in the event-based session. The hemodynamic responses or BOLD measures were collected from all the subjects (n=12), and they were pooled, averaged, and mapped to the surface area of the brain in order to facilitate interpretation of the resulting neurological response. As can be seen in the Figure 5, the neurological impact of scanning for relevant items is clearly differentiated from the resting modes (also known as fixation modes).

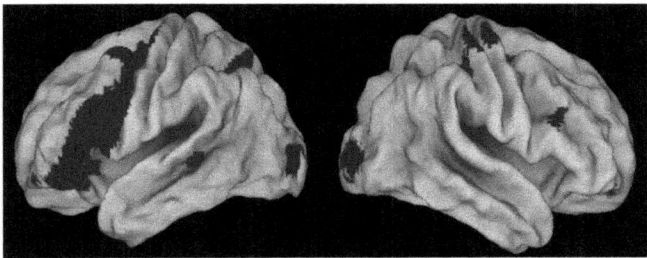

Figure 5. Brain-surface area mapping of fMRI BOLD signals collected from 12 subjects contrasting fixation with the search result scanning. The left and right lateral views of the brain surfaces are shown. The large dark patches on the brain surfaces represent those areas that were active during scanning modes but NOT active during the resting or fixation modes.

A fulsome description of the fMRI pilot study is out-of-scope for this position paper. Additional details on the experimental design, results, and analysis can be found in a recently published paper [40]. Here, we only provide a small glimpse of the fMRI results to point to the potential application of fMRI for generating NP evidence for investigating the impact of search related activities on the brain. As can be seen in Figure 5, a highly active area while the scanning tasks were being completed is the prefrontal cortex (PFC). It is known that the lateral PFC is generally associated with working memory and decision making; particularly, in the PFC the ventral regions are associated with working memory and the dorsal regions are associated with decision making process. Given that the scanning task is strongly verbal in nature, which involves reading and interpreting the search question and the search results, it is not a surprise to find the dominant role of various PFC regions while subjects execute the scanning tasks.

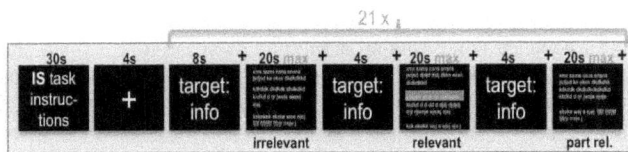

Figure 6. Experimental Design of the second pilot study.

In another pilot fMRI experiment conducted by one of the paper authors, a difference in brain activations between reading relevant and not-relevant short text documents was investigated [22]. The fMRI environment and the essentials of this experimental design bear many similarities with the first study described above. The

experimental design was also event-based, but in this case it consisted of 21 trials that contained irrelevant, partially relevant and topical text documents in randomly changing order (Figure 6).

The findings from this experiment indicated that reading and deciding on relevance of relevant vs. not-relevant documents was characterized by increased activity in middle front gyrus, an area of frontal lobe that has been generally associated with executive mechanisms and decision-making. This finding also comes with little surprise, since judging relevance certainly involves areas of brain responsible for decision-making. While this early results shed some light on cognitive processes engaged in relevance judgments, we are just at the beginning of this new research territory.

In order to establish more precisely the contributions of specific brain regions to execute search tasks, it would be necessary to examine full search cycles: starting with a question, to query formulation, to execution, to revision, and finally to interpretation stages. As far as we know, no one has examined full search cycles inside fMRI machines. Additionally, of course, the association of search types (i.e., tasks) and search difficulty with specific brain regions also remain unexamined. To be sure, we must note here, the challenges associated with applying fMRI as a tool for generating NP evidence are immense and some are potentially impossible to overcome. We will discuss some of the key challenges associated fMRI and the other two modalities in the next section.

4. PROMISES AND PERILS OF NP EVIDENCE

In this section, we will discuss some fundamental advantages and disadvantages associated with NP-based methods in investigating search interactions.

4.1 Balancing the Good with the Bad

When researchers study search behavior, either retroactively by scrutinizing search log data or proactively by collecting data from search performance, the analysis is always strongly dependent on the context of the search (e.g., task scenario, time allocated, and even location of experiments). It is also well-known that search experiments that involve collecting self-report data face the risk that the nature of interactions or relationship between the experimenter and the searcher may impact the quality of the experimental data generated (i.e., the risk of response bias). Thus, any insights to be gained from such behavior-oriented experiments regarding critical cognitive and psychological factors, causal or associated, must always be achieved second-hand, based on assumptions or stipulations regarding what the data represents about the user's actual mental condition or physical status.

Neuro-physiological signals as indicators of human engagement and responses to search tasks comes with the great promise of "lifting the lid" of the black-box that is the searcher's state-of-mind or his/her physical condition. If NP data are collected carefully and with appropriate level of control, while subjects engage in search tasks, it may reveal a wide array of additional clues regarding factors such as level of cognitive effort (e.g., load), type of effort (e.g., verbal vs. motor planning), anxiety, stress, curiosity, arousal, and even pleasure. We contend that a particularly powerful approach to amplify and clarify the clues regarding searching is to collect and correlate behavioral data with NP data. Such an approach may lead to more precise prediction of search activities and the quality of search performance, based only on monitoring behavioral responses during the search process[3]. Last but not least, NP approaches open up the possibility of gathering evidence that are not directly expressed (or even expressible) by the searcher. Thus, it may be possible via an NP-driven approach to unearth deeper and more nuanced insights regarding a subject's response to a search task and arguably such evidence is immune from being tainted by response bias.

We would, however, like to end this paper with a strong note of caution regarding problems associated with NP methods. First and foremost, it should be amply clear by now that NP approaches may be extremely intrusive, and while they may reduce or eliminate one type of problem (e.g., contamination of data due to response bias), at the same time they may introduce new type of problems. How a researcher should set up an experiment to elicit useful NP evidence while preserving realism of the search context remains a great barrier. Applying NP approaches may involve transforming the search context to such a degree that it becomes an artificial or unrealistic condition, thus compromising external validity and generalizability of the findings. Second, a big obstacle is the wide variety of standards and metrics that NP tools employ in categorizing and reporting the critical interaction data. For example, we know fixation durations and pupil dilations are important parameters that are employed in measuring eye movement activities during interactions, however, much more evidence is needed as to what they actually represent in terms of cognitive processing and mental load associated with specific types of search tasks. The lack of clarity regarding these metrics remains, in large part, due to the opacity and obstacles researchers face when they seek information from NP tool vendors. Third, although one may be able to pinpoint a specific a physiological location associated with an NP signal, it may not actually translate to a clear understanding of what that signal means. The challenge in associating a specific function to a location is particularly relevant to the brain. Researchers must be cautious to avoid reverse inferencing [44]; that is, after already being aware of functions that are associated with specific brain locations, based on evidence collected by past studies, the inclination is to attribute the causality of, or the association with specific triggering factors in the new experimental condition (i.e., specific stages or activities of a search task) to those brain regions. Given that a brain region is actually capable of playing different roles for different human activities, additional research is needed to identify the functions those regions dominantly or consistently represent and how they contribute to search tasks. It has to be emphasized here that functional mapping of the brain is still an emerging area, and, particularly, the knowledge of connectivity among brain regions and the information exchange among specific regions is just beginning to be established. Therefore, establishing contributions of specific brain regions to a high-level cognitive activity such as search needs to be approached extremely cautiously. Fourth and the final point we would like to make is regarding the parameters and settings associated with instruments, both software and hardware, used during NP experiments and the lack of a tradition in sharing key details regarding these parameters. Utilizing each NP instrument and the software demands manipulation and appropriate initialization of a large number of parameters. The omission of details along with published results deters reproducibility, makes validation difficult, and may delay further advances in the field.

---

[3] We referred to such behavioral indicators as "markers" earlier in this article.

5. AN ILLUSTRATIVE EXAMPLE

One example will serve as an illustration of how one might move from considering information retrieval phenomena to the space of NP concepts and then to NP markers. Historically, dwell time has been suggested as a good indicator of user interest in a document and thus of its relevance [8]. Subsequent research showed that the length of time a user spends viewing a document does not correlate significantly with the user's explicit relevance assessments [33]. Ambiguity of dwell time comes from its association with user interest in information as well as with problems encountered by users in processing this information. Total dwell time on a document includes periods of actual reading and processing a document and periods of not attending to the document. We translate interest into attention given to a document and possible problems associated with reading difficulty or lack of attention (e.g., mind wandering) and model dwell time on a document as composed of several critical components,

$$t_d = t_{tr} + t_{dr} - t_{mw} + \varepsilon$$

where t_d is dwell time on a document; t_{tr} is typical reading time; t_{dr} is additional time required for reading of difficult text; t_{mw} is time spent on mind wandering; and, ε is error term.

At a simple level, attention can be assessed by considering time spent on reading. This metric can be obtained from eye-tracking as total duration of eye fixations on text. Prior research showed that using eye-tracking measures improves document relevance classification as compared to using dwell time alone (Gwizdka 2014). Let us now consider text difficulty (readability) and word frequency. These metrics can help to account for individual differences in reading time between users as well as for differences between documents. We can further improve measurement of dwell time components by detecting and subtracting periods of mind wandering ("daydreaming"). Mind wandering is defined as decoupling attention from perception and from immediate task. During reading, when the mind wanders to unrelated feelings and thoughts, the eyes continue to scan the words but without close attention to their meaning. The periods of mindless reading that result are characterized by longer fixations and reduced sensitivity to lexical features [48, 51]. Application of these measures requires building a model of text, making it somewhat difficult to apply the measures. However, a few other NP markers, can be applied without considering text features. Larger pupil dilation (PD) was found as a NP marker of mind-wandering while reading [14]. Other NP markers of potential interest include spectral features of EEG signal and ERPs. For example, mind wandering was shown to generally reduce brain signal responses to perceptual events (within 100ms) and to task related events (the aforementioned P300 wave patterns) [50]. Furthermore, mind wandering was found to be characterized by a power amplitude increase in the theta and delta frequency bands and an amplitude decrease in the alpha and beta frequency bands. The alpha-peak frequency increase was found to be a likely marker of the attentional switch between mind wandering and the focused task [4]. These NP markers may be potentially helpful in developing a "cleaner" measure of dwell time on documents. IR researchers who plan to take advantage of NP metrics presented in the example here should take into consideration some key factors associated with them. While some NP markers were obtained based on search activities (e.g., PD during reading) and are thus directly applicable, others such as the EEG metrics were obtained in different contexts (e.g., based on simple visual and auditory tasks). This points out the difficulty of translating research findings from cognitive neuroscience to IR and the need for further studies that exclusively concentrate on NP metrics associated with search tasks .

6. CONCLUSION

Despite the challenges, NP approaches hold immense promise in advancing human-information interaction scholarship. Beyond IR, NP approaches are finding wider usage in domains such as learning, entertainment, and health care. Some of the press releases and video announcements describing the amplification of human capacities can be quite seductive (e.g., children playing computer games by wearing EEG skull caps). Generally, we do hope that human-information interaction researchers would look beyond IR and would investigate and learn from a wide variety of interaction modalities in related domains. Such a broad approach in studying interaction, however, should be conducted with some caution, as the contexts of user engagement, their roles, and the goals can vary greatly.

In this paper, we focused exclusively on investigating the prospects of pursing NP approaches as they pertain to information retrieval. We end this position paper with a list of goals as a way to integrate NP approaches into mainstream research and methods in HII that focus on search. First, researchers need to concentrate on establishing standardized search tasks. These search tasks need to be carefully established in terms of individual steps and realistic contexts. Second, there is a strong need to evaluate the standardized search tasks and generate baseline NP data. The latter line of research could be driven with the goal of creating a solid foundation of behavioral markers and their NP correlates. Third, whenever possible, the NP outcomes and their interpretations (e.g., cognitive load or stress) should be cross-validated with more than one NP modalities. For example, EEG can be combined with Eye-tracking while the subjects are engaged in the same set of tasks [15]. Fourth and the final recommendation is to conduct NP-oriented research as transparently and as openly as possible by sharing details regarding the environmental contexts such as software and device settings and other critical details regarding the experimental conditions.

7. REFERENCES

[1] Ajanki, A. et al. 2009. Can eyes reveal interest? Implicit queries from gaze patterns. *User Modeling and User-Adapted Interaction.* 19, 4 (2009), 307–339.

[2] Ajanki, A. 2013. Inference of relevance for proactive information retrieval. (2013).

[3] Allegretti, M. et al. 2015. When Relevance Judgement is Happening?: An EEG-based Study. *Proceedings of the 38th International ACM SIGIR Conference on Research and Development in Information Retrieval* (New York, NY, USA, 2015), 719–722.

[4] Braboszcz, C. and Delorme, A. 2011. Lost in thoughts: Neural markers of low alertness during mind wandering. *NeuroImage.* 54, 4 (Feb. 2011), 3040–3047.

[5] Bui, A.A.T. and Taira, R.K. 2009. *Medical Imaging Informatics.* Springer Science & Business Media.

[6] Bulling, A. and Roggen, D. 2011. Recognition of visual memory recall processes using eye movement analysis. *Proceedings of the 13th international conference on Ubiquitous computing* (New York, NY, USA, 2011), 455–464.

[7] Buscher, G. et al. 2012. Attentive documents: Eye tracking as implicit feedback for information retrieval and beyond. *ACM Trans. Interact. Intell. Syst.* 1, 2 (2012), 9:1–9:30.

[8] Claypool, M. et al. 2001. Implicit Interest Indicators. *Proceedings of the 6th International Conference on Intelligent User Interfaces* (New York, NY, USA, 2001), 33–40.

[9] Cutrell, E. and Guan, Z. 2007. What are you looking for?: an eye-tracking study of information usage in web search. *Proceedings of the SIGCHI Conference on Human Factors in Computing Systems* (New York, NY, USA, 2007), 407–416.

[10] Duchowski, A.T. 2007. *Eye Tracking Methodology: Theory & Practice.* Springer-Verlag.

[11] EEG: Instructions (by Carl Rosenkilde): *http://www.rosenkilde.com/EEG--Instructions.html.* Accessed: 2015-09-05.

[12] Eickhoff, C. et al. 2015. An Eye-Tracking Study of Query Reformulation. *Proceedings of the 38th International ACM SIGIR Conference on Research and Development in Information Retrieval* (New York, NY, USA, 2015), 13–22.

[13] Eugster, M.J.A. et al. 2014. Predicting Term-relevance from Brain Signals. *Proceedings of the 37th International ACM SIGIR Conference on Research & Development in Information Retrieval* (New York, NY, USA, 2014), 425–434.

[14] Franklin, M.S. et al. 2013. Window to the wandering mind: Pupillometry of spontaneous thought while reading. *The Quarterly Journal of Experimental Psychology.* 66, 12 (Dec. 2013), 2289–2294.

[15] Frey, A. et al. 2013. Decision-making in information seeking on texts: an Eye-Fixation-Related Potentials investigation. *Frontiers in Systems Neuroscience.* 7, 39 (2013).

[16] Gomathi, P.M. and Nasira, G.M. 2014. Detection Of Dyslexia From Eye Movements Using Anfis & Bbwpe Feature Extraction Methods. *International Review on Computers and Software (IRECOS).* 9, 3 (Mar. 2014), 526–532.

[17] Granka, L.A. et al. 2004. Eye-tracking analysis of user behavior in WWW search. *Proceedings of the 27th annual international ACM SIGIR conference on Research and development in information retrieval* (New York, NY, USA, 2004), 478–479.

[18] Greef, T. et al. 2009. Eye Movement as Indicators of Mental Workload to Trigger Adaptive Automation. *Foundations of Augmented Cognition. Neuroergonomics and Operational Neuroscience.* D.D. Schmorrow et al., eds. Springer Berlin Heidelberg. 219–228.

[19] Guan, Z. and Cutrell, E. 2007. An eye tracking study of the effect of target rank on web search. *Proceedings of the SIGCHI Conference on Human Factors in Computing Systems* (New York, NY, USA, 2007), 417–420.

[20] Gwizdka, J. 2014. Characterizing Relevance with Eye-tracking Measures. *Proceedings of the 5th Information Interaction in Context Symposium* (New York, NY, USA, 2014), 58–67.

[21] Gwizdka, J. 2010. Distribution of cognitive load in Web search. *Journal of the American Society for Information Science and Technology*. 61, 11 (2010), 2167–2187.

[22] Gwizdka, J. 2013. Looking for Information Relevance In the Brain. *Gmunden Retreat on NeuroIS 2013* (Gmunden, Austria, Jun. 2013), 14.

[23] Gwizdka, J. and Zhang, Y. 2015. Towards Inferring Web Page Relevance – An Eye-Tracking Study. *Proceedings of iConference'2015* (Mar. 2015), 5.

[24] Hoeks, B. and Levelt, W.J.M. 1993. Pupillary dilation as a measure of attention: a quantitative system analysis. *Behavior Research Methods, Instruments, & Computers*. 25, 1 (Mar. 1993), 16–26.

[25] Hofmann, K. et al. 2014. An Eye-tracking Study of User Interactions with Query Auto Completion. *Proceedings of the 23rd ACM International Conference on Conference on Information and Knowledge Management* (New York, NY, USA, 2014), 549–558.

[26] Holland, C. and Komogortsev, O.V. 2011. Biometric identification via eye movement scanpaths in reading. *2011 International Joint Conference on Biometrics (IJCB)* (Oct. 2011), 1–8.

[27] Holmqvist, K. et al. 2011. *Eye Tracking: A comprehensive guide to methods and measures*. Oxford University Press.

[28] Jacob, R.J.K. 1991. The use of eye movements in human-computer interaction techniques: what you look at is what you get. *ACM Trans. Inf. Syst.* 9, 2 (Apr. 1991), 152–169.

[29] Just, M.A. and Carpenter, P.A. 1980. A theory of reading: From eye fixations to comprehension. *Psychological Review*. 87, 4 (1980), 329–354.

[30] Kahneman, D. and Beatty, J. 1966. Pupil Diameter and Load on Memory. *Science*. 154, 3756 (Dec. 1966), 1583–1585.

[31] Kandel, E. 2013. *Principles of Neural Science, Fifth Edition*. McGraw Hill Professional.

[32] Kasprowski, P. and Ober, J. 2004. Eye Movements in Biometrics. *Biometric Authentication*. D. Maltoni and A. Jain, eds. Springer Berlin / Heidelberg. 248–258.

[33] Kelly, D. and Belkin, N.J. 2004. Display Time As Implicit Feedback: Understanding Task Effects. *Proceedings of the 27th Annual International ACM SIGIR Conference on Research and Development in Information Retrieval* (New York, NY, USA, 2004), 377–384.

[34] Krugman, H.E. 1964. Some applications of pupil measurement. *JMR, Journal of Marketing Research (pre-1986)*. 1, 000004 (Nov. 1964), 15.

[35] Luck, S. 2005. *An introduction to the event-related potential technique*. MIT Press.

[36] Makeig, S. 2009. Electrophysiology: EEG and ERP Analysis. *Encyclopedia of Neuroscience*. Academic Press. 879–882.

[37] Mitra, B. et al. 2014. On User Interactions with Query Auto-completion. *Proceedings of the 37th International ACM SIGIR Conference on Research & Development in Information Retrieval* (New York, NY, USA, 2014), 1055–1058.

[38] Moshfeghi, Y. et al. 2013. Understanding Relevance: An fMRI Study. *Advances in Information Retrieval*. P. Serdyukov et al., eds. Springer Berlin Heidelberg. 14–25.

[39] Moshfeghi, Y. and Jose, J.M. 2013. An effective implicit relevance feedback technique using affective, physiological and behavioural features. *Proceedings of the 36th international ACM SIGIR conference on Research and development in information retrieval* (New York, NY, USA, 2013), 133–142.

[40] Mostafa, J. et al. 2015. Identifying Neurological Patterns Associated with Information Seeking: A Pilot fMRI Study. *Information Systems and Neuroscience*. F.D. Davis et al., eds. Springer International Publishing. 167–173.

[41] Oliveira, F.T.P. et al. 2009. Discriminating the relevance of web search results with measures of pupil size. *Proceedings of the 27th international conference on Human factors in computing systems* (Boston, MA, USA, 2009), 2209–2212.

[42] Onorati, F. et al. 2013. Characterization of affective states by pupillary dynamics and autonomic correlates. *Frontiers in Neuroengineering*. 6, (2013), 9.

[43] Pavlidis, G.T. 1985. Eye Movements in Dyslexia Their Diagnostic Significance. *Journal of Learning Disabilities*. 18, 1 (Jan. 1985), 42–50.

[44] Poldrack, R.A. 2006. Can cognitive processes be inferred from neuroimaging data? *Trends in Cognitive Sciences*. 10, 2 (Feb. 2006), 59–63.

[45] Preuschoff, K. et al. 2011. Pupil dilation signals surprise: evidence for noradrenaline's role in decision making. *Frontiers in Decision Neuroscience*. 5, (2011), 115.

[46] Rayner, K. et al. 2011. *Psychology of Reading*. Psychology Press.

[47] Regan, D. 1989. *Human brain electrophysiology: evoked potentials and evoked magnetic fields in science and medicine*. Elsevier.

[48] Reichle, E.D. et al. 2010. Eye Movements During Mindless Reading. *Psychological Science*. 21, 9 (2010), 1300–1310.

[49] Salojärvi, J. et al. 2005. Implicit Relevance Feedback from Eye Movements. *Artificial Neural Networks: Biological Inspirations – ICANN 2005*. W. Duch et al., eds. Springer Berlin Heidelberg. 513–518.

[50] Smallwood, J. et al. 2007. Going AWOL in the Brain: Mind Wandering Reduces Cortical Analysis of External Events. *Journal of Cognitive Neuroscience*. 20, 3 (Nov. 2007), 458–469.

[51] Smallwood, J. 2011. Mind-wandering While Reading: Attentional Decoupling, Mindless Reading and the Cascade Model of Inattention. *Language and Linguistics Compass*. 5, 2 (2011), 63–77.

[52] Ward, J. 2015. *The Student's Guide to Cognitive Neuroscience*. Psychology Press.

[53] Wierda, S.M. et al. 2012. Pupil dilation deconvolution reveals the dynamics of attention at high temporal resolution. *Proceedings of the National Academy of Sciences*. 109, 22 (May 2012), 8456–8460.

Investigating the Role of User Engagement in Digital Reading Environments

Heather L. O'Brien
School of Library, Archival and
Information Studies
University of British Columbia
Vancouver, Canada
1-604-822-6365
h.obrien@ubc.ca

Luanne Freund
School of Library, Archival ard
Information Studies
University of British Columbia
Vancouver, Canada
1- 604-822-0825
Luanne.Freund@ubc.ca

Richard Kopak
School of Library, Archival and
Information Studies
University of British Columbia
Vancouver, Canada
1- 604-822-2898
r.kopak@ubc.ca

ABSTRACT

User engagement is recognized as an important component of the user experience, but relatively little is known about the effect of engagement on the learning outcomes of such interactions. This experimental user study examines the relationship between user engagement (UE) and comprehension in varied academic reading environments. Forty-one university students interacted with one of two sets of texts presented in 4 conditions in the context of preparing for a class assignment. Employing the User Engagement Scale (UES), we found evidence of a relationship between students' comprehension of the texts and their degree of engagement with them. However, this association was confined to one of the UES subscales and was not consistent across levels of engagement. An examination of additional variables found little evidence that system and content characteristics influenced engagement; however, we noted that all students' reported increased knowledge, but topical interest for non-engaged students declined. Results contribute to existing literature by adding further evidence that the relationship between engagement and comprehension is complex and mediated.

Keywords
User engagement; comprehension; digital reading environments

1. INTRODUCTION

In digital information environments, user engagement (UE), "a user's response to an interaction that gains, maintains and encourages attention" [18], is viewed as a positive and necessary component of human information interaction. It is a widely held belief that UE mediates outcomes such as knowledge acquisition, yet there is conflicting evidence to support this claim. While we do know that UE is pivotal in fostering long-term relationships between users and systems [43], most work has focused on users' interaction preferences. For example, [19] noted that users preferred more "engaging" educational multimedia systems, but that modality preferences were mediated by task type (searching versus browsing). Other researchers have focused on the role of

UE in the adoption of learning technologies [17, 44] and the effect of interactive computer-mediated environments on learning [36, 10]. Yet drawing any larger conclusions about the relationship between UE and learning is inhibited by a lack of consistency in how researchers define and measure both UE and learning.

Research on human information interaction and retrieval has tended to focus on user-system interaction outcomes such as the retrieval of relevant documents or user satisfaction, rather than comprehension or learning per se. While some studies measure self-reported topical knowledge and search expertise to document cognitive changes during the search process [20], more robust methods are needed to ascertain the extent to which users develop cognitively and affectively through their interactions with systems. Comprehension, the process of extracting meaning from information [30], is a critical indicator of success for information systems, yet largely under-researched in interactive information retrieval (IIR).

In this research, we focused specifically on comprehension as an outcome of interacting with digital texts. Drawing upon prior research on the design of digital reading environments [36, 23, 26], we created a reading interface with different modes of interaction (note-taking and annotation) and text representation. We investigated whether UE affected comprehension outcomes and whether features of these reading environments influenced UE. Our initial conjecture was that more engaged readers would score higher on comprehension tests and that more interactive and visually rich reading environments would be more engaging. While there was a relationship between UE and comprehension, we found that it was more nuanced than we predicted, leading us to explore the role of user, system and content characteristics to interpret the findings. In this paper, we review relevant prior research and outline our methodology, and then describe our findings in detail. We conclude with a discussion of the findings and illuminate future directions for examining the relationship between UE and comprehension in human information interaction research and applications.

2. PRIOR RESEARCH
2.1. User Engagement (UE)

This research builds upon the work of [33] that defined user engagement as a multidimensional construct comprising the interaction between cognitive (e.g., attention), affective (e.g., emotion, interest), and behavioral (e.g., propensity to re-engage with a technology) characteristics of users, and system features (e.g., usability). UE is characterized by a number of interrelated factors: attention, motivation, control, hedonic and utilitarian

CHIIR'16, March 13–17, 2016, Carrboro, North Carolina, USA
Copyright is held by the owner/author(s). Publication rights licensed to ACM.
ACM 978-1-4503-3751-9/16/03…$15.00.
DOI: http://dx.doi.org/10.1145/2854946.2854973

needs, perceived time, attitudes, interest, sensory and aesthetic appeal, interactivity, novelty, challenge and feedback [19, 33]. Researchers are developing and applying various self-report, analytic and physiological methods to capture UE [24]. The User Engagement Scale [35] has been used extensively to investigate UE in various computer-mediated environments, including search, educational technologies, haptic interfaces, and social and communication media, and has found to be reliable and valid [31].

Within computer-mediated environments UE can be distinguished from *student engagement*, which looks at the extent to which a student is involved and invested in his or her own learning [13]. Research on student engagement has shown that more engaged students are more likely to succeed academically, and less likely to drop out of school [12]. In this study, we acknowledge that student engagement serves as the broader context in which UE with digital learning applications takes place. Whereas student engagement measures socio-economic, classroom and student variables that contribute to academic success, UE is more concerned with system (e.g., usability) and user (e.g., motivation) attributes as they relate to interactions with digital media. UE is equated with "stickiness," that is, continued engagement or re-engagement with systems [33, 43]. However, continued engagement with digital technologies cannot be assumed to foster outcomes such as comprehension and learning: the UE "equation" is not well-defined: unlike student engagement, we do not have a good understanding of what predicts UE or its outcomes, and how this varies across different types of systems.

Yet, the general consensus is that UE fosters better outcomes: more products sold, increased loyalty to a search engine, more invested e-learners, etc. Furthermore, interactive system features (e.g., links), embedded multimedia (e.g., video), and social annotation (e.g., "likes" or comments embedded within news websites) are believed to foster UE [3]. However, there is a dearth of literature that explicitly examines the relationships between UE, system features and user outcomes. Does greater engagement with digital systems make us better learners, more productive employees, or more efficient information seekers? In the current study we focus specifically on the relationship between UE and comprehension in a digital reading environment and the role UE plays in facilitating the understanding of texts.

2.2. User Engagement and Digital Learning Environments

Studies of digital learning environments are numerous and span multiple disciplines. Here we focus on a few examples that have explored UE within learning systems. These studies examined the presentation of content, compare different kinds of digital media, or contrast computer and non-computer mediated media. Webster and Ho [44] for instance, sought to determine characteristics of presentation software that were valued by students (challenge, variety, control and feedback), and whether these characteristics could be manipulated in the design of a computer-mediated lecture. The authors captured students' design preferences for presentation software over the duration of two iterative studies, but did not look specifically at the relationship between UE and learning outcomes, e.g., students' comprehension or retention of content. More recently, Denny [7] found that badge-based achievement systems lead to increased participation in an online course management system, as measured by the number of days students interacted with the system and the number of questions posed and answered by students. Denny concluded that badges increased student motivation, but made little difference in student learning, based on the number of questions formulated by students.

Results were inconclusive regarding the relationship between learning, UE and interactions with the course management system.

Other work has focused on comparing "human" versus computer-mediated instruction. Hu and Hui [17], for example, compared face-to-face versus computer-mediated (i.e., 20-minute video) instruction on students' ability to perform tasks using Adobe Photoshop. They found that face-to-face instruction resulted in more learning activities than video instruction. Yet, regardless of the medium of instruction, learning engagement predicted learning effectiveness and learning satisfaction. In other words, engaged students were more effective learners, independent of the medium of interaction. Sung, et al. [40] explored the depth of students' interactions with museum exhibits, comparing use of an interactive guidebook with a print worksheet. Results indicated longer and more positive interactions with museum exhibits for those in the interactive guidebook condition; however, there were no differences in learning outcomes as measured by concept maps created by students. Taking another approach, Jacques, et al. [19] drew upon the findings of four studies of multimedia learning software and concluded that users' perceptions of media depended on its type (e.g., videos, animations, photographs), presentation (e.g. aesthetic qualities such as font, color, sound quality) and their perceived control when using the system. However, perceptions were mediated by the user's interaction task and level of interest.

In summary, studies have manipulated how material is presented and showed that students preferred specific modes of interaction or design features, but have not found significant differences in terms of the quality of the output generated by students (concept maps [40], or discussion questions constructed [7]). In light of such findings, it is clear we need not only to understand the effects of specific technologies, but also how individual (e.g., motivation) and contextual (e.g., content, task) factors interact with system characteristics to produce experiential outcomes.

2.3. Digital Reading Environments

The shift from reading in print to reading in digital formats has received considerable attention in recent decades. Early work demonstrated that reading from screens was slower, less accurate, and resulted in performance and comprehension deficits in comparison to print reading [9]. More recent studies have characterized digital reading as non-linear, selective and antithetical to deep and sustained attention [6], running counter to the goals of "active reading", as framed by Adler [1]. Support for active and focused reading has been identified as an important challenge in designing digital reading environments [36]. Hence, many digital reading environments attempt to enable active reading by implementing various modes of interaction, e.g., browsing, scanning, skimming and keyword extraction [6, 25] through affordances such as note-taking, linking and annotating. Interfaces are designed with attention to features such as page layout, legibility, typology [26, 36] and structural cues (e.g. hierarchies, link definitions, etc.) [29]. The main thrust of these efforts is to help readers transition from reading to writing [29] and, more importantly, to engage in active reading that facilitates comprehension. Much of this work is based on an implicit assumption that heightened user engagement in a reading task will foster greater learning outcomes.

Comprehension is the process of extracting meaning from information [30] and is an essential component of learning from texts. Of the many models of text comprehension utilized in this context, Kintsch's Construction-Integration (C-I) Model is widely referenced and well-suited for investigating comprehension in information interaction research [4; 21]. In this model, comprehension results from a multi-staged process where propositions are first formed into a plausible interpretation of linguistic input [construction of a textbase], and then integrated with existing knowledge into a situation model. The text-base relies on micro-level (e.g., decoding, remembering facts) and macro-level (e.g., more global processing of the gist or topic) inferences within the text. Reading consists of increasingly sophisticated parsing of text-based propositions to form a mental representation of the content. This, coupled with prior knowledge and experience, evokes imagery, emotions, and intentions that create the "situation model" and guide current and future text interactions [22].

The C-I Model has been previously applied in IIR research. Cole and Mandelblatt [4] devised an information retrieval (IR) model based on Shannon and Weaver's Communication System Model with three sub-systems: perception, comprehension, and application, and mapped these sub-systems to Kintsch's layers of mental representation (e.g., propositions, micro-level representation, macro-level representation, situation model). At the perceptual level, the information searcher must perceive the signal or series of propositions from the IR system, input the information, and encode it in such a way that it can be processed by the comprehension sub-system. The comprehension system receives this microstructure output and transforms it into macrostructure output and situation model. Finally, the situation model is applied when it reaches the application sub-system. At this stage, the searcher is able to use his/her altered cognition to communicate with the IR system, for example, by refining query terms to achieve more relevant results. The C-I Model was used to guide the design of an information system for undergraduate students in the preliminary stages of their research. It was believed that helping students to articulate their information need and represent it to the IR system would aid in promoting more successful searching behaviors.

While [4] saw the potential of Kintsch's work in IR system development, we envisioned it could assist with the evaluation of IIR experiences, both in terms of its ability to help us construct an instrument to measure comprehension and to understand the relationship between learning outcomes and readers' perceptions of enjoyment and engagement.

Utilizing the C-I model of comprehension in this study, we hypothesized that one way that UE may contribute to comprehension and learning is through its relationship with the concept of flow, a state characterized by deep absorption in an activity [5]. UE shares qualities with flow, including intrinsic motivation, focused attention and control [19]. Kintsch [22] articulated the relationship between learning and flow saying, "flow is not the goal of instruction, learning is, which is hard work, but the flow may provide motivation to engage in the hard work of deliberate practice" (p. 230). Thus UE, like flow, may be a mediating variable in the learning equation, inspiring learners to invest in the "hard work" of learning.

2.4. Current Study
UE is a desirable goal for interactive systems and is believed to foster positive user outcomes. The reviewed literature suggests that people interact more in more engaging computer-mediated environments. But such systems do not necessarily affect greater gains in learning [7, 40]. Student motivation [17], interest, and the nature of the learning task [19] may intervene between UE and learning outcomes.

One of the dilemmas in documenting learning outcomes is that studies are focused on different technology-mediated interactions (presentation software, course management software), settings and time frames. The latter is particularly crucial if we consider that learning is a process. Another issue is the variety of measures employed in attempting to measure learning. Some researchers have focused on perceptions of UE and learning, rather than on more objective indicators. Comprehension, which is of interest to us, is typically assessed through fact-based questions in multiple-choice or true and false formats that ask readers to recall information or make inferences [27] or to create written text summaries [39]. A major challenge with comprehension measures is that the variable content of the learning environment makes it impossible to develop standardized metrics.

We adopted Kintsch's C-I Model to guide us in the development of suitable measures of micro (local) and macro (global) level comprehension. We created a digital reading environment with four reading conditions that varied in interactivity (note-taking, linking) and text presentation (plain versus in-context cues). Based on the inconsistencies in the literature regarding the relationship between UE and learning outcomes, we sought to address the following questions: Do more engaged readers achieve better comprehension outcomes? What role do user, system and content characteristics play in facilitating UE?

3. METHOD
This study was conducted with 41 student participants. We designed a simulated task scenario based on a typical academic task of preparing for class by completing assigned readings. Readings were focused on a general interest "Technology and Society" theme. Students interacted with three digital readings of mixed genres (journal article, website, and popular press article) from one of two article sets: Digital Activism (7874 words) and Human-Robot Interaction (8325 words). Groups of students were assigned to interact with one article set, and with one of four versions of the experimental reading interface (see Table 1). The reading interface manipulated the level of interactivity (presence or absence of interactive features) and presentation style ("plain text" or "in-context"). The interactive conditions included a small number of hyperlinks that connected relevant ideas within the reading set, and had the Diigo Toolbar installed so that participants could annotate and highlight text; the non-interactive interface had neither of these features. The "in-context" condition presented the texts in their original format together with images and any original formatting features, whereas the "plain text" interface displayed articles in a single font and standard format with no images. Articles were presented as individual Web pages in a browser with a vertical scrollbar available for within-page navigation. A menu page contained the task description and hyperlinks to each article in the set and was used to navigate between readings.

3.1. Participants
The students recruited for this study (21 F; 17 M; 4 not specified) were 19-24 ($n=21$) and 25-29 ($n=14$) years old. There were undergraduate ($n=22$), masters ($n=10$) and doctoral students ($n=5$) who were enrolled in a range of degree programs; four did not specify student status. The majority reported spending more than 30 minutes per day reading for academic ($n=39$) or personal ($n=30$) purposes. Participants used digital media about half the time for academic reading ($M=49\%$; range: 10-95%).

Table 1. Summary of experimental conditions

Interface Condition	Human Robot Interaction	Digital Activism
Plain text with interactive features	Group 1 (*n*=5)	Group 2 (*n*=4)
Plain text without interactive features	Group 3 (*n*=5)	Group 4 (*n*=6)
In-Context with interactive features	Group 5 (*n*=5)	Group 6 (*n*=6)
In-Context without interactive features	Group 7 (*n*=5)	Group 8 (*n*=5)

3.2. Instruments

We used a variety of performance, self-report, and comprehension measures. In this paper, we focus specifically on the self-report measures for UE, topical knowledge, interest, and motivation, and comprehension. Students were asked to rate their knowledge and interest (4-items) on a 7-point Likert scale before and after the reading task. These were intended to gauge whether students perceived changes in their topical knowledge or interest as a result of interacting with the texts.

The User Engagement Scale (UES), consisting of 31-items rated on a 7-point Likert scale, was used to measure UE [35]. The UES comprises six sub-scales: perceived usability, aesthetic appeal, felt involvement, novelty, focused attention and endurability. It has been used to measure UE in computer-mediated domains such as web search, e-commerce, social networking systems and online news, and has demonstrated good reliability and validity; however, the use of factor analysis in some studies has pointed to a four-factors, rather than a six-factor UES [34, 46]; we elaborate on the implications of this below in the "data analysis and preparation" section.

The Adult Reading Motivation Scale (ARMS) (21 items rated on a 5-point Likert scale) was used to investigate attitudes toward reading [38]. It includes dimensions of reading for recognition, reading to do well in other areas of life, reading for efficiency, and reading as part of one's self identity. Motivation has been shown to precipitate UE [19, 33, 44], and is an affective component of learning experiences. The Nelson-Denny Standardized Reading Test was used to assess students' general reading level [2], and allowed us to collect baseline reading ability data of participants.

We developed and refined a reading comprehension test based on Kintsch's C-I model [21]. Comprehension questions for each article set were designed to assess microstructural and macrostructural text comprehension. For all of the comprehension questions there were "correct" and "incorrect" responses. *Microstructural items* tested recall (eight factual true or false items) and understanding of the concepts presented in the texts through the Sentence Verification Technique (SVT) [37]. The SVT for each set of articles consisted of twelve sentences (four per article), two of which accurately represented the semantics of the text in the form of one exact phrase and one paraphrase, and two of which falsely represented the content of the article by changing the meaning or inserting something incongruous. Participants were asked to indicate whether or not each sentence accurately represented the content. *Macrostructural items* asked students to connect ideas presented in the three texts and consisted of six

summary statements (SS) that varied in centrality and importance [21, 42]. Students were asked to select the three statements that best depicted the central themes in the article set.

3.3. Procedure

Each two-hour session took place in a seminar room. Morae software recorded on-screen activity, including URLs visited (task menu and articles), time spent on each page, scrolling, typing, and mouseclicks. Laptops were pre-set to display the texts in one of the four conditions per session. All other materials (instructions, questionnaires) were provided in print format. A researcher was present to greet students and facilitate the session. Following completion of the informed consent procedure, students (in groups of 4-6) completed a demographic and reading habits questionnaire, and the ARMS. Following this, those in the interactive conditions participated in a tutorial of the Diigo Toolbar. Next, participants were asked about their pre-task knowledge and interest in the topic of the assigned article set. They then moved on to the reading task, beginning from an online menu page that contained the task scenario and links to the three articles. They were asked to browse the readings within a 30-minute time frame. Immediately after the reading task, students completed a post-task questionnaire consisting of items related to their knowledge of and interest in the topic *after* interacting with the readings, the UES, and the comprehension test related to each reading set. Lastly, students completed the Nelson-Denny Standardized Reading Test. At the conclusion of the study, participants were thanked and paid an honorarium.

4. DATA ANALYSIS AND PREPARATION

4.1. User Engagement Scale (UES)

Responses to the UES were first examined to assess data quality and consistency of the sub-scales. Missing values ranged from 0 to 2 per item. The exception to this was one aesthetic appeal item ("I liked the graphics and images in this set of readings") that had nine missing items. The lower response rate was likely due to the fact that readings did not contain graphics and images in some conditions; this item was removed from further analysis.

A standard approach when using an experiential scale such as the UES would be factorization to test its robustness before proceeding to data analysis. Factorization was not appropriate here given the small sample size. Therefore, we based our groupings of items on prior work [34, 46] that recommend the use of four-factors, rather than six, as most appropriate for the UES. Specifically, three of the six sub-scales (perceived usability, aesthetic appeal, and focused attention) have consistently resulted in distinct factors across various administrations of the UES, but the endurability, felt involvement, and novelty sub-scales have tended to combine to form one factor, which we refer to here as "Interest" (INT). Thus, we grouped the 31 items as follows: 1) endurability + felt involvement + novelty (INT) (2) perceived usability (USAB), 3) aesthetic appeal (AESTH), and 4) focused attention (ATTEN), and checked the reliability of these groupings.

AESTH and ATTEN had excellent Cronbach's alpha values [7]. The value of USAB was not optimal (0.66). Through an examination of the inter-item correlations for this sub-scale, two items were removed ("I could not do some of the things I needed to do during this reading experience" and "This experience was mentally taxing"); internal consistency was subsequently improved (0.704). Although INT had a good Cronbach's alpha value (0.9), the Endurability item, "This reading experience did not work out the way I had planned," was poorly correlated with other items in the grouping, and was therefore removed. This increased the alpha value to 0.914, which indicated some redundancy. One further item was removed ("This experience was worthwhile") after examining the inter-item correlations to reduce the amount of overlap for this factor. Thus 26 items were used to create four groupings. The descriptive and correlation statistics for the sub-scales are summarized in Tables 2 and 3, respectively, for the four UES groupings.

Table 2: Descriptive statistics of UES item groupings

UES	*M* (*SD*)	# items	α	Skewness (*SE*)	Kurtosis (*SE*)
INT	4.37 (0.96)	9	0.898	0.075 (0.338)	-0.218 (0.75)
USAB	5.25 (0.81)	6	0.704	-0.06 (0.374)	-0.254 (0.733)
AESTH	4.01 (1.24)	4	0.84	0.147 (0.378)	-0.146 (0.741)
ATTEN	2.51 (0.73)	7	0.894	-0.204 (0.378)	-0.593 (0.741)

Table 3: Correlations for UES groupings (Sig. at *p*<0.001)**

UES	INT	USAB	AESTH
INT	1		
USAB	0.512**	1	
AESTH	0575**	0.348**	1
ATTEN	0.74**	0.206	0.291

Score distributions were then examined to determine appropriate approaches to data analysis. Kurtosis statistics showed a fairly flat distribution for all of item groupings, but INT and AESTH were positively skewed, whereas USAB and ATTEN were negatively skewed. The mean USAB score was high, whereas ATTEN was quite low (based on the seven-point Likert scale range). This analysis confirmed it was best to examine sub-sets of the UES as opposed to calculating a composite score for engagement based on all 26 items, and, given these findings and the small sample size, that non-parametric statistics were most appropriate.

We examined the validity of the UES by looking at the association between the UES item groupings and a single post-task self-report item: "What was your level of engagement with the content of the articles that you read for the experimental task?" Spearman's rank correlation coefficient showed positive associations between responses to the level of engagement question and the UES item groupings: INT (r_s=0.662, p=0.00), ATTEN (r_s=0.5, p=0.001), and USAB (r_s=0.48, p=0.002); AESTH was marginally significant (r_s=0.309, p=0.056). These correlations validated the use of these groupings in subsequent analyses.

4.2. Comprehension assessments

Table 4 shows descriptive statistics for the comprehension measures. Responses to the comprehension questions were scored by comparing them with the correct responses to the true or false (T/F), sentence verification technique (SVT) and summary statements (SS) questions. We looked at the number of errors made by students for each of the T/F, SVT and SS assessments. Scores were calculated by subtracting the number of errors from the maximum number of correct answers. Since there were different maximum scores for each test based on the number of questions, we attempted to give each test equal weight in computing the microstructural and total comprehension scores. For *microstructural comprehension*, T/F and SVT each comprise half of the score, and T/F, SVT and SS were equal to a one third of the *total comprehension score*. These latter measures are expressed as percentages.

Table 4. Descriptive statistics for total comprehension, true/false, SVT and summary statements

Comprehension	*M(SD)*	Median	Range	Max Score
T/F	6.04 (1.53)	6	3-8	8
SVT	7.92 (1.63)	8	4-11	12
SS	5.09 (1.13)	6	2-6	6
T/F + SVT	70.83 % (14.39)	72.91%	41.67-95.83%	100%
T/F + SVT + SS Score	73.35 % (12.59)	76.92%	46.15-96.15%	100%

The UES results were converted into low, medium and high engagement groups using the percentiles of each variable based on the median. This approach was chosen given the non-normal distribution of the item groupings, as previously described. As shown in Table 2, the mean for ATTEN was low (2.51) compared to USAB (5.01); AESTH and INT closer to the middle of the seven-point Likert scale range.

5. RESULTS

5.1. User Engagement and Comprehension

A summary of the means and standard deviations for the overall comprehension score for the three levels of engagement on each of the factors is presented in Table 5. The means vary by group, but a strong general trend is not discernable. Kruskal Wallis Tests show a significant difference in the Total Comprehension score for the INT factor, but not for ATTEN, USAB, and AESTH. A more fine-grained analysis of comprehension outcomes across levels of INT (Table 6) shows that scores on the True/False questions varied significantly (P=0.052), which affected the overall Microstructural comprehension (T/F + SVT) and Total Comprehension scores (Table 5). The SVT and SS scores did not vary significantly. The means and standard deviations indicate a non-linear relationship in which the T/F scores were higher for the High and Low INT groups than in the Medium group. A similar pattern repeats across all comprehension measures, with the highest mean scores achieved by those with the lowest level of INT.

Table 5. Descriptive statistics for total comprehension for three levels of user engagement

	INT M (SD)	AESTH M (SD)	ATTEN M (SD)	USAB M (SD)
Low	76.92 (12.3)	70.9 (14.09)	73.84 (10.69)	71.94 (13.44)
Medium	62.01 (12.4)	78.84 (10.13)	78.32 (11.7)	71.67 (12.55)
High	72.43 (9.25)	69.93 (10.71)	70.19 (11.72)	75.96 (12.06)

Table 6. Descriptive statistics (M, SD) and Kruskal Wallis Test (df=2) for low, medium and high INT for comprehension measures

INT	T/F	SVT	SS	T/F + SVT	Total Compre-hension
Low	6.25 (1.43)	8.37 (1.45)	5.37 (1.2)	73.95 (13.6)	76.92 (12.40)
Medium	4.62 (1.59)	6.75 (1.83)	4.75 (1.03)	57.03 (14.81)	62.01 (12.4)
High	6.25 (1.28)	7.66 (1.49)	4.91 (1.16)	71 (10.63))	72.43 (9.96)
Kruskal Wallis	x^2=5.91, p=0.052	x^2=4.68, p=0.09	x^2=2.73, p=0.25	x^2=6.57, p=0.037	x^2=6.61 p=0.037

In response to our first research question, these results provide some evidence that engagement and comprehension are related, in that participants with either a high or low level of Interest (INT), measured in terms of their felt involvement, and the endurability and novelty of the reading experience, achieved better outcomes on the comprehension test than those with a medium level of interest. Specifically, they had better outcomes on the True and False questions, an indication of surface level comprehension and recall. Other dimensions of engagement, specifically the aesthetic appeal and perceived usability of the reading environment, and the extent to which the readers focused their attention on the task, were not associated with comprehension outcomes.

5.2. User, System and Content Characteristics

This section presents the results of analyses to determine whether characteristics of participants (demographic variables, reading ability, and general reading motivation), the experimental system (interactivity and text presentation style), or content (reading set, pre- and post-task knowledge and interest) offer insights into the findings with respect to engagement and comprehension. We test for relationships between these variables and engagement, focusing on the INT dimension of engagement, which displayed an association with comprehension.

5.2.1. User Characteristics

We were interested in whether student status or age affected self-reported engagement. Older or more advanced students may have greater familiarity with the task of preparing for class, the scenario featured in our experiment; one might assume they have developed efficient strategies for navigating texts and could therefore become more engaged. Six participants (two in the low and one in the medium groups) did not provide their age, gender or student status. Chi-square tests showed no significant differences in INT for student status (e.g., undergraduate, Masters, etc.), x^2=5.62(6), p=0.443; gender, x^2=3.62(2), p=0.163; or age group, x^2=5.08(4), p=0.278. However, it is worth noting that 4 of the 5 doctoral students who participated in the study were in the High INT group.

We also examined the relationship between INT scores and reading ability and motivation. We might hypothesize that people with lower reading ability or lower motivation would be less engaged in the reading task scenario due to the cognitive challenge of engaging with the texts or disinterest in reading. We saw no difference between INT ratings and students' Nelson Denny reading grade, x^2=1.985(2), p=0.371, or reading strength, x^2=0.695(2), p=0.707. Despite the fact that this was a sample of university students, there was a range of reading abilities amongst participants. The mean Nelson Denny reading grade was 14.24 (range: 4.09-18.8). Thus, the sample did not consist solely of "strong readers" according to the Nelson Denny Test, yet this variability in reading grade and strength did not affect perceived engagement. Schutte and Malouff saw motivation as a "central feature" of reading engagement that impacts reading competency and both the function and social components of reading [38, p. 470]. We expected a positive association between participants' reading motivations, as measured by the Adult Reading Motivation Scale and their engagement in the texts, but this was not supported, x^2=3.53(2), p=0.171.

5.2.2. System Characteristics

Chi-square tests also showed no significant differences according to whether students were assigned to an interactive or non-interactive condition, x^2=3.96(2), p=0.138, nor a plain text or in-context condition, x^2=0.76(2), p=0.682. However, the frequency distributions across the four system environments are suggestive of some trends (Table 7). Almost half of those in the Low INT group were in the simplest reading environment and the majority of those in the High INT group were in one of the interactive conditions, in which they were provided with tools for highlighting and annotating text while reading.

5.2.3. Content Characteristics

Aspects of content, such as the topic, format or writing style, may influence UE [32]. In this study there were no statistically significant differences in INT between the two sets of articles, x^2=4.77(2), p=0.092. However, more participants were in the high INT group for the human-robot interaction article set, which had four people in the medium, and nine people in the high group. The digital activism set of readings had twelve people in the low, four in the medium, and five in the high INT groups. This suggests that the content of the readings had some impact on participants' engagement.

When comparing participants' self-reported interest in the content (post-task) with their level of engagement based on the UES, Kruskal Wallis tests show significant differences between the low, medium and high INT groups, x^2=9.45(2), p=0.009 (Table 8). This result validates our interpretation of the UES INT factor as representing the user interest component of engagement. Further, patterns across the three groups in pre and post task reports of interest in and knowledge of the content offer some insight into this finding (Tables 8 and 9). Mean pre-task levels of interest and knowledge in the topic of the articles are lowest for the Medium

INT and highest for the High INT groups, but the level of interest of both groups increased after reading. In contrast, the mean level of interest among those in the Low INT group, which started out quite high, decreased after reading.

Table 7: Frequency of system conditions by levels of INT

INT	n	Non-Inter-active, Plain	Inter-active, Plain	Non-Inter-active, In-Context	Inter-active, In-Context
Low	16	7	1	3	5
Medium	8	1	2	4	1
High	14	3	5	1	5

Table 8: Pre- and post-task interest for low, medium and high INT groups

INT	n	Pre-task interest M(SD)	Post-task Interest M(SD)	Change in Interest
Low	16	4.69 (1.44)	3.44 (1.36)	-1.25 (1.52)
Medium	8	4.25 (1.5)	4.88 (0.99)	0.62 (1.4)
High	12	4.83 (1.68)	5.58 (0.99)	0.75 (2.09)

The difference between students pre- and post-task self-reported knowledge was not statistically significant: x^2=5.008(2), p=0.082, and all groups, on average, reported gaining knowledge over the course of the study (Table 9). This gain was less pronounced for the low INT group, which had lost interest over the course of the readings, as compared to the medium and high groups, which both became more interested as they read (Table 9). It is worth noting that the Medium INT group, which achieved the lowest outcomes on the comprehension tests, reported a lower level of topical knowledge prior to reading and the highest knowledge gains of all the groups. Thus, while they may have scored lowest on the comprehension measures, they evaluated their own learning as having increased from when they began the experiment.

It is recognized that prior knowledge is key to formulating queries and devising tactics in information search [41]. Extrapolating to the digital reading environment, students' lack of topical knowledge may have resulted in less understanding of how to interact effectively and efficiently with these particular sets of readings. The effort they expended to make sense of the texts in the limited time frame of the study may have affected their INT ratings. In this case, learning gains were made, but they may have experienced more cognitive load than either the low or high INT groups, who began with higher self-reported topical knowledge, and evaluated their experience as less engaging. Their comprehension score may have been equally affected by their lack of prior subject knowledge. If digital reading strategies are comparable to information seeking more generally, where there is movement from the general to the specific [41], students may have spent their time orienting themselves to the topic rather than focusing on the detailed information of the texts which they were required to understand to complete the comprehension tests.

Table 9: Pre- and post-task knowledge for low, medium and high INT groups

INT	n	Pre-task knowledge M(SD)	Post-task Knowledge M(SD)	Change in knowledge
Low	16	2.44 (1.2)	3.56 (1.2)	1.12 (1.14)
Medium	8	2.00 (0.92)	4.25 (1.48)	2.25 (1.28)
High	12	2.83 (2.16)	4.75 (1.54)	1.91 (1.67)

In response to our second research question, we found limited evidence of an influence of user, system or content characteristics on user engagement. Statistical testing on this small sample showed no significant results for most of the variables tested; however, the descriptive data suggest some possible trends that merit further investigation: doctoral student participants were primarily in the High INT group, as were the majority of those in the Interactive System condition, and more of the readers of one article set (human-robot interaction) than the other. Different patterns with respect to levels of topical knowledge and interest across the three INT groups and over time point to a possible explanation for the non-linear relationship between INT and comprehension observed in this study.

6. DISCUSSION

We examined the relationship between user engagement, as measured by the User Engagement Scale, and comprehension, as measured through true/false and sentence verification items that addressed micro-level (local) comprehension, and sentence summaries intended to capture macro-level (global) understandings of texts. We reiterate here that our sample was relatively small and our findings should be treated as exploratory. Rather than identifying a strong effect of engagement on comprehension, our results echo those of previous research in the educational domain, summarized in section 2, which found partial or inconclusive associations between engagement and learning. Nevertheless, these results contribute to our understanding of human information interaction as a complex phenomenon, and offer some insights for future research.

We observed a positive association between one of the four UES subscales – INT – and comprehension at the micro-level and overall. Given that this was a reading task conducted in a relatively simple and familiar web environment, it makes sense that the INT factor, representing the novelty, felt involvement and endurability of the reading experience, would be associated with comprehension, while the more system-oriented components of engagement, AESTH and USAB, were not. If we had compared highly complex systems with more pronounced design features, it is possible that these factors would have had an effect. The lack of an association between comprehension and focused attention (ATTEN) is more surprising. We had anticipated that a higher degree of perceived focus during the study would contribute to comprehension, in keeping with the notion that text comprehension is associated with effort on the part of the reader [20]. It may be that, given the relatively low scores on this factor (M=2.91, SD=0.73), there was not enough variation to see a difference between groups.

The only individual test score associated with INT was the True/False questions, which measure surface learning [11]. From this, we can infer that readers who were highly engaged in the textual content were more likely to remember facts gleaned from the texts; however, this association only held true for the Medium and High INT groups. Surprisingly, the Low INT group performed as well as the High INT group on the True/False questions, indicating that the relationship between engagement and comprehension may be non-linear or mediated by other variables.

To better understand the relationship between UES ratings and comprehension, we looked at user characteristics (demographics, reading ability and reading motivation), the experimental condition to which people were assigned and content characteristics (article sets, user interest and prior knowledge). We hypothesized that people who were farther along in their academic careers, stronger readers, or those who rated reading as a more favorable (enjoyable) activity would be more engaged [38]. Further, we expected that the experimental condition to which people were assigned would affect UE based on how the different reading environments shaped the user experience. Surprisingly, clear relationships between these variables and engagement did not emerge, although trends in the data suggest that level of education, the provision of interactive reading tools, and the nature of the content may be associated with engagement. Thus designing reading and learning environments requires consideration of many variables beyond the system's affordances [17], and experience may be shaped by factors beyond the developer's control.

Data on participants' knowledge of and interest in the content of these texts provided the most insight into the observed association between engagement and comprehension. While all participants reported similar levels of knowledge and interest before starting the reading task, the Low INT group lost interest during the task and reported learning less, while the Medium and High groups increased in both interest and knowledge. Two important questions arise from this: what caused the decline in interest for the Low INT group, and how did they manage in spite of this, to achieve comprehension outcomes as good as or better than the other groups?

One explanation for this is that students in the Low INT group may have been working hard to learn [22] and had good outcomes, but a less positive experience. The effect of that experience may have caused them to under-estimate how much they actually learned. This conjecture is supported by the observation that many of the participants in the Low INT group were in the simplest, and possibly least engaging, reading environment (plain text/non-interactive), and from Whitman's [45] findings of students' experiences with either a baseline or interactive tutorial: learning gains were achieved for students using both systems, but the interactive tutorial resulted in faster completion without sacrificing their ability to succeed or their enjoyment. Results of a separate analysis of the current study's dataset showed that readers in the plain text/non-interactive system condition had the strongest comprehension outcomes overall, but also tended to spend more time reading [14]. Future work should include assessment of cognitive effort to measure the effects of challenge on UE and comprehension in digital reading environments.

Another explanation is that students in the low INT group, who had quite a high level of prior knowledge, lost interest because the texts failed to add anything new to their existing knowledge of the topic, resulting in boredom, disengagement and a negative self-perception of their learning. Despite this, they completed the assigned task and their knowledge of the topic enabled them to do well on the comprehension tests. This corresponds to findings in the online news domain showing that novel content was

imperative for initiating and sustaining engagement for some news readers [32]. Finally, it is possible that there were different types of motivations inherent within these groups. For example, the low INT group may have been motivated by the extrinsic reward of the honorarium at the end of the experiment, whereas the high INT group may have been intrinsically motivated or interested in the subject matter of the texts. The concentration of doctoral students, predominantly highly self-motivated learners, in the High INT condition suggests this may be one factor at play.

If we focus on evidence of learning, rather than comprehension, the Medium and High INT groups reported higher gains in knowledge than the Low INT group, even though the Medium group was least successful on the comprehension test. This supports a relationship between UE and learning, at least in terms of self-perception: those who rated their novelty, felt involvement and endurability higher claimed to have learned more. This also points to the limitations of comprehension as a static outcome measure and the need to employ more individualized process measures to assess learning in the context of human information interaction. For example, recent work [16] used students' facial expressions and postures to disambiguate engagement and frustration with intelligent tutoring systems over seven sessions, defining specific expressions, postures and event sequences, such as interactions with human and non-human tutors, that characterized the nature of students' experiences; these were corroborated with self-reports. This research shows the potential for designing more responsive systems, but also for triangulating process and outcome, and subjective and objective data.

Clearly, prior knowledge plays a key role in comprehension generally, and, although we did not observe differences at the macro-level of comprehension through the Sentence Summary questions, we expect that it is particularly important for these (the?) more integrative components of comprehension [22]. However, due to sample size, it was not possible to perform regression analysis using prior knowledge as a co-variate. Another limitation of our experiment is that we looked at comprehension over a two-hour period, rather than an actual academic class where scaffolding content and collecting data at multiple points in time might provide more accurate measures of comprehension at the macro-level. Future work should address these limitations.

Interest in content, and how it affects learning, is also worthy of further exploration. This study pointed to interest, whether measured through self-report data or through the UES INT factor, as a key component of both engagement and learning for human information interaction tasks. Flowerday, et al. [11] distinguished topical (trait) and situational (state) interest; both promote deeper learning and engagement with reading materials. They examined self-reported topical and situational interest in an experiment that manipulated perceived choice in the reading of an expository text. Situational interest, more so than topical interest, increased UE and resulted in more positive affect. In our study, we used the scenario of preparing for class to create situational interest and observed that some aspects of UE were positively associated with pre and post task changes in knowledge and interest. In considering how to stimulate interest, designers of digital reading environments should focus on situational interest, particularly since topical knowledge is largely unpredictable. This may mean going beyond retaining the visual or structural features of genre, as we did in this study, and experimenting with visual salience through the size and placement of text [28]. More guidance on manipulating visual salience and attention, specifically in the area of academic reading environments, could be better revealed through eye tracking; recent research has demonstrated the success of this method for examining other IIR phenomena, including relevance [15].

One important aspect of human information interaction that was not addressed in this study is persistence: the motivation and willingness to continue interacting with the learning environment and to complete the task. Because of the experimental setting, participants were unlikely to stop reading, whether or not they were highly engaged in the task. However, in a real world academic setting, persistence is more likely to be intertwined with engagement, and may then have a more direct effect on comprehension and learning: a student who stops reading, or skips more quickly through a text, is much less likely to learn from it. This points to the need to conduct more naturalistic studies of the relationship between engagement and learning in the context of digital reading, as has been done in the past in information seeking research [for example, 41].

7. CONCLUSION
In this paper, we found that students in the low and high INT groupings had comparable microstructural and total comprehension scores; we did not find a relationship between macro-level (global) comprehension and UE. We explored connections between UE and individual (demographics, reading ability, general reading motivation), and system (interactivity, para-textual cues) characteristics, and the article sets, but no significant differences were detected. This may be due to our sample size and the small number of participants in each condition. However, we did note statistical differences when we examined self-reported INT and pre and post task interest and knowledge. While all groups reported increased knowledge as a result of interacting with the texts, the interest of the low INT group declined. Overall, the directionality of the relationship amongst the variables in not clear: for some participants, interest in the texts and engagement with the task was associated with text comprehension, while for other students there was no association between their perceived experience and comprehension scores.

Results suggest that engagement, arising from a user's interest in content, can facilitate comprehension and learning in academic environments, but that engagement is not an essential component for learning to occur. It is therefore not appropriate to assume that more engaging systems will necessarily produce better learning outcomes: the relationship is more complex than this. As these results are not conclusive, more research is needed to explore other factors, such as motivation, with larger samples and in more naturalistic settings. Future work might focus on design features that increase visual salience as a way to increase situational interest, measuring cognitive load as a means of interpreting users' perceptions of the interaction, and using eye-tracking methods to better appreciate readers' experiences. Replicating this research with a larger sample would allow for the construction and testing of predictive models to better articulate the connection between UE and comprehension in digital reading environments.

In this research we opted to examine students' reading experiences quantitatively, and the group administration of our experiment prevented us from collecting qualitative post-session interviews to learn more about students' perceptions of the tasks, reading environments, and levels of engagement. The combination of qualitative and quantitative methods in future work will facilitate a more holistic understanding of the relationship between engagement, interest, and learning. However, as noted in other research [14; 46], measuring learning in IIR contexts is challenging and has been limited to quizzes and written summaries that test recall and recognition rather than learning. Here we

sought to build a measure rooted in the learning sciences that was specific to the texts students were exposed to in the study; the UES and Adult Reading Motivation Scale are established measures against which to examine this novel comprehension measure. As research interests in this area continue to grow, so do the possibilities for validating measurement approaches with physiological and qualitative data.

8. ACKNOWLEDGMENTS
Thank you to our research participants and graduate research assistance Florian Ehrensperger, Elizabeth Shaffer, Kimberly Buschert, Ariel Deardorff and Devin Soper. This research was generously supported by a Hampton Fund Research Grant from the University of British Columbia.

9. REFERENCES
1. Adler, M.J. 1940. *How to Read a Book: The Art of Getting a Liberal Education*. Simon and Schuster, New York, NY.

2. Brown, J.A., Fishco, V.V., and Hanna, G. 1993. *Nelson–Denny Reading Test: Manual for Scoring and Interpretation*. Riverside Pub, Rolling Meadows, IL.

3. Chung, D. S. 2008. Interactive features of online newspapers: Identifying patterns and predicting use of engaged readers. *J J Comput Mediat Commun, 13*, 658–679.

4. Cole, C. and Mandelblatt, B. (2000). Using Kintsch's discourse comprehension theory to model the user's coding of an informative message from an enabling information retrieval system. *JASIS&T, 51*(11), 1033-1046.

5. Csikszentmihalyi, M. 1990. *Flow: The Psychology of Optimal Experience*. Harper and Row, New York, NY.

6. Cull, BW. 2011. Reading revolutions: Online digital text and implications for reading in academe. *First Monday, 16*(6).

7. Denny, P. 2013. The effect of virtual achievements on student engagement. In *Proceedings of the SIGCHI Conference on Human Factors in Computing Systems* (pp. 763-772). ACM. DOI= 10.1145/2470654.2470763.

8. DeVellis, R. F. (2003). *Scale Development: Theory and Applications* (2nd ed). Sage, Thousand Oaks, CA.

9. Dillon, A. 1992. Reading from paper versus screens: An empirical review of the literature. *Ergonomics, 35*, 1297-1326.

10. Eysink, T.H.S. and de Jong, T. 2012. Does instructional approach matter? How elaboration plays a crucial role in multimedia learning. *J Learn Sci, 21*(4), 583-625.

11. Flowerday, T., Schraw, G., and Stevens, J. 2004. The role of choice and interest in reader engagement. *J Exp Educ, 72*, 93–114.

12. Fredricks, J. A., Blumenfeld, P. C., and Paris, A. H. 2004. School engagement: Potential of the concept, state of the evidence. *Rev Educ Res, 74*, 59–109.

13. Fredricks, J. A., McColskey, W., Meli, J., Montrosse, B., Mordica, J. and Mooney, K. 2011. *Measuring student engagement in upper elementary through high school: A description of 21 instruments*. Greensboro, NC. http://ies.ed.gov/ncee/edlabs/regions/southeast/pdf/rel_2011098.pdf.

14. Freund, L., Kopak, R. & O'Brien, H.L. (in press). The effects of textual environment on reading comprehension: implications for searching as learning. *J Inform Sci.*

15. Gwizdka, J. 2014. Characterizing relevance with eye-tracking measures. In *Proceedings of the Information Interaction in Context Symposium* (pp. 58-67). ACM.

16. Grafsgaard, J.F. (2014). Multimodal Affect Modeling in Task-Oriented Tutorial Dialogue. Unpublished Doctoral Dissertation, North Carolina State University. Raleigh, North Carolina.

17. Hu, P.J-H. and Hui, W. 2012. Examining the role of learning engagement in technology-mediated learning and its effect on learning effectiveness and satisfaction. *Deci Support Syst, 53*, 782-792.

18. Jacques, R.D. 1996. *The nature of engagement and its role in hypermedia evaluation and design.* Unupblished doctoral dissertation, South Bank University, London.

19. Jacques, R., Preece, J. and Carey, T. 1995. Engagement as a design concept for multimedia. *Cdn J. Educ. Comm.* 24,1, 49-59.

20. Kelly, D. 2009. Methods for evaluating interactive information retrieval systems with users. *Foundations and Trends in Information Retrieval, 3*(1-2), 1-224.

21. Kintsch, W. 1998. *Comprehension: A Paradigm for Cognition.* Cambridge University Press, New York, NY.

22. Kintsch, W. 2009. Learning and constructivism. In Tobias, Sigmund and Duffy, Thomas M. (Eds), *Constructivist Instruction: Success or Failure?* (pp. 223-241). Routledge, New York, NY.

23. Kopak, R. and Chiang, C 2007. Annotating and linking in the Open Journal Systems. *First Monday*, 12(10). http://firstmonday.org/article/view/1961/1838

24. Lalmas, M., O'Brien, H., and Yom-Tov, E. 2014. *Measuring User Engagement.* Morgan Claypool Pub.

25. Liu, Z. 2006. Reading behavior in the digital environment: changes in reading behavior over the past ten years. *J Doc, 61*(6), 700-712.

26. Marshall, C. 2009. *Reading and Writing the Electronic Book.* Synthesis Lectures on Information Concepts, Retrieval, and Services 1:1, pp. 185. Morgan Claypool Pub.

27. McCay-Peet, L., Lalmas, M., and Navalpakkam, V. 2012. On saliency, affect and focused attention. In *Proceedings of Conference on Human Factors in Computing Systems* (pp. 541-550). ACM.

28. Maynard S. and McKnight, C. 2001. Children's comprehension of electronic books: An empirical study. *New Rev Children's Lit. Libr., 7*, 29-53.

29. McNamara, D.S. and Shapiro, A.M. 2005. Multimedia and hypermedia solutions for promoting metacognitive engagement, coherence, and learning. *J Educ Comput Res, 33*(1), 1-29.

30. McNamara, D. S. and Magliano, J. P. 2009. Towards a comprehensive model of comprehension. In B. Ross (Ed), *The Psychology of Learning and Motivation, vol. 51,* (pp. 297-284). Elsevier Science, New York, NY.

31. O'Brien, H.L. Translating Theory into Methodological Practice. In H.L. O'Brien and P. Cairns (Eds). *Why Engagement Matters: Cross-Disciplinary Perspectives and Innovations on User Engagement with Digital Media.* Springer, forthcoming.

32. O'Brien, H.L. 2011. Exploring engagement in online news interaction. In *Proceedings of the Annual Meeting of the Association for Information Science and Technology*, New Orleans, LA.

33. O'Brien, H.L., and Toms, E.G. (2008). What is user engagement? A conceptual framework for defining user engagement with technology . *JASIS&T*, 59(6), 938-955.

34. O'Brien, H.L. and Toms, E.G. 2013. Measuring engagement in search systems using the User Engagement Scale (UES). *Inform Process Manag, 49*(5), 1092-1107.

35. O'Brien, H.L. and Toms, E.G. 2010. The development and evaluation of a survey to measure user engagement in e-commerce environments. *JASIS&T, 61*(1), 50-69.

36. Pearson, J., Buchanan, G. and Thimbleby, H. 2013. *Designing for Digital Reading.* Synthesis Lectures on Information Concepts, Retrieval, and Services 5(4), 1-135.

37. Royer, J. M., Greene, B. A. and Sinatra, G. M. 1987. The sentence verification technique. *J Reading*, 30(5), 414-422.

38. Schutte, N. S. and Malouff, J. M. 2007. Dimensions of reading motivation: Development of an adult reading motivation scale. *Read Psychol*, 28(5), 469-489.

39. Shannon S. and Winterman B. 2012. Student comprehension of primary literature is aided by companion assignments emphasizing pattern recognition and information literacy. *Issues in Science and Technology Librarianship* http://istl.library.ucsb.edu/12-winter/refereed3.html

40. Sung, Y-T., Chang, K-E., Hou, H-T., and Chen, P-F. 2010. Designing an electronic guidebook for learning engagement in a museum of history. *Comput Hum Behav, 26,* 74-83.

41. Vakkari, P/ (2001). A theory of the task-based information retrieval process: a summary and generalisation of a longitudinal study. *J Doc, 57* (1), 44 – 60.

42. van Dijk, T.A. 1980. Story comprehension: An introduction. *Poetics, 9*(1), 1-21.

43. Webster, J. and Ahuja, J. S. 2006. Enhancing the design of web navigation systems: The influence of user disorientation on engagement and performance. *MISQ, 30*(3), 661-678.

44. Webster, J. and Ho, H. 1997. Audience engagement in multimedia presentations. *ACM SIGMIS Database, 28*(2), 63-77.

45. Whitman, L. 2013. *The Effectiveness of Interactivity in Multimedia Software Tutorials.* Unpublished Doctoral Dissertation, North Carolina State University, Raleigh, NC.

46. Wiebe, E. N., Lamb, A., Hardy, M., and Sharek, D. 2014. Measuring engagement in video game-based environments: Investigation of the User Engagement Scale. *Comput Hum Behav, 32*, 123-132.

47. Wilson, M. J., and Wilson, M. L. (2013). A comparison of techniques for measuring sensemaking and learning within participant generated summaries. *JASIS&T, 64*(2), 291-306.

User Experience Dimensions:
A Systematic Approach to Experiential Qualities for Evaluating Information Interaction in Museums

Marianne Lykke
Aalborg University
Rendsburgsgade 14
DK – 9000 Aalborg, Denmark
(+45) 9940 8157
mlykke@hum.aau.dk

Christian Jantzen
Aalborg University
Rendsburgsgade 14
DK – 9000 Aalborg, Denmark
(+45) 9940 9023
jantzen@hum.aau.dk

ABSTRACT

The present study develops a set of 10 dimensions based on a systematic understanding of the concept of experience as a holistic psychological. Seven of these are derived from a psychological conception of what experiencing and experiences are. Three supplementary dimensions spring from the observation that experiences apparently have become especially valuable phenomena in Western societies. The 10 dimensions are tried out in a field study at the Center for Art and Media (ZKM) in Germany with the purpose to study their applicability in the evaluation of interactive sound archives. 29 walk-alongs were carried out with 58 museums visitors. Our analysis showed that it was possible to identify the 10 experience dimensions in the study material. Some dimensions were expressed more frequently than others. The distribution of expressed dimensions and the content of the user comments provided a clear picture of how the two sound archives differed in respect to the experiential qualities.

1. INTRODUCTION

Is user experience (UX) "old wine in new bottles"? This was the rhetorical question posed by [2] after having examined 51 empirical research publications on UX. User experience is a relatively new research area, and the authors' goal was thus to examine 3 key issues related to the study and assessment of user experience: *dimensions,* what experiential qualities to examine, *methodology,* what study methods to apply, and *context,* what products and use cases to study [15]. Altogether the publications examined show a shared understanding of user experience as a non-instrumental, hedonic or non-task oriented quality as opposed to the notion of usability stressing instrumental, practical or task-oriented qualities [2].

There seems to be a common understanding that hedonic as well as task-oriented qualities are essential for the user's perception and evaluation of an interactive system that a person can interact with through a user interface. As described by [15] usability refers

to the system's practical goals, the do-goals, such as finding a book in an online bookstore or accessing sounds in a digital sound archive, whereas user experience refers to the system's hedonic qualities, the be-goals such as feeling competent in retrieving the book or feeling engaged when looking for sounds in the sound archive. Usability makes a task or system easy and intuitive whereas user experience makes it meaningful and valuable.

A large and varied set of dimensions is used as indication of the experiential quality of interactive systems with affect, aesthetics, emotion, and enjoyment being the most common. Many other dimensions or variations of already known dimensions have been introduced: e.g. relevance, engagement. But this is typically done without a clear relation between such dimensions making it difficult to compare studies that investigate similar phenomena within UX. Many studies use two or fewer dimensions, e.g. [8, 38, 40]. Although there seems to be a common agreement that experiences are multidimensional, only few studies analyze the interrelatedness of several experiential qualities.

Among these are [41] that looked at the concept of experience from a human-computer perspective and build on a holistic, pragmatic view on experience. This study worked from the position that experience stands for an orientation toward life as lived and felt in all its particulars. Experience is a dynamic inter-relationship between people and environment, made up of four intertwining threads: the sensual, the emotional, the compositional, and the spatio-temporal thread. Experience is constituted by continuous engagement by being what individuals bring to the interaction, which implies that it is not possible to engineer or control experience in technology. The authors dealt with experience as a rich concept with many varieties for which one might seek to design, including curiosity, frustration, anger, joy, enchantment, and sadness. Interaction, dialogue, empathy, engagement, and enchantment are key dimensions of experience.

A study by [15] likewise stressed the richness in experiencing and situatedness – "experiences are never alike, neither between nor within experientors" [15:16]. At the same time, following [32] notion of experience, this author argued that experiences could be categorised in terms of their generic emerging properties. In a study with 52 participants, the author used three core human needs (competence, autonomy, and relatedness) combined with five positive dimensions of feeling (inspired, alert, excited, enthusiastic, determined) as well as five negative dimensions (afraid, upset, nervous, scared, and distressed) to study and model user experiences with a technology. The study showed that

CHIIR'16, March 13–17, 2016, Carrboro, North Carolina, USA .
© 2016 ACM. ISBN 978-1-4503-3751-9/16/03...$15.00.
DOI: http://dx.doi.org/10.1145/2854946.2854965

experienced autonomy and competence was a source for positive experiences, whereas relatedness only played a minor role.

In [14] is introduced a multidimensional framework for user judgement of user interface quality. In line with [15] the authors distinguished between task-oriented and hedonic qualities. This framework covers a range of quality attributes: usability, content/functionality, aesthetics, customisation and engagement. Inspired by [26] they differentiate the aesthetic dimension between classical aesthetic, referring to orderly and clear design and expressive aesthetic associated with creativity and originality and the ability of the design to challenge, fascinate and surprise users. The findings reinforced the importance of knowing the preferences and expectations of the users. Another result showed that usability is important, but good aesthetic design can overcome some usability problems. Regarding framework and experience dimensions the results of this study point to the necessity of a closer examination of the relative strengths of experience dimensions on users' overall quality judgement and of exploring the interactions between them. In addition, the authors recommend further research on the concept of attractiveness to encompass interaction and engagement.

The purpose of this paper is to outline a set of experiential qualities for exploring and assessing user experience. The study aims at contributing to what UX basically is all about by deducing a set of experiential dimensions based on a systematic understanding of the concept of experience. Experiences are complex and dynamic, and experiential qualities are multiple. But many of these dimensions, we argue, can be related systematically to the psychological structure of experiencing.

We frame this study with the purpose that developers and designers could use this multidimensional model as a basics to analyze the effect and improve the quality of user experience in interactive systems where both pragmatic and hedonic qualities are essential, e.g. virtual archives [24], museum exhibits [17], or a living museum research studio [11]. In order to illustrate the dimensions and to test their applicability they have been utilized in an analysis of interactive sound archives at the ZKM, Zentrum für Kunst und Medientechnologie, in Karlsruhe (Germany).

The remainder of this paper will proceed as follows. Section 2 presents the concept of experience and section 3 the dimensions developed to study the user's experiences based on this concept. Section 4 describes the characteristics of two sound archives. In section 5 an overview is provided of the research design used for the user experience study. Section 6 presents the results, and section 7 discusses the findings. The paper closes with concluding remarks in section 8 summing up findings about experiential dimensions and their applicability in the analysis and evaluation of interactive museum systems and archives.

2. A PSYCHOLOGICAL CONCEPT

Experiencing is a holistic psychological process. This implies, firstly, that an experience consists of physiological, perceptual, emotional and cognitive parts and is more than the sum of these parts. Secondly, holism means that experiencing something pleasurable or painful may make one become (more) experienced. Linguistically, this holism is expressed in the dual purport of the noun "experience", which in most Germanic languages is translated into two different words: e.g. the German *Erlebnis* (an experience you are having right now) and *Erfahrung* (an experience you have acquired by interacting with the world). *Erlebnis* is what is happening here and now, *Erfahrung* is the

digesting of key *Erlebnisse*, which make 'me' into what 'I' am [6: 7]. Erlebnisse lead to *Erfahrungen*. And in reverse: past experiences (*Erfahrungen*) may guide, frame or tune future experiences (*Erlebnisse*). The quality and valuation of the present process of experiencing (*Erleben*) is colored by past experiences (*Erfahrungen*) setting expectations as to what is going to occur [35]. This process may again generate new experiences (*Erfahrungen*), thus influencing future experiencing (*Erleben*) by adjusting or expanding the set of expectations.

This holism was addressed by early psychology (18, 42). The rise of behaviorism as the paradigmatic approach to psychology in the first decades of the 20th century meant an orientation away from holism towards scientific reductionism, atomizing the wholeness of the concept of experience into separate sub-disciplines like emotional, cognitive and social psychology [6, 10]. As a consequence, the conceptualization of what experiences fundamentally are has stagnated since these early advances.

A systematic approach to the field tries to restore this holism by conceptualizing experiences as a dynamic complex generated by the interaction of perception, emotion and cognition [15]. An experience could hence be defined as a change in an individual's physiological (pleasure or pain) and/or affective state (relief, anger, anxiety, excitement etc.), bringing about perceptual and/or behavioral changes (e.g. heightened awareness or altered conduct), which may challenge or charge previous experiences potentially leading to new understandings or expanding existing ones [19]. Learning something new may therefore be the outcome of the experiencing process.

This interaction is seminal for identity formation. To a large degree, the "I" is the sum of past experiences (*Erfahrungen*), which are stored in autobiographical memory [3]..But also semantic memory, i.e. the knowledge of what to expect and how to behave in specific situations [39],, depends crucially on this complexity. Experiences (as *Erfahrungen*) are the memorable and meaningful outcomes of experiencing (as *Erleben*), contributing to identity (e.g. in the form of autobiographical memory) and to learning about the world (which may become semantic memory). This learning outcome could be conceptualized as accommodation, a modification of existing cognitive structures and behavioral patterns to match the new experience [27].

The holistic take thus implies that the concept of experience comprises more than sensations and emotions. Experiential qualities are not only about fun, pleasure and wellbeing (or their opposite). They are also about expectations and about learning something new: i.e. about cognition and identity. A further implication of this holism is that the quality of a particular experience in the present (*Erlebnis*) always depends on past experiences (*Erfahrungen*) and that future experiences (*Erlebnisse*) may change the value of the present ones. In evaluating experiences, the quality of present experiencing (*Erleben*) should be related to past and future outcomes.

A frame for understanding this complex dynamics of bodily and cognitive aspects of experiencing and experiences is aesthetics. In the German tradition of the philosophy of aesthetics, aesthetics is cognition through the senses ("sinnliche Erkenntnis") [22]. The purpose of aesthetics is not to produce pleasing sentiments but to generate an understanding of the world and the self through bodily involvement: through sensations and emotions. Aesthetics is thus cognition by other means than ordinary reasoning. This captures the holism of experiencing being an on-going flux of experiencing (*Erleben*) as well as past and future outcomes (*Erfahrungen*).

Dewey pointed out this intrinsic connection between aesthetics and experiences [9]. Importantly, he pointed out that true experiences just like art presuppose a balance between reacting to the world and acting in the world: i.e. of passively undergoing stimuli from the environment and of actively doing something in respect to this environment. The user's activity is just as seminal to experiencing as indulging in pleasurable stimuli. This corresponds with insights from motivation psychology indicating that experiential value is derived from hedonic pleasures (passive) as well as from engagement (active) [16] Another important contribution from motivation psychology sheds more light on the nature of "doing" in art as well as experiencing. Contrary to activities directed towards an external purpose (e.g. "do"-goals in [15]), "doing" in the aesthetic mode has no purpose outside the activity. Whereas goal-directed activities are "telic", aesthetic activity having no ordinary utility is "paratelic" [1]. Like in playing one "does" for the pleasure of "doing". In a famous wording in the philosophy of aesthetics, purely experiential activities could be seen as "purposefulness without a purpose" [22]. The concept of "flow" seems to capture the aesthetics of these experiential "doings" [8].

In brief, experience could be defined as the transposition of affect into cognition. In experiencing attention is directed towards otherwise automatic acts of sensing and feeling [19]. These acts take on a quality of their own.. They become "aesthetic generating awareness of potentially attractive or harmful opportunities in the surroundings, and thereby diverting the ordinary course of action. Experiences – of the world or one's self - are the memorable and meaningful outcomes of experiencing.

The importance of this definition for UX is threefold. Firstly, a systematic approach is holistic, thereby stressing the dynamic interaction of sensations, affects, cognitions as well as learning and identity issues in experiencing something. Evaluating the experience dimensions of an interactive system should therefore delve into the extent in which it arouses (sensations), generates pleasure, pain, relief or frustration (emotions), is comprehensible and memorable (cognitions) and contributes to understanding (learning and identity).

Secondly, experiencing happens in "the immediate flux of life" furnishing "the material of our later reflections" [18 :117]. The present of experiencing (*Erleben*) is a building block for future experiences (*Erfahrungen*). But this present relies on past experiences (*Erfahrungen*) made of prior *Erlebnisse*. This temporal aspect implies that in positive experiences (outcomes: *Erfahrungen*) not every instant of the experiential process (*Erleben*) has to be pleasurable. Moments of frustration or even anxiety may also help generating memorable and cherished experiences. Dimension like "pleasure" and "enjoyment" should therefore not be used as prime criteria in evaluating the design. It moreover implies that the evaluation of the experiential qualities of a system ideally should capture the immediacy of experiencing and relate this to prior expectations and later reflections. A further implication of this temporality, one critically affecting the value of present experiencing, is "hedonic adaptation": i.e. the routinizing of once exciting experiences [21]. Repeat exposure leads to adaptation, thereby turning novelty into habits and reducing the experiential qualities of these stimuli. Therefore, dimensions expressing the novelty, unexpectedness or originality

of the experience at the perceptual and emotional levels as well as on the cognitive level should be introduced.

Thirdly, the scope of experiencing and experiences is more profound than hedonics understood ad passively undergoing pleasant stimuli. Experiential value is also created by actively engaging with the system. This "doing" is of an aesthetic nature and deals with learning through active engagement with the world [23]. This learning may be explicit, as in adjusting existing mental structures (accommodation), or it may be implicit, as in habit formation (implicit memory). The implication for evaluating interactive systems is that dimensions expressing "affect" and "emotion", although important, are far from sufficient in evaluating the design.

3. DIMENSIONS FOR EVALUATION

From this psychologically defined concept of experience a set of relevant dimensions for evaluating users' experiences can be deduced [19]. Experiencing being a universal phenomenon, these dimensions are independent of the technological characteristics of the object that is being experienced.

Experiencing is a bodily process engaging the senses and arousing emotions. This fact is expressed in two dimensions. A design has to be *involving*: i.e. it has to be entertaining, which implies mood management by increasing positive moods or by reversing a negative mood [43]. On the physiological level involvement implies a change in the body's arousal level: a decrease leading to relaxation or an increase of stress heightening awareness. On the emotional level such changes broaden the scope of attention and may further a seeking behavior (i.e. curiosity) [13]. The apex of involvement is the user's immersion in the design.

Next a design has to divert the user from his or her pre-planned goals. The design becomes the goal in itself and not a utility for reaching an external goal. The design becomes playful and the user's behavior (a "doing") is oriented towards this play. It becomes "paratelic" [1]. The dimension *spontaneous* captures this dimension: i.e. in how far is the design able to promote non-goal-directed behavior?

Experiences are the outcomes (*Erfahrungen*) of a bodily process of experiencing (*Erleben*) by which affects are transformed into cognitions. This fact is expressed in two further dimensions. A design has to be *interesting*: i.e. it has to challenge expectations formed by prior experiences. This dimension puts ordinary perceptions and conceptions of the world at stake. It could be called "cognitive involvement" whereby otherwise familiar assumptions are "made strange", unfamiliar. This diversion of habitual awareness is a main characteristic of aesthetics [36].

The companion of this de-automatization of expectations is the dimension *relevant*. Relevance assures that the challenge remains understandable as well as manageable. The deviation disrupts expectations, but it can nonetheless be handled within the established cognitive structures, the experience based mental models [20], schemata [31] or scripts [37]. A relevant design without interest is not experiential. An interesting design without relevance will at best have only very few users. UX-design thus has to find a delicate balance between these twin dimensions. To use an analogy: interesting and relevant experience design is like a riddle. A "good" riddle should beg to be solved (be interesting). But it should also convey the impression on its audience that they are actually capable of solving it and that the problem solving will be worthwhile (be relevant).

Experiences are "lessons" learnt from experiencing. A further dimension is thus *learning*: i.e. the ability of the design to integrate interest and relevance in revised cognitive structures. This dimension evaluates in how far the entertaining qualities of the design contribute to the user's development, to identity and habit formation. New experiences expand the existing ones. This elaboration of cognitive structures is "accommodation" [27].

A sixth dimension is *unique*. This dimension is a quality in the design as perceived by the user and is related to the "novelty" aspect of those experiences that deviate from the routine. The design's degree of attributed singularity and originality may be a motivating factor for user involvement and interest. The unique is exceptional by being non-repeatable (e.g. events), non-reproducible or strictly time and space defined (e.g. rituals and sanctuaries). Exceptional designs provoke awe and admiration even after they have lost their novelty. They become known "time-outs" from ordinary existence thereby maintaining strong experiential qualities.

The dialectics of "undergoing" and "doing" in experiencing, pointed out by [9], leads to the final psychologically derived dimension: *interactive*. An experience is not something bought and sold or designed and used by two distinct agencies. In fact, viewed as psychological phenomena, experiences are actively produced by the user, who utilizes both the design and own expectations in this process. The core of experience design is therefore not only a matter of involvement, but also of user participation. Such participation is mental as well as corporeal. And the quality of this dimension is expressed by the degree in which this participation alters the mental representation and physical shape of the design. The importance of interactive qualities has been stressed in managerial studies as well as in design theory under the labels of "co-creation" and "co-design" [29, 33].

A very plausible reason why UX-design has become *en vogue* is that this practice explicitly caters for the last dimension. Interactivity in a stricter sense than implied in our description is obviously a defining feature of HCI-systems. Another reason might be that broader tendencies of societal, economic and technological change have created a push from usability towards "experientiability" as a determining factor for the design's success. An early analysis of how these changes generated a new notion of what the meaning of life basically is, is Schulze's seminal sociological study [35]. The main assumption of this study may be summarized as follows. In the "experience society" experiences are no longer contingent by-products of processes of social exchange (e.g. production and consumption). Instead, experiences become either the very goal of these exchanges (e.g. in hedonism) or a token of proof that the user is existentially on course towards some non-material goal (e.g. self-actualization). This latter utilization of experiences in everyday behavior could be dubbed a neo-romantic tendency [30], whereas the former could be called a symptom of neo-utilitarian materialism. In this case people use design for the sake of optimizing pleasure. High scores of the dimensions *involving*, *spontaneous* and *interesting* will be indicative for the pleasure optimizing goal. A supporting, supplementary dimension could be *fun*.

On the other hand will high scores on *interesting, relevant* and *learning* indicate that experiences are meaningful testimonies in the pursuit of self-development. Another two supplementary dimensions express this evidence-oriented utilization of experiences in identity-projects: *close* and *authentic*. A high score

on *close* expresses that the design is felt to address issues and concerns that the user finds significant for his or her life and that this address seems to be tailored to match the user personally. Examples of how this dimension is being practiced are customization and social media communication. *Authentic* expresses that the purpose of the design is felt to be "for real" and that its intentions are trustworthy and reliable. Authenticity is a (neo-romantically inspired) demand in that it prefers scrutinizing motives of acts at the cost of examining their possible consequences. It is preoccupied with the sincerity of a specific statement and of its utterer..

The three supplementary dimensions could be said to be culturally specific. They are relevant for evaluating designs circulating in societies where experiences are valued as if they were commodities, i.e. in experience economies [5, 29, 34], or where technology significantly enhances the production of experiences [41]. On the other hand, we assert that the first seven, psychologically derived dimensions have a universal character. They are independent of societal and cultural issues, economic agendas and technological innovations. We therefore consider them to be the basic dimensions.

The ten experience dimensions are summarized in table 1:

Table 1. Experience dimensions

Dimension	Key issues
Involving	Does the user feel physiologically and emotionally engaged? Is the design entertaining? Is it relaxing or exhilarating? Does it generate positive or negative emotions? Does the user get immersed in the design?
Spontaneous	Does the user feel that the design invites to divert from goal-directed behavior? Is it playful?
Interesting	Does the user feel a challenge? Does the design present something unexpected, an obstacle? Is it surprising? Does it pose a riddle to be solved?
Relevant	Does the user feel capable using existing cognitive structures? Does the design relate to previous experiences? Is it a riddle that can be solved in a meaningful manner?
Learning	Does the user feel empowered by the design? Does the design expand the user's horizon? Does it contribute to (self-)development, to identity and habit formation?
Unique	Does the user feel confronted with an exceptional design? Is the design original? Is the design something never encountered before or something that cannot be encountered anywhere else?
Interactive	Does the user feel that he or she is an active part of the design? Does the design invite the user to become co-creators or co-designers?
Fun	Does the user find the design inherently enjoyable? Is the design primarily meant to be pleasurable?
Close	Does the user feel that the design "talks to him or her"? Is the design tailored to meet the user's specific demands? Is it personalized?
Authentic	Does the user feel that the design is sincere, true to its purpose?

These dimensions are systematic. Seven of them are derived from a psychological conception of the holism of experiencing and experiences. It is our ambition that these dimensions should cover the complexity of the concept without atomizing its inherent holism. Moreover, three supplementary dimensions spring from the observation that experiences seemingly have become especially valuable phenomena in society. They try to capture socially and culturally ascribed qualities in experiential commodities: one related to hedonism, two to self-actualization.

One of the dimensions frequently used in other studies is "aesthetics". In a philosophical tradition stemming from [22], aesthetics is the field of "cognition through the senses" (German *sinnliche Erkenntnis*). It is thus more than beautification, ornament or a pleasurable expression. Therefore aesthetics cannot meaningfully be reduced to only one dimension when evaluating experiential qualities. It implies such different aspects as physiological and emotional involvement, the twin dimensions of interest and relevance, playful spontaneity (the paratelic mode), interactivity and not least learning. The holism of an experience is hence matched by the complexity of aesthetic operations.

4. THE VENUE OF THE STUDY

Our research was conducted at the Center for Art and Media (ZKM), Karlsruhe (Germany) in 2012. The object of our research was a special exhibition *The Unheard Avant-Garde [in Scandinavia]*, curated by Morten Søndergaard. It was part of a larger sound art exhibition *Sound Art. Sound as Medium of Art* that ran as the main activity at ZKM from March 2012 until January 2013. The larger exhibition consisted of works by 90 artists giving a retrospect impression of tendencies and developments in 20th and 21st century sound art. The special exhibition on Scandinavian avant-garde was located in a corner section of the main exhibition in two rooms slightly separated by walls from the rest. The smaller room covering approximately 20% of the space for the special exhibition had 1 entrance, while the larger room had 3 entrances (cf. Fig. 1). At each entrance a sign on the floor read "The Unheard Avant-Garde [in Scandinavia]", thus indicating to the public that they were about to enter a special section of the overall exhibition.

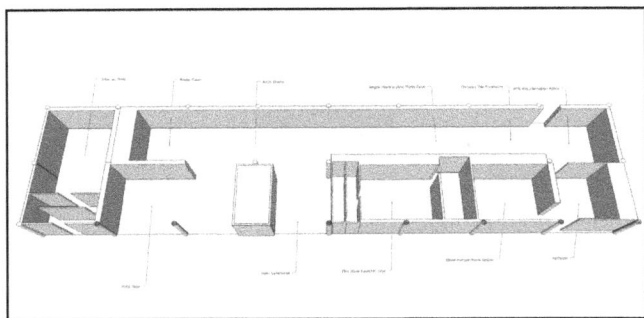

Figure 1. Floor plan of the special exhibition The Unheard Avant-Garde [in Scandinavia] (ZKM).

The theme of the special exhibition was the avant-garde movement in Scandinavia in the 1960s, which has been quite influential for the international development of sound art. The Finnish pioneer Errki Kurenniemi was celebrated in the separate room. The larger room exhibited 11 works: 3 of them where archives making works of sound art available to the public, the other ones where either remakes of sonic artworks from the 1960ies or installations constructed to give the audience not only information but also a tangible experience of the milieu and the debates characterizing the avant-garde of the 1960ies.

In our research we used multiple methods in studying audience responses to all 11 works in the larger room. 5 of these works, including the 3 archives, were wholly or partly interactive, the rest were not. For our present study we have selected the responses to 2 of these works, both interactive archives allowing the visitor to search for and interact with sound information and objects.

The first one, *Hørbar* by Mogens Jacobsen and Morten Søndergaard (2007), was the odd man out. It differed from the rest of the special exhibition in two respects: unlike the rest of the exhibits it was an already existing archive and furthermore it was the only piece not explicitly related to the theme. The title of the archive is a pun, *Hørbar* meaning both "Audible" and "Audio-bar" in Danish. This work intends to give the public access to the sound archive of the Museum of Contemporary Art, Roskilde (Denmark), covering works from 1910 up to 2000. This is achieved in quite an idiosyncratic way. The sound archive consists of 260 glass bottles neatly placed on shelves. Each bottle apparently "contains" a piece of recorded poetry read by the poet or of avant-garde music performed by the composer, the information objects. When placed on a round bar table, the ghost in the bottle is released. The piece becomes audible. Several metadata are used to describe the sound works. The title of the work and the name of the artist are shown on a playlist of the 10 latest pieces, displayed on a screen on the wall. The bottles have labels in 12 different colors, each color indicating a category. This categorization is wildly unsystematic. Some categories are time periods: e.g. 1910-1920 or 1960-1965. Others seem to indicate musicological properties: e.g. "slow/quick" or "staccato/legato". And there are categories apparently indicating a mood or a theme: e.g. "cold/warm", "man/machine" etc. The labels do not hold any further information on the piece. And it is not transparent to the public, which pieces each category consists of. So when placing the bottle on the bar the public does not now what precisely to expect. The piece performed is to a high degree random. The retrieval system, namely, picks one chance piece from the category. The repeat placement of the bottle on the bar does therefore not guarantee that the piece will be repeated. If the piece is not to one's liking the performance can be aborted by placing a new bottle on the bar. At ZKM this feature led to frequent "bottle battles" between members of the same group of visitors: i.e. one member of the group interrupting the piece activated by another member by putting a competing bottle on the bar.

Just on the other side of a wall was the second archive selected for the present study: a display on *Elektronmusikstudion* (EMS), designed by Sanne Krogh Groth and Mats Lindström. This archive documented the early years of the still operational EMS, which was conceived by Knut Wiggen in 1962 to promote the production of avant-garde electronic music in Sweden. The archive consisted of three basic elements. Firstly, 3 screens on the wall with video footage from the 1960ies. Each screen displayed one program, showed in a continuous loop. The audience could watch these programs on a bench opposite the screen. The bench had three headphones, one for each screen. Secondly, photos and copies of manuscripts on the wall conveyed further historical documentation about the establishment of EMS, its pioneers and its relationship with Swedish public service broadcast. Thirdly, in one corner there was a digital, interactive archive of early EMS productions made available via a playlist on an iPad placed on a tripod. The audience could listen to selected sound objects from this list by using the headphone connected to the device. The objects were searchable by title.

To sum up: *Hørbar*, one might assume, seems to cater for dimensions like *spontaneous, interesting* and *interactive* due to the "wild" categorization and random retrieval. In comparison, the EMS is more like a "proper" archive representing and making available significant moments of a past that has once been. This work thus seems to be aiming at the *learning* dimension.

5. RESEARCH DESIGN

Two researchers and two research assistants from Aalborg University carried out the sensory-ethnographic walk-along study between Friday June 1 and Sunday June 3 2012. The aim of the study was to record the visitors' perceptions, emotions and sense-making while walking the museum and interacting with the interactive sound artworks. In the present study we use findings from the study to examine whether the developed experiential dimensions capture and describe the users' experiences of the works.

5.1.1 Walk-along

The principal reason for choosing the walk-along method as a UX study method is that this method, originally developed in urban geography, allows researchers to follow participants closely and to track their route and actions while talking to them and getting involved in their experiences [25]. The objective was to get detailed information about how museum visitors are experiencing and making sense while interacting with, seeing, hearing, feeling, touching and smelling the works. 58 museum visitors participated: 10 visitors were in single-person walks and the remaining 48 visitors were distributed on 19 in-group walks. 3 participants were seniors, 23 adolescents, 22 youngsters, and 10 children. The majority was German, but the participants also included visitors from USA, Romania, Italy, Austria and Spain. 19 visitors declined the invitation to participate.

Working independently, the researchers and research assistants came into contact with visitors at one of the three entrances of the special exhibition (cf. Fig. 1). When inviting them to participate, the interviewers gave an oral presentation of the research project and the research team and handed out a written consent letter describing the project and the walk-along method in German or English (depending on the participant's native language). As an encouragement, the visitors agreeing to participate were offered free drinks in the museum café for their involvement. After having signed the consent letter, the participants were told that they were free to decide the pace and route through the special exhibition. While some participants explored all the works, others only explored a few. The durations of the walk-alongs therefore differed between 7 and 90 minutes.

During the walk-alongs the participants were stimulated to comment on the works and describe their experiences and viewpoints. The interviewers used an interview guide including 6 themes to inspire and prompt the informal talks (cf. Table 3). These themes touch upon characteristics, identified as defining features of sound works in a museum context: i.e. interactivity, de-centeredness, immediacy in presence, engrossment, multi-perspectivism, and embodiment [4]. The participants were also questioned as to the influence of the interaction on learning and on coming to understand the works and on whether the interaction

had any influence on their experience of and feelings about the works. When a participant decided to leave the special exhibition, the interviewer closed the conversation with some factual, demographic questions including participant's age, nationality, level of knowledge about sound and media art works on a 5 point scale, and whether he or she had a professional or layman relationship to sound and media works.

The walk-along conversations were tape-recorded and then transcribed and coded. The coding was carried out in two steps. First the transcribed conversations were divided into excerpts of meaning, each representing a single statement about the work. In the analysis we call these excerpts of meaning for user comments. Thereafter the excerpts were read and analyzed with the purpose of identifying and coding what experience the participants expressed while commenting on the sound art work: e.g. did they feel physiologically and emotionally engaged, did they feel empowered. The 10 dimensions from Table 1 were used to code the experience of the participants. It was furthermore noted whether the excerpts reflected a positive or negative experience. One of the senior researchers carried out the coding along with the two research assistants. First, the coders conducted the analysis separately; next, the results of the coding were compared; and finally, the differences were discussed and resolved during a group discussion. The final definition and use of the coding categories was established during the discussions. The coding was hence primarily used as an access point to dig into the data with the purpose to get an understanding of the user experience.

Additionally, after each walk-along the interviewers made structured notes on observations about the sound artworks and the influence of interaction and on the participants' experiences with the walk-along method (e.g. advantages and challenges). The notes were later compared and discussed among the interviewers, and used as background information for the analysis and interpretation of the walk-along findings.

6. FINDINGS ON USER EXPERIENCE

In the following we will present what we learnt about user experience based on the conversations and observations during the 29 walk-alongs. The results are primarily based on the 145 user comments (excerpts of meaning) concerning the sound archives *Hørbar* and EMS extracted from the transcriptions. Information from the researcher notes is used when it provides background information to the findings. 84 user comments are on *Hørbar* and 61 comments on the EMS archive.

The most frequent experiences associated with *Hørbar* are *interactive, involving,* and *interesting,* each are expressed in 18 comments. This is not surprising considering the nature of the archive. Less frequent, but still significant are the experiences of *relevance* (9), *learnability* (8), and *fun* (6). Only few informants express experiences that *Hørbar* is *close* to them (3) or *authentic* (2). One single informant perceives it as *unique* (1) or *spontaneous* (1).

Concerning the experience of feeling *interactive,* the users' comments tell us several interesting things about user experience. Firstly, it is a quality in itself that users feel *interactive:*

107F: *"Yeah, and because they are such an ordinary thing, but very handy? that's also really nice. I'm actually the bad person in museums, because I am always trying to touch things or just... no one is looking, and so I like the fact that it's touchable, but not... I think when they offer you to touch things, they want to give you something funny or something? This is... The bottles are a nice choice."*

One user emphasize that interaction is a constituent part of the archive:

104b: *"We are part of the artwork. We are part of the work because the piece doesn't function without us, because it needs us mediator.*
Researcher: You are not passive?
104b: *That's right. We are active and that I find cool, because you yourself have to do something for the art to emerge.*
[Translated from German]"

Another informant highlights that interaction helps her to keep interest:

Researcher: *In overall, what's your impression of this part of the museum?*
202F: *I like the bottle installation very much, because it was colorful and enjoyable and you could do things - it was interactive. And then I lost interest relatively quickly. These things following, not the round the screen and sound installation, but this corner, the corner in the back, this is specialized in a way that is not interesting for me. I'm not into electronic music or, so it doesn't attract me.*

One of the users points at the importance of having multiple means of interaction:

106M: *Yeah! It takes some time, and you get something really awesome! (Laugh) That's cool. I like it. The different colors, and then you can sort of figure it out, and you have a lot of different possibilities. So not only the different colors, but also on the scale, can pick different things... Yeah, combinations.*

Others stress the importance, not only of interaction, but also of participation and co-creation:

203F: *Should I put in on?*
203F: *Choose another one ... ?*
Researcher: *What is your first thought about this one?*
203F: *Colourful... And it's nice, because you can do whatever you like. *Laughing**
Researcher: *What do you think about the concept that you are taking bottles and placing them ?*
203F: *What makes one feel a bit like mixing a cocktail as a bar person.*

Most informants express positive feelings of being interactive, but a single informant is critical and emphasizes that there should be a clear connection between the interactive parts:

102: *I just see bottles and colors and words again. It looks... For me the same... looks like surface because no depth. First impression because it's, it's, it's, it's like joke, very short idea. Hm hm. And of course the words correspond to the music and words and things from acoustics, but I think there is no connection really. It's ?just/lost?... People do not go deep in the material make things like this, I think.*

Sometimes the experiences are interrelated, and the fact that Hørbar is interactive makes the informant feel emotionally involved:

108M: *I ask myself how it works, how it functions? It's very good?*
Researcher: *So it's a little, you know... Is it exciting for you? Do you want to find out..?*
108M: *Yeah, yeah, yeah. Find out which sound the bottle makes. I want to find it. Is there a difference whether I take one or two or three bottles? I have to try it myself, I can't ask her (the archive), she doesn't answer me.* [last sentence translated from German]

Not only the interactivity involves the audience, but also the colors:

202: *And I think the fact that it is so colorful invites you, and it makes it interesting.*

The informants mostly evaluate the experiential qualities *interactive* and *involving* as positive experiences. The same goes for the experience of *fun*.

Researcher: *What do you think about this, that you can be part of the art? That you can take bottles and put them there.*
303: *It's kind of fun. I love music where you can ...As a visitor, like a musician *laughs**

Fun provides a positive feeling, but not necessarily any understanding or learning:

Researcher: *Do you believe that this ?makes it more inspiring to look at, or do you learn more?*
303F: *It makes fun, but it's not learning.*
Researcher: *It makes fun?*
303F: *Yeah. It's not a kind of learning I think.*

Researcher: *Do you like it.*
308: *Hmm. A little bit.*
Researcher: *A little bit. And what do you like about it?*
308: *I don't know. I don't understand it.*
Researcher: *No.*
308: *It's entertaining, but it has no sense.*
Concerning the experience of *interesting* and *relevant*, we can see from the comments that the informants feel interest and relevance in positive as well as negative settings. It is apparent that for several of the informants it is positive when they feel challenged, when they need to work with the archive in order to understand it:

However, the informants still feel interest even though they are incapable of relating to existing cognitive structure or although it is difficult to handle the bottles. The cognitive problems may even spur a stronger experience of *interest*.

Researcher: *It is frustrating that you don't know ... Are you curious?*
104a: *Curious. But I would like to know, I would really like to know what it ...? How the system is? Why this is placed here, for example? [translated from German]*

One informant likes to solve puzzles, but time is an issue, and the experience should be *fun*.

106M: *I think it's kind of hard. I'm usually the kind of person that if I see artwork, then I try to understand it, and if it takes me longer than a certain amount of time, it doesn't get too hard for me, but I just get bored quickly. So I try to understand and grasp it, because for me, artwork that I can quickly understand and adapt, is more interesting, so... Yeah, it depends on the kind of artwork. This kind of art... I like it when it's fast and when it's entertaining.*

The experience of *relevance* is important for several of the informants. They need to relate to previous experiences to learn and to feel interest:

108M: *Okay. I keep asking myself how it functions. I don't understand it.* [translated from German]
Researcher: *It's a little...bewildering?* [Last word translated from German]
108M: *I ask myself, I don't know how it functions, how it works.*
Researcher: *So... Is it too complex?*
108M: *Complex, yes.*

Several informants express a feeling of learning, thus the *Hørbar* seems both to inform and to entertain although the quality of involvement and engagement is mostly expressed:

303: *Yes. But I think it is interesting to learn about that music, the modern music.*
Researcher: *Yeah, so it's actually a way to learn about modern music.*
303: *Yeah.*

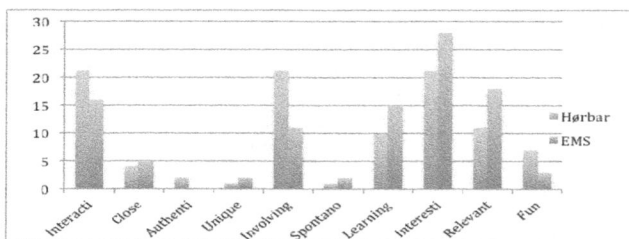

Figure 2. Relative distribution of experience dimensions for *Hørbar* and *EMS* (in percentage).

In Figure 2 we can see that the relative distribution of experience dimensions is different for the two archives studied. The informants express more *interactive* and *involved* experiences when they interact with *Hørbar* compared to EMS. On the other hand the experience is found more *interesting*, *relevant* and *learning* when they interact with the EMS archive. The differences are largest when it comes to *relevant* and *involved*. EMS seems to relate better to the informants' previous knowledge, whereas they feel more physiologically and emotionally engaged by *Hørbar*.

In general, the EMS seems to appeal more to the cognitive perspective of museum visits compared to *Hørbar* that triggers feeling of involvement and participation. The most frequent experiences associated with the EMS archive are *interesting* (17), *relevant* (11) and *interactive* (10). For all three dimensions, the informants express positive as well as negative experiences. Some informants find the sound archives interesting, others not at all, some see the relatively simple possibilities of interaction as an advantage, others not, some relate easily to the archive by activating previous knowledge, others not. The experience of *learning* (9) and *involving* (7) appears less, *close* (3), *fun* (2), *unique* (1) and *spontaneous* (1) only few times, and *authentic* (0) is not present at all.

Interesting is the most common experience, and reading the comments we learn what produces interest or challenges the user.

Different aspects attract the user, e.g. the mere topic, form, or cognitive or emotional contribution (for instance information versus entertainment):

Topic as provider of interest
102: *This looks more interesting to me because 70s and the machines and the studio and the colors and the old videos. I would be interested to hear it (short laugh)*

Form as provider of interest
102: *The differences are also something I like because I like something like a collage.*

Contribution as provider of interest
Researcher: *What is your first impression of this part?*
203F: *Information.*
Researcher: *Lots of information?*
203F: *Lots of information, yeah! It looks like the beginnings of the technology, it is explaining .... sound electronic development...* 'Technorama'... 'Principle'.
203F: *Puts headset on*.
203F: *Takes headset off* Oh no, that I do not like.*

Other comments emphasize the importance of time and space. The more informative form is interesting, but it is time demanding and presupposes a more private environment:

102: *But I think the problem with a lot of this media like DVD, films or music that you have better a situation at home to listen a piece of twenty minutes. Not here. It's just to walk around very fast and maybe you buy a catalogue or you inform you afterwards. It's not the place here to stay for two days, maybe.*

7. DISCUSSION AND IMPLICATIONS
The findings show that it is possible to identify the 10 experience dimensions in the study material. Some experiences are expressed far more frequently than others, for instance *interesting*, *interactive*, *relevant* and *involving* compared to *authentic*, *unique*, *close*, *spontaneous* and *fun*. Most dimensions appear in relation to both works, only *authentic* emerges in only one of the works.

The dimensions have provided us with nuanced insight into users' ways of dealing with the archives. Feeling interested, involved and interactive have emerged as the most important qualities for the users in this particular museum setting, followed by the feeling of learning and being able to understand and capture the meaning of the archive: i.e. to grasp the purpose of the artist. Uniqueness, authenticity or closeness did not have a high impact on user experience at ZKM. Interestingly, in this particular context with interactive, dialogical archives the experience of surprise and challenge seems more important than joy and fun. From a design perspective it is furthermore interesting that we do not only gain knowledge about the relative presence and importance of experience dimensions, but also insight into factors that may increase or decrease the experience: e.g. that *interacting* may help to maintain interest, that *interesting* is stimulated and depends on form and genre, that space and place may be requirements, that *close* and *relevant* are related to *interesting* and *involving*.

Our research has focused on two archives that are rather distinct in nature. The differences in the relative distribution of dimensions between these archives (cf. figure 2) show the cognitive and emotional responses to this distinction. The EMS-archive could be labeled a proper archive making artworks retrievable and providing relevant contextual information. Scoring high on the *learning, interest* and *relevant* dimensions, it could be characterized as a relatively well functioning archive for its users. Hørbar, on the other hand, could be labeled as an artwork that uses the archival logic of retrieval to accentuate, demonstrate and challenge this logic in a playful manner (i.e. by randomizing the output). Scoring relatively lower on *learning, relevant* and also on *interesting*, its instrumental functionality seems lower than EMS. In contrast, it scores higher on some of the emotional dimensions related to play: *involving* and *interactive*. Its purpose is to make the users play with archival material. It is "paratelic" [1]. Hørbar is a relatively well functioning artwork, but as an archive it doesn't function that well. It does not provide the user with systematic information. EMS is not an artwork. Its purpose is to make information accessible in a systematic way.

Thus, besides knowledge about the users' perception and assessment of the experiential qualities, we also obtained useful knowledge of why a dimension is important, and indications of how to design the experience. As such the dimensions have also proved operational. The analysis whether the experience was positive or negative contributed to obtaining these nuances in the understanding of experience.

The analysis did not reveal any new dimensions of experience, but the informants' enthusiasm about the possibility of being co-creative indicate that it might be worthwhile to consider *co-creative* as an independent experiential experience and not as a specification of *interacting*. Co-creation is mentioned by several other UX researchers, e.g. [12] describing the concept of *co-experience* where experiences are created together or shared with others, and defining *co-creation* as the participation of the user in generating and designing an experience [5, 41]. In the present study the informants looked at co-creation from another perspective. Instead of emphasizing co-experience or co-creation with other human actors, they express experiences about their co-creation with the archives, e.g. 303 who describes herself as a "bottle musician" or 203 who sees herself as a bartender "mixing cocktails" at *Hørbar*.

In our analysis of the walk-along data, we have tried to deduce the user experience, whether physiological, emotional or cognitive, from a combination of user comments (utterances) and the researchers' remembered perceptions and (co)experiences. As such, there is a chance that we refer to posteriori rationalizations rather than immediate and unmediated experiences. Co-experiencing allows the researcher to sense the user's sensing and affective reactions, but although the researcher and informant sense the same stimuli, the awareness is cognitive, and they may not share the same physiological or emotional experience. In addition, the data collection methods, audio recordings and notes, will never completely capture the physiological, the emotional or the cognitive aspects of experiencing. Multiple dimensions require multiple data collection methods. As a matter of fact, the study reported in this paper was therefore part of a larger mixed method study, which furthermore consisted of non-obtrusive observations, GSR measurements and a survey based on semantic differentials.

Concerning the basis of data we consider the possibility of transforming the qualitative data about user experience to quantitative measurements as a strong advantage. The frequencies

and relationships that appeared through the quantitative measurements and diagrams acted as important pointers to the qualitative data in the interpretive process.

8. CONCLUSION

This paper has presented a coherent concept of experience. From a psychological perspective the act of here-and-now experiencing is interrelated with prior experiences and emerging memories of this act. Experiences are thus complex, dynamic and holistic. This complexity has been outlined in order to develop a multidimensional framework that might serve as criteria for evaluating the whole gamut of experiential qualities. Our contention is that this framework not only captures the strictly psychological aspects of experiencing (e.g. the involving and interesting qualities related to physiological, emotional and cognitive aspects) but also identity issues related to learning, understanding (i.e. relevance) and interactivity as well as social aspects of community creation and maintenance implied by the spontaneity of play-like behavior. Furthermore the dimension "unique" is meant to capture the event-like quality of many experiences, whereas the dimensions of authenticity, closeness and fun are coined to highlight functions and purposes often attributed to experiences in popular discourse.

We have tried out the dimensions in a field study at the Center for Art and Media (ZKM), Karlsruhe (Germany). Four researchers walked along with 58 museum visitors, talked to them and co-experienced their perceptions, emotions and sense-making while walking the exhibition and interacting with the sound artworks. 29 walk-alongs were carried out, 10 single person walks and 19 in–group walks. The walk-along conversations were tape-recorded, transcribed, and analyzed for the experiential qualities they expressed. The analysis showed that it was possible to identify the 10 experience dimensions in the study material. Some experiences were expressed more frequently than others. Most dimensions appeared in relation to both sound archives studied, but the distribution of expressed dimensions and the content of the user comments provided a clear picture of the experiential differences between the two archives. We also obtained useful knowledge why an experience dimension is important, what factors may influence the user experience, and how to modify an experience design. Thus, besides knowledge about the users' perception and assessment of experiential qualities, we also gained insight into how to design for user experiences.

Experiences are complex and dynamic, experiential qualities are multiple, and to provide a rich picture of user experience require multiple data collection methods. Future research should therefore explore the potential of doing larger mixed-method studies.

9. REFERENCES

[1] Apter, M. J. 1989. *Reversal theory: Motivation, emotion and personality*. Taylor and Frances/Routledge, London.

[2] Bargas-Avila, J.A. and Hornbæk, K. 2011. Old Wine in New Bottles or Novel Challenges? A Critical Analysis of Empirical Studies of User Experience. In *Proceedings of the CHI 2011* (Vancouver, Canada, May 07-12, 2011). ACM, New York, NY, 2689-2698.DOI=10.1145/1978942.1979336.

[3] Berntsen, D. and Rubin, D. C. 2012. *Understanding autobiographical memory: Theories and approaches*. Cambridge University Press, Cambridge.

[4] Bishop, C. 2010. *Installation Art. A Critical History*. Tate Publishing, London.

[5] Boswijk, A., Peelen, E., Olthof, S., and Beddow, C. 2012. *Economy of experiences*. European Centre for the Experience and Transformation Economy, Bilthoven.

[6] Bradley, B. S. 2005. *Psychology and experience*. Cambridge University Press, Cambridge.

[7] Chonchúir, M. N. and McCarthy, J. 2008. The enhanting potential of technology: a dialogical case study of enchantment and the Internet. *Personal and Ubiquitous Computing*, 12, 401-409. DOI=10.1007/s00779-007-0157-0

[8] Csikszentmihalyi, M. 1991. *Flow: The psychology of optimal experience*. Harper Perennial, New York.

[9] Dewey, J. 1934. *Art as Experience*. Minton Balch, New York, NJ.

[10] Diriwächter, R. 2008, Genetic Ganzheitspsychologie. In *Striving for the whole: Creating theoretical syntheses*, R. Diriwächter and J. Valsiner, Eds. Transaction Publishers, New Brunswick, NJ, 21–46.

[11] Edmonds, E., Zafer, B. and Muller, L. 2009. Artist, evaluator and curator: three viewpoints on interactive art, evaluation and audience experience. *Digital Creativity*, 20 3, 141-151.

[12] Forlizzi, J., Battarbee, K. 2004. Understanding Experience in Interactive Systems. In *Proceedings of the DIS2004* (Cambridge, Mass, August 01-04,). ACM, New York, NY, 261-268. DOI=10.1145/1013115.1013152

[13] Fredrickson, B. L. 2001. The role of positive emotions in positive psychology: The broaden-and-build theory of positive emotions. *American psychologist*, 56 3, 218-226.

[14] Hartmann, J., Sutcliffe, A. and De Angeli, A. 2008. Towards a theory of user judgement of aesthetics and user interface quality. ACM Transactions on Computer-Human Interaction (TOCHI), 15 4. DOI=10.1145/1460355.1460357

[15] Hassenzahl, M. 2010. *Experience design: Technology for all the right reasons*. Morgan&Claypool Publishers, San Rafael, CAL.

[16] Higgins, E. T. 2006. Value from hedonic experience and engagement. *Psychological review*, 113 3, 439-460. DOI=10.1037/0033-295X.113.3.439

[17] Hornecker, E. and Stifter, M. 2006. Learning from interactive museum installations about interaction design for public settings. In *OZCHI 2006* (Sydney, Australia, November 20-24, 2006) ACM, New York, NY, 135-142. DOI=10.1145/1228175.1228201

[18] James, W. 1912, *Essays in Radical Empiricism*, Longmans, Green and Co., London.

[19] Jantzen, C. 2013. Experiencing and experiences: A psychological framework. In *Handbook on the experience economy*, J. Sundbo and F. Sørensen, Eds., Edward Elgar, Cheltenham, 146-170.

[20] Johnson-Laird, P. N. 1983. *Mental models: Towards a cognitive science of language, inference, and consciousness*. Harvard University Press, Cambridge, MA.

[21] Kahneman, D. 2003. Objective Happiness. In D. Kahneman, E. Diener & N. Schwarz Eds., *Well-being: Foundations of hedonic psychology*. Russell Sage Foundation, 3-25.

[22] Kant, I. 1973/1790. *The Critique of Judgement*. Clarendon Press. Oxford.

[23] Kolb, D. A. 1984. Experiential learning: Experience as the source of learning and development. Prentice-Hall, Englewood Cliffs, NJ.

[24] Krause, M., & Yakel, E. (2007). Interaction in virtual archives: the polar bear expedition digital collections next generation finding aid. *The American Archivist*, 70(2), 282-314.

[25] Kusenbach, M. 2003. Street Phenomenology. The Go-Along as Ethnographie research Tool. *Ethnography* 4 3, 455-485.

[26] Lavie, T. and Tractinsky, N. 2004. Assessing dimensions of perceived visual aesthetics of web sites. *International Journal of Human-Computer Studies*, 60 3. 269-298. DOI=10.1016/j.ijhcs.2003.09.002

[27] Piaget, J. 1985. *The equilibration of cognitive structures: The central problem of intellectual development*. University of Chicago Press. Chicago.

[28] Pine, B. J., and Gilmore, J. H. 1999. *The experience economy: Work is theatre and every business a stage*. Harvard Business Press, Boston.

[29] Prahalad, C. K., and Ramaswamy, V. 2013. *The future of competition: Co-creating unique value with customers*. Harvard Business Press, Boston.

[30] Reckwitz, A. 2006. *Das hybride Subjekt*. Velbrück, Weilerswist.

[31] Rumelhart, D. E., and Ortony, A. 1977. The representation of knowledge in memory. In *Schooling and the acquisition of knowledge*, R. C. Anderson, R. J. Spiro, R. J. and W. E. Montague, Eds. Lawrence Erlbaum, Hillsdale, NJ.

[32] Russel, J. A. 2003. Core effect and the psychological construction of emotion. *Psychological review*, 55, 68-78. DOI=10.1037/0033-295X.110.1.145 17

[33] Sanders, E. B. N. and Stappers, P. J. 2008. Co-creation and the new landscapes of design. *Co-design*, 4 1, 5-18.

[34] Schmitt, B. H. 2003. *Customer experience management: a revolutionary approach to connecting with your customers*. John Wiley and Sons.

[35] Schulze, G. 1992. *Die Erlebnisgesellschaft: Kultursoziologie der Gegenwart*. Campus Verlag. Frankfurt/M.

[36] Shklovsky, V. 1965/1917. Art as technique. In *Russian formalist criticism*. L. T. Lemon and M.J. Reiss, Eds., University of Nebraska Press, Lincoln, 3-24.

[37] Schank, R. C. and Abelson, R. P. 1977. *Scripts, plans, goals, and understanding: An inquiry into human knowledge structures*. Psychology Press.

[38] Swallow, D., Blythe, M., Wright, P. 2005. Grounding Experience: relating theory and method to evaluate the user experience of smartphones. In *Proceedings of the EACE05*, University of Athens, 91-98.

[39] Tulving, E. 1985. Elements of episodic memory. Clarendon Press, Oxford.

[40] Wakkary, R. and Hatala, M. 2007. Situated play in a tangible interface and adaptive audio museum guide. Personal and Ubiquitous Computing, 11, 171-191. DOI=10.1007/s00779-006-0101-8

[41] Wright, P., and McCarthy, J. 2004. *Technology as experience*. MIT Press, Cambridge, MASS.

[42] Wundt, W. 1896. *Grundriss der Psychologie*. Engelmann, Leipzig.

[43] Zilmann, D. 1988. Mood management: Using entertainment to full advantage. *Communication, social cognition, and affect*, L. Donohew, H. E. Sypher and E. T. Higgins, Erlbaum, 135-168.

Knowledge Graphs versus Hierarchies: An Analysis of User Behaviours and Perspectives in Information Seeking

Bahareh Sarrafzadeh
University of Waterloo
bsarrafz@uwaterloo.ca

Alexandra Vtyurina
University of Waterloo
avtyurin@uwaterloo.ca

Edward Lank
University of Waterloo
lank@uwaterloo.ca

Olga Vechtomova
University of Waterloo
ovechtomova@uwaterloo.ca

ABSTRACT

In exploratory search, how information is presented to the user and how the user interacts with the presented information heavily influence the user's success. In this paper, we examine two different spatial representations of search results: knowledge graphs and hierarchical trees. Through interaction logs we show that knowledge graphs can effectively reduce the need to read source content with no reduction in the quality of the information gathered by the user. Through qualitative interviews and thinkalounds we explore factors that influence user perception of different search results representations including biases, task, perceived structure of the data, and problem-solving approach. Overall, these results enhance our understanding of the role each of these representations can play in information seeking.

1. INTRODUCTION

In the domain of on-line search, the output of current search engines is normally sufficient for many well-defined online tasks, including navigational queries, transactional queries, and many types of informational queries. However, when information is sought to address broad curiosities, e.g. for learning and other complex mental activities, retrieval is necessary but may not be sufficient [35], [1].

One type of complex search that is of increasing interest to researchers is *exploratory search*, where the goal involves "learning" or "investigating", rather than simply "look-up" [20]. In characterizing searching that involves learning or investigating, Marchionini (referencing Bloom's taxonomy of educational objectives) notes that the goal of these searches involves "knowledge acquisition, comprehension of concepts or skills, interpretation of ideas, and comparisons or aggregation of data and concepts" [20].

There are many open research questions about how to design interfaces to support exploratory search using techniques that organize the retrieved information into mean-

ingful structures. Search results presented by modern search engines are an example of an ordered list sorted by relevance, i.e. a *vectorial model* [19]. However, information seekers often express a desire for a user interface that organizes search results into meaningful groups to help make sense of the results, to infer relationships between concepts, and to help decide what to do next [13], [20]. As a result of this desire for organization, *spatial models* [23], i.e. hierarchies and networks, have also been used to organize information and support sensemaking [19]. While both hierarchies and networks have been shown to be useful in the structuring of content (e.g. [9], [22], [10]) little work has explored the similarities and differences between these two representations. The goal of this paper is to explore how two specific visualizations of information – Knowledge Graphs (or Knowledge Maps) and Hierarchical Trees – support exploratory search tasks.

We present the quantitative and qualitative results of a study contrasting participants' perspectives on the use of knowledge graphs versus hierarchical trees to support exploration of data for the purpose of developing an answer for informational queries. We describe the design of interfaces and our evaluation of the use of network and hierarchical data structures during exploratory search tasks. Log data indicates that knowledge graphs result in participants viewing source documents fewer times and spending less time reading those documents with no effect on overall quality of information gleaned to satisfy queries. Data from thinkalouds and a post-task interview are synthesized using a grounded theory approach, yielding observations on biasing factors, task effects, data relationships, and problem solving approaches which discriminate between use-cases for our hierarchical tree-based interface versus our knowledge graph interface. Overall, despite some statistical advantages of knowledge graphs in our study, our goal is not to argue that one presentation of information is better than another; information visualization research would argue that different visualizations serve different purposes [34] and our goal with this work is to better understand the purposes that each of these two interfaces serve with respect to exploratory search.

The remainder of this paper is organized as follows. First, we provide an overview of related work, focusing on different categorizations of search tasks and goals, organizing search results, and evaluation of different search results visualizations. Next, we briefly describe our interface design process, beginning with low-fidelity prototypes and culminating with the two tested interfaces. We then present our study design

CHIIR '16, March 13 - 17, 2016, Carrboro, NC, USA

© 2016 Copyright held by the owner/author(s). Publication rights licensed to ACM.
ISBN 978-1-4503-3751-9/16/03...$15.00

DOI: http://dx.doi.org/10.1145/2854946.2854958

and our results. Finally, we conclude with a discussion on the implications of our work in the design of exploratory search interfaces.

2. RELATED WORK

2.1 Understanding Web Search Queries

Studies of user search behaviour have a long history in Information and Library Science. Specifically with respect to web search, Broder [5] proposed a taxonomy of Web Search in 2002. He was motivated by the idea that the traditional notion of an "information need" might not adequately describe web searching. Broder's taxonomy classifies web searches into navigational, informational and transactional. Similarly, Rose and Levinson [27] analyze user goals to classify web searches into Navigational, Informational and Resource. Drawing upon earlier work by Campbell [8] and Byström [7], web searches can broadly be classified into "Simple" and "Complex" searches. Simple search tasks are similar to "known-item" search tasks and usually involve looking up some discrete, well-structured information object: for example numbers, names and facts [20]. Complex search tasks, on the other hand, involve investigating, learning and synthesizing of information [36].

In contrast to Broder's and Rose and Levinson's taxonomies, Marchionini [20] focuses specifically on a process he terms *exploratory search*. Marchionini broadly separates web search into three categories: Look-up, which includes fact retrieval, navigation and transaction; Learn, which includes knowledge acquisition, comprehension, and comparison; and Investigate, which includes analysis, synthesis and evaluation. The latter two categories, Learn and Investigate, he groups under the umbrella of exploratory search. There are two activities which mediate the process of exploratory search: information foraging theory [25], which describes how searchers collect relevant pieces of information, and sensemaking [11], which describes the process through which people assimilate new knowledge into their existing understanding.

Marchionini notes that there are interactive aspects to exploratory search, rather than simply viewing the query satisfaction or information retrieval problem as optimally matching documents to a query. Characteristics of these interfaces, drawn from research in human-computer interaction, include the use of high-level overviews and rapid previews to facilitate sensemaking during the exploratory process. The incorporation of overviews argues for some organization of search results that both presents this overview and allows the user to explore the data and its interconnected relationships more fully through filtering and the examination of user-selected details [32].

2.2 Organizing Search Results

Any system that supports information seeking must structure information to make it accessible. The way information is organized and made available affects the strategies used to access this knowledge and thus information-seeking performance [21]. For example, Capra et al. [9], in their study on the relationships between search tasks, information architecture and interaction style, note, among other observations, that users gain benefits from support for facets and topic organization implemented in a flexible style.

Given the observation that organization of search results benefits users, one might then ask what organizations of search results exist. A taxonomy of techniques for organizing search results was proposed by Wilson et al. [37]. They identify two main classes of approaches: (1) Using annotations or classifications to organize results into groups (e.g. faceted search which uses a hierarchy structure to enable users to browse information by choosing from a pre-determined set of categories). (2) Directly organizing results which visualizes a result set to help users find the specific results they are looking for. As well, Ltifi et al [19] proposed a classification of visualization techniques for knowledge discovery including visualizations for linear data (e.g. timelines), multi-dimensional data (e.g. scatterplots), vectorial models (e.g. relevance-ordered results), hierarchies (trees, tables of contents) and networks (e.g. knowledge graphs). Given the non-numerical characteristic of web search results, the latter three types of visualizations (vectorial, hierarchical, and network) are particularly useful for displaying search results. While the vectorial representation presents results as a ranked list, hierarchical and network representations can be used to display grouping, similarity or relationships among search results.

Fully elaborating on all of the organization techniques or visualizations for search results is beyond the scope of this paper, and the interested reader is referred to the above taxonomies. However, some visualizations of search result data are specifically salient to our research, in particular, Ltifi et al.'s [19] vectorial model, hierarchies and networks. Trees are a common tool for representing hierarchies. A hierarchical structure is mainly made up of organizational links that organize the information into categories (topics) with no or few cross-links between categories. Google's "Knowledge Graph" enhances basic search results with structured data, essentially presenting a network organization of search results [33]. Google claims the knowledge graph enhances search in three main ways: query disambiguation, a summarization of related facts, and exploratory search suggestions (based on what other users explored next).

Most network visualizations tend to provide a global perspective on a graph by attempting to represent an overview of the information space so no information is missing and the data can speak for itself. Most of these techniques are based on Shneiderman's Visual Information Seeking Mantra [32]: "Overview first, zoom and filter, then details on demand". For example Sanchez and Llamas [29] followed this principle to visualize a large combination of concept maps to distinguish between an interface for the author and an interface for the end user that facilitates the exploration tasks.

2.3 Evaluating Search Results Visualizations

Novick and Hurley [23], working in the field of education, performed extensive research on the use of spatial models such as networks, hierarchies, and matrices. In particular, they were interested in the properties of these spatial models that were particularly suited to problem solving. Our work differs in its focus on information retrieval and the representation of search results. As well, our work differs in that Novick and Hurley do not develop interfaces that support problem solving; instead, they use questionnaire data to elicit from participants which representations participants think might best support information representation.

More recently, researchers in information retrieval have performed evaluations of techniques for representing search results, examining both hierarchical structures (e.g. [9], [22],

[12]) or networks ([31]). However, these results investigate how different properties of one structure may affect users' behaviour, whereas our work aims at understanding the type of support provided by two inter-related structures for different types of search tasks on the Web.

Other recent work in search results representation focuses on a single visualization (e.g. concept maps) that seeks to represent both hierarchies and networks ([3], [2], [10]) to support information seeking and finding. However, the focus of this research was on comprehension of the representations through a quantitative study. Our focus is on understanding how hierarchical versus network representations support different types of search tasks.

Most similar to our work, Sarrafzadeh et al. [31] investigated the effects of combining a knowledge graph with textual documents. Their goal, like ours, was to understand user behaviour with respect to different search tasks. They argue that a hybrid approach that combines the coherent content of text with the organized structure of graphs may better support information finding and sense making. They conclude that utilizing graphs of concepts and relationships which are derived from documents can be effective for finding relevant information when the information need is well defined. Their findings also demonstrate that providing meaningful relations that explain how different entities of a domain are connected are crucial for supporting more complex search task. Our work broadens this work by looking specifically at the contrast between hierarchical representations (e.g. trees) and network representations (e.g. knowledge graphs).

3. APPLICATION DESIGN

One challenge with any application that presents search results from an exploratory query to users is that the goal is rarely a static representation of the content returned by a user's query. Instead, the goal is to develop an interface that allows a user to interact with the content, to filter and select specific content, essentially to explore the information returned. As a result, the representation is linked to the interface that contains it and supports manipulation and exploration of it [13]. To develop an interface for exploratory search that would allow us to explore the characteristics of hierarchical and network visualizations, we engaged in an iterative process using a series of walkthoughs, thinkalouds, and pilot studies.

3.1 Prototype Development

To develop our representations and interface, we began with a low-fidelity design, where paper prototypes were used to explore user perception of representations of data and user interaction with those representations. We initially designed two low fidelity interfaces. The first interface employed a graph structure in which the entities from each article were the nodes and the sentences describing a semantic relation between them were the edges. In order to investigate how users navigate through large graphs to find information, our knowledge-graph-based prototype was designed such that the user would start from the overview page that contained all the nodes that had a high number of connections to other nodes in the graph. These nodes could be considered as representatives of different components of the graph and would help distribute different sub-graphs into different pages. The user was able to expand any of the nodes on the overview

page and would proceed to a new page that contained the selected node and all the nodes that had a link to this node. The user could expand a new node on this page or collapse the expanded node and go back to the previous page.

The second interface utilized a hierarchy (or a tree) structure to organize headings and sub-headings of the articles, as observed in each page's table-of-contents. Each tree was in a collapsed format initially and the user would expand and collapse nodes to drill down into document content. We also created an overview node that linked all the trees in our collection. Interfaces were seeded with data gleaned from Wikipedia pages on Canadian capital cities.

We conducted a thinkaloud study to evaluate our paper prototypes with six participants (two female) to gather a set of features required for these interfaces. Data was presented in both graph and tree form to each participant. We asked participants to think aloud about what the data represented and how they would interact with the data. We also collected qualitative data on different use cases of these interfaces with respect to different search tasks. From this initial study, we redesigned our interfaces.

3.2 Final Design

The qualitative data and participants' feedback helped refine both the design of our search result presentation and our interface for manipulating the representation of the search results. We used force and pack layouts (as part of the D3 library[1]) to visualize the graphs and trees respectively.

When the user launches the graph-based application (Figure 1, top), they are presented with a knowledge graph containing labelled nodes and unlabelled links between nodes. Nodes that represent entities with low frequency are hidden in the initial view, and only appear once a higher-frequency, connected node is clicked. This ensures that the graph does not become too cluttered. Once the user clicks on a node, that node and all connected nodes are highlighted, while the remainder of the graph is alpha-blended into the background. By hovering over any connected node in highlighted portion of the graph, the user can see the relationship(s) between the two nodes in the snippet window located on the left side of the interface (Figure 1. top). For each relationship in the snippet region, participants have a link that allows them to view the corresponding Wikipedia article.

The tree interface is shown in Figure 1, bottom. When the user launches the application, the user is presented with a fully expanded tree. By clicking on any node within the tree, that portion of the wikipedia document corresponding to the node is presented in the preview area at the left of the interface. Under the snippet in question, there is a link to view article, allowing users to access the article in question.

4. EXPERIMENTAL DESIGN

To detail our experimental design, we first discuss the data extraction method that we used to populate our interface with data. Next, we present the tasks in our study and describe our participant population. Finally, we describe the data we capture from each participant.

4.1 Data Extraction

To populate our interactive applications, we created two distinct data sets: one focusing on history and the second on global politics. For the history data set, we used the previous
[1]http://d3js.org/

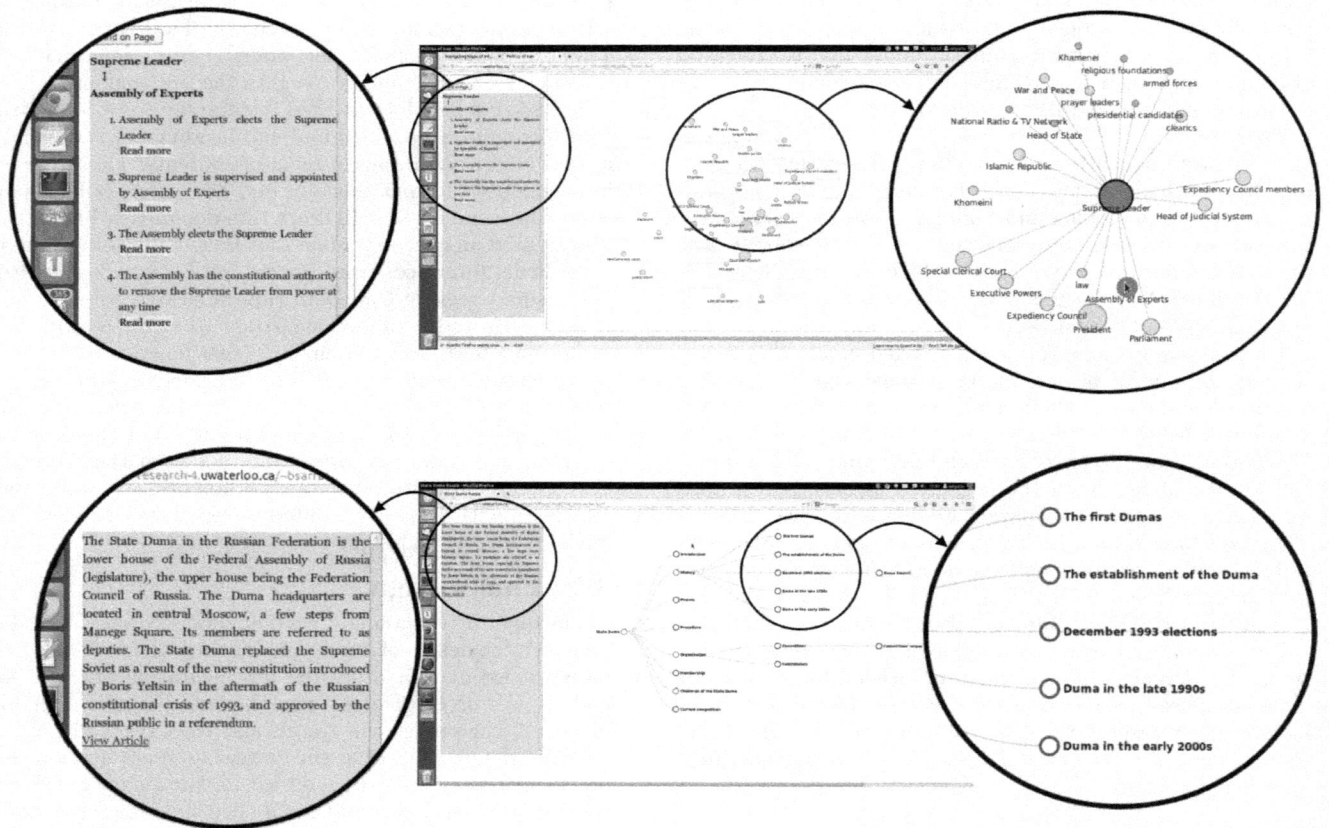

Figure 1: The graph and tree visualization interfaces. Note the callouts of nodes and document snippets.

search task exploring former capital cities of Canada. For the politics search task, we created a data set representing governmental structures in Iran and Russia.

To create this data set, we first collected a set of Wikipedia articles by querying the Web using a popular search engine. We retrieved the top 10 articles in Wikipedia based on their relevance to three queries corresponding to three topics: "Former Capital Cities of Canada", "Political System of Iran" and "Political System of Russia".

To create our knowledge graph, we designed an Open Information Extraction system that processes a text collection and generates (entity-relation-entity) triples [30]. This module is implemented in four phases. During the first phase we create the input corpus by collecting retrieved documents based on a given query. Next, we extract entities from text using state-of-the-art entity taggers [2]. We then select the sentences that contain at least two entities in them and parse them using Stanford Dependency Parser. For each sentence, we extract meaningful relations between the entities by finding the shortest path in the corresponding parse tree. For example we extract *The Constitutional Act divided the Province of Quebec into Upper and Lower Canada* as a relationship between the entities *Constitutional Act* and *Upper Canada*. We constructed a set of patterns based on dependency triples that lead to semantically meaningful relations. In the final phase we generate labels for the ex-

[2]https://cogcomp.cs.illinois.edu/page/software_view/NETagger

tracted relations and rank them based on relevance to the query and the informativeness of the extraction. Once the knowledge graph is generated, we hand-tune some aspects of the graph by correcting minor errors caused by the extraction of entities and relations.

For the tree based interface, we extracted the Tables of Content (TOCs) embedded in each Wikipedia article. We then manually extended the table-of-contents by adding subheadings to each section in order to provide a richer structure for the trees. Overall, our goal was to create visualizations that could realistically be created by computer algorithms while ensuring equivalent, high-quality for each of the generated visualizations.

4.2 Search Tasks

We noted earlier that researchers have defined search queries as simple or complex. With respect to the complexity level, each participant performed one Simple (i.e. question answering) and one Complex (i.e. essay writing) task. We also used two different topics (i.e. History and Politics) to investigate the relation between the topic and content knowledge with the structure used to organize the retrieved information. The queries we asked people to find information to satisfy in our study were the following:

Simple Politics: What governmental body or bodies are involved in the impeachment of the President of Iran and of Russia?

Complex Politics: Imagine you are a high school student who is going to write an essay on the Political Systems of Iran and Russia. Knowing little about the presidents of these two countries, you wish to determine which president has more power. Find at least 3 arguments to justify your answer."

Simple History: As a result of which act were Upper and Lower Canada formed?

Complex History: Imagine you are a high school student who is going to write an essay on the History of Canada. Knowing little about Canadian History, you wish to know which cities have served as a capital for Canada. You would also like to understand the reasons behind moving the capital from one city to another.

To assess the study design, we piloted with four participants. The pilot ensured that the usability of the system was sufficient to support interaction and provided guidance on the semi-structured interview to collect qualitative data on distinctions and use cases of the designed interfaces.

To limit study length and ensure coverage of simple and complex queries within subjects, our final study design was a $2 \times 2 \times 2$ [interface, interface-topic, topic-complexity] mixed design with interface as a within subjects factor, topic to interface assignment and complexity to topic assignment as between subject factors. This resulted in eight different groupings of participants. Each participant saw both interfaces. In the first interface, they had either politics or history, with the other topic in the second interface. For the two topics, each participant saw a complex query on one topic and a simple query on the other. In order to control for order effects, we rotated the order in which the tasks and the interfaces were assigned to the participants. That is, participants were randomly divided into 8 groups.

4.3 Participants

Once the study design was final, we recruited 26 (13 female) participants from different areas of Science, Math and Engineering for this study, all of whom use the Internet on a regular basis to search for information.

4.4 Procedure and Data Collection

The study proceeded as follows. After a brief introduction to the study, participants were given an initial questionnaire that evaluated their knowledge of the first query's topic. Participants were then presented with their first interface, were given an introduction to the features of the interface demonstrating how each feature of the interface worked, and were then given some time to manipulate the interface.

Once participants had developed some comfort with the features of the interface (approximately three minutes), participants were given the query and told to manipulate the interface as if they did not know the answer to the query and wished to locate it. To capture data on participants' actions, participants were asked to "think aloud" during each task and share their thoughts and strategies with the researcher. For both tasks, the participants were given 15 minutes and were required to find relevant information by providing a reference sentence or sentences from the interface or document collection to justify their arguments or answers. The need to find specific information ensured that each participant manipulated the interface to find relevant information.

After providing an answer to the query, participants completed a post-task questionnaire that evaluated the expe-

rience they just had. We used questionnaires provided by TREC-9 Interactive Searching track [3] and modified them to fit into our experiment design. At the end of each task, via a semi-structured interview participants were asked to reflect on their experience with using the assigned interface for performing the assigned task. They were encouraged to think about the conceptual usability of the type of structure utilized for information organization as well as the technical usability of the application. At the end of the second task a semi-structured interview format was used to elicit comparison between the two interfaces with respect to the different types of search tasks and to reflect on the design of an "ideal" interface that could support them more efficiently. Participants received a $10 incentive for their participation.

Data was captured in a variety of ways. Each interface was instrumented with a logger which monitored participants during the search sessions. Both movement on the computer screen and participants' interactions with the system were captured. Interactions we collected included clicking on nodes or edges, reading snippets, viewing articles, and the time they spent reading the articles. The activity logs for two of the participants were corrupted so we excluded their data from our activity log analysis. Experimental blocks and a post-task semi-structured interview were audio recorded. Finally, two assessors evaluated the quality of answers provided by the participants for each of the search tasks independently. Simple queries were rated as either correct or incorrect. To receive a correct rating, both answer and referenced document section were required to be correct. Complex questions were rated on a scale. Scores for all queries were normalized to reflect a value in the range $[0, 1]$. Inter-assessor reliability was evaluated using Pearson coefficient and an overall value of 0.8 for simple queries and 0.9 for complex queries was found.

4.5 Analysis

Log and Questionnaire Data were extracted and analyzed for statistical patterns. Interviews were all transcribed and analyzed using affinity diagramming. Data were clustered collaboratively by two researchers using open coding, producing 14 clusters. Clusters were then analyzed using axial coding to identify overall themes in the data.

We found that saturation for our qualitative data occurred approximately mid-way through our participant sample – after 14 participants, no new clusters of information were identified. However, to allow statistical analysis of log data, we continued to cluster interview data for the remaining participants, particularly attuned to data that might expand our clusters or add nuance to our analysis.

5. MAIN OBSERVATIONS

In this section, we present an analysis of data collected during the study. We first present some numerical data collected from search logs which provides a broad overview of participants' contrasting behaviours given different interfaces and given queries of differing complexity. Next, we present the results of our qualitative analysis, clustered into four broad themes: Biasing Factors, Task Effects, Data Relations, and Problem Solving Approach.

---

[3] www-nlpir.nist.gov/projects/t9i/qforms.html

5.1 Validating Search Tasks

In any study where the goal is to explore search result representations for exploratory search, one concern is whether or not the search tasks are representative of exploratory search tasks. In our task design, we were guided by Marchionini's work on exploratory search [20]. Leveraging two task domains, politics and history, we created one look-up task and one exploratory search task within each domain using Marchionini's definitions, yielding four tasks overall. The politics tasks asked participants to compare two different governmental structures, Iran and Russia, rationalizing and providing citations for answers they provide. Similarly, the history tasks asked participants to discover something about the history of Canada and, again, rationalize and provide citations for their answers. For our complex tasks, in particular, we argue that the tasks combine aspects of knowledge acquisition or comparison (the *learn* subcategory of exploratory search) with analysis, synthesis, and evaluation (the *investigate* subcategory).

Another concern is whether the actual topics are of sufficiently similar complexity that topic effects do not overwhelm other factors in our results. To address this, beyond ensuring counterbalancing of topics, we analyzed topic effects vis a vis our dependent variables to determine whether either the history or politics task resulted in statistically significantly varying behaviours. Interestingly, our *look-up tasks* in both history and politics, where participants returned a factoid, differed in quality of answers, time reading, and document views ($F_{1,24} = 6.02, p < 0.05$ for quality; $F_{1,24} = 6.00, p < 0.05$ for reading; and $F_{1,24} = 21.22, p < 0.001$ for document views). However, for our *exploratory tasks*, i.e. our complex tasks where participants were asked to learn or investigate, scores did not differ significantly between the two topics areas of history and politics ($p > 0.05$ in all cases). Because our primary interest is supporting exploratory search, we argue that our complex tasks are of sufficiently similar complexity as to limit topic effects.

Finally, alongside care designing our search tasks and a analysis of topic effects on dependent numerical measures, we also examined our qualitative data to determine whether participants found the tasks to be aligned with their conceptualization of exploratory search. The comments made by our participants when they were presented by the tasks descriptions indicated that these tasks were indeed complex, i.e. that they were ambiguous and open ended in nature. As well, different participants interpreted the task descriptions differently and came up with different strategies based upon their interpretation, further validating the open-ended, exploratory nature of the search tasks.

5.2 Log Data Analysis

As noted earlier, our data logged all user action with the system. Of particular interest to us was information on the scoring of participant responses, the number of nodes clicked in each interface, the number of documents read, and the amount of time spent reading documents. Table 1 summarizes this data. The Mark column contains scoring of participant responses. Clicks is a count of the number of nodes clicked on. Views is the number of instances when a participants used the interface to view the actual Wikipedia document (as opposed to relying on the information contained in the interface). Finally, ViewTime is the amount of time in seconds spent reading documents (as opposed to

manipulating the interface).

We performed a repeated measures ANOVA with interface (tree versus graph) as a within subject effect and query complexity as a between subjects effect. Dependent variables were scoring of query results, clicks with the interface, number of document views, and time spent viewing documents. Overall, RM-ANOVA indicated that interface had a statistically significant effect on dependent variables ($F_{4,20} = 5.83, p < 0.01, \eta^2 = 0.54$). Query complexity was not significant, nor was there any interaction between complexity and interface. Univariate tests of dependent variables with respect to interface (tree versus graph) show statistically significant effect on number of document views ($F_{1,23} = 26.29, p < 0.001, \eta^2 = 0.53$) and on time spent viewing documents ($F_{1,23} = 6.01, p < 0.05, \eta^2 = 0.21$). Marks and Clicks were not significant.

	Marks	Clicks	Views	ViewTime
Graph	0.74 (0.27)	18.7 (3.2)	1.6 (0.43)	131 (37)
Tree	0.43 (0.04)	17.9 (2.2)	4.9 (0.49)	1228 (444)

Table 1: Mean (Standard Deviation) values for marks (average independent evaluator scores), clicks on nodes, document views, and document view time.

Overall, our data indicate that the knowledge-graph visualization allows participants to glean more information from the data structure (67% fewer document views, on average) in less time (almost 90% less time reading documents). The knowledge graph is designed to represent the information in the document in a way that obviates the need to read extensively, and it was very successful at accomplishing this. Over half of all participants examined either 0 or 1 documents while using the knowledge graph (mean of 1.6 documents), whereas all except one participant examined at least three documents with the tree structure (mean of 4.9 documents). Qualitatively, we note that the knowledge graph also fared better in score, though not statistically significantly better. As well, the workload in both documents (as measured by node clicks) was very similar (18.7 versus 17.9 clicks per query on average).

5.3 Qualitative Data

Given the statistical advantage enjoyed by the graph representation, the next question we wished to explore involved participant perspectives on each of these representations of search results. How did they differ? What were the advantages and disadvantages of each from a user perspective? We present four themes arising from our qualitative data analysis in this section.

5.3.1 Biasing Factor: A Willingness to Explore

Exploratory behavior, defined by the National Library of Medicine as "the tendency to explore or investigate a novel environment", is driven by curiosity and is evident in most exploratory searches. Both lookup and exploratory searches use curiosity in their search models, though the actual curiosity which drives each type of search is slightly different [4]. *Specific curiosity* is the desire for a particular piece of information, as typified by an attempt to solve a problem or puzzle. *Diversive curiosity* is a more general seeking of stimulation or novelty, for example a television viewer flipping between channels. In information seeking, specific curiosity corresponds to well-defined goals and directed searching, while diverse curiosity corresponds to ill-defined goals and exploratory browsing [24].

In our thinkaloud data and in our follow-up interview data, we identified specific versus diversive curiosity as a factor that influenced participants' perceptions of each web interface. Essentially, some participants preferred an interface over the other based on the amount of time they were willing to spend in exploratory browsing. Linking to specific curiosity, if an interface is effective in accomplishing a search task but required extensive time browsing, the participant would rather use a different interface. Participants patience with the search task was influenced by the tension between the drive to solve the problem (specific curiosity) versus the tolerance for browsing (diversive curiosity):

"For specific questions, it depends on how much time I'm willing to spend. If I have more time I'd like the tree, because it's more scattered and I can learn more objectively." [P4]

"So I feel like the Tree would be good if I wanted to sit down and spend time reading about a topic and I wasn't looking for something specific. Whereas if I was looking for something very specific, for that, I think I would like the other one [graph] better. Cause it was already doing the keyword search and it was easier to pick out things." [P8]

"If I need a fast way, I go to the graph. I use the tree only when I'm learning deep about a new domain." [P4]

This observation is in line with the initial work on information foraging; Pirolli and Card [25] defined the profitability of an information source "as the value of information gained per unit cost of processing the source." Cost is defined in terms of time spent, resources utilized and opportunities lost when pursuing a search strategy instead of others [28]. We find that diversive curiosity biases toward the tree structure, whereas specific curiosity biases toward the graph.

5.3.2 Task Effects: Finding Versus Learning

The Web has provided the opportunity to browse and navigate through an extensive information space. However, beyond simply finding basic answers, web searchers also engage in learning and discovery [20].

As noted in our study design, we incorporate two tasks with different levels of complexity. Given these two levels of complexity, in post-experiment interviews the participants were able to compare the two interfaces based on the specificity of the information they were looking for. Interestingly, however, participants were divided on which interface was better for simple versus complex search tasks.

Overall, most participants found the graph interface more practical for finding specific information and simple question answering tasks. Both question-answering and keyword-based tasks were typically perceived of as advantaging the graph structure:

For the question-answering task I'd rather use the graph. Because I want to know exactly if this word is linked to that word. If there are two words appear in the same sentence you can quickly find an answer and I don't have to read the whole article. [P9]

When I was searching for specific keywords, with the tree interface I actually had to go to the article itself to search. so it wasn't useful. Whereas the other one [graph] actually gives me access to the keywords. [P14]

To learn I think the hierarchy interface is good if I want to learn say about history of Canada, because then you start from step 1 and the you go to the next level. [P10]

This is not to say that our participants were universal in their beliefs about data visualizations. Some participants found that the tree was significantly better for finding a specific piece of information. P2, P3, and P6 all articulated variants of this belief:

But when you are trying to find a specific answer to a question, then the tree structure is good, because it helps you traverse from the root to a leaf node. [P2]

I like the tree better for specific questions. It categorizes things better.[P3]

Tree is pretty good for finding exact information. [P6]

To try to understand this phenomenon better, we looked at other demographic data collected from our participants, and found an intersection between the belief that a tree was better suited to search tasks and our participants self-rated prior knowledge of the topic being examined. Participants were biased toward a tree structure for broad learning of the task domain particularly when they had low prior knowledge. This result seems to replicate findings by Amadieu et al. [3] on the use of network structures versus hierarchical structures in the education domain, i.e., that low knowledge learners benefited from hierarchical structures in free recall performance and exhibited reduced disorientation, whereas high knowledge learners performed better and followed a more coherent reading sequence given a network structure. Participants, too, noted this phenomenon:

So if you are an expert in a domain, you want the view very focused [knowledge graph]. But if you don't know much about a domain, you want to see an overview first [tree]. [P6]

5.3.3 Data Relations: Derivative Versus Multifaceted, Local Versus Global

Visualizations of structures, i.e. of entities and relationships, inherent in large data sets can help users understand the structure of the data and make information more accessible. However, participants may perceive a domain to have a derivative/hierarchical structure or a multi-faceted structure. If the representation of search results mimics that perceived structure, participants prefer that structure:

If you are searching for something that is already structured and we already know the names of these categories, then the tree is helpful. [P2]

For the [tree] interface, if I was using it for a topic like Geography, then I'm looking for continents, countries, cities, states, capitals, ... Then I know the headings and then I know which path to take.[P3]

I think [tree] would also be useful if you had some sort of notion of how things are laid out, like if there was a chronological order. Yeah, if that was chronological that would be nice cause you could gauge where you needed to click. Like you saw something that was really-really previous and two nodes down to find something more recent, even if you don't know exactly which one.[P8]

To clarify, the data relations in question are those perceived to be salient *by the participant*. If salient relationships are viewed as derivative or hierarchical (e.g. 'is-a' relationships), then a tree can best capture this view of data, whereas if salient relationships are more heterogeneous and resist structure as a hierarchy, that advantages the graph-based representation.

Beyond the specific relationships between entities, another theme that appeared in our data involved the scope of information required to satisfy a query. The tree structure seems to provide a comprehensive overview for the information space. Even if we provide groupings and overviews for our graphs, the graph interface best serves exploration at the entity-relationship level. As a result, several participants liked the tree structure for cases where they needed a comprehensive overview of the domain:

If I'm learning about a new domain, in the case that I want to cover the entire domain and get a general understanding of everything but at the surface, I'd like the tree. [P7]

5.3.4 Problem Solving Approach: Depth-First Versus Breadth-First

According to Brown [6] information seeking is a goal-driven activity in which needs are satisfied through problem solving. This view is comparable to Wilson's model of information seeking [38], which considers information seeking as a problem-solving process with the goal of reducing uncertainty about the information being searched.

... if you have a large amount of data then you're kind of confused, you don't know which part to look at, which connection to look at. ... I would use hierarchy to get an idea of how everything is organized and then maybe I go and try to dig in more, find out the relations between terms.
- For digging more would you use the graph?
- Yes. But again, even in the graph, it should be the specific, the focused one. Not the whole thing. [P21]

In unpacking this quote, we note that the process of directly addressing a problem is essentially a depth-first process where the knowledge graph allows a focused exploration of a region. On the other hand, with confusion the breadth-first or tree-based exploration is beneficial as it allows the user to iteratively reduce confusion, obtain an overview, and only slowly exploit detail. Many participants indicated similar concepts of confusion, nervousness, or inadequacy as a rationale for their preference for the tree structure:

[The graph interface] is not friendly. Too many things! [P2]
Because I get frustrated jumping from one node to the other for a while and don't get any information I want. ... If the graph is too big, I get scared of it! ... Too many things, so I don't know where to look [P26]
when the graph is too big, I don't know where to look ... and I don't also know where to start. Because I'm not familiar with most of the information .. the Councils, the positions, the names, ... So I don't know where to start. [P26]

More generally, many research domains argue for overview and structuring of content to permit sense-making and reduce confusion. Information visualization is founded on the techniques people use to structure and cluster visual stimuli (see, for example, [34], Chapter 1). Problem solving research in psychology connects aspects of visual perception and structuring of content to comprehension [26]. Designing for visually impaired readers argues for well-structured hierarchical content to allow more rapid sense-making [14], even in the absence of vision. Essentially, overviews are invaluable when people feel a need to orient themselves within data.

Alongside confusion and the need to orient ones-self within a domain, one's problem-solving strategies may bias behaviour. Research into problem solving strategies has a long history in the psychology domain. One well-known characterization of *coping* or problem-solving strategies identifies two groups of individuals: Problem-focused and Emotion-focused [18]. Problem-focused individuals tend to directly

address a problem, whereas those with an emotion-focused strategy seek to reduce the effects of the problem. In web search, Kim [17] found that problem-solving style had some impact on navigational patterns. Emotion-focused subjects traversed several layers of nodes before returning to the starting page (i.e. a depth-first navigation), whereas problem-focused subjects spent more time checking nodes available in the same level (i.e. a breadth-first navigation). Acknowledging the lack of personality-testing in our questionnaires [17], the link between confusion, nervousness, or fear and a desire for a hierarchical structure that allows depth-first exploration may merit further inquiry.

6. DISCUSSION

6.1 Understanding Tree Versus Graph Visualizations

As we note in the introduction, our goal with this research was to explore the differences between graph and tree visualization, specifically to understand their similarities and differences with respect to the search process. Our results explore these differences, triangulating both quantitative data from log files and qualitative data from participant interviews to understand how search result representations influence search behaviour.

From our log data, we note that the hierarchical structures in our study serve as pointers to passages in a document due to their similarity to tables-of-contents. Essentially, they simplify the process of locating topics, but the monotonic relationship that they represent – for example an is-a relationship – limits the information they can represent. The end result is that hierarchies result in a greater need to read the document rather than find the information contained within the visualization, shown, in our log data, by more instances of reading documents, and a longer period of time reading documents. Specifically, participants read documents three times more frequently and spent almost ten times more time reading. Our data also highlights the advantages and disadvantages of gleaning information from a knowledge-graph versus finding the relationship within source material and generating an abstract version of the knowledge graph for oneself. However, it is also clear that one representation is not better than the other in any subjective sense. Many of our participants expressed a need for combining both interfaces into one interface which enables switching between a global and a local view of the information space.

6.2 Design Implications

When designing search interfaces, the process of creating a view of search results remains challenging. Information visualization tools such as the InfoVis Toolkit[4], SpotFire[5] and InfoZoom[6] typically support multiple representations of search results. Our work does not dispute the accepted practice of recognizing that heterogeneous, interactive visualizations are the best way to allow exploration of a data set generated by search queries.

Our study highlights the complementary nature of hierarchical structures and knowledge graphs as representations of data. Our data indicates that hierarchies allow a more grad-

[4]http://sourceforge.net/projects/ivtk/
[5]http://spotfire.tibco.com/
[6]http://www.softlakesolutions.com/

ual depiction of and immersion into the domain, essentially fostering sense-making of the overall content (see Section 5.3.3). On the other hand, participants note that graphs are "more engaging" (P4), yield "more control over exploration" (P8), or are "similar to my mind" (P16). This, then begs the question of whether hierarchies and knowledge-graphs could be combined, but the challenge with combining hierarchical structures with knowledge-graphs is that hierarchies represent topics within a corpus, whereas nodes in a knowledge graph represent entities and their relations. Any one entity in a knowledge graph can map onto several topics in a hierarchy: For example, a political figure or governmental structure (e.g. the Guardian Council) or a historical event (e.g. the War of 1812) may be mentioned in all topics in a hierarchy, depending on how pervasive that entity is to the overall corpus.

On the other hand, within our knowledge graphs, nodes have different prominence based upon the number of edges they connect to. Entities that are more pervasive in the document have more connections and, hence, can be assumed to be more central to the topic. One alternative to hierarchical structures is to consider central entities within a knowledge graph, those entities that have a higher connectivity to the graph. By setting thresholds, one might be able to structure a multi-level view of a knowledge graph around central entities. We are exploring this option as one way to effectively combine the advantages of knowledge graphs and hierarchies into a single view. Rather than breaking down topics or concepts as in our tree view or in concept maps, the multi-level view of knowledge graphs focusing on central entities simply introduces information seekers to those entities or objects most central to a retrieved corpus.

6.3 Limitations

In designing any study, compromises must be made. In this section, we discuss three potential confounds: interface effects versus information representations; the effect that hand-tuning may have had on results; and the generalizability of our results given corpus size and topic/task selection. In this section, we address each of these concerns.

Any time one conducts a user study comparing two artifacts, it is always possible to bias the study through selective design. A poor user interface or poor interaction design can disadvantage one experimental option, leading to biased results. To limit this confound, we conducted multiple rounds of pilot studies and made modification to ensure that each representation was sufficiently rich that participants could perform a significant portion of the information seeking task within the visualization. In analyzing our data, we found that participants in our study data indicated no dissatisfaction with the interaction within the visualizations, and, instead, focused on the visualizations themselves. Even on probing during de-briefing interviews, participants would frequently discuss the advantages and disadvantages of knowledge representations (hierarchies versus graphs) when asked to comment on each interface.

A second concern revolves around the ecological validity of our results, particularly in light of hand tuning. As we noted in our experimental design section, we used automated algorithms to generate knowledge graphs [30] and extracted hierarchies from tables-of-contents or headings within documents. However, we then performed some refinement of the hierarchies (adding low-level sectioning to documents) and

knowledge graphs (mainly refinement of coreferencing). We address this point in two ways. First, arguably, to ensure that confounds are *not* present in our results, hand-tuning (or at least manual verification) is essential. Otherwise, error-prone algorithms and poorly structured data could influence the effectiveness of any individual representation of search results, focusing the data around the algorithmic failures as opposed to the nature of hierarchies versus graphs. Second, it is important to note that the manual refinement we performed was very limited. In hierarchies, we created a richer set of leaf nodes, but did not modify the overall structured content of the document; in knowledge-graphs, a small set of entities (less than 10%) needed to be combined when coreference resolution failed. As research in automatic summarization and coreference resolution continues, these problems will hopefully be addressed by researchers working in natural language processing.

Finally, task and corpus has been a concern in past iterations of this paper. Our tasks and topic effects are discussed in Section 5.1. We argue that the 10 most relevant documents from Wikipedia represents a set of documents similar to the number explored in real-world web searching tasks. First, while web searches return more results, work on information seeking argues that the effective size of a *relevant* document set for web search results is significantly smaller that all documents returned – on the order of six documents – hence the importance of ranking algorithms in information retrieval [16] [15]. Second, not every retrieved document is directly relevant to any specific information seeking task. A user may look within any individual document within a set of top ranked documents, and he or she may also combine information from multiple sources to satisfy his or her information needs.

7. CONCLUSION

In this paper, we present the results of a study evaluating knowledge graphs and trees as spatial representations of Web search results. Our analysis includes both log data gleaned from participant interactions with data representations and qualitative interview data gleaned from thinkalouds and semi-structured interviews. Overall, we find that knowledge graphs are effective in capturing the entities and relationships in a corpus in a way that reduces participant reliance on actual retrieved documents, i.e. participants viewed significantly fewer documents for significantly less time. As well, the quality of participant responses to pre-specified queries (a measure of how effective visualizations are at representing data) was statistically unaffected by representation. Finally, from the perspective of our participants, we find that tree-based representations are better suited to learning, provide better overviews of a domain, and are more approachable for participants who are confused. Graphs, in contrast, work best for directly seeking answers, and appear to be a more playful mechanism for exploring the details of individual entities and their relationships.

8. REFERENCES

[1] J. Allan, B. Croft, A. Moffat, and M. Sanderson. Frontiers, challenges, and opportunities for information retrieval: Report from swirl 2012. In *ACM SIGIR Forum*, volume 46, pages 2–32. ACM, 2012.

[2] F. Amadieu and L. Salmerón. Concept maps for comprehension and navigation of hypertexts. In

Digital Knowledge Maps in Education, pages 41–59. Springer, 2014.

[3] F. Amadieu, A. Tricot, and C. Mariné. Interaction between prior knowledge and concept-map structure on hypertext comprehension, coherence of reading orders and disorientation. *Interacting with computers*, 22(2):88–97, 2010.

[4] D. E. Berlyne. Conflict, arousal, and curiosity. 1960.

[5] A. Broder. A taxonomy of web search. In *ACM Sigir forum*, volume 36, pages 3–10. ACM, 2002.

[6] M. E. Brown. A general model of information-seeking behavior. In *Proceedings of the ASIS Annual Meeting*, volume 28, pages 9–14. ERIC, 1991.

[7] K. BystrÖm. Information and information sources in tasks of varying complexity. *Journal of the American Society for information Science and Technology*, 53(7):581–591, 2002.

[8] D. J. Campbell. Task complexity: A review and analysis. *Academy of management review*, 13(1):40–52, 1988.

[9] R. Capra, G. Marchionini, J. S. Oh, F. Stutzman, and Y. Zhang. Effects of structure and interaction style on distinct search tasks. In *Proceedings of the 7th ACM/IEEE-CS joint conference on Digital libraries*, pages 442–451. ACM, 2007.

[10] M. Carnot, P. Feltovich, R. Hoffman, J. Feltovich, and J. Novak. A summary of literature pertaining to the use of concept mapping techniques and technologies for education and performance support. 2003.

[11] B. Dervin. Sense-making theory and practice: an overview of user interests in knowledge seeking and use. *Journal of knowledge management*, 2(2):36–46, 1998.

[12] N. Ducheneaut and V. Bellotti. E-mail as habitat: an exploration of embedded personal information management. *interactions*, 8(5):30–38, 2001.

[13] M. A. Hearst. Clustering versus faceted categories for information exploration. *CACM*, 49(4):59–61, 2006.

[14] M. Hersh and M. A. Johnson. *Assistive technology for visually impaired and blind people*. Springer Science & Business Media, 2010.

[15] T. Joachims, L. Granka, B. Pan, H. Hembrooke, and G. Gay. Accurately interpreting clickthrough data as implicit feedback. In *Proc. of SIGIR*, pages 154–161. ACM, 2005.

[16] D. Kelly and L. Azzopardi. How many results per page? a study of serp size, search behavior and user experience. 2015.

[17] K.-S. Kim. Searching the web: Effects of problem solving style on information-seeking behavior. In *World Conference on Educational Multimedia, Hypermedia and Telecommunications*, volume 1999, pages 1541–1542, 1999.

[18] R. S. Lazarus and S. Folkman. Stress. *Appraisal, and coping*, 725, 1984.

[19] H. Ltifi, M. Ben Ayed, A. M. Alimi, and S. Lepreux. Survey of information visualization techniques for exploitation in kdd. pages 218–225. IEEE, 2009.

[20] G. Marchionini. Exploratory search: from finding to understanding. *CACM*, 49(4):41–46, 2006.

[21] G. Marchionini and B. Shneiderman. 3.1 finding facts vs. browsing knowledge in hypertext systems. *Sparks of innovation in human-computer interaction*, page 103, 1993.

[22] K. L. Norman and J. P. Chin. The effect of tree structure on search in a hierarchical menu selection system. *Behaviour & Information Technology*, 7(1):51–65, 1988.

[23] L. R. Novick and S. M. Hurley. To matrix, network, or hierarchy: That is the question. *Cognitive Psychology*, 42(2):158–216, 2001.

[24] S. Pace. A grounded theory of the flow experiences of web users. *International journal of human-computer studies*, 60(3):327–363, 2004.

[25] P. Pirolli and S. Card. Information foraging. *Psychological review*, 106(4):643, 1999.

[26] R. M. Ratwani, J. G. Trafton, and D. A. Boehm-Davis. Thinking graphically: Connecting vision and cognition during graph comprehension. *Journal of Experimental Psychology: Applied*, 14(1):36, 2008.

[27] D. E. Rose and D. Levinson. Understanding user goals in web search. In *Proceedings of the 13th international conference on World Wide Web*, pages 13–19. ACM, 2004.

[28] D. Russell, M. Stefik, P. Pirolli, and S. Card. The cost structure of sensemaking. In *Proc. of INTERACT'93 and CHI'93*, pages 269–276. ACM, 1993.

[29] F. Sanchez-Zamora and M. Llamas-Nistal. Adaptive concept maps: Issues on design and navigation. In *Concept Mapping: Connecting Educators. Proceedings of the Third International Conference on Concept Mapping. Tallinn, Estonia & Helsinki, Finland*, 2008.

[30] B. Sarrafzadeh, R. Guttikonda, K. Suleman, J. Thomas, and O. Vechtomova. Automatic discovery of related concepts. Technical report, March 2013.

[31] B. Sarrafzadeh, O. Vechtomova, and V. Jokic. Exploring knowledge graphs for exploratory search. In *Proceedings of the 5th Information Interaction in Context Symposium*, pages 135–144. ACM, 2014.

[32] B. Shneiderman. The eyes have it: A task by data type taxonomy for information visualizations. In *Visual Languages, 1996. Proceedings., IEEE Symposium on*, pages 336–343. IEEE, 1996.

[33] A. Singhal. Introducing the knowledge graph: things, not strings, 2012. *Official Blog (of Google)*.

[34] C. Ware. *Information visualization: perception for design*. Elsevier, 2012.

[35] R. W. White and R. A. Roth. Exploratory search: Beyond the query-response paradigm. *Synthesis Lectures on Information Concepts, Retrieval, and Services*, 1(1):1–98, 2009.

[36] B. M. Wildemuth and L. Freund. Assigning search tasks designed to elicit exploratory search behaviors. In *Proc. of HCIR 2012*, page 4. ACM, 2012.

[37] M. L. Wilson, B. Kules, B. Shneiderman, et al. From keyword search to exploration: Designing future search interfaces for the web. *Foundations and Trends in Web Science*, 2(1):1–97, 2010.

[38] T. D. Wilson. Models in information behaviour research. *Journal of documentation*, 55(3):249–270, 1999.

Exploring the Use of Query Auto Completion: Search Behavior and Query Entry Profiles

Catherine L. Smith
School of Library and
Information Science
Kent State University
csmit141@kent.edu

Jacek Gwizdka
School of Information
University of Texas at Austin
chiir2016@gwizdka.com

Henry Feild
Computer Science
Department
Endicott College
hfeild@endicott.edu

ABSTRACT

Query auto completion (QAC) is nearly ubiquitous in modern search systems, however, there are few published studies on how searchers use QAC query suggestions. This study describes the use of QAC by 29 searchers working on eight assigned search topics in a lab setting. We found that our subjects had differing propensities to use QAC, with some searchers rarely using it, while others used QACs for about half their queries. This study extends prior work by examining the use of QAC in the context of whole search sessions across multiple topics, and by comparing search behavior and visual attention for queries that used QAC and those that did not. The study concludes with an exploration of differences in QAC usage and query behavior among searchers, which reveals six possible query entry profiles.

Keywords

Query suggestion, query auto completion, interactive information retrieval, search behavior, eye-tracking.

1. INTRODUCTION

Modern search systems assist their users by identifying and suggesting useful query terms during interaction. Where the system has contextual information such as query and click history, GPS location, etc., the system can produce suggestions with a great deal of relevance to the searcher's situation. While this assistance mechanism has become nearly universal in systems such as Web search engines, library catalogs, and academic databases, relatively little is known about how searchers use this feature during interaction. In contrast, there is a large body of research on searcher interaction with results pages. Much of this work has been motivated by the need to understand behavioral data observed in query logs, with the objective of improving results rankings [4, 7, 8].

More recently, motivated by similar objectives with respect to the performance of query suggestion mechanisms, a

CHIIR'16, March 13–17, 2016, Chapel Hill, North Carolina, USA.

© 2016 ACM. ISBN 978-1-4503-3751-9/16/03...$15.00

DOI: http://dx.doi.org/10.1145/2854946.2854975

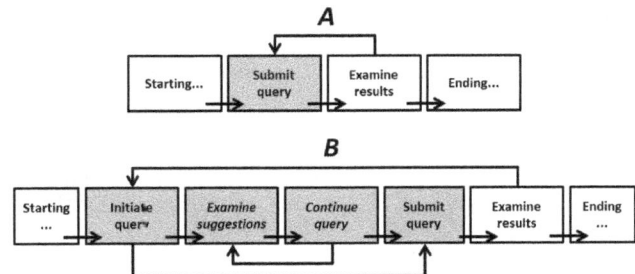

Figure 1: (A) the standard searcher interaction model and (B) the model with QACs offered during query formulation.

small but growing stream of research has focused on interaction with a specific form of query suggestion: query auto completion, or QAC. This work has examined search engine logs, visual attention, typing behavior, and the effect of QAC rankings on QAC usage. Prior experimental work reporting uptake for modern QAC has examined a single topic [15], or the first query of a search session [6]. Our paper extends this work by examining QAC usage during complete query sessions across several topics, and within the context of alternative query forms (typed queries and spelling suggestions). Our goal was to gain insight into factors in QAC uptake among individual searchers, particularly factors not explained by the quality of QACs or QAC rankings. We have examined typing, clicking, and visual scanning behaviors, as well as the length of QAC lists. Our findings suggest that uptake is affected by visuomotor factors associated with preferences between use of the mouse or keyboard. This insight has implications for models of QAC quality and utilization, as well as for system design.

2. RELATED WORK

Query auto completion (QAC) provides assistance at the time of query formulation, by dynamically revising suggested queries as a searcher types into a query box. Typically, the suggestions appear immediately under the query box, and a list of suggestions is refreshed with every keystroke. QAC changes the standard interaction sequence, so that formulation now includes the possible additional step of examining a suggestion list before query submission (see Figure 1).

While QAC has been deployed in commercial systems since 2007 [1], little research has been reported on the uptake of QAC outside lab settings and possible factors affecting usage, however, as discussed below, evidence suggests that searchers often ignore suggestions. Understanding how QAC is used, and factors associated with its disuse, are important to continued improvement in system design and evaluation.

QAC is one form of query suggestion. The earliest types of suggestion were a form of feedback, requiring an initial query. Terms derived via pseudo-relevance feedback were provided to searchers for use in query reformulation; studies revealed that searchers were unlikely to use individual suggested terms [9]. The second generation of query suggestion presented full phrases in a static form, where the whole intact query might be submitted by clicking. In lab studies, searchers have been found to prefer phrases over individual terms, and to prefer phrases created as real queries over phrases generated algorithmically [9]. Niu and Kelly [14] found that when static suggestions were available, 41% of submitted queries were clicked suggestions, and another 15% were typed copies of suggestions. The suggestions helped subjects locate more relevant documents, particularly on difficult topics. The third generation of query suggestion presented terms and phrases that changed as the searcher typed [1]. In an early lab study using an experimental dynamic suggestion system, White and Marchionini found that 44% of all queries used a dynamic suggestion and 57% of query reformulations used at least one suggested term [17].

QAC is the modern iteration of dynamic suggestion. While QAC usage rates have not been widely reported, several recent studies provide insight. The recent lab study of Hofmann et al. [6] found that searchers used a suggestion on 29% of the initial queries submitted in a search session. Hofmann's finding is consistent with the large log study of Li et al. [11], which reports that searchers do not submit a QAC on approximately 60% of queries. Two log studies have found that usage is dependent on the position of a QAC in the list of suggestions [10, 13]. Mitra et al. [13] also found that the probability of using a suggestion was affected by the type and subject matter of the searcher's goal (e.g., navigational, image search, autos, celebrities).

Three recent studies support the assumption that searchers interact with QAC in ways similar to their interaction with SERPs: visual attention focuses at the top of the list. Hofmann et al. [6] found that searchers scan some part of the QAC list almost invariably, and that visual attention generally focuses on the top suggestion. Consistent with that finding, Mitra et al. [13] found that when searchers use QAC, they are over twice as likely to click on the top-ranked suggestion relative to the second suggestion, and they are very unlikely to click suggestions further down the list. These results support the conclusion that searchers are biased favorably toward QACs at the top of the suggestion list, much as they are for SERP rankings.

Recently, work on improving QAC ranking models has focused on exploiting behavioral signals for QAC quality. The study of Zhang et al. [19] tested a QAC model that incorporates implicit negative feedback derived from QAC dwell time and rank position, which are shown to be indicators of QAC relevance. The model resulted in superior performance over prior models, however, the authors point to large variability in their results, and the need to better understand searchers' behavior when using QAC. The model of Li et al. [10] used searchers' interaction history and other features to predict QAC relevance. Both models make explicit assumptions about query behavior and the visual attention searchers give to QACs.

The present study contributes a description of searchers' interactive behavior and visual attention over iterations of query formulation. We focus specifically on the query formulation interval (QFI), during which decisions about when to look at QACs, and when to use them, are made. We explore factors affecting usage, and differences in the characteristics of query formulation resulting in QAC queries and non-QAC queries. The larger objective is to understand how interaction may shape searchers' decisions on using QAC so that more effective query assistance mechanisms may be designed and developed.

3. METHOD

We conducted an exploratory laboratory study of web search with N=31 subjects. Client-side logs were collected as subjects engaged in searching on assigned topics. Retrospective evaluations of search easiness and success were also gathered in two short questionnaires. Below we describe the study, subjects, and design, as well as the topics, system, instruments, and procedures used.

3.1 Participants

Volunteers were recruited from an undergraduate student research pool and received course credit for participation. Forty subjects were recruited, of which 33 attended the appointments, with data retained for 29 subjects (62% female; 97% 18–24 years old). Two subjects were excused with credit due to problems with calibration and two subjects reported that English was not their native language; all data from these subjects are excluded from analysis.

3.2 Design

Each subject completed one practice topic and eight additional searches on eight of twelve topics, in one of nine assigned orders, which comprised an incomplete Williams design [18], such that every topic was used in each position once in nine orders, and no topic order repeated . Because the design was incomplete, not all subjects searched on the same topics.

3.3 Topic construction

The twelve topics were selected from an initial set of 30 designed with the objective of minimizing variability due to task demands. Each topic started with context information on a hypothetical prior association between the searcher and the topic, where the association and an explicit statement of affect (e.g., worry, excitement) motivated the information need. Each topic contained two related but specific simple sub-needs, stated as a question or request. These were designed with the goal that each search require more than one query yet be simple enough to complete in less than ten minutes. All topic descriptions were between 58–65 words in length. The system disallowed copying the topic text. Topic summaries are listed in Table 1.

3.4 Systems

The data were collected using a modified version of the CrowdLogger extension (CL) for Google Chrome.[1] CL administered the study and logged subject interactions with the browser and system responses [3, 2]. A Tobii T60 eye-

---

[1]https://github.com/hafeild/crowdlogger

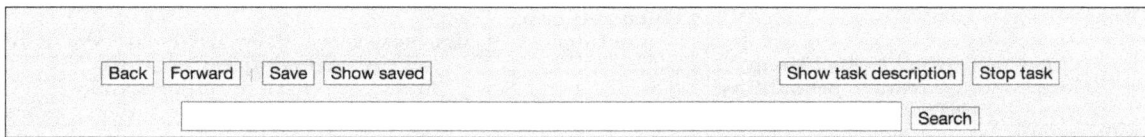

Figure 2: Shows the CrowdLogger interface. The study toolbar is presented at the top of every page and the content of the page (Figure 3, right) is placed in the area below.

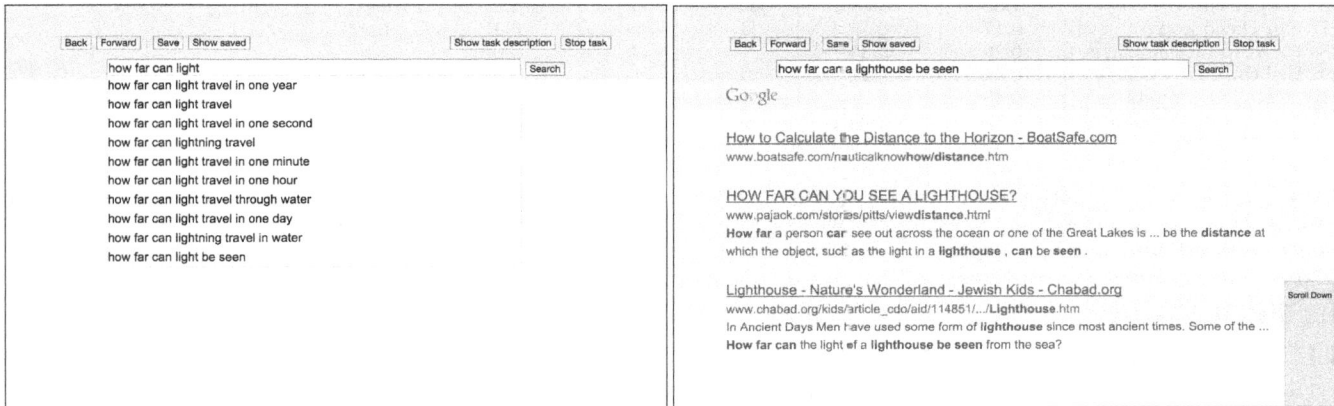

Figure 3: An example of a QList (left) and the top pane of results for an altered Google SERP (right).

tracker,[2] running at 60 Hz, recorded eye gaze and also logged mouse and keyboard events. I-VT fixation filter, which is built into Tobii Studio software (ver.3.03), was used to detect fixation events.[3] We used the algorithm's default settings (velocity threshold $30°/s$; min. fixation duration 60 ms).

3.5 System interface and SERP presentation

In order to obtain sufficient accuracy for fixations on individual words and on elements of the search interface, we used an enlarged and simplified search interface based on the standard Google interface to present search topic, QAC lists, and search results. A toolbar controlled the study (see Figure 2), and by placing Chrome in full screen, the browser omni-box (combined address line and query entry box) was hidden, as were any tabs. The toolbar included standard browser forward and back buttons, as well as a query entry box (QBox) and button for submitting queries. QAC lists (QLists, see Figure 3, left) were displayed immediately below the QBox. Other buttons controlled the study, including functions that saved the current page to a list of good information sources for the topic, unsaved the current page from the list, showed the current topic description, ended the current topic, or started the next topic. As in modern QAC, QLists were altered dynamically with every keystroke in the QBox. The QACs were generated using the Google QAC API, and were unaltered except to increase the font size and line spacing. It is important to note that the QACs were not necessarily those that would be displayed by Google in native operation, and they did not include more advanced features such as completion of individual terms, substitution of prefixes, personalization, and localization. Native SERPs

returned by Google were automatically cleaned of image, shopping, and news results as well as advertising before organic items were reformatted with order retained.

Because of reduced eye-tracking accuracy at the edge of a screen, all screen elements were placed within a 100-pixel boundary from the screen edge. For the toolbar, query box, QAC lists, and SERP, the line height, including whitespace, was 36 pixels, resulting in 0.84° of horizontal visual angle, at a typical distance from the monitor of 65cm. A 24 pixel font was used for everything but surrogate titles, resulting in approximately 0.56° of horizontal visual angle on each character. Surrogate titles used a 28 pixel font, yielding roughly 0.65° of horizontal visual angle. With the 100 pixel boundary, the toolbar at the top of the screen, and the larger-than-normal font and line spacing, the available screen size only allowed for two or three results to be shown at once. To allow for all of the results to be viewed, SERPs were split into three or more sub-pages, which were navigated by use of large scroll buttons located on the right side of each sub-page (see Figure 3, right). All non-SERP pages were displayed unaltered below the toolbar, with normal scrolling enabled.

3.6 Data collection and processing

In addition to cleaning and formatting Google SERPs, the CL extension also logged searcher interaction and data displays in the browser, including: keypresses; QACs displays; reformatted SERPs; SERP scrolling and paging (e.g., from page 1 to 2); all queries submitted, toolbar buttons, and links clicked, including spelling corrections; SERP and QAC content; and page loads, focuses, and blurs. The Unix Epoch timestamp of each logged event was also recorded. The Tobii T60 recorded fixation locations and durations, and its own internal timestamp. For fixations below validity threshold on both eyes, the data were discarded. In analysis, the Tobii and CL timestamps were synchronized.

---

[2]http://www.tobii.com/en/eye-tracking-research/global/products/hardware/tobii-t60t120-eye-tracker
[3]http://www.tobii.com/eye-tracking-research/global/library/white-papers/the-tobii-i-vt-fixation-filter

Topic	Mean NDCG@3	Mean probability of QacQ	Open response mentions[†]		Easiness score "How hard/easy was it to…"			
			easiest	hardest	find information	come up with words	understand the topic	average
1. Keurig coffee recall	0.29	0.49	2	0	6.4	6.2	6.0	6.2
2. Theft at Louvre	0.22	0.20	2	1	5.9	5.6	5.6	5.7
3. Importing tulips	0.26	0.28	1	0	5.9	5.3	5.5	5.5
4. Rail-trail conversion	**0.15**	**0.09**	**0**	**11**	**4.7**	**4.0**	**3.4**	**4.0**
5. Mexico health	0.85	0.52	5	0	6.7	6.4	6.6	6.5
6. Depression	**0.38**	**0.59**	**12**	**0**	**6.9**	**6.6**	**6.5**	**6.7**
7. San Diego Zoo	0.17	0.35	3	2	6.4	5.9	5.1	5.8
8. Fly-trap mechanism	0.26	0.38	1	3	6.0	5.3	4.8	5.4
9. Lighthouses	0.44	0.21	0	1	6.0	5.9	5.6	5.9
10. Catalina Mountains	0.48	0.21	1	2	5.7	5.8	5.2	5.5
11. Dahomey warriors	0.33	0.29	0	2	5.8	5.5	5.2	5.5
12. Colored honey	0.43	0.13	1	6	5.9	4.9	5.0	5.3

Table 1: Per-topic statistics, including QacQ uptake rates (mean probability) and easiness ratings collected from subject responses. Easiness scores were reported on a 7-point scale between 1 (very hard) and 7 (very easy). Easiest and hardest topics are bolded.

† Note: one subject did not respond to "hardest" question and two did not respond to "easiest".

4. PROCEDURE

4.1 Experimental sessions

Two-hour experimental sessions were conducted individually in a quiet room with a single researcher present. Subjects were not told that the study was about QAC. There were no time limits on searching, but most sessions lasted well under 80 minutes. After being greeted by a researcher, consent was obtained and a PowerPoint presentation explained the study in detail. The eye-tracking system was then calibrated. CL administered the search topics in the assigned order, and after completing each topic, subjects responded to questions on topic easiness in a questionnaire booklet (see Table 1). After the first five topics and an optional break, the eye-tracker was recalibrated before the final topics. An online questionnaire was then completed, which included questions on demographic information and details related to eyewear.

4.2 Topic sessions

Each topic session started with the "Start task" button. The topic appeared in a pop-up box, which was closed with a button. The description could also be reviewed by showing the topic again. After submitting queries, reviewing results, and examining items, useful Web pages were saved, and possibly reviewed and unsaved. When the sought information was found, the "Stop task" button was used to complete the topic before starting the next topic. In presenting results, we refer to work on a topic as a *session*.

5. ANALYSIS

The results presented below are from the 8 non-practice tasks completed by 29 subjects, with a total of 707 queries submitted in 232 topic sessions. Log data were extracted and processed, along with questionnaire responses. The extracted log data included epoch-stamped records for each of 21 different search actions (e.g. click button, click link, scroll) as well as all keystrokes in the search box and the content of all QAC lists displayed during the query formulation interval (QFI), where the QFI starts with the first keystroke or mouse click of a query, and ends with query submission by click or enter key. Data processing resulted in a detailed record describing behavior, system response, and performance for each query submitted. These data were ag-

gregated for analysis at the level of a session (all interaction between "start task" and "end task") and across sessions for each subject. For analysis of visual attention, the locations of areas of interest (AOIs) were computed from the pixel offsets of each page, which were used to define visual bounding boxes for each toolbar element and the QLists. The QList AOIs are thus dynamic, and change as the length of the QList changes during typing.

In preparing data for analysis, three query types (QType) and two query submission types (SubType) were defined. Qtypes include: *Box queries*—**BoxQs** were created by typing in the QBox, as well as by pasting text into the QBox, using the back button to return to a previously submitted query, or by editing a previously submitted query; *QAC queries*—**QacQs** used query suggestion text displayed in a current QList; and *Spelling correction queries*—**SpellQs** used spelling correction hyper links displayed in SERPs. SubTypes include: *click queries*—**ClickQs** were submitted by clicking the search button in the toolbar or a SpellQ link; and *enter queries*—**EnterQs** were submitted using the enter key on the keyboard. QType and SubType were then used to define the cross between these types as **XQTypes**: clicked QAC (CQ), keyed QAC (KQ), clicked Box (CB), and keyed box (KB). For keyed QACs, the enter key was generally used after the QAC was highlighted using arrow keys.

Table 2 lists extracted and derived variables reported in the paper. These include count data, time intervals, and ratios, all of which required transformation before using an analysis of variance. Other variables, such as NDCG@3, have irregular distributions that required non-parametric analysis, as noted in each section.

6. RESULTS

We report results of four analytical approaches. The first analysis describes QAC usage across subjects and topics. We then describe differences in query behavior and system response for QAC and Box queries, followed by an analysis of visual attention. Finally, we explore characteristics of searchers and associations between query behavior and visual attention, which we characterize as *query entry profiles*.

6.1 QAC usage

BoxQs vs. QacQs As detailed in Table 3, of the 707 queries submitted, 184 (26%) were QacQs and 498 (70%)

Variable	Definition
QueryLength (chars)	The number of characters in the query.
NDCG@3	Normalized Discounted Cumulative Gain at rank 3, with relevance determined by number of times an item was saved as good for the task.
QFT (secs)	Elapsed query formulation time during the query formulation interval—note that spelling queries and queries submitted after return via back key, QFT=0.
TotalQueryKeystrokes	The number of keystokes (including deletions) used to formulate the query.
KeystrokesPerSecond	The average number of keystrokes per second during the QFT.
SizeFirstQList	# QACs in first list displayed in the QFI, where more than one QAC displayed.
SizeLastQList	# QACs in last list displayed in the QFI, where more than one QAC displayed.
QueryLastQAC	Similarity (lexical or semantic) between a submitted query and the bottom ranked QAC for that query.
FirstQACLastQAC	Similarity (lexical or semantic) between a the top and bottom ranked QAC for a submitted query.
TGD (secs)	Total gaze duration for all fixations detected during the query formulation interval .

Table 2: Query variables and their definitions.

QType	SubType		Total
	Clicked	Enter Key	
BoxQ	49	415	464
QacQ	106	78	184
Spelling Correction	25	0	25
Resubmitted no action	1	33	34
Total Queries	181	526	707

Table 3: Distribution of queries, by type (QType) and submission mode (SubType).

were BoxQs. This rate of QAC usage is comparable to Hofmann's reported 29% of queries [6]. In addition, our data included 25 (3.5%) queries submitted by clicking on a spelling suggestion. Among the BoxQs, 34 (4.8%) were resubmissions of the prior query after a click on the back button, with no change to the query. These query types didn't involve typing in the QBox or selecting a QAC and had short or zero formulation times, therefore we view them as different query forms and exclude them from our analyses.

Table 3 also details the submission mode for each query, with 526 (74%) of the 707 queries submitted using the enter key on the keyboard, and 181 (26%) submitted by clicking the submit button with the mouse. The table clearly shows strong preference to submit BoxQs using the enter key (89%), while for QacQs there is a very weak preference for submission by click (57%). Further analysis indicates that submission mode plays a role in visual attention, which we discuss in Section 6.3.

Effects due to topics. Because not all subjects searched on the same topics, understanding topic effects was particularly important. Also, our preliminary analysis revealed large differences in the use of QTypes among subjects. For example, several participants used BoxQs to the near exclusion of QacQs. In order to examine the effect of these two factors on the probability of using a QAC (*usage rate*) we used an ANOVA model with subject and topic as fixed factors. Both factors were significant (for subjects: $F(28,192)=3.7$, $p<.001$, partial $\eta^2 = 0.35$; topics: $F(11,192) = 5.9$, $p<.001$, partial $\eta^2 = 0.25$). The estimated marginal usage rates for topics (subject effects removed) are listed in Table 1. For subjects, the probability of using a QAC ranged from a low of under 5% to a high of 68%. Others were distributed as follows: 4 had a probability between 5% and 10%, 6 were between 11% and 20%, 13 were between 21% and 50%, and 5 were over 50% but lower than 68%. Post-hoc analysis with Scheffe's test found that differences between the extreme ends of the range were significant.

We were also interested in how searchers' perceptions of the topics related to QAC usage. After completing each topic, subjects reported their impressions of topic easiness

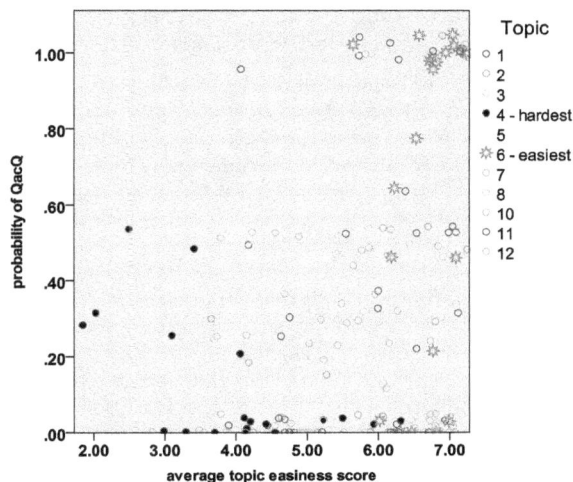

Figure 4: Topic easiness.

using three scales on: finding information, coming up with words, and understanding the topic, as presented in Table 1. Also, after finishing all searches, subjects identified the topics that were hardest and easiest for them. The table lists counts for these mentions. Topic 6, which asks for information about depression symptoms and psychologists, was identified as the easiest and had the highest probability of a QacQ. Topic 4, on rail-trail conversions, was hardest, and had the lowest probability of a QacQ. Figure 4 displays the averages of the three scores and the unadjusted probability of a QacQ for each of the 232 sessions. In the parametric analyses that follow, we use models that account for subject and topic effects, as noted.

6.2 Characterizing QAC and Box queries

In describing QacQs and BoxQs, we examine system performance, search behavior, and characteristics of QLists. Table 4 lists descriptive statistics, and results from comparisons. Comparisons were made using ANOVA with a model that included main effects due to topic, subject, query order, SubType, and QType. Where analysis of variance was inappropriate due to non-normal distribution, we use non-parametric tests, as noted by the dagger symbol in Table 4. The specific tests used are noted in each section.

Sytem performance. In comparing system peformance for BoxQs and QacQs we find greater performance for QacQs, with relevant results more likely to appear in the top three positions of the SERP, as indicated by NDCG@3 (p<.05, sign test). Because an association was found between the

	Variable	QAC Queries		BOX Queries		difference	
		n	mean (sd)	n	mean (sd)		
Performance	NDCG@3†	184	0.39 (0.41)	396	0.29 (0.36)	*	+0.1
Effort	QFT (secs)	184	12.0 (9.0)	464	11.8 (8.3)	***	−0.2
	QueryLength (chars)	184	28.0 (11.1)	464	37.3 (13.9)	***	−9.3
Query behavior	TotalQueryKeystrokes	184	21.1 (12.6)	454	36.2 (22.1)	*	−15.1
	KeystrokesPerSecond	184	2.0 (0.9)	454	3.2 (1.2)	***	−1.2
QList characteristics	SizeFirstQList†	184	9.7 (1.4)	396	9.2 (2.4)	**	+0.5
	SizeLastQList†	184	7.7 (3.5)	396	4.2 (3.7)	***	+3.5
Lexical similarity	QueryToLastQAC	166	0.49 (0.18)	246	0.41 (0.16)	***	+0.08
(trigram overlap)	FirstQACToLastQAC	166	0.49 (0.15)	246	0.53 (0.18)	**	−0.04
Semantic similarity	QueryToLastQAC	166	0.56 (0.29)	246	0.56 (0.28)		0
	FirstQACToLastQAC	166	0.58 (0.28)	246	0.65 (0.27)	***	−0.07

Table 4: **Measures of system performance, effort and QAC dynamic for BOX and QAC queries, mean (sd), and p-values of tests; * $p<.05$, ** $p<.01$, *** $p<.001$. Note: 25 spelling suggestion queries, and 34 back-key resubmissions are excluded from these data. † Sign test, with QType the only factor.**

topic of a search and the probability of using a QAC, we were interested in any association between topic and performance, which we tested using the Durbin test for incomplete block designs. The result was not significant. The mean performance of each topic is listed in Table 1. No significant correlation between topic performance and the probability of QacQ usage was found ($p=.131$).

Search behavior. Compared with BoxQs, QFT for QacQs was longer by two-tenths of a second ($F(1,596)=48.7$, $p<.001$). Submission of a QAC saved our subjects typing an average of 7 characters per query (28.0 characters - 21.1 keystrokes = 6.9, s.d.=11.4). QacQs required 15 fewer keystrokes ($F(1,586) = 5.9$, $p<.05$) and QacQs were shorter than BoxQs ($F(1,596) = 16.8$, $p<.001$). It follows that the longer BoxQs, formulated with more keystrokes and taking less time, were typed at a faster pace ($F(1,586) = 16.3$, $p<.001$). The finding is consistent with the log study of [10], which found that not using a QAC (skipping) was associated with faster typing speed. These findings present a complex picture of interaction in which it takes more time to submit a query that has been formulated with fewer keystrokes. For our subjects, on average, there was a cost in query formulation time for the use of QacQs. This implies that there should be an offsetting future expected utility for the cost of the time. We revisit this question in our discussion.

QList characteristics As mentioned above, QACs are displayed in lists that change dynamically with each keystroke. In the QAC engine used in our study, as a typed query grew in length, the longer prefix caused fewer QACs to be displayed and the QList to be shortened as typing continued. The length of QLists is of interest because it is a visual indicator of change in the match between searcher's representation of a need and the system's understanding. Comparing QacQ and BoxQ formulations, we find that QLists were shorter on average for BoxQ formulations. This was true for the first QList displayed ($p<.01$, sign test), and the last QList displayed for a query ($p<.01$, sign test). The average final QList of a BoxQ contained only about 4 QACs, while the last QLists for QacQs contained about 8 QACs. For 63% of BoxQs there was no QList displayed at the time of query submission.

The content of QLists is a direct indicator of the match between the query and the system's understanding. For QacQs, the last QList displayed contains the QAC submitted. For BoxQs, the last QList displayed indicates the system's final understanding of the query, before the searcher has decided to use the content of the QBox. We explored

differences in the content of the final QList displayed, first by examining the similarity of the first and last QACs in final lists, and then by examining the similarity of the query and QAC at the bottom of the final list.

Measures of lexical and semantic similarity were computed. For lexical similarity, we report results of analysis using the Jaccard Coefficient at the level of character trigrams. We also tested a word-level Jaccard Coefficient and length-normalized Levenshtein distance with similar results, not reported here. For semantic similarity, we used the August 2015 version of Wiktionary,[4] indexed with the Galago search engine.[5] For each of the input strings (QAC or query), we computed its tf-idf similarity to each of the Wiktionary entries via Galago. Semantic similarity was then calculated as the cosine between the tf-idf score vectors. Where a QList had only one suggestion, similarity within the list was not computed. Results are shown in Table 4.

In examining the last QLists displayed, for both lexical and semantic similarity, we find greater similarity between first and last QACs for BoxQs and less similarity for QacQs. There is a small but significant negative correlation between the length of the QList and the lexical similarity of the first and last QACs on the list ($r(409)=-0.286$, $p<.001$); the correlation is similar for the semantic measure. As the list shrinks in size, similarity increases. This result is likely due to the similarity of longer QAC prefixes and the smaller number of QAC variations for those prefixes, as reflected by the shorter lists. We also find that QacQs have greater similarity to the last QACs in the list than do BoxQs. This follows from the fact that for QacQs, the last QList displayed contains the query, and also from the fact that 63% of BoxQs are long enough to exhaust the prefix store so that the QList disappears. Interestingly, the semantic similarity of the query and the last QAC is the same for both QacQs and BoxQs.

We speculate that for some searchers, a shrinking QList may signal greater specificity of the QACs in the list. Also, because the similarity of the QACs grows as the QList shrinks, the change in size may signal that there is little variation in the highly specific QACs. In effect, these dual signals may reduce expected utility of the the entire list, motivating the searcher to keep typing without expending the effort of giving visual attention to the QList. We revisit these ideas in our discussion.

---

[4] https://www.wiktionary.org
[5] http://www.lemurproject.org/galago.php, Galago v3.2 with default settings.

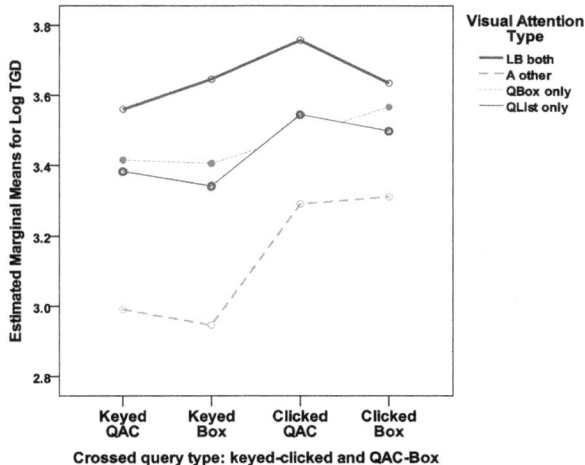

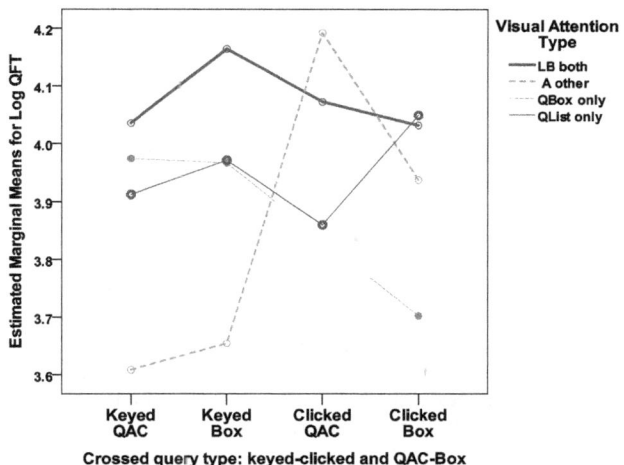

Figure 5: TGD means (left) and QFT means (right).

		#Queries with expected fixations	missing fixations	Total
QType	BoxQ	347	117	464
	QACQ	144	40	184
SubmitType	Clicked	129	17	146
	Enter Key	362	115	477
	Total Queries	491	132	623

Table 5: Missing fixations by QType and SubType.

6.3 Visual attention in QAC and Box queries

As discussed in Section 2, recent work on behavioral models for QAC rankings have used simplifying assumptions on searchers' visual attention to QACs [10, 19]. Several prior findings reveal the complexity of attention to QACs. Hofmann [6] found that 48% of study subjects were touch-typists who monitored the screen while typing; others looked down at the keyboard while typing. In examining logs of QAC usage, Li et al. [10] found that some searchers rarely used QACs, with the assumption that these searchers skipped viewing the QACs. In this section we use two approaches to investigate visual attention during query formulation, with the goal of describing differences for QacQs and BoxQs.

As in the analysis in Section 6.1, 59 spelling and zero keystroke queries are excluded. In addition, 25 queries had no fixations recorded during the QFI, indicating that the subject did not look at the screen or data recording failed. The 25 queries were distributed across 13 subjects, with one subject accounting for 8 of the 25. Because these queries may be due to error in data recording, we exclude them from analysis in this section, with no effect on the findings.

"Missing" fixations. In our first approach to exploring visual attention, we looked for any association between QTypes, SubTypes, and "missing" fixation points, expecting missing fixations for queries typed while looking at the keyboard. Because submitting a QAC requires selecting a QAC from the QList, one may expect that subjects will fixate at least once on the submitted QAC. Similarly, for BoxQs one may expect that the query box will be fixated at least once during formulation. Queries with missing expected fixations were detected by determining whether a submitted QAC had been fixated at least once, in the case of QacQs, and by determining whether the QBox was fixated at least once for

BoxQs. Table 5 details the distribution of 132 queries for which no expected fixation data was recorded.

We tested for significant differences in miss rates for Q-Types and SubTypes by aggregating the data by subject and computing the probability of a miss for each type. The sign test indicated no significant differences in the probability of a missing fixation among QTypes (p=.089) or SubTypes (p=.170). The association between missing fixations and query behavior is explored further in our analysis of query entry profiles in Section 6.4.

Visual attention allocation. Our second approach to visual attention focused on how attention was allocated between the QList and QBox during query formulation and differences in attention associated with QType and SubType. We make a simplifying assumption that the total duration of eye fixations on a visual element reflects the amount of attention given to this element. The assumption is safe for interactions with text when a word to be processed needs to be in the area of high visual acuity—where our eyes are focused. Because queries with missing fixations have zero total gaze durations (TGD), they cause a large skew in distributions, making the analysis complex. Therefore, we partitioned the queries into four attention types (*AType*). Of the 623 queries with recorded fixation in any AOI, 334 have fixation data for both QLists and the QBox: we label these as *LBBoth*. For another 74 queries, fixations are recorded for QLists with no QBox fixations (*QListOnly*), and for another 150, fixations are recorded for the QBox but not QLists (*QBoxOnly*). For the other 65 queries, the only fixations recorded are in other areas of the screen (*Aother*). Table 7 lists the ATypes, with the probability of an XQType for each (P(XQType | AType), along with the mean QFT and TGD for each XQ-Type. Note that for all ATypes, even when attention was on QListOnly, a keyed box query was the most likely outcome. Also note that 6 of the possible 16 outcomes have Ns under 5 cases.

The comparisons discussed below were made using ANOVA with a model that included the main effects of AType, topic, subject, and XQType. The interaction of AType and XQ-Types was also included. Post-hoc analysis was performed using Scheffe's test.

Analysis revealed significant differences in gaze duration (TGD) between the four attention types (F(3,569)=12.8,

		Cluster 1	Cluster 2
QType	QacQ	.54	.13
	BoxQ	.45	.83
SubType	Click	.39	.18
	Enter Key	.60	.79
	N (sessions)	104	128

Table 6: Usage rates for QType and SubType (unadjusted mean probabilities), by cluster.

p<.001), as well as between XQTypes (F(3,569)=3.6, p<.05) and subjects (F(28,569)=10.9, p<.001). The effect of topic approached significance (F(11,569)=1.8, p=.05) and the interaction was not significant (p=.536). Estimated marginal means for log(TGD) are depicted in Figure 5 (left). The post-hoc Scheffe test of attention type resulted in four separate subsets, one for each type. TGD was longest for queries with fixations found on both QList and QBox (mean=6.6 secs, s.d.=4.7), shortest for queries where the only fixations recorded were on other AOIs (mean=1.7 secs, s.d.=2.5). QBoxOnly (mean=4.2 secs, s.d.=4.0) and QListOnly (mean=2.9 secs, s.d.=2.4) were in separate subsets between these extremes. The post hoc Scheffe test of XQType identified three separate subsets, with clicked QACs in the subset with the longest TGD (mean=7.1 secs, s.d.=4.8) and clicked box queries in a separate subset (mean=4.9 secs, s.d.=3.4). Keyed QACs (mean=3.6 secs, s.d.=3.1) and keyed Box queries (mean=4.8 secs, s.d.=4.6) were in one subset, with the shortest durations.

The analysis of QFT reveals a somewhat different pattern of results. Estimated marginal means are depicted in Figure 5 (right). XQType (p=.491) and topic (p=.105) were not significant factors in the model, however, attention type (F(3,569)=4.6, p<.001) and subject (F(28,569)=4.8, p=.001) were. As with TGD, QFT was longest for queries where both the QList and QBox are fixated (mean=14.1, s.d.=8.3) and shortest where only other AOIs are fixated (mean=8.1, s.d.=11.7). Where only QBox or QList are fixated there is no significant difference in mean QFT. The interaction was significant (F(8,569)=2.6, p<.01); however it was due to cells with small Ns and high variability, so we draw no conclusion from the result.

Figure 5 (left) presents a clear picture of the longer fixation-time used when the searcher attended to both the QBox and the QList. This suggests that, relative to looking at only one option, additional time was used for decision making between QacQ and BoxQ, and this additional time is similar no matter the outcome. For queries where subjects focused on only one area, TGD is very similar for each XQType, with clicked submissions requiring additional fixation time relative to keyed submissions. The pattern across XQtypes is similar for the AOther state. The additional TGD used for clicked QACs suggests an extra load on visual attention in order to coordinate cursor movement to the selected QACs. Figure 5 (right) shows a similar pattern in the additional query formulation time used when attention focused on both the QList and the QBox. This suggests that the time cost of visual attention to the QBox and QList has an expected utility other than time-savings for formulation.

6.4 Exploring query entry profiles

Our results on QAC usage (see Section 6.1) reveal large differences among searchers. Recent behavioral models of QAC usage also suggest that searchers have differing propensities to use QAC [11, 10]. Factors associated with these preferences are not well understood. The analysis presented in this section sought insight into associations between the search behavior, visual attention, and the use of QACs. We used a three-step process to bin subjects according to QAC usage rates and then analyzed the characteristics of each bin. We describe the procedure and then present results.

Because subjects searched different subsets of the 12 search topics, in order to further explore differences associated with usage rates we used a linear model to isolate and extract variability in QAC usage due to differences in the topics [5, 16]. In this first step, topic identifiers were used as the only factor in the model, which estimated, for each of 232 search sessions, the effect of topic on the probability of using a BoxQ. These effects were then extracted from the actual probabilities, which resulted in a topic-adjusted probability for each session. The same procedure was also used to estimate and extract topic effects on the probability of using a QacQ in the session. In the second step, the two adjusted probabilities were used to cluster the 232 sessions using a TwoStep cluster analysis procedure in SPSS. A two-cluster solution was obtained. Table 6 lists the unadjusted mean probabilities for each Qtype and SubType within each cluster. As can be seen, sessions in cluster 1 are characterized by greater use of QacQs and clicked queries, while sessions in cluster 2 are much less likely to use a QacQ or a click, with greater use of BoxQs and the enter key. In the final step, we binned the subjects according to the frequency of cluster membership for their sessions, as detailed in Table 8. For example, 5 subjects had only 1 session in cluster 1 and 7 sessions in cluster 2; these subjects were assigned to Bin A. A profile was then created for each bin, as detailed next.

A GLM, with bin as a fixed factor and topic as a random factor, was used to analyze main effects on general and specific measures of query behavior. The 13 measures found to be significantly different between bins are listed across the top of Table 9. For these features, Scheffe's post hoc test was used to find significant subsets among the six bins. Where a bin was found to be in only one subset, this was noted in Table 9, along with the position of the subset in the range of all subsets for the measure. The positions were labeled according to the nature of the measure. For example, for QFT, bins in the subset with the shortest time of were labeled *fast*, and those with the longest time were labeled *slow*. Table 9 is the outcome of that analysis, with empty cells representing bins found in more than one subset, and therefore, not at an extreme of the measure. Using this information, we then drew tentative profiles of the searchers in each bin, as follows.

Searchers in Bin A (fast Boxers) work quickly, submitting box queries to the exclusion of QAC queries, using the enter key almost exclusively, with very little attention to the screen other than to the QBox. Those in Bin B (touch typists) are similar to A, working quickly and mostly using BoxQs and the enter key, but not to the exclusion of QacQs and clicks. They look at the QList very rarely but they do focus on the QBox, as they rarely have a missing fixation. Searchers in Bin C (slow and methodical typists) work slowly to create many long queries in the query box. Although they tend to focus a great deal of attention to all parts of the screen, they are likely to focus on the QBox alone for many queries, and rarely focus on only the QList. Searchers in Bin D (Agnostic mousers) use both BoxQs and QacQs, attending to both the QBox and QLists, but using more time focused on QLists than the query box. Queries

Attention Type (AType)	QType	SubType	XQType	N	P(XQType | AType)	QFT	TGD
Box GD > 0 QAC GD > 0 LBBoth	QAC	click	CQ	90	27%	14.6 (1.2)	7.8 (4.7)
		key	KQ	43	13%	9.0 (0.8)	4.2 (3.3)
	Box	click	CB	20	6%	17.0 (2.0)	5.5 (3.8)
		key	KB	181	54%	14.8 (0.6)	6.7 (4.9)
Box GD > 0 QAC GD = 0 QBoxOnly	QAC	click	CQ	0	0%	–	–
		key	KQ	4	3%	7.1 (1.2)	1.8 (1.6)
	Box	click	CB	16	11%	12.8 (2.0)	4.8 (3.1)
		key	KB	130	87%	10.8 (0.6)	4.2 (4.2)
Box GD = 0 QAC GD > 0 QListOnly	QAC	click	CQ	13	13%	10.8 (1.0)	2.7 (2.6)
		key	KQ	25	25%	7.6 (0.7)	3.3 (2.8)
	Box	click	CB	2	2%	15.2 (0.8)	3.1 (2.4)
		key	KB	34	34%	9.7 (0.8)	2.7 (2.2)
Box GD = 0 QAC GD = 0 Aother	QAC	click	CQ	3	3%	37.7 (45.0)	2.8 (2.4)
		key	KQ	3	3%	3.5 (0.9)	0.5 (0.1)
	Box	click	CB	2	2%	12.0 (10.6)	1.8 (<.1)
		key	KB	57	57%	6.7 (5.6)	1.7 (2.6)

Table 7: Gaze analysis by attention type.

Bin	N (subjects in bin)	Number of sessions in: Cluster 1	Cluster 2
A	5	1	7
B	5	2	6
C	4	3	5
D	5	4	4
E	4	5	3
F	5	6	2
F	1	7	1

Table 8: Cut-points for assigning subjects to bins.

are submitted by clicking the mouse, to the near exclusion of the enter key. The high visual attention to the screen may be explained by the reliance on the mouse and the need to track the mouse cursor visually. Those in Bin E (fast and unfocused agnostics) work quickly to submit a lot of QacQs, but they also use BoxQs. Although a lot of their visual attention is given to QLists and very little is given elsewhere, they have a lot of missed fixations and may be focused on the keyboard. Finally, searchers in Bin F (fast QACers) also work quickly, but create very short queries that are likely to be QacQs. Their attention often focuses on the QList only, and rarely on the QBox.

7. DISCUSSION

We find that the propensity to use QACs differs among searchers, and that search topics have a large effect on QAC usage. For our subjects, search was easiest for the topics with the highest QAC usage. We also found that system performance, as measured by NDCG@3, was greater when a QAC was used. In examining gaze fixations during query formulation, we found that attention was focused on the QList, the query box, or somewhere else. Total gaze duration was longest when attention was shared between a QList and the QBox, and this was true for all four types of queries. We hypothesize that some of the additional time was due to the decision on whether to use a QAC. Gaze was longer when a query was submitted using a mouse click. We hypothesize that this was due to visuomotor coordination required to move the cursor to a QAC. Also, when the type of submission and the location of visual attention were included in the model for query formulation time, we found the gaze location was associated with QFT but the type and submission mode of the query were not.

Perhaps counter-intuitively, when a QAC was used, it took subjects longer to formulate a query, but with less typing. Consistent with the finding of Li et al. [10], typing was faster when a QAC was not used; however, our results on gaze duration and query formulation time suggest that additional formulation time was not used for typing. While over the whole formulation interval the average typing speed was faster when QACs were not used, it may be that for clicked QAC queries, typing speed is no slower if we take into account the time spent selecting and then clicking a QAC.

These findings suggest a time cost for visual attention to QACs and for using the mouse for submission, which is the most likely entry mode for using a QAC. The cost of the time spent in focusing on the screen is not gained back by a reduction in the formulation time. We speculate that the value of using a QAC is realized later, perhaps by reducing the number of additional queries needed or by increasing the value of the information found. Our data supports this last idea: QacQs resulted in significantly higher NDCG@3 than BoxQs.

Considering the difference in QAC usage among searchers, we explored associations between the search behavior, visual attention, and the use of QACs to identify six profiles of query entry. Due to the exploratory character of our study, these findings raise questions for future research.

Our findings have implications for the development of behavioral models for QAC quality and learning-to-rank for QACs. Recent modeling of QAC "skip bias", or the likelihood of not using a QAC, has found that typing speed was the most important predictive feature [11, 10]. These models do not include the searcher's preference for query submission types (click vs key), which may be a stable and informative feature. Further, if visuomotor factors limit the usability of QACs for some searchers, this has implications for interface design. More generally, our findings are a reminder that the searcher is expending cognitive resources on more than query term selection, relevance judgments, and attendant visual processes. Interaction involves the keyboard, mouse, visual design, and associated affordances, which engage the whole searcher. This motivates consideration of embodied cognition in work on interactive information retrieval [12].

This work has several limitations. Our analysis is exploratory; the data guided our questions and statistical tests, which are not confirmatory. The study itself was relatively small and our design was not balanced, making some analysis cumbersome. We altered the scale of the interface and

Bin	Profile name	Behavior QFT	Query length	SubType Click	Enter key	Qtype QAC	Box	Fixation duration Qlist	Qbox	Other AOI	Total	Attention Location Box only	QAC only	Missed fixations
A	Fast Boxers	fast		few	many	few	many	short		short	short			
B	Touch typists	fast		few		few							few	few
C	Slow and methodical typists	slow	long				many	long	long	long	long	many	few	
D	Agnostic mousers			many	few			long		long				
E	Fast unfocused agnostics	fast				many		long	short	short				many
F	Fast QACers	fast	short			many	few	long	short			few	many	

Table 9: Query entry profiles

removed noise from search results (ads, images), all of which reduce the generalizability of our findings.

8. CONCLUSIONS

This paper contributes to better understanding of the use of query auto completion and factors that affect use. Our findings extend prior work by examining QAC usage in the context of completed search sessions across multiple topics, and by comparing search behavior and visual attention for queries that used QAC to queries that did not. We also contribute a set of exploratory profiles for QAC usage, which raise questions about the role of typing skill and visuomotor effort in the propensity to disuse QAC. There are many directions for future work, including a more detailed analysis of how QAC usage changes over the course of a search session and the temporal dynamics of interaction, such as typing speed, and how these affect visual attention. We speculate that, much as searchers have developed strong habits with respect to ranked lists, they have similarly developed habits with respect to suggestion. Also of interest are effects due to various possible signals of QAC quality, such as the length of QAC lists. The ultimate goal of these questions is a deeper understanding of how query assistance fails or succeeds, so that more effective mechanisms may be designed.

9. REFERENCES

[1] P. Anick and R. G. Kantamneni. A Longitudinal Study of Real-time Search Assistance Adoption. In *Proc. of SIGIR'08*, pages 701–702, New York, NY, 2008. ACM.

[2] H. A. Feild and J. Allan. Using CrowdLogger for in Situ Information Retrieval System Evaluation. In *Proc. of the 2013 Workshop on Living Labs for Information Retrieval Evaluation*, LivingLab '13, pages 15–18, New York, NY, 2013. ACM.

[3] H. A. Feild, J. Allan, and J. Glatt. CrowdLogging: Distributed, Private, and Anonymous Search Logging. In *Proc. of SIGIR'11*, pages 375–384, New York, NY, 2011. ACM.

[4] L. A. Granka, T. Joachims, and G. Gay. Eye-tracking analysis of user behavior in WWW search. In *Proc. of SIGIR'04*, pages 478–479, New York, NY, 2004. ACM.

[5] J. Gwizdka. Distribution of cognitive load in Web search. *J. of the American Society for Info. Sci. and Tech.*, 61(11):2167–2187, 2010.

[6] K. Hofmann, B. Mitra, F. Radlinski, and M. Shokouhi. An Eye-tracking Study of User Interactions with Query Auto Completion. In *Proc. of CIKM'14*, pages 549–558, New York, NY, 2014. ACM.

[7] T. Joachims, L. Granka, B. Pan, H. Hembrooke, and G. Gay. Accurately interpreting clickthrough data as implicit feedback. In *Proc. of SIGIR'05*, pages 154–161, New York, NY, 2005. ACM.

[8] T. Joachims, L. Granka, B. Pan, H. Hembrooke, F. Radlinski, and G. Gay. Evaluating the accuracy of implicit feedback from clicks and query reformulations in Web search. *ACM Trans. Inf. Syst.*, 25(2), Apr. 2007.

[9] D. Kelly, K. Gyllstrom, and E. W. Bailey. A Comparison of Query and Term Suggestion Features for Interactive Searching. In *Proc. of SIGIR'09*, pages 371–378, New York, NY, 2009. ACM.

[10] L. Li, H. Deng, A. Dong, Y. Chang, H. Zha, and R. Baeza-Yates. Analyzing User's Sequential Behavior in Query Auto-Completion via Markov Processes. In *Proc. of SIGIR'15*, pages 123–132, New York, NY, 2015. ACM.

[11] Y. Li, A. Dong, H. Wang, H. Deng, Y. Chang, and C. Zhai. A Two-dimensional Click Model for Query Auto-completion. In *Proc. of SIGIR'14*, SIGIR '14, pages 455–464, New York, NY, 2014. ACM.

[12] C. P. Lueg. The missing link: Information behavior research and its estranged relationship with embodiment. *Journal of the Association for Information Science and Technology*, 66(12):2704–2707, Dec. 2015.

[13] B. Mitra, M. Shokouhi, F. Radlinski, and K. Hofmann. On User Interactions with Query Auto-completion. In *Proc. of SIGIR'14*, pages 1055–1058, New York, NY, 2014. ACM.

[14] X. Niu and D. Kelly. The use of query suggestions during information search. *Info. Proc. & Mgmt.*, 50(1):218–234, Jan. 2014.

[15] C. Shah, J. Liu, R. González-Ibáñez, and N. Belkin. Exploration of dynamic query suggestions and dynamic search results for their effects on search behaviors. *Proc. of ASIST'12*, 49(1):1–10, Jan. 2012.

[16] C. L. Smith and P. B. Kantor. User Adaptation: Good Results from Poor Systems. In *Proc. of SIGIR'08*, pages 147–154, New York, NY, 2008. ACM.

[17] R. W. White and G. Marchionini. Examining the effectiveness of real-time query expansion. *Info. Proc. & Mgmt.*, 43(3):685–704, 2007.

[18] E. Williams. Experimental Designs Balanced for the Estimation of Residual Effects of Treatments. *Australian J. of Chem.*, 2(2):149–168, Jan. 1949.

[19] A. Zhang, A. Goyal, W. Kong, H. Deng, A. Dong, Y. Chang, C. A. Gunter, and J. Han. adaQAC: Adaptive Query Auto-Completion via Implicit Negative Feedback. In *Proc. of SIGIR'15*, pages 143–152, New York, NY, 2015. ACM.

What Affects Word Changes in Query Reformulation During a Task-based Search Session?

Jiepu Jiang
Center for Intelligent Information Retrieval
College of Information and Computer Sciences
University of Massachusetts Amherst
jpjiang@cs.umass.edu

Chaoqun Ni
School of Library and Information Science
Simmons College
chaoqun.ni@simmons.edu

ABSTRACT

This paper performs an analysis on the influence of different factors on users' choices of specific word changes in query reformulation during a search session. We study three types of word changes: whether to remove or retain a word in the current query; whether or not to add a brand-new word to the query; whether or not to reuse a word (included in previous queries, but removed in the current query). Three types of factors are examined: session-level factors measuring task and user characteristics; query-level factors related to past user activities in a session; word-level factors for the characteristics of the examined word and its relation to the current query and search results. Statistical analysis suggests that: word-level factors strongly influence all three types of word changes; query-level factors only show a clear influence on retaining or removing a word; task-level factors exhibit limited direct influence on all three types of word changes. Analysis also disclose reasons for different word changes: users remove a word to stop exploring a subtask, or to correct bad performing queries; they look for related, unused words from recently viewed result summaries and add to queries; reusing a word usually indicates reverting from a subtask to the main task or another subtask.

Keywords

Query reformulation; search session; context; task.

1. INTRODUCTION

Some simple information needs such as finding home pages may be satisfied by a single query and one click, but it usually requires multiple searches to solve more complex tasks. The reasons vary. For example, sometimes it is the user who employs a divide and conquer strategy, using each query to deal with a part of the task [3]. Sometimes it is the user's limited knowledge about the problem that makes search and query formulation difficult [4]. For whichever reason, a complex search problem usually involves more than one query (a search session).

CHIIR '16, March 13-17, 2016, Carrboro, NC, USA

© 2016 ACM. ISBN 978-1-4503-3751-9/16/03...$15.00

DOI: http://dx.doi.org/10.1145/2854946.2854978

The activity to modify an existing query and perform a new search is called *query reformulation*. Previous work [1, 5, 11, 12, 26] studied patterns of reformulation at query level, such as adding, deleting, and replacing words. These patterns provide insights on how query reformulations look like, but they also have a few limitations:

- They do not look into specific words, e.g., why users add or remove a specific word instead of others.

- They are patterns for the *outcome* of users' query reformulations, but are not necessarily indicative of users' decisions in query reformulation or the reasons for reformulation.

In contrast, we focus on individual and specific word changes in query reformulation. All vocabulary differences in query reformulation can be decomposed into three types of word changes: to retain or remove a word in the current query; to add a brand-new word to the next query or not; whether or not to reuse a word that was involved in previous queries, but removed in the current query. These word changes stand for finer-grained decisions compared with the query-level reformulation patterns.

We examine the influence of three categories of factors on word changes: session-level factors measuring task and user characteristics; query-level factors related to past user activities in a session; word-level factors for the characteristics of the examined word and its relation to the current query and search results.

2. RELATED WORK

2.1 Query Reformulation

Query reformulation, in the scope of this paper, refers to the activity of formulating a query that is different from an existing one. We focus on the difference of the two queries.

Previous work characterized patterns of reformulation at query level [1, 5, 11, 12, 26]. Some are characterized from the lexical aspect, for example: adding words, removing words, replacing words by synonyms, spelling correction, stemming, case change, and using acronyms. Some are concerned with syntactic differences, for example: punctuation, reordering words, and using search operators. Some patterns may imply users' intents, for example: specification, generalization, and subtopic change. These patterns are not exclusive of each other. For example, one can reformulate a more specific query (specification) either by adding words, or replacing words with more specific ones.

In contrast to previous work, we look into changes in query reformulation at word level—the unit of analysis in our study is a specific word, and whether users will remove, retain, or add the word in query reformulation. This is also relevant to previous work on choices of words in query reformulation and interactive relevance feedback.

Spink et al. [30] studied five sources of query terms in mediated online searching. Among the sources they examined, question statement is similar to task description in our study, and we also consider relevance feedback as a source for new terms. In addition, the content of search results is also an important source of knowledge for query reformulation [18]. Yue et al. [33] examined possible sources of query words in collaborative search. Some of them may also be applied to other types of searches, including users' past queries and viewed search results. Another source we examined is query suggestions displayed on the SERP. Kelly et al. [17] compared term and query suggestions, where users reported that query suggestions provide ideas for manually formulating queries; Jiang et al. [13] reported that before query reformulation, searchers viewed task description and query suggestions more frequently.

The word changes we examined in this paper were rarely studied in previous work from the user's perspective. However, some work built technical solutions for contextual search and query suggestion based on these word changes. Guan et al. [10] separately considered added, retained, and removed words in relevance feedback; Dang et al. [8] generated synthesized query suggestions by considering similar patterns.

2.2 Search Session and Search Task

We study query reformulation in the context of a *search session*—a period that the user searches consecutively for the same search task. This definition is ideal. Practically a user may perform multiple tasks in an interleaved way [29]. In such case, one needs to identify and concatenate queries for each unique task [14] to obtain such sessions.

Search task [31] is a widely studied factor influencing user interaction in a search session. Li et al. [19] classified task from six facets: source, task doer, time, products, process, and goal. We examine the influence of task goal and product on word changes. Other ways of characterizing search tasks exist [16, 32], but we do not consider them in this study.

Much previous work studied search behavior variation in sessions with different task goals [6, 7, 13, 20, 24], products [6, 7, 13, 20, 24], complexity [6, 7, 24], and at different stages [22, 23], and etc. However, few studied the influence of tasks on query reformulation, especially on word changes in query reformulation. Liu et al. [21] compared the frequencies of using different reformulation patterns in different tasks.

3. APPROACH

3.1 Dependent Variables

We use S for a session, q_i for the ith query of a session, and $q_k \rightarrow q_{k+1}$ for the reformulation from q_k to q_{k+1}. We do not consider query reformulations where any of the two queries are query suggestions. When discussing $q_k \rightarrow q_{k+1}$, we call q_k *the current query* and q_{k+1} *the next query* or *the next query*. We consider a query as *a set of words* and ignore word sequence. We also do not consider multiple occurrences of the same word in a query, because this only happens in 2 out of 388 queries in the collected data.

We decompose a user's decisions in $q_k \rightarrow q_{k+1}$ into the following two types of events:

- For each word in q_k, to decide whether to retain or remove the word in the next query (q_{k+1}).

- For each word in C, to decide whether or not to add the word to the next query (q_{k+1}).

Here C stands for a candidate set of words in the user's mind being considered for adding to the next query or not. In this paper we consider two types of words added to the next query. The first type is words that are brand-new in the session, i.e., none of the previous queries included the word. We refer to this case as *adding a new word* and use C_{new} for its candidate set. The second type is words that were involved in past queries (from q_1 to q_{i-1}), but removed in q_i. We refer to this case as *reusing a word* and use C_{reuse} for its candidate set. We separately consider these two types of words because they may stand for different intentions of users. Any added words should belong to either type. We discuss choices of the candidate sets in Section 6.

Any vocabulary changes in a query reformulation can be categorized into the two types of events. Words in the current query are either retained or removed in the next query. Words in C_{new} and C_{used} are either added or not.

Formally, we study three binary dependent variables:

- For $w \in q_k$, $Y_{rmv}(w, q_k, q_{k+1}) = 1$ if the user removes w in $q_k \rightarrow q_{k+1}$, or 0 otherwise.

- For $w \in C_{new}$, $Y_{new}(w, q_k, q_{k+1}) = 1$ if the user adds w to q_{k+1} in $q_k \rightarrow q_{k+1}$, or 0 otherwise.

- For $w \in C_{used}$, $Y_{used}(w, q_k, q_{k+1}) = 1$ if the user adds w to q_{k+1} in $q_k \rightarrow q_{k+1}$, or 0 otherwise.

3.2 Independent Variables

The purpose of this study is to analyze the influence of different factors on word changes, as characterized by the three dependent variables. Table 1 lists all independent variables considered in this paper. We divide them into three groups depending on their relations to the dependent variables.

3.2.1 Session-level Variables

Session-level variables measure factors related to the characteristics of the task and the searcher. Within a search session, every word change in each query reformulation shares the same influence from session-level variables.

We follow Li and Belkin's faceted task classification framework [19] and consider three characteristics of search tasks: the goal of a search task is either clear or amorphous (`goal`); the product of a search task is either factual information, or enhanced intellectual understanding of the user (`product`); user's self-rated familiarity on the task using a five-point Likert scale (`familiarity`).

In addition, we suspect that users' choices of word changes in a query reformulation may also depend on individual preference. Some searchers may prefer to add or remove words in general. In order to capture this factor, we compute the average number of added (`avg_num_add`) and removed words (`avg_num_rmv`) during a query reformulation in other sessions performed by the same searcher as surrogates for the users' preferences for adding or removing words.

Table 1: Independent variables for analyzing word changes in query reformulation.

Group	Variable	Explanation
session	goal	0 if the goal of the search task is clear, or 1 if it is amorphous [19].
	product	0 if the task looks for factual information, or 1 if for intellectual understanding [19].
	familiarity	User's self-rated familiarity regarding the topic of the task using a five-point likert scale.
	avg_num_rmv/add	Average number of removed/added words in other sessions by the same user.
query	q_length	Length of the current query (excluding stop words).
	q_duration	Time duration from the submission of the current query to that of the new query.
	q_clickpos	Position of the lowest ranked clicked results on the SERP, or 0 if no click.
	num_query	Number of submitted queries in the session (including the current query).
	num_click	Number of past clicks in the session (including clicks on the current query's SERP).
	duration	Time duration from the beginning of the session to the submission of the new query.
word	idf	IDF of the word in the ClueWeb09 collection.
	p(w|pastq)	Probability of the word appearing in past queries of the session.
	avg_jaccard	Average Jaccard similarity of the word with other words in the current query.
	#click_hasw	Number of clicked results whose title/snippet/URL contains the word.
	#skip_hasw	Number of skipped results whose title/snippet/URL contains the word.
	freq_w_suggest	Frequency of the word in query suggestions if users viewed the area, or 0 otherwise.

3.2.2 Query-level Variables

Query-level variables measure factors related to past user activities in a session. These factors apply to a query reformulation as a whole. Each word change in a query reformulation shares the same influence from query-level variables.

We suspect users' choices of word change in a query reformulation is directly influenced by the most recent search. We include variables for the characteristics of the current query, such as q_length, and user activities on its SERP, including q_duration and q_clickpos. In addition, we include variables for the time of a session when the reformulation happened, including num_query, num_click, and duration.

3.2.3 Word-level Variables

Word-level variables measure factors directly related to the word being examined. Different words in the same query reformulation can be affected differently by these variables.

idf indicates word specificity [28], i.e., whether the word is general or specific. p(w|pastq) is the probability that the word w was included in past queries of the session (from q_1 to q_i). We use p(w|pastq) to measure the centrality of a word to the task. Example 1 shows queries in a session, where the task is to find information on the symptoms and treatments of depression. "Depression" is included in every query and expresses the main theme of the task, which is unlikely to be removed in query reformulation.

Example 1	
1	**depression** symptoms
2	**depression** definition
3	**depression** treatment
4	**depression** treatment cost

avg_jaccard measures the connection between the word being examined and other words in the current query using their co-occurrences in documents. Here we define the Jaccard similarity of two words as that between the sets of documents containing each word. When examining a word w, we calculate its Jaccard similarity with each word that is not w in the current query, and use the mean value as an independent variable (avg_jaccard). If there is no other

words in the query, we set the value to the mean value of avg_jaccard in other query reformulations.

In addition, we examine variables measuring occurrences of the word in results displayed on the current query's SERP. We separately consider clicked results (#click_hasw) and skipped results (#skip_hasw). Here we use *skipped results* to refer to those that users viewed their summaries but did not click on. We rely on eye movement to determine skipped results. We separately examine different elements of result summaries, including their titles, snippets, and URLs.

Moreover, we measure occurrences of words in query suggestions displayed on the current query's SERP and viewed by the user (freq_w_suggest). We consider the screen area for query suggestions as a whole. If the SERP provides query suggestions and we observed the user's eye fixations on that area, the variable's value is set to the frequency of the word in all query suggestions. Otherwise, we set its value to 0. We do not consider users' visual attention for individual query suggestions due to the limited accuracy of our device in tracking eye fixations on small items.

3.3 Analysis Approach

We examine the influence of independent variables on the dependent variables using hierarchical (multilevel) logistic regression, a technique that models variables with more than one variance component [9]. More specifically, it deals with a regression model with binary outcome (dependent variable), and varying coefficients of independent variables. This study performs analysis using SPSS 23.

We use hierarchical logistic regression instead of vanilla logistic regression because the observations in this study are nested—we examine multiple word changes nested within a query reformulation, and there can be multiple query reformulations nested within a session as well. In such case, the observations are not independent of each other, because some of them share the same contexts at the query and/or session levels. This violates the independence assumption to apply vanilla logistic regression. In contrast, hierarchical models can handle such issues. We use a hierarchical model with three levels to study word changes (level 1) during a query reformulation (level 2) in a search session (level 3).

However, it should be noted that our approach does not

consider another type of dependency issue in word changes—decisions on one word may depend on those on other words. This is a limitation of our approach.

4. DATA

4.1 User Study

We use data from a previous user study [13] to analyze the proposed questions. The purpose of the user study was to compare search activity patterns in sessions of different types of tasks. The experiment controlled two characteristics of search tasks in Li et al.'s framework [19]: goal (specific or amorphous) and product (factual or intellectual). We did not consider tasks with a mixed goal and other types of product (e.g., image, mixed product) in Li et al.'s framework. Different combinations of task goal (two levels) and product (two levels) define four types of tasks. This is identical to the settings of the TREC session tracks [15] and is similar to many related studies [13, 20, 22, 24].

The experiment used a 2×2 within-subject design. Each subject performed four tasks of different types using an experimental search system. We employed 20 formal subjects and divided them into 5 groups. We assigned different tasks to each group to increase task diversity. Subjects in the same group performed the same 4 tasks, and we rotated task sequence using a Latin square. These tasks were developed by and used in the TREC 2012 session track [15]. In total, we collected 80 sessions from 20 unique subjects on 20 tasks.

The experimental search system provides modified Google search results. It redirects user queries to Google and returns the "10-blue links" and query suggestions (related searches). It removes other results such as sponsored links and direct answers. The system displays search results in the same way Google would display, e.g., the highlight of query terms are retained. The system records user search activities, including queries and clicks. In addition, we collected searchers' eye-movement on the screen using a Tobii 1750 eye-tracker. In this study, we determine that a user viewed a result summary or query suggestions if we observed an eye fixation on the corresponding area on the screen. We set the minimum duration of an eye fixation to 100 milliseconds, a common value adopted in many previous studies of web search behaviors using the same series of eye-tracker.

During experiments, the subjects were first introduced to the experimental search system and a training task. Then, they worked on four formal tasks. After finishing two formal tasks, they took a 10-minute break. For each task, they spent about 10 minutes to search information to solve the task. After each task, they answered post-search questionnaires (we only use their self-rated task familiarity in this study) and judged relevance of results. We required all the subjects to be English native speakers (to reduce the influence of language efficiency) and to have a perfect eyesight without glasses or lens (to ensure accuracy of eye tracking). More details were introduced in a previous article [13].

4.2 Dataset Statistics

The collected dataset includes 80 sessions and 388 requests in total. Among them, 39 are query suggestions, and 36 are turning to different pages of results for the same query. After removing these 75 requests, the rest of the dataset includes 313 queries formulated by the searchers and 203 query reformulations where both queries are formulated by the searchers. The average length of a query is 3.37 words excluding stop words (we use the stop words list in Indri). Among the 203 query reformulations, 158 removed at least one word from the current query, and 186 added at least one word to the next query. On average searchers removed 1.56 words and added 1.68 words during a query reformulation.

5. REMOVING OR RETAINING A WORD

This section reports results for whether to remove or retain a word in query reformulation (Y_{rmv}). As discussed in Section 3.1, we examine each word in the current query (q_i) when studying $q_i \rightarrow q_{i+1}$. This is to assume that users consider each word in the current query and make decisions on whether to remove or retain the word in the next query. This yields 687 observations of Y_{rmv} from 203 query reformulations, where 304 (44%) are positive ($Y_{rmv} = 1$).

Table 2 reports results for hierarchical logistic regression, where Y_{rmv} is the dependent variable. $\exp(B) > 1$ suggests a positive influence of the independent variable on Y_{rmv}, and $\exp(B) < 1$ indicates a negative one. Model 1 includes only session-level variables and constant. Model 2 further includes query-level variables. Model 3 includes all variables.

We transform some variables by taking natural log values to make them linear, including: `q_length`, `q_duration`, and `avg_jaccard`. We examine multicollinearity using the variance inflation factor (VIF). A value greater than 5 suggests a cause for concern, and a value greater than 10 indicates a serious collinearity problem [25]. We exclude `avg_num_add` due to its high correlation with `avg_num_rmv` ($r = 0.85$). Similarly, we remove `#click_url_hasw` because of its correlation with `#click_title_hasw` ($r = 0.86$) and `#skip_url_hasw` ($r = 0.83$ with `#skip_title_hasw`). All variables included in Table 2 satisfy VIF < 5.

5.1 Influence of Session-level Variables

Session-level variables show certain influence on whether to remove or retain a word in query reformulation. Model 1 explains the collected data significantly better than a baseline model including only constant ($p < 0.001$ by the Omnibus test). However, the magnitude of change in -2 log likelihood is small, indicating only a mild influence.

Among these variables, only the user's average number of removed words in other sessions (`avg_num_rmv`) consistently shows a significant positive effect in all three models—users are more likely to remove a word in a session if they removed words more frequently in other sessions. This suggests that a user's overall preference to remove a word may affect their decisions on removing or retaining a word in a specific session. Some users may prefer to remove words in query reformulations in general, and they are likely to do so in a specific session. But it is unclear whether such preference is related to other factors, e.g., search expertise.

Task product (`product`), goal (`goal`), and topic familiarity (`familiarity`) have no significant effects in any models. This indicates that the examined task characteristics may not directly affect removing or retaining a word.

5.2 Influence of Query-level Variables

Query-level variables also show certain influence on Y_{rmv}. After including query-level variables, Model 2 significantly improves over Model 1 ($p < 0.001$). Over half of the query-level variables show significant effects in both Model 2 and Model 3. This suggests that removing or retaining a word

Table 2: Results for hierarchical logistic regressions: Y_{rmv} as dependent variable.

Step	Variable Name	Model 1 exp(B)		Model 2 exp(B)		Model 3 exp(B)		95% CI	
1	constant	0.236	***	0.039	***	0.068	***	-	-
	product (intellectual)	0.974		0.682		0.825		0.545	1.250
	goal (amorphous)	1.001		0.926		0.929		0.638	1.353
	familiarity	1.018		1.064		1.085		0.917	1.283
	avg_num_rmv	2.123	***	1.626	**	1.559	*	1.063	2.285
2	q_length (log)			2.067	***	1.675	*	1.117	2.511
	q_duration (log)			1.334	**	1.570	***	1.236	1.993
	q_clickpos			1.042		1.130	**	1.038	1.230
	num_query			1.213	***	1.165	***	1.077	1.261
	num_click			0.953		0.959		0.897	1.026
	duration			0.905	*	0.885	*	0.804	0.974
3	idf					0.928		0.845	1.019
	p(w|pastq)					0.216	***	0.123	0.378
	avg_jaccard (log)					0.851	*	0.749	0.966
	#click_title_hasw					0.734	**	0.590	0.912
	#click_snippet_hasw					0.946		0.767	1.165
	#skip_title_hasw					0.921		0.797	1.065
	#skip_snippet_hasw					0.916		0.813	1.032
	freq_w_suggest					0.941		0.844	1.049
	−2 Log Likelihood (baseline 943.3)	917.3		877.1		802.5			
	Omnibus Tests of Model Coefficients	$p < 0.001$		$p < 0.001$		$p < 0.001$			

*, **, and *** indicate statistical significance at 0.05, 0.01, and 0.001 levels, respectively.

can be influenced by past user interaction in the session.

The length of the current query (q_length) shows a significant positive effect—users are more likely to remove a word in relatively longer queries. This is not surprising considering longer queries are more likely to include words that are unnecessary for the task.

Results also suggest that users are more likely to remove a word if they spent a relatively longer time on the current query (q_duration shows a significant positive effect) and clicked on results on the current query's SERP (q_clickpos shows a significant positive effect). This indicates a situation that the current query retrieved some relevant information (such that users would spend time on examining the results, instead of quickly reformulating to the next query without clicking). We further examined the collected data and found that this is probably because the majority of the removal happened when users had (successfully) finished exploring a facet of the task (a subtask) and switch to another subtask. Section 5.4 discusses more details.

In addition, results suggest that users are more likely to remove a word if they submitted many queries in a session (a significant positive effect of num_query), but they are less likely to do so with the time goes by in a session (a significant negative effect of duration). The two trends are seemingly conflicting with each other, since the time spent in a session (duration), unsurprisingly, has a moderate correlation with the number of issued queries (num_query) ($r = 0.52$). But the two variables may also stand for two different factors.

Submitting more queries does not necessarily mean a better search progress, because querying and SERP examination themselves provide limited relevant information. Submitting many queries may even indicate limited search performance, e.g., previous studies reported that users will compensate limited search performance by searching more frequently [2, 27]. The number of clicks (num_click), in con-

trast, may better indicate the amount of relevant information acquired in a search session, even though not all clicked results are relevant. In the collected data, duration better correlates with num_click ($r = 0.61$), while num_query only slightly correlates with num_click ($r = 0.33$).

As such, we believe results for num_query, num_click, and duration in Table 2 indicate two possible factors for whether to remove or retain a word in query reformulation. On the one hand, users are more likely to remove a word when the session has limited search effectiveness, which is supported by the significant positive effect of num_query and its connection with limited search performance reported in previous studies [2, 27]. On the other hand, searchers are less likely to remove a word after acquiring more relevant information, as suggested by the negative effect of duration and num_click. Note that in Table 2, num_click shows no significant effect, but this is in fact influenced by the relatively high correlation between num_click and duration ($r = 0.61$). After excluding duration, num_click shows a significant negative effect (exp(B) = 0.917, $p = 0.005$).

5.3 Influence of Word-level Variables

Word-level variables show a strong influence on whether to remove or retain a word in query reformulation. After including word-level variables, Model 3 significantly improves over Model 2 ($p < 0.001$). The −2 log likelihood reduces by 74.6 compared with Model 2. The magnitude is greater than that for the combination of session and query-level variables (66.2). This suggests word-level variables are more salient factors than session and query-level variables for removing or retaining a word in query reformulation.

The frequency of using a word in past queries of the same session (p(w|pastq)) has a significant negative effect on removing the word—users are less likely to remove a word that appeared frequently in previous queries. As we discussed in

Table 3: Mean values (S.E.) of variables for removed and retained words (post-hoc analysis).

Variables	Removed	Retained	
`#click_title_hasw`	0.63 (0.06)	1.03 (0.08)	***
`#click_snippet_hasw`	0.97 (0.08)	1.27 (0.09)	**
`#click_url_hasw`	0.46 (0.05)	0.78 (0.06)	***
`#skip_title_hasw`	1.17 (0.09)	1.75 (0.09)	***
`#skip_snippet_hasw`	2.02 (0.11)	2.49 (0.11)	**
`#skip_url_hasw`	0.82 (0.07)	1.30 (0.08)	***
`#unclick_title_hasw`	2.69 (0.16)	3.85 (0.15)	***
`#unclick_snippet_hasw`	4.25 (0.15)	5.15 (0.13)	***
`#unclick_url_hasw`	2.03 (0.13)	2.91 (0.13)	***
`freq_w_suggest`	0.35 (0.08)	0.64 (0.10)	*

*, **, and *** indicate significance at 0.05, 0.01, and 0.001 levels, respectively, by a two-tail Welch's t-test.

Section 3.2.3, this is probably because words repeatedly used in a session indicate the main theme of the task, which is less likely to be excluded in queries.

Results also suggest that users are more likely to remove a word that does not co-occur frequently with other words in the current query (`avg_jaccard` shows a significant negative effect on Y_{rmv}). This usually happens when the word is off-topic, overspecific, or misspelled. In these cases, the word co-occurs with other query words only in a limited number of (if any) documents, causing a low value of `avg_jaccard`.

In addition, results for `#click_hasw` and `#skip_hasw` suggest that searchers are more likely to remove a word in query reformulation if the word appeared less often in the current query's results. Although only `#click_title_hasw` shows a significant negative effect in Table 3, this is affected by the correlations among these variables ($r = 0.77$ between `#click_title_hasw` and `#click_snippet_hasw`, and $r=0.68$ between `#skip_title_hasw` and `#skip_snippet_hasw`). After we removed `#click_title_hasw` and `#skip_title_hasw`, both `#click_snippet_hasw` ($\exp(B) = 0.798$, $p = 0.010$) and `#skip_snippet_hasw` ($\exp(B) = 0.876$, $p = 0.003$) show significant negative effects. Similarly, `#skip_title_hasw` will show a significant negative effect ($\exp(B) = 0.861$, $p = 0.006$) if we remove `#skip_snippet_hasw`.

Results from post-hoc analysis also confirms this finding. Table 3 compares occurrences of the removed and retained words in different result elements. In addition to the clicked and skipped results, we also examine *unclicked* results—any results displayed on the SERP that users did not click on, regardless of whether or not they viewed the results. Table 3 clearly suggests that removed words appear significantly less often in the current query's results compared with the retained words. This applies to all clicked, skipped, and unclicked results, and is consistent among different elements of the results. Therefore, we do not hope to over-emphasize the significant effect of word occurrences in clicked result titles (`#click_title_hasw`) in Table 2. It seems in general users are more likely to remove words that appeared less often in the retrieved results. This may happen when the word is ineffective (cannot retrieve any results containing the word when combining with other query words), or when the word is not central to the main theme of the task.

5.4 Qualitative Analysis

To better interpret results in Table 2, two authors of this article manually examined all 304 cases of word removal and divided them into two groups: removing with satisfaction (SAT remove), and removing due to dissatisfaction (DSAT remove). The Cohen's κ is 0.72. They further discussed the disagreements in annotation and came into a final decision. 199 (65%) removed words are classified as SAT remove, and 105 (35%) are DSAT remove. SAT remove is more frequent than DSAT remove in the collected data.

SAT remove stands for the case that a word has successfully served its purpose in a query and is removed afterwards. It usually happens when users finished exploring one facet of the task (a subtask) and plan to switch to another. Example 2 shows queries, the number of clicks, and the time spent on each query in a session. Removed words are highlighted. Removed words in the third, fourth, fifth, and sixth queries were labeled SAT removes. These words all indicate different subtopics related to sunspot, the main theme of the task. The user clicked on some results and spent relatively longer time on each of these queries, indicating they might have acquired some useful information, and the removed words might have successfully served their purposes.

Example 2			#click	time
1	what are sunspots	-	1	93s
2	are sunspots a **new phenomena**	DSAT	0	14s
3	when were sunspots **first observed**	SAT	2	103s
4	are sunspots **random** or **patterned**	SAT	2	150s
5	sunspots and **earths climate**	SAT	1	142s
6	sunspots **11 year cycle**	SAT	1	94s
7	sunspots magnetic fields	-	1	-

In contrast, DSAT remove stands for the case that a word did not fulfill the searcher's purpose of using it in the query. The query usually retrieves low quality results, such that the user did not click on any results and spent only a short duration on the SERP. In the second query of Example 2, *new* and *phenomena* were labeled DSAT removes. The searcher showed a similar intent in the second and the third queries, but did not click on any results for the second query. We examined the second query's SERP and found that the retrieved results seem not useful—none include both *new* and *phenomena* in the summaries. Therefore, the user rephrased the query and removed the two words in the next query.

The greater popularity of SAT remove in the collected data explains why results in Table 2 suggest that users tend to remove a word when they spent a relatively longer time on the current query (`q_duration`) and clicked on its results (`q_clickpos`). However, we did also observe a substantial number of DSAT removes (35%). This is concealed by the positive effects of `q_duration` and `q_clickpos`.

5.5 Summary

To summarize, results in this section suggest that users remove a word mainly for two reasons. Firstly, the word has already fulfilled its purpose and becomes less useful (SAT remove)—users need to remove the word in query reformulation in order to move forward in the session. This is supported by: users spent a longer time on the current query (`q_duration`) and clicked on results on the current query's SERP (`q_clickpos`) before they remove a word; removed words appeared less frequently, but still quite often, in the retrieved results (`#skip_snippet_hasw`; searchers are less likely to remove a word if it is related to the main theme of the task (`p(w|pastq)`). Secondly, the word caused limited search performance in the current query (DSAT remove). This conflicts with the positive effects of `q_duration` and `q_clickpos`, but is supported by the qualitative analysis. DSAT remove is also consistent with the observed effects of `avg_jaccard_log` and `#skip_snippet_hasw`. Moreover, removing a word may also be influenced by individual preference in query reformulation (`avg_num_rmv`), query length (`q_length`), overall search performance of the session (`num_query`), and the amount of acquired relevant information in the session (`duration` and `num_click`).

6. ADDING A WORD

6.1 Candidate Sets

For a query reformulation $q_i \rightarrow q_{i+1}$, we examine two types of added words: brand-new word (Y_{new}) that was not used in any previous queries; used words (Y_{reuse}) that was included in past queries (from q_1 to q_{i-1}), but removed in the current query (q_i). We separately study these two cases, because they may stand for different intentions of users.

We can observe all added words in query reformulations, but it is difficult to determine the words that users considered but did not added. We refer to the set of words that users consider for whether or not to add to the new query as *candidate set*. In this study, we implement the candidate sets for Y_{new} and Y_{reuse} as follows:

The candidate set for Y_{reuse} includes all words in previous queries (from q_1 to q_{i-1}) excluding those in the current query (q_i). This is to assume that during a query reformulation, users reconsider each previously used word that was excluded in the current query, and decide whether or not to reuse it in the next query. For each session, we apply this rule to extract Y_{reuse}'s candidate set for query reformulations starting from $q_2 \rightarrow q_3$. On average the candidate set for Y_{reuse} includes 4.4 words. This yields 668 observations of Y_{reuse} among 151 query reformulations, where 53 (7.9%) are positive ($Y_{reuse} = 1$).

The candidate set for Y_{new} includes words from three sources: task description, result summaries (both titles and snippets) viewed by the user, and query suggestions viewed by the user. Here we only consider result summaries and query suggestions displayed on the current query's SERP. By definition, the candidate set for Y_{new} excludes words from q_1 to q_i. This is to assume that in a query reformulation, users consider whether or not to add new words related to the task (in task description) and those they recently viewed in result summaries and query suggestions. We extract candidate sets for each query reformulation. On average the candidate set has 71.0 words. In total, we extract 14,413 observations from 203 query reformulations, where 152 (1.05%) are positive ($Y_{new} = 1$).

As Table 4 shows, Y_{new}'s candidate set (all three sources) covers about half (54.9%) of the observed added new words. Task description and viewed result summaries are the major two sources of added new words. In contrast, query suggestions viewed by the users include only 1.3% of the added new words. In this study, we restrict our scope to this candidate set when examining Y_{new}. We do not consider words from clicked result web pages, because at the time of the user experiment [13], we did not store a copy of the visited web pages for that moment. This is a limitation of our study.

6.2 Models

We estimate models for Y_{new} and Y_{reuse} separately. Table 5 reports the results. Similarly, Model 1 includes only

Table 4: Percentage of new words in query reformulations found in different sources.

Source	Percentage
Task description	43.3%
Result summaries viewed by the user	26.7%
Query suggestions viewed by the user	1.3%
All three sources	54.9%
Result titles viewed by the user	15.2%
Result snippets viewed by the user	23.5%

session-level variables and constant, Model 2 further includes query-level variables, and Model 3 uses all variables. We only report coefficients of variables for Model 3 due to limited space. For Model 1 and Model 2, we only report changes in -2 log likelihood (LL) and results for the Omnibus tests.

For Y_{new}, we exclude `p(w|pastq)` from independent variables because by definition, all words in the candidate sets should not appear in previous queries. For both Y_{new} and Y_{reuse}, we exclude `avg_num_rmv` to avoid serious multicolinearity issues (VIF ≥ 5), because it has a high correlation with `avg_num_add` ($r = 0.85$ for Y_{new} and $r = 0.91$ for Y_{reuse}). Similarly, we exclude `click_url_hasw` ($r = 0.71$ with `click_title_hasw`) and `skip_url_hasw` ($r = 0.87$ with `skip_title_hasw`) in Y_{reuse}. The variables included in the reported models all satisfy VIF < 5.

6.3 Influence of Session-level Variables

Results in Table 5 suggest that session-level variables have no significant influence on adding a word or not in query reformulation. This is consistent for both adding a new word (Y_{new}) and reusing a word (Y_{reuse}). None of the session-level variables show any significant effects on Y_{new} or Y_{reuse} in Model 1, Model 2, or Model 3. In addition, for both Y_{new} and Y_{reuse}, Model 1 cannot explain the collected data significantly better than baseline models involving only constant ($p = 0.073$ for Y_{new} and $p = 0.122$ for Y_{reuse}). This indicates that the included task and user characteristics may not directly affect users' decisions on whether or not to add a word in query reformulation.

6.4 Influence of Query-level Variables

Results show that the query-level variables have limited influence on adding a word or not in the next query. This applies to both adding a new word (Y_{new}) and reusing a word (Y_{reuse}). As Table 6 shows, only one query-level variables shows a significant effect on adding new words (Y_{new}) in Model 3, and none have any significant effects on reusing (Y_{reuse}). For Y_{new}, Model 2 significant outperforms Model 1 at 0.05 level, but the magnitude of change in -2 log likelihood is small. For Y_{reuse}, Model 2 does not significantly improve over Model 1 ($p = 0.172$). Even taking into account the limited sample size for Y_{reuse}, we believe results suggest limited influence of the query-level variables on adding a new word and reusing a word in query reformulation.

The length of the current query (`q_length`) shows a significant negative effect on adding a new word (Y_{new}) in Model 3. This is not surprising because longer queries are usually more specific. Adding a new word can make it overspecific.

6.5 Influence of Word-level Variables

Word-level variables show relatively strong influence on whether or not to add a new word to the next query (Y_{new}),

Table 5: Results from hierarchical logistic regressions: Y_{new} and Y_{reuse} as dependent variables.

Variable Name	Y_{new}: Adding a New Word exp(B)		95% CI		Y_{reuse}: Reusing a Word exp(B)		95% CI	
constant	**0.048**	***	-	-	**0.006**	**	-	-
product (intellect)	0.916		0.618	1.357	1.031		0.337	3.153
goal (amorphous)	0.801		0.557	1.153	1.155		0.403	3.313
familiarity	1.059		0.909	1.233	0.847		0.566	1.267
avg_num_add	1.317		0.899	1.930	2.703		0.799	9.143
q_length (log)	**0.615**	*	0.426	0.890	0.913		0.487	1.712
q_duration (log)	1.051		0.824	1.339	1.386		0.878	2.188
q_clickpos	1.031		0.961	1.106	0.902		0.731	1.114
num_query	1.009		0.925	1.101	1.067		0.946	1.205
num_click	0.958		0.898	1.023	0.980		0.821	1.168
duration	0.952		0.867	1.046	0.851		0.681	1.064
idf	1.092		0.990	1.203	1.020		0.860	1.209
p(w|pastq)	-		-	-	**4.663**	*	1.003	21.68
avg_jaccard (log)	**1.395**	***	1.202	1.619	0.965		0.740	1.259
#click_title_hasw	**2.399**	***	1.688	3.410	1.693		0.458	6.253
#click_snippet_hasw	**0.688**	*	0.494	0.957	2.253		0.891	5.694
#click_url_hasw	1.281		0.957	1.717	-		-	-
#skip_title_hasw	**1.442**	*	1.045	1.990	0.824		0.443	1.530
#skip_snippet_hasw	**0.752**	*	0.575	0.985	1.364		0.821	2.268
#skip_url_hasw	0.775		0.548	1.097	-		-	-
freq_w_suggest	0.317		0.049	2.058	3.152		0.810	12.27
−2 LL & Omnibus Tests, Model 1	$1686.2 \rightarrow 1677.6$		$p = 0.073$		$370.3 \rightarrow 363.0$		$p = 0.122$	
−2 LL & Omnibus Tests, Model 2	$1677.6 \rightarrow 1666.8$		$p = 0.036$ *		$363.0 \rightarrow 356.3$		$p = 0.172$	
−2 LL & Omnibus Tests, Model 3	$1666.8 \rightarrow 1598.1$		$p < 0.001$ ***		$356.3 \rightarrow 339.5$		$p < 0.030$ *	

*, **, and *** indicate differences are significant at 0.05, 0.01, and 0.001 levels, respectively.

and they also show a clear influence on reusing words in query reformulation (Y_{reuse}). After including the word-level variables, Model 3 for both Y_{new} and Y_{reuse} significantly improve over Model 2 ($p < 0.001$ for Y_{new}, and $p < 0.030$ for Y_{reuse}). This indicates that the word-level variables are more salient factors for adding a word in query reformulation compared with the session and query-level variables.

Results suggest that users are more likely to add new words that co-occur frequently with existing words in the current query (avg_jaccard shows a significant positive effect on Y_{new}). This is not surprising because words with low avg_jaccard values are more likely off-topic and may retrieve low quality results.

Results also show that users are more likely to add a new word to the next query if it appeared frequently in result titles they viewed on the current query's SERP, regardless of whether or not they clicked on the results (both #click_title_hasw and #skip_title_hasw show significant positive effects on Y_{new}). On the contrary, users are less likely to add a new word if it appeared frequently in the result snippets they viewed on the current query's SERP (both #click_title_hasw and #skip_title_hasw show significant negative effects on Y_{new}). Post-hoc analysis (Table 6) also agrees with these trends. The new words added to the next query ($Y_{new} = 1$) appeared in significantly more clicked ($p < 0.01$) and skipped result titles ($p < 0.05$) compared with other words in the candidate sets ($Y_{new} = 0$). The added new words also appeared in significantly fewer skipped result snippets ($p < 0.05$), although the difference is not significant for clicked result snippet.

This indicates that the occurrences of a new word in result

Table 6: Mean values (S.E.) of variables for new words added and not added to the next query.

Variables	$Y_{new} = 1$	$Y_{new} = 0$	
#click_title_hasw	0.243 (0.054)	0.079 (0.003)	**
#click_snippet_hasw	0.270 (0.058)	0.286 (0.005)	
#click_url_hasw	0.224 (0.050)	0.108 (0.004)	*
#skip_title_hasw	0.257 (0.056)	0.186 (0.004)	*
#skip_snippet_hasw	0.487 (0.074)	0.605 (0.006)	**
#skip_url_hasw	0.191 (0.047)	0.221 (0.006)	

*, **, and *** indicate significance at 0.05, 0.01, and 0.001 levels, respectively, by a two-tail Welch's t-test.

titles may play a more important role on users decisions of whether or not to add the word to the next query. This is probably because result titles are more eye-catching than other elements on the SERP, as most current search engines show result titles using a larger font size than other SERP elements. However, as Table 4 shows, we can only locate 15.2% of the added new words in result titles, in contrast to 23.5% in snippets and 26.7% in summaries (both titles and snippets). This indicates result snippets still provide valuable ideas for new words in query reformulation, but the new words do not necessarily appear more often than other words in result snippets. In fact, both results in Table 5 and Table 6 suggest that they appear less often in snippets compared with other words that were not added to the next query. This is probably because result snippets are noisy, including both relevant and off-topic words.

In contrast, only p(w|pastq) (how frequently the word was used in past queries of the session) shows a significant effect on reusing a word (Y_{reuse}). None of the other word-level variables show any significant effects. This indicates that while reusing a word, users usually simply reuse the word associated to the main theme of the task.

We manually examined the cases of reusing a word in the collected data. We found that reusing a word in query reformulation mostly happens when users revert from a subtask to the main task, or to another subtask. The following table shows an example. The user first explored differences in dehumidifiers in the first two queries, and then switched to look for information related to hygrometer in the third and the fourth queries. After finishing exploring hygrometer, the user reverted back to continue to explore dehumidifier and thus reused the word **dehumidifier** in the fifth query. This example explains why users are more likely to reuse words related to the main theme of the task (with high $p(w|pastq)$ values).

No.	Query
1	differences in dehumidifier
2	differences in dehumidifier 500 sq ft room
3	hygrometer
4	hygrometer amazon
5	**dehumidifier** ACH

6.6 Summary

To summarize, results in this section suggest that adding a brand-new word (Y_{new}) and reusing a word (Y_{reuse}) stand for different intentions of users. Such distinctions were not identified in previous studies. Users exploit highly related, unused words from the results they viewed and include them into the next query, as suggested by the positive effects of `avg_jaccard`, `#click_title_hasw`, and `#skip_title_hasw`. In contrast, they reuse a word when reverting from a subtask to the main task or another subtask, as suggested by the positive effect of $p(w|pastq)$ and manual analysis.

Compared with removing or retaining a word, results show that adding a word is less likely influenced by the session and query-level variables, as suggested by the limited effects of session and query-level variables on both Y_{new} and Y_{reuse}. This indicates that users may make decisions on whether or not to add a word mostly based on local factors that are directly related to the word itself. Such decisions are less likely influenced by task characteristics or past user activities in the session.

7. CONCLUSION

7.1 Findings and Implications

Using both hierarchical logistic regression and qualitative analysis, this paper provides insights on how different factors may affect specific choices of word changes in query reformulations during a task-based search session. This advances the state-of-the-art understanding of query reformulation from query-level patterns [1, 5, 11, 12, 26] to word-level and finer-grained users decisions related to specific words.

Results suggest that word-level variables may strongly influence all three types of word changes. This is not surprising because word-level variables are word-specific, while other two types of factors are not. In contrast, query-level variables only show certain influence on removing or retaining a word, but limited influence on adding and reusing a

word. This indicates that removing or retaining a word may more likely be affected by past user interaction and situation in a session, while adding and reusing a word may not. Session-level variables exhibited limited *direct* influence on all types of word changes. However, we believe they still influence word changes in a session in an *indirect* way. This is based on the fact that much previous work found that task type and user characteristics can affect search behavior patterns in a session [6, 7, 13, 20, 24]. Therefore, session-level variables may affect query and word-level variables and consequently influence word changes in query reformulation.

Comparing the three categories of factors, word-level factors show the strongest influence on all three types of word changes compared with the other two types of factors. Query-level factors show less influence, and session-level factors only exhibit limited direct influence. Results also suggest that these variables may influence different word changes in different ways. For example, word occurrences in result summaries show different patterns for all three types of word changes. This implies the different nature of these word changes In addition, our analysis also help identify effective sets of features for predicting such word changes in an on-going search session. Such techniques may potentially help develop and evaluate interactive search systems.

Moreover, our study also discloses typical scenarios for different types of word changes. Users remove a word in query reformulation for two possible reasons. Firstly, it happens when users finished exploring a subtask and move forward to another. Secondly, it also happens when users try to correct bad performing queries (e.g., removing off-topic or ambiguous words). In our collected data, the former is more prevalent. In contrast, adding a new word usually happens in relevance feedback—users exploit related, unused words from recently viewed result summaries and add them to new queries. Reusing a word mostly happens when searchers revert back from a subtask to the main task, and the reused words are highly related to the main theme of the task.

7.2 Limitations

Our study has a few limitations. Firstly, we study three types of word changes and each individual word change separately. This ignores dependencies among word changes—users' decisions to remove or add a word may depend on the removal or addition of another. Whereas analyzing such dependencies may enlarge the problem space exponentially—most notably it may require a substantially greater amount of data to examine these issues.

Secondly, the approach of generating candidate sets, especially that for adding a new word, is limited. This also resulted in a biased dataset for Y_{new} and Y_{reuse}, where over 90% of the cases are negative. This may be one reason for the limited influence of the session and query-level variables in our analysis. However, we also believe that, as long as the influence of a variable is strong enough, it should still be able to show a significant effect. Yet we may have missed a few variables with slight or moderate effects on word changes.

Thirdly, it should be noted that the search tasks searchers performed in the user study are typically more complex than daily web search information needs. For example, no simple tasks such as navigational searches were included. Results and findings from this study should be generalized with cautious to other tasks with a substantially different nature.

8. ACKNOWLEDGMENT

This work was supported in part by the Center for Intelligent Information Retrieval and in part by NSF grant #IIS-0910884. Any opinions, findings and conclusions or recommendations expressed in this material are those of the authors and do not necessarily reflect those of the sponsor. We thank the anonymous reviewers for their thoughtful and constructive comments.

9. REFERENCES

[1] P. Anick. Using terminological feedback for web search refinement: A log-based study. In *SIGIR '03*, pages 88–95, 2003.

[2] L. Azzopardi. Modelling interaction with economic models of search. In *SIGIR '14*, pages 3–12, 2014.

[3] M. J. Bates. The design of browsing and berrypicking techniques for the online search interface. *Online review*, 13(5):407–424, 1989.

[4] N. J. Belkin, R. N. Oddy, and H. M. Brooks. ASK for information retrieval: Part I. background and theory. *Journal of Documentation*, 38(2):61–71, 1982.

[5] P. Bruza and S. Dennis. Query reformulation on the internet: Empirical data and the hyperindex search engine. In *RIAO '97*, pages 488–499, 1997.

[6] M. J. Cole, J. Gwizdka, C. Liu, R. Bierig, N. J. Belkin, and X. Zhang. Task and user effects on reading patterns in information search. *Interacting with Computers*, 23(4):346–362, 2011.

[7] M. J. Cole, C. Hendahewa, N. J. Belkin, and C. Shah. Discrimination between tasks with user activity patterns during information search. In *SIGIR '14*, pages 567–576, 2014.

[8] V. Dang and B. W. Croft. Query reformulation using anchor text. In *WSDM '10*, pages 41–50, 2010.

[9] A. Gelman and J. Hill. *Data analysis using regression and multilevel/hierarchical models.* Cambridge University, 2006.

[10] D. Guan, S. Zhang, and H. Yang. Utilizing query change for session search. In *SIGIR '13*, pages 453–462, 2013.

[11] J. Huang and E. N. Efthimiadis. Analyzing and evaluating query reformulation strategies in web search logs. In *CIKM '09*, pages 77–86, 2009.

[12] B. J. Jansen, D. L. Booth, and A. Spink. Patterns of query reformulation during web searching. *Journal of the American Society for Information Science and Technology*, 60(7):1358–1371, 2009.

[13] J. Jiang, D. He, and J. Allan. Searching, browsing, and clicking in a search session: Changes in user behavior by task and over time. In *SIGIR '14*, pages 607–616, 2014.

[14] R. Jones and K. L. Klinkner. Beyond the session timeout: Automatic hierarchical segmentation of search topics in query logs. In *CIKM '08*, pages 699–708, 2008.

[15] E. Kanoulas, B. Carterette, M. Hall, P. Clough, and M. Sanderson. Overview of the TREC 2012 session track. In *the Twenty-First Text REtrieval Conference (TREC 2012) Proceedings*, 2012.

[16] D. Kelly, J. Arguello, A. Edwards, and W.-C. Wu. Development and evaluation of search tasks for IIR experiments using a cognitive complexity framework. In *ICTIR '15*, pages 101–110, 2015.

[17] D. Kelly, K. Gyllstrom, and E. W. Bailey. A comparison of query and term suggestion features for interactive searching. In *SIGIR '09*, pages 371–378, 2009.

[18] J. Koenemann and N. J. Belkin. A case for interaction: A study of interactive information retrieval behavior and effectiveness. In *CHI '96*, pages 205–212, 1996.

[19] Y. Li and N. J. Belkin. A faceted approach to conceptualizing tasks in information seeking. *Information Processing & Management*, 44(6):1822–1837, 2008.

[20] C. Liu, N. J. Belkin, and M. J. Cole. Personalization of search results using interaction behaviors in search sessions. In *SIGIR '12*, pages 205–214, 2012.

[21] C. Liu, J. Gwizdka, and N. J. Belkin. Analysis of query reformulation types on different search tasks. In *iConference 2010*, pages 477–485, 2010.

[22] J. Liu and N. J. Belkin. Personalizing information retrieval for multi-session tasks: The roles of task stage and task type. In *SIGIR '10*, pages 26–33, 2010.

[23] J. Liu and N. J. Belkin. Personalizing information retrieval for multi-session tasks: Examining the roles of task stage, task type, and topic knowledge on the interpretation of dwell time as an indicator of document usefulness. *Journal of the Association for Information Science and Technology*, 66(1):58–81, 2015.

[24] J. Liu, M. J. Cole, C. Liu, R. Bierig, J. Gwizdka, N. J. Belkin, J. Zhang, and X. Zhang. Search behaviors in different task types. In *JCDL '10*, pages 69–78, 2010.

[25] S. Menard. *Applied logistic regression analysis, Second Edition.* SAGE publications, 2002.

[26] S. Y. Rieh and H. Xie. Analysis of multiple query reformulations on the web: The interactive information retrieval context. *Information Processing & Management*, 42(3):751–768, 2006.

[27] C. L. Smith and P. B. Kantor. User adaptation: Good results from poor systems. In *SIGIR '08*, pages 147–154, 2008.

[28] K. Spärck Jones. A statistical interpretation of term specificity and its application in retrieval. *Journal of Documentation*, 28(1):11–21, 1972.

[29] A. Spink, M. Park, B. J. Jansen, and J. Pedersen. Multitasking during web search sessions. *Information Processing & Management*, 42(1):264–275, 2006.

[30] A. Spink and T. Saracevic. Interaction in information retrieval: Selection and effectiveness of search terms. *Journal of the American Society for Information Science*, 48(8):741–761, 1997.

[31] P. Vakkari. Task-based information searching. *Annual Review of Information Science and Technology*, 37(1):413–464, 2003.

[32] W.-C. Wu, D. Kelly, A. Edwards, and J. Arguello. Grannies, tanning beds, tattoos and NASCAR. In *IIIX '12*, pages 254–257, 2012.

[33] Z. Yue, S. Han, D. He, and J. Jiang. Influences on query reformulation in collaborative web search. *Computer*, 47(3):46–53, 2014.

Understanding User Satisfaction with Intelligent Assistants

Julia Kiseleva[1,*]   Kyle Williams[2,*]   Jiepu Jiang[3,*]   Ahmed Hassan Awadallah[4]
Aidan C. Crook[4]   Imed Zitouni[4]   Tasos Anastasakos[4]

[1]Eindhoven University of Technology, j.kiseleva@tue.nl
[2]Pennsylvania State University, kwilliams@psu.edu
[3]University of Massachusetts Amherst, jpjiang@cs.umass.edu
[4]Microsoft, {hassanam, aidan.crook, izitouni, tasos.anastasakos}@microsoft.com

ABSTRACT

Voice-controlled intelligent personal assistants, such as Cortana, Google Now, Siri and Alexa, are increasingly becoming a part of users' daily lives, especially on mobile devices. They introduce a significant change in information access, not only by introducing voice control and touch gestures but also by enabling dialogues where the context is preserved. This raises the need for evaluation of their effectiveness in assisting users with their tasks. However, in order to understand which type of user interactions reflect different degrees of user satisfaction we need explicit judgements. In this paper, we describe a user study that was designed to measure user satisfaction over a range of typical scenarios of use: controlling a device, web search, and structured search dialogue. Using this data, we study how user satisfaction varied with different usage scenarios and what signals can be used for modeling satisfaction in the different scenarios. We find that the notion of satisfaction varies across different scenarios, and show that, in some scenarios (e.g. making a phone call), task completion is very important while for others (e.g. planning a night out), the amount of effort spent is key. We also study how the nature and complexity of the task at hand affects user satisfaction, and find that preserving the conversation context is essential and that overall task-level satisfaction cannot be reduced to query-level satisfaction alone. Finally, we shed light on the relative effectiveness and usefulness of voice-controlled intelligent agents, explaining their increasing popularity and uptake relative to the traditional query-response interaction.

Keywords: intelligent assistant, user satisfaction, user study, user experience, mobile search, spoken dialogue system

1. INTRODUCTION

Spoken dialogue systems [35] have been around for a while. However, it has only been in recent years that voice controlled intelligent assistants, such as Microsoft's Cortana, Google Now, Apple's Siri, Amazon's Alexa, Facebook's M, etc, have become a daily used feature on mobile devices. A recent study [12], executed by Northstar Research and commissioned by Google, found out that 55% of the U.S. teens use voice search every day and that

CHIIR '16, March 13 - 17, 2016, Carrboro, NC, USA

© 2016 Copyright held by the owner/author(s). Publication rights licensed to ACM.
ISBN 978-1-4503-3751-9/16/03...$15.00

DOI: http://dx.doi.org/10.1145/2854946.2854961

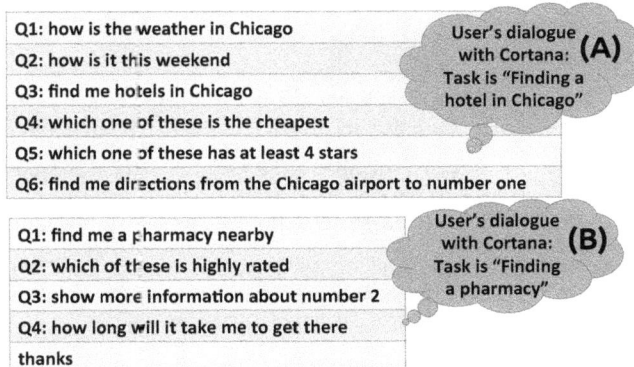

Figure 1: Two real examples of users' dialogues with a intelligent assistant: In the dialogue (A), a user performs a 'complex' task of planning his weekend in Chicago. In the dialogue (B), a user searches for the closest pharmacy.

89% of teens and 85% of adults agree that voice search is going to be 'very common' in the future. One of the reasons for the increased adoption is the current quality of speech recognition due to massive online processing [36], but perhaps more important is the added value users perceive: the spoken dialogue mode of interaction is a more natural way for people to communicate and is often faster than typing.

Intelligent assistants enable new mechanisms of information access, that are very different from traditional web search. Figure 1 shows two examples of dialogues with intelligent assistants sampled from the interaction logs. They are related to two tasks: (**A**): searching things to do on a weekend in Chicago, and (**B**): searching for the closest pharmacy. Users express their information needs in spoken form to an intelligent assistant. The user behavior is different compared with standard web search because in this scenario an intelligent assistant is expected to maintain the context throughout the conversation. For instance, our user anticipates intelligent assistants to understand that their interaction is about 'Chicago' in the transitions: $Q_1 \rightarrow Q_2, Q_3 \rightarrow Q_4$ in Figure 1(A). These structured search dialogues are more complicated than standard web search, resembling complex, context-rich, task-based search [43]. Users expect their intelligent assistants to understand their intent and to keep the context of the dialogue—some users even *thank* their intelligent assistant for its service, as in example in Figure 1(B).

Users communicate with intelligent assistants through voice commands for different scenarios of use, ranging from controlling their device—for example to make a phone call, or to manage their cal-

Figure 2: An example of mobile SERPs that might lead to 'good abandonment'.

Figure 3: An example of a 'simple' task with a structured search dialogue.

endar—to complex dialogues as shown in Figure 1. These interactions between users and intelligent assistants are more complicated than web search because they involve:

- automatic speech recognition (ASR): users communicate mostly through voice commands and it has been shown that errors in speech recognition negatively influence user satisfaction [23];

- understanding user intent: an intelligent assistant needs to understand user intent in order to take action on the intended task, or to provide an exact answer when possible;

- dialogue-based interaction: users expect an intelligent assistant to maintain the context of the dialogue;

- complex information needs: users express more sophisticated information needs while interacting with intelligent assistants.

This prompts the need to better understand success and failure of intelligent assistant usage. When are users (dis)satisfied? How can we evaluate intelligent assistants in ways that reflect perceived user satisfaction well? Can we resort to traditional methods of offline and online evaluation or do we need to take other factors into consideration?

Evaluation is a central component of many web search applications because it helps to understand which direction to take in order to improve a system. The common practice is to create a 'gold' standard (set of 'correct' answers) judged by editorial judges [21]. In case of intelligent assistants, there may be no general 'correct' answer since the answers are highly personalized and contextualized (e.g., by the user's location, prior queries or interactions) to fit user information needs. Another way to evaluate web search performance is through implicit relevance feedback such as clicks and dwell time [3, 11, 16, 26, 27]. However, we know that user satisfaction for mobile web search is already very different [33].

In the examples in Figure 2, different types of answers are shown for queries such as *'Location Answer'*, *'Image Answer'* or *'Knowledge Pane Answer'*. Users can find required information directly on the search result page (SERP) and they do not need to perform any further interactions (e.g. clicks). So we cannot assume that users who do not interact with the SERP are dissatisfied. This problem of 'good' abandonment received a lot of interest in recent years [6–8, 34]. An example of a users' dialogue about *'weather'* is shown in Figure 3. All information about the weather is already shown to the users and they do not need to click. In case of structured dialogue search, the lack of standard implicit feedback signals emerges even more because users talk to their phones instead of making clicks. One example of this is the transition $Q_2 \rightarrow Q_3$ in Figure 1(B).

In light of the current work, this paper aims to answer the following main research question:

> *What determines user satisfaction with intelligent assistants?*

We breakdown our general research problem into five specific research questions. Our first research question is:

> **RQ 1:** *What are characteristic types of scenarios of use?*

Based on analysis of the logs of a commercial intelligent assistant; and from previous work [25], we propose three types of scenarios of intelligent assistant use: **(1)** controlling the device; **(2)** searching the web; and **(3)** perform a complex (or 'mission') task in a dialogue interaction. We characterize key aspects of user satisfaction for each of these scenarios.

Our second research question is:

> **RQ 2:** *How can we measure different aspects of user satisfaction?*

We set up user studies with realistic tasks derived from the log analysis, following the three scenarios of use, and measuring a wide range of aspects of user satisfaction relevant to each specific scenario.

Our third research question is:

> **RQ 3:** *What are key factors determining user satisfaction for the different scenarios?*

In order to understand what the key components of user satisfaction are, we analyze output of our user studies for different intelligent assistants scenarios. We aim at understanding what factors influence user satisfaction the most: speech recognition quality, complexity of the task, or the amount of effort required to complete the task.

Our fourth research question is:

> **RQ 4:** *How to characterize 'abandonment' in the web search scenario?*

'Good abandonment' makes it difficult to measure user satisfaction with web search scenario using conventional implicit feedback behavioral signals. We analyze the way in which users interact with the intelligent assistant following a web search; we characterize user satisfaction in general, and over the number of issued queries, and types of answers found.

Our fifth research question is:

RQ 5: *How does query-level satisfaction relate to overall user satisfaction for the structured search dialogue scenario?*

The structured search dialogue scenario introduced a new mechanism for users to interact with intelligent assistants which has not received a lot of attention in the literature. We analyze the data for the search dialogue interactions, and investigate satisfaction over tasks with increasing complexity; we consider how sub-task level satisfaction relates to overall task satisfaction.

The remainder of this paper is organized as follows. Section 2 describes earlier work and background. Then, Section 3 introduces scenarios of user interaction with intelligent assistants, discusses differences and similarities in user behavior. Section 4 describes different types of user studies developed to evaluate user satisfaction for intelligent assistants different scenarios. Finally, Section 5 reports our results and findings. We summarize our findings, discuss possible extensions of the current work in Section 6.

2. RELATED WORK

In this section, we will discuss related work relevant to the research described in this paper, covering three broad strands of research. First, methods for evaluating user satisfaction in web search systems are presented in Section 2.1. Research on spoken dialogue systems is discussed in Section 2.2. Finally, we focus on user studies for the evaluation of intelligent assistants in Section 2.3.

2.1 Evaluating User Satisfaction

User behavioural signals have been extensively studied and used for the evaluation of web search systems [1, 2, 14–16, 24, 30, 45]. Historically, the key objective of information retrieval systems is to retrieve relevant information (typically documents) or references to documents containing required information [37, 38]. Given this query-document relevance score, many metrics have been defined: MAP, NDCG, DCG, MRR, P@n, TBG, etc. [21]. For such setup we have a collection of documents and queries that are annotated by human judges. It is a common setup used at TREC[1]. In this case we evaluate system performance at the *query-level* for the pair $\langle Q, SERP \rangle$. Building such data collections needed for this type of evaluation is both expensive and time consuming. There is a risk that such collections may be noisy, given that third-party annotators have limited knowledge of an individual user intent.

User satisfaction is widely adopted as a subjective measure of search experience. Kelly [28] proposes a definition: *'satisfaction can be understood as the fulfillment of a specified desire or goal'.* Furthermore, recently researchers studied different metrics reflective of user satisfaction such as effort [48] and it has been shown that user satisfaction at the query-level can change over time [31, 32] due to some external influences. These changes lead to the necessity of updating the data collection. Unfortunately, *query-level* satisfaction metrics ignore the information about a user's 'journey' from a question to an answer which might take more than one query [22]. Al-Maskari et al. [4] claim that *query-level* satisfaction is not applicable for informational queries – users can run followup queries if they are unsatisfied with the returned results; reformulations can lead users to an answer; this scenario is called *tasklevel* user satisfaction [9, 16]. Previous research proposed different methods for identifying successful sessions: Hassan et al. [16] used a Markov model to predict success at the end of the task; Ageev et al. [1] exploited an expertise-dependent difference in search behavior by using a Conditional Random Fields model to predict a

search success – authors used a game-like strategy for collecting annotated data by asking participants to find answers to non-trivial questions using web search. On the other hand, situations when users are frustrated have also been studied: Feild et al. [10] proposed a method for understanding user frustration. Hassan et al. [17] and Hassan Awadallah et al. [18] have found that high similarity of queries is an indicator of an unsuccessful task. All described methods focus on analyzing user behavior when users interact with traditional search systems.

2.2 Spoken Dialogue Systems

The main difference between traditional web search and intelligent assistants is their conversational nature of interaction with users. In the considered scenarios of usage of intelligent assistants, the technology can refer to the users' previous requests in order to understand the context of a conversation. For instance, in the dialogue (A) in Figure 1, the user asks for Q_2 and assumes that the intelligent assistant will 'remember' that he is interested in Chicago. Therefore, the spoken dialogue systems [35] are closely related to intelligent assistants because the spoken dialogue systems understand and respond to the voice commands in a dialogue form. This area has been studied extensively over the past two decades [40–42]. Most of these studies focused on systems that have not been deployed in a large scale and hence did not have the necessary means to study how users interact with these systems in real-world scenarios. However, intelligent assistants are different from traditional spoken dialogue systems because they also support interactions and 'understand' user intent. Furthermore, intelligent assistants display an answer which users can interact with and they are not purely based on speech—users can type in responses as well. From these perspectives, intelligent assistants are similar to multi-modal conversational systems [19, 44].

2.3 User Studies of Intelligent Assistants

In recent years voice-controlled personal assistants have become available to the general public. There are few studies researching intelligent assistants, and there is only one earlier paper that organizes a user study [25]. Jiang et al. [25] focus on simulated tasks for device control, as well as chat and web search, and identify satisfactory and unsatisfactory sessions based on features used in predicting satisfaction on the web, as well as acoustic features of the spoken request. Our work extends this study focusing on a wider range of scenarios of intelligent assistant use, including complex dialogues, and analyzing crucial aspects determining user satisfaction under these different conditions.

More broadly, intelligent assistants are often used for longer sessions and tasks that involve sub-tasks and complex interactions, and task complexity has been studied in many user studies. Wildemuth et al. [46] reviewed over a hundred interactive information retrieval studies in terms of task complexity and difficulty, and found that the number of sub-tasks, the number of facets, and the indeterminably were the main dimensions of task complexity. The structured search tasks we use in our study score high on these dimensions. Recently, Kelly [29] linked perceived task complexity with effort, suggesting that user satisfaction may depend on the amount of effort required to complete a complex task. We also look specifically at the role of effort relative to task-level user satisfaction.

To summarize, the key distinctions of our work compared to previous efforts are: we studied how users interact with intelligent assistants; we studied how we can use these interactions to understand *'good abandonment'*; we explored three main scenarios of user interactions with intelligent assistants and a definition of user satisfaction for these scenarios.

---

[1] Text REtrieval Conference: http://trec.nist.gov/

3. USER INTERACTION WITH INTELLIGENT ASSISTANTS

This section reports our study findings pertaining to the **RQ 1**: *What are characteristic types of scenarios of use?* In order to answer our research question we used the Microsoft intelligent assistant — Cortana. Historically, the scenario of controlling devices through voice commands was implemented first. It is described in detail in Section 3.1. From a user-satisfaction perspective, the main difference of this scenario compared with an information seeking task is that the 'right answer' is clear; in order to satisfy a user, an intelligent assistant needs to interpret requests correctly and give access to the correct functionality. In contrast, for information seeking tasks [20, 47] users exhibit different behaviour. Cortana responds to a general search scenario by returning a variant of the Bing Mobile SERP, which may include answers or tiles from the knowledge pane as well as organic search results (see Figure 2); we discuss this scenario in Section 3.2. Another mechanism by which users interact with information systems that some intelligent assistants support is the 'structured search dialogue' (Figure 1). In this case, intelligent assistants are able to maintain the context of a conversation as the system engages with the user in a dialogue; it is definitely more complex (for the system) but at the same time more natural (for the user) form of 'communication' between users and information systems. This scenario is presented in Section 3.3.

3.1 Controlling a Device

The first scenario of using intelligent assistants that we study is the direct access of on-device functionality – e.g., call a contact, check the calendar, access an app, etc. This scenario is useful because, ordinarily, it takes several actions to complete on existing smartphones. For example, in order to make a phone call, the user needs to first access a contact list on the phone and then identify the desired person. The ordinary process is time consuming, especially when the user is not familiar with the device. Instead, one can directly talk to the intelligent assistant to solve the problem, e.g., 'call Sam'. As long as the intelligent assistant can correctly recognize the user's words and task context, this largely reduces the user's effort.

Our user study includes the following types of on-device tasks that are popular in Cortana's usage logs:

- Call a person;
- Send a text message;
- Check on-device calendar;
- Open an application;
- Turn on/off wi-fi;
- Play music.

We group these tasks into one category because they share the similarity that users try to access these on-device functions through the intelligent assistants. These functions are normally not provided by the intelligent assistants, but offered by the device hosting it. In these tasks, intelligent assistants serve as a quick and efficient interface for accessing on-device functionality.

3.2 Performing Mobile Web Search

Another popular usage scenario for intelligent assistants is the general web search scenario. For this scenario, input can be either speech or text and there is no need for the system to be state-aware since it does not provide a multi-turn experience. During web search on mobile devices, the intent can be ambiguous. Therefore, the search result page (SERP) is very diverse and may include different types of answers such as:

- *'Answer Box'*. A box such as the knowledge pane (Figure 2(A)) or directions to a location (Figure 2(C)). These answer boxes are present for specific query intents.

- *'Image'*. In this case, just seeing an image may have satisfied a user's information need (e.g. Figure 2(A,B)).

- *'Snippet'*. The user's information need is satisfied by a snippet of text appearing below an organic search result (e.g. Figure 2(B)).

These different elements on a SERP can all lead to user satisfaction. For instance, the knowledge pane might contain the answer that the user is looking for or a user may be satisfied by the text in a snippet.

In some cases, the SERP is able to directly satisfy the user's information need and it can lead to the absence of one of the most studied user interaction signals (i.e. clicks on the SERP). Previous work on general web search has shown that presenting these types of answers affects user behavior [33] and leads to 'good abandonment' [7, 34] where the user appears to have abandoned the results but was actually satisfied without the need to engage with the SERP using clicks.

3.3 Structured Search Dialogue

In the structured search dialogue scenarios, the users are engaged in a conversation with the system using voice as we show in Figure 1. Cortana returns a structured answer that is distinguishably different from the usual SERP (Figure 2). The key component of this scenario is the ability of the intelligent assistant to maintain the context of the conversation. Examples of tasks where this scenario is activated include places (e.g. restaurants, hotels, travel, etc.) and weather. There are two types of tasks that fall under this scenario: *'simple'* and *'mission'* tasks. We discuss *'simple'* tasks in Section 3.3.1 and *'mission'* tasks in Section 3.3.2.

3.3.1 Simple Tasks

'Simple' tasks have one underlying atomic information need and mostly consist of one query and one answer. An example of a 'simple' task is the weather-related task shown in Figure 3. 'Simple' tasks can be very similar to web search scenarios. We expect that they can be evaluated using a paradigm of *query-level* satisfaction because 'simple' task usually consists of one query and one answer.

3.3.2 Mission Tasks

'Mission' tasks consist of multiple interactions with Cortana that lead towards one final goal (e.g. 'find a place for vacation'). The final task can be divided into sub-tasks; the complexity of 'missions' is dependent on the need to understand the context of the conversation.

The example of a places-related 'mission' dialogue is presented in Figure 4. A user makes the following transitions:

- **(1)** 'asking for a list of the nearest restaurant' → **(2)** 'sorting the derived list to find best restaurants';

  (***Comment for the transition*** $1 \to 2$: *Cortana 'knows' that a user is working on the same list of restaurants*)

- **(2)** → **(3)** 'selecting the restaurant from the list and asking for the directions';

  (***Comment for the transition*** $2 \to 3$: *Cortana 'knows' that a user is working with the sorted list of restaurants*)

Figure 4: An example of a structured search dialogue (mission task).

Table 1: Demographics of the user study participants: gender (A), native language (B), and field of education (C)

Gender		Native language		Field of education	
Male	75%	English	55%	Computer science	82%
Female	25%	Other	45%	Electrical engineering	8%
				Mathematics	7%
				Other	2%

This type of interaction can be viewed as a sequence of user requests ('user journey towards a information goal') where each request is a step towards user satisfaction or frustration. Much of the frustration happens when Cortana is not able to keep the context and users need to re-attempt the task from the start. Going back to the example in Figure 1 (B), if Cortana did not carry the context across the transition $Q_3 \rightarrow Q_4$ (e.g. due to ASR error) then the user has to restart the task. Overall, user satisfaction goes down dramatically in this case, especially because the mistake happens at the end of the session.

To summarize, in this section, we categorized three distinct scenarios of user interactions with intelligent assistants. Cortana was used as an intelligent assistant example. We discussed difficulties in evaluating user satisfaction in each of these scenarios. For the controlling a device scenario, users' requests cannot be characterized by information needs. In order to satisfy users' needs the system is required to recognize their speech correctly and map a request to the right functionality. The web search and structured search dialogue are more complex because a comprehensive information seeking process is involved. The effect of good abandonment makes it difficult to measure user satisfaction. The structured search dialogue is a novel way of users' interactions that support complex tasks which consist of more than one singular objectives. We refer to these complex tasks as 'mission' tasks.

4. DESIGNING USER STUDIES

This section addresses **RQ 2:** *How can we measure different aspects of user satisfaction?* by describing the design of user study to collect user interaction data and ratings for different intelligent assistant scenarios. We start by characterizing the participants of our study in Section 4.1 followed by a description of the environment of the studies in Section 4.2. The general procedure for the study is presented in Section 4.3. Then, we present the detailed tasks and user study procedure for the different scenarios separately: device control in Section 4.4, structured search dialogue in Section 4.6, and mobile web search in Section 4.5. While designing the user study tasks we follow two requirements: **(1)** the simulated tasks should be realistic and as close as possible to real-world tasks ; **(2)** according to Borlund [5] we construct the simulated tasks so that participants could relate to them and they would provide '*enough imaginative context*.'

4.1 Participants

We recruited 60 participants through emails sent to a mailing list of an IT company located in the United States. All participants were college or graduate students interning at the company or

full time employees. They are reimbursed $10 gift card for participating in an experiment. The average age of participants is 25.53 ($\pm$ 5.42). The characteristics of participants regarding gender (A), field of education (B) and native language (C) are presented in Table 1.

4.2 Environment

Participants performed the tasks on a Windows phone with the latest version of Windows Phone 8.1 and Cortana installed. If the task needed to access some device resources, functions or applications (e.g. maps), they are installed to make sure users would not encounter problems. The experiment was conducted in a quiet room, so as to reduce the disturbance of environment noise. Although the real environment often involves noise and interruption, we eliminate those factors to simplify the experiment.

4.3 General Procedure

The participants were first asked to watch a video introducing the different usage scenarios of Cortana, and then complete a background questionnaire with demographics and previous experience with using intelligent assistants. Then, they work on one training task and eight formal tasks. We instructed participants that they could stop a task when they had accomplished the goal or if they became frustrated and wanted to give up. Finally, they were asked to answer an extensive questionnaire on their experience and share further details during a short interview.

For each task, we asked participants to listen to an audio recording that verbally described the task objective. We did not show the participants the task description while they were working on the task, because in an earlier pilot study, many participants directly used the sentences shown in task descriptions as requests. We strongly want to avoid such outcome because our goal is to simulate real user behavior. After completing the task, participants were directed to the questionnaires. The questions depend on the objectives of the experiment and vary per user study. Participants answered all questions using a standard 5-point Likert scale.

4.4 User Study for Controlling Device

The first user study is to conduct the most basic scenario–controlling a device. We will now describe the tasks (Section 4.4.1) and the specific procedure for this study (Section 4.4.2).

4.4.1 Tasks

In total we develop nine device control tasks. We rotated the assignment of tasks using a Latin square such that 20 participants worked on each unique task. Some examples of these tasks are:

- Ask Cortana to play a song by Michael Jackson (a song by the artist is downloaded on the device prior to the task).

- You are on your way to a meeting with James, but will be late due to heavy traffic. Send James Smith a text message using Cortana and explain your situation.

- *Create a reminder for a meeting with James next Thursday at 3pm.*

- *Ask Cortana to turn off the Wi-Fi on your phone.*

- *Ask Cortana to open WhatsApp (the name of a popular App, and the App is installed on the device prior to the task).*

4.4.2 Procedure

The instructional video about the controlling device scenario is about 2 minutes long. Our informal observation is that the video instructions were effective and felt like a natural extension of the speech interaction of the study, framing the study for the participants better than written instruction would do. When the participants worked on this user study, they were asked to use mostly voice for interactions. After terminating a task, they answer questions regarding their experience, including:

1. *Were you able to complete the task?*

2. *How satisfied are you with your experience in this task?*

3. *How well did Cortana recognize what you said?*

4. *Did you put in a lot of effort to complete the task?*

The total experiment time was about 20 minutes.

4.5 User Study for Web Search

The next use-case for the user study is general web search. There has already been significant research involving search on mobile phones [33, 39]; however, *'good abandonment'* in mobile search has had limited investigation. It is a particularly interesting problem to investigate as queries in mobile search have been described as *quick answer types* and previous research has shown that users formulate mobile queries in such as way so as to increase the likelihood of the query being satisfied directly on the SERP [34]. For this reason, in this user study we choose to focus on tasks that have an increasing likelihood of leading to good abandonment. Section 4.5.1 introduces the used tasks . The specific procedure for this study is presented in Section 4.5.2.

4.5.1 Tasks

The tasks for web search were designed to encourage answer-seeking behavior and increase the likelihood of good abandonment. The tasks involved:

- *A conversion from the imperial system to the metric system.*

- *Determining if it was a good time to phone a friend in another part of the world.*

- *Finding the score of the user's favourite sports team.*

- *Finding the user's favourite celebrity's hair colour.*

- *Finding the CEO of a company that lost most of its value within the last 10 years.*

After data cleaning, we retained the data from 55 users who completed a total of 274 tasks, 194 of which were labeled as SAT, while the remaining 70 were labeled as DSAT. There were a total of 607 queries for these tasks of which 576 were abandoned, thereby indicating that we were successful in designing tasks that had a higher potential of leading to good abandonment.

4.5.2 Procedure

The user study starts with the instructional video (about 3 minutes long) that contains an example task for general web search. After completing each task, users were asked:

1. *Were you able to complete the task?*

2. *Where did you find the answer?*

   (**Suggested Answers:** *In an answer box*; *On a website that I visited*; *In a search result snippet*; *In an image.*)

3. *Which query led you to finding the answer?*

   (**Suggested Answers:** First; Second; Third; Fourth or later)

4. *How satisfied are you with your experience in this task?*

5. *Did you put in a lot of effort to complete the task?*

The purpose of the second question was to allow us to better understand where users find information that they are looking for. The option *'On a Website that I visited'* means a user clicked on a search result and visited a website to find the information that they were looking for.

The purpose of the third question was to allow us to tie a success event within a task to a specific query for future evaluation. We did not ask users about ASR quality because we gave users the option of using text input instead of speech. The reason for doing this is that, since we wanted to study good abandonment, we tried to reduce the level of frustration due to speech recognition errors. However, even though that was the case, we still found that most of the participants used voice input because they found it more convenient. The total experiment time was about 20 minutes.

4.6 User Study for Structured Search Dialogue

This Section introduces the design of the user study to explore user satisfaction for the structured search dialogue. First, we describe the way we create tasks for our user study and tasks examples in Section 4.6.1. The specific procedure for this study is described in Section 4.6.2.

4.6.1 Tasks

In order to come with the list of tasks for participants, Cortana's logs (over 400K requests) are analyzed. We look at the terms distribution to get an idea for what kind of places users are looking for. Based on our analysis we come up with eight tasks that designed to cover a large portion of topics used by Cortana's users.

Among these eight tasks we have:

- *(A) one simple task that is related to the weather where almost all participants are satisfied;*

- *(B) four 'mission' tasks that include two sub-tasks;*

- *(C) three 'mission' tasks that require at least three switches in a subject.*

Tasks are given to participants in a free/general form in order to get query diversity and stimulate use satisfaction or frustration with returned results. For instance, let us consider the 'mission' task with 3 sub-tasks: *'You are planning a vacation. Pick a place. Check if the weather is good enough for the period you are planning the vacation. Find a hotel that suits you. Find the driving directions to this place.* By giving a free-form task we stimulate the information need of participants (they need to come up with their own goal and they are more involved in the tasks) so this scenario should lead to satisfaction or frustration. For instance, out of 60 responses for the described task we get 46 unique places.

As a result of free-form task-formulation we obtained a diverse query set, characterized by the following: participants performed a total of 540 tasks that incorporated $2,040$ queries, of which $1,969$ were unique and the average query-length is 7.07. The simple task generated 130 queries in total; five (B)-type tasks generated 685 queries; three (C)-type tasks generated $1,355$ queries.

4.6.2 Procedure

The introductory video for this user study is about 4 minutes long and informs participants how to use the structured search dialogue. During this user study, we instruct participants to verbally interact with Cortana. We instruct them to use text input only if Cortana does not understand their requests more than three times. Only after completing a task are they then redirected to questions regarding their experience in this task session. For 'mission' tasks, users are asked to indicate their satisfaction with both the sub-tasks and the whole task in general. In order to stimulate participant involvement in the tasks, we asked them to answer clarifying questions. For instance, if the task was *what is the weather tomorrow'*, the user also needed to indicate the temperature; this way we keep participants engaged.

Participants answer the following four questions after completing the tasks:

1. *Were you able to complete the task?*

2. *How satisfied are you with your experience in this task in general?*

   If the task has sub-tasks participants indicate their graded satisfaction e.g. **a.** *How satisfied are you with your experience in finding a hotel?* **b.** *How satisfied are you with your experience in finding directions?*

3. *Did you put in a lot of effort to complete the task?*

4. *How well did Cortana recognize what you said?*

The total experiment time was about 30 minutes.

To summarize, we described how we designed user study with the objective of understanding user satisfaction with different scenarios of intelligent assistants, measuring relevant variables as speech recognition quality, task completion, and the effort taken. The introductory videos designed for the user study are available.[2] Detailed descriptions of the tasks and the recording on the task can be accessed.[3]

5. RESULTS AND FINDINGS

This section presents the results and findings from the user studies, investigating our three remaining research questions (RQ3–5). In Section 5.1, we focus on the user satisfaction relative to the different usage scenarios, and in relation to other measures like the speech recognition, task completion and effort taken. In Section 5.2, we analyze 'good abandonment' in web search, in short sessions where answers may be shown without the need for further interaction. In Section 5.3, we focus on structured search dialogues and how session- or task-level satisfaction relates to subtask-level satisfaction for longer sessions.

5.1 Scenarios of Use

[2]https://goo.gl/6Gv5Y5
[3]https://goo.gl/0jXu2J

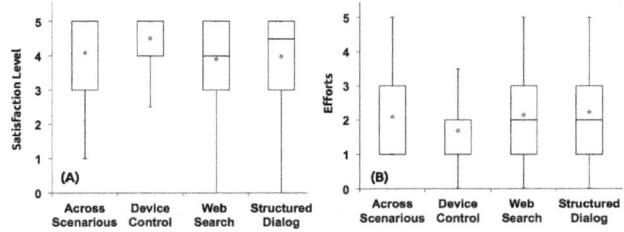

Figure 5: User satisfaction (A) and effort (B) across scenarios and in three discussed scenarios separately. Mean is red dot. Median is horizontal line.

Table 2: Correlations of user satisfaction with other measures: ASR quality, Task Completeness, User Efforts. The sign * stands for statistically significant results ($p < 0.05$)

Measures	All	Device Control	Web Search	Struct. Dialogue
SAT vs. ASR	0.57*	0.57	$-$[†]	0.56*
SAT vs. Completion	0.18*	0.59*	0.10	0.10*
SAT vs. Effort	-0.75*	-0.64*	-0.65*	-0.80*
ASR vs. Completion	-0.22*	-0.27*	$-$[†]	-0.19*
ASR vs. Effort	-0.54*	-0.56*	$-$[†]	-0.51*
Completion vs. Effort	-0.11*	-0.39*	-0.08*	-0.05*

[†]ASR was not calculated for web search as both spoken and typed queries were used.

We will now investigate **RQ 3**: *What are key factors determining user satisfaction for the different scenarios?* The scenarios of use differ considerably in terms of complexity, session duration, type of outcome, and more, suggesting that different factors may play a role in determining user satisfaction.

We first discuss the distribution of user satisfaction across all aforementioned mechanisms of intelligent assistant use, both over the entire session and broken down by scenario—device control, web search on a mobile device, and structured search dialogue — which is presented in Figure 5(A). The user satisfaction is very high with means around 4 on a 5-point scale, both overall sessions and for each of the three scenarios. The high level of satisfaction showcases the maturity of the current generation of intelligent assistants, and explains the increasing adoption. As a case in point, many participants had (almost) never used the service, and were impressed by its effectiveness. We can see that user satisfaction with the device controlling tasks (mean of 4.5) is somewhat higher on average than with the information seeking tasks (mean of 3.7), plausibly because the information seeking tasks are open domain and more complex.

We also show the distribution of user effort, both across scenarios and separately, in Figure 5(B). Here we see relatively low scores for effort overall, consistent with high levels of satisfaction.[4] When we break down the effort over the scenarios, a similar picture emerges as with user satisfaction: participants spend more effort on search tasks, especially structured search.

We now perform a correlation analysis of user satisfaction and its components. Table 2 presents the correlation of user satisfac-

[4]To be precise, this is based on the response to the question 'was a lot of effort was required to complete the task?', measured on a Likert scale, where low scores indicate disagreement with the statement, hence that not much effort was required.

Figure 6: User satisfaction in the web search scenario: satisfaction over the number of queries that users run to find a required answer (A), and over where users find a required answer (B). The mean is represented by the dot and the median is the horizontal line.

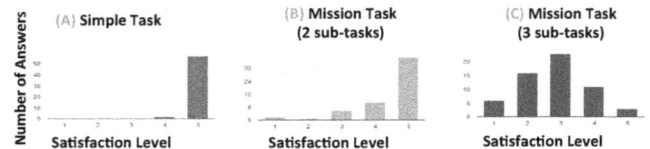

Figure 7: A distribution of overall user satisfaction for different types of tasks: 'simple' tasks, and 'mission' tasks with two and three objectives.

tion with (1) speech recognition quality (ASR), (2) task completion (participants indicate if they are able to complete the suggested task), and (3) effort spent (participants report the perceived effort to complete the task). We also look at the correlation between effort and completion. An obvious finding is that user satisfaction depends on ASR quality which is consistent with previous research [25]. Hence ASR quality is a key component of user satisfaction. We find a more interesting pattern for task completion: there is a high correlation with satisfaction for device control, but a low correlation for the information seeking scenarios. This suggests that users are able to find the required information and complete their tasks even in cases where their user satisfaction is suboptimal. And the strong negative correlation between satisfaction and effort shows that users spend a considerable amount of effort to complete their task.

This has important methodological consequences: we cannot equate 'success' in terms of task completion with user satisfaction for the informational scenarios, and have to incorporate the effort taken as a key component of user satisfaction across the different intelligent assistant scenarios. This finding is in line with recent work on task complexity or difficulty and effort, which postulates that satisfaction is low (high) for tasks that take more (less) effort than expected [29]. In addition, ASR quality is of obvious influence on user satisfaction. However, speech recognition is improving constantly and reached the levels that users can recover from misrecognition within a dialogue and still complete their task, at the cost of some extra effort and frustration.

5.2 Good Abandonment for Web Search

We continue with investigating our **RQ 4**: *How to characterize 'abandonment' in the web search scenario?* Whilst intelligent assistants can encourage highly interactive sessions, many results are provided as answers in speech or on the screen, requiring no further interaction of the user (e.g. no need to open a web page and read further to extract the requested information). Hence many sessions stop without an explicit user action, making it hard to discern good and bad search abandonment from interaction log data.

We analyze the phenomenon of *'good abandonment'* from two perspectives: (1) the session length and (2) where users find the answer addressing their intent. Figure 6(A) presents the dependency of user satisfaction and how much effort was required to find an answer. Effort is associated with the number of queries that participates issued to find the required information. Our observations suggest that user satisfaction is higher if users use fewer queries to reach their goal. Figure 6(A) suggests that if users cannot find an answer after their first query their satisfaction goes down dra-

matically. Longer sessions lead to user frustration; however, task completion levels are high for the web search scenario, indicating that unnecessary effort was spent in completing the task.

Figure 6(B) shows the dependency of user satisfaction on the place where users find the desired answer. Furthermore, users are more satisfied if they can find a required result directly ('Answer Box' and 'Image') without the need to interact with the SERP such as (1) finding an answer in snippets ('SERP'); (2) clicking on SERP ('Visited Website'). Hence, cases without further interaction ('Answer Box' and 'Image') lead to higher levels of satisfaction than those requiring interaction ('SERP' and 'Visited Website'). This has important methodological consequences: we have to consider cases of *'good abandonment'*. To measure user satisfaction in this case we need to investigate the other forms of interaction signals that are not based on clicks, such as touch or swipe interactions.

5.3 Analyzing Structured Search Dialogues

We now investigate our **RQ 5**: *How does query-level satisfaction relate to overall user satisfaction for the structured search dialogue scenario?* Structured search dialogues are complex interactions with a longer session and different sub-tasks and changes of focus within the same context. This is very different from traditional search in the query-response paradigm, and session context becomes of crucial importance.

We start our analysis of the collected user interactions with structured search dialogues by introducing the satisfaction distribution for the different types of tasks presented in Figure 7. We see that users are more satisfied with the simple tasks (A), where almost all participants give the highest possible rating. The 'mission' tasks (B and C), that are more complex have a less skewed satisfaction distribution. This immediately shows the complexity of context in structured search dialogues: when viewed independently the quality of the results is comparable for each step of the interaction, and the high levels of satisfaction for the simple task confirm that the quality is high, yet the satisfaction levels go down considerably when tasks are of increasing complexity. This suggests that the intelligent assistant loses context of a conversation, and requires more effort and interaction to restart the dialogue and get back on track. This observation is in line with our previous finding that the amount of effort users spend on a task is a principal component of user satisfaction.

We look now in greater detail at the mission tasks that contain 2 or more sub-tasks, and try to find out how overall user satisfaction is related to user satisfaction per sub-task. Table 3 presents the correlation between the overall *task*-level satisfaction and the minimum, mean, and maximum *query*-level satisfaction per sub-task. The results suggest that overall user satisfaction with the 'mission' tasks depends more on either user frustration—some sub-task results in low satisfaction and frustration dragging down the overall satisfaction fast—or on user success—high levels of satisfaction with the

Table 3: Correlations of overall task user satisfaction and different summations over sub-tasks satisfaction. All presented results are statistical significant ($p < 0.05$)

Measures	Mission tasks
Overall SAT vs. *Average* Sub-task SAT	0.50
Overall SAT vs. *Minimum* Sub-task SAT	0.69
Overall SAT vs. *Maximum* Sub-task SAT	0.71

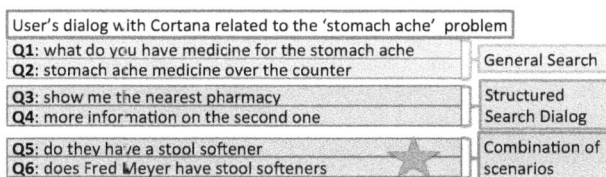

Figure 8: Example of a mixed dialogue.

main sub-task solving the problem lead to high levels of overall satisfaction. This has important methodological consequences: user satisfaction with the structured search dialogues cannot be measured by averaging over satisfaction with sub-tasks, suggesting that task-level satisfaction is different from sub-task or query-level satisfaction, and session-level features are a crucial component.

To summarize, this section show the main results of the user study. We first looked at user satisfaction and found high levels of satisfaction throughout, but important differences between the scenarios on the factors contributing to overall satisfaction: the device control scenario completion correlates well with user satisfaction—it either worked or it did not—but the informational scenarios effort has a much higher correlation with user satisfaction than completion. We then looked in detail at the web search scenario. We found satisfaction dropping fast with the number of issued queries. We also found that direct answers (not requiring interaction) had higher levels of user satisfaction than SERP or web-page results (requiring further interaction) making 'good abandonment' a frequent case and necessitating to take other features (e.g., touch, swipe, acoustic) into account to discern good and bad abandonment. Finally, we zoomed in on the structured search dialogues, and found high level of satisfaction per sub-task but a drop in overall satisfaction for 'mission' tasks with multiple sub-tasks addressing different aspects, showing the importance of preserving session context and demonstrating that task-level satisfaction cannot be reduced to query- or impression-level satisfaction.

6. DISCUSSION AND CONCLUSIONS

This paper aimed to answer the following main research question: *What determines user satisfaction with intelligent assistants?*, by investigating key aspects that determine user satisfaction for different scenarios of intelligent assistant usage. Our first research question was: **RQ 1:** *What are characteristic types of scenarios of use?* We proposed three main types of scenarios of use: **(1)** device control; **(2)** web search; and **(3)** structured search dialogue. The scenarios were identified on the basis of three factors: their proportional existence in the logs of a commercial intelligent assistant; the way requests are handled at the intelligent assistant backend (e.g. user requests are redirected to the different services and they serve different interfaces); and the way scenarios were defined in previous works [25]. Next, we investigated: **RQ 2:** *How can we measure different aspects of user satisfaction?* We designed a series of user studies tailored to the three scenarios of use, with questionnaires on variables potentially related to user satisfaction. The used tasks were based on an extensive analysis of logs of a commercial intelligent assistant.

The data collected in the user study was used to investigate the remaining research questions. First, we looked at: **RQ 3:** *What are key factors determining user satisfaction for the different scenarios?* We collected participant's responses on their satisfaction with the task, their ability to complete a task, and the estimated

effort it took. Our main conclusion is that effort is a key component of user satisfaction across the different intelligent assistants scenarios. Second, we focused on the web search interactions: **RQ 4:** *How to characterize 'abandonment' in the web search scenario?* We clearly demonstrated a 'presence' of 'good abandonment' in the web search scenario, and concluded that to measure user satisfaction we need to investigate the other forms of interaction signals that are not based on clicks or reformulation. Third, we zoomed in on the structured dialogue interactions: **RQ 5:** *How does query-level satisfaction relate to overall user satisfaction for the structured search dialogue scenario?* We looked at user satisfaction as 'a user journey towards an information goal where each step is important,' and showed the importance of session context on user satisfaction. Our experimental results show that user satisfaction cannot be measured by averaging over satisfaction with sub-tasks. Hence, frustration with some steps in a user's 'journey' can greatly affect their overall satisfaction.

Our general conclusion is that the factors contributing to overall satisfaction with a task are different between the scenarios. Task completion is highly correlated with user satisfaction for the device control scenario—it either worked or it did not. For information seeking scenarios, user satisfaction is more related to effort than task completion. We demonstrated that task-level satisfaction cannot be reduced to query or impression-level satisfaction for information seeking scenarios.

Research on intelligent assistants for mobile devices is a new area, and this paper addresses some of the important first steps. This work can be extended in two main directions. First, our taxonomy of three types of scenarios could be extended in various ways. In the logs we noticed that users use a mix of scenarios in order to satisfy their information needs. Consider for example the dialogue in Figure 8, in which the user combined multiple different scenarios in order to accomplish his/her task: The user started by using general web search (Step 1: $Q_1 \rightarrow Q_2$) to get information about his/her problem. Then he/she used the structured search dialogue (Step 2: $Q_3 \rightarrow Q_4$) to find a pharmacy. Afterwards, he/she attempted to combine the information from the prior steps through complex requests (Step 3: $Q_5 \rightarrow Q_6$). Unfortunately, this led to dissatisfaction as the intelligent assistant failed to process Step 3. Therefore, it is essential to study user satisfaction when users use the mix of scenarios. Second, we found that typical behavioral signals in interaction logs (e.g., clicks) are not sufficient to infer user satisfaction with intelligent assistants. Going forward, therefore, it will be important to make use of other types of interactions such as touch or swipe, or acoustic signals to predict user satisfaction. It has been shown [13, 25, 33] that these signals are promising to detect user satisfaction with intelligent assistants and hold the potential to construct accurate predictions of task-level user-satisfaction based on behavioral data. Ultimately, such signals can be used in production systems to improve the quality of human interaction with intelligent assistants.

Acknowledgments

We thank Sarvesh Nagpal and Toby Walker for the help in collecting the internal API data for the user study. We also thank the participants in the study.

References

[1] M. Ageev, Q. Guo, D. Lagun, and E. Agichtein. Find it if you can: a game for modeling different types of web search success using interaction data. In *SIGIR*, 2011.

[2] M. Ageev, D. Lagun, and E. Agichtein. Improving search result summaries by using searcher behavior data. In *SIGIR*, pages 13–22, 2013.

[3] E. Agichtein, E. Brill, and S. T. Dumais. Improving web search ranking by incorporating user behavior information. In *SIGIR*, pages 19–26, 2006.

[4] A. Al-Maskari, M. Sanderson, and P. Clough. The relationship between ir effectiveness measures and user satisfaction. In *SIGIR*, pages 773–774, 2007.

[5] P. Borlund. The iir evaluation model: a framework for evaluation of interactive information retrieval systems. *Inf. Res. (IRES)*, 8(3), 2003.

[6] A. Chuklin and P. Serdyukov. How query extensions reflect search result abandonments. In *SIGIR*, pages 1087–1088, 2012.

[7] A. Chuklin and P. Serdyukov. Good abandonments in factoid queries. In *WWW (Companion Volume)*, pages 483–484, 2012.

[8] A. Diriye, R. White, G. Buscher, and S. T. Dumais. Leaving so soon?: understanding and predicting web search abandonment rationales. In *CIKM*, pages 1025–1034, 2012.

[9] A. Dong, Y. Chang, Z. Zheng, G. Mishne, J. Bai, R. Zhang, K. Buchner, and C. L. F. Diaz. Towards recency ranking in web search. In *WSDM*, pages 11–20, 2010.

[10] H. A. Feild, J. Allan, and R. Jones. Predicting searcher frustration. In *SIGIR*, pages 34–41, 2010.

[11] S. Fox, K. Karnawat, M. Mydland, S. T. Dumais, and T. White. Evaluating implicit measures to improve web search. *ACM Trans. Inf. Syst. (TOIS)*, 23(2):147–168, 2005.

[12] Google Inc. Teens use voice search most, even in bathroom, google's mobile voice study finds, 2015. http://prn.to/1sfiQRr.

[13] Q. Guo, H. Jin, D. Lagun, S. Yuan, and E. Agichtein. Towards estimating web search result relevance from touch interactions on mobile devices. In *CHI Extended Abstracts 2013*, pages 1821–1826, 2013.

[14] A. Hassan. A semi-supervised approach to modeling web search satisfaction. In *SIGIR*, pages 275–284, 2012.

[15] A. Hassan and R. W. White. Personalized models of search satisfaction. In *CIKM*, pages 2009–2018, 2013.

[16] A. Hassan, R. Jones, and K. L. Klinkner. Beyond DCG: user behavior as a predictor of a successful search. In *WSDM*, pages 221–230, 2010.

[17] A. Hassan, X. Shi, N. Craswell, and B. Ramsey. Beyond clicks: query reformulation as a predictor of search satisfaction. In *CIKM*, pages 2019–2028, 2013.

[18] A. Hassan Awadallah, R. W. White, S. T. Dumais, and Y.-M. Wang. Struggling or exploring?: disambiguating long search sessions. In *WSDM*, pages 53–62, 2014.

[19] L. P. Heck, D. Hakkani-Tür, M. Chinthakunta, G. Tür, R. Iyer, P. Parthasarathy, L. Stifelman, E. Shriberg, and A. Fidler. Multi-modal conversational search and browse. In *SLAM@INTERSPEECH*, pages 96–101, 2013.

[20] P. Ingwersen and K. Järvelin. *The Turn: Integration of Information Seeking and Retrieval in Context (The Information Retrieval Series)*. Springer-Verlag New York, 2005.

[21] K. Järvelin and J. Kekäläinen. Cumulated gain-based evaluation of ir techniques. *ACM Trans. Inf. Syst. (TOIS)*, 20(4):422–446, 2002.

[22] K. Järvelin, S. L. Price, L. M. L. Delcambre, and M. L. Nielsen. Discounted cumulated gain based evaluation of multiple-query ir sessions. In *ECIR*, pages 4–15, 2008.

[23] J. Jiang, W. Jeng, and D. He. How do users respond to voice input errors?: lexical and phonetic query reformulation in voice search. In *SIGIR*, pages 143–152, 2013.

[24] J. Jiang, A. H. Awadallah, X. Shi, and R. W. White. Understanding and predicting graded search satisfaction. In *WSDM*, 2015.

[25] J. Jiang, A. Hassan Awadallah, R. Jones, U. Ozertem, I. Zitouni, R. G. Kulkarni, and O. Z. Khan. Automatic online evaluation of intelligent assistants. In *WWW*, pages 506–516, 2015.

[26] T. Joachims. Optimizing search engines using clickthrough data. In *KDD*, pages 133–142, 2002.

[27] T. Joachims, L. Granka, B. Pan, H. Hembrooke, and G. Gay. Accurately interpreting clickthrough data as implicit feedback. In *SIGIR*, pages 154–161, 2005.

[28] D. Kelly. Methods for evaluating interactive information retrieval systems with users. *Foundations and Trends in Information Retrieval (FTIR)*, 3(1-2):1–224, 2009.

[29] D. Kelly. When effort exceeds expectations: A theory of search task difficulty (keynote). In *SCST'15: Proceedings of the First International Workshop on Supporting Complex Search Tasks*, volume 1338 of *CEUR Workshop Proceedings*, 2015.

[30] Y. Kim, A. Hassan, R. W. White, and Y.-M. Wang. Playing by the rules: mining query associations to predict search performance. In *WSDM*, pages 133–142, 2013.

[31] J. Kiseleva, E. Crestan, R. Brigo, and R. Dittel. Modelling and detecting changes in user satisfaction. In *CIKM*, pages 1449–1458, 2014.

[32] J. Kiseleva, J. Kamps, V. Nikulin, and N. Makarov. Behavioral dynamics from the serp's perspective: What are failed serps and how to fix them? In *CIKM*, 2015.

[33] D. Lagun, C.-H. Hsieh, D. Webster, and V. Navalpakkam. Towards better measurement of attention and satisfaction in mobile search. In *SIGIR*, pages 113–122, 2014.

[34] J. Li, S. B. Huffman, and A. Tokuda. Good abandonment in mobile and pc internet search. In *SIGIR*, pages 43–50, 2009.

[35] M. F. McTear. Spoken dialogue technology: enabling the conversational user interface. *ACM Computing Surveys (CSUR)*, 34(1):90–169, 2002.

[36] M. Negri, M. Turchi, J. G. C. de Souza, and D. Falavigna. Quality estimation for automatic speech recognition. In *COLING*, pages 1813–1823, 2014.

[37] T. Saracevic. Relevance: A review of and a framework for the thinking on the notion in information science. *Journal of the American Society for Information Science*, 26:321–343, 1975.

[38] T. Saracevic, P. B. Kantor, A. Y. Chamis, and D. Trivison. A study of information seeking and retrieving. I. background and methodology. II. users, questions and effectiveness. III. searchers, searches, overlap. *Journal of the American Society for Information Science and Technology*, 39:161–176; 177–196; 197–216, 1988.

[39] M. Shokouhi and Q. Guo. From queries to cards: Re-ranking proactive card recommendations based on reactive search history. In *SIGIR*, pages 695–704, 2015.

[40] G. Tür. Extending boosting for large scale spoken language understanding. *Machine Learning (ML)*, 69(1):55–74, 2007.

[41] G. Tür, Y.-Y. Wang, and D. Z. Hakkani-Tür. Techware: Spoken language understanding resources [best of the web]. *IEEE Signal Process. Mag. (SPM)*, 30(3):187–189, 2013.

[42] G. Tür, Y.-Y. Wang, and D. Z. Hakkani-Tür. Understanding spoken language. *Computing Handbook*, 3rd ed(41):1–17, 2014.

[43] P. Vakkari. Task-based information searching. *ARIST*, 37:413–464, 2003.

[44] W. Wahlster. Smartkom: Foundations of multimodal dialogue systems. *Springer*, 2006.

[45] Y. Wang and E. Agichtein. Query ambiguity revisited: Clickthrough measures for distinguishing informational and ambiguous queries. In *HLT-NAACL*, pages 361–364, 2010.

[46] B. Wildemuth, L. Freund, and E. G. Toms. Untangling search task complexity and difficulty in the context of interactive information retrieval studies. *Journal of Documentation*, 70:1118–1140, 2014.

[47] T. Wilson. Models in information behaviour research. *Journal of Documentation*, 55(3):249 – 270, 1999.

[48] E. Yilmaz, M. Verma, N. Craswell, F. Radlinski, and P. Bailey. Relevance and effort: An analysis of document utility. In *CIKM*, pages 91–100, 2014.

Playing Your Cards Right: The Effect of Entity Cards on Search Behaviour and Workload

Horaţiu Bota
University of Glasgow
h.bota.1@research.gla.ac.uk

Ke Zhou
Yahoo Labs London
kezhou@yahoo-inc.com

Joemon M. Jose
University of Glasgow
joemon.jose@glasgow.ac.uk

ABSTRACT

In addition to merging results of different types (e.g. images, videos, news items) into a ranked list of Web documents, modern search engines have also started displaying *entity cards (ECs)* on the results page. Entity cards are intended to enhance search experience in several ways: *(i)* they help searchers navigate diversified results, *(ii)* provide a summary of relevant content directly on the results page and *(iii)* support exploratory search by highlighting relevant entities associated with a given user query. We conducted a large-scale crowd-sourced user study, with more than 700 unique searchers, to investigate the effects of entity cards on search behaviour and perceived workload. We find that the presence of ECs has a strong effect on both the way users interact with search results and their perceived task workload. Furthermore, by manipulating EC properties (*content, coherence* and *vertical diversity*), we uncover different effects and interactions between card properties on measures of search behaviour and workload. Our study contributes an in-depth analysis of the effects of entity cards on user interaction with modern Web search interfaces.

Keywords: Entity cards; User behaviour; Task workload

1. INTRODUCTION

Current search engines (e.g. Yahoo, Bing or Google) provide users with access to a wide range of specialised search services, in addition to Web search. These specialised services, also known as *verticals*, allow users to direct their searches towards specific types of documents, such as *images*, *videos*, *news* and others. To help users explore relevant heterogeneous content, modern Web search engines merge results from different verticals into a single results page (SERP). This search paradigm is known as *aggregated search* [17] in the research community.

Recently, besides aggregating results, modern search engines have started displaying complex information objects, or *entity cards* [20] (ECs), on the results page. Similar to aggregated search, entity cards are intended to augment search

CHIIR '16, March 13-17, 2016, Carrboro, NC, USA

© 2016 ACM. ISBN 978-1-4503-3751-9/16/03. . . $15.00

DOI: http://dx.doi.org/10.1145/2854946.2854967

results with structured information, gathered from a variety of heterogeneous sources [6]. Unlike aggregated search, they are assembled using different *semantic* retrieval techniques available to search engines[1] and are displayed as a contextual element (at the top-right on the SERP), rather than an in-line result or block of results. Figure 1 shows the results page generated for the query *"castro"* by the Google search interface, which contains an entity card displayed in parallel to the organic Web results.

Entity cards are intended to enhance search experience in several ways. Firstly, they help disambiguate underspecified information needs by highlighting different facets of a user's query. For instance, figure 2(b) shows the example of an entity card displayed for the query *"Castro"* on our experimental search interface. Although the central component of the card focuses on one particular facet of the query (in this case "Fidel Castro"), the *"See Results About"* component allows the users to easily navigate search results about other facets of the query (e.g. "Castro" the fashion company). Secondly, entity cards summarise relevant content about a given topic by aggregating information from a variety of sources, such as images, maps, Wikipedia or social media. Lastly, they support exploratory search by highlighting relationships between different entities associated with a given query.

Several factors suggest that studying the effect of entity cards on search behaviour is an important practical problem. Firstly, ambiguous queries are frequent – Sanderson [21] examined a commercial search engine query log and found that 16% of all head queries issued by searchers are ambiguous. Entity cards are increasingly being used by modern search engines to assist users in disambiguating their information need. Given the frequent ambiguous queries modern search engines receive and because *ECs* are becoming a tool frequently used to help users navigate diversified search results, understanding the impact of *ECs* on search behaviour is crucial. Secondly, users' perception of entity cards can potentially influence their interaction with the search system as a whole. In fields other than information retrieval, research has shown that people can associate attributes of a contextual stimulus to an object being judged. This effect has been observed in people's judgements on the quality of products [19] or businesses [18], and is known as the *assimilation effect*. In information retrieval, this effect has been studied in connection to aggregated search, where the ver-

---

[1] For example, Google uses its Knowledge Graph to create this type of information objects; similarly, the Satori Knowledge Base is used by Bing.

Figure 1: Entity card in context, as shown on Google

tical search result blocks merged into SERPs were treated as contextual stimuli and Web results as the objects being judged [1, 2, 15]. Given ECs' contextual placement on the SERP, we intend to determine whether *ECs* trigger an assimilation effect and influence searchers' perception of the Web results, as reflected in their search interactions, which has not been studied by previous research. Therefore, we focus on studying the effect entity cards have on user search behaviour and perceived workload by conducting a large-scale, crowd-sourced user study. We aim to answer the following research questions (**RQs**):

- (**RQ1**) How does card presence and content influence users' search behaviour and perceived workload?
- (**RQ2**) Do knowledge card properties (*coherence, vertical diversity*) moderate the effect cards have on workload and search behaviour?

The contributions of our work are twofold: (**i**) we examine the effect of ECs on user search interactions by analysing 11 different search behaviour signals, and 6 components of perceived task workload, in a study with more than 700 unique searchers; (**ii**) we conduct a detailed analysis on the influence of entity card properties (*coherence* and *vertical diversity*) on search behaviour.

2. BACKGROUND

Understanding user search behaviour is a key component of modelling and evaluating search engine performance. Numerous recent studies have investigated different aspects of user search behaviour in information seeking tasks [1, 9, 10, 14, 20]. Extending these, our study brings together two different lines of research on user behaviour in information seeking: (i) the effect of *aggregated search* on user behaviour, with focus on aggregated search *coherence*; and (ii) searcher behaviour on *non-linear results pages* in the context of heterogeneous information access.

Aggregated Search In the context of aggregating heterogeneous information on the results page, user behaviour has been shown to differ significantly compared to the more traditional ten blue links environment. For example, in a study

analysing click-through rates in an aggregated search scenario, Sushmita et al. [24] found users click more on vertical results that are relevant to the task, shown higher in ranking and more visually salient. Diaz et al. [10] mined users' mouse movement interactions from a commercial search engine log and found that different results presentation strategies create various biases with respect to user attention and browsing sequence. In an eye-tracking study, Wang et al. [25] and recently Liu et al. [15] showed that different vertical blocks lead to various biases on users' eye movement behaviour, which in turn lead to different results examination patterns for both organic and vertical results. All previously mentioned studies investigate aggregated search scenarios in which heterogeneous content is displayed as a block of items, embedded into the organic Web results list. Overall, the presence of heterogeneous content displayed on the results page has been shown to influence user behaviour in various ways. Unlike aggregated search, ECs merge results from different sources into a single contextual block that is usually shown at the top right of the results page, in parallel to the list of organic Web results. There is limited understanding of search behaviour in this context and we review previous studies on non-linear results pages later in this section.

Aggregated search coherence, the extent to which heterogeneous content on the SERP focuses on the same query-sense as the organic results, and its effect on search behaviour has been investigated in recent work. Arguello et al. [1] found that the query-sense reflected by images on the results page significantly influences user interaction with organic Web results. They show that, in general, the effect of the images on users' decision to interact with organic results is likely to be greater when Web results are highly diversified. Even more, in a follow-up study, Arguello et al. [3] show that different types of vertical results lead to varying levels of spill-over interaction with Web results, and that users generally make the assumption that heterogeneous content and organic results are related and coherent.

Our approach is similar to prior work [4] in which the effects of task complexity and vertical display are investigated. In their study, Arguello et al. [4] use task duration, number of queries issued, number of clicks on Web and vertical results, and user explicit preferences to analyse the various effects of task complexity and vertical display on search behaviour. Similarly, our work studies the effect of entity cards on user search behaviour, but also looks at different EC coherence and diversity manipulation in a novel search scenario: SERPs displaying entity cards shown as contextual, non-linear elements. We also report the users' subjective assessments on different dimensions of task workload, operationalised through the application of the NASA TLX questionnaire [11]. Workload measurements using a similar technique have been used widely to understand search tasks in interactive information retrieval [8].

Non-linear results pages Web search interfaces are becoming increasingly complex, on both desktop and mobile, displaying heterogeneous results, entity cards, query suggestions and ads in non-linear layouts. Understanding user behaviour on these novel interfaces is becoming essential for modelling and evaluating search engine performance. With an eye and mouse tracking study, Navalpakkam et al. [20] found that the flow of user attention on non-linear page layouts (with entity cards shown at the top-right corner of the SERP) is different from the widely believed, top-down linear examination of search results. In addition, they show that the relevance of ECs can also significantly affect user attention, and that the users tend to pay more attention to relevant cards. At the same time, cards that are relevant to a user's search task generally lead to lower overall task duration. In the context of mobile search, Lagun et al. [14] performed a similar study in understanding how user attention is distributed between entity cards and Web results in a mobile context – in this scenario, EC content was embedded into the ranked list of Web results. They found that users scroll past ECs faster and pay more attention to the organic results right below the card when the entity card is irrelevant. Similar to the above mentioned studies, our work focuses on studying the effects of entity cards on user search behaviour. In addition to previous work, our study goes into more detail with regard to card content and structure, given that we manipulate not only card relevance, but also card coherence and diversity. Even more, our study examines additional search behaviour signals, such as mouse hovers, scroll depth, query reformulations and task duration.

3. METHOD

We conducted a crowd-sourced experiment to investigate the effects of entity cards on search behaviour. In the following sections, we provide an overview of the experiment (3.1), a discussion on the experimental variables, including search tasks (3.2), and give details on the crowd-sourcing methodology we employed (3.4).

3.1 Overview

A practical scenario that relates to our study is the following: a user issues an ambiguous query to a search engine, either because: *(i)* their information need is well defined (e.g. "Find info about Fidel Castro, the Cuban president"), but their query is underspecified (e.g. "castro"); or because *(ii)* their information need is ambiguous (e.g. "What does Castro mean?") and their query reflects this ambiguity (e.g. "castro"). In response to the ambiguous query, the search interface displays an entity card that focuses on a particular entity (e.g. "Fidel Castro"). In this context, the user must decide to interact with the entity card or Web results, or to reformulate the query. Our research questions focus on whether cards, and their properties (*topical focus* or *content*, *coherence* and *vertical diversity*), influence users' behaviour and workload during their search tasks.

Our study participants were given access to a live Web search engine and asked to find results that were relevant to a search task defined by us. Our primary goal was to study user behaviour when the SERP displays an entity card. We followed a similar experimental protocol as previous work on aggregated search coherence [2]. In addition, we also manipulated card coherence and card diversity, as described in section 3.2. After being given general instructions for their tasks, participants were redirected to our search engine, where they were shown an *initial SERP*, which contained a list of results and an entity card. The initial SERP was the only part of the experiment in which participants interacted with the entity card, and it was where all experimental manipulation took place. In addition, the initial SERP displayed a standard querying interface, a topic accompanied by a detailed description and an *initial query* for which the results on the page had been retrieved. On the initial SERP, we displayed the top-50 results returned by the Bing Web

Initial query	Task description
colt	Find information about colt, the animal.
dido	Find information about Dido, the singer.
ck	Find information about CK, the fashion company.
jaya	Find information about Jaya, the singer.
doom	Find information about Doom, the videogame.

Table 1: Example task descriptions

Search API, without pagination support or vertical results. We decided to show additional results on the page, and not just the traditional ten blue links, because we wanted to assess the effect of entity cards on the effort searchers are willing to expend during their tasks, as reflected by scroll depth.

Participants were asked to "find information" about their assigned topic, by indicating the results they considered to be relevant. Clicking on a Web result displayed a dialogue which contained some information about the result – title, URL and highlighted snippet – and two buttons for labelling the result as either "Relevant" or "Not Relevant". Clicking on different blocks of the entity card displayed a similar dialogue, containing a highlighted version of the card block.

Participants were told to search freely, by issuing their own queries or by inspecting the results on the initial SERP. A button in the top-right corner of the search interface allowed participants to end their task when they had "found enough information" about their given topic. Clicking this button displayed a post-task questionnaire, where they were asked to fill in their subjective workload assessments. The task ended after participants submitted their responses.

Before discussing experimental manipulations, it is worth reviewing card structure and components. The cards that we used in our experiment are made up of four major blocks: *Images*, *Wiki*, *Related Entities* and *See Results About*. Each individual block contains several items from its respective vertical. The *Wiki* block displays, in addition to a brief summary about a given entity, a list of short facts specific to that particular entity – for example, the entity card for "Fidel Castro' displays a list of facts about his *date of birth*, *height*, *siblings*, and others. In our experiment, all manipulations of the *Wiki* block refer to manipulations on this list of facts. Figure 2 shows several examples of entity cards manipulations, together with a card structure diagram. More details on card content and structure are provided in the following sections.

3.2 Input Variables

In this section, we describe our experimental manipulations. The variables we control relate to card *content* – or topical focus – and card *properties and structure*. The user interaction outcome measures that we employed as a proxy for search behaviour and our approach to assessing workload are described in this section as well.

3.2.1 Tasks

For our study, we chose to select 40 different ambiguous search topics and attach task descriptions to each individual topic. The topics used in our experiment were selected by following a procedure similar to Sanderson et al. [21], and employed in several studies on aggregated search [1, 2, 9]. Firstly, we selected a set of ambiguous entities by identifying all Wikipedia disambiguation pages. On Wikipedia, a disambiguation page is a page that displays links to specialised articles related to different meanings of an ambiguous entity,

Figure 2: Card examples for different experimental conditions

(a) Card structure   (b) On-topic card   (c) Off-topic card   (d) Non-coherent card   (e) Non-diverse card

and serves as a navigational hub[2]. A total of $162,987$ Wikipedia disambiguation pages were identified. Secondly, we selected only the ambiguous entities that appeared in the AOL query-log: $36,910$ ambiguous entities (roughly 22% of the initial set) had an exact match in the AOL query-log. We then sorted the set based on entity popularity[3] and selected the top 10% most popular ambiguous entities on Wikipedia that appear in the AOL query-log as our selection pool. Even though entity cards are displayed for non-ambiguous queries as well, we chose to focus on ambiguous queries because this allows us to realistically explore the effects on search interactions of both *on-topic* and *off-topic* entity cards.

Because we wanted to select topics that potentially trigger the presence of entity cards, we issued each entity in our set of $3,691$ entities to a popular commercial search engine and, using a scraper, downloaded all the corresponding SERPs. Using regular expressions, we identified a total of $2,485$ entities (roughly 67% of our filtered set) that triggered entity cards on the results page. The high percentage of ambiguous queries that trigger cards further supports our assertion that ECs are increasingly being used by commercial search engines to enhance user experience and that studying their effect on search behaviour is an important practical problem.

Finally, we randomly selected 40 entities that had at least two different senses determined by the presence of a *See results about* block on the EC, which allows searchers to navigate to a different sense of a given query. For each search task, we manually assembled entity cards, containing similar information[4], displayed in the same style, as the cards shown on the commercial SERPs we scraped, whereas the *off topic* cards contain information about the related topic, shown in the *See results about* of the scraped card. All card content, including images, was cached on our servers.

---

[2] For example http://en.wikipedia.org/wiki/Castro

[3] The number of page visits for its top-3 most visited disambiguated pages, from https://dumps.wikimedia.org

[4] There is some variation in the way different cards are presented. Some cards contain results from the maps or social media verticals. For our experiment, we decided to investigate only cards that follow the structure outlined in figure 2, and, where necessary, replaced maps with images, as well as removed social media content.

3.2.2 Cards and Card Properties

In this section, we describe our experimental manipulations of cards and card properties. We explored three different dimensions of card manipulation: *(i)* card content – whether the card is *on-topic* or *off-topic* with regard to the user's assigned search topic; *(ii)* card coherence – whether card blocks are coherent and all focus on the same topic of a user's assigned topic; *(iii)* card diversity – whether cards contain visually salient blocks of elements, such as *Images*.

The **card content** variable manipulated information displayed on the entity card and the card's presence on the SERP. For our tasks, *EC*s were either (i) *on-topic*, displaying information about the user's assigned search topic, (ii) *off-topic*, displaying information about a different facet of the user's assigned topic, or (iii) completely *absent* from the SERP. Figure 2 shows examples of *on* and *off-topic* entity cards for the topic "Castro". Our decision to manipulate card content is primarily motivated by the frequency with which entity cards are being displayed for ambiguous user queries, as previously discussed. Inferring intent from ambiguous queries has been widely studied in recent work [5, 7], and remains one of the important problems of modern Web search. Given that query disambiguation is problematic, and that entity cards are becoming widely used as disambiguation helpers, understanding user interaction with *on* and *off-topic* cards is an important aspect of user modelling.

In addition to card content, we also manipulated **card coherence** to study the assimilation effects of unreliable cards on user behaviour and workload. In aggregated search, if Web results and vertical results on a SERP focus on different senses of a given query, then the overall results can be described as having *low* coherence [1]. Unlike aggregated search, our manipulation of card coherence refers to the internal components of the card, and not the card's relation to Web results. In our work, a card is *non-coherent* when it contains both *on-topic* and *off-topic* content within the same card. This exploration of card coherence is partially motivated by previous work on aggregated search [1], and also by our empirical observations that cards scraped from commercial search engines (as described in the previous section) can contain non-coherent elements. To create *non-coherent*

134

Card Interactions	
num_card_clicks	Number of clicks on card.
num_card_hovers	Number of hovers on card.
frac_card_hovers	Proportion of task time (time_init_serp) spent hovering over card.
Web Interactions	
num_web_clicks	Number of organic Web results clicked on the initial SERP.
num_web_hovers	Number of organic Web results hovered over on the initial SERP.
num_rel_web_docs	Number of organic Web results marked as relevant on the initial SERP.
num_reform_queries	Number of user issued queries.
web_scroll_depth	Max rank of inspected (hover or click) Web results, on the initial SERP.
time_init_serp	Time spent on the initial SERP.
time_to_web_click	Time to first click on organic Web document on the initial SERP.
frac_web_hovers	Proportion of task time (time_init_serp) spent hovering over Web documents.
Workload	
workload_<dimension>	User assessment on different <dimensions> of perceived workload.

Table 2: Experimental output measures used to investigate user search behaviour and workload

Card content	Card coherence	Card diversity
Absent	-	-
Off-topic	Coherent	Non-diverse
Off-topic	Coherent	Diverse
On-topic	Coherent	Non-diverse
On-topic	Coherent	Diverse
On-topic	Non-coherent	Diverse

Table 3: Experimental conditions

cards, we replaced two individual elements within each card block – *Images*, *Wiki* and *Related entities* – on the on-topic card, with corresponding elements from the off-topic card. Figure 2d shows an example of a *non-coherent* card for the search topic "Castro": each individual block within the card contains both *on-topic* and *off-topic* elements. In our investigation of card coherence, we only manipulated the top three blocks of each card, without modifying the *See Results About* block. *Coherent* cards are *on-topic* cards with unmodified content – all elements within their blocks focus on the same aspect of a user's assigned search topic.

In addition to card coherence, we also manipulated card **vertical diversity** to determine the effect of cards' content diversity and visual saliency on user behaviour. In our study, *diverse* cards displayed all the blocks, whereas *non-diverse* cards displayed the *Wiki* block, but not the *Images* or *Related Entities* blocks, as shown in figure 2e. Note that our definition of card *vertical diversity* may also imply that non-diverse cards contain less information than diverse cards. Both types of cards displayed the *See Results About* block.

3.3 Output Variables

In this section, we describe the interaction measures we used to investigate user search behaviour and the way we operationalised workload assessments.

Search behaviour was investigated only on the initial SERP, given that our main goal was to investigate the effect of entity cards on user interaction with Web results and ECs were only shown on the initial SERP. A full list of experimental output measures is shown in table 2. These measures extend prior work on aggregated search that considered only clicks and bookmarks[1, 3], and indicate different levels of engagement with Web results and entity cards.

Workload was operationalised by applying the *raw NASA Task Load Index (TLX)*[11] questionnaire. The TLX is a tool used to assess perceived workload, and measures various types of demands imposed on participants during their task, as well as self-assessed effort, frustration and performance. It is one of the most widely used workload measurement scales[16] and has been applied in various studies related to information seeking[8, 22, 23]. Our study participants com-

pleted the workload questionnaire at the end of each task, answering 6 questions on a 5-increment 100 point scale (low to high). The overall workload was computed as the mean of individual responses.

3.4 Study Details

Our crowd-sourcing study was run as an external task, using both Amazon's Mechanical Turk (MTurk) and Crowd-Flower (CF) platforms. We decided to publish the study on both platforms because we wanted a diverse pool of workers attempting our tasks. On both platforms, we employed similar quality control mechanisms, as outlined below.

Each Human Intelligence Task (HIT) corresponded to a single search task. Because we wanted to increase the number of individual participants attempting our tasks, workers were allowed to complete no more than 5 of our HITs. The study design was not fully crossed, because we wanted to investigate the effect of card coherence only on cards that can potentially improve search experience (i.e. *on topic* cards). Similarly, we only studied the effect of card diversity on coherent cards, both *on* and *off-topic*. Table 3 shows a list of all experimental conditions and variable manipulations in our study. In total, we had 240 experimental conditions: 6 different conditions for card presence and properties × 40 search topics. For each card experimental condition, we collected 10 redundant data points, for a total of 2400 HITs. Each HIT was priced at $0.15 USD. Our tasks were completely *external* to the crowd-sourcing platforms they were deployed on, meaning that only worker recruitment and compensation was managed by the platforms. Our system assigned workers to experimental conditions, logged user interaction, and dynamically managed quality control. This allowed us to capture all the user interaction measures described in table 2. Additionally, each worker was assigned a different search topic for each task attempted. In total, we collected data from 730 unique workers.

Quality control is one of the major components of running crowd-sourcing tasks. We approached quality control from several angles. Firstly, on both platforms we allowed only workers from English speaking countries[5] to attempt our tasks. Secondly, we only allowed workers with acceptance rate above 85% on AMT, or Level 2 on CF, to complete our task. Thirdly, because entity cards occupy a large area on the SERP, we needed to ensure that searchers can at least view them. Therefore, we disabled access to our HITs from mobile devices, or from browser windows with display width lower than 800 pixels. Finally, because our tasks were external to the crowd-sourcing platforms, we were able to dynamically manage quality control on two dimensions. Firstly, we inserted two results retrieved for a different query on each individual SERP, at random positions between ranks 3 and 10. Workers marking any of these results as relevant were labelled as unreliable and were not

---

[5]USA, UK, IRL, AU, NZ, CAN

	Absent (A)	On-topic (On)	Off-topic (Off)	MANOVA	ANOVA	Post-hoc
num_card_clicks		0.216 (0.593)	0.100 (0.518)	~$F(1, 689) = 2.922$ $p = 0.033$	$F(1, 689) = 7.425$, p = 0.007	—
num_card_hovers		0.571 (1.057)	0.386 (0.891)		$F(1, 689) = 6.137$, p = 0.013	—
frac_card_hovers		0.011 (0.026)	0.008 (0.028)		$F(1, 689) = 2.208$, p = 0.138	—
num_web_clicks	13.668 (16.678)	13.338 (16.282)	11.552 (14.872)	~$F(2, 1031) = 1.922$ $p = 0.015$	$F(2, 1031) = 1.734$, p = 0.177	—
num_web_hovers	15.321 (15.667)	15.938 (16.005)	14.649 (15.653)		$F(2, 1031) = 0.576$, p = 0.562	—
num_rel_web_docs	6.099 (7.128)	5.719 (6.125)	5.192 (5.746)		$F(2, 1031) = 1.749$, p = 0.174	—
num_reform_queries	0.111 (0.350)	0.097 (0.349)	0.168 (0.466)		$F(2, 1031) = 3.213$, p = 0.041	On < Off
web_scroll_depth	24.099 (20.230)	23.153 (19.986)	22.218 (19.415)		$F(2, 1031) = 0.763$, p = 0.467	—
time_on_initial_serp	172.797 (134.723)	165.737 (129.479)	165.223 (131.490)		$F(2, 1031) = 0.354$, p = 0.702	—
time_to_web_click	22.005 (33.992)	24.050 (42.310)	27.682 (50.634)		$F(2, 1031) = 1.537$, p = 0.216	—
frac_web_hovers	0.148 (0.109)	0.170 (0.117)	0.178 (0.134)		$F(2, 1031) = 5.508$, p = 0.004	A < On, Off
workload_mental	44.417 (29.481)	46.420 (28.173)	49.985 (29.006)	~$F(2, 1031) = 1.607$ $p = 0.083$	$F(2, 1031) = 3.249$, p = 0.039	A < Off
workload_physical	24.431 (24.769)	25.284 (25.065)	26.740 (26.056)		$F(2, 1031) = 0.726$, p = 0.484	—
workload_temporal	38.163 (27.641)	38.040 (26.967)	43.083 (27.916)		$F(2, 1031) = 3.740$, p = 0.024	A, On < Off
workload_performance	15.918 (18.188)	17.060 (19.184)	17.345 (18.796)		$F(2, 1031) = 0.556$, p = 0.573	—
workload_effort	53.834 (31.437)	54.517 (29.019)	60.605 (29.603)		$F(2, 1031) = 5.260$, p = 0.005	A, On < Off
workload_frustration	28.834 (25.463)	28.196 (26.392)	29.218 (25.733)		$F(2, 1031) = 0.138$, p = 0.871	—

Table 4: Main effect of card content (diverse, coherent cards)

allowed to attempt any other HITs. Secondly, the workload questionnaire contained an additional question, ranked low to high, asking workers "How much attention are you paying right now?". For each task, the question was displayed at a random position in the list of questions. All workers with answers below 50% for this question were not allowed to attempt other HITs.

4. RESULTS

Our goal was to investigate the effect of entity cards on searchers' interactions with the results page. We intended to answer the following questions:

- **(RQ1)** How does card presence and content influence users' search behaviour and perceived workload?
- **(RQ2)** Do card properties, such as card *coherence* and *vertical diversity*, moderate the effect cards have on search behaviour and workload?

For our analysis, user search behaviour is defined as the interaction with different components of the *initial SERP*, as quantified by the measures outlined in section 3.3. Similarly, perceived workload is operationalised through post-task questionnaire responses, as described in the same section. We separate our user interaction outcome measure into three different groupings, each containing conceptually interrelated variables: *Card Interactions*, which refers to users' engagement with entity cards; *Web Interactions*, which focuses on searchers' engagement with organic Web results displayed on the SERP, and *Workload*, which focuses on several dimensions of searchers' perceived workload. Table 2 shows the assignment of outcome measures to individual groupings. This separation of outcome measures is primarily motivated by our interest in identifying and analysing overall main effects of ECs on underlying components of search interaction: card interactions, Web interactions, and perceived workload. Thus, in the following sections we report the results of multivariate analysis of variance (MANOVA) tests on conceptually interrelated outcome variables. In addition, we report univariate analysis of variance (ANOVA) test results to better understand the effect of ECs on individual measures. An in-depth discussion on multivariate versus univariate analysis approaches and their limitations, that is pertinent to our study, is available in Huberty et. al [13]. All post-hoc analyses reported in the following sections make use of the Holm-Bonferroni correction[12]. In our significance tests, we reject the null hypothesis at $p < 0.05$.

4.1 Card Content

Card content has a strong effect on user interaction with both entity cards and organic Web results, as shown by results in table 4. From the MANOVA test, we found that users interact significantly more (p = 0.033) with cards that reflect their intended search topic (on-topic cards), and this trend is supported by univariate analysis of outcome measures (num_card_clicks (p = 0.007), num_card_hovers (0.013)).

With regard to Web interactions, our multivariate analysis suggests that card content has a significant effect ($p = 0.015$) on searcher behaviour, with searchers interacting less with organic Web results when the card is off-topic, compared to on-topic or absent. In particular, univariate analysis reveals significant effects on num_reform_queries ($p = 0.041$) and frac_web_hovers ($p = 0.004$). Post-hoc analysis suggests that searchers issue significantly fewer queries when the entity card displayed on the SERP is on-topic as opposed to off-topic. With regard to time spent inspecting documents (frac_web_hovers), post-hoc comparisons reveal that the presence of entity cards on the SERPs, on or off-topic, significantly increases users interaction with organic Web results, as reflected in their document hover durations. This suggests that searchers tend to inspect organic Web results more carefully when an entity card is present on the results page. Although not significant, it is interesting to observe that when the card is off-topic, searchers click less on Web results (num_web_clicks $p = 0.177$) and mark fewer results as relevant (num_rel_web_docs $p = 0.174$). This suggests a weak *spill-over effect*, implying searchers interact less with organic Web results when the entity card displayed on the SERP is off-topic.

Multivariate analysis reveals no significant main effect of card content on perceived workload. Univariate tests suggest off-topic cards can increase different types of workload (workload_mental ($p = 0.039$), workload_temporal ($p = 0.024$), workload_effort ($p = 0.005$)), but this is not reflected in the overall trend. Users are not frustrated (workload_frustration) or perceiving worse performance in accomplishing their task (workload_performance) even when the card is absent or off-topic. It is also interesting to note that, based on our findings, on-topic entity cards do not affect perceived workload, compared to the absent condition, which suggests that even though they have an impact on search behaviour, this impact is not reflected in users perceived workload. This can be attributed to the fact that searchers are able to find relevant information in both the organic

	Absent	Coherent	Non-coherent	MANOVA	ANOVA	Post-hoc
num_card_clicks		0.216 (0.593)	0.183 (0.501)	~F(1, 688) = 0.728 p = 0.536	F(1, 688) = 0.601, p = 0.438	–
num_card_hovers		0.571 (1.057)	0.624 (1.129)		F(1, 688) = 0.409, p = 0.523	–
frac_card_hovers		0.011 (0.026)	0.012 (0.028)		F(1, 688) = 0.199, p = 0.656	–
num_web_clicks	13.668 (16.678)	13.338 (16.282)	12.754 (16.308)	~F(2, 1030) = 0.524 p = 0.839	F(2, 1030) = 0.221, p = 0.638	–
num_web_hovers	15.321 (15.667)	15.938 (16.005)	15.524 (15.690)		F(2, 1030) = 0.118, p = 0.732	–
num_rel_web_docs	6.099 (7.128)	5.719 (6.125)	5.447 (6.449)		F(2, 1030) = 0.323, p = 0.570	–
num_reform_queries	0.111 (0.350)	0.097 (0.349)	0.077 (0.318)		F(2, 1030) = 0.598, p = 0.440	–
web_scroll_depth	24.099 (20.230)	23.153 (19.986)	22.825 (19.670)		F(2, 1030) = 0.047, p = 0.828	–
time_on_initial_serp	172.797 (134.723)	165.737 (129.479)	176.743 (145.794)		F(2, 1030) = 1.101, p = 0.294	–
time_to_web_click	22.005 (33.992)	24.050 (42.310)	25.187 (34.066)		F(2, 1030) = 0.150, p = 0.698	–
frac_web_hovers	0.148 (0.109)	0.170 (0.117)	0.171 (0.123)		F(2, 1030) = 0.015, p = 0.903	–
workload_mental	44.417 (29.481)	46.420 (28.173)	48.121 (28.226)	~F(2, 1030) = 1.065 p = 0.382	F(2, 1030) = 0.627, p = 0.429	–
workload_physical	24.431 (24.769)	25.284 (25.065)	28.609 (27.291)		F(2, 1030) = 2.782, p = 0.096	–
workload_temporal	38.163 (27.641)	38.040 (26.967)	42.574 (27.769)		F(2, 1030) = 4.735, p = 0.030	–
workload_performance	15.918 (18.188)	17.060 (19.184)	16.997 (18.224)		F(2, 1030) = 0.002, p = 0.965	–
workload_effort	53.834 (31.437)	54.517 (29.019)	57.175 (29.054)		F(2, 1030) = 1.444, p = 0.230	–
workload_frustration	28.834 (25.463)	28.196 (26.392)	30.178 (25.445)		F(2, 1030) = 1.007, p = 0.316	–

Table 5: Main effect of card coherence (on-topic, diverse cards)

Web results or the on-topic card. Presenting off-topic cards can generate more workload because of the additional (non-relevant) information users need to examine while scanning the results page.

4.2 Card Properties

In addition to main effects related to card content, we examined the effect of card properties on users' interactions and perceived workload. The two card properties we investigated were *card coherence* and *card (vertical) diversity*, experimentally manipulated as described in section 3. In this section, we analyse the main effects associated with card properties on different components of search interactions and perceived workload.

Card Coherence.

Our results show that card coherence does not have a significant effect on any components of search behaviour we observed in our study: card or Web engagement, and perceived workload. As shown in table 5, some weak trends are suggested by consistently higher mean values on all workload dimensions when *non-coherent* entity cards are displayed on the SERP – overall workload for coherent cards *mean* = 45.899, *sd* = 18.106 versus non-coherent *mean* = 48.714, *sd* = 18.394 – but these trends are not supported by our significance tests. Our tests suggest that perceived temporal demand is the only measure which card coherence has a significant influence on (workload_temporal, *p* = 0.030). We attribute the weaker main effect of card coherence on search interaction to the fact that users were assigned clearly formulated information seeking tasks, and therefore were able to quickly extract useful information even from cards that displayed non-coherent information.

Card Diversity.

In addition to card coherence, we examined the main effect of card *vertical diversity* on search interaction, and our results are presented in table 6. We find that card diversity has no overall main effect on card engagement. Users had similar card click and hover patterns irrespective of card vertical diversity. With regard to Web engagement, our results suggest that card diversity has a stronger effect overall, but univariate post-hoc analysis does not reveal any significant trends. As in the case of card content, the presence of both diverse and non-diverse cards significantly increase searchers attention on Web results, reflected by frac_web_hovers

(*p* = 0.031). Another interesting (but weaker) observation is that, although not significant, users tend to reformulate more queries (num_reform_queries, *p* = 0.051) when the card is non-diverse, compared to the cases when the card is absent or diverse.

On the other hand, our results show that card diversity has a significant overall effect on user perceived workload (multivariate *p* = 0.022), with diverse cards present on the SERP generating less workload on users than non-diverse card. Based on our analysis of individual outcome measures, several dimensions of workload are perceived to be lower by searchers when cards contain heterogeneous content: mental (workload_mental *p* = 0.000), physical (workload_physical *p* = 0.006), temporal (workload_temporal *p* = 0.006) and effort (workload_effort *p* = 0.004).

4.3 Interaction Effects

Our analysis of the main effect of *card (vertical) diversity* on search interaction shows that heterogeneous content (contained by the *Images* and *Related Entities* blocks) displayed within entity cards has a strong effect on user perceived workload. To better understand the interaction between card *content* and card *diversity*, we used two-way analysis of variance tests with both card content and card diversity categorical variables. In other words, we wanted to investigate whether the effect of card diversity on interaction outcome measures varies with different types of card content. The underlying linear regression model for our tests is of the form: $outcome = \beta_0 + \beta_1 * Content + \beta_2 * Diversity + \beta_3 * (Content \times Diversity) + \epsilon$. Note that we follow the same regression analysis model used in the previous work [2] and all predictors were treated as categorical and encoded using dummy variables. The interaction effects revealed by our analysis are shown in table 7, where we report F and p-values associated with both main effect variables (*Content*, *Diversity*, respectively) and the interaction variable (*Content* × *Diversity*).

For outcome measures regarding user interaction with entity cards, card *Content* is significantly the most reliable predictor of card engagement (*p* < 0.01), and our analysis does not reveal any significant interactions between card diversity and card content. In contrast, for outcome measures regarding user engagement with Web results, our multivariate analysis reveals that the interaction variable *Content* × *Diversity* is the most reliable predictor of Web engagement (*p* = 0.078), as compared to the individual variables, *Content* (*p* = 0.852) and *Diversity* (*p* = 0.365). Even more,

	Absent (A)	Diverse (D)	Non-diverse (N)	MANOVA	ANOVA	Post-hoc
num_card_clicks		0.216 (0.593)	0.187 (0.484)	~F(1, 693) = 0.384 p = 0.765	F(1, 693) = 0.508, p = 0.476	—
num_card_hovers		0.571 (1.057)	0.586 (0.960)		F(1, 693) = 0.038, p = 0.845	—
frac_card_hovers		0.011 (0.026)	0.012 (0.029)		F(1, 693) = 0.227, p = 0.634	—
num_web_clicks	13.668 (16.678)	13.338 (16.282)	12.157 (14.697)		F(2, 1035) = 0.856, p = 0.425	—
num_web_hovers	15.321 (15.667)	15.938 (16.005)	14.892 (15.548)		F(2, 1035) = 0.388, p = 0.679	—
num_rel_web_docs	6.099 (7.128)	5.719 (6.125)	5.983 (6.752)		F(2, 1035) = 0.297, p = 0.743	—
num_reform_queries	0.111 (0.350)	0.097 (0.349)	0.163 (0.429)	~F(2, 1035) = 1.715; p = 0.038	F(2, 1035) = 2.994, p = 0.051	—
web_scroll_depth	24.099 (20.230)	23.153 (19.986)	22.962 (19.226)		F(2, 1035) = 0.324, p = 0.723	—
time_on_initial_serp	172.797 (134.723)	165.737 (129.479)	156.017 (120.043)		F(2, 1035) = 1.481, p = 0.228	—
time_to_web_click	22.005 (33.992)	24.050 (42.310)	23.168 (33.692)		F(2, 1035) = 0.268, p = 0.765	—
frac_web_hovers	0.148 (0.109)	0.170 (0.117)	0.166 (0.120)		F(2, 1035) = 3.499, p = 0.031	A < D, N
workload_mental	44.417 (29.481)	46.420 (28.173)	52.464 (26.095)		F(2, 1035) = 7.713, p = 0.000	A, D < N
workload_physical	24.431 (24.769)	25.284 (25.065)	30.233 (27.342)		F(2, 1035) = 5.091, p = 0.006	A, D < N
workload_temporal	38.163 (27.641)	38.040 (26.967)	43.819 (26.157)	~F(2, 1035) = 1.990; p = 0.022	F(2, 1035) = 5.180, p = 0.006	A, D < N
workload_performance	15.918 (18.188)	17.060 (19.184)	16.778 (17.173)		F(2, 1035) = 0.369, p = 0.692	—
workload_effort	53.834 (31.437)	54.517 (29.019)	60.539 (27.203)		F(2, 1035) = 5.469, p = 0.004	A, D < N
workload_frustration	28.834 (25.463)	28.196 (26.392)	30.496 (26.367)		F(2, 1035) = 0.717, p = 0.488	—

Table 6: Main effect of card diversity (on-topic, coherent cards)

univariate analysis suggests that the interaction variable is a significantly more reliable predictor for the number of Web clicks (num_web_clicks, $p = 0.024$) and the number of user issued queries (num_reform_queries, $p = 0.007$). This suggests that card diversity affects Web search behaviour in significantly different ways, depending on card content. Figures 3(a) and 3(b) show the interaction effect on the number of organic Web clicks (num_web_clicks) and the number of user issued queries (num_reform_queries), respectively. It is interesting to note that *diverse* cards generate more organic Web clicks when they are on-topic, whereas *non-diverse* cards generate more organic Web clicks when they are off-topic, as shown in figure 3(a) – the effect is reversed in the case of num_reform_queries, shown in figure 3(b). This suggests that when users are highly confident the entity card is not relevant (i.e. the card is *off-topic* and *diverse*, occupying a large fraction of the SERP with salient but non-relevant content), they perceive the whole SERP as being "low-quality", and this leads to fewer interactions overall. In turn, this could potentially lead to an assessment of poor search engine performance from the searchers, prompting them to reformulate the query and obtain a new SERP for inspection. On the other hand, when searchers know the card is off-topic, and does not occupy a large part of the SERP (*non-diverse*), the card assimilation effect is lower, and users tend to examine more of the organic Web results. When the card is on-topic, but does not provide heterogeneous information (non-diverse), searchers tend to issue more queries.

In addition to Web engagement, our results suggest that there is also a significant interaction between card content and card diversity with regard to searcher perceived workload. Both multivariate ($p = 0.022$) and univariate analyses on several workload dimensions (workload_mental, $p = 0.003$, workload_temporal $p = 0.012$, workload_effort $p = 0.001$) suggest that card diversity significantly interacts with card content, and affects user perceived workload in different ways, strongly dependent on card content. As shown in figures 3(c) and 3(d), we can see that on-topic, diverse cards decrease perceived workload, as compared to their off-topic counterparts, whereas on-topic, non-diverse cards increase perceived workload, as compared to their off-topic equivalents. This is consistent with our findings relating to variable interaction effects in Web engagement (figures 3(a) and (b)).

5. DISCUSSION

In this section we discuss the implications of our findings. We follow a similar structure as in the previous section, discussing our findings regarding card content followed by the implications of our results on card properties.

Card content.

In the previous sections, we reported on the effects of card content on search interactions. With respect to **RQ1**, our results suggest that the presence of entity cards on the SERP influences searchers' behaviour. Furthermore, we show that users interact more with entity cards that contain information relevant to their search task (on-topic cards). Even though this result is not surprising, it does explicitly show that searchers perceive this novel component of the SERP as engaging and useful when it contains relevant information.

More interestingly, our results suggest that entity cards influence searchers' interaction with organic Web results on several dimensions. Firstly, they spend more of their task time inspecting Web results (frac_web_hovers) when an entity card is present on the SERP, regardless of card content (on-topic or off-topic). This suggests that entity cards, beyond their informative value, contribute towards making results pages more engaging than pages displaying only the traditional ten blue links. This can potentially be attributed to the novelty aspect of entity cards and further research is required to better understand subjective preferences on the use of non-linear SERP layouts. Our findings differ from previous work on aggregated search coherence [1, 2], where only on-topic aggregated vertical blocks, displayed on highly diversified results pages, increased user engagement with organic Web results. In our case, both on and off-topic entity cards increase user engagement with Web results. This suggests that, although similar to aggregated search, entity cards – through their non-linear display and more diverse, composite content – influence searchers in different ways than aggregated search. Additional research is required to better understand the differences between aggregated search and entity cards regarding their effects on search behaviour. Secondly, our results show that users issue fewer queries when entity cards displayed on the SERP are on-topic, which suggests that users perceive certain aspects of their information need as being satisfied directly on the initial results page, by the entity card, without needing to seek further information, when the card is on-topic.

Figure 3: Interaction effects between card content and card diversity

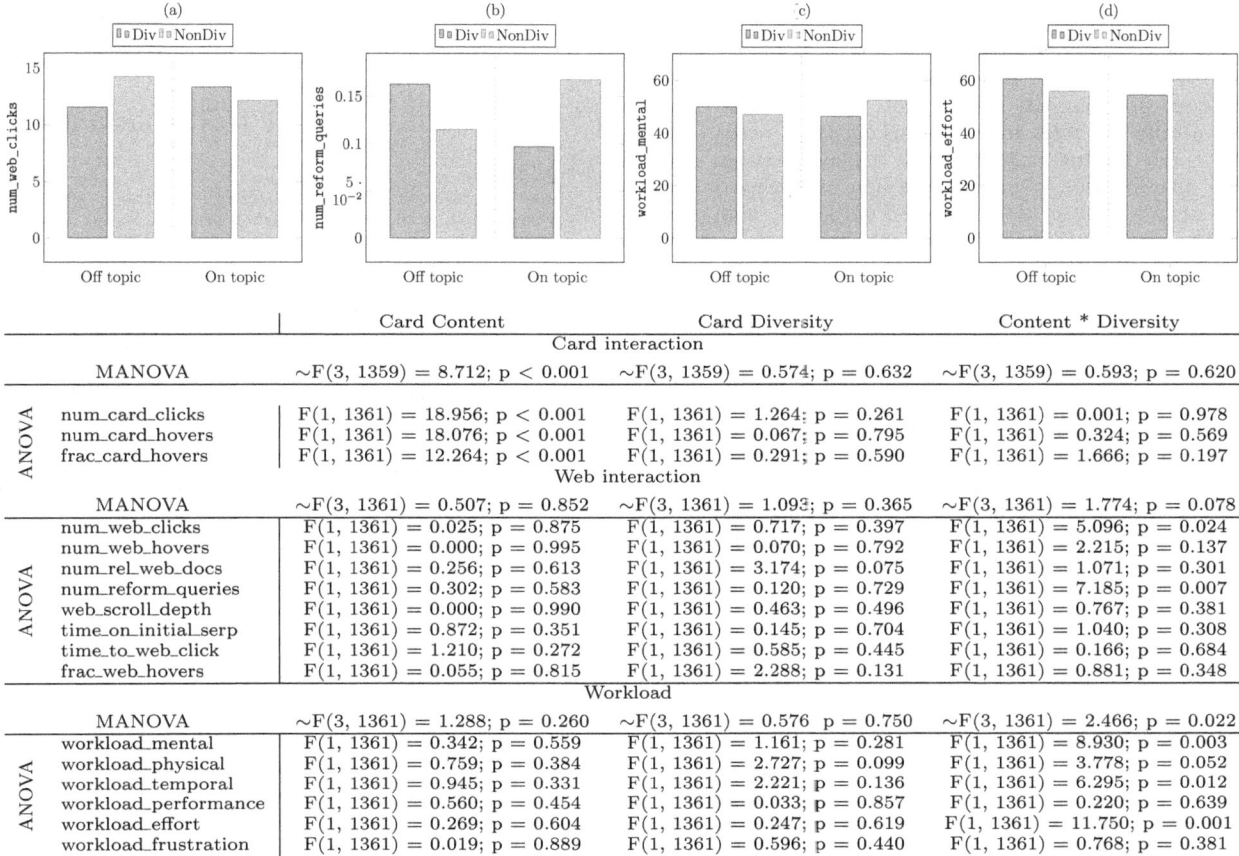

(a) num_web_clicks · (b) num_reform_queries · (c) workload_mental · (d) workload_effort — bar charts comparing Div and NonDiv conditions across Off topic and On topic.

		Card Content	Card Diversity	Content * Diversity
		Card interaction		
MANOVA		~F(3, 1359) = 8.712; p < 0.001	~F(3, 1359) = 0.574; p = 0.632	~F(3, 1359) = 0.593; p = 0.620
ANOVA	num_card_clicks	F(1, 1361) = 18.956; p < 0.001	F(1, 1361) = 1.264; p = 0.261	F(1, 1361) = 0.001; p = 0.978
	num_card_hovers	F(1, 1361) = 18.076; p < 0.001	F(1, 1361) = 0.067; p = 0.795	F(1, 1361) = 0.324; p = 0.569
	frac_card_hovers	F(1, 1361) = 12.264; p < 0.001	F(1, 1361) = 0.291; p = 0.590	F(1, 1361) = 1.666; p = 0.197
		Web interaction		
MANOVA		~F(3, 1361) = 0.507; p = 0.852	~F(3, 1361) = 1.093; p = 0.365	~F(3, 1361) = 1.774; p = 0.078
ANOVA	num_web_clicks	F(1, 1361) = 0.025; p = 0.875	F(1, 1361) = 0.717; p = 0.397	F(1, 1361) = 5.096; p = 0.024
	num_web_hovers	F(1, 1361) = 0.000; p = 0.995	F(1, 1361) = 0.070; p = 0.792	F(1, 1361) = 2.215; p = 0.137
	num_rel_web_docs	F(1, 1361) = 0.256; p = 0.613	F(1, 1361) = 3.174; p = 0.075	F(1, 1361) = 1.071; p = 0.301
	num_reform_queries	F(1, 1361) = 0.302; p = 0.583	F(1, 1361) = 0.120; p = 0.729	F(1, 1361) = 7.185; p = 0.007
	web_scroll_depth	F(1, 1361) = 0.000; p = 0.990	F(1, 1361) = 0.463; p = 0.496	F(1, 1361) = 0.767; p = 0.381
	time_on_initial_serp	F(1, 1361) = 0.872; p = 0.351	F(1, 1361) = 0.145; p = 0.704	F(1, 1361) = 1.040; p = 0.308
	time_to_web_click	F(1, 1361) = 1.210; p = 0.272	F(1, 1361) = 0.585; p = 0.445	F(1, 1361) = 0.166; p = 0.684
	frac_web_hovers	F(1, 1361) = 0.055; p = 0.815	F(1, 1361) = 2.288; p = 0.131	F(1, 1361) = 0.881; p = 0.348
		Workload		
MANOVA		~F(3, 1361) = 1.288; p = 0.260	~F(3, 1361) = 0.576 p = 0.750	~F(3, 1361) = 2.466; p = 0.022
ANOVA	workload_mental	F(1, 1361) = 0.342; p = 0.559	F(1, 1361) = 1.161; p = 0.281	F(1, 1361) = 8.930; p = 0.003
	workload_physical	F(1, 1361) = 0.759; p = 0.384	F(1, 1361) = 2.727; p = 0.099	F(1, 1361) = 3.778; p = 0.052
	workload_temporal	F(1, 1361) = 0.945; p = 0.331	F(1, 1361) = 2.221; p = 0.136	F(1, 1361) = 6.295; p = 0.012
	workload_performance	F(1, 1361) = 0.560; p = 0.454	F(1, 1361) = 0.033; p = 0.857	F(1, 1361) = 0.220; p = 0.639
	workload_effort	F(1, 1361) = 0.269; p = 0.604	F(1, 1361) = 0.247; p = 0.619	F(1, 1361) = 11.750; p = 0.001
	workload_frustration	F(1, 1361) = 0.019; p = 0.889	F(1, 1361) = 0.596; p = 0.440	F(1, 1361) = 0.768; p = 0.381

Table 7: Interaction effect between card content and card diversity.

With respect to perceived workload, we observe that off-topic cards tend to generate higher demand on searchers than both on-topic or absent cards. Increased workload is expected when the EC is off-topic, given the higher dissonance between the information searchers are required to find and the information displayed on the initial SERP. It is interesting to note that on-topic cards do not have a significant effect on workload, compared to the *absent* condition, even though they add to the information searchers need to process on the results page, and also increase users' attention to organic Web results (as indicated by frac_web_hovers and discussed previously). This suggests entity cards are informative and engaging elements of the results page, that can be easily integrated into users' search strategies without generating additional demand.

Overall, with respect to **RQ1**, our findings suggest that the presence of entity cards on SERPs can lead to increased searcher engagement with organic Web results, irrespective of card topic, and that in terms of workload, off-topic cards tend to increase searcher task demand. Our findings have implications for different areas of information retrieval research, in particular cross-component coherence for search interface design. Understanding how non-linear components of the SERP influence user behaviour is critical for developing informative user models and comprehensive evaluation metrics, and our work contributes an essential understanding of the role entity cards play in modern search interaction.

Card properties.

The results of our experimental manipulation of card properties suggest several trends. Firstly, our analysis reveals that *card coherence* does not seem to have a significant effect on the different components of search interaction we explored (card. Web interaction and workload). This can be attributed to the fact that users were assigned clearly formulated search tasks and were able to extract useful information from entity cards and use them as reference points even when their content was not completely coherent. This also suggests that cards with "imperfect" content or intent prediction (e.g. 70% relevant on-topic content) do not necessarily have a negative impact on user experience, compared to solely presenting organic Web results. Additional exploration is required to fully understand the role of card coherence in tasks of varying complexity and ambiguity. We hypothesise there might be a stronger assimilation effect related to card coherence when search tasks are more cognitively demanding and require the user to refer to all SERP elements before deciding on appropriate search strategies. We leave the exploration of card effects in complex or ambiguous search tasks for future work.

Secondly, our results show strong effects of card *vertical diversity* on perceived task workload. In particular, our analysis reveals that when the card is on-topic, non-diverse cards significantly increase workload compared to their diverse counterparts. This suggests that heterogeneous content displayed within cards is not only informational, but also diverting from task demand. Our findings have implications for designers of search interfaces, and suggest that displaying more diverse content within entity cards is to be preferred. Even more, our interaction analysis between card content and card diversity shows that heterogeneous content plays different roles in *on* versus *off-topic* cards. In particular, our findings suggest that displaying either off-topic but diverse cards or on-topic but non-diverse cards are suboptimal in terms of user perceived workload, and user interactions with the SERP. Users tend to reformulate more and interact less with the initial SERP in these cases, and from this perspective, off-topic but diverse cards perform the worst. In comparison, based on our findings, promoting on-topic diverse cards is an optimal solution, followed by displaying non-diverse off-topic cards. This suggests that, for optimal user experience, search engines should promote diverse contents within the card when they have fair confidence in card and query intent. However, when confidence in intent prediction is low, search engines should still present the card (even if there is a chance for it being off-topic), but only with non-diverse contents. Even if the card is off-topic, this can determine users to continue exploring the organic Web results, and overall perceive relatively low workload.

Overall, with respect to **RQ2**, our results suggest that card diversity plays a larger role than card coherence in moderating the effects entity cards have on search interactions.

6. CONCLUSIONS

We report on a large-scale, crowd-sourced user study that investigates the effects of entity cards on search behaviour and perceived workload. Our results show that the presence of an entity card on the results page influences searcher behaviour in terms of both engagement with organic Web results, as well as perceived task demand. Our analysis of card properties suggests that card *vertical diversity* is more influential on search behaviour and workload than card *coherence*. Furthermore, we uncover interaction effects between card *content* and card *diversity* which suggest that heterogeneous components of entity cards influence users in different ways, significantly dependent on card topical focus. Our findings have important practical implications for modern Web search. In particular, our findings can help develop more accurate user models and evaluation approaches for non-linear results pages. Areas for future work include exploring the effects of entity cards in tasks of varying complexity, exploiting user engagement patterns for card layout and content optimisation, as well as analysing searcher engagement with entity cards in mobile Web search.

7. REFERENCES

[1] J. Arguello and R. Capra. The effect of aggregated search coherence on search behavior. ACM CIKM '12, pages 1293–1302.

[2] J. Arguello and R. Capra. The effects of vertical rank and border on aggregated search coherence and search behavior. ACM CIKM '14, pages 539–548, 2014.

[3] J. Arguello, R. Capra, and W.-C. Wu. Factors affecting aggregated search coherence and search behavior. ACM CIKM '13, pages 1989–1998.

[4] J. Arguello, W.-C. Wu, D. Kelly, and A. Edwards. Task complexity, vertical display and user interaction in aggregated search. ACM SIGIR '12, pages 435–444.

[5] A. Ashkan, C. Clarke, E. Agichtein, and Q. Guo. Classifying and characterizing query intent. In M. Boughanem, C. Berrut, J. Mothe, and C. Soule-Dupuy, editors, *Advances in Information Retrieval*, volume 5478 of *Lecture Notes in Computer Science*, pages 578–586. Springer Berlin Heidelberg, 2009.

[6] R. Blanco, B. B. Cambazoglu, P. Mika, and N. Torzec. Entity recommendations in web search. In *The Semantic Web–ISWC 2013*, pages 33–48. Springer, 2013.

[7] D. J. Brenes, D. Gayo-Avello, and K. Pérez-González. Survey and evaluation of query intent detection methods. In *Proceedings of the 2009 Workshop on Web Search Click Data*, WSCD '09, pages 1–7, New York, NY, USA, 2009. ACM.

[8] K. Brennan, D. Kelly, and J. Arguello. The effect of cognitive abilities on information search for tasks of varying levels of complexity. ACM IIiX '14, pages 165–174.

[9] R. Capra, J. Arguello, and F. Scholer. Augmenting web search surrogates with images. ACM CIKM '13, pages 399–408, 2013.

[10] F. Diaz, R. White, G. Buscher, and D. Liebling. Robust models of mouse movement on dynamic web search results pages. ACM CIKM '13, pages 1451–1460.

[11] S. G. Hart and L. E. Staveland. Development of nasa-tlx (task load index): Results of empirical and theoretical research. In P. A. Hancock and N. Meshkati, editors, *Human Mental Workload*, volume 52 of *Advances in Psychology*, pages 139 – 183. North-Holland, 1988.

[12] S. Holm. A simple sequentially rejective multiple test procedure. *Scandinavian Journal of Statistics*, 6(2):pp. 65–70, 1979.

[13] C. J. Huberty and J. D. Morris. Multivariate analysis versus multiple univariate analyses. *Psychological Bulletin*, 105(2):302 – 308, 1989.

[14] D. Lagun, C.-H. Hsieh, D. Webster, and V. Navalpakkam. Towards better measurement of attention and satisfaction in mobile search. In *ACM SIGIR '14*, pages 113–122.

[15] Z. Liu, Y. Liu, K. Zhou, M. Zhang, and S. Ma. Influence of vertical result in web search examination. SIGIR '15, pages 193–202, New York, NY, USA, 2015. ACM.

[16] T. Megaw. The definition and measurement of mental workload. In J. R. and E. N. Corlett, editors, *Evaluation of Human Work*. CRC Press, 2005.

[17] M. Melucci and R. Baeza-Yates. Advanced topics in information retrieval. pages 109–123. Springer Publishing Company, 2011.

[18] J. Meyers-Levy and B. Sternthal. A two-factor explanation of assimilation and contrast effects. *Journal of Marketing Research*, 30(3):pp. 359–368, 1993.

[19] A. C. Morales and G. J. Fitzsimons. Product contagion: Changing consumer evaluations through physical contact with "disgusting" products. *Journal of Marketing Research*, 44(2):272–283, 2007.

[20] V. Navalpakkam, L. Jentzsch, R. Sayres, S. Ravi, A. Ahmed, and A. Smola. Measurement and modeling of eye-mouse behavior in the presence of nonlinear page layouts. In *ACM WWW '13*, pages 953–964.

[21] M. Sanderson. Ambiguous queries: Test collections need more sense. ACM SIGIR '08, pages 499–506.

[22] C. Speier and M. G. Morris. The influence of query interface design on decision-making performance. *MIS Q.*, 27(3):397–423, Sept. 2003.

[23] L. L. D. Stasi, A. Antoli, M. Gea, and J. J. Canas. A neuroergonomic approach to evaluating mental workload in hypermedia interactions. *International Journal of Industrial Ergonomics*, 41(3):298 – 304, 2011.

[24] S. Sushmita, H. Joho, M. Lalmas, and R. Villa. Factors affecting click-through behavior in aggregated search interfaces. In *ACM CIKM '10*, pages 519–528. ACM, 2010.

[25] C. Wang, Y. Liu, M. Zhang, S. Ma, M. Zheng, J. Qian, and K. Zhang. Incorporating vertical results into search click models. ACM SIGIR '13, pages 503–512.

Impacts of Time Constraints and System Delays on User Experience

Anita Crescenzi
School of Information and
Library Science, University of
North Carolina
Chapel Hill, NC, USA
amcc@email.unc.edu

Diane Kelly
School of Information and
Library Science, University of
North Carolina
Chapel Hill, NC, USA
dianek@email.unc.edu

Leif Azzopardi
School of Computing Science,
University of Glasgow
Glasgow, United Kingdom
leif@dcs.gla.ac.uk

ABSTRACT

During information search, people often experience time pressure. This might be a result of a deadline, the system's performance or some other event. In this paper, we report results of a study with forty-five participants which investigated how time constraints and system delays impacted the user experience during information search. We randomly assigned half of our study participants to a treatment condition where they were only allowed five minutes per search task (the other half were given no time limits). For half of participants' search tasks, five second delays were introduced after queries were submitted and SERP results were clicked. We used multilevel modeling to evaluate a number of hypotheses about the effects of time constraint, system delays and user experience. We found those in the time constraint condition reported significantly greater time pressure, experienced higher task difficulty, less satisfaction with their performance, increased importance of working fast and engaged in more metacognitive monitoring. We found when experiencing system delays participants reported slower system speeds when encountering delays on the second task. This work opens a new line of inquiry into how time pressure impacts the search experience and how tools and interfaces might be designed to support people who are searching under time pressure. It also presents an example of how multilevel modeling can be used to better understand and model the complex interactions that occur during interactive information retrieval.

Keywords Search Experience, Time Pressure, System Delays

1. INTRODUCTION

Time has figured prominently in many information-seeking models [23]. Information needs and behaviors have been modeled at specific moments in time (e.g., [9]) and as evolving over time (e.g., [3]). Models have also represented the information-seeking process as a series of events or stages that occur over time in a linear, iterative or cyclical sequence (e.g., [16]). Despite the inclusion of time in these models, few empirical studies have investigated the relationship between time and information-seeking behaviors and experiences.

In this work, we investigate the impact of time constraints and system delays on user experience using a constructivist view of time Following Ordoñez and Bensen [21], we use *time constraint* to refer to an external stimulus that places a limit on how long a person has to search and *time pressure* to refer to a person's internal response to a time constraint. As time is subjectively experienced [4], it is not sufficient to make assumptions about how people will behave as a result of time constraints during information search; rather, if and how time constraints impact search is an open question that requires empirical investigation.

We report results describing the impact of time constraints and system delays on users' experiences of time pressure, and how this effects their overall experiences. This work extends our previous work where we found participants who experienced time pressure accelerated their information processing: they queried at higher rates, viewed fewer documents per query, had shallower hover and view depths, and spent less time examining documents [7].

In this paper, we explore several hypotheses about time and the user's experience (Section 3). As is typical in interactive information retrieval (IIR) studies, we collect data about many aspects of the user's experience through self-report questionnaires and scales. These types of data are central to studies of IIR as users are the only ones who can tell us about their attitudes, feelings and experiences. Self-report measures offer a critical perspective to understanding IIR, and when properly constructed, can provide both a valid and reliable signal.

Analyzing self-report data in the context of other aspects of the experimental design, including other variables, can be challenging in part because of the way data is typically analyzed in IIR experiments. In Kelly and Sugimoto's [15] review of forty years of IIR experiments, they found the most common statistical tools used to analyze data were t-tests and ANOVAs, with little use of modeling techniques that allow for the investigation of larger numbers of variables in a single analysis. This is consistent with Toms and O'Brien's [28] call for the exploration of more sophisticated models and use of more powerful analysis techniques.

CHIIR '16, March 13 - 17, 2016, Carrboro, NC, USA

© 2016 Copyright held by the owner/author(s). Publication rights licensed to ACM.
ISBN 978-1-4503-3751-9/16/03...$15.00

DOI: http://dx.doi.org/10.1145/2854946.2854976

This discussion leads us to the second goal of this paper: to demonstrate the usefulness of multilevel modeling (MLM) as a technique for analyzing data from IIR experiments [22]. MLM is similar to many other modeling techniques, such as regression, where there exists several predictor variables and one outcome (or dependent) variable. MLM allows for analysis of data to multiple levels. In an IIR context, repeated-measures (e.g., task) would be modeled at Level 1 and the group variable (e.g., individual) would be modeled at Level 2. Using multiple levels, researchers can explicitly model the effect of task-level variables (e.g., task sequence or topic) as well as individual-level variables (e.g., demographics). In addition, multilevel models provide an estimation of the strength, direction and magnitude of each included variable as well as estimates of the variance attributable to task versus individual. We assume that most IIR researchers have little experience with MLM and therefore use this paper as an opportunity to demonstrate the potential usefulness of this technique.

2. BACKGROUND

Savolainen [23] notes "we lack conclusive empirical studies of the significance of time affordance," in information-seeking (p. 116). While time is recognized as an important part of information search, there are few studies investigating how limited time impacts search behaviors and perceptions (e.g., [6, 17, 18, 20, 27]). In their study of relevance criteria, Tombros et al. [27] found participants who had a 15 minute time limit used "more obvious" features (e.g., presence of query terms, number of links) to assess website usefulness and used a higher percentage of the allowed time than participants with a 30 minute time limit. Participants in the 15 min. time limit group reported lower levels of perceived task completion and satisfaction with the search outcomes as well as higher task complexity and stress than participants with 30 minutes.

Other work has found that a lack of time or desire to save time can influence information source selection (e.g., [11, 14, 31]) and the selection of a "strategic satisficing" strategy to find information as quickly as possible (e.g., [30]. For example, Julien and Michels [14] found that for short-term searches (answer needed within days), participants considered more of the sources they found as useful or very useful than for long-term (within a few weeks), crisis (same day) or searches of an undeterminable timeframe. They suggest the low proportion of useful sources under very low or very high timeframes might be as a result of differences in relevance thresholds and motivation in the face of different search timeframes. Mishra et al. [20] found when people search for time-critical information they were often dissatisfied with the quality and quantity of results.

Liu and colleagues [17, 18] sought to understand how time constraints and task type impact search behaviors and experiences. Study participants conducted two fact-finding and two information understanding tasks, half with a 5 minute time constraint and the other half with unlimited time. Results showed that when searching with no time constraint, participants spent more time completing information understanding tasks than fact finding tasks but produced and gained similar amounts of information, while in the time constraint condition they acquired less knowledge in the information understanding tasks. Time constrained participants also reported lower search confidence, worse search

performance and more negative affective states although no difference in perceived task difficulty was found [17]. In our previous examination of time constraints and delay on search behaviors, we found evidence of accelerated information processing in participants who experienced time constraints: they queried at higher rates, viewed fewer documents per query, had shallower hover and view depths, and spent less time examining documents [8].

Research on the impact of time constraints and time pressure on behavior in the decision-making and cognitive psychology literature often differentiates between time constraints and time pressure. This distinction recognizes that there may be individual differences in how a time constraint is experienced and a time constraint does not necessarily cause people to feel the same amount of time pressure. This distinction has not been made in many studies of information search, although we see some recognition of the differences. For example, Heinström [13] described the use of a "fast surfing" strategy that "seemed to be a reaction to stress and lack of time" by students who "tended to have a sensitive personality with a vulnerability to feelings of pressure" (p. 1447). In an experimental study in which all participants were given the same amount of time to complete a task, we found higher levels of perceived time pressure was associated with lower satisfaction with search results and higher levels of task difficulty [7].

Another way time has been investigated in information search is through manipulating system delays [1, 2, 19, 25, 26]. Users of systems with slower query response times have been found to have lower perceptions of system usability and helpfulness [1] and increases in subconscious physiological responses [2]. User sensitivity to delay has been shown to vary among individuals, the average speed of the system used [1], and how the information is presented [25].

Maxwell and Azzopardi [19] found that searchers who experienced query and document response delays marked a higher proportion of viewed documents as relevant but viewed fewer documents overall. They found no significant impact of response delay on the number of queries issued, the number of documents marked as relevant, the depth of results inspection or the accuracy of the searchers.

In an experimental study examining navigational searches, Arapakis et al. [1] added latency to systems that varied in general system speed. Users of a consistently fast search system were able to detect smaller levels of added latency (as small as 750ms) and reported higher levels of perceived usability and more focused attention than users of a slower system. Users of the slower system found the system as less usable and helpful when there was high latency added (1750ms) compared to no added latency.

Taylor, Dennis and Cummings [25] examined the depth of information processing when browsing for information. They found significantly lower website satisfaction when delay reached a tipping point around 7-11 seconds as well as changes in information processing patterns. They found no evidence of a difference in decision time, decision quality, or perceived effort as a result of delays.

Of note, several studies investigating delay also offered financial incentives related to performance: finishing the most searches [1], finding the most relevant documents (and least not relevant) [19] or finding the right answer in the shortest time [25]. While the goal of these types of instruction was likely to motivate people to search, these types of instruction might have also caused participants to feel time pressure.

3. HYPOTHESES

Based on our review of the literature, we posit several hypotheses about the effects of time constraint and system delays on search experience. Our manipulations and variables are described in the next section.

H1: Participants who are given a task time limit will report greater time pressure than those with no time limit.

H2: For tasks with added system delay, participants will rate the system speed as slower than those without added delay.

Hypotheses 1 and 2 also serve as manipulation checks.

H3: Participants who are given a time limit will report higher perceived task difficulty than those with no time limit.

H4: Participants who are given a time limit will report lower satisfaction with their search performance than those with no time limit.

H5: Participants who are given a time limit will report higher importance of working quickly than those no time limit.

H6: Participants who are given a time limit will report higher metacognitive monitoring (i.e., monitoring time remaining, task performance and task progress) than those with no time limit.

H7a: Participants who are given a time limit will report the system performance lower than those with no time limit.

H7b: For tasks with added system delay, participants will rate the system performance lower than those without added delay.

We test these hypotheses using average marginal effects of multilevel models to isolate the effect of our experimental treatments by partially out the effects of potentially confounding variables relating to task, search behavior and participant demographics.

4. METHOD

We conducted a laboratory experiment with two independent variables: type of time constraint and system response time. Type of time constraint was a between-subjects variable that consisted of two levels: a task time limit and no task time limit. All participants were given a session time limit of one hour and 15 minutes, which was communicated to them at the time they signed-up for the study and at the start of the experimental session when they signed the consent form.

Half of our participants were given a task time limit of 5 minutes per task intended to induce perceived time pressure. The five minute time limit represented approximately half the mean task completion times from a previous study [10] where participants completed three of the same tasks used in this study with the same system, without time limits. Participants in the no time limit group were given no instruction for how to allocate their time within the experimental session. Participants were randomly assigned to time constraint condition.

System response time was a within-subjects variable that consisted of two levels: delay and non-delay. In the delay condition, for half of participants' search tasks (n=2), 5 second delays were introduced after they submitted queries

and clicked on SERP results. Half of our participants experienced delays during their first and third tasks and the other half experienced delays during their second and fourth tasks. Our choice of a 5 second delay was based on prior research which has shown a delay of 4 seconds changed behaviors but not attitudes and is usually considered acceptable to users (delays of 7-10 seconds have been found to be unacceptable by users [25]). In the non-delay condition, the response time was the normal system response time.

Since the presence of a researcher has been found to induce time pressure in experimental settings [24], the researcher sat in an adjacent room while the participant completed the study. The task time limit was introduced after participants completed a practice task with the system (described below). To ensure participants with no task time limit would have adequate time to complete the exit questionnaire and debriefing, the researcher entered the experimental room and stopped participants if they were still working when approximately 10 minutes remained in the experimental session.

4.1 Scenario, Tasks and Procedures

As recommended in [5], a search scenario situated participants' searching within the context of a project in which a research team is comparing the news coverage about four topics during three U.S. presidential terms: Clinton, Bush and Obama. Participants were told their assignment was to examine the news during Clinton's second term, 1996-2000, which corresponded to the date range of the collection (AQUAINT corpus [29]). We wanted the scenario to provide participants with a rationale for searching articles from this time period and to make this characteristic salient to help ground participants' relevance judgments. The scenario indicated that participants should find 8-12 articles per topic.

We selected tasks from the collection with contemporary relevance and where prior studies have reported that participants found the tasks at least moderately interesting, but not too difficult [10]. After the task scenario was displayed on screen, participants completed one practice task; no time constraints were given and no system delay was included in the practice task. Four experimental tasks were used: wildlife extinction (347), journalist risks (354), piracy (367) and population growth (435). Because we did not plan to use the TREC relevance assessments, we only presented the topic descriptions without the narratives. Topic order and system delay were counterbalanced.

After participants finished the practice task, they were shown one of two messages. Those in the task time constraint group were shown a message that alerted them that their meeting with the research team had just been rescheduled and they would only have five minutes to complete their searching for each topic (Figure 1). We wanted this message to simulate a situation where a person receives an urgent notification, through email, chat or text, that changes his/her prior expectations about the amount of time available to complete a task. Those with only a session time limit saw a message that said they were ready to begin their first task.

4.2 Search System

All participants used the same search system which resembled a standard search engine. The Whoosh IR Toolkit was used as the core of the retrieval system, with BM25 as the retrieval algorithm, using standard parameters, but with an implicit ANDing of query terms to restrict the retrieval set.

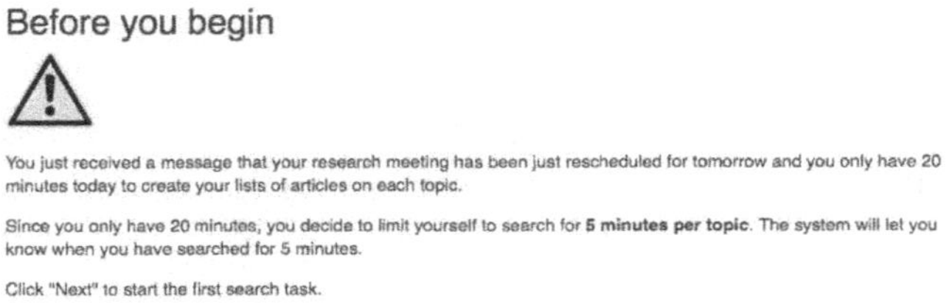

Figure 1: The task time constraint manipulation explained to participants that they only had enough time to spend 5 minutes per search task.

Only a portion of the collection was indexed to ensure that the natural response time of the system was quick and constant. This was so we could control and isolate the effects of the delay times as much as possible (both the natural delay and the one we introduced). The documents included in the index consisted of all the TREC pooled documents for the given topics, along with the top 100 documents retrieved from the full index given a set of user generated queries from a past study (approximately 100-200 queries per topic). In total over 200,000 documents were indexed providing good coverage of the topics used. In both conditions, the search system displayed a spinning wheel when it was busy. For those with a task time limit of five minutes, the system popped up a message when five minutes expired.

Participants' interactions were logged by the system and from these logs a number of measures were computed including time taken to complete tasks, number of queries issued and number of documents viewed. Analyses of search behavior data were reported in a previous paper [8]. We include a small subset of these measures as covariates in the analyses reported in this paper to demonstrate how MLM allows one to integrate these types of measures with self-report data.

4.3 Search Questionnaires

The primary data used in the analyses reported in this paper were self-report data from questionnaires. This includes data about participant demographics (e.g., age, highest degree earned), participants' pre-search evaluations of tasks (e.g., topic interest, expected difficulty) and their post-search evaluations which contained items about perceived tim pressure, perceived system speed, experienced task difficulty, satisfaction with search performance, metacognitive task monitoring and system performance. Items from the pre- and post-search questionnaires can be viewed in Tables 1 and 2. These tables show the specific construct being measured (e.g., time pressure) and the items used to measure the construct. Participants also completed an exit questionnaire, but these data are not included in the analyses reported in this paper because none of the models using these variables were significant.

As our pre- and post-task questionnaires contained multiple questions for some constructs, we created composite variables for each construct using exploratory and confirmatory factor analysis. To determine whether the items loaded on the intended factors, we conducted an exploratory factor analysis using principle factors with an oblique (promax) rotation to allow for correlation between extracted factors. Our analysis resulted in two retained factors for the pre-task questionnaire (task difficulty and task definition) and four

factors for the post-task questionnaire (time pressure, system speed, task difficulty and searcher performance). The analysis did not support the creation of composite variables for speed/accuracy, metacognitive monitoring and system performance.

To create the composite variables, we estimated a confirmatory factor model for each latent factor (construct) using the retained items. We used the estimated factor loadings to scale the contributions of each individual question to the composite variable representing the latent construct (see online Appendix: http://bit.ly/1Nm9iRo for details). Cronbach's alpha is reported in Tables 1 and 2 for the composite variables.

4.4 Participants

Forty-five people were enrolled in this study. Participants were from a major research university and consisted of undergraduate students (n=13), graduate students (n=8) and staff (n=22) representing many different majors and occupations. Participants ranged in age from 18-59 years (M=32.1, SD=12.8) and 31 were female. Participants reported conducting an average of 42.65 (SD=55.09) searches per week. Participants rated their online search ability fairly high (M=5.33, SD=1.10) on a 7-point scale (1=novice; 7=expert). Participants were compensated $20USD.

4.5 Multilevel Modeling

We analyzed pre-and post-task questionnaires using a multilevel modeling (MLM) approach. Similar to a repeated-measures ANOVA, this approach allows us to estimate main effects and interaction effects of our experimental conditions with nested data at two levels of analysis: task at level 1 and participant at level 2. A multilevel model provides multiple advantages over a repeated-measures ANOVA: (a) the ability to include multiple covariates related to task (e.g., sequence, task time, etc.), (b) coefficient estimates indicate the strength, direction and significance of effects of each variable while partialling out the effects of the other covariates in the model, and (c) effect size estimates of variance attributable to differences between tasks within an individual (i.e., variance in residual, level 1) and between individuals (i.e., variance in intercept, level 2). To test for differences between values of categorical predictor variables (e.g., topic number), we used post-hoc marginal contrasts with Bonferroni correction. We estimated our models in Stata 14 using maximum likelihood estimation with robust standard errors.

We analyzed pre-task questionnaire responses to identify which task-related covariates to include when modeling the post-task questionnaire items. For each construct in the pre-task questionnaire, we estimated multilevel models with post-hoc marginal contrasts to determine if there was a significant impact of experimental conditions (time constraint, delay), task characteristics (topic, sequence), and demographic factors (education level, status, age). There was no significant effect of time constraint or delay on pre-task questionnaire responses, but we did find significant effects of topic, sequence, age and education level. As a result of these differences, we include task-related variables (topic number, sequence) as well as pre-task knowledge, interest, expected difficulty and task definition in our analysis of our post-task questionnaire.

Already we see the benefit of using MLM in that it allows us to examine the effects of the experimental set-up (topic

	Time Limit		Response Time	
	No Limit	5 min. Lim.	No Delay	5 sec. Delay
Pre-task Questionnaire				
Topic knowledge	2.21 (1.17)	2.62 (1.50)	2.51 (1.42)	2.36 (1.34)
I know a lot about this topic.				
Topic interest	4.50 (1.59)	4.86 (1.49)	4.75 (1.55)	4.65 (1.54)
I am interested in this topic.				
Task definition (3 questions, α=.85)	5.63 (0.97)	5.34 (1.18)	5.44 (1.08)	5.49 (1.13)
It is clear how much information I need to complete the task.				
It is clear which steps I need to take to complete this task.				
It is clear what information I need to complete the task.				
Difficulty (3 questions, α=.79)	3.59 (1.43)	3.61 (1.39)	3.55 (1.39)	3.66 (1.42)
Overall, I think this will be a difficult task.				
I think it will be difficult to search for information using this system.				
I think it will be difficult to find relevant items for this task.				
Diff finish	2.97 (1.41)	3.49 (1.70)	3.39 (1.62)	3.14 (1.56)
I think it will be difficult to determine when I have enough information to finish the task.				
Search behaviors reported in [8]				
task time (min)	4.60 (.98)	9.04 (6.12)	2.51 (1.42)	2.62 (1.50)
total delay (min)	0.78 (1.01)	0.52 (0.56)	0	1.28 (0.70)
# queries	4.83 (5.15)	4.24 (2.87)	4.71 (3.89)	4.29 (4.21)
# docs viewed	15.82 (7.7)	10.18 (3.92)	13.48 (6.95)	11.83 (5.96)
# docs marked rel.	10.00 (2.76)	7.64 (3.30)	8.90 (3.26)	8.45 (3.44)

Table 1: Pre-task questionnaire, search behaviors by experimental conditions; Cronbach's α for composite variables; 1-7 scale (1=strongly disagree, 7=strongly agree) unless otherwise noted

number and sequence) and people's tasks evaluations (e.g. knowledge, interest) on the dependent variables (e.g., self-reported time pressure, difficulty, satisfaction). This technique also allows us to consider the impact of process measures (i.e., search behaviors) on these dependent variables. If we examine Tables 1 and 2 we can see how this analysis technique goes beyond what we can learn from the standard methods of analyses (i.e., ANOVA), which would require us to look for separate main and interaction effects for time constraint and delay on each of the different questionnaire and behavioral measures.

5. RESULTS

Our final dataset includes 163 tasks completed by 43 participants. Data from two participants who did not complete any search tasks were excluded. In addition, nine tasks were excluded: two tasks in which the participant unintentionally ended their task early by pressing the wrong button and seven tasks in which participants reached the end of the experimental session before completing the tasks.

Although we randomly assigned participants to condition, we found participants in the time constraint group to be younger (tc: M=29.17, SD=11.32; ntc: M=35.73, SD=13.76; $t(40)$=1.7, $p<.05$). The time constraint group also contained more undergraduate students (39 vs 12), fewer graduate students (12 vs. 16) and fewer staff (36 vs. 41); these differences were statistically significant ($\chi^2(2)$=13.29, $p<.001$). We found no differences in the self-reported search ability or the number of searches conducted per week. As a result of these differences, we include education level, status and age (categorized as <25, 25-34, 35-44, 45+) as covariates in subsequent analysis. One of the benefits of using MLM in that we can include a variety of demographic variables in our analysis, including both continuous and discrete variables, and for discrete variables those that do not have uniform distributions across category.

We analyzed post-task questionnaire responses to test our hypotheses for effects of time constraint and delay. For each construct/dependent variable, we report descriptive statistics (Table 2) and present the results of our multilevel models (Table 3). In Table 3, the columns represent multilevel models used to test our hypotheses. For H3, H5, H6 and H7, we estimated multiple models as we had multiple dependent variables. Each model had the same set of independent variables (rows). The fixed effects included in the models are at the top of Table 3: experimental variables (time limit and delay), task variables (pre-task interest, pre-task difficulty, task definition and task order), and search interaction variables as well as terms for the interaction effects and the model intercept. Due to space considerations, we do not include the fixed effects of the categorical variables for topic, age group, status and education level in Table 3 although we discuss the significant contrasts within the text.

The second section of Table 3 provide the random effects (variance estimates attributable to differences between individuals and between tasks) and information about the model fit and explanatory power of the model. A larger interclass correlation (ICC) indicates that more variability observed in the dependent variable is attributable to differences between individuals than between tasks. This section also reports estimates of R^2 for level 1 and level 2, which indicate the variance explained by the model (with independent variables) compared to a null model (random intercept only) at each level. The final section provides the Average Marginal Effects which show the average difference in the dependent variable due to the experimental manipulation taking into account all of the model variables and interaction effects.

Time Pressure (H1). We found overall moderate levels of reported time pressure (M=4.38, SD=1.71). In our multilevel model (column H1 in Table 3), we found significant effects of time constraint and delay on the composite perceived time pressure variable. Starting with the average marginal effects, we found that time limits lead to higher time pres-

Post-task questionnaire items	Time Limit		Response Time	
	No Limit	5 min. Lim.	No Delay	5 sec. Delay
Time pressure (3 questions, α=.91)	3.31 (1.42)	5.23 (1.43)	4.30 (1.75)	4.45 (1.67)
I felt time pressure when completing this task.				
I felt hurried or rushed when completing this task.				
I needed to work fast to complete this task.				
System speed (3 questions, α=.91)	4.34 (1.52)	4.66 (1.79)	4.98 (1.56)	4.05 (1.68)
The system retrieved and displayed search results pages quickly.				
The system displayed the individual news articles quickly.				
Difficulty (3 questions, α=.89)	3.23 (1.52)	3.64 (1.62)	3.36 (1.58)	3.56 (1.59)
Overall, I thought this was a difficult task.				
I thought it was difficult to search for information on this topic.				
I thought it was difficult to find relevant information on this topic.				
Diff finish	3.35 (1.54)	3.74 (1.87)	3.58 (1.81)	3.55 (1.68)
I thought it was difficult to determine when I had enough information to finish the task.				
Performance satisfaction (3 questions, α=.88)	5.09 (1.23)	4.72 (1.83)	5.05 (1.58)	4.72 (1.61)
I found enough information about the search topic.				
I am satisfied with the amount of information I found for the topic.				
I am satisfied with the steps I took to find information about the topic.				
Speed/accuracy				
It was important to me to complete this task quickly.	3.94 (1.40)	5.58 (1.27)	4.77 (1.67)	4.96 (1.44)
It was important to me to complete this task accurately.	6.04 (0.96)	5.99 (0.85)	6.01 (0.96)	6.01 (0.83)
Metacognitive monitoring				
While I was working on this task, I thought about how much time I had left.	3.78 (1.62)	4.91 (1.78)	4.39 (1.88)	4.44 (1.72)
While I was working on this task, I thought about how well I was doing.	4.76 (1.49)	4.96 (1.56)	4.83 (1.55)	4.91 (1.51)
While I was working on this task, I thought about how much information I had already found and how much more I still needed.	5.56 (1.21)	5.56 (1.34)	5.59 (1.29)	5.53 (1.28)
System performance				
This system provided me with a great deal of relevant information.	4.49 (1.53)	4.65 (1.80)	4.75 (1.74)	4.40 (1.62)
I am satisfied with how the system performed for this task.	4.51 (1.56)	4.52 (1.84)	4.72 (1.76)	4.30 (1.66)
I found all of the information about the search topic in the search system.	4.39 (1.85)	4.21 (1.97)	4.43 (1.93)	4.14 (1.90)

Table 2: Post-task questionnaire items by experimental conditions; Cronbach's α for composite variables; 1-7 scale where 1=strongly disagree, 7=strongly agree

sure (2.04, $p<.001$) while system delay lead to lower levels of time pressure (-1.11, $p<.05$). To better understand these results, we examine fixed effects coefficients. The effect of time constraint interacted with task time: time pressure increased as participants in the time constraint group spent more time on the task (β=.37, $p<.01$).

Although delay was associated with lower time pressure overall (β=-1.53, $p<.05$), time pressure increased as more cumulative delay was experienced (β=.99, $p<.01$). In addition, interaction effects between delay and task sequence indicated higher time pressure if delay was experienced on the second (β=2.19, $p<.01$) or fourth task (β=1.87, $p<.01$) compared to the first task – situations in which a participant's first task was completed without system delay.

Higher time pressure was predicted for more interesting topics (β=.15, $p<.05$) and less well defined tasks (β=-.23, $p<.05$). Participants with a high school diploma reported higher time pressure than those with a bachelor's or master's degree (BS: 1.56, $p<.001$; MS: 1.62, $p<.01$). There were no significant effects of age, status or topic.

Slightly more than half (53%) of the variance in time pressure was attributable to differences between individuals and 47% to differences at the task level (ICC=.53). Compared to a random-intercept only model (i.e., with no experimental, task, demographic or search behavior predictor variables), the fixed effects variables in the model explained 60% of the variance in time pressure at the task level (R^2 Level 1=.6) and 67% at the individual level (R^2 Level 2=.67).

System Speed. Overall, participants slightly agreed that the system displayed search result and articles quickly

(M=4.52, SD=1.68). As shown in column H2 in Table 3, we found no significant overall marginal effects of time limit (.25, $p=.57$) or delay (-.80, $p=.20$) on perceived system speed. As we found significant fixed effects of task delay (β=-2.37, $p<.01$), task sequence (2: β=-1.62, $p<.01$; 3: β=-1.73, $p<.001$; 4: β=-1.15, $p<.05$) and an interaction between delay and task sequence (delay*task 3: β=1.92, $p<.001$), we ran additional post-hoc marginal contrasts. We found that participants who did not experience delay in task 1 reported significantly lower system speed for task 2 with delay (-2.63, $p<.001$) and even task 3 without delay (-1.51, $p<.001$). We found no sequence effect for participants who experienced delay on their first task.

There were no significant differences due to topic number, pre-task questionnaire or demographic variables although fewer queries (β=-.1, $p<.01$) and more document views (β=.09, $p<.05$) were associated with lower perceived system speed.

The fixed effects variables in the model explain 43% and 36% of the variance at the task and individual levels compared to a random-intercept only model (R^2 Level 1=.43, R^2 Level 2=.36) and 43% of the variance in perceived system speed is at the task level (ICC=.43).

Difficulty. Overall, participants thought tasks were slightly difficult (M=3.46, SD=1.58) and it was somewhat difficult to determine when to finish working on the task (M=3.26, SD=1.59). As shown in H3 in Table 3, we found significant marginal effects of time limit on task difficulty (1.27, $p<.001$) and the effect of delay was not significant (-.45, $p=.46$). Examining the fixed effects, we found time limit (β=-2.23, $p<.01$), time limit interacted with task time (β=.47, $p<.001$)

and delay interacted with task time (β=.10, $p<.05$) were significant predictors of reported task difficulty. This suggests that reaching the end of the allowed time might have contributed to participants finding tasks more difficult.

Higher levels of post-task difficulty were also predicted by higher pre-task difficulty (β=.36, $p<.01$), more queries issued (β=.14, $p<.001$), and fewer docs marked relevant (β=-.15, $p<.001$). Marginal contrasts predicted higher task difficulty for participants with a high school diploma than those with a bachelor's degree (1.18, $p<.01$) and for staff versus undergraduate students (.88, $p<.05$).

We found similar results for difficulty determining when to stop. There was a significant marginal effect of time limit (2.03, $p<.001$) and the average marginal effect of delay was not significant (-.93, $p=.17$). The interaction of time limit and task time was significant in the model (β=.52, $p<.01$). Marginal contrasts indicate more difficulty determining when to stop for participants with PhDs compared to high school diplomas or bachelor's degrees (HS: 2.8, $p<.01$; BS: 2.36, $p<.001$).

Nearly all variability in reported difficulty was due to differences at the task level (ICC<.01) while individual differences also contributed to variability in difficulty determining when to stop (ICC=.23). Both the models for difficulty and difficulty determining when to stop have similar explanatory power over a random-intercept only model (48-50% of the variance at Level 1 and 64-67% at Level 2).

Searcher Satisfaction with Performance. Overall, participants were somewhat satisfied with their search performance (the amount of information found, their steps and they found enough information; M=4.89 (SD=1.60)). We found significant marginal effects of time limit on searcher satisfaction (-1.54, $p<.001$) and the marginal effect of delay was not significant (-.38, $p=.53$). The model coefficients for time limit (β=2.81, $p<.01$) and the interaction between task time and time limit (β=-.63, $p<.001$) were significant indicating that searchers with a time limit who completed their task early were more satisfied with their search performance than those who took the entire 5 minute task time.

The population growth topic (435) had lower performance evaluations than ocean piracy (367) (-.88, $p<.01$) and staff rated their search performance lower than undergraduate students (-1.36, $p<.001$). Most of the variance in searcher satisfaction was attributable to the task (ICC=.02) and the model explained between 61% and 71% of the variance at the task and individual levels.

Working Fast and Accurately. Overall, participants slightly agreed that it was important to work fast (M=4.86, SD=1.55) and accurately (M=6.01, SD=.90). We found significant marginal effects of time limit on the importance of working fast (1.44, $p<.001$) indicating that working fast was more important to time limited participants. The marginal effect of delay was not significant (-.95, $p=.14$). No other significant predictors were found. ICC was .6 indicating considerable individual variability, and 44-49% of the variance in working fast at the task and individual levels was explained by the model.

We found no significant marginal effects of time limit (-.02, $p=.96$) or delay (.05, $p=.84$) on working accurately. Examining the fixed effects, we found working accurately to be less important when participants complete tasks with a delay and a time constraint (β=-.32, $p<.05$), tasks they thought to be less difficulty pre-task (β=.12, $p<.05$) and tasks in

which they issued more queries (β=-.03, $p<.05$) and viewed more documents (β=-.05, $p<.05$). Low R^2 for both Level 1 (.18) and Level 2 (.17) indicate little explanatory power in the model.

Metacognitive Monitoring. In H3 in Table 3, we provide the results of models for each of the three questions for metacognitive monitoring as factor analysis did not support the creation of a composite variable. Monitoring time remaining in the task was significantly higher for time limited participants as indicated by average marginal effects (1.81, $p<.001$) and the marginal effect of delay was not significant (-.42, $p=.56$). We found a significant fixed effect of the time constraint and task time interaction (β=.54, $p<.05$) indicating participants were running out of time they were monitoring their time remaining. Marginal contrasts indicate more time monitoring for participants with high school diplomas compared to bachelor's or master's degrees (BS: 1.76, $p<.001$; MS: 2.05, $p<.05$) and for graduate students compared to undergraduate students or staff (Undergrad: 2.14, $p<.01$; Staff: 1.62, $p<.01$). The ICC of .38 indicates considerable variability between tasks and R^2 ranges from .32 to .40 for level 1 (task) and level 2 (individual).

We found similar results for monitoring how well the task was progressing: significant marginal effects of time limit (.84, $p<.05$) and nonsignificant marginal effects of delay (-.39, $p=.64$). A significant interaction between time limit and task time (β=.34, $p<.05$) indicated that participants monitored task progress more as they neared the end of time. An interaction effect of time limit and sequence indicates that more progress monitoring was predicted for the second task than first in the time limit group (β=1.07, $p=.05$). The ICC of .33 indicates considerable variability between tasks and the model explains approximately 25% of the variance over a random-intercept only model. The model predicting monitoring the amount of information found did not have good explanatory power (R^2 Level 1=.16, R^2 Level 2=.07).

System Performance. Overall, participants agreed that the system contained many relevant documents (M=4.57, SD=1.69), were satisfied with how the system performed (M=4.51, SD=1.71), and thought they found all relevant documents within the system (M=4.29, SD=1.91). We found no significant marginal effects of time limit on thinking there were many relevant items in the system (-.31, $p=.44$) or satisfaction with system performance (-.70, $p=.10$) nor marginal effects of delay (.3, $p=.64$; 1.51, $p=.053$). There was a significant effect of time limit on thinking they found all documents in the system (-1.11, $p<.05$), this effect was only present when delay was also present (-1.43, $p<.05$).

Although there were significant fixed effects of time limit (many relevant: β=3.6, p<.001; satisfaction with system performance: β=2.02, p<.05; found all: 2.6, p<.05), interactions between time limit and task time (β=-.56, p<.001; β=-.4, p<.01; β=-.45, p<.01) indicate that the positive system perception in the task time limit group decreased as the end of the task approached. In addition, participants over 35 thought the system had fewer relevant documents than participants under 25 (45+: -2.14, p<.01; 35-44: -2.35, p<.05).

6. DISCUSSION AND CONCLUSIONS

We found significant impacts of task time constraint and delay on participants' search experience using a multilevel modeling approach to isolate the effects of our experimen-

	H1	H2	H3		H4	H5		H6			H7		
	time press.	system speed	task diff.	diff finish	search satis.	work fast	accur.	time	monitor well	info	many rel.	system satis.	found all
Fixed effects													
Experimental var.													
time limit	-.43	1.16	**-2.23†**	-1.27	**2.81†**	**1.50***	-.03	-1.54	-1.65	**-2.27***	**3.60‡**	**2.02***	**2.60***
delay	**-1.53***	**-2.37†**	-1.38	-.51	.63	.00	.59	-.57	-.28	-1.72	.96	.01	.76
Task var.													
knowledge	-.08	-.06	-.11	-.08	.13	.05	.04	.10	.11	.07	.00	.09	-.00
interest	**.15***	.11	.01	.14	-.10	.01	.06	-.05	.10	.11	.12	-.08	-.07
diff. (pre)	.18	-.16	**.36†**	.12	-.16	.04	**.12***	.20	-.09	-.15	-.09	-.10	-.20
task def.	**-.23***	-.04	.14	-.19	-.13	.01	.08	.04	.05	.00	-.14	-.12	-.14
task order													
task 2	-.77	**-1.62†**	-.39	.07	.11	-.05	-.12	-.71	-.68	**-1.36†**	-.47	-.99	.34
task 3	.09	**-1.73‡**	.57	.61	-.29	.08	-.02	-.01	-.50	**-.87***	-.93	**-1.46†**	.57
task 4	-.78	**-1.15***	.20	.03	.36	.03	-.01	.04	-.28	**-1.38†**	-.04	-.64	.65
Search interaction var.													
task time (m)	-.06	-.13	-.05	.17	-.07	-.04	**.07†**	-.05	-.09	-.09	.06	**-.28‡**	-.06
delay (m)	**.99†**	.02	.36	.46	.26	.94	-.11	.36	.47	.64	-.48	**-1.11***	-.16
# queries	-.03	**-.10†**	**.14‡**	-.03	**-.08***	-.02	**-.03***	-.03	-.09	-.05	**-.14‡**	-.05	-.06
# doc views	.01	**.09***	.00	-.08	.05	.00	**-.05***	.04	**.10***	.03	-.02	**.12***	.08
# marked rel	-.04	-.04	**-.15‡**	-.04	**.19‡**	.08	.03	-.01	.01	.05	**.19‡**	**.19‡**	**.15†**
Interaction effects													
time limit													
* delay	-.28	.10	.67	-.14	-.86	-.34	**-.32***	-.46	-.60	-.06	**-1.07***	-.20	-.64
* task 2	.27	.12	.78	.06	-.50	.23	.07	.52	**1.07***	**.73***	-.25	-.46	-.80
* task 3	.48	.38	-.30	-.07	.86	.40	.25	.13	.88	.77	1.04	.09	-.36
* task 4	.28	-.06	.34	.33	.00	.28	.24	.04	.68	.47	-.11	.10	-1.02
* task time	**.37†**	-.17	**.47‡**	**.52†**	**-.63‡**	-.02	.01	**.54***	**.34***	.36	**-.56‡**	**-.40†**	**-.45†**
delay													
* task 2	**2.19†**	.74	.20	-.38	.24	.14	.39	1.45	.52	**1.84***	.37	.99	-.03
* task 3	-.15	**1.92‡**	-.09	-.59	.33	-.47	-.13	.29	.63	.48	.47	**1.03***	.12
* task 4	**1.87†**	1.48	-.43	-.64	-.16	-.29	.14	.19	.27	1.34	.61	.75	.66
* task time	-.06	.08	**.10***	.01	-.10	-.10	**-.07***	-.01	-.02	.00	-.06	.15	-.06
Intercept	**4.77‡**	**6.80‡**	**2.26***	2.52	**5.56‡**	**3.32‡**	**4.92‡**	**3.55†**	**4.19‡**	**6.64‡**	**4.04†**	**5.68‡**	**5.14†**
Random effects													
var(Intercept)	.62	.68	.00	.37	.03	.78	**.46‡**	.81	.56	.66	**.21***	.26	.82
var(Residual)	**.55†**	.91	1.25	1.28	1.01	**.51†**	**.15‡**	1.32	1.15	.76	1.18	1.33	1.11
Overall model													
Observations	152	152	152	152	152	151	151	152	149	152	152	149	152
Wald $\chi^2(34)$	2554‡	2745‡	3575‡	1242‡	2225‡	627‡	509‡	1751‡	998‡	293‡	2054‡	2287‡	1002‡
BIC	587	651	645	679	617	584	427	702	664	628	658	667	681
ICC	.53	.43	.00	.23	.02	.60	.75	.38	.33	.47	.15	.16	.43
R^2 Level 1	.60	.43	.50	.48	.61	.44	.18	.32	.26	.16	.53	.49	.50
R^2 Level 2	.67	.36	.67	.64	.71	.49	.17	.40	.24	.07	.59	.53	.54
Average Marginal Effects													
time limit (vs. none)													
overall	**2.04‡**	.25	**1.27‡**	**2.03‡**	**-1.54‡**	**1.44‡**	-.02	**1.81‡**	**.84***	.50	-.31	-.70	**-1.11***
in no delay	**2.18‡**	.20	.94	**2.10‡**	**-1.12‡**	**1.60‡**	.15	**2.03‡**	**1.14***	.53	.21	-.60	-.79
in delay	**1.9‡**	.30	**1.61‡**	**1.96‡**	**-1.98‡**	**1.29†**	-.18	**1.58‡**	.54	.48	-.86	-.79	**-1.43***
delay (vs. none)													
overall	**-1.11***	-.80	-.45	-.93	-.38	-.95	.05	-.42	-.39	-.85	.30	1.51	.17
in no tc	-.95	-.86	-.83	-.85	.11	-.75	.23	-.15	-.05	-.81	.91	1.63	.53
in tc	**-1.23***	-.76	-.16	-.99	-.75	-1.09	-.91	-.61	-.64	-.87	-.16	1.42	-.11

Table 3: Multilevel model results for dependent variables. Average marginal effects include Bonferroni-corrected p-values. R^2 provides an estimate of variance explained by the model compared to a random-intercept only. Post-hoc contrasts for topic and demographic categorical variables (topic, status, education level and age) described in the text. * p<.05, † p<.01 ‡ p<.001.

Construct	Time Constraint	Delay
H1: Time pressure	↑ (supported)	
H2: System speed		↓ (partial)
H3: Task difficulty	↑ (supported)	
H4: Satis. with search perf.	↓ (supported)	
H5: Speed/Accuracy		
Work fast imp.	↑ (supported)	
Accuracy imp.		
H6: Metacog. monitoring	↑ (partial)	(supported)
H7: System quality	↓ (partial)	↓ (not supported)

Table 4: Hypothesis summary. ↑=sig. increase, ↓=sig. decrease.

tal variables (time constraint and delay) from task-related (topic, sequence) and demographic (age, education level, and status) variables while estimating between- and within-individual variance. Table 4 summarizes our major findings; we discuss each one below.

H1: Time Pressure. We found mixed support for Hypothesis 1: participants experienced more time pressure with a time constraint; the effect of delay varied based on the amount of time spent on the search. Although few IIR studies have examined time pressure, our findings are consistent with Tombros et al. [27] who found time constraints made the search more stressful. We also found considerable individual variation in experienced time pressure which is consistent with Heinström's [13] suggestion that some individuals have a more "sensitive personality" that makes them experience more pressure. In the post-MANOVA univariate ANOVA tests , we found a significant effect of system delay on one of three time pressure-related questions; however, we do not find a significant effect of delay using a composite time pressure variable. It is possible that the time pressure composite variable might measure multiple underlying constructs, or be due to measurement error in the composite variable or in the single indicator question.

H2: System Speed. We found partial support for Hypothesis 2: participants thought the system was slower when they experienced delay in the second task, but not when they experienced delay for the first task. This suggests a lingering effect of the perceived system speed of their first task.

H3: Task Difficulty. We found support for Hypothesis 3: time-constrained participants reported that tasks were more difficult (consistent with [7]). System delay did not contribute to increased task difficulty.

H4: Satisfaction with Search Performance. We also found support for Hypothesis 4: time-constrained participants were less satisfied with their search performance. There was no effect of system delay on search performance even for time-constrained participants. Our finding of lower perceptions of search performance under time constraints is consistent with [7, 17, 27].

H5: Speed/Accuracy Trade-off. We found support for Hypothesis 5: time-constrained searchers rated the importance of working fast higher than non-time constrained searchers. We found no effect of delay even within the time constrained group. In addition, we found no significant differences in the importance of completing the task accurately. Our data suggests that our searchers did not believe that they had to sacrifice accuracy due to time limits, or at least were not willing to admit this.

H6: Metacognitive Monitoring. We analyzed the three questions separately as our factor analysis did not support the creation of a composite variable. We found time constraint to be a significant predictor of monitoring time and task progress but not of monitoring the information found. We found no effects of delay.

H7: System Quality. We found mixed support for H7. We found a significant effect of time limit on participants' perceptions that they found all of the relevant documents but no effect on perceiving many relevant items in the system and satisfaction with system performance. Contrary to our hypothesis, we found no effect of delay.

Limitations, Implications and Future Work. One limitation of our study is that we experimentally manipulated time pressure in a laboratory setting. Our manipulation worked to induce time pressure; however, even participants in the no time constraint group mentioned being aware of the experiment time limit and/or pacing their tasks to finish in time. Observing naturally occurring time constraints and time pressure might produce different findings. We also structured the scenario and tasks to focus on the behaviors and perceptions of information search rather than information-seeking; however, possible adaptation to time constraints in an information-seeking or work task might involve differences in time allocation to different subtasks (e.g., search) or use of more accessible information sources.

The findings from our study have implications for the design of IIR experiments as participants reported some time pressure and adapting their behavior (i.e., working faster) even when they were not given time limits. In addition, our findings suggest that task difficulty is, in part, a function of contextual factors (e.g., time) as well as properties of a task.

We found few effects of delay on the search experience. These findings are consistent with other studies [1, 19] but it is possible that selecting different delay lengths could produce different results. The intermittent nature of system delay may have impacted our results [1].

Future work will examine the relationship between metacognitive monitoring [12], task regulation activities and search behavior. While past research has not investigated the relationship between time constraint and metacognitive monitoring, we think it is worthwhile because dedicating more attentional resources to metacognitive monitoring means that less is available for the primary task (i.e., searching). Is there a relationship between good search process or outcomes and metacognitive monitoring? If so, there might be an opportunity to create tools to support an individual's metacognitive monitoring so that more cognitive resources can be allocated for the primary cognitive task.

We also found considerable variance attributable to individual differences for time pressure, difficulty determining when to finish the task, and metacognitive (time) monitoring. Future work might investigate additional factors that contribute to an individual's search experience (e.g., domain knowledge, pacing style, cultural differences).

A better understanding of time also has significance for IIR experiments, where it is common to give participants search task time limits to restrict the total time required for participation. Kelly and Sugimoto [15] found researchers reported giving task time limits to participants in about 40% of the papers they studied. In some cases, participants were instructed to search quickly or offered incentives for fast completion times. Providing such time constraints might induce time pressure in some participants, potentially confounding results. Additional aspects of the method, which might seem innocuous such as displaying a clock to help participants keep track of the time, popping up time reminders or being present in the room, might inadvertently induce feelings of time pressure in participants and require special consideration.

Finally, this paper provides a demonstration of how multi-level modeling can be used to better understand and model the complex interactions that occur during interactive information retrieval. We hope our presentation has helped readers gain a better understanding of the potential usefulness of MLM in the context of IIR and provided insight about how this technique can be used.

7. REFERENCES

[1] I. Arapakis, X. Bai, and B. B. Cambazoglu. Impact of response latency on user behavior in web search. In *Proc. of SIGIR Conference*, pages 103–112, 2014.

[2] M. Barreda-Ángeles, I. Arapakis, X. Bai, B. B. Cambazoglu, and A. Pereda-Baños. Unconscious physiological effects of search latency on users and their click behaviour. In *Proc. of SIGIR Conference*, pages 203–212, 2015.

[3] M. Bates. The design of browsing and berrypicking techniques for the online search interface. *Online review*, 13(5):407–424, 1989.

[4] A. Bluedorn and R. Denhardt. Time and organizations. *J. of Management*, 14(2):299–320, 1988.

[5] P. Borlund. The IIR evaluation model: A framework for evaluation of interactive information retrieval systems. *Information Research*, 8(3):1–34, 2003.

[6] S.-Y. M. Chen and S. Y. Rieh. Take your time first, time your search later: How college students perceive time in web searching. *Proc. of ASIST Conference*, 46(1):1–19, 2009.

[7] A. Crescenzi, R. Capra, and J. Arguello. Time pressure, user satisfaction and task difficulty. *Proc. of ASIST Conference*, 50(1):1–4, 2013.

[8] A. Crescenzi, D. Kelly, and L. Azzopardi. Time Pressure and System Delays in Information Search. In *Proc. of the 38th ACM SIGIR conference*, pages 767–770, 2015.

[9] B. Dervin. *An overview of sense-making research: Concepts, methods, and results to date.* 1983.

[10] A. Edwards, D. Kelly, and L. Azzopardi. The impact of query interface design on stress, workload and performance. In *Proc. of ECIR*, pages 691–702, Vienna, Austria, 2015.

[11] R. Fidel and M. Green. The many faces of accessibility: engineers' perception of information sources. *IP&M*, 40(3):563–581, 2004.

[12] J. Flavell. Metacognition and cognitive monitoring: A new area of cognitive–developmental inquiry. *American Psychologist*, 34(10):906, 1979.

[13] J. Heinström. Broad exploration or precise specificity: Two basic information seeking patterns among students. *JASIST*, 57(11):1440–1450, 2006.

[14] H. Julien and D. Michels. Intra-individual information behaviour in daily life. *IP&M*, 40(3):547–562, 2004.

[15] D. Kelly and C. Sugimoto. A systematic review of interactive information retrieval evaluation studies, 1967-2006. *JASIST*, 64(4):745–770, 2013.

[16] C. Kuhlthau. Inside the search process: Information seeking from the user's perspective. *JASIS*, 42(5):361–371, 1991.

[17] C. Liu, F. Yang, Y. Zhao, Q. Jiang, and L. Zhang. What does time constraint mean to information searchers? In *Proc. of IIIX Conference*, pages 227–230, 2014.

[18] C. Liu, L. Zhang, Q. Jiang, F. Yang, and Y. Zhao. The influence of task type on search experience from the perspective of time constraint. In *Proc. of ASIST Conference*, pages 1–4, 2014.

[19] D. Maxwell and L. Azzopardi. Stuck in traffic: How temporal delays affect search behavior. In *Proc. of IIIX Conference*, pages 155–164, 2014.

[20] N. Mishra, R. White, S. Ieong, and E. Horvitz. Time-critical search. In *Proc. of SIGIR Conference*, pages 747–756, 2014.

[21] L. Ordóñez and L. Benson. Decisions under time pressure: How time constraint affects risky decision making. *Org. Beh. and Human Decision Processes*, 71(2):121–140, 1997.

[22] S. Rabe-Hesketh and A. Skrondal. *Multilevel and longitudinal modeling using Stata.* Stata Press, College Station, TX, 3rd edition, 2012.

[23] R. Savolainen. Time as a context of information seeking. *LISR*, 28(1):110–127, 2006.

[24] D. Stone and K. Kadous. The joint effects of task-related negative affect and task difficulty in multiattribute choice. *Org. Beh. and Human Decision Processes*, 70(2):159–174, May 1997.

[25] N. Taylor, A. Dennis, and J. Cummings. Situation normality and the shape of search: The effects of time delays and information presentation on search behavior. *JASIST*, 64(5):909–928, 2013.

[26] J. Teevan, K. Collins-Thompson, R. W. White, S. T. Dumais, and Y. Kim. Slow search: Information retrieval without time constraints. In *Proc. of HCIR*, pages 1–10, New York, New York, USA, 2013.

[27] A. Tombros, I. Ruthven, and J. M. Jose. How users assess web pages for information seeking. *JASIST*, 56(4):327–344, 2005.

[28] E. Toms and H. O'Brien. The ISSS Measurement Dilemma. *Computer*, 42(3):48, 2009.

[29] E. Voorhees. Overview of the trec 2005 robust retrieval track. In *Proceedings of TREC-14*, 2006.

[30] C. Warwick, J. Rimmer, A. Blandford, J. Gow, and G. Buchanan. Cognitive economy and satisficing in information seeking: A longitudinal study of undergraduate information behavior. *JASIST*, 60(12):2402–2415, 2009.

[31] S. Wilkinson, W. Reader, and S. Payne. Adaptive browsing: Sensitivity to time pressure and task difficulty. *Int. J. of Human-Computer Studies*, 70(1):14–25, 2012.

Interactive Information Retrieval:
An Evaluation Perspective

Pia Borlund
University of Copenhagen
Fredrik Bajers Vej 7K
DK-9220 Aalborg East
(+45) 98 77 30 51
pia.borlund@hum.ku.dk

ABSTRACT

This presentation addresses methodological issues of interactive information retrieval (IIR) evaluation in terms of what it entails to study users' use and interaction with IR systems, as well as their satisfaction with retrieved information. In particular, the presentation focuses on test design, and it takes a look into the toolbox of IIR test design with reference to data collection methods and test procedure. It calls for careful and well-planned studies to qualify the knowledgebase generated as a result of the conducted IIR studies.

The presentation further reflects on the need for an updated theoretical framework to describe partly the various types of IIR, and partly how IIR nowadays often is carried out in a seamless task switching IT environment on various platforms, including via apps. This type of environment furthermore calls for new methodologies to study the IIR behaviour in the habitat of the users to ensure a complete and realistic picture to enhance our understanding of IIR.

The presentation also reflects on whether a re-thinking of the concept on an information need is necessary. One may ask whether it still makes sense to talk about types of information needs. Or should we rather study IIR from the perspective of search dedication and task load in order to also include everyday life information seeking?

With this presentation, the IIR community is invited to an exchange of ideas and is encouraged to engage in collaborations with the solving of these (and other) issues to our joint advantage.

CHIIR'16, March 13–17, 2016, Carrboro, North Carolina, USA
ACM ISBN: 978-1-4503-3751-9/16/03.
DOI: http://dx.doi.org/10.1145/2854946.2870648

A Usefulness-based Approach for Measuring the Local and Global Effect of IIR Services

Daniel Hienert and Peter Mutschke
GESIS – Leibniz Institute for the Social Sciences
Cologne, Germany
{firstname.lastname}@gesis.org

ABSTRACT

In Interactive Information Retrieval (IIR) different services such as search term suggestion can support users in their search process. The applicability and performance of such services is either measured with different user-centered studies (like usability tests or laboratory experiments) or, in the context of IR, with their contribution to measures like precision and recall. However, each evaluation methodology has its certain disadvantages. For example, user-centered experiments are often costly and small-scaled; IR experiments rely on relevance assessments and measure only relevance of documents. In this work we operationalize the usefulness model of Cole et al. (2009) on the level of system support to measure not only the local effect of an IR service, but the impact it has on the whole search process. We therefore use a log-based evaluation approach which models user interactions within sessions with positive signals and apply it for the case of a search term suggestion service. We found that the usage of the service significantly often implicates the occurrence of positive signals during the following session steps.

Keywords

Usefulness; IIR; Evaluation; Term Suggestion; Query Suggestion

1. INTRODUCTION

There are numerous services which support users in their information seeking process such as term or query suggestions, personalization, faceted navigation, relevance feedback, visual representations, re-ranking mechanisms, browsing facilities or related items. Different methodologies are available to evaluate the applicability, usability, effectiveness or performance of such services. User-centered studies aim to identify usability or interaction problems which are based on the user's interaction with the system. This reveals the human's view on an IR service [cp. 20]. In classical IR the focus is on document relevancy which is measured by variables such as precision and recall on the basis of available relevance assessments. Accordingly, the influence of supporting services is measured by their positive impact to these traditional measures.

As a novel approach Cole et al. [4] introduced the notion of *usefulness* as a general criterion of "how well the user is able to achieve his goal" in the system under study. The authors present an IIR evaluation model which asks for usefulness on three different levels: a) the entire information seeking episode and the leading task, b) each interaction and its contribution to the leading task and c) the system support toward the goal of each interaction and of each information seeking strategy (ISS). This perspective takes "both task success and the value of support given over the entire information seeking episode" [4] into account. This represents a novel paradigm in IR evaluation insofar as it expands the perspective to the entire search process instead of just evaluating single search results with respect to relevancy [cp. 5]. However, it remains difficult in a complex environment to answer these questions, especially if the user's task and subtasks remain unclear. Moreover, there is still a lack of computational methods that can be applied to evaluate interactive IR systems.

In this work we try to operationalize the usefulness model on a local and global level in the form of a computational model that can be applied in large-scale evaluation studies. Following the different evaluation levels described by [4] we focus on the usefulness of a single service of an IR system for supporting a single ISS (local usefulness of the service) as well as its contribution to the usefulness of the entire system in accomplishing the user's information seeking goal (global usefulness of the service). Following [4] which introduces usefulness as a concept "suited to interaction measurement" we use a log-based approach focusing on interaction events that indicate a positive impact of the service. We then apply this evaluation methodology to the case of a search term suggestion service and discuss the results.

2. BACKGROUND AND RELATED WORK

2.1 Evaluation Models

The measurement of document relevancy with evaluation initiatives such as TREC [31] has been the predominant evaluation methodology over the last decades. However, the field of IR opens to a more holistic view of the search and information process and puts the user in context. Ingwersen & Järvelin [13] present an evaluation model that asks beside the (a) IR context, for the (b) seeking-, (c) work task and (d) socio-organizational/cultural context. That automatically leads to other evaluation criteria such as usability, quality of information process, quality of information and work process/results, socio-cognitive relevance and quality of work task result.

The usefulness model as a holistic evaluation model [cp. 4] assumes a *problematic situation* a user has by lacking knowledge about a topic. The general information seeking *goal/task* is then to achieve this knowledge. This overall goal can be subdivided into several *sub-goals*, each described by an *information interaction* to achieve the subgoal and, to this end, the general goal, e.g.

collecting information, learning about the material or comparing results. Therefore, each information seeking episode can be seen as a sequence of *information seeking strategies* (IIS, [3]), e.g. querying, receiving results or evaluating documents which the IR system can support. Accordingly, usefulness can be measured on three levels as mentioned above.

This makes the model a good starting point for IIR evaluation because it describes the information seeking process from the user's point of view and how the IR system can support it. For the broad application of the model there are some challenges: (1) the users' overall goal and sub goals are often unknown in real world applications, (2) until now it has not been shown how the theoretical model of usefulness can be transformed into practice and how it can be operationalized.

As regards (1), it must be pointed out that the usefulness model is very much designed around precise knowledge about the leading goal and the following tasks of a particular user [34]. However, the overall task and sub tasks are often only available in a laboratory setting where evaluation studies are conducted in direct contact with users. In real-world systems, in contrast, knowledge about tasks is hard to collect. One possible solution is to explicitly ask the user for the task by some system dialogues, another is the extraction of tasks from log files by clustering search queries from web search engines [23,32]. The task-based session then contains all search queries for a particular search intention. However, the overall goal and task is still missing, especially with more complex and longitudinal information problems as in IIR.

As regards (2), Cole et al. [4] provide a non-exclusive list of questions at the different levels, such as "How *useful* were suggested queries/terms for formulating queries?" or "How *well* does the system support evaluation of retrieved documents?". The intention of Cole et al. [4] is to let the user give the answers within user studies. However, user studies are often small-scaled and very much specific to a particular system. In a large-scale evaluation setting, however, which needs a computational model, most of the evaluation questions proposed by [4] are hard to answer since adjectives such as "useful" or "well" are hard to capture by computational measures.

The central research question of our paper therefore is: "How can usefulness of a particular IR service under study be approximated in the form of log data based measures?" The availability of a reliable approach for this would allow large-scale experiments and the application in very different contexts and IR systems.

2.2 Evaluation Methodologies

For the field of Interactive Information Retrieval (IIR) Kelly [20] gives a good overview of existing and established evaluation methodologies and measures. She proposes a research continuum which has on the one side TREC-style studies which build the system focus on IIR evaluation and on the other side the observation of information-seeking in context which build the most human focus on IIR evaluation. The archetypical IIR evaluation study is represented by the TREC Interactive Track. Seen from there log analysis studies are situated one step towards the system focus. According to Kelly "search engine logs look at queries, search results and click-through behavior" [20] and log analysis is more descriptive than explanatory, also "it is possible to model user behavior and interactions for certain situations" [20].

For the basic possibilities and limitations of search log analysis Jansen [14] gives a good overview. Log analysis can identify trends and typical interactions, but cannot record the user's

perception of the task, the underlying information need or the underlying situation and context of the search. A review of log analysis literature is given in [1]. The authors distinguish explicitly between Web search engine log analysis (WSE) and digital library log analysis (DLS) as in WSE the retrieved documents are web pages and in DLS documents with a quality maintained by professionals. Additionally, in DLS document collections are mostly organized and structured by a knowledge organization system and users in DL search are much more specific around a community of a domain or a certain topic.

2.3 Interaction Measurement

Interaction measurement as a methodic approach to solve IR problems is in line with current works addressing whole user sessions and multiple sessions. For example, Wildemuth [33] examined search tactics behavior of medical students searching a database in microbiology. She found patterns of search tactics where users added and deleted concepts to their search queries and shows that domain knowledge influences search tactics behavior. Jansen et al. [15] found analog to prior results that in web search main transition patterns are generalization and specialization. Additionally, different measures have been found as signals for session behavior. For example, Fox et al. [7] found in a user study that a combination of click-through, time spending on the search result page and how a user exited a result of a search session correlates best with user satisfaction. Liu et al. [22] identified three main behavioral measures as important for document usefulness in a laboratory experiment: dwell time on documents, the number of times a page has been visited during a session and the timespan before the first click after a query is issued. Predictive models have then been applied to the TREC 2011 Session Track and showed improvement over the baseline by using pseudo relevance feedback on the last queries in each session. Azzopardi [2] suggested different effectiveness measures for IR systems based on a stream-based view of documents in the IR process including a window-based approach. Thomas [29] uses positive and negative signals of web sessions such as session duration or scrolling events to determine if users are struggling. Navigation patterns that correlate with these signals can then help website authors to reveal navigational problems. Kelly [21] gives an overview of related work which utilizes implicit feedback from users, mainly applied for query expansion or user profiling. Implicit feedback is given by user behavior such as viewing, printing or quoting a document. Zhang & Kamps [36] for example used email correspondence between archivists and users which reference documents for specific topics as ground-truth. For the approach of click-through data, it is assumed that a document has certain relevance if the user clicks on it. Joachims et al. [16,17] analyzed click-through data as implicit feedback in web search and found that on average click data is reasonable accurate but biased by the trust in the retrieval function and the quality of the result set. Kamps et al. [18] compared click-through and user judgements on the base of different test collections and manually created and assessed topics. They found that in their comparison the agreement is only small and have some biases. For example the number of relevant documents for a topic depending on the test collection can differ.

2.4 Search Term Suggestion

Typically there is a gap between the user's natural language and the vocabulary an information system uses to index its documents which is described as the "vocabulary problem" [8]. Knowledge organization systems (KOS) such as thesauri, classifications and ontologies contain knowledge structures which can help improve the search process, for instance by expanding the search query (e.g. [35]) with near-by concepts for better retrieval results. On the user interface, users can be supported with a list of query or term suggestions. Search term recommenders today are widely implemented, from web search engines to e-commerce platforms. Terms proposed to the user can derive from a number of different sources. Efthimiadis [6] distinguishes between (1) collection dependent and independent knowledge structures such as thesauri and (2) knowledge from search results. Vechtomova [30], for example compared two approaches based on a co-occurrence analysis on the entire document collection and on a subset from the retrieved results and found that the local approach performed clearly better for query expansion. But also other sources such as query logs [12] have been used as vocabulary for term recommendation. Schatz et al. [28] compared term recommenders based on a subject thesauri and from a co-occurrence list. They conclude that a combination of both in one interface with multiple views can be advantageous for users to choose recommendations from multiple sources. Nowadays, term suggestion services are used in a lot of information systems especially on commercial platforms, but larger digital libraries such as the ACM Digital Library or Google Scholar are still struggling offering them (compare [25] for a short list). One of the reasons can be the broad content or a missing knowledge organization system to structure it.

The use of search term recommenders can improve the retrieval performance in the sense of document relevancy. So, it has been shown that query expansion based on a local subset of documents from the result list [26,35] or discipline-specific query expansion [24,27] can result in significantly better results. Thus, term suggestion services in digital libraries (especially in domain-specific ones with organized content) seem to be useful insofar as they can help to suggest the user query terms, titles, authors, journals and so on. However, beyond document relevancy, it is difficult to measure which effect an IR system or a particular service of the system has on the entire search or interaction process.

3. APPROACH
In contrast to many other measures, which evaluate single elements of a retrieval system (such as the quality of its ranking), usefulness aims at evaluating the degree to which the system under study helps the user in solving his/her information seeking problem. This includes the quality of the entire search process consisting of functionalities beyond pure searching offered by many digital libraries, such as navigating through link structures, structuring, sharing, storing and exporting information, which broaden the amount of possible user-system interactions. Given this, user-system-interactions lead to valuable data for a better understanding of user needs and information behavior. Following [4] usefulness "is suited to interaction measurements". Thus, we suppose that by a particular analysis of interaction measurement usefulness can be approximated beside from relevancy.

Cole et al. [4] consider usefulness on the level of the entire "information seeking episode" as well as on the level of each single ISS (given by an interaction) and its contribution to achieve the leading information seeking goal. Accordingly, we differentiate between local and global usefulness of the service that implements the ISS in question. Following the overview of Kelly [21] and also Thomas [29] which describe implicit feedback as indicators of user preference, user satisfaction and interests, an intuitive notion of local usefulness is the amount of positive choices of a particular ISS, given by invoking a single interaction

such as the selection of a term provided by a term suggestion service. Therefore, we utilize the frequency of interactions that stand for the particular service under study to define *local usefulness* as the percentage of the services usage in all search processes. This is basically a usage-based notion of usefulness providing a clue of how useful the service is considered by users to achieve a certain sub goal (such as selecting a proper search term by the help of a search term recommender), and it is a local measure since it refers to the *current* phase of the search process: The more often the service has been used, the greater its (expected) usefulness for supporting the user on the local level of a single ISS.

On the level of the entire search session we can then ask for the degree to which the use of the service contributes to successfully accomplish the leading information seeking goal. An approach for estimating global usefulness is to count the amount of positive signals emanating from the (local) use of the service in question. Thus, we define *global usefulness* as the degree to which the use of a certain service on the local level leads to positive signals of search success in the succeeding phase of the search session. In contrast to local usefulness this is a success-based notion of usefulness, and it is a global measure since it refers to the entire search session: The more often the service in question leads to positive signals in a later phase of the session, the greater its usefulness in supporting the user on the level of the entire information seeking episode.

Formally, we define the *retrieval system R* to consist of a set D of *documents*, a set E of possible *interaction events* and a set U of different *users*:

$R = (D, E, U)$, where $D = \{d_1, \ldots, d_n\}$, $E = \{e_1, \ldots, e_n\}$ and $U = \{u_1, \ldots, u_n\}$

A *search process p* is a sequence of search events $e \in E$ invoked by a user $u \in U$, starting with a start search event, e.g. *enter_search_term* and ending with either a terminal event of the session, such as *logout*, or the last event preceding a new start search event which indicates the start of a new search process:

$p_u = (enter\_search\_term, e_2, \ldots, e_n)$

The explicit usage of a particular IR service by the user (e.g. choosing a term from a recommender) is indicated by the dedicated event $e_{IRService} \in E$.

Success events $SE \subset E$ are a subset of events indicating positive signals of success in a search process, e.g.

$SE_i = \{print\_record, export\_record, bookmark\_record\}$

A window of events $w(n)$ is a sequence of interaction events, starting with a particular initial event $e_{Initial} \in E$, followed by n succeeding events:

$w(n) := (e_{Initial}, \ldots, e_n)$

$e_{IRService}^+(w(n))$ indicates search success in terms of incidence of positive signals following the use of the IR service in question. The function returns 1 if the usage of the IR service is followed by at least one success event within a window of n succeeding events (for $e_{Initial} = e_{IRService}$), otherwise 0. However, a value of 1 does not mean that the use of the IR service causes the positive signal. But it points to the co-incidence of the two events in question during the search process. Our intention is to enable comparisons between different services as well as different searches with/without usage of a particular service as regards their effect on search success.

Similarly, $e_{Search}^+(w(n))$ is 1 if a search is followed by at least one success event in a window of n succeeding events, otherwise 0.

The *local usefulness* of an IR service is then defined as the ratio of the count of all IR service usages to the number of all search processes:

$$LocalUsefulness\,(IRService) = \frac{\sum (e_{IRService})}{|p|}$$

The *global usefulness* of an IR service is defined as the ratio of the count of all IR service usages followed by a positive signal within a window of n succeeding events to the number of all usages of the IR service.

$$GlobalUsefulness\,(IRService) = \frac{\sum (e_{IRService}^+(w(n)))}{|e_{IRService}|}$$

Both metrics provide numbers in the range [0:1].

This can be compared to the global usefulness of a search without the usage of the IR service which is defined as the ratio of the count of search events followed by a positive signal in a window of n succeeding events to all search events:

$$GlobalUsefulness\,(Search) = \frac{\sum (e_{Search}^+(w(n)))}{|e_{Search}|}$$

The values of global usefulness for *IRService* and *Search* can then finally be compared in order to find the smallest window of actions where the difference in values is significant. Consider for example the log of a retrieval system is the following:

Table 1. Local/Global Usefulness Example

Search process	Events
1	enter_search_term→select_term_from_recommender→search →view_record_1→view_record_2→view_record_3→ export_record
2	enter_search_term→select_term_from_recommender→search →view_record_1→view_record_2→logout
3	enter_search_term→search→view_record_1→view_record_2 →view_record_3
4	enter_search_term→search→view_record_1→view_record_2 →view_record_3→view_record_4→view_record_5
5	enter_search_term→select_term_from_recommender→search →view_record_1→view_record_2→bookmark_record→ view_record_3
6	enter_search_term→search→view_record_1→export_record

In the given example (see Table 1) the *LocalUsefulness* (*select_term_from_recommender*) is then 0.5 as in three out of six search processes the recommender was used.

The *GlobalUsefulness* (*select_term_from_recommender*) is 0.66 in a window of five succeeding actions as two out of three search processes with term recommender usage are followed by a positive signal in a window of five actions. We can furthermore compare the effect of using and non-using the term recommender on search success. Given this example, the ratio of searches without term recommender usage but incidence of a positive signal is just one out of three (0.33), which differs immensely from the global usefulness of 0.66 found for the term recommender. This result emphasizes the positive effect of the search term recommender on search success, i.e. its usefulness. The values furthermore show that this positive effect correlates not very well with the usage rate (50%) on the local level which

may indicate some potential for improvements of the service locally.

A strength of this approach is that it does not need to know the concrete task of the user but appropriate interaction logs. For measuring local usefulness we just need to count the interactions that stand for the service in question. To estimate global usefulness of a service we need to define the set of interactions representing positive signals of search success. This is surely the crucial point of the proposed approach since we need to make some assumptions about positive signals of search success. However, we believe that for each IR system a domain-specific set of positive signals can be defined on the ground of the purpose of the system in question. For the case of a scholarly information portal, for instance, downloading found publications is certainly a strong indication of search success.

In the following we present a case study with a search term recommender provided by a digital library of the Social Sciences where we apply the above introduced measures of local and global usefulness. Our focus in this study is on the occurrence of positive signals in search processes using vs. not using the term recommender.

4. EXAMPLE OF USE

4.1 Use Case: The Combined Term Suggestion Service

A search term recommenders is a value-added IR service which aims at improving retrieval quality by proposing the user more proper search terms. In [11] we have tested search term recommenders with different vocabularies (user terms, terms from a heterogeneity service, thesaurus terms, co-word analysis) in Sowiport and found that a combination of thesaurus terms and co-word analysis terms works best with respect to user acceptance. The service has been used in about 14% of 3,604 search queries submitted by 1,000 unique users. In this work we build on these results and have implemented an extended recommender service which combines (1) thesaurus terms, (2) additional related thesaurus terms and (3) terms from the Search Term Recommender (STR). The STR works on the basis of co-word analysis from titles and abstracts to thesaurus terms.

The combined search term suggestion service (CTS) [11] is integrated in the Social Science Digital Library Sowiport[1] [10]. The portal contains more than 8 million literature references, full texts and research projects from 18 different databases and reaches more than 20,000 unique users per month. The CTS has been integrated into the search bar on the start page and above the result list for the search form field types "All Fields" and "Keywords". For the other types (Title, Institution, Numbers, Date) we use the autocomplete functionality of the underlying VuFind[2] framework based on the Solr index. On the user interface, in the upper part of the CTS (see Figure 1), users are proposed up to five descriptors from the thesaurus that autocomplete already entered characters. Additionally, for each thesaurus term, all thesaurus terms with a semantic relation like broader, narrower or related are shown in a line underneath in a lighter font color. In the lower part, under the heading "Alternative keywords", the recommender suggests up to five

---

[1] http://sowiport.gesis.org

[2] http://vufind.org

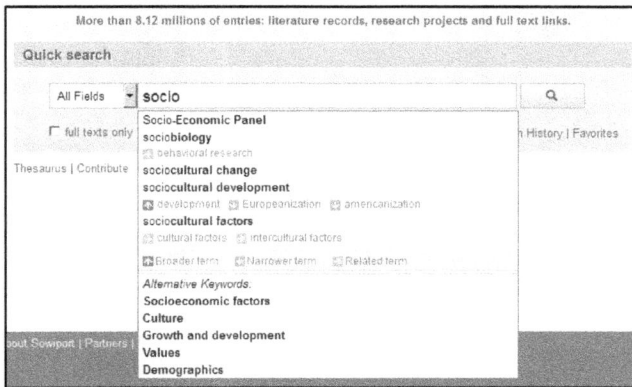

Figure 1. A screenshot of the term suggestion service in Sowiport. The service recommends more appropriate terms from controlled vocabulary (such as "Socio-Economic Panel" for the search term "socio") as well as alternative terms returned by a co-word analysis (here, "Socioeconomic factors").

terms from the STR. Figure 1 shows a screenshot of the CTS included in Sowiport.

4.2 Data Set & Methodology

Given our definition of usefulness described above, in this case study we count the frequency to which the CTS has been used (to measure local usefulness) and the degree to which term selections from the CTS co-occurs with positive signals of search success in the following search process. For this, we first need to define the set of positive signals indicating search success. In the case of Sowiport there are a number of interactions on the hit list of a search and in the detailed document view that can be considered as positive indications of a successful search, for example downloading the full text from a record in the result list. See Table 2 for a list of all positive signals and their descriptions.

We then measure the co-occurrence between CTS usages and positive signals on the basis of log data. For this we have used the WHOSE log analysis tool for IIR [9]. The tool allows to load log data from a digital library and to examine user session data with filters, visualizations and a detailed session list with all interactions. We used the tool for the preparation of session data with log data from Sowiport from 15th July 2014 to 15th July 2015

Table 2. Positive Signals in Sowiport

Short	Description
goto_fulltext	Follow an external link which leads to a full text in PDF or HTML format
goto_google_scholar	Search the record in Google Scholar
goto_google_books	Search the record in Google Books
goto_local_availability	Check for availability in a local library
view_description	View the record's abstract
view_citation	View the record's citation data
view_references	View the record's references
export_cite	View record in different citation styles
export_bib	Export the record to different citation formats
export_mail	Send the record via email
save_to_multiple_favorites	Check several records in the result list and save them to favorites
to_favorites	Save a single record to favorites
export_search_mail,	Send the search via email
save_search	Save the search to favorites
save_search_history	Save a search from the history to favorites

including all user interactions, e.g. a term selection from the CTS by a user is logged by the event CTS_select. See Table 3 for some basic search interactions.

Table 3. Some basic search interactions in Sowiport

Short	Description
CTS_select	A user selects a term from the CTS
CTS_search	A search from a search form with the field type selected to "All Fields" (default setting) or "Keywords"
search	A general search from a search form, an internal link or by URL from a search engine etc.
view_record	A click on a record in the result list to see the detailed view of a record

The result is a database that contains all user sessions with its actions and parameters. The tool also prepares session patterns containing the sequence of actions of a session in the form "*action_1>>action_2>>action_3*". To measure local usefulness we used the count of CTS_select occurrences in the data set. To compute the global usefulness of the CTS we measured the co-occurrence between CTS_select and positive signals within a certain event window. For this, we defined a regular expression to identify relationships between CTS_select and positive signals within an event window of n actions, for all $n \leq 17$. By this, we obtained both information on the relationship between the occurrence of CTS_select (the use of the term suggestion service) and positive signals of search success as well as information on the point in time (in terms of interactions) in which a positive signal occurs after submitting CTS_select. For the comparison to searches without CTS usage we defined a regular expression to get all event windows with the starting event CTS_search ("CTS usage would be possible...") not preceded by CTS_select ("...but has not been used"). This makes the comparison between event windows with vs. without CTS usage more precise as no general searches e.g. from internal links or URLs are included.

5. RESULTS

5.1 Local Usefulness

In the evaluation period 59,568 sessions with 192,024 search queries from search forms with the field type selected to "All Fields" or "Keywords" have been performed, among them 21,448 selected recommendations from the CTS. Figure 2 shows the development of the CTS usage in Sowiport in relation to conducted searches. After the integration of the CTS service in Sowiport in July 2014 in just about 4% of the searches the service has been used. In August/September 2014 the service showed a large increase in usage to 9-10% because of a major speed and cache improvement. Since that time there is a relatively stable usage of around 10% of all searches. Thus, locally (in the query formulation phase) in 10% of searches the CTS service has been considered as useful by users. Without having a reference value or other comparative information it is difficult to judge 10% as a low or a high value. Thus, at first glance, a pure usage rate based notion of usefulness does not appear as a very valuable metric of system quality. However, its benefit opens up if we complement it with global usefulness.

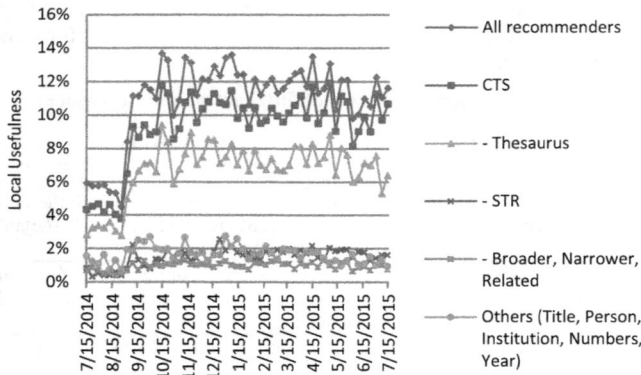

Fig 2. Recommender usage in Sowiport in percent of all conducted searches

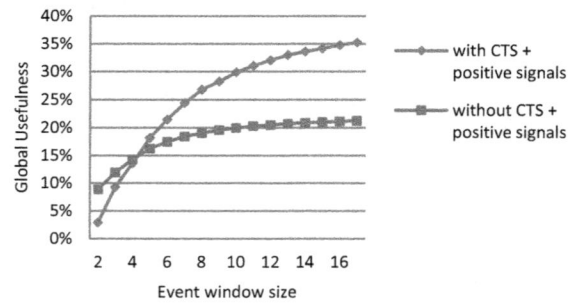

Fig 5. The global usefulness of searches with vs. without use of a combined term suggestion service (CTS)

5.2 Global Usefulness

To analyze the global usefulness of the CTS we follow the evaluation methodology from Section 3. Figure 3 gives an overview of extracted patterns for CTS_select followed by at least one positive signal within an event window of seven succeeding actions (4,569 sessions). Positive signals are color-coded in green. The main pattern which leads to a positive signal is: "CTS_select>>CTS_search>>(view_record)+>>{positive_signal}". Figure 4 then shows the analog diagram for searches without the use of CTS_select in advance and positive signals within an event window of seven actions (21,712 sessions). Here, the main starting point is CTS_search (one event less than for CTS_select). Figure 3 and 4 show that the main path patterns differ not very much between the two search variants. However in Figure 5 it can be seen that searches with CTS usage lead much more frequently to positive signals than searches without (statistically significant for *window size≥5* with Chi-Squared-Test, *p<0.001*). About 14% of the searches lead to positive signals after four interactions, independently of having CTS used before or not. Beginning with

step 5, however, the amount of CTS usage followed by at least one positive signal differs significantly from searches without the usage of CTS. The success rate of searches where the CTS has been used increases to a value of 30% (after 10 interactions, and increases further to a value of around 35%) whereas searches where the CTS has not been used achieve a value of 20% (after 10 interactions and do increase only slightly). Within an event window of seven interactions searches *with* CTS usage achieved a global usefulness of 0.24 whereas searches *without* CTS usage achieved a global usefulness of 0.18. This is clearly a significant difference in favor of the CTS service. The CTS service improves the search success at a rate of about 20-35%. Thus, the CTS service seems to be – globally – a useful service since it shows a high potential in increasing retrieval quality in terms of search success. The interesting finding now is that from the perspective of the user the "true" usefulness of the CTS service is not evident at the local level, in the moment when the user has to make a choice of using or leaving the search term recommender. Its benefit becomes apparent in a later phase of the session. This discrepancy may provide a clue to system developers to improve transparency of the service at the local level (e.g. by providing a preview of search results).

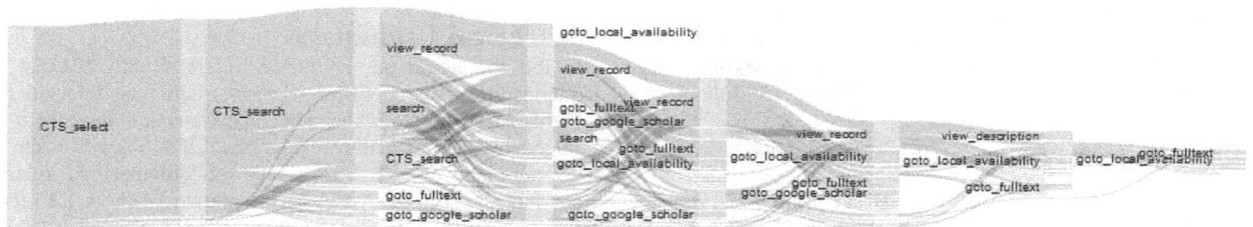

Fig 3. Path patterns for searches with the use of the CTS + positive signals (green colored) within an event window of seven actions (Node labels for p>0.02 and positive signals with p>0.005)

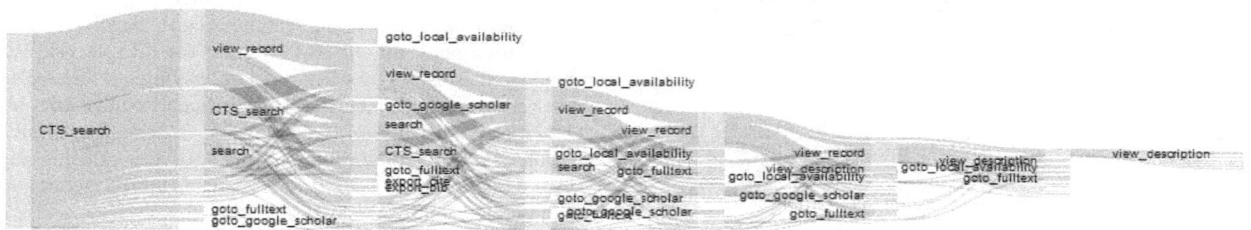

Fig 4. Path patterns for searches without the use of CTS + positive signals (green colored) within an event window of seven actions (Node labels for p>0.02 and positive signals with p>0.005)

Table 4. Mean P@20 and MAP@20 for different session units. An asterisk (*) indicates that the means are significantly different with a two-sample Z-Test and p<0.0001. The numbers in parentheses show the average count of searches per session unit.

Session unit	Mean P@20 without CTS	Mean P@20 with CTS	MAP@20 without CTS	MAP@20 with CTS
All whole sessions	0.0685 (9.5)	0.0677 (13.1)	0.1177	0.1112
Sessions with searches > 1 click-through signal	0.1853 (3.5) *	0.1886 (4.7) *	0.3183	0.3099
Succeeding search process	0.0624 (1.0)	0.0551 (1.0)	0.1904 *	0.1692 *
Window (7) - split to single searches - Click-through signals	0.0515 (1.5) *	0.0476 (1.9) *	0.1550	0.1403
Window (7) - split to single searches - All positive signals	0.0562 (1.5) *	0.0513 (1.9) *	-	-
Window (7) - split to single searches - with searches >1 signal - Click-through signals	0.1478 (0.5) *	0.1371 (0.7) *	0.4452 *	0.4040 *
Window (7) - split to single searches - with searches >1 signal - All positive signals	0.1599 (0.5) *	0.1465 (0.7) *	-	-
Window (7) - no split to single searches - Click-through signals	0.0709 (1.0) *	0.0869 (1.0) *	0.2062 *	0.2440 *
Window (7) - no split to single searches - All positive signals	0.0779 (1.0) *	0.0541 (1.0) *	-	-

6. COMPARISON TO STANDARD IR MEASURES

In the following we compare the results for global usefulness from the previous section to traditional IR measures such as precision (P@k) and mean average precision (MAP). The underlying research question addresses the difference between sessions with and without CTS usage (analog to the results for global usefulness) to measure the usefulness of the CTS service.

Thereby, we evaluate both precision measures with variable parts: (1) the *session unit* to which the measure is applied to. For different *session units* we use the *whole session* itself, the *succeeding search process* after the use of an IR service and a growing *window of actions* after the usage of the IR service.

(2) the *type of signals* the measures use. For global usefulness we have used the set of positive signals listed in Table 2. For precision measures relevance judgements for document relevancy from real users are needed as ground truth. However, in the case of log-based evaluation these are most times missing. There are several ways to recover them: (1) referring to an external source of user judgments, (2) asking a set of users subsequently to rate document relevancy for topics or (3) click-through data as implicit user feedback for the relevancy of documents can be used. In the following we use different signals for implicit user feedback.

Precision measures describe the number of relevant documents in a search result. P@k takes only the first k positions into account. Mean precision (MP) takes the mean of precision values for multiple search results. Average precision (AP) additionally takes the position of a relevant document into account. Mean average precision (MAP) then takes the mean of average precision values for multiple search results.

The result list in Sowiport shows twenty documents. Accordingly, we use P@20 as a first precision measure and MAP@20 as a second measure. For P@20 we use five actions on the result page for *click-through signals*: click on the title for a detailed view of the record (view_record, see Table 3), click on the full text link, click on the Google Scholar link, click on the Google Books link, and adding the document to favorites. Thus, the set of *all positive signals* contains the positive signals from Table 2 plus the view_record signal. For MAP we use only the click to the detailed view as all other actions have no rank information in our logs. All click-through signals appear on the initial result page directly after the search commit and are directly connected to a single document. It should be noted that these signals surely provide no reliable indications of relevance, but some clues of search success

in terms of getting the user to start a more detailed inspection of the information retrieved. Thus, we just apply precision measures to the incidence of positive signals among the top 20 documents.

Table 4 shows the results for different session units. The first row shows the mean P@20 and MAP@20 over *all whole sessions* with and without CTS usage. The sessions were split into single search processes. Then, in each search process we look for click-through signals. As one can see in the table the precision and MAP values are relatively low. A deeper look into the data showed a very high number of query reformulations and actions on the result list such as filtering with facets before looking at a document in detail. Theoretically, for session-based mean precision measures all query reformulations need to be merged to a topic and all clicked documents over the session need to be assigned to the topics. This forms an own complex problem which has been already addressed in research [e.g. 19]. As a naïve approach we computed the sessions' precision only with search processes which include at least one click-through signal (see Table 4, second row). Here, the precision values increase strongly. For P@20 the difference between searches with CTS usage and searches without CTS usage are statistically significant but the absolute difference is still very low. The numbers in parentheses show the average count of searches per session unit. By comparison to the first row we find that only every third search process includes at least one click-through signal. This is a further indication for a high number of query reformulations.

As already mentioned, precision and average precision are related to a single search result. We accordingly tested the precision of the *search process* which directly follows the events CTS_search and CTS_select. The table's third row shows that the results are again very low for P@20 and low for MAP@20. Here, the same problem as in sessions as a unit occurs: the first query after submitting from a search form is often only the starting point for a set of several query reformulations and search adaptions.

Similarly to our procedure for global usefulness we then tested with the *event window approach*, which takes the first seven succeeding actions after submitting a search (either with or without CTS usage). This window has then been *split to single searches*. The window involves on average 1.9 searches for windows with CTS usage and 1.5 searches for windows without CTS usage. We can see in the fourth and fifth row that the mean precision values are still very low. By counting again only searches with more than one following signal the precision increases strongly. Finally, taking all positive signals into account the precision increases additionally by about 1%. So far, with the window-based approach and splitting to single searches we found statistical differences (mainly because of the high sample size), but the precision values are very low. Also, the number of searches per window are different (1.9 searches for CTS_select, 1.5 for Search). This makes it hard to compare the two kinds of sessions.

Therefore, in the next approach we did *not split the window to single searches*, but look the whole window as a single search. This means, we count all signals inside the window and do not assign the signals to single searches which will give us a different view. The last two rows in the table show that there is a significant difference for both P@20 and MAP@20 in favor of sessions with CTS usage.

To understand how the MAP measure evolves over increasing window sizes we show the precision graphs in Figure 6. It shows MAP@20 with a window of growing size, once for the window split to searches, and once not split to searches. The curves for the "with CTS split" remain at 0.14, for "without CTS split" slightly higher at 0.15. The curves for the no-split window diverge. Differences between MAP@20 for "with CTS no-split" and "without no-split" are significant for a window size≥6 with a two-sample Z-Test and $p<0.0001$. Here it can be seen that with the window-based approach and not splitting the window to single searches the differences between sessions with and without CTS usage are getting larger by increasing the window size. This means for MAP that significantly more top-ranked documents are viewed after CTS usage than without it and the effect becomes larger in the following steps of the session. If we normalize the effect of more searches per window for CTS sessions not split to searches, the difference between sessions with and without CTS usage becomes really measurable also with the MAP measure.

7. DISCUSSION

The case study showed a local usefulness of 10% for the CTS. When we contrast this value with the global version of usefulness it turned out that the local usage of the service under study does not correspond with its positive effect on search success (in terms of positive signals). Thus, the "true" usefulness of the CTS service becomes apparent in a later phase of the session, but is not shown to the user at the local level. Usefulness therefore is a concept that obviously needs both a local and a global version contrasting the effect of a local ISS to the global benefit of the system in helping the user accomplishing his/her information seeking goal.

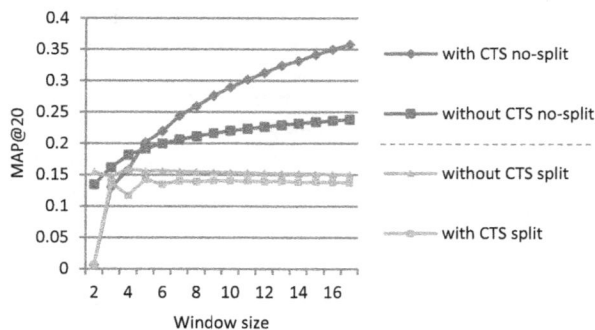

Fig 6. MAP@20 for a window of succeeding actions with growing size. One time the window has been split to searches (split), the other time not (no-split).

7.1 Signals and their variations

A critical point of our approach is surely the definition of a set of positive signals. In our case study positive signals are either bounded to search results (email, save, RSS) or documents (download full text, view abstract, save, export etc.). Positive signals on the document level can be an approximation of document relevance in the case where explicit relevance assessments are not available. This way, relevance can be computed with a log file-based approach. However, in other use cases probably positive signals exist which are bounded to different artefacts of the search process (such as query formulation, results scanning, working with favorite documents and searches, browsing in the document space etc.). Choosing different categories of positive signals can adopt the use case, but also makes the usefulness measure applicable to the whole search process. Another factor is the weighting of signals. In this case study we weighted every signal equally. However, one could argue that exporting or saving a record weights more than just viewing the abstract or its references. Here, definitely more research in the field of (positive) signals in the search and browsing process needs to be carried out.

In our study we utilized actions from log files as indications for positive signals. Research showed (compare Section 2.3) that more complex actions such as a record view with a certain dwell time represent well document usefulness or user satisfaction. Additionally, there are also signals from other eye-, mouse- or keyboard tracking that can identify user satisfaction. There is no difficulty to use these signals in our approach, however signals may vary from system to system, may not be available in every log and computability could increase.

Depending on the type of the IR Service there can also be a set of signals which indicates a negative impact of the service, for example, by a quick exit of the session or by dropping a document from the favorite list. An obvious solution to this problem is to compute global usefulness for these "negative" sessions separately and then subtract it from the global usefulness of the "positive" sessions.

7.2 Path patterns

A deeper look into path patterns might reveal insight which typical action sequences lead to positive signals. In our case searches seem to follow a relatively straightforward pattern, such as CTS_select>>CTS_search>>view_record>>{positive_signal}. This observation raises further research questions: "Are there any regularities in search path patterns?", "Causes the use of particular IR services differences in patterns?", "Are there any differences between different kind of users?", and so on. More insights as regards search patterns can reveal a ground for optimization of IR services.

7.3 Differences to standard IR measures

Global usefulness measures the observation of at least one positive signal (like bookmarking a record) within a fixed window of actions after the use of an IR service (like a search term recommender). In contrast, P@k and MAP measure the quality of a search result by the presence and ranking of relevant documents. Thus, there are a number of differences between global usefulness and classical measures such as precision or MAP: (1) Global usefulness measures *success* of an IR service in terms of occurrence of positive interaction signals, P@k/MAP measures the *quality* of a search result in terms of relevance; (2) Global usefulness evaluates interactions in a fixed window of actions whereas P@k/MAP evaluates a specific search result. (3) Global usefulness uses positive signals obtained from log data whereby P@k/MAP uses relevance assessments usually obtained from human experts. In Section 6.1 we have analyzed these differences by substituting relevance assessments by click-through signals and applying different session units (wrt 2.) and different signals (wrt 3.) to the precision measures.

(Regarding 2.) Precision measures are per definition bound to a single search result. Because in our data set we found a high number of query reformulations and adaptions this leads to low mean values because not in every search process users clicked on documents. The succeeding search directly after the usage of the IR service also seems to be inappropriate as it is only the starting point for a number of reformulations. We then choose a window approach which allows to go further into the sessions and captures about 1.9 search processes for windows with CTS usage in a window of 7 actions. But here again the number of searches keeps the precision values on the same low level and significant differences between sessions with or without CTS usage are difficult to prove. Not splitting the window to single searches then shows a strong increase in precision and MAP. Additionally, a significant difference between sessions with/without CTS usage appears to be similar to the results for global usefulness.

(Regarding 3.) Global usefulness uses a set of positive signals (without the view_record signal) whereby MAP uses only the view_record signal. However, both lead to significant differences for sessions with and without CTS usage. This seems to measure the same but it does not: the CTS usage led to more relevant documents (MAP) and these subsequently to more positive signals (global usefulness). However, global usefulness can measure also signals apart from document relevancy, e.g. when a user exports the whole search result.

8. CONCLUSION

In this paper we propose a specific log data based methodology that measures how useful an IR service is for the user. Corresponding to the model of Cole et al. [4] usefulness is measured on several levels. In our approach we distinguish between local and global usefulness of the IR service. Local usefulness asks for "the systems support toward the goal of each interaction", i.e. we measure how often the IR service is used at the local level and which patterns of usage occur. Our case study turned out that the service under study (a combined term suggestion service (CTS)) was used in about 10% of cases. On the level of global usefulness Cole et al. ask for the contribution of each information interaction to accomplishing the sub goal and the overall task or goal. Since the user's task is often difficult to capture our approach is to approximate usefulness by looking at positive signals in the search process and investigating how well the search service's local usage co-occurs with positive signals. Our case study showed that CTS usage has a significantly stronger relationship with positive signals than searches without it.

In general, our attempt can contribute to a new approach of measuring usefulness of IR supporting services with regard not only to its usage, usability or its influence on search results but encompassing the whole search process. Unlike user-oriented studies our approach is based on log files and scales well on thousands of users and sessions. Nevertheless, the users will not be lost of sight, as their individual behavior is stored in the log files.

The work done in this paper is insofar only theoretical, as we take positive signals in search sessions as indications of user's preference. A critical next step is to compare our findings and

measures from this work with insights from user studies where we intend to compare user feedback on usefulness with log-based findings.

ACKNOWLEDGMENTS

This work was partly funded by the DFG, grant no. MA 3964/5-1; the AMUR project at GESIS. The authors thank the focus group IIR at GESIS for fruitful discussions and suggestions.

9. REFERENCES

1. Maristella Agosti, Franco Crivellari, and Giorgio Maria Di Nunzio. 2011. Web log analysis: a review of a decade of studies about information acquisition, inspection and interpretation of user interaction. *Data Mining and Knowledge Discovery* 24, 3: 663–696. http://dci.org/10.1007/s10618-011-0228-8

2. Leif Azzopardi. 2009. Usage Based Effectiveness Measures: Monitoring Application Performance in Information Retrieval. *Proceedings of the 18th ACM Conference on Information and Knowledge Management*, ACM, 631–640. http://doi.org/10.1145/1645953.1646034

3. Nicholas J. Belkin, Colleen Cool, Adelheit Stein, and Ulrich Thiel. 1995. Cases, Scripts, and Information-Seeking Strategies: On the Design of Interactive Information Retrieval Systems. *EXPERT SYSTEMS WITH APPLICATIONS* 9: 379–395.

4. Michael Cole, Jingjing Liu, Nicholas Belkin, et al. 2009. Usefulness as the criterion for evaluation of interactive information retrieval. *Proceedings of the Workshop on Human-Computer Interaction and Information Retrieval*, 1–4.

5. S. Dumais. 2012. Whole-session evaluation of interactive information retrieval systems. *Compilation of Homework, NII Shonan Workshop*. Retrieved from http://research.microsoft.com/en-us/um/people/sdumais/niishonanworkshop-web/NII-Shonan-CompiledHomework_Final.pdf

6. Efthimis N Efthimiadis. 1996. Query expansion. *Annual review of information science and technology* 31: 121–187.

7. Steve Fox, Kuldeep Karnawat, Mark Mydland, Susan Dumais, and Thomas White. 2005. Evaluating Implicit Measures to Improve Web Search. *ACM Trans. Inf. Syst.* 23, 2: 147–168. http://doi.org/10.1145/1059981.1059982

8. G. W. Furnas, T. K. Landauer, L. M. Gomez, and S. T. Dumais. 1987. The Vocabulary Problem in Human-system Communication. *Commun. ACM* 30, 11: 964–971. http://doi.org/10.1145/32206.32212

9. Daniel Hienert, Wilko van Hoek, Alina Weber, and Dagmar Kern. 2015. WHOSE – A Tool for Whole-Session Analysis in IIR. *Proceeding of ECIR 2015*, Springer, 172–184.

10. Daniel Hienert, Frank Sawitzki, and Philipp Mayr. 2015. Digital Library Research in Action - Supporting Information Retrieval in Sowiport. *D-Lib Magazine* 21, 3/4. http://doi.org/http://dx.doi.org/10.1045/march2015-hienert

11. Daniel Hienert, Philipp Schaer, Johann Schaible, and Philipp Mayr. 2011. A Novel Combined Term Suggestion Service for Domain-Specific Digital Libraries. *Proceedings of the 15th International Conference on Theory and Practice of Digital Libraries (TPDL)*. Retrieved from http://dl.acm.org/citation.cfm?id=2042564

12. Chien-Kang Huang, Lee-Feng Chien, and Yen-Jen Oyang. 2003. Relevant Term Suggestion in Interactive Web Search Based on Contextual Information in Query Session Logs. *J. Am. Soc. Inf. Sci. Technol.* 54, 7: 638–649. http://doi.org/10.1002/asi.10256

13. P. Ingwersen and K. Järvelin. 2007. On the holistic cognitive theory for information retrieval: Drifting outside the border of the laboratory framework. *Studies in the Theory of Information Retrieval (ICTIR 2007), Foundation for Information Society*, 135–147.

14. Bernard J. Jansen. 2006. Search log analysis: What it is, what's been done, how to do it. *Library & Information Science Research* 28, 3: 407 – 432. http://doi.org/http://dx.doi.org/10.1016/j.lisr.2006.06.005

15. Bernard J. Jansen, Mimi Zhang, and Amanda Spink. 2007. Patterns and transitions of query reformulation during web searching. *International Journal of Web Information Systems* 3, 4: 328–340. http://doi.org/10.1108/17440080710848116

16. Thorsten Joachims, Laura Granka, Bing Pan, Helene Hembrooke, and Geri Gay. 2005. Accurately Interpreting Clickthrough Data As Implicit Feedback. *Proceedings of the 28th Annual International ACM SIGIR Conference on Research and Development in Information Retrieval*, ACM, 154–161. http://doi.org/10.1145/1076034.1076063

17. Thorsten Joachims, Laura Granka, Bing Pan, Helene Hembrooke, Filip Radlinski, and Geri Gay. 2007. Evaluating the Accuracy of Implicit Feedback from Clicks and Query Reformulations in Web Search. *ACM Trans. Inf. Syst.* 25, 2. http://doi.org/10.1145/1229179.1229181

18. Jaap Kamps, Marijn Koolen, and Andrew Trotman. 2009. Comparative Analysis of Clicks and Judgments for IR Evaluation. *Proceedings of the 2009 Workshop on Web Search Click Data*, ACM, 80–87. http://doi.org/10.1145/1507509.1507522

19. Evangelos Kanoulas, Ben Carterette, Paul D. Clough, and Mark Sanderson. 2011. Evaluating Multi-query Sessions. *Proceedings of the 34th International ACM SIGIR Conference on Research and Development in Information Retrieval*, ACM, 1053–1062. http://doi.org/10.1145/2009916.2010056

20. Diane Kelly. 2009. Methods for Evaluating Interactive Information Retrieval Systems with Users. *Found. Trends Inf. Retr.* 3, 1—2: 1–224. http://doi.org/10.1561/1500000012

21. Diane Kelly and Jaime Teevan. 2003. Implicit Feedback for Inferring User Preference: A Bibliography. *SIGIR Forum* 37, 2: 18–28. http://doi.org/10.1145/959258.959260

22. Chang Liu, Nicholas J. Belkin, and Michael J. Cole. 2012. Personalization of Search Results Using Interaction Behaviors in Search Sessions. *Proceedings of the 35th International ACM SIGIR Conference on Research and Development in Information Retrieval*, ACM, 205–214. http://doi.org/10.1145/2348283.2348314

23. Claudio Lucchese, Salvatore Orlando, Raffaele Perego, Fabrizio Silvestri, and Gabriele Tolomei. 2011. Identifying Task-based Sessions in Search Engine Query Logs. *Proceedings of the Fourth ACM International Conference on Web Search and Data Mining*, ACM, 277–286. http://doi.org/10.1145/1935826.1935875

24. Thomas Lüke, Philipp Schaer, and Philipp Mayr. 2012. Improving Retrieval Results with Discipline-Specific Query Expansion. *TPDL*, Springer, 408–413. Retrieved from http://arxiv.org/abs/1206.2126

25. Thomas Lüke, Philipp Schaer, and Philipp Mayr. 2013. A Framework for Specific Term Recommendation Systems. *Proceedings of the 36th international ACM SIGIR conference on Research and development in information retrieval*, ACM, 1093–1094. Retrieved from http://arxiv.org/abs/1407.1539

26. Mandar Mitra, Amit Singhal, and Chris Buckley. 1998. Improving Automatic Query Expansion. *Proceedings of the 21st Annual International ACM SIGIR Conference on Research and Development in Information Retrieval*, ACM, 206–214. http://doi.org/10.1145/290941.290995

27. Peter Mutschke, Philipp Mayr, Philipp Schaer, and York Sure. 2011. Science models as value-added services for scholarly information systems. *Scientometrics* 89, 1: 349–364. http://doi.org/http://dx.doi.org/10.1007/s11192-011-0430-x

28. Bruce R. Schatz, Eric H. Johnson, Pauline A. Cochrane, and Hsinchun Chen. 1996. Interactive Term Suggestion for Users of Digital Libraries: Using Subject Thesauri and Co-occurrence Lists for Information Retrieval. *Proceedings of the First ACM International Conference on Digital Libraries*, ACM, 126–133. http://doi.org/10.1145/226931.226956

29. Paul Thomas. 2014. Using Interaction Data to Explain Difficulty Navigating Online. *ACM Trans. Web* 8, 4: 24:1–24:41. http://doi.org/10.1145/2656343

30. Olga Vechtomova, Stephen Robertson, and Susan Jones. 2003. Query Expansion with Long-Span Collocates. *Inf. Retr.* 6, 2: 251–273. http://doi.org/10.1023/A:1023936321956

31. Ellen M. Voorhees and Donna K. Harman. 2005. *TREC: Experiment and Evaluation in Information Retrieval (Digital Libraries and Electronic Publishing)*. The MIT Press.

32. Hongning Wang, Yang Song, Ming-Wei Chang, Xiaodong He, Ryen W. White, and Wei Chu. 2013. Learning to Extract Cross-session Search Tasks. *Proceedings of the 22Nd International Conference on World Wide Web*, International World Wide Web Conferences Steering Committee, 1353–1364. Retrieved from http://dl.acm.org/citation.cfm?id=2488388.2488507

33. Barbara M. Wildemuth. 2004. The Effects of Domain Knowledge on Search Tactic Formulation. *J. Am. Soc. Inf. Sci. Technol.* 55, 3: 246–258. http://doi.org/10.1002/asi.10367

34. Iris Xie. 2009. Dimensions of tasks: influences on information-seeking and retrieving process. *Journal of Documentation* 65, 3: 339–366.

35. Jinxi Xu and W. Bruce Croft. 1996. Query Expansion Using Local and Global Document Analysis. *Proceedings of the 19th Annual International ACM SIGIR Conference on Research and Development in Information Retrieval*, ACM, 4–11. http://doi.org/10.1145/243199.243202

36. Junte Zhang and Jaap Kamps. 2010. A Search Log-based Approach to Evaluation. *Proceedings of the 14th European Conference on Research and Advanced Technology for Digital Libraries*, Springer-Verlag, 248–260. Retrieved June 30, 2015 from http://dl.acm.org/citation.cfm?id=1887759.1887795

Assessing Learning Outcomes in Web Search: A Comparison of Tasks and Query Strategies

Kevyn Collins-Thompson[1], Soo Young Rieh[1], Carl C. Haynes[2], Rohail Syed[1]

[1]School of Information, University of Michigan, Ann Arbor, MI U.S.A. 48109
[2]School of Information Studies, Syracuse University, Syracuse, NY U.S.A. 13244
{kevynct, rieh, rmsyed}@umich.edu, cchaynes@syr.edu

ABSTRACT

Users make frequent use of Web search for learning-related tasks, but little is known about how different Web search interaction strategies affect outcomes for learning-oriented tasks, or what implicit or explicit indicators could reliably be used to assess search-related learning on the Web. We describe a lab-based user study in which we investigated potential indicators of learning in web searching, effective query strategies for learning, and the relationship between search behavior and learning outcomes. Using questionnaires, analysis of written responses to knowledge prompts, and search log data, we found that searchers' perceived learning outcomes closely matched their actual learning outcomes; that the amount searchers wrote in post-search questionnaire responses was highly correlated with their cognitive learning scores; and that the time searchers spent per document while searching was also highly and consistently correlated with higher-level cognitive learning scores. We also found that of the three query interaction conditions we applied, an intrinsically diverse presentation of results was associated with the highest percentage of users achieving combined factual and conceptual knowledge gains. Our study provides deeper insight into which aspects of search interaction are most effective for supporting superior learning outcomes, and the difficult problem of how learning may be assessed effectively during Web search.

Keywords: Learning; search behavior; exploratory search; user study.

1. INTRODUCTION

Users often turn to Web search when their goal is to learn [5]. These learning-related search tasks range from basic factual knowledge questions, to more in-depth needs that seek information about 'how' or 'why' [8]. While researchers have recognized the importance of learning as a search outcome, [2][3] current Web search engines are optimized for generic relevance,

CHIIR '16, March 13-17, 2016, Carrboro, NC, USA
© 2016 ACM. ISBN 978-1-4503-3751-9/16/03...$15.00
DOI: http://dx.doi.org/10.1145/2854946.2854972

not learning outcomes. To build search engines that provide better support for learning-related tasks requires progress in several areas. First, systems need more effective algorithms for retrieving documents that are optimal for a particular learning goal. Second, we need better understanding of how different query strategies affect different types of learning. Third, we need reliable assessment methods that can detect when and how different types of learning occur.

Toward these goals, we conduct a user study of an interactive search system with which searchers accomplish different learning tasks within one of three between-subjects querying frameworks. Using data from background surveys, pre- and post-search questionnaires, written responses to prompts, and search interaction logs, we explore the effect of different query and exploration strategies on learning, and characterize effective indicators of learning outcomes in Web search. Specifically, this study addresses the following research questions:

- **RQ1**: What kinds of measures and indicators can be developed to demonstrate learning experiences and outcomes in interactive search systems?
- **RQ2**: What query strategies – submitting a single query, multiple queries, or multiple queries with intrinsically diverse results – do best support human learning experiences and outcomes?
- **RQ3**: To what extent is searchers' search behavior correlated with learning experiences and outcomes?

The idea that search technology can and should play a more central role in supporting deeper learning experiences has been attracting renewed interest with researchers. At both the SWIRL 2012 workshop [3] and the 2013 Dagstuhl Seminar on Evaluation in IR [2] participants proposed ideas for moving "from searching to learning" that emphasized the importance of learning as a search outcome. While these venues discussed the possibilities of a new research agenda for searching as learning, they did not present specific research advances.

This study aims to conceptualize searching as learning by expanding the concept of learning not only in terms of search tasks but also as a part of cognitive activities occurring during the search process. Thus, this study explores new methods and measures for assessing learning across multiple stages of the search process, starting from query formulation, selection of documents, and saving documents to writing summaries at different learning levels, reflecting users' perceived learning and searching experiences and outcomes after searching.

2. RELATED WORK

Previous studies providing context for our work can be divided into four major themes: learning-related search tasks, learning-oriented exploratory search, expertise and learning, and assessment of learning in searching.

Learning-related search tasks. Learning-related search tasks can be complex, requiring multiple queries and significant time spent searching and browsing. A study by Bailey et al. [5] of how users engage in such tasks using commercial search engines described a task taxonomy of web search, based on 4 months of search log data that captured query events to Google, Yahoo, and Bing. This taxonomy included some learning-related tasks, spanning topic exploration, fact-finding, and procedural learning. In a later study, Eickhoff et al. [8] analyzed the fraction of sessions that involved a procedural or declarative knowledge intent. Both studies found that learning-related tasks accounted for a non-trivial proportion of all search sessions, and a disproportionally larger fraction of time spent searching: many learning-related tasks each accounted for 1-2% of all search sessions, but 4-5% of time spent searching. Raman et al. [18] had a similar finding for *intrinsically diverse* (ID) search tasks, which are exploratory Web searches intended to explore and learn about multiple aspects of a specific topic. Jansen et al. [12] applied revised Bloom's taxonomy of learning [4] to classify search tasks and described how searching needs could be classified into an appropriate learning model based on searching behavior. Other recent work has attempted to assess the motivation that users exhibit in completing information-seeking tasks, e.g. Kim et al. [14] characterized this motivation in terms of how willing a user was to search and browse documents that were far above their 'typical' reading level.

Learning-oriented exploratory search. Learning-based search activities often involve multiple interactions in the search process and processing of multiple sets of search results that need to be interpreted deeply by searchers. Marchionini [17] claims that search activities that support learning in particular focus on "knowledge acquisition, comprehension of concepts or skills, interpretation of ideas, and comparisons, or aggregations of data and concepts" (p. 43). Therefore, searching activities that support learning require human participation in more continuous and exploratory ways during the search process.

Exploratory search, which focuses on broader information-seeking strategies that emphasize deeper understanding over quick factual answers, has emerged as an alternative paradigm to foster learning and investigation in search [17][22]. Heinström [9] gathered empirical evidence comparing exploratory vs precise information-seeking patterns among students and their relationship to students' learning. She observed that students often undertake broad explorations when exploring new research topics or to get a wide overview of the topic, switching to more precise strategies to fill in specific facts once a topic has been initially explored. Learning outcomes have been proposed as an important future evaluation method for exploratory search [22].

Expertise and learning. Expertise is a dynamic characteristic of users that reflects learning over time. Wildemuth [24] examined how domain expertise was reflected in users' choice of search strategies, finding that domain novices tended to exhibit increasingly similar search strategies to those of more expert users as the novices learned more about the topic. Previous work [23][26] has characterized domain expertise and search behavior in terms of metrics that can be derived from search logs, typically focusing on longer-term behavior patterns across sessions. In one of the first large-scale search log-based studies to examine session-level features of tasks where people are explicitly searching for new knowledge, Eickhoff et al. [8] looked at within-session changes for these expertise metrics. They focused on two specific types of knowledge acquisition: procedural knowledge

(how to do something) vs. declarative knowledge (knowing facts about something). The authors found evidence both for learning progress within single session, and for persistence of learning across sessions. Significant proportions of new query terms came from result page snippets and recently visited pages, showing that the search process itself contributed to augmenting the user's domain knowledge. Other recent studies, e.g. [26] have attempted to predict domain knowledge from user search behavior.

Assessment of learning in searching. A few studies have attempted to identify indicators of learning during the search process. Vakkari et al. [21] found that students' level of knowledge about their topic can predict patterns of search queries, in that students who know less about the topic are likely to use fewer, broader, more vague search terms as their queries. In a study with medical students, Vakkari and Huuskonen [20] found that effort put into the search process did not lead to better search outcomes (the products delivered by a system), but did improve task outcomes (the benefits the system produced). Several IR researchers designed research methods to investigate learning as a measure of search outcome. In one of the earlier studies measuring learning, Hersh et al. [10] showed how searching enabled students to answer more questions in a post-search quiz. Instead of a quiz, Kammerer et al. [15] asked their study participants to write a summary about the topic after using the exploratory search interface, MrTaggy, to assess learning. Summary quality was evaluated based on topic-specific criteria including the number of reasonable topics, overall quality of the topic description, and number of arguments. Wilson and Wilson [25] developed systematic techniques to measure the depth of learning at three levels: quality of facts, interpretation of data into statements, and use of critique. These previous studies indicate that traditional measures in information retrieval, such as recall and precision, can be effectively complemented with alternative measures that pay more attention to search behavior, process, and task outcomes beyond basic search results.

3. METHODS

We conducted a user study with an interactive Web search system in a laboratory setting, controlling two conditions: query strategy and search tasks. By controlling 'query strategy' we mean constraining or expanding the space of possible query interactions available to users in the search environment. As we were interested in finding out to what extent query strategies have an effect on users' learning outcomes and experiences from searching, we decided to compare search-related and learning-related measures by controlling users' query strategies as follows:

Single Query (SQ) condition: subjects are asked to select a single query from a given set and to use the results of this query for the remainder of the search session;

Multiple Query (MQ) condition: after selecting an initial query from a given set, subjects may run and use the results from multiple queries of their own design;

Intrinsic Diversity (ID) condition: subjects are allowed to run multiple queries, as in the MQ condition, but additionally the results are *intrinsically diverse*, covering a range of subtopics related to the query and providing query suggestions associated with subtopics that they may have not initially considered [18].

For all three conditions, subjects were instructed to select an initial query out of 10 queries that were pre-determined by the authors for each of two search tasks. This restriction was to minimize the variance of results that might occur due to differences in users' abilities to formulate a good initial query which in turn could influence the assessment of learning.

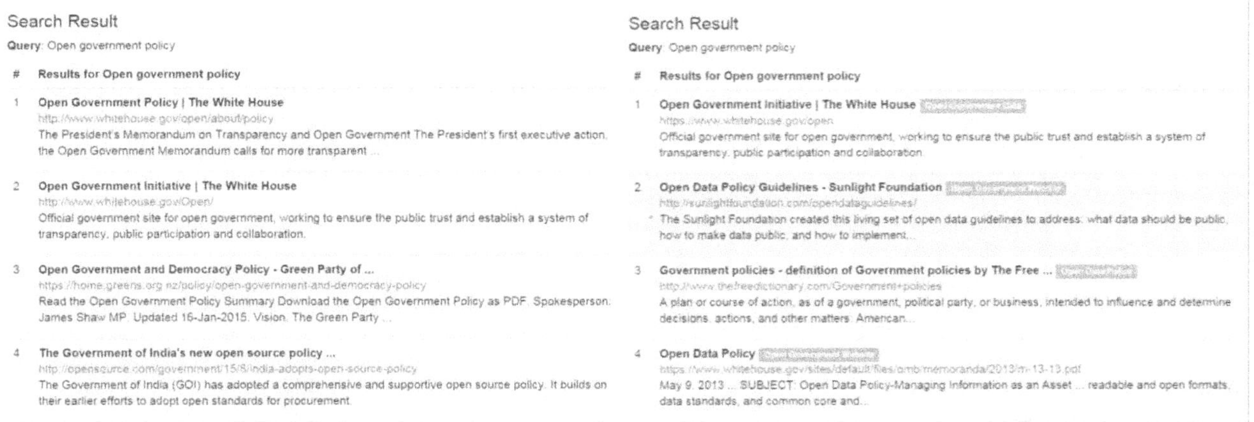

Figure 1. Search results interface for single & multiple query conditions (left) and intrinsically diverse condition (right).

After the initial query, subjects were allowed either to create their own queries or select one of the topics offered by the Intrinsic Diversity (ID) condition. The study used a mixed between- and within-subject design, the between-subject factor being query strategy and within-subject factor being search tasks. The order of the two search tasks was rotated to avoid any ordering bias, learning effect or potential fatigue issues. Subjects were randomly assigned to one of the three query formulation conditions and compensated US $20.00 for participation.

3.1 Study Participants

A recruiting email was sent to a University of Michigan School of Information mailing list. Undergraduate students, graduate students, and alumni can opt in to subscribe to the list. A total of 44 study subjects (30 female, 14 male) signed up for the study. We offered 10 different session timeslots in which we accepted up to 10 people for each session. Participants ranged in age from 19 to 38 years old. Participants also varied in their academic standing: there were 34 graduate students, 7 undergraduate students, 2 doctoral students, and 1 alumnus; 36 of the recruited subjects were affiliated with the University of Michigan.

Subjects were assigned to one of the three query conditions in a randomly-initialized, round-robin fashion to ensure balanced numbers for each condition. Two subjects were later removed due to technical issues with incomplete data gathering, leaving 42 subjects for analysis. The final counts of subjects in each query condition were: Single Query (SD): 12, Multiple Query (MQ): 15, Intrinsic Diversity (ID): 15.

3.2 Search System and Interface

The search system was hosted on Amazon EC2 and used an architecture derived from uFindIt [1] that logs user events such as queries and clicks to a MySQL database. The baseline ranked document lists for the single and multiple query conditions were provided by the Google Custom Search API[1]. The intrinsically diverse (ID) condition was implemented using the ranking algorithm by Raman et al. [18] that jointly finds a set of diverse subtopics, and a set of main results representing the best results that cover those subtopics[2]. The ID result candidates were obtained using the same Google Custom Search API to obtain ranked lists for the main query and subtopics. Since the ID algorithm requires a source of subtopic candidates, in our implementation we used section headings of Wikipedia articles if

one existed for a given query, and otherwise used query suggestions provided by the Bing Related Query API.

In the user interface, each ID subtopic was displayed as a rectangular button to the right of the corresponding document title in the search engine results page (SERP). Users could click on the subtopic button to launch a new query using that subtopic as the query, whose results would be a simple baseline ranking (not another ID ranking). Figure 1 shows screenshots of the search results interface used for the study conditions.

3.3 Tasks and Procedures

We developed two tasks as "simulated work task situations" [7] in which we gave scenarios that simulate real life information needs. Subjects were asked to conduct searches on a topics for a course term paper. We developed two search tasks that could be characterized differently in terms of complexity and domain/non-domain knowledge. At the same time, we tried to create tasks that required students to explore multiple aspects of the topic. We made such expectations clear by saying "present your views on this topic" and "save all the webpages, publications, and other online sources that are helpful for you to write a paper." The task descriptions as shown to the participants were as follows.

Task 1 description (Oil Spill): Suppose you are taking an introductory Environmental Science course this term. For your term paper, you have decided to write about what chemicals can be used to clean up oil spills. You also would like to learn what environmental effects oil spills have in the ocean and on shore.

Task 2 description (Open Data): For a course you are taking this term, you have decided to write a term paper about government open data policy. You know that it is about how government agencies manage information as an asset throughout the life cycle to promote openness.

General descriptions for both tasks: The professor requires all students to demonstrate what they learn about a particular topic by conducting searches online and presenting their views on this topic. To prepare your term paper, you need to collect and save all the webpages, publications, and other online sources that are helpful for you to write a paper. After your search is completed, you will be asked to answer six questions about this topic. Questions include answering

---

[1] With personalization and 'safe search' filtering not activated.

[2] Using default ID algorithm parameters of $\beta = 0.5$, $\lambda = 0.3$.

questions and writing an outline and completing a survey based on what you have learned from this search. To be able to answer these questions, you may want to take some notes during the searching.

The first "oil spill" task dealt with a scientific topic about which students were unlikely to have extensive domain knowledge, but for which the basic concept was not especially abstract or difficult to understand. The second "open data" task addressed a topic about which participants might have a certain level of prior exposure and some domain knowledge, but the basic concept itself was more abstract and could be rather complex.

The study took approximately 1 hour to complete. When subjects arrived at the laboratory, they received a one-page set of written instructions that outlined the 13 steps for subjects to take step-by-step. Subjects were presented with their first search task both on screen and in hard copy. Next, after they completed reading the task description, they were asked to fill out a Pre-Search Questionnaire which had three scale-based questions and one writing question about subjects' knowledge level in the topic. They were then guided to follow instructions for one of the three query conditions. Their search continued without time constraints. When subjects found a document they liked in the search results page (SERP), they would click a document URL to view the document. After they finished reading the document, they would come back to the SERP, at which point they were presented with a new button "Was this helpful?" that was associated with that particular document. They were given to a choice to save the document by clicking that button or to click on the X icon. They would then return to looking at the search results page. When they wanted to stop their searching, they would click "I completed my search for this topic" button, which would take them to the next screen displaying a Post-Search Questionnaire, which had 23 questions in total. Once they completed the Post-Search Questionnaire, they were allowed to start the same process for the second search task. When they completed searching and filling out questionnaires for both tasks, they were taken to the screen showing a Background Questionnaire, which was the last step in their participation.

3.3.1 Questionnaires

We now discuss the motivation and methods for our question design in each portion of the study. A complete inventory of the question set described here is given in Table 3. The content of the Pre-Search Questionnaire was identical for the two search tasks. The first three questions were closed questions designed to assess subjects' prior knowledge level (**P1**), interest in the topic (**P2**), and perceived difficulty of searching (**P3**). These three questions were assessed using a 5-point scale (1 = not at all and 5 = very likely). The fourth question (**P4**) asked participants to summarize their topic knowledge.

The Post-Search questionnaire was composed of two parts: (1) A set of 15 questions investigating learning and searching experiences on a 5-point scale (1= not at all and 5=very likely). Questions covered variables related to search experiences for the purpose of information exploration, user experiences with system usability, and learning attitudes focusing on interest, motivation, and willingness to learn more. The on-screen order of these 15 questions was rotated for each subject. (2) Two questions assessing subjects' perceived search and learning outcomes based on a self-reported learning score on a scale of 0 to 100. All responses were collected using Google Forms, and exported to Excel and Stata for analysis.

3.3.2 Post-Search Written Tests

In addition to the above 17 questions, the Post-Search Questionnaire also included a set of six learning assessment questions that were developed using Bloom's revised learning taxonomy [4]. Each question addressed one of Bloom's learning levels such as remembering (**Q1**), understanding (**Q2**), applying (**Q3**), analyzing (**Q4**), evaluating (**Q5**), and creating (**Q6**). Out of six questions, the first three questions focused on *lower-level cognitive learning* (Q1–Q3) while the other three questions focused on *higher-level cognitive learning* (Q4–Q6).

The lower-level learning questions Q1–Q3 were tailored for the nature of the specific search tasks. For the Oil Spill task, the first three questions designed to assess lower-level learning were:

Q1: What are the kinds of materials that can be used as a sole cleanup method in small spills?

Q2: When workers decide which methods are most effective to clean up oil spills, what are some factors that they should consider to make decisions for recovery methods?

Q3: Why do you think that oil spills are important environment issues? Describe its effects and impacts on human and environment.

For the Open Data task, the corresponding questions were:

Q1: Is copyright protection available for works of the United State Government?

Q2: In 2007, a number of open government advocates got together and claimed that government data shall be considered open if it is made public in a way that complies with some fundamental principles. Others added more principles since then. What are some examples of principles of open government data?

Q3: What kinds of individuals, communities, or organizations could be benefited as a result of accessing open data provided by government?

The higher-level learning questions Q4–Q6 were identical across tasks and were as follows:

Q4: Based on what you have learned from your searching, please write an outline for your paper.

Q5: Please write what you learned about this topic from your searching with 3-5 sentences.

Q6: Based on your searching, what questions do you still have about this topic?

We used Google Forms to collect subjects' written responses to these six questions.

3.4 Coding of Written Summaries

To analyze the written responses to the one pre-search summary question (P4) and six post-search questions (Q1-Q6) described above, we derived the following three assessment variables, the first of which was based on a detailed coding scheme designed to be a sensitive measure of knowledge acquisition.

1. **Cognitive Learning Scores**. For each question Q1-Q6, we defined seven criteria for assessing different dimensions of knowledge that might be observed in the participant's response. These criteria ranged from assessing factual knowledge by checking whether subjects could recall factors, issues, and elements, to assessing conceptual knowledge by looking at subjects' written responses to see whether they could identify themes and integrate multiple concepts. The criteria were derived from cognitive processes identified by Anderson & Krathwahl [4] as being associated with each of the six main learning levels in Bloom's Revised Taxonomy.

Each written response was assigned a raw score in the range 0–7 by counting how many of these seven learning criteria were demonstrated. If a written response showed no evidence of knowledge about the topic, the lowest score (0) was given. If a response exhibited every knowledge dimension listed in all seven learning criteria, it was given the highest score (7).

Two coders independently applied this coding scheme comprising 84 different learning criteria (7 criteria for each of the 6 written tests, Q1–Q6, for both tasks) to analyze the written responses of all 42 valid subjects. There were 87 written summary responses in total to Q1–Q6. Inter-coder agreement was computed between the two coders. We used Holsti's coefficients [11] to measure the consistency of coder judgments by calculating the ratio of coding agreements to the total number of coding decisions for each of the six questions. For both search tasks, we reached a high level of agreement: the mean inter-coder reliability across Q1–Q6 for the Oil Spill Task was 0.914 and for the Open Data task was 0.797.

From the raw scores we derived 3 cognitive learning scores:
- *Lower-level cognitive learning score*: The sum of raw scores coded from Q1–Q3 responses.
- *Higher-level cognitive learning score*: The sum of raw scores coded from Q4–Q6 responses.
- *Overall cognitive learning score*: The sum of raw scores coded from Q1–Q6 responses.

2. **Knowledge Level Gain**. To capture the nature of a subject's gain in knowledge during a task, we also coded written responses for P4 (prior knowledge) and Q5 (current knowledge) with a level score based on the highest of three levels of knowledge judged to have been exhibited in the writing (0=no knowledge, 1=factual knowledge, and 2=conceptual knowledge). If we observed a gain in this score from P4 to Q5, we considered that the subject had increased their level of knowledge for that task.

3. **Written Response Length**. This was simply the number of characters submitted by a subject for each of the written tests.

In Section 4, we examine these observed variables and their relationships to those derived from other sources in the study.

3.5 Logging of Search Interaction

To identify implicit indicators of learning from search interaction, we collected and analyzed the following variables that captured important aspects of time-related interaction, clicking behavior, and judgments of "usefulness" for each document viewed:

Unique docs clicked in search results: Total unique document clicks from the SERP (Search Engine Results Page) for each query entered.

Total time spent on assessing SERP: The time difference between when subjects returned to a SERP and when they switched to another page.

Average time spent on assessing SERP: Total time spent on assessing SERP divided by total queries entered.

Total time spent viewing documents: The difference from the time that subjects left a SERP to the time that they returned to the SERP.

Average time spent viewing documents: Total time spent viewing documents divided by count of unique clicks.

Average time spent viewing documents per query: Total time spent viewing documents divided by total queries.

Number of useful documents saved: Total documents users marked as useful.

Table 1. Log-based variables

Variable	Task	SQ	MQ	ID
Unique documents clicked in search results	Open	5.07	6.40	7.00
	Oil	4.91	6.66	5.73
Total time assessing SERP (sec)	Open	146.85	98.13	276.77
	Oil	83.42	137.07	176.07
Average time assessing SERP per query (sec)	Open	146.85	45.38	133.93
	Oil	83.42	85.42	81.95
Total time viewing documents (sec)	Open	973.64	964.4	1810.38
	Oil	787.33	1410.4	1399.06
Average time spent per document (sec)	Open	196.66	228.38	270.23
	Oil	146.52	272.29	246.87
Average time viewing documents/query (sec)	Open	973.64	505.18	865.72
	Oil	787.33	652.69	723.52
Number of useful documents saved	Open	3.00	4.00	4.08
	Oil	2.33	4.00	4.00

In analyzing document selection behavior, we investigated how many links on the SERP page the user clicked, what position each link was ranked at and how a binary judgment (a document was useful or it was not useful) the user gave to the corresponding document after viewing it. Table 1 summarizes observed values of these variables per task and condition, averaged across users.

4. DATA ANALYSIS

We now summarize our main results regarding self-reported outcomes, learning measures and indicators, the relationship of query strategy conditions to learning outcomes, and the relationship between learning outcomes and search behavior.

4.1 Self-Reported Searching and Learning Experiences

Before searching, subjects were asked about their topic knowledge and perception for each task (P1-P3). There was a significant difference in their perceived difficulty (P3) between the two tasks. Subjects perceived that the information searching required for the Open Data Task (M=3.10, SD=.81) would be more difficult than that required for the Oil Spill Task (M=2.53, SD=.93), p<0.01. However, their perceived interest and prior knowledge did not show any difference between the two tasks.

After subjects completed their searches, they were asked to respond to 15 items in the Post-Search Questionnaire. Overall, subjects seemed have more positive search and learning experiences with the Oil Spill Task than the Open Data Task across the three query conditions: this is not surprising, as subjects perceived the Open Data Task would be more difficult even before they began searching. Subjects did not report that their search experiences differed significantly depending on the perceived difficulty of tasks. For instance, subjects responded that they felt that search time was spent productively (Oil Spill M=3.87, Open Data M=3.62) and they were cognitively engaged in the search task (Oil Spill M=3.85, Open Data M=3.75), showing no difference between the tasks. However, they responded that they had more positive learning experiences after searching when they perceived the task as easier. For instance, they rated that they were able to develop new ideas and perspectives more highly in the Oil Spill Task (M=3.65) than in the Open Data Task (M=3.17), p<.05. They also reported understanding the topic at a higher level in the Oil Spill Task (M=2.82) than in the Open Data Task (M=2.37), p<.05, although

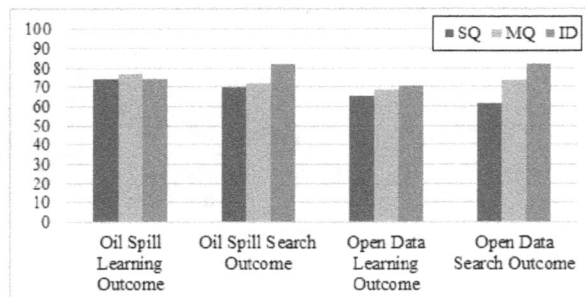

Figure 2. Users' self-reported perceived search and learning success by query condition and task.

their overall rating for this question was lowest out of the 15 items in the Post-Search Questionnaire.

We next examined how subjects' responses to searching and learning experiences might differ depending on the query condition to which they were exposed. An analysis of individual items revealed that subjects' learning and search experiences were not significantly different across the three query conditions (SQ, MQ, and ID) except in relation to one question. After subjects completed searching about Open Data, those subjects who were assigned to the ID condition (M=3.85) reported feeling able to synthesize the various pieces of information together at significantly higher levels than those subjects who were in the other two conditions (SQ=3.14, MQ =2.85), p<.05.

Cross-question factor analysis. To investigate possible aspects that shaped subject's responses to questions about their searching and learning experiences, we conducted a factor analysis of responses across questions: specifically, principal component factor analysis using Varimax with Kaiser Normalization, based on the responses to the 15 items with 5-scale rating (Q7-Q21) from the Post-Search Questionnaire. This analysis revealed three distinct factors, which we term 'Experience Factors' that characterized aspects of subjects' responses:

Experience Factor 1 (Search for Information Exploration) focuses on users' experiences with searching itself, examining their effort, engagement, feeling of time well-spent, and perception of knowledge expansion as a result of searching.

Experience Factor 2 (User Experience with Search Systems) deals with users' experience with respect to learning by investigating whether searching helps people to increase their interest in the topic or develop new ideas and a willingness to find and share more information.

Experience Factor 3 (Learner Interest and Motivation) is related to the use and usability of search systems.

Internal consistency for each of the scales was examined using Cronbach's alpha. The alphas were 0.855 for Search for Information Exploration (6 items), 0.846 for User Experience with Search Systems (4 items), and 0.814 for Learner Interest and Motivation (5 items). Factor 1 explains 25.76% of the total variance, and Factor 2 explains 20.52% of the total variance. Factor 3 explains 17.60% of the total variance. Table 3 (the question inventory), shows questions (Q7-Q21) grouped by these three Experience Factors.

Subjects rated their learning experience with the search systems (Experience Factor 2) lower than their search experience for information exploration (Experience Factor 1) and their perceived learner interest and motivation (Experience Factor 3) across the

two tasks. The results of ANOVA (df=39) comparing the three factors across the three query conditions (SQ, MQ, and ID) showed that there was no statistical difference in subjects' experiences of search for information exploration, user experience with search systems, and learner interest and motivation across query strategies.

Self-reported outcomes. Two questions in the Post-Search Questionnaire (Q22, Q23) asked subjects to grade their own learning and search outcomes on a scale of 0-100. Overall, subjects gave lower scores to both learning and searching outcomes related to the more difficult task – Open Data. The results of ANOVA showed that subjects self-reported learning outcomes did not differ significantly in both tasks depending on search strategies. However, while the mean of self-reported searching outcomes across the three query formulation conditions (SQ, MQ, and ID) were not significantly different in the case of the Oil Spill task, they were different for the Open Data task (F(2,37) = 4.68, p<.02): subjects who used the intrinsically diverse (ID) search system reported the highest search outcomes (M=81.92), compared with those subjects from the SQ (M=73.69) and MQ conditions (M=61.50). Also, those subjects who were allowed to reformulate their queries (MQ) reported higher search outcome scores than those who had to use a limited query formulation (SQ). Figure 2 summarizes the analysis of perceived learning and search outcomes across tasks and query conditions.

4.2 Learning measures and indicators

The analysis of data collected from the logs, questionnaires, and written tests described in Section 3 revealed a number of explicit and implicit indicators potentially useful for measuring learning in web searching (RQ1).

4.2.1. Explicit Measures

(1) Assessment of High- and Low-Level Cognitive Learning. When subjects engaged in searching for an easier task (Oil Spill), they demonstrated more evidence of lower-level cognitive learning (M=7.21) than higher cognitive learning (M=5.88) in their written summaries. When searching for a more difficult task (Open Data), they provided summaries with slightly more evidence of higher cognitive learning (M=5.31) than that of lower-level cognitive learning (M=4.55). Overall, we did not find that there was a significant difference in overall cognitive learning scores across the three query conditions.

(2) Perceived Learning and Searching Outcomes. When we examined the correlation between perceived learning outcome scores (Q22) and actual cognitive learning scores, we found that for both tasks, perceived learning outcome positively correlated with both lower-level cognitive learning scores on Q1–Q3 (r=.33, r=.38) and higher-level cognitive learning scores on Q4–Q6, (r=.32, r=.37). Aggregating both lower and higher cognitive learning scores, the overall correlation was even stronger (r=.40, r=.45). This result implies that subjects were able to assess their own learning outcomes reasonably well, and thus perceived learning outcome scores could be used as a measure for learning in searching. While the perceived searching outcome variable (Q23) was useful in comparing subjects' perceived outcomes across two tasks and three query conditions, we found that perceived searching outcomes were not correlated with learning scores from written responses.

4.2.2. Implicit Indicators

(1) Knowledge Level Gain. Of the 42 subjects who wrote valid answers to questions P4 and Q5, 16 showed no knowledge level

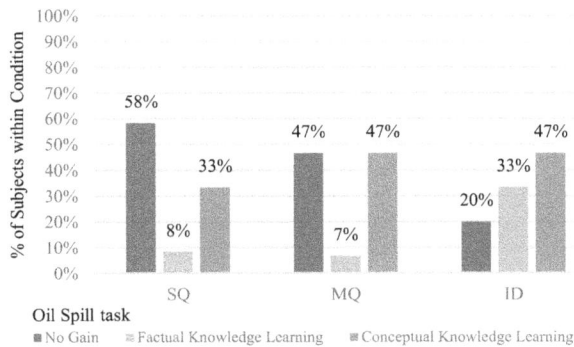

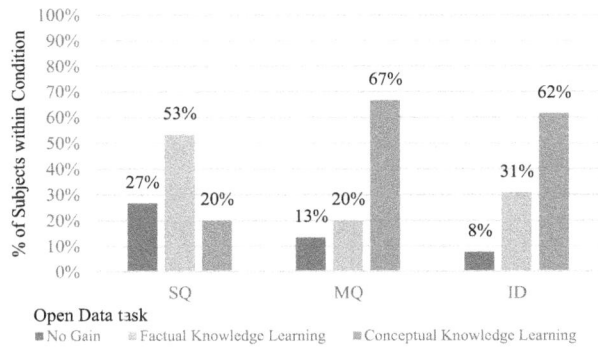

Figure 3. Percentage of Subjects Gaining in Knowledge Level in each Query Condition, for Oil Spill and Open Data tasks.

gain, 15 had a +1 gain, and 10 had a +2 gain. One participant had a negative gain (exhibiting conceptual knowledge in the pre-test but only describing factual knowledge in the post-test). We found a strong positive correlation between perceived learning outcomes and actual knowledge level gain in the ID condition, for both the Open Data (r=0.69) and Oil Spill (r=0.64) tasks.

(2) **Length of Written Responses.** We found that the length of written responses was another potential indicator of learning: the total combined length of all six post-written responses (Q1-Q6) had a strong positive correlation with the overall cognitive learning score for each task (r=.75, r=.90). The total combined response length for the lower-level cognitive learning assessment questions (Q1-Q3) was strongly correlated with the corresponding lower-level cognitive learning score for both the Open Data and Oil Spill tasks (r=.75, r=.86). Similarly, the total combined length of the written responses to the higher cognitive learning questions (Q4-Q6) was correlated with the higher-level cognitive learning score for both tasks (r=.66, r=.83). In sum, longer responses were more likely to exhibit more evidence of cognitive learning as measured by the coding scheme.

(3) **Interaction Speed.** Although time has been used in IR evaluation as an indicator of efficiency [13][19], we took a different approach to time-related measures, focusing on the relationship between interaction speed and learning outcomes. We hypothesized that time spent searching might be positively correlated with increased learning. Indeed, we found that the average viewing time spent per document had positive correlations with overall cognitive learning scores in both Open Data (r=.44) and Oil Spill (r=.39) conditions. Thus, regardless of the nature of tasks and query strategies, subjects who spent more time reading documents were more likely to receive higher scores on their writing summaries.

(4) **Interaction with Documents.** We also hypothesized that the more subjects saved documents they judged to be useful, the more they were learning through searching, which would lead to higher quality written responses. We observed a correlation between interaction with documents and learning only for the Open Data task: there was a positive correlation (r=0.385) between the number of unique documents clicked from the SERP and lower-level cognitive learning score. The number of useful documents saved was also strongly correlated with the lower-level cognitive learning score (r=.45) and with perceived search outcome (Q23), (r=0.34). This provides some evidence that document interaction variables could be useful as implicit indicators of learning.

4.3 Relationships of query strategies to learning outcomes

To help answer RQ2, we compared knowledge level gain across query conditions. In the Open Data task, subjects' gain in knowledge level was relatively consistent across interaction conditions, with ANOVA results showing no significant differences (SQ=0.928, MQ=1.33, ID=1.153). However, in the Oil Spill task, we found a statistically significant difference between conditions (SQ=0.41, MQ=0.73, ID=1.20: p=.031): the ID condition offered the highest learning gains compared with both the SQ and MQ conditions. We also observed that prior knowledge scores in this task also showed significant differences (SQ=1.08, MQ=0.8, ID=0.2, p=.004). For all three conditions, the post-search knowledge level (Q5) is almost the same (SQ=1.5, MQ=1.53, ID=1.4).

We also found a general trend that the average time users spent per query in terms of reading documents and in terms of assessing the SERP page was much higher in the SQ and ID conditions compared to the MQ condition (Table 1). Users in the MQ and ID conditions also tended to select more unique documents in the SERP than users in the SQ condition.

An analysis of knowledge level gain across the three query conditions, shown in Figure 3, shows that subjects exhibited different patterns in gaining knowledge depending on the query condition. For the Oil Spill task, 58% of the subjects who were assigned to the SQ condition did not gain any new knowledge as a result of searching, while 33% gained knowledge at the conceptual level of learning. In contrast, only 20% subjects in the ID condition showed no gain in knowledge after searching, and 47% achieved conceptual-knowledge-based learning for the same task. For the Open Data task, most subjects showed conceptual knowledge gains in both the MQ condition (67%) and ID condition (62%), compared to the SQ condition (20%). The ID condition gave the best combined factual + cognitive knowledge gain score on both tasks in terms of the percentage of users achieving a gain (Oil Spill: 80%; Open Data: 93%). The SQ and MQ conditions achieved gains of (41%, 73%) and (54%, 80%) of users respectively. Thus, of the three query conditions, there was some evidence that the intrinsically diverse (ID) query condition gave the best support to learning for these tasks.

One limitation of our study was that, while subjects might exhibit similar levels of knowledge about a topic, they might also have different learning abilities, which could interact with variables such as their assigned query strategy condition. A future study could add specific assessments to track and account for individual differences in learning ability. Also, since the intrinsically diverse (ID) condition both modified the results ranking and added query suggestions, additional experiments would help understand how each of these modifications contributed to our observed results.

4.4 Relationships between key variables and learning outcomes: user factor analysis

Finally, to understand the relationships between key learning-related variables in this study as they relate to users' search behavior (RQ3), we conducted a second factor analysis across users based on their search behavior and learning outcomes (in contrast to the first factor analysis in Sec. 4.1 based on experience-oriented questions Q7-Q21). Specifically, each participant was represented by their responses to learning-oriented questions P1-P4, Q1-Q6 and the log-based search behavior variables TimePerDoc (Table 1, average time spent viewing documents per query) and TotalClicks (Table 1, unique documents clicked in search results). For space reasons we omit analysis of the remaining 15 variables, which also showed less consistent contrasts between factors than the ones included here. We used $k=2$ factors in order to examine whether at least two main groups of potentially different types of users were evident from the data. We did one factor analysis for each query formulation condition.

Figure 4 shows the resulting factor biplots. A biplot shows users and variables in the same factor space: users are shown as numeric points plotted by their factor scores, and each variable is shown as a vector whose coordinates are the factor coefficients of the variable. Thus, points that are close together represent users with similar factor scores, and vectors of similar length with small angle between them represent highly correlated variables.

Across all conditions, the lower-level cognitive learning variables (Q1-Q3) generally clustered together, as did higher-level cognitive learning variables (Q4-Q6). Of these two groups, the lower-level cognitive learning scores were most consistently correlated across conditions (Q1,Q2: r= 0.42; Q2,Q3: r=0.33; Q1,Q3: r=0.46; all p< 0.001). For higher-level cognitive learning scores, there was consistent but weaker correlation (Q4,Q5: r=0.41, p<0.001; Q4, Q6: r=0.24, p<0.04). For pre-search scores, none of P1-P4 were correlated with either TimePerDocs or TotalClicks. However, P2 scores (interest in learning more about the topic) were correlated with Q2-Q5 scores. For the log-based variables, we can refine our initial finding in Sec. 4.2.2 that time

Table 2. User factor analysis of key variables, for each of the three query conditions.

Condition	SQ		MQ		ID	
User Factor	F1	F2	F1	F2	F1	F2
TotalClicks	**0.71**		-0.47	-0.10	-0.31	**0.70**
TimePerDoc		-0.19	**0.76**	0.31	**0.36**	
P1		**0.44**	0.14	0.20	-0.10	**0.36**
P2	0.33	0.65	-0.22	-0.29	**0.39**	
P3	-0.20	**-0.74**		**-0.39**	-0.20	
Q1	0.53	0.78		**0.37**	0.11	**0.61**
Q2	**0.62**		0.35	0.36	0.19	**0.85**
Q3	**0.57**		0.17	**0.42**	0.32	0.38
Q4	**0.56**	0.22	0.15	**0.73**	**0.70**	
Q5	**0.58**		0.34	**0.78**	**0.65**	
Q6	0.16	-0.32	**0.98**	0.18	**0.10**	
%Variance	*21%*	*18%*	*19%*	*18%*	*17%*	*13%*

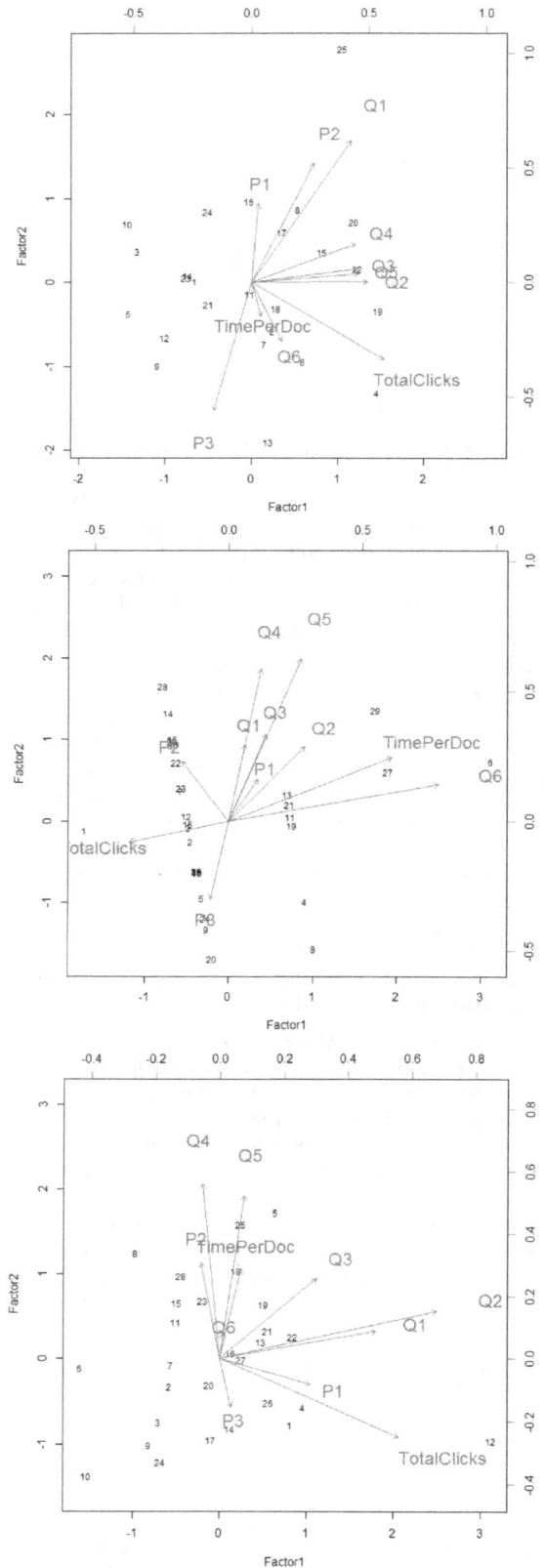

Figure 4. User factor biplots showing correlation of key learning and search behavior variables (red arrows) and clustering of subjects in factor space (numeric points) for Single Query (top), Multiple Query (center), and ID conditions (bottom). Vectors of similar length with small angle between them represent highly correlated variables.

170

spent per document is correlated with overall cognitive learning scores. Figure 4 makes clear that TimePerDoc is consistently correlated with Q6 scores (creative question-asking) across all query conditions (r=0.56, p<0.001), and to a lesser extent, the other high-level cognitive learning scores (Q4: r=0.26; Q5: r=0.29, p < 0.01) but not with lower-level cognitive learning scores (Q1-Q3). TotalClicks was most strongly correlated with Q2 (r=0.22; p<0.05) that assessed users' understanding of the topic. To examine the nature of the user groups found by the user factor analysis, we inspected the factor loadings (shown as User Factors F1, F2 in Table 2), with the following interpretations.

Single Query Condition. The group of users associated with User Factor 1 had greater positive loading on TotalClicks and cognitive learning scores (Q2-Q6). User Factor 2 subjects were characterized by high loadings on background knowledge (P1), interest level (P2), factual recall (Q1) and lower negative loading on perceived difficulty (P3).

Multiple Query Condition. User Factor 1 users had higher positive loading for time spent per document, and writing creative questions (Q6). User Factor 2 users had high positive loading on existing knowledge (Q1) and negative loading on perceived difficulty (P3), and strong positive loading on both lower and higher-level cognitive learning scores (Q3-Q5). These two clusters of users are evident on Fig. 4 (center).

Intrinsically Diverse Condition. Users associated with User Factor 1 were characterized by higher positive loading on time spent per document, level of interest (P2), and the three higher-level cognitive response scores (Q4-Q6). In contrast, User Factor 2 users had higher positive loading on clicks (TotalClicks), existing topic knowledge (P1), and response scores for the lower-level cognitive, factual questions (Q1, Q2).

In sum, our user factor analysis showed the existence of distinct groups of users exhibiting complementary search strategies: one group chose a broader strategy, tending to click and explore more results while obtaining higher lower-level cognitive learning scores, while the other group tended to read fewer results more deeply while obtaining higher scores on the higher-level cognitive learning assessment questions. These differences were evident in the richer query environments of both the MQ and ID conditions.

5. CONCLUSION

In this paper we described a lab-based user study in which we investigated potential indicators of learning in web searching, effective query strategies for learning, and the relationship between search behavior and learning outcomes. We developed and analyzed a rich set of implicit and explicit learning measures based on behavioral data from search logs, questionnaires, and written responses to knowledge questions. The written responses were coded using a new, carefully developed scheme based on Bloom's revised learning taxonomy. Our examination of potential learning indicators, and how search behavior correlated with learning outcomes, found that searchers' perceived learning outcomes closely matched their actual learning outcomes; that the amount searchers wrote in the post-search survey was highly correlated with their cognitive learning question scores; and that the time searchers spent per document while searching was also highly and consistently correlated with higher-level cognitive learning question scores. To investigate which search paradigms best support human learning experiences and outcomes our study incorporated three distinct between-subjects query strategies – submitting a single query, using multiple queries, and using multiple queries with intrinsically diverse (ID) subtopics. We

found that the ID condition gave a large advantage over the SQ and MQ conditions, for both search tasks, in terms of the percentage of users able to achieve combined factual and conceptual knowledge gains. Our study provides deeper insight into the problem of how learning may be assessed effectively during web search, and which aspects of search interaction are most effective for supporting superior learning outcomes.

Acknowledgements. We thank Yi-Yin Alison Wang, Kuan-Chun David Cheng, and Gracie Mu-Yun Chien for their study contributions; the University of Michigan Office of Research and School of Information for support of this work; and the anonymous reviewers for their comments.

6. REFERENCES

[1] Ageev, M., Guo, Q., Lagun, D., and Agichtein, E. 2011. Find it if you can: a game for modeling different types of web search success using interaction data. In *Proc. of SIGIR '11*. ACM, 345-354.

[2] Agosti, M., Fuhr, N., Toms, E., and Vakkari, P. 2014. Evaluation methodologies in Information Retrieval Dagstuhl seminar 13441. *ACM SIGIR Forum*. 48, 1 (June 2014), 36-41.

[3] Allan, J., Croft, B., Moffat, A., & Sanderson, M. 2012. Frontiers, challenges, and opportunities for information retrieval: Report from SWIRL 2012: the second strategic workshop on information retrieval in Lorne. *ACM SIGIR Forum*. 46, 1 (May 2012), 2-32.

[4] Anderson, L. W. and Krathwohl, D. R. 2001. *A Taxonomy for Learning, Teaching, and Assessing: A Revision of Bloom's Taxonomy of Educational Objectives*. Longman, New York.

[5] Bailey, P., Chen, L., Grosenick, S., Jiang, L., Li, Y., Reinholdtsen, P., Salaca, C., Wang, H., and Wong, S. 2012. User task understanding: a web search engine perspective. In *NII Shonan Meeting on Whole-Session Evaluation of Interactive Information Retrieval Systems, Kanagawa, Japan*. (Oct. 2012).

[6] Bloom B. 1956. *Taxonomy of Educational Objectives*. David McKay Company, New York.

[7] Borlund, P. 2000. Experimental components for the evaluation of interactive information retrieval systems. *Journal of Documentation*. 56, 1, 71-90.

[8] Eickhoff, C., Teevan, J., White, R., and Dumais, S. 2014. Lessons from the journey: a query log analysis of within-session learning. In *Proc. of WSDM 2014*. ACM, New York, NY, 223-232.

[9] Heinström, J. 2006. Broad exploration or precise specificity: Two basic information seeking patterns among students. *JASIST*. 57, 11 (Sept. 2006), 1440-1450.

[10] Hersh, W. R., Elliot, D. L., Hickam, D. H., Wolf, S. L. and Molnar, A. 1995. Towards new measures of information retrieval evaluation. In *Proc. of SIGIR 1995*. ACM, 164-170.

[11] Holsti, O. R. 1969. *Content Analysis for the Social Sciences and Humanities*. Addison-Wesley, Reading, MA.

[12] Jansen, B. J., Booth, D., and Smith, B. 2009. Using the taxonomy of cognitive learning to model online searching. *Information Processing & Management*. 45, 6 (Nov. 2009), 643-663.

[13] Kelly, D. 2009. Methods for evaluating interactive information retrieval systems with users. *Foundations and Trends in Information Retrieval*. 3, 1—2 (Jan. 2009), 1-224.

[14] Kim, J. Y., Collins-Thompson, K., Bennett, P. N., and Dumais, S. T. 2012. Characterizing web content, user interests, and search behavior by reading level and topic. In *Proc. of WSDM 2012*. ACM, New York, NY, 213-222.

[15] Kammerer, Y., Nairn, R., Pirolli, P., and Chi, E. H. 2009. Signpost from the masses: Learning effects in an exploratory social tag search browser. In *Proceedings of SIGCHI 2009*. ACM, 625–634.

[16] Krathwohl, D. R. 2002. A revision of Bloom's taxonomy: An overview. *Theory into practice*. 41, 4, 212-218.

[17] Marchionini, G. 2006. Exploratory search: from finding to understanding. *Comm. of the ACM*. 49, 4 (April 2006), 41-46.

[18] Raman, K., Bennett, P. N., and Collins-Thompson, K. 2014. Understanding intrinsic diversity in Web search: Improving whole-session relevance. *ACM Trans. Info. Systems.* 32, 4 (Oct. 2014).

[19] Smucker, M., and Clarke, C. 2012. Time-based calibration of effectiveness measures. In *Proc.of SIGIR 2012,* ACM, 95-104.

[20] Vakkari, P., and Huuskonen, S. 2012. Search effort degrades search output but improves task outcome. *J. American Society for Information Science and Technology.* 63, 4 (April 2012), 657-670.

[21] Vakkari, P., Pennanen, M. and Serola, S. 2003. Changes of search terms and tactics while writing a research proposal. *Information Processing & Management.* 39, 3 (May 2003), 445-463.

[22] White, R. W., and Roth, R. A. 2009. Exploratory search: Beyond the query-response paradigm. *Synthesis Lectures on Information Concepts, Retrieval, and Services.* 1, 1 (2009), 1-98.

[23] White, R. W., Dumais, S. T., and Teevan, J. 2009. Characterizing the influence of domain expertise on web search behavior. In *Proceedings of WSDM 2009.* (Barcelona, Spain, February 2009). WSDM '09. ACM, New York, NY, 132-141.

[24] Wildemuth, B. M. 2004. The effects of domain knowledge on search tactic formulation. *J. of the American Society for Information Science and Technology.* 55, 3 (Feb. 2004), 246-258.

[25] Wilson, M. J., and Wilson, M. L. 2013. A comparison of techniques for measuring sensemaking and learning within participant-generated summaries. *J. of the American Society for Information Science and Technology.* 64, 2 (Feb. 2013), 291-306.

[26] Zhang, X., Cole, M., and Belkin, N. 2011. Predicting users' domain knowledge from search behaviors. In *Proceedings of SIGIR '11.* ACM, New York, NY, 1225-1226.

Table 3. Inventory of all questions used in this study, along with their response types and source

Category	Variable	ID	Question text	Scale or unit	Source
Topic knowledge	Perceived knowledge	P1	How much do you know about this topic?	1= nothing; ... 5=I know a lot	Pre-search
	Interest in topic	P2	How interested are you to learn more about this topic?	1= not at all; ... 5=very much	
	Perceived difficulty	P3	How difficult do you think it will be to search for information about this topic?	1= very easy; ... 5=very difficult	
	Prior knowledge	P4	Please write what you know about this topic with 3-5 sentences.	Knowledge level coded as 0, 1, 2.	
Search for information exploration (Experience Factor 1)	Engagement in search	Q8	I was cognitively engaged in search task.	Rating on 5-point scale: 1= not at all; 2=unlikely; 3=somewhat; 4=likely; 5=very likely	Post-search
	Search effort	Q9	I made an effort at performing the search task.		
	Time well spent	Q7	The time for search was spent productively on meaningful tasks.		
	Concept relations	Q11	I was able to explore relationships among multiple concepts.		
	Topic scope expanded	Q12	I was able to expand the scope of my knowledge about the topic.		
	Synthesis	Q20	I feel that I was able to put together pieces of information into one big concept.		
User experience with search system (Experience Factor 2)	Like using system	Q16	I liked using this system to find information I needed.	Rating on 5-point scale: 1= not at all; 2=unlikely; 3=somewhat; 4=likely; 5=very likely	Post-search
	Needs well expressed in system	Q17	I feel that my needs were fully expressed using this system.		
	Easy to use the system	Q18	It was easy to use the system to express what I was looking for.		
	Topic understanding	Q21	I feel that I have full understanding of the topic of this task		
Learner interest and motivation (Experience Factor 3)	Increased interest	Q13	I became more interested in this topic.	Rating on 5-point scale: 1= not at all; 2=unlikely; 3=somewhat; 4=likely; 5=very likely	Post-search
	Willingness to find more information	Q14	I would like to find more information about this topic.		
	Willingness to share	Q15	I would like to share what I learned with my friends.		
	Learning useful information	Q19	I feel that I learned useful information as a result of this search.		
	Developing new ideas	Q10	I was able to develop new ideas or perspectives.		
Perceived learning	Self-reported learning score	Q22	How would you grade your learning outcome?	Score on 0-100 scale	Post-search
Perceived search success	Self-reported searching score	Q23	How would you grade your search outcome?	Score on 0-100 scale	Post-search
Lower-level cognitive learning assessment	Remember	Q1	Assessing to what extent a subject can remember specific elements about the topic.	Written response was analyzed by checking off 7 criteria	Post-search written test
	Understand	Q2	Assessing to what extent subjects could construct meaning about the topic.		
	Apply	Q3	Assessing to what extent subjects could carry out the concept in a given situation		
Higher-level cognitive learning assessment	Analyze	Q4	Assessing to what extent subjects could break content into an outline of a paper	Written response was analyzed by checking off 7 criteria	Post-search written test
	Evaluate	Q5	Assessing to what extent subjects could write what they learned from searching		
	Create	Q6	Assessing to what extent subjects could write creative questions		

A Comparison of Primary and Secondary Relevance Judgements for Real-Life Topics

Simon Wakeling[1]   Martin Halvey[2]   Robert Villa[1]   Laura Hasler[1]

[1] University of Sheffield
Information School, Regent Court,
Sheffield, United Kingdom.

[1] {first initial.surname}@sheffield.ac.uk

[2] University of Strathclyde,
Department of Computer and Information Sciences,
Glasgow, Scotland, United Kingdom

[2] martin.halvey@strath.ac.uk

ABSTRACT

The notion of relevance is fundamental to the field of Information Retrieval. Within the field a generally accepted conception of relevance as inherently subjective has emerged, with an individual's assessment of relevance influenced by numerous contextual factors. In this paper we present a user study that examines in detail the differences between primary and secondary assessors on a set of "real-world" topics which were gathered specifically for the work. By gathering topics which are representative of the staff and students at a major university, at a particular point in time, we aim to explore differences between primary and secondary relevance judgements for real-life search tasks. Findings suggest that while secondary assessors may find the assessment task challenging in various ways (they generally possess less interest and knowledge in secondary topics and take longer to assess documents), agreement between primary and secondary assessors is high.

CCS Concepts

• **Information systems~Test collections**   • **Information systems~Relevance assessment**

Keywords

Assessment; Secondary; Primary; Judgement; Test Collection.

1. INTRODUCTION

The notion of relevance is central to Information Science research and there exists a vast body of literature on the subject. Whilst research into the notion of relevance is on-going, with many perspectives and open/unanswered questions, a generally accepted conception of relevance as inherently subjective has emerged, with an individual's assessment of relevance influenced by a myriad of contextual factors [16]. In particular understanding and measuring relevance is of the utmost importance to the evaluation of information retrieval (IR) systems. There are many views on evaluation with the IR community, where user-focused evaluation and system focused evaluation can be considered as two extreme points on a continuum of IR evaluation [11], with many points in

between. An integral component of the system-orientated evaluation process is the generation of annotated test-collections. There are many successful initiatives in this area including TREC, CLEF, INEX etc. While processes vary between test collections, the method of creating a test collection typically consists of expert assessors creating a series of topics against which to assess the relevance of documents in a collection. In recent years there has been an increasing focus on this aspect of the evaluation process, particularly in terms of the accuracy and efficiency of the judgement process. Investigating ways in which this type of system focussed evaluation can be improved is an on-going effort, and has been the subject of much debate (e.g. [1]) and long-term critique, especially concerning the lack of user interactivity [15].

At the other end of the spectrum, from a user centred perspective, work lead by Borlund has noted the importance of task creation in the evaluation process, in particular that "an information need ought to be treated as a user-individual and potentially dynamic concept" [6]. In proposing the simulated work task situation as a method of stimulating that information need, Borlund argues that measures of system interaction and judgements of situational relevance better reflect real-life when the information need is truly realistic and engaging. She argues that this approach can lead to a more effective evaluation of a system.

While the topics created for TREC style relevance assessments may be user-individual, we argue that they do not in practice always represent "real-life" information needs. While a growing body of research has examined differences between primary and secondary relevance judgements for these synthetic tasks [2; 17], little has been done to investigate how the use of real-life search tasks might affect relevance judgements for test-collections. This paper aims to address this deficit by exploring the differences between primary and secondary relevance judgements for real life non-synthetic tasks gathered from staff and students at a large University. More specifically, we seek to answer the following research questions in relation to real-life search-tasks:

RQ 1: How does relevance assessment behaviour differ between primary and secondary assessors?
RQ 2: To what extent do secondary assessments agree with primary judgements?
RQ 3: To what extent do interest in and knowledge of the topic affect relevance judgements?
RQ 4: Does the length of the topic description affect secondary relevance judgements?
RQ 5: How does confidence in judgements differ between primary and secondary assessors?

To address these questions a two-part study was conducted where participants' real world information needs were gathered, and used to generate document sets. These were then assessed by both the initial participant and a number of secondary assessors. A mixed methods approach was taken, where quantitative data relating to the judgement and assessment process was integrated with qualitative data collected during post-task interviews.

The rest of this paper is structured as follows: first, a short literature review of the recent and relevant material is provided, followed by a description of the study carried out. This includes a description of the data collected, with an emphasis on the qualitative data collected. Results are provided in Section 4, which is followed by a discussion of our findings and finally our conclusion. The proceedings are the records of the conference. ACM hopes to give these conference by-products a single, high-quality appearance. To do this, we ask that authors follow some simple guidelines. In essence, we ask you to make your paper look exactly like this document. The easiest way to do this is simply to download a template from [2], and replace the content with your own material.

2. RELATED WORK

2.1 Primary vs. Secondary Assessments

Voorhees [20] used TREC data to compare differences between the original relevance judgements of topic authors, and subsequent secondary relevance assessments. While significant variation in relevance judgements were observed, these were found to not meaningfully effect the subsequent evaluation of retrieval performance. Webber & Pickens [21] examined disagreements between primary and secondary assessors of a text classifier, finding that while the use of secondary assessors lowered the classification quality this had little practical effect on results rankings. Alonso & Mizzaro [3] examined agreement between TREC assessors and crowd workers on Mechanical Turk. They found that while agreement varied for individual assessors, collective agreement levels were high. Al-Harbi and Smucker [2] also compared the original judgements of TREC assessors with those of secondary assessors, focusing particularly on the assessment process. Using a think-aloud protocol they identified three general reasons for disagreements between primary and secondary assessments; *topic* (the secondary assessor having difficulty understanding or applying the topic description to the documents), *document* (difficulty processing the document), and *assessor* (the secondary assessor lacking knowledge or concentration).

It should be noted that while the primary assessments used in [20; 21] represent the judgement of the "creators" of a topic, these topics do not necessary represent real-life information needs. Chouldechova & Mease [7] in contrast, compared the relevance judgements of primary and secondary assessors for results sets returned by real-life search engine queries. They found that using primary assessments led to more valuable relevance judgements, attributing this to the superior background knowledge of primary assessors. The authors do however note some of the practical difficulties of eliciting such real-life primary judgements.

2.2 Impact of Domain Knowledge

Bailey et al. [4], Kinney et al. [12], Ruthven et al. [14] all found evidence that an assessor's level of topic knowledge positively correlated with judgement quality, with [14] also finding that interest in the topic was similarly related. Clough et al. [8] compared crowdsourced relevance judgements of search engine rankings with expert assessments, and concluded that while overall rankings were comparable, experts were able to better distinguish between different levels of highly accurate results. In contrast to these studies, Efthimiadis and Hotchkiss [9] compared expert and non-expert judgements for search topics within the TREC legal track, finding that the judgements of assessors without legal expertise were of higher quality than those of experts. Research has also suggested a link between domain knowledge and confidence in a judgement. Ruthven et al. [14] found that an assessor's prior confidence in their ability to judge documents for a topic was linked to their knowledge of the topic, and that this confidence level was found to influence their judgements. Al-Harbi and Smucker [2] suggest that secondary assessors are frequently uncertain about their judgement, which in extreme cases results in the assessor decision is being a guess. They advocate the collection of a certainty measure with each relevance judgement.

2.3 Impact of Topic Description

Al-Harbi and Smucker [2] found some evidence that the length of the topic description influenced differences in judgement between primary and secondary assessors. In particular they suggest that a short topic description may encourage a higher number of relevant judgements from secondary assessors, who are able to interpret the criteria for relevance more liberally. This contrasts with the work of Webber et al. [22], who found that in the context of the TREC legal track more detailed descriptions did not improve assessor reliability. It is also useful to note that reviews of variations in topic description structure and length across TREC programmes reveal an acknowledgement of the influence descriptions have on the judgement process. We note for example that TREC-4 shortened the length of descriptions, and removed the "narrative" section, which was found to greatly impact performance [10].

3. USER STUDY

3.1 Overview

The overall aim of the study was to explore differences between primary and secondary relevance judgements for real-life search tasks. As such the study was split into two parts: an initial questionnaire to gather real-life "search tasks" from participants, and an in-lab study which involved participants judging the relevance of documents to both their own and other participants' tasks. The first part was based on library search forms and the procedure is described in Section 3.1. From these search forms a document collection was generated (Section 3.2). These documents were then utilised in a lab study to gather assessments (Section 3.3 and 3.4).

While full details of the study design are below, several key decisions were made early in the study design that merit discussion here. Since it was necessary to generate documents relating to real-world search tasks, which would naturally cover a diverse range of topics, the web was used as a source for documents. It was also decided to elicit specific types of search-task from respondents to the phase one survey. The vast literature on information seeking has resulted in a variety of ways of categorising search-tasks, but the evaluation of the impact of all possible task types is beyond the scope of the research presented here. For the purposes of this study it was deemed sufficient to explicitly distinguish between two fundamental types of task – open (a task in which the searcher will likely need to access and synthesise information from several sources to address their information need, and for which there may not be a single definitive answer) and closed (a task which likely has a single unambiguous solution) [13].

The structure of the topic description was modelled on early TREC protocols [10], and consisted of three sections: a basic description of the topic, an outline of the context for the search, and an explicit summary of the criteria for assessing relevance. The assessment itself took the form of a binary relevant/not relevant judgement. Since results presented in related studies (e.g. [2; 17]) are also based on binary judgements, we determined that the use of a scale or continuum would potentially affect the comparability of our results. A binary judgement was therefore collected for each document. Finally the collection of qualitative data was done through post-session play-back interviews rather than the think-aloud protocol used by [2]. This was to allow for the collection of temporal and behavioural data relating to the judgement process, using a think aloud protocol could have potentially skewed the data collected.

3.2 Task Generation

Participants were initially recruited via an introductory email sent to volunteer mailing lists at the University of Sheffield. This email explained what would be required of participants, and offered compensation of £24 for those completing both stages of the research project. Those interested in participating were asked to email the investigators directly, and the first 20 respondents were then sent two links; to an online calendar to book a date and time for the lab session, and to an online task form. This form first gathered some background information about participants (age, gender, educational background etc.), and then asked for details of two search tasks the participant either was about to undertake, or had recently undertaken. The form specified that the first task should be a closed search task, and the second an open search task. Explanations of both terms and example search tasks were provided to ensure participants understood what was required. To elicit details of each search task, participants were asked to respond to four requests for information about the search task. These are presented below, along with an example response from a participant:

1. Please describe what you are searching for, in one clear and precise sentence.
   What led to the recession that began in 2008?

2. Please describe your search situation in more detail (e.g. the context of your search, the purpose of seeking this information, why you are interested in it, etc.) A good way of approaching this is to consider what someone else would need to know in order to conduct this search on your behalf.
   The economic recession that suddenly occurred throughout the world in 2008 made little sense to anybody outside of economics/finance. I want to get a better understanding of how such an event can occur i.e. what features of current economics/finance allowed such a problem to happen.

3. Please specify what would constitute a relevant or non-relevant document or webpage relating to this search situation. You might want to use the format "A relevant document or website would include information about X or Y. Pages that include only information about Z are not relevant".
   A relevant document or website would include information about the recession and what principles of current economics allowed the propagation of the problem throughout the world. Pages that include only information about the period during which the recession took place are not relevant.

4. Please provide any key words or search terms you remember using or you think might be useful in searching for your topic.

21st century recession; financial crisis 2008; financial crisis UK; Economics of recession

While the majority of respondents provided clear and detailed answers to these questions, in three cases participants described search tasks that were not clearly closed or open in nature. In these cases it was necessary to request alternative search tasks from the participants, with further guidance on the type of tasks required. The resulting data-set consisted of forty search tasks, one closed and one open from each of the twenty participants. In order to allow for comparison between primary and secondary relevance judgements, it was necessary to select eight participants at random for whose topics relevance judgements would be made by five other participants (a full explanation is provided in Section 3.4). The responses to question 1-3 were used verbatim as the structured topic description presented to participants during the lab study (see Sections 3.3 and 3.4).

3.3 Document Generation

For each participant topic, the keywords provided by participants were used as a query to conduct a web search. To present a range of different documents with potentially different degrees of relevance to the user's topic, 3 search results were sampled from each page of 10 links provided by Google, i.e. three random results were selected from page 1, then page 2, etc. until a total of 30 document results were downloaded. As far as possible, any non-HTML documents in the result list were removed from consideration during this process.

Each of these documents was then processed using the "Readability" API[1], which removed advertising and other superfluous webpage information. The aim here was to ensure that documents would be presented in a similar text and image form to each other, in order to remove issues around differing website designs. Not all of the resulting documents necessarily contained data, and so a final manual scan of the documents was carried out to remove empty documents. A final stratified sampling of 15 documents was then taken from this list, across each Google result page. This process was derived from a number of pilot tests which investigated different methods of downloading documents of different degrees of relevance. While "relevance" is not being controlled in this study, we did wish to maximise the chances of both relevant and non-relevant documents being presented to participants. Techniques to dilute search results were not found to be useful in this particular study, with the simpler assumption that documents further down the ranking were less likely to be relevant being found to provide a range of material expected by assessors. Beyond removing non-HTML documents, no attempt was made to control other document characteristics like length.

The result of this process was that for each participant topic, 15 documents were downloaded, the collection as a whole consisting of 600 unique documents. Across all topics the mean document word length was 1977 words (SD 3840). The majority of documents were less than 5000 words long (545 documents), with one document of over 50,000 words, over twice as long as any other document in the collection, belonging to topic number 8-2. A copy of all topics and documents is available for download[2].

3.4 Experimental Interface

The task description was displayed first, along with the question "How much do you know about this topic?" and the associated 7

---

[1] https://readability.com/developers/api

[2] http://dx.doi.org/10.15129/317def18-5702-407e-9cf4-a92ed4e6c081

point scale. On pressing the "view document" button the first page to be judged would be displayed. On the top right hand side of the screen a fixed dialog box asked the three questions "Is this document relevant to the topic?", "How confident are you in making this judgement?", and "Have you seen this document before?" It should be noted that participants were able, by design, to complete and submit these questions without viewing the entire document. The title of the current topic was displayed at the top of the window along with a "click to view topic" button which would allow the participant to return to the full topic description

Table 1: Measures used in the study.

Measure	Description
For each document judged:	
Relevance	Binary relevance judgement (0/1).
Confidence	Degree of confidence in the relevance judgement (1 = no confidence, 7 = very confident).
Time	Time taken to make the relevance judgement.
View Topic	Number of times a user "returned" to the topic description.
For each topic:	
Knowledge	Knowledge of the topic (1 = no knowledge, 7 = expert). Recorded before judgements made.
Interest	Degree of interest in the topic (1 = not interesting at all, 7 = extremely interesting). Recorded after all judgements have been made for a topic.

At the very start of the study a single "practice" task/document was displayed, which allowed the participant to become familiar with the interface before the study topics were displayed. On commencing the study proper, the first topic description was presented. All 15 documents for each topic were then displayed in turn, with order of document presentation being randomised. After all documents for the topic had been judged the participant would then be asked "How interesting was this topic to you?" The system then moved on to the next topic, displaying the topic description followed by 15 documents. This was repeated for all 6 topics judged by each participant. All participants used the interface under the same conditions (screen/interface size and computer). The system logged mouse movement, button clicks, question responses, and other measures such as time taken for each judgement (a list of the measures used in this paper, and a subset of the full list used, is provided in Table 1). Morae was also used to record the screen of the computer.

3.5 Laboratory Protocol

The laboratory sessions were conducted in the University of Sheffield's iLab. Each participant was required to judge the relevance of fifteen documents for each of six search tasks; two being their own (one open and one closed), and four being the open and closed tasks of two other users. This meant that each participant judged the relevance of 90 documents.

Once the practice task had been completed, Morae screen recording software was started, and the participant was instructed to begin the tasks proper. No time limit was imposed for any stage of the process, and the order of tasks, and of documents within each task, was randomised for each participant. The investigator observed the session via a remote Morae connection in the iLab control room, and was able to add markers to the Morae screen recording on occasions when the participant exhibited interesting or note-worthy

behaviour (for example changing their relevance judgement, making very speedy or slow judgements, or assigning a low confidence value to their judgement).

On completion of all six tasks, the investigator returned to the lab and loaded the Morae screen recording onto the participant's PC. The participant was then asked to watch back their session and describe their behaviour and the rationale behind their relevance judgements. Due to time constraints it proved impractical for the participant to watch the whole of their session. Instead particular attention was paid to the first documents for each task, and other documents that the investigator had marked as noteworthy. Participants were also asked explicitly for their perspective on the differences between completing their own and other participants' tasks, and on the perceived effects of topic knowledge and interest. Attention was also paid to their interpretation of the confidence scale. All replay and interview sessions were recorded, and the audio recordings transcribed. The transcriptions were then subjected to Qualitative Content Analysis.

3.6 Demographics

The experiment had 20 participants, who were predominantly staff and students at the University of Sheffield. The participants had an average age of 27.9 (std. dev. = 8.17), the youngest participant was 19 and the oldest 54. 9 of the participants were male and 11 female. 12 of the participants were native English speakers; the other native languages were Indonesian, Japanese, Hindi, Chinese, Arabic and Italian. Of the non-native speakers, 5 rated their English as fluent and 3 at an intermediate level. In terms of search experience, 14 participants reported that they had high search experience, with the remaining 6 reporting medium experience. In the experiment 1800 relevance assessments were made in total. Of those 1200 were secondary assessments and 600 primary. 240 documents received more than 1 assessment, and each of those documents received 1 primary and 5 secondary assessments, giving a total of 1440 assessments.

4. RESULTS

4.1 How does relevance assessment behaviour differ between primary and secondary assessors?

4.1.1 Quantitative Results

Table 2: Summary of results for primary and secondary judgements. Significant differences in bold

	Primary		Secondary	
	Median	Mean (SD)	Median	Mean (SD)
Relevant	0	0.448 (0.498)	0	0.447 (0.497)
Time (millisecs)	23687	34630 (33982)	26496	38727 (40263)
Milliseconds per word	**34.045**	**53.482 (96.137)**	**38.336**	**68.349 (123.152)**
View Topic	**0**	**0.04 (0.212)**	**0**	**0.135 (0.388)**

Table 2 presents a summary of some assessor behaviour statistics, showing the number of documents marked relevant, absolute time to make a judgement, time to make a judgement scaled by the word length of the document, and number of times the 'view topic' button was pressed. As the data was not normally distributed Wilcoxon Rank Sum tests were used to compare between conditions. Significant differences were found for scaled time (p = 0.01, W = 386670) and number of view topic button presses (p < 0.001, W = 390312). We show absolute times in addition to scaled time since previous work has shown that document length can affect effort (e.g. [18]). It was found that assessors pressed the 'view topic' button more often on secondary topics, although the relatively rarity of this action results in very small per-session numbers. In total, across the whole data set, there were 162 button presses for secondary topics (out of 1200 document sessions) versus only 24 button presses for primary topics (out of 600).

4.1.2 Qualitative Results

Several participants stated during the post-session interview that they felt other people's tasks took longer to complete. A number of different explanations for this were given. A common theme related to difficulties understanding the scope and details of the topic instructions, which led to extra time considering the relevance of individual documents as well as time taken to review the topic description. Lack of familiarity with the subject of the topic was also mentioned as a factor, leading to difficulties unravelling complex vocabulary and terminology, and determining the most appropriate keywords for which to scan documents. In practice this often meant that documents had to be read in closer detail, or scanned several times for different terms:

"I just had to like put in a lot of effort. I needed to try and work out what words to look for, or I needed to go through the entire thing to be sure if it's relevant."

It should also be noted that a number of participants also stated that they felt their speed increased over the course of the experiment as they became more comfortable with the requirements of the study.

4.2 To what extent do secondary assessments agree with primary judgements?

4.2.1 Quantitative Results

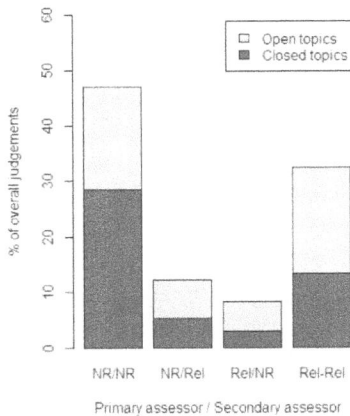

	NR/NR	NR/Rel	Rel/NR	Rel-Rel
Closed topics	57%	11%	6%	27%
Open topics	37%	14%	11%	38%
All topics	47%	12%	8%	32%

Figure 1: Overall agreement between primary and secondary assessors.

Within the data set there are 16 topics (8 closed and 8 open) which have a primary judgement and a total of 5 other secondary judgements by other assessors. Figure 1 shows the overall

percentage agreement between primary and secondary assessors, plus the split between the open and closed tasks. Over all topics, the overall agreement was 79%, rising to 84% for closed topics and falling to 75% for open topics. This agreement is somewhat higher than that reported by Alonso and Mizzaro [3] when using crowdsourcing.

The first column of Table 3 gives the Fleiss' kappa between all assessors (column 1) and between secondary assessors only (column 2). Both follow a similar pattern, with an overall kappa value of 0.545 for all topics, indicating fair to good agreement. Again, this was higher than the study of Alonso and Mizzaro [3]. Overlap was also calculated (the intersection between secondary and primary assessors divided by the union of the relevance assessments), following Voorhees [20] with results presented in the final column of Table 3. The overall overlap was 0.61, which is a higher agreement than that reported by Voorhees [20].

Table 3: Fleiss' kappa for all assessors (primary + secondary), only secondary assessors, plus the overlap between primary and secondary.

	Kappa (all)	Kappa (secondary)	Overlap
Closed topics	0.589	0.565	0.62
Open topics	0.483	0.469	0.61
All topics	0.545	0.526	0.61

There was considerable variation in the number of documents considered relevant for each topic (Figure 2). Topics such as 5-1 and 9-1 contained many "non-relevant" documents judged by the primary assessor, as indicated by the dark bars. Other topics contained far more relevant documents, e.g. topic 16-2 or 6-2. These differences are at least partly due to the quality of the search engine results presented to assessors, and potentially suggests that the data set contains a range of different topic difficulties.

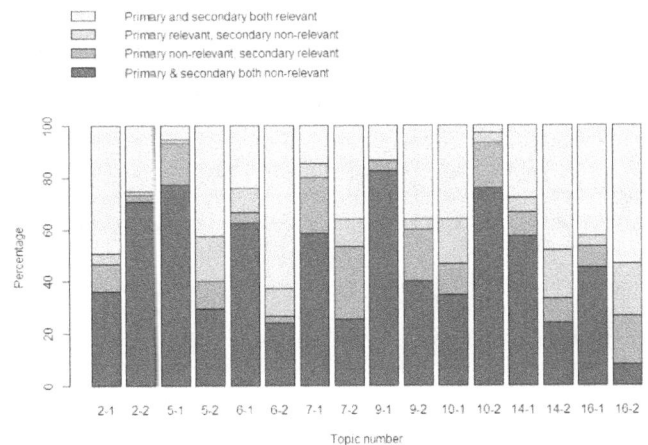

Figure 2: Percentage agreement across topics. Closed topics are 2-1, 5-1, etc., open topics are 2-2, 5-2, etc. The first number is the ID of the participant.

Following Alonso and Mizzaro [3], we also show the group agreement in Figure 3. This is calculated by subtracting the mean relevance judgement of all 5 secondary assessors from the primary relevance judgement (which can be 0 or 1). E.g. if the primary assesses a document as being non-relevant and the mean of the secondary assessors is 0.6 (3 relevant and 2 non-relevant, or 3/5), then the "error" is -0.6. As can be seen in Figure 4, in many cases all 5 secondary assessors exactly agree with the primary (in 49% of all cases). In 23% of cases (ranging from -0.2 to +0.2 in Figure 3, only a single assessor disagrees with the primary, while in 7% of cases two assessors disagree with the primary. If we were to use a "majority vote" to determine relevance from the 5 secondary judgements, in 79% of all cases the majority would match the primary assessment. For comparison with Alonso and Mizzaro [3], the solid red box and dotted red box represent where one assessor (solid box) or two assessors (dashed box) have disagreed with the other assessors (and the primary assessor).

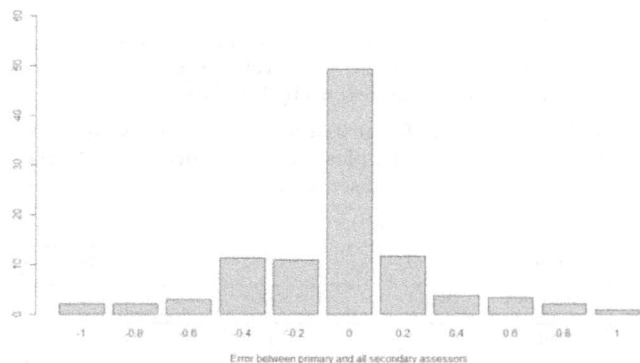

Figure 3: Difference between all secondary assessors and the primary.

4.2.2 Qualitative Results

The post-session interviews provided a rich source of data relating to perceived differences in the primary and secondary judgement processes. Perhaps most interesting were participants' comments about their interpretation of other people's topics, and in particular determining the appropriate criteria for a relevant document. As one participant put it:

"Sometimes I found it really hard to work out what they wanted. It would seem clear at first but then you'd see a document and get confused about whether was on exactly what they were looking for"

For many participants this became a question of whether to take a literal or broad interpretation of the topic description. Several participants described encountering documents that they felt might be useful and relevant to the general topic, but that did not meet the precise criteria laid out in the description. The following extract is typical of several exchanges during the post-session interview and replay assessments:

Interviewer: I think I noticed that you judged this document as relevant.
Participant: Yes, I just felt, well it's got quite a lot of useful information in it.
Interviewer: But if we look at what the actual task was...
Participant: I don't think it does actually have the exact information I was looking for, does it?
Interviewer: Yes, right, you were looking for the release dates of these two films.
Participant: Yes, but I thought, "Oh that's interesting." I think this would be useful for the person doing the search even if it didn't have everything they wanted.

This had interesting implications when primary assessors encountered such situations. They described consciously deciding whether to limit themselves to the confines of the topic description, or taking a more "real-life" approach: *I was almost thinking, "Am I*

coming at it from being me and knowing what I was looking for or am I coming at it being a participant going off the description of what it was?"

Primary assessors frequently admitted some prior experience of evaluating documents on a similar topic to the one in the study. This led to situations where the novelty of a document became a factor in the relevance assessment, something which was clearly not applicable to secondary judgements.

In almost all cases, secondary judgements were deemed to be more difficult than primary ones. Aside from issues relating to topic scope, and the keyword identification issues described above, the characteristics of the documents themselves were sometimes a cause of difficulties. Some participants stated they were unsure whether the reliability or source of a document should be considered. These assessors spoke of doubts about whether documents that were recognisable as blogs or opinion pieces should be considered relevant even if they appeared to be topical:

"I think it does affect how you look at the document, how much weight you put to it and the confidence you would take from it. So ultimately whether it's relevant or not."

It should also be noted that participants described substantial differences between open and closed tasks. Closed tasks were almost universally perceived as easier, with the Open tasks were viewed as more subjective, and as such were more prone to the secondary judgement issues described above:

"Open tasks were just more open to interpretation, just what you wanted as a person to find out. Which was hard when it's not what you specifically want to find out."

4.3 How do contextual factors such as interest in the topic and knowledge of the topic affect relevance judgements?

4.3.1 Quantitative Results

Table 4: Differences between primary and secondary assessors for topic knowledge and interest.

	Primary		Secondary	
	Median	Mean (SD)	Median	Mean (SD)
Knowledge	6	5.25 (1.375)	1	2.062 (1.461)
Interest	6	5.475 (1.55)	4	3.513 (1.636)

Summary statistics for topic knowledge and interest in the topic for all assessors are shown in Table 4. Wilcoxon rank sum tests found that there were significant differences between primary and secondary assessors for both knowledge ($p < 0.001$, $W = 60522$) and interest ($p < 0.001$, $W = 136688$). As can be seen in Table 4 primary assessors were significantly more knowledgeable and interested in their own topics. Figure 4 shows the relationship between knowledge and interest as reported by secondary assessors versus the Cohen Kappa agreement between these secondary judgements and the primary judgements. Kruskal-Wallis tests were used to investigate significant relationships, with none being found, i.e. neither greater interest nor greater knowledge in the topic resulted in greater agreement between the secondary and primary assessors. This analysis was also repeated for open and closed tasks, again with no significant results being found. Histograms showing the distribution of secondary topic knowledge and interest are also shown in Figure 4. Few secondary assessors used the top of the knowledge scale, it being highly skewed right with both a median and mode of 1. For topic interest the distribution is almost constant through the first six levels with the exception of the top 7 rating which not selected by any secondary assessor. This would suggest secondary assessors were reluctant to indicate that they were "experts/knowledgeable" in a topic, but were much more likely to indicate that they were "interested" in the same topic, but not "extremely interested".

4.3.2 Qualitative Results

Two key themes emerged during the post-session interviews. First, that participants were generally much more interested in their own tasks, which meant they were happy to spend longer reading documents where necessary, and were less likely to feel frustrated during the judgement process. Two participants described instances of encountering documents that would be of use in real-life:

"I was bored before I started this task. I've just got no interest in it so it was hard to care whether a document was relevant or not."

"So I just took a while and I was like, "Okay. Let me note that. I will go home and look for them." (Laughter)

Second, that participants were clear that they were likely to have greater topic knowledge for their own tasks. Participants frequently saw this factor as the main cause of it being easier to identify keywords for their own tasks, and were less likely to be troubled by specialist vocabulary present in some documents: *"It's easier for me to absorb because I know more about environmental issues than I do about international finance and banking structures."*

4.4 Does the length of the topic description affect secondary relevance judgements?

Table 5 shows the word length of the different components of the topics, the description, situation, and criteria parts, as well as the mean topic length in words. On average topic size was roughly in line with TREC-5 (mean 82.7 words per topic) and TREC-6 (mean 88.4 words per topic [19]). On average open topics were slightly longer than closed.

Table 5: Mean (SD) length of topic in words, spit be different section of topic and open/closed

	Description	Situation	Criteria	All
Closed	9.8 (4.3)	41.6 (8.8)	28.4 (11.5)	79.8 (13.1)
Open	11.9 (5.3)	43.1 (16.8)	36.9 (11.5)	91.9 (18.5)
All	10.8 (5.0)	42.4 (13.3)	32.6 (12.2)	85.8 (17.1)

Al-Harbi and Smucker [2] suggested that there may be a relationship between topic length and number of documents judged relevant by assessors, arguing that shorter descriptions resulted in broader interpretations of relevance criteria, and therefore a higher number of documents judged relevant. Figure 5 illustrates this relationship (for all assessors, and also split between primary and secondary assessments). Spearman's rank correlation coefficients were used to test these relationships and no significant correlations were found, i.e. the length of the topic description did not appear to affect the number of documents marked relevant by assessors. A similar analysis for carried out for only open and closed topics, and again no relationship was found.

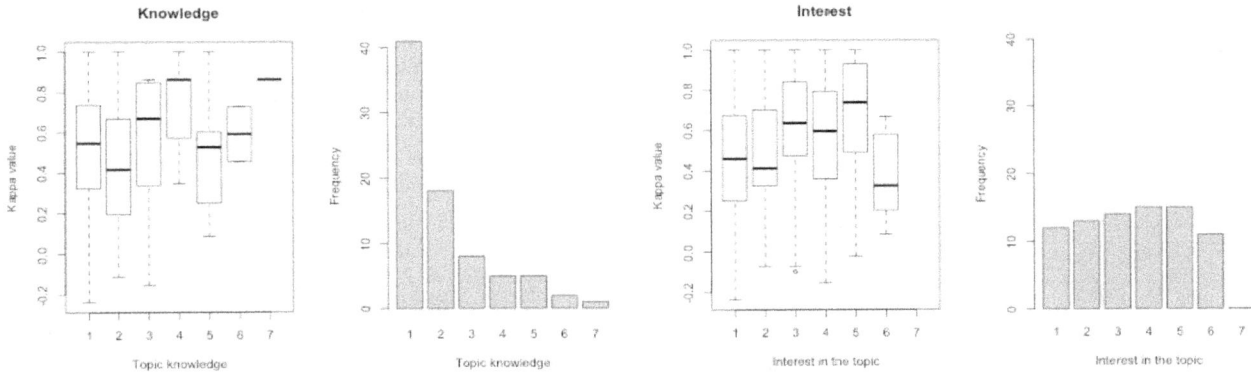

Figure 4: Secondary assessor agreement with primary by topic knowledge and topic interest. The distribution of knowledge and interest for all secondary judgements are also shown.

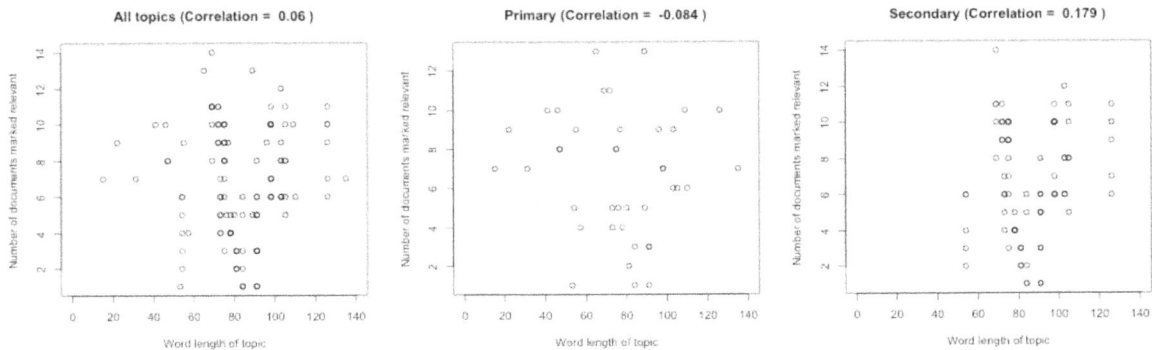

Figure 5: Number of documents marked relevant versus the length of the topic description (all, primary judgements only, and secondary judgements only, from left to right)

4.5 How does confidence in judgements differ between primary and secondary assessors?

4.5.1 Quantitative Results

Table 6: Confidence values for assessors who have judged primary and secondary documents, Mean (SD). Significant differences in bold.

User	Primary	Secondary	P value	W
2	6.867 (0.434)	6.683 (0.624)	0.132	1020.5
5	**6.9 (0.403)**	**5.667 (1.515)**	**< 0.001**	**1376**
6	**6.667 (0.606)**	**5.333 (1.515)**	**< 0.001**	**1371**
7	6.267 (1.143)	6 (1.414)	0.485	974
9	**6.833 (0.747)**	**6.5 (0.893)**	**0.022**	**1091.5**
10	**6.133 (1.306)**	**5.283 (1.151)**	**< 0.001**	**1315.5**
14	6.933 (0.365)	6.75 (0.571)	0.057	1031.5
16	5.9 (1.125)	5.9 (1.298)	0.698	856.5
All	*6.302 (1.036)*	*5.712 (1.4)*	*< 0.001*	*273891*

Table 7: Confidence for primary vs secondary assessors for the 16 topics with secondary assessments, mean (SD). Significant differences in bold, "closed" topics are 2-1, 5-1, etc., "open" topics numbered 2-2, 5-2, etc.

Topic	Primary	Secondary	p-value	W
2-1	6.8 (0.561)	6.373 (1.148)	0.201	653.5
2-2	**6.933 (0.258)**	**6.533 (0.741)**	**0.042**	**710.5**
5-1	**6.933 (0.258)**	**5.467 (1.711)**	**< 0.001**	**878**
5-2	**6.867 (0.516)**	**5.827 (1.288)**	**< 0.001**	**845.5**
6-1	**6.8 (0.561)**	**5.987 (1.257)**	**0.007**	**792.5**
6-2	6.533 (0.64)	5.96 (1.38)	0.244	661.5
7-1	**6.733 (0.594)**	**5.28 (1.122)**	**< 0.001**	**964.5**
7-2	**5.8 (1.373)**	**4.973 (1.174)**	**0.012**	**787**
9-1	6.933 (0.258)	6.88 (0.366)	0.639	585.5
9-2	**6.733 (1.033)**	**5.613 (1.46)**	**<0.001**	**866**
10-1	6.133 (0.99)	5.4 (1.533)	0.114	703.5
10-2	**6.133 (1.598)**	**5.587 (1.347)**	**0.043**	**742.5**
14-1	**6.867 (0.516)**	**6.107 (1.247)**	**0.007**	**783**
14-2	**7 (0)**	**4.613 (1.895)**	**< 0.001**	**1012.5**
16-1	6 (1.134)	5.587 (1.14)	0.167	685.5
16-2	**5.8 (1.146)**	**5.2 (1.027)**	**0.027**	**759**

Overall it was found that primary assessors were more confident in their judgements when compared to secondary assessors (Wilcoxon rank sum test was significant W = 273891, p < 0.001). Table 6 shows the overall mean and SD confidence values for all users (final row), and also for the assessors who have judged both primary and secondary documents. As can be seen, for four assessors confidence on primary assessments was significantly higher when compared to that assessor's confidence on the secondary assessments. For the four other assessors, however, there were no differences in confidence between primary and secondary

assessments. While confidence was generally high across all users, this also varied (e.g. user 16 in Table 6).

Looking at confidence by topic, Table 7 shows the confidence split by the 16 topics for which there are primary and secondary assessments. Wilcoxon rank sum tests were used to compare primary and secondary confidence values, with significant differences being found for 11 topics (p-values and W test statistics are shown in Table 7). It should be noted that while Table 6 compares a single assessor's confidence on primary topics vs. the same assessor's confidence on secondary topics, Table 7 compares the confidence of the primary assessor against the other five secondary assessors.

Across topics confidence is generally high, but there are some striking differences between primary and secondary assessments, such as Topic 14-2. Topic 14-2 was an open topic, with description "What led to the recession that began in 2008?" While the primary assessor was obviously confident in his/her judgements, the same could not be said of the secondary assessors. For other topics confidence was almost equal between primary and secondary assessors, e.g. topic 9-1, a closed topic with description "What year was the original Vienna State Opera House completed?" In this case both primary and secondary assessors indicated that they were uniformly confidence in their relevance judgements. Overall, it was found that confidence on closed and open tasks did vary significantly (Wilcoxon rank sum test p < 0.001, W = 453304), although as can be seen in Table 7 this also varied by topic. For the 16 topics in Table 7 in 5 cases there was no significant difference between primary and secondary assessors, four out of the five being closed topics. For the other 11 topics where differences were found 7 were open topics and 4 closed.

4.5.2 Qualitative Results

A number of interesting findings emerged from the qualitative data. It was notable that in many cases, participants struggled to explain both how they interpreted the confidence scale, and the factors that influenced their confidence judgement:

"It was very difficult. I think it was just subjective, I think it was just depending on what I felt."

Those participants who were able to articulate their assessment of confidence described a range of factors influencing their confidence score, including the speed with which they were able to make their relevance judgement, the reliability of the source, how well they felt they understood the document, and how clearly they understood the topic description:

"How easy it was to relate to what the situation was, what they were searching for. I think I was confident in most of them and close to very confident in most of all my judgements."

"If I find something that is relevant but I cannot totally understand the document, I will choose less confident."

"It was partly down to just how reliable I thought the document was."

Perhaps most striking was the number of participants who described using the confidence scale as a proxy for graded relevance:

"In many ways I was using that confidence scale as more of a precise relevance scale. It was how relevant I thought it was."

In total over half of participants equated the confidence value with a measure of the document's relevance.

5. DISCUSSION

Before addressing the question of agreement levels between primary and secondary assessors for real-life search tasks, it is instructive to review results of this study relating to the judgement process itself. Looking first at speed of judgement, we note that when scaled by document length, primary assessors were found to be significantly quicker in making their judgements. Substantial differences in speed were also observed between open and closed search-tasks. Participants were quicker to judge the relevance of documents relating to closed tasks, and differences between the two types of task were also mentioned by participants in the post-task interviews. Judgements for open tasks were seen as more difficult to make, and the judgement process itself was considered more taxing. This was in part due to the additional factors perceived as influencing relevance for open tasks such as the reliability of the document. Given Yilmaz et al.'s [26] findings showing the relationship between effort, relevance, and utility we observe that using open search tasks for judging relevance within test collections may result in relevance judgements based on factors beyond topicality.

Results of this study also confirm that for real-life search tasks, knowledge of and interest in the topic are greater for primary assessors than secondary. However, as shown in Section 4.3, no results were found which suggested that an increase in the interest or knowledge of a secondary assessor would increase the chance of the secondary agreeing with a primary. While this may partially be a consequence of self-reporting scales (we note for example that even primary assessors rarely ranked their knowledge of a topic highly), our results do suggest that secondary assessors are generally well able to make topical relevance judgements even while professedly unsure of the full scope, context or background to a topic.

The post-session interviews revealed that the form and complexity of the topic description was a key factor affecting secondary assessment. The topic descriptions which were gathered in this study turned out to be roughly the same length as many TREC topics (Table 5). It has been suggested that topic length may be related to number of documents marked relevant, but we could find no evidence of this in our data set. However given the qualitative results in Section 4.2.2, taking a simple word count for a topic may not be a good representation of the complexity or difficulty of that topic to an assessor, a view supported by Bell and Ruthven [5]. A key theme to emerge from the interviews was the difficulty secondary assessors had in interpreting the context and scope of other participants' open tasks from the task description text. It seems likely that many of the disagreements in relevance judgement were a consequence of how secondary assessors chose to construe the task description. This is supported by the data showing secondary assessors were significantly more likely than primary assessors to review the topic description while undertaking relevance judgement, and suggests that the form and content of task descriptions can play an important role in minimising the interpretative challenges faced by secondary assessors. We suggest that further research investigating the precise effect of variations in task description structure and content could provide valuable insight into optimising task descriptions for secondary relevance assessments. A significant difference was found between the confidence of relevance judgements between primary and secondary (see Figure 7), with primary assessors being generally more confident in their judgements. However the difference was not large, and assessors in general were found to be confident in their judgements. This is a somewhat surprising finding given that the use of a binary rather than graded relevance scale forced

assessors to resolve doubts about a borderline document one way or the other. One explanation for this can be found in the interview data, which suggests that the confidence scale used was problematic: different assessors used the scale in different ways, and some found it extremely difficult to articulate both the factors influencing the certainty of their judgement, and the way in which the confidence scale was interpreted. Although not the original focus of this research, we conclude that for many assessors, understanding and measuring judgement certainty is problematic, particularly if required to use a Likert-type scale. We suggest that further work investigating more effective means of soliciting a measure of judgement confidence might be of considerable value.

We find then that when judging the relevance of documents for real-life search tasks, secondary assessors are less knowledgeable, find the process slower and more demanding, perceive the topic as less interesting, and are less confident in their judgements. They also face substantial problems interpreting the scope of the topic, and determining the criteria for relevance. Yet despite these apparently confounding factors, agreement levels between primary and secondary assessors were found to be high. Comparing our results with studies investigating non-real-life search tasks, we observed a greater overall level of agreement with the primary (79%) than [3] (68%), and a similar level of majority agreement. We also found a higher level of judgement overlap (.61) than [20] (.30). There is little doubt that this is at least in part due to the nature of the topics and documents under consideration, which of course differed from standard TREC evaluations used in [3; 23], and the characteristics of the assessors and assessment environment (we note in particular here that [3] were utilising crowd-workers). Nonetheless, we have shown that secondary assessors produce high levels of agreement with the creators of real-life search tasks. Put another way, we find that the judgements of assessors for whom the topic does not represent a real-life information need are generally the same as those for whom it does. Given the many practical difficulties of obtaining test-collection judgements from real-life topic owners, it is reassuring to conclude that using synthetic search tasks is unlikely to affect judgement quality, and by extension the accuracy of laboratory evaluations.

6. CONCLUSIONS AND FUTURE WORK

The concept of relevance continues to be of importance to information retrieval and information science research. Much research in this area has involved the use of TREC topics. Unfortunately, as pointed out elsewhere [2], these topics are dated. One of the aims of this work has been to revisit relevance assessment using up to date "real-life" topics gathered from staff and students at a major university. From the data collected, it is possible to gain a greater understanding of such real-life assessments, and enables us to compare our results to the large volume of previous work which has used TREC.

While behavioural differences were found between primary and secondary assessors (e.g. time to judge when scaled by document length) agreement between primary and secondary assessors was generally high. Self-reported contextual factors (topic interest and knowledge) did not appear to affect assessor agreement. This was despite secondary assessors generally assessing themselves as being less knowledgeable and less interested in the topics, and qualitative results suggesting that assessors found the relevance assessment task difficult. In attempting to interpret these results it is important to acknowledge some limitations of this study. In particular we note that while primary assessors were assessing the relevance of documents to their real-life search tasks, the judgement process itself was essentially artificial, since it occurred under laboratory conditions and using a constructed document set. We therefore emphasise that these results are most usefully interpreted within the context of the standard relevance assessment process for IR system test collection development. In this sense, our results support the notion that the use of synthetic topics for relevance assessment, as typified by TREC, result in judgement sets of no lower quality than those for real-life topics.

One final result of this work worthy of discussion concerns the instruments which we use to gather more information about the relevance judgement process itself. While measuring the confidence of an assessor in a relevance judgement is an intuitively attractive proposition, results here suggest that in practice its use can be problematic. Assessors were found to interpret a simple seven point scale in very different ways, including as a proxy for graded relevance. We believe that investigating novel ways of measuring factors such as confidence which do not themselves become proxies for relevance is a subject for future work.

7. ACKNOWLEDGEMENTS

This work was funded by a UK Arts and Humanities Research Council grant to the second and third authors (grant AH/L010364/1).

8. REFERENCES

[1] Agosti, M., Fuhr, N., Toms, E., and Vakkari, P. 2014. Evaluation methodologies in information retrieval (Dagstuhl Seminar 13441). *SIGIR Forum* 48, 1, 36-41.

[2] Al-Harbi, A.L. and Smucker, M.D. 2014. A qualitative exploration of secondary assessor relevance judging behavior. In *Proceedings of the 5th Information Interaction in Context Symposium* (IIiX '14). ACM, New York, NY, USA, 195-204.

[3] Alonso, O. and Mizzaro, S. 2012. Using crowdsourcing for TREC relevance assessment. *Inform. Process. Manag.* 48, 6, 1053-1066.

[4] Bailey, P., Craswell, N., Soboroff, I., Thomas, P., De Vries, A.P., and Yilmaz, E. 2008. Relevance assessment: are judges exchangeable and does it matter. In *Proceedings of the 31st annual international ACM SIGIR conference on Research and development in information retrieval* (SIGIR '08). ACM, New York, NY, USA, 667-674.

[5] Bell, D.J. and Ruthven, I. 2004. Searcher's assessments of task complexity for web searching. In *Proceedings of the 26th Annual International European Conference on Information Retrieval* (ECIR 2004), Springer-Verlag, Berlin, Germany, 57-71.

[6] Borlund, P. 2003. The IIR evaluation model: a framework for evaluation of interactive information retrieval systems. *Information Research* 8, 3.

[7] Chouldechova, A. and Mease, D. 2013. Differences in search engine evaluations between query owners and non-owners. In *Proceedings of the sixth ACM international conference on Web search and data mining* (WSDM '13). ACM, New York, NY, USA, 103-112.

[8] Clough, P., Sanderson, M., Tang, J., Gollins, T., and Warner, A. 2013. Examining the limits of crowdsourcing for relevance assessment. *Internet Computing, IEEE.* 17, 4, 32-38.

[9] Efthimiadis, E.N., and Hotchkiss, M.A. 2008. Legal discovery: Does domain expertise matter? *P. AM. SOC. INFORM. SCI.* 45, 1, 1-2.

[10] Jones, K.S. 1998. Further reflections on TREC. *Inform. Process. Manag.* 36, 1, 37-85.

[11] Kelly, D. 2009. Methods for evaluating interactive information retrieval systems with users. *Foundations and Trends in Information Retrieval 3*, 1—2, 1-224.

[12] Kinney, K.A., Huffman, S.B., and Zhai, J. 2008. How evaluator domain expertise affects search result relevance judgments. In *Proceedings of the 17th ACM conference on Information and knowledge management* (CIKM '08). ACM, New York, NY, USA, 591-598.

[13] Marchionini, G. 1989. Information-seeking strategies of novices using a full-text electronic encyclopedia. *J. Am. Soc. Inf. Sci. Tec.* 40, 1, 54-66.

[14] Ruthven, I., Baillie, M., and Elsweiler, D. 2007. The relative effects of knowledge, interest and confidence in assessing relevance. *J. Doc.* 63, 4, 482-504.

[15] Saracevic, T. 1995. Evaluation of evaluation in information retrieval. In *Proceedings of the 18th annual international ACM SIGIR conference on Research and development in information retrieval* (SIGIR '95), ACM, New York, NY, USA, 138-146.

[16] Saracevic, T. 2007. Relevance: A review of the literature and a framework for thinking on the notion in information science. Part III: Behavior and effects of relevance. *J. Am. Soc. Inf. Sci. Tec.* 58, 13, 2126-2144.

[17] Smucker, M.D., and Jethani, C.P. 2011. Measuring assessor accuracy: a comparison of nist assessors and user study participants. In *Proceedings of the 34th international ACM SIGIR conference on Research and development in Information Retrieval* (SIGIR '11). ACM, New York, NY, USA, 1231-1232.

[18] Villa, R. and Halvey, M. 2013. Is relevance hard work?: evaluating the effort of making relevant assessments. In *Proceedings of the 36th international ACM SIGIR conference on Research and development in information retrieval* (SIGIR '13). ACM, New York, NY, USA, 765-768.

[19] Voorhees, E., and Harman, D. 2000. Overview of the Seventh Text Retrieval Conference. In *Proceedings of the Seventh Text REtrieval Conference (*TREC-7*)*, NIST Special Publication, 1-24.

[20] Voorhees, E. 2000. Variations in relevance judgments and the measurement of retrieval effectiveness. *Inform. Process. Manag.* 36, 5, 697-716.

[21] Webber, W., and Pickens, J. 2013. Assessor disagreement and text classifier accuracy. In *Proceedings of the 36th international ACM SIGIR conference on Research and development in information retrieval* (SIGIR '13). ACM, New York, NY, USA, 929-932.

[22] Webber, W., Toth, B., and Desamito, M. 2012. Effect of written instructions on assessor agreement. In *Proceedings of the 35th international ACM SIGIR conference on Research and development in information retrieval* (SIGIR '12). ACM, New York, NY, USA, 1053-1054. |

[23] Yilmaz, E., Verma, M., Craswell, N., Radlinski, F., and Bailey, P. 2014. Relevance and effort: an analysis of document utility. In *Proceedings of the 23rd ACM International Conference on Conference on Information and Knowledge Management* (CIKM '14). ACM, New York, NY, USA, 91-100.

History by Diversity: Helping Historians search News Archives

Jaspreet Singh, Wolfgang Nejdl, Avishek Anand
L3S Research Center, Leibniz Universität Hannover.
Appelstr. 9a
30167 Hanover, Germany
{singh,nejdl,anand}@L3S.de

ABSTRACT

Longitudinal corpora like newspaper archives are of immense value to historical research, and time as an important factor for historians strongly influences their search behaviour in these archives. While searching for articles published over time, a key preference is to retrieve documents which cover the important aspects from important points in time which is different from standard search behavior. To support this search strategy, we introduce the notion of a *Historical Query Intent* to explicitly model a historian's search task and define an aspect-time diversification problem over news archives.

We present a novel algorithm, HɪsᴛDɪv, that explicitly models the aspects and important time windows based on a historian's information seeking behavior. By incorporating temporal priors based on publication times and temporal expressions, we diversify both on the aspect and temporal dimensions. We test our methods by constructing a test collection based on *The New York Times Collection* with a workload of 30 queries of historical intent assessed manually. We find that HɪsᴛDɪv outperforms all competitors in subtopic recall with a slight loss in precision. We also present results of a qualitative user study to determine wether this drop in precision is detrimental to user experience. Our results show that users still preferred HɪsᴛDɪv's ranking.

1. INTRODUCTION

Newspaper articles encode history as it happens by capturing events and their immediate impact on society, politics, business and other important spheres. These are of immense value to historians, sociologists, and journalists who rely on fairly reliable, accurate and time-aligned information sources. Specifically for historians, whose desired corpus of study is an archive, browsing and searching such archives has emerged as an important aspect in their research [44]. Consequently, designing access methods and retrieval models tailored to their search patterns and information need is an important problem.

The information seeking behavior of a historian is slightly different from the traditional user search behavior, for which classical retrieval tasks are designed, in two respects. First, historians are interested in obtaining an overview of the topic they wish to research in order to contextualize results. They desire to look at

CHIIR'16, March 13–17, 2016, Carrboro, North Carolina, USA.

© 2016 ACM. ISBN 978-1-4503-3751-9/16/03. . . $15.00

DOI: http://dx.doi.org/10.1145/2854946.2854959

relevant results from *important subtopics* from the most *relevant time points of interest*. Currently, this is realized by issuing an underspecified broad query on the topic and then trying to identify relevant articles from important subtopics by applying various filters which are time, source, region or domain-based. Secondly, the major preoccupation of historians is in finding *primary sources* of information (accounts/reports/documents made by an observer of an event). Secondary information sources (accounts made in retrospect) are also important, however they are intrinsically used to identify primary information sources.

Consider a historian interested in Rudolph Giulaini, a U.S. Republican politician, in the period between 1987 and 2007. Giuliani started out as an attorney and rose to prominence to challenge for the mayorality of New York City in 1989. Though he lost that year to David Dinkins he went on to win in 1993, again in 1997 and stayed mayor until 2001. He was known for his tough stance on crime, his efforts after 9/11 and is responsible for many forward reforms in the city. In 2000, he ran for senate against Hilary Clinton before being diagnosed with cancer. At the same time he was involved in an extramarital affair with Judith Nathan. He then decided to run for president in 2007. Identifying the New York Times newspaper archive[2] as the best source of primary material, the historian formulates her intent of finding information related to Giuliani with the keywords `rudolph giuliani` and sets the publication date filter to 1987 − 2007 only to get the following results:

Rank	Year	Headline
1	2007	In His Own Words
2	2007	Giuliani Is Expected to Sell One of His Three Businesses
3	2007	Giuliani Is Selling Investment Firm
4	2007	'08 Candidacy Could Shake Up Giuliani's Firm
5	2006	Giuliani Building Network of Donors, a Backer Says

None of the result documents mention his stance on crime, cancer, Hilary Clinton, World Trade Center, David Dinkins or his reforms. Arguably a better set of results for her to scope out her topic is a diversified set of top documents covering important aspects which could be entities like Hilary Clinton and David Dinkins but also from important time points so that she can contextualize or reformulate her query.

Learning from the experiences of our colleagues at the British Library and the Institute of Historical Research in London (cf. Section 2), in this work, we propose a novel document retrieval task which intends to present the most relevant results from a topic-temporal space. This problem can be seen as a generalization of the classical diversity problem by adding a temporal dimension. The topical diversity focuses on presenting results from different subtopics while the temporal diversity ensures that the documents returned are primary in nature. However, the challenge in adapting existing diversity-based approaches is the following. Firstly, traditional diversity approaches [14, 41, 3, 15, 23] tend to diversify typically on the topical aspect and do not take time into account. As a result, documents retrieved might still cover a good number of aspects but (a) might be from the same time period disregarding the temporal salience of the aspect and (b) might return secondary sources even when more relevant primary sources are present. For the query `rudolph giuliani`, such methods would not guarantee that documents are from the important time periods like '89, '93, '00, '01 and '07.

Time-aware approaches which take into account latent topics or aspects like [37] are optimized to present results which are valid at querying time or in other words reward recency. On the other hand [7] diversifies based on time without explicitly considering topical aspects. Although this ensures that results are temporally distant from each other, as a consequence of the inherent topic-agnostic nature they still might belong to similar aspects. In our example, if the historian uses a temporal diversification retrieval model there is no guarantee that results returned from 2000 and 2001 will definitely cover the WTC, cancer, Hilary Clinton and Judith Nathan. Finally, multi-dimensional approaches to diversity treat both time and aspects similarly which is not always desirable since both these dimensions have different semantics. We on the contrary, explicitly model both the topical and temporal aspects of a document by treating time as a first-class citizen in our model. In our approach, called HistDiv, the temporal space is based on primary (publication times) and secondary sources (temporal references in text) and the topic space is based on the entities present in the news article. We then jointly diversify both in the aspect and time dimensions discounting each of these dimensions based on semantics unique to each. In sum we make the following contributions:

- We introduce the notion of *Historical Query Intents* and model this as a search result diversification task on both the aspect and time dimensions for historical search.

- We develop a novel retrieval algorithm called HistDiv which jointly diversifies both dimensions by appropriately discounting the contribution of aspects and time.

- We establish the effectiveness of our method by building a test collection based on the 20 years of the *New York Times Collection* as a dataset and a workload of 30 manually judged queries which will be made available to the community. The quantitative results show we outperform our competitors in subtopic recall at the cost of precision.

- Finally, we conducted a qualitative study with the target users to confirm if this loss in precision truly harms the quality of the overview derived from the ranking.

2. HOW DO HISTORIANS SEARCH?

A historian's corpus of study is often an archive. Archives consist of time annotated records, from the distant and recent past, categorized as primary and secondary sources.

Need for Overview and Context: A vital step in a historians search process is to browse the archive in order to get an *overview* of material available on a topic. This allows them to identify potential areas of interest which subsequently lead to more focused queries in the next search phase. Undoubtedly, the onset of digital archives has greatly improved information access but a key requirement of historians still is to obtain an overview of multiple aspects of the topic [43]. This overview allows them to not only find more specific topics of study but also to contextualize their results by studying the temporal and spatial vicinity of the topic.

Focus on primary sources: The main preoccupation of historians is the reading of primary sources while secondary sources

are useful when no primary evidence exists and for tracing references to cited primary sources [16]. Even with the onset of digital archives, [43] re-enforces the historian's preference and focus on primary sources.

Historian Search Behavior: Based on existing literature and a short survey in collaboration with the British Library (BL) and the Institute of Historical Research in London, we found that the current way of searching digital archives is a two-stage iterative querying process. In the first stage, keyword queries on broader topics are issued and further reformulated by the use of a combination of filters (time, source, entity, etc.) and facets to gain an overview of the results. Subsequently, more specific queries on each aspect are prepared to serve their information need. [10] finds keyword search (labeled a *blunt instrument*) in archives to be most effective when the user is very precise and focused in his search. Hence, the initial stage is indeed the most cumbersome, firstly because it leads to a large number of results which then have to be read in its entirety, and secondly because of the increased usage of filters. Examples of such general queries are queries about entities, recurring events, conflicts etc.

In general, historians working with physical archives are privy to themed sub-collections created by archivists. An entity search in these smaller collections may produce plenty of results but nearly all tend to be relevant. On the other hand, a news archive is a single large collection only subdivided based on time, hence searching for entities, especially popular ones, can return many records.

As we will show in the remainder of this paper, the joint diversification of aspects and time can lead to better ranking of documents for the initial search phase, involving these broad keyword queries, in newspaper archives.

3. HISTORICAL SEARCH TASK

A *Historical Query Intent* is the moniker we choose to describe a user's intent to cover as many historically relevant subtopics and time windows for a given topic. According to [33], a temporal query intent is used to specify queries which are either atemporal, temporally ambiguous or unambiguous. We however deal with a special case of temporally ambiguous queries which have an explicit information need for the past. Additionally, historical query intents also deal with ambiguity with respect to the aspect and time dimensions. In this section we formally present our input model and define our historical search task problem based on historical query intents, and discuss how to measure the effectiveness of proposed approaches.

3.1 Model

Document Model: We operate on a document collection $\mathcal{D}$ where each document $d_p \in \mathcal{D}$ has a publication time point p. The content of d_p, for instance "<u>Dinkins</u> pulls negative ad about <u>Giuliani</u> as the race for Mayor draws closer", can be represented by a set of aspects such as {David Dinkins, Rudolph Giuliani}. The set of aspects describing the content of d_p is denoted by the set $A(d_p) = \{a_1, \ldots a_n\}$ where a_i is a single aspect like David Dinkins. The document can also contain temporal references such as "last year" or "2001" which can be useful indicators of important time intervals. The set of temporal expressions contained in d_p is given by $E(d_p) = \{I_1, I_2, \ldots I_n\}$ where I is an arbitrary time interval with a definite begin and end timestamp.

Temporal Model: We adopt a discrete notion of time for the collection and assume that a time-stamp t_i is a positive integer and is computed periodically, with a fixed granularity Δ, from a reference point in the past t_0. The discretized time span of the collection is denoted by an ordered set $W = \langle t_0, t_1, \ldots t_n \rangle$ such that $\Delta = t_{i+1} - t_i$. We define $\delta_i = [t_i, t_{i+1})$ as the elementary time in-

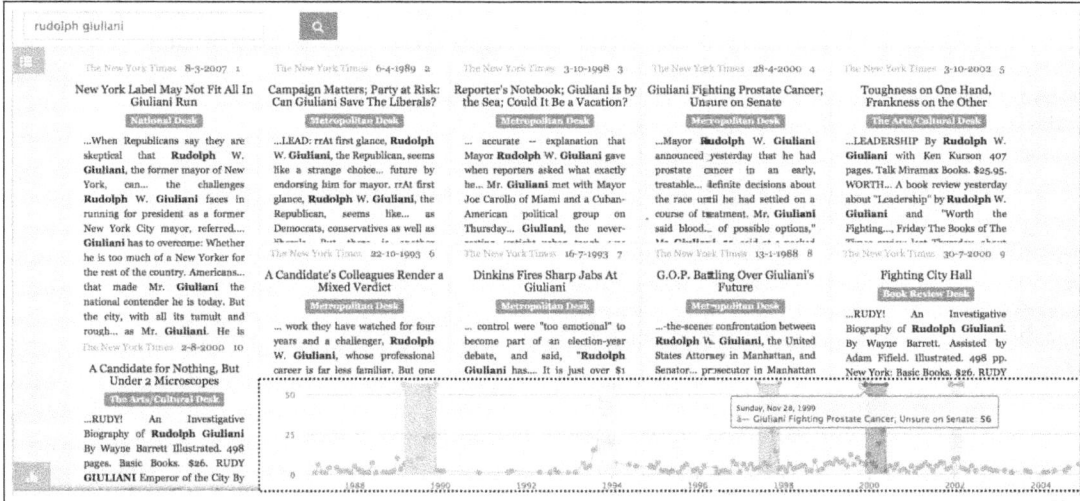

Figure 1: The HISTDIV search system. The search results are layed out to mimic a newspaper. The coloured areas in the timeline represent bursts detected from the temporal distribution. Results shown are for the top 10 out of 26,000 results returned for the query Rudolph Giuliani.

terval between two consecutive time points. A document d_p is published in the interval δ_i if $t_i \leq p < t_{i+1}$ and is given by the function $\Lambda(p) = \delta_i$. The set of all elementary time intervals of size Δ in W is called the temporal space $\mathcal{T} = \{\delta_i \mid \delta_i \in \bigcup_{d_p \in \mathcal{D}} \Lambda(p)\}$.

Aspect-Time Space: For a given query q, $\mathcal{R}_q$ is set of top-K documents retrieved such that $\mathcal{R}_q \subseteq \mathcal{D}$. The time space relevant to q is the set $\mathcal{T}_q = \{\delta_i \mid \delta_i \in \bigcup_{d_p \in \mathcal{R}_q} \Lambda(p)\}$ such that $\mathcal{T}_q \subseteq \mathcal{T}$. Similarly we define the aspect-space of q as the set of all aspects found in documents from $\mathcal{R}_q$ denoted by $\mathcal{A}_q = \{a_i \mid a_i \in \bigcup_{d_p \in \mathcal{R}_q} A(d_p)\}$ where $\mathcal{A}_q \subseteq \mathcal{A}$. However, not all aspects are relevant in all time intervals. For example, the aspect World Trade Center for the query rudolph giuliani is historically irrelevant for time intervals before 2001. To this end, we define a combined aspect-time space $\mathcal{AT}_q \subseteq \mathcal{A}_q \times \mathcal{T}_q$ which contains aspect-time pairs encoding subspaces which are both temporally and aspect-wise relevant.

$$\mathcal{AT}_q = \{(a_i, \delta_j) \mid a_i \in \mathcal{A}_q \wedge \delta_j \in \mathcal{T}_q\}.$$

A result document d_p for query q with aspects $A(d_p)$ and temporal expressions $E(d_p)$ is said to be relevant to an aspect-time pair $(a_i, \delta_j) \in \mathcal{AT}_q$ if $a_i \in A(d_p)$ and $\Lambda(p) = \delta_j$.

3.2 Problem Definition

The historical search result diversification problem or simply the *historical search task* intends to find a re-ranking S of an initial result set $\mathcal{R}_q$ that has maximum coverage and minimum redundancy with respect to different aspect-times underlying q. In other words, it is the standard search result diversification task but over the $\mathcal{AT}_q$-space which encodes the historical query intent of obtaining relevant documents from the most important aspects from the time-period/s it is important in. As shown by [3], search result diversification is a bi-criterion optimization problem which can be reduced from the maximum k-coverage problem and hence is $\mathcal{NP}$-hard.

3.3 Evaluation Measures

Given that we define a new two-dimensional solution space, we could re-use the standard diversity-based retrieval measures for evaluating approaches to the historical search task, considered on the $\mathcal{AT}_q$-space. Subtopic-recall $\mathsf{SBR}_{q,k}$, for instance, for $\mathcal{R}_q$ at depth

k, can be computed as:

$$\frac{\left| \bigcup_{d_p \in \mathcal{R}_q^k} \{(a_i, \delta_j) \mid a_i \in A(d_p) \wedge \Lambda(p) = \delta_j\} \right|}{|\mathcal{AT}_q|}.$$

Similarly for other diversity metrics suggested in [25] like intent aware ERR (IA-ERR), intent aware precision (IA-P), mean average precision MAP and α-NDCG (NDCG) we can substitute the subtopic space with the $\mathcal{AT}_q$-space.

4. RELATED WORK

Before we describe the HISTDIV approach for historical search tasks, in this section we outline the relevant existing literature. Our problem has overlap with areas relating to temporal representation and temporal retrieval models under temporal IR, and with works on search result diversification.

4.1 Temporal Information Retrieval

Temporal IR has emerged as an important subfield in IR with the goal to improve search effectiveness by exploiting temporal information in documents and queries [12]. The value of the temporal dimension was clearly identified in [4] and has led to a plethora of work which utilizes temporal features in query understanding [33, 36], retrieval models [8, 26, 27, 11], temporal indexing [9, 6], clustering [5] and query modelling [40, 39, 17]. A survey by Campos et. al. [12] gives an elaborate overview of the field.

Improving Ranking using temporal features One of the first algorithms to incorporate time in search result ranking was suggested in [34]. They used a temporal language model approach where time and term importance are handled implicitly. Various approaches have been suggested that consider time more explicitly. [8] proposes a language modelling approach taking into account the temporal expressions in the query and document text. [11] on the other hand, taking a non-probabilistic interpretation of relevance, defines *temporal scope similarity* between queries and documents in *metric spaces*. In both these works, similarity between the temporal references in the query and documents are used to rank documents. In our query model, we never make any assumptions on the presence of temporal references nor do we model the similarity of query and document based on temporal references. Another line of work in this domain considers the freshness or recency of a document when ranking [26].

Finding important time periods An important ingredient in our retrieval model is finding temporal priors for different time points. [33] estimates a probability distribution over different time points for each query called the temporal query profiles using publication times of the documents. In [42], the authors exploit the publication dates to identify important time points for a given query by contrasting rankings for adjacent time points. However, neither of them utilize secondary sources or temporal references in text. Recently, [30] suggests using temporal references for ranking time intervals for a given temporal query. In our work, we use both publication dates (primary sources) and temporal references (secondary sources) to assign temporal priors to each granular time window akin to a temporal profile [33].

4.2 Search Result Diversification

Diversity in search (both explicit and implicit) has seen a rich body of literature lately in [22, 14, 3, 41, 15, 47, 35, 23]. Search result diversification aims to maximise the overall relevance of a document ranking to multiple query aspects, while minimising its redundancy with respect to these aspects. Existing approaches differ in the way they model different query aspects. Implicit approaches, like [14], assume similar documents cover similar aspects and do not model aspects. Explicit approaches model aspects in a variety of ways using query logs, taxonomies etc. We also model aspects explicitly by using entities found in text documents as their aspects. Also, none of the previous approaches take time into account or model the historical information intent.

Temporal diversification [7] proposes a diversification model which considers time windows as a set of intents for a query while modeling the importance of each intent as the weight of its burst. In traditional aspect-based diversification tasks like [20, 18], intent importance is considered static over time. However, intent importance was shown to vary across time; thus affecting the diversity evaluation of queries issued at different time points [46]. Keeping this in mind, [37] considers the time at which the query is issued to diversify intents based on their temporal significance at that time. Their approach also explicitly models time and aspects, although latent, but rewards recency. HISTDIV, on the other hand, is query-time agnostic, since it is intended for historical search, and seeks to diversify documents based on both time and aspects.

5. THE HISTDIV APPROACH

5.1 Approach Overview

The challenge in designing a retrieval model for the historical search task is to identify important time intervals and aspects. More importantly, the documents which optimize both dimensions and are relevant to the user intent. Towards this, we first model the temporal space for the initial result set $\mathcal{R}_q$. We build a probability distribution $P(\delta_i|q)$ for $\delta_i \in \mathcal{T}_q$ over the entire time span W taking into account the publication times and temporal references (mined from document text). Such a temporal profile, as shown in Figure 1 helps us isolate the important time-periods in the result timeline (described in Section 5.2). Next in Section 5.3, we detail how we build priors for the aspects of the documents. Finally in Section 5.4, we present our diversification algorithm HISTDIV which takes into account textual relevance, temporal sensitivity and aspect importance along with the *typical semantics* of the temporal and aspect domains to maximize coverage in the $\mathcal{AT}_q$ space.

5.2 Building Temporal Priors

To find important time intervals, we build a probability distribution $P(\delta_i|q)$ over the entire time span by projecting both the

---

Algorithm 1: The HISTDIV Algorithm

Input: $k, q, \mathcal{A}_q, \mathcal{R}_q, \mathcal{T}_q, V(d|q), S = \emptyset$
Output: Set S of diversified documents

1   $\forall a \in \mathcal{A}_q$, $\forall \delta_i \in \mathcal{T}_q$, $U_{aspect}(a|q, S, \delta_i)$ = refer Eqn. 1
2   $\forall \delta_i \in \mathcal{T}_q$, $U_{time}(\delta_i|q, S)$ = refer Eqn. 2
3   **while** $|S| \leq k$ **do**
4   **while** $d \in R$ **do**
5       $g(d|q, S) \leftarrow \alpha.V(d|q) + (1 - \alpha).(\beta. \sum_a^{A(d)} U_{aspect} + (1 - \beta).U_{time}$
6     $d^* \leftarrow argmax_d \; g(d|q, S)$
7     $S \leftarrow S \cup \{d^*\}$
8   **return** S

---

publication times and the reference times into $\mathcal{T}_q$. The temporal references are treated as secondary sources and can be used as indicators of relevant primary sources. For computing the distributions we use the document counts published in a time interval δ_i (contrary to using top-k relevance scores for profile generation [33]). The probability $P_{pub}(\delta_i|q)$ is the fraction of all documents in $\mathcal{R}_q$ published in δ_i. To compute $P_{ref}(\delta_i|q)$ we first estimate the contribution of an interval $I \in E(d_p)$ as $\frac{1}{|I|}$ for all constituent time intervals δ_i. Finally, we employ a language modeling strategy to smooth the probability distribution of the publication times P_{pub} with the background distribution of the temporal references P_{ref} with a mixing parameter θ to arrive at a distribution $P(\delta_i|q)$:

$$P(\delta_i|q) = \theta.P_{pub}(\delta_i|q) + (1 - \theta).P_{ref}(\delta_i|q).$$

In our experiments we demonstrate the value of estimating the time prior by comparing it to a temporal diversification baseline that assumes equal distribution of δ_i called EQT.

5.3 Aspect Modeling

Historians are particularly interested in events which can be described using groups of entities associated with specific time intervals. Keeping this in mind, we use entities mentioned in the document text as our aspects. Traditional aspect-space diversification methods, like IA-SELECT [3] and PM2 [23], estimate the probability $P(a_i|q)$ assuming the collection is static. For historical search, time is an essential factor and needs to be considered when estimating $P(a_i|q)$. Consider a document d_p published in time interval $\Lambda(p) = \delta_j$; an aspect $a_i \in A(d_p)$ can be temporally diverse if it occurs in documents from different time intervals. Hence the aspect a_i has a probability distribution across time intervals $\delta_j \in \mathcal{T}_q$. Consequently, the prior probability of an aspect $a_i \in \mathcal{A}_q$ in a time interval $\delta_j \in \mathcal{T}_q$ is given by:

$$P(a_i|q, \delta_j) = \frac{\left|\{d_{a_i,p} \mid a_i \in A(d_p) \land \Lambda(p) = \delta_j\}\right|}{\left|\{d_p \mid \Lambda(p) = \delta_j\}\right|}$$

where $d_{a_i,p}$ is a document tagged with aspect a_i published in the interval δ_j. Notice in the Figure 1 that the event mayoral campaigns is recurring every 4 years. Hence the aspects representing mayoral campaigns will have a higher $P(a_i|q, \delta_j)$ in certain time intervals $\{\delta_{1989}, \delta_{1993}, \delta_{1997}\}$ when compared to the others.

5.4 The HISTDIV Algorithm

In classical diversification approaches like [3, 23, 28], each document is assigned a utility score computed using textual relevance (denoted as $V(d|q)$ in Algorithm 1) and aspect importance. Most approaches employ a greedy algorithm which selects the candidate documents that maximize utility with respect to the uncovered aspects in each iteration. HISTDIV considers both aspect and time dimensions (with their special semantics) and operates in a similar manner treating both the topical and temporal aspects as sets thereby retaining the $(1 - 1/e)$ approximation guarantee. However, we differ significantly from previous approaches in the way we interpret and compute the utility of each dimension. Traditional diversification algorithms model only aspects and maximize coverage in the space $\mathcal{A}_q$. Since the objective is to maximize coverage in the $\mathcal{AT}_q$ space we first consider how they can be adapted to model the required space $\mathcal{AT}_q$.

Temporally augmented aspect space: A naïve approach to introduce time could be to enrich the aspect space by adding time intervals as new aspects. For instance for d_p published in δ_i we can add δ_i to $A(d_p)$. In our experiments we use this method to create two variations of IA-SELECT and PM2 called E-IA-SELECT and E-PM2.

Linearizing aspect space with time: Since we deal with two dimensions we can project or *linearize* the temporal dimension onto the aspect dimension. More formally, the result of linearization is the set of m aspects $\{a_1 \delta_i, \ldots, a_m \delta_i\}$ for document $d_p \in \delta_i$ which is used to alter IA-SELECT and PM2. We name these two variations T-IA-SELECT and T-PM2 and also use them as baselines in our experiments.

An alternative would be to keep the dimensions separate like the multi-dimensional approach proposed in [28] (referred to as MDiv henceforth). In this general framework, for the diversification of n arbitrary dimensions, the utility score $g(d|q, S)$ computation reflects how the dimensions are combined. The marginal utility of aspects given a document d is computed based on rank of d for the given aspect a_i. We can naturally add time as a second dimension and use it for diversification. We use MDiv as a competitor in our experiments.

A key drawback of both these approaches is that they do not consider the fact that: (a) temporal aspects are ordered and thus have special semantics (b) temporal and topical aspects are interrelated. Hence MDiv's assumption of dimensional independence and identical discounting function for both dimensions might not yield optimal results. A retrieval model designed for a historical search task however should take this into account while computing the utility of aspects and time intervals to optimize coverage of the $\mathcal{AT}_q$ space (see Section 3).

In HISTDIV, the utility of a document in the aspect space is measured by $U_{aspect}(a_i|q, S, \delta_j)$ with the exception that we treat an aspect in various time windows differently. We discount aspects in a neighborhood defined by the w so that $P(a_i|q, \delta_j)$ is strongly discounted if δ_j is temporally closer to a document $d_p \in S$ and $a_i \in A(d_p)$. We use the decay function suggested in ONLYTIME [7] to discount aspects across time. In this way, we avoid the time agnostic property of standard topical diversification retrieval models which may select the right aspects but will discount the aspect for the entire span of the collection thereby reducing the probability of selecting documents for the same aspect from other important time intervals. The utility of an aspect, $U_{aspect}(a_i|q, S, \delta_j)$, is

$$P(a_i|q, \delta_j) \prod_{d_p \in S} \left(1 - \frac{1}{1 + e^{-w + |t_j - p|}} \right) \quad (1)$$

t_j denotes the boundary time point of δ_j. Like ONLYTIME we can set w to the size of Δ. The limitation of modeling utility this way is that we are restricted by the fixed w. Consider bursts, where a high number of documents from multiple consecutive δ typically discuss a single event (especially if Δ is small). If we select a document about this event from the edge of the burst then we face two potential issues: (i) we may assign high utility to documents which are about similar aspects from two temporally distant intervals but still refer to the same event (ii) we heavily discount documents just outside the burst (temporally close but sufficiently different) unfavorably. Both of these issues lead to a potential drop in subtopic

recall which we address by using the burst detection technique suggested in [38]. To detect the set of bursts B_q, this technique utilizes the mean and standard deviation of a fixed width sliding window across W.

We can now vary w depending on the position of d_p within its corresponding burst ($b_i \in B_q$) or non-bursty interval ($b_i \in \hat{B}_q$) and use $U_{aspect}(a_i|q, S, \delta_j)$ as before. w is then computed as follows:

$$w = \begin{cases} |p - begin(b_i)| & : p \geq t_j \\ |p - end(b_i)| & : p < t_j \end{cases}$$

In the time dimension, we need to be wary of discrediting a time interval too heavily. ONLYTIME produces a result set with high temporal diversity by selecting relevant documents from important intervals and discounts those intervals heavily with the aforementioned decay function. This approach to discounting bursts doesn't consider the fact that a single burst could consist of many diverse aspects. For example, in 2000-2001 Giuliani was divorced, diagnosed with cancer and was involved in helping New York recover from 9/11. Hence unlike ONLYTIME, we discount the interval in the time dimension of $d_p \in S$ by the weighted proportion of aspects covered by it. The utility of time, $U_{time}(\delta_i|q, S)$, is

$$P(\delta_i|q) \prod_{d_p \in S} \left(1 - \frac{|(d_{a_j, p^*} \mid a_j \in A(d_p) \wedge \Lambda(p^*) = \delta_i)|}{|(d_{p^*} \mid \Lambda(p^*) = \delta_i)|} \right) \quad (2)$$

With burst detection, for all $d_p \in S$ we simply discount all time intervals δ_i contained in it's corresponding bursty / non-bursty interval.

The essence of our approach lies in our temporal interpretation of aspect utility and aspect aware interpretation of time utility. This interpretation helps us maximize coverage in the joint space $\mathcal{AT}$, as shown in our experiments, when compared to pure aspect based diversification, pure time based diversification and multidimension diversification. Algorithm 1 shows the iterative process in which documents are selected in to result based on the utility g, where aspect and temporal utilities are traded-off by the parameter β. The parameter α trades-off the impact of document relevance $V(d|q)$ with the utility of the two dimensions.

6. TEST COLLECTION

In this section we detail the test collection which we constructed to evaluate our approach. There exist well known collections for the standard diversification task (diversity tasks in the TREC Web track), temporal information retrieval (Temporalia'14 [32]) as well as web archives [21]; however to the best of our knowledge there are no established test collections to measure the effectiveness of retrieval models designed for diversification of the $\mathcal{AT}_q$ space in news archives. Hence we choose to build our own collection guided by the target user group - historians, whose judgments will be made available to the research community.

Metrics: The evaluation metric for a search task should reflect the user's goal. For users with historical query intents the objective is to find primary sources of information from all the important aspects and time periods. The primary metric we choose to measure the effectiveness of a retrieval model is SBR (subtopic recall) in the joint aspect-temporal space $\mathcal{AT}_q$ because of the recall oriented nature of historical query intents.

Document Corpus: As a corpus we use the *Annotated New York Times* collection [2] which qualifies as a suitable news archive since it spans for 20 years, i.e., 1987 - 2007. Although there exists larger news corpora, they span for a shorter time duration reducing the likelihood of having ample primary sources .Also, the timestamps associated with the articles are accurate and do not have to be estimated as in other web collections. The corpus consists of 1.8

million articles from all sections of the newspaper including the editorial desk, arts, technology and literature making it replete with various aspects interesting for historians.

Search topics: Topics, with a historical intent, for our test collections are derived from experts who held discussions with historians at the Institute of Historical Research as well as from insights in Section 2. These experts first described the intents verbosely and then proceeded to identify keywords that represent it. Since our corpus is a newspaper daily for the USA, topics are chosen from a set of historically relevant issues related mostly to the USA and a few from more global issues. To define the *subtopics* of each topic the experts were guided by the history sections from the relevant Wikipedia articles. To confirm or modify subtopics, they explored the corpus with a simple keyword search interface whenever necessary. The chosen subtopics are also qualified by a set of relevant time periods. The experts chose time periods of relevance to the subtopic by consulting relevant Wikipedia articles and defined the interval size as the period in which they found primary sources in the corpus. Depending on the type of subtopic the time interval can span months (Giuliani's efforts in the aftermath of 9/11) or years (Giuliani's senate run). Each subtopic can also have multiple time intervals like Giuliani's mayoral election campaigns which are relevant during 1989,1993 and 1997. Time intervals can also overlap each other, for instance Giulaini's personal life (struggle with cancer) and his senate run.

Listing 1: Excerpt of a topic in the workload

```
<topic>
 <query>rudolph giuliani</query>
 <desc>I want to know the history of Rudolph Giuliani</desc>
 <subtopics>
  <subtopic>
   <desc>Mayoral campaigns</desc>
   <time>[{01.01.1989 — 31.12.1989}, {01.01.1993 — 31.12.1993}, {01.01.97 —
         31.12.1997}]</time>
  </subtopic>
  <subtopic>
   <desc>Senate race</desc>
   <time>[{01.01.2000 — 31.12.2000}]</time>
  </subtopic>
  <subtopic>
   <desc>Efforts after 9/11</desc>
   <time>[{11.09.2001 — 01.04.2002}]</time>
  </subtopic>
   .
   .
   .

 </subtopics>
</topic>
```

We have a total query workload of 30 topics. On average there are 5 subtopics per topic and each subtopic has at least one relevant time interval. The types of topic chosen are inspired by the characteristics defined in Section 2, i.e, broad topics related to entities like Rudolph Giuliani and the Atlantic City, major events like the reunification of germany and team usa soccer world cup as well as controversial subjects like gay marriage and sarin gas. A key assumption made when creating subtopics is the omission of historical facts that lie outside of the 20 year time period of the NYT corpus.

Pooling: We devise suitable baselines (detailed in Section 7.1.2) and "submit" runs for each baseline corresponding to all possible parameter settings. By doing so we increase the coverage of documents for each topic and improve the diversity of the pool. We chose a run size of top 20 for all topics and the pool size was set to 300 documents per topic. We overall generated nine competitors which produced on average 20 runs per baseline. To gather relevance judgments we use the Cranfield paradigm [45]. Trained evaluators were instructed to assign binary relevance judgments to topic, subtopic, document triples. Each document was judged once with high confidence. Once the pools were evaluated, a standard robustness test was carried out with SBR over $\mathcal{AT}_q$ as the primary measure. We selected 25% of the query workload at random and

split them into two equal sets. We selected 50% of the runs at random for retrieval depth 10 and ranked the system runs for both sets of queries by SBR. We found that the rankings were consistent (high Kendal's tau) for p<=0.05.

7. EXPERIMENTAL EVALUATION

Before we present our results, we detail our experimental setup in which we describe how we mine our aspects and select baselines. Then to assess the effectiveness of our approach we first present in Section 7.2 the overall retrieval effectiveness across different retrieval depths, assess the impact of varying the granularity Δ and also highlight certain drawbacks. Next, in Section 7.3 we discuss interesting insights from a user study to estimate the quality of an overview produced by different rankings and finally summarize take-aways from our experiments.

7.1 Setup

7.1.1 Modeling Aspects and Time

Since we model aspects of a documents as the entities therein we consider the named-entity tagging system AIDA [31] for our experiments. AIDA is the state-of-art approach for *named entity disambiguation* which canonicalizes mentions of named entities (person, locations, organizations) into Wikipedia pages. Note, there are certain entities like United States that occur in nearly all documents and distort the performance of aspect based diversification methods. To overcome this we remove non-salient entities using an IDF filter and set the threshold to 0.2. To extract the temporal references mentioned in the article text and populate $E(d)$ we use *Tarsqi*. We consider two granularities of time intervals for the experiments – $\Delta = \{$month, year$\}$.

7.1.2 Baselines

We evaluate the effectiveness of HISTDIV at diversifying the search results produced by four effective classes of baselines:

Non-temporal Baselines : The first baseline that we considered is the standard unigram language model with dirichlet smoothing (LM, $\mu = 1000$). The other approaches use the top 1000 documents returned by LM for diversification. Though not designed for the historical search task we also consider IA-SELECT [3] and PM2 [23] which are pure aspect-based diversification methods. It allows us to better highlight the nature of the task and the challenges faced when diversifying across a joint aspect-time space.

Temporal Diversification Baselines : First, to create baselines more suited to the task we create temporal variants of IA-SELECT and PM2 by (a) linearizing the aspects with the time window corresponding to the publication date of the document respectively denoted as T-IA-SELECT and T-PM2; (b) augmenting the aspect space by including temporal aspects. Temporal aspects are represented by time-intervals and contain documents which were published in that interval. These variations are named E-IA-SELECT and E-PM2 respectively. Next, we consider two approaches that take time into account directly while diversifying: ONLYTIME [7] and MDIV [28]. ONLYTIME [7] diversifies results purely in the time dimension, denoted by $\mathcal{T}_q$. MDIV [28] is a multi-dimensional diversification approach that treats both dimensions equivalently. Finally, we also have a variant of ONLYTIME called EQT which, unlike its counterpart, assumes equal distribution for the prior and does 0/1 discounting of the time windows. We do not consider XQUAD [41] due to (a) the absence of a reasonable query log for this time period and (b) the lack of clarity regarding its' adaptation without an external log for the historical search task.

HistDiv : We compare both the original HISTDIV and its burst-aware version HISTDIV-BURST to the aforementioned baselines. For

	k=10			k=15			k=20		
	A	T	AT (W/L%)	A	T	AT (W/L%)	A	T	AT (W/L%)
Lm	0.706	0.060	0.428	0.752	0.085	0.491	0.780	0.091	0.518
Ia-Select°	0.722	0.039	0.442 (23/23)	0.766	0.047	0.491 (20/26)	0.841	0.055	0.516 (20/23)
Pm2*	0.707	0.069	0.429 (16/20)	0.794	0.082	0.471 (20/23)	0.817	0.097	0.509 (16/26)
Tia-Select•	0.614	0.039	0.380(23/36)	0.717	0.047	0.433 (20/43)	0.770	0.055	0.470 (20/26)
T-Pm2'	0.551	**0.088**	0.308 (13/50)	0.680	0.106	0.408(20/43)	0.761	0.128	0.453 (16/33)
E-Ia-Select‡	0.700	0.062	0.435 (23/23)	0.776	0.084	0.501 (23/23)	0.837	0.095	0.524 (23/20)
E-Pm2†	0.692	0.061	0.422 (6/16)	0.766	0.083	0.469 (6/26)	0.816	0.098	0.495 (10/26)
EqT	0.714	0.076	0.440 (16/13)	0.766	0.097	0.503 (13/6)	0.802	0.117	0.542 (20/6)
Mdiv▲	0.720	0.060	0.460 (33/33)	0.764	0.079	0.515 (23/16)	0.823	0.096	0.552 (29/3)
OnlyTime◊	0.729	0.068	0.426 (20/26)	0.807	0.092	0.497 (26/26)	0.826	0.115	0.534 (26/20)
HistDiv	0.761°	0.07	0.497▲ (40/13)	0.814	0.085	0.542▲ (36/26)	**0.864‡**	0.101	0.583▲(43/13)
HistDiv-Burst	**0.777°**	0.087	**0.509▲** (33/6)	**0.830◊**	**0.113'**	**0.560▲** (46/20)	0.860‡	**0.132**	**0.601▲** (43/16)

Table 1: SBR at varying depths for Δ =month. Win-Loss percentages are presented in brackets next to the $\mathcal{AT}$ scores. The superscript denotes a statistically significant difference when compared to the closest competitor (p<=0.5). For example ° represents statistically significant difference from OnlyTime.

HistDiv-Burst we fix the the moving window size used to detect bursts to 24 months in all experiments.

To get the best performance and avoid over fitting we tune each variant for SBR in $\mathcal{AT}_q$ and present results using 5-fold cross validation. We evaluated all baselines for metrics mentioned in Section 6 at variable retrieval depths. Similar to the TREC diversity track we assumed equal distribution of subtopics for all topics. For the temporal space $\mathcal{T}_q$ each time window in the ground truth was divided into partitions of size Δ and then given equal importance akin to [7]. Consequently, for the $\mathcal{AT}_q$ space each subtopic and relevant time interval pair is given equal importance. Note, in the joint space we do not divide the qualifying intervals into partitions. We assumed equal distribution of the qualifying intervals associated with a single subtopic.

7.2 Results

In this section we first analyze the performance of all baselines for historical query intents using subtopic recall or SBR since our goal is to optimize SBR. Even though the measure of choice for a historical search task is SBR in the $\mathcal{AT}-$ space, observing the component spaces $\mathcal{A}$ and $\mathcal{T}$ provides a clearer explanation of our results. Note, since each space uses a different set of subtopics, the range of values in each varies considerably. Table 7.2 summarizes the effectiveness of all baselines at Δ = month with respect to SBR in the aspect space $\mathcal{A}$, temporal space $\mathcal{T}$ and aspect-temporal space $\mathcal{AT}$ at $k = \{10, 15, 20\}$. Remember that we have a nested representation of important subtopics and times in our topics definition (cf. Section 6). A document d is relevant to a subtopic in the ground truth, irrespective of its corresponding time interval, is said to be relevant in aspect space $\mathcal{A}$. Similarly d, if published in a time interval I in the ground truth, is said to be relevant in the temporal space $\mathcal{T}$ irrespective of which subtopic it is relevant to.

First, we look at the performance of the non-temporal baselines. Not surprisingly, the diversity-unaware Lm fares worse than most baselines. Ia-select performs better than Lm in the aspect space $\mathcal{A}_q$ but since it does not account for time, we find that SBR in the temporal space $\mathcal{T}_q$ is lower compared to the temporal baselines. Consequently it performs poorly in $\mathcal{AT}_q$. The proportionality-based approach Pm2 also performs poorly suggesting that choosing aspects proportionally is detrimental to historical query intents.

Next, we consider the temporal variants of the standard diversification approaches. We find that the linearized variant T-Ia-select performs consistently worse than its non-temporal counter part in all spaces across all retrieval depths. This shows that linearizing aspects with time leads to over-specification of aspects especially for smaller time granularities. E-Ia-select addresses this problem leading to significantly better results in all spaces when compared to T-Ia-select. It also performs significantly better in $\mathcal{T}_q$ when compared to Ia-select. As a consequence of the inherent temporal nature of aspects alluded to earlier, the subtopic recall of E-Ia-select in the $\mathcal{AT}_q$ improves and is either better or comparable to Ia-select along with performance in the other metrics showing marked improvement (shown in Table2). Now we consider the other temporal baselines OnlyTime and Mdiv in comparison to the temporal baselines discussed above. We observe that Mdiv has comparable to the best performance (although not the best) in both $\mathcal{T}_q$ and $\mathcal{A}_q$ and therefore is easily the best performing temporal baseline in $\mathcal{AT}_q$. Surprisingly, for Δ = month, OnlyTime does not perform as well as we expected in $\mathcal{T}_q$ even though it optimizes for temporal coverage. However, for Δ = year, it significantly outperforms all competitors in $\mathcal{T}_q$ including HistDiv (results omitted from Table 2 for space reasons) which leads us to believe that OnlyTime is sensitive to the underlying granularity Δ. Expectedly, both OnlyTime and EqT perform worse than Mdiv. Since subtopics need not be from mutually exclusive time intervals, OnlyTime struggles to cover the relevant $\mathcal{AT}_q$ space properly. Mdiv, on the other hand, by virtue of modeling aspects (albeit independently) reconciles both dimensions better and is our closest competitor.

Lastly, we turn to HistDiv and its burst-aware version HistDiv-Burst. HistDiv outperforms all classes of competitors in the $\mathcal{AT}_q$ space and is significantly different from its closest competitor Mdiv by an achieved significance levelËIJ[24] of $p \leq 0.05$. The results vindicate our choice of mining aspects temporally and considering time period granularities as aspect proportions for $\mathcal{AT}_q$. A key point to note is that methods which perform comparably to HistDiv in spaces $\mathcal{A}_q$ and $\mathcal{T}_q$ like Ia-select and T-Pm2 are significantly outperformed in the space $\mathcal{AT}_q$ meaning that we achieve the right trade-off between these two seemingly conflicting yet interdependent dimensions HistDiv-Burst is the best performing variant in all spaces for all depths. The improvement over HistDiv can be attributed to the accurate identification of important time intervals pertaining to long running events. HistDiv-Burst which also has the advantage of being granularity free and as evidenced by our results, is a better retrieval model to find relevant documents from important aspects during important time intervals. In Table 1 we also show the win-loss percentage of queries in $\mathcal{AT}$ compared to

	IaP		SBR		NDCG		IA-ERR		MAP	
	M	Y	M	Y	M	Y	M	Y	M	Y
Lм	0.099	0.099	0.428	0.428	0.402	0.402	0.201	0.201	0.228	0.228
Ia-Select°	0.101	0.101	0.442	0.442	0.415	0.415	0.180	0.180	0.215	0.215
Pм2*	0.100	0.100	0.429	0.429	0.388	0.388	0.213	0.213	0.241	0.241
Tia-Select•	**0.120**▲	**0.113**‡	0.380	0.361	**0.497**‡	**0.468**°	0.195	0.179	0.242	0.232
T-Pм2′	0.064	0.091	0.308	0.410	0.232	0.368	0.123	0.176	0.152	0.167
E-Ia-Select‡	0.106	0.102	0.435	0.430	0.478	0.412	0.183	0.177	0.219	0.214
E-Pм2†	0.103	0.099	0.422	0.417	0.419	0.379	0.217	0.204	0.227	0.239
EqT	0.096	0.078	0.441	0.426	0.360	0.331	0.203	0.200	0.229	0.213
Mdiv▲	0.109	0.096	0.460	0.428	0.389	0.370	0.204	0.203	0.236	0.236
OnlyTime°	0.089	0.076	0.426	0.415	0.354	0.297	0.196	0.189	0.236	0.220
HistDiv	0.096	0.087	0.497▲	0.459°	0.383	0.339	0.229*	0.208	**0.255**•	0.231
HistDiv-Burst	0.096	0.096	**0.509**▲	**0.509**°	0.375	0.375	**0.231***	**0.231***	0.244	**0.244**

Table 2: Effect of granularity Δ (M = month; Y = year) at $k = 10$. The superscript denotes a statistically significant difference when compared to the closest competitor (p<=0.5). For example ° represents statistically significant difference to OnlyTime.

the baseline LM. We see that HistDiv improves a sizable portion of the workload (around 43% at $k = 20$) but more importantly under performs only in a small set of queries (16%).

Unlike HistDiv-Burst the other retrieval models that incorporate time are dependent on the granularity of the time window used to discretize the time dimension. To examine the effect of granularity on the baselines we report scores in $\mathcal{AT}_q$ at $k = 10$ in Table 2 using all intent-aware metrics mentioned earlier in Section 6 for $\Delta = \{Year, Month\}$. We find that a yearly granularity works best for certain retrieval models because, for the given workload, a smaller granularity causes temporally-aware diversification methods to *over represent* relevant time periods. HistDiv-Burst on the other hand is more robust against over representing long running subtopics like Giuliani's mayoralty. However for queries like reunification of germany, temporal spread is not key to diversity but instead it is imperative to diversify within a small set of time intervals. Here T-Pм2, irrespective of granularity, is able to focus on to the dominant time window "1989" and covers as many aspects as possible within this window. On the other hand, HistDiv covers enough important aspects in the important time intervals and subsequently diversifies to find aspects in other less relevant intervals. Although with sufficient tuning HistDiv can perform as good or if not better than T-Pм2.

Interestingly, HistDiv also performs the best in $\mathcal{A}_q$ which leads us to believe that temporal aspects guide us to make the right choice of subtopics for temporally ambiguous queries. However this is achieved at the cost of precision. In Table 2, we can also see the performance of all retrieval models for the other metrics. Historical search is cast as a recall-oriented task and hence it is not surprising to find HistDiv is not the best in IA-P. The baseline Tia-Select consistently outperforms other competitors but does so by producing aspect-redundant documents indicated by the low SBR score. We also notice that Ia-Select and Mdiv achieve good precision with satisfactory subtopic recall. Balancing precision and recall is key to satisfying the target user group. In the next section we choose to focus on the intended users of our search system. We first briefly highlight the quantitative results from user-centric metrics. We then take a more qualitative approach to study if this drop in precision for HistDiv is detrimental to user satisfaction in historical search tasks. Finally for completeness, though not included in Table 1, we considered two other competitors – the search engine on the official New York Times portal and a commercial search engine using the appropriate site (nytimes.com) and date filters (1987-2007) on June 9, 2015. The SBR scores achieved by them were the lowest – 0.288 and 0.312 at $k = 10$ respectively. Such low recall can be attributed

to the fact that commercial search engines favor recency and more popular information needs reaffirming the need for specialized retrieval models designed for historical intents.

7.3 User Study

We now turn our attention to the target users to get a deeper understanding of what they perceive is a good historical overview from search results. In this section we attempt to answer the following research question: *Despite a loss in precision, are users satisfied with the quality of the overview derived from HistDiv when compared to its competitors?* In traditional IR, to quantify if search results are satisfactory for users (who inherently examine a result list from top to bottom) metrics such as IA-ERR and α-NDCG are used. From Table 2 we see that HistDiv performs well in IA-ERR, which is one of the primary metrics for TREC's diversity web track, due to its ability to not only rank diverse documents higher but also cover more subtopics in the top 10 results. The lack of precision is reflected in the low NDCG(α set to 0.5) scores although HistDiv has the highest MAP score. What these results do not indicate however is the overall satisfaction of the user when trying to discern an overview from the top-K search results as a whole. We see quantitatively that we cover more subtopics at important time periods but how good is the overview from a user perspective? Is the lack of precision detrimental to the overall user experience?

Study design: We attempt to answer the research question by comparing HistDiv against Ia-Select because Ia-Select exhibits high precision coupled with good recall. It is also distinctly different from HistDiv since it is a pure aspect based diversification algorithm. Due to the sheer number of baselines, comparing against all is prohibitive. We used a within-subjects study design to determine which approach produces a better overview. We had a total of 10 participants comprised of 3 senior historians, 1 humanities researcher and 6 computer science graduate students. The historians and the humanities researcher represent the expert opinion. Participants were required to compare and contrast both approaches for a subset of the query workload from the test collection. Of the three historians two were from the United States and the other from the United Kingdom. All of them cited previous experience using news archives for their research. The non-expert users were from three different nationalities and possessed strong proficiency in the English language. All participated voluntarily in the study.

We selected 15 topics at random from our workload and generated the top 10 results for each from both approaches. Each participant was given between 2-5 topics to evaluate. To take into account the varying familiarity of participants with their designated topics we instructed them to first read the history section of the relevant Wikipedia page for the topic. We suggested a period of 5-15 minutes for this preparation. Following this period, participants were shown the top 10 results from both methods and asked the following question : "Which result ranking gives you a better overview of the history for the given topic and why?". The approaches were anonymized and presented to the users as "X" (IA-SELECT) and "Y" (HISTDIV). Participants were instructed to argue their choice in the form of free text. We opted against structured questions since a good overview can be subjective and many unforeseen nuances cannot be captured. Each topic from the randomly selected subset was evaluated by 3 different participants to account for inter-rater agreement. Participants were instructed to complete each topic sequentially in no particular order. Note that the same interface was used to display both result lists.

Outcomes: We obtained complete results (3 distinct raters for each topic) for 14 out of the 15 topics. The average duration was 25 minutes per topic. Participants emailed their responses individually at the end of the study. They resorted to using either bullet points or paragraphs when explaining their choices. For the evaluation, we consider an approach is superior to the other when the majority of raters vote in its favor. For the sake of readability we de-anonymize the approaches in the participants' responses in the proceeding discussion. Overall we found that participants preferred HISTDIV's ranking in order to get a historical overview for 10 out of 14 topics. 5 out of the 14 topics had 100% agreement with 4 of those being in favor of HISTDIV. The positive comments from the participants often mentioned good coverage and a better ranking of subtopics within the top 10. Some participants explicitly stated "*good diversity in results*" while others justified their choices with examples of subtopics covered exclusively by the winning approach. HISTDIV's span of coverage was immediately apparent to the participants. One of the topics where HISTDIV out performed IA-SELECT is Bob Dole. Participants felt that the increased coverage provided a more rounded picture when compared to IA-SELECT ("*Histdiv mentions an article which talks about the role his wife plays which provides a more complete representation of Bob Dole*") showing that emphasis on recall is justified for this task. Al Gore was another such topic - "*HistDiv has articles about the Oscar winning movie but the other doesn't*" - indicating that an important subtopic was uncovered. The same participant also noted that "*Ia-Select has 7 articles from the year 2000 -> not diverse*". This redundancy is due to over-specification of the time period caused by IA-SELECT's lack of temporal awareness.

Even though participants were instructed to judge the quality of overview from the top 10 as a whole there was a tendency to be critical of the ranking. While two participants indicated that chronological ordering in the top 10 would be easier to understand, the others preferred seeing documents from the most important subtopic towards the top. For Bob Dole, a participant stated that "*HistDiv is better as it returns his presidential campaign as the top ranked document which highlights the pinnacle of his political career*". For the topic Oklahoma City, an expert remarked that the results from HISTDIV were more "*on point*". He argued that while both approaches rightly picked articles about the Oklahoma city bombing at the top, HISTDIV returned the more relevant result from the most relevant time period - "BOMB SUSPECT IS HELD, ANOTHER IDENTIFIED; TOLL HITS 65 AS HOPE FOR SUR-VIVORS FADES" vs "Oklahoma City, a Year Later". The former headline from HISTDIV is a vital primary source whereas the latter from IA-SELECT is a less relevant secondary source. Here HISTDIV's superior modeling of document utility helps it pick highly relevant documents from the more important historical subtopics first. This difference in importance between subtopics is not captured in the

quantitative results due to our classical assumption of equally relevant subtopics. For the topics where participants agreed that IA-SELECT did better than HISTDIV, lack of precision was cited as the main factor. Seven participants cited the number of relevant articles as the deciding factor which is a valid concern. We found from the responses that there were two types of irrelevant articles: articles completely unrelated to the topic and articles seemingly less relevant than the others that explicitly covered important historical facts. We observed this bias towards precision almost exclusively from the non-experts although for cases like Landon Donovan (the former captain of the U.S. mens soccer team) both sets of users agreed that articles about politicians with similar names hurt the overview. Similarly for Charlie Sheen participants responded with comments such as "*HistDiv includes a few articles which do not seem to be about Charlie Sheen at all or concern him only very marginally (articles ranked 2,3,7) , hard to get overview if a third of articles are not really about Charlie Sheen*" upon encountering articles about movie listings or his father Martin Sheen.

An interesting topic that divided opinion was Rudolph Giuliani. In HISTDIV's ranking there was an article regarding an interview on Giuliani's personal life that non-experts considered irrelevant. An expert on the other hand acknowledged the presence of less relevant results but mentioned that for certain topics these documents are not as irrelevant as they first seem since you can find valuable contextual information – "*(For Giuliani) HistDiv is better than Ia-Select because it provides a better mix of political and personal information*". This tendency to evaluate the overview from multiple perspectives was also observed in other topics. For the topic Atlantic City, a participant stated that "*HistDiv gives a more well argued discussion about the political choices that have been taken in order to reinvent the city*". This shows that the lack of precision is detrimental to user satisfaction although it is highly dependent on the topic. When the inherent aspect diversity of the topic is low, HISTDIV's tendency to increase recall ranks irrelevant documents higher. An interesting direction for future work is to design methods that allow automatic adjusting of parameters to increase precision rather than recall for certain types of queries.

From the observations in both experiments we can conclude that (a) HISTDIV is consistently better at finding primary sources by best diversifying the aspect-time space indicated by high subtopic recall (b) HISTDIV shows promise for pure aspect-based diversification of temporally ambiguous queries (c) In isolated cases users feel that the lack of precision hurts HISTDIV but in the majority of cases the emphasis on recall provides a more holistic overview.

8. CONCLUSION & OUTLOOK

In this paper we introduced the notion of a historical query intent over longitudinal news collections like news archives. We cast the problem as diversification task in a new aspect-time space. To evaluate the task we built a new temporal test collection based on 20 years of the *New York Times* collection. We introduced HISTDIV which shows improvements over temporal and non-temporal methods for most of the time-aware diversification methods. We also outperform all competitors in subtopic recall over the joint space showing the suitability of our approach for historical query intents. We observe that HISTDIV works well for topics which have aspects that span across multiple time intervals and have fluctuating importance at different times. It trades-off nicely between important aspects and important times which we perceive as important in historical search. HISTDIV does not perform quite as well for queries which only one dominant aspect at a certain time window. HISTDIV also acheives lower precision than some of its competitors although the user study showed that only in isolated cases there is a loss in overview quality. In the future, for more practical settings where training data is little to none, we want to investigate the usage of query related features like the degree of temporal variance of aspects, the number of bursts, etc. to estimate the parameters used. This opens up exciting future work opportunities to automatically identify queries of different historical intents and evaluate them accordingly.

9. ACKNOWLEDGMENT

This work was carried out under the context of the ERC Grant (339233) ALEXANDRIA. We thank Prof. Jane Winters and her colleagues from the Institute of Historical Research at the University College of London for their help and cooperation.

10. REFERENCES

[1] British newspaper archive http://www.britishnewspaperarchive.co.uk/.
[2] New york times archives, http://timesmachine.nytimes.com/browser.
[3] R. Agrawal, S. Gollapudi, A. Halverson, and S. Ieong. Diversifying search results. In *WSDM* 2009.
[4] O. Alonso, M. Gertz, and R. Baeza-Yates. On the value of temporal information in information retrieval. *SIGIR Forum*, 2007.
[5] O. Alonso, M. Gertz, and R. Baeza-Yates. Clustering and exploring search results using timeline constructions. In *CIKM* 2009.
[6] A. Anand, S. Bedathur, K. Berberich, and R. Schenkel. Index maintenance for time-travel text search. In *SIGIR* 2012.
[7] K. Berberich and S. Bedathur. Temporal diversification of search results. In *SIGIR Workshop TAIA*, 2013.
[8] K. Berberich, S. Bedathur, O. Alonso, and G. Weikum. A language modeling approach for temporal information needs. In *ECIR*, 2010.
[9] K. Berberich, S. Bedathur, T. Neumann, and G. Weikum. A time machine for text search. In *SIGIR*, 2007.
[10] A. Bingham. The digitization of newspaper archives: Opportunities and challenges for historians. *Twentieth Century British History*, 2010.
[11] M. Brucato and D. Montesi. Metric spaces for temporal information retrieval. In M. d. Rijke, T. Kenter, A. P. d. Vries, C. Zhai, F. d. Jong, K. Radinsky, and K. Hofmann, editors, *Advances in Information Retrieval* 2014.
[12] R. Campos, G. Dias, A. M. Jorge, and A. Jatowt. Survey of temporal information retrieval and related applications. *ACM Comput. Surv.*, 2014.
[13] R. Campos, A. M. Jorge, G. Dias, and C. Nunes. Disambiguating implicit temporal queries by clustering top relevant dates in web snippets. In *WI-IAT*, 2012.
[14] J. Carbonell and J. Goldstein. The use of mmr, diversity-based reranking for reordering documents and producing summaries. In *SIGIR*, 1998.
[15] B. Carterette and P. Chandar. Probabilistic models of ranking novel documents for faceted topic retrieval. In *CIKM*, 2009.
[16] D. O. Case. The collection and use of information by some american historians: a study of motives and methods. *The Library Quarterly*, 1991.
[17] J. Choi and W. B. Croft. Temporal models for microblogs. In *CIKM*, 2012.
[18] C. Clarke, N. Craswell, I. Soboroff, and E. Voorhees. Nist, overview of the trec2011 web track. In *Proceedings of TREC*, 2011.
[19] C. Clarke, N. Craswell, I. Soboroff and A. Ashkan. Nist, overview of the trec2011 web track. In *Proceedings of WSDM*, 2011.
[20] C. L. Clarke, N. Craswell, and I. Soboroff. Overview of the trec 2009 web track. Tech. report, DTIC Document, 2009.
[21] M. Costa and M. J. Silva. Evaluating web archive search systems. In *WISE*, 2012.
[22] V. Dang and B. W. Croft. Term level search result diversification. In *SIGIR*, 2013.
[23] V. Dang and W. B. Croft. Diversity by proportionality: An election-based approach to search result diversification. In *SIGIR* 2012.
[24] D. Anthony C. and D. V. Hinkley. Bootstrap methods and their application. *Vol. 1. Cambridge university press* 1997.
[25] Clarke, C. A and Kolla, M and Cormack, G and Vechtomova, O. and Ashkan, A. and Büttcher, S. and MacKinnon, I.. Novelty and diversity in information retrieval evaluation. In *SIGIR*, 2008.
[26] A. Dong, Y. Chang, Z. Zheng, G. Mishne, J. Bai, R. Zhang, K. Buchner, C. Liao, and F. Diaz. Towards recency ranking in web search. In *WSDM*, 2010.
[27] A. Dong, R. Zhang, P. Kolari, J. Bai, F. Diaz, Y. Chang, Z. Zheng, and H. Zha. Time is of the essence: Improving recency ranking using twitter data. In *WWW*, 2010.
[28] Z. Dou, S. Hu, K. Chen, R. Song, and J.-R. Wen. Multi-dimensional search result diversification. In *WSDM*, 2011.
[29] W. M. Duff and C. A. Johnson. Accidentally found on purpose: information-seeking behavior of historians in archives. *The Library Quarterly*, 2002.
[30] D. Gupta and K. Berberich. Identifying time intervals of interest to queries. In *CIKM*, 2014.
[31] J. Hoffart, M. A. Yosef, I. Bordino, H. Fürstenau, M. Pinkal, M. Spaniol, B. Taneva, S. Thater, and G. Weikum. Robust disambiguation of named entities in text. In *EMNLP*, 2011.
[32] H. Joho, A. Jatowt, and R. Blanco. Ntcir temporalia: a test collection for temporal information access research. In *companion publication of the 23rd WWW*, 2014.
[33] R. Jones and F. Diaz. Temporal profiles of queries. *ACM Trans. Inf. Syst.*, 25(3), July 2007.
[34] X. Li and W. B. Croft. Time-based language models. In *CIKM*, 2003.
[35] S. Liang, Z. Ren, and M. de Rijke. Fusion helps diversification. In *SIGIR*, 2014.
[36] D. Metzler, R. Jones, F. Peng, and R. Zhang. Improving search relevance for implicitly temporal queries. In *SIGIR*, 2009.
[37] T. N. Nguyen and N. Kanhabua. Leveraging dynamic query subtopics for time-aware search result diversification. In *ECIR*, 2014.
[38] M. Peetz, M. Edgar and M. de Rijke. Using temporal bursts for query modeling. In the *Springer Journal of Information Retrieval*, 2014.
[39] M.-H. Peetz, E. Meij, M. de Rijke, and W. Weerkamp. Adaptive temporal query modeling. In *Advances in Information Retrieval*, 2012.
[40] K. Radinsky, K. M. Svore, S. T. Dumais, M. Shokouhi, J. Teevan, A. Bocharov, and E. Horvitz. Behavioral dynamics on the web: Learning, modeling, and prediction. *TOIS* 13.
[41] R. L. Santos, C. Macdonald, and I. Ounis. Exploiting query reformulations for web search result diversification. In *WWW*, 2010.
[42] V. Setty, S. Bedathur, K. Berberich, and G. Weikum. Inzeit: Efficiently identifying insightful time points. *In VLDB Endow.*, 2010.
[43] C. Johnson and W. Duff. Chatting up the archivist: Social capital and the archival researcher. *The American Archivist*, 2005.
[44] H. R. Tibbo. The philosophy of information retrieval evaluation *Evaluation of cross-language information retrieval systems*, 2002.
[45] H. R. Tibbo. Primarily history in america: How us historians search for primary materials at the dawn of the digital age. *The American Archivist*, 2003.
[46] K. Zhou, S. Whiting, J. M. Jose, and M. Lalmas. The impact of temporal intent variability on diversity evaluation. In *Advances in Information Retrieval*, 2013.
[47] Y. Zhu, Y. Lan, J. Guo, X. Cheng, and S. Niu. Learning for search result diversification. In *SIGIR'*14.

How Writers Search

Analyzing the Search and Writing Logs of Non-fictional Essays[*]

Matthias Hagen   Martin Potthast   Michael Völske   Jakob Gomoll   Benno Stein

Bauhaus-Universität Weimar
99421 Weimar, Germany
<first name>.<last name>@uni-weimar.de

ABSTRACT

Many writers of non-fictional texts engage intensively in exploratory web search scenarios during their background research on the essay topic. Though understanding such search behavior is necessary for the development of search engines that specifically support writing tasks, it has neither been systematically recorded nor analyzed. This paper contributes part of the missing research: We report on the outcomes of a large-scale corpus construction initiative to acquire detailed interaction logs of writers who were given a writing task on 150 pre-defined TREC topics. The corpus is freely available to foster research on exploratory search. Each essay is at least 5000 words long and comes with a chronological log of search queries, result clicks, web browsing trails, and fine-grained writing revisions that reflect the task completion status. To ensure reproducibility, a fully-fledged, static web search environment has been created on top of the ClueWeb09 corpus as part of our initiative.

In this paper, we present initial analyses of the recorded search interaction logs and overview insights gained from them: (1) essay writing behavior corresponds to search patterns that are rather stable for the same writer, (2) fact-checking queries often conclude a writing task, (3) recurring anchor queries are often submitted to not lose the main themes or to explore new directions, (4) query terms can be learned while searching and reading, (5) the number of submitted queries is not a good indicator for task completion.

1. INTRODUCTION

The web has fundamentally changed how writers of non-fictional texts approach their task. In the past, research on a topic and writing about it typically happened separately in time and space (e.g., research in the library, writing at home). Nowadays, both can be done more or less simultaneously, since web search engines retrieve relevant information on almost any topic. Therefore, writers cab easily switch between search and writing whenever they perceive gaps of

---

[*]Extended version of our EuroHCIR 2013 workshop contribution [23].

knowledge (i.e., information needs). This situation has accelerated the rate at which non-fictional texts are written as well as significantly decreased the costs of doing so, which is particularly true in cases where the resulting texts are not expected to be award-worthy, but merely publishable.

This paper studies the writing process and search behavior of writers in action: we hired 12 authors to write a total of 150 essays on that many topics, at least 5,000 words each, while recording a fine-grained log of text revisions, search queries, result clicks, and browsing. To attain reproducibility, we chose topics from the TREC web track and set up a static web search environment based on the ClueWeb09. Our search engine employs BM25F as the retrieval model, its user interface resembles those of commercial search engines, and its performance was optimized to allow for an average retrieval time of less than five seconds. While the retrieval model of our search engine obviously does not compete with those of commercial search engines in terms of retrieval quality, that may be to our advantage since our writers had to engage with our search engine to find sufficient material to write an essay of the aforementioned length. Given budget limitations, we further attempted to shift the attention of our writers toward searching for information, rather than spending time pondering over formulations, by allowing them to reuse in their essays the texts they found in the ClueWeb09. Nevertheless, the final essays were still required to be coherent and consistent—often resulting in reformulations of copy-pasted texts. Altogether, despite the outlined limitations, we created the largest and most realistic resource available to date to study the search behavior of writers at scale. The corpus is freely available.

We present the results of an exploratory corpus analysis. After a review of related work, Section 3 describes our corpus. Section 4 then discusses analyses of various aspects of the logs and the observed writers' search behavior. We examine the structure of the submitted queries, reveal and distinguish between two elementary search strategies employed that also reflect the writing behavior, and analyze how different working phases relate to each other. Section 5 summarizes our findings and gives directions for future work.

2. RELATED WORK

Marchionini [17] distinguishes closed-ended and open-ended search tasks, where the former is a search for a particular fact, and the latter does not necessarily have a an unequivocal result. For example, compare the search for a date of birth with that for the best hotel for an upcoming trip. Open-ended tasks are often referred to as *exploratory search* since they do not necessarily lead to only one correct answer but they help to build a mental model of a topic [30]. White and Roth [33] describe exploratory search as an iterative, multi-tactical process, where the user explores the information space as extensively as necessary to fulfill an open-ended information need. Closed-ended searchers may iteratively refine their queries as well, but they usually zero in on a specific, targeted piece of information. Exploratory searchers, instead, explore the information space extensively; while examining search results, they obtain clues for their next steps [35]. The challenge of exploratory search is to design retrieval models that support users in these tasks. Web search engines are typically tuned towards precision, which limits the chance of finding loosely related information. But exploratory search is more recall-oriented [17]. This can be supported via rapid query refinement in the early phase of a search [32], supporting facets such as search result clustering [28], and leveraging the searcher's context, e.g., via pseudo-relevance feedback [36]. The task of writing an essay on a given topic is open-ended and exploratory.

The query logs of search engine users are a valuable resource to study their goals. However, Kurth [15] argued early on that no measure that can be derived from user interactions alone explains the user's intentions. Researchers nevertheless rely on such measures for the lack of a better alternative. Typical measures found in the literature include the number of queries submitted by a user, the average number of terms and clicks per query, and the time between query and first click [3]. Log analyses often measure further attributes from a more global context, such as the number of physical sessions to complete a task. Machine learning algorithms then exploit a wide range of such and similar measures [1, 2, 7, 5, 20]. For example, Agichtein et al. [2] predict whether a user is likely to resume a suspended session within the next few days. After determining the dominant topic of the majority of the queries using data from the Open Directory Project, their approach is able to automatically decide for each query whether it is related to the task or not. Such approaches face the typical dilemma of machine learning, namely that the results obtained often do not reveal *why* the classifier works. User behavior is hardly ever characterized, which is the goal of our work. Also, the reproducibility of these studies is often limited by the fact that query logs cannot be shared for privacy reasons. In our case, we can safely share the entire query logs, since they are not interspersed with personal queries.

While log analyses have been conducted for a long time, exploratory search has shifted into focus only recently: to the best of our knowledge, Qu and Furnas [24] were the first to design a corresponding study. Based on the sense-making model [9, 26], they studied the relation between information seeking and construction of a mental representation. In this regard, not only the interactions of their 30 participants with the search system were recorded, but participants were also asked to prepare an outline for a 1-hour talk. Interestingly, Qu and Furnas found that the resulting talk structure strongly correlated with that of the participant's bookmark folders. Human judges rated the topical similarity between consecutive queries and assigned each query to one of the bookmark folders. Qu and Furnas visualized this information on a timeline to show when which query occurred, which folder it referred to, and which web page was bookmarked in this context. The visualizations for all 30 subjects reveal

the influence of emerging structure on the following search. Moreover, 14 out of 30 participants used their folder structure as a roadmap for subsequent search. The authors conclude that search engines should support users, for instance, by analyzing the structure of their bookmark folders.

Egusa et al. [11] pursued a similar approach asking 35 undergraduate students to produce a concept map of their understanding of a given topic before and after searching. A concept map is a graph consisting of named entities and labeled connections between them. By analyzing the differences between the before- and after-maps, Egusa et al. develop a new task performance measure for exploratory search tasks. Such a measure goes beyond traditional IR measures in assessing not only precision but also the *benefit* a user has from a set of search results [33]. In this regard, Vakkari [30] differentiates between evaluating *search engine output*—the precision of a result list with regard to the submitted query—and *task outcome*, which describes how well the system supported the user in fulfilling the task. A high precision does not necessarily lead to good overall task performance. Egusa et al. performed their experiments on only two very broad (i.e., open-ended) topics, namely "Politics" and "Media." The task was to find and compare different opinions about these topics. The before- and after-maps were analyzed with respect to the number of kept, discarded and inserted nodes, links and labels. Among other findings, nearly as many deletions as insertions occurred. This indicates that people not only gather new information while exploring a topic but also adjust their existing knowledge. However, the authors conclude that applying descriptive statistics on concept maps cannot serve as a measure for the performance of an exploratory search system. They argue that one has to conduct more qualitative analyses of the described concepts and users' searching behavior.

Vakkari and Huuskonen [31] designed a study that concentrates on the search process, especially the effort that users put into the search, and how it is interlinked with the task outcome. Within the scope of a term's course, medical students were asked to find information with a domain-specific search engine in order to write an essay on a medical topic. The search log interactions were examined with respect to the applied search tactics (narrowing and broadening of queries, use of logical operators, etc.) and effort variables (like number of sessions or the number of read, but not cited articles). The essays' grades as awarded by the course's instructors were used as a performance measure for task outcome. Vakkari and Huuskonen show several interesting relationships between search process, output and outcome variables. They report a negative correlation between diversity of queries, search engine precision, and essay scores: the broader the queries were formulated, the lower the system's precision, yet the higher the essay scores. A very similar correlation was observed for search effort: the more sessions a student needed to write the essay, the lower was the system's overall precision because of the larger result set, but the higher was the quality of the essay.

Liu and Belkin [16] investigated the association between newspaper article writing and information search in a study with 24 undergraduate students. The participants worked on one of two writing tasks, with intermediate stages of task completion recorded at the end of each of three sessions. As such, this study approaches what is possible with our own log, albeit at a much lower level of granularity.

Our efforts to construct a corpus for exploratory search have been guided by the aforementioned approaches, addressing several shortcomings: *(a) Task diversity.* Qu and Furnas [24], Egusa et al. [11] as well as Liu and Belkin [16] employed only two different topics. Vakkari and Huuskonen [31] employ eleven topics, but all of them from the medical domain. We employ 150 topics, derived from the TREC web track, which are diverse and can be understood by laymen. *(b) Connection of search and task outcome.* Qu and Furnas [24] and Egusa et al. [11] do not provide revisions of task outcomes. Our study aligns all search interactions with text revisions on a time line, which allows fine-grained analysis of the connection between search and task outcome, as proposed by Järvelin et al. [14]. *(c) Experimental setup and reproducibility.* Qu and Furnas [24], and Liu and Belkin [16], asked participants to use a search system in their lab—a maximally obtrusive setting [13]—whereas our participants could work from home. Unlike the other studies, we employ a well-known web corpus frequently used for evaluation purposes to create a static search scenario, that can be reproduced even after years. *(d) Incentives and motivation.* All four studies recruit undergraduate students as study subjects, which often introduces bias with regard to diversity and motivation. Vakkari and Huuskonen ensure proper motivation, since their participants were graded and had the chance of earning credit points by completing the course; Liu and Belkin's participants received monetary compensation. In our case, we hired (semi-)professional writers from all over the world with a diversity of backgrounds, we had them sign a contract, and paid them on an hourly basis.

3. DATASET DESCRIPTION

Our Webis Text Reuse Corpus 2012 (Webis-TRC-12)[1] consists of fine-grained interaction logs for the writing of 5,000 word long essays on 150 different topics—147 essays with a few pre-defined documents that the authors should use, 150 essays for which the authors were actually asked to search for relevant information. The dataset consisting of the latter 150 essays and their writing process (i.e., the so-called "search" subset of the Webis-TRC-12) forms the basis of the analyses in this paper. Each topic was derived from the TREC Web track topics of the years 2009–2011; reformulated to result in an essay writing task on the topic instead of information finding only. Since most topics are rather broad, the authors had to resort to exploratory search for their research using the ClueWeb09 search engine ChatNoir [21] based on the BM25F retrieval model [25]. All search interactions are logged in the Webis-TRC-12 alongside the revisions of the actual texts. A new revision was added whenever the authors stopped typing for 300ms in our online editor provided for their essay writing. This way, the dataset allows to complement analyses of the task progress in form of essay completion with a fine-grained search behavior log. The authors were allowed to reuse passages from the found web documents but instructed to indicate the sources. The whole process of the essay revision logging and the framework involved was discussed in much detail in our previous publication focusing on the writing behavior [22]. In the paper at hand, we focus on the search interactions to gain insights on how writers search. To be rather self-contained,

we give some key figures on the essays first but then concentrate on the search log. The dataset is freely available for use by other researchers.[2]

3.1 The Essays in the Webis-TRC-12

The outstanding property of the essays compared to other corpora is that very fine-grained intermediate states from the beginning up to essay completion are synchronized with the writer's search behavior. Most essays are around 5,000 words long as requested—there are only two shorter ones due to difficulties in finding useful documents in the ClueWeb09. For example, one author should write about the HP Mini 2140 notebook but since its market launch falls in the crawling period of the ClueWeb09 [6] only few announcements of the product could be found. About half of the essays contain reused text from 11 up to 21 different ClueWeb09 documents, only one fourth of the essays contain less than 11 sources, with a minimum of only 3. Section 4.5 will later show that writers with many sources can be considered slightly more dedicated to the task than writers with only few sources. For more details on the corpus creation process, we refer to our previous publications [22, 23].

3.2 The Search Log of the Webis-TRC-12

The search log consists of 150 files, each containing all search interactions for one essay. There are three different types of interactions in the log: (1) queries submitted by the user along the shown ranked results including snippets; (2) document views, characterized by the visited URL and a type (click on a search result, a trail click, or a revisit via some bookmark);[3] (3) revision numbers of text-writing interactions, serving as a cross reference to the actual essays.

Each interaction has a timestamp and an anonymized IP address, which may give a clue about different workstations that writers worked with. Documents are referenced by both their ClueWeb09 IDs, as well as their real URLs.

Table 1 summarizes important statistics on our dataset. The search log contains 13,609 queries, 16,698 document views and 6,123 text-writing interactions by 12 different authors. All interactions took place in about half a year, spanning 166 days. The longest time period spanned by one essay is 56 days, yet the author actually worked on only 12 of these days and paused work on the other 44 days. The majority of authors worked for about 6 days on a topic before essay completion, whereof 5 days involve actual working phases and 1 day involves no working hours at all (median values).

When separating all interactions into physical sessions with a cut-off time of 15 minutes—i.e., an author is considered to be inactive after a gap of 15 minutes—the log contains 2,797 physical sessions, resulting in an average of 18.6 sessions per essay or 3.4 sessions per working day, respectively. The shortest sessions only span a couple of minutes and often involve only a few edits, whereas the longest sessions last up to 253 minutes (more than four hours). A more detailed analysis of these sessions and a visualization scheme is provided in Section 4.2.

A rather surprising number is the ratio of unique queries among all submitted queries, which is about one quar-

---

[1]The name's inspiration is the utilization of the final essays in the PAN lab's shared task on text reuse detection.

[2]http://webis.de/corpora
[3]Result clicks are views of search results. Followed links in such documents form the trail clicks. All other document views are bookmark clicks when the document has been visited before; otherwise, they are categorized as "unknown."

Table 1: Key figures of searching and writing for all essays in the Webis-TRC-12 "search" subset.

	Min	Q1	Mdn	Avg	Q3	Max	Sum
Queries							
– per essay	4.0	40.0	68.0	90.7	117.0	612.0	13,609
– per essay (unique)	1.0	12.0	20.0	23.6	31.5	121.0	3,538
– per physical session	0.0	0.0	0.0	4.9	4.0	231.0	13,609*
Clicks							
– per essay	12.0	55.0	87.0	111.3	144.5	431.0	16,698
– per essay (unique)	8.0	44.5	67.0	74.5	101.0	259.0	1,181
– per physical session	0.0	0.0	1.0	6.0	6.0	164.0	16,698*
– per query	0.0	0.0	0.0	0.2	0.0	76.0	8,779
Clicks per essay							
– on results	5.0	30.5	49.0	58.5	75.5	280.0	8,779*
– trail clicks	0.0	13.5	33.0	52.8	73.0	332.0	7,919
Writing sessions							
– per essay	11.0	28.0	42.0	46.3	59.5	178.0	6,943
– revisions (thousands)	0.2	1.8	2.9	2.9	3.8	6.8	–**
– words (thousands)	0.7	4.8	5.0	5.0	5.2	13.9	–**
– paste events	0.0	13.0	25.0	28.6	39.0	134.0	4,291
– references	3.0	11.0	16.0	18.4	21.0	69.0	2,761
Work time per essay							
– days passed	1.0	4.0	6.0	8.6	9.0	56.0	–**
– working days	1.0	4.0	5.0	5.5	7.0	17.0	–**
– working hours	1.8	5.2	7.5	7.9	9.8	23.0	1,191
– physical sessions	2.0	11.5	16.0	18.6	23.0	55.0	2,797
Minutes spent							
– reading per click	0.0	0.1	0.4	0.7	0.8	15.0	11,236
– writing per session	0.0	0.5	2.2	7.4	8.9	145.2	51,126

*Equal to some above value by definition.
**Sum not given to avoid misinterpretation.

ter (3,538 to 13,609). About half of this effect is explained by the interface of the search engine: Writers were shown the top ten results first, and could request 100 results by clicking a "more"-button. This accounts for 6,874 queries with 10 results and 6,727 follow-up queries requesting 100 results. Almost always, the authors clicked "more." A further explanation why there is only about one fourth of unique queries is provided in Section 4.3: many authors submit identical queries in different sessions or even in a row.

It is also remarkable that more than half of the physical sessions contain no query submission. In fact, the third quartile of queries per session is 4, meaning that 2,097 sessions contain ≤ 4 queries. Almost all queries (12,094 of 13,609) were submitted in 700 sessions only. The document views are similarly distributed: 14,421 of 16,698 views take place in only 700 sessions. This indicates that text-writing interactions form the largest part of most physical sessions.

A closer inspection of the statistics reveals two other interesting aspects. First, the number of result and trail clicks is quite balanced, which indicates that the writers genuinely followed exploratory search strategies and not just entered look-up queries. Second, the writers did not spent too much time reading the clicked documents. With a median value of 0.4 minutes ($\cong$ 24 seconds) and a third quartile of 0.8 minutes ($\cong$ 48 seconds) only few clicked documents seem to be worth reading in-depth. For example, only 661 documents, which is about 4% of all clicks, were viewed for two and a half minutes or longer. One reason could be that the writers just copy-pasted content from some of the results and only read the content while editing it in the essay editor.

4. WRITERS' BEHAVIOR

The following analyses of our dataset aim to shed some light on how to characterize and understand the writers' behavior in exploratory search tasks.

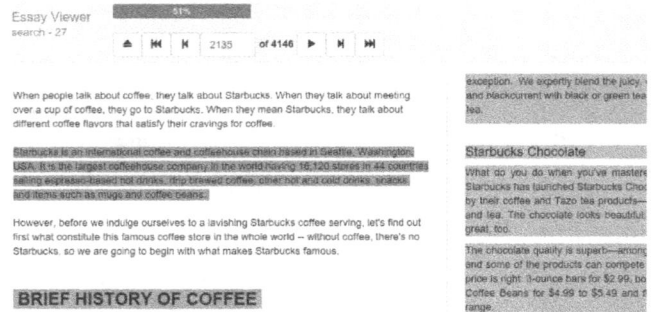

Figure 1: Screenshot of the essay viewer interface.

4.1 Visualizing Essay Writing

In order to better understand the essay writing process, we implemented a web application that shows all revisions of a given essay in sequence. A screenshot of the interface is shown in Figure 1: The controls at the top of the page allow stepping forward and backward through the essay revisions, or jumping to a specific revision. The rest of the page shows the current state of the essay. Different colors indicate different ClueWeb09 sources for copied or paraphrased text. We envision extending this tool to include information from the query log, such that queries occurring at a given point in time can be correlated with their contemporary writing interactions. The tool is available alongside the corpus.

4.2 Visualizing Writer Interactions

In a visual illustration of the logged interaction, we examine the temporal course of actions that the authors took during their essay writing task. To this end, the physical working sessions are determined based on a 15 minutes inactivity gap. However, only the text-writing interactions have an exactly known end time; for query and click interactions, we estimate the durations. For queries, we apply a threshold of 60 seconds, because we assume that a writer would not stare on the result list for more than one minute without clicking any result. For clicked documents, we estimate the reading time based on the document length and an assumed reading speed of 250 words per minute [8]. A solid (green) line further shows the development of essay length in the sessions. Figure 2 shows examples of three topics—visualizations for all topics are available alongside the corpus. Each row depicts a physical session, and the horizontal dashed lines divide different working days (most of the sessions in the plots are about one hour). The beige blocks represent text-writing interactions, and the blue and red ones depict queries and document views, respectively.

The author of the essay on topic 29 submitted rather few queries but seems to have worked very purposeful. Writing often directly follows document views and it seems that the author deliberately decided to learn and write about some particular aspect and visited a couple of documents in order to collect the needed information. In contrast to this, the author of the essay on topic 27 has a very different working style. Starting with a couple of sessions in which the author foraged all possibly needed information, almost all sessions from the third working day on deal with rewriting and removing content from the priorly collected sources. Following our previous notation [22], we call the first type a "build-up" writer and the second a "boil-down" one. In Section 4.4, we will also relate this to different searching behavior.

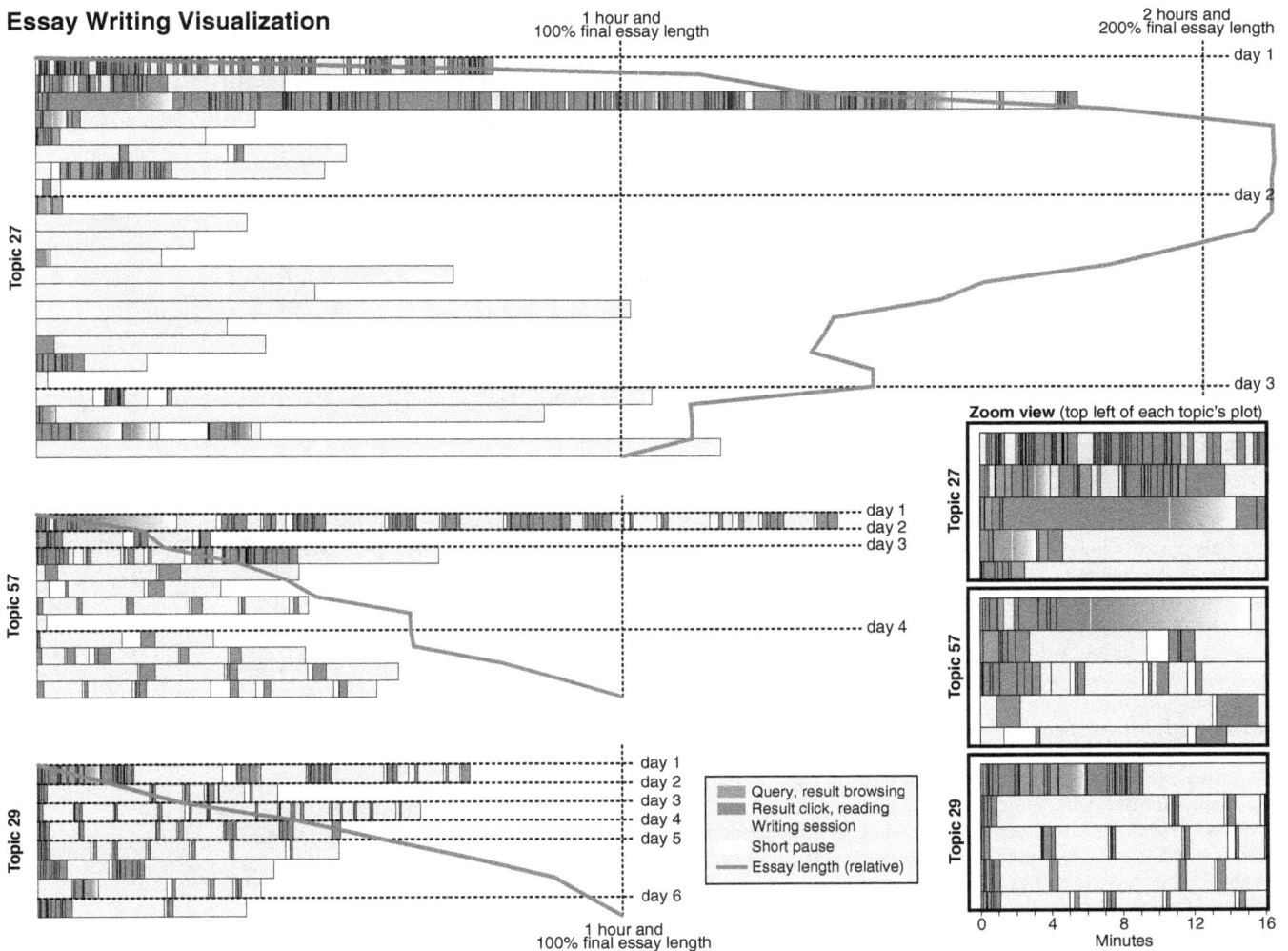

Figure 2: Visualization of the interactions for a selection of three of the 150 essays. Each stacked bar denotes an uninterrupted working session (15 minutes inactivity gap). Bar lengths indicate work time in minutes, blue boxes indicate querying and result browsing, red boxes indicate document views, and beige boxes indicate writing. White boxes and gradients in red or blue boxes indicate short pauses. The solid green line denotes the current essay length relative to the final essay.

There is another interesting detail about the essay on topic 27: In the session before the last, a couple of document views are followed by very short writing interactions that influence the essay length only marginally. This can be observed for many topics and different authors and was also recognized by Vakkari et al. [30]. One explanation could be that writers check their essay for possibly missing but important text passages from priorly selected sources or that they double-check the facts in their essays.

4.3 Query Formulation

In exploratory tasks searchers learn and extend or adapt their knowledge about a topic [11]. We expect the queries for an essay to also develop over time and examine when in the process specific terms occur and where they might stem from. For each query term entered for the first time, we assign it to one of the possible origins: the task description, a previously clicked document, the title or snippet of a previously shown search result, or the writer's initial knowl-

Table 2: Origins of learned query terms.

Prior knowledge	Task description	Search Results		
		Title	Snippet	Clicked doc.
312 (8.4%)	902 (24.3%)	291 (7.8%)	1,067 (28.7%)	1,147 (30.8%)

edge. If a term has not occurred during any of the prior interactions, it is classified as *prior knowledge* only.

Table 2 shows the origins of all 3,719 distinct query terms that appeared in the queries for the 150 topics. Almost all terms could potentially be learned during work on the topic. Figure 3 (middle and right) shows when in the search process a writer introduced new terms and where they are likely to come from for topic 29 and 133. On the x-axis, one can see the current query number. The y-axis displays all clicked documents, and the staircase-shaped line depicts which click(s) happened as a result of which query. For topic 29, the first three clicks happened for the sixth query, another click followed after submitting the ninth query, and so on. The dots indicate a new term in the query and all previously clicked documents that contain this particular term.

197

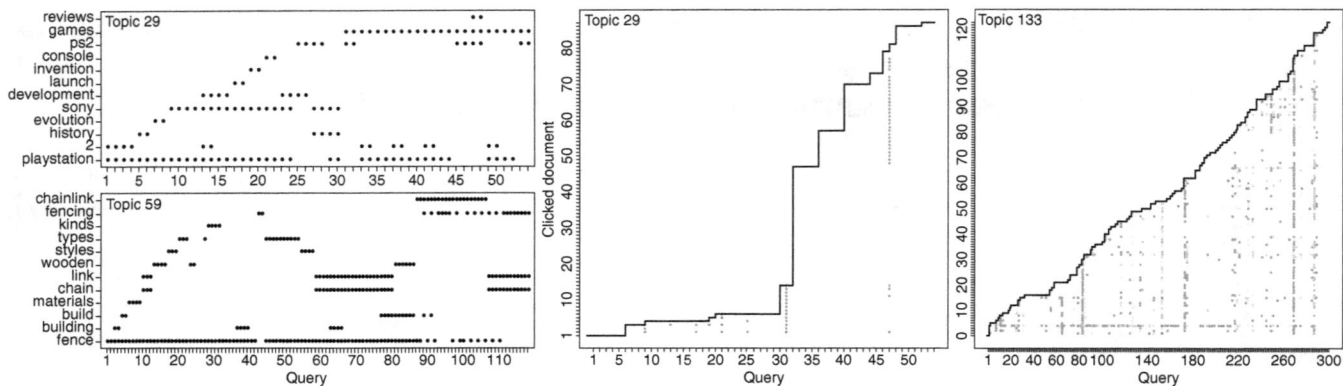

Figure 3: Query composition for topics 29 and 59 (left). Learned terms for topic 29 (middle) and 133 (right).

If two or even more terms were introduced in only one query, each of the terms is represented by another color. For instance, in topic 29 the queries 31 and 47 introduce the terms "games" and "reviews." These terms were contained in almost all of the clicked documents that were visited before the respective queries. Such a vertical line of dots can be interpreted as a change of subtopic because the writer ignored an often occurring term for quite a long time and then decided at some point to finally search for it. About 70 of the topics contain such clear subtopic changes based on recently visited documents. Topic 133 also shows another interesting pattern: a horizontal line (Figure 3 (right)). This indicates that document number 4 was influential for many queries (it is a detailed overview on the Declaration of Independence, the main theme of the topic).

With respect to what terms were used in which queries, also the left part of Figure 3 visualizes usage: the terms on the y-axis and the queries on the x-axis. From the two example topics it is obvious that many queries have numerous identical, immediate follow-up queries. Half of it can be explained through clicks on the "more"-button requesting 100 instead of 10 results. Often a query is submitted more than twice when there was a session break in between and the writer started with the same query again. However, there are also some oddities like the query `chain link fence` that is submitted ten times in a row for topic 59 (queries 67 to 76 in topic 59). We have no satisfying explanation for this behavior; maybe the search engine was slow at this time such that the writer submitted the query again before having seen any result.

We consider the identical queries that are submitted from time to time to be *anchor* queries. The results of such a query can point to many directions for further investigations and a writer might return to this query as soon as the work on one subtopic is finished. Second, anchor queries can serve to keep track of the main theme at any time and keep the writer on course. And third, writers might bring recently acquired knowledge into line with older knowledge structures and therefore want to return to previously seen documents. Typical anchor queries for many topics reflect the main theme of the task (i.e., the TREC topic itself).

4.4 Search Strategies

We now focus on elementary differences in writers' searching strategies. Figure 4 shows the extreme cases of submitted queries over essay revisions for four authors (axes normalized to percentages). The curves are organized to high-

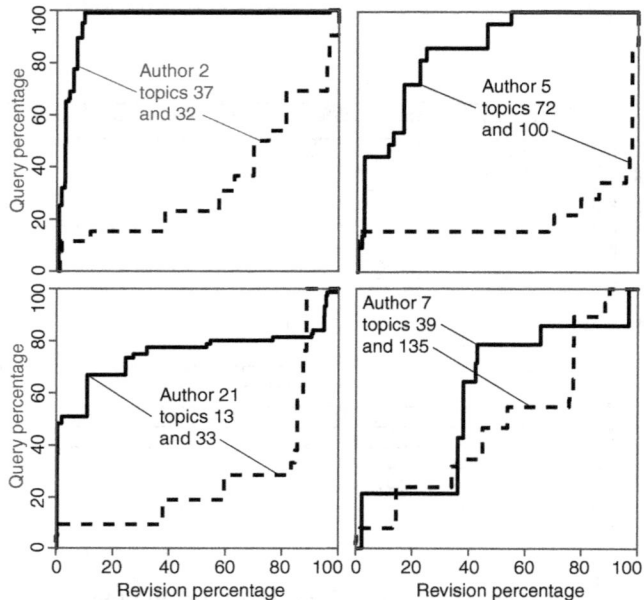

Figure 4: Examples for the spectrum of writer search behavior. Each curve shows the percentage of submitted queries (y-axis) per percentage of essay revisions (x-axis). For each author, we show the topics with the largest and smallest area under the curve (i.e., early queries vs. late queries).

light the spectrum of different search behavior for individual authors. Authors 2, 5, and 21, for instance, have topics for which they submit most of the queries rather early, but also topics with most queries at the end only (i.e., probably fact checking). Typically, sets of queries are submitted in short "bursts," followed by extended periods of writing, which can be inferred from the plateaus in the curves. For author 7, all the topics show a more linear increase of queries over the whole writing time for all topics, indicating continuous switching between searching and writing. From these observations, it can be inferred that query frequency alone is not a good indicator of task completion or the current stage of a task even within a single author. Moreover, exploratory search systems have to deal with a broad behavior spectrum and be able to make the most of few queries, or be prepared that writers interact only a few times with them.

To further distinguish search behavior, we focus on the number of queries and clicks. As observed in Section 3.2,

198

Table 3: Median values for essays of clickers and queriers (Mann-Whitney U-test).

	Clickers	Queriers	Significance of difference
Queries	47.0	107.0	$U = 1058.5$, $z = -6.148$, $p < 0.01$
Clicks	102.5	79.5	$U = 2074.0$, $z = -2.136$, $p < 0.05$
Pastes	39.0	19.0	$U = 1361.5$, $z = -4.952$, $p < 0.01$
References	17.5	15.0	$U = 1876.0$, $z = -2.921$, $p < 0.01$

some authors submit only few queries but follow long click trails; others submit a variety of queries but rarely click on search results. We call the authors following one of these two strategies *clickers* and *queriers*. To distinguish between clickers and queriers, we count the number of queries and clicks that are performed until a document is clicked that is also used in the essay. It is not important how many queries and clicks occurred overall but only how many of them occur between two clicks on such reference documents. The analysis for all essays reveals the two groups among our authors. Authors 5, 7, 20, 21 and 04 are clickers, and the authors 2, 6, 17 and 18 are queriers. Authors 1, 14 and 25 have worked on at most two topics only, yet the trend shows that they tend to be clickers.

Table 3 highlights the differences between clickers and queriers. Except for the number of clicks, which is also fairly high for queriers, all differences between both groups are highly significant as shown by a Mann-Whitney U-test (the data is not normally distributed). The fairly high number of clicks in the querier group simply seems to depend on the number of queries submitted. After all, the distributions of clicks for both groups differ not as much as the distributions of queries, pastes and references. This underpins the assumption that writers in exploratory search tasks consume some informative content before considering themselves to have learned enough. It is notable that clickers paste about twice as often as queriers do. It seems plausible that clickers pick up several possibly useful text passages during their information exploration phase, which they retain in their essays for later use. The number of used references confirms this trend and it can be stated that queriers seem to be more selective with their reference documents than clickers.

4.5 Writer Dedication

Besides different search strategies, we also want to explore whether our data allows us to measure the degree of *writer dedication* to the exploratory search task. We try to reflect writer dedication by the effort a writer puts into the treatment of the task, which can be a valuable information for a search engine. For example, a truly dedicated writer might be interested in additional resources beyond the original query, whereas a writer who works only unwillingly on a task like essay writing might be only interested in overview pages without too many details. Recent studies investigating user engagement [18, 19] go beyond the simple features we can explore below, but we think that our search log-derivable measures can still be useful.

To distinguish "lazy" from more dedicated writers, we use the following nine features per essay: number of distinct queries, number of distinct clicks, number of copy-paste interactions, number of used references, total working hours, time spent for reading documents, time spent for writing, number of physical sessions, number of handled subtopics (determined by the number of session IDs a search mission detection algorithm returned [12]). In a next step, a ranking of all topics is produced for each feature individually, and

Table 4: Essays with topic (T) and author IDs (A) ranked (R) by the writer dedication score (S).

R	T	A	S	R	T	A	S	R	T	A	S
1	58	2	551	51	150	24	334	101	73	24	201
2	53	2	538	52	138	2	331	102	81	17	200
3	110	2	524	53	57	5	330	103	24	14	196
4	13	21	523	54	36	5	326	104	100	5	196
5	67	2	503	55	48	18	323	105	66	20	194
6	27	2	499	56	50	2	320	106	102	24	194
7	49	2	498	57	117	2	320	107	69	24	191
8	144	2	493	58	55	21	319	108	126	6	191
9	10	2	484	59	137	5	317	109	14	5	189
10	22	2	479	60	65	17	314	110	40	17	188
11	133	17	476	61	47	2	313	111	15	20	186
12	80	2	470	62	1	17	311	112	94	17	184
13	88	2	469	63	63	5	311	113	90	18	178
14	51	2	468	64	107	17	308	114	95	5	178
15	139	5	467	65	25	17	304	115	83	18	173
16	45	21	466	66	92	18	304	116	4	18	170
17	37	2	455	67	115	5	301	117	103	20	169
18	71	21	448	68	12	5	298	118	20	5	168
19	127	2	448	69	39	7	296	119	140	18	165
20	86	21	446	70	105	7	295	120	85	17	163
21	42	17	444	71	64	2	291	121	34	18	162
22	8	2	441	72	75	2	289	122	46	7	159
23	120	21	430	73	99	7	285	123	16	18	155
24	141	2	422	74	109	7	282	124	148	20	155
25	106	21	417	75	125	21	279	125	72	5	152
26	17	2	414	76	60	18	276	126	101	24	152
27	82	2	414	77	145	17	273	127	104	7	150
28	98	21	406	78	19	20	267	128	9	17	149
29	87	17	404	79	54	6	263	129	142	20	147
30	11	24	403	80	30	2	262	130	136	7	139
31	114	5	399	81	41	7	252	131	61	18	135
32	59	2	394	82	77	5	252	132	129	6	131
33	76	21	394	83	35	5	248	133	123	1	127
34	5	17	393	84	118	25	248	134	84	18	126
35	70	20	392	85	6	17	247	135	132	24	126
36	74	2	389	86	29	5	246	136	91	20	125
37	96	18	383	87	121	17	246	137	113	5	125
38	119	2	378	88	131	7	243	138	112	18	122
39	135	21	376	89	78	5	235	139	130	24	117
40	31	2	375	90	149	17	235	140	38	18	116
41	26	1	374	91	62	17	233	141	89	7	115
42	128	2	372	92	122	2	233	142	32	2	113
43	18	2	366	93	97	6	226	143	3	24	111
44	2	17	357	94	56	18	220	144	124	18	104
45	7	7	355	95	79	24	218	145	23	24	89
46	44	18	355	96	28	18	216	146	147	6	74
47	33	21	354	97	143	17	213	147	116	6	63
48	93	17	344	98	52	18	207	148	43	20	62
49	108	17	342	99	134	17	205	149	146	6	45
50	68	24	336	100	111	18	202	150	21	24	40

each essay gets a score depending on its rank. For example, the essay on topic 133 contains the most distinct queries and thus obtains 121 points (it is not 150 because 29 essays share the same number of distinct queries and obtain the same score). For the feature "distinct clicks," the essay on topic 133 is only on rank 18 and obtains 77 points. This is done for all features and the scores are summed up per essay; the resulting ranking is shown in Table 4. Remarkably, nine of the top-10 essays were written by author 2, who seems to have worked with high dedication on many essays, whereas authors 6 and 24 seem to have worked with little enthusiasm—even though the authors picked their favorite topic from the remaining ones when starting a new essay.

To identify the most and the least dedicated writers, we simply compute the average for each writer in order to bypass the different numbers of treated topics. It turns out that author 2 indeed belongs to the most dedicated writers with an average score of 403.5 but is slightly outperformed by author 21 with an average of 404.8. Note that author 2 worked on 33 different topics and the range of scores is distributed, whereas author 21 worked on only 12 topics, which all achieved quite high dedication scores. The least dedicated writers in our collection are author 6 and author 20 with an average score of 141.9 and 188.6, respectively. Note that the dedication ranking does not imply any conclusions on the quality of the essay itself but only about the effort that the authors spent for writing. The quality of the essay has to be determined in a separate step—an idea could be to run the essays through text reuse detection software and assign higher quality scores to essays from which the ClueWeb09 sources cannot be really detected anymore, similar to the source-based writing analyses of Sormunen et al. [27]. This could then also be used to confirm previous findings on how effort correlates with the task outcome [31].

4.6 Searching and Writing Styles

In our previous study focusing on the writing process, we found two different writing styles: build-up and boil-down [22]. The first is characterized by a rather continuous lengthening of the essay over the whole period of writing while the second style is characterized by a first quick length growth and subsequent reorganization and shortening. The essay on topic 27 reflects a typical boil-down writing while the essays on the topics 29 and 57 are build-up essays (cf. Figure 2). In our writing style study, we characterized 65 build-up essays, 65 boil-down essays, and 20 that mix both styles by a manual visual inspection [22]. Here, we now compare the writing style (essay length growth) to the search and copy-pasting behavior. The hypothesis is that in build-up essays text passages are copy-pasted in rather regular intervals (and almost immediately adapted to fit into the essay structure) while in boil-down essays most of the background research is hypothesized to happen at the beginning and thus most copy-paste interactions are to be expected at the beginning of working on a task.

As a simple measure of the search behavior, we use the regularity of copy-paste events over the course of the writing process. One could argue that queries are a better search behavior measure but with the copy-paste events we focus on the search and web interactions that actually led to some change in the essay. As for the regularity, we count the number of revisions between each consecutive pair of copy-paste events and compute the observed variance. For example, a 50-revisions essay with paste events in the revisions 10, 22 and 40, would result in the list $\langle 10, 12, 18, 10 \rangle$ (also containing the revisions prior to the first and after the last paste). A low variance in this list means that the paste events are rather equally distributed over the essay revisions, whereas a high variance indicates that a writer pasted very irregularly.

As a measure for the development of essay length, we check whether at least one full word was added or removed for all subsequent revision pairs. If either is the case, a respective counter is increased. Note that for simplicity we do not count how many words have been added or removed; only the trend matters (i.e., how many revisions lengthen the essay vs. how many shorten it). In an example 50-revision essay, this might result in 20 revisions in which content was removed and 30 in which content was added. The essay thus tends to grow, as 60% of the revisions lead to a longer essay. Yet, naturally each of the essays has to grow in total to reach a 5,000-words length. Therefore, a low value like 60% rather is an indication of a boil-down writing style.

Figure 5 shows the plot resulting from the essay length development and the paste regularity for each topic. Different symbols (and colors) indicate different authors, thus revealing trends for each author's writing style. The x-axis ranges from about 50% to almost 100%; the essays more to the right are from the more lazy writers that hardly ever rephrased something they copy-pasted. The two authors 6 and 20 who are isolated from all other authors by reaching

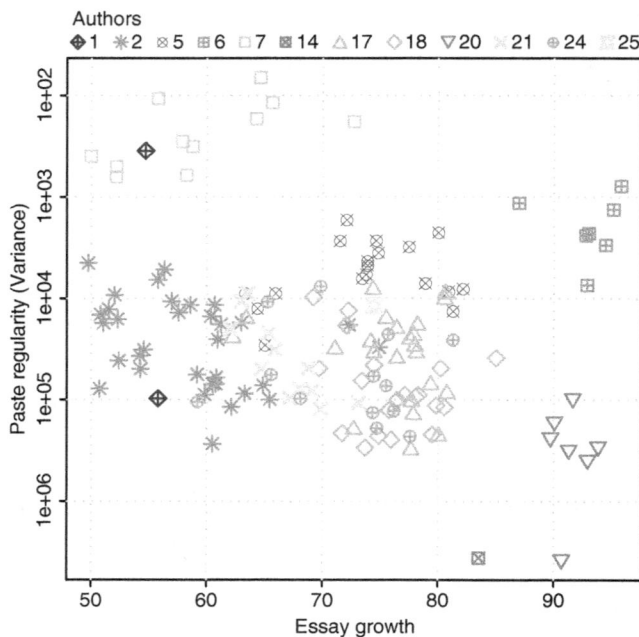

Figure 5: Authors' searching and writing style in form of the essay growth (x-axis, percentage of revisions of an essay that lengthen it) vs. the regularity of copy-pasting content from search results (log-scaled y-axis, variance of the copy-paste revision number differences, low variance = high regularity). Each essay is a data point; essays from the same author typically have similar characteristics.

an essay growth of $\geq 85\%$ also are the least dedicated authors in Section 4.5. Many authors range in a 70% to 85% essay growth showing a build-up pattern in our earlier observations, while most essays with a growth below 70%, here especially those by author 2, are those that show the boil-down pattern. Yet, as can be seen on the y-axis, even a boil-down pattern might come with rather regular paste events (low variance with high regularity is on the top of the y-axis) meaning that some authors boiled down individual fragments rather than all useful passages at once. Interestingly, different authors' essays form clusters in our plot contrasting search behavior with the writing progress (copy-paste regularity vs. essay growth). Knowing to which category a writer belongs can help the search engine to better tailor its results. For instance, later follow-up queries are likely for build-up writers. The search engine could take some time while the author is writing to already prepare appropriate results in a slow search fashion [29].

4.7 Comparison of Working Phases

Finally, we investigate whether the authors work in distinct phases. Do they submit more queries early? Does writing form the major load at the end? Any patterns may inspire ideas to support writers in their respective working phases. In the beginning, a search engine could present not only results for the submitted query but also suggest short-cut queries [4] that helped other users finding relevant documents on the treated topic. While this is helpful to quickly acquire an overview of different aspects of a topic, it might not be desirable in a later phase in which a writer is only interested in specific details or just checking some facts.

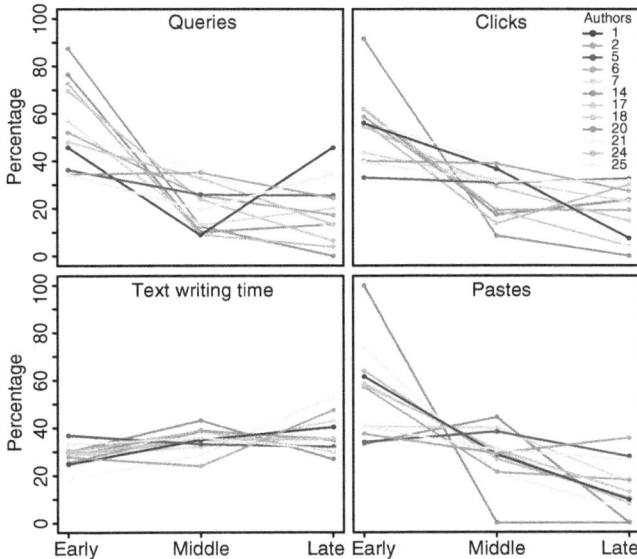

Figure 6: Work load in different working phases for all authors.

For the sake of simplicity, we subdivide each topic into three working phases—early, middle and late—by splitting up the interactions in the actual working time into three parts of equal duration. For each phase, we measure the percentage of queries, clicks, writing and copy-paste interactions that happened in that phase. For example, if 25 queries out of 50 appeared in the very beginning, the query dimension score is 50% for the early phase etc. For each author and each phase, we take the median value over all their essays to "average" the scores. Figure 6 shows the plots for all authors. The general trend is that most queries, clicks and paste interactions happen in the early phases while writing in general seems to happen more in the later phases. This is not too surprising given the fact that most authors wrote essays on topics they were not familiar with and had to search for useful content to first explore the structure of the information space [33]. Still, some authors (and even more essays) show a V-pattern in their query or click load indicating that a large portion of queries also was submitted in the last phase (e.g., authors 1, 7, and 21). Interestingly, these authors did not have a high paste load in the last phase. This indicates that the authors might have checked the essay for possibly missing text passages from previously clicked documents or that they fact-checked some of their content before completion. Interestingly, for most authors the percentages of clicks and pastes over the different phases approximately correlate. At first glance, this might indicate that the authors did no improve their precision (i.e., clicks vs. found relevant content in form of copy-pasting) over the time spent on the topic. However, an in-depth analysis of this issue is left for future work.

5. CONCLUSION AND OUTLOOK

To examine user behavior in exploratory search tasks, we analyze the search interaction logs of authors writing a 5,000-word essay for which we have a fine-grained revision history. We consider our results to constitute one more step towards understanding exploratory search and building an ideal search engine that fulfills the user's needs in

such situations. Since our corpus is freely available and is related to widely used resources like TREC topics and the ClueWeb09 web crawl, replicability is ensured and comparisons can foster research on exploratory search.

In order to analyze the behavior, we propose a visualization scheme that provides a fast and easily graspable overview of all interactions throughout the writing of an essay. Although being informative for any single essay, it is difficult to draw general conclusions about user behavior just from visualizations. To this end, we conduct analyses of our dataset with respect to the search behavior complementing our previous observations on the writing process [22].

As for the querying, we find many writers submitting identical rather general "anchor" queries from time to time while working on an essay. Reasons might be to guide the exploration of the information space, to keep track of the main essay theme, or to bring recently acquired knowledge into line with earlier knowledge structures.

As for the overall search strategy, we identify two types: the *clickers* and the *queriers*. Clickers tend to visit more results and follow long click trails, whereas queriers submit significantly more queries, and often click on only few results. However, both can be very dedicated to the task.

In our analysis of writer dedication, we rank the different essays based on several features. The number of clicks, the overall reading time and the number of copy-pastes are the most discriminating features for writer dedication in our setting. Since we do not have quality assessments for the written essays yet, we did not correlate writer dedication with the quality of the essays. However, contrasting dedication with the analysis of how well automatic text reuse detection systems identify the ClueWeb09 sources of the reused passages could be a promising way in that direction. The underlying hypothesis is that easy-to-detect sources probably were not rewritten that much indicating a lower essay quality. Such writers can be considered rather "lazy" or less dedicated than writers of essays with fewer detected sources.

As for the general search behavior, we find a relationship to the build-up and boil-down writing styles [22]. By a thorough grounding on a machine derivable score for essay growth, we could relate the author types to the regularity of copy-pasting from the search results. The resulting plot shows that authors rather stick to their habits of paste-regularity and writing style over different essays. However, interestingly most authors had differences in their search behavior close to essay completion. For some essays they invoke a rather extensive querying phase at the end (e.g., fact-checking) while for other essays, the same authors submitted all queries way ahead of essay completion. Search engines could leverage that knowledge to support writers with pre-processed search results aimed at supporting fact-checking close to essay completion—a "slow search" way of exploiting the "idle" times when the author is writing. Another idea would be to offer very diverse search results for the first queries of a boil-down writer while build-up writers probably benefit more from more similar search results for their individual queries.

Finally, we also examine different working phases during essay writing and how they influence querying. Although the number of queries alone is a bad predictor for task completion, a general trend is that the number of queries, clicks and pastes decrease over time and the number of writing interactions increases—late fact-checking as an exception.

As for future work, we envision support tools for writers involved in exploratory search tasks as an interesting direction. First steps could be tried along our above described findings (treating build-up and boil-down writers differently, pre-computed fact-checking results for the final phase, etc.). Testing such tools probably then again requires similar studies but our embedding in the TREC environment (topics and the ClueWeb09 corpus) should make comparisons to our findings rather straightforward.

Another interesting direction would be to further analyze the documents the authors used as references and how they were found in the process and to what extent they inspired the final text. Potentially, this kind of analyses can result in better usefulness prediction approaches. Interestingly, on most longer click trails that contain one document the author used as a reference, the authors did find other reference documents, too. These documents not contained in the initial results are good candidates for shortcuts that may be provided to other search engine users in similar situations. A future investigation could also more deeply examine why queriers select their reference documents more carefully than clickers seem to do. It would also be interesting to test the conjecture that authors are not really able to improve their precision in terms of needed queries and clicks to find further reference documents in the course of writing even though having acquired topic knowledge along the process.

References

[1] E. Agichtein, E. Brill, S. Dumais, and R. Ragno. Learning user interaction models for predicting web search result preferences. In *SIGIR 2006*, pp. 3–10.

[2] E. Agichtein, R. White, S. Dumais, and P. Bennet. Search, interrupted: Understanding and predicting search task continuation. In *SIGIR 2012*, pp. 315–324.

[3] J. Arguello. Predicting search task difficulty. In *ECIR 2014*, pp. 88–99.

[4] R. Baraglia, F. Cacheda, V. Carneiro, D. Fernández, V. Formoso, R. Perego, and F. Silvestri. Search shortcuts: a new approach to the recommendation of queries. In *RecSys 2009*, pp. 77–84.

[5] P. Bennett, R. White, W. Chu, S. Dumais, P. Bailey, F. Borisyuk, and X. Cui. Modeling the impact of short- and long-term behavior on search personalization. In *SIGIR 2012*, pp. 185–194.

[6] J. Callan, M. Hoy, C. Yoo, and L. Zhao. The ClueWeb09.

[7] H. Cao, D. Jiang, J. Pei, E. Chen, and H. Li. Towards context-aware search by learning a very large variable length Hidden Markov Model from search logs. In *WWW 2009*, pp. 191–200.

[8] M. De Leeuw and E. De Leeuw. *Read better, read faster*. Penguin Books, 1965.

[9] B. Dervin. From the mind's eye of the user: The sense-making qualitative-quantitative methodology. In *Qual. Res. in Inf. Managm.*, 9:61–84, 1992.

[10] E. Efthimiadis. Query expansion. *ARIST*, 31:121–187, 1996.

[11] Y. Egusa, H. Saito, H. Takaku, H. Terai, M. Miwa, and N. Kando. Using a concept map to evaluate exploratory search. In *IIiX 2010*, , pp. 175–184.

[12] M. Hagen, J. Gomoll, A. Beyer, and B. Stein. From search session detection to search mission detection. In *OAIR 2013*, pp. 85–92.

[13] B. Jansen, A. Spink, and I. Taksa. Research and methodological foundations of transaction log analysis.

In *Handbook of Res. on Web Log Analysis*, pp. 1–16, 2008.

[14] K. Järvelin and P. Ingwersen. Information seeking research needs extension towards tasks and technology. *Information Research*, 10(1), 2004.

[15] M. Kurth. The limits and limitations of transaction log analysis. *Library Hi Tech*, 11(2):98–104, 1993.

[16] J. Liu and N. Belkin. Searching vs. writing: Factors affecting information use task performance. *ASIST*, 49 (1):1–10, 2012.

[17] G. Marchionini. Exploratory search: From finding to understanding. *CACM*, 49(4):41–46, 2006.

[18] H. O'Brien and E. Toms. What is user engagement? A conceptual framework for defining user engagement with technology. *JASIST*, 59(6):938–955, 2008.

[19] H. O'Brien and E. Toms. The development and evaluation of a survey to measure user engagement. *JASIST*, 61(1):50–69, 2010.

[20] U. Ozertem, O. Chapelle, P. Donmez, and E. Velipasaoglu. Learning to suggest: A machine learning framework for ranking query suggestions. In *SIGIR 2012*, pp. 25–34.

[21] M. Potthast, M. Hagen, B. Stein, J. Graßegger, M. Michel, M. Tippmann, and C. Welsch. ChatNoir: A search engine for the ClueWeb09 corpus. In *SIGIR 2012*, p. 1004.

[22] M. Potthast, M. Hagen, M. Völske, and B. Stein. Crowdsourcing interaction logs to understand text reuse from the web. In *ACL 2013*, pp. 1212–1221.

[23] M. Potthast, M. Hagen, M. Völske, and B. Stein. Exploratory search missions for TREC topics. In *EuroHCIR 2013*, pp. 11–14.

[24] Y. Qu and G. Furnas. Model-driven formative evaluation of exploratory search: A study under a sensemaking framework. *IPM*, 44(2):534–555, 2008.

[25] S. Robertson, H Zaragoza, and M. Taylor. Simple BM25 extension to multiple weighted fields. In *CIKM 2004*, pp. 42–49.

[26] D. Russell, M. Stefik, P. Pirolli, and S. Card. The cost structure of sensemaking. In *CHI 1993*, pp. 269–276.

[27] E. Sormunen, J. Heinström, L. Romu, and R. Turunen. A method for the analysis of information use in source-based writing. *Information Research*, 17(4): paper 535, 2012.

[28] B. Stein, T. Gollub, and D. Hoppe. Beyond precision@10: Clustering the long tail of web search results. In *CIKM 2011*, pp. 2141–2144.

[29] J. Teevan, K. Collins-Thompson, R. White, and S. Dumais. Slow search. In *CACM*, 57(8):36–38, 2014.

[30] P. Vakkari. Exploratory searching as conceptual exploration. In *HCIR 2010*, pp. 24–27.

[31] P. Vakkari and S. Huuskonen. Search effort degrades search output but improves task outcome. *JASIST*, 63 (4):657–670, 2012.

[32] R. White and G. Marchionini. Examining the effectiveness of real-time query expansion. *IPM*, 43(3): 685–704, 2007.

[33] R. White and R. Roth. *Exploratory search: Beyond the query-response paradigm*. Morgan & Claypool, 2009.

[34] R. White, B. Kules, S. Drucker, and M. Schraefel. Introduction. In *CACM*, 49(4):36–39, 2006.

[35] R. White, G. Marchionini, and G. Muresan. Evaluating exploratory search systems. *IPM*, 44(2):433–436, 2008.

[36] J. Xu and B. Croft. Improving the effectiveness of information retrieval with local context analysis. *ACM TOIS*, 18(1):79–112, 2000.

You Can Check It Out But It Will Never Leave: Characterising Ebook Borrowing Patterns

Dana McKay
University of Melbourne
Parkville 3010
Australia
dmckay1@student.unimelb.edu.au

George Buchanan
Centre for HCI Design, City University London
Northampton Square
London, EC1V 0HB
+44 20 7040 8469
george.buchanan.1@city.ac.uk

ABSTRACT

What does it mean for a reader to borrow an ebook? Ebook technology means that borrowing can take different forms, for example printing and reading. We do not know, though, which of these options readers actually use. Ebook technology generates logs that allow us to understand ebook borrowing patterns over time, both by individual readers and in aggregate. Despite the ready availability of ebook logs, this area remains under-researched. In this paper we present an exploratory log analysis of ebook borrowing, comparing printing and reading, discovery patterns, single- and multiple-book sessions and identifying specific borrowing patterns.

Keywords

Ebooks; log analysis; reading; information behaviour

1. INTRODUCTION

When a reader borrows a print book from a library, they check it out, and—we assume—read it before returning it. The book is a physical thing, and while it is checked out to one reader cannot be borrowed by another. Similarly individual readers (usually) leave little trace of what they did with borrowed books, though cumulative wear will appear over time. Books are borrowed from shelves, where—in academic libraries at least—they are shelved near books on similar topics. Within library opening hours, readers may sample books in the library for any length of time, even completing a reading. Finally, with the exception of copying for later, books can only be read in one medium—the printed pages they contain.

As Marshall rightly notes, ebooks represent a different proposition [35]. They can have numerous simultaneous users, and never show any signs of wear. Ebook providers typically require readers to take out a loan within a short time of beginning to read, though this process is largely transparent to readers. Ebooks are not shelved at all, and generally only accessible using search: ebook browsing capabilities, especially those for academic ebooks, are relatively poor. Most importantly for this

paper, though, ebook providers can (and often do) record all ebook usage, even down to the page level. This data allows us to study ebook use in a way that would be so obtrusive as to be 'creepy' [35] to do for print books.

Data on ebook use has been leveraged at a basic level, both to allow patron driven acquisition [13] and to compare raw loans between print and ebooks [7; 8]. It has also been used less widely to study how readers triage ebooks [39; 40], and once to study reading behaviour [37]. The capacity for logging, though, has not (to our knowledge) been used to study what it means to borrow an ebook given the technological differences between ebooks and print books outlined above. There is also a dearth of literature on ebook borrowing patterns (outside of a small number of comparisons with print borrowing [8; 29; 42]). In this paper we aim to understand how reading and printing interact in ebook borrowing; how individual readers borrow over time, and what the differences are between sessions where readers borrow a single ebook and sessions where they borrow more than one. By looking at these facets of ebook use we hope to characterise what it means to borrow an ebook.

This paper is organised as follows: Section 2 addresses the background literature, Section 3 outlines our research method. Section 4 compares printing and reading in ebook borrowing, and Section 5 describes the differences between sessions where readers borrow a single ebook, and those where they borrow many. Section 6 discusses these results in view of the literature in the field; finally we draw conclusions and provide avenues for future work in Section 7.

2. BACKGROUND LITERATURE

This paper builds on both the literature on book borrowing (Section 2.1), and the literature on ebook usage (Section 2.2). It also builds on the literature on reading—both ebooks and print books (Sections 2.3 and 2.4 respectively).

2.1 Book Borrowing

There is a long but sparse history of studying print borrowing in libraries. The most common traditional method has been the materials availability survey, where library users are asked whether they found what they were looking for [22]. The advent of online cataloguing allowed more detailed analysis of borrowing, though apart from examining users' search behaviour [11; 26; 61] this was poorly leveraged until recently. One early study based on borrowing logs exists; it found that relative shelf location (and thus browsing) was an strong predictor of borrowing for a few small subject areas, at least [30]. This assertion is supported by a contemporaneous study of the impact of a new online catalogue on reader behaviour, which found that over 50%

CHIIR '16, March 13-17, 2016, Carrboro, NC, USA.
Copyright is held by the owner/author(s). Publication rights licensed to ACM.
ACM 978-1-4503-3751-9/16/03…$15.00.
DOI: http://dx.doi.org/10.1145/2854946.2854970

of users who found one book they had identified in the catalogue on the shelves also borrowed at least one further book [12].

More recent studies of borrowing behaviour have tended to use an observational approach [16; 17; 31; 56] or interviews [48; 53]. These studies have typically investigated how readers find books rather than aiming to understand broader borrowing patterns.

Finally, we have recently used transaction log analysis to demonstrate borrowing patterns more widely. An initial study found that proximal books were more likely than distant books to be borrowed together [41]; this was followed up by a study demonstrating that browsing appears to be a better predictor of borrowing than search, that day of the week affects borrowing rates, and that books are more likely to be borrowed together within classification boundaries than across them [38].

The one finding common to studies of print borrowing is the prevalence and importance of shelf location in borrowing patterns: readers value the opportunity to browse [5; 17; 31; 51], and log analysis demonstrates they leverage it willingly [38; 41; 42]. This is not to say that the shelves are perfect—readers are well aware that books can be checked out or misshelved [5]. Even so, given the dominance of shelves as an influencer in print borrowing, what does this mean for ebooks, where—dependent on one's viewpoint—either there are no shelves, or they are infinitely re-arrangeable? We aim to address this question in this paper.

2.2 Ebook usage

The equivalent studies to the browsing studies above are ebook usage studies. These studies typically have been used to establish that ebooks are used at all, rather than how they are used. In this vein, early studies of ebook usage typically compared ebook circulation with print circulation [8; 29]. These circulation comparisons found that ebooks were used more than equivalent print books in some disciplines—usually tech and science related—but not others. A similar study that looked solely at the use of ebooks found similar discipline effects, and that ebooks were used in a power-law distribution—some were very popular, but popularity tails off exponentially [7].

These studies were followed up by a spate of reader surveys to find out what proportion of users was using ebooks, and—where possible—whether these groups had any identifying characteristics. These studies found a number of things— undergraduates were more likely to prefer ebooks than other users, as were men and those in technical fields [27; 52]. Similar studies asked users what advantages and disadvantages they saw in ebooks [15; 52; 54]; results were fairly consistent. Users appreciated the ability to search within ebook content anytime anywhere access and but were irritated by DRM and usage restrictions and poor annotation capacity.

Finally our own very recent study of ebook and print book use compared borrowing patterns [42]. This study found that ebooks were more likely to be borrowed in single-book transactions than print and that groups were more loosely topic clustered. The total number of unique books borrowed by each user was marginally higher for ebooks than print, suggesting convenience is a factor in book use.

None of these studies address what actually happens during an ebook loan, however, nor whether there are patterns of behaviour with repeated loans. We aim to address this gap in this paper.

2.3 Reading Ebooks

Studies of how people read ebooks can be roughly divided into three groups: usability studies, experimental studies, diary or interview studies of some particular aspect of ebook reading, and log studies.

Usability studies of ebook reading have compared print and screen reading, or focused on ereader technology. Comparisons of print and screen reading initially suggested that screen reading was more difficult than print [10], though this difference has been ameliorated by the introduction of e-ink technology [35]. Usability studies of ereaders have identified a number of issues, including poor navigation and annotation capabilities [47; 50]. Ereaders are still more usable than attempting to read from the screen of a larger device, however [35].

Experimental studies have examined a number of aspects of ebook reading. Berg [4] and Malama [32] both studied navigation within ebooks, and found that readers used table of contents and index frequently, but that they struggled with ebook navigation. Liesaputra et al noted that a realistic book presentation somewhat ameliorates these difficulties [28]. Thayer et al gave readers the choice of print or e-textbooks, and found that print was generally preferred, but that ebooks were more frequently used on the move [59].Takano and colleagues have looked at a range of aspects of ereading in comparison with print (for example [55; 57; 58]), notably document handling and navigation. These studies have consistently found print to be more usable, particularly for navigation. Finally, Mangen compared recall in readers of a print novel and its ebook equivalent, and found almost no difference [33]. The one exception was event order in the story: print readers recalled this better than ebook readers. These studies focus on individual aspects of ereading, however, and do not allow for the long term examination that ebook logging technology affords.

Two studies have used logs to examine ebook selection, though not deep reading [39; 40]. These studies found that triage behaviour looks similar in ebooks to print books, and that cover and table-of-contents are important in book selection. Finally, two studies have used logs to address reading specifically. The first examined navigation during reading, and found significant flicking backwards and forwards and some use of the electronic table of contents [37]. The other dates from 2009 [9], and reports that the typical ebook reading session covers only a handful of pages (usually fewer than 7) in a few minutes.

No study has harnessed the power of ebook logging to examine not just reading, but printing, nor has any study attempted to use logs to characterise user behaviour over time. This paper attempts to address some of these gaps.

2.4 Print Reading

Marshall rightly notes that it is difficult and to study long form print reading [35], however the use of videotape and diary studies have allowed some insight into this area.

Video recordings of reading [36] show that readers move around a lot while reading print, that they flick backwards and forwards within a text regularly, and that they use tables of contents—the latter two have also been seen in ebooks, as noted above.

A diary study of work-related reading notes that there are a number of types of reading, including deep reading, scanning, and fact checking [1]. This work also notes that annotation and navigation are core parts of these activities.

These studies are fairly representative of the studies of print reading, and identify the major problem with studying it: it is simply not possible to do unobtrusively in the way that ebook logs allow. For the first time in history ebook logs allow us to watch readers at work; this paper leverages that capability to further our understanding of academic reading patterns.

3. METHOD

In this section we first describe our dataset, then define the meaning of an ebook loan, and then outline our approach to analysing this data.

3.1 The Dataset

This paper is based on two sets of ebook log data provided by the library at Swinburne University of Technology, a small, research-active Australian university. The datasets are from 2013 and 2015, each from April to July (inclusive); this is core term time in Australia.

The collection's technology and access policy has been stable over two years; hence changes will primarily reflect changes in behaviour, rather than alterations in response to, for example, changes in search interfaces or the reading experience.

The system being used is EBL, an established ebook platform used in many academic libraries. The interface for this platform is shown in Figure 1. The configuration of EBL at Swinburne does not allow for PDF downloads of ebooks. Readers must instead view ebooks online, print them or copy content. The system logs user behaviour anonymously, using a patron identifier that is unique to each user, but cannot be de-anonymised. We can thus track the behaviour of individual readers over time.

Each log entry reflects a single ebook loan. Loans only occur after one of a number of conditions is met. Most commonly, this is because the reader views the book for longer than a set period (ten minutes for books pre-purchased by the library, or five minutes for other books). Other loan conditions include reading or more than 20% of the pages of a book, copying (via cut-and-paste) part of the content of a page, or printing one or more pages. Each log entry records the book, patron identifier and a range of information, including the date and time of the loan, the duration of user activity, the quantity and page numbers of any pages viewed, printed or copied, and other bibliographic information.

Loans are not automatically generated; readers must confirm (by clicking 'yes' in a click through box) that they wish to borrow a book. This confirmation is lightweight—it requires only a single click, and does not have any financial implications for readers.

We cleaned the data prior to analysis; removing 1281 loans that recorded no usage activity, and over 70 loans that were exact duplicates of other loans.

3.2 Our analysis

Our overall methods draw from previous log-based analyses of library and information behaviour, for example [7; 21; 26; 41; 45]. To avoid over-testing, and allow for the evaluation of interaction between factors, we used log-linear analysis—a non-parametric test for population frequencies.

Our first aim was to understand the contrasting role of printing versus online viewing, and the degree to which these were co-occurring actions. A high reliance on print would indicate that ebooks are primarily used as a fast delivery method for paper, whereas a high level of online viewing would be more suggestive of a 'born digital' ebook culture. Different researchers have

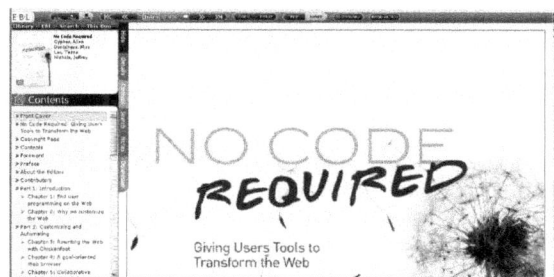

Figure 1. The ebook reading interface. Note the interactive table of contents at left.

argued passionately for opposing viewpoints [20; 43], but we lack data to support either view. We similarly do not know if printing and viewing are of the same material, or of distinct content.

Examining individual page sequences of views can further reveal the degree to which reading is either sequential or non-linear. Again, our current research data is sparse. Though Marshall observes that strictly linear reading is rare even in print [36], non-linear reading is both more common and more random online [37].

As with any novel technology, practise will vary in early adoption. With access to data from two separate years, we could identify changes in behaviour across time. Determining which factors are stable and which are in flux gives us clearer insight into user behaviour.

To provide a foundation for our analysis, we established a global view of the data, counting the number of loans that included every possible combination of printing, viewing and copying to identify the relative frequency of these actions. We grouped loans that occurred within 30 minutes of each other and had a single reader to form co-borrowing sessions; in line with our earlier work [42]. All other loans were singleton loan sessions. For both co-borrowing and singleton loans the frequency of printing and viewing were established. Where a loan included both, we tested for any overlap in the pages used, to determine if these were interconnected or distinct activities.

One property of digital books is the potential for direct copying. As the public data on digital copying is minimal, we tallied the volume of both the number of loans that included copying, and the number of pages copied. The rates of copying in co-borrowing and singleton sessions were counted separately. We also counted the proportion of copying that was accompanied by printing and viewing.

We then embarked on three separate analyses, comparing co-borrowing versus single-book sessions; second and subsequent readings of the same book by individual users; and book-specific patterns across all readers. For each ebook, we measured:

- The total duration of a loan
- The total number of pages viewed, their sequence both in time and in page order, and the number of times each was viewed.
- The total pages printed, and again sequence and frequency.
- The number of pages copied

First, we compared the co-borrowing sessions against single-book sessions to identify any differences in the four measures above.

Previous research on reading has reported that reading of pages is often non-linear, with considerable skipping of pages. For both co-borrowing and singleton loans, we established the span of pages both viewed and printed. These measures were then compared by loan type and year.

Second, we examined renewal (repeat) readings of individual ebooks by single users, again using the four measures above. This would show if renewal readings differed with each renewal. We gathered the profile for the co-borrowings in each sequence, to determine if the earlier loans would vary from the later ones in terms of time, printing and viewing preferences, etc. Again, 20 individual books were analysed by hand.

Third, we aggregated all the sessions for each ebook, and identified which of its pages that were repeatedly used by different readers for printing, viewing and copying. This enabled us to see if different readers used the same ebook in similar ways, and determine commonly accessed material. We sampled the 100 most loaned ebooks and collated the number of times each page was printed or viewed. This was further consolidated into contiguous groups of pages that were used the same number of times. A subset of 20 was manually inspected to identify the content of the pages in terms of the book structure (chapters, front matter) and page content (tables, diagrams etc.).

To conclude the analysis, we finally turned to assess the impact of topic on co-borrowing. We created a further sample set that excluded any book that was loaned fewer than ten times (to minimise data noise). This set allowed us to investigate the impact of (a lack of) physical shelves on borrowing patterns. Our recent work [38; 41; 42] strongly suggests that browsing on physical shelves increases co-borrowing (borrowing more than one book at a time) where books are shelved close together. Topic is a confounding factor in shelf proximity; academic library shelves are organised according to topic. Our recent comparison of ebook and print borrowing has shown that ebook loan clustering around topic occurs, but that it is looser than print clustering [42]. To further understand this phenomenon, we created a virtual shelf of the ebooks available in our collection sorted by Dewey decimal number, then by title (sadly the author metadata needed to replicate library practice was not available). We examined ebook co-borrowings according to their nominal shelf distance to assess the impact of topic (clearly relevant in ebook borrowing) versus browsing, which does not exist for this collection.

4. RESULTS

From the 40708 loans in the two years, 36064 (89%) included viewing of pages, 10170 (25%) included printing, and 4034 (10%) included the copying of content from one or more pages. A small residue of 281 loans (0.7%) recorded only the copying of one or more pages, but no viewing of pages. 1281 loans recorded no activity whatsoever, and these were omitted from these totals.

Our first interest was the relationship between the volume of pages users viewed and printed. For the overall set, there was no significant correlation between the number of pages printed and viewed in a single loan (r=0.06). If we examine only those loans where both printing and viewing took place, there is a moderately significant correlation between the number of printed and viewed pages (r=0.39, df=4541, p<0.001).

There was no significant correlation between the number of pages where content was copied in a loan and the number of pages accessed in any other way.

4.1 Co-borrowing and single- ebook sessions

We separated loans into two sets: singleton loans, where readers accessed only a single book, and co-borrowing sessions, where the readers accessed two or more ebooks each within 30 minutes of finishing the last.

Table 1. Patterns of loans: single and co-borrowing sessions

Loans	2013	2015	Total
Co-borrowing sessions	856	2161	3017
Co-borrowing ebook loans	1864	4898	6812
Single loans	11623	22274	33897
Total loans	13487	27222	40709
Total sessions	12479	24435	36914
Unique users	4945	6752	11697

This basic summary revealed both that the number of both sessions and loans nearly doubled across the two years, and the number of unique users rose by over 35%. While the number of ebooks loaned per session was relatively stable, the number of sessions and loans per user increased.

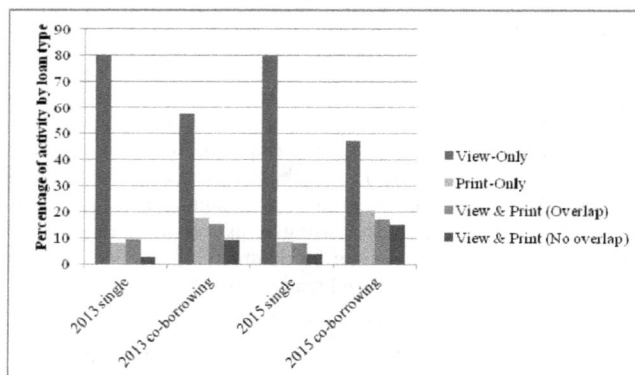

Figure 2: Types of use activity according to loan type

We then examined whether singleton and co-borrowing sessions were associated with different types of user activity. There was a marked difference in the balance of viewing and printing activity (see Figure 2). It is clear from our data that co-borrowing involves a much higher degree of printing than singleton borrowing, behaviour that looks somewhat like checking a number of books out of a library to read later. There is also a slight increase in printing in 2015 over 2013. This data shows that despite the cost of printing to users (where viewing is free), there are clearly times where the goal of ebook activity is to locate and print content from a number of books.

Analysing the data using a log-linear test across the three factors (loan activity, year and session type), produced p<0.0001 (G^2=2853.61, df=13). The strongest interaction was between session type and loan activity, (G^2 = 2577.86, df=4), but all interactions were significant (G^2=157.38, df=4; G^2=126.1, df=1; p<0.0001).

4.2 Copying Content

The collection permits copying of small portions of a book, creating a loan when readers do so. Between 2013 and 2015, while the total volume of copying was similar, the proportion of sessions that included copying fell markedly (see Table 2).

The likelihood of copying was not affected by the temporal length of loans, but the number of pages copied increased with longer reading. Loans under 5 minutes that included any copying had an average of 1.6 pages copied; this rose to 2.4 pages by 10 minutes, and quickly plateaued at around 3 pages.

Table 2. Copying rates and activity

Loan Type	2013		2015	
	Single	Co-Borrow	Single	Co-Borrow
Included Copy	33.9%	23.4%	13.0%	18.1%
Copy only	103	10	143	25
Copy & print	33	5	53	21
Copy & view	1432	185	1730	345

4.3 Session activity and length

The time readers spent on each loan decreased markedly between 2013 and 2015. The average time per book in 2013 was 29m36s for singleton loans, and 19m20s for co-borrowed books. In 2015 this fell to 17m8s and 8m40s respectively. While it may seem counterintuitive that session time shortens with co-borrowing, one explanation for this is the increase in printing with co-borrowing seen in Section 4.1; printing takes less time than reading.

Figure 3 shows the average number of pages accessed and page span (distance from first to last page accessed) for each loan type.

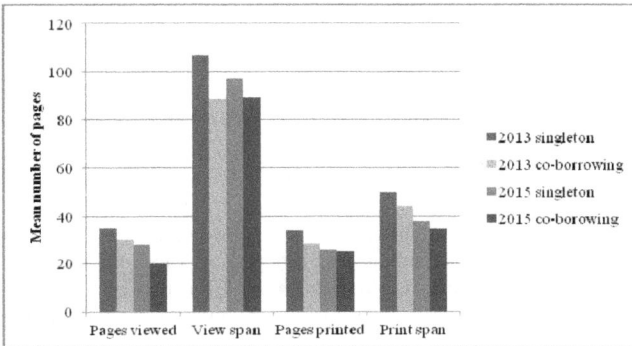

Figure 3: Number of pages viewed and printed by loan type

The most obvious feature of this graph is that the span of pages accessed is much greater than the number of pages accessed— readers are skipping past a great deal of content, in common with earlier work in the area [37]. For printing, the number of skipped pages is smaller than for viewing, this discrepancy is likely to be a result of the viewing interface presenting single-click options for skipping multiple pages.

The next thing to note is that for co-borrowings the span viewed and printed is largely the same in 2015 as 2013, but the number actually accessed dropped substantially: users are examining a smaller number of pages within a similar span.

4.4 Viewed pages per loan

Over 30% of viewing loans started on the first page, however a similar number started beyond the 33rd page. This distribution is, as with so many information behaviours, Zipfian. This distribution also applies to the span of pages covered by each reading session: 33% are shorter than 18 pages, and the same proportion longer than 101. The later in the ebook viewing began, the fewer pages were read, a correlation which is marginally significant ($r^2=-0.2$).

Viewing was primarily linear, but perfectly continuous reading was rare, as has been observed in print and previous studies of ebooks [36; 37]. While there were many jumps of 4-5 pages (mean 4.53 pages for all loans), the mean longest jump per book

was over 50 pages for both years, a result also seen in 2011 [37]. These big leaps explain most of the difference between the span of pages and the smaller number of pages read seen in Figure 3.

We also analysed different activity factors—total page counts, and time per page—by time, initially separating sessions by bands of five minutes.

Loans under 5 minutes (close to 50% of all loans in both years) were less likely to be linear than longer ones; the mean number of consecutive pages viewed was 2.3 in 2013 and 2.55 in 2015.Sessions that exceeded 10 minutes typically included sequences of 8 pages (mean 7.83 pages) and when reading lasted over an hour, runs of 15 pages or more were commonplace.

The average length of time spent on each page echoes this difference. For loans under 5 minutes the mean was a bare 6.4s per page; for loans over 15 minutes, this was 28.75s and beyond an hour, the mean time per page rises to 93.14s. It is quite likely that the latter figure includes a much higher proportion of idle time than with a short viewing time.

Bearing in mind that loans generated by the library only commence after a large number of initial pages, or several minutes, short loans are perhaps surprisingly more similar to triage-like skim reading than might be expected. Conversely long loans begin to look like deep reading.

4.5 Patterns in co-borrowing

We wanted to know whether readers' behaviour changed as they moved through the books borrowed in a co-borrowing sequence. We were particularly interested in the proportion of printing and viewing over time; after all co-borrowing could just be long-form triage or there may be some other pattern. To understand the nature of co-borrowing, we examined both the overall behaviour in borrowing sequences and the behaviour in the final book in particular. Results are shown in Figure 4.

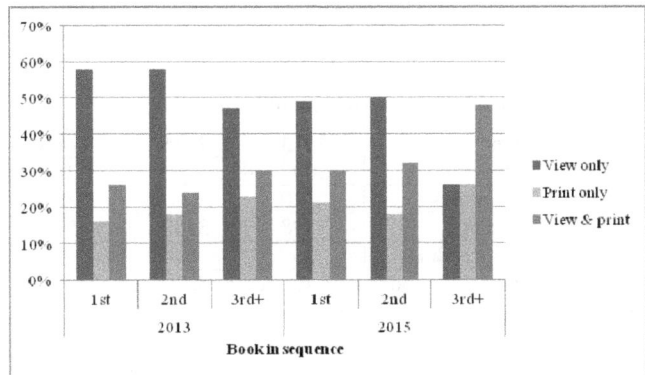

Figure 4: Actions by order of co-borrowing sequence

There is a drop in the rate of view-only loans over time, particularly by the third or greater book in a sequence. This suggests that readers viewing three or more books are either triaging books and printing material for later, or that readers run out of time to read everything they need from the screen. It is also clear that there is more printing generally in 2015 than 2013. . Testing these differences for significance using a log-linear test, produced p<0.0001 ($G^2=354.1$; df=31), confirming that both the difference between years and the fall in view-only loans across a sequence are reliable.

When examining whether readers showed access preferences over the course of a session, we found a marked result. 95% of view-only loans were followed by another view-only loan, where random distribution would have predicted around 60%. For print-only loans, 49% were followed by another print-only loan, 49% by a print-and-view loan, and only 2% by a view-only loan. For loans with both viewing and printing, there was less than a 10% chance of a view-only loan for the next book.

Overall, co-borrowing sessions were either printing- or viewing-focused. Manual inspection of a sample of books revealed that the number of viewed pages was limited in print-focussed sessions. Viewed pages in print session mostly appeared in the front matter, with a small number (3-4 pages) being located in the printed region, usually towards the very beginning. This appears strongly to suggest that viewing can be target-acquisition task, used identify material for printing.

In contrast to session behaviour, most users both printed and viewed ebooks over the course of their usage: The behaviour focus in sessions represents user tasks for those sessions, rather than a preference by individual users for printing or viewing.

4.6 Re-reading ebooks

Given the short loan period of ebooks in this collection (24 hours), the restrictive online reading environment (ebooks are not downloadable) and the possibility that readers were using books for reference materials it seems likely that individual readers would borrow books in this collection more than once. We examined whether this behaviour occurred, and what actions readers took with individual books over a number of re-readings.

It is clear in the data that readers return to books: every page read had a 56% chance of being re-read by the same reader in later sessions. 7825 ebooks were borrowed more than once by a single user; 58.4% of all loans were repeat borrowings (see Table 3). Repeat borrowings account for more loans than co-borrowing sessions.

There was a rise in repeat borrowings in 2015: 56% of all loans being part of multiple readings of an ebook, compared to 37.5% in 2013 ($p<0.0001$, $\chi^2=2511.2$; df=1).

Table 3. Renewed ebook behaviours

Loans	2013	2015	Total
Books re-read	2005	5280	7285
Total re-readings	5170	15874	21044
Two readings	1398	3102	4500
Largest # of re-readings	23	50	n/a

With each reading, the odds of a further reading increased: 41% of 2nd readings were followed by a third, 50% of those by a fourth, and 56.9% of those, in turn, by a fifth. The actions taken during each loan influenced this progression. The likelihood of a print-only loan being the last in a sequence was 13-16% greater than a view-only loan. For example, 56.5% of view-only second loans were the last, 71.3% of print-only loans were, a difference that is significant ($G^2=806.65$; df=28, $p<0.001$ for 3rd to 6th loans). Loans with both printing and viewing fell in the middle of this range. The high rate of termination with printing suggests again that print is being used for long-term reference or record. The number of printed pages, in contrast, was highest in the first loan—28.7 pages; later loans show an average of around 22 pages printed.

Conversely, the ratio of viewing-only loans rose from under 80% to over 90% of later readings. The average number of pages viewed grew from 23.9 pages, up to a plateau of approximately 35 pages (later re-readings varying from 34.8 to 35.3 pages). The

length of sessions also increased, from 15m 28s (first reading) to 25m 55s (5th reading or later). This suggests that later readings are usually in depth, rather than brief access for reference.

Readers showed preferences for interacting with each book: viewing is disproportionately followed by viewing, and printing begets further printing. When examining variations between first and second readings with respect to activity—print-only, view-only, and print-and-view—consistency of access method is statistically significant. ($p<0.0001$, $\chi^2=1381.95$, df=4).

Readers do return to previously borrowed books, and they have behavioural preferences when doing so—viewing begets viewing, and printing begets printing. Final loans, though, show more printing than other loans—possibly readers saving material for later review or reference.

4.7 Co-borrowing sessions & re-read ebooks

Having examined behaviour in co-borrowing sessions and re-read ebooks separately, we then investigated interactions between the two. To recap, c. 15% of books are read in co-borrowing sessions, whereas repeatedly read books account for just under 60% of total loans. When examining only those books that were re-read, 48.6% of all first readings occurred as part of a co-borrowing session. The prevalence of co-borrowing decreases as the number of borrowings goes up: second readings show co-borrowing at around 33%, third readings 30%. Given the overall low rate of co-borrowing, these numbers seem higher than chance would predict.

We tested this relationship with a 3-way log-linear test of year, reading (1st to 3rd) and session type (co-borrowing or single-book), producing $p<0.0001$ ($G^2=780.3$, df=7). All 2-way interactions proved significant. In 2015, co-borrowing was more frequent in the first reading, and dropped off more by the third: suggesting that initial readings are more often part of a "triage" activity, and that if read, focus turns more onto the individual text.

4.8 Ebooks as reference material

Given the prevalence of reading lists as part of the academic experience [33; 51; 59], it seemed likely that we would be able to identify books or parts of books that were accessed in similar ways (reading a specific page or chapter, for example) by groups of readers.

To investigate this likelihood we aggregated the data of all users for each ebook, looking at which pages were printed and viewed. Using a sample of the 100 most frequently borrowed ebooks, we noted the ten most popularly viewed and printed pages in each. These lists had surprisingly little overlap: only 25% of pages were found in each list, even when omitting the first 10 pages of each book from the 'viewed' lists. This disparity was not universal, some books had a strong correlation between viewed and printed material; one such example is *Lessons on the war on terror*, all printing was between pages 92 to 120, and no page outside that range was viewed more than once.

Conversely, nearly 40% of these books had no pages that were both printed and viewed. "The Magic of Mathematics" was one—the most printed span of pages consisted of the first full chapter (p. 3-32), however, the most viewed content consisted of the fore-matter and preface, and the fourth chapter; indeed only two of the pages of the much-printed chapter (printed 51 times) were viewed by any user. Similarly, only four of the 29 pages comprising the second-most printed part of the book were ever viewed. Considering that this book was borrowed 400 times it is striking that there were no views of numerous pages that were regularly printed. In books demonstrating this pattern of use, viewing is typically confined to early pages in the book, or pages that could help readers identify the material they wish to print.

Many books showed printing that repeatedly covered one or more whole chapters. "Extending Thought in Young Children: A Parent - Teacher Partnership" was a popular text in 2015, with over 150 separate loans, 39 of which included printing. While three printed extracts started from other pages, the other thirty-six began at the start of Chapter 5. All but three were for the chapter's full 52 pages; one omitted the last (incomplete) page, one the last five pages, and one covered only the first nine pages. Similarly, "Promoting Emotional and Social Development in Schools: A Practical Guide" had 42 prints in 185 loans, with 37 starting on the same page; and "Alone Together" by Sherry Turkle had every print run begin on the first page of Chapter 10. In some cases— just over 10% of the total prints of whole chapters—two or more contiguous chapters were printed; we coded these multi-chapter prints as a special case of the whole-chapter case.

Another recurring pattern was the printing of self-contained content within a chapter, usually comprising one or two pages. In "Sociology, the basics", patrons printed 11 individual chapters, but 16 of the 29 prints were of single pages. 14 of these were of a page containing a set of guidelines, and the other two contained a list: one of websites, one a checklist. Similarly, "SPSS Survival Guide" had 25 printing loans, of which 12 printed out a three-page set of instructions, and 15 one or more complete chapters (2 printing a table and the immediately following chapter). Printing short excerpts was more commonly found in instructional textbooks, and reference material. In both types of book, pages held distinct content, separate from a longer span of flowing text. While we cannot offer direct proof, it appears plausible that these extracts were printed for reference.

It is clear, then, when we examine behaviour aggregated across users, that ebooks are being used for reference and assigned reading purposes. This represents a digital behaviour that many have argued makes sense [20] or is likely to happen [59], but which has never before been positively shown in usage data.

4.9 Topic versus Keyword Clustering

Browsing at the physical shelves is something readers profess to value [17; 31; 44], and that arguably affects loan patterns. Browsing—or topic clustering—is a more contested issue online. It has proved inferior when compared to keyword search for focussed discovery [14], leading some to claim its possible redundancy. However, others say browsing is both important and under-researched [23; 41]. We analysed the loan histories, taking all co-borrowing sessions : those sessions when two books are checked out of a library at the same time (by the same reader)..

The distance between books in all 3017 co-borrowing sessions was calculated three different ways. First, we counted the nominal distance between co-borrowed books in a Dewey-sorted list of all books; this count represented topic distance. Second, a search was done using the title of the ebook to identify search neighbours. Third, we did pairwise searches of shared keywords between books in each co-borrowing session allowing us to maximise the chances of a search match. Both search calculations were on an index using metadata only, not full text. Co-borrowed books were only considered neighbours by any of these measures if they fell within ten books of each other consistent with our previous work in this area [38]. We then compared search distance and shelf or topic distance as explanations for co-borrowings: as shown in

Table 4, search clearly explains more co-borrowings than topic (even within the low number of co-borrowings explained by any of these methods).

Table 4. Closest Neighbour, Co-Loans

Year	Search Only	Browse Only	Search Closest	Tie	Browse Closest
2013	88	70	78	22	46
2015	196	54	38	96	31

Clearly serendipitous discovery in this collection is low, echoing readers' worries about the rise of ebooks (see Section 2.3).

5. DISCUSSION

Copying was, in all contexts, surprisingly rare. One regularly stated concern of publishers is securing their content sometimes far more than they would be able to with print [20]. Others have complained of the negative impact of rights management on fair use [19] and prior research has demonstrated how DRM can frustrate users [18; 35; 54]. However, the low rate of copying seen by us suggests that literal reuse is in fact low, and DRM may be unnecessarily raising barriers to use.

The trade-off between online viewing and printing is complex. In any co-borrowing session, readers tended to focus either on printing encountered ebooks, or viewing them online. However, there was so sign of a clear division between readers who print and readers who view. Instead, individual readers used both strategies at different times. This reflects other work about individuals' book seeking behaviour, which suggests few users adhere strictly to a single strategy; the majority of users employ mixed approaches over time [42; 51].

It is interesting to note the high proportion of co-borrowings that are either exclusively or mostly print sessions, with little viewing;. This behaviour begins to look like print borrowing— triaging at the shelves and taking the books away for later, more extensive use [5; 17; 31]. While readers who printed did not (and indeed cannot, due to usage restrictions imposed by publishers) print entire books, there is similarly no indication that those who check out print academic books read them from cover to cover.

The regular use of printing indicates that digital books are often used as a delivery mechanism for print reading. This has been previously reported by Marshall [35], but there is no evidence of any shift away from print in 2015. The role of ebooks as print source material is probably going to endure for some time, despite many arguments that a new generation of students read exclusively online, and in spite of the associated individualized cost of printing[1] . Conversely, arguments that only print reading is deep or academic reading also do not hold true, with many readers displaying behaviours that look like deep reading over time in view mode, without printing.

We saw many types of loan activity. Similar to the JISC report on ebook reading [9], we saw many short loans with limited time-on-page; this looks like Adler et al's 'checking' reading or Marshall's triage reading [1; 36]. In contrast, there were a number of loans where the time-on-page was over a minute and a large number of pages read; these loans look very like the 'deep reading' as described by Adler et al. and Marshall. This deep reading could occur over multiple sessions; in contrast with print

---

[1] See http://www.swinburne.edu.au/library/study-spaces-computers/print-copy-scan/ for print costs at Swinburne.

loans which (usually) persist for a number of days, each ebook loan lasts only 24 hours.

We examined two types of sequence: co-borrowing, and renewal-type sequences, where an individual reader returned to a book on a number of occasions. Neither of these are well addressed in the literature. Many quick co-borrowing sessions seem again to be in many cases a form of triage, particularly for print. As just noted, renewals may involve checking, but also longer-term multi-chapter reading, in contrast to the chapter-focussed printing and viewing that occurred in many popular documents. This style of reading, probably driven by reading lists, is absent from Adler's categories, which are built on professional work.

Co-borrowing sessions came in two main forms: viewing-focussed, and print-focussed. There was minimal occurrence of printing in sessions that commenced with viewing, but not printing, a document; conversely there were a number of print-focussed sessions. Previous research has articulated the likely existence of 'print-to-read' strategies [35], and that seems a plausible explanation for the behaviours we observed here. However, elements of our data show other approaches, too. Some printing is of specific, atomic content such as tables or guidelines, which appears to be for reference purposes. Printing is often the last action in a series of loans of the same book, but it frequently has little overlap with the pages viewed online in a book. These facts suggest that this 'final' printing is not simply a method for preserving materials that have been viewed online for later offline reading. Printing and online reading appear to be complementary, rather than competing actions. Most users deploy both strategies in their reading, rather than turning exclusively to one or other.

Our data shows that, in contrast to recent studies of browsing in the physical library [38; 41], search appears a more likely explanation of co-borrowing of ebooks than traditional topic clustering. Indeed, compared to that data on co-borrowing in the physical library, rates of co-borrowing seem surprisingly low. Given that much of a library's reading occurs in the building, the print data almost certainly under-reports co-use. As noted by previous ebook studies [6; 35], the advantages of the print medium could explain part of this gap, the difference in discovery behaviour suggests that finding related ebooks is part of the challenge.

There has been a spate of recent research on how to provide browsing and non-search discovery for books online [23; 49; 60]; our findings underline the importance of this work. Search is not an analogue of, nor a replacement for browsing—not even faceted search [2; 25; 62], which is a search narrowing behaviour rather than a breadth strategy. We have known that search is not enough since the publication of early information seeking behaviour studies [3; 24; 34]. While some Similarly, given the dearth of topical co-borrowing in ebook collections topical similarity seems unlikely to entirely explain the value of browsing the library shelves, though a closer understanding of user cognition and approach is needed. Log-based analyses, as presented here, cannot address that gap in our scientific knowledge.

6. CONCLUSIONS

Logs have always had the potential to reveal new behaviours and validate users' self-reports. This potential for analysis of ebook data was noted in 2010 [35], however studies of ebook logs remain stubbornly limited in both number and scope. The majority of such studies address only that ebook borrowing takes place at all [7-9; 29]; the capacity to study user activity beyond

simple borrowing has only been leveraged in our own earlier work [37; 39; 40] to the best of our knowledge. Readers' use of and attitudes to ebooks have been studied almost entirely using survey methods [15; 27; 46; 52] and experimental approaches [28; 32] limiting our capacity for understanding actual ebook use.

Our data reveals a range of user behaviours. Some of these behaviours, such as apparent deep reading and reference use, mimic print borrowing (in many cases to the point that readers are using ebooks as a print delivery service). Conversely some behaviours—such as the preponderance of singleton loans, and the heavy reliance of co-borrowing on search—appear to confirm the stated reservations readers have about ebooks, such as the loss of browsing and serendipitous discovery. 'Born digital' activities such as text copying are seen only on a limited basis, despite users claiming to value them. This means that born digital responses such as DRM are likely unduly heavy handed.

Overall, we now know that ebook borrowing is increasing in popularity, and includes both printing and viewing actions. Printing tends to involve a smaller proportion of each book than viewing; this is likely due to the interface support (or lack thereof) for each action. Similarly books that are borrowed together are more likely to share keywords than a Dewey classification; interface support for topic browsing in this collection is limited. Individual readers employ both printing and viewing in their interactions with ebooks, putting paid to both the argument that print is obsolete and that electronic reading simply doesn't happen—even individuals are not so strict about their preferences. Readers return regularly to books they have previously used, either examining new content and reading further, or returning to the same content for reference purposes. Some books are clearly being used as assigned reading, with the majority of content remaining untouched in favour of single pages or chapters. In summary, our analysis has revealed some facets of ebook use we might have suspected, some that mimic what we know about print use, some that are born digital, and some that are entirely surprising.

We have only grazed the tip of the iceberg with this analysis, however; the logs give us the capability to, for example, explore the impact of interface changes, to understand the relative value to users of different classification schemes, and to follow the behaviour of individual readers and books over much longer than a semester, to name a few. These and other interesting challenges remain future work.

7. ACKNOWLEDGMENTS

The authors thank Kim Tairi, Tony Davies and Justin Kelly at Swinburne University of Technology for access to the data that forms the basis of this paper.

During the writing of this paper, one of the authors said goodbye to Satchmo, one of the best cats who ever lived. They would like to thank him for 16 years of companionship, and dedicate this paper to his memory.

8. REFERENCES

[1] Adler, A., Gujar, A., Harrison, B.L., O'Hara, K., and Sellen, A., 1998. A diary study of work-related reading: design implications for digital reading devices. In *Proc. CHI 98* (Los Angeles, California, United States, 1998), ACM Press, 241-248. DOI= http://dx.doi.org/10.1145/274644.274679.

[2] Ballard, T. and Blaine, A., 2011. User search-limiting behavior in online catalogs: Comparing classic catalog use to search behavior in next-generation catalogs. *New Library World 112*, 5, 261-273.

[3] Bates, M.J., 2002. Toward an integrated model of information seeking and searching. *The New Review of Information Behaviour Research 3*, 1-15.

[4] Berg, S.A., Hoffmann, K., and Dawson, D., 2010. Not on the Same Page: Undergraduates' Information Retrieval in Electronic and Print Books. *J Acad Libr 36*, 6, 518-525. DOI= http://dx.doi.org/10.1016/j.acalib.2010.08.008.

[5] Blandford, A., Rimmer, J., and Warwick, C., 2006. Experiences of the Library in the Digital Age. In *Proc. CCCDT 06* (Tavros, Greece, 2006), Foundation of the Hellenic World.

[6] Brown, L., 2009. *Ebooks and the academic library: their usage and effect*, Masters Thesis, Aberystwyth University.

[7] Christianson, M., 2005. Patterns of use of electronic books. *Libr Collect Acquis 29*, 4, 351-363. DOI= http://dx.doi.org/10.1080/14649055.2005.10766084.

[8] Christianson, M. and Aucoin, M., 2005. Electronic or print books: Which are used? *Libr Collect Acquis 29*, 1, 71-81. DOI= http://dx.doi.org/10.1080/14649055.2005.10766034.

[9] CIBER, 2009. *Scholarly e-books usage and information seeking behaviour: a deep log analysis of MyiLibrary*.

[10] Dillon, A., 1992. Reading from paper versus screens: A critical review of the empirical literature. *Ergonomics 35*, 10, 1297-1326. DOI= http://dx.doi.org/10.1080/00140139208967394.

[11] Hancock-Beaulieu, M., 1993. A comparative transaction log analysis of browsing and search formulation in online catalogues. *Program: electronic library and information systems 27*, 3, 269-280. DOI= http://dx.doi.org/10.1108/eb047145.

[12] Hancock-Beaulieu, M., 1993. Evaluating the impact of an online library catalogue on subject searching at the catalogue and at the shelves. *J Doc 46*, 4, 318-338. DOI= http://dx.doi.org/10.1108/eb026863.

[13] Hardy, G. and Davies, T., 2007. Letting the patrons choose: using EBL as a method for unmediated acquisition of ebook materials. In (Sydney, Australia, 2007), ALIA.

[14] Hearst, M.A. and Pedersen, J.O., 1996. Reexamining the cluster hypothesis: scatter/gather on retrieval results. In *Proc. SIGIR 96* (Zurich, Switzerland, 1996), ACM, 76-84. DOI= http://dx.doi.org/10.1145/243199.243216.

[15] Hernon, P., Hopper, R., Leach, M.R., Saunders, L.L., and Zhang, J., 2007. E-book Use by Students: Undergraduates in Economics, Literature, and Nursing. *J Acad Libr 33*, 1, 3-13. DOI= http://dx.doi.org/10.1016/j.acalib.2006.08.005.

[16] Hinze, A., Alqurashi, H., Vanderschantz, N., Timpany, C., and Alzahrani, S., 2014. Social Information Behaviour in Physical Libraries: Implications for the design of digital libraries. In *Proc. DL 14* (2014), IEEE, 107-116. DOI= http://dx.doi.org/10.1109/JCDL.2014.6970156.

[17] Hinze, A., McKay, D., Vanderschantz, N., Timpany, C., and Cunningham, S.J., 2012. Book selection behavior in the physical library: implications for ebook collections. In *Proc. JCDL '12* (Washington, DC, USA, 2012), ACM, 305-314. DOI= http://dx.doi.org/10.1145/2232817.2232874.

[18] Holt, K., 2010. E-book Sales Statistics from BISG Survey. In *Publishing Perspectives*.

[19] Houghton, S., 2011. Ebook Users' Bill of Rights. In *Librarian in Black*, San Rafael, CA.

[20] Hull, R. and Lennie, M., 2010. Why E-Textbooks Just Make Sense: An Academic and a Literary Agent Explain In *Publisher's Weekly Soapbox* PWxyz, New York NY.

[21] Jones, S., Cunningham, S.J., and McNab, R., 1998. An Analysis of Usage of a Digital Library. In *Proc. ECDL 98* (Heraklion, Crete, 1998), Springer, 261-277.

[22] Kantor, P.B., 1976. Availability analysis. *JASIST 27*, 5, 311-319. DOI= http://dx.doi.org/10.1002/asi.4630270507.

[23] Kleiner, E., Rädle, R., and Reiterer, H., 2013. Blended shelf: reality-based presentation and exploration of library collections. In *Proc. CHI 13* (Paris, France, 2013), ACM, 577-582. DOI= http://dx.doi.org/10.1145/2468356.2468458.

[24] Kuhlthau, C.C., 1999. Inside the Search Process: Information Seeking from the User's Perspective. *JASIST 42*, 5, 361-371. DOI= http://dx.doi.org/10.1002/(SICI)1097-4571(199106)42:5<361::AID-ASI6>3.0.CO;2-#.

[25] Kules, B., Capra, R., Banta, M., and Sierra, T., 2009. What do exploratory searchers look at in a faceted search interface? In *Proc. JCDL 09* (Austin, TX, USA, 2009), ACM, 313-322. DOI= http://dx.doi.org/10.1145/1555400.1555452.

[26] Lau, E.P. and Goh, D.H.-L., 2006. In search of query patterns: A case study of a university OPAC. *Inform Process Manag 42*, 5, 1316-1329. DOI= http://dx.doi.org/10.1016/j.ipm.2006.02.003.

[27] Li, C., Poe, F., Potter, M., Quigley, B., and Wilson, J., 2011. *UC Libraries Academic e-Book Usage Survey*. University of California, Springer, California Digital Libraries.

[28] Liesaputra, V. and Witten, I.H., 2008. Seeking information in realistic books: a user study. In *Proc. JCDL 08* (Pittsburgh PA, 2008), ACM, 29-38. DOI= http://dx.doi.org/10.1145/1378889.1378896.

[29] Littman, J. and Connaway, L.S., 2004. A Circulation Analysis of Print Books and E-Books in an Academic Research Library. *Libr Resour Tech Serv 48*, 256-262.

[30] Losee, R.M., 1993. The relative shelf location of circulated books: A study of classification, users, and browsing. *Libr Resour Tech Serv 37*, 2, 197-209.

[31] Makri, S., Blandford, A., Gow, J., Rimmer, J., Warwick, C., and Buchanan, G., 2007. A library or just another information resource? A case study of users' mental models of traditional and digital libraries. *JASIST 58*, 3, 433-445. DOI= http://dx.doi.org/10.1002/asi.20510.

[32] Malama, C., Landoni, M., and Wilson, R., 2004. Fiction Electronic Books: A Usability Study. In *Proc. ECDL 04* (2004), Springer Berlin / Heidelberg, 69-79. DOI= http://dx.doi.org/10.1007/978-3-540-30230-8_7.

[33] Mangen, A. and Kuiken, D., 2014. Lost in an iPad: Narrative engagement on paper and tablet. *Scientific Study of Literature 4*, 2 (//), 150-177. DOI= http://dx.doi.org/10.1075/ssol.4.2.02man.

[34] Marchionini, G., Dwiggins, S., Katz, A., and Lin, X., 1993. Information Seeking in Full-Text End-User-Oriented Search Systems: The Roles of Domain and Search Expertise. *Libr Inform Sci Res 15*, 1, 35-69.

[35] Marshall, C.C., 2010. *Reading and Writing the Electronic Book*. Morgan & Claypool, Chapel Hill, NC USA.

[36] Marshall, C.C. and Bly, S., 2005. Turning the page on navigation. In *Proc. JCDL 05* (Denver, CO, USA, 2005), ACM, 225-234. DOI= http://dx.doi.org/10.1145/1065385.1065438.

[37] McKay, D., 2011. A jump to the left (and then a step to the right): reading practices within academic ebooks. In *Proc. OzCHI 11* (Canberra, Australia, 2011), ACM, 202-210. DOI= http://dx.doi.org/10.1145/2071536.2071569.

[38] McKay, D., Buchanan, G., and Chang, S., 2015. Tyranny of Distance: Understanding Academic Library Browsing by Refining the Neighbour Effect. In *Proc. TPDL 15* (Poznan, Poland, 2015), Springer, 280-294. DOI= http://dx.doi.org/10.1007/978-3-319-24592-8_21.

[39] McKay, D., Buchanan, G., Vanderschantz, N., Timpany, C., Cunningham, S.J., and Hinze, A., 2012. Judging a book by its cover: interface elements that affect reader selection of ebooks. In *Proc. OzCHI 12* (Melbourne, Australia, 2012), ACM, 381-390. DOI= http://dx.doi.org/10.1145/2414536.2414597.

[40] McKay, D., Hinze, A., Heese, R., Vanderschantz, N., Timpany, C., and Cunningham, S.J., 2012. An Exploration of ebook Selection Behavior in Academic Library Collections. In *Proc. TPDL '12* (Paphos, Cyprus, 2012), Springer, 13-24. DOI= http://dx.doi.org/10.1007/978-3-642-33290-6_2.

[41] McKay, D., Smith, W., and Chang, S., 2014. Lend me some sugar: Borrowing rates of neighbouring books as evidence for browsing. In *Proc. DL 2014* (2014), 145-154. DOI= http://dx.doi.org/10.1109/JCDL.2014.6970161.

[42] McKay, D., Smith, W., and Chang, S., 2015. Down the Superhighway in a Single Tome: Examining the Impact of Book Format on Borrowing Interactions. In *Proc. OzCHI 15* (Parkville, VIC, Australia, 2015), ACM, 517-525. DOI= http://dx.doi.org/10.1145/2838739.2838766.

[43] Megarrity, L., 2010. Books Matter: The Place of Traditional Books in Tomorrow's Library. *ALJ 59*, 1/2, 6-11.

[44] Mikkonen, A. and Vakkari, P., 2012. Readers' search strategies for accessing books in public libraries. In (Nijmegen, The Netherlands, 2012), ACM, 214-223. DOI= http://dx.doi.org/10.1145/2362724.2362760.

[45] Nicholas, D., Huntington, P., Jamali, H.R., and Tenopir, C., 2006. Finding Information in (Very Large) Digital Libraries: A Deep Log Approach to Determining Differences in Use According to Method of Access. *J Acad Libr 32*, 2, 119-126. DOI= http://dx.doi.org/10.1016/j.acalib.2005.12.005.

[46] Nicholas, D., Rowlands, I., and Jamali, H.R., 2010. E-textbook use, information seeking behaviour and its impact: Case study business and management. *J Inf Sci 36*, 2 (April 1, 2010), 263-280. DOI= http://dx.doi.org/10.1177/0165551510363660.

[47] O'Hara, K. and Sellen, A., 1997. A comparison of reading paper and on-line documents. In *Proc. CHI 97* (Atlanta, Georgia, United States, 1997), ACM. DOI= http://dx.doi.org/10.1145/258549.258787.

[48] Ooi, K., 2008. *How Adult Fiction Readers Select Fiction Books in Public Libraries: A Study of Information Seeking in Context*, Masters Thesis, Victoria University of Wellington.

[49] Pearce, J. and Chang, S., 2014. Exploration without Keywords: The Bookfish Case. In *Proc. OzCHI 2014* (Sydney, Australia, 2014), ACM, 76-79. DOI= http://dx.doi.org/10.1145/2686612.2686639.

[50] Pearson, J., Buchanan, G., and Thimbleby, H., 2010. HCI design principles for ereaders. In *Proc. Booksonline '10* (Toronto, ON, Canada, 2010), ACM. DOI= http://dx.doi.org/10.1145/1871854.1871860.

[51] Rowlands, I. and Nicholas, D., 2008. Understanding Information Behaviour: How Do Students and Faculty Find Books? *J Acad Libr 34*, 1 (1//), 3-15. DOI= http://dx.doi.org/10.1016/j.acalib.2007.11.005.

[52] Rowlands, I., Nicholas, D., Jamali, H.R., and Huntington, P., 2007. What do faculty and students really think about e-books? *Aslib Proceedings 59*, 6, 489-511. DOI= http://dx.doi.org/10.1108/00012530710839588.

[53] Saarinen, K. and Vakkari, P., 2013. A sign of a good book: readers' methods of accessing fiction in the public library. *J Doc. 69*, 5, 736-754. DOI= http://dx.doi.org/10.1108/JD-04-2012-0041.

[54] Shelburne, W.A., 2009. E-book usage in an academic library: User attitudes and behaviors. *Libr Collect Acquis 33*, 2-3, 59-72.

[55] Shibata, H. and Takano, K., 2014. Reading from paper versus reading from a touch-based tablet device in proofreading. In *Proc. DL 14* (London, United Kingdom, 2014), IEEE Press, 433-434.

[56] Stelmaszewska, H. and Blandford, A., 2004. From physical to digital: a case study of computer scientists' behaviour in physical libraries. *IJDL 4*, 2, 82-92. DOI= http://dx.doi.org/10.1007/s00799-003-0072-6.

[57] Takano, K., Shibata, H., and Omura, K., 2015. Effects of paper on cross-reference reading for multiple documents: Comparison of reading performances and processes between paper and computer displays. In *Proc. OzCHI '15* (Parkville, VIC, Australia, 2015), ACM, 497-505. DOI= http://dx.doi.org/10.1145/2838739.2838745.

[58] Takano, K., Shibata, H., Omura, K., Ichino, J., Hashiyama, T., and Tano, S.i., 2012. Do tablets really support discussion?: comparison between paper, tablet, and laptop PC used as discussion tools. In *Proc. OzCHI '12* (Melbourne, Australia, 2012), ACM, 562-571. DOI= http://dx.doi.org/10.1145/2414536.2414623.

[59] Thayer, A., Lee, C.P., Hwang, L.H., Sales, H., Sen, P., and Dalal, N., 2011. The imposition and superimposition of digital reading technology: the academic potential of e-readers. In *Proc. CHI 11* (Vancouver, BC, Canada, 2011), ACM. DOI= http://dx.doi.org/10.1145/1978942.1979375.

[60] Thudt, A., Hinrichs, U., and Carpendale, S., 2012. The bohemian bookshelf: supporting serendipitous book discoveries through information visualization. In *Proc. CHI 12* (Austin, Texas, USA, 2012), ACM, 1461-1470. DOI= http://dx.doi.org/10.1145/2207676.2208607.

[61] Wallace, P.M., 1993. How do patrons search the online catalog when no one's looking? Transaction log analysis and implications for bibliographic instruction and system design. *RQ 33*, 2, 239-253.

[62] Yee, K.-P., Swearingen, K., Li, K., and Hearst, M., 2003. Faceted metadata for image search and browsing. In *Proc. CHI 03* (Ft. Lauderdale, Florida, USA, 2003), ACM, 401-408. DOI= http://dx.doi.org/10.1145/642611.642681.

Interactive Topic Modeling for aiding Qualitative Content Analysis

Aneesha Bakharia
Queensland University of
Technology
Brisbane, Australia
aneesha.bakharia@gmail.com

Peter Bruza
Queensland University of
Technology
Brisbane, Australia
p.bruza@qut.edu.au

Jim Watters
Queensland University of
Technology
Brisbane, Australia
j.watters@qut.edu.au

Bhuva Narayan
University of Technology
Sydney
Sydney, Australia
bhuva.narayan@uts.edu.au

Laurianne Sitbon
Queensland University of
Technology
Brisbane, Australia
laurianne.sitbon@qut.edu.au

ABSTRACT

Topic Modeling algorithms are rarely used to support the qualitative content analysis process. The main contributing factors for the lack of mainstream adoption can be attributed to the perception that Topic Modeling produces topics of poor quality and that content analysts do not trust the derived topics because they are unable to supply domain knowledge and interact with the algorithm. In this paper, interactive Topic Modeling algorithms namely Dirichlet-Forrest Latent Dirichlet Allocation and Penalised Non-negative Matrix Factorisation, are evaluated with respect to their ability to aid qualitative content analysis. More specifically, the relationship between interactivity, interpretation, topic coherence and trust in interactive content analysis is examined. The findings indicate that providing content analysts with the ability to interact with Topic Modeling algorithms produces topics that are directly related to their research questions. However, a number of improvements to these algorithms were also identified which have the potential to influence future algorithm development to better meet the requirements of qualitative content analysts.

Keywords

Topic Modeling; Content Analysis; Latent Dirichlet Allocation; Non-negative Matrix Factorisation

1. INTRODUCTION

Krippendorff [10] describes content analysis as a "careful, detailed, systematic examination and interpretation of a body of material to identify patterns, themes, biases and meanings". Content analysis is an important inference technique used within qualitative research methodologies. Ad-

CHIIR '16, March 13-17, 2016, Carrboro, NC, USA

© 2016 ACM. ISBN 978-1-4503-3751-9/16/03. . . $15.00

DOI: http://dx.doi.org/10.1145/2854946.2854960

vanced computational techniques are rarely used as qualitative content analysis aids. More specifically, there has been a lack of mainstream adoption of Topic Modeling algorithms by qualitative researchers even though these algorithms are capable of accurately finding latent topics (themes) within document collections [8]. Most qualitative researchers still prefer to conduct their analysis manually or with the aid of data management and tagging software such as Atlas.ti [12]. In recent years however, with the increase in textual data emerging from social media platforms, it is impossible for a single researcher or even a team of researchers to perform manual content analysis. The need to address the issues that have affected the mainstream adoption of computational techniques for qualitative content is becoming imperative. The research presented in this paper aims to review the issues affecting the adoption of computational techniques for content analysis and then evaluate the extent to which recently proposed interactive topic modeling algorithms meet the needs of qualitative content analysts.

The main reasons for the lack of mainstream adoption and user acceptance relates to the researchers ability to trust the algorithm [11]. Researchers perceive the topics generated by a Topic Modeling algorithm to be of poor quality or lose confidence in the algorithm when topics of varying quality are produced (i.e., topics that are made up of a mix of unrelated words) [11, 13] and when topics do not relate to the researchers research questions. In many instances an algorithm may derive statistically valid topics, but these topics may be of no relevance to the research questions the analyst is seeking to answer [10]. Researchers don't trust algorithms that they are unable to interact with. Denzin and Lincoln [7] describe interactivity in terms of the support for situated and contextualized analysis from an analyst's perspective. Interactivity is seen as a means by which a content analyst can provide domain knowledge specifically related to the research question that the analyst is seeking to answer. When interactivity is viewed in this way, the interactive use of a Topic Modeling algorithm would entail reviewing the derived topics, supplying additional domain knowledge as required and repeating the process. The lack of trust in algorithms means that researchers do not believe that credible research findings can be obtained by using Topic Modeling algorithms as an aid to content analysis. Semantic validity is important in establishing credibility. Semantic validity is the degree to which textual statements (document, paragraphs, text segments) correspond to the topics that they have been derived by the algorithm.

This paper investigates the interactive use of Topic Modeling algorithms for aiding content analysis. The research questions are:

- **Can content analysts use interactive Topic Modeling algorithms to include domain knowledge and improve the semantic validity of the topics produced in relation to their research?**

- **How do topic coherence (i.e., quality), interpretation and interactivity relate to a content analysts perception of trust?**

2. INTERACTIVE TOPIC MODELING FOR CONTENT ANALYSIS

Topic Modeling algorithms, such as Non-negative Matrix Factorisation (NMF) [14] and Latent Dirichlet Allocation (LDA) [5] have properties that are ideally suited to the task of grouping similar documents or shorter textual responses together. Both algorithms are able to simultaneously group words and documents into topics (also known as themes or clusters) and allow documents to be assigned to more than one topic. A number of extensions to NMF and LDA that support interactivity have also been proposed.

Although NMF and LDA are motivated from different mathematical perspectives, NMF from linear algebra and LDA from probabilistic graphical models, both algorithms have properties that make them applicable to support the inductive content analysis process. Both NMF and LDA are unsupervised machine learning algorithms and are therefore suitable aids for inductive content analysis [9]. Directed content analysis is not addressed in this paper as supervised machine learning algorithms are not evaluated.

NMF and LDA produce the latent topics that are present in a document collection. The output of both algorithms can be interpreted as a network that links documents to topics and topics to words. The link values are only positive. The topics derived from NMF and LDA can easily be interpreted and this will essentially allow content analysts to gather supporting evidence for the existence of a topic.

Various extensions also exist that facilitate the addition of domain knowledge by allowing users to provide information about documents that should be grouped together in the same topic. These variants are examples of semi-supervised algorithms and support the addition of domain knowledge via constraints [4]. These algorithms have the potential to meet the interactivity requirements of qualitative content analysts.

3. SELECTION OF INTERACTIVE TOPIC MODELING ALGORITHMS

Interactive Topic Modeling algorithms are beneficial as qualitative content analysis aids because the algorithms are able to uncover latent topics (themes) that exist in a corpus and are also able to be directed by domain knowledge provided by the content analyst to discover new topics. There are two main types of interactive Topic Modeling algorithms, namely variants of NMF and LDA. In the previous section,

it was illustrated that both NMF and LDA are able to structurally (i.e., in terms of mapping topics to documents and topics to words in a corpus) produce similar output however both of the algorithms are motivated from a different mathematical basis. NMF is inspired by an auto-associative neural network and uses linear algebra while LDA is a probabilistic graphical model. In this paper, comparable interactive variants of NMF and LDA will be evaluated to gauge whether the mathematical underpinning of the algorithm affects the quality (i.e., topic cohesion) of derived latent topics and whether the way interactivity is incorporated into the algorithm affects semantic validity and the ability for qualitative content analysts to address their research questions.

Interactivity within Topic Modeling algorithms is defined by a set of rules that must be provided to the algorithms. The main types of rules are specified in the form of must-link and cannot-link constraints which emerged from early research into semi-supervised clustering [15, 4]. Most interactive variants of NMF and LDA use a combination of must-link and cannot-link constraints to create more complex rules. Rules that were deemed essential within the context of qualitative content analysis were:

Topic Creation Allowing the analyst to provide a list of seed words for a topic.

Topic Merging Allowing the analyst to provide a list of words from 2 derived topics with the aim of combining the topics. Uses a must-link rule between each set of words.

Topic Splitting Allowing the analyst to provide 2 sets of words that occur in a single topic with the aim of splitting the topic into 2 topics. Uses a must-link rule for words that must appear together and a cannot-link between the sets of words that must not appear together.

Various NMF and LDA interactive variants were reviewed for support of the 3 key types of rules. The algorithms included, Graph Regularised Non-negative Matrix Factorisation (GNMF) [6], Penalised NMF (PNMF) [16], Dirichlet Forest LDA (DF-LDA) [1] and Logic-LDA [2]. PNMF and DF-LDA were found to be similar in terms of rule support and selected for evaluation. Logic-LDA allowed the addition of complex rules based on first order logic but was not selected because there was no equivalent functionality available in an NMF variant.

4. STUDY DESIGN

The study was designed as a between-subjects experiment in order to compare the results for the 2 selected interactive Topic Modeling algorithms namely, PNMF and DF-LDF. The aim of the study was to determine whether allowing content analysts to incorporate domain knowledge via an iterative and interactive process, improved the semantic validity of the derived topics in relation to the analysts research questions. Twenty participants were split into 2 groups of 10 participants, with each group assigned to evaluate a single interactive Topic Modeling algorithm (i.e., either PNMF or DF-LDA). Participants were not made aware of which algorithm they were assigned to evaluate. Both groups of participants performed their analysis on the same corpus (described in Section 4.1) and were provided with a set of research questions (described in Section 4.3).

Participants were given access to a purpose built web-based tool that provided a user interface for participants to review derived topics and provide domain knowledge (via the specification of create, merge and split rules). Each participant had to:

1. Read an introduction to the corpus and was provided with a set of research questions

2. Read a step-by-step tutorial on using the interface to add domain specific rules to create, merge and split topics

3. Specify the number of topics to be generated

4. Review the generated topics

5. Add create, merge and split rules; and annotate the rules to specify the related research question

6. Review, rate and match topics to research questions

7. Repeat steps 5-6 until research questions are answered

8. Complete a questionnaire with sections on interactivity, interpretation, topic coherence and trust

Steps 1 - 8 and all participant entered data was tracked as part of the experiment. This allowed data on the number of iterations and type of manipulations to be collated for further analysis. After settling on the rules that needed to be added and the number of topics to be generated, participants were required to rate the derived topics and link them to a research question and specified rule. At the completion of the activity, participants were also required to complete a questionnaire.

4.1 Corpus Selection

The corpus consisted of 100 free text responses to a survey question from a larger study on First Year Mathematics and Science Teacher Professional Development. The survey question was: "What types of support does your school provide to beginning science or mathematics teachers?". The length of responses varied from between one line to four lines of text. The corpus was chosen because it contained a good spread of respondents views, had been used in a previous study involving manual content analysis and shown to contain complex topics based upon word relationships (e.g., sets or synonyms) [3].

4.2 Participant Recruitment

Due to the domain specific nature of the the corpus (i.e., professional development for beginning mathematics teachers), participants were recruited that had a background in education and experience in conducting qualitative content analysis either at a Masters or Doctoral level. A total of twenty four (24) participants accessed the interactive web-based tool with 4 participants unable to complete all the required tasks as specified in steps 1-8 in Section 4. Group A consisted of 3 post-graduate masters students, 4 participants with a masters degree and 3 participants with a PhD. Group B consisted of 5 post-graduate masters students, 3 participants with a masters degree and 2 participants with a PhD. Participants were assigned to either Group A or Group B based upon their level of expertise in a round robin manner.

4.3 Research Questions for Participants

All participants were provided with 3 research questions that they were required to address in relation to the provided corpus while using the interactive variants of NMF and LDA as content analysis aids. The research questions provided to participants were determined from the review of topics found inductively by manual coders in a prior research study [3]. The following research questions were provided to participants in Group A and Group B:

Research Question 1 (RQ1)
What are the different forms of support that are provided to beginning teachers?

Research Question 2 (RQ2)
Is collegial support in terms of peer mentoring and buddying mentioned?

Research Question 3 (RQ3)
Is Workload Balance (i.e., efforts to lighten teaching load for beginning teachers) or release time for professional development mentioned?

4.4 Interface Design

Both the PNMF and DF-LDA algorithms are executed from the command line with a custom text file format used to specify the topic creation, merging and splitting rules, which would present usability challenges to the recruited participants. In order to conduct the experiment and make the interactive algorithms accessible to the recruited qualitative content analysts, a simple intuitive web-based interface was designed. The web-based design had the advantage of allowing participants to complete the specified research task at a convenient time using their own computer. Detailed step-by-step instructions for all aspects of the research task was provided. As the interactive features available from both the PNMF and DF-LDA were similar, a single user interface was used for both algorithms.

The interface was designed to allow participants to select the number of generated topics as well as specify create, merge and split topic rules. The tabbed rule creation interface is shown in Figure 1. The rule creation component of the interface was crucial to the experiment as it allowed participants to provide domain knowledge that could potentially improve the semantic validity of topics in relation to their own research questions. Within the create a topic tab, participants were able to enter the multiple seed words that must be included in a topic. An autocomplete user interface control was used to assist participants in entering words that were within the corpus vocabulary. Within the Merge topics tab, the multiple topic seed words could be added with the aid of an autocomplete control for the two topics to be merged. The Split topics tab allowed the seed words for the two topics that must be split apart to be entered via an autocomplete control.

For each generated topic, the participants had the ability to view the main words and text responses in the topic (see Figure 2). The main topic words when clicked, highlighted all matching word occurrences in the survey text responses that were mapped to the topic (i.e., keyword-in-context functionality).

Participants were instructed to increase the number of generated topics as additional rules to create, merge and split topics were added. This was an important instruction

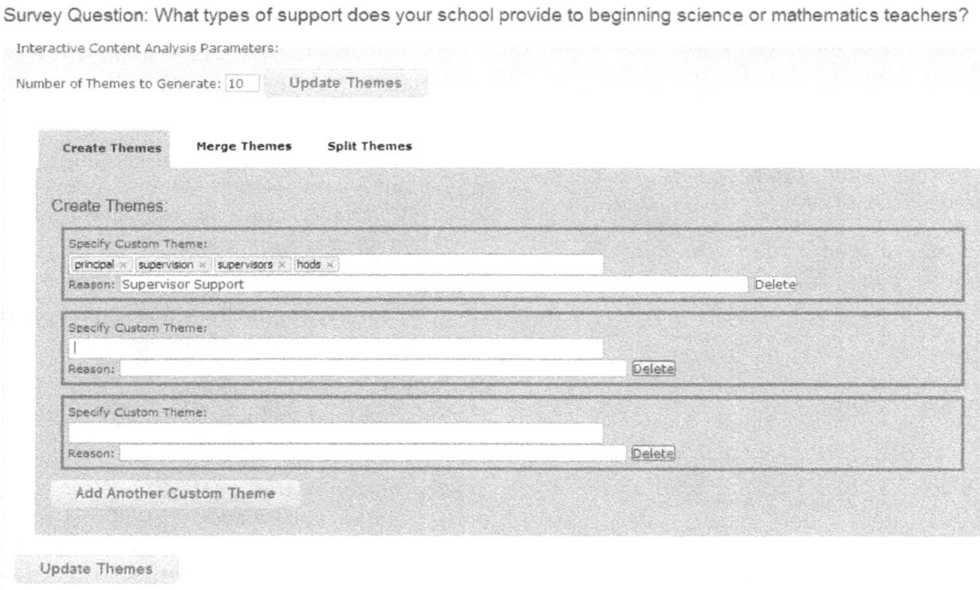

Survey Question: What types of support does your school provide to beginning science or mathematics teachers?

Figure 1: The rule entry interface provided to participants in Group A and Group B.

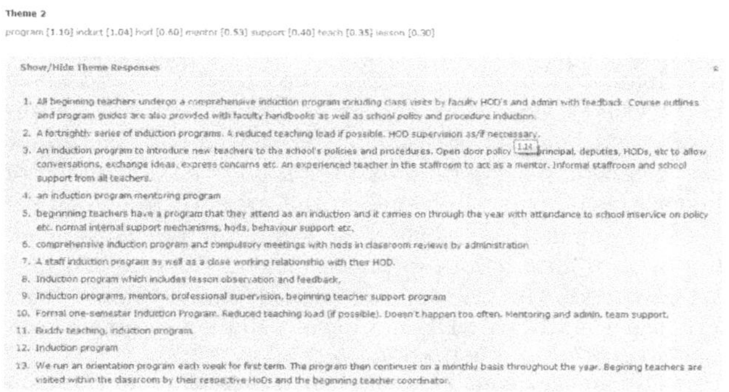

Figure 2: Keyword-In-Context functionality included within the user interface provided to participants.

to participants as without increasing the number of generated topics there was a possibility that topics matching rules may not have been generated. A summary of the specified rules was also included above the display of the generated topics for participants review and reuse across their iterative interaction with the algorithms.

Participants were also instructed that when they were satisfied with the number of generated topics and the topics influenced by the create, merge and split rules, that they needed to rate all the topics. Participants could provide feedback for a topic and suggest a title (label) for the topic.

4.5 Participant Session Tracking

The following interaction data was tracked during each participant session: Creation of topics (i.e., the specification of words within a topic), merging of topics (i.e., must-link words), splitting of topics (i.e., can-not link words), changing of the number of topics to be generated, participant rating of each topic in terms of coherence on a scale of -2 to 2,

participant rating of each topic in terms of research question relevance on a scale of -2 to 2, and textual feedback on each generated topic (optional).

4.6 Evaluation Model for Interactive Content Analysis Questionnaire

A questionnaire with categories of questions dedicated to Topic Coherence, Interpretability, Interactivity and Trust that was designed for interactive content analysis applications was used [3]. All participants were required to complete the questionnaire after they had generated and rated topics. The questionnaire was designed to gauge how the categories related to each other as well as the importance the qualitative content analysts would place on each of the four categories. Likert Scale questions were used with a range between Strongly Agree to Strongly Disagree (i.e., Strongly Agree, Agree, Neutral, Disagree and Strongly Disagree). Each section also included a free text feedback question.

4.6.1 Topic Coherence Questions

Topic Coherence is an indicator of topic quality. The key questions for Topic Coherence relate to the whether the responses were grouped together in a meaningful manner, whether the topics were easy to interpret, and whether the generated topics were relevant to the research questions.

4.6.2 Interpretability Questions

The questions in the Interpretability section were designed to gauge the usefulness of the topic display and whether this assisted the participants in interpreting and understanding the derived topics. The questions in this section therefore focused on the the list of main words derived from the topic and the inclusion of the keyword-in-context tool. A question was also included to determine the relationship between the Interpretability and Trust categories.

4.6.3 Interactivity Questions

The questions in the the the Interactivity section of the questionnaire focused on domain knowledge input to the algorithms. There were questions on the usefulness of the create, merge and split rules; and the relationship between Interactivity and the other sections namely Trust, Interpretability and Topic Coherence.

4.6.4 Trust Questions

The questions in the Trust section were designed to determine whether the participants trusted the generated topics. Trust was gauged by questions on whether the participant would use the derived topics as a basis for their own research, whether the participant would recommend the use of the interactive algorithms to other researchers and whether the participant after reviewing topics had confidence in the interactive algorithms.

5. ANALYSIS

In the sub-sections that follow, the participant sessions and questionnaire responses will be analysed. The relationship between Interactivity, Trust, Interpretability and Topic Coherence will also be discussed.

Summary statistics for Group A (DF-LDA) and Group B (PNMF) in terms of the average duration of participant sessions, the number of generated topics and the types of rules used is included in Table 1. Participant session behaviour across both Group A and Group B were similar. Participants from Group A took on average 27 minutes to complete the research task and participants from Group B took on average 31.3 minutes.

Step plot visualisations for participants in Group A (DF-LDA) and Group B (PNMF) are provided in Figure 3 and Figure 4. The step plots show the duration of each participants session, the changes in the number of topics that the participant choose to generate, the time between each change in the number of generated topics, the type of interactivity rules that were provided to the algorithm at each iteration as well as the number of topics and rules that were specified for the final iteration. In the final iteration participants were required to rate and match the generated topics with the research questions provided that were provided as part of the research task.

5.1 Selection of the Number of Topics

Participants experienced difficulty with specifying the number of topics, which is a required parameter for all Topic Modeling algorithms and this difficulty increased when participants added their domain knowledge in the form of rules. Participants from both Group A and Group B, changed the number of topics to be generated multiple times before beginning to add rules. Participants investigated topics across a range of values (i.e. between 5 - 20 topics). Extensions to the Topic Modeling algorithms are therefore needed that are able to provide a good estimate of the number of topics to allow qualitative content analysts to review topics that are representative of the corpus without needed to explore parameter selection. The inclusion of an automatically selected default would allow qualitative content analysts to focus on linking the latent topics to their research questions.

The addition of domain knowledge in the form of create, merge and split rules increased the complexity of selecting the number of topics. There are instances where participants kept the rules constant and increased the topics for the algorithm to generate, because with a lower number of topics specified it was unlikely for a topic that was influenced by a rule to be included. Certain participants kept the number of topics generated constant while they experimented with different rules and variations of rules because specifying a rule did not always result in a related topic relevant to the research question. Interactive Topic Modeling algorithms need to incorporate strategies to ensure that where topics can be generated based on the entered rules, that these topics are guaranteed to be included in the output and can be directly linked back to the rule.

5.2 Rule Usage

Allowing participants to specify rules and thereby incorporate their domain knowledge was crucial in helping participants to find topics that corresponded to their assigned research questions. Participants from both Group A and Group B entered their domain knowledge as a rule, generated topics, reviewed topics for a match to a rule (i.e., a topic related to a research question) and repeated the process until they had refined their specified rules and the number of generated topics.

In the final iteration where topics were rated and linked to a research question, 9 participants from Group A and 9 participants from Group B used rules to direct the output of the topics. Table 2 contains a summary of the create rules linked to a research questions and the number of resulting topics that were linked to a research question for each participant. In Group A, 8 participants used a create rule associated with RQ2 and 6 of these participants were able to find a topic related to RQ2. In Group A, 8 participants used a create rule associated with RQ3 and 7 of these participants were able to find a topic related to RQ3. In Group B, 8 participants used a create rule associated with RQ2 and all 8 of the participants were able to find a topic related to RQ2. In Group B, 7 participants used a create rule associated with RQ3 and 5 of these participants were able to find a topic related to RQ3. The two interactive variants of NMF and LDA were therefore able to support the addition of domain knowledge in an iterative manner and improved semantic validity.

A majority of participants specified create rules, particularly in relation to responding to RQ2 and RQ3, with RQ1 being matched with latent topic generated naturally by the algorithms. Only 2 participants, one from each group of participants did not specify any rules across the duration of their entire session.

It is evident that participants from both groups used the create rule predominantly. Example create topic rules as defined by participants for "Research Question 2: Is collegial support in terms of peer mentoring and buddying mentioned?" included: "buddy, colleagues, mentors"; "support, colleagues, collegiality, buddy, mentors"; "colleagues, collaborative, collegiality"; "colleagues, collegiality, peer, mentors, buddy, shadowing" and "resources, share, collaborative".

There was little usage of the merge and split rules with only 5 participants across both groups specifying merge and split rules in the final iteration of topic generation. Although merge and split rules were rarely used, it is interesting to review where and why they were used. The reason for the use could be deduced from the annotation (i.e., text to describe the rule) provided by the participant. As an example, a participant wanted to merge the "Lesson Observation" and

Table 1: Summary statistics for Group A and Group B participant sessions.

	Group A (DFLDA)	Group B (PNMF)
Average Session Duration	27 minutes	31.3 minutes
Total Number of Rules Used by Participants	38	61
Number of Create Rules Used by Participants	34	53
Number of Merge Rules Used by Participants	2	3
Number of Split Rules Used by Participants	1	4
Number of Create Rules Used by Participants in Final Iteration	22	21
Number of Merge Rules Used by Participants in Final Iteration	1	2
Number of Split Rules Used by Participants in Final Iteration	1	2
Range of Topics Selected by Participants in Final Iteration	6 - 20	6 - 20

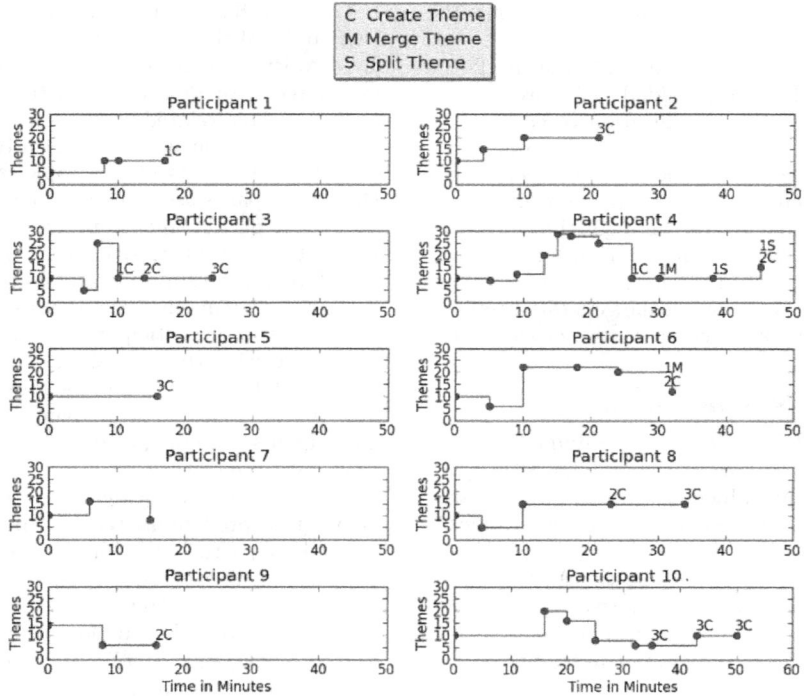

Figure 3: Group A Participant Sessions (DF-LDA).

218

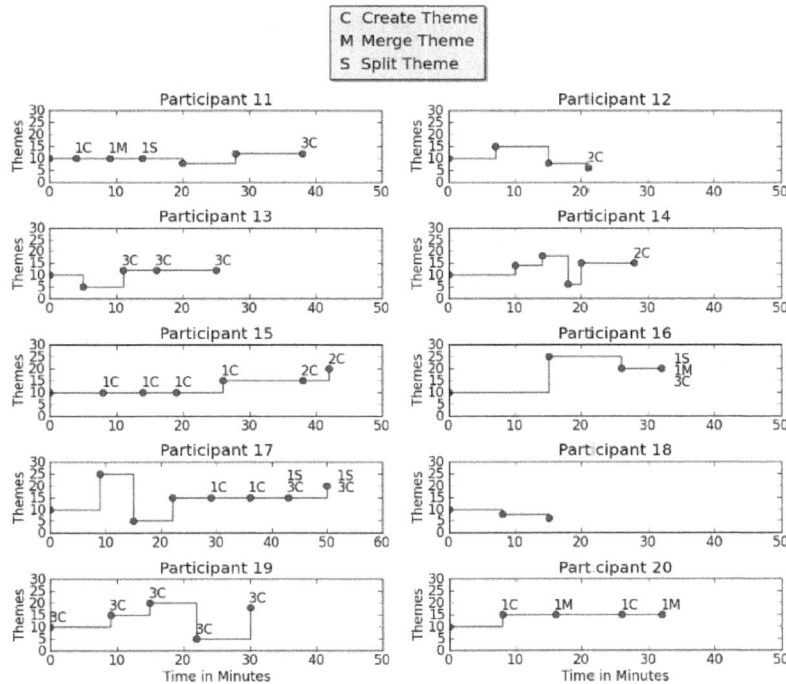

Figure 4: Group B Participant Sessions (PNMF).

"Teacher Observation" topics because they both referred to the same core concept. A common split rule that participants used involved splitting topics that mentioned the word "teacher" into topics that focused on "Beginning Teachers" and "Experienced Teachers" with the aim of deriving topics that were more fine grained. Example merge and split rules included:

Merge Rule observation, lesson : observation, teaching: These two topics relate to the same thing (i.e., lesson observations)

Split Rule beginning, teachers : experienced, teachers : Useful to separate

Split Rule beginning, teachers : experienced, teachers : would like to see beginning teachers in topics separated from experienced teachers

Questionnaire feedback also revealed that participants found it difficult and time consuming to find the topics that were influenced by the domain knowledge that was being specified using the rule interface. In particular participants had to review all the generated topics, searching for those that might have been influenced by a rule (i.e, Create Topic Rule, Merge Topic Rule or a Split Topic Rule).

Analysis of questionnaire feedback revealed that participants, that did not know how to use the rule interface, did not experiment with adding any rules even though they felt that this functionality would be useful to aid qualitative content analysts. A participant suggested designing a more intuitive interface specifically for specifying the words in the merge or the split rules.

5.3 Topic Coherence

After participants had completed their interaction with the Topic Modeling algorithm, they were required to complete a questionnaire which included a section on Topic Coherence with questions designed to gauge the quality of generated topics. In terms of the Topic Coherence questions, no substantial differences between Group A and Group B participants were found:

- 80% of participants from both groups either strongly agreed or agreed that the survey responses were grouped together in a meaningful way.

- 90% of participants from Group B and 80% of participants from Group A either strongly agreed or agreed that topics containing meaningfully grouped together responses were easier to interpret and understand.

- 70% of participants from both Group A and Group B either strongly agree or agreed that the derived topics were relevant to the research questions. Further analysis revealed that the remaining 30% of participants chose to generate a small number of topics in their final iteration.

5.4 Interpretability

The Interpretability section of the questionnaire was designed to gauge the usefulness of including tools to help analysts interpret topics. The results indicate that the inclusion of tools to aid with topic interpretation such as the provided keyword-in-context tool improved the participants confidence in the derived topics. This indicates a strong relationship between Interpretability and Trust. No substantial differences between Group A and Group B participants were found.

Table 2: Linking create rules to research questions for Group A and Group B participants.

Group	Participant	No. Topics	Rules Used			Topics Matched		
			RQ1	RQ2	RQ3	RQ1	RQ2	RQ3
A	1	10	1C	-	-	-	0	0
	2	20	1C	1C	1C	-	1	1
	3	10	1C	1C	1C	5	1	1
	4	15	-	1C	1C	-	1	1
	5	10	1C	1C	1C	-	1	1
	6	12	-	1C	1C	6	0	1
	7	8	-	-	-	6	-	-
	8	15	1C	1C	1C	10	1	1
	9	6	-	1C	1C	-	0	0
	10	10	1C	1C	1C	6	1	1
B	11	12	-	2C	1C	7	1	0
	12	6	-	1C	1C	-	1	0
	13	12	1C	1C	1C	-	1	0
	14	15	-	1C	1C	6	2	1
	15	20	-	1C	-	-	1	1
	16	20	1C	1C	1C	-	3	2
	17	20	-	1C	1C	-	2	1
	18	6	-	-	-	-	0	0
	19	18	1C	1C	1C	-	2	1
	20	15	-	-	-	-	0	0

- 60% of participants from both Group A and Group B agreed that they were able to get an indication of the type of responses that were grouped together in a topic by reviewing the main words that were displayed.

- 80% of all participants were able to interpret and understand topics by using the provided keyword-in-context functionality. This functionality allowed participants to click on a main word in a derived topic and view the occurrences within the survey responses.

- 90% of Group A and 80% of Group B either strongly agreed or agreed that the ability to interpret a topic improved their confidence in the derived topics.

In terms of suggestions for improvements in topic display and interpretation tools participants requested the following:

- The ability to simultaneously highlight multiple words using the keyword-in-context functionality.

- The ability to search for words or phrases within the topic display interface.

- The ability to see a visual representation of the size of the derived topics in relation to each other.

- The ability to highlight words across topics and get an indication of how many times a word appeared in a topic.

5.5 Interactivity

The Questionnaire section on Interactivity contained seven Likert Scale questions and one open free text question. Participants found the ability to create topics more useful in terms of answering research questions than the ability to merge and split topics. The findings for the Interactivity section of the questionnaire are summarised as follows:

- 80% of participants either strongly agreed or agreed that the ability to define topics by specifying the words that must appear within a topic was a useful way to discover topics relevant to research questions.

- 60% of participants agreed that the ability to merge topics was a useful technique for conducting qualitative content analysis and answering research questions. 40% of likert scale responses however fall within the neutral to disagree range.

- 40% of Group B and 50% of Group A participants agreed that the ability to split topics was useful for conducting qualitative content analysis and answering research questions.

Only 20% of participants from both Group A and Group B thought that Interactivity (encompassing the creation of topics; and merging and splitting of topics) increased their confidence (i.e., trust) in the derived topics. This is perhaps the most surprising finding from the questionnaire analysis. Interactivity was initially seen as a way to improve qualitative content analysts trust in algorithmic aids. The ability to interpret a topic has a stronger relationship with building an analysts trust.

Participant feedback to enhance interactivity is summarised below:

User Interface Usability A participant expressed difficulty in understanding how to use the interface to add rules. The participant thought that interactivity had the potential to be useful but that they required more of an understanding of how to use the interface.

Interface Design for Merging and Splitting A participant mentioned that merging and splitting of topics could be made more intuitive with the design of a custom interface. The participant described an interface that allowed the user to drag the responses from multiple topics together to specify the contents of the merged topic.

Finding Topics Resulting from a Rule Five participants mentioned that they found it difficult to locate the topics that were influenced by a rule. It was time consuming for these participants to read all of the generated topics and match these topics to the rules they entered in order to evaluate whether the resulting topics were of relevance to the research questions.

5.6 Trust

Participants from both Group A and Group B after using their assigned interactive algorithm indicated that they had trust in the algorithm, because they would use derived topics as a foundation for their own qualitative research and recommend the algorithms to other qualitative researchers. A summary of the findings for the Trust section of the questionnaire is as follows:

- 90% of all participants either strongly agreed or agreed that they would use the derived topics as a foundation for their qualitative content analysis.

- 80% of participants felt that using the the keyword-context functionality (i.e., a key topic interpretation tool) helped to improve their confidence in finding evidence to support the existence of a topic.

- 80% of participants either strongly agreed or agreed that they would recommend the software program (i.e., algorithm, topic display and interface to support interactivity) to other researchers.

6. DISCUSSION

In this section the findings from the analysis of participant sessions and responses to the questionnaire which included sections on Trust, Interactivity, Interpretability and Topic Coherence will be used to answer the research questions:

- **Can content analysts use interactive Topic Modeling algorithms to include domain knowledge and improve the semantic validity of the topics produced in relation to their research?**
  The findings indicated that interactive Topic Modeling algorithms are useful qualitative content analysis aids. Both the LDA and NMF algorithms were shown to produce latent topics (themes) that were useful in providing analysts with an overview of the representative topics in a corpus and some of these latent topics were directly related to an analysts research questions. From this we conclude that there is evidence that semantic validity is being algorithmically enforced. Even though the aim of this study was not framed to investigate the relative performance of LDA and NMF, our impression is that there is no basis to chose between them in relation to both research questions that were studied.

  The interactive variants of NMF and LDA both provided a means for the analyst to incorporate domain knowledge by specifying rules to create, merge and split topics. Participants were able to specify rules to direct the algorithm to derive topics to answer more specific and complex research questions. Participant

interaction with the algorithms was also done in an iterative manner involving cycles of review and rule refinement.

Analysts use a model (known as an analytical construct), to operationalise the knowledge that the analyst has in relation to the context of the research. The analytical construct is a key element in Krippendorff's conceptual foundation for content analysis [10, pp. 35]. The analytical construct is used by the analyst to make the appropriate inferences in order to answer the research questions. In simplistic terms, the analytical construct can be thought of as a set of rules that the analyst employs. The ability for interactive Topic Modeling algorithms to support the inclusion of rules means that the algorithms are better able to match the analytical constructs of content analysts and make appropriate inference.

- **How do topic coherence (i.e., quality), interpretation and interactivity relate to a content analysts perception of trust?**
  There was a strong link between Interpretability and Trust but not between Interactivity and Trust. This research finding was initially surprising as interactivity was seen as the key issue contributing to the lack of trust. It is however important to note that a distinction was made to separate interactivity relating to the display and interpretation of topics derived from the interactivity provided to incorporate domain knowledge by an algorithm. It makes sense that there is a strong link between Interpretability and Trust because interpretation tools such as the keyword-in-context tool allows analysts to find evidence to support their research claims. Interactivity in the form of rules to create, merge and split topics on the other hand, has a strong link with Topic Coherence and provides a means for the analyst to directly address their research questions.

Numerous issues specific to the requirements of qualitative content analysts were also identified. The following enhancements to the NMF and LDA interactive variants are therefore recommended:

- Automated selection of the default number of topics to display to the qualitative content analyst. This feature will reduce the time the analyst spends trying to locate the optimum number of topics.

- Linking of topics to their associated create, merge or split rules. This feature will allow analysts to easily find topics that emerged from their provided domain knowledge and provide a traceable model for collating evidence to support research findings.

The findings also indicate that a holistic approach needs to be employed in the development of software that implements interactive Topic Modeling algorithms as qualitative content analysis aids. While the algorithm is the central element and interactivity plays an important role in helping the analyst to answer their research questions, the incorporation of tools to help the analyst interpret the derived topics are equally important and affect trust. Analysis of the questionnaire responses in particular revealed that tools such as the keyword-in-context tool helped the analyst to interpret topics and improved the analysts trust in the algorithm as qualitative analysis aid.

Interface design is also crucial particularly in relation to the merge and split rule interface. Analysts were found to mainly use create rules and while these create rules were successful in helping direct the algorithm to to answer a research question for the majority of analysts, there are scenarios where merging and splitting topics would be required. Participants felt that interface provided as part of the experiment was too simple and would have preferred a visual drag and drop interface.

7. CONCLUSION

To the best of our knowledge the research presented in this paper is the first to evaluate interactive NMF and LDA Topic Modeling algorithms as qualitative content analysis aids. A between-subjects study was designed to evaluate both an NMF and LDA Topic Modeling variant. Participants were provided with a corpus and research questions that they needed to address; and given access to an interactive Topic Modeling algorithm via a custom designed web-based interface which allowed participants to supply domain knowledge in the form of create, merge and split rules. The findings indicated that participants were able to use the provided interactivity to direct the algorithms to derive topics related to their research questions thereby improving semantic validity. Analysis of participant questionnaire responses provided a clearer understanding of how interactivity with a Topic Modeling algorithm, the inclusion of tools to allow analysts to interpret topics, and the quality of topics (i.e. topic coherence) impacts on a content analysts ability to trust the algorithm. Interactivity was important in allowing the analyst to derive topics that were directly related to their research questions but was found not to improve an analysts trust in the algorithm. However, evidence gathering tools such as the keyword-in-context tool that were included to help the analyst interpret topics were shown to improve the analysts trust in the algorithm as an qualitative analysis aid.

This study also uncovered a number of requirements for interactive Topic Modeling algorithms which can be used to guide the future development of algorithms. These include the ability to automatically determine the number of topics as a starting point for the content analyst and a way to link the domain knowledge specified as rules to the derived topics, in order to aid the analyst in finding topics influenced by a rule and provide traceable models for the collation of supporting evidence. We hope that the suggested requirements will influence the development of Topic Modeling algorithms and eventually increase the adoption of interactive algorithms as qualitative content analysis aids.

8. REFERENCES

[1] D. Andrzejewski, X. Zhu, and M. Craven. Incorporating domain knowledge into topic modeling via dirichlet forest priors. In *Proceedings of the 26th Annual International Conference on Machine Learning*, pages 25–32. ACM, 2009.

[2] D. Andrzejewski, X. Zhu, M. Craven, and B. Recht. A framework for incorporating general domain knowledge into latent dirichlet allocation using first-order logic. In *Proceedings of the Twenty-Second international joint conference on Artificial Intelligence-Volume Volume Two*, pages 1171–1177. AAAI Press, 2011.

[3] A. Bakharia. *Interactive content analysis: evaluating interactive variants of non-negative Matrix Factorisation and Latent Dirichlet Allocation as qualitative content analysis aids*. PhD thesis, Queensland University of Technology, Brisbane, Australia, 8 2014.

[4] S. Basu, I. Davidson, and K. Wagstaff. *Constrained clustering: Advances in algorithms, theory, and applications*. CRC Press, 2008.

[5] D. M. Blei, A. Y. Ng, and M. I. Jordan. Latent dirichlet allocation. *the Journal of machine Learning research*, 3:993–1022, 2003.

[6] D. Cai, X. He, J. Han, and T. S. Huang. Graph regularized nonnegative matrix factorization for data representation. *Pattern Analysis and Machine Intelligence, IEEE Transactions on*, 33(8):1548–1560, 2011.

[7] N. K. Denzin and Y. S. Lincoln. *The Sage handbook of qualitative research*. Sage Publications, Incorporated, 2005.

[8] T. L. Griffiths and M. Steyvers. Finding scientific topics. *Proceedings of the National academy of Sciences of the United States of America*, 101(Suppl 1):5228–5235, 2004.

[9] H.-F. Hsieh and S. E. Shannon. Three approaches to qualitative content analysis. *Qualitative health research*, 15(9):1277–1288, 2005.

[10] K. Krippendorff and M. A. Bock. *The content analysis reader*. SAGE Publications, Incorporated, 2008.

[11] D. Mimno, H. M. Wallach, E. Talley, M. Leenders, and A. McCallum. Optimizing semantic coherence in topic models. In *Proceedings of the Conference on Empirical Methods in Natural Language Processing*, pages 262–272. Association for Computational Linguistics, 2011.

[12] T. Muhr. Atlas.ti-a prototype for the support of text interpretation. *Qualitative Sociology*, 14(4):349–371, 1991.

[13] D. Newman, Y. Noh, E. Talley, S. Karimi, and T. Baldwin. Evaluating topic models for digital libraries. In *Proceedings of the 10th annual joint conference on Digital libraries*, pages 215–224. ACM, 2010.

[14] D. Seung and L. Lee. Algorithms for non-negative matrix factorization. *Advances in neural information processing systems*, 13:556–562, 2001.

[15] K. Wagstaff, C. Cardie, S. Rogers, and S. Schrödl. Constrained k-means clustering with background knowledge. In *ICML*, volume 1, pages 577–584, 2001.

[16] F. Wang, T. Li, and C. Zhang. Semi-supervised clustering via matrix factorization. In *SDM*, pages 1–12, 2008.

The Information Network: Exploiting Causal Dependencies in Online Information Seeking

Prasanta Bhattacharya
Department of Information Systems
National University of Singapore
prasanta@comp.nus.edu.sg

Rishabh Mehrotra
Department of Computer Science
University College London
r.mehrotra@cs.ucl.ac.uk

ABSTRACT

The Internet has emerged as a leading source of information about the world and its daily occurrences. Platforms like Wikipedia act as information conduits through which informational elements (e.g. topic pages) cater to the information seeking needs of users worldwide. While usage data from these informational elements help us to predict the information seeking behavior of users, especially in reaction to external news events, what has been largely ignored in past literature is the predictive value of the underlying informational network that connects these elements. In this study, we uncover causal linkages in information seeking behavior among related informational elements on Wikipedia. We demonstrate that incorporating this causal information leads to better predictions of page view counts of relevant Wikipedia pages, when compared to models that ignore such underlying causal linkages. We also provide additional evidence about the efficacy of our approach from the real world, by performing a judgment study with human annotators. This research is among the first to investigate and uncover the value of understanding the underlying relationships among informational elements.

Keywords

Granger Causality, Information Seeking, Recommendations

1. INTRODUCTION

The Internet has emerged as a leading source of information about the world we live in. Over 3 billion of the 7.2 billion people in this world, depend on the Internet to satisfy their informational needs in various forms [1]. Wikipedia, the largest free and multilingual encyclopedia on the Internet, has over 4 million articles on its English version as of July 2015 and experiences an addition of 1200 articles on average each day [2]. Other online platforms including Q&A

[1] http://www.internetworldstats.com/stats.htm
[2] https://en.wikipedia.org/wiki/Wikipedia:Size_of_Wikipedia

CHIIR '16, March 13-17, 2016, Carrboro, NC, USA

© 2016 ACM. ISBN 978-1-4503-3751-9/16/03. . . $15.00

DOI: http://dx.doi.org/10.1145/2854946.2854974

sites (e.g. Stack Exchange and Quora), Blogs (e.g. Blogger and Tumblr) and Social Network Sites (SNS) (e.g. Facebook and Twitter) have also emerged as complementary sources of information for users on the Internet.

Given the rising popularity of information seeking behavior on the Internet, it has becomes crucial for platform owners to predict informational needs of its users in advance, and if possible, recommend sources to satisfy these needs. Predicting user interest in trends and events has been the subject of some recent analysis in this area [25]. However, predicting information seeking behavior and the subsequent recommendations are complicated by the fact that there often exists significant heterogeneity in user tastes online, and that the informational needs are quite dynamic in nature, showing fluctuations and seasonal trends.

The key intuition we exploit in the current study is that the Internet is composed of informational elements which cater to specific informational needs of its users. Examples of informational elements could be a Wikipedia page, a Tumblr blog or an entity on Freebase. By analyzing the usage patterns of these informational elements, we can not only make inferences about the informational needs of Internet users, but also make better predictions and recommendations that would benefit the users. While a number of recent studies have looked at Wikipedia [27], search queries [13] and information entities [20] to study related questions, none of them exploit the fact that these informational elements are often linked to each other and there often exist non-obvious causal interactions among these elements that can be exploited to make better predictions of information seeking behavior. For instance, an increase in information seeking propensity on the topic of "Ebola" might be a direct result of an increase in information seeking propensity of a related informational element e.g. "Recent Outbreaks". Further, this increase can potentially trigger a further increase in user interest and subsequent readership of related informational elements, like "World Health Organization (WHO)". Either way, what is important is to acknowledge that there exists an underlying network of relatedness between informational elements, that can be intelligently exploited to improve inferences about information seeking.

In the current study, we use longitudinal data on daily page views of Wikipedia pages for 4 popular world events to create a relatedness-graph of linked informational elements on Wikipedia. For each event, we uncover hidden and non-obvious causal links among related informational elements. We then show that by incorporating information about these uncovered links in our predictive model, we are able to achieve lower error rates on predicting page view counts as compared to a baseline model which ignores such causal links. We also validate the recommendations made from our causal model using a real-world user judgment study which establishes the efficacy of our approach. Finally, we make a point about the temporal adaptiveness of our causal model by showing that the causal graphs we construct evolve in reaction to external events, by demonstrating distinct network characteristics for the different temporal phases (e.g. before and after an event).

2. RELATED WORK

There are two distinct lines of work related to the current research viz. extant work on information seeking and popularity prediction and research on drawing causal insights from observational data via statistical models. We next review relevant literature in both these areas.

Information Seeking & Popularity Dynamics:
Predicting trends in information access and content popularity finds application in many areas, including support facilitation, media advertising, content caching, revenue estimation, traffic management and macro-economic trends forecasting, to name a few. Some prior work [10, 30] show that there is a correlation in views that contents receive over time. There are, however, relatively fewer studies that forecast a value for the actual popularity of content. Lee et al. [16, 17] use survival analysis to evaluate the probability that a given content will receive more than some x number of hits. Jamali and Rangwala [15] predict the popularity of content using an entropy measure based on the "user-interest peak"and the "co-participatory network". Szabo and Huberman [30] present a linear regression model based on the number of views. This method was also applied by [32, 5] to create predictive popularity models in different feature spaces.

These existing information seeking models fail to capture the interdependencies between the different informational elements, something we focus on in the current piece of work.

Causality Models & Analysis:
Advancements in causal inference has led to the development of a plethora of new methods, both for causal structure learning and for making causal predictions (i.e., predicting the aftermath of interventions). Causal relations among time series data have been modeled with Granger causality [31], lagged correlation [19], Bayesian networks [36], among others. Granger causality measures a cause in terms of whether it passes Granger Test, i.e., whether a variable helps in predicating the future events for a related variable, beyond what can be predicted by using only historical events for the latter variable alone. Lagged correlation characterizes causal relations with the correlation between two time series shifted in time relative to one another. Causal Bayesian networks interpret causal relations with graphical models, in which the predecessors of a node are interpreted as directly causing the variable associated with that node.

A variety of causality mining techniques have been studied in past work. Chang et al. [11] propose a Granger causality based influence model for Twitter context summarization. Qui et al. [23] propose Granger graphical models as an effective and scalable approach for anomaly detection. Non-parametric generalization of the Granger graphical models called Generalized Lasso Granger (GLG) were

proposed by Bahadori et al.[3] to uncover the temporal dependencies from irregular time series. More recently, Zong et al. [37] leveraged the causal and dependency structure among alerts sequences in data center monitoring systems. Finally, Granger causality has also been used to compute the cause and effect relationships for pairs of motion trajectories of a video [21].

In this work, we enrich the information seeking models with Granger causal dependencies and show that incorporating insights from predictive causal linkages between informational elements helps improve predictive performance and enables making better recommendations.

3. PROBLEM FORMULATION

Information seeking has emerged as one of the leading activities of users on the Internet today [7, 28]. The informational needs of a user can be very specific (e.g. searching for the capital of a particular country) or more navigational and exploratory (e.g. knowing more about the Ebola outbreak across the globe) [20, 6]. On the web, this information is supplied to users via a multitude of distribution platforms e.g. information repositories like Wikipedia, social media platforms like Twitter and Facebook, and Q&A sites like Quora and Stack Exchange. Each of these platforms, in turn, is an agglomerate of several informational elements which provide information on a multitude of topics and entities e.g. Pages on Wikipedia, Subjects on Stack Exchanges etc. More formally, we define Informational Elements as follows:

Definition: An *informational element* can broadly be defined as digital atomic units which have some informational value associated with them. Examples of informational elements could be various named entities, Facebook pages, Twitter handles, blogs, topics, Wikipedia pages, etc.

While the approaches discussed in this work are broadly applicable for any informational element, we make use of Wikipedia pages as the specific instance in this work. The usage activity logs from these informational elements provide a useful proxy to both measure and predict the informational needs of users.

While there have been past work that predicts the popularity of topics and news events on social media platforms [33], we argue that the predictive power can be improved by exploiting causal linkages among related informational elements. The intuition behind this is that the popularity of a particular informational element, say after an important event, would increase popularity of related informational elements too. Hence, by incorporating popularity information from related elements, we should be able to make better predictions about the popularity of our focal informational element. Predicting popularity of informational elements is not only instrumental at illuminating our understanding of how individuals search for information on the Internet, but is also of key value to advertisers and platforms who wish to anticipate users' information needs and evolving preferences [24] following major events.

In the current study, we demonstrate our approach of identifying causal linkages, that are often non-obvious at times, using page-view logs from the English edition of Wikipedia [3]. We select a total of four Wikipedia pages corresponding

---

[3]https://en.wikipedia.org/wiki/Main_Page

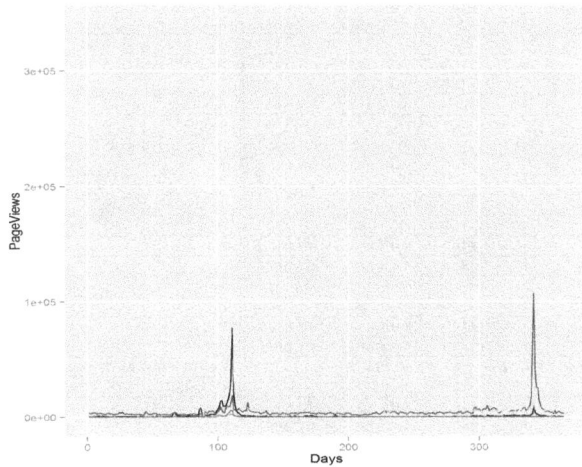

(a) Scotland Time Series

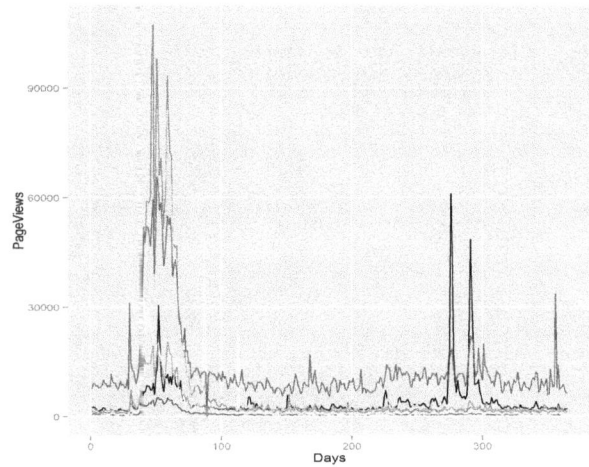

(b) Hamas Time Series

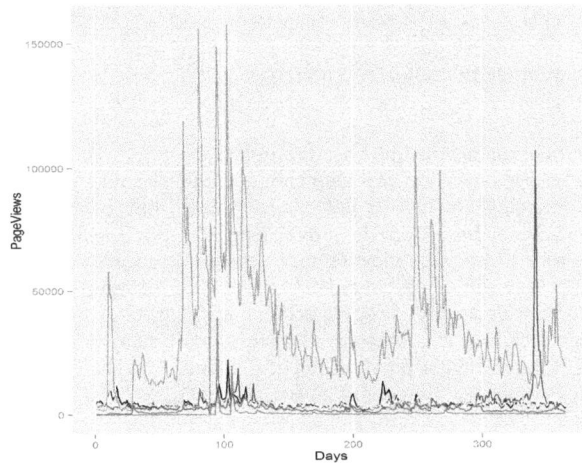

(c) ISIS Time Series

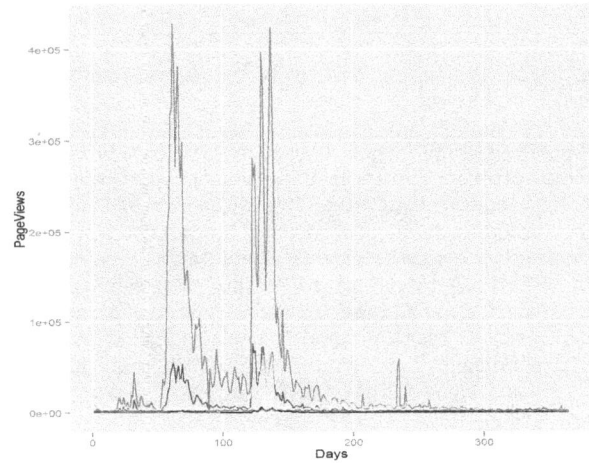

(d) Ebola Time Series

Figure 1: Time series of page views for the various informational elements considered in the different world events.

to major world events in recent history viz. The Scottish referendum on Independence, the Ebola outbreak, the rise and spread of ISIS militancy, and the rise of Hamas the Palestinian Islamic organization. Using an entity-tagging approach [9] that we describe in the following section, we identify a set of related Wikipedia pages for these four events. These are illustrated in Table 1 below. We then gather time series data on page view logs for each of these Wikipedia pages and visually inspect these to see if there is any evidence of the information seeking trends that co-evolve with each other.

Figures 1a, 1b, 1c and 1d illustrate the number of page views for each of the four events over a period of 1 year from June 1, 2014 to May 31, 2015. Interestingly, we find that for each of the focal events, while some related informational elements co-evolve in popularity, others don't. This poses an interesting problem of candidate selection when making predictions for the focal event as it is not obvious as to which informational elements might be useful to include in the pre-

dictive models. Specifically, we seek to answer the following two questions in this study, (i) "Can the predictive power of an informational element be improved by incorporating information from related informational elements?" and (ii), "Can we identify "causally" related informational elements from a set of all related elements?"

4. MODELING INTERACTION RELATION-SHIPS BETWEEN INFORMATIONAL ELEMENTS

In this section, we hypothesize that informational elements such as topic pages on Wikipedia are often causally related to each other in terms of information seeking patterns. We employ a Granger causality based approach to model these interactions between the elements.

4.1 Causality: Prior Art

Drawing causal conclusions for a set of observed variables

Event	Event Description	Informational Element (node ID)	Wikipedia Page
Scotland	The Scottish independence referendum on Scottish independence that took place in Scotland on Sept 18, 2014	Yes Scotland (1)	https://en.wikipedia.org/wiki/Yes_Scotland
		Edinburgh Agreement (2)	https://en.wikipedia.org/wiki/Edinburgh_Agreement_%282012%29
		Royal Bank of Scotland (3)	https://en.wikipedia.org/wiki/The_Royal_Bank_of_Scotland
		Scotland (4)	https://en.wikipedia.org/wiki/Scotland
		David Cameron (5)	https://en.wikipedia.org/wiki/David_Cameron
		Alex Salmond (6)	https://en.wikipedia.org/wiki/Alex_Salmond
ISIS	On 29th June 2014, ISIS proclaimed itself to be a worldwide caliphate.	Islamic State of Iraq (1)	https://en.wikipedia.org/wiki/Islamic_State_of_Iraq_and_the_Levant
		Syria (2)	https://en.wikipedia.org/wiki/Syria
		Iraq (3)	https://en.wikipedia.org/wiki/Iraq
		David Cawthrone Haines (4)	https://en.wikipedia.org/wiki/David_Cawthorne_Haines
		Islamic State (5)	https://en.wikipedia.org/wiki/Islamic_state
		Al-Qaeda (6)	https://en.wikipedia.org/wiki/Al-Qaeda
		Iraq War (7)	https://en.wikipedia.org/wiki/Iraq_War
		David Cameron (8)	https://en.wikipedia.org/wiki/David_Cameron
Ebola	The Ebola outbreak began in Guinea in December 2013 & then spread to Liberia & Sierra Leone	Ebola virus (1)	https://en.wikipedia.org/wiki/Ebola_virus
		Ebola Disease (2)	https://en.wikipedia.org/wiki/Ebola_virus_disease
		Ebola River (3)	https://en.wikipedia.org/wiki/Ebola_River
		WHO (4)	https://en.wikipedia.org/wiki/World_Health_Organization
		Ebola Epidemic in Africa (5)	https://en.wikipedia.org/wiki/Ebola_virus_epidemic_in_West_Africa
		Malaria (6)	https://en.wikipedia.org/wiki/Malaria
Hamas	Israeli air force attacks Hamas targets in central Gaza Strip	Israel (1)	https://en.wikipedia.org/wiki/Israel
		Gaza Strip (2)	https://en.wikipedia.org/wiki/Gaza_Strip
		Hamas (3)	https://en.wikipedia.org/wiki/Hamas
		State of Palestine (4)	https://en.wikipedia.org/wiki/State_of_Palestine
		Benjamin Netanyahu (5)	https://en.wikipedia.org/wiki/Benjamin_Netanyahu
		Fatah (6)	https://en.wikipedia.org/wiki/Fatah
		West Bank (7)	https://en.wikipedia.org/wiki/West_Bank
		Iron Dome (8)	https://en.wikipedia.org/wiki/Iron_Dome
		UN (9)	https://en.wikipedia.org/wiki/United_Nations

Table 1: World events and related informational elements on Wikipedia

from a given sample from their joint distribution is a fundamental problem. Statistical associations are often due to underlying causal structures [26]. Research in causal discovery has led to the identification of fundamental principles and methods for causal inference, including a complete algorithm, the PC algorithm, that identifies all possible orientations of causal dependencies from observed conditional independencies [29]. Identifying such causal relations helps uncover dependencies between variables which could be leveraged for different applications, in our case, making better predictions.

We first introduce the problem of causal inference on iid data, as with the case with no temporal structure. Let therefore X_i, $i \in V$, be a set of random variables and let G be a directed acyclic graph (DAG) on V describing the causal relationships between the variables. The *Causal Graphical Models* are usually thought of as joint probability distributions on the variables $X_1, ..., X_n$ with arrows indicating direct causal influences. The causal Markov assumption states that each vertex X_i is independent of its non-descendants in the graph, given its parents. Crucially, this links causal semantics, which is important for predicting how a system reacts to interventions, to something that has empirically measurable consequences. Given observations from a joint distribution, it allows us to test conditional independence statements and thus infer which causal models are consistent with an observed distribution, subject to a genericity assumption referred to as faithfulness.

We now turn to the case of time series data - which is of interest in the present study, and describe a popular framework to infer causal dependencies in temporal data.

4.2 G-Causality

Granger Causality [14] or "G-Causality", is one of the earliest methods developed to quantify the temporal-causal effect among multiple time series. It is based on two major principles: (i) the cause happens prior to the effect and (ii)

the cause makes unique changes in the effect [4]. Such a formulation is based on the idea that a cause should be helpful in predicting the future effects, beyond what can be predicted solely based on their own past values. Specifically, a time series (or "page view count" series in the terminology of the present paper) x is said to *Granger cause* another time series y, if and only if regressing for y in terms of both past values of y and x is statistically significantly more accurate than doing so with past values of y alone.

More specifically, consider two vector autoregressive processes:

$$x_t = \Sigma_{i=1}^{\infty} a_{1i} x_{t-i} + u_{1t}; \quad var(u_{1t}) = \Sigma_1 \quad (1)$$

and

$$y_t = \Sigma_{i=1}^{\infty} b_{1i} y_{t-i} + v_{1t}; \quad var(v_{1t}) = \Gamma_1 \quad (2)$$

which can be viewed as linear projections of x_t and y_t on their own past values, which we denote as X_{t-1} and Y_{t-1}, respectively. The linear projection of x_t on both X_{t-1} and Y_{t-1} and of y_t on both X_{t-1} and Y_{t-1} can be obtained from the joint auto-regressive process:

$$x_t = \Sigma_{i=1}^{\infty} a_{2i} x_{t-i} + \Sigma_{i=1}^{\infty} c_{2i} y_{t-i} + u_{2t}; \quad var(u_{2t}) = \Sigma_2 \quad (3)$$

and

$$y_t = \Sigma_{i=1}^{\infty} b_{2i} y_{t-i} + \Sigma_{i=1}^{\infty} d_{2i} x_{t-i} + v_{2t}; \quad var(v_{2t}) = \Gamma_2 \quad (4)$$

The variance Σ_1 represents the error in predicting the present value of x_t from its own past, while the variance Σ_2 represents the error in predicting the present value of x_t from the past values of both X_{t-1} and Y_{t-1}. If Σ_2 is less than Σ_1, then Y is said to cause X. This intuition is captured by the causal measure [14]:

$$F_{Y \to X} = ln(\frac{|\Sigma_1|}{|\Sigma 2|}) \quad (5)$$

A similar measure of causality from X to Y can be computed by symmetry. However note that in general $F_{Y \to X} \neq F_{X \to Y}$, due to the directionality of the flow of time.

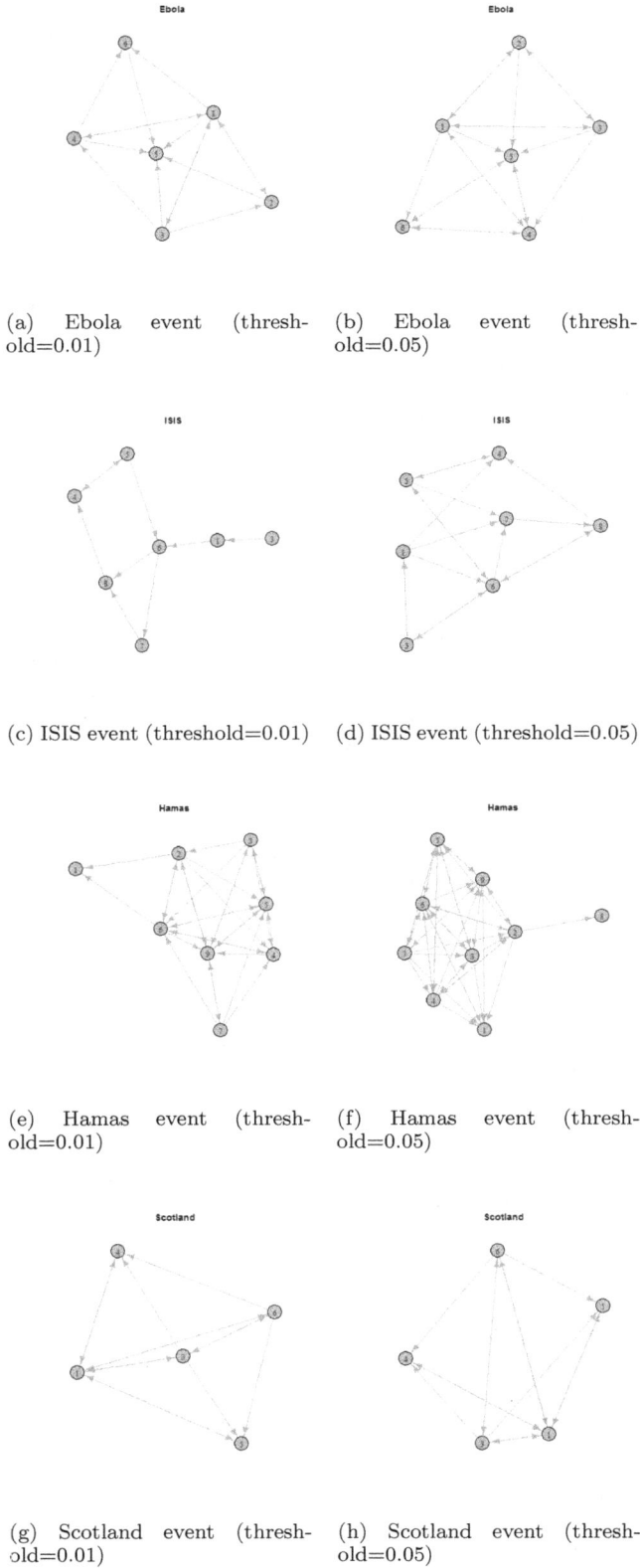

(a) Ebola event (threshold=0.01)

(b) Ebola event (threshold=0.05)

(c) ISIS event (threshold=0.01)

(d) ISIS event (threshold=0.05)

(e) Hamas event (threshold=0.01)

(f) Hamas event (threshold=0.05)

(g) Scotland event (threshold=0.01)

(h) Scotland event (threshold=0.05)

Figure 2: Causal network between various informational elements for the different events considered.

In spite of offering an enhanced degree of flexibility, parametric models of regression as formulated above suffer from potential exacerbation of performance inadequacy in cases where the true forms of correspondence between the response and the regressors may be non-linear. Non-parametric pairwise Granger causality is calculated as follows: given two point processes N_X and N_Y, a power spectral matrix S_{XY} is defined as the Fourier transform of covariance of two point processes N_X, N_Y, which is estimated using the multitaper function $h_k(t_j)$ [22]:

$$S_{XY}(f) = \frac{1}{2\pi KT}\Sigma_{k=1}^{K}\overline{N_X}(f,k)\overline{N_Y}(f,k)^* \qquad (6)$$

where

$$\overline{N_X}(f,k) = \int_0^T h_k(t)exp(i2\pi ft)dN_X(t) \qquad (7)$$

and S_{XY} is factorized by Wilson's algorithm [35] as follows:

$$S_{XY}(f) = H_{XY}(f)\Sigma_{XY}H_{XY}^*(f) \qquad (8)$$

where H_{XY} is the transfer function which corresponds to the coefficients of an AR model, Σ corresponds to covariance matrix of error term of AR model and $*$ represents a conjugate transpose. Non-parametric pairwise Granger causality of $F_{N_Y \to N_X}$ for frequency f is finally calculated as:

$$F_{N_Y \to N_X}(f) = ln\frac{S_{XX}(f)}{S_{XX}(f) - (\Sigma_{YY} - \frac{\Sigma_{XY}^2}{\Sigma_{XX}})|H_{XY}(f)|^2} \qquad (9)$$

We next describe our approach of using this notion of temporal causality in analyzing the interdependencies among the different informational elements.

5. EXPERIMENTAL SETUP

To investigate the implications of incorporating causal linkage information among informational elements, we consider a set of worldwide events as described in Table 1. For each of these events, we take a New York Times summary article which provides a descriptive summary of the event and use the content of the NYT article to extract the set of informational elements via entity extraction as described in Subsection 5.2 below. We next describe in detail the dataset construction and causal graph construction technique.

5.1 Dataset Description

The data used for this study is a time-series dataset on the number of daily page views for the English version of Wikipedia. Wikipedia not only allows its users instant access to information on virtually any topic of interest, but also provides usage metadata (e.g. page views, page edits etc.) through its periodic data dumps. The page view statistics we use for our study were collected from Wikimedia data servers [4] which were made more accessible through an external web application [5]. We collect daily page views for the period of June 1, 2014 to May 31, 2015 for the event pages on Wikipedia, as well as for the related pages as listed in Table 1 earlier.

---

[4]http://dumps.wikimedia.org/other/pagecounts-raw/
[5]http://stats.grok.se/

	1%		5%		10%		Common Baselines	
	G-Causal	Shuffle	G-Causal	Shuffle	G-Causal	Shuffle	Shuffle (all edges)	No edges
Scotland	**1693.8**	3536.1	**1693.8**	3550.4	**1693.8**	2484.4	4715.3	5001.9
ISIS	**1395.2**	1419.2	**1395.2**	1419.2	**1395.2**	1419.2	3405.2	3575.1
Ebola	**295.6**	302.02	295.6	294.8	**295.6**	302.0	6171.6	6152.5
Hamas	**3419.5**	3463.2	3419.56	3419.5	**3419.5**	3446.5	2652.1	2705.9

Table 2: Prediction estimates on the different events considered. RMSE values are reported for the proposed Causal approach and the different baselines considered. Row headers indicate the level of statistical significance considered.

5.2 Entity Extraction

The entity linking task aims at identifying all the small text fragments in a document referring to a particular entity contained in a given knowledge base, e.g., Wikipedia. The annotation is usually organized in three tasks. Given an input document, the first task involves discovering the fragments that could refer to an entity. Second, since an individual mention could refer to multiple entities, it is necessary to perform a disambiguation step, where the correct entity is selected among all possible candidates. Third and finally, discovered entities are ranked by some measure of relevance. More specifically, we use Dexter [8, 9] to link the events considered with entities. Dexter, in turn relies on DBPedia for entities and their type information.

The entities extracted via this technique are mapped to corresponding Wikipedia pages and the page view statistics are obtained for each of these entities. As discussed before, we treat these Wikipedia entities as the specific instance of informational elements and base our work on predictions and recommendations around these Wikipedia entities.

5.3 GCausal Graph Construction

We formalize our set of 4 focal events using a vector Event {Scotland, Ebola, ISIS, Hamas}. Each element $Event_i$ is associated with a list of related informational elements as listed earlier in Table 1. Drawing on our discussion of Granger causality in Sec. 4.2, we perform bivariate Granger casuality tests on every pair of informational elements in $Event_i$ and obtain a $n(Event_i) \times n(Event_i)$ causal adjacency matrix (CAM) for each focal element $Event_i$ where $n(Event_i)$ is the number of informational elements related to the focal event, including the informational element for the page itself. Each entry (m,n) in CAM represents the statistical significance of the non-parametric G-causality test between informational elements m and n. Next, we prune this adjacency matrix to remove all edges where the statistical significance is below certain level of significance. The resulting G-causal graphs for the four events at 1% and 5% levels of significance are shown in Fig. 2 where the node labels correspond to the IDs mentioned within parentheses alongside the informational elements in Table 1.

6. PREDICTION EXPERIMENT

In this section, we implement a G-Causality model based on the causal network identified, and fit it to the observed page-view data from Wikipedia. In order to emphasize the value proposition of incorporating the causal linkages, we baseline our results against that from a shuffle-test which replaces the causal predictors with a randomly selected, but informationally related predictor.

6.1 Predicting Page Popularity

In this section, we illustrate the predictive value of incor-
porating causal relationships between related informational elements as depicted in Fig. 2. For each informational element in $Event_i$, we choose the best predictor based on the G-causality test results as explained in Sec. 4.2. The best predictor for each target node is selected by comparing the F-statistics across the bivariate causality tests for every pair of nodes. We apply a time-series technique, namely, Vector Autoregressive Model (VARX) which captures dynamic feedback effects [12, 18, 1]. The model specification has been described earlier in Sec. 4.2.

This modeling approach allows us to explain the volume of page views for a particular informational element as a function of the volume of page views from past years of the same informational element, as well as the volume of page views of the "most related" informational element. The "most related" informational element is selected as the best predicting element, mentioned above. The root-mean-square of the estimation residuals are described in Table 2 above.

6.2 Baselines: Shuffle Test

We emphasize the benefits of uncovering causal predictors, using an edge shuffle test, similar to the one described in [2]. Specifically, we randomize the predictor nodes for each target node in our G-causal graph, by choosing randomly from a set of all candidate predictors including but not limited to the best predictor. We hypothesize that if there is no advantage to including best predictors from related informational elements, the shuffle test should not provide any significant reduction in predictive accuracy. The RMSE of model residuals from the shuffle test are provide alongside the RMSE of our G-causal model in Table 2 above. The common baselines include two cases viz. first, when the causal graph is not pruned based on the significance level and shuffling is performed on all edges, and second, when no causal graph is constructed and each variable is predicted only using an auto-regressive model.

6.3 Results & Discussions

As evident from our experiment results, incorporating information about related best predicting information elements provides an improvement in prediction accuracy over related but weak predicting information elements. Thus, while we contend that related information elements are useful predictors of popularity of the focal information element, it is important to identify the best predicting elements from the pool of all related elements. The choice of the best predicting element is often non-obvious and requires statistical causality tests for its identification. We show in Table 2 that the results from our causal prediction model outperforms results from the shuffle test model for all information elements, across almost all levels of significance.

	Causal 0.01	Causal 0.05	Shuffle	Content
	Relatedness			
Related	**70%***	63%	60%	67%
Somewhat Related	20%	23%	17%	30%
Not Related	10%	14%	23%	3%
	Interestingness			
Interesting	**73%***	67%	57%	63%
Somewhat Interesting	20%	23%	17%	20%
Not Interesting	7%	10%	26%	17%
	Informativeness			
Informative	**63%***	**63%***	50%	57%
Somewhat Informative	33%	27%	40%	37%
Not Informative	4%	10%	10%	6%

Table 3: Performance in terms of Relatedness, Interestingness & Informativeness for the Wikipedia page recommendation task. The results highlighted with * signify statistically significant difference between the proposed Causal recommendation framework and the best performing baseline using χ^2 test with $p \leq 0.05$.

7. RECOMMENDATION JUDGMENT STUDY

In addition to the prediction experiments, we evaluate the prowess of the proposed causal graph in making causal recommendations. We build the causal graph and use the methods proposed in Section 4, along with other baselines to generate Wiki page recommendations and perform a judgment study to evaluate the quality of recommendations. Next, we discuss the methodology and findings from the judgment study in detail.

7.1 Research Questions

To assess the quality of our casual graph for content recommendation, we performed crowd-sourced assessments with human annotators to seek answers to the following research questions:

RQ1: Relatedness: Are the recommended Wiki pages related to the original page? Relatedness is important since readers are unlikely to be interested in unrelated suggestions.

RQ2: Interestingness: Will readers be interested in exploring the recommended Wiki page given their original Wiki page visit? Interestingness is important since we are not trying to propose replacement or surrogates of the current page. Hence, a reader is likely to be interested in the suggestions if they are both related and novel.

RQ3: Informativeness: Are the recommendations intrinsically informative? Informativeness is an important characteristic since and it is preferable to avoid redundancy in recommendations, while at the same time suggest Wiki pages which provide some additional information to the reader who was interested in reading the original Wiki page.

7.2 Study Methodology

Given an event, we have a list of related informational elements and the Granger causal graph among these elements. The premise of this study is to show that these causal graphs can be used to improve content recommendations. In order to do so, we structure this judgment study in the following way: a user is shown contents from an initial wiki page (i.e. a base Wiki page) following which she is shown one recommended Wiki page based on the method being evaluated. We populate the set of recommend Wiki pages using the proposed Granger Causal graph as well as the baselines. The suggestions were labeled by judges who were recruited to participate in the judgment study. We used hidden quality control questions to filter out poor-quality judges. We had three judges in total, with each judge being shown a base Wiki page and asked to rate the recommended Wiki page on a number of measures evaluating the different aspects of recommendations. The procedure involving all the 30 informational elements, 4 different methods and the three measures yielded a total of 360 judgments.

The objective of this judgment study was to evaluate the quality of the recommendations, and answer RQ1 - RQ3 described above. As comparator methods, we generate and compare suggestions using the following techniques, which includes variations of the parameters in the proposed methods and some other methods used as baselines in the study.

- **Granger Causal graph based (2 variants):** Using the Granger Causal graph constructed, we take note of the directed relationships from the original Wiki page shown to the user and select the recommended page from the set of elements (Wiki pages) which had a directed link from the original wiki page in the causal graph constructed for the event (Fig. 2).

- **Content based:** Making use of content overlap between the base Wikipedia page and the recommended Wiki page, this baseline makes recommendations based on the most similar page to the current base Wiki page being viewed by the user. Intuitively, such recommendations should score well in terms of relatedness based measures and provide informative resources to users.

- **Shuffle Test based:** For this baseline, we make use of the linkage graph obtained via the shuffle test and recommend Wiki page which has a directed link from the original base Wiki page in the graph obtained in the Shuffle test as described in 6.2.

For every method, we show a maximum of 4 recommendations to judges and the judges were asked to judge the

3-9 Nov, 2011	12-18 Jan, 2012	20-26 Jan, 2012	29 Mar-4 Apr, 2012
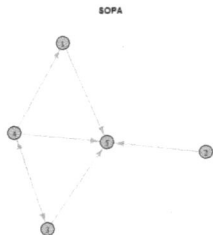	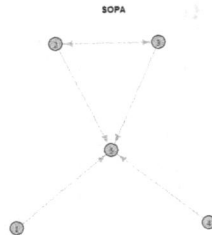	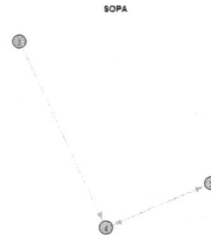	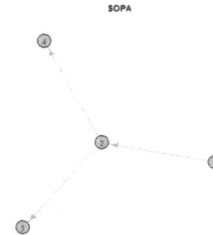

Figure 3: Analyzing the temporal evolution of causal linkages.

	1%				5%				10%			
	Pre 1	Pre 2	Post 1	Post 2	Pre 1	Pre 2	Post 1	Post 2	Pre 1	Pre 2	Post 1	Post 2
Degree	2.8	2.4	2	1.5	2.8	2.4	2	1.5	2.8	2.4	2	1.5
Closeness	0.06	0.064	.75	0.75	0.082	0.068	0.278	0.133	0.139	0.092	0.133	0.188
Betweenness	0	0	0	0	0.2	0	0.33	0.5	0.8	0.4	0.25	0.25

Table 4: Centrality measures for the different stages of SOPA event.

recommendations on the following dimensions on a three-point scale:

Relatedness: Suggestions are: (1) *Related*: all suggestions are related to the original Wiki page; (2) *Somewhat Related*: many suggestions are related to the original Wiki page; or (3) *Not Related*: most or all of the suggestions are not related to the original Wiki page.

Interestingness: Suggestions are: (1) *Interesting*: all suggestions are interesting given the original page; (2) *Somewhat Interesting*: many suggestions are interesting; or (3) *Not Interesting*: most or all suggestions are uninteresting.

Informativeness: Suggestions are: (1) *Informative*: all suggestions are informative given the original page; (2) *Somewhat Informative*: many suggestions are informative; or (3) *Not Informative*: most or all suggestions are uninformative given the contents of the original Wiki page.

Since most judges label largely disjoint sets of aspects, we do not report the standard Cohen's kappa for inter-annotator agreement. Instead, we report label agreement, which was 89.4%, 81.4% and 84.0% for relatedness, interestingness and informativeness respectively. This level of agreement demonstrates that judgment variance is quite small, and increases our confidence in the reliability of the judgments for evaluating our methods.

7.3 Findings

Table 3 shows the percentage of each response for the proposed methods and baselines in terms of relatedness, interestingness and informativeness.

Relatedness: The table shows that the causality based methods perform the best in terms of relatedness of the recommended Wiki page with the best performing method being Causal model with threshold 0.1. It is interesting to note that the content based recommendation performs better than Shuffle test based recommendation and Causal 0.5.

This is not as surprising since a method that tries to find a related Wiki page which overlaps with the base Wiki page in terms of words, is bound to find a page which is very similar in terms of content. However, incorporating the causal aspect improves the score further to 70%.

Interestingness: Interestingness is a more important measure than relatedness given that one of the contributions of this user study is in devising techniques to better recommend Wikipedia pages to read. Like relatedness, we notice that the proposed causality based methods outperform all other baselines and with a bigger difference. Unlike Relatedness, both the causality based approaches beat the Content based and Shuffle test based recommendation baselines. This shows that incorporating causal linkages information while making recommendation indeed helps recommend more *interesting* content.

Informativeness: In terms of informativeness, the overall percentages obtained are less than those for relatedness and interestingness: 63% as compared to 70% & 73% but we do observe that the proposed causal based approaches outperform the baselines and hence recommend Wiki content which is more informative.

Overall, the findings of this analysis show that the Wiki page recommendations generated using our methods yield significant gains over the baselines in a number of important measures of recommendation value. This supports our claim that incorporating causal linkage information embedded in the information seeking behavior of the crowd helps uncover hidden insights which could be leveraged to make better recommendations of content.

8. TEMPORAL EVOLUTION OF CAUSAL LINKAGES

In the previous sections, we have established the importance of understanding causal linkages between related informational elements in predicting the information seeking behavior of Internet users. However, we also hypothesize that these linkages are highly dynamic and often sensitive to major external events. To put it in different words, the causal networks for the focal events would evolve in a way that new linkages would emerge, while older linkages would lose strength and gradually disappear. To empirically investigate whether the causal graphs are indeed dynamic, we exploit a major World event to analyze whether the information seeking of event related pages show any short-run and long-run changes.

8.1 Event Context

On Jan 18, 2012, a number of major Internet-based organizations including Google, Wikipedia, Reddit etc. coordinated a series of protests against two proposed laws in the US Congress viz. the Stop Online Piracy Act (SOPA) and the Protect IP Act (PIPA). As part of the protest, some of the websites shut down their services and directed their users to a page displaying a protest message. This effect was clearly noticed, and within hours, other companies like Mozilla and Flickr joined in. The event triggered significant public participation with over 8 million people looking up their representatives on Wikipedia, and Twitter recording over 2.4 million anti-SOPA tweets. Giving in to popular opinion, both bills were finally removed from further voting by Jan 20, 2012.

8.2 Causal Linkages

Using our methodology as described in Sec.5.3, we constructed Granger causal graphs for the SOPA-blackout related informational elements, as shown in Fig. 3. In order to investigate the evolution of the causal graphs, we constructed these graphs at four different time stamps viz. (i) two months before the blackout (Pre 1) , (ii) a week before the blackout (Pre 2), (iii) a week after the blackout (Post 1), and (iv) two months after the blackout (Post 2). A simple visual inspection of the Figure 3 uncovers significant changes in the causal nature of linkages across the four periods. Beyond the change in network composition, we also perform centrality analysis [34] on the information elements in the graphs to verify if the overall centrality of the causal graph also changes over time. The centrality measures of degree, betweenness and closeness have been popularly used in the social networks literature as proxies to characterize the importance of the members of the social network. The results for the sociometrics are illustrated in Table 4 and confirm our hypothesis that both the composition of the causal graph, as well as the relative importance of the nodes change in response to major external events.

9. CONCLUSION & FUTURE WORK

Our research offers an early attempt at proposing a method to identify and incorporate causal linkages among informational elements on the Internet. The user access logs on information repositories like Wikipedia offer an invaluable source of data about the information seeking behavior of users. We demonstrate that such logs can be effectively exploited to uncover causal relationships among informational elements, that are not always obvious from a model-free analysis of the data. We highlight the incremental benefits to incorporating such causal information in our predictive model, over baseline approaches that ignore such causal linkages by randomizing the causal network. We then pro-

vide converging evidence from a judgment study where we asked human annotators to judge pairs of Wikipedia pages on Relatedness, Interestingness and Informativeness. Consistent with our predictions, we found that when users were exposed to pairs of pages that had causal linkages, they rated their experience more favorably as compared to those users who were exposed to a random pair of pages.

In addition to the predictive value of causal linkages, we also emphasize that this causal network among informational elements is not static, and is sensitive to major external events. Using the much popularized SOPA internet blackout as a test case, we demonstrated how the causal network changed at 4 different time periods before and after the event. An important recommendation we make based on this observation is that any predictive model for information seeking on the Internet must inherently be a dynamic one, and would need to be updated after major world events that are likely to influence the focal informational element.

10. REFERENCES

[1] G. Adomavicius, J. Bockstedt, and A. Gupta. Modeling supply-side dynamics of it components, products, and infrastructure: An empirical analysis using vector autoregression. *Information Systems Research*, 23(2):397–417, 2012.

[2] A. Anagnostopoulos, R. Kumar, and M. Mahdian. Influence and correlation in social networks. In *Proceedings of the 14th ACM SIGKDD international conference on Knowledge discovery and data mining*, pages 7–15. ACM, 2008.

[3] M. T. Bahadori and Y. Liu. Granger causality analysis in irregular time series. In *SDM*, pages 660–671. SIAM, 2012.

[4] M. T. Bahadori and Y. Liu. An examination of practical granger causality inference. In *Proceedings of the SIAM International Conference on Data Mining, May*, pages 2–4, 2013.

[5] R. Bandari, S. Asur, and B. A. Huberman. The pulse of news in social media: Forecasting popularity. In *ICWSM*, pages 26–33, 2012.

[6] A. Broder. A taxonomy of web search. In *ACM Sigir forum*, volume 36, pages 3–10. ACM, 2002.

[7] D. O. Case. *Looking for information: A survey of research on information seeking, needs and behavior.* Emerald Group Publishing, 2012.

[8] D. Ceccarelli, C. Lucchese, S. Orlando, R. Perego, and S. Trani. Dexter: an open source framework for entity linking. In *Proceedings of the sixth international workshop on Exploiting semantic annotations in information retrieval*, pages 17–20. ACM, 2013.

[9] D. Ceccarelli, C. Lucchese, S. Orlando, R. Perego, and S. Trani. Learning relatedness measures for entity linking. In *Proceedings of the 22nd ACM international conference on Conference on information & knowledge management*, pages 139–148. ACM, 2013.

[10] M. Cha, A. Mislove, and K. P. Gummadi. A measurement-driven analysis of information propagation in the flickr social network. In *Proceedings of the 18th international conference on World wide web*, pages 721–730. ACM, 2009.

[11] Y. Chang, X. Wang, Q. Mei, and Y. Liu. Towards twitter context summarization with user influence

models. In *Proceedings of the sixth ACM international conference on Web search and data mining*, pages 527–536. ACM, 2013.

[12] M. G. Dekimpe and D. M. Hanssens. Sustained spending and persistent response: A new look at long-term marketing profitability. *Journal of Marketing Research*, pages 397–412, 1999.

[13] N. G. Golbandi, L. K. Katzir, Y. K. Koren, and R. L. Lempel. Expediting search trend detection via prediction of query counts. In *Proceedings of the sixth ACM international conference on Web search and data mining*, pages 295–304. ACM, 2013.

[14] C. W. Granger. Investigating causal relations by econometric models and cross-spectral methods. *Econometrica: Journal of the Econometric Society*, pages 424–438, 1969.

[15] S. Jamali and H. Rangwala. Digging digg: Comment mining, popularity prediction, and social network analysis. In *Web Information Systems and Mining, 2009. WISM 2009. International Conference on*, pages 32–38. IEEE, 2009.

[16] J. G. Lee, S. Moon, and K. Salamatian. An approach to model and predict the popularity of online contents with explanatory factors. In *Web Intelligence and Intelligent Agent Technology (WI-IAT), 2010 IEEE/WIC/ACM International Conference on*, volume 1, pages 623–630. IEEE, 2010.

[17] J. G. Lee, S. Moon, and K. Salamatian. Modeling and predicting the popularity of online contents with cox proportional hazard regression model. *Neurocomputing*, 76(1):134–145, 2012.

[18] X. Luo. Quantifying the long-term impact of negative word of mouth on cash flows and stock prices. *Marketing Science*, 28(1):148–165, 2009.

[19] A. A. Mahimkar, Z. Ge, A. Shaikh, J. Wang, J. Yates, Y. Zhang, and Q. Zhao. Towards automated performance diagnosis in a large iptv network. In *ACM SIGCOMM Computer Communication Review*, volume 39, pages 231–242. ACM, 2009.

[20] I. Miliaraki, R. Blanco, and M. Lalmas. From selena gomez to marlon brando: Understanding explorative entity search. In *Proceedings of the 24th International Conference on World Wide Web*, pages 765–775. International World Wide Web Conferences Steering Committee, 2015.

[21] S. Narayan and K. R. Ramakrishnan. A cause and effect analysis of motion trajectories for modeling actions. In *Computer Vision and Pattern Recognition (CVPR), 2014 IEEE Conference on*, pages 2633–2640. IEEE, 2014.

[22] A. G. Nedungadi, G. Rangarajan, N. Jain, and M. Ding. Analyzing multiple spike trains with nonparametric granger causality. *Journal of computational neuroscience*, 27(1):55–64, 2009.

[23] H. Qiu, Y. Liu, N. Subrahmanya, W. Li, et al. Granger causality for time-series anomaly detection. In *Data Mining (ICDM), 2012 IEEE 12th International Conference on*, pages 1074–1079. IEEE, 2012.

[24] K. Radinsky, F. Diaz, S. Dumais, M. Shokouhi, A. Dong, and Y. Chang. Temporal web dynamics and its application to information retrieval. In *Proceedings of the sixth ACM international conference on Web search and data mining*, pages 781–782. ACM, 2013.

[25] K. Radinsky, K. Svore, S. Dumais, J. Teevan, A. Bocharov, and E. Horvitz. Modeling and predicting behavioral dynamics on the web. In *Proceedings of the 21st international conference on World Wide Web*, pages 599–608. ACM, 2012.

[26] H. Reichenbach and M. Reichenbach. *The direction of time*, volume 65. Univ of California Press, 1991.

[27] A. T. Scaria, R. M. Philip, R. West, and J. Leskovec. The last click: Why users give up information network navigation. In *Proceedings of the 7th ACM international conference on Web search and data mining*, pages 213–222. ACM, 2014.

[28] C. Shah. Collaborative information seeking: understanding users, systems, and content. In *Proceedings of the fifth ACM international conference on Web search and data mining*, pages 765–766. ACM, 2012.

[29] P. Spirtes, C. N. Glymour, and R. Scheines. *Causation, prediction, and search*, volume 81. MIT press, 2000.

[30] G. Szabo and B. A. Huberman. Predicting the popularity of online content. *Communications of the ACM*, 53(8):80–88, 2010.

[31] J. Tian and J. Pearl. Probabilities of causation: Bounds and identification. *Annals of Mathematics and Artificial Intelligence*, 28(1-4):287–313, 2000.

[32] M. Tsagkias, W. Weerkamp, and M. De Rijke. News comments: Exploring, modeling, and online prediction. In *Advances in Information Retrieval*, pages 191–203. Springer, 2010.

[33] M. Tsytsarau, T. Palpanas, and M. Castellanos. Dynamics of news events and social media reaction. In *Proceedings of the 20th ACM SIGKDD international conference on Knowledge discovery and data mining*, pages 901–910. ACM, 2014.

[34] S. Wasserman and K. Faust. *Social network analysis: Methods and applications*, volume 8. Cambridge university press, 1994.

[35] G. T. Wilson. The factorization of matricial spectral densities. *SIAM Journal on Applied Mathematics*, 23(4):420–426, 1972.

[36] C. Yuan, X. Liu, T.-C. Lu, and H. Lim. Most relevant explanation: properties, algorithms, and evaluations. In *Proceedings of the Twenty-Fifth Conference on Uncertainty in Artificial Intelligence*, pages 631–638. AUAI Press, 2009.

[37] B. Zong, Y. Wu, J. Song, A. K. Singh, H. Cam, J. Han, and X. Yan. Towards scalable critical alert mining. In *Proceedings of the 20th ACM SIGKDD international conference on Knowledge discovery and data mining*, pages 1057–1066. ACM, 2014.

Are Secondary Assessors Uncertain When They Disagree About Relevance Judgements?

Aiman L. Al-Harbi
School of Computer Science
University of Waterloo
Waterloo, Ontario, Canada
a2alharb@uwaterloo.ca

Mark D. Smucker
Department of Management Sciences
University of Waterloo
Waterloo, Ontario, Canada
mark.smucker@uwaterloo.ca

ABSTRACT

The collection of relevance judgements by assessors is important for many information retrieval (IR) tasks. In addition to the construction of test collections, relevance judging is critical to e-discovery and other applications where many assessors are hired to perform relevance judging. It is well known that assessors may differ in their judgements for a given document. One possible cause of a judgement difference is that an assessor may be uncertain in their judgement and thus may in effect be guessing the document's relevance. If assessors are aware of their uncertainty and can self-report their level of certainty, then uncertain relevance judgements can be targeted for adjudication by additional assessors. In this paper, we conducted a user study with 48 participants to test our hypothesis that assessors will be uncertain about their relevance judgements when the assessors are likely to disagree with each other. We found that for low consensus documents, i.e. documents known for assessor disagreement, assessors judge these documents with almost as much certainty as high consensus documents. In particular, assessor self-reported uncertainty is predictive of disagreement only for high consensus documents and not for low consensus documents.

CCS Concepts

•Information systems → Information retrieval; Users and interactive retrieval; Search interfaces; Evaluation of retrieval results; Test collections; Relevance assessment; Retrieval effectiveness;

Keywords

Search, relevance judging, evaluation, secondary assessors

1. INTRODUCTION

Assessor disagreements about relevance judgements has been observed since the 1960s and 1970s [5, 3, 8]. While early research emphasized on if the disagreement between

CHIIR'16, March 13–17, 2016, Carrboro, North Carolina, USA.

© 2016 Copyright held by the owner/author(s). Publication rights licensed to ACM.
ISBN 978-1-4503-3751-9/16/03...$15.00

DOI: http://dx.doi.org/10.1145/2854946.2854993

different assessors could have impact on the performance of IR systems, more recent studies have investigated the causes of these disagreement [2, 10, 11].

In a recent qualitative study [1], we observed secondary assessors' behaviour when making relevance judgements. A secondary assessor is an assessor who has not originated the search topic or information need. In the remainder of the paper, we simply refer to secondary assessors as assessors. We found that assessors judge the relevance of documents with different certainty levels. These levels of certainty range from very uncertain judgements to very certain ones. We divided assessor expressions of certainty into three levels: low, medium, and high. Firstly, the low level certainty relevance judgements are judgements made when assessors are entirely unsure of their judgements. When assessors produce low level certainty relevance judgements, they are very uncertain and may be guessing. Secondly, medium certainty relevance judgements are the judgements made with a degree of certainty but which lack complete certainty. Lastly, high certainty relevance judgements are those made with complete or near complete certainty. In our previous study [1], we used documents for which we knew from prior studies [4, 7, 6] that assessors either tended to agree or disagree on the documents' relevance. *Low consensus* documents are those that lack a majority agreement on their relevance while *high consensus* documents are those that reach a majority agreement on their relevance.

Based on our earlier findings, we hypothesized that assessors would tend to be uncertain in their relevance judgements when they were likely to disagree with other assessors. To test our hypothesis, we used the same documents and their consensus labels from our earlier study and conducted a user study where we asked participants to both judge the relevance of a document and report their certainty in their judgement.

In this paper we report our preliminary findings. We found that assessors demonstrate a tendency towards high certainty relevance judgements regardless of the consensus level of documents. Assessors produce more high certainty relevance judgements than medium or low certainty relevance judgements. We only see a slight trend for assessors to be more uncertain for low consensus documents as compared to high consensus documents. Likewise, for low consensus documents, self-reported certainty is not predictive of disagreement with the NIST assessor's judgment. These results refute our hypothesis that assessors would be uncertain when the consensus level of documents is low. However, when assessors judge high consensus documents, their reported certainty reflects their judgement accuracy. In other words, high consensus documents judged with low certainty are more likely to be incorrect judgements than high consensus documents judged with high certainty. For low consensus documents, judgement certainty does not appear to reflect judgement accuracy. Thus, we found that our hypothesis holds for high consensus documents but not for low consensus ones.

2. METHODS AND MATERIALS

In our earlier study [1], we conducted a think-aloud study with only 9 participants and a single user interface. However, in this study, we designed 4 different user interfaces and conducted a between subjects experiment using 12 different participants per user interface for a total of 48 participants. Each of our user interfaces collected both a binary relevance judgement and the user's self reported certainty of their relevance judgement.

2.1 Study Protocol

The study consisted of two parts: a practice part and the main task. On average, the required time to complete the whole study was an hour. Before working on the main search tasks, assessors practised on one search topic (Search Topic 427: UV Eye Damage). The aim here was to give the assessors the experience of what they would work on during the main task. In the practice part, assessors judged the relevance of four documents to the given search topic. Two of the documents were relevant to the search topic, while the other two were not relevant. Assessors were told if their judgments were correct or not, and they were allowed to ask questions or seek more clarification when necessary. In the main task part, assessors were given 4 search topics. For each search topic, there were 9 documents to judge. In total, every assessor produced 36 relevance judgments. Also, since this part was the main part of our data collection process, the research facilitator did not intervene. Assessors were working on their own.

2.2 Search Topics and Documents

We used the same search topics and documents as in our previous study [1]. To summarize what we did there, we used 4 search topics from the TREC 2005 Robust Track [9]. The topics are: 310 (Radio Waves and Brain Cancer), 336 (Black Bear Attacks), 383 (Mental Illness Drugs), and 436 (Railway Accidents). For each topic, participants judged the relevance of 3 low consensus documents and 6 high consensus documents. The high consensus documents consisted of 3 NIST judged non-relevant and 3 NIST judged relevant documents. The low consensus documents were a mix of NIST judged relevant and non-relevant documents. We determined the consensus level of documents based on data collected in other studies. We defined a document to have a probability of relevance. For example, if a document was judged relevant by 5 assessors out of 100, then this documents has a probability of relevant of 0.05. A high consensus document must have a probability of relevance ≤ 0.2 or ≥ 0.8 while a low consensus one must have a probability of relevance ≥ 0.4 and ≤ 0.6.

2.3 User Interfaces

We designed four user interfaces for this study. These interfaces fall into two groups, with two interfaces in each group: binary certainty interface group, and the ternary certainty interface group. These two groups represent our first variable in the study, which is the interface type. All of the interfaces (in spite of their certainty levels) have the same answers for the first question about relevance judgements, either relevant or not relevant. However, the answers for the second question, which is about level of certainty, differs in each interface.

In the binary certainty and ternary certainty groups, assessors were given different choices of words and phrases that represent their certainty level. These choices represent our second variable in the study. For example, in the binary certainty interface group, assessors were given only two choices. However, those choices were different in the two interfaces in the binary group. In the first interface, we gave assessors only two words: Guessing and Definitely. Each word represents a different certainty level. Guessing refers to low certainty level while Definitely refers to a high certainty level. For example, if an assessor chooses Guessing when answering the second question, it means the assessor does not know the answer and the answer is just a guess. In contrast, if Definitely is chosen, it means the assessor is highly certain about the produced relevance judgment. The certainty's choices answers in the other interface in the binary certainty interface group, which is the third interface, is represented by either low or high levels of certainty. We grouped a number of words and phrases under each level. The aim here is to give all possible words/phrases that might come to assessors' minds while judging relevance of documents. Therefore, the third interface offered more expressions than the first interface. On the other hand, the ternary certainty interface group also contained two interfaces: the second interface and the fourth interface. Both of these interfaces are composed of three levels of certainty. However, the second interface gave assessors a single word in each level to choose from. Guessing referred to the low certainty level, Maybe to the medium certainty level and Definitely to the high certainty level. Instead of giving single words, as in the second interface, in the fourth interface, assessors were given levels: low, medium and high. Under each level, we grouped all the words and phrases we found assessors to use in [1] study to express certainty of relevance judgments. Figure 1 illustrates the four interfaces.

2.4 Participants

After obtaining ethics clearance from our university, we recruited participants via different means: emails, posters and in-person invitations. We recruited 48 participants from different departments and programs. Of the 48 participants, 26 were male and 22 were female. We targeted both graduate and undergraduate students. The participants' range of age was 18 to 42 years old, and the average age was 24 years old. For most participants, using search engines is a daily activity. 83% of participants considered themselves experts in finding information. Participants did not have any training in information retrieval with the exception of basic search training sessions.

2.5 Study Design

In order to eliminate any influence of exposing the participants to all conditions of the experiment, we decided to use the between-subjects design where each participant is exposed to only one level of our two variables in the study.

Binary Interfaces

Ternary Interfaces

1. Please judge the document below as relevant or not relevant to the search topic on the right.

[Relevant] [Not Relevant]

2. Please determine your level of certainty about your judgment of the document's relevance to the search topic.

[Guessing] [Definitely]

(a) First Interface

1. Please judge the document below as relevant or not relevant to the search topic on the right.

[Relevant] [Not Relevant]

2. Please determine your level of certainty about your judgment of the document's relevance to the search topic.

[Guessing] [Maybe] [Definitely]

(b) Second Interface

1. Please judge the document below as relevant or not relevant to the search topic on the right.

[Relevant] [Not Relevant]

2. Please determine your level of certainty about your judgment of the document's relevance to the search topic.

I guess that serves	Relevant for sure	Definitely relevant
	Pretty sure	Super relevant
	Relevant/Not relevant	Certainly relevant
I do not see how this is relevant	Not related	Very relevant
	It does not count	Not related at all
I am not sure	Pretty relevant	Definitely not relevant
Low		High

(c) Third Interface

1. Please judge the document below as relevant or not relevant to the search topic on the right.

[Relevant] [Not Relevant]

2. Please determine your level of certainty about your judgment of the document's relevance to the search topic.

	I say it is	I would say		
	I am going with	I still think		
	Slightly relevant	I am going with	Relevant for sure	Definitely relevant
	That would be	That sounds	Pretty sure	Super relevant
	Should be relevant	That might be	Relevant/Not relevant	Certainly relevant
I guess that serves	There is some relevancy	Maybe slightly relevant	Not related	Very relevant
I do not see how this is relevant	I will say	a bit relevant	It does not count	Not related at all
I am not sure	It looks like	That makes it	Pretty relevant	Definitely not relevant
Low		Medium		High

(d) Fourth Interface

Figure 1: Certainty Relevance Judgements Interfaces.

Therefore, we used a Latin Square to balance the order of the topics in the study. Since we used the between-subjects design, we only balanced the order of topics and this was done to ensure it would not have any impact on the way participants completed the study. Also, for each search topic and each participant, document order was randomized. We used 3 blocks of Latin Squares for each interface. The reason for this is that we have 4 topics and in order to create a Latin Square for 4 topics we must create a 4x4 square. As such we needed 4 participants in each block. We assigned participants in round robin fashion to the 4 interface conditions. For example, each of the first four participants were assigned to one of the interfaces, and likewise for each subsequent group of 4 participants.

3. RESULTS

Table 1 shows the results of our experiment. All computations are done by aggregating the judgements for the given set of conditions. For example, in total there were 432 judgements made with each interface. A third of the judgements made were for low consensus document, i.e. 144 per interface. Continuing our example, for the first interface, of the 144 low consensus documents judged, 40 judgements where made with low certainty (27.8%) and 104 with high certainty (72.2%). Of the 40 low certainty judgements, 23 were correct, i.e. agreed with the NIST relevance judgement, and thus had an accuracy of 57.5%, which is little better than guessing. Of the 104 judgements made with high certainty for low consensus documents using the first interface, 60 were correct for an accuracy of 57.7%.

Our hypothesis was that for low consensus documents, i.e. those documents with high levels of disagreement, our study participants would report low certainty in their judgements. Our experimental results largely do not support our hypothesis. As Table 1 shows, for all four interface conditions, the study participants overwhelmingly said they were more certain than uncertain for both low and high consensus documents. There is some support for our hypothesis when we compare the rates at which documents were judged with the different levels of certainty for low and high consensus documents. For all interfaces, high consensus documents are judged with more certainty than low consensus documents. For example, with the first interface, 72.2% of low consensus documents are judged with high certainty while 77.8% of high consensus documents are judged with high certainty. Thus while we cannot directly use an assessor's reported certainty to identify documents that will be low consensus, it does appear that in general low consensus documents will be judged with slightly less certainty than high consensus documents.

The right side of Table 1 shows the accuracy of the relevance judgements. For low consensus documents, we see little to no evidence that the assessors' certainty reflects their accuracy. For example, on the first interface, low consensus documents judged with low or high certainty are judged with effectively the same accuracy of 58%, which is only slightly better than random judging. The other interfaces have similar results for low consensus documents. In contrast to the low consensus document, the high consensus documents show that when the assessors judge these documents with high certainty, their accuracy is much higher than when they judge them with medium or low certainty. For example, using the first interface, accuracy is 90.2% when high consensus documents are judged with high certainty, and accuracy drops to 70.3% for low certainty judgements.

These results imply that low consensus documents are not the result of assessors being unsure in their judgements, but that some property of the documents in combination with the search topic causes assessors to be divided in their relevance judgements. In addition, these results show that collection of judgement certainty may help assessors self identify documents that should be judged by additional assessors.

Unfortunately, the collection of judgement certainty does not appear to be helpful in the identification of judgement errors on low consensus documents nor in the identification of low consensus documents.

	Percent of Judgements			Relevance Judgement Accuracy		
	Certainty Level			Certainty Level		
Interface Type	Low	Medium	High	Low	Medium	High
Low Consensus Documents						
Binary Certainty Interfaces:						
First Interface	27.8%	NA	72.2%	57.5%	NA	57.7%
Third Interface	20.8%	NA	79.2%	50.0%	NA	48.3%
Ternary Certainty Interfaces:						
Second Interface	8.3%	36.8%	54.9%	66.7%	47.2%	53.2%
Fourth Interface	13.2%	25.7%	61.1%	36.6%	51.4%	52.3%
High Consensus Documents						
Binary Certainty Interfaces:						
First Interface	22.2%	NA	77.8%	70.3%	NA	90.2%
Third Interface	17.4%	NA	82.6%	62.0%	NA	90.0%
Ternary Certainty Interfaces:						
Second Interface	1.0%	22.9%	76.0%	66.7%	66.7%	95.4%
Fourth Interface	9.4%	22.9%	67.7%	66.7%	83.3%	89.2%
All Documents						
Binary Certainty Interfaces:						
First Interface	24.1%	NA	75.9%	65.4%	NA	79.9%
Third Interface	18.5%	NA	81.5%	57.5%	NA	76.4%
Ternary Certainty Interfaces:						
Second Interface	3.5%	27.5%	69.0%	66.7%	58.0%	84.2%
Fourth Interface	10.7%	23.8%	65.5%	54.4%	71.8%	77.7%

Table 1: Results. This table reports the percent of judgements made with different levels of certainty as well as the accuracy of the relevance judgements. Results are shown separately for low and high consensus documents as well as for all documents.

4. CONCLUSION

We conducted a study where we asked assessors to declare their certainty levels when judging the relevance of documents. We designed four different interfaces which included the uncertainty factor along with the binary relevance scale. We found that assessors tend to judge low consensus, high consensus, and all documents with high levels of certainty. The high certainty relevance judgements are the dominant ones. In other words, to a large extent, assessors are unaware that their judgements of low consensus documents are likely to be little better than random judgements. We also found that for high consensus documents, low judgement accuracy is reflected in a correspondingly low certainty of judgement, and when assessors are certain in their judgement, their judgements tend to be correct and agree with the NIST assessor. For low consensus documents, assessors have low accuracy regardless of their certainty.

5. ACKNOWLEDGMENTS

This work was supported in part by King Saud bin Abdulaziz University for Health Sciences (KSAU-HS), in part by the Natural Sciences and Engineering Research Council of Canada (NSERC), and in part by the University of Waterloo. We thank Gaurav Baruah for his valuable comments on the paper.

6. REFERENCES

[1] A. L. Al-Harbi and M. D. Smucker. A Qualitative Exploration of Secondary Assessor Relevance Judging Behavior. In IIiX, pages 195–204, 2014.

[2] P. Bailey, N. Craswell, I. Soboroff, P. Thomas, A. P. de Vries, and E. Yilmaz. Relevance Assessment: Are Judges Exchangeable and Does it Matter? In SIGIR, pages 667–674, 2008.

[3] C. W. Cleverdon. The Effect of Variations in Relevance Assessments in Comparative Experimental Tests of Index Languages. Tech. report, Cranfield Univ.; Aslib, 1970.

[4] C. Jethani. Effect of Prevalence on Relevance Assessing Behavior. Master's Thesis, University of Waterloo, 2011.

[5] M. E. Lesk and G. Salton. Relevance Assessments and Retrieval System Evaluation. Information Storage and Retrieval, 4(4):343–359, 1968.

[6] M. D. Smucker and C. Jethani. Human Performance and Retrieval Precision Revisited. In SIGIR, pages 595–602, 2010.

[7] M. D. Smucker and C. Jethani. The Crowd vs. the Lab: A Comparison of Crowd-Sourced and University Laboratory Participant Behavior. In Proc. of the SIGIR 2011 Workshop on Crowdsourcing for IR, 2011.

[8] E. M. Voorhees. Variations in Relevance Judgments and the Measurement of Retrieval Effectiveness. Information Processing & Management, 36(5):697–716, 2000.

[9] E. M. Voorhees. Overview of the TREC 2005 Robust Retrieval Track. In TREC, 2005.

[10] J. Wang and D. Soergel. A User Study of Relevance Judgments for E-discovery. In ASIST, 47(1):1–10, 2010.

[11] W. Webber, P. Chandar, and B. Carterette. Alternative Assessor Disagreement and Retrieval Depth. In CIKM, pages 125–134, 2012.

Developing a Measure of Search Expertise

Earl Bailey and Diane Kelly
School of Information and Library Science
University of North Carolina at Chapel Hill
Chapel Hill, North Carolina, USA
earl.bailey@gmail.com, dianek@email.unc.edu

ABSTRACT

While search expertise has long been considered an important variable in the study of online information search, the creation of a robust measure to characterize it has eluded researchers. Instead, those wishing to measure search expertise often include a single item that asks people to indicate how often they search or for how long they have been searching. In this paper, we report initial results of a four-phase study aimed at developing a measure of search expertise. Interviews and focus groups were conducted with nine professional searchers and an inventory of items related to online search expertise was created. While participants identified a number of usual items for determining search expertise, such as prior search experience, domain knowledge and resource knowledge, they also identified a large number of items related to personality characteristics such as persistence, flexibility, curiosity, adaptability and humility. These results suggest that measuring personality characteristics in addition to experience and knowledge might help determine who will be a more successful searcher. In today's search environments, where many people describe themselves as experts, representing these types of characteristics in a measure of search expertise might allow researchers and practitioners to observe more variation in populations of interest, design more effective instruction and make better predictions about search outcomes.

CCS Concepts

• **Information systems**→**Users and Interactive retrieval**
• **Human-centered Computing**

Keywords

Search Expertise; Measurement; Information Search

1. INTRODUCTION

Search expertise has been studied extensively in information search research, both as a fundamental concept and as a method of comparing groups of users. Search expertise has long been a difficult concept to define or measure, often equated with system experience, web experience, or computing experience. This difficulty stems in part from the complicated nature of expertise itself, which has been defined a number of ways in a number of different domains. While some argue that expertise is based primarily upon natural talent [13], others believe that acquisition of skills plays a key role [7]. Many, like Glaser [8] theorize that

CHIIR '16, March 13-17, 2016, Carrboro, NC, USA.
Copyright is held by the owner/author(s). Publication rights licensed to ACM.
ACM 978-1-4503-3751-9/16/03...$15.00.
DOI: http://dx.doi.org/10.1145/2854946.2854983

expertise develops over time, and that experience teaches experts how to organize and represent information differently than novices, leading to an increased ability to see patterns in information. If experience plays a key role in expertise, then it is particularly important in search expertise, where differences in experiences could have an impact on search success.

Sternberg [13] argued that expert abilities could be measured behaviorally, including time spent to solve problems, accuracy in solving problems, use of strategies to solve problems, and creation of schemas to represent problems. This is the perspective taken by many researchers who have devised procedures to measure search expertise. Markey [11] listed accepted and demonstrated qualities of less experienced end-user searchers such as few queries, few query terms and few uses of BOOLEAN operators or quotes. Hölscher and Strube [9] conceptualized search expertise as a kind of media competence, or "the knowledge and skills necessary to utilize the World Wide Web and other Internet resources successfully to solve information problems" (p. 338). Similarly, Chen [4] used experience searching on the Web, experience with point and click interfaces, and experience with online catalogs to separate experts from novices. In a recent study, Smith [12] studied search behaviors of searchers formally trained in the use of Dialog, specifically examining domain independent search expertise and found similarities in how people monitored the search space as well as progressed through the search task. She proposed that gaining this procedural knowledge allowed trained searchers to focus and shift their attention during a search.

Measuring the search expertise of the typical Web user presents many challenges. The Web population is vast and diverse, and includes casual users as well as professional users [1]. Hsieh-Yee argues no typical Web user even exists because the target is not stationary, and the online population constantly grows and changes [10]. While some have stressed the need for training Web users as a way to create a more homogeneous user base, others have called for changes in the design of search engines to better encourage effective searching [1].

Much of the early study of search expertise was done using card catalogs and databases, the primary means of locating information at that time. The extent to which these results and measurement practices generalize to today's searchers and search environments is questionable. Additionally, search expertise has been inconsistently defined and measured by researchers. For example, years of experience has often been used to divide searchers into novice and expert groups. Experts defined by this division in one study might be considered novices in another study, making it impossible to compare results among studies. There is currently no valid and reliable instrument that can be used to measure search expertise and which can possibly be used to make research results from different studies more commensurable. The lack of such a measure also complicates the development of information literacy programs and techniques to evaluate such programs.

In this paper, we report on Phases 1 and 2 of a four-phase study designed to develop a measure of search expertise. The goal of Phases 1 and 2 is to develop an initial set of items that can potentially be used to measure search expertise. This was accomplished through one-on-one interviews and focus group interviews with professional searchers. In Phase 3, the initial instrument will be tested using cognitive interviews and in Phase 4 the initial version of the instrument will be tested using quantitative means to establish validity and reliability.

2. METHOD

Nine participants were recruited for both Phase 1 and Phase 2 simultaneously. All participants completed both phases. Each participant was given two ten-dollar gift cards for a local coffee shop as an honorarium. Participants were professional librarians with MLS or MLIS degrees currently working in a university environment, recruited using snowball sampling. All participants held positions where they searched on a regular basis: four in medical research, two in humanities research, two in archival research and metadata, and one in economic research. Three participants each had more than 20 years of experience in positions using search regularly. Participants were also published authors in their fields of study.

2.1 Phase 1 Interviews

Phase 1 consisted of 60 minute, one-on-one, semi-structured interviews with participants. Before coming to the interview, participants were told:

For the interview, please consider your experiences around online search. I will be asking you to discuss what online search expertise means to you, as well as different aspects of online search expertise that you consider to be important.

During the interview, they were asked to list important dimensions of online search expertise, including both general ideas and specific items. Interviews were initiated by a script listing possible questions and guided by participants' responses. Specifically, participants were asked: What do you think it means to be an expert searcher?; Can you tell me what search expertise means to you?; and Considering your thoughts on what search expertise means and what an expert searcher means, can you tell me some specific ways you would measure search expertise? These primary questions were also explored further with clarifying questions based upon the responses. Interviews were recorded and transcribed. The dimensions and items that emerged from these interviews were used in Phase 2.

2.2 Phase 2 Focus Groups

For Phase 2, participants were organized into three 90-minute focus groups of three participants each and given the combined dimensions and items from their interviews before the focus group meeting for consideration. This organization was done by convenience: when 3 participants completed Phase 1 a focus group was organized with these three participants. The listing of items and dimensions from Phase 1 was sorted alphabetically and sent to participants before the focus group. During each focus group, participants performed two exercises. In the first exercise, they were given each item written on an index card. Then, as a group, participants performed a free-form card sorting exercise to sort the cards into categories. Cards with items that they

considered to represent the same idea were clipped together. Participants were also instructed to add cards for missing concepts or remove cards for items they considered unimportant. In the second exercise, participants rated the concepts listed on each card according to how important the concept was in defining expertise.

2.3 Data Analysis

Interview data from Phase 1 was examined for mention of concepts, measures, or items related to online search expertise. These were listed without ordering or sorting in order to obtain as comprehensive a list as possible for each participant. Only duplicate items were discarded. For Phase 2, the lists for each participant in a specific focus group were merged and sorted alphabetically. Only duplicates were removed. After the focus groups, the categories used were noted, as well as the items listed in each category and the concepts determined by participants to be similar. These categories and items were then compared across focus groups for similarities and differences.

Items from Phase 1 and categories from Phase 2 were also compared to a proposed model of online search expertise, created by examining the literature and shown in Figure 1. In the model, search expertise is defined as an ability that is derived from prior experiences, but also modified in any particular moment by the searcher's current affective and cognitive states and capabilities. The results from the focus groups were compared to this model, noting both places where they correlated and differed.

Figure 1. Proposed Model of Online Search Expertise

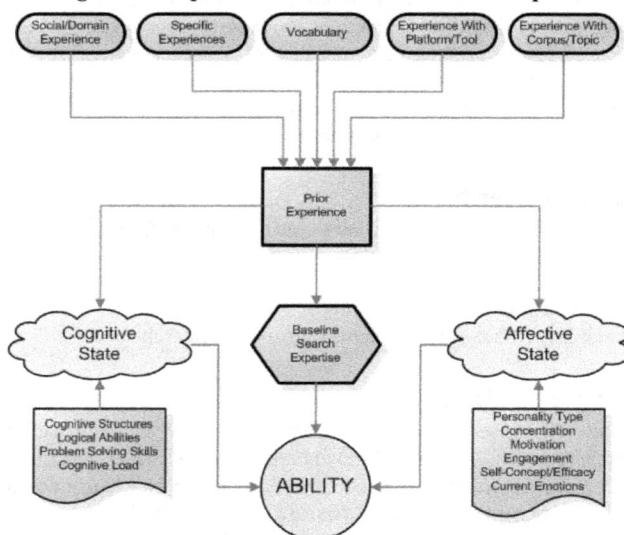

3. FINDINGS AND DISCUSSION

Many of the items identified by participants during Phase 1 interviews were similar. Items related to experience were most prevalent and included domain experience, experience with tools and platforms, experience with databases, education, and some specific experiences. Participants also focused on items related to personality and abilities, including concentration, creativity, intuition, tenacity, patience, and confidence. Many of these items were expected as specific examples of factors shown in Figure 1. Below, we elaborate our findings.

3.1 Phase 1 Interviews

As expert searchers, participants were asked to think about online search expertise before the interviews, and many of them came with particular ideas, even notes. The initial responses they gave focused on the practical aspects of being an expert searcher, for example understanding the tools being used or their limitations.

P1-2: *"I think to be an expert searcher, it's important to be able to understand something about what's going on behind the search box. So I think to be an expert searcher it really involves having enough knowledge of the technology or the database or whatever it is to understand what you're searching when you type in words, how the search box interprets your responses on the back end and then how the results that come out reflect the words that you've typed in."*

P2-3: *"So expert searcher...someone who understands the structure of the database. The way in which the search engine searches the contents, how language is used in storage and searching..."*

Other practical aspects that were mentioned by participants in initial statements were keeping up to date on search skills, understanding questions, especially questions from others, and focusing on both the process of searching as an interaction and also the end result needed.

P2-2: *"...so being able to think about in terms you're searching for what each term actually means, how to combine them in ways that's not just guessing or not letting the tool guess for you but deliberately being able to combine terms in a way that anyone can see a meaningful result."*

P2-2: *"I think it is a combination of experience, knowledge of the tool, knowledge of the subject... teamwork. ... knowing how to get help, knowing where to go, knowing where to look outside yourself..."*

This focus on the practical skills and process of search supports the idea of 'deliberate practice' in expertise research [6] as well as fitting into the varied types of experience shown in Figure 1.

After their initial thoughts, participants were encouraged to add other aspects of online search expertise that seemed important to them. Here, participants referred to personal characteristics of the searcher, including persistence or tenacity, curiosity, patience, confidence, intuition, and analytic ability.

P2-3: *"...analytic ability, patience and persistence in terms of kind of innate traits, curiosity."*

While these traits of the searcher were mentioned after their ideas on tools and databases and other practical ideas, when asked to consider the most important part of online search expertise, participants selected these traits rather than practical experiences.

P3-1: *"I could teach somebody to do that. I can't really teach somebody patience and flexibility. ...sometimes people are sort of innately good at more or less innately able to analyze a situation, state the information need and to be able to plan and prepare."*

It is also interesting to note that participants often seemed hesitant to state unequivocally that any particular experience with a tool or database would lead to search expertise. On the other hand, for traits of the person, they were more certain.

P2-3: *"No I think, I mean, certainly, they're more likely to be an expert searcher if you spend a lot of time searching one database, you'll usually try to understand why it does what it does and if you also have the ability to transfer that knowledge and use it as a tool when you go someplace else and some people do and some people don't. If you don't, they'll know you're not an expert searcher in my opinion, you may be an expert ex-database searcher..."*

P2-3: *"...curiosity is a big key because you can't create it, either someone has it or they don't. If they don't have it, they're not going to be a good librarian let alone an expert searcher."*

Participants were also asked how they might measure online search expertise without resorting to using a specific task. Their responses to this question once again showed their focus on the practice of search; generally, participants had a difficult time identifying methods for measuring search expertise.

At the end of the interview, participants were asked whether their ideas on search expertise had changed after talking about it. Their answers here focused on both the ongoing nature of expertise, as well as the traits of the searcher.

P3-3: *"So expertise is...ongoing and...one part of fluidity is this willingness to learn and to grow and sort of a curiosity maybe that makes an expert searcher and sort of willingness to ... fail and to consider alternatives."*

3.2 Phase 2 Focus Groups

The focus groups began with a randomized set of items written on index cards, with 79 individual items for Focus Group 1, 123 individual items for Focus Group 2, and 78 individual items for Focus Group 3. The number of items per group was a function of the items identified by group participants during the one-on-one interviews. After the groups sorted the cards, Focus Group 1 had 10 categories and 78 individual items; Focus Group 2 had 13 categories and 113 individual items; and Focus Group 3 had 7 categories and 58 individual items. The items were combined into a single list and duplicates were eliminated, resulting in 125 individual items. Combining the three lists together showed some clear patterns in the words that participants used to talk about online search expertise.

All three groups sorted items related to experience differently than the model, but used many of the same dimensions. Focus Group 1 split experience into: General Search Experience, containing basic online experience; Interacting With Search Systems, containing tool and controlled vocabulary experience; Knowledge of Sources, including corpus and culture; and Subject Knowledge. Focus Group 2 identified: Experience in Searching Specific Subjects, Knowledge of Specific Databases, Non-Search Related Experience, Knowledge of a Variety of Databases, Acquiring Subject Knowledge, and Maintaining/Improving Search Skill. Focus Group 3 used a more general Experience category along with Training and Understanding Tools.

All three groups included items related to Social/Domain Experience, Vocabulary, Experience with Platform/Tool, and Experience with Corpus/Topic. All three also considered updating skills to be an important part of search expertise. Training was also mentioned as important. All three groups also focused on specific ways in which tools could be manipulated to enhance results, including Boolean, iteration, quotes, and synonyms.

None of the focus groups differentiated Cognitive State from Affective State, instead combining the two into a category they named Personality or Personal Characteristics. Within that category, for all three focus groups the most explicit items were items related to Motivation and Engagement, including terms like: Passion for Searching, Enjoys Search Process, and Curiosity.

Aspects of Cognitive State were represented by specific items within Personality rather than being separated into a distinct category for two of the focus groups. Items included Creativity, Adaptability, Self-awareness, Analytical and Problem Solving skills, and Organizational Skills. Focus Group 2 grouped items like these into Analytical Skills, although that grouping also contained items related to evaluation of results. Evaluation of Results was a concept seen in all three groups, with multiple items including judging search results, judging information quality, analyzing results, understanding relevance and fine-tuning results.

All three focus groups also touched upon another area related to dealing with others, either specific experience searching for others or more general people skills. For two groups, these skills were placed into Personality, but Focus Group 2 separated them into a separate group, including skills in negotiation, communication, teamwork, marketing, and training.

Not all of the listed concepts were used by the focus groups. Focus Group 1 discarded the most items, the majority of which were specific kinds of experience they did not consider to be important such as experience with bibliographies, professions, academic sources, bibliographic tools, specific platforms, and reference. These discards were not seen in the other focus groups, each of which discarded only one item they deemed unimportant.

4. CONCLUSIONS

The listing of items provides support for the categories shown in the model, although the focus groups did not always use the same categories. The very different ways in which items were grouped by the three focus groups suggests that many of these concepts are intertwined and that the individual items might be of more interest than the exact way in which those items are arranged.

Within the model, Prior Experience showed the strongest support, with many of the items and groups mapping directly to the model. The addition of continual skill improvement and training experience to the model was identified in all three focus groups. Planning could also be supported in some search environments as well, although it should be noted that planning was often mentioned in conjunction with searching on behalf of others.

It is interesting to note the support for both the cognitive and affective aspects of online search expertise, especially from the individual interviews. While Prior Experience as an overall category dominated in terms of number of items, statements from the interviews indicated a hesitancy to support those items as necessary. On the other hand, items sorted as Personality Traits or Analytical Abilities, including persistence, flexibility, curiosity, adaptability, and humility, were given stronger support in interviews as necessary traits for the expert searcher.

Of course, the idea that personality characteristics influence search is not new. Bellardo [2] sought to determine and measure the cognitive or personality traits that led to success in searching. She collected information on each participant including GRE scores to measure intelligence, Interpersonal Disposition

Inventory scores to measure personality traits, and the Khatena-Torrance Creative Perception Inventory to measure creative orientations. While her results showed no clear indication that cognitive or personality traits could be used to predict search success, there were indications that both creativity and analytical ability could influence search results. Borgman [3] combined concepts of inherent individual personality differences with training in systems use and suggested that while technical aptitude played a role in executing search strategies, personality could influence the actual selection of those strategies. Chi [5] noted that while experts could often be expected to surpass non-experts, individual differences in cognition could impair expert performance. However, to our knowledge, no one has created a measure of search expertise that incorporates these factors. The strong support for these factors by the experts shows how important these factors are in moving forward with the creation of a more diverse measure of online search expertise.

Our next step is to create an initial instrument to measure online search expertise and evaluate it with cognitive interviews. Following this, we will invite several hundred people to complete the instrument and conduct factor and reliability analyses. We will include participants who are search experts by virtue of specialized degree and job duties, and those new to online searching to help test validity. Creating a measure of search expertise will allow for a better understanding of this important ability, and provide researchers with a robust way to measure this construct and incorporate it into their research models. This will also allow future research results to be more commensurable. Finally, as a diagnostic tool, such a measure can assist in the development and evaluation of information literacy programs.

5. REFERENCES

[1] Aula, A. & Nordhausen, K. (2006). Modeling successful performance in Web searching. *JASIST*, *57*, 1678–1693.

[2] Bellardo, T. (1985). An investigation of online searcher traits and their relationship to search outcome. *JASIS*, *36*, 241-250.

[3] Borgman, C.L. (1989). All users of information systems are not created equal: An exploration into individual differences. *IP&M*, *25*(3), 237-252.

[4] Chen, C. (2000). Individual differences in a spatial-semantic virtual environment. *JASIS*, *51*(6), 529–542.

[5] Chi, M. (2006). Two approaches to the study of experts' characteristics. In K.A. Ericsson, N. Charness, P.J. Feltovich, & R.R. Hoffman (Eds.), *The Cambridge handbook of Expertise and Expert Performance* (pp. 21-30). Cambridge, UK: Cambridge Univ. Press.

[6] Ericcson, K., Krampe, R., & Tesche-Romer, C. (1993). The role of deliberate practice in the acquisition of expert performance. *Psychological Review, 100*, 363–406.

[7] Ericsson, K. & Charness, N. (1994). Expert performance: its structure and acquisition. *Amer. Psych.*, *49*(8), 725-747.

[8] Glaser, R. (1987). Thoughts on expertise. In C. Schooler & W. Schaie (Eds.) *Cognitive functioning and social structure over the life course.* Norwood, NJ: Ablex.

[9] Hölscher, C. & Strube, G. (2000). Web search behaviour of Internet experts and newbies. *Proc. of WWW Conference.*

[10] Hsieh-Yee, I. (2001). Research on Web search behavior. *Library and Information Science Research*, 23, 167-185.

[11] Markey, K. (2007). Twenty-five years of end-user searching, Part 1: Research findings. *JASIST*, *58*(8), 1071- 1081.

[12] Smith, C. (2014). Domain-independent search expertise: A description of procedural knowledge gained during guided instruction. *JASIST*, *66*(7), 1388-1405.

[13] Sternberg, R. J. (2006). *Cognitive psychology* (4th ed.). Belmont, CA: Thomson Wadsworth.

Factor Analysis of a Search Self-Efficacy Scale

Kathy Brennan, Diane Kelly, Yinglong Zhang
School of Information and Library Science
University of North Carolina at Chapel Hill
Chapel Hill, NC, 27599-3360
[kbrennan, diane.kelly, yinglongz] @ unc.edu

ABSTRACT

Participants in information search studies are often asked to characterize their search expertise using questionnaires provided by researchers. These questionnaires often contain ad hoc sets of items in part because there are no valid and reliable measures of search experience. In this paper, we present results of an exploratory factor analysis of 327 responses to a 14-item Search Self-Efficacy scale (SSE) that we have been using as a way to measure search experience in our research. The responses come from eight different interactive information retrieval (IIR) studies, which we have conducted over the last six years, with a variety of participant types: university students, participants from the general adult population and crowd-sourced participants. The purpose of this analysis is to understand the variation in search self-efficacy scores across different types of people and to evaluate the potential of the SSE scale as a tool for measuring search experience. Overall, participants from all eight studies reported similar levels of search self-efficacy; the overall average from all eight studies was 7.47 (items scored on a 10-point scale) with little variance (standard deviation=1.36). Both the lowest and highest scores (7.1 and 7.8) were observed in studies involving the general adult population. A factor analysis showed that the questionnaire items load onto six factors, although only four had sufficient numbers of items loading on them. These four factors represent overall task success, effective use of time, query development skills, and advanced search skills.

Keywords

Search behavior; self-efficacy; search experience; measures

1. INTRODUCTION

In many studies of online search behavior, it is common for researchers to ask participants to provide an indication of their search experience. This is typically done with one or more items that ask searchers to indicate the frequency with which they perform searches, the length of time they have used search engines, or their general expertise (from novice to expert). The basic idea is that differences in search experience may cause differences in search behaviors and outcomes [4, 13, 14].

CHIIR'16, March 13-17, 2016, Carborro, NC, USA.
Copyright is held by owner/author(s). Publication rights licensed to ACM.
ACM 978-1-4503-3751-9/16/03$15.00.
DOI: http//dx.doi.org/10.1145/2854946.2855002

Measuring search experience was important in early studies of interactive searching as online information systems often required searchers to have extensive knowledge of search syntax and query languages, and were designed primarily for search experts such as librarians. After search went 'public' in the form of Web search engines, more and more people had an opportunity to search, to develop search skills and, more importantly, to develop ideas about the quality of their skills, even to the point of overestimating their skills [6]. Although it is unlikely that today's average Web searcher's skills are equivalent to the skills of a trained searcher, it is reasonable to assume that the public's general search abilities have increased during the past 20 years and that a greater range of expertise exists. This implies that more nuanced measures of search experience are needed if researchers would like to use search experience as a variable in their studies.

Previous measures used to characterize search experience have been coarse and general, and there are no contemporary measures of search experience that are valid and reliable (at least not demonstratively). Typically, researchers create reasonable sounding self-report instruments on an ad-hoc basis [12], or ask questions that greatly simplify search experience, such as how frequently one conducts online searching. Past measures have also not been particularly predictive of behaviors. For example, when distinguishing between search novices and experts, some studies have found that expert searchers submit longer queries than novice searchers [1, 8], while results from other studies have contradicted these findings [2]. Examples of conflicting results in studies of expert versus novice searchers can also be found related to other search behaviors such as number of queries submitted to the system, number of items opened, and speed of querying (see [13] for a review). Smith [13] suggests that these conflicts occur because expert searchers dynamically adapt their search behaviors to their contexts. Thus, behavioral signals alone do not provide an accurate characterization of search ability and also do not allow a person to be characterized before they commence searching.

Self-report instruments are one of the primary methods for gathering information from people (regardless of field of study), so creating measures that are valid, reliable and discriminating are important concerns. One of the only examples of a validated measure of search experience is the work of Debowski, Wood and Bandura [5], who used Bandura's concept of self-efficacy as the basis for search experience [3]. Bandura posited that the main cognitive drivers of behavior are: (1) beliefs about behavioral outcomes leading to favorable consequences and (2) beliefs about one's ability to perform particular behaviors (self-efficacy). Bandura [3] provides a succinct definition of self-efficacy as "People's judgments of their capabilities to organize and execute courses of action required to attain designated types of performances. It is not concerned with the skills one has but with one's judgments of what one can do with whatever skills one possesses" [p. 391]. Notice the focus is on a person's *beliefs* and *perceptions* not their *actual* skill. The underlying assumption behind using search self-efficacy as a surrogate for search experience is people who have greater confidence in their abilities to accomplish specific search tasks will be more likely to successfully execute these tasks even if through several attempts.

In Debowski, et al.'s [5] 21-item instrument, a list of items was presented and individuals first indicated whether they could perform the task (yes or no) and then indicated the amount of confidence they felt about their abilities to perform the tasks (10-point scale). Debowski, et al. [5] used classic library science research to identify items for their search self-efficacy scale and performed validity and reliability testing, although it is not described in detail in their paper. For the past six years, we have used a modified version of Debowski, et al.'s scale in our research to characterize participants' search experience. Before we started using the scale, we reviewed the items, deleting some that were no longer relevant (e.g., searching CD-ROMs) and updating others; this reduced the number of items on the scale from 21 to 14. We also changed the format of the response, eliminating the binary question asking participants if they felt they could perform the task described. Since people were asked to indicate how confident they were they could execute the task, we assumed if an individual did not feel they could execute a particular task, they could express this through the confidence scale. The modified version of the SSE scale is shown in the Appendix: Table 1.

While we were able to do some reliability testing in the past, none of our previous studies had sufficient sample sizes for conducting a more substantial inquiry such as can be done with factor analysis. In this paper, we describe results of a factor analysis of the pooled search self-efficacy data collected in eight studies with a combined total of 327 participants. The purpose of this analysis is to understand the variation in search self-efficacy scores across different types of people and to evaluate the potential of the SSE scale as a tool for measuring search experience. Table 2 (Appendix) provides a description of the datasets. All studies used general information search tasks, either using online web search engines or TREC collections with custom search applications.

2. RESULTS

Descriptive statistics (means and standards deviations) for each dataset as well as the statistics for the pooled data are shown in Table 3 (Appendix). Ten participants' data were eliminated because they either did not respond to all of the questions or answered all 14 questions with the highest value. There were no significant differences detected among participants' average search self-efficacy scores according to study, $F(7, 319)=.978$, $p=0.447$, which provides support for combining the datasets. It is also the case that this scale was completed at the start of all studies, before any experimental variables were introduced.

Overall, participants reported similar levels of search self-efficacy; the average from all eight studies was 7.47 with little variance (SD=1.36). Both the lowest and highest scores (7.1 and 7.8) were observed in studies involving the general adult population. The pooled averages for the individual questionnaire items range from 6.41 to 8.17. There were three scores greater than 8.0: identify requirements, distinguish relevant, and competent effective. The lowest scores (<7.0) were on four items: special syntax, like a pro, few irrelevant, and focus query.

2.1 Factor Analysis

Before performing Exploratory Factor Analysis (EFA), we conducted Mayer-Olkin (KMO) measure of sampling adequacy and Bartlett's test of Sphericity to test whether the sample size in

our study could support a valid EFA. The result of the KMO was 0.92, with Bartlett's Test yielding 357.88 ($p<0.001$). Both values indicated that our sample satisfies the requirement assumptions for proceeding with EFA [7].

To determine the number of factors to keep in the EFA, we used a procedure called parallel analysis, which is a Monte Carlo simulation technique for determining how many factors to extract during factor analysis [10]. In parallel analysis, one generates a random dataset with the same number of responses and variables as in the sample data. A correlation matrix is then created and eigenvalues computed. Analyses of the eigenvalues allow researchers to determine the appropriate number of factors to extract. The scree plot with an induced parallel analysis using our data indicated that six factors should be kept for the EFA.

We adopted oblique (Promax) rotation because responses to different items were highly correlated. The principal axis factoring (PAF) method was used to extract factors. Readers will likely be more familiar with principal components analysis (PCA) for factor analysis; however, Hatcher [7] argues that PCA should only be used for data reduction as it has limited capability for discovering underlying factor structures. Hatcher [7] argues that PAF provides a better way to identify underlying latent structures, especially when the assumption of multivariate normality in the manifest variables cannot be strictly met.

The item loadings on the six factors are shown in Table 4. All loadings (highlighted in gray shadow and bold typeface) ranged in value from 0.626 to 0.818. The final communality estimate, h^2, of each item is larger than 0.40, indicating that each item is moderately correlated with its corresponding factor. Unlike PCA, the factor loadings for PAF are not always as distinctive, which is why, for example, Item 7, loads on multiple factors. In PAF, it is recommended in these cases to also examine all factor matrices and consider the logical agreement between items [15]. For example, we ultimately grouped Item 7 with Items 3 and 4, rather than Items 14 and 9 because the latter items were about time management, while the former were about advanced search skills and Item 7 asked people to indicate the extent to which they could find results similar to a professional.

Table 4: Principal Axis Factoring of Self-Efficacy Data

Item	F_1	F_2	F_3	F_4	F_5	F_6	h^2
6	**0.818**	0.593	0.488	0.553	0.581	0.460	0.68
5	**0.812**	0.572	0.499	0.586	0.588	0.704	0.83
12	**0.812**	0.742	0.589	0.650	0.765	0.400	0.74
13	**0.795**	0.582	0.519	0.613	0.610	0.324	0.65
14	0.622	**0.954**	0.548	0.601	0.621	0.450	0.62
9	0.591	**0.769**	0.526	0.518	0.582	0.438	0.60
8	0.402	0.403	**0.775**	0.365	0.373	0.499	0.63
10	0.523	0.606	**0.767**	0.492	0.499	0.360	0.61
2	0.666	0.637	0.528	**0.982**	0.595	0.531	0.97
1	0.572	0.599	0.421	**0.677**	0.590	0.447	0.97
11	0.626	0.596	0.479	0.522	**0.902**	0.404	0.83
3	0.329	0.407	0.466	0.405	0.341	**0.626**	0.43
4	0.596	0.532	0.408	0.566	0.613	**0.638**	0.57
7	0.603	0.677	0.633	0.491	0.509	**0.630**	0.62

Note: h^2 = communalities of the measured variables

While the PAF produced a solution using six factors, one factor did not have a sufficient number of items loading on it (F_5). One (F_3) had items loading on it that were similar to another factor (F_4), so we decided to eliminate this factor. We believe the four remaining factors represent: overall task success (F1), effective use of time (F2), query development skills (F4) and advanced

242

search skills (F6). The Pearson correlations observed among the six factors are shown in Table 5, and ranged from 0.45 to 0.74. All correlations were significant ($p<0.001$).

Table 5. Pearson Correlations of Six Factors

Factor	F_1	F_2	F_3	F_4	F_5	F_6
F_1	1.00					
F_2	0.72	1.00				
F_3	0.59	0.65	1.00			
F_4	0.69	0.67	0.53	1.00		
F_5	0.74	0.71	0.54	0.66	1.00	
F_6	0.46	0.51	0.50	0.50	0.45	1.00

3. DISCUSSION

Overall, levels of search self-efficacy were similar across the eight studies, with little variance. The descriptive statistics show a positive skew of individual and pooled questionnaire data, which is not surprising, given the known tendency for people to overestimate their search abilities [6]. Since self-efficacy is based on people's beliefs about their abilities to accomplish tasks rather than their actual abilities, such a scale might simply reflect this bias. At the same time, however, there is a clear trend in the data showing that when it comes to more sophisticated search skills such as use of special syntax or skills associated with professional searchers, people are able to recognize and acknowledge their more limited abilities. This is particularly the case with studies involving student participants (S4, S5, S8); despite Gross and Latham's finding [6] that students express inflated self-efficacy, the fact that the lowest scores for the item "like a pro" are from the three student studies suggests that people can differentiate between layperson search skills and professional search skills. It may be the case that more directed questions related to search-specific skills are needed to elicit more accurate self-appraisal from study participants. The positive skew might also reflect the supposition that people are getting better at search, or people's interpretation of the number 7 as average. In regard to the lack of variance, the study reporting the largest variance (S7) had the smallest sample size (N=20) and was of the general adult population. The lack of variance in the remaining studies may be the product of a homogeneous sample or an indicator that the samples were of adequate size to reduce sample size-related variance issues. The lack of variance also is a sign that the items may not be particularly discriminating.

We believe our results and analysis extend the original work of Debowski et al. [5] in several ways. First, Debowski et al. investigated search behaviors in a structured, CD-ROM database of bibliographic records, while our studies have all included evaluation of full text documents and Web searching. Our increased scope of information behaviors to include full text evaluation provides a more complete representation of current-day information searching. Second, in all of our studies, participants were provided search tasks and allowed to search either the open web or a document collection based on their own knowledge of searching and using natural language queries. This is different from Debowski et al. [5], where participants were provided search instructions to conduct searches in a structured system that required the use of defined keywords and search syntax. Experimental manipulations in our studies focused on interfaces, whereas the manipulation in [5] involved the instructions given to participants. Finally, in terms of the factor analysis, we can compare our results to Debowski et al. [5]. Debowski et al. identified four subfunctions of electronic search: problem definition, keyword identification, structured search statement

construction, and personal beliefs about performance. It is possible to see how three of our four factors map roughly to the four subfunctions: our overall task success to Debowski et al.'s problem definition, query development skills to both keyword identification and structure search statement construction, and advanced search skills to people's beliefs in their abilities to achieve different levels of search performance. In addition, we identified one new factor related to time.

4. CONCLUSION

We presented results of an exploratory factor analysis of data pooled from eight IIR studies using a 14-item SSE scale. The work makes two main contributions: (1) it provides data describing how a variety of different types of people characterize their search self-efficacy; and (2) it suggests four possible factors which might be used in a measure of search expertise. While these factors represent some activities that might distinguish different levels of search expertise they are not exhaustive and are limited to a particular search context; that is, searching for documents to resolve information-gathering tasks. Our results also showed that the scale in its current form is unlikely to be sensitive enough to discriminate amongst people with different levels of search expertise. Thus, additional work needs to be done to enhance the content and discriminant validity of the instrument. This line of research is important as the development of a valid and reliable measure of search expertise would facilitate more in-depth investigations of the relationship between search experience, search interfaces and search behaviors.

5. ACKNOWLEDGEMENT

Thanks to Henry Feild for sharing the data from S1 and everyone who helped gather the data in S2-S8.

6. REFERENCES

[1] Aula, A. & Käki, M., 2003. Understanding expert search strategies for designing user-friendly search interfaces. In *ICWI 2003*, 759-762.

[2] Aula, A. & Nordhausen, K., 2006. Modeling successful performance in Web searching. *JASIS&T*, 57, 12, 1678-1693.

[3] Bandura, A., 1986. *Social Foundations of Thought and Action: A Social Cognitive Theory*. Prentice-Hall, Englewood Cliffs, N.J.

[4] Bates, M. J., 1990. Where should the person stop and the information search interface start? *IP&M*, 26, 5, 575-591.

[5] Debowski, S., Wood, R., & Bandura, A., 2001. Impact of guided exploration & enactive exploration on self-regulatory mechanisms & information acquisition through electronic search. *J Appl Psychol*, 86, 6, 1129-1141.

[6] Gross, M. & Latham, D., 2013. Addressing below proficient information literacy skills: Evaluating efficacy of evidence-based educational intervention. *L&ISR*, 35, 3, 181.

[7] Hatcher, L., 2013. *Advanced Statistics in Research: Reading, Understanding and Writing Up Data Analysis Results*. Shadow Finch Media, LLC.

[8] Hölscher, C. & Strube, G., 2000. Web search behavior of Internet experts and newbies. *Compu Netw*, 33, 1-6, 337-346.

[10] Ledesma, R. & Valero-Mora, P., 2007. Determining the number of factors to retain in EFA: An easy-to-use computer program for carrying out parallel analysis. *Pract Assess Res Eval*, 12, 2, 1-11.

[12] Moore, J. L., et al., 2007. The search experience variable in information behavior research. *JASIS&T*, 58, 10, 1529-1546.

[13] Smith, C. L., 2015. Domain-independent search expertise: A description of procedural knowledge gained during guided instruction. *JASIS&T*, *66*, 7, 1388-1405.

[14] Wildemuth, B. M., 2004. The effects of domain knowledge on search tactic formulation. *JASIS&T*, *55*, 3, 246-258.

[15] Worthington, R. & Whittaker, T., 2006. Scale development research: A content analysis and recommendations for best practices. *Couns Psych*, *34*, 6, 806-838.

APPENDIX

Table 1. Questionnaire items, labels, and questionnaire language (10-point scale, where 1=Totally Unconfident; 5-6=Reasonably Confident; 10=Very Confident)

Item	Label	Questionnaire language: "How confident are you that you can ..."
1	Identify requirements	Identify the major requirements of the search from the initial statement of the topic.
2	Develop queries	Correctly develop search queries to reflect my requirements.
3	Special syntax	Use special syntax in advanced searching (e.g., AND, OR, NOT).
4	Evaluate list	Evaluate the resulting list to monitor the success of my approach.
5	Many results	Develop a search query which will retrieve a large number of appropriate articles.
6	Enough results	Find an adequate number of articles.
7	Like a pro	Find articles similar in quality to those obtained by a professional searcher.
8	Few irrelevant	Devise a query which will result in a very small percentage of irrelevant items on my list.
9	Structure time	Efficiently structure my time to complete the task.
10	Focus query	Develop a focused search query that will retrieve a small number of appropriate articles.
11	Distinguish relevant	Distinguish between relevant and irrelevant articles.
12	Competent effective	Complete the search competently and effectively.
13	Little difficulty	Complete the individual steps of the search with little difficulty.
14	Allocated time	Structure my time effectively so that I will finish the search in the allocated time.

Table 2: Description of eight studies used in analysis[1]

Year	Code	Purpose of study	N	Participant type	Corpus
2010	S1	Search behaviors	100	Crowdworkers	Open web
2012	S2	Search interface study	29	General pop. adults	Open web
2012	S3	User evaluations of queries	40	General pop. adults	Open web
2013	S4	Search interface study	36	University students	TREC 2005 robust
2014	S5	Use of query suggestions	29	University students	TREC 2005 robust
2014	S6	Individual differences and search behaviors	47	General pop. adults	Open web
2014	S7	Individual differences and search behaviors	20	General pop. adults	Open web
2015	S8	Search interface study	36	University students	TREC 2005 robust

Table 3: Descriptive statistics from each of eight studies and overall pooled

	S1	S2	S3	S4	S5	S6	S7	S8	Pooled
Sample size (N)	97	29	39	36	29	46	19	32	327
1.Identify requirements	7.8 (2.0)	8.3 (2.1)	8.1 (1.5)	8.3 (1.2)	8.0 (1.6)	8.7 (1.4)	8.5 (2.4)	8.5 (0.9)	8.17 (1.59)
2.Develop queries	8.1 (1.8)	8.3 (1.6)	7.8 (1.7)	7.6 (1.7)	7.8 (1.4)	8.3 (1.4)	8.2 (2.5)	8.0 (1.8)	7.98 (1.58)
3.Special syntax	6.8 (2.2)	6.8 (2.6)	6.8 (2.4)	6.7 (2.1)	6.6 (2.1)	7.5 (2.1)	5.4 (3.1)	6.6 (2.1)	6.82 (2.29)
4.Evaluate list	7.7 (1.9)	7.8 (2.3)	8.1 (1.6)	7.4 (1.9)	7.8 (1.5)	8.5 (1.5)	7.3 (3.1)	7.9 (1.2)	7.73 (1.88)
5.Many results	8.2 (1.8)	8.0 (1.9)	7.8 (1.9)	7.6 (1.7)	7.7 (1.4)	8.1 (1.5)	7.4 (2.9)	7.9 (1.1)	7.68 (1.84)
6.Enough results	7.3 (2.0)	8.1 (1.5)	7.9 (1.5)	7.8 (1.6)	7.8 (1.6)	8.2 (1.6)	8.2 (2.3)	8.2 (1.1)	7.90 (1.68)
7. Like a pro	8.1 (1.7)	6.3 (2.4)	6.7 (2.1)	6.3 (2.1)	6.5 (1.7)	7.3 (1.6)	6.4 (2.8)	6.0 (1.2)	6.69 (1.99)
8.Few irrelevant	7.7 (1.9)	6.2 (2.0)	6.3 (2.1)	6.5 (1.5)	5.8 (1.7)	6.7 (1.7)	6.0 (2.8)	6.8 (1.4)	6.41 (1.95)
9.Structure time	7.6 (2.0)	7.1 (2.1)	6.9 (1.8)	6.9 (1.7)	7.0 (1.9)	7.3 (1.7)	6.6 (2.9)	7.3 (1.7)	7.21 (1.94)
10.Focus query	6.9 (2.1)	6.5 (2.5)	6.2 (2.1)	6.5 (1.8)	6.7 (1.6)	6.9 (1.8)	5.9 (2.5)	6.6 (1.9)	6.54 (2.00)
11.Distinguish relevant	7.6 (1.9)	8.4 (1.9)	7.9 (1.8)	8.1 (1.5)	7.9 (1.7)	8.2 (1.7)	7.5 (2.8)	8.2 (1.1)	8.04 (1.75)
12.Competent effective	7.2 (2.2)	8.1 (1.7)	7.9 (1.6)	7.8 (1.7)	7.8 (1.7)	8.2 (1.6)	8.2 (2.2)	8.3 (1.1)	8.03 (1.64)
13.Little difficulty	8.0 (1.5)	8.0 (2.0)	7.7 (1.8)	7.8 (1.7)	7.8 (1.5)	8.0 (1.8)	7.9 (2.5)	8.0 (1.3)	7.77 (1.81)
14.Allocated time	7.9 (1.7)	7.3 (2.6)	7.3 (1.7)	6.9 (1.8)	7.8 (1.5)	7.6 (1.7)	6.7 (3.0)	7.6 (1.3)	7.49 (1.93)
Total	7.6 (1.4)	7.5 (1.6)	7.4 (1.4)	7.3 (1.2)	7.3 (1.3)	7.8 (1.3)	7.1 (2.1)	7.5 (1.0)	7.47 (1.36)

---

[1] List of studies is available online at http://ils.unc.edu/ssestudies

Generalized Group Profiling for Content Customization

Mostafa Dehghani[1]   Hosein Azarbonyad[2]   Jaap Kamps[1]   Maarten Marx[2]

[1]Institute for Logic, Language and Computation, University of Amsterdam, The Netherlands
[2]Informatics Institute, University of Amsterdam, The Netherlands
{dehghani,h.azarbonyad,kamps,maartenmarx}@uva.nl

ABSTRACT

There is an ongoing debate on personalization, adapting results to the unique user exploiting a user's personal history, versus customization, adapting results to a group profile sharing one or more characteristics with the user at hand. Personal profiles are often sparse, due to cold start problems and the fact that users typically search for new items or information, necessitating to back-off to customization, but group profiles often suffer from accidental features brought in by the unique individual contributing to the group. In this paper we propose a generalized group profiling approach that teases apart the exact contribution of the individual user level and the 'abstract' group level by extracting a latent model that captures all, and only, the essential features of the whole group.

Our main findings are the followings. First, we propose an efficient way of group profiling which implicitly eliminates the general and specific features from users' models in a group and takes out the abstract model representing the whole group. Second, we employ the resulting models in the task of contextual suggestion. We analyse different grouping criteria and we find that group-based suggestions improves the customization. Third, we see that the granularity of groups affects the quality of group profiling. We observe that grouping approach should compromise between the level of customization and groups' size.

Keywords: Group Profiling, Contextual Suggestion, Content Customization.

1. INTRODUCTION

Context is pervasive on the modern web, due to cloud-based and mobile applications, making every information access interaction part of an eternal user session. Effective ways to leverage this context are key to further enhancing the user experience, both in terms of better quality of results as in terms of easier ways to articulate complex information needs. This requires both effective ways of personalization

to an individual user as well as customization to a profile based on groups of users. For group level analysis, there is a need for extracting a group profile that captures the essence of the group, separate from the sum of the profiles of its individual members. This profile should be "specific" enough to distinguish the preferences of the group from other groups, and in the same time, "general" enough to capture all shared tastes, expectations, and similarities of its members.

Group profiling can help understand both explicit groups, like Facebook groups, and implicit groups, like groups extracted by community detection algorithms. There is a wide range of applications for group profiling, like understanding social structures [9], network visualization, recommender systems [1, 4, 8], and direct marketing [3]. One of the important applications of group profiling is in the content customization problem. Content customization is the process of tailoring content to individual users' characteristics or preferences. However, using individual preferences for content customization is not always possible. For example sometimes there is a new user in the system with no historical interactions and no rich information about the preferences, or sometimes the user is not able to determine his/her preferences explicitly. In these situations, group based content customization would be beneficial to suggest content to the user based on the preferences of the groups that the user belongs to.

The main aim of this paper is *to develop a language model for a group of users based on the group preferences, which contains all, and only, essential shared commonalities of the group members, and to employ such a group profile to customize content suggestion for individual users.* We break this down into three concrete research questions:

RQ1 *How to estimate models for group profiles capturing exactly the shared commonalities of their members?*

RQ2 *How effective are group profiles to customize content suggestion for individual users?*

RQ3 *How does the user's group granularity affect the quality of the group's profile?*

There is various research done on the task of group profiling which, given the individual attributes and preferences, aims to find out group-level shared preferences [6, 7]. Tang et al. [9] presented three different methods for group profiling: *Aggregation*, which tries to find features that are shared by the whole group; *Differentiation*, which tries to extract features that can help to differentiate one group from others; and *Egocentric differentiation*, which tries to extract features that can help to differentiate members of one group from the neighbour members. In recent work, Hu et al.

[4] proposed a deep-architecture model to learn a high level representation of group preferences.

For group recommendation there is research on building a model of a group by forming a linear combination of the individual models [5]. Some of them construct the group's preference model on the basis of individual preference models, using a notion of distance between preference models [10]. Some approaches try to divide the group into several categories of homogeneous users and specify the preference model for each subgroup. Then they create the group model as a weighted average of the subgroup models, with the weights reflecting the importance of the subgroups [2].

In this paper, we assume that the model of a user's preferences is a mixture of general, specific and his/her group preferences, and we try to extract the latent group model. We utilize the extracted profile in the task of contextual suggestion to improve content customization based on a user's group memberships.

The rest of the paper is structured as follows. First, in Section 2, we explain our approach for group profiling in detail. Section 3 presents the results of our experiments on the task of group-based contextual suggestion as well as some analysis on the effect of group granularity on the quality of group profiling. Finally, Section 4 concludes the paper and discusses possible extensions and future work.

2. GROUP PROFILING

In this section, we investigate our first research question: "How to estimate models for group profiles capturing exactly the shared commonalities of their members?"

Group profiling refers to the task of extracting a descriptive model for a group of users which addresses the particular aspects that bind group members together. The goal of the proposed method for group profiling is to extract the latent common language model of the group which represents the shared group preferences. We assume that there are three different models from which the group members sample to express their preferences: *group* model, *general* model, and *specific* model. The group model is supposed to represent the shared preferences of the group. The general model represents the general terms that anybody may use (very common observed terms), and specific model represents the terms that are attached to an individual user's preferences but not others (partially observed terms).

Each model is a distribution over terms. We consider collection language model θ_c as the general model:

$$p(t|\theta_c) = \frac{c(t, C)}{\sum_{t' \in V} c(t', C)} \quad (1)$$

This way, terms that are well explained in the collection model get high probability and are considered as general terms. To estimate the probability of terms given the specific model, θ_s, we use the Equation 2 and normalize all the probabilities to form a distribution:

$$P(t|\theta_s) = \sum_{u_i \in G} \left(P(t|\theta_{u_i}) \prod_{\substack{u_j \in G \\ j \neq i}} (1 - P(t|\theta_{u_j})) \right) \cdot idf_G(t) \quad (2)$$

where u_i is the user i in group G, and θ_{u_i} is the language model representing the user's preferences. Here, $idf_g(t)$ represents inverse document frequency of term t in group G. Equation 2 calculates probability of term t to be an specific

term. To this end, it simply considers the probability of a term to be important in one of the user models but not others, marginalized over all user models as well as considering group document frequency. In this way, terms that are well explained in only one user model but not others get high probability and are considered as specific terms.

Based on the generative model, each term in a user model is generated by sampling from a mixture of these three models—group, general (or collection), specific—independently. Thus, the probability of generating term t in user model u would be:

$$p(t|u) = \lambda_{u,g} p(t|\theta_g) + \lambda_{u,c} p(t|\theta_c) + \lambda_{u,s} p(t|\theta_s), \quad (3)$$

where $\lambda_{u,x}$ stands for $p(\theta_x|u)$ which is the probability of choosing model θ_x given the user u.

The goal is to fit the log-likelihood model of generating all terms in the user models to discover the exact term distribution of the group model, θ_g. Let $G = \{u_1, \ldots u_n\}$ be a group of users. The log-likelihood of the group would be:

$$\log p(G|\Lambda) = \sum_{u \in G} \sum_{t \in V} c(t, u) \log \Big(\sum_{x \in \{g,c,s\}} \lambda_{u,x} p(t|\theta_x) \Big), \quad (4)$$

where $c(t, u)$ is the frequency of term t in user model u and Λ determines the set of all parameters:

$$\Lambda = \{\lambda_g, \lambda_c, \lambda_s\}_{u \in G} \cup \{\theta_g\} \quad (5)$$

As we have mentioned, we estimate θ_c and θ_s based on the collection language model as well as the patterns of terms occurrences in the documents and we make them fixed in the model. Finally, to fit our model, we estimate the parameters using the maximum likelihood (ML) estimator. So we solve the following problem:

$$\Lambda^* = \underset{\Lambda}{\operatorname{argmax}} \, p(G|\Lambda) \quad (6)$$

Assuming $X_{u,t} \in \{g, c, s\}$ as a hidden variable indicating which model has been used to generate term t in user model u, we can compute the parameters efficiently using Expectation-Maximization (EM) algorithm. The stages of EM algorithm would be:

E-Step

$$p(X_{u,t} = x) = \frac{\lambda_{u,x} p(t|\theta_x)}{\sum_{x' \in \{g,c,s\}} \lambda_{u,x'} p(t|\theta'_x)} \quad (7)$$

M-Step

$$p(t|\theta_g) = \frac{\sum_{u \in G} c(t, u) p(X_{u,t} = g)}{\sum_{t' \in V} \sum_{u \in G} c(t', u) p(X_{u,t'} = g)} \quad (8)$$

$$\lambda_{u,x} = \frac{\sum_{t \in V} c(t, u) p(X_{u,t} = x)}{\sum_{x' \in \{g,c,s\}} \sum_{t \in V} c(t, u) p(X_{u,t} = x')} \quad (9)$$

After convergence of the EM algorithm, all the parameters are estimated including the group model, θ_g, which is a distribution over terms representing shared group preferences as well as $\lambda_{u,g}$, $\lambda_{u,c}$, and $\lambda_{u,s}$ for each user u which determine the contribution of each model in each user's preferences.

In this section, we proposed a generative user model as a mixture of group, general (or collection), and specific models, and showed that the latent distribution of group model over terms can be extracted as the group's profile.

3. EXPERIMENTS

In this section, we present our experiments to evaluate the effectiveness of the estimated language model of groups in the task of contextual suggestion. Furthermore, we analyse the effect of group granularity on group profiling. We first explain the data collection used in our experiments and then present the evaluation results.

3.1 Data Collection

In this research, we have made use of the TREC 2015 contextual suggestion[1] Batch task dataset. Contextual suggestion is the task of searching for complex information needs that are highly dependent on both context and user interests. The dataset contains the information from 207 users including their age, gender, and set of rated places or activities as the user preferences (rates are in the range of -1 to 4). The task is to generate a list of ranked suggestions from a set of candidate attractions, by giving the user information as well as some information about the context, including location of trip, trip season, trip type, tripe duration, and the type of group the person is travelling with. For each user, we consider rated suggestions that are annotated with rates of more than 2 as relevant. Furthermore, we generate the user language models as a mixture of their relevant preferences considering the rates. Based on the information in the dataset, we divide users into several groups. Groupings are based on the users information and context information. Table 1 presents grouping criteria, the groups, and number of users in each group.

3.2 Group Profiling for Contextual Suggestion

In this section, we investigate our second research question: "How effective are group profiles to customize content suggestion for individual users?"

We generate group-based rankings of suggestions to evaluate the quality of group profiles in content customization. To this end, one of the grouping approaches given in Table 1 is chosen, e.g. based on users' age. Then we estimate language model of each group employing the approach explained in Section 2. Afterward, regarding the information of the given request, i.e. the user information and context information, the group which the user belongs to is selected and based on the similarity of the language model of the selected group and the language model of candidate, the ranked list of the suggestions is generated.

Beside the group-based ranking, we generate a ranked list of suggestions based on the preferences of the user as a baseline. To do so, a language model is estimated as the mixture of the model of user preferences regarding their ratings and based on the similarity of the preferences language model and the candidate language model, a ranked list is generated.

Furthermore, according to the explanation in Section 2, the contribution of each of *specific*, *group*, and *general* models in each user model is learned as the model parameters, i.e. $\lambda_{u,s}$, $\lambda_{u,g}$, and $\lambda_{u,c}$. Having these parameters empowers us to efficiently combine the group-based model with the preferences-based model for content customization. To this end, we smooth the preferences-based model of user with both the group model and the general model using JM-smoothing employing the learn parameters. To evaluate

[1]https://sites.google.com/site/treccontext/trec-2015

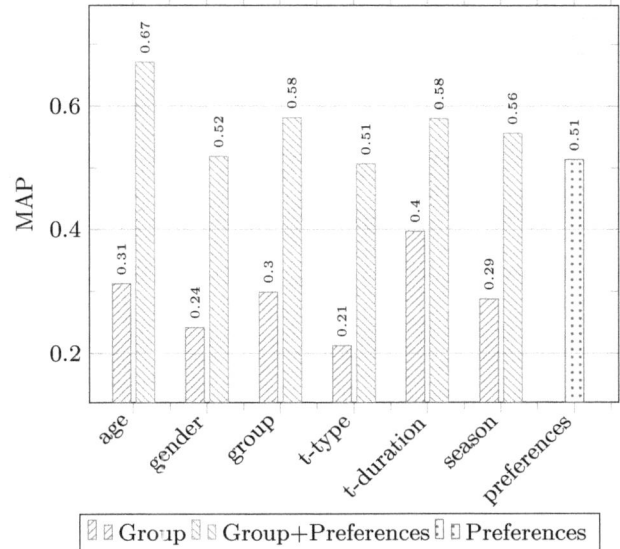

Figure 1: Performance of employing user preferences-based and group-based customization on contextual suggestion task. Improvements of combining group-based and preferences-based approach over the preferences-based approach and corresponding group-based approaches are statistically significant based on one-tailed t-test, with p-value < 0.05.

the quality of the combination, we have done experiments considering different grouping criteria.

Figure 1 presents the performance of employing different grouping approaches for group-based suggestion as well as preferences-based suggestion. The combinations of preferences-based suggestion and group-based suggestion are also reported.

As can be seen, among the group-based strategies, suggestions based on the duration of the trip is the most effective strategy. Also age of the user and the type of the group the user travels with, are rather important while type of the trip is not so important. This could be due to the fact that most of the time, the user's interests and beloved attractions do not change based on the type of trip which could be "business" or "holiday". On the other hand, combining the preferences-based suggestions with group-based suggestions in all grouping strategies leads to improvement. This means in case of incompleteness of user's profile, customizing the content based on the groups that user belongs to, implicitly fills the missing information and improves the performance of suggestions. However, this depends on the quality of the groups profiles that should reflect essential common (not general, not specific) characteristics of the groups.

3.3 Effect of Group Granularity

In this section, we investigate our third research question: "How does the user's group granularity affect the quality of the group's profile?"

In the grouping stage, sometimes users can be grouped based on different levels of granularity. For example, having the age of users, discretization can be done using binning with different sizes of bin. In this section, we analyse the effect of granularity of groups, and consecutively the size of the groups with a fixed volume of train data, on the quality of group profiling.

Table 1: Statistics of users groups resulted by grouping based on different critera

Grouping Criterion	Age					Gender		Group Type				Trip Type			Trip Duration				Season			
Groups	<20	20-30	30-40	40-50	>50	male	female	alone	family	friends	other	holiday	business	other	night out	day trip	weekend	longer	spring	summer	autumn	winter
Group Size (#users)	9	87	60	22	23	107	91	23	101	65	4	176	7	12	8	17	99	74	20	99	52	22

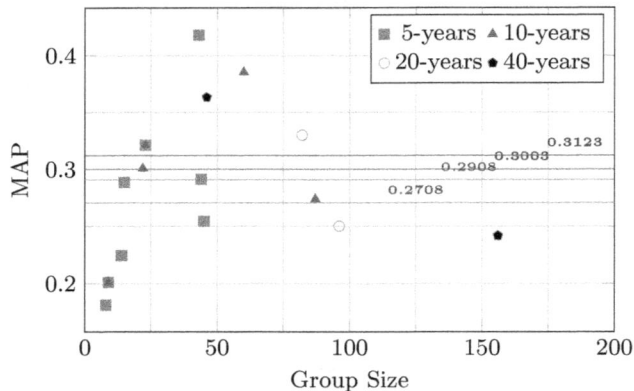

Figure 2: Effect of groups granularity on the performance group profiling

We have selected "age" of users as the grouping criterion and tried different bin sizes for discretization: 5 years, 10 years, 20 years and 40 years. Figure 2 shows the quality of groups profiles on different levels of granularity and consequently on different sizes of groups in the task of contextual suggestion. Each point in the figure represents a group of users and its position determines its size and the performance of group-based contextual suggestion for the users within the group. Moreover the horizontal lines represent overall performance of different levels of granularity. As can be seen, since the number of sample users is limited fine-grained grouping leads to having smaller groups. So small number of samples affects the group profiling quality and slightly decreases the performance. While coarse-grained grouping leads to having large groups that leads to not being able to adequately customize the group profile.

In our dataset, 10 years granularity for "age" has the best performance since the formed groups are big enough so that the group profiling approach is able to estimate high quality models, and they are small enough so that the group profiles are easily distinguishable which leads to a more effective customization.

4. CONCLUSIONS

In this paper, we dealt with the problem of group profiling. The main aim of this paper was *to develop a language model for a group of users based on the group preferences, which contains all, and only, essential shared commonalities of the group members, and to employ such a group profile to customize content suggestion for individual users*

Our first research question was: *How to estimate models for group profiles capturing exactly the shared commonalities of their members?* We proposed to consider each user preferences as a mixture of general, specific and its group preferences and estimated the latent group preferences as the shared concerns among all group members.

Our second research question was: *How effective are group profiles to customize content suggestion for individual users?* We utilized the proposed group profiling approach for the task of contextual suggestion, and our experimental results showed that considering group-based suggestions along with user preferences-based suggestions can improve the content customization.

Our third research question was: *How does the user's group granularity affect the quality of the group's profile?* We designed an experiment to investigate how group granularity may affect the group profiling quality. We found that the grouping approach should result in groups that are big enough to enable group profiling to infer high quality models and small enough to enable the extracted model to make customization for group members.

As the future work, we are going to find a way for learning how to employ group-based suggestions on the basis of different grouping criteria simultaneously. For example, how to combine suggestions based on the age with suggestions based on the gender. A further development would be to evaluate the proposed group profiling approach on other tasks and other kinds of data including non-textual data.

Acknowledgments This research is funded in part by the European Community's FP7 (project meSch, grant # 600851) and the Netherlands Organization for Scientific Research (WebART project, NWO CATCH # 640.005.001; ExPoSe project, NWO CI # 314.99.108; DiLiPaD project, NWO Digging into Data # 600.006.014).

References

[1] S. Amer-Yahia, S. B. Roy, A. Chawlat, G. Das, and C. Yu. Group recommendation: Semantics and efficiency. *VLDB*, 2:754–765, 2009.

[2] L. Ardissono, A. Goy, G. Petrone, M. Segnan, and P. Torasso. Intrigue: personalized recommendation of tourist attractions for desktop and hand held devices. *Applied Artificial Intelligence*, 17(8-9):687–714, 2003.

[3] B. Custers. Effects of unreliable group profiling by means of data mining. In *Discovery Science*, pages 291–296, 2003.

[4] L. Hu, J. Cao, G. Xu, L. Cao, Z. Gu, and W. Cao. Deep modeling of group preferences for group-based recommendation. In *AAAI*, 2014.

[5] A. Jameson and B. Smyth. The adaptive web. chapter Recommendation to Groups, pages 596–627. 2007.

[6] J. Masthoff. Group recommender systems: Combining individual models. In F. Ricci, L. Rokach, B. Shapira, and P. B. Kantor, editors, *Recommender Systems Handbook*, pages 677–702. Springer US, 2011.

[7] C. Senot, D. Kostadinov, M. Bouzid, J. Picault, and A. Aghasaryan. Evaluation of group profiling strategies. In *IJCAI*, pages 2728–2733, 2011.

[8] S. Shang, Y. Hui, P. Hui, P. Cuff, and S. Kulkarni. Beyond personalization and anonymity: Towards a group-based recommender system. In *SAC*, pages 266–273, 2014.

[9] L. Tang, X. Wang, and H. Liu. Group profiling for understanding social structures. *TOIS*, 3(1):15:1–15:25, 2011.

[10] Z. Yu, X. Zhou, Y. Hao, and J. Gu. Tv program recommendation for multiple viewers based on user profile merging. *User Modeling and User-Adapted Interaction*, 16 (1):63–82, 2006.

How does Interest in a Work Task Impact Search Behavior and Engagement?

Ashlee Edwards and Diane Kelly
School of Information and Library Science
University of North Carolina at Chapel Hill
Chapel Hill, NC, USA
{aedwards, diane.kelly}@unc.edu

ABSTRACT

One goal of using simulated work tasks in interactive information retrieval (IIR) experiments is to create a more relevant and interesting search experience for study participants. However, there is not much guidance about how to identify interesting tasks or how interest in a task impacts search behaviors and experiences, which is the purpose of this study. In this study, we created eight work tasks and asked forty participants to rank these tasks from most interesting to least interesting before they came into the lab for an IIR experiment. During the experiment, we asked participants to conduct searches for the two tasks they ranked as most interesting and the two they ranked as least interesting. Participants completed pre- and post-search questionnaires to characterize their interests in the tasks and their search experiences, including engagement. Participants rated their interest, prior knowledge and search experience, and the relevancy of interesting tasks significantly higher than uninteresting tasks. They also predicted these tasks would be significantly less difficult to complete. Participants reported significantly greater engagement with interesting tasks and they spent longer completing these tasks. However, there were no significant differences in participants' search behaviors including number of queries issued, number of SERPs, or number of documents bookmarked. These results provide evidence that our method of assigning tasks to participants that would interest and engage them, at least cognitively, if not behaviorally, was somewhat successful. This method can be used by others conducting laboratory IIR studies.

Keywords
Engagement; Interest; Assigned Search Tasks; IIR Experiments

1. INTRODUCTION

A key component of interactive information retrieval (IIR) studies is the work task participants are asked to perform. The work task forms the basis of participants' searches and allows them to exercise systems. Typically, work tasks are assigned to participants in order to allow for more control over the situation [5]. For example, the assignment of work tasks helps ensure tasks have the same scope and are of the same type. In this work, we use the term *work task* to refer to the job participants are given during an experiment, where a single work task might spawn several search tasks [4]. Over time, work tasks have become

increasingly important in IIR research and are often included as a variable to be analyzed in the research model [13].

Many researchers have discussed the potential limitations of assigning work and search tasks to study participants [1, 5, 11]. Some limitations include challenges associated with making relevance assessments, a participant's lack of interest in the task, and the potential lack of relevance of the task to the participant. To address some of these limitations, Borlund [1] proposed the use of simulated work tasks, which provide a short "cover story that describes an IR requiring situation" (p. 76) and are tailored to target participants. The simulated work task allows participants to direct their own searches, while providing a common scenario to anchor experimental comparisons. Vakkari [11] states that simulated work tasks help bring greater validity to IIR evaluation, while also offering experimental control. Simulated work tasks are increasingly used in IIR evaluations because of their utility in fostering more authentic search behavior, although they are not always implemented as recommended [2].

One goal of using simulated work tasks is to better motivate people during search by providing them with tasks that interest them. Previous work on genuine and assigned tasks has shown that participants generally indicate greater interest in genuine tasks than assigned tasks [2, 10]. Borlund, Dreier and Byström [2] found that interest was one of the main indicators of time spent searching. Participants in this study rated their genuine tasks more interesting, spent more time searching, and generally found genuine tasks more difficult than simulated work tasks. Poddar and Ruthven [10] found participants had greater positive emotions, made more use of various search strategies, and had more confidence in their ability to succeed on their own tasks versus assigned tasks. Some researchers have attempted to generate greater task interest by allowing participants to select tasks from a predefined set (e.g., [12]).

While there are certainly many authentic search scenarios where a person lacks interest in the task, interest can be important in keeping people active during laboratory IIR studies. In particular, interest is especially critical for research contexts where engagement is important, as it is more difficult to become engaged if one lacks interest in the search task [7]. If participants lack interest in the first place, then it will be difficult to create, observe and study engaging search situations.

In this research, we focus on the *interest* dimension of the simulated work task in order to promote more engaging laboratory search experiences. We created eight tasks using the same basic template and asked participants to rank these tasks from most interesting to least interesting the day before they came into the lab. We assigned participants the two tasks they ranked as most interesting and the two they ranked as least interesting. Our main research questions are: (1) Can this method be used to assign tasks

CHIIR'16, March 13–17, 2016, Carrboro, North Carolina, USA
Copyright is held by the owner/author(s). Publication rights licensed to ACM.
ACM 978-1-4503-3751-9/16/03...$15.00.
DOI: http://dx.doi.org/10.1145/2854946.2855000

to participants that interest them? (2) How does participant interest in a task impact search behavior and engagement?

The results reported in this paper are from a larger study whose goal is to understand how search behavior differs when people are engaged versus frustrated. In this larger study, we attempted to induce engagement by manipulating task interest and frustration by starting the search results lists at rank 500. The study was designed such that the frustrator was introduced during one interesting task and one uninteresting task. In this initial paper, we focus on our method of inducing engagement during search by manipulating task interest.

2. METHOD

A laboratory experiment was conducted with 40 undergraduate participants, which represents a typical type of subject in IIR experiments. The average age of participants was 20.45 (1.77) and most were female (n=31). A variety of majors were represented across the natural sciences (n=13), social sciences (n=8), humanities (n=11), and professional schools (n=7). One person was undecided. Most participants reported having between 7-9 years of search experience, and conducting online searches for information more than 7 times a day.

2.1 Tasks and Task Interest

The tasks used in this study were modeled after *evaluate* tasks we used in previous work [6]. This task type asked participants to search in order to evaluate several options, make a selection among the options and justify the selection (see Figure 1 for an example). This type of task was chosen because in the previous work, participants ranked these types of tasks as interesting and engaging [6]. From these tasks, we extrapolated a basic template, slightly modifying four original task descriptions to fit the template and creating four new tasks. The basic template can seen in Figure 1: each task started with 1-2 statements to situate the need and then followed with four questions that asked participants to list and describe, compare, select and justify. The task topics were from four domains we believed would potentially appeal to at least some members of the target population for the experiment (health, science, technology, and entertainment). All tasks can be viewed online at: http://bit.ly/1OINo6e.

You recently heard a story on National Public Radio about the use of biomass as fuel. Biomass refers to material created from living organisms. What are different types of biomasses that are used as fuels and how are they created? How do biomass fuels compare with fossil fuels when it comes to environmental impact? Which do you think is better? Why?

Figure 1. Example Task

To identify tasks that did and did not interest participants from the set, we asked them to rank the tasks the day before they completed the experiment. Participants completed an online form which presented the task topics using a two word task description (Table 1) and asked them to rank the topics based on interest, where 1=most interesting and 8=least interesting. The presentation order of the topics was randomized to avoid selection bias. During the experiment, participants were given four tasks to complete: the two tasks they ranked as most interesting and the two tasks they ranked as least interesting. The tasks were counterbalanced such that all task rankings appeared in all positions.

2.2 Questionnaires

Throughout the experiment, participants completed several questionnaires including a demographic questionnaire and pre-

and post-search questionnaires. The pre-search questionnaire assessed items such as prior knowledge. We also included a question about task interest on the pre-search questionnaire as a manipulation check and to evaluate the first research question (i.e., just because a participant ranks one task as more interesting than another does not mean they find the task interesting). The post-search questionnaire assessed items such as difficulty and satisfaction. The pre- and post-search questionnaire items were evaluated with 5-point scales and coded so that higher values indicate more of the construct being evaluated (e.g., more difficult, more success).

The post-search questionnaire also measured engagement and frustration. Engagement was measured using the User Engagement Scale (UES) [8]. This scale includes several subscales: perceived usability (7 questions), felt involvement (2 questions), novelty (2 questions), endurability (6 questions), and focused attention (5 questions), for a total of 21 questions. The aesthetics subscale was not used in this study. Participants responded to each UES item on 5-point Likert scale where 1=strongly disagree and 5=strongly agree. Frustration was also measured using a three-item scale that participants responded to after each task [9]. This instrument used a 5-point scale, where 1=strongly disagree and 5=strongly agree. Paired-sample t-tests, with alpha=0.05, were used for analyses of the questionnaire data.

2.3 Search System

The search system consisted of a standard interface with a query box and list of search results, each of which could be selected. We used the Bing API to retrieve results and provided 50 results per query. Participants' searching was not limited to the search results pages and they could enter as many queries as desired. Participants were asked to bookmark relevant pages and provide a short annotation describing why they bookmarked pages. Interactions with the system were logged. Morae was also used to capture participants' search interactions. Paired-sample t-tests, with alpha=0.05, were used for analyses of the interaction data.

A cover story was used to motivate the experiment. This cover story explained to participants that they were using four different experimental search systems, and that they would complete questionnaires to evaluate each of the four search systems. Each interface was labeled "System A," "System B," and so forth, in different colors, to differentiate between the systems.

3. RESULTS

Table 1 shows the number of people that ranked each of tasks as interesting (rank 1 and 2) and uninteresting (rank 7 and 8). We do not report all the rankings for space reasons. Table 1 also shows which tasks were actually completed by our participants. The online communication task was the most popular, followed by energy sources, lupus and endurance sports. Tattoo removal and vehicle purchasing were the least popular tasks, followed by biomass fuel and video game violence.

3.1 Pre-Search Questionnaire

Table 2 shows the results of the pre-search questionnaire. The first item shows that participants rated their interest in tasks they ranked as most interesting significantly higher than their interest for uninteresting tasks, so the relative rankings did translate into differences in absolute judgments. Participants also rated their prior knowledge of interesting tasks significantly higher than uninteresting tasks and rated interesting tasks significantly more relevant. Participants had searched for information significantly more frequently in the past for interesting tasks, and predicted interesting tasks would be significantly less difficult to complete.

Table 1. Participant rankings by task topic and interest

Task	Interesting	Uninteresting
Online Communication	25	3
Energy Sources	11	6
Lupus	9	10
Endurance Sports	10	8
Vehicle Purchases	8	15
Tattoo Removal	7	13
Video Game Violence	4	12
Biomass Fuel	6	13

Table 2. Means, standard deviations, and t-test results of pre-search questionnaire, df=79, ***$p<.001$

	Interesting Tasks	Uninteresting Tasks	t-values
Interest	4.01 (0.96)	2.77 (1.15)	7.39***
Prior Knowledge	3.00 (1.13)	2.20 (1.80)	5.27***
Relevance	3.61 (1.23)	2.24 (1.23)	7.06***
Search Frequency	2.44 (1.20)	1.64 (0.94)	4.69***
Difficulty	3.35 (1.15)	3.81 (0.93)	2.72***

3.2 Post-Search Questionnaire

Participants rated interesting tasks as slightly more difficult than uninteresting tasks, as well as rated their skill higher for interesting tasks (Table 3). Participants rated the system's ability to retrieve documents as slightly higher for interesting tasks than uninteresting tasks, felt slightly less successful during interesting tasks than uninteresting tasks and reported less frustration. However, none of the differences were significant.

Table 3. Means, standard deviations and t-test results for post-search questionnaire (all non-sig), df = 79

	Interesting Tasks	Uninteresting Tasks	t-values
Difficulty	3.61 (0.83)	3.38 (0.89)	1.35
Skill	3.85 (0.70)	3.62 (0.85)	1.57
System Ability	3.40 (0.86)	3.35 (1.04)	0.27
Success	3.77 (0.69)	3.80 (0.77)	-0.17
Frustration	2.45 (0.56)	2.52 (0.84)	-0.65

3.3 Engagement

Participants reported higher scores for three of the engagement subscales for interesting tasks, with the exception of perceived usability and endurability, which is not too surprising since these components focus more on the interface (Table 4). Participants also reported significantly higher overall engagement for tasks they ranked as interesting.

3.4 Search Behaviors

Participants spent significantly more time completing interesting tasks than uninteresting tasks (Table 5). In addition, participants spent more time on SERPs for interesting tasks than uninteresting tasks and slightly more time examining documents, but these differences were not significant. Participants submitted similar

numbers of queries for interesting and uninteresting tasks and there were no differences in query length between the task types. Participants made about one more click per query for interesting tasks than uninteresting tasks and they viewed slightly more SERPs, but these differences were not statistically significant. The number of pages bookmarked per condition was also similar.

Table 4. Means, standard deviations and t-test results for User Engagement Scale, df = 79, **$p<.01$, ***$p<.001$

	Interesting Tasks	Uninteresting Tasks	t-values
Perceived Usability	3.63 (0.60)	3.56 (0.79)	0.50
Focused Attention	2.87 (0.79)	2.64 (0.66)	2.70**
Felt Involvement	3.61 (0.50)	3.27 (0.72)	3.00***
Endurability	3.41 (0.58)	3.20 (0.76)	1.60
Novelty	3.72 (0.67)	3.09 (0.90)	4.43***
Total Engagement	3.45 (0.42)	3.15 (0.64)	3.04***

Table 5. Means, standard deviations, and t-test results of search behaviors, df = 79, *$p<.05$

	Interesting Tasks	Uninteresting Tasks	t-values
Total Time (in minutes)	6.86 (3.84)	5.88 (3.06)	2.06*
Time on SERP	2.04 (1.80)	1.74 (1.30)	1.40
Time on Docs	2.72 (2.25)	2.33 (1.79)	1.45
Queries	5.65 (4.45)	5.06 (4.13)	1.01
Query Length (in words)	2.56 (1.77)	2.55 (1.78)	0.94
Clicks Per Query	7.77 (4.77)	6.79 (3.97)	1.66
SERPs viewed	13.80 (9.16)	12.29 (7.88)	1.42
Bookmarks	3.60 (2.06)	3.42 (1.83)	0.63

4. DISCUSSION & CONCLUSIONS

In this study, we focused on increasing research participants' interests in assigned search tasks. We created eight tasks and asked participants to rank these tasks from most interesting to least interesting the day before they came into the lab. During the experiment, we assigned participants the two tasks they ranked as most interesting and the two they ranked as least interesting. We addressed the following questions: (1) Did participants evaluate these tasks as more interesting and relevant (i.e., did our method work)? (2) Did participants search differently for these tasks and rate their engagement higher?

The results indicate that our manipulation was successful. Participants evaluated tasks they ranked most interesting as more interesting and personally relevant than uninteresting tasks. Results from the pre-search questionnaire also revealed that participants had more prior knowledge of tasks they rated as interesting. Participants also rated their skill at finding documents for interesting tasks greater, likely because they had searched more frequently for information about interesting tasks in the past. These results demonstrate participants were more interested in tasks they felt were personally relevant, despite the tasks being researcher-generated. This finding also suggests that incorporating more genuine tasks can enhance a person's ability to make authentic relevance judgments [1].

With respect to the second research question, the post-search evaluations indicated that participants were significantly more engaged with interesting tasks than with uninteresting tasks. The subscales of the UES serve to confirm and support participants' pre-search evaluations of interesting tasks. Participants had greater focused attention and felt more involved in interesting tasks, similar to their pre-search ratings of relevance. They also reported significantly higher levels of novelty. These results provide evidence that it is more than just the mechanics of the system that fosters engaging situations – the relationship between the person and the content is equally, if not more, important. These results provide support for the notion that task interest is an important component of engagement and that it can influence the extent to which a person becomes engaged during search. Other post-search evaluations revealed no differences in participants' ratings of task difficulty, their own skill, the system's performance, overall success or frustration.

There were no differences in participants' search behaviors except for total time. The result regarding time is consistent with past work that found that people spend more time searching for genuine tasks [2, 10]. In this study, this difference amounted to about one minute, which may or may not be important. Participants might have spent this additional time reading documents [8]. Overall, though, participants executed more search behaviors for interesting tasks and it might be that if this study were done in a natural setting, significant differences would occur. Given the lab setting, participants likely had an upper bound on the amount of time they were willing to spend per task.

The results reported in this paper are from a larger study whose goal is to understand how search behavior differs when people are engaged versus frustrated. The study was designed such that participants experienced a frustrator during one interesting task and one uninteresting task. We look forward to analyzing the post-search evaluations and search behavior to see if there are any significant interaction effects between interest and frustration. For example, when searching for interesting tasks, participants might persevere longer after becoming frustrated than when searching for uninteresting tasks. Task interest might also help participants overcome any unexpected irritation caused by the frustration, or the effect of the frustration might be greater when participants complete interesting tasks versus uninteresting tasks. In this larger study, we also collected physiological data and look forward to seeing if participants exhibit physiological differences when searching for interesting versus uninteresting tasks.

One of the major limitations of this study is that participants ranked tasks from a prescribed set, so it might be the case that participants did not find any of the tasks particularly interesting. While the ratings from the pre-search questionnaires for interesting and uninteresting tasks were significantly different for all items, including task interest, task knowledge, relevance, amount of prior searching and expected difficulty, the mean ratings for most items were around the scale mid-point. For example, participants' average prior knowledge for interesting tasks was a 3, and average prior knowledge for uninteresting tasks was rated at 2.20. Thus, the differences in interest could be due in part to comparison among a limited set of task topics and not

because of a genuine interest on the part of the participant. Still, we believe this study presents some interesting findings with regards to fostering interest and engagement using simulated tasks during laboratory IIR studies and presents a fairly lightweight method for doing so that can be used by others.

5. ACKNOWLEDGMENTS

We thank Dr. Rob Capra for providing the search system and Drs. Rob Capra, Jaime Arguello, Heather O'Brien, and Ioannis Arapakis, as well as doctoral student Anita Crescenzi for their feedback on the design of this research.

6. REFERENCES

[1] Borlund, P. (2003). The IIR evaluation model: a framework for evaluation of interactive information retrieval systems. *Information Research*, 8.

[2] Borlund, P., Dreier, S., & Byström, K. (2012). What does time spent on searching indicate? *Proc. of IIiX*, 184-193.

[3] Borlund, P., & Schneider, J. W. (2010). Reconsideration of the simulated work task situation: A context instrument for evaluation of information retrieval interaction. In *Proceedings of the Third Symposium on Information Interaction in Context*, 155-164.

[4] Byström, K. & Hansen, P. (2005). Conceptual framework for tasks in information studies. *JASIST, 56*, 1050–1061.

[5] Kelly, D. (2009). Methods for evaluating interactive information retrieval systems with users. *Foundations and Trends in Information Retrieval, 3(1-2)*.

[6] Kelly, D., Arguello, J., Edwards, A., & Wu, W. C. (2015). Development and evaluation of search tasks for IIR experiments using a cognitive complexity framework. *Proc. of ICTIR*, 101-110.

[7] O'Brien, H.L., & Toms, E.G. (2008). What is user engagement? A conceptual framework for defining user engagement with technology. *JASIST*, 59, 938-955.

[8] O'Brien, H.L., & Toms, E.G. (2013). Examining the generalizability of the User Engagement Scale (UES) in exploratory search. *IP&M*, 49, 1092-1107.

[9] Peters, L. H., O'Connor, E. J., & Rudolf, C. J. (1980). The behavioral and affective consequences of performance-relevant situational variables. *Organizational Behavior and Human Performance*, 25, 79-96.

[10] Poddar, A., and Ruthven, I. (2010). The emotional impact of search tasks. *Proc. of IIiX*, 35-44.

[11] Vakkari, P. (2003). Task-based information searching. *ARIST*, 37, 413-464.

[12] White, R. W., Ruthven, I., & Jose, J. M. (2005). A study of factors affecting the utility of implicit relevance feedback. In *Proceedings of the 28th Annual International ACM SIGIR Conference on Research and Development in Information Retrieval*, 35-42.

[13] Wildemuth, B. W., Freund, L. & Toms, E. G. (2014). Untangling search task complexity and difficulty in the context of interactive information retrieval studies. *Journal of Documentation, 70*, 1118-1140.

A Spoken Dialog System for Coordinating Information Consumption and Exploration

Shinya Fujie
Chiba Institute of Technology
Tsudanuma 2-17-1, Narashino, Chiba, Japan
shinya.fujie@p.chibakoudai.jp

Ishin Fukuoka   Asumi Mugita   Hiroaki Takatsu
Waseda University
Waseda-Cho 27, Shinjuku-ku, Tokyo, Japan
{fukuoka, mugita, takatsu}@pcl.cs.waseda.ac.jp

Yoshihiko Hayashi
Waseda University
Waseda-Cho 27, Shinjuku-ku, Tokyo, Japan

Tetsunori Kobayashi
Waseda University
Waseda-Cho 27, Shinjuku-ku, Tokyo, Japan

ABSTRACT

Passive consumption of information is boring in most cases and even painful in some cases, especially when the information content is delivered by employing speech media. The user of a speech-based information delivery system, for example a text-to-speech system, usually cannot interrupt the ongoing information flow, inhibiting her/him to confirm some part of the content, or to pose an inquiry for further information exploration. We argue that a carefully designed spoken dialog system could remedy these undesirable situations, and further enable an enjoyable conversation with the users. The key technologies to realize such an attractive dialog system are: (1) pre-compilation of a dialog plan based on the analysis of a source content, and (2) the dynamic recognition of user's state of understanding and interests. This paper illustrates technical views to implement these functionalities, and discusses a dialog example to exemplify the technical merits of the proposed system.

1. INTRODUCTION

A novel framework for coordinating passive information consumption and active information exploration exploiting speech interaction is proposed. In the rest of this paper, we use the term "mixed information consumption" to denote the information behavior that intermingles the two modes of information behavior.

Most of our information consumption behaviors in everyday life are performed by employing visual media, such as articles on newspapers, smart-phones, and so on. Take an example of newspaper reading: a reader can skip unwanted information simply by drifting his/her attention to the neighboring area. Thanks to its random-accessibility, visual media naturally facilitate a dynamic information interaction even if the content itself is static. On the other hand, information consumption with speech media has its own upside and downside. Take an example of radio listening: a listener can simply go with the information flow, but never be able to interrupt it to make a confirmation or pose

CHIIR '16, March 13-17, 2016, Carrboro, NC, USA

© 2016 ACM. ISBN 978-1-4503-3751-9/16/03. . . $15.00

DOI: http://dx.doi.org/10.1145/2854946.2854995

an inquiry to explore the evoked interests. News reading services made possible by adopting a text-to-speech technology involve almost the same problem. At the other extreme, a voice QA (question and answering) system can be thought of. The existing spoken dialog systems[8, 2, 11] can provide relevant information, when an explicit information request is clearly uttered by the user. However, as the dialog provided by such a system basically consists of a series of one-shot Q&A turns, the user cannot comfortably come and go the two modes of information access.

We argue in this paper that a carefully designed spoken dialog system can facilitate mixed information consumption, and further enable an enjoyable conversation with the users. Two issues have to be addressed to achieve this goal. First, the system has to accurately interpret a user's instant response, which may convey various intentions: No matter explicit or implicit, we often acknowledge our particular mental state with a back-channel feedback, such as "uh-huh," or asking back, such as "huh?" after or during the interlocutor's utterance. Second, the system has to promptly respond to a user's response. The promptness is highly important for a conversation with rhythm. To achieve the promptness, we propose to pre-compile a dialog plan by analyzing the source content. A dialog plan consists of a primary plan and subsidiary plans. The primary plan basically summarizes the content, and enables a user's passive information consumption. The subsidiary plans are generated to promptly respond to a user's inquiry that could be evoked by the main line of the content.

2. SYSTEM ARCHITECTURE

2.1 System overview

Figure 1 shows the overview of the proposed system. The system components are divided into two major parts, "preprocessing part" which processes news articles and generates utterance plans in advance, and "dialog system part" which actually talks with a user following the generated plans.

The preprocessing part consists of "information structure analysis" module and "plan generation" module. The former analyzes news articles in plain text and extracts the structure of information the articles contain, and the latter makes utterance plans using the extracted structure.

The dialog system part performs an actual dialog with a user using utterance plans which the preprocessing part generated. The augmented speech recognizer recognizes users' short instant responses, such as back-channel, asking back,

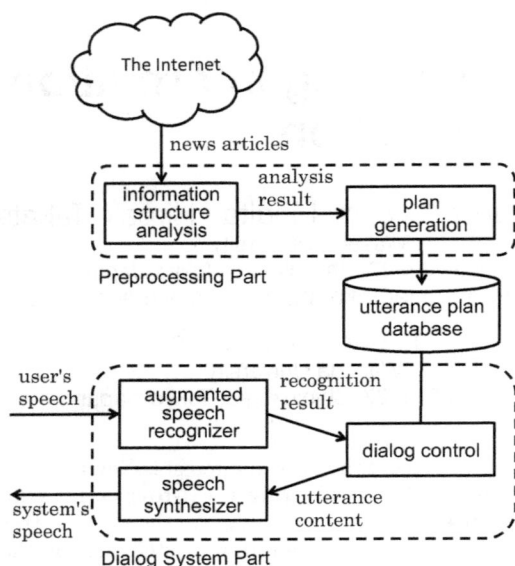

Figure 1: System Overview

and repetition, as well as linguistic information[1]. The dialog control module outputs a system utterance content to the speech synthesizer according to the plan. As user's short instant response is captured by the recognizer, it alters the system's utterance responding to the user's demand. That is done by selecting a subsidiary plan included in the pregenerated plan. The speech synthesizer generates speech signal of utterance content given by the dialog control module.

2.2 Utterance plan and dialog control

The proposed system generates utterance plans including user's responses in advance, and information consumption is performed by the system controlling the dialog according to them. This section describes what kind of information an utterance plan contains and how a dialog proceeds using it.

Figure 2 shows an example of utterance plan. As shown in this figure, an utterance plan is in a state transition structure. The variables $U_{i,j}$ and $S_{i,j}$ on arcs indicate user utterance and system utterance respectively. User utterance $U_{i,j}$ is assumed as one of the following short responses.

Positive Reaction encourages proceeding of the dialog, for example "yes," and "uh-huh"

Negative Reaction shows that the user has a doubt or uncomprehension on the preceding system utterance, for example "what?"

Repetition also shows a doubt but also gives the focus by repeating a word in the preceding system utterance.

Note that ϵ means that the system ignores user's response. Though effects of negative reaction and repetition are similar, repetition can give a focus of user's doubt by looking at the word contained in the response. Because system utterance $S_{i,j}$ contains concrete words that should be delivered to the user, it is directly transferred to the speech synthesizer. In the figure, bold arcs represent a primary plan which consists of utterances the system should give to a user at first. If the user gives neither negative reaction nor repetition during the system utterance, the system just provides information following the primary plan.

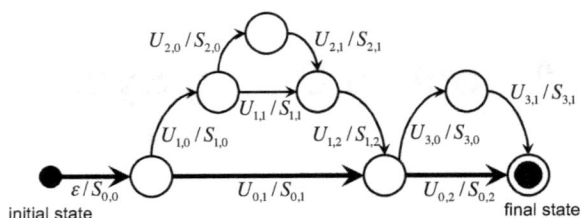

Figure 2: An example of utterance plan. $U_{i,j}$ is user's utterance and $S_{i,j}$ is system's utterance.

The state transits after the system outputs content of $S_{i,j}$ given to the arc to the speech synthesizer. At each state, the system waits for user's response and performs the next transition depending on the given response. Since it seems to be preferred that the dialog proceeds without any responses given by the user on the primary plan, at the states before $U_{0,1}$ and $U_{0,2}$ the transition automatically occurs after any arbitrary duration, 0.6 seconds for example, passed without any reactions from the user. In the case that a negative reaction or a repetition, for example $U_{3,0}$, is given, the system switches to the subsidiary plan that can compliment the previous utterance, $S_{0,1}$ and $S_{1,2}$, and generates precise information providing utterance, $S_{3,0}$. Thus, a dialog control following utterance plans with expected user's short responses realizes information consumption reflecting user's demands using speech interaction.

An ordinary question may be given by a user instead of a short instant response. If that's the case, one idea is that we treat it as an exception and activate another dialog control module that can perform a conventional QA dialog. This dialog control switching is in our future work.

3. PREPROCESSING

3.1 Information structure analysis

Information structure analysis module makes information structure for plan generation from news articles retrieved via the internet. The purpose of this module is extracting useful information to generate utterance plans from news articles in plain text. An utterance plan consists of a primary plan, which provides a main content of a news article, and subsidiary plans, which compliment the primary plan. Thus, the analysis result should contain hints to classify the information into several groups and assign them to each plan. For simplicity, we make one utterance plan for one sentence in an article in this study.

To analyze structure, phrase dependency analysis is adopted. Japanese morphological analyzer Juman[1] and parser KNP[2] are used in this study. Figure 3 shows the result of phrase dividing on a sentence in a news article from a web news site. Then, a structured tree is constructed from the result. Here, each phrase becomes each node in the tree one by one. Figure 4 shows the structured tree constructed from the result in Fig. 3. Every phrase has a node on which it depends and grammatical information of its own. For example, in Fig. 4, the phrase "Yuzuru Hanyu" depends on the phrase "has cancelled" and has its grammatical information such as "person" and "topic."

---

[1] http://nlp.ist.i.kyoto-u.ac.jp/index.php?JUMAN
[2] http://nlp.ist.i.kyoto-u.ac.jp/index.php?KNP

ソチオリンピック、(Sochi Olympic) ／フィギュアスケート男子の (figure skating games male) ／金メダリスト、(gold medalist) ／羽生結弦選手が (Yuzuru Hanyu) ／腰の (in lower back) ／痛みの (pain) ／ため、(because of) ／今シーズンの (of this season) ／初戦と (the first match) ／して、(as) ／来月 (next month) ／フィンランドで (in Finland) ／出場を (participation) ／予定していた (had been planned) ／国際大会を (the international competition) ／欠場することになりました。(has cancelled)

Figure 3: Result of phrase dividing of a sentence.

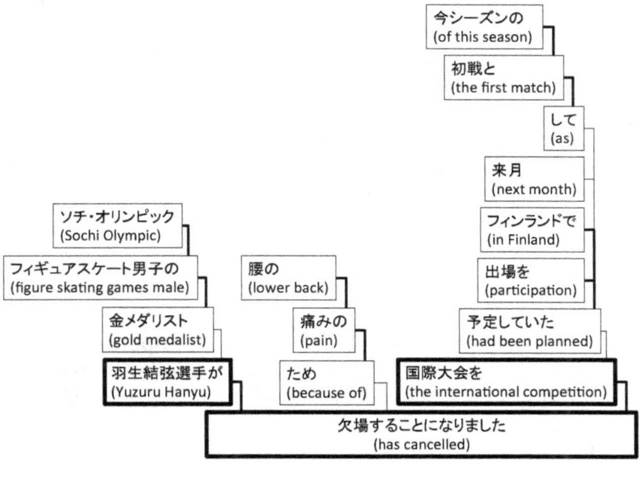

Figure 4: Dependency tree generated from a sentence in Fig. 3

In the figure, nodes with bold squares represent the primary information in the sentence. As the primary information, the final predicate in the sentence and the important phrases are selected. Importance of a phrase is calculated with the statistical method similar to one Matsuo proposed[6]. A bold line between two nodes means that the node cannot be skipped in the case that the node on which it depends is included in an utterance. For example, since the phrase "because of" does not construct a meaningful utterance alone, the two depending phrases "the pain" and "in lower back" cannot be skipped. This study employs a text summarization technique[7] to decide whether if a phrase is skippable or not.

3.2 Plan generation

The plan generation module generates utterance plans from the results of information structure analysis. Here, we describe how it generates the primary plan and the subsidiary plans shown in Fig. 5 from the information structure described in the previous section.

Figure 5: An example of generated utterance plan.

S:	Yuzuru Hanyu ...	[Pri. Plan]
U:	Yes	[Positive]
S:	has cancelled the international competition.	[Pri. Plan]
U:	What?	[Negative]
S:	He has cancelled because of pain in lower back.	[Sub. Plan]
U:	Uh-huh	[Positive]
S:	And the Skating Federation announced ...	[Pri. Plan]
U:	Yes	[Positive]
S:	"His condition is not so bad that he cannot practice at all. His target is the competition held in China ...	[Pri. Plan]
U:	China?	[Repetition]
S:	Yes, the part of the Grand Prix Series.	[Sub. Plan]
U:	Okay	[Positive]
S:	This cancellation is for preparation for that competition."	[Pri. Plan]

Figure 6: A dialog example of the proposed system. "S:" and "U:" indicate a system utterance and a user utterance respectively. System utterances are tagged with which plan they are generated from. User utterances are tagged with the type of short instant response

The primary plan must contain the main content of the news, which is just the same as the primary information described in the previous section. Thus, the primary plan includes three phrases, "Yuzuru Hanyu," "the international competition," and "has cancelled" in this case.

A sentence can be constructed as concatenating the phrases in the primary plan. However, if the system simply speaks it, the user has no chance to give a short instant response. On the other hand, if the system utters each phrase one by one with inserting short pause between every single pair of them, the user must feel annoyance and inconvenience. Thus, grammatical rules are applied to connect several phrases and construct sentences appropriate as utterances. In the proposed system, the pause insertion rules proposed by Kaiki[3], which checks the branch direction of the dependency tree and the comma existence, is referred. A sentence is divided at which the rules match. As applying the rules to the abovementioned example, two phrases, "Yuzuru Hanyu" and "has cancelled the international competition," are generated.

Among the nodes in structured information, the nodes depending on the nodes in the primary information are used to construct subsidiary plans. The subsidiary plan nodes are picked up recursively from each node in the primary information with checking unskippability. In the example of Fig. 4, to generate the subsidiary plan complementing the phrase "the international competition," the directly depending phrase "had been planned" is selected and other depending phrases such as "participation" and "in Finland" are selected because of their unskippability. Consequently the three phrases "In Finland," "participating," "had been planned" are selected as the subsidiary plan to "the international competition." Subsidiary plans are generated recursively and the utterances of them are generated with the same way as the primary plan.

4. EXAMPLE AND DISCUSSION

4.1 Dialog example

An example of a dialog between the proposed system and a user is shown in Fig. 6. As the system generates utterances

> S: Yuzuru Hanyu has cancelled the international competition. The Skating Federation announced "His condition is not so bad that he cannot practice at all. His target is the competition held in China. This cancellation is for preparation for that."
> U: Why has he cancelled the competition?
> S: Because of pain in lower back.
> U: What is the competition held in China?
> S: It is one competition of the Grand Prix Series."

Figure 7: An example dialog of conventional question answering spoken dialog system.

following the primary plan, the user can retrieve the main content of the news just giving back-channels or keeping silence. When the user faces an unknown word or an incomprehensible phrase, he/she can insert a negative feedback and a repetition to request the supplementary information to the system. The system switches to the subsidiary plan and provides detailed information matching to the user's demand. Thus, the proposed system realizes dynamic information interaction synchronized with user's interest and knowledge, using speech interaction.

4.2 Discussion

In this section, we discuss the difference between the proposed system and conventional question answering spoken dialog systems by comparing dialog examples about the same news article. An example dialog of a conventional system is shown in Fig. 7.

In the figure, the conventional system gives the user a whole summary of the news article, and it answers to the questions the user asks. The user might have various demands even while the system is giving the summary. In fact, in this example, the user reveals two of his/her demands. One is the reason the skater cancelled the participation, and the other is the detailed information of the "the competition held in China." Although the dialog seems to proceed smoothly because the user asks the questions explicitly in this example, it might be hard for the user to keep all the demands in mind until the system finishes giving the summary. If things comes to the worst, the user forgets some of the demands so that he/she cannot ask them to the system. As the result, the information consumption will finish incompletely. Additionally, the user has to indicate the focus explicitly because question answering is performed after the whole summary. For example, the user must ask with a complete sentence like "why has he cancelled the participation?" because the focus has not been resolved, while simply asking with "why?" is enough if the focus is obvious. The spoken dialog systems generating utterances depending on users' personality[5, 10] and changing its behavior corresponding to dialog history and context[9] have been proposed. These systems, however, still expect their users to ask questions explicitly.

In comparison, during the dialog with the proposed system, the user can show the demand as soon as it is evoked. Since the user does not have to wait for the system to finish the summary, he/she does not have to keep the requests in mind until his/her turn to say them as questions. Moreover, because a short instant response is given after the system utterance which is the cause of the demand, the focus has already been resolved and a simple asking back such as "what?" is enough for the system to catch the focus. As

a whole, thanks to its ability to process the implicit information request from the user, the proposed system realized smooth information consumption with speech interaction. The system is one actual system employing the conversation protocols we previously discussed[4].

5. CONCLUSIONS

This paper described a spoken dialog system that can coordinate passive information consumption and active information exploration. It was particularity emphasized that promptly responding to a user's implicit information request is highly demanded.

Although the technical bottom lines to this issue have been presented in the paper, there remains several challenges, including: to precisely identify the focus of interest that is being latent in a user's response; and to adequately prepare the providing information by considering user model and the ongoing dialog context. In addition, establishing a way to evaluate an accomplished dialog is vital, as a number of factors could affect the quality of a dialog.

6. REFERENCES

[1] S. Fujie, R. Miyake, and T. Kobayashi. Spoken dialogue system using recognition of user's feedback for rhythmic dialogue. In *Speech Prosody 2006*, May 2006. paper 147.

[2] S. Janarthanam, et al. Integrating location, visibility, and question-answering in a spoken dialogue system for pedestrian city exploration. In *SIGDIAL '12*, pages 134–136, 2012.

[3] N. Kaiki and Y. Sagisaka. Study of pause insertion rules based on local phrase dependency structure. *IEICE Trans. (D-II)*, 79(9):1455–1463, Sept. 1996.

[4] T. Kobayashi and S. Fujie. Conversational robots: An approach to conversation protocol issues that utilizes the paralinguistic information available in a robot-human setting. *Acoustical Science and Technology*, 34(2):64–72, 2013.

[5] K. Komatani, S. Ueno, T. Kawahara, and H. Okuno. User modeling in spoken dialogue systems to generate flexible guidance. *User Modeling and User-Adapted Interaction*, 15(1-2):169–183, 2005.

[6] Y. Matsuo and M. Ishizuka. Keyword extraction from a single document using word co-occurrence statistical information. *International Journal on Artificial Intelligence Tools*, 13(01):157–169, 2004.

[7] T. Nomoto. A generic sentence trimmer with CRFs. In *ACL2008*, June 2008.

[8] S. Seneff and J. Polifroni. Dialogue management in the mercury flight reservation system. In *ANLP/NAACL ConvSyst '00*, pages 11–16, 2000.

[9] H. Sugiyama and Y. Minami. Information provision-timing control for informational assistance robot. In *HRI '11*, pages 259–260, 2011.

[10] K. Yoshino and T. Kawahara. News navigation system based on proactive dialogue strategy. In *IWSDS2015*, Jan. 2015.

[11] K. Yoshino, S. Mori, and T. Kawahara. Spoken dialogue system based on information extraction using similarity of predicate argument structures. In *SIGDIAL '11*, 2011.

The Role of Language Skills in Interactive Social Book Search Sessions

Maria Gäde
Berlin School of Library and Information Science
Humboldt-Universität zu Berlin
Dorotheenstr. 26, 10117 Berlin
Germany
maria.gaede@ibi.hu-berlin.de

Mark M. Hall
Department of Computing
Edge Hill University
St Helens Road, L39 4QP
United Kingdom
mark.hall@edgehill.ac.uk

ABSTRACT

When searching for books, people frequently have to deal with content that is in a language different from their own. However, research on multilingual systems has generally focused on the user interface's language rather than the content language. In this paper, we describe and compare early results from the multilingual aspects in the Interactive Social Book Search (iSBS) task at CLEF 2014 and 2015. A preliminary analysis of usage patterns for native English and non-native English speakers indicates an influence of language skills on search behaviour during goal-oriented and casual leisure tasks. Based on previous experiences and results, strengths and challenges of IIR studies are discussed.

CCS Concepts

•Information systems → Users and interactive retrieval; Search interfaces; •Human-centered computing → HCI design and evaluation methods;

Keywords

Social Book Searching, Casual Leisure Behaviour, Multilingual Information Access, Interface Design

1. INTRODUCTION

Ideally, information systems provide boundless access to information, irrespective of the user's origin, linguistic background and search strategy [12]. While a lot of effort has gone into the implementation of multilingual user interfaces, less research has focused on the impact of the content language on the interaction between the user, the system, and the content [14]. Previous research assumed that differences in search behaviour are based on the level of cognitive effort the user needs to access a website [7]. It is thus likely that language skills should influence search strategies, and preferences [13].

CHIIR '16, March 13-17, 2016, Carrboro, NC, USA

© 2016 ACM. ISBN 978-1-4503-3751-9/16/03. . . $15.00

DOI: http://dx.doi.org/10.1145/2854946.2854990

Research in these areas has generally focused on professional work scenarios, where there is a specific, focused goal that the user is attempting to satisfy. However, particularly in book search contexts, users will frequently have no specific goal or only a very rough aim of what they might want to achieve in their search session and will frequently be searching in a personal and leisure context. To be able to support exploring and discovering strategies we need to understand the characteristics of such open-ended, leisure-focused sessions and possible language barriers within those.

2. INTERACTIVE SOCIAL BOOK SEARCH (ISBS)

The overall goal of the Social Book Search lab at CLEF (Conference and Labs of the Evaluation Forum) in 2014 [1] and 2015 [6] was to investigate how professional metadata (title, authors, ...) can be combined with social meta-data (tags, reviews) to satisfy an information need. Within this the Interactive Social Book Search Task (iSBS) looked at how the two types of meta-data can be combined in the search interface and in what way users make use of the two meta-data searches when interacting with the interface to complete a task.

To investigate this two search user interfaces (SUI) were created and two tasks defined that would be used with the two SUIs. The experiment was set up using SPIRES [5], which provides standardised pre- and post-task and pre- and post-session questions. The SUIs were created using PyIRE [4], which allows detailed data on the user interaction to be collected even if the experiment participants are located remotely.

Using the interfaces and tasks two user experiments were conducted using participants recruited from across Europe. In this paper we will focus only on the following research question:

RQ1 What role do language skills play in *goal-oriented* and *non-goal* tasks using an interactive multi-stage interface?

2.1 Tasks

In both experiments each participant used one of the two interfaces to complete both tasks. A latin-square setup was used to ensure a balanced distribution of interface use and task ordering. In both 2014 and 2015 participants had to complete a *goal-oriented* and a *non-goal* task. In both years the following *non-goal* task from [11] was used:

Imagine you are waiting to meet a friend in a coffee shop or pub or the airport or your office. While waiting, you come across this website and explore it looking for any book that you find interesting, or engaging or relevant.

In 2014 the following "simulated leisure task" [10] was used for the *goal-oriented* task:

Imagine you are looking for some interesting physics and mathematics books for a layperson. You have heard about the Feynman books but you have never really read anything in this area. You would also like to find an "interesting facts" sort of book on mathematics.

This generated very short sessions, thus to increase session length in 2015 the following *goal-oriented* task was used:

Imagine you participate in an experiment at a desert-island for one month. There will be no people, no TV, radio or other distraction. The only things you are allowed to take with you are 5 books. Please search for and add 5 books to your book-bag that you would want to read during your stay at the desert-island:

- Select one book about surviving on a desert island
- Select one book that will teach you something new
- Select one book about one of your personal hobbies or interests
- Select one book that is highly recommended by other users (based on user ratings and reviews)
- Select one book for fun
- Please add a note (in the book-bag) explaining why you selected each of the five books.

Additionally in 2015 participants were first given a training task that introduced them to the functionality available in the SUI they would be using to complete the two tasks.

2.2 Interfaces

Two SUIs were developed, with both providing a monolingual English interface [3].

The baseline (BL) interface implemented a standard SUI, consisting of a search box, the search result list, the item details display, and an area in which to collect the books that fulfill their task. It represents a standard interface that participants are likely to be familiar with.

The multi-stage (MS) interface implemented a novel SUI that consisted of three linked pages that implemented the pre-focus, focus, and post-focus phases of [12]. The first page provided an interface aimed at supporting less focused exploration of the collection, the second page a focused SUI that included the ability to restrict results by a given facet, and the third page a review interface that allowed participants to review the books they had collected and add or remove as required.

In 2015 the MS interface was updated and re-designed according to previous results and user comments [2].

Table 1: Number of participants by language using the multi-stage interface

Year	Native English	Non-Native (Other)
2014	8	14
2015	16	79

2.3 Data

For all tasks a monolingual English subset of the INEX Social Book Search's Amazon/LibraryThing book collection was used, consisting of approximately 1.5 million books. Each book consisted of publisher-supplied meta-data (title, author(s), publisher, publication year, etc.), subject meta-data (classification codes, subject headings), user-generated content (Amazon user reviews, LibraryThing user tags), and a thumbnail image.

2.4 Participants and Data Gathering

In 2014 and 2015 participants from different countries and language backgrounds were recruited. A total of 233 users, 41 in 2014 and 192 in 2015, from 36 different countries and 30 different mother tongues participated in the experiment. Participants' mother tongues included amongst others Afrikaans, German, Dutch, English, Danish, Romanian, Farsian, Russian, Turkish, Chinese or Portuguese. Those that did not select English as their mother tongue will for the purpose of the analysis be grouped together as non-native English speakers.

The SPIRE system's latin-square functionality balances participants across the task/interface combinations, but this does not take into account the participants' mother tongue. As a result in 2014 all but one of the English-language participants used the multi-stage interface, making a comparative analysis of the baseline SUI impossible. From this point forward we will only be considering the participants who used the multi-stage interface (Table 1).

The SPIRE system collected the following data points for each participant, which form the basis of the analysis:

- user profile (questionnaires), e.g. age, gender, level of education, first language, all languages used in web-search, country of residence;
- user – system interactions (from logs), e.g. queries, books collected, facets selected, UI elements interacted with;
- post-task motivation (questionnaires), e.g. why did you select these books, usefulness of UI elements, usefulness of meta-data elements;
- user engagement (questionnaires) based on [8].

3. THE IMPACT OF LANGUAGE SKILLS ON SEARCH BEHAVIOUR

To investigate the language impact, the log data collected during the participants' use of the MS interface was automatically processed and the following five characteristics extracted for both of the tasks:

- Session length: Total length of the session;
- First interaction: Time from the interface loading to the first user activity;

- First query: Time from the interface loading to when the first query was executed;

- First book: Time from the interface loading to when the first book was collected;

- Books: Total number of books collected.

No tests were done for language impact on task ordering, search behaviour, or engagement, as [9] found no language impact on any of these aspects. However, in both experiments the qualitative responses of many of the German language participants stated that they encountered a significant language barrier when exploring the English language content, which is the motivation for the analysis presented here.

3.1 Goal-oriented Task

2014.

In the *goal-oriented* task English native speakers were faster in their first interaction with the system and faster to run their first query (Wilcoxon signed rank $p < 0.05$). No statistical differences were found in the time needed to collect their first book, the total number of books collected, and the total session length.

2015.

The only statistically significant difference was in the total session length (Wilcoxon signed rank $p < 0.05$). English native speakers' median session length was approximately four minutes faster than the non-native speakers'.

Comparing the two years, in the second year non-English speakers seem to have less difficulties dealing with the interface and task. The most likely reason for this is the introduction of the training task, which gives the non-native speakers the opportunity to get to know the SUI and reduces language and system knowledge impact on the initial interactions. This strongly indicates that for multi-lingual IIR experiments a training task is a necessity to minimise the language learning effects of the interface itself.

At the same time in 2015 the non-native speakers spent significantly more time on the *goal-oriented* task than the native speakers. Considering that there was no difference in the number of books selected and the initial speed of interaction, it is likely that the non-native speakers needed more time to inspect and select content. While not statistically significant, the 2014 experiment shows a similar trend, but due to the simpler task the individual differences mask the language impact. However, especially for casual leisure situations, longer session duration does not always indicate a poorer experience or dissatisfaction, but could also indicate a good user experience.

3.2 Non-goal Task

There are no statistically significant differences in the total session length in either year.

2014.

In the *non-goal* task English native participants were faster to issue their first query, collect their first book, and collected more books overall (Wilcoxon signed rank $p < 0.05$). However, they did not take less time for their first interaction.

2015.

Unlike in 2014, there is no difference on the time to the first query or collect the first book. However, English native participants were faster with their first interaction (4 seconds faster). Interestingly in 2015 the English native participants actually collected less books than the non-native participants.

As in the *goal-oriented* task, the introduction of the training task reduces much of the language impact of the interface. However, the slower time for the first interaction indicates that the impact of the content language remains. On the initial page, participants saw a hierarchical tree of topics that they could browse. While this had no impact in the *goal-oriented* task, in the *non-goal* task it seems that because participants have to come up with their own goal, the non-native speakers take a bit longer to translate their goal into the appropriate part of the topic tree, leading to a slower initial interaction.

The training instructions were designed so as not to have any direct connection to either the two tasks. To test this, we checked the queries issued by users in the training task against the queries used in the two main tasks. Only 6 of the 192 users (3%) reused at least one training query in either the *goal-oriented* (3 users) or *non-goal* (3 users) task. 5 re-users were English non-native speakers and 1 was an English native speaker. 3 participants re-used in their first task, 3 in their second. Overall this indicates that while the training instructions can act as direct prompts, potentially influencing the results, they can also simply act as reminders of topics the user is interested in in any case.

The differences in the number of books collected in the *non-goal* task is puzzling. The task did not change between the two years and none of the changes to the user-interface explain why in 2015 the non-native speakers collect more books than the native speakers, while in 2014 the situation is reversed.

4. CONCLUSIONS AND OUTLOOK

The results from two years iSBS data indicate differences between native and non-native speakers facing *goal-oriented* and *non-goal* casual leisure tasks. In particular they indicate that non-native English speakers require additional time to process the, for them, foreign-language content, which was to be expected.

However, the more interesting aspect is that the introduction of a training task in the second year reduced many of the language-specific differences. This gives a strong indication that it is possible to run experiments investigating multilingual issues in a mono-lingual environment, as long as participants are trained on the environment, so that only the content language impacts the results. There is of course a danger that the training task influences the results of the experiment itself, however our results show that only a small number of participants (3%) are influenced by the training task.

One of the difficulties with (multilingual) IIR studies is that they often struggle to reproduce and explain effects. In our analysis we see this with the number of books collected in the *non-goal* task. Here, although many non-native speaker participants reported finding the task difficult in both years, in the second year they collected significantly more books than the native speakers. A brief review of the annotations provided for most of the collected books also does not reveal any issues such as collecting books they are not interested in just to complete the task.

One issue for further work that this raises is whether the metrics we are using are stable enough and have a clear enough interpretation to enable conclusions to be drawn. In the case of the books, perhaps in the *non-goal* task individual differences such as age or education are actually much stronger than the language aspects and the difference between the two years is pure chance. Other situation or context indicators might only appear during an experiment. Using thinking aloud protocols in smaller studies might help detecting and understanding the influence of additional factors we are currently not aware of.

Additionally as indicated [5] the variety of indicators and metrics that are used to characterise user behaviour remain a problem within, but also between studies. For example, session duration and selection of books could be interpreted in multiple ways. Both longer and shorter durations could be argued as being better. The same goes for the number of books. The user engagement scale [8] represents a stable metric across the two years of the experiment. However, [9] suggest that they see no language effects that could explain the differences we see in our results.

As far as the comparability between studies goes, the heterogeneity of the user groups, tasks, and interfaces, which create a more realistic setting and are one of the strengths of IIR compared to classic IR, also make comparison between studies difficult. Part of the iSBS track's goal was to create a common baseline and set of experiments that different research groups could use to investigate different research questions while maintaining comparability. However, as the results presented here show, we are still some way from creating such a stable baseline that would enable reliable comparisons. Therefore, the major challenge in IIR remains to identify and establish suitable interactive IR infrastructures that support comparable long-term studies.

5. REFERENCES

[1] BELLOT, P., BOGERS, T., GEVA, S., HALL, M., HUURDEMAN, H., KAMPS, J., KAZAI, G., KOOLEN, M., MORICEAU, V., MOTHE, J., ET AL. Overview of inex 2014. In *Information Access Evaluation. Multilinguality, Multimodality, and Interaction.* Springer, 2014, pp. 212–228.

[2] GÄDE, M., HALL, M., HUURDEMAN, H., KAMPS, J., KOOLEN, M., SKOV, M., TOMS, E., AND WALSH, D. Overview of the sbs 2015 interactive track. In *CEUR Workshop Proceedings* (2015).

[3] HALL, M. M., HUURDEMANN, H., SKOV, M., WALSH, D., ET AL. Overview of the inex 2014 interactive social book search track.

[4] HALL, M. M., KATSARIS, S., AND TOMS, E. A pluggable interactive ir evaluation work-bench. In *European Workshop on Human-Computer Interaction and Information Retrieval* (2013), pp. 35–38.

[5] HALL, M. M., AND TOMS, E. Building a common framework for iir evaluation. In *CLEF 2013 - Information Access Evaluation. Multilinguality, Multimodality, and Visualization* (2013), pp. 17–28.

[6] KOOLEN, M., BOGERS, T., GÄDE, M., HALL, M., HUURDEMAN, H., KAMPS, J., SKOV, M., TOMS, E., AND WALSH, D. Overview of the clef 2015 social book search lab. In *Experimental IR Meets Multilinguality, Multimodality, and Interaction.* Springer, 2015, pp. 545–564.

[7] KRALISCH, A. The impact of culture and language on the use of the internet: Empirical analysis of behaviour and attitudes, 2005.

[8] O'BRIEN, H. L., AND TOMS, E. G. The development and evaluation of a survey to measure user engagement. *Journal of the American Society for Information Science and Technology 61*, 1 (2010), 50–69.

[9] SKOV, M., AND BOGERS, T. The influence of language proficiency on book search behaviour. In *CLEF2015 Working Notes* (2015).

[10] SKOV, M., AND INGWERSEN, P. Exploring information seeking behaviour in a digital museum context. In *Proceedings of the second international symposium on Information interaction in context* (2008), ACM, pp. 110–115.

[11] TOMS, E., AND HALL, M. The chic interactive task (chici) at clef2013. CLEF.

[12] VAKKARI, P. A theory of the task-based information retrieval process: a summary and generalisation of a longitudinal study. *Journal of documentation 57*, 1 (2001), 44–60.

[13] VASSILAKAKI, E., AND GAROUFALLOU, E. Multilingual digital libraries: A review of issues in system-centered and user-centered studies, information retrieval and user behavior. *The International Information & Library Review 45*, 1 (2013), 3–19.

[14] ZHANG, J., AND LIN, S. Multiple language supports in search engines. *Online Information Review 31*, 4 (2007), 516–532.

Effects of Topic Familiarity on Query Reformulation Strategies

Debanjan Ghosh
School of Communication and Information, Rutgers University, NJ, USA
debanjan.ghosh@rutgers.edu

ABSTRACT

Users employ various Query Reformulation (QR) Strategies to improve their search experiences as well as to retrieve the better results. In this exploratory research, we investigate the association of topic familiarities with such QR strategies. We design a user study where 38 participants with different levels of Topic Familiarity (TF) took part in the TREC Genomics Search Track (a total of five search tasks). We conducted two experiments: 1) we evaluate a set of predefined QR strategies to discover if participants with a specific level of TF tends to use a specific QR strategy. 2) we propose a supervised classification system that classifies consecutive queries made by the participants with different levels (low, medium, and high) of topic familiarity. Various lexical and distributional semantic features are implemented and feature analysis shows that participants with low familiarity tend to alter the spelling and use stemming for QR whereas participants with medium or higher familiarity are inclined to add new terms and phrases to reformulate queries.

1. INTRODUCTION

Studies in search behaviors and user interactions have demonstrated that users consistently attempt to utilize their topic familiarity (TF) during the search activities to improve the quality of the retrievals [5]. Previous research has demonstrated that surface features, such as bag-of-words and phrases are able to identify the main concepts in the search and these features can improve the query reformulation performances [3].

In this exploratory research, we utilize the results of a user study to analyze the association of users' TF with their QR strategies. We define various lexical and distributional semantic features based on the *subsequent* queries made by the users. We analyze the QR strategies as described in [3, 4]. Following that, we propose a supervised classification setup where every training data instance represents the difference between two consecutive queries in the form of lexical as well as semantic features. User's self-reported TF is regarded as the gold label for training. During the evaluation, given a pair of consecutive unseen queries from a participant, the classifier attempts to predict the TF, of the participant.

The data for our study is extracted from the trace files generated

CHIIR '16, March 13-17, 2016, Carrboro, NC, USA

© 2016 ACM. ISBN 978-1-4503-3751-9/16/03. . . $15.00

DOI: http://dx.doi.org/10.1145/2854946.2855001

during a TREC Genomics Track (TGT) interactive study [1]. This study contains search tasks centered on genomics and biomedical data collection. A total of 38 participants, with different levels of TF participated in the study. We discuss the search tasks in detail in the next section.

Our research has two major contributions. First, lexical and semantic feature analysis reveals that certain strategies (i.e., forming a query with *new* words) have a strong association to participants with high TF whereas participants with low TF tend to alter only the spellings of words to refine their queries. Second, the classifier consistently achieves a 10-15% improvement in predicting the TF of the participant over a majority baseline, which shows that QR strategies have a strong link with topic familiarity.

2. RESEARCH DATA AND SEARCH TASKS

One of the main motifs of the TREC Genomics Track is to analyze how participants can query a medical document repository to extract information related to their needs. Based on this motif, we design an user study that requires participants to search, view and save documents to assist in gathering information for specific search tasks (a total of five search tasks). The medical repository contains MEDLINE abstracts. MEDLINE is a bibliographic database that includes bibliographic information from articles published in academic journals of life sciences and related fields in health care.

38 participants with different levels of topic familiarity took part in the search tasks. These participants have different levels of education in biology discipline. Queries formulated by the participants are extracted from the trace files generated during their interactions with the TREC search tasks. They were provided with a short explanation of the task that includes Medical Subject Headings (MeSH) description of related biological terms [2]. MeSH is consists of comprehensive vocabulary for the purpose of indexing articles and books in life sciences. For instance, for the task - "correlation between DNA repair pathways and oxidative stress" - participants were introduced to MeSH terms, such as "Genetic Process" and "DNA Repair". Finally, participants completed presearch questionnaires, which assessed participants' self-reported *familiarity* with each search topic. The familiarity was assessed via a 1 to 7 point Likert scale, where 1 was not at all familiar, 3-4 was somewhat/medium familiar, and 7 was extreme familiar.

3. ANALYSIS OF QR STRATEGIES

In this section, we discuss the two experiments we conducted to assess the association of QR strategies with topic familiarities.

---

[1] http://trec.nist.gov/data/genomics.html
[2] https://en.wikipedia.org/wiki/Medical_Subject_Headings

Familiarity Level	QR Strategies	
	Strategy	% of Queries
LTF	Common	**29.77**
	NewWords	23.26
	AddWords	21.86
	Same	12.56
MTF	Common	**25.83**
	NewWords	25.42
	AddWords	20.83
	RemoveWords	10.42
HTF	NewWords	**35.29**
	Common	29.41
	AddWords	17.65
	Same	11.76

Table 1: % of QR strategies for all tasks (word based)

Familiarity Level	QR Strategies	
	Strategy	% of Queries
LTF	SamePhrase	**26.98**
	AddPhrase	26.51
	NewPhrase	21.86
	Remove	13.95
MTF	SamePhrase	**28.75**
	NewPhrase	26.25
	AddPhrase	17.08
	Remove	15.83
HTF	NewPhrase	**44.12**
	SamePhrase	23.53
	AddPhrase	20.59
	Common	8.82

Table 2: % of QR strategies for all tasks (phrase based)

First, we analyze the different queries made by the participants using a set of predefined QR strategies. We evaluate the queries to discover whether participants with different topic familiarities undertake different QR strategies during their search activities. In the second experiment, we have presented a supervised *text classification* framework to study the link between participant's TF with QR strategies.

3.1 QR Strategies and Topic Familarity

Existing research in QR strategy analysis has shown how participants employ query refinements in web search [4, 3]. Given two consecutive queries q_i and q_j (q_j occurs after q_i), [4] introduced a list of query reformulation strategies (i.e., "Same", "AddWord", "Common" etc.) to categorize q_j by comparing it to q_i. We considered some of these strategies to discover how they are linked to the TF of the participants. In the TGT search task, not many participants self-identified them with high familiarity with search tasks. Thus, to avoid data sparsity problem, we combine the familiarity scores to three categories (e.g. scores of 1 and 2 to *Low Topic Familiarity (LTF)*, scores of 3 and 4 to *Medium Topic Familiarity (MTF)*, and 5, 6, and 7 to *High Topic Familiarity (HTF)*) instead of using every familiarity score as a different category. Below is a short description of the strategies we implemented[3].

- **Same:** Both q_i and q_j queries are same.

- **Reorder:** q_j is word reordering of q_i.

- **AddWords:** q_j has all the words of q_i and new word(s).

- **RemoveWords:** Removing words from q_i returns q_j.

- **Substring:** q_j is a substring of q_i or vise versa.

- **Stem:** q_j contains "stemming" of words of q_i or vise versa.

- **Common:** q_i and q_j share common words.

- **NewWords:** q_j is composed of entirely new words.

Table 1 shows the *top* QR strategies employed by the participants. We observe that participants usually take three QR strategies - add new word/words, create a new query with common words from the previous query, and third, create an entirely different (new) query. We also observe that participants with HTF employ more new words than MTF or LTF participants.

[3] mentioned that lexical similarity between queries often introduces many false negatives and to overcome such problem, queries are first segmented into important "phrases" and then similarity is

---

[3]For further details of these QR strategies, please refer [4].

measured between the phrases. Similar to [3], we adopt the pointwise mutual information (PMI) technique to discover the query segments. For a query q, which is composed of words $q = q_1, q_2, \ldots, q_n$, PMI between any two successive words q_i and q_{i+1} is computed as,

$$PMI(q_i, q_{i+1}) = log \frac{p(q_i, q_{i+1})}{p(q_i)p(q_{i+1})} \qquad (1)$$

where $p(q_i, q_{i+1})$ is the joint probability of occurrence of the bigram (q_i, q_{i+1}) and $p(q_i)$ and $p(q_{i+1})$ are the individual occurrence probabilities of the two words, respectively [4]. We consider only those bigrams as *phrases*, where the PMI score is above a certain threshold τ. The threshold we used, $\tau = 4.0$ is set empirically [5]. Since the TGT search task is about biological document retrievals, instead of using any Web N-Gram repository, we utilize the MEDLINE abstract repository to compute the joint and individual probabilities [6]. If a word q_{i+1} is present in two phrases, we choose the phrase with higher PMI score. We adopt the QR strategies as described in [4] for phrases (see Table 2) and repeated the experiment for phrases similar to Table 1.

The results from Table 2 shows that participants with LTF and MTF tend to either utilize same phrases or add new phrases to the previous queries. However, participants with HTF prefer to create new queries with specific biological terms. For instance, 44.12% of all query formulations are with new phrases for HTF participants (see the rows in Table 2 for familiarity = HTF). Similarly, [9] also observed that HTF participants use their domain knowledge to use specific search terms. In the next section, we define a set of lexical and distributional semantic features based on the queries and identify the top discriminative features associated with different levels of TF.

3.2 Classification Experiment for QR

We present a supervised *text classification* framework to discover the link between user's topic familiarity with query reformulation strategies. Any training data is represented as q_{ij}, where q_i and q_j are the two consecutive queries formulated by a participant who took part in the TGT search task. Training data contains queries from all the search tasks. TF of the participant is regarded as the gold label for q_{ij}. Each training data q_{ij} represents the lexical and semantic similarities between q_i and q_j as features that may capture the QR strategy. For instance, suppose a participant made two consecutive queries q_i ("glyphosate tolerance") and q_j ("glyphosate

---

[4]Here, we only considered bigram phrases, although phrases can be longer.
[5]Lower threshold resulted in many non-grammatical bigrams.
[6]http://mbr.nlm.nih.gov/Download/

Word Based Features
Normalized Levenshtein edit distance
Number of characters in common (starting from left)
Number of characters in common (starting from right)
Number of common words
Jaccard Similarity score

Table 3: Word Based Features

Phrase Based Features
Number of common phrases
Number of phrases in q_i missing in q_j
Number of phrases in q_j missing in q_i
If all phrases in q_i is present in q_j (boolean feature)
If all phrases in q_j is present in q_i (boolean feature)

Table 4: Phrase Based Features

tolerance gene sequence") to create a report on "glyphosate tolerance". A feature can capture that q_j has "added" new words (i.e., the "gene sequence") to the previous q_i query. Note, same participant may express different TF for different search tasks. This would not be a problem in our training setting, since we are not training on each participant separately. Below is a short description of all the lexical and semantic features we have utilize.

3.2.1 Lexical Features

We consider two types of lexical features - *word* based and *phrase* based, to capture the similarities between q_i and q_j. Word based edit features are useful in identifying QR strategies since consecutive queries q_i and q_j may have many overlapping words to show how the queries are related. The features are in Table 3. Once we computed the PMI scores for each bigram and identified the phrases (i.e. $PMI > \tau$) for each query we create the following features for phrases (Table 4).

Finally, we also adopt the QR strategies as described in [4] for words as well as for phrases. That is, we define a set of boolean features to capture the intent of the q_j in comparison to q_i. This is similar to the description in previous section (i.e., "AddWords", "RemoveWords", "AddPhrase" etc.) but now we use these strategies as boolean features for words and for bigram phrases. Altogether, we have created 29 features.

3.2.2 Semantic Features

Ontologies like WordNet [7] is useful in measuring semantic similarities between texts. However, we cannot use WordNet here since TGT search tasks contain terms taken from biology and medical domain (i.e., gene names) that are absent in WordNet. Thus, we utilize - "distributional semantic" - based method where a target word is represented by a vector of its context (e.g., co-occurring words) that appear in a corpus, as a proxy for meaning representation [2]. For instance, words such as "effector", enzyme name -"dioxygenase", and chemical process - "hydroxylase", co-occur very frequently with the word "gene" in MEDLINE abstracts and these words can act like a proxy for the meaning of "gene". To measure similarity between two words i.e., "gene" and "dna", geometric interpretations, such as cosine similarity are then applied between corresponding vectors of "gene" and "dna".

Recently, neural network-inspired vector representations (also denoted as "word embeddings") have seen tremendous success in finding semantic similarity between words [8, 6] and they are applied in many Natural Language Processing (NLP) problems [7]. To build a similar distributional model for words, we utilize - "GloVe",

---

[7]Word embeddings and word vectors are used interchangeably.

a word embedding model that is based upon weighted least-square model trained on global word-word co-occurrence [8]. We utilize a snapshot of MEDLINE abstracts (780k abstracts) to build a word-word co-occurrence model (window of ten words) via GloVe [8]. Given two consecutive queries q_i and q_j, we first represent the words in the queries via word embeddings that are learned via GloVe and then apply cosine similarity to measure the semantic similarity between the queries. We create two features from word embeddings. First, we extract all the words from q_i and q_j and then measure cosine similarity between the word embeddings of the words (first feature). Second, we extract only the phrases from q_i and q_j and then measure cosine similarity between the words of the phrases (second feature).

4. EXPERIMENTS

Recall, each training instance q_{ij} represents the lexical and semantic similarities between q_i and q_j. We collected a total of 632 such data instances from the queries made by the participants in the TGT search tasks. Out of 632 instances, 286 instances belong to LTF, 203 instances belong to MTF, and remaining 143 instances belong to HTF. We conducted a five-fold cross-validation experiment via Support Vector Machines (SVM) algorithm to predict the topic familiarity category of each data instance q_{ij}. We ran separate binary classification experiments for each topic familiarity category (positive category) where as the negative category is comprised of the other two topic familiarity category. We utilize the [1] toolkit for experiments with SVM while choosing linear kernel for classification. Given, the number of data instances are imbalanced, cost parameter for each TF category is proportional to the number of data instances for that category.

5. RESULTS AND DISCUSSION

Table 6 shows the results for the classification experiments using lexical and semantic features. Average results of the cross-validation is reported throughout via precision (Prec.), recall (Rec.), and F1 scores. Baseline (BL) for each of the category - LTF, MTF, and HTF - is the % accuracy of the instances that belong to the familiarity category during test time. For instance, the Avg. number of test instance (in each fold) is 29 for HTF, and the number of negative instances (comprised of LTF and MTF) is 98. Thus the BL for HTF is 29/(98+29) or 22.8%. *Word* and *Phrase* represent the results from lexical features described in Section 3.2.1. *WE* denotes Word Embedding results.

We observe that the features derived from phrases as well as the WE approach have better performance than the BL and simple word-based features for each of the TF category. Also, the combination of the features (i.e., word and phrase) often produces better results. For instance, for LTF, the combination of word and phrase result in 61.22% (F1) which is more than 15% (absolute value) than the baseline. Recall the WE approach contains only two features that measure the cosine similarity between word embeddings (Section 3.2.2). It is remarkable to see even with only two semantic similarity features, WE approach is comparable to phrase based features and better than word based features for each of the TF category.

One aspect we are investigating here is whether there are linguistic constructions that are consistently shown in queries that belong to specific TF category. To answer that question, we utilize the weight vectors for each feature from SVM training and use the

---

[8]The algorithm is freeely availabe at: http://nlp.stanford.edu/projects/glove/

TF	Best Results	Top Features
LTF	Word + Phrase	QR_Spelling, QR_Stem, QR_Remove
MTF	Word + Phrase + WE	Leven_Dist, QR_Substring, Common_Words, QR_Phrase_New
HTF	Word + Phrase + WE	WE_Sim, QR_Substring, QR_New

Table 5: Top Features for Topic Familiarity

TF	Features	Prec.	Rec.	F1
	BL	-	-	45.31
	Word	47.69	53.45	50.41
	Phrase	49.33	63.79	55.64
LTF	WE	41.9	75.86	53.99
	Word + Phrase	50.56	77.59	**61.22**
	Word + Phrase + WE	48.89	75.86	59.46
	BL	-	-	32.28
	word	33.33	43.9	37.89
	Phrase	36.59	73.17	48.78
MTF	WE	34.48	73.17	46.88
	Word + Phrase	31.25	73.17	43.8
	Word + Phrase + WE	33.96	87.8	**48.98**
	BL	-	-	22.8
	Word	26.32	51.72	34.88
	Phrase	24.68	65.52	35.85
HTF	WE	27.59	55.17	36.78
	Word + Phrase	24.47	79.31	37.4
	Word + Phrase + WE	24.07	89.66	**37.96**

Table 6: Evaluation of QR Stratigies for Topic Familiarity

scores of the weights to decide the relevancy of a feature. For example, for LTF category, features with the highest positive weights are selected as most discriminative features for the LTF category, and so on.

As shown in Table 6 we have conducted many different combinations of features for the classification experiments. For brevity, in Table 5, we only report the *top* features where we have achieved the best F1 scores in Table 6. Observe that for the LTF category, the top features for Query Reformulation are QR_Spelling and QR_Stem. This shows the fact that participants who have LTF for the search task create the query q_j by altering the spelling of the previous query q_i (or utilize stemming/root form of a word) without making a completely new query q_j. For instance, LTF participants attempt to change spellings such as "genes" to "gene" or "mice" to "mouse" during formulating new queries instead of using new words. On the other hand, for MTF and for HTF, it is more common to bring new words or utilize substring of the previous query. For MTF, QR_Phrase_New and QR_Substring denote that participants use new phrases or use substring of the previous phrase while formulating new queries. For example, a participant with MTF created a query q_i as "glyphosate tolerance gene sequence" and then the modified subsequent query q_j was "DNA sequence". Similarly, for HTF, QR_New is a top feature that shows participants with HTF prefer new words in making queries.

6. CONCLUSION AND FUTURE WORK

Identifying QR strategies is a useful application in Information Retrieval research because it is directly related to the quality of the retrievals and user experiences. Previous research has shown that surface word features can reliably predict the type of QR. In this research, we discover the association of QR strategies with different levels of TF of participants. Our results show that participants with LTF are tended to alter the spellings of the queries to formulate new queries where as HTF participants are able to formulate queries with new terms and phrases.

This study was not without limitations. Traditionally, supervised research tends to perform better with large training data, where as we have collected only a few hundreds of query pairs for each TF category. Moreover, we need participants to create many queries for each search task because we are analyzing the textual difference between two consecutive queries made by the same participant. For future work, we plan to ask more participants to take part in the search tasks. We also observe that HTF participants are more keen in using abbreviations, such as "ros" ("reactive oxygen species"), where currently we do not have any resource that can map such abbreviations to their actual forms. Thus, we plan to study the word embeddings more closely to model such abbreviations.

7. REFERENCES

[1] C.-C. Chang and C.-J. Lin. Libsvm: A library for support vector machines. *ACM TIST*, 2(3):27, 2011.

[2] Z. S. Harris. *Distributional structure*. Springer, 1970.

[3] A. Hassan. Identifying web search query reformulation using concept based matching. In *Proceedings of the EMNLP 2013*, 2013.

[4] J. Huang and E. N. Efthimiadis. Analyzing and evaluating query reformulation strategies in web search logs. In *Proceedings of CIKM 2009*, pages 77–86. ACM.

[5] D. Kelly and J. Teevan. Implicit feedback for inferring user preference: a bibliography. In *ACM SIGIR Forum*, volume 37, pages 18–28. ACM, 2003.

[6] T. Mikolov, I. Sutskever, K. Chen, G. S. Corrado, and J. Dean. Distributed representations of words and phrases and their compositionality. In *NIPS 2013*, pages 3111–3119.

[7] G. A. Miller. Wordnet: a lexical database for english. *Communications of the ACM*, 38(11):39–41, 1995.

[8] J. Pennington, R. Socher, and C. D. Manning. Glove: Global vectors for word representation. *EMNLP 2014*, 12:1532–1543.

[9] H. Rong, L. Kun, and S. Joo. Effects of topic familiarity and search skills on query reformulation behavior. In *Richard B II. Pro-ceedings of the 76th ASIST Annual Meeting. Silver Spring: ASIST*, pages 1–9, 2013.

Evaluating Touch-Based Interactions in an Image Search Task

Roberto González-Ibáñez   Carlos Barrera-Pulgar   José Luis Varela-Otárola

Departamento de Ingeniería Informática
Universidad de Santiago de Chile
Avenida Ecuador #3659, Estación Central, Santiago, Chile
{roberto.gonzalez.i, carlos.barrerap, jose.varela}@usach.cl

ABSTRACT

Current technologies provide users different ways to interact with digital content, nevertheless, a physical gap between these two interaction components exists. In particular, touch-based interfaces enable users to use their own fingers to manipulate and interact with digital objects in a more direct fashion than mouse-based interactions. However, it is not clear yet to what extent, if any, this type of interaction could help bridge the gap between users and the digital world in particular information-related contexts such as information search. In this paper we report preliminary results of a user study designed to compare mouse and touch-based interactions in the context of an image search task. This study is part of a larger research project focused on immersive interaction with digital information objects. Our results show that in spite of the novelty, high adoption rates, and tangible nature of touch-based interfaces, no significant differences exist with prevalent technology (i.e., mouse) in terms of performance; nevertheless, user experience was found to better in touch-based interactions.

1. INTRODUCTION

Interacting in the digital world implies a physical gap between users and digital objects. While in the real world most people can freely interact with physical objects through their hands and experience such interaction through their senses, in the digital world, interaction capabilities and the participation of human senses are subject to system constraints. This particular phenomenon can be observed in different digital interaction settings including information search. In this context, users interact with different types of digital information objects in order to evaluate its usefulness or relevance with respect to an information need.

Interacting with digital information objects is a rather common activity these days. The prevalent interaction technology for this has been mouse and keyboard, however, in the past ten years or so, touch-based interfaces – in particular touchscreen devices – have become increasingly popular [1]. Today several devices such as computer screens, smartphones, and tablets, have built-in touch capabilities and some of them may also embed haptics technology. Unlike traditional interactions through mouse where users control a digital pointer, in touch-based interfaces people can use their own fingers to virtually touch digital content.

In information-related contexts such as information search, touch interfaces should, at least in principle, provide a more natural experience. However, it is not clear yet to what extent, if any, this type of interface contributes to bridge the interaction gap between users and digital information objects. In the context of this research problem, we present preliminary results from a user study designed to compare mouse and touch-based interactions. In particular, we hypothesize that touch-based interactions should contribute not only to improve performance but also user experience (UX). The rest of this paper is organized as follows. In the next section we present some related work. Then, in the third section, we describe our methodological approach. Following, in the fourth section, we present preliminary results focused on performance and UX. Finally, in the fifth section, we conclude our paper with discussion, implications, and future work.

2. RELATED WORK

Touchscreen technology has been around for the past 50 years or so, however, only until the last decade the proliferation of devices with built-in touch capabilities has been evident. This technology explosion has grabbed researchers' attention, especially those from the human-computer interaction community. Despite the vast amount of work focused on touch-based interfaces, little is known about the implications of such interaction technology in the particular domain of information search.

In an early work by Ostroff et al. [2], three interfaces (i.e., keyboard, mouse, and touchscreen) were investigated. The authors compared the effects of these interfaces in terms of speed, error rates, and timing in a task that consisted in the selection of information from an interactive encyclopedia. Results from this study suggested that effectiveness of a given interface depends on both task and users' skills. Moreover, the authors found that touchscreen was the preferred interface among the participants, the fastest one, but the least accurate one. Note that by the time this study (late '80s) was carried out, computer interactions were less common than today, and touchscreen were in an early development stage, hence, these factors could be determining in the authors' findings.

Along the lines of this work, Liming et al. [3] conducted a user study with 30 participants in order to compare usability implications of mouse and touch-based interactions. Researchers used three types of tasks, namely, drag and drop, pointing and selection, and assembling a bike. Results from this study showed that mouse interactions were significantly faster than those performed through touch, less subtle to errors, and the preferred option among the participants.

In the context of Web-based interactions, Wu et al. [4] compared touchscreen and mouse interactions in the navigation of digital

CHIIR '16, March 13-17, 2016, Carrboro, NC, USA.
© 2016 ACM. ISBN 978-1-4503-3751-9/16/03...$15.00.
DOI: http://dx.doi.org/10.1145/2854946.2854999

maps. Participants in this study were asked to search points of interest in a map. To complete this task, the participants were able to perform actions such as zoom in/out, and scroll. Results from this study indicated that mouse interactions were more successful than those performed through touchscreen. According to the authors, these results could be explained by the predominant familiarity of users with mouse-operated user interfaces.

In a follow up study, Wu et al. [5] adjusted the graphic user interface used in [4] – which was designed for traditional interfaces – in order to better support touch-based interactions. Unlike the above study, performance in touch interactions was found to be as good as that achieved through mouse.

Finally, in the context of information search, recent work by Klouche et al. [6] introduced the Exploration Wall (EW), a touch-based interface for supporting exploratory search. According to the authors, the proposed design – which integrates different aspects from information exploration and sense-making – is better suited for this type of search task. A comparison of the EW and a traditional interface showed that the former led to significantly higher recall without affecting precision. Additionally, the EW was better rated in terms of satisfaction and engagement levels. We note that unlike the study presented in this paper, Klouche's et al. work contrasted completely different user interfaces (i.e., both graphic and interaction interfaces), therefore it is not clear if using Exploratory Wall through mouse would lead to results similar to those obtained using touchscreen.

3. METHOD
3.1 Study Design

We addressed the research problem introduced above through a user study that follows a crossover design in order to evaluate within and between-subjects effects. The study was designed to compare two interactions interfaces (independent variable) in terms of performance and UX (dependent variables). More specifically, we contrasted interactions through mouse and touchscreen – in a common graphic interface – in the context of an image search task. Note that in this study we consider a user interface to be defined in terms of two key components, namely, (1) graphic interface and (2) interaction apparatus.

Participants in the study were randomly assigned to two groups associated to interaction sequences in accordance to the crossover design. The participants in the first group (M_1-T_2) began the interaction sequence by performing a search task using a traditional interface (M1: mouse operated). Following, the participants performed the same search task – with a different collection of information objects – using a touchscreen interface (T_2: touch operated). On the other hand, the participants in the second group (T_1-M_2) performed the same search task used in M_1-T_2, but with the interaction interfaces in the opposite order.

3.2 Search Task
An image search task about the British Petroleum (BP) Gulf oil spill that took place in April 2010 was designed for this study. The topic of the task has been previously used in individual and collaborative information seeking studies [7], thus demonstrating its adequacy for an exploratory search task. The task description required the participants to find, select, and organize relevant images about: (1) impact on flora and fauna, (2) damaged areas, (3) structural damages, and (4) mitigation maneuvers.

In order to simplify the search process and focus on interactions, the task was designed to simulate an asynchronous-role-based collaborative search process [8]. More specifically, an artificial context – in which each participant and a fictitious collaborator were working on a report about the BP oil spill for a prestigious magazine – was presented to the participants. In this artificial context, the participants were required to complete the search process by selecting and organizing relevant images for each subtopic using a specialized graphic interface (details provided in the system section), which displayed a set of images previously collected by the fictitious collaborator using a popular search engine and different queries linked to the above four subtopics.

Finally, the study was presented as a competition (with prizes for the three best performing participants). This approach has proven effective in other studies (e.g., [7]) in terms of recruitment and participants' performance.

3.3 Image Collection
Following the search task description, we created an image collection that represents the set of images gathered by the fictitious collaborator. This set of images was split into two subsets that were used in the two stages of each interaction sequence. Images included in this collection were obtained from Google images using the Extreme Picture Finder software and 13 queries linked to the four subtopics stated above. Additionally, images were automatically filtered in order to remove duplicates (using the VisiPics software) and select images with a resolution equal or higher than 600x600 pixels.

We performed an additional process to introduce noise to the sets by including images retrieved using unrelated queries. This was done in order to produce a more realistic set of images. Following, three human judges classified images in the four subtopics (Fleiss' Kappa=0.53, $p<.01$). Note that images were classified as relevant for one or multiple subtopics. Following, a ranking of relevance was defined in which images classified in a single category were ranked higher than those that fitted in more than one category. In other words, the more specific the image, the more relevant to the subtopic. It is noteworthy that relevant images were classified as such only if the three judges agreed in their assessment.

The resulting image collection was comprised of 881 images with approximately 66% of noise. From this set of images, 442 were used in the first interaction (i.e. M_1 and T_1) and 439 in the second one (i.e. M_2 and T_2). The number of images for each subtopic was roughly balanced and the order of images used in the two interactions was randomly assigned. Finally, no significant differences were found in the distribution of images (relevant and not relevant) in the two subsets, which ensures that task difficulty in the two interactions was equivalent.

3.4 Participants
We recruited 21 participants (all volunteers) from two Chilean universities. One participant was used as pilot run. For the analyses conducted in this paper, we only used data from 20 participants (12 men and 8 women). The participants were students from different fields such as education, engineering, and health services. Their age ranged between 19 and 26 (M=23.55, SD=2.50) years old.

Finally, with regard to their experience using touch-based interfaces, all the participants reported having previous experience with touch devices. More specifically, smartphones and tablets – Android (70%), iOS (20%), and Windows Phone (10%). Furthermore, most participants (90%) reported using such interfaces quite often.

3.5 System

To better support our study design, experimental protocol, session workflow, and data collection, we developed TIIES (Touch-based Information Interaction Evaluation System). This system was developed as an Android App that was deployed on a 10.5" tablet device. The graphic interface was designed to be operated either by mouse or through touchscreen.

In terms of data collection, TIIES was designed to log all participants' actions in the user interface (e.g. selection, drag and drop, and clicks) and survey responses. A screenshot of TIIES is presented in Figure 1.

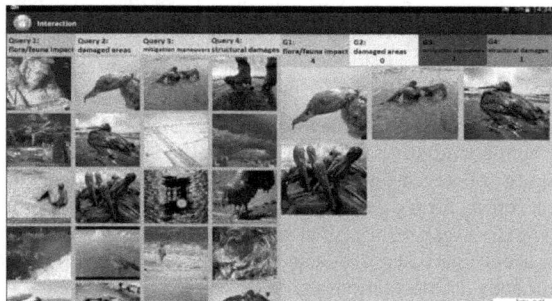

Figure 1. A screenshot of TIIES with its main components.

3.6 Session Workflow

The experimental sessions lasted approximately one hour. Time and session workflow were semi-automatically managed by TIIES. At the beginning of the sessions, the participants were required to sign a consent form. Then, we provided general instructions about the study and the system. Next, physiological sensors and other instruments were calibrated. The participants in both groups were given 10 minutes in each interaction. Additional time was given for practicing with each interaction interface. In accordance to the experimental design, the search task was approached using the two interaction interfaces in a predefined order (i.e., M_1-T_2 and T_1-M_2). Additionally, participants were required to respond different surveys before and after each interaction. More specifically, we measured effects on the affective dimension using the Self-Assessment Manikin (SAM) [9], effects on cognitive workload through the NASA TLX [10], and effects of usability perception using the Computer Usability Satisfaction Questionnaire (CUSQ) [11]. Sessions concluded with a brief interview to gather additional information about the interaction experiences.

3.7 Instruments

In addition to the instruments mentioned above, we collected data through a demographic survey, the Positive and Negative Affect Schedule (PANAS) [12], and short pretest-posttest questionnaires to evaluate prior knowledge, task difficulty, and confidence on the work done. To take a closer look at the participants' internal experiences during the search tasks, we also collected physiological data with the Bitalino board [13]. In particular we captured electrocardiogram (ECG) and electrodermal activity (EDA). On the other hand, to investigate participants' experience at the expressive level, we used a webcam for capturing their facial expressions. Finally, we used Rec.[1] for screen recording. Note that the system time of the tablet in which the study was conducted, was used to synchronize all data collected.

---

[1] https://play.google.com/store/apps/details?id=com.spectrl.rec&hl=es_419

4. RESULTS

As reported earlier in this paper, our preliminary results focus on performance and UX measures computed at the end of each interaction.

4.1 Performance

Performance was evaluated in terms of precision, recall, and F-Measure from the participants' perspective. To do so, images collected by the participants' were analyzed with respect to classified images in the collection introduced in section 3.3. The normality of the distributions were evaluated with the Shapiro-Wilk test. As a result, analyses were conducted with the two-sample t-test or Wilcoxon rank-sum test (between subjects), and paired-sample t-test or Wilcoxon signed-rank test (within subjects). Depending on the test applied, means (M) or medians (Mdn), and standard deviations for the three measures are presented in Table 1.

Table 1. Precision, recall, and F-measure for touch and mouse interactions.

Interface	Order	Mean or Median (Standard Deviation)		
		Precision	Recall	F-Measure
Touch (T_1)	1	M = 0.60 (0.19)	Mdn = 0.21 (0.14)	M = 0.36 (0.16)
Mouse (M_2)	2	M = 0.64 (0.18)	Mdn = 0.27 (0.12)	M = 0.40 (0.14)
Mouse (M_1)	1	M = 0.58 (0.18)	M = 0.22 (0.12)	M = 0.31 (0.14)
Touch (T_2)	2	M = 0.68 (0.12)	M = 0.38 (0.18)	M = 0.47 (0.16)

4.1.1 Precision

As shown in Table 1, precision means were rather similar. Increments from the first to the second interaction could be attributed to learning effects. Despite such variations, no significant differences at $p<.05$ were found for this particular measure as indicated by two-sample t-test and paired-sample t-test. In other words, regardless of the interaction interface (i.e., mouse or touchscreen), the participants were able to achieve similar ratios between relevant images and the total number of images selected for each subtopic.

4.1.2 Recall

Results for recall only reported significant differences at $p<.01$ in the M_1-T_2 group (as informed by paired-sample t-test). However, such difference was not observed in the opposite interaction order (i.e., T_1-M_2). Moreover, regardless of the interaction order, an increment in recall was observed. Therefore, we associate this finding to a learning effect as a result of familiarization with the graphic interface and the search task.

4.1.3 F-Measure

Not surprisingly, the significant variation found for recall also contributed to a significantly higher F_1 score ($p<.01$) for the touchscreen interaction in the M_1-T_2 sequence (as reported by paired-sample t-test). However, such significant effect was not found in the alternate order (i.e., T_1-M_2).

4.2 User Experience (UX)

To evaluate UX we analyzed data from three dimensions: cognitive, affective, and usability. Statistical tests were selected depending upon data distribution (tested with the Shapiro-Wilk test). In particular we used two-sample t-test or Wilcoxon rank-sum test for between-subject comparisons, and paired-sample t-test or Wilcoxon signed-rank test for within-subject comparison. A summary of descriptive statistics for the cognitive and usability dimensions are listed in Table 2.

Table 2. UX measures for touch and mouse interactions.

Interface	Order	Cognitive (NASA TLX)	Usability (CUSQ)
		Mean or Median (Standard Deviation)	
Touch (T₁)	1	M = 47.94 (11.61)	M = 5.81 (0.60)
Mouse (M₂)	2	M = 50.48 (18.00)	M = 5.04 (1.20) Mdn = 4.89
Mouse (M₁)	1	M = 50.73 (11.01)	M = 4.76 (1.27) Mdn = 4.37
Touch (T₂)	2	M 56.83 (17.15)	Mdn 6.16 (1.71)

4.2.1 Cognitive dimension

First of all, we analyzed cognitive workload effects of each interaction interface. For doing so, we used participants' responses to the NASA TLX instrument. Regardless of the interaction sequences, no significant differences ($p<.05$) were found between or within subjects in the use of the two interfaces.

4.2.2 Affective dimension

At the affective level, we analyzed responses to the SAM questionnaire, which consider three affective components (i.e., valence, activation, and dominance). Results from paired-sample t-test revealed significant difference ($p<.01$) in terms of the dominance experienced by the participants after completing each interaction. In this case, participants who used touchscreen in the second task (T₂) felt more in control (M=1.60, SD=1.51) than when using mouse during the first task (M₁) (M=0.30, SD=1.49). Note that this finding was not consistent in the reverse order (i.e., no significant difference between T₁ an M₂), however, results showed that dominance levels also increased from T₁ (M=0.40, SD=1.96) to M₂ (M=1.40, SD=1.84) (borderline significant level, $p=.05$). Therefore, this particular effect could be related to participants' feeling more confident and also in control of the situation as a result of experience gained during the first interaction.

4.2.3 Usability dimension

Finally, in terms of usability, results consistently showed better experiences with touchscreen. For instance, two-sample t-test – when comparing T₁ and M₁ – showed significantly higher satisfaction levels at $p<.05$ (as measured through CUSQ) for users interacting through touchscreen. Then, in the second interaction (T₂ vs M₂), though differences persisted, these were not significant (Wilcoxon rank-sum test). Likewise, within-subject analyses showed that satisfaction levels were significantly higher in T₁ than in M₂ (paired-sample t-test, $p<.05$). However, in the reverse order (i.e., M₁-T₂), though such difference was consistent (i.e., T₂>M₁), this was not found to be significant (Wilcoxon signed-rank test).

5. DISCUSSION

In this paper we compared two interaction interfaces (i.e., mouse and touchscreen) in the context of an image search task. In particular, we presented preliminary results from a user study focused on the effects of performance and UX.

On the one hand, our results did not show significant effects on performance (in terms of precision, recall, and F-Measure) that can be attributed to the interaction interfaces. On the other hand, results for UX suggested that usability was better rated when interacting through touchscreen than with mouse.

Although our findings are somehow consistent with what has been reported in the general human-computer interaction literature, these constitute interesting contributions in the particular study of human-information interaction in specific contexts such as information search. In particular, we showed that touch-based interactions do not help nor hurt performance, however, it provides a boost in UX. Furthermore, this latter finding supports the idea that this type of interaction could help bridge the gap between users and digital information.

As reported by other authors, an adequate design can have further implications in the UX and performance of search tasks [6]; however, we showed that such impact can be linked not only to graphic and interaction design, but also to the interaction device (e.g. touch and mouse). This has both theoretical and practical implications for the design of search interfaces in order to provide users with more natural or immersive experiences with information objects.

Our future work will focus on examining process-level data – using both quantitative and qualitative methods – in order to better explain the observed differences in UX. Additionally, we will also explore other forms of immersive interactions (e.g. augmented reality and virtual reality), that can provide users not only with a better user experience, but also to contribute to improving their performance in information search tasks.

6. ACKNOWLEDGEMENTS

The work described in this article was in part supported by Proyecto DICYT, Código 061519GI, Vicerrectoría de Investigación, Desarrollo e Innovación, Universidad de Santiago de Chile.

7. REFERENCES

[1] Meyyarasu, N., Dalton, G. and Abinaya, S. 2015. A review on touch sensor screen system. *National conference on recent trends in communication & information technologies*. Tamilnadu, India, 1-12.

[2] Ostroff, D. and Shneiderman, B. 1988. Selection devices for user of an electronic encyclopedia: an empirical comparison of four possibilities. *IP&M*. 24, 6, 665–680.

[3] Liming Luke Chen, D.R.M., Dr Matthias Steinbauer, P., Travis, C. and Murano, P. 2014. A comparative study of the usability of touch-based and mouse-based interaction. *International Journal of Pervasive Computing and Communications*. 10, 1, 115–134.

[4] Wu, F.-G., Lin, H. and You, M. 2011. Direct-touch vs. mouse input for navigation modes of the web map. *Displays*. 32, 5, 261–267.

[5] Wu, F.-G., Lin, H. and You, M. 2011. The enhanced navigator for the touch screen: A comparative study on navigational techniques of web maps. *Displays*. 32, 5, 284–295.

[6] Klouche, K., Ruotsalo, T., Cabral, D., Andolina, S., Bellucci, A. and Jacucci, G. 2015. Designing for Exploratory Search on Touch Devices. *Proc of the 33rd ACM Conference on Human Factors in Computing Systems*. New York, NY, USA, 4189–4198.

[7] Shah, C. and González-Ibáñez, R. 2011. Evaluating the Synergic Effect of Collaboration in Information Seeking. In *Proceedings of the 34th Int'l ACM SIGIR Conference on Research and Development in Information Retrieval*. Beijing, China, 913–922.

[8] Golovchinsky, G., Qvarfordt, P. and Pickens, J. 2008. Collaborative information seeking. *Information Seeking Support Systems*.

[9] Bradley, M.M. and Lang, P.J. 1994. Measuring emotion: the self-assessment manikin and the semantic differential. *Journal of behavior therapy and experimental psychiatry*. 25, 1, 49–59.

[10] Hart, S.G. and Staveland, L.E. 1988. Development of NASA-TLX (Task Load Index): Results of empirical and theoretical research. *Advances in psychology*. 52, 139–183.

[11] Lewis, J.R. 1995. IBM computer usability satisfaction questionnaires: psychometric evaluation and instructions for use. *Int'l Journal of Human-Computer Interaction*. 7, 1, 57–78.

[12] Watson, D., Clark, L. A. & Tellegen, A. 1998. Development and validation of brief measures of positive and negative affect: the PANAS scales. *JPSP*. 54, 6, 1063–1070.

[13] Da Silva, H.P., Guerreiro, J., Lourenço, A., Fred, A. and Martins, R. 2014. BITalino: A novel hardware framework for physiological computing. *Int'l Conference on Physiological Computing Systems (PhyCS)*, 246-253.

Evaluating Body-Centered Interactions in an Image Search Task

Roberto González-Ibáñez   José Luis Varela-Otárola   Carlos Barrera-Pulgar

Departamento de Ingeniería Informática
Universidad de Santiago de Chile
Avenida Ecuador #3659, Estación Central, Santiago, Chile
{roberto.gonzalez.i, jose.varela, carlos.barrerap}@usach.cl

ABSTRACT

Interacting with information in digital environments involves a physical gap between people and information. Although current advances in interaction technology provide the means for helping bridge this gap, little is known about whether this gap affects user experience and performance in the context of information-related tasks such as information search. In this paper we present preliminary results from a larger study focused on immersive interaction with digital information objects. In particular, we report those derived from a user study designed to evaluate interactions with digital information objects through body gestures in the context of an image search task. Our results suggest that compared to traditional interactions through mouse, this type of interaction not only helps lessen cognitive workload, but also leads to achieve similar precision in terms of the information collected.

General Terms
Experimentation, Human Factors, Performance

Keywords
Body Gestures, Kinect, Image Search, Exploratory Search

1. INTRODUCTION

With the advent of new technologies, interactions with digital systems are quickly changing. People often use technology to search and interact with information for different reasons. Not surprisingly, today, interaction with digital information objects (e.g. Web pages, online content, etc.) may be more frequent than with physical ones (e.g. paper-based documents). However, each form of interaction implies both advantages and disadvantages. For instance, finding particular fragments of text on a digital document may be more efficient than in a physical one. On the other hand, manipulation of the latter may be more natural as a result of little to no restrictions on how to interact with it and the active participation of human senses (e.g. quickly flip a book, removing pages and throwing them away, and feeling how old or heavy a book is, etc.). Such interaction differences constitute a gap between the experiences in digital and physical environments.

Current technologies such as augmented reality, touch and touchless interfaces, and virtual reality, among others, could help bridge this gap. Nevertheless, most information-related research efforts during the last decades have used traditional interfaces (i.e., mouse and keyboard) as interaction technology between users and information systems. In this context, we present preliminary results from a study focused on comparing traditional and body-centered user interfaces. We hypothesize that in particular interaction contexts of information search (e.g. image search in open spaces), body-centered interaction may be a more suitable means for performance and user experience (UX).

The rest of this paper is organized in four parts. In the second section we present a selection of related work. In the third section we describe our methodological approach. In the fourth section we present our preliminary results. Finally, in the fifth section, we conclude this paper with discussion, implications, and future work.

2. RELATED WORK

Body-controlled user interfaces have been used for different applications in order to provide a more intuitive way for interacting with digital systems. However, to the best of our knowledge, there are no studies about body-centered interactions in the context of information search.

Although applications and evaluations have been focused mainly on entertainment and health (e.g. [1], [2]), there are some studies focused on evaluating the interaction with digital information objects. For instance, Fang et al. [3] compared the use of the Microsoft Kinect sensor and mouse with respect to performance variations in a spatial perception task, in particular, the two-string problem [4]. In this study, no significant differences were found between the two interfaces.

Others have investigated body-controlled user interfaces in interaction, signaling, and selection tasks. For example, Kouroupetroglou et al. [5] used the Nintendo Wiimote for interacting with objects in bidimensional and tridimensional spaces. The authors compared both mouse and Wiimote in terms of throughput (i.e., number of tasks completed per time), number of errors, and duplicated selections, among others. Results from this study were significantly better for mouse interactions. However, as the authors pointed out, poor results obtained with the Wiimote could be attributed to (1) technical problems or (2) unexperienced participants.

In addition to performance, some studies have investigated other interaction dimensions such as UX, engagement, and entertainment. For instance, Van Beurden et al. [6] compared mouse and interfaces operated through body gestures in the context of a task for exploring tridimensional objects using actions such as rotation, selection, and zoom. Results from this study showed that body gestures led to achieve a better UX than that achieved when using mouse. However, in terms of performance, interactions through the latter led to better results.

3. METHOD

3.1 Study Design

To address the research problem introduced above, we designed and conducted a user study based on a crossover design. This study design was intended to evaluate between- and within-subjects effects in order to compare groups and also to control for participants' learning effects with respect to the user interface and the topic of the task. More importantly, this study was designed to compare two interaction approaches (independent variable) on performance and UX (dependent variables). In this work we consider user interfaces to be defined in terms of two key components, namely, (1) graphic interface and (2) interaction apparatus. Based on this conceptual division, we devised a user interface with a common graphic interface that can be operated either by a traditional interaction device (i.e. mouse) or by a body-centered interaction sensor (i.e. first-generation Kinect sensor).

As part of the crossover design, we defined two groups of participants. Each group was assigned to an interaction sequence. The participants in group M_1-K_2, initiated the interaction sequence by performing a search task using a traditional interface (M_1: mouse operated). Then, participants performed the same search task – with a different collection of information objects – using a body-centered interface (K_2: Kinect operated). Conversely, the participants in group K_1-M_2 performed the same search task used in M_1-K_2 but with the interaction interfaces in the reverse order.

3.2 Search Task

For this study we designed an image search task that fits in the scope of exploratory search. We chose as a topic for this task the British Petroleum (BP) Gulf oil spill that took place in April 2010, which has been previously used in studies focused on individual and collaborative information seeking [7]. For this search task, participants were asked to find, select, and organize relevant images related to: (1) impact on flora and fauna, (2) damaged areas, (3) structural damages, and (4) mitigation maneuvers.

Additionally, the task was designed to simulate an asynchronous-role-based collaborative search process [8]. In particular, the participants were situated in a fictional context in which each of them and a fictitious collaborator were preparing a report about the BP oil spill for a prestigious magazine. In this context, the fictitious collaborator performed an initial search process in order to gather images using a search engines and queries associated to the above four subtopics. Then, the participants' objective focused on completing the search process by selecting and organizing only relevant images for each subtopic using only the collection of images gathered by the fictitious collaborator and a specialized user interface (details provided in the system section).

In order to encourage participants to perform well in the search task, the study was designed to be a competition in which the best three performing participants received prizes. Similar approaches have proven effective in previous studies [7].

3.3 Image Collection

To simulate the set of images gathered by the fictitious collaborator in the search task, we created a set of images retrieved from Google Images using the Extreme Picture Finder software and 13 queries derived from the four subtopics stated above. Besides queries, another selection criterion for this automatic process was image resolution, which set a lower bound of 600x600 pixels. Following, images were automatically filtered to remove duplicates using the VisiPics software.

To create a more realistic set, we introduced noise by incorporating images retrieved using queries unrelated to the topic. All images were manually classified in the four subtopics by three judges (Fleiss' Kappa=0.53, p<.01). Images were coded as relevant for a single or multiple subtopics. As a result, we created a ranking of relevance, that is to say, the more specific the image (e.g. single match with the structural damages subtopic), the more relevant to the subtopic. Images that fitted in more than one subtopic were ranked lower. Note that for this study, we considered images as relevant only if all the coders agreed on that.

Overall, the image collection consisted of 881 images with approximately 66% of noise. This set was split into two subsets to be used in each stage of the interaction sequences. As a result, 442 were used in the first interaction (i.e. M_1 and K_1) and 439 in the second one (i.e. M_2 and K_2). The number of images for each subtopic was roughly balanced in each set. Moreover, the order of images in each set was randomly assigned. Finally, no significant differences were found in the distribution of images (relevant and not relevant) in the two subsets, which ensures that task difficulty in the two interactions was equivalent.

3.4 Participants

Overall, we recruited 26 undergraduate students (all volunteers) from three Chilean universities. From this sample, four participants were used as pilot runs. Only the remaining 22 participants (16 men and 6 women) were considered in the analyses reported in this work.

Participants' age ranged between 18 and 26 years old (M=23, SD=2.62). Their field of study included engineering, law, education, health services, and chemistry, among others.

Finally, with regard to their experience using body-centered interfaces, such as the Kinect sensor, Wiimote, and Sony Move, to name a few, 59% of the participants reported having previous experience using this type of interface.

3.5 System

To conduct the study we developed BGIIES (Body-Gesture Information Interaction Evaluation System), a system for supporting the experimental design, session workflow, and data collection. In terms of user interface, the graphic interface was implemented as an interactive Web page using HTML5, jQuery,

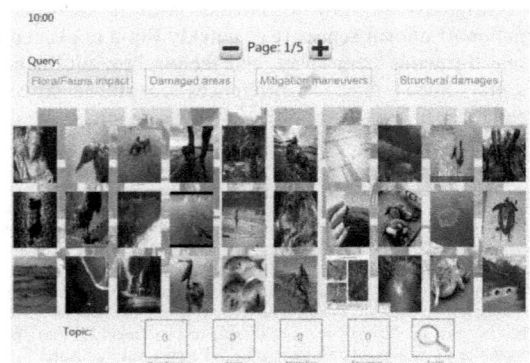

Figure 1. A screenshot of BGIIES with its main

and ThreeJS. This graphic interface was presented to users using a DLP projector in order to provide users with a larger screen. On the other hand, the interface was designed to be operated either by mouse or through the Microsoft Kinect sensor (in standing position, using both hands, and predefined gestures). Note that for the latter, a specialized communication service (to enable the use of Kinect in Web environments) using websockets was developed.

In terms of data collection, BGIIES was designed to log all participants' actions in the user interface (e.g. selection, drag and drop, and clicks), body gestures, and survey responses. A screenshot of BGIIES is presented in Figure 1.

3.6 Session Workflow

Each session lasted approximately 60 minutes. The session workflow was semi-automatically controlled by BGIIES. Prior to starting sessions, participants were required to sign a consent form. Following, general instructions were given and sensors were calibrated (details provided in the instruments section). During the 60 minutes, participants completed the search task (with the two collections of images) using the two interaction interfaces in the order assigned to the corresponding groups. For each interaction, participants were given 10 minutes. Moreover, prior to starting each interaction, participants were allowed to practice with the corresponding interface. Before and after each interaction, participants completed surveys, in particular the Self-Assessment Manikin (SAM) [9], NASA TLX [10], and the Computer Usability Satisfaction Questionnaire (CUSQ) [11], in order to evaluate effects of the two interfaces at the affective, cognitive, and usability levels respectively. At the end of the sessions, participants were briefly interviewed to obtain additional information about their interaction experiences.

3.7 Instruments

Besides BGIIES and the surveys mentioned above, we also used a demographic survey, the Positive and Negative Affect Schedule (PANAS) [12], two short tests to evaluate prior knowledge, task difficulty, and confidence on the work done. Additionally, we used a Bitalino board [13] for capturing physiological data, and two webcams for capturing facial expressions and body gestures. Finally, complementary software was used for capturing screen and mouse activity. All data were synchronized with respect to system time of the local computer in which the study was carried out.

4. RESULTS

In this study we focused on specific performance and UX measures. We only conducted analyses to evaluate within- and between-subjects factors in terms of participants' outcomes at the end of each interaction.

4.1 Performance

To measure performance we used traditional IR measures (i.e., precision, recall, and F-Measure) adapted to evaluate participants' performance. More specifically, the images selected by the participants were contrasted with the coded images in the collection described in section 3.3. Due to the normal distribution of data – according to the Shapiro-Wilk test – comparison analyses were conducted with two-sample t-test (between subjects) and paired-sample t-test (within subjects). Descriptive statistics for the three measures are summarized in Table 1.

4.1.1 Precision

In terms of precision, our results for within- and between-subjects did not show significant differences between the two interaction interfaces. Regardless of the order in which the two interfaces were

Table 1. Precision, recall, and F-measure for Kinect and mouse interactions.

Interface	Order	Mean (Standard Deviation)		
		Precision	Recall	F-Measure
Kinect (K)	1	0.50 (0.12)	0.06 (0.03)	0.11 (0.04)
Mouse (M)	2	0.55 (0.20)	0.23 (0.09)	0.32 (0.12)
Mouse (M)	1	0.52 (0.13)	0.20 (0.06)	0.28 (0.06)
Kinect (K)	2	0.47 (0.17)	0.10 (0.05)	0.16 (0.07)

used, the mean for precision ranged between 0.47 and 0.55. In other words, ratios between the number of relevant images and the overall number of images selected by the participants in the different experimental conditions were similar.

4.1.2 Precision
In terms of precision, our results for within- and between-subjects did not show significant differences between the two interaction interfaces. Regardless of the order in which the two interfaces were used, the mean for precision ranged between 0.47 and 0.55. In other words, ratios between the number of relevant images and the overall number of images selected by the participants in the different experimental conditions were similar.

4.1.3 Recall
When it comes to recall, our results showed consistent differences at the level of subjects and groups. Indeed, within-subject analyses indicated that, regardless of the order assigned to each user interface (i.e., K_1-M_2 and M_1-K_2), recall was significantly higher at $p<.01$ for mouse interactions. Likewise, between-subject analyses showed that recall was significantly higher at $p<.01$ for mouse interactions (K_1-vs-M_1 and K_2-vs-M_2).

4.1.4 F-Measure
The last performance measure analyzed was F-measure. Results were consistent with those obtained for recall. Thus, F-Measure was found to be significantly lower ($p<.01$) when the search task was performed using Kinect as interaction interface.

4.2 User Experience (UX)
User experience was evaluated in terms of three dimensions: cognitive, affective, and usability. Depending on the distribution of the data (tested with the Shapiro-Wilk test), analyses were carried out using two-sample t-test or Wilcoxon rank-sum test for between-subject comparisons, and paired-sample t-test or Wilcoxon signed-rank test for within-subject comparison. Descriptive statistics for the cognitive and usability dimensions are summarized in Table 2.

Table 2. UX measures for Kinect and mouse interactions.

Interface	Order	Mean (Standard Deviation)	
		Cognitive (NASA TLX)	Usability (CUSQ)
Kinect (K)	1	40.55 (9.74)	4.29 (0.60)
Mouse (M)	2	52.50 (8.95)	5.98 (0.55)
Mouse (M)	1	51.46 (7.92)	5.80 (0.74)
Kinect (K)	2	51.14 (8.92)	4.66 (0.90)

4.2.1 Cognitive dimension
To evaluate UX at the cognitive level, we analyzed responses to the NASA TLX. Results showed that for the first interaction, Kinect (K_1) led participants to experience significantly lower cognitive workload than that experienced by the participants who used mouse (M_1) ($p<.01$). However, this finding did not show up in the second interaction (K_2-vs-M_2). More interestingly, within-subject analyses revealed that while a significant increment in cognitive workload was reported from K_1 to M_2 ($p<.01$) (which could be related to

intervening factors such as tiredness), cognitive workload presented a slight decrement from M_1 to K_2. Although the latter result was not statistically significant, this could indicate that body-centered interactions with information may help lessen cognitive workload.

4.2.2 Affective dimension

To measure the affective dimension, we used responses to the SAM questionnaire. In particular, we evaluated the three components measured by this instrument (i.e., valence, activation, and dominance). In general, our results suggest that the participants' affective experiences are rather similar when using any of the two interaction devices. In fact, between- and within-subject analyses did not report significant differences for valence and activation. However, in terms of dominance (or control), participants who used mouse in the first interaction, felt more in control than when using Kinect in the second interaction ($p<.01$). Although this finding could be related to the interaction interface itself, results obtained in the K_1-M_2 group (where no significant differences were reported) suggest that such difference may be better explained by the intervention of the researcher before starting the second interaction in order to provide additional instructions about the use of the body-centered interface.

4.2.3 Usability dimension

This dimension was measured through CUSQ. Results from this questionnaire can be evaluated in terms of its global value or with respect to its main components (i.e., system use, information quality, and interaction quality). Either way, results showed that usability was significantly better ($p<.01$) for participants who used mouse interactions (regardless of the order in which the two interfaces were used).

5. DISCUSSION

In this paper we presented preliminary results from a user study designed to compare two interaction interfaces (i.e., mouse and Kinect) in the context of an image search task. The comparison focused on performance and UX effects of the two interfaces.

Regarding performance, our results showed that Kinect interactions led the participants to achieve lower recall and F-measure than that achieved through mouse. However, when looking at the quality of the work in terms of precision, no significant differences were reported between the two interfaces. These findings suggest that while the amount of work performed through Kinect is lower than that achieved through mouse (on average, 23 images were classified using Kinect and 72 using mouse), the former allowed the participants to achieve similar quality of work expressed by the ratios between relevant images and the total amount of images collected.

In terms of UX, our results indicated that usability was significantly better rated in mouse-based interactions. Nevertheless, Kinect-based interactions were found to lessen cognitive workload. This particular effect could be attributed to factors such as (1) positive effects of physical activity in cognition and brain functioning (e.g. [14]), (2) a more immersive experience when using body-centered interfaces, or (3) as discussed above, it could be also related to the participants performing less amount of work when interacting through body gestures.

Although immersive interactions in the context of information-related tasks such as information search has not been widely studied, it is possible to consider a variety of practical applications. While most research in information search has been conducted using traditional interaction interfaces (i.e., mouse and keyboard), there are scenarios in which interactions do not take place at desktop computers. For instance, interactive museums and libraries have the potential to provide to their users more immersive experiences to interact with digital information objects. This could be contextualized on specific processes such as browsing and searching. However, further research is necessary in order to design better user interfaces that fully use state-of-the-art interaction technology, which includes touch and touchless interfaces.

This paper presented preliminary results of a larger project focused on immersive interaction with digital information objects. Therefore, our next steps include taking a closer look at the interaction between users and information by analyzing interaction, physiological, and expressive data captured through the user study described in previous sections. We will also explore other interaction and information presentation forms, such as virtual reality and haptics, among others.

6. ACKNOWLEDGEMENTS

The work described in this article was in part supported by Proyecto DICYT, Código 061519GI, Vicerrectoría de Investigación, Desarrollo e Innovación, Universidad de Santiago de Chile.

7. REFERENCES

[1] Chang, Y. J., Der Chou, L., Wang, F. T. Y. and Chen, S. F. 2013. A kinect-based vocational task prompting system for individuals with cognitive impairments. *Pers. Ubiquitous Comput.* 17, 2, 351–358.

[2] Chang. Y. J., Han, W. Y. and Tsai, Y. C. 2013. A Kinect-based Upper Limb Rehabilitation System to Assist People with Cerebral Palsy. *Res. Dev. Disabil.* 34, 11, 3654–3659.

[3] Fang, W.-C., Lin, Y.-L., Sheu, F.-R., & Chen, N.-S. 2013. Exploring Problem Solving Performance through Natural User Interfaces. *IEEE 13th Int. Conf. on Adv. Learning Tech.* (Jul. 2013). 232–234.

[4] Landrum, R.E. 1990. Maier's (1931) Two-String Problem Revisited: Evidence for Spontaneous Transfer? *Psych. Reports.* 67, 1079-1088.

[5] Kouroupetroglou, G., Pino, A., Balmpakakis, A., Chalastanis, D., Golematis, V., Ioannou, N., & Koutsoumpas, I. 2012. Using Wiimote for 2D and 3D Pointing Tasks: Gesture Performance Evaluation. In *Gesture and Sign Language in Human-Computer Interaction and Embodied Communication* SE – 2. 7206, 13–23.

[6] Van Beurden, M. P. H., Ijsselsteijn, W., & de Kort, Y. W. 2012. User Experience of Gesture Based Interfaces: A Comparison with Traditional Interaction Methods on Pragmatic and Hedonic Qualities. In *Gesture and Sign Language in Human-Computer Interaction and Embodied Communication* SE - 4. 7206, 36–47.

[7] Shah, C., & González-Ibáñez, R. 2011. Evaluating the Synergic Effect of Collaboration in Information Seeking. In *Proceedings of the 34th Int'l ACM SIGIR Conference on Research and Development in Information Retrieval* (2011). Beijing, China, 913–922.

[8] Pickens, J., Golovchinsky, G., Shah, C., Qvarfordt, P., & Back, M. 2009. Collaborative Information Seeking. *Computer* (Long. Beach. Calif). 42, 3, 47–51.

[9] Bradley, M. M. 1994. Measuring emotion: The self-assessment manikin and the semantic differential. *Journal of Behavior Therapy and Experimental Psychiatry.* 25, 1, 49–59.

[10] Hart, S. G., & Staveland, L. E. 1998. Development of NASA-TLX (Task Load Index): Results of Empirical and Theoretical Research. *Advances in Psychology.* 52, C, 139–183.

[11] Lewis, J. R. 1995. IBM computer usability satisfaction questionnaires: Psychometric evaluation and instructions for use. *International Journal of Human-Computer Interaction.* 7, 1, 57–78.

[12] Watson, D., Clark, L. A., & Tellegen, A. 1998. Development and validation of brief measures of positive and negative affect: the PANAS scales. *Journal of personality and social psychology.* 54, 6, 1063–1070.

[13] Silva, H., Guerreiro, J., Lourenço, A., Fred, A. and Martins, R. 2014. BITalino: A novel hardware framework for physiological computing. In *Proc. of the Int'l Conf. on Physiological Computing Systems* (PhyCS). 246-253.

[14] Hillman, C. H., Erickson, K. I., & Kramer, A. F. 2008. Be smart, exercise your heart: exercise effects on brain and cognition. *Nature Review Neuroscience.* 9, 1, 58–65.

TwIST: A Mobile Approach for Searching and Exploring within Twitter

Radhika Gopi
Department of Computer Science
University of Regina
Regina, SK, Canada S4S 0A2
gopi200r@uregina.ca

Orland Hoeber
Department of Computer Science
University of Regina
Regina, SK, Canada S4S 0A2
orland.hoeber@uregina.ca

ABSTRACT

Popular user-generated content services like Twitter have made it easy for people to post and browse short messages while on the go. However, the ability to search is limited by the query box and search results list paradigm. In this paper, we propose TwIST (Twitter Information Search Tool), which has been designed to support interactive search and exploration within Twitter. TwIST is a mobile application that works in two modes: simple search and exploratory search. The searcher can easily change between these modes by rotating the device, making it easy to access the mode that will support the desired search activity. While the simple search mode is dominated by the common search results list format, the exploratory search mode uses topic modelling, visualization, and interactive filtering to support the searcher in finding the information they are seeking.

CCS Concepts

•Information systems → Search interfaces; Information extraction; Retrieval on mobile devices;

Keywords

Search interfaces, topic modelling, mobile computing

1. INTRODUCTION

Social networking services such as Twitter serve as an important source for user-generated content. Their public, unfiltered, and open aspects make them a valuable source for public opinion on a wide range of topics. However, finding useful information on Twitter is limited by a search interface that follows the traditional list based representation, requiring the user to evaluate the search results tweet by tweet. While list based displays can be effective when presenting topically focused search results, they are less effective when there is ambiguity within the information displayed [7]. Due to the short and cryptic nature of tweets and the breadth of information posted within Twitter, search results that

CHIIR '16, March 13-17, 2016, Carrboro, NC, USA

© 2016 ACM. ISBN 978-1-4503-3751-9/16/03. . . $15.00

DOI: http://dx.doi.org/10.1145/2854946.2854991

include a mix of relevant and irrelevant posts are commonplace. As such, we suggest that searching within such data may be more effective if visual and interactive tools are provided that allow the searcher to focus their efforts on the intended topic, filtering out irrelevant tweets.

While mobile devices are constrained in terms of memory, processing power, and screen size, they have become extremely popular as information seeking tools due to their portability, connectivity, and intuitive operation. When designing a mobile search app, it is important to provide an interface that makes it easy to identify and navigate among the information presented, and to remain focused on why one might want to search for information in a mobile context. In terms of searching within Twitter, we have observed that one may be interested to know three things: (1) What are the most recent posts that use the search term? (2) What are the major topics mentioned in these posts? and (3) How are the posts related in terms of the topics?

In this paper, we propose TwIST, a Twitter Information Search Tool that provides both simple search and exploratory search modes, enabling the searcher to address these questions as they seek relevant tweets that satisfy their information seeking goals. The simple search mode was designed to support the lookup-based IR model [2], which is useful when the search strategy focuses on the lookup of specific information [12] or the verification of facts [20]. It allows the user to issue query and inspect the tweets in a list based representation. The exploratory search mode was designed to support the exploratory search model [12], which extends the search activities beyond information lookup towards learning and investigation. This mode helps the user to recognize relevant information by displaying a set of topics extracted from the tweets, along with their relative importance within the search results. Interactive selection of relevant topics allows for the exploration of the search results and a comparative analysis of the topics. These topics can subsequently be used to interactively refine the query.

2. RELATED WORK

2.1 Search within User Generated Content

In a systematic comparison of search behaviour in Twitter and the web, Teevan et al. found that searching within user generated content generally focuses on temporally relevant information (e.g., related to current news and events) and social information (e.g., related to opinions and the posts of people of interest) [17]. Traditional search interfaces may not be the best option in these cases; there is a need to develop new interfaces that focus on supporting complex search activities using machine learning to extract relevant information and visualization to convey this information to the searcher[11]. Approaches that use faceted browsing to leverage existing or dynamically extracted data attributes can be an effective method for supporting information seeking tasks [1]. Hearst et al. has demonstrated that such facets can help structure the search results and aid in the reformulation of queries [8].

Topic modelling has been shown to be an effective technique for summarizing user generated content. Methods for extracting topics by aggregating hashtags has helped to identify topically relevant streams of posts [13]. However, the over-reliance on hashtags require that posters use them effectively. Other topic-based approaches, such as Eddi [4] and TweetMotif [5], follow a clustering approach to extract the topics, and display them to the user for further exploration. A common theme among these approaches is the use of topics to summarize the results, and as a tool to help the searchers to refine their queries.

2.2 Mobile Based Search Applications

Although conducting searches using mobile devices is more difficult than on a computer, people have shown an interest in using mobile devices to perform complex information behaviours such as browsing, downloading, and sharing content [16]. Amidst the advantage of the immediacy of information, there are a limited number of mobile applications supporting search activities. For those that do exist, displaying the results in categories provides an effective overview of the information, and has resulted in an increase in retrieval performance [6, 9]. Such categorical views help the searcher to find relevant information faster than list based views. Visual representations of search results [10] may also help the searcher in their information seeking processes, even with limited prior knowledge about the information being shown.

3. TWIST

TwIST has been designed to support the searcher's knowledge discovery and decision making activities [10] through interactive visualization of the search results, leveraging topic modelling, dynamic categorization, faceted browsing, and interactive query refinement. Two modes of operation are available, depending on the orientation of the device. The details of these two modes are explained in the remainder of this section.

3.1 Simple Search Mode

When the device is held in upright position (portrait mode) TwIST defaults to the simple search mode, with the primary interface elements following the query box and search results list paradigm (see Figure 1). This orientation provides more vertical than horizontal space, and is dominated by the list of tweets that match the searcher's query. The overall design is meant to replicate the search interface currently used by the Twitter app, but with some simple modifications and additions. Upon submitting a query, the app fetches the most recent 100 posts using the Twitter API [18], with the results sorted by their submission date and time (most recent first). These are displayed in a scrollable list, and include relevant metadata such as author information and date/time. In order to help the searcher to decide on the relevance to the query, any use of the query terms within the tweet contents

Figure 1: The simple search mode provides a query box and search results list, as well as a timeline visualization.

are highlighted in bold.

Given the importance of the temporal aspect of the tweets, a timeline is provided to allow the searcher to observe such patterns visually. This timeline represents time on the x-axis and the aggregated frequency of the tweets on the y-axis. The aggregation scale is chosen automatically depending on the temporal range of the tweets within the search results. The timeline supports interactive zoom and filter operations, allowing the searcher to dynamically adjust the timeframe of the tweets shown in the search results list. The simplicity and familiarity of the overall interface was designed to enable learnability.

3.2 Exploratory Search Mode

When the device is rotated to landscape mode, the search interface is transformed into the exploratory search mode (see Figure 2). This orientation provides more horizontal than vertical space, making room to provide interactive visualization features to support exploration and analysis activities. The exploratory search mode was designed following Shneiderman's information seeking mantra: "overview first, zoom and filter, then details-on-demand" [15]. Topics automatically extracted from the search results provide a framework for the overview of the search results. Both temporal zooming and topic-based filtering are supported. At any time, the searcher can view the specific details of any of the tweets. The primary goal is to support information filtering tasks [3], which can help the searcher to focus the search results on the specific topics that are of interest at the specific point in time. In addition, the exploratory search activities of learning the topics hidden in the search results, investigating the relationship between the topics, and looking up of results with respect to the topics [12] are all supported.

Due to the limited processing power of the mobile device, the computing necessary to perform topic modelling on the

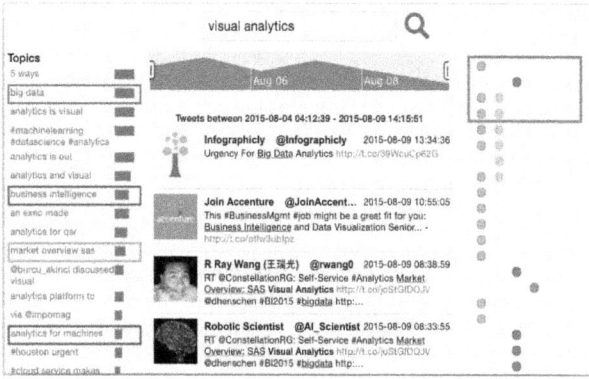

Figure 2: The exploratory search mode provides an overview of the topics (left), the list of tweets (middle), and a comparison view (right). A timeline filter is included at the top.

tweets is implemented on a server. The TwIST app communicates with this server using REST, loading the search results first, and the additional information regarding the topics once the modelling is complete. The topic modelling algorithm itself operates in three steps, which are described in the following subsections.

3.2.1 Preprocessing of Tweets

Given that the topic modelling is meant to extract meaningful textual topics from the set of search results, it is important to first clean the data to remove any content that may result in meaningless topics. All symbols, emoticons, incomplete URLs, and single characters other than numbers are removed from the data. Since retweets may result in significant repetition within the data, distinct tweets are selected for the topic modelling process.

Many tweets include links to external content, so we use this information to supplement the topic modelling process. All URLs included within the tweets are followed, and the titles of the corresponding web pages are added to the tweet. In the cases where this information was already written in the body of the tweet itself, the information is not duplicated.

3.2.2 Clustering

The next step in the process is to group similar tweets into topic clusters, such that each cluster represents a specific and independent topic. Given the variability within the search results sets, it is necessary to perform such clustering in an unsupervised manner, and without a predetermined number of clusters. As such, nearest neighbour clustering [14] is used. The clustering begins by computing the similarities between tweets, where each tweet is represented as a feature vector of terms, weighted using TF-IDF. The distance is computed using cosine similarity according to the following formula:

$$sim(FV_i, FV_j) = \frac{FV_i \cdot FV_j}{||FV_i|| \; ||FV_j||}$$

where FV_i and FV_j are feature vectors of tweets i and j in the collection.

Calculating the pair-wise similarity between all tweets results in a similarity matrix n × n where n is the number of tweets in the collection (for this work, $n = 100$). This similarity matrix is then sorted in ascending order over each column, with any entries greater than a pre-defined similarity constant removed. At this point, each column of the matrix will represent a cluster of tweets that are most similar to each tweet. Since this representation will include multiple repetitive clusters, the final step is to merge similar clusters. Each column of the matrix is compared to all other columns to find the overlapping clusters that are sufficiently close in terms of overall per-tweet similarity. Duplicates found in this way are merged into the original.

3.2.3 Topic Extraction

Using the tweet contents that produced the clusters in the previous step, uni-grams, bi-grams, and tri-grams are extracted from the text. The bi-grams and tri-grams are computed in consideration of any content that was removed from the original tweet (e.g., punctuation, emoticons), as well as the boundary between the tweet itself and the titles of any URLs added to the tweet in the pre-processing step. For each such n-gram, its frequency within the cluster is calculated.

Part-of-speech (POS) tagging is then used to identify key n-grams that can be used as topic-describing phrases. With each term in each n-gram tagged in this way, the n-grams are then passed to a syntactic filter that only retains those n-grams that contain at least a single noun phrase. This noun phrase is considered a subject descriptor, and is therefore a good representation of some topic within the search results. All n-grams remaining after this filtering are sorted by their frequency within the cluster and then their length. As a final step, the top n-gram from each cluster is chosen as topic, and the frequency of occurrence of each topic is calculated within the entire search results set.

3.2.4 Displaying Topics

The topics extracted in the previous step are displayed along with an horizontal histogram that visually depicts the relative importance of each topic in relation to the search results set. Tapping on any topic will filter the search results to only show those that make use of the selected phrase. Doing so for multiple topics will produce a combined list, sorted chronologically. If the searcher recognizes any topic that is particularly relevant to what is being sought, a new search using this topic as the query can be initiated with a long-tap on the topic.

3.2.5 Visual Comparison of Topics

When multiple topics are activated within the exploratory search mode, it may be useful to help the searcher to understand the relationship between these topics and the tweets from which they were extracted. Visual encoding within the search results list, along with a visual comparison view are provided in the exploratory search mode for this purpose. Each topic selected is encoded using a distinct colour [19] and the use of these topics within the tweets are underlined using this same colour. This allows the searcher to visually identify where these topics are being used in the tweets. In the case where the topic came from the URL, the URL within the tweet is underlined.

Within the comparison view, the tweets of the selected topics are displayed in a table format, with each column representing a topic and each row representing the tweets. Each tweet belonging to a topic is represented as a coloured circle that corresponds to the topic. This visual representation makes it easy to visually compare the topics to one another (e.g., viewing the column similarities and differences) as well as compare the tweets (e.g, viewing the row similarities and differences). A scrollable box is placed over the comparison view to show which tweets are being displayed in the search results list, providing context to what will be found if the searcher scrolls within the filtered search results.

4. CONCLUSIONS

In this paper, we have presented our work on the development of a mobile Twitter search interface. TwIST is a dual-mode search app that can be transformed from a simple search interface to an exploratory search interface simply by rotating the orientation of the device. Within the exploratory search mode, the topics are automatically extracted from the search results, with the importance of each in the search results visually encoded. Interactive selection of a topic filters the search results, and when multiple topics are selected, a comparison view is provided to support the searcher in understanding the relationships between topics and tweets.

The key limitation in this work is the efficiency of the unsupervised topic modelling. Given the limited computing capacity of mobile devices, we have moved this computation to a server. Even so, the system must still download all of the tweets, follow any embedded links, and then iterate over the data multiple times to discover the topics. With a search results set of 100 tweets, the system currently takes approximately 12 seconds to display the topics that are necessary for the exploratory search mode. In order to hide this delay from the searcher, the topic modelling is initiated even while searching within the simple search mode.

There are three elements of future work that are ongoing. We are working to improve the efficiency and accuracy of the topic modelling aspect of this work. A comprehensive user evaluation of the TwIST interface is currently in the planning stages. Finally, we plan to make it possible for a Twitter user to provide their login credentials in order to support searching and exploration within their personalized Twitter feed.

5. REFERENCES

[1] F. Abel, I. Celik, G.-J. Houben, and P. Siehndel. Leveraging the semantics of tweets for adaptive faceted search on Twitter. In *Proceedings of the International Conference on The Semantic Web*, pages 1–17, 2011.

[2] M. J. Bates. The design of browsing and berrypicking techniques for the online search interface. *Online Review*, 13(5):407–424, 1989.

[3] N. J. Belkin and W. B. Croft. Information filtering and information retrieval: Two sides of the same coin? *Communications of the ACM*, 35(12):29–38, 1992.

[4] M. S. Bernstein, B. Suh, L. Hong, J. Chen, S. Kairam, and E. H. Chi. Eddi: Interactive topic-based browsing of social status streams. In *Proceedings of the Annual ACM Symposium on User Interface Software and Technology*, pages 303–312, 2010.

[5] B. O. Connor, M. Krieger, and D. Ahn. TweetMotif: Exploratory search and topic summarization for Twitter. In *Proceedings of the International AAAI Conference on Weblogs and Social Media*, pages 2–3, 2010.

[6] E. W. De Luca and A. Nürnberger. Supporting information retrieval on mobile devices. In *Proceedings of the International Conference on Human Computer Interaction with Mobile Devices & Services*, pages 347–348, 2005.

[7] S. Dumais, E. Cutrell, and H. Chen. Optimizing search by showing results in context. In *Proceedings of the SIGCHI Conference on Human Factors in Computing Systems*, pages 277–284, 2001.

[8] M. Hearst, A. Elliott, J. English, R. Sinha, K. Swearingen, and K.-P. Yee. Finding the flow in web site search. *Communications of the ACM*, 45(9):42–49, 2002.

[9] T. Heimonen. Mobile Findex: Facilitating information access in mobile web search with automatic result clustering. In *Proceedings of the International Conference on Human Computer Interaction with Mobile Devices and Services*, pages 397–404, 2007.

[10] O. Hoeber. Human-centred web search. In C. Jouis, I. Biskri, J.-G. Ganascia, and M. Roux, editors, *Next Generation Search Engines: Advanced Models for Information Retrieval*, pages 217–238, 2012.

[11] O. Hoeber. Visual search analytics: Combining machine learning and interactive visualization to support human-centred search. In *Proceedings of Beyond Single-Shot Text Queries: Bridging the Gap(s) Between Research Communities Workshop*, pages 37–43, 2014.

[12] G. Marchionini. Exploratory search: From finding to understanding. *Communications of the ACM*, 49(4):41–46, 2006.

[13] K. D. Rosa, R. Shah, B. Lin, A. Gershman, and R. Frederking. Topical clustering of tweets. In *Proceedings of the SIGIR Workshop on Social Web Search and Mining*, pages 1–8, 2011.

[14] N. Roussopoulos, S. Kelley, and F. Vincent. Nearest neighbor queries. In *Proceedings of the International Conference on Management of Data*, pages 71–79, 1995.

[15] B. Shneiderman. The eyes have it: A task by data type taxonomy for information visualizations. In *Proceedings of the IEEE Symposium on Visual Languages*, pages 336–343, 1996.

[16] A. Smith. The best (and worst) of mobile connectivity, 2012. http://www.pewinternet.org/files/old-media/ Files/Reports/2012/PIP_Best_Worst_Mobile\ _113012.pdf Accessed: 2015-08-22.

[17] J. Teevan, D. Ramage, and M. R. Morris. #TwitterSearch: A comparison of microblog search and web search. In *Proceedings of the International Conference on Web Search and Data Mining*, pages 35–44, 2011.

[18] Twitter. Twitter search API. https://api.twitter.com/1.1/. Accessed: 2015-08-18.

[19] C. Ware. *Information visualization: Perception for design*. Elsevier, 2nd edition, 2012.

[20] R. W. White and R. A. Roth. Exploratory search: Beyond the query-response paradigm. *Synthesis Lectures on Information Concepts, Retrieval, and Services Series*, 3(1):1–98, 2009.

Effects of Position and Time Bias
on Understanding Onsite Users' Behavior

Seyyed Hadi Hashemi   Wim Hupperetz   Jaap Kamps   Merel van der Vaart

University of Amsterdam, Amsterdam, The Netherlands
{hashemi|W.M.H.Hupperetz|kamps|M.J.vanderVaart}@uva.nl

ABSTRACT

The existence of different biases in logged users' behavior makes it difficult to extract realistic topical and social information from users' interaction logs (e.g., query logs). To understand users' behavior and their interests in the cultural heritage domain, we have logged onsite user interaction logs of visits in a museum. This prompts the question on the reliability of the social information being gathered from the onsite logs: How does the position of museum objects affect users' behavior in the museum? How does order of visiting point of interests affect their dwell-time in front of each point of interest? How do different users' characteristics affect their behavior in the museum? In short, what are different kinds of biases that should be considered in the onsite logs? Our main findings are the following: First, there is a considerable position bias, which is due to the design of the exhibition and should be considered during extraction of social signals from the log. Second, there is a bias in the amount of time that users spend for interacting with the point of interests and the order of picking them to visit. This shows a fatigue on users' interactions while they are reaching to the end of the exhibition. Third, we find out some variations among the users' visit, which shows context is an important factor to consider while using onsite logs for different purposes.

Categories and Subject Descriptors: H.3.3 [**Information Storage and Retrieval**]: Information Search and Retrieval— *Query formulation, Search process, Selection process*

Keywords: Behavioral dynamics; Bias; Internet of things; Onsite logs

1. INTRODUCTION

In modern search, interaction logs are one of the main sources of information about user behavior, form a key feature for training ranking algorithms, and are crucial for online and offline evaluation. However, due to existence of different kinds of biases in different kinds of human information interaction logs, extracting realistic behavioral information

CHIIR'16, March 13–17, 2016, Carrboro, NC, USA

© 2016 Copyright held by the owner/author(s). Publication rights licensed to ACM.
ISBN 978-1-4503-3751-9/16/03. . . $15.00

DOI: http://dx.doi.org/10.1145/2854946.2855004

from the logs and understanding users' actual behavior is so challenging. Due to the adoption of mobile devices and the 'internet of things,' interaction logs have gained a physical component posing additional constraints on observed user behavior.

In the search domain, biases in query logs has been studied for a long time [2, 4]. Eye tracking studies for understanding how users interact with search results show that users tend to click on the top of the rank list (i.e., position rank bias) and not continuing search after finding a relevant page [2]. Trust bias is another kind of bias, which is studied for using clickthrough data as implicit feedback [4]. Biases have also been studied in user click models studies, helping to better understand users' behavior [5].

In this paper, we introduce new kinds of biases in human information interaction logs that should be considered while using onsite logs to understand users' behavior and use it for different purposes, like for improving the museum's collection search engine or for unseen object recommendation at the museum. These new onsite biases are different from the ones introduced above. Moreover, unlike the users' behavior in search task where they end their search session after finding a relevant page, museum visitors tend to keep on exploring the museum, willing to visit as many interesting objects as possible.

We observe a number of biases in the onsite logs that might affect on understanding users' behavior. The first one is walk-through bias, in which visitors usually follow a path from a check-in station to a check-out station. The second one is the position rank bias, in which visitors tend to spend more time in front of the first object being shown to them in the museum. The last one is the time rank bias, in which visitors tend to spend more time in front of objects they decided to visit first, regardless of the position of those objects. We have also observed variation in users' behavior based on the context of their visit, which is important to be considered as well.

In this paper, our main aim is to study the question: *What are different kinds of biases in onsite logs that might affect on extraction of users' interests based on their onsite behavior?* Specifically, we answer the following research questions:

1. *How do position of objects and time of the visit affect on users' behavior?*

   (a) *How do users tend to walk through real objects in museums?*

   (b) *How does a position rank bias affect users dwell-time in front of each point of interest?*

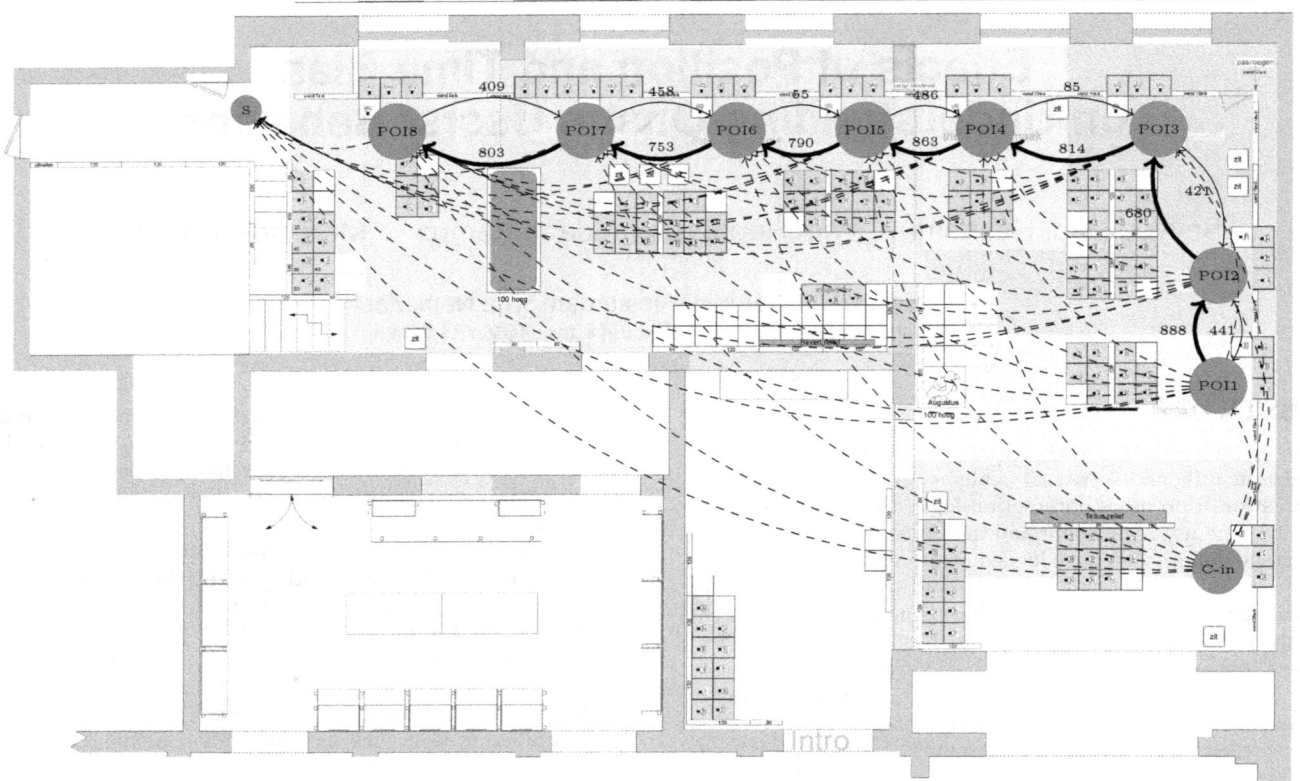

Figure 1: Walk through position bias: dominant transitions from check-in (C-in) to check-out (S). Numbers on the edges show count of users' movements between point of interests.

(c) *How does a time rank bias affect users dwell-time in front of each point of interest?*

2. *What is the effect of users' profile and their visit context on the position bias?*

The rest of the paper is organized as follows. Section 2 details the experimental data being used in this research. In Section 3, we introduce biases in the onsite logs. Section 4 is devoted to studying users' variation and the effect of biases on them. Finally, we present the conclusions and future work in Section 5.

2. EXPERIMENTAL DATA

In our archeological museum, RFID cards are provided as a key to access to some additional information about objects being shown in the museum. Visitors enter their preference at the beginning of the museum exhibition in order to personalize the content being shown in all of the point of interests. These preferences are perspectives of the narratives, language and the user's age range.

After checking in, users are free to put their keys on RFID readers of point of interests to unlock contents being shown about point of interests. They are free to interact with point of interests in any order. They can watch short movies, interacting with 3D photos of point of interests' objects, or read contents about objects being shown at POIs. At last, users might check out in a summary station, in which they might leave their name, birth date and email. In this paper, we

5 months onsite logs of the museum with more than 21,000 sessions is used.

3. BIASES IN ONSITE LOGS

This section studies biases in onsite logs, aiming to answer our first research question: *How do position of objects and time of the visit affect on users' behavior?*

3.1 Walk Through Position Bias

We first look at the question: *How do users tend to walk through real objects in museums?* Specifically, we study visitors walking path by tracking users' activity inside the museum. To this aim, we logged users' interaction with each system using RFID cards. In this experiment, we filtered sessions without interacting with the summary station, and we use more than 5,000 out of 21,000 sessions of the logs. According to Figure 1, there are many moves between different point of interests, but the most frequent ones are bold in the Figure. Although users are free to visit any POI at any order during their visit, they tend to visit point of interests one after the other from check-in to check-out stations. The second most frequent transition is to the previous POI, consistent with location proximity as a driving force. This makes a considerable bias in users' behavior extracted from onsite logs. More positively, the bias in onsite logs makes visitors behave more closely to simple click models [1].

The users walk through bias causes two other kinds of biases, namely position rank bias and time rank bias, which will affect on understanding users' behavior and their interests based on their dwell-time in front of POIs.

278

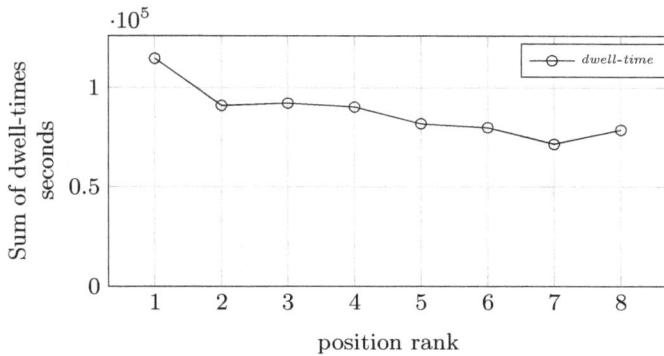

Figure 2: Position rank bias: dwell-time over POIs in exhibition order.

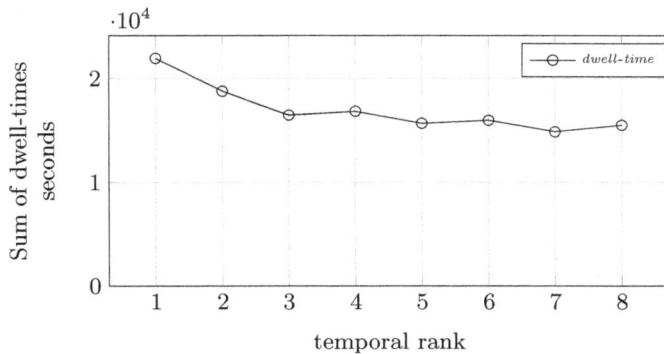

Figure 3: Time rank bias: dwell-time over POIs in order of visit.

3.2 Position Rank Bias

We next look at the question: *How does a position rank bias affect users dwell-time in front of each point of interest?* One of the important social signals in the onsite logs is the dwell-time of each user in front of each point of interests. This information indicates the degree of interest in objects being presented at each point of interests. However, walk-through bias causes a position rank bias, in which users spending more time in front of point of interests installed in the beginning of the exhibition, and the dwell-time decreases by reaching step by step to the end of the exhibition. As it is shown in Figure 2, dwell-time is inverse-proportional to the position rank of the objects in the museum, and the highest dwell-time is for the first object after check in station. Therefore, this bias should be considered while dwell-time is being used as a social signal to understand users' interests. According to this experiment, position of objects affects on the dwell time of users in front of them, which shows the dwell-time should be used with some care.

3.3 Time Rank Bias

As it is mentioned in previous experiments, users are free to visit any point of interest at anytime of their visits. As a result, they are free to not follow objects based on their position order. In this experiment, we analyzed dwell-time of users in each rank of point of interest based on users' visit order. In order to do this experiment, we filter all the sessions that do not interact with all the point of interests.

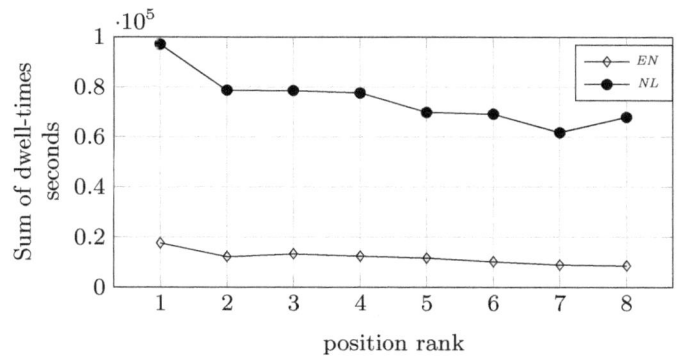

Figure 4: Position rank bias: English versus Dutch language.

According to Figure 3, users tend to spend more time in their earliest stage of their visit. In fact, the dwell-time is decreasing while the time rank of objects are increasing. It is also observed that users tend to spend less time at the end of exhibition, and users' fatigue of using technology in the museum affect on the dwell-time of their visit.

This experiment shows that spending less time at the last stage of the exhibition does not show that users are less interested in the last points of interests in comparison to the first ones; rather, they are less interested in interacting with technology or staying at museums.

4. IMPACTS OF CONTEXTS AND PROFILES

This section answer our second research question: *What is the effect of users' profile and their visit context on the position bias?*

As it is shown in the previous section, dwell-time of users in front of each object has a position and time rank bias. However, it is questionable that visits of which type of users are more affected by the position or time rank bias. To this aim, we stored gender, age, language, time and some other contexts in each session. In the following, some interesting observations based on users' profile are detailed.

Language We first look at differences between behaviors of users who decided to see Dutch content in comparison to users preferred English contents. According to Figure 4, we see a considerable difference in time spent by Dutch and English visitors (with identical content shown in each case) possibly due to foreign visitors spending more time with museum objects. People who preferred to see Dutch contents are less interested in POI7, which is about death. On the other hand, among sessions with English content preference, as expected by the position rank bias, people were more interested in spending time at POI7 rather than POI8. This experiment indicates that different variation of contents being prepared to be shown in deferent contexts affect differently on position rank bias.

Age We now study contributions of age groups in position rank bias. We log 2 different values for age in this log data, namely, adult and child. Figure 5 shows that children do not like POI7 (which is about death) and spend less time in front of death point of interest. Figure 4 and 5 indicate that children and Dutch content of POI7 contribute more on the lower dwell-time of POI7 in comparison to the POI8.

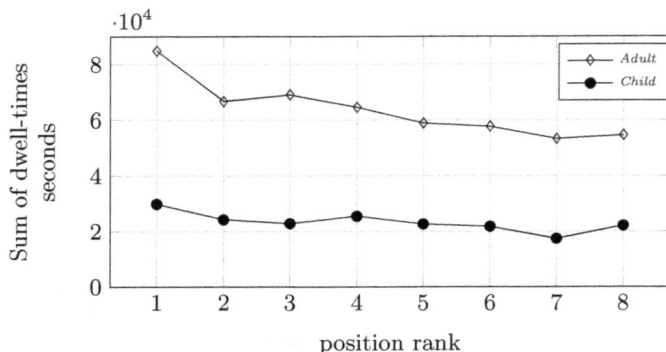

Figure 5: Position rank bias: adults versus children.

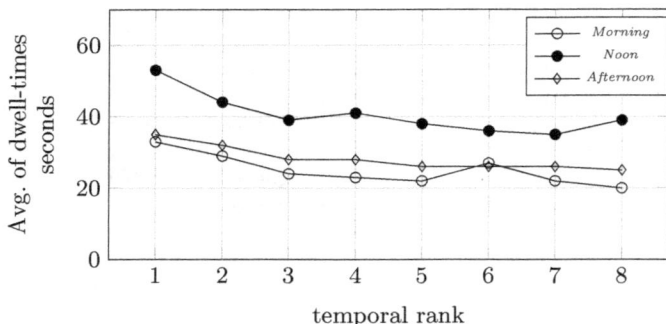

Figure 6: Time rank bias: visit time of day.

This experiment indicates that although adults' dwell-time at each POI shows a position rank bias in their behavior, children's behavior is less predictable and their dwell-time are less affected by the position rank bias.

Visit Time At last, we look at behavior of users in different time of a day. Basically, we answer the question: how long users in average tend to stay in front of each point of interests at different time of a day (i.e., morning, noon and afternoon)? We consider morning as a time from 10:00 to 12:00, noon as a time from 12:00 to 14:00, and afternoon as a time from 14:00 to 17:00. As it is shown in Figure 6, users are staying longer and interacting more with systems at noon in comparison to visits in the morning or afternoon. This experiment shows that due to museums opening hours in the afternoon and next activities users might plan to do after their visit in the morning, users might like to finish their visit earlier in morning or afternoon in comparison to others visits at noon.

Moreover, while users are willing to spend plenty of time in the museums, they are less affected by the time rank bias. As it is shown in the diagram of sessions at noon, users in average stayed longer in their last choice of museum object visit in comparison to their 3rd, 5th, 6th and 7th choices. However, this behavior is not true for morning and afternoon sessions.

Variations of users' behavior in different contexts show that the context of information interaction is an important factor to consider in using the onsite social information. However, similar to other research on using contextual information for search and recommendation [3], using contextual

information increases the variation of users' behavior and makes it difficult to have a system satisfy different users' information needs in all contexts, and consequently complicates the evaluation of contextual search systems. In fact, different users behave differently in different contexts, which leads to different degree of biases in each context in the onsite interaction logs. As it is shown in this section, context of visits has some consequences on the time or position rank bias in the onsite logs. Therefore, contexts should be considered as a factor in the rank bias smoothing process for understanding users' behavior, and evaluation of the contextual suggestion systems going to be used in museums.

5. CONCLUSIONS

We have studied different kinds of biases in onsite logs that could affect on the information extracted for understanding users' behavior for different purposes like post-visit online search tasks. Specifically, we analyzed how users tend to walk through the exhibition based on a logging their interactions at different POIs.

An analysis based on more than 21,000 sessions shows that they tends to follow point of interests from entrance to the end of the exhibition. In addition, we have analyzed how position rank bias affects dwell-time of visitors in front of each point of interest. An analysis based on more than 5,000 sessions indicates that users tend to interact with the system at the first point of interests more than the others, and the dwell-time is inverse-proportional to the order of objects being shown to the users. Moreover, effects of time rank bias on the dwell-time is also studied, which shows users tend to spend less time in front of objects when they are reaching to the end of their visits, and users' fatigue is an important factor in understanding users' behavior based on the onsite logs. Finally, we looked at the effect of context and users' profile on users' behaviors. We observed that children are less sensitive to the position bias. We also observed that time of the day play an important role in the amount of time users tend to spend for interacting with point of interests.

Our general observation is that we cannot use dwell-time information of onsite logs without care, and we should consider position and time rank bias as two important factors for smoothing their effects on the dwell-time as a source of evidence of users' interests.

Acknowledgments This research is funded by the European Community's FP7 (project meSch, grant # 600851).

References

[1] N. Craswell, O. Zoeter, M. Taylor, and B. Ramsey. An experimental comparison of click position-bias models. In *WSDM*, pages 87–94, 2008.

[2] L. A. Granka, T. Joachims, and G. Gay. Eye-tracking analysis of user behavior in www search. In *SIGIR*, pages 478–479, 2004.

[3] S. H. Hashemi, C. L. Clarke, A. Dean-Hall, J. Kamps, and J. Kiseleva. On the reusability of open test collections. In *SIGIR*, pages 827–830, 2015.

[4] T. Joachims, L. Granka, B. Pan, H. Hembrooke, and G. Gay. Accurately interpreting clickthrough data as implicit feedback. In *SIGIR*, pages 154–161, 2005.

[5] Y. Zhang, W. Chen, D. Wang, and Q. Yang. User-click modeling for understanding and predicting search-behavior. In *KDD*, pages 1388–1396, 2011.

Rationale and Architecture for Incorporating Human Oculomotor Plant Features in User Interest Modeling

Sampath Jayarathna and Frank Shipman
Computer Science & Engineering, Texas A&M University
College Station, TX 77843-3112
(Sampath, shipman)@cse.tamu.edu

ABSTRACT

We present a conceptual framework expanding the use of eye movement as a source of implicit relevance feedback. While gaze time has been the primary feature to be incorporated in interest modeling, this work constructs a model of human oculomotor plant features during user's interaction with multiple everyday applications with the goal of better interpreting user gaze data. The following presents the anatomical reasoning behind incorporating additional gaze features, the integration of the additional features into an existing interest modeling architecture, and a plan for assessing the impact of the addition of the features.

Keywords

User interest modeling, eye movements, oculomotor plant, implicit feedback

1. INTRODUCTION

Accurate models of user interest are valuable in personalizing the presentation of the often large quantity of information relevant to a query or other form of information request. We have previously developed and evaluated a software framework for capturing user activity across multiple applications and combining this activity data in a user interest model to aid information delivery. In this paper, we present the extension of this user modeling framework based on the non-visible anatomical structure and its characteristics of the human eye.

The human eye already provides a plethora of information useful for user modeling. Eye tracking has been employed in studying user attention on the web. Yarbus et al. show that visual behavior is closely correlated to the user task when looking at a visual scene [23]. A variety of uses of gaze data have been explored as a source of implicit relevance feedback for IR. Previous work has primarily focused on identifying visual attention to make user interest predictions [1, 3], interactive image retrieval [5, 9, 16] and more recently to predict a target in search results [2, 8, 20, 24]. In cognitive and perceptual psychology, eye tracking has been established as a mean of analyzing user attention as well as information processing tasks [21]. The human-computer interaction and information retrieval communities have shown that eye-tracking

have investigated trends and differences in user attention patterns and cognitive processing including correlations to the relevance of reading text [4], identifying pattern differences [7], tasks types [10], and user accuracy in alternative interfaces [19].

1.1 Motivation and Hypothesis

The motivation behind our work is that not all gazes are created equal. Thus, systems should not treat focus activity equally when using gaze information for user interest modeling. We hypothesize that the anatomical characteristics of the human eye may be utilized to estimate oculomotor plant features that can then be used to alter user interest modeling techniques. The research presented here presents a more comprehensive description of oculomotor plant features and an initial hypothesis as to what features will be of most use in conjunction with traditional implicit relevance feedback indicators. To the best of our knowledge, very few studies have used oculomotor plant characteristics [14, 15] in the context of biometrics. This study attempts to use eye movements and these oculomotor plant characteristics to identify the relevance of content.

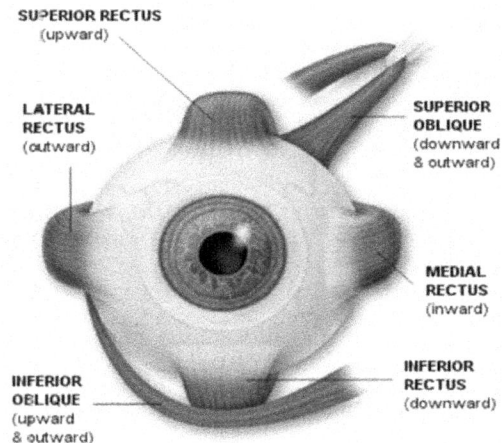

Figure 1. Human Oculomotor Plant

2. HUMAN OCULOMOTOR PLANT

The human oculomotor plant (OP) consists of the eye globe and six extraocular muscles and its surrounding tissues, ligaments each containing thick and thin filaments, tendon-like components and liquids (see Figure 1). In general there are six major eye movement types: fixations, saccades, smooth pursuits, optokinetic reflex, vestibule-ocular reflex and vergence [17]. An eye-tracker provides eye gaze position information as well as other gaze related parameters (pupil dilation etc.) so that algorithmic derivation in terms of two primary eye movements, *fixations* (relative gaze position at one point on the screen), and *saccades* (rapid eye movements of gaze from one fixation point

CHIIR '16, March 13-17, 2016, Carrboro, NC, USA.
© 2016 ACM. ISBN 978-1-4503-3751-9/16/03...$15.00.
DOI: http://dx.doi.org/10.1145/2854946.2854992

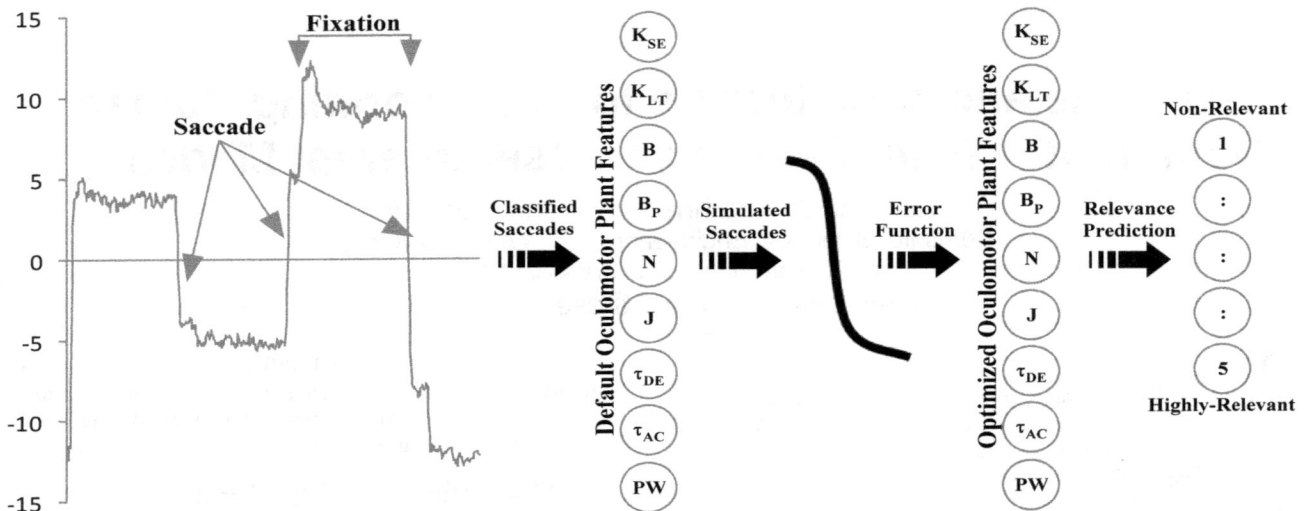

Figure 2. Raw eye movement signal before classification (Left). OPF vector default values and the simulated saccade trajectory (Middle). Optimized OPF vector and Relevance prediction task (Right)

to another) can be analyzed to derive the users attention patterns. The retinal image is transmitted to the brain during fixations but not during saccades. The static and dynamic characteristics of the human OP are represented by the series elasticity, viscosity, active-state tension, length-tension and force-velocity relationships and the frequency characteristics of the neuronal control signal sent by the brain to the extraocular muscles and the speed of propagation of this signal.

We next present details of the underlying oculomotor plant features, the integration of these features into an existing interest modeling architecture and then how the features are expected to provide value during user modeling.

2.1 Oculomotor Plant Features (OPF)

The following subset of oculomotor plant features was empirically selected as a feature-set to represent saccadic eye movement during both horizontal and vertical trajectories. The 18-parameter OPF listed below includes, *series elasticity* – resistive properties of an eye muscle, *length-tension* – the relationship between the length of an extraocular muscle and the force it is capable of exerting, *force velocity* – the relationship between the velocity of an extraocular muscle during extension/contraction and the force it is capable of exerting, *passive viscosity* – damping component coefficient for the viscosity of the eye-orbit and surrounding tissues, *muscle tension* – that ensures an equilibrium state during an eye fixation at primary eye position including the tension slope, *neuronal pulse-step* – represented as neuronal discharge from the brain.

More information about the 2D Oculomotor Plant and its mathematical derivation of the features can be found in [13].

1. Series Elasticity (AG) [K_{AG_SE} = 2.5 g/°]
2. Series Elasticity (ANT) [K_{ANT_SE} = 2.5 g/°]
3. Length-Tension Relationship (AG) [K_{AG_LT} = 1.2 g/°]
4. Length-Tension Relationship (ANT) [K_{ANT_LT} = 1.2 g/°]
5. Force-Velocity Relationship (AG) [B_{AG} = 0.046 g•s/°]
6. Force-Velocity Relationship (ANT) [B_{ANT} = 0.022 g•s/°]
7. Passive Viscosity [B_P = 0.06 g•s/°]
8. Tension Slope (AG) [N_{AG_C} = 0.8 g]
9. Tension Slope (ANT) [N_{ANT_C} = 0.5 g]
10. Inertial Mass [J = 0.000043 g•s2 /°]

11. Activation Time (AG) [τ_{AG_AC} = 11.7]
12. Activation Time (ANT) [τ_{ANT_AC} = 2.4]
13. Deactivation Time (AG) [τ_{AG_DE} = 2.0]
14. Deactivation Time (ANT) [τ_{ANT_DE} = 1.9]
15. Tension Intercept [N_{FIX_C} = 14.0 g]
16. Neural Pulse (AG) [N_{AG_SAC} = 55 g]
17. Neural Pulse (ANT) [N_{ANT_SAC} = 0.5 g]
18. Neural Pulse Width [PW = |A| + 6 ms]

Numbers in the brackets represent default values, and g – grams, s – seconds, ° – degrees of the visual angle, A – amplitude of the recorded saccade. The agonist (AG) muscle contracts, rotates the eye globe and stretches the antagonist (ANT) muscle.

2.2 Oculomotor Plant Module

By estimating oculomotor plant features (OPF) via the recorded eye position signal, these OPF values can alter how gaze data is incorporated into the evolving user interest model.

We next present (see Figure 2) the step-by-step process of obtaining OPF vectors and then applying these in the user modeling system to predict relevance values.

During a search task, the recorded eye movement signal from the user is supplied to the Eye Movement Classification module that classifies these position signals into fixations and saccades. We employ Velocity-Threshold (I-VT) algorithm to automatically and reliably identify and classify each recorded saccade's approximate beginning (onset) and ending (offset) from the noisy eye position signal. A threshold of 70^0/s is empirically selected to split the eye movement recording into fixations and saccades. The detected saccades trajectories represented by the onset and offset coordinates of the eye position and amplitude (length) of the saccade are used in the Oculomotor Plant Mathematical Model (OPMM) [11], which generates simulated saccade trajectories based on the default oculomotor plant feature (OPF) values. Each individual classified saccade is then compared with the simulated saccade and the corresponding OPF values are extracted by minimizing the error between each pair. After several iterations, these optimum OPF feature vectors are then supplied to the user interest estimation module for relevance prediction.

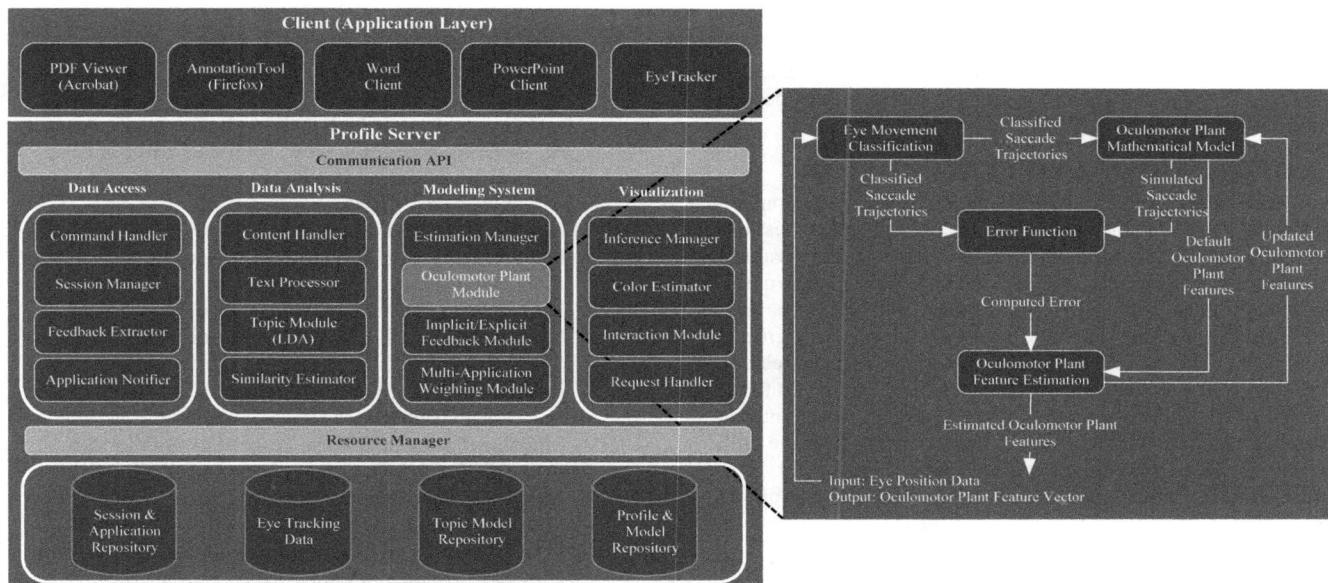

Figure 3. User Modeling Architecture (Left), Oculomotor Plant Module (Right)

2.3 Can OPF Reveal Relevance?

Eye movement fixations provide information about attentional states because the only way to acquire information visually is by placing the eye gaze position on the location [6]. It is also possible to measure the pupil dilation to infer the relevance on content with increase pupil dilation indicates fixations on relevant information content. A saccade itself is not an effective source of relevance, since visual perception is suppressed during a saccadic movement where eye is in motion. However, fixations require preceding saccades help to place the gaze in the stimuli to gather information from the target location. We believe that these small but significant movements can provide important cumulative clues in order to understand the underlying deployment of visual attention.

A variety of research in non-human primates has shown that executing saccades quicken when they are employed to a rewarded (positive outcome) location compared to an alternative unrewarded (non-positive outcome) locations [22]. These findings implicate an important role in cognitive learning, cognitive load and reinforcements in order to execute saccades to both rewarding and unrewarding target locations. Studies of task-driven saccades in the absence of a clear visual clue exhibited through slower eye movements [18]. This finding suggests existence of larger cognitive load to identify a cue and then calculate necessary target location to send the gaze position. Compared to an alternative simple eye movement to a visual clue, higher cognitive load may costs oculomotor system and possibly, loss of saccadic speed and accuracy. If these cognitively demanding decisions do influence the movement trajectories of saccades in simple tasks, a natural next step is to look into how relevance may be reflected in oculomotor plant features in more challenging search tasks.

3. AN OPF-AWARE USER INTEREST MODELING SERVER

Our interest modeling system [12] incorporates user activity data from multiple applications within a personal profile server (see Figure 3) to support personalized information presentations. The user activity data collected includes a combination of implicit

and semi-explicit interest information. It also shares the inferred user interests with registered applications that ask for it.

The profile server currently communicates with a web browser (Mozilla-Firefox) to present search results and also to visualize recommendations, and three other content reading and authoring applications: a PDF reader, Microsoft Word, and Microsoft PowerPoint. Records of user activity in PDF documents, Mozilla Firefox, MS Word and MS PowerPoint are stored in the server and drive the visualizations that the server generates for each of the applications registered for relevant notification request.

The Oculomotor Plant module provides OPF features that are expected to provide insight into the user's assessment of content to the modeling system. The eye tracker provides a continuous eye movement signal during the user activity and (as shown in the Resource Layer of Figure 3) an eye tracking data repository saves session data to be used for relevance prediction. An interest profile is made up of the aggregated heterogeneous interest evidence collected from these different clients that is generated based on all the features, including the new OPF features. The server defines the XML communication interface so that other application clients can interact via TCP/IP. A detailed description of the server and its modules are beyond the scope of this paper and can be found in [12].

4. FUTURE WORK: GATHERING OPF DATA FOR REAL INFORMATION TASKS

Saccades are integral parts of visual attention. The above framework and architecture incorporates OPF data capture, storage and analysis techniques to explore the value of saccades in determining the relevance of encountered content. Going forward, we will perform controlled studies to capture OPF data during information gathering tasks. By giving the user a specific search task and a set of documents of known relevance, we can initially explore the hypothesis that OPF data will be distinguishable between the relevant and non-relevant documents. The subjects' task will be to (i) read the search task assigned and decide whether each document associated with the task is relevant to the task assignment. (ii) Select the relevance score for each document on a 5-point scale (1-Non-Relevent, 5-Higly Relevant), for content relevance assessment. Eye movements will be recorded during reading the associated documents. The resulting data will lead to an assessment of if and how OPF data can be used as implicit relevance feedback in future systems.

5. DISCUSSION AND CONCLUSION

We have introduced a framework for enhancing implicit relevance feedback by including oculomotor plant features during the use of eye tracking data. In order to further evaluate the proposed architecture, we are currently designing a multi-application user study that will gather user activity data, including eye tracking data, and post-task relevance judgments from users. This will allow us to assess user behavior in relation to the relevance of documents in order to build and evaluate the possibility of using oculomotor plant features in user interest modeling context. We believe that understanding how the OPF values change over the course of user engagement with information resources will be valuable in the pursuit of developing more accurate user interest models.

There is a wide range of follow-on work related to the user modeling approach explored here. We limited our approach to features that could be computed from oculomotor plant data. Understanding how saccades relate to the fixations they precede is also an important part of moving towards a richer account of relevance learning in the context of user modeling. Most theories and models are based on fixation patterns that lack an understanding of how saccadic eye movements preceding these fixations are affected by the task environment.

6. ACKNOWLEDGMENTS

This work was supported in part by National Science Foundation grant DUE-0938074.

7. REFERENCES

[1] Borji, A. and Itti, L., "Defending Yarbus: Eye movements reveal observers' task," *Journal of vision,* vol. 14, p. 29, 2014.

[2] Borji, A., Lennartz, A., and Pomplun, M., "What do eyes reveal about the mind?: Algorithmic inference of search targets from fixations," *Neurocomputing,* vol. 149, pp. 788-799, 2015.

[3] Borji, A., Sihite, D. N., and Itti, L., "Probabilistic learning of task-specific visual attention," in *Computer Vision and Pattern Recognition (CVPR), 2012 IEEE Conference on,* 2012, pp. 470-477.

[4] Buscher, G., Dengel, A., and van Elst, L., "Eye movements as implicit relevance feedback," in *CHI'08 extended abstracts on Human factors in computing systems,* 2008, pp. 2991-2996.

[5] Coddington, J., Xu, J., Sridharan, S., Rege, M., and Bailey, R., "Gaze-based image retrieval system using dual eye-trackers," in *Emerging Signal Processing Applications (ESPA), 2012 IEEE International Conference on,* 2012, pp. 37-40.

[6] Cole, M. J., Gwizdka, J., Bierig, R., Belkin, N. J., Liu, J., Liu, C.*, et al.,* "Linking search tasks with low-level eye movement patterns," in *Proceedings of the 28th Annual European Conference on Cognitive Ergonomics,* 2010, pp. 109-116.

[7] Goldberg, J. and Helfman, J., "Eye tracking for visualization evaluation: Reading values on linear versus radial graphs," *Information visualization,* 2011.

[8] Haji-Abolhassani, A. and Clark, J. J., "A computational model for task inference in visual search," *Journal of vision,* vol. 13, p. 29, 2013.

[9] Hussain, Z., Klami, A., Kujala, J., Leung, A. P., Pasupa, K., Auer, P.*, et al.,* "PinView: Implicit Feedback in Content-Based Image Retrieval," *arXiv preprint arXiv:1410.0471,* 2014.

[10] Iqbal, S. T. and Bailey, B. P., "Using eye gaze patterns to identify user tasks," in *The Grace Hopper Celebration of Women in Computing,* 2004, pp. 5-10.

[11] Jayarathna, S., "Two Dimentional Oculomotor Plant Mechanical Model (2DOPMM)," Texas State University–San Marcos, 2010.

[12] Jayarathna, S., Patra, A., and Shipman, F., "Unified Relevance Feedback for Multi-Application User Interest Modeling," presented at the Proceedings of the 15th ACM/IEEE-CS Joint Conference on Digital Libraries, Knoxville, Tennessee, USA, 2015.

[13] Komogortsev, O. V., Holland, C., and Jayarathna, S., "Two-Dimensional Linear Homeomorphic Oculomotor Plant Mathematical Model," 2012.

[14] Komogortsev, O. V., Jayarathna, S., Aragon, C. R., and Mahmoud, M., "Biometric identification via an oculomotor plant mathematical model," in *Proceedings of the 2010 Symposium on Eye-Tracking Research & Applications,* 2010, pp. 57-60.

[15] Komogortsev, O. V., Karpov, A., Price, L. R., and Aragon, C., "Biometric authentication via oculomotor plant characteristics," in *Biometrics (ICB), 2012 5th IAPR International Conference on,* 2012, pp. 413-420.

[16] Kozma, L., Klami, A., and Kaski, S., "GaZIR: gaze-based zooming interface for image retrieval," in *Proceedings of the 2009 international conference on Multimodal interfaces,* 2009, pp. 305-312.

[17] Leigh, R. J. and Zee, D. S., *The neurology of eye movements*: Oxford University Press, 2015.

[18] McColeman, C. M. and Blair, M. R., "Task relevance moderates saccade velocities to spatially separated cues."

[19] Plumlee, M. D. and Ware, C., "Zooming versus multiple window interfaces: Cognitive costs of visual comparisons," *ACM Transactions on Computer-Human Interaction (TOCHI),* vol. 13, pp. 179-209, 2006.

[20] Rajashekar, U., Bovik, A. C., and Cormack, L. K., "Visual search in noise: Revealing the influence of structural cues by gaze-contingent classification image analysis," *Journal of Vision,* vol. 6, p. 7, 2006.

[21] Rayner, K., "Eye movements and cognitive processes in reading, visual search, and scene perception," *Studies in Visual Information Processing,* vol. 6, pp. 3-22, 1995.

[22] Takikawa, Y., Kawagoe, R., Itoh, H., Nakahara, H., and Hikosaka, O., "Modulation of saccadic eye movements by predicted reward outcome," *Experimental brain research,* vol. 142, pp. 284-291, 2002.

[23] Yarbus, A. L., Haigh, B., and Rigss, L. A., *Eye movements and vision* vol. 2: Plenum press New York, 1967.

[24] Zelinsky, G. J., Peng, Y., and Samaras, D., "Eye can read your mind: Decoding gaze fixations to reveal categorical search targets," *Journal of vision,* vol. 13, p. 10, 2013.

Correlation Between System and User Metrics in a Session

Jiepu Jiang
Center for Intelligent Information Retrieval
College of Information and Computer Sciences
University of Massachusetts Amherst
jpjiang@cs.umass.edu

James Allan
Center for Intelligent Information Retrieval
College of Information and Computer Sciences
University of Massachusetts Amherst
allan@cs.umass.edu

ABSTRACT

We investigate the correlations between system-oriented evaluation metrics and a few user experience metrics for a search session. The system-oriented metrics include session-based DCG (sDCG), normalized sDCG (nsDCG), estimated session nDCG (esNDCG), and a few variants of these metrics. We also look into statistics (e.g., the mean, maximum, and minimum values) of individual queries' nDCG scores, as well as the first and the last query's nDCG in a session. These system-oriented metrics are compared with users' self-rated search performance and task difficulty for a session. Experimental results show that nsDCG and esNDCG have reasonable but weak correlations with the user metrics, while the worst and the last query's nDCG in a session have comparably strong correlations. This suggests future work may better measure users' search experience in a session by modeling each query in the session differently.

Keywords

Search session; evaluation metric; user experience

1. INTRODUCTION

A challenge in the information retrieval community is to develop robust and reusable automatic evaluation approaches for interactive search, usually spanning multiple queries (a *search session*). One of the most critical issues is to find and design metrics for the quality of a search session. Such metrics can provide guidance to the design and optimization of search techniques for a session.

Existing approaches include two types. The first type directly predicts user experience based on behavioral signals. Previous studies predicted search success [1, 5], frustration [4], satisfaction [6, 9], and task difficulty [2, 15]. This approach requires user interaction as inputs and can only be performed in an online manner. The second type extends the Cranfield-style evaluation to a search session. It relies on relevance judgments and session-level evaluation metrics [8, 12] to assess search quality. The second approach is reusable,

CHIIR '16, March 13-17, 2016, Carrboro, NC, USA
© 2016 ACM. ISBN 978-1-4503-3751-9/16/03...$15.00
DOI: http://dx.doi.org/10.1145/2854946.2855005

but it is unclear how well existing metrics correlate with user perceptions on search quality.

In this paper, we examine the issue of the second approach by correlating system-oriented evaluation metrics for a session with user-rated search performance and task difficulty.

2. METRICS

2.1 sDCG

Järvelin et al. [8] proposed the session-based discounted cumulated gain (sDCG) metric. sDCG sums up discounted cumulated gain (DCG) [7] for each query, but penalizes the contribution of later queries in a session. Järvelin et al. [8] believe that results retrieved by later queries in a session are less valuable, because query reformulation costs effort.

Here we examine the version of sDCG used by Kanoulas et al. [12] in order to be consistent with the normalized sDCG metric (discussed in Section 2.2). It is calculated as in Equation 1. For a session of n queries, sDCG sums up the DCG for each query, and applies a discount factor $1/\log_{bq}(i + bq - 1)$ to later queries in a search session. The DCG of the ith query q_i is calculated as in Equation 2, where $rel(q_i, r)$ stands for the relevance grade for the rth result on q_i's search result page (SERP). Following Kanoulas et al.'s work [12], we set $b = 2$ and $bq = 4$. When $b = 2$, the DCG in Equation 2 is identical to the one usually adopted for evaluating a single query's performance.

$$\text{sDCG}(q_1, q_2, ..., q_n) = \sum_{i=1}^{n} \frac{\text{DCG}(q_i)}{\log_{bq}(i + bq - 1)} \quad (1)$$

$$\text{DCG}(q_i) = \sum_{r=1}^{k} \frac{2^{rel(q_i, r)}}{\log_b(r + b - 1)} \quad (2)$$

2.2 nsDCG

Kanoulas et al. [12] proposed a normalized version of the sDCG metric—normalized session DCG (nsDCG). A version of this metric tailored for two queries was used in the TREC 2010 session track [11]. nsDCG assumes an ideal ranked list for each query (q_{ideal}) where the judged relevant results are sorted by their relevance grades in a descending order. A session achieves the ideal performance if each query retrieves results with relevance grades equivalent to those in the ideal ranked list. The ideal session's sDCG is used for normalization, as in Equation 3.

$$\text{nsDCG} = \frac{\text{sDCG}(q_1, q_2, ..., q_n)}{\text{sDCG}(q_{\text{ideal}}, q_{\text{ideal}}, ..., q_{\text{ideal}})} \quad (3)$$

2.3 esNDCG

Kanoulas et al. [12] also proposed the estimated session family of metrics. This family of metrics model different possible scan paths of users in a session. For example, a user may first examine two results on the first query's SERP, and then reformulate to the second query and examine four results. In this case, the scan path consists of the six examined results from the two queries' SERPs. The estimated session metrics evaluate each scan path by treating it as a virtual ranked list of results, and applying conventional IR evaluation metrics (such as nDCG and average precision) to assess the quality of the scan path. The metrics evaluate a search session by summing up each possible scan path's quality scores, weighted by the probability of the scan path.

Here we use nDCG to evaluate the quality of a scan path (to be consistent with other metrics examined in this paper). The metric is thus called esNDCG. Equation 4 computes esNDCG, where ω is a scan path, and $P(\omega)$ is ω's probability. $P(\omega)$ depends on two parameters: P_{ref}, the probability that users will reformulate to the next query after viewing the current SERP, instead of stopping and exiting the session, and P_{down}, the chances that users, after examining a result, will continue to examine the next one on the SERP.

$$\text{esNDCG} = \sum_{\omega} P(\omega)\text{nDCG}(\omega) \qquad (4)$$

We also examine a variant of esNDCG that uses normalized cumulated gain (nCG) to evaluate the quality of a scan path. We call this metric esNCG. nCG is similar to nDCG, except that it does not apply the position-based discount to results at different ranks. The motivation of examining esNCG is that the estimated session family metrics already penalize lower ranked results and later queries in a session by modeling scan path (controlled by P_{ref} and P_{down}). Lower ranked results and those from later queries are less likely to be involved in a scan path. In such cases, it seems redundant to further penalize lower ranked results in each scan path.

2.4 sDCG/q

sDCG/q is an alternative way of normalizing sDCG. A session's sDCG is normalized by simply the number of queries in the session, instead of an ideal session's sDCG. Equation 5 computes sDCG/q, where n is the number of queries.

This metric comes from Jiang et al.'s work for predicting user satisfaction in a session [9]. They reported in a dataset that a similar metric highly correlates with user satisfaction in a session. Their metric does not discount later queries in a session (and is thus referred to as sCG/#queries in their article [9]). Another difference is that they computed sCG as simply the sum of all queries' ratings by external annotators rather than based on relevance judgments. The purpose of their work is to verify that user satisfaction can be modeled as the ratio of search outcome to effort. They measured search outcome by sCG, and effort by the number of queries in a session (n). The latter is motivated by Azzopardi's economic model of search interaction [3], where the cost of a search session is proportional to the number of queries in that session. Here our metric is different in that we calculate sDCG and sDCG/q based on relevance judgments, but they summed up assessors' query ratings.

$$\text{sDCG/q} = \frac{\text{sDCG}(q_1, q_2, ..., q_n)}{n} \qquad (5)$$

2.5 Alternatives Without Query Discount

sDCG, nsDCG, sDCG/q, and esNDCG all penalize results retrieved by later queries in a session. However, Jiang et al. [9] showed that a variant of sDCG/q without discounting later queries better correlates with user satisfaction. Therefore, we also examine alternatives of these metrics that do not penalize later queries in a session.

We compute a variant of sDCG that does not discount later queries as in Equation 6. For nsDCG and sDCG/q, we replace sDCG by $\text{sDCG}_{\text{no\_query\_discount}}$ to remove the query discount component. It seems unclear how to exclude the query discount component in esNDCG, because both P_{ref} and P_{down} can affect the discounting. Thus, we do not consider its variant without query discount in this study.

$$\text{sDCG}_{\text{no\_query\_discount}} = \sum_{i=1}^{n} \text{DCG}(q_i) \qquad (6)$$

2.6 Individual Queries' nDCG

A seemingly reasonable idea for evaluating a search session is to consider statistics of individual queries' quality in the session. For example, a session may be satisfactory if each query retrieved good results. However, we know few use of these statistics as evaluation metrics for a session. We evaluate the quality of individual queries using nDCG [7], and then use the sum, mean, maximum, and minimum of the queries' nDCG scores in a session as metrics for that session's quality. In addition, we also use the first and the last queries' nDCG scores as indicators for the whole session's quality. This is suggested by Huffman et al.'s work [6] that showed search satisfaction in a session can be predicted using the first query's quality, while we examine both the first and the last query.

2.7 User Metrics

These system-oriented metrics are compared with two user-oriented metrics measured using the following two questions after users finished a search session. Responses to the first and the second questions are referred to as user-rated performance and task difficulty in this study.

- **Performance**: *how well do you think you performed in this task?* Options are: *very well (5), fairly well (4), average (3), rather badly (2),* and *very badly (1).*

- **Task Difficulty**: *how difficult do you think the task is?* Options are: *very difficulty (5), difficulty (4), average (3), easy (2),* and *very easy (1).*

3. DATASET

We use data from an existing user study[1] [10] to examine the system-oriented metrics for a session. We adopt this dataset because it collected both relevance judgments and users' ratings on their search experience when using an interactive search system. We restrict our scope to user-rated performance and task difficulty because the user study only collected these two user experience measures.

The original purpose of that user study was to compare search activity patterns in four types of tasks that vary in search goal (clear or amorphous) and product (factual or

---

[1] The dataset and source code can be accessed at https://github.com/jiepujiang/ir_metrics.

Table 1: Correlations between system-oriented metrics and user-rated performance and task difficulty.

Block	Metrics	Performance				Task Difficulty			
		Pearson		Spearman		Pearson		Spearman	
A	Performance	-		-		−0.787	***	−0.788	***
	Difficulty	−0.787	***	−0.788	***	-		-	
	Number of queries	−0.256	*	−0.241	*	0.305	**	0.301	**
B	sDCG	0.009		−0.056		0.065		0.063	
	nsDCG	0.350	**	0.326	**	−0.324	**	−0.300	**
	sDCG/q	**0.401**	***	**0.349**	**	**−0.388**	***	**−0.336**	**
	esNDCG ($P_{\text{ref}} = 0.9$, $P_{\text{down}} = 0.7$)	0.325	**	0.285	*	−0.246	*	−0.224	*
	esNCG ($P_{\text{ref}} = 0.8$, $P_{\text{down}} = 0.7$)	0.357	**	0.335	**	−0.261	*	−0.253	*
C	sDCG (no query discount)	−0.020		−0.104		0.092		0.118	
	nsDCG (no query discount)	0.353	**	0.323	**	−0.332	**	−0.305	**
	sDCG/q (no query discount)	**0.399**	***	**0.330**	**	**−0.374**	***	**−0.315**	**
D	sum nDCG	−0.018		−0.115		0.094		0.136	
	mean nDCG	0.352	**	0.320	**	−0.332	**	−0.302	**
	max nDCG (best query)	0.269	*	0.204		−0.191		−0.177	
	min nDCG (worst query)	0.348	**	**0.358**	**	−0.364	***	−0.379	***
	first query's nDCG	0.259	*	0.227	*	−0.177		−0.156	
	last query's nDCG	**0.371**	***	0.354	**	**−0.436**	***	**−0.419**	***

*, **, and *** indicate the correlation is significant at 0.05, 0.01, 0.001 levels, respectively.
Bold font indicates the strongest correlation of its column in each block.

informational) [14]. These tasks were developed by and used in the TREC 2012 session track [13]. The study recruited 20 subjects. Each worked on four tasks for about 10 minutes using an experimental search system. The system is similar to existing search engines, except that it shows only 9 results per page (to facilitate analysis of eye-movement data). The study collected 80 sessions (4.9 queries per session).

Relevance of results were judged at three levels: *Highly Relevant* (2), *Relevant* (1), or *Non-relevant* (0). Users rated 22 sessions' performance as *very well*, 27 as *fairly well*, 22 as *average*, 7 as *rather badly*, and 2 as *very badly*. They rated 3 sessions' difficulty as *very difficult*, 14 as *difficult*, 25 as *average*, 14 as *easy*, and 24 as *very easy*.

4. RESULTS

We evaluate the collected 80 sessions using the system-oriented metrics, and correlate the metrics' values with user-rated performance and task difficulty. esNDCG and esNCG include two parameters. We set their values by a brute force scan to optimize Pearson's r with user-rated performance. Table 1 reports Pearson's r and Spearman's ρ between the system-oriented metrics and the user metrics. Block A shows that performance and task difficulty have a strong negative correlation. This indicates that search performance and task difficulty are closely related but different. The number of queries, as an indicator of search cost [3, 9], has a positive correlation with task difficulty and a negative one with user-rated performance.

4.1 Existing Session Evaluation Metrics

Block B examines and compares the correlations of sDCG, nsDCG, esNDCG, esNCG, and sDCG/q with user metrics.

sDCG does not have any significant correlations with user-rated performance or task difficulty. We suspect it is because sDCG only measures how much information are retrieved in a session, but ignores the cost—as long as searchers issue more queries, they can find more information. Since sDCG sums up DCG for each query, it naturally correlates with

the number of queries in a session ($r = 0.67$). But the latter has a negative correlation with user-rated performance.

The two normalized versions—nsDCG and sDCG/q—both significantly correlate with user-rated performance and task difficulty. It should be noted that the normalization factor of nsDCG (the ideal session's sDCG) also correlates with the number of queries, because it sums up the ideal DCG for each query. Thus, after normalization, both nsDCG and sDCG/q set off the cost factor in sDCG.

Both esNDCG and esNCG show significant correlations with the two user metrics, but esNCG consistently has relatively stronger correlations. This suggests that for the estimated session family metrics, discounting lower ranked results in each scan path may be harmful.

Except sDCG, other metrics in Block B all show significant positive correlations with user-rated performance. This verifies that existing metrics for a search session's performance are reasonable to some extent. But the correlations remain weak (Pearson's $r \leq 0.4$ and Spearman's $\rho \leq 0.35$), indicating the limited status of existing system-oriented metrics in measuring potential search experience of users.

sDCG/q, a variant of nsDCG that normalizes sDCG simply by the number of queries, has the strongest correlation with both user-rated performance and task difficulty in the collected data. We do not want to over-generalize this finding due to the limited size of the collected data. We require further studies to fully validate this metric.

4.2 Discounting Later Queries in a Session

Block C examines variants of sDCG, nsDCG, and sDCG/q that do not discount results from later queries in a session. Compared with their corresponding metrics in Block B, these variants have very similar correlations with both user-rated performance and task difficulty. For nsDCG and sDCG/q, the differences in r and ρ between Block B and Block C do not exceed 0.02. This indicates that the query discounting component in sDCG, nsDCG, and sDCG/q may not be necessary. At least our collected data do not show clear benefits of discounting results from later queries.

4.3 Individual Queries' Performance

Block D examines the connections between search experience in a session and individual queries' quality.

The sum of all queries' nDCG scores (sum nDCG) does not show any significant correlations with user-rated performance or task difficulty. The reason is similar to that for sDCG. The metric also highly correlates with the number of queries in a session ($r = 0.72$). Similar to sDCG/q, the mean value of individual queries' nDCG in a session (mean nDCG) shows significant correlations with user metrics. It should be noted that in our collected data, "sum nDCG" and sDCG have an almost perfect correlation ($r = 0.98$). The correlations of "mean nDCG" with nsDCG ($r = 0.99$) and sDCG/q ($r = 0.92$) are almost perfect as well. This means that many existing system-oriented session evaluation metrics, such as sDCG and nsDCG, are not much different from the sum or average performance of individual queries.

The worst query's nDCG in a session (min nDCG) has the strongest Spearman's correlation with user-rated performance among all the system-oriented metrics we examined. The Pearson's correlation ($r = 0.348$) is also comparable to those for nsDCG and esNDCG. In contrast, the best query's nDCG in a session (max nDCG) does not show clear correlations with the two user metrics. This indicates that a few underperforming queries in a session may substantially affect user experience, while it is common to find well-performing queries in any session.

The last query's nDCG has significant correlations with both user metrics. In fact, it has the strongest correlation with task difficulty among all system-oriented metrics we examined. In contrast, the first query's nDCG does not correlate much with user metrics. This suggests that failing to formulate effective queries in later stages of a session may be an indicator of task difficulty.

To conclude, results in Block D suggest that further studies may rely on individual queries to evaluate a search session. In addition, some queries such as the worst and the last query may have stronger influence on users' search experience in a session compared with other queries. This suggests that future work may better measure users' search experience in a session by modeling each query differently.

5. CONCLUSION

We examined the correlations between system-oriented evaluation metrics and user-rated performance and task difficulty in a search session. We found that a few existing metrics such as nsDCG and esNDCG have significant but weak correlations with user metrics. This verifies that these metrics are reasonable evaluation surrogates to some extent. However, results also indicate limited value of existing metrics. For example, we found that metrics such as sDCG and nsDCG are not much different from the sum or mean values of individual queries' nDCG. The worst query and the last query's nDCG values generally show stronger correlations with user metrics than existing system-oriented metrics such as sDCG, nsDCG, and esNDCG in our dataset.

This work, however, is limited by the small number of sessions we had evaluated (80). Due to the limited sample size, we also did not examine task effects on these metrics. In addition, we also did not examine a few other metrics in this work, such as the time-biased gain [17] and U-measure [16]. We leave these issues for future work.

6. ACKNOWLEDGMENT

This work was supported in part by the Center for Intelligent Information Retrieval and in part by NSF grant #IIS-0910884. Any opinions, findings and conclusions or recommendations expressed in this material are those of the authors and do not necessarily reflect those of the sponsor.

7. REFERENCES

[1] M. Ageev, Q. Guo, D. Lagun, and E. Agichtein. Find it if you can: A game for modeling different types of web search success using interaction data. In *SIGIR '11*, pages 345–354, 2011.

[2] J. Arguello. Predicting search task difficulty. In *ECIR '14*, pages 88–99, 2014.

[3] L. Azzopardi. Modelling interaction with economic models of search. In *SIGIR '14*, pages 3–12, 2014.

[4] H. A. Feild, J. Allan, and R. Jones. Predicting searcher frustration. In *SIGIR '10*, pages 34–41, 2010.

[5] A. Hassan, R. Jones, and K. L. Klinkner. Beyond DCG: User behavior as a predictor of a successful search. In *WSDM '10*, pages 221–230, 2010.

[6] S. B. Huffman and M. Hochster. How well does result relevance predict session satisfaction? In *SIGIR '07*, pages 567–574, 2007.

[7] K. Järvelin and J. Kekäläinen. Cumulated gain-based evaluation of IR techniques. *ACM Transactions on Information Systems*, 20(4):422–446, 2002.

[8] K. Järvelin, S. L. Price, L. M. L. Delcambre, and M. L. Nielsen. Discounted cumulated gain based evaluation of multiple-query IR sessions. In *ECIR '08*, pages 4–15, 2008.

[9] J. Jiang, A. Hassan Awadallah, X. Shi, and R. W. White. Understanding and predicting graded search satisfaction. In *WSDM '15*, pages 57–66, 2015.

[10] J. Jiang, D. He, and J. Allan. Searching, browsing, and clicking in a search session: Changes in user behavior by task and over time. In *SIGIR '14*, pages 607–616, 2014.

[11] E. Kanoulas, B. Carterette, P. Clough, and M. Sanderson. Overview of the TREC 2010 session track. In *TREC 2010*.

[12] E. Kanoulas, B. Carterette, P. D. Clough, and M. Sanderson. Evaluating multi-query sessions. In *SIGIR '11*, pages 1053–1062, 2011.

[13] E. Kanoulas, B. Carterette, M. Hall, P. Clough, and M. Sanderson. Overview of the TREC 2012 session track. In *TREC 2012*.

[14] Y. Li and N. J. Belkin. A faceted approach to conceptualizing tasks in information seeking. *Information Processing & Management*, 44(6):1822–1837, 2008.

[15] C. Liu, J. Liu, and N. J. Belkin. Predicting search task difficulty at different search stages. In *CIKM '14*, pages 569–578, 2014.

[16] T. Sakai and Z. Dou. Summaries, ranked retrieval and sessions: A unified framework for information access evaluation. In *SIGIR '13*, pages 473–482, 2013.

[17] M. D. Smucker and C. L. Clarke. Time-based calibration of effectiveness measures. In *SIGIR '12*, pages 95–104, 2012.

The Role of the Unconscious in Information Retrieval: What User Perception Tells Us

Jingjing Liu, Kendra Albright, Hassan Zamir

School of Library and Information Science, University of South Carolina
1501 Greene Street, Columbia, SC 29208

jingjing@sc.edu, albright@sc.edu, mhzamir@gmail.com

ABSTRACT

Increasing evidence from psychoanalytic and psychodynamic research suggests that the unconscious influences our daily decisions, and psychologists have suggested that as much as 85-95% of decision making occurs outside our conscious awareness. For information science, it is important to understand how these unconscious processes play a role in information seeking. The current study uses subliminal psychodynamic activation (SPA), through the use of subliminal messages that appeared below the threshold of conscious awareness, to investigate the influence of the unconscious in information searching. Twenty-four college students participated in a controlled laboratory experiment, each searching freely on the Internet for information for three search tasks, with various SPA messages appearing in each search. Participants were systematically assigned to one of the four SPA conditions with various subliminal messages. Users' perceptions of search task topic interest, topic knowledge and task difficulty was examined between different SPA conditions, as well as the change of users' perceptions on topic interest, knowledge, and difficulty before and after searching in different SPA conditions. Findings suggested that users' pre- and post-task ratings of topic interest, knowledge, and difficulty did not show significant differences among the 4 SPA conditions. However, the change in users' perceptions of topic interest and topic knowledge before and after searching showed significant differences when SPA messages were present. Our findings inspire future research in this underexplored field.

Keywords

Unconsciousness; subliminal message; information search; user behaviors.

1. INTRODUCTION

Human behavior is seen as the outcome of underlying motives, drives, needs, and conflicts, some of which are not even realized by individuals, i.e., and fall in the unconscious domain. Pervin & John [8] noted that unconscious processes influence the ways in which we think and feel. Westen [11] also pointed out that the underlying thoughts and feelings of human beings direct much of our emotional life and guide our decisions, which are not always the result of cognitive reasoning, and that the way we feel can exert a stronger influence on decisions than the way we think.

CHIIR '16, March 13-17, 2016, Carrboro, NC, USA
© 2016 ACM. ISBN 978-1-4503-3751-9/16/03...$15.00
DOI: http://dx.doi.org/10.1145/2854946.2854986

As one type of human behavior, information behavior can be influenced by mental and emotional processes that occur outside of conscious awareness [1]. Information seeking involves obtaining information through physical actions and behaviors, It also involves affective and emotional aspects, as Kuhlthau [7] pointed out in her famous ISP (information search process) model. How the unconscious may play a role in users' affective and emotional aspects, therefore, is also important and calls for more research. In the current study, we were particularly interested in exploring how the unconscious may influence users' perceptions of their information searching in the aspects of search task topic interest, topic knowledge, and task difficulty.

One way to operationalize the unconscious that has been used in the literature is the method of Subliminal Psychodynamic Activation (SPA). SPA refers to the use of subliminal visual stimulation to activate unconscious processes that can then be studied (e.g., [3], [9]). Given this operationalization method, four specific research questions in the current study were generated, as follows:

1. Does the use of SPA messaging have an influence on users' perceptions of information search task topic interest, topic knowledge, and task difficulty?
2. Does the use of SPA messaging have an influence in changes on users' perceptions before and after the search in the aspects of topic interest, topic knowledge, and task difficulty?
3. Do different SPA messages show an influence on users' perceptions of information search task topic interest, topic knowledge, and task difficulty?
4. Do different SPA messages show an influence in changes on users' perceptions before and after the search in the aspects of topic interest, topic knowledge, and task difficulty?

2. LITERATURE REVIEW

Much of the research in information behavior has focused on cognitive behaviors, i.e., behaviors that are directed by rational and cognitive decision-making. While cognitive attitudes are important, Westen [11] suggests that emotions that lie in the unconscious have a greater influence on decisions than cognitive attitudes. Harmon & Ballesteros [5] also noted the unconscious in their research regarding the problems with accuracy of user's needs. They suggested that "unconscious cognition plays a key role in the framing of inquiry, (and for that matter, of discovery in the communication chain), and it persists throughout the entire inquiry cycle, whether it be formal reasoning of casual day-to-day problem solving" (p. 423). They further noted the importance of the unconscious in query formation, suggesting that "attempts to address only those queries that are expressed in a conscious mode may treat the symptoms of the problem rather than the true problem itself. Such attempts can even give the illusion of problem resolution, and can hence be misleading, counter-productive, or even dangerous" (p. 424).

Despite the dominant perspective, Information Science literature has observed the role of the unconscious, either directly or inadvertently. Taylor [10] describes "the actual, but unexpressed need for information," (i.e., a visceral need) where the individual recognizes "the conscious or even unconscious need for information not existing in the remembered experience of the inquirer" (p. 182). Kulthau [7] built information seeking models with three aspects involved: physical actions (behaviors), cognitive aspects, and affective and emotional aspects. The unconscious, while not as easy to articulate, describe, measure, and evaluate in such a tangible way as cognitive reasoning, calls for research effort regarding its influence on information seeking and decision-making involved in the information seeking process.

As the use of subliminal visual stimulation to activate unconscious processes, the SPA method was developed and refined by Lloyd Silverman and his colleagues from the 1960s through the 1980s as a way to test psychoanalytic processes experimentally [2]. Silverman hypothesized that through the presentation of stimuli below the threshold of conscious awareness, psychological effects could be generated that would be consistent with psychoanalytic theories. Silverman further believed that these effects could have an impact on longer term behavioral change. Based on the earlier work of Margaret Mahler, Silverman used the subliminal phrase, "Mommy and I are one," to activate feelings of attachment and oneness, based on early mother-child relationships, a foundational concept in psychoanalysis [11]. Silverman reported positive behavior changes in eleven of fourteen studies, some of whose participants were schizophrenic; other studies included obese women and smokers.

Additional work in SPA is also found in advertising and brand research. For example, in 1957, James Vicary, a private market researcher, claimed to have substantially increased sales of Coca Cola and popcorn in a movie theatre, by flashing the subliminal messages, "Drink Coca Cola" and "Eat Popcorn" [6].

Although SPA research is not without controversy, SPA studies continue to produce some very interesting and important findings and inspired continuous research interest and effort. The current study was inspired by these research findings, and applied to the information science field.

3. METHOD

3.1 Experiment Design

To explore our research questions and test our hypotheses, a 4*3 controlled laboratory experiment was conducted with 4 different subliminal message conditions as the between-subject factor, and 3 different information tasks as the within-subject factor. Details about the experiment are introduced below.

3.2 Conditions

To apply the SPA conditions using subliminal messages, we used the software Subliminal Blaster[1]. Messages were input in the software application and then showed up following the duration and frequency as set by the experimenter. We used the recommended setting in this study, with the messages appearing for 0.02 seconds every 4 seconds.

---

[1] http://sourceforge.net/projects/sublaster/

The condition was a between-subject factor. Each participant was assigned to one of the four SPA conditions. The condition messages and participants assignment were shown as below (Table 1). Since the participants were randomly recruited and scheduled only according to their availability and no other factors were considered, the assignment could be treated as random.

Table 1. SPA condition messages and participants assignment

Condition	Message	Participants
C1	No messages flashing	p01-p06
C2	"People walking"	p07-p12
C3	"Mommy and I are one"	p13-p18
C4	"I am enlightened"	p19-p24

The determination of these messages was based on the previous work of Lloyd Silverman (1985), using different kinds of messages of various emotional states. The design of the messages was based on the following consideration: "People walking" was an emotionally neutral but an action oriented message, which may influence people to take active actions. "Mommy and I are one" was an emotionally positive message, which may make people feel comfortable and secure. "I am enlightened" was a positive and encouraging message, which may enhance one's confidence in their searching abilities.

3.3 Participants

Participants were students in the authors' university. They were recruited by flyers posted at dorms and campus cafeteria, as well as email discussion lists of randomly selected academic programs. Each was paid $15 for participation.

There were a total of 24 participants (14 female), with an average age of 22. They had various academic backgrounds such as English, psychology, exercise science, business, mechanical engineering, etc. They had an average of 10.3 years of searching experience, and 2.3 hours per day doing online searching.

3.4 Tasks

We designed tasks with a simulated task environment as proposed by Borlund [4], i.e., that selected topics were selected that were familiar to college students. Doing so aimed to maintain participants' information searching to be as natural as possible, despite a controlled laboratory experiment.

We designed three tasks for each participant to finish. One training task was added and administered in the beginning to familiarize the participants with the process of information searching and saving. The tasks were:

- Training task: How long is the Nile River?
- Summer job (JOB): Should I get a job this summer?
- Apartment finding (APT): My roommate is a slob and I need to find a new place to live.
- Sexually transmitted disease (STD): You are worried that you might have a sexually transmitted disease (STD).

Table 2. Pre- and post-task questionnaire comparison.

		C1	C2	C3	C4	Condition comparison F(p)
Topic interest	Pre-task rating Mean (SD)	5.28 (1.13)	4.83 (1.30)	5.44 (1.20)	5.00 (1.46)	0.83 (0.48)
	Post-task rating Mean (SD)	5.83 (0.92)	5.39 (1.29)	5.33 (1.37)	5.33 (1.33)	0.69 (0.56)
	Pre- & Post- comparison F(p)	**-2.56 (.020)**	-1.61 (.126)	0.62 (.542)	-1.14 (.269)	--
Topic knowledge	Pre-task rating Mean (SD)	4.44 (1.15)	4.17 (2.18)	4.22 (1.59)	4.44 (1.85)	0.13 (0.94)
	Post-task rating Mean (SD)	5.17 (1.20)	5.56 (1.29)	5.56 (0.98)	5.50 (0.86)	0.52 (0.69)
	Pre- & Post- comparison F(p)	-1.91 (.073)	**-4.03 (.001)**	**-3.37 (.004)**	**-2.64 (.017)**	--
Task difficulty	Pre-task rating Mean (SD)	3.06 (1.59)	2.67 (1.61)	3.17 (1.54)	2.44 (1.46)	0.85 (0.47)
	Post-task rating Mean (SD)	2.78 (2.02)	2.89 (1.68)	2.61 (1.72)	1.78 (1.44)	1.54 (0.21)
	Pre- & Post- comparison F(p)	0.70 (.491)	-0.47 (.646)	1.61 (.126)	1.41 (.175)	--

Table 3. Further comparison of SPA conditions with message presence

	C2	C3	C4	F(p)
Topic interest rating change Mean (SD)	-0.56 (1.46)	0.11 (0.76)	-0.33 (1.24)	1.40 (0.25)
Topic knowledge rating change Mean (SD)	-1.39 (1.46)	-1.33 (1.68)	-1.06 (1.70)	0.65 (0.59)
Task difficulty rating change Mean (SD)	-0.22 (2.01)	0.56 (1.46)	0.67 (2.00)	0.87 (0.46)

Each participant completed the training task and three formal tasks. In order to reduce possible order effects, the three formal tasks' orders were rotated following a Latin Square design.

3.5 Data Collection

Multiple data collection methods were used in this study including questionnaires and logging software. Questionnaires were administered both before (eliciting users' background information, knowledge with the tasks, and previous experience) and after each task (eliciting their perception of the search experience, degrees of satisfaction, and success). The last question asked the participants if they noticed the subliminal messages during information searching. All questions in the questionnaire asked users to respond based on a 7-point Likert scale. For example, "How knowledgeable are you with the topic of this task?" 1 stands for "not at all", 4 for "somewhat", and 7 for "extremely".

Logging software Morae[2] was used to record participants' interaction with the search system, including queries, clicks, webpage viewing and saving, dwelling time on webpages, and so on. The screen was also recorded by Morae using the video format.

3.6 Procedures

Each participant was invited individually to an on-campus information interaction lab. Each experiment session took about one hour. After signing the consent form, the participants were given the training task to become familiar with the information search, starting with a blank Internet Explorer window. They

---

[2] http://www.techsmith.com

were also familiarized with how to save useful webpages using the browser's bookmark function, to experimenter-pre-created folders for each task. They then performed the three search tasks in the assigned task order. Before and after each task, the participants were given the pre- and post-task questionnaires.

Although the experiment setting was controlled, for each task, participants were allowed to search freely on the Web for information for up to 15 minutes. Those who finished the task within 15 minutes moved on to the post-task questionnaire and then the following task, and those who did not finish the task at the 15-minute point was asked to stop working on the task, and move on to the post-task questionnaire and then the following task. After completing all three tasks, the final questionnaire was administered and a debriefing session was conducted.

4. RESULTS

4.1 About the subliminal messages

Data collected from the final questionnaire revealed that 5 out of 24 participants, in 11 out of 72 task sessions, noticed the flash messages. However, none of them was able to read the words in the message correctly. Some believed that the messages had useful information relevant to the search topic. Since the messages actually had no direct relationship with the search topics, it seems safe for us to accept that the subliminal messages were in the unconscious, or played only the emotional roles but did not help with decision-making in an explicit and conscious way.

4.2 Results about user perception

We examined the pre- and post-task questionnaires regarding searchers' perceptions of topic interest, topic knowledge, and task difficulty. Table 1 shows the results of one-way ANOVA analysis for participants' perceptions of these aspects in the four conditions (compared horizontally in Table 2), as well as the paired t-test comparison in different conditions (compared vertically in Table 1).

As can be seen from the "Condition comparison F(p)" values, there were no statistical differences found among the four conditions for any of the pre- or post-task perception elicited by the questionnaires.

However, as can be seen from the "Pre- & Post- comparison F(p)" results, statistical significance was found for the comparison of the pre- and post-task perception rating. Specifically, for topic interest, those with no SPA messages (C1) rated higher topic interest after working with the tasks, and those which had SPA messages (C2, C3, and C4) all showed no differences in their topic interest ratings before and after working with the tasks. Topic knowledge change also showed a difference in the patterns regarding SPA messages being present or absent, although the pattern was opposite with what was found for topic interest. Specifically, users with no SPA messages (C1) did not have differences in their topic interest ratings before and after working with the tasks, but those who had SPA messages (C2, C3, and C4) all rated higher topic knowledge after working with the tasks.

For the perceived task difficulty, users' pre- and post-task ratings did not show significant differences in any of the 4 conditions. No statistical significance was found in the comparison between pre- and post-task ratings, either.

Further analysis was done to compare the three conditions with SPA messages present (i.e., C2, C3, and C4). For each task done by each user, 3 new variables were computed to denote the change of ratings before and after the task on topic interest, topic knowledge, and task difficulty, by having the pre-task rating score to minus the post-task rating score. The one-way ANOVA test was then used to examine possible significant differences. As can be seen from Table 3, no significant differences were detected.

5. DISCUSSION & CONCLUSIONS

Our results showed that users' pre- and post-task ratings on topic interest, topic knowledge, and task difficulty did not have significant differences among the four conditions. Meanwhile, our results also revealed that the change users' perceptions of topic interest and topic knowledge before and after searching, showed different patterns, depending on the presence or absence of SPA. Users with subliminal messages did not have significantly different changes in their topic interest ratings but gave significantly higher topic knowledge ratings after the search. Users with no subliminal messages showed significantly higher topic interest ratings after the search, although their topic knowledge ratings remained the same level, i.e., having no significant differences. Regarding the three SPA conditions with subliminal messages present, further analysis did not find significance in the change of ratings before and after users worked with the tasks on topic interest, topic knowledge, or task difficulty.

While the sample size is limited to only 24 participants and care needs to be taken when generalizing our results, one interpretation of our results could be that those with the subliminal messages felt that they learned more than those with no subliminal messages, even though they did not feel topic interest changes after

searching. As introduced above, the three subliminal messages, "People walking" was action-oriented, "Mommy and I are one" was a positive and comforting message, and "I am enlightened" was a positive and encouraging message which may influence one's confidence of knowledge. All three messages could have positive influences on one's self-assessed knowledge gain. However, how the different messages play these roles requires further research. Future studies will consider having negative messages in order to better understand how different messages play these roles.

Our study, although limited by the sample size and messages used, was the first step to attempt understanding the role that the unconscious may play in information seeking, learning, as well as decision making. The results shed light on this generally unexplored field and calls for more research in this area.

6. ACKNOWLEDGMENTS

We thank Caitlin Creel for her assistance with data collection.

7. REFERENCES

[1] Albright, K. S. (2010). Multidisciplinarity in Information Behaviour: Expanding Boundaries or Fragmentation of the Field? *Libri, 60*(2), 98-106.

[2] Balay, J. & Shevrin, H. (1988). The subliminal psychodynamic activation method: A critical review. *American Psychologist, 43*, 161-174.

[3] Birgegakd, A. & Sohlberg, S. (2001). Methodology in Subliminal Psychodynamic Activation: The Next Step in the Debate. *Perceptual and Motor Skills, 92*, 504-506.

[4] Borlund, P. (2003). The IIR evaluation model: A framework for evaluation of interactive information retrieval systems. *Information Research, 8*(3), paper no. 152.

[5] Harmon, G. & Ballesteros, E. R. (1997). In P. Vakkari, R. Savolainen & B. Dervin (Eds.), *Information Seeking in Context*, (pp. 422-433). London: Taylor Graham Publishing.

[6] Karremans, J.C., Stroebe, W., & Claus, J. (2006). Beyond Vicary's fantasies: The impact of subliminal priming and brand choice. *Journal of Experimental Social Psychology*, 42, 792-798.

[7] Kuhlthau, C. C. (1991). Inside the search process: Information seeking from the user's perspective. *Journal of the American Society for Information Science, 42*, 361-371.

[8] Pervin, L. A. & John, O. P. (2001). Personality: theory and research. 8th ed. New York, NY: John Wiley & Sons, Inc.

[9] Silverman, L. H. & Weinberger, J. (1985). Mommy and I are one: Implications for psychotherapy. *American Psychologist, 40*(12), 1296-1308.

[10] Taylor, R. S. (1968). Question negotiation and information seeking in libraries. *College and Research Libraries, 29*(3), 178-194.

[11] Weinberger, J., & Smith, B. (2011), Two experimental programs for studying unconscious processes. *Journal of the American Psychoanalytic Association, 59,*553-570.

[12] Westen, D. (2007). *The political brain: the role of emotion in deciding the fate of the nation.* New York, NY: Public Affairs.

Manipulating Time Perception of Web Search Users

Cheng Luo*°, Fan Zhang*□, Xue Li*°, Yiqun Liu*°, Min Zhang*°, Shaoping Ma*°,
Delin Yang*+
*Tsinghua National Laboratory for Information Science and Technology
°Department of Computer Science and Technology, □Department of Physics,
+School of Economics and Management
Tsinghua University
Beijing 100084, China
luochengleo@gmail.com

ABSTRACT

Time is an important factor in information retrieval studies including search evaluation, user behavior analysis and query understanding. In most of the previous works, time is usually an objective factor measured by timing devices. However, the time perceived by user seems more intuitive to describe the impact of time because search user's opinion is considered subjective. Psychological researches have reported that time perception can be affected by many physical and psychological factors. In this work, a laboratory study with 50 participants was adopted to investigate the impact of *Temporal Relevance*, e.g., the awareness of elapsed time, on time perception of Web search users. Experimental results show that participants in high temporal relevance environments tend to perceive significantly longer task durations than the actual ones. It shows that the perception of time can be manipulated in Web search scenario and reveals the necessity to take the factor of user perception into consideration in time-related Web search researches such as effort-based evaluation.

CCS Concepts

•**General and reference** → **Evaluation**; *Performance;*
•**Information systems** → **Information retrieval;**

Keywords

time perception, temporal relevance, search engine

1. INTRODUCTION

Time plays an essential role in multiple areas of Information Retrieval (IR) researches, such as search evaluation, user behavior analysis and search query understanding.

In a typical Web search scenario, a user issues a query to the search engine and hope to fulfill his/her information need with reasonable effort (search duration shouldn't be too long). From the system's perspective, the time reflects the

CHIIR '16, March 13 - 17, 2016, Carrboro, NC, USA
© 2016 Copyright held by the owner/author(s). Publication rights licensed to ACM.
ISBN 978-1-4503-3751-9/16/03...$15.00
DOI: http://dx.doi.org/10.1145/2854946.2854994

effectiveness of the retrieval system. The users with slower response would have lower perceptions of system usability [1]. From the user's perspective, the user's expected and actual efforts spent on search task provide important implicit feedback of the experience in the search process, user variability and IR system evaluation [2].

In *search evaluation*, time-biased gain (TBG) [11] computes the benefits obtained by the users and accounts for user effort taken to achieve those benefits in terms of time. As a more recent instantiation of TBG, time well spent (TWS) [3], expressed as the total time spent consuming relevant material v.s. the total time spent searching, measures both benefits and effort in meaningful units. In *user behavior analysis*, click dwell time is one of the most important features used to identify satisfied clicks. The clicks with dwell time longer than 30s are usually assumed to be more likely from users who are reading relevant results than short clicks (shorter than 15s) [6]. In *query understanding*, the time factor should also be taken into consideration. First, queries with temporal intents should be identified so that search engines can decide whether it should rank results based on timeliness or not. Second, search engine should be able to identify situations where users have urgent information needs in the context of an acute problem [9].

To the best of our knowledge, time mentioned in previous works is the objective time, measured by timing devices in experiments or systems. However, the perceived time seems more intuitive to describe the impact of time on IR evaluation where user behavior is considered subjective.

Time perception, referring to the subjective experience of time, is a construction of the brain that is manipulable and distortable under certain circumstances. In the field of psychology, substantial studies indicated that many aspects of our cognitive and behavioral functioning are based on processing temporal information to some extent [10]. Psychologists have found that the perception of the passing of time is influenced by many subjective factors, such as body temperature, emotion and etc [7].

As a factor that has an impact on interval length estimation in psychology, *Temporal Relevance* (TR) was defined by Zakay [13] as the *"level of relevancy and importance of time dimension in a specific state required for the optimal adaptation to the external environment"*. TR is one of the main determinants of the level of temporal awareness [8].

From this definition, we can see that different tasks may lead to different levels of TR in Web search scenario. For example, users who are supposed to meet urgent information needs (e.g. collecting information for an unfamiliar topic in a few minutes as described in the cases from [4]) should have high TR in their tasks. However, it remains uninvestigated whether TR will affect the time perception of Web search users and further have influence on the perception of system effectiveness.

In this paper, we report preliminary results of a study investigating the impact of TR on time perceiving and user experience in Web search scenario. Especially, we focus on the impact of TR on time perception in completing search tasks. We conduct an experimental study by manipulating temporal relevance for different groups of participants and measure their time perceptions while completing search tasks. Experimental results show that participants in high TR scenario tend to perceive longer durations than they actually spent in tasks, which suggests that we could make a better inference of user experience by considering the scenario the user involves in. This result also accords with existing findings in more general settings [12], which shows the probability of extending more findings in human time perception to Web search related studies.

2. EXPERIMENT SETUP

We conducted a laboratory study where TR is manipulated by specific signals in search interface. Users were asked to estimate the time they have spent in each search task under different manipulation settings.

There were 16 informational search tasks adopted in the experiment. For each task, we first randomly selected a medium-frequency (1,000 to 10,000 monthly) query from the log of a commercial search engine. Then a backstory was created as suggested in [2] to explain the information need of the task. Three annotators worked together to create the backstories based on the original query and corresponding clicked results. The backstories were carefully discussed until agreements were reached. In our experiment, the backstories were read and recorded by one of the authors and the same recordings were played to all the participants to ensure that they receive the same task information.

To encourage the participants to engage more into the tasks, the assessors organized a question for each task which required the participants to summarize the information gained in the search process. Participants had to answer the question correctly to get the payment to guarantee quality. An example of our tasks is shown in Table 1.

Table 1: An example of search tasks

Query	Miranda Warning
Backstory	There is a famous concept called Miranda Warning in the law of the U.S. Please search for the explanation and history.
Question	Briefly explain what is Miranda Warning with your own words.

We built an Web-based experimental search system to provide modified search results from a popular commercial search engine. All ads and sponsors' links were removed. We also removed the vertical results and query suggestions to reduce possible behavior biases during searching. Besides these changes, the search system looked just like a traditional commercial search engine. The users could issue

a query, click results and switch to the landing pages in the Web page as they wish. Query reformulation was not allowed in our system to ensure that users get the same results from the search engine and TR would not be affected by other factors such as result quality.

We randomly assigned half of our participants to a treatment condition where they were shown a "timing block", a flashing colored block, on top-right corner of the search result page (SERP). The Web-based search system is represented on an Dell workstation with a 17" display running at 1366*768. The timing block was 200*20 pixels in size. A coloration and flashing scheme was applied to better visually inform the user about elapsed time: the colored block was initially in green and flash slowly. In the search process, as time goes on, the bar would subsequentially turn to orange, red and it would flash more and more frequently. An example of user interface is shown in Figure 1(a). The other half of participants were given no suggestion about the purpose of the experiment and the timing block was not shown on their SERPs. We did not use the progress bar to prevent the participant estimate the duration based on the distance of progress bar. According to their findings, the coloration and flashing scheme adopted in our work would strengthen the time pressure during search process significantly.

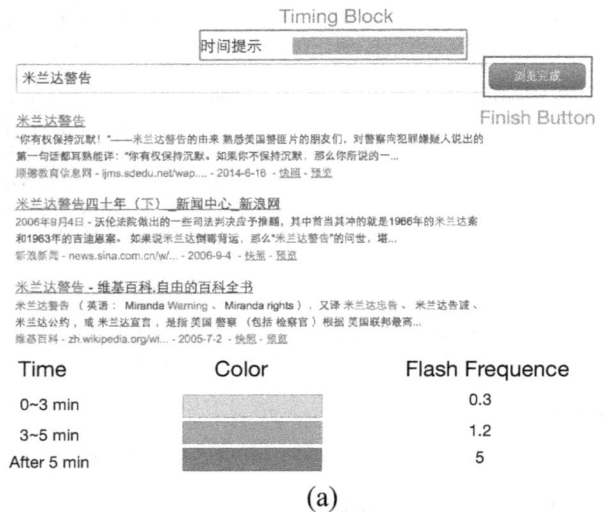

(a)

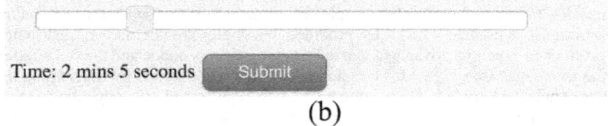

(b)

Figure 1: User interface for the treatment group (The length of the timeline is 10 mins because each task was expected to be finished in 10 mins, but not had to be finished in 10 mins)

Before the experiments began, we first asked the participants to take off their watches or other timing devices such as cellphones, tablets and music players. The clock on computer desktop was also removed. During the experiment, the participants were not allowed to acquire time from external environments. Then they were shown a video instruction of the experiments. The only difference in the instruction video between the treatment and control groups was the introduction to the timing block on SERPs. For both groups of participants, we had no time limit for the tasks. For each task, first the backstory was read to them via a voice element on the Web page. The backstory could be repeated for multiple times until the participant understood the intent. Then the participant could search for relevant information with the given query and corresponding SERP. He/she could finish the search by clicking the finish button on the SERP. After searching, the participant was required to estimate the time spent during the task in seconds, e.g., the duration of the whole search session as shown in Figure 1(b). Since they never knew how their perceived time varied from actual time, their ability of estimating time wouldn't improve. Then he/she was asked to answer the predefined question and annotate his/her satisfaction in five-point scale. After 6 tasks, he/she was asked to take a short break in case of fatigue. After the completion of all the tasks, an interview was performed to investigate their experience in the experiment.

We recruited 50 undergraduate students (23 females and 27 males) from a university. All of them reported that they were familiar with basic usage of search engines. For each participant, he/she was randomly assigned to the control/treatment group and required to finished 12 of the 16 tasks. We dynamically selected tasks for them to make sure all the tasks were finished in a balance way. A Latin-Square arrangement was used to minimize the order effects. All the interactions such as mouse clicks and mouse movements were recorded by the experimental system for further analysis. Each participant was compensated $20 USD.

3. RESULTS AND ANALYSIS

We first look into the average of objective dwell time (dtime) and perceived time (ptime) in both groups. Both dtime and ptime are the time spent during each task in seconds. The results in Figure 2 show that the average dwell time in treatment group is shorter ($p\text{-}value < 0.01$) than that in control group. A potential reason is that the participants in high TR environment would perceive more time pressure and spend less time processing individual information pieces [5].

The user perceived time (ptime) in the treatment group is significantly longer (10.36% with $p\text{-}value < 0.01$) than the dwell time while no significant difference is observed between dwell time and perceived time in the control group, which means that in high TR situation, human beings are more sensitive to the time effort and they attend to perceive longer durations than usual. This result also accords with previous psychological experiments in general settings [12].

We also compare the difference between average dwell time and user perceived time of each task in Figure 3. For 15 of the 16 tasks, the average perceived time in treatment group is longer than the average dwell time. While in the control group, the perceived time is very close to the dwell time. In both control group and treatment group,

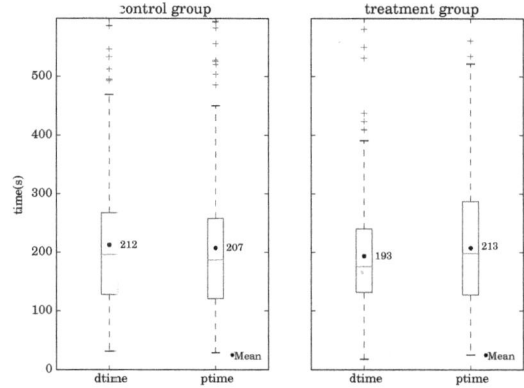

Figure 2: The comparison between average dtime and average ptime

the variance of dwell time and perceived time between users is very great, which means that the actual dwell time and perceive time on each task varies significantly across users and tasks.

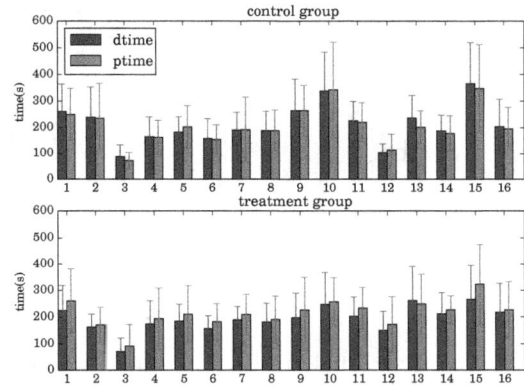

Figure 3: The comparison between dtime and ptime on each task

For each individual participant, we calculate the *average estimation offset* (AEO) on all the tasks finished by the participant. Figure 4 shows that there are more participants whose AEO are positive in the treatment group than in the control group. The difference of a user's time perception in different TR settings might be helpful for us to understand the ability and variability of the time perception. We would like to leave this problem in our future work.

$$AEO = \sum_{t \in tasks} \frac{ptime_t - dtime_t}{dtime_t} \qquad (1)$$

For each individual task, we count the number of users whose perceived times longer or shorter than dwell time in the control/treatment group. The results are represented in Figure 5. In the treatment group, for 14 of the 16 tasks, there are more users who have longer perceived time than dwell time. While in the control group, the participants in two conditions (dtime>ptime, dtime<ptime) follow a more balanced distribution.

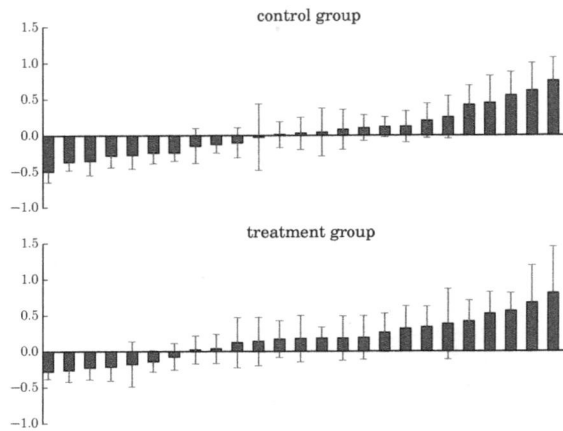

Figure 4: The Average Estimation Offset (AEO) of participants from control/treatment groups

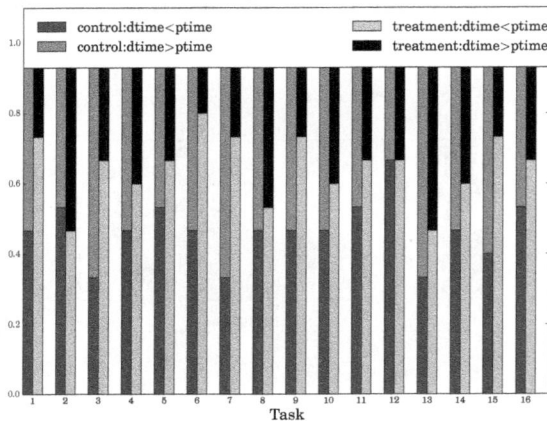

Figure 5: The distribution of users whose perceived times are longer/shorter than dwell times

Based on these results, we can conclude that the TR, e.g., the awareness of elapsed time, would have a significant effect on time perception in Web search environment. The users in high TR settings tend to perceive longer time than the participants in low TR settings. This finding may present a potential way to improve time based evaluation frameworks (such as TBG, etc.) by replacing the objective measured time with the user perceived time.

4. CONCLUSION AND FUTURE WORK

In this work, we investigate the impact of TR on users' time perception in Web search environment. Results showed that the participants who were in a high TR settings had longer perceived time than the ones in low TR settings, which accords with the previous findings in psychology, which means that we could make better inference of user experience by considering the temporal features of search tasks and the scenario the users involved in. In the future work, we plan to explore the relationship between TR, time perception and user satisfaction and improve the time-based measurements by incorporating the user perception information into existing frameworks.

5. ACKNOWLEDGMENTS

This work was supported by Tsinghua National Laboratory for Information Science and Technology (TNList) Cross-discipline Foundation, National Key Basic Research Program (2015CB358700) and Natural Science Foundation (61532011, 61472206) of China. Part of the work has been done at the Tsinghua-NUS NExT Search Centre, which is supported by the Singapore National Research Foundation & Interactive Digital Media R&D Program Office, MDA under research grant (WBS:R-252-300-001-490).

6. REFERENCES

[1] I. Arapakis, X. Bai, and B. B. Cambazoglu. Impact of response latency on user behavior in web search. In *Proceedings of the 37th international ACM SIGIR'14*, pages 103–112. ACM, 2014.

[2] P. Bailey, A. Moffat, F. Scholer, and P. Thomas. User variability and ir system evaluation. In *Proceedings of the 38th International ACM SIGIR'15*, pages 625–634, New York, NY, USA, 2015. ACM.

[3] C. L. A. Clarke and M. D. Smucker. Time well spent. In *Proceedings of the 5th Information Interaction in Context Symposium*, IIiX '14, pages 205–214, New York, NY, USA, 2014. ACM.

[4] A. Crescenzi, R. Capra, and J. Arguello. Time pressure, user satisfaction and task difficulty. *Proceedings of the American Society for Information Science and Technology*, 50(1):1–4, 2013.

[5] A. Crescenzi, D. Kelly, and L. Azzopardi. Time pressure and system delays in information search. In *SIGIR'15*.

[6] S. Fox, K. Karnawat, M. Mydland, S. Dumais, and T. White. Evaluating implicit measures to improve web search. *ACM Trans. Inf. Syst.*, 23(2):147–168, Apr. 2005.

[7] S. Grondin. Timing and time perception: a review of recent behavioral and neuroscience findings and theoretical directions. *Attention*, 2010.

[8] F. Macar, V. Pouthas, and W. J. Friedman. *Time, action and cognition: Towards bridging the gap*. Number 66. Springer Science & Business Media, 1992.

[9] N. Mishra, R. W. White, S. Ieong, and E. Horvitz. Time-critical search. In *Proceedings of the 37th International ACM SIGIR'14*, pages 747–756, New York, NY, USA, 2014. ACM.

[10] E. Pöppel. Lost in time: historical foundations and the 3-second-window of temporal integration. *Acta Neurobiol Exp (Wars)*, 64:295–301, 2004.

[11] M. D. Smucker and C. L. Clarke. Time-based calibration of effectiveness measures. In *Proceedings of the 35th International ACM SIGIR'12*, pages 95–104, New York, NY, USA, 2012. ACM.

[12] M. Sucala, B. Scheckner, and D. David. Psychological time: interval length judgments and subjective passage of time judgments. *Current psychology letters. Behaviour, brain & cognition*, 26(2, 2010), 2011.

[13] D. Zakay. *On prospective time estimation, temporal relevance and temporal uncertainty*. Springer, 1992.

Characterizing Users' Multi-Tasking Behavior in Web Search

Rishabh Mehrotra
Dept. of Computer Science
University College London
r.mehrotra@cs.ucl.ac.uk

Prasanta Bhattacharya
Dept. of Information Systems
National University of
Singapore
prasanta@comp.nus.edu.sg

Emine Yilmaz
Dept. of Computer Science
University College London
emine.yilmaz@ucl.ac.uk

ABSTRACT

Multi-tasking within a single online search sessions is an increasingly popular phenomenon. In this work, we quantify multi-tasking behavior of web search users. Using insights from large-scale search logs, we seek to characterize user groups and search sessions with a focus on multi-task sessions. Our findings show that dual-task sessions are more prevalent than single-task sessions in online search, and that over 50% of search sessions have more than 2 tasks. Further, we provide a method to categorize users into focused, multi-taskers or supertaskers depending on their level of task-multiplicity and show that the search effort expended by these users varies across the groups. The findings from this analysis provide useful insights about task-multiplicity in an online search environment and hold potential value for search engines that wish to personalize and support search experiences of users based on their task behavior.

CCS Concepts

•Information systems → Web mining; Task models;

Keywords

Task extraction, Task multiplicity, Web search interests, User types

1. INTRODUCTION

Search engine users' information needs tend to span a broad spectrum [4]. While simple needs, such as homepage finding, can mostly be satisfied via a single query, users may also issue a series of queries to collect, filter, and synthesize information from multiple sources to solve a task. Given the inherent diversity in information needs, users engage with search systems in varied ways. Further, and as a direct result of the increasingly complex informational environment around us, users are increasingly engaged in multitasking and information task switching behaviors. Multitasking is

CHIIR '16, March 13-17, 2016, Carrboro, NC, USA

© 2016 ACM. ISBN 978-1-4503-3751-9/16/03. . . $15.00

DOI: http://dx.doi.org/10.1145/2854946.2855006

the ability of humans to simultaneously handle the demands of multiple tasks through task switching [1, 5]. However, many interactive technologies do not provide effective support for managing multitasking behaviors of users.

Web search engines offer a typical environment where users perform multiple tasks across diverse contexts. For example, a programmer searching for solutions to a bug in his code, might take a brief hiatus to listen to some music. The two tasks described here need not be at the same level of importance for the user, nor must they be performed in parallel. While such situations are commonly observed in our daily search behavior, not much is understood about the kind of users who indulge in such multi-tasking behavior or even the extent or nature of such multi-tasking behavior in major search engines. This research gap stems mainly from the difficulty in identifying and quantifying multiple task completions from observational data. In the current study, we leverage search logs from a large-scale search engine to provide a detailed analysis of multi-tasking behavior for different user groups, and across multiple session sessions over a 30-day period. We seek to provide evidence that multi-tasking has emerged as a dominant characteristic of online search behavior and that users have varying propensities to indulge in such multi-tasking.

Different from existing studies on multi-tasking which have used topics of queries as proxies for tasks, we make use of an explicit search task extraction framework to extract the task information from web search sessions. This allows us to provide richer insights on the prevalence of task multiplicity in search sessions. Making use of real world search logs, we first quantify the extent of multi-tasking behavior in search sessions and show the existence of user groups based on multi-tasking behaviors. We go a step further in analyzing the user groups on a number of search interaction metrics and quantify the differences in these user groups based on how they interact with search systems. Our results motivate the need for designing search interfaces specifically catered to the needs and multi-tasking behavior of users.

2. RELATED WORK

Recent studies suggest that users' information search may have multiple goals or topics and occur within the broader context of their information-seeking behaviors [3]. Through an online survey, Wang *et al.* [9] show that 92% of the participants reported to have participated in online sessions where they accessed several sites, to perform between 2 to 8 tasks. In the context of web search sessions, most work on multi-tasking has been based on user studies [4, 7]. Other

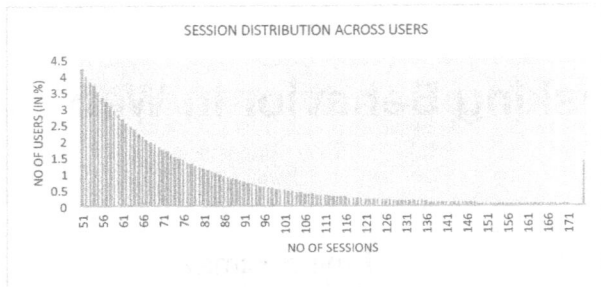

Figure 1: The variations of number of sessions per user across the user population.

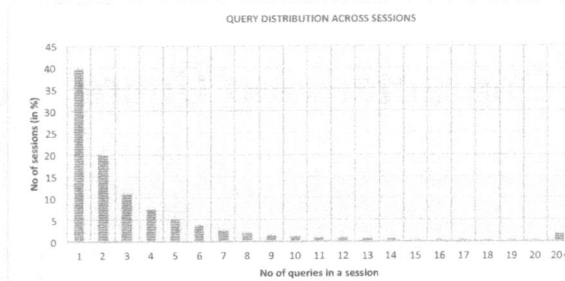

Figure 2: The variations of the number of queries across sessions.

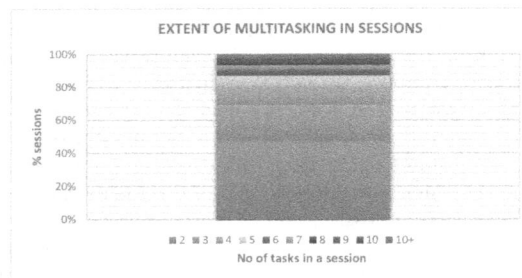

Figure 3: Quantifying the extent of multi-tasking in search sessions: .

studies do not explicitly refer to online multi-tasking, but provide useful insights. For instance, users access different sites during a session [2] and a large proportion of pages are visited more than once. In addition, the frequency at which a page is revisited differs depending on user habits and the type of website [2, 6], or in other words, the web tasks a user accomplishes on the site.

All these provide a strong evidence that multi-tasking during online sessions exists and depends on the web tasks. We depart from existing work that rely on using topics as a proxy to identify tasks by making use of an explicit task identification algorithm to identify users' search tasks. This approach enables us to provide estimates and qualitative insights on the extent of multi-tasking behavior in web search tasks.

3. CHARACTERISING TASK BEHAVIOR ACROSS SEARCH SESSIONS

In this study, we seek to characterize user behavior in online search sessions based on task specificity and multiplicity. While users generally perform a single task in a single search session, the task process might get interrupted by other competing tasks that become salient in the particular context. For example, a programmer attempting to search for bug solutions on the search engine, might choose to take a short break to listen to music from her favorite musician or band. The search session, in this case, would transform into a multi-task session. Given this backdrop, we contend that it is imperative for the search engine to understand the type of users who might be more prone to multi-tasking within a single session, and also the type of tasks that might be more susceptible to interleaving or interference by competing tasks. In the current study, We formulate the following 3 research questions, and offer preliminary evidence from a large scale observational dataset on search behavior to answer these questions.

RQ1: *Quantifying the Extent of Multi-tasking in Online Search Sessions.*: While it is well known that online search sessions often tend have interleaving of multiple tasks, but what has been largely ignored are the heterogeneities at a user level and/or a search session level. Specifically, we aim at quantifying, first, the prevalence of multi-tasking behavior in online search sessions (i.e. *how common is multi-tasking?*), and second, the extent of multi-tasking behavior in multi-task sessions (i.e. *how many tasks on average are there in multi-task search sessions?*).

RQ2: *Uncovering User-level Heterogeneities in Multi-tasking Behavior*: Through the current study, we also seek to uncover the presence of user-level idiosyncrasies in multi-tasking behavior in search sessions. Specifically, we attempt to understand the proportion of sessions per user that are single tasked vs. multi-tasked. Consequently, we seek to uncover any underlying categorizations among the users based on the extent of their multi-tasking behavior (i.e. *Can we identify and classify groups of users who demonstrate similar proportions of multi-tasking behavior?*. Uncovering such user groups would pave the way for the search engine to provide better personalized search assistance based on the group-level features and characteristics.

RQ3: *Characterizing Task Effort across User Groups*:The presence of competing or interfering tasks within a single session could accentuate or attenuate the search effort expended by the users. Specifically, we wish to understand the relationship between task multiplicity and total effort expended by the users (i.e. *do users who multitask more(less) expend more effort than users who multitask less(more)?*. In the context of the current study, we operationalize search effort using the query time, the average length of queries etc.

4. DATA CONTEXT

We use backend search logs for users of a major US-based search engine for a period of 30 days from May 1, 2015 to May 31, 2015 and choose a random sample of over 2 million users where each user is identified by a unique IP address. Over the 30-day period, the users participated in a total of over 200 million search sessions comprising one or more search queries, as illustrated in Fig. 2. We also observe that most users participate in 50 to 100 sessions in the 30-day period as clear from Fig. 1. We filter out inactive users from our dataset who participate in <50 sessions, and focus instead on the more active user population.

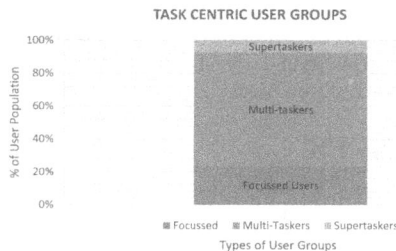

Figure 4: User groups based on multi-tasking behaviors.

User Type	Example Queries from a Typical Session
Focused User	"test guide.com", "CNA Practice Test", "CNA State Board Exam", "CNA Testing Schedule and Locations", "CNA State Board Practice Test", "CNA Practice Test 2014", CNA 50 Questions Test", "Free GED Practice Test 2014"
Multi-Tasking User	"Gravity FSX 2.0", "Full Suspension Mountain Bikes", "Walmart Cards", "Walmart Instant Card Application", "Gravity FSX 2.0 price", "full suspension bike sale"
Supertasking User	"hairstyles for women over 50", "thin wavy hairstyles for women", "facebook", "fb sign in", pulled pork crock pot recipe easy", "Slow-Roasted Pulled Pork", "barefoot contessa", "miley cyrus hair styles", "hairstyler.com"

Table 1: Example query sessions from different types of users.

5. EXPERIMENT SETUP

We next describe our experimental setup wherein we first extract search tasks from search logs and then proceed to analyze the multi-tasking behavior of searchers.

5.1 Task Extraction

Search tasks, comprising a series of search queries serving the same information need, have recently been recognized as an accurate atomic unit for modeling user search intent. For our analysis, we make use of the Latent Structural SVM framework [8] for task identification. Given query sequences within sessions, search tasks are identified by clustering queries into tasks by find the strongest link between a candidate query and queries in the target cluster (*bestlink*). This is achieved by making use of a structural learning method with latent variables, i.e., latent structural SVMs, to utilize the hidden structure of query inter-dependencies to explore the dependency among queries within the same task.

Given a query sequence $Q = q_1, q_2, ..., q_M$, a feature vector for the task partition y is specified by the hidden best-link structure h as $\psi(Q, y, h)$. Based on $\psi(Q, y, h)$, the bestlink SVM is a linear model parameterized by w, and predicts the task partition by,

$$(y*, h*) = argmax_{y,h} w^T \psi(Q, y, h) \qquad (1)$$

where Y and H represent the sets of possible structures of y and h respectively. $y*$ becomes the output for cross-session tasks and $h*$ is the inferred latent structure. A detailed overview of the approach can be found in Want *et al.* [8].

5.2 Analysis of Multi-task Search Behavior

Fig. 3 illustrates the prevalence and extent of multi-tasking behavior in our data. In our dataset, we find close to 90 million search sessions which have 2 or more completed tasks. Among these 90 million search sessions, there is a varied distribution of task multiplicity as described by Fig. 3. Specifically, we observe that while over 60% of the sessions have 2 or 3 tasks, about 20% of the sessions have 5 or more tasks. On an average, however, each user participates in 76 sessions in which she performs an average of 2 tasks.

Next, we look at the user-level heterogeneities in search sessions. Specifically, we categorize users based on the average number of tasks completed by the user across all sessions in the 30-day period. We observe that a sizable number of users (>20%) perform just a single task on average across their session history. We call such users *focused users*, as their search behavior is focused on a specific task, free from interference of competing tasks. On the other extreme, we also find a small group of users who perform 4 or more tasks on average across their session history. We call such users *supertaskers* who perform several tasks within a single session. We categorize all the other users as *multi-taskers* who completed between 2 and 3 tasks on average in their session history. The density of users across each of the three groups has been better depicted in Fig. 4. Interestingly, from Fig. 4, we observe that most users are not focused in their search behavior, and tend to complete at least 2 tasks within a session. This is not entirely unsurprising, given that one of the tasks could be the primary (e.g. search for solution to a programming bug on the Internet) or important task, while the others might be ancillary tasks (e.g. listen to music, check weather updates). Table 1 provides a list of sample queries executed by users across the three user groups.

Finally, we analyze search effort across the three user groups identified in the study. We characterize search effort using 4 different metrics viz. *(i) Time to First Click (TTFC), (ii) Time to Last Click (TTLC), (iii) Page Click Count (PCC), (i) Pagination Click Count (PgCC)*. The TTFC metric measures the time elapsed before the user clicks the first link on the query result page. A longer TTFC is an indication of user surprise or confusion with the search results, and hints at a more extensive cognitive elaboration process as the user decides which link to click on. The TTLC metric, on the other hand, measures the time elapsed before the user clicks the final link in her search session. The TTLC is a more direct measure of search effort expended by the user within a particular session. A higher TTLC could indicate that the user dissatisfaction with the early results provided by the query results, or a heightened motivation on part of the user to search more about the particular topic of interest.

The PCC metric measures the total number of clicks made by the user on the query result page, while the PgCC metric measures the number of times the search page was incremented or decremented by the users. Both these metrics are direct measures of the search intention of the user, and are hence good proxies to capture the different facets of search effort. We compute each of these metrics across each of the user groups as defined earlier, and highlight our findings in Figure 5.

Our analysis indicates that Supertasking users have a much higher TTFC and TTLC scores, but a lower PCC score than the Focused and Multi-Tasking groups. This supports our conjecture that most supertaskers perform multiple tasks in a master-slave fashion, where they focus bulk of their attention on a focal task, while being periodically distracted by ancillary tasks (e.g. music, weather updates). This periodic distraction causes a decrease in attention span on the focal

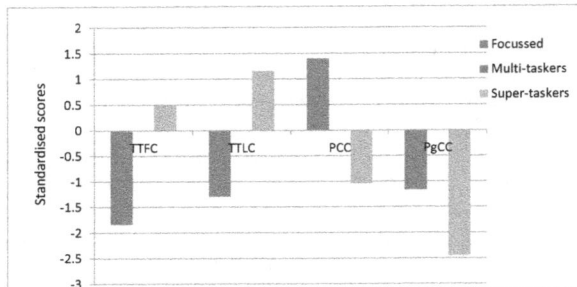

Figure 5: Differences in user groups quantified via effort based metrics. The scores reported are deviations from the Multi-taskers group which is held as baseline. All numbers are standard scores (Z-scores).

task, which is manifested by a decrease in click count, and an increase in click delays on the focal task. We do not, however, find any noticeable difference in the PgCC scores across the groups.

6. CONCLUSION AND FUTURE WORK

This study is among the first to analyze task behavior in web search sessions using large-scale and objective search logs. Specifically, we emphasize that, contrary to popular understanding, most users on search engines are multi-task users performing 2 or more tasks within a single search session. We also provide evidence of "Supertaskers" who perform onwards of 4 tasks within a single session. This widespread prevalence of task multiplicity makes it imperative for search engines to refocus their personalization and recommendation strategy towards a task-oriented view. For example, if search engines can fully identify and characterize the number and types of tasks performed by a given population of users on the engine, they could potentially optimize the session to better fit specific user- and task-based needs, while also making potential task-recommendations to reduce the search effort, as quantified in this paper.

Yet another finding we wish to highlight through our study is the characterizing of multiple tasks into a combination of a single primary and multiple ancillary tasks. Our task effort scores provide preliminary evidence to suggest that such categorization of multiple tasks into a task-hierarchy might indeed be plausible. Such insights are useful for search engines in that they could reduce task-transition delays and make design improvements to reduce cognitive loads in such multi-task sessions.

In future work, we wish to perform a deeper task-level analysis to uncover possible topical differences among tasks that occur frequently in multi-task sessions, versus those that occur frequently in single-task sessions (i.e. *Are tasks in single-task sessions qualitatively different than tasks prevalent in multi-task sessions?*). Understanding such task-level differences would provide a stepping stone towards understanding specific task-characteristics that might make it more or less susceptible to interference and/or distraction. Yet another direction of future work is about making more accurate task-predictions within a single search session, as well as across multiple sessions for a given user. With a steadily improving understanding of task and search behavior online, we envision a day when the search engine would be able to infer user-,task- as well as session- level characteristics based on just the first query issued by the user, and personalize the search experience accordingly.

7. REFERENCES

[1] M. A. Just, P. A. Carpenter, T. A. Keller, L. Emery, H. Zajac, and K. R. Thulborn. Interdependence of nonoverlapping cortical systems in dual cognitive tasks. *NeuroImage*, 14(2):417–426, 2001.

[2] R. Kumar and A. Tomkins. A characterization of online browsing behavior. In *Proceedings of the 19th international conference on World wide web*, pages 561–570. ACM, 2010.

[3] J. Lehmann, M. Lalmas, G. Dupret, and R. Baeza-Yates. Online multitasking and user engagement. In *Proceedings of the 22nd ACM international conference on Conference on information & knowledge management*, pages 519–528. ACM, 2013.

[4] C. Lucchese, S. Orlando, R. Perego, F. Silvestri, and G. Tolomei. Identifying task-based sessions in search engine query logs. In *Proceedings of the fourth ACM international conference on Web search and data mining*, pages 277–286. ACM, 2011.

[5] M. Miwa. User situations and multiple levels of user goals in information problem solving processes of askeric users. In *Proceedings of the ASIST Annual Meeting*, volume 38, pages 355–71. ERIC, 2001.

[6] H. Obendorf, H. Weinreich, E. Herder, and M. Mayer. Web page revisitation revisited: implications of a long-term click-stream study of browser usage. In *Proceedings of the SIGCHI conference on Human factors in computing systems*, pages 597–606. ACM, 2007.

[7] A. Spink, M. Park, B. J. Jansen, and J. Pedersen. Multitasking during web search sessions. *Information Processing & Management*, 42(1):264–275, 2006.

[8] H. Wang, Y. Song, M.-W. Chang, X. He, R. W. White, and W. Chu. Learning to extract cross-session search tasks. In *Proceedings of the 22nd international conference on World Wide Web*, pages 1353–1364. International World Wide Web Conferences Steering Committee, 2013.

[9] Q. Wang and H. Chang. Multitasking bar: prototype and evaluation of introducing the task concept into a browser. In *Proceedings of the SIGCHI Conference on Human Factors in Computing Systems*, pages 103–112. ACM, 2010.

Vapor Engine: Demonstrating an Early Prototype of a Language-Independent Search Engine for Speech

Douglas W. Oard,
Rashmi Sankepally
University of Maryland
College Park, MD USA
{oard|rashmi}@umd.edu

Jerome White
New York University
Abu Dhabi, UAE
jerome.white@nyu.edu

Craig Harman
Johns Hopkins HLTCOE
Baltimore, MD USA
craig@craigharman.net

ABSTRACT

Typical search engines for spoken content begin with some form of language-specific audio processing such as phonetic word recognition. Many languages, however, lack the language tuned preprocessing tools that are needed to create indexing terms for speech. One approach in such cases is to rely on repetition, detected using acoustic features, to find terms that might be worth indexing. Experiments have shown that this approach yields term sets that might be sufficient for some applications in both spoken term detection and ranked retrieval experiments. Such approaches currently work only with spoken queries, however, and only when the searcher is able to speak in a manner similar to that of the speakers in the collection. This demonstration paper proposes Vapor Engine, a new tool for selectively transcribing repeated terms that can be automatically detected from spoken content in any language. These transcribed terms could then be matched to queries formulated using written terms. Vapor Engine is early in development: it currently supports only single-term queries and has not yet having been formally evaluated. This paper introduces the interface and summarizes the challenges it seeks to address.

1. INTRODUCTION

The best present approach to searching naturally occurring spoken content is to tune the vocabulary, the pronunciation model, and the language model of a Large-Vocabulary Continuous Speech Recognition (LVCSR) system to generate terms using Automatic Speech Recognition (ASR) [10]. By recognizing words in the spoken content to be indexed, typed text queries become possible. This is an expensive process however, requiring thousands of US dollars in some cases for languages in which state-of-the-art LVCSR systems already exist. For languages for which no LVCSR systems exist—several thousand, worldwide—that cost can balloon by an order of magnitude or more. Given the expense, alternatives involving phonetic recognition have been developed. Phonetic recognition is less language-specific than

CHIIR '16, March 13–17, 2016, Carrboro, NC, USA

© 2016 Copyright held by the owner/author(s). Publication rights licensed to ACM.
ISBN 978-1-4503-3751-9/16/03. . . $15.00

DOI: http://dx.doi.org/10.1145/2854946.2854987

word recognition, but, because they operate with fewer constraints, phonetic recognizers suffer from low accuracy; and as the size of the phonetic inventory grows that accuracy degrades further. Going even further in the direction of language generality (although at some cost in the ability to generalize over speakers with dissimilar voices), a so-called zero-resource term discovery technique has been developed that is capable of using (approximate) acoustic repetition as a way of identifying indexing terms. Early work with this technique found roughly 50% term recall at a 10% false alarm rate. Recent work has found that, when sufficiently rich spoken queries are available, indexing terms generated in this way can also be useful as a basis for ranked retrieval. This paper describes an early prototype system for selectively transcribing some of those terms, which can then be used as single-term queries. This work is a first step toward the development of a fully functional system for interactive exploration of speech collections in languages for which no LVCSR systems are available.

We build on previously published work in which the "zero-resource spoken term detection" method for automatically detecting indexable terms based on acoustic repetition has been described [4]. In this paper, the focus is on the design of the collection exploration tool that we propose to demonstrate, which we call Vapor Engine. Vapor Engine is an interface for interactively examining, annotating, and using terms detected using zero-resource spoken term detection to explore a collection of recorded speech. The zero-resource spoken term detection runs as a batch process prior to indexing, building a mapping of terms to their respective recordings. Vapor Engine then presents the user with an interface for interactively browsing the term space and the recording (i.e., the "document") space, for replacing some term identifiers with readable strings, and for using those readable strings to facilitate selection of recordings that contain content that is of interest. The present version of Vapor Engine implements the following capabilities for interaction: a) a simple term cloud visualization of the terms detected in the collection as a whole, as well as in specific recordings; b) a facility to rapidly play a sequence of variants for a specific term and to manually annotate every occurrence of that term in the collection by making a single entry of a readable text representation for that term (which is similar in spirit to an approach that has been proposed to rapidly annotate clustered images [3]); and c) a primitive single-term query facility that displays a selectable list of recordings that contain any specified term.

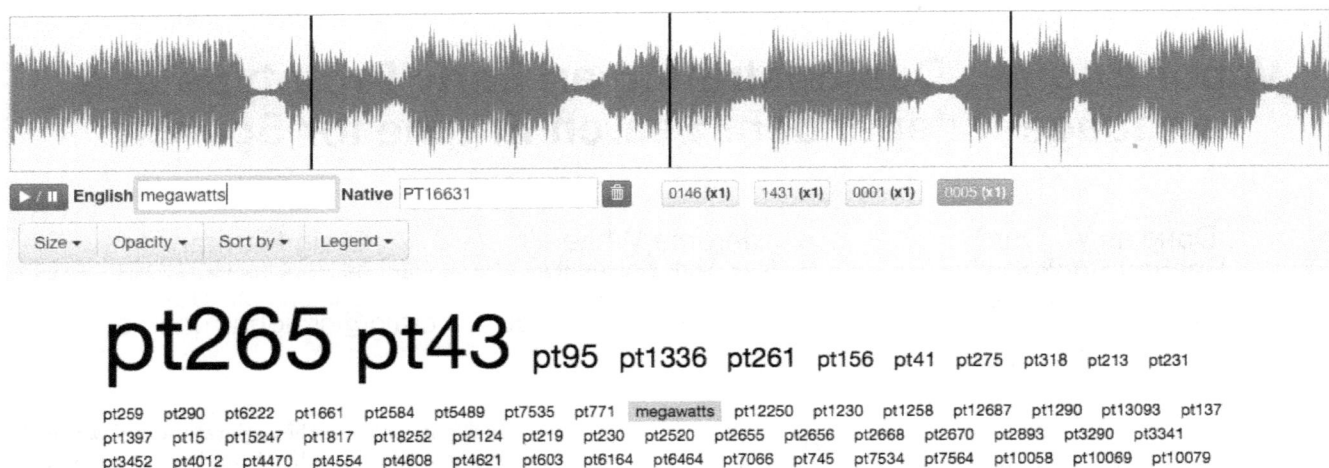

Figure 1: Vapor Engine word cloud view. Terms (indicated by the characters "PT" followed by a number), are presented at the bottom of the view. In this case, they are sized based on their frequency. Selecting a single term plays that term across all recordings in the corpus; the waveforms at the top of the view are each such instance. Terms can be renamed to something more linguistically familiar to the user. In this case, term "PT16631" was selected; there four instances of the term in the corpus. Playback revealed that it as the word "megawatt," so the term was renamed (English/Native below the waveform). In doing so, the term name is updated in every recording view where that term appears.

Vapor Engine is currently available on the Web.[1] That version indexes a freely redistributable collection of Enron phone calls in English [5]. We propose to demonstrate the system using that collection and two other licensed collections: a Gujarati collection from MediaEval for which ranked retrieval results have been reported [16], and the English Buckeye linguistics research collection from the Linguistic Data Consortium [14].

The remainder of this paper recaps how zero-resource spoken term detection works, reviews prior work on access to spoken content, describes the design of Vapor Engine and its principle use-case and outlines planned next steps.

2. ZERO RESOURCE TERM DISCOVERY

Zero-resource term discovery uses unsupervised learning to locate repeated units from digitized speech [6, 9, 13, 18]. Vapor Engine was designed, specifically, for the zero-resource spoken term discovery system developed by Dredze et al. [4]. Given a set of audio recordings, the system detects regions of similar speech patterns across those recordings. It assigns unique identifiers, or *terms*, to such sets of matching regions. The regions are identified by their acoustic patterns, as opposed to higher-level linguistic features, such as phonemes, syllables or words. Because of this, terms do not necessarily respect word boundaries; and their time occurrences can overlap. Indeed, it is not uncommon to have a single time point in a speech signal associated with dozens of terms. In an analogy with text, consider the terms 'periodicity,' 'period,' 'per,' 'city,' and 'it'; without spaces or other evidence, it might be wise to generate them all, which is essentially what zero-resource spoken term detection does.

Recorded speech can thus be represented as a set of terms that are found in this way. With appropriate attention to the temporal structure of term overlap, these terms can be indexed as a basis for retrieval [12, 16]. Vapor Engine, by

contrast, simply views each recording as a bag of terms, which it conventionally label as "PT" followed by a unique numeric identifier.

3. RELATED WORK

This review of related work focuses on interactive exploration of spoken content, mostly with an eye toward illustrating the rather basic state of Vapor Engine's present development. SCAN [17] is an interface for audio navigation that addresses common user deficiencies in perusing audio data. Specifically, it allows users to search content based text transcriptions, as well as hear summaries and read text. One of the key underlying contributions of the work is the concept of, "what you see is almost what you hear," in which audio summaries are formatted in ways that are commonly used only in textual representations—varying text size, for example, which do not have a one-to-one correspondence to raw audio. Such features are incorporated into Vapor Engine based on statistical analysis of zero-resource output.

SpeechLogger [2] is a tool for searching and browsing transcripts from speech recognition. The interface allows users to search transcripts, and quickly playback audio from corresponding hits. SpeechLogger was designed to offer good search experience irrespective of transcription quality; thus, a major focus of the work was on integration and presentation of various retrieval systems to the end user.

Ranjan et al. [15] attempt to improve audio transcription through a specialized audio browser. The browser presents a transcription of the audio to the user; the user can then click on various text segments to hear the corresponding audio. Part of what the authors wanted to study was whether such an interface could aid in search tasks, even when transcription was erroneous.

Abdulhamid and Marshall [1] use a modified treemap to display ordered segments of audio. Each segment presents its underlying audio as a word cloud, with text presented based on its frequency within the segment. Users can play

---
[1]http://vapor.umiacs.umd.edu

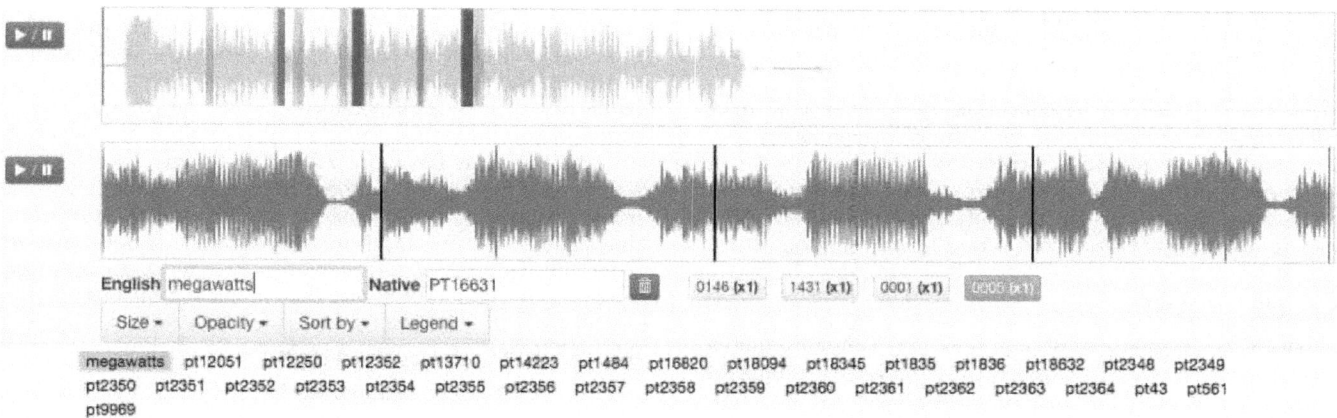

Figure 2: Vapor Engine recording view. The top-most waveform is the audio from the recording itself; the lower waveform is that of the selected term (in this case term "PT16631," renamed "megawatts."). Terms comprising the recording make up the lower portion of the screen, with the currently selected term highlighted.

audio from the segment while also seeing how that audio relates to the overall recording. The authors found that the use of word clouds as a presentation device aided in user topic selection; Vapor Engine takes a similar approach.

Each of the audio browsing methods relies on some transcription of underlying audio, a layer of processing that zero-resource systems do not provide. Thus, Vapor Engine can also be compared to interfaces specifically designed for audio transcription. Amazon Mechanical Turk has been a popular platform for transcription. Efforts over naturally occurring speech, such as what is studied in this work, include that of Novotney and Callison-Burch [11] for conversational speech, and Marge et al. [8] for meeting speech. Task organizers present segments of audio for workers to transcribe. This requires manual segmentation on the part of the organizer, along with a decision on how much audio to present versus the number of jobs to advertise. Presenting terms in this setting would likely be suboptimal due to the number produced, and their relationship to the underlying audio.

Luz et al. [7] turn the transcription task into a game. The primary focus of the game is to refine the output of speech recognition by allowing user corrections. Sentence-level transcription lattices are continuously presented to the user. The user's task is to select the correct word within portions of the lattice containing ambiguities. Because there are not always gold-standards for transcription, player scores are based on communal agreement. Thus, the game is similar to a crowdsourced task in which the incentive is non-monetary.

4. ARCHITECTURE

Vapor Engine is a term organization and display tool, capable of maintaining metadata about the terms themselves. It can be used by developers to enhance understanding of how zero-resource systems categorize matching regions of audio, or by searchers to explore a collection. Here we focus on that collection exploration use case. When started, Vapor Engine first builds a database of term information; most notably, each term's duration and recording association. Vapor Engine relies on having the original audio files analyzed by the zero-resource engine so that it can facilitate playback at arbitrary—term specific—points within each file. Vapor Engine also calculates document frequency for each term to build an understanding of how terms relate to each other.

5. PRESENTATION

At the top-level, Vapor Engine provides two corpus-level views: a word cloud, and a recording list. Each view allows a user to play a given term and alter the default name of the term. As will be discussed later, name alteration plays an important role in the utility of the system overall.

5.1 Collection View

The collection view presents a flat list of all terms; essentially a simple word cloud. By default, terms are initially listed alphabetically using a font size that is proportional to their collection frequency (i.e., the sum of the term frequency over all recordings); they can be re-sorted based on document frequency (i.e., the number of recordings in which a term occurs) if desired. Figure 1 shows the word cloud view sorted by document frequency.

Each term is presented as a link. By following the link, a subwindow is loaded with each occurrence of the term. Occurrences are displayed using their waveform, taken directly from the portion of the respective recording. In addition, each recording that contain the term appears as a link.

Users have the option to play all occurrences of a term in sequence. They can also annotate the label for a term to something more meaningful than the Vapor Engine default (which is PT followed by a unique identifier that is otherwise meaningless). An edit to the label for a term occurrence in any recording will be automatically reflected for the same term in all other recordings.

5.2 Recording View

The second view is the recording view (Figure 2). When the recording view is selected, Vapor Engine presents all recordings in the collection as a set of links. By following a link, users are taken to a page similar to that displayed in the collection view, but populated only with terms from the respective recording. The recording view has the same options for sorting and resizing terms as the collection view.

The recording view shows the entire recording as a light-red waveform with vertical indigo-colored lines that indicate the occurrence of terms. As the recording is played, the waveform turns red. When the indigo colored lines are encountered, all term occurrences to which it pertains are highlighted yellow.

As was the case in the collection view, when a term is selected, all instances of that term are displayed as a waveform and can be played. Further, all recordings in which the term appears are listed as hyperlinks, thus essentially providing a single-term query functionality. This allows the user to move between recordings that share common terms.

6. USE CASE

One of the primary uses envisioned for Vapor Engine is corpus exploration. To explore the hundreds of hours of audio that our present zero-resource spoken term detection system can index without Vapor Engine, users would have to randomly select portions for listening. Even then, without any easy way of seeing how different portions of the audio collection are related, that understanding would be fragmented at best.

Zero-resource term detection simplifies this task by linking similar content in different recordings and by essentially allowing efficient note-taking—any time content in one recording is understood, its meaning is noted in all recordings. Through this process, it is expected that users will build out regions in the collection that are well enough summarized by the relatively few manually labeled terms that have been heard to provide a basis for navigation between recordings. Such a summary will allow users to recognize when other recordings share several of the same terms and potentially even topics. Moreover, as users gain experience with the system, there is the possibility that they will develop a sense for what cues—collection frequency, document frequency, term duration, etc.—are useful guides to prioritizing their labeling effort.

Ultimately, we seek to help users maximize their ability to characterize the contents of a collection from the specific perspective(s) that interest them, for any given level of effort. We seek to support that in three ways: a) minimizing the users listening requirement; b) minimizing the users transcription effort; and c) streamlining the interface so that, for example, many instances of the same term can be played while labeling that term. Through creative management of terms, Vapor Engine allows users to focus on more cognitively demanding activities and be more efficient with their retrieval efforts.

7. CONCLUSION AND FUTURE WORK

About half the world's population speak a language for which no LVCSR system currently exists; and approximately one fifth of that half can speak and hear, but cannot read or write. For those users—10% of the world's population—zero-resource spoken term detection offers the promise of some degree of information access. In their raw form, however, zero-resource systems require some amount of effort to navigate. Vapor Engine is a means to lower the barrier of entry, improving the technologies' accessibility. This work presents an early prototype of Vapor Engine based on an actual working system. Much work remains, but the design of a tool for exploring spoken content using zero-resource term detection is no longer a blank slate. Going forward, it is imperative to learn whether users find Vapor Engine simple, intuitive, and effective in its present form—a usability

study is currently being conducting toward this end. The tool should also be extended to support multi-term queries using techniques that have been shown to be effective in batch experiments. Such multi-term queries require annotation of several terms, which in turn requires new ways of prioritizing terms for annotation; that is, methods beyond the sizing of terms by document frequency. Ultimately, that prioritization should be sensitive to factors such as overlap that could minimize duplicate effort, and to factors such as co-occurrence with already-annotated terms that could foster the construction of highly discriminating queries.

8. ACKNOWLEDGMENTS

This work has been supported in part by NSF 1218159.

References

[1] F. Abdulhamid and S. Marshall. Treemaps to visualise and navigate speech audio. In *OZCHI*, 2013.

[2] L. Begeja et al. A system for searching and browsing spoken communications. In *NAACL-HLT*, 2004.

[3] J. Cui et al. Easyalbum: an interactive photo annotation system based on face clustering and re-ranking. In *CHI*, 2007.

[4] M. Dredze et al. NLP on spoken documents without ASR. In *EMNLP*, 2010.

[5] J. Goldstein et al. Annotating subsets of the enron email corpus. In *CEAS*, 2006.

[6] A. Jansen and B. Van Durme. Efficient spoken term discovery using randomized algorithms. In *ASRU*, 2011.

[7] S. Luz et al. Supporting collaborative transcription of recorded speech with a 3D game interface. In *KES*, 2010.

[8] M. Marge et al. Using the Amazon Mechanical Turk to transcribe and annotate meeting speech for extractive summarization. In *NAACL-HLT*, 2010.

[9] A. Muscariello et al. Unsupervised motif acquisition in speech via seeded discovery and template matching combination. In *ICASSP*, 2012.

[10] K. Ng. *Subword-Based Approaches for Spoken Document Retrieval*. PhD thesis, MIT, 1990.

[11] S. Novotney and C. Callison-Burch. Cheap, fast and good enough: Automatic speech recognition with non-expert transcription. In *NAACL-HLT*, 2010.

[12] D. Oard et al. The FIRE 2013 question answering for the spoken web task. In *FIRE*, 2013.

[13] A. Park and J. Glass. Unsupervised pattern discovery in speech. In *ICASSP*, 2008.

[14] M. A. Pitt et al. The Buckeye corpus of conversational speech: Labeling conventions and a test of transcriber reliability. *Speech Communication*, 2005.

[15] A. Ranjan et al. Searching in audio: the utility of transcripts, dichotic presentation, and time-compression. In *CHI*, 2006.

[16] J. White et al. Using zero-resource spoken term discovery for ranked retrieval. In *NAACL-HLT*, 2015.

[17] S. Whittaker et al. SCAN: Designing and evaluating user interfaces to support retrieval from speech archives. In *SIGIR*, 1999.

[18] Y. Zhang and J. Glass. Towards multi-speaker unsupervised speech pattern discovery. In *ICASSP*, 2010.

On Identifying the Bounds of an Internet Resource

Faryaneh Poursardar and Frank Shipman

Computer Science and Engineering

Texas A&M University

College Station, TX 77843-3112

1-979-862-3216

{faryaneh,shipman}@tamu.edu

ABSTRACT

Systems for retrieving or archiving Internet resources often assume a URI acts as a delimiter for the resource. But there are many situations where Internet resources do not have a one-to-one mapping with URIs. For URIs that point to the first page of a document that has been broken up over multiple pages, users are likely to consider the whole article as the resource, even though it is spread across multiple URIs. Comments, tags, ratings, and advertising might or might not be perceived as part of the resource whether they are retrieved as part of the primary URI or accessed via a link. Similarly, whether content accessible via links, tabs, or other navigation available at the primary URI is perceived as part of the resource may depend on the design of the website. We are examining what people believe are the bounds of Internet resources with the hope of informing systems that better match user perceptions. To understand this challenge we explore a situation where the user is assumed to have identified a resource by a URI, particularly for archiving. To begin to answer these questions, we asked 110 participants how desirable it would be for web contents related to an identified archived resource to also be archived. Results indicate that the features important to this decision likely vary considerably from resource to resource.

CCS Concepts

• Applied computing→Digital libraries and archives • Information systems→Web searching and information discovery; Information retrieval.

Keywords

Resource identification; digital preservation; web archiving

1. INTRODUCTION

We live a world in which information is expected to be always at hand. Search engines and archiving tools mediate access to much of the content available on the Internet. Whether indexing the contents to enable search or determining what contents need to be saved for archiving, systems need an accurate model of what content is and is not part of a resource.

Misidentification of resource boundaries results in false positives in search results when components of a web page unrelated to the main resource (e.g. advertising, off-topic comments) are indexed

with the resource. But it also affects users through false negatives that occur when the contents of a resource are spread across multiple web pages. Figure 1 shows the first page of a news article spread across multiple URIs. Without understanding what is part of the article, what is advertising, and what is site-oriented navigation, systems will incorrectly index or archive such resources.

Our work explores the question of how users perceive the bounds of Internet resources. We do this in the context of archiving, where it is more straightforward to ask users about what is and is not part of a resource. The next section further discusses archiving Internet resources how the bounds of resources can be challenging to define. After this we describe a pilot study and its findings. This leads to a discussion of implications and future work.

2. WHAT IS AN INTERNET RESOURCE?

When we point to a resource, we expect that resource to be available as a whole. But what does it mean to be whole? When

Figure 1. First page of a multi-page article on the Web. Systems need to determine if the website navigation components, advertisements, related articles, and story pages 2 and 3 are part of the resource being indexed or archived.

people point to the main page of a web site, do they expect the site as a whole to remain available? When pointing to an item on Amazon, should all the comments and ratings also be available? In contexts where the receiver has access to the Internet and where the resource is from a reliable provider, there is no issue. But when the reference is being used to either create a temporary offline version of the resource or to create a copy for long-term archiving [16], the question of which content is expected to be part of the resource becomes a central consideration.

The answers to the above questions are complicated by the fact that the content visible on web pages is rarely fetched through a single http request. Web pages include frames and other methods for generating a page based on a variety of static and dynamic content. This content takes the form of links to external web pages, audio, video, advertisements based on user interest, comments, tags, likes, etc. When people refer to the web page as a resource, it is unclear how many of these components they are identifying as part of the resource. Also, it is dependent on the particular situation; most reuse contexts would not require the same advertising so be shown beside a news story with embedded images and video but there are contexts where this would matter. It might be the juxtaposition that was being preserved – such as recording the perceived irony of an advertisement for vacations in Florida appearing next to a story about a Florida hurricane.

Beyond the question of how much of a visible page is expected to be part of a referenced resource there can be expectations for related content. A reference to the first page of an article on the Web may well be expected to include the content for the remaining pages of the article. Similarly, navigation bars on web pages can be designed to imply a page is composed of content separated into components available through tabs even though they are retrieved through independent URIs. Some references to the resource might expect to include the content on these tabs even though they are not visible when going to the initial URI.

How can systems identify, or at least estimate, the boundaries of a resource automatically? To help answer this question we performed a pilot study asking people about the value of related content in the context of an archive. Before discussing the study we describe work from the archiving community that relates to these issues.

2.1 Related Work

Information on the Web becomes a thing to be addressed, linked to, organized and placed into larger contexts. But Fetterly et al. [2] estimates that about two percent of the Web disappears from its current location every week. To have access to the content of these missing pages, Internet Archive (IA) [7] and other institutions save materials to preserve their availability. But such sites are limited in what they can capture due to limits in their capacity, legal rights, and access to the original content. On the other hand, Web sites and services are not static: a service can be shut down or an account can became inactive. Indeed, loss on the Web has been attributed to many sources other than technology failure [10].

Missing information on the web is often not lost completely; it can be moved from one URI to another for a number of reasons [14]. Phelps and Wilensky [15] and Dalel et al. [1] investigated the effectiveness of saving identifying search terms and phrases respectively for relocation. In [8], Klein and Nelson examine four retrieval methods for discovering missing web pages: 1. lexical signatures, 2. page titles, 3. social bookmarking tags, and 4. link neighborhood lexical signatures (LNLS). Preserving features of resources is part of the solution to their relocation. Once identifying features are discovered, there remains alternative methods for effectively using those features. The Warrick system restores lost resources by crawling web repository crawlers [13]. All of these systems make assumptions about what is and what is not within a particular internet resource. Our work aims to revisit these assumptions.

Others have pointed out much that is on the Web does not behave like a traditional information resource. Harper et al. [6] points to social media as things that one might wish to download or otherwise act upon, but that do not support the simple range of actions normally associated with files. One cannot, for example, simply save a status update as a standalone object, or copy a photo that integrates the social metadata that is associated with it. Harper et al. suggest new actions are needed, which better enable users to act upon, and thus feel in control of, their online content. They suggest that such actions are essential if users are to have a greater sense of control, and ability to manage, digital content in a socially-networked world. Variations in perceptions of what is and is not part of a resource also influence how people react to scenarios of archiving and reusing social media content [11,12]. While the ambiguity of resource bounds is more obvious in social media, we explore this question with more traditional internet resources, resources that we have known are somewhat more fluid [9] than paper based resources but that archives still tend to treat as relatively fixed.

3. STUDY APPROACH AND METHOD

A study was performed to identify patterns in user expectations and desires when archiving resources. We asked 110 participants to indicate the value of archiving a second page when archiving an initial page. The pages were selected with an eye towards features likely to be part of an automatic approach to identifying resource bounds. Before describing the study method, we first provide some background regarding the context in which we are asking these questions.

3.1 PathCompiler

As part of the Walden's Paths project, we developed a tool that enables users to archive Internet resources, called *PathCompiler* [5]. PathCompiler was originally developed to let a variety of users "freeze" a set of web pages for later use by others. This was a simple first approach for coping with change to resources [3,4]. When users point to a resource by its URI, PathCompiler saves all necessary content of a web page on the local machine along with the context necessary in order to show the Web pages off-line. Since the modern Internet is not just static pages, but is full of multimedia materials, pictures and scripts, PathCompiler traverses the links within a page to retrieve embedded content.

Upon initial use, it became clear that when users pointed to a resource via a URI they might mean only that page but often times they mean to provide access to a set of pages. Because of the challenge of identifying the bounds of a resource, a feature was added to [PathCompiler to capture content at a number of links away from the original URI. But this approach is not efficient – the amount of network traffic and storage required is a function of the number of links on a page raised to the power of the chosen maximum link distance. If there are on average 30 links on a page and the distance selected is 2, there are on the

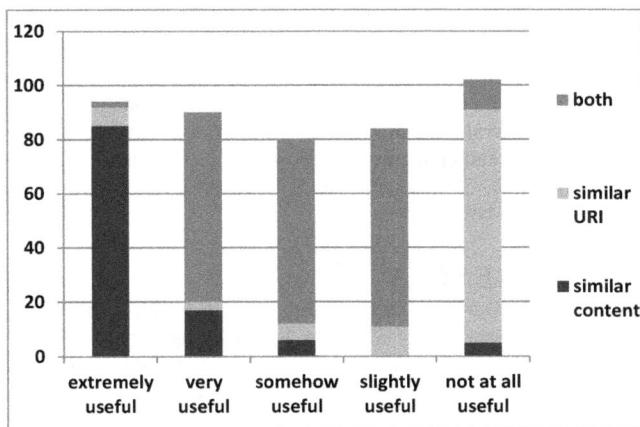

a.) Health topic results

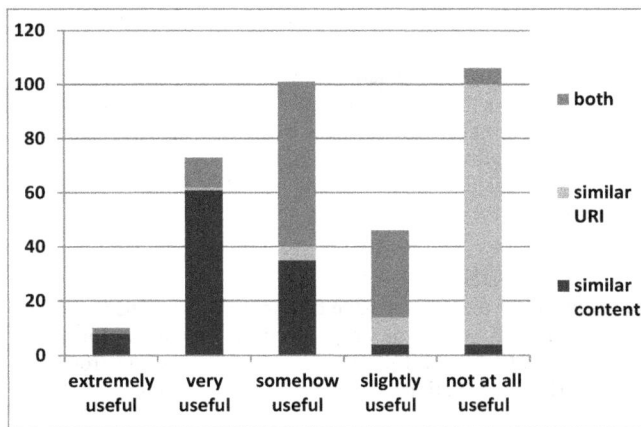

b.) Business topic results

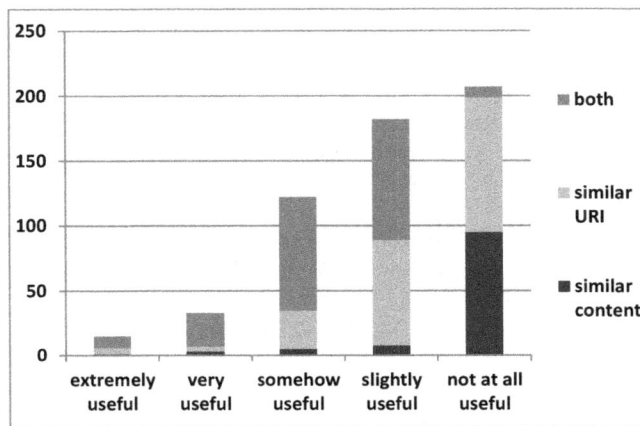

c.) Technology topic results

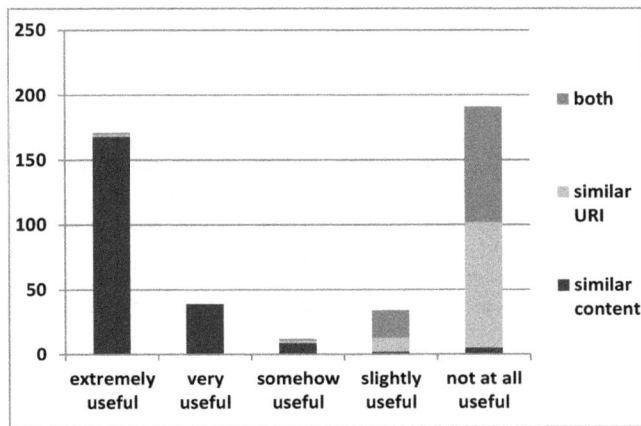

d.) Daily news topic results

Figure 2. Distribution of ratings for each topic shows variation but that similar content is more important than similar URI.

order of 900 additional resources being archived for each original resource.

Thus, PathCompiler needs techniques to determine what are the likely bounds for a resource. The following heuristics were considered for archiving resources existing in a web page: 1) Save linked materials that have content similar to the originally referenced resource, 2) Save links that have URIs similar to the referenced resource, and 3) Save links which have both similar content and similar URIs.

3.2 Study Method

The study involved the development of a corpus of initial Internet resources and content potentially related to or part of those resources and the assessment of pairs of the initial resource and potentially-related pages by participants.

Corpus Development. For the purpose of this pilot study, we developed a corpus of four groups of web resources in subjects shown in Table 1. All selected Internet resources were in English. Using PathCompiler we crawled each original source page (the Base URI in Table 1) to extract all the links in the page. The contents of these linked pages constituted the corpus of potentially co-archived pages for assessment for that resource. Each of these pages was then categorized as being either similar in content or not and similar in URI or not. The cosine similarity

of the term vectors for the original resource and the linked page (with a threshold of 0.7) was used to categorize them as having similar content or not. Resources from the same web site (same root URI) were considered to have similar URIs. Better techniques could be used for both classifications but initial results with these simple techniques could indicate where such effort should be spent.

Table 1. Original primary web page resources

Subject	Base URI
Technology	http://www.economist.com/news/science-and-technology/21573089-ambitious-project-map-brain-works-possibly-too-ambitious-hard
Daily news	http://shine.yahoo.com/love-sex/teenage-sweethearts-prove-it-s-never-too-late-as-they-and-reunite-and-marry-in-their-70s-163409359.htm
Health	http://www.naturalnews.com/033414_cancer_cures documentary.html
Business	http://www.economist.com/news/briefing//21574489-britain-has-many-options-providing-extra-airport-capacity-its-capital-going-need

Participant Selection. Our one hundred and ten (110) participants were identified among friends, neighbors, family members, friends of friends, etc. Participants ranged in age from 26 to 70 and had a wide range of educational levels.

Participant Tasks. Each of the participants assessed 16 page pairs. For each pair, participants were simultaneously shown the primary resource and the potentially valuable content. They were asked to rate on a 5-point Likert scale the value in archiving the second page. In total, 1760 web page pairs were assessed which is the sum of all ratings shown in Figure 2. Participants were not shown anything other than pair pages, no URLs and no data about how the pages were related.

4. FINDINGS

The results show that people have different expectations based on what the original content is and how it is presented. Figure 2 shows the results for the four data sets. As is apparent from the highly varied distributions, each topic had a unique outcome. Where the health topic (figure 2a) had a relatively flat distribution of assessments across the five ratings, the technology topic distribution was heavily skewed to the negative (very few pages were viewed as part of the resource) and the daily news topic was classically bimodal with nearly all pages rated at the extremes.

The data in Figure 2 also shows which features correlated with high ratings vary across the four topic areas. While the highest rated content for the daily news group was overwhelmingly similar content from other servers, the ratings of the health and business topics were comparable among the pages with similar content on other servers and similar content from the same server (although in both cases the content from the same server was rated as slightly less valuable). For the technology topic, there was a strong preference for materials that were from the same server.

Overall, the results show that while there was a relatively strong overall preference in preserving similar content, whether the URI of that content mattered varied across the four data sets. The primary lesson for those developing systems that preserve web-based resources from this study is that there is no simple answer to what is related to a resource.

5. DISCUSSION AND CONCLUSIONS

What might be going on? One answer is that participants intermixed information value assessments with their ratings of expectations of having the content available – and this was exacerbated by the imprecise wording of the Likert-scale statement in the pilot study. The second answer is that the features that make a difference in whether people expect to have access to content are more nuanced than simply having similar content or a similar URI.

The results of this pilot study show that content similarity is likely a viable feature for systems when deciding the bounds of a resource. The results also show that further study is needed to help design techniques to automatically identify the bounds of a resource.

Based on these preliminary results, we are in the process of generating a corpus to evaluate a broader set of features used to compare pages and to design a more rigorous assessment concerning the perception of resource bounds. The results of this work will better answer what it takes to save copies of resources and also indicate what content needs to be considered when assessing resource change.

While our focus has been on identifying the bounds of a resource for the purposes of archiving, the results of such investigations have broader implications. Search engines and recommender systems also benefit from more accurate assessments regarding Internet resource boundaries due to potential improvements to the content used when developing the indexes and content models used for retrieval. We hope this pilot study leads to greater interest in the dual challenges of determining what users perceive as the bounds of resources and techniques for systems to determine such bounds.

6. REFERENCES

[1] Dalal, Z., Dash, S., Dave, P., Francisco-Revilla, L., Furuta, F., Karadkar, U., and Shipman, F. Managing distributed collections: evaluating web page changes, movement, and replacement, *Proc. JCDL 2004*, pp. 160-168.

[2] Fetterly, D., Manasse, M., Najork, M., and Wiener J. A large-scale study of the evolution of web pages. *Proc. WWW.* 2003. pp. 669-678.

[3] Francisco-Revilla, L., Shipman, F., Furuta, R., Karadkar, U., and Arora, A. Managing change on the web, *Proc. JCDL 2001*, 67-76

[4] Francisco-Revilla, L., Shipman, F., Furuta, F., Karadkar, U., and Arora, A. Perception of content, structure, and presentation changes in Web-based hypertext. *Proc. HT 2001*, 205-214.

[5] Furuta, R., Shipman, F., Marshall, C., Brenner, D. and Hsieh, H. Hypertext paths and the World-Wide Web: experiences with Walden's Paths, *Proc. HT 1997*, 167-176.

[6] Harper, R., Lindley, S., Thereska, E., Banks, R., Gosset, P., Smyth, G., Odom, W., Whitworth, E. What is a File? *Proc. CSCW.* 2013. pp. 1125-1136.

[7] Jaffe, E., Kirkpatrick, S. Architecture of the Internet Archive. *Proc. SYSTOR 2009.* Article No. 11.

[8] Klein, M. and Nelson, M. Moved but not gone: an evaluation of real-time methods for discovering replacement web pages. *Int. J. on Digital Libraries*, 2014. 14(1-2): pp. 17-38.

[9] Levy, D. Fixed or fluid?: document stability and new media. *Proc. ECHT 1994*, pp. 4-31.

[10] Marshall, C.C., Rethinking personal digital archiving, Part 1: Four challenges from the field. *D-Lib Magazine*, 2008. 14(3): pp. 2.

[11] Marshall, C.C., Bly, S., and Brun-Cottan, F. The long term fate of our digital belongings: Toward a service model for personal archives. *Proc. of Archiving.* 2006. ASIST. pp. 25-30.

[12] Marshall, C.C., McCown, F., and Nelson, M. Evaluating personal archiving strategies for Internet-based information. *Proc. of Archiving.* 2007. ASIST. pp. 151-156.

[13] McCown, F., Marshall, C.C., and Nelson, M. Why Web Sites Are Lost (and How They're Sometimes Found). *Communications of the ACM*, 2009. 52(11): pp. 141-145.

[14] Meneses, L., Furuta, R., and Shipman, F. Identifying "Soft 404" error pages: analyzing the lexical signatures of documents in distributed collections, *Proc. of TPDL*, 2012, Springer. pp. 197-208.

[15] Phelps, T.A. and Wilensky, R. Robust hyperlinks and locations. *D-Lib Magazine*, 2000. 6(7/8): pp. 1082-9873.

[16] Toyoda, M. and Kitsuregawa, M. The History of Web Archiving. *Proc. of the IEEE*, 2012. 100, 1441-1443.

Video Test Collection with Graded Relevance Assessments

Weng Qiying
University of Strathclyde
Department of Computer and
Information Sciences
Glasgow, United Kingdom.
weng-qiying.2014@uni.strath.ac.uk

Martin Halvey
University of Strathclyde
Department of Computer and
Information Sciences
Glasgow, United Kingdom.
martin.halvey@strath.ac.uk

Robert Villa
University of Sheffield
Information School
Sheffield, United Kingdom.
r.villa@sheffield.ac.uk

ABSTRACT

Relevance is a complex, but core, concept within the field of Information Retrieval. In order to allow system comparisons the many factors that influence relevance are often discarded to allow abstraction to a single score relating to relevance. This means that a great wealth of information is often discarded. In this paper we outline the creation of a video test collection with graded relevance assessments, to the best of our knowledge the first example of such a test collection for video retrieval. To directly address the shortcoming above we also gathered behavioural and perceptual data from assessors during the assessment process. All of this information along with judgements are available for download. Our intention is to allow other researchers to supplement the judgements to help create an adaptive test collection which contains supplementary information rather than a completely static collection with binary judgements.

CCS Concepts

• **Information systems~Test collections** • **Information systems~Relevance assessment**

Keywords

Video; Variable; Graded; Relevance; Assessment; Test Collection.

1. INTRODUCTION

Judgment of relevance is a heavily studied topic within Information Retrieval. Relevance judgment is important to both the search process itself [14], and in the creation of test collections [3; 12]. With regard to the latter, there is a considerable body of work which has investigated the criteria assessors use to judge relevance for the creation of test collections [3; 12]. However the generation of test collections is not without its drawbacks. On one hand, when generating relevance assessments for test collections, the behavior of assessors is not normally considered as important [8], beyond the overall time taken to create a set of relevance judgments [12; 16]. Given the importance of relevance assessment to the information seeking process, the relative lack of research studying assessors is perhaps surprising. On the other hand, often by necessity, relevance assessments are reduced down to a binary decision which ignores the many facets of relevance [11]. There are some exceptions to

CHIIR '16, March 13-17, 2016, Carrboro, NC, USA © 2016 ACM.
ISBN 978-1-4503-3751-9/16/03...$15.00
DOI: http://dx.doi.org/10.1145/2854946.2854980

this. TREC HARD considered multiple levels of relevance in their assessments [1]. Whilst in the area of image retrieval, previous ImageCLEF tasks have considered the variance within tasks [4; 5]. Although these initiatives have gone some of the way to addressing this shortcoming for text and image retrieval to the best of our knowledge there has been no such effort for video retrieval. Thus in this paper we attempt to address the issue of a lack of details on the creation assessments and provide a test collection with variable levels of relevance assessment for video retrieval, this is addressed in our 2 research objectives:

1. Create a video test collection with graded relevance assessments
2. To capture behavioural and perceptual information about the judgment process to augment the judgments.

In relation to the second objective, all data captured as part of the judgment process described in this paper is available for download (http://dx.doi.org/10.15129/7f16e19f-794a-4cd5-a9d7-caba4e2bcf2a). It is hoped this repository will not be a static resource, but rather we welcome other researchers to download and use this resource, which will be updated with future results from future evaluations of others. The remainder of this paper is organised as follows. In the next section we describe the corpus used for evaluation. We follow this with a description of the topics used for assessment. We follow this with an outline of the judgement process and information gathered. Finally we provide a conclusion section.

2. CORPUS

The British Universities Film and Video Council Roundabout Collection (http://bufvc.ac.uk/newsonscreen/roundabout) was used as a corpus. This collection contains a total of 660 videos showcasing Britain and Asia during the 1960s to the late 1970s. The videos have a mixed time duration, from about 44 secs up to about 10 minutes in duration. The videos are categorised based on their topics and each video contains additional metadata including a title, keywords, location, date and summary (see Table 1).

3. TOPICS

To identify topics all of the text from all of the documents was downloaded and placed into a tag cloud (see Figure 1) to visualise commonly occurring words and themes. This resulted in an initial list of 17 topics. To help narrow down the topics we created HITs on CrowdFlower which required users to create search terms. We wanted to see how diverse the range of search terms would be. After discussion of the topics amongst the research team and also analysis of the search terms returned, a final list of 10 topics was decided upon, those topics (and descriptions are):

1. Manufacturing in Britain: Identify products that Britain was manufacturing during the 1960s and 70s

2. Outdoor Water Activities: Identify water sports well-known to the world or equipment used for the water sports
3. South East Asia Country Development: Identify countries in South East Asia and their development in areas of either education, industry, agriculture or society in the 1960s and 70s
4. British Exhibitions: Identify famous exhibitions you can see in Britain (including Scotland, England and Wales)
5. Asian Culture Events: Identify events, festivals or cultural exchanges between Asia and Britain
6. Industrial Research: Identify industries in Britain that have students studying and learning, Industrial experts investigating their industry through site visits can also be included.
7. Aviation Display: Identify demonstrations and events associated with aircraft.
8. Educational Visit for Children: Identify events where children or students visit other countries or take part in educational events such as learning new skills and supporting educational campaigns.
9. Transport for People: Identify the modes of transport commonly used by people in Asia and Britain.
10. Military Events: Identify well-known military ceremonies or events in Britain.

Table 1: Example of metadata provided for each video.

ID	327511
URL	http://bufvc.ac.uk/newsonscreen/search/index.php/story/327511
Start Time	17
End Time	166
Title	Treble One Squadron
Series Name	Roundabout
Issue No.	1
Date Released	May-62
Story within the issue	01-Mar
Summary	COI synopsis: Treble One Squadron, famous aerobatic unit of the Royal Air Force making its last public appearance before reconstituting as a fighter unit, in a breathtaking display of precision flying.
Keywords	Displays; Aviation; Air force
COI Ref	MI 1072/1

Figure 1: Tag cloud describing metadata from Roundabout Collection.

4. JUDGEMENT PROCESS

4.1 Procedure

Gathering assessments involved two stages. The first stage involved collecting search terms and the second involved collecting relevance assessments. For the first stage each participant was sent an online form. This form contained each of the search topics, for each topic the participants were asked to provide 4 queries that they would use to satisfy the information need exemplified in the topic. The participants were also asked to rate the perceived the difficulty of the topic on a 5 point scale.

In the second stage participants were assigned to groups. Each group was given a set of 2 topics and for each topic had to provide a relevance assessment for the top 5 ranked videos (see next section for explanation of ranking). Each set of relevance assessments was collected individually in our lab. The participants were asked to rate the relevance of each video on a four point scale. A four point scale has previously been proposed for gathering relevance assessments [9]. For our scale we used the 3 options from the TREC HARD track, namely not relevant, partially relevant and highly relevant. We also gave the participants the option to say that they are not sure.

After each judgment the participants were presented with a questionnaire. This questionnaire asked questions about effort which are inspired by the NASA TLX [7], which has previously been used to measure effort for both TREC HARD [15] and ImageCLEF [6]. Following the procedure of Kelly and Azzopardi [10] we used a 7 point Likert scale for our questions rather than the standard TLX scale. We also removed the question about performance, as this question reverses the scale. After each topic we also asked participants to judge their knowledge of the topic and how interesting the topic was on a 7 point Likert scale. An additional benefit of gathering this information is that it allows us to make some comparisons between the effort involved in making those assessments for video retrieval with the effort for text [15] and image [6] assessment.

4.2 Ranking Videos

To rank the videos we used the search terms gathered in the first part of the assessment. Each search query was used to rank the documents using TFIDF (based on the metadata associated with each video), the each document in top 10 documents of each rank was assigned a score from 10 for top rank down to 1 for 10th rank. These scores was aggregated across all queries and the videos with the 5 highest scores were used for assessment. The variance in search terms gathered in the first stage of the assessment insures a variance in returned videos. In this way we simulate the pooling that normally occurs when creating a test collection [13].

4.3 Participants

In total 20 participants were recruited as assessors. 12 male and 8 female, with an average age of 30. 10 were International students studying at the University of Strathclyde, 8 workers, 1 self-employed and 1 homemaker. For stage 1, a total of 80 distinct search terms were contribute by the participants across all 10 topics. For stage 2, a total of 50 videos were judged across all 10 topics, resulting in a total of 200 relevance judgements.

5. DATA GATHERED

In this section we outline some of the data gathered during the relevance assessments.

5.1 Relevance Assessments

In Table 2 we can see that there is a reasonably even distribution of assessments throughout the three relevance categories. We can also see differences in the results returned from our pooling approach, topics 2,3 and 10 have a high number of highly relevant documents, whereas topics 8 has only 1. Overall for only 2 videos were individual assessors unable to make a judgement. In terms of assessor agreement we plot agreement (see Figure 2) in a similar way to Alonso and Mizzaro [2], where we plot error distribution. For ground truth we consider the majority decision. Column 0 represents complete agreement, +1 represents 1 assessor having a positive assessment outside the consensus, -1 represents 1 assessor having a negative assessment outside the consensus. In our figure we have to additional columns, a tie represents when an equal number of assessors have differing assessments, n/a represents where there is a majority (2) and 2 other assessors disagree, 1 being more positive and 1 more negative in assessment. We can see only for a small number of documents is there a consensus (32%). This helps demonstrate the difficulty in getting a consensus and perhaps why multiple assessments a range of assessments may be beneficial in test collections.

Table 2: Choice of relevance assessment per topic.

Topic	Not Sure	Not Relevant	Partially Relevant	Highly Relevant
1	0	6	7	7
2	0	4	5	11
3	0	2	7	11
4	0	5	9	6
5	0	10	5	5
6	1	1	11	7
7	0	13	3	4
8	1	12	6	1
9	0	8	5	7
10	0	6	3	11
Total	2	67	61	70

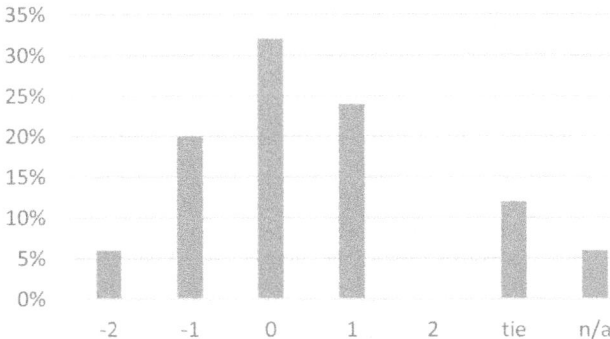

Figure 2: Agreement between reviewers Table 1 the number of responses given for each of the topics.

5.2 Time

Table 3 shows the average duration of videos judged for each topic. In comparison we present the average judgement time per video. It can be seen that for most judgements that the assessors do not watch

the entire video. We can also see high variance in judgement time, with some topics taking a lot less time than other topics.

Table 3: Average duration for all videos in each topic

Topic Number	Avg. Duration (secs)	Avg. Judgement (secs)
1	373	140
2	264	54
3	352	156
4	364	163
5	214	58
6	401	85
7	294	126
8	212	145
9	262	55
10	329	64

Table 4: Video duration classification, sample mean and sample standard deviation

Time duration (sec)	Number of Videos judged	Mean (Std Dev.)
Short (0-200 sec)	68	63.49 (5.62)
Medium (201-400 sec)	56	121.61 (11.01)
Long (>401sec)	76	130.16 (12.27)

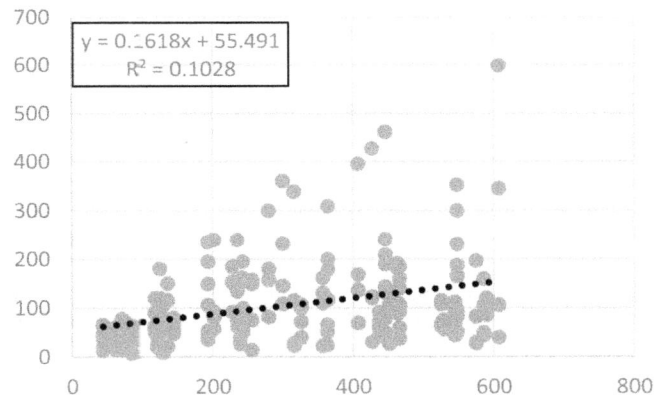

Figure 3: Scatter plot of video duration against judgement time per participant across all topics

We also considered if video length has any impact on assessment time. Initially we segmented videos in short (0-200 secs), medium (201-400 secs) and (401-600 secs) segments (see Table 4). It was found that longer videos took longer to judge on average in comparison with shorter videos. This finding is in keeping with previous research on text documents [15]. To look at this in more detail we plotted time duration of the video and the time per judgement in a scatter plot (see Figure 3). We can observe from the plot that there is only a weak correlation ($R^2 = 0.1028$) between the video duration and the judgement time. This suggests that as video time increase in video duration does not always produce a linear increase in the time taken for relevance judgement. Based on the scatter plot, most relevance judgements across the collection are made within 200 secs while some judgements took more than 300 seconds to complete.

5.3 Workload

Table 5 presents the average responses for the 7 point Likert scales that measure work load and interest. The not sure category only has responses from 2 participants, but it clearly has higher workload and lower interest than any other assessment. In terms of workload we see that the more clear categories i.e. not relevant and highly relevant, have lower workload in almost all categories in comparison to partially relevant. Again this is in keeping with other research which has found that less clear relevance assessments have higher workloads [15].

Table 5: Average responses for post judgement questionnaires. All on a 7 point Likert scale. Higher=better.

Question	Not Sure	Not Relevant	Partially Relevant	Highly Relevant
Mental	4.5	3.0	3.4	2.29
Physical	5	2.15	1.94	1.9
Temporal	5.5	2.42	2.68	2
Effort	5.5	3.05	3.37	2.41
Frustration	4	2.86	3.06	1.94
Interest	3.5	3.77	3.94	4.59

6. CONCLUSION

In our introduction we set out two research objectives, namely:

1. Create a video test collection with graded relevance assessments
2. To capture behavioural and perceptual information about the judgment process to augment the judgments.

In this paper we have described the topics, document collection and judgment process that were used to create our test collection. As part of the judgment process we gathered feedback from the assessors on their assessments as well as measuring time taken to make judgments. All of this data is made available to other researchers. Researchers can use this test collection for video search evaluations, to the best of our knowledge a video test collection with variable relevance judgments is not available. We will also maintain this test collection and encourage supplementary data to be gathered by researchers.

7. ACKNOWLEDGEMENTS

This work was funded in part by a UK Arts and Humanities Research Council (grant AH/L010364/1) grant to the second and third authors.

8. REFERENCES

[1] ALLAN, J., 2005. HARD track overview in TREC 2003 high accuracy retrieval from documents. DTIC Document.

[2] ALONSO, O. and MIZZARO, S., 2012. Using crowdsourcing for TREC relevance assessment. Information Processing & Management 48, 6, 1053-1066.

[3] CARTERETTE, B., ALLAN, J., and SITARAMAN, R., 2006. Minimal test collections for retrieval evaluation. In Proceedings of the 29th annual international ACM SIGIR conference on Research and development in information retrieval ACM, 268-275.

[4] GRUBINGER, M., 2007. Analysis and evaluation of visual information systems performance Victoria University.

[5] GRUBINGER, M., CLOUGH, P., HANBURY, A., and MÜLLER, H., 2008. Overview of the ImageCLEFphoto 2007 photographic retrieval task. In Advances in Multilingual and Multimodal Information Retrieval Springer, 433-444.

[6] HALVEY, M. and VILLA, R., 2014. Evaluating the effort involved in relevance assessments for images. In Proceedings of the 37th international ACM SIGIR conference on Research & development in information retrieval ACM, 887-890.

[7] HART, S.G. and STAVELAND, L.E., 1988. Development of NASA-TLX (Task Load Index): Results of empirical and theoretical research. Advances in psychology 52, 139-183.

[8] HASLER, L., HALVEY, M., and VILLA, R., 2015. Augmented Test Collections: A Step in the Right Direction. arXiv preprint arXiv:1501.06370.

[9] KEKÄLÄINEN, J. and JÄRVELIN, K., 2002. Using graded relevance assessments in IR evaluation. Journal of the American Society for Information Science and Technology 53, 13, 1120-1129.

[10] KELLY, D. and AZZOPARDI, L., 2015. How many results per page?: A Study of SERP Size, Search Behavior and User Experience. In Proceedings of the Proceedings of the 38th International ACM SIGIR Conference on Research and Development in Information Retrieval, ACM, 2767732, 183-192.

[11] SARACEVIC, T., 1975. Relevance: A review of and a framework for the thinking on the notion in information science. Journal of the American Society for Information Science 26, 6, 321-343.

[12] SORMUNEN, E., 2002. Liberal relevance criteria of TREC-: Counting on negligible documents? In Proceedings of the 25th annual international ACM SIGIR conference on Research and development in information retrieval ACM, 324-330.

[13] SPARCK JONES, K. and VAN RIJSBERGEN, C.J., 1976. Information retrieval test collections. Journal of Documentation 32, 1, 59-75.

[14] TANG, R. and SOLOMON, P., 1998. Toward an understanding of the dynamics of relevance judgment: An analysis of one person's search behavior. Information Processing & Management 34, 2, 237-256.

[15] VILLA, R. and HALVEY, M., 2013. Is relevance hard work?: evaluating the effort of making relevant assessments. In Proceedings of the 36th international ACM SIGIR conference on Research and development in information retrieval ACM, 765-768.

[16] WANG, J., 2011. Accuracy, agreement, speed, and perceived difficulty of users' relevance judgments for e-discovery. In Proceedings of SIGIR Information Retrieval for E-Discovery Workshop, 1.

Usability Evaluation of Electronic Health Record System (EHRs) using Subjective and Objective Measures

Prithima Reddy Mosaly	Lukasz Mazur	Lawrence B. Marks
University of North Carolina, Chapel Hill	University of North Carolina, Chapel Hill	University of North Carolina, Chapel Hill
101 Manning Dr.	101 Manning Dr.	101 Manning Dr.
UNC Cancer Hospital, CB295	UNC Cancer Hospital, CB295	UNC Cancer Hospital, CB295
Chapel Hill, NC 27599	Chapel Hill, NC 27599	Chapel Hill, NC 27599
1-984-974-8418	1-984-974-8418	1-984-974-8418
prithima_mosaly@med.unc.edu	lukasz_mazur@med.unc.edu	lawrence_marks@med.unc.edu

ABSTRACT

The objective of this pilot study was to explore the applicability of various evaluation methods (subjective and objective) for assessing usability of electronic health record system (EHRs) during physician interaction on simple vs. complex tasks. Five physicians performed two simulated clinical scenarios consisting of 9 tasks using the EHR. Tasks were categorized into simple vs. complex tasks based on the user, task and context characteristics by the subject matter expert. Usability was assessed using four methods, (1) subjectively using subject's informal feedback and usability expert's heuristics, (2) workload measures using eye tracking, (3) behavior measures using clicks and navigation windows, and (4) performance measures using actual time on task and predictive time based on CogTool ©. Overall, the results suggest that heuristic methods (1) are highly effective in identifying usability issues, with other methods (2-4) providing complementary analysis to identify differences is task complexly and user experience with EHRs.

Keywords

Usability; Cognitive workload (CWL); User feedback, Electronic Health records (EHR); Pupillary dilations (PD); Task Evoked Pupillary Response (TEPR); Behavior; Performance

1. INTRODUCTION

There is an increasing reliance on computer-based systems (health Information Technology [HIT]) to perform routine clinical tasks. Providers are required to essentially-continually interact with multiple computer screens to enter/view/extract information (e.g. electronic health record [EHR], etc.). HIT clearly provide unparalleled opportunities for improved patient care (e.g. more ready access to patient-specific information, data integration, decision support, etc.), and thus need to be vigorously embraced. Nevertheless, many EHR-type systems are not optimally designed (poor usability) to enable physicians to perform routine tasks quickly and accurately. For example, more than 1,000 adverse events associated with EHRs were reported to the Pennsylvania Patient Safety Authority in 2011 [1]. Further, poor usability of EHR design can "create new hazards in the already complex delivery of health care" [2], and increase user workload [3].

CHIIR'16, March 13–17, 2016, Carrboro, North Carolina, USA
© 2016 ACM. ISBN 978-1-4503-3751-9/16/03…$15.00.
DOI: http://dx.doi.org/10.1145/2854946.2854985

Usability is defined as how useful, usable and satisfying a system is for the intended users to accomplish goals in the work domain by performing certain sequence of tasks [4]. Due to a significant increase in growth of the EHR market, there is a need for improved usability evaluation and measurement methods to help guide researchers, developers and users to choose/design proper EHR systems [5]. There exists many usability evaluation methods and of all, laboratory based techniques are considered to be gold standard due to the advantage of collecting both subjective and objective data [6]. Heuristic evaluation technique is one of the most commonly used discount evaluation method due to its low cost [7]. Laboratory based heuristic evaluation (subjective data) will be useful since both domain and usability experts can interact in identifying the major issues related to user's experience with EHRs and EHR design. However, it may be time consuming and expensive. Previous reports suggested that a combination of different techniques that complement one another should be used for better usability evaluation [8]. Many objective data collection techniques may be of a great advantage due to its capability to collect user workload, behavior and performance data (e.g., eye tracking, clicks, detailed time studies, and error rates), which are limited in heuristic evaluation technique.

Thus, the objective of this study was to explore the applicability of various usability techniques (subjective and objective measures) in assessing usability of EHRs during physician-EHR interaction under two different task types (simple vs. complex).

2. METHODS
2.1 Study and Subjects

The study was conducted within the Human Factors Laboratory in the Department of Radiation Oncology at University of North Carolina (UNC), where we have created a simulated environment that closely mirrors the environment required for physician-computer interaction. Five physicians (two faculty and three physician residents) performed two simulated clinical scenarios consisting of total 9 tasks using EMR (Table 1). Based on user, task and context characteristics of (e.g., knowledge required to perform the task, degree of difficulty in using the EHR, type of task [i.e., simple, decision making, problem solving or judgement], degree of urgency), the 9-tasks were divided into two categories for data collection and analysis (simple vs. complex) [4, 9-10]. These categories were done based on usability expert's and the subject-matter expert's feedback. Five simple (1A, 1C, 1E, 2A, 2B) and four complex tasks (1B, 1D, 2C, 2D) were evaluated for usability. The study was approved by Internal Review Board (IRB).

2.2 Procedure

The study was carried out in three phases, first: participants were trained and walked through the tasks to be performed in the new version of a familiar EMR (~50mi); second, simulation of 9 tasks (~12min); third, revisiting the tasks (~50min) with expert. Subjective feedback was collection in phase 1; all objective measures were collected using eye tracking (Tobii x2-60) and screen video capture (Eyeworks, Inc.) during phase 2; and usability heuristics were conducted in phase 3. The nine tasks were divided into two categories, simple vs. complex tasks [9].

2.3 Measures and Assessment

Subjectively, participants assessed usability using informal feedback on their experience with the EHR, and usability expert guided heuristics. Objectively, usability was assessed for cognitive workload (CWL) [pupillary dilations (PD) and eye fixations]; behavior [mouse clicks and windows]; and performance measures [task-completion-time: real and predictive methods], while comparing participants' measures to a subject-matter "expert set standard" (Δ, expert in EHR use and clinical tasks). That is, the subject matter expert performed the clinical tasks initially during which the objective measures of CWL, behavior, and performance were collected. These measures were then compared to the individual subject's CWL, behavior, and performance measures as change from "expert-set standard".

Table 1 Two scenarios and tasks

Scenario 1: You have completed a consult (Level 4) with a female patient for a primary breast cancer to the upper outer quadrant of the left breast. Your decision is to treat the patient curatively to an initial dose of 50Gy. The patient is menopausal, has a pacemaker, and no prior RT. A cardiology consult has been scheduled, please document.	
You will need to complete 5 tasks	
1A	Charge the consult
1B	Complete the diagnosis (designate as the primary)
1C	Enter a brief Tx Plan note
1D	Enter a Care Plan with intent and Rad Rx
1E	Complete a 3P (**P**rior radiation, **P**regnancy, **P**acemaker) assessment
Scenario 2: This patient is under treatment for a LL Lung RT and has asked to be seen in the clinic.	
You will need to complete 4 tasks	
2A	Add a Quick Order for Labs
2B	Review Lab results
2C	Add Pharmacy Orders for Medication
2D	Update Problem List

2.3.1 Feedback from participants and expert guided heuristics

After training, participants were asked informally to provide feedback on the tasks. The responses were recorded in the form of free text (notes). At the end of the experiment, participants re-watched the recoded video (along with their eye behavior) and identified usability issues. The percentage of issues agreed by the experts was calculated for comparison between simple and complex tasks. The main purpose of using heuristics was to identify whether or not there was a difference in the percentage agreed by usability experts between the two task categories.

2.3.2 Cognitive Workload (CWL)

CWL was assessed using pupillary dilations (PD) and eye fixations. Data was collected using Tobii x2-60, 60Hz, and was processed according to the procedure recommended by [11]. Processed data was averaged to 1 sample/second (task PD). A baseline task was administered prior to the clinical tasks in which participants were required to memorize 3-letters presented at the rate of 1 letter/second followed by a recall test (repeated 10 times). A baseline PD was then calculated as 1 second PD data prior to the recall-test, averaged across 10 trails. Task evoked pupillary dilations (TEPR) was calculated by subtracting the baseline PD from the task PD. Eye fixations were computed using Eyeworks (Eye Tracking Inc®, Sweden) and total number of fixations were calculated for each task. The criteria for counting a fixation was set to 250msec (5x5 pixel; [12, 13]).

2.3.3 Behavior

The total number of mouse clicks and windows open (number of screens open) to perform the task was obtained using video analysis through Eyeworks.

2.3.4 Performance

Task completion time (actual) was obtained from the video analysis. For predictive time, CogTool [14] was used to prototype each task flow for each subject as observed in the recorded videos. CogTool is a user interface (UI) prototyping tool that can produce quantitative predictions of how users will behave when the prototype is ultimately implemented. It is used to simulate the cognitive, perceptual and motor behavior of humans interacting with the system prototype to accomplish tasks. The program calculates the amount of time an expert user will use to complete the task [13]. For the current study, the "think time" component (as measures by CogTool; set to 1.2sec default) was manually inputted based on the video analysis.

2.3.5 Data Analysis

For usability heuristics, we quantified and compared the percentage of usability issues that were identified for simple vs. complex tasks by participants and agreed by the usability experts. Two set of statistical analysis was performed for objective measures. A two-sample t-test was used to (1) assess the difference between simple and complex task; (2) assess the differences in mean deviations from "expert set standard" for simple and complex tasks respectively. An alpha of 0.05 was used to set the significance.

3. RESULTS

Figures 1 to 6 present the data on objective measures for simple and complex tasks.

3.1 Feedback from users and expert guided heuristic evaluations

The users identified 51 (27 vs. 24 for simple vs. complex tasks) usability issues. Usability experts agreed with 93% (92% vs. 94% for simple and complex tasks respectively) of the issues based on heuristics.

3.2 Cognitive Workload (CWL)

Participants experienced significantly high CWL as measured using number of fixation for complex vs simple tasks (mean: 28 vs. 15; t-stats =-2.2, p=0.02), but not for TEPR (mean: 0.06 vs. 0.05 mm, p=0.6). There was a significant deviation from "expert set standard" for both simple and complex tasks on TEPR (Δ=0.02, 0.01mm; t-stats=6, 3.4, p<0.001, 0.003 for simple and complex task respectively; Figure 1); and fixations (Δ=10, 22; t-stats=1.7, 2.4, p=0.04, 0.03 for simple and complex tasks respectively; Figure 2).

3.3 Behavior

Participants used significantly more number of clicks (mean: 13 vs. 9; t-stats=-2.3, p=0.03) and windows (mean: 3 vs. 2; t-stats=-2.3, p=0.001) for complex vs. simple task. There was no significant deviation from "expert set standard" for number of clicks and windows for simple tasks (p>0.05), but there was a significant deviation for complex tasks for both clicks (Δ=3, 1; t-stats=2.4, 4; p=0.03, 0.001; Figures 3), and windows (Δ=1; t-stats=3.7, p=0.001; Figure 4).

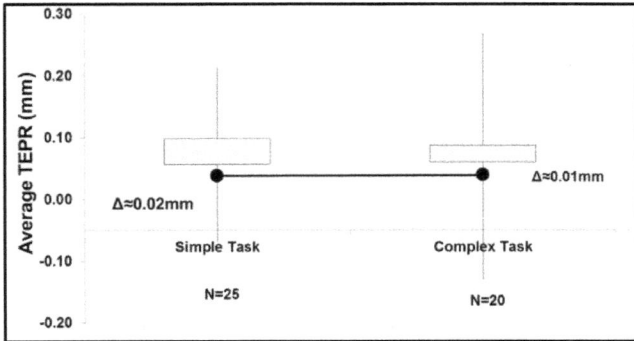

Figure 1 Spread (box plot) and deviation from "expert set standard" (line plot) of participants' CWL measured using task evoked pupillary response (TEPR).

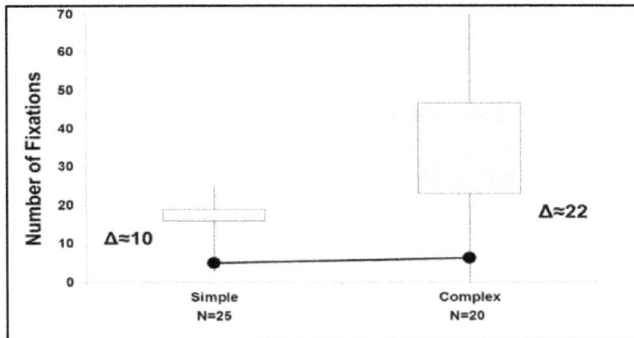

Figure 2 Spread (box plot) and deviation from "expert set standard" (line plot) of participants' CWL measured using Fixations.

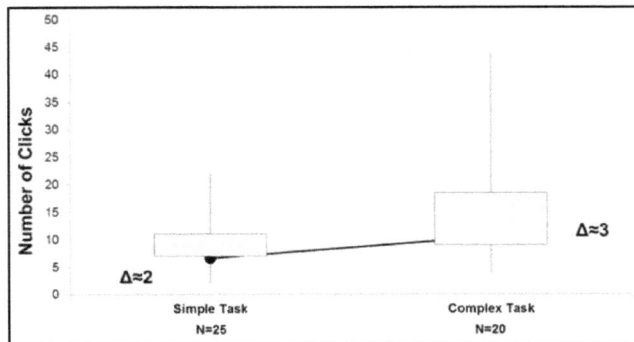

Figure 3 Spread (box plot) and deviation from "expert set standard" (line plot) of participants' behavior using number of clicks.

3.4 Performance

Participants took significantly more time in completing the complex tasks vs. simple tasks (mean: 105 vs. 36sec; t-stats=-2.96, p=0.008). Similarly, CogTool predicted longer completion time for complex tasks vs. simple tasks (=42 vs. 25sec; t-stats= -2.5, p=0.01). As compared to "expert set standards", there was a significant deviation in task completion time (Δ=65sec; t-stats=3.2, p=0.004; Figure 5) and CogTool predicted time (Δ=19sec; t-stats=3.6, p=0.002; Figure 6) for only complex task only.

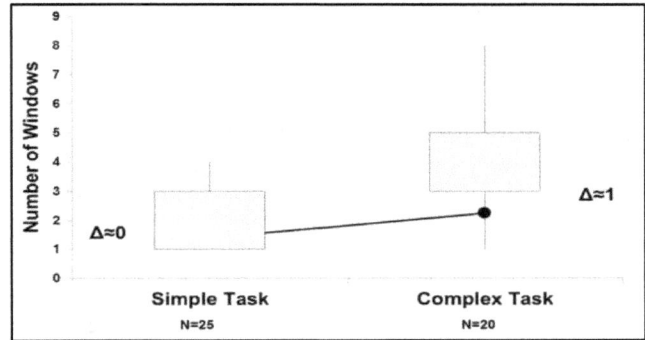

Figure 4 Spread (box plot) and deviation from "expert set standard" (line plot) of participants' behavior using number of windows (or screens).

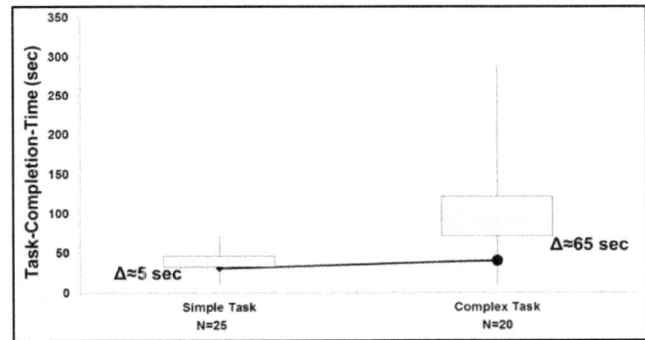

Figure 5 Spread (box plot) and deviation from "expert set standard" (line plot) of participants' Performance using task-completion time.

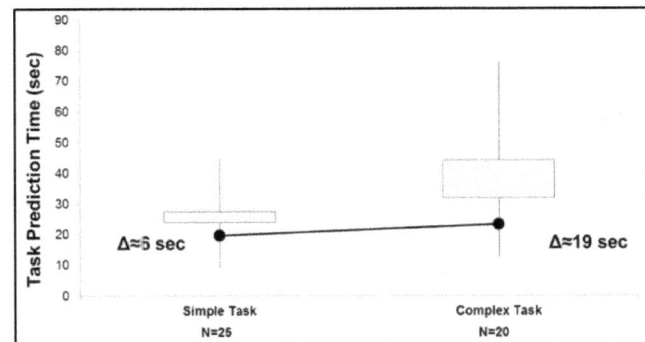

Figure 6 Spread (box plot) and deviation from "expert set standard" (line plot) of participants' Performance using CogTool prediction.

4. DISCUSSION

The study explored the applicability of subjective (heuristics and subject feedback), and objective (CWL [TEPR and fixations], behavior [clicks and windows] and performance [total time, both actual and predicted]) methods to assess usability of EHRs during physician interaction on simple vs. complex tasks. All methods identified usability issues; however, the applicability of these methods differed based on simple vs. complex tasks.

4.1 Feedback from users and expert guided heuristics.

Overall, usability experts agreed on 92% and 94% if usability issues for simple and complex task respectively, indicating applicability of heuristic evaluations for EHR tasks.

4.2 Cognitive Workload (CWL)

Results indicated that the total number of eye fixations were sensitive in identifying differences between simple vs. complex tasks. TEPR and total number of fixations were effective in identifying deviations from "expert set standards" for both simple and complex tasks. This suggests that CWL measures may be applicable in identifying usability issues related to task complexity and user's EHR experience within task complexity.

4.3 Behavior

Behavior methods (clicks and window analysis) were sensitive in identifying differences between simple and complex tasks and between participants and "expert set standards" for complex tasks only. This suggests that both click and window analysis may be applicable in identifying usability issues related to task complexity and user's EHR experience within task complexity.

4.4 Performance

As expected, complex tasks took longer time vs. simple tasks for both actual and predictive performance. Also, in comparison to "expert set standards", subjects took significantly longer time for complex task only. In line with CWL and behavior measures, the performance measures may also be sensitive in identifying usability issues related to task complexity and user's EHR experience within task complexity.

5. Conclusions

Table 2 summarizes the applicability of subjective and objective measures for assessing EHRs during physician-EHR interactions on simple vs. complex tasks. Overall, results suggest that feedback from users and expert guided heuristics are highly effective in identifying usability issues, with other methods (CWL, behaviors, and performance) providing complementary analysis in identifying differences is task complexly and user experience with EHRs.

Despite the limitations (small sample size, 2 basic task categories, etc.), the current study findings highlight the applicability of various measures to assess usability and to better understand the interactions of physicians with EHR systems. Further research is needed to investigate the applicability of other eye tracking measures (saccades, blinks, eye gaze etc.) in addition to current CWL metrics based on TEPR and eye fixations, As there is increasing reliance on computer-based systems to perform routine clinical tasks, additional research efforts to assess applicability of various methods to detect usability issues in EHRs is needed.

6. ACKNOWLEDEMENT

This project was supported by Elekta Inc® and their EMR for Radiation Oncology "Mosaiq" was evaluated for usability assessment.

Table 2 Summary of applicability (Applicable vs. Not Applicable) of subjective and objective methods for assessing usability of EHRs during physician-EHR interaction with simple vs. complex tasks

Task		Subjective	Cognitive Workload		Behavior		Performance	
		Heuristics	PD (mm)	Fixations (#)	Clicks (#)	Windows (#)	TTC (sec)	CogTool Prediction (sec)
Simple vs. Complex		Applicable	Not Applicable	Applicable	Applicable	Applicable	Applicable	Applicable
Deviation from "Expert set standard"	Simple		Applicable	Applicable	Not Applicable	Not Applicable	Not Applicable	Not Applicable
	Complex		Applicable	Applicable	Applicable	Applicable	Applicable	Applicable

7. REFERENCES

[1] Sparnon, E., & Marella, W. M. 2012. The role of the electronic health record in patient safety events. *Pennsylvania Patient Safety Advisory*, 9(4), 113-121

[2] Lin, H. S., & Stead, W. W. (Eds.). 2009. *Computational Technology for Effective Health Care: Immediate Steps and Strategic Directions.* National Academies Press.

[3] Mazur, L.M., Mosaly, P., Hoyle, L., Jones, E., and Chera, B., and Marks, L.B. 2014. Relating Physician's Workload with Errors during Radiotherapy Planning, accepted to *Practical Radiation Oncology*, accepted for publication.

[4] Zhang, J., & Walji, M. F. 2011. TURF: Toward a unified framework of EHR usability. *Journal of biomedical informatics*, 44(6), 1056-1067.

[5] Armijo, D., McDonnell, C., & Werner, K. (2009). Electronic health record usability: interface design considerations. *AHRQ Publication*, 9(10), 0091-2.

[6] Hartson, H. R., Andre, T. S., & Williges, R. C. (2001). Criteria for evaluating usability evaluation methods. *International journal of human-computer interaction*, 13(4), 373-410.

[7] Johnson, C. M., Johnston, D., & Crowle, P. K. (2011). EHR Usability Toolkit: A Background Report on Usability and Electronic Health Records. *Rockville, MD: Agency for Healthcare Research and Quality.*

[8] Jaspers, M. W. (2009). A comparison of usability methods for testing interactive health technologies: methodological aspects and empirical evidence. *International journal of medical informatics*, 78(5), 340-353.

[9] Gill, T. G., & Hicks, R. C. (2006). Task Complexity and Informing Science: A Synthesis. Informing Science, 91-30.

[10] Institute of Medicine (US). Committee on Patient Safety and Health Information Technology. 2012. *Health IT and patient safety: Building safer systems for better care.* National Academies Press.

[11] Beatty, J., & Lucero-Wagoner, B. 2000. The pupillary system. *Handbook of psychophysiology*, 2, 142-162.

[12] Solé Puig, M., Puigcerver, L., Aznar-Casanova, J. A., & Supèr, H. 2013. Difference in visual processing assessed by eye vergence movements. *PloS one*, 8(9), e72041.

[13] Underwood, G., Schmitt, N., & Galpin, A. 2004. The eyes have it. *Formulaic sequences: Acquisition, processing, and use*, 9, 153.

[14] Card, S. K., Newell, A., & Moran, T. P. 1983. The psychology of human-computer interaction.

Modeling Optimal Switching Behavior

Mark D. Smucker
Department of Management Sciences
University of Waterloo, Canada
mark.smucker@uwaterloo.ca

Charles L. A. Clarke
School of Computer Science
University of Waterloo, Canada
claclark@plg.uwaterloo.ca

ABSTRACT

Recently developed retrieval effectiveness measures have incorporated models of user behavior, but have limited themselves to predicting user performance over a single query and response. Accurate prediction of user performance with search systems must incorporate a means to model how users switch between different information sources. For example, a search session may consist of multiple queries with the user making decisions of when to switch from evaluating the current result list to a new result list produced by a query reformulation. Likewise, users may switch to a result list produced by a query suggestion or other interaction mechanism that produces a new search result list. In this paper, we simulate user behavior and investigate optimal switching behavior for a user who must decide when and if to issue their current query to another search engine. As a first step in understanding the problem space, we restrict our investigation and discussion to two top performing runs submitted to the TREC 2005 Robust track. We find four classes of switching behavior that a user would be faced with in making a decision about whether to switch from one result list to another.

Keywords

Search; evaluation

1. INTRODUCTION

Searching requires decision making. After deciding on a search system to use, the searcher must pose a query and interact with the system. Many search engines respond to the query with a result list of query-biased summaries, which the searcher traverses, sometimes deciding to skip over a summary, sometimes deciding to click and view a full document, and then afterwards deciding whether to return to the list.

Some queries work better than others. While traversing a result list, the searcher must decide whether to continue on the current list, or to switch to another source of potentially relevant information. After deciding to stop processing the

CHIIR '16, March 13 - 17, 2016, Carrboro, NC, USA

© 2016 Copyright held by the owner/author(s). Publication rights licensed to ACM.
ISBN 978-1-4503-3751-9/16/03. . . $15.00

DOI: http://dx.doi.org/10.1145/2854946.2854981

current list, the searcher could reformulate their query and pose it to the same search engine, or the searcher could take their information need to another search engine, or to another person, or to some other source that might help them satisfy their need.

When should the searcher decide to quit working with one source of information and find another? If the searcher decides to quit, time must be invested in switching to the new resource. For a reformulation, the searcher must conceive of a new query, submit it, and wait for the results. If the query reformulation derives from a query suggestion feature, or a similar mechanism, the user must read the suggestions and select one. For a switch to a new search engine, the searcher must navigate to the new engine and then enter a query, which might be their original query or a reformulation. All of these decisions and actions cost the user time, and may have different mental costs.

In this short paper, we examine the simple scenario of a searcher switching from one search engine to another. Building on our earlier simulation studies [11], which used simulation as a method of evaluating individual result lists, we consider simulations of searcher behavior when it is possible for them to switch from the result list of one engine to that of another. Applying a central idea from reinforcement learning [12] and foraging theory [3, 9] that an agent will strive to maximize its gain, we focus on optimal switching behavior. Consideration of optimal behavior produces insights into what a searcher could gain from switching and what the searcher might need to know to obtain those gains. For example, we discover that an optimal policy for switching, i.e., when to switch, can be highly dependent on the total time available to search.

A central goal of information retrieval evaluation is to make valid predictions about how changes to search systems will impact system performance and user satisfaction. Offline, batch-style IR evaluation has long sought to move beyond the ranked list to consider query reformulations, query suggestions, and searcher behavior across full search sessions [4–7, 10, 15]. At the SWIRL 2012 Strategic Workshop [1], simulation of interaction was identified as a promising approach, provided that the complexities of user decision making could be managed. Although consideration of optimal behavior has its own limitations, we demonstrate that it also produces insights. While we focus on a simple scenario in this short paper, our ongoing and future work extends these efforts to more complex scenarios.

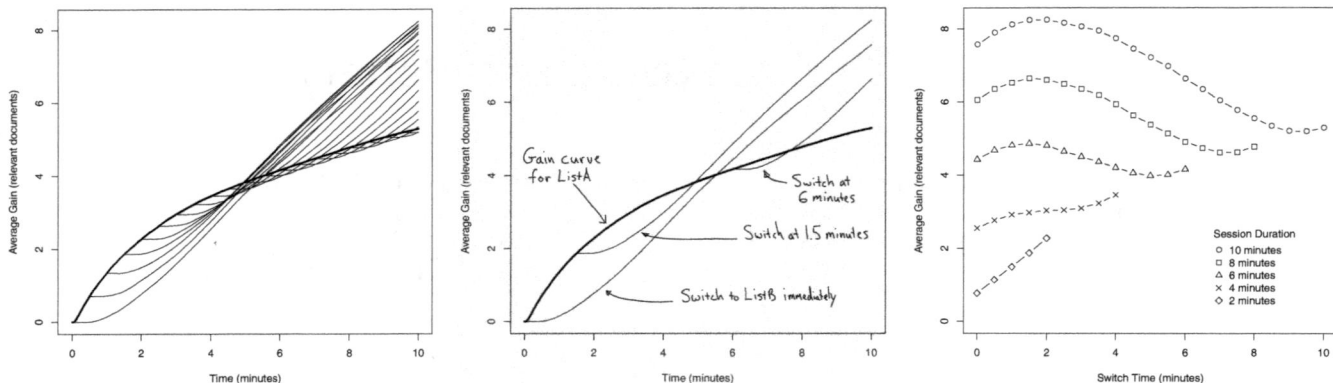

Figure 1: In this example, List A is the sab05ror1 run and List B is the uic0501 run from the TREC 2005 Robust track and the topic number is 389. The average gain for List A is shown in the left and center figures as the thicker curve. The average gain achieved by switching to List B at various times is shown with the thinner lines. The center plot highlights a select set of switching times. The right plot shows the average cumulative gain for search sessions of 2, 4, 6, 8, and 10 minutes for switching times of 0, 30, ..., 600 seconds.

2. SIMULATION

In this paper we simulate users who process two ranked lists of documents, where each ranked list is produced by a different search engine. The user starts on a list produced by one engine ("*List A*") and may potentially switch to a list produced by a second engine ("*List B*"). We assume that the hypothetical user interfaces for each engine are identical, and are simplified versions of typical search interfaces. In response to a user query, the engine displays a ranked list of search results with clickable summaries. When clicked, a summary takes the user to a full document.

For our user model, we adopt the time-biased gain (TBG) user model [11], modified to allow the simulated user to switch from List A to List B. The TBG user model has the simulated user proceed through a ranked list in rank order, with the simulated user spending T_S seconds reading each summary, where T_S is a random deviate drawn from a Weibull distribution. TBG assumes that each document has a known relevance value, derived from some evaluation experiment, and this known relevance is used in part to drive the simulation. Given the known relevance of a document, the user with some probability will click on the summary. Because it is possible, and indeed quite likely, that List B will contain documents in List A, we modify the original TBG model to set the probability of clicking on an already clicked on document to be zero.

If a user does not click on a summary, they proceed to the next summary in the ranked list. After clicking on a summary, the simulated user will spend T_D seconds reading a document, where T_D is a random deviate drawn from a log-normal linear distribution parameterized by document length. Unlike our earlier work [11], we do not provide special handling in the case of distinct documents containing duplicate or near-duplicate content. While we have simplified and adapted the TBG model to some extent, we retain its key features, including the parameter values derived from actual user data.

After reading the document, and given its known relevance, the simulated user will with some probability decide

that the document is or is not relevant. If the simulated user decides the document is relevant, and the known relevance value indicates that document is indeed relevant, then the user's cumulative gain over the ranked list will increase by one relevant document. The simulated user then returns to the search engine results page and begins to read the next summary in the ranked list. At any point in time, the simulated user may switch from List A to List B. Switching incurs a time cost. For all of our experiments, we arbitrarily set the switching cost to 10 seconds, allowing a reasonable time for the user to navigate from one engine to another. For simplicity, if a user is in the middle of reading a document when the switch occurs, the user does not receive any gain for that document.

We use the same values for the user model parameters as in our earlier work [11], which separately modeled each of 48 users. Each user is simulated separately by setting the parameter values accordingly and then simulating that user's behavior with List A and B, recording cumulative gain vs. time over a search session of up to 10 minutes to produce a *gain curve*. The simulated users are stochastic and spend varying amounts of times on summaries and documents and probabilistically click on summaries and decide that documents are relevant. For each user, we simulate its interaction with List A and List B 100 times. We take the multiple gain curves produced for all of the 48 simulated users and compute an average gain curve. To produce an average gain curve we simply average the cumulative gain of the individual curves at one second intervals.

3. EXPERIMENTS

Our experiments are derived from the TREC 2005 Robust Track data [13]. We selected the uic0501 and sab05ror1 runs to represent two high quality search engines. Of the submitted runs, these two runs achieve the highest expected cumulative gain as per the TBG measure [11]. We consider switching times of 0, 30, 60, 90, ..., and 600 seconds. Figure 1 shows an example of the average gain curves that are produced by our 48 simulated users as they process List A

Never Switch: In this example (topic 409), over the course of 10 minutes of searching, List A has a consistently faster rate of gain than List B. The thicker line is List A and the thinner lines represent the gain resulting from switching from A to B at 30 second intervals. Switching from A to B would only slow the average user's rate of gain.

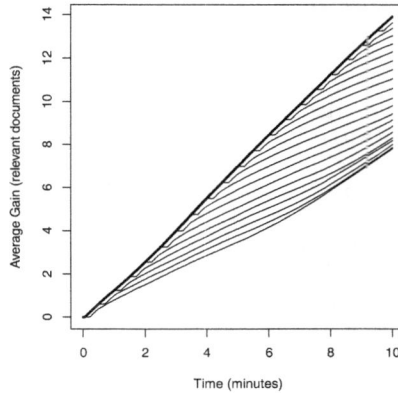

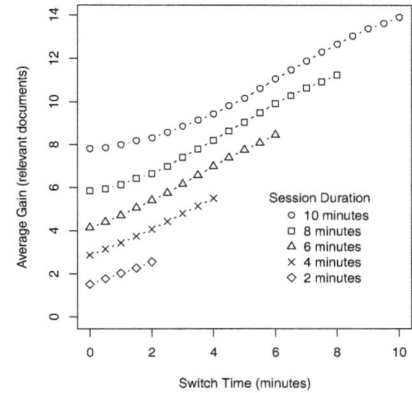

Switch Immediately: For topic 419, the average simulated user is unable to accumulate much of any gain within 10 minutes via List A. As a result, for all search sessions within the simulated 10 minutes, the average user should switch immediately to List B. The *switch immediately* class is the opposite of the *never switch* class. In both cases, the user is faced with two result lists that each produce consistent — but different — rates of gain over the length of the search session.

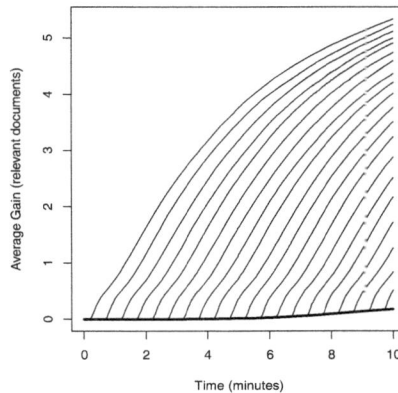

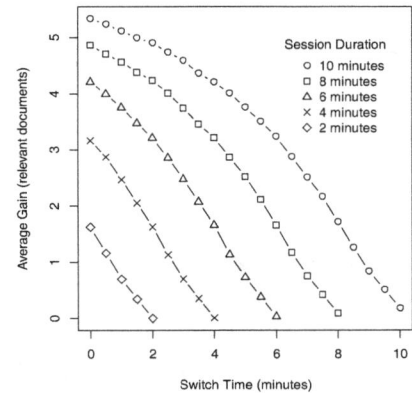

Moot Switch: Simulated users have similar performance on topic 625 with either List A or List B. Switching from List A to List B neither helps nor hurts user performance.

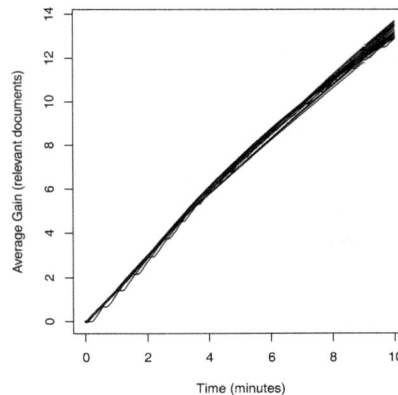

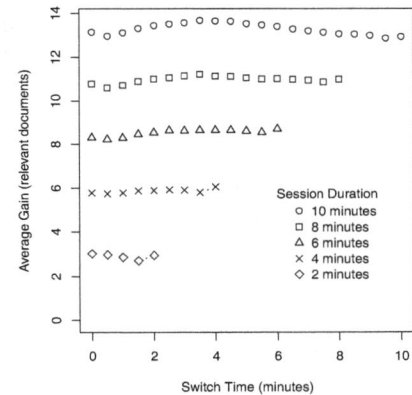

Complex Switch: To achieve maximum cumulative gain on topic 651 requires a user to stay on List A for differing amounts of time depending on the search session duration. For example, the far right plot shows that the average simulated user with a search duration of 10 minutes should switch from List A to List B at about 6 minutes to maximize gain. These sorts of complex switches appear to occur when one list has a high rate of gain initially that is not sustained over the duration of the search session.

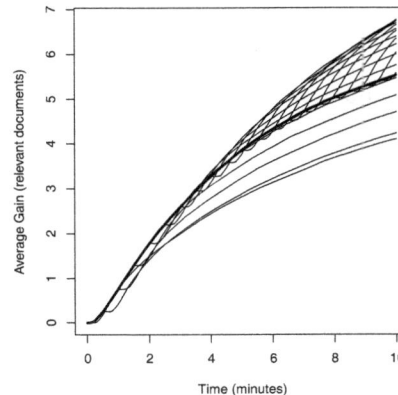

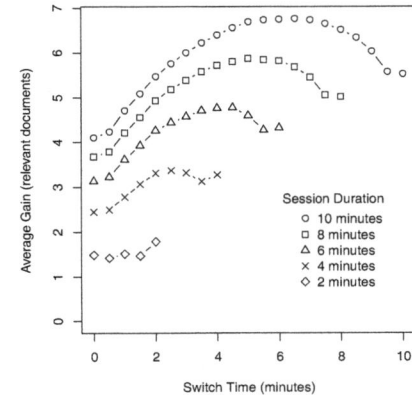

Table 1: **Four classes of gain curve switching behavior. Each class is illustrated with an example. Each example is a separate search topic. In all examples, List A is sab05ror1 and List B is uic0501.**

and then switch to List B at the different switching times. The left plot in Figure 1 shows the average gain curves for all possible switching times.

The middle plot illustrates a select set of average gain curves. The average cumulative gain of a user that never switches from List A to List B is shown with the thicker curve. For this topic, we see that if the average user was to switch immediately to List B, the average user would not match the gain of a user who stayed on List A until approximately 5 minutes. Indeed, for these search results, an average user with a search session less than 295 seconds would be best served by never switching to List B. For search sessions of 295 seconds and longer, it is advantageous for the average user to switch to List B after taking advantage of the well placed relevant documents at the top of List A.

The rightmost plot shows the average cumulative gain achieved for search sessions of different durations. The plot shows, for shorter sessions, that it is best to stay on List A, but for longer search sessions, there is an optimal time to switch to List B to maximize gain. When we examined the average gain curves for all 50 topics in the runs sab05ror1 and uic0501, we saw four classes of switching behavior stand out. Table 1 describes the four classes and shows an example of each one.

4. DISCUSSION

While we can compute optimal switching behavior, a user would need complete knowledge about both search lists to make the optimal decision. Users making decisions about when to switch will have available their experience with the current result list and also past experience with search engines and the quality of results that they are able to produce.

Assuming that search users want to maximize their cumulative gain during a search session, we have seen that there are likely four different situations that a user will be faced with when trying to decide if and when to switch from one result list to another list. Looking at the four classes of switching behavior in Table 1, all point to users developing the ability to discern when a result list's rate of gain is below or has fallen below what they would expect from another search engine's result list or other method of generating new search results [2].

While we do not know the mechanism by which users decide to abandon a given result list and switch to another search engine or reformulate their query, etc. it seems that models of this decision function will involve some user computable measure of the current rate of gain, i.e. the slope of the user's gain curve. For example, a possible user computable measure of the current rate of gain could be the number of relevant documents found in the last 3 examined results or perhaps the number of relevant documents found in the last 2 minutes, or some of the strategies proposed by Maxwell et al. [8]. White and Dumais [14] conducted a study and found that 24% of search engine switches were a result of dissatisfaction and 23% were because of an expectation of better results, and many of the other reasons reflect some desire for more or different information.

We see two complimentary approaches to developing models that will allow us to simulate these sorts of switching decisions. The first approach involves various user studies to collect behavioral data, e.g. eye-tracking data and other user interaction behavior, and also qualitative data, e.g. think-aloud while searching. The second approach is to learn decision functions given limited state information that a user could realistically utilize to make a decision. In this second approach, reinforcement learning (RL) seems particularly well suited to the task.

5. CONCLUSION

Search is inherently interactive and filled with decisions to be made by searchers. Simulation gives us the ability to predict user performance with retrieval systems, but to date, the majority of our simulations restrict themselves to single query response pairs. To make our simulations more realistic and thus more predictive of actual user performance, we need to begin modeling decisions such as when a user decides to switch from one result list to another. We found that models of user switching behavior will likely need to simulate some user computable rate of gain and its comparison to an expected rate.

6. ACKNOWLEDGMENTS

This work was supported in part by the Natural Sciences and Engineering Research Council of Canada (NSERC), in part by Google, and in part by the University of Waterloo.

7. REFERENCES

[1] J. Allan, B. Croft, A. Moffat, and M. Sanderson. Frontiers, challenges, and opportunities for information retrieval: Report from SWIRL 2012 the second strategic workshop on information retrieval in Lorne. *SIGIR Forum*, 46(1):2–32, May 2012.

[2] E. L. Charnov. Optimal foraging, the marginal value theorem. *Theor. Population Biology*, 9(2):129–136, 1976.

[3] W.-T. Fu and P. Pirolli. SNIF-ACT: A cognitive model of user navigation on the world wide web. *Human-Computer Interaction*, 22(4):355–412, 2007.

[4] K. Järvelin, S. L. Price, L. M. L. Delcambre, and M. L. Nielsen. Discounted cumulated gain based evaluation of multiple-query IR sessions. In *ECIR*, pages 4–15, 2008.

[5] E. Kanoulas, B. Carterette, P. Clough, and M. Sanderson. Session track overview. In *TREC*, 2010.

[6] E. Kanoulas, B. Carterette, P. D. Clough, and M. Sanderson. Evaluating multi-query sessions. In *SIGIR*, pages 1053–1062, 2011.

[7] H. Keskustalo, K. Järvelin, T. Sharma, and M. L. Nielsen. Test collection-based IR evaluation needs extension toward sessions: A case of extremely short queries. In *AIRS'09*, 2009.

[8] D. Maxwell, L. Azzopardi, K. Järvelin, and H. Keskustalo. An initial investigation into fixed and adaptive stopping strategies. In *SIGIR*, 2015.

[9] P. Pirolli. *Information Foraging Theory*. Oxford University Press, 2007.

[10] T. Sakai and Z. Dou. Summaries, ranked retrieval and sessions: a unified framework for information access evaluation. In *SIGIR*, pages 473–482, 2013.

[11] M. D. Smucker and C. L. A. Clarke. Modeling user variance in time-biased gain. In *HCIR*, pages 1–10, 2012.

[12] R. S. Sutton and A. G. Barto. *Reinforcement Learning: An Introduction*. MIT Press, 1998.

[13] E. M. Voorhees. Overview of the TREC 2005 Robust Retrieval Track. In *TREC*, 2005.

[14] R. W. White and S. T. Dumais. Characterizing and predicting search engine switching behavior. In *CIKM*, pages 87–96, 2009.

[15] Y. Yang and A. Lad. Modeling expected utility of multi-session information distillation. In *ICTIR*, pages 164–175, 2009.

Individual Differences and Online Health Information Source Selection

Yalin Sun
School of Information
The University of Texas at Austin
1616 Guadalupe Street
Austin, Texas 78701
clairesun05@utexas.edu

Yan Zhang
School of Information
The University of Texas at Austin
1616 Guadalupe Street
Austin, Texas 78701
yanz@ischool.utexas.edu

ABSTRACT

Online information sources are become increasingly diverse. The selection of sources for health information has significant implications for people's healthcare decision-making. However, little is known about how individual differences influence users' selection of online sources for health information. This study intends to fill this gap by exploring the impact of a number of individual characteristics on users' selection of five online sources (search engines, social Q&A sites, SNSs, online health communities, and crowdsourcing sites) for three distinct types of health search task (factual, exploratory, and personal experiences). We found that individuals' health literacy and frequency of using a source are the most significant predictors of their source selections across task types. Preference for information has an impact on users' selection of SNSs for exploratory tasks. Extraversion personality has an impact on users' selection of search engines for tasks that seek personal experiences. Nevertheless, demographic factors, including gender, income, and health status, do not predict users' selection of online sources for health information.

Keywords

Individual differences; information sources; health information seeking; search tasks; preference for information; health literacy.

1. INTRODUCTION

Search engines have been a primary venue for consumers to seek health information online. With the emergence of Web 2.0, including social media and human computing (e.g., social networking sites (SNSs) and social Q&A), information seekers also increasingly turn to these "social" sources to fulfill their health information needs [7, 12, 20]. The types of information available at different sources vary, so does the quality. Given the increasing importance that information plays in consumers' participation in their healthcare, the use

CHIIR '16, March 13-17, 2016, Carrboro, NC, USA

© 2016 ACM. ISBN 978-1-4503-3751-9/16/03. . . $15.00

DOI: http://dx.doi.org/10.1145/2854946.2854989

of different information sources has an impact on people's health decision making, and subsequently their health outcomes [10, 16]. Therefore, it is important to understand what factors affect people's selection of online health information sources.

Studies have pointed out that people's selection of sources is affected by a wide range of factors, including source attributes, user-source relationships, characteristics of individual users, and characteristics of the problematic situation that prompts the information seeking [23]. In this study, we focus on exploring the impact of individual differences on their selections of online sources for different types of health search task. Prior studies have found that individual characteristics, such as age, education, ethnicity, health status, and health beliefs affect their source selections (e.g., [2, 4]). However, these studies primarily focus on the selection of different source channels (e.g., the Internet, TV, and healthcare providers), with few examining the selection of Internet-based sources, such as search engines and social media sites.

Studies have suggested that characteristics of the search tasks (e.g., factual information, recommendations, and opinions) affect information search behaviors [6, 15], but little is known about how tasks moderate the impact of individual differences on a specific information search behavior - selection of sources. This study intends to fill these gaps to contribute to a better understanding of user's source selection behavior in the context of health information seeking. The knowledge gained can inform the personalization of users' health information search experience.

2. THEORETICAL FRAMEWORK

Figure 1 shows the theoretical framework of this study. It was drawn from three major theoretical sources: 1) the comprehensive model of information seeking [13], which postulates that demographics and direct health experience impact people's health information seeking actions, 2) the integrative model of ehealth use [3], which delineates that personality, demographics, health literacy, and source use history affect people's online health behaviors, 3) the stress and coping theory [8], which suggests that preference for information, as a trait, influences people's health information seeking. Considering the impact of different search tasks on search behaviors [18], we treated it as a moderator factor.

Our specific research question is: How do individual characteristics (including personality, preference for information, health literacy, source experience, health status, and de-

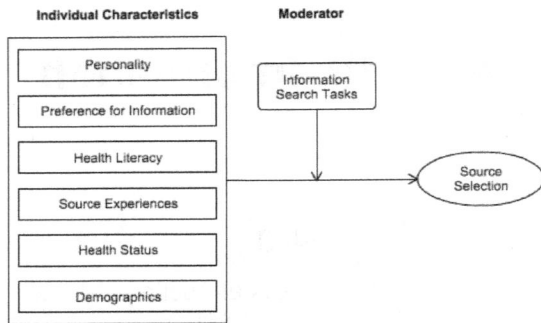

Figure 1: Conceptual Model

mographic factors) impact users' selection of Internet-based sources for different types of health-related tasks (factual, exploratory, and personal experiences)?

3. METHODS

3.1 Measures

3.1.1 Dependent Variables

The dependent variables are people's selections of five online sources (search engines, social Q&A sites, SNSs, online health communities, and crowdsourcing sites) for three different types of health-related search task (factual, exploratory, and personal experiences). We selected these five online sources because they are either already often used by health information seekers or becoming popular among online users.

3.1.2 Independent Variables

There are 11 independent variables, all of which are individual characteristics, including age, gender, education, ethnicity, income, health status, personality, preference for information, health literacy, source familiarity, and frequency of source use.

Questions eliciting age, gender, education, ethnicity, income, and health status were adopted from the Health Information National Trends Survey (HINTS). The Ten-Item Personality Inventory [11] was adopted to measure the Big-Five personality. Krantz Health Opinion Scale [14] was used to measure preference for information, and the NVS Health Literacy Assessment Tool [19] was used to measure health literacy. Source familiarity was measured by asking users to indicate their familiarity with a particular source on a scale from 1 to 5 (1-extremely familiar; 5-not familiar at all). Frequency of use was measured by asking users to report their frequency of using each source on a 1-5 scale (1-a great deal; 5-never).

3.1.3 Moderator: Tasks

Three types of health information search task that represent three major types of health information needs were used: factual, exploratory, and tasks seeking personal experiences [22]. For each task type, three different tasks were created to minimize the potential impact of any particular task on source selections (e.g., topic familiarity). The tasks were adapted from prior studies [21] or user-posted questions in Yahoo! Answers, a social Q&A site. For each task

based on the latter source, the two authors made independent judgment of the task type. Those selected for this study were those agreed by both authors.

3.2 Data Collection

An online survey was launched using Qualtrics subscribed by the university. Recruitment was conducted through an email post on the university's campus-wide email listserv and a task request on Amazon Mechanical Turk (AMT). Individuals were required to be at least 18 years old to participate and the consent to participation was sought at the beginning of the survey. Then, participants completed questions and scales that measure their demographics, personality, preference for information, health literacy, familiarity with each source, and the frequency of using them. The participants were then presented with the nine search tasks (three tasks for each task type). For each task, they were asked to select one or multiple sources that they would use to solve the task. An "other" field was provided to allow them to list sources that they would choose but were not on the list. As incentive for participation, we provided a drawing of two $20 amazon gift cards for those who participated through the university listserv. For participants recruited through AMT, we compensated $0.35 for each participant. The data collection took place between January 29 and March 30, 2015.

3.3 Data Analysis

The dependent variables, selections of sources, were treated as binary variables. For a particular source, its value was 1 if it was selected for one or multiple tasks of the same type, indicating that a respondent would select the source for this type of task; its value was 0 if it was not selected for any tasks of the same type, indicating that the respondent would not select the source for this type of task. For example, if "social Q&A sites" is selected for one or multiple factual tasks, the value of the dependent variable, the selection of social Q&A for factual tasks, would be 1; it would be 0 if the source was not selected for any factual tasks. In total, there were 15 binary dependent variables (5 online sources x 3 search task types).

Respondents' selections of sources and their individual characteristics were first analyzed using descriptive statistics. Logistic regressions were performed to examine the relationships between source selections and individuals' characteristics. We used SAS 9.2 (SAS Institute Inc., Cary, NC, USA) to perform the analyses. The rates of missing data for every variable in our analysis were less than 3%. The data analysis is ongoing and the results reported in this short paper are preliminary.

4. RESULTS

4.1 Sample Characteristics

In total, 393 individuals started the survey and 350 completed it (202 were from AMT, 148 from the listserv). Among the respondents, 63.8% were female, and 65.1% belonged to the age group 18-34. Most respondents were non-Hispanic White (66.0%), and had attended some college (88.3%). In terms of health status, 19.7% self-reported to be excellent, 39.4% very good, 31.1% good, and 9.7% either fair or poor. The mean score of preference for information (total 7 points)

Table 1: Percentage of respondents who selected each source for each task type (%)

	Factual	Exploratory	Personal
Search Engines	96.5	95.9	92.4
Social Q&A Sites	49.0	57.6	63.7
SNSs	42.3	25.9	48.6
Online Health Communities	75.8	82.0	86.6
Crowdsourcing Sites	14.6	9.6	11.3

was 4.23 (SD=2.25) and the mean of health literacy (total 6 points) was 5.27 (SD=1.23).

4.2 The Selection of Sources by Task Types

Respondents were asked to select as many sources as they would consult in real life for each task. Table 1 shows the number of respondents who selected each source for at least one task of each task type. It was not surprising that search engines were selected by the most respondents for all three task types: factual (96.5%), exploratory (95.9%), and personal experiences (92.4%), followed by online health communities. The source selected by the least number of respondents was crowdsourcing sites, with only about 10% selecting it for any task type.

4.3 Prediction of Source Selections

Because demographic variables including ethnicity, education, and age, were highly skewed towards one category, we only reported descriptive results. Logistic regression analyses were performed on the remaining demographic factors: gender, income, and health status. The results indicated that none were significant predictors of the selection of any source for any type of task.

Logistic regressions revealed that the selection of search engines for factual tasks is significantly associated with individual's health literacy (adjusted odds ratio [OR] 2.26, 95% CI 1.61-3.15, P<.0001) and the frequency of search engine use (adjusted [OR] 0.02, 95% CI 0.01-0.12, P<.0001). This means one unit increase in health literacy is associated with a 125.6% increase in the predicted odds of selecting search engines. Compared with people who used search engines very often, people who used search engine occasionally is associated with a 97.6% decrease in the predicted odds of selecting that. For factual tasks, the selection of SNSs and crowdsourcing sites can also be significantly predicted by health literacy. Nevertheless, their relationships were negative: one unit increase in health literacy is associated with a 23.2% decrease in the predicted odds of selecting SNSs and a 22.5% decrease in crowdsourcing sites. The selection of social Q&A sites for factual tasks can be significantly predicted by the frequency of use (adjusted [OR] 0.28, 95% CI 0.12-0.61, P<.0014) and the familiarity (adjusted [OR] 0.32, 95% CI 0.17-0.60, P<.0004). However, when controlling the effect of the frequency of use, the effect of familiarity is not significant anymore. The analysis suggests that if people used social Q&A a lot, the predicted probability of selecting this source is 72.7%; whereas if they only used it occasionally, the probability goes down to 11.9%.

Similar to that for factual tasks, the selection of search engines for exploratory tasks can also be predicted by the frequency of use (adjusted [OR] 0.06, 95% CI 0.01-0.48, P<.0081) and health literacy (adjusted odds ratio [OR] 2.20, 95% CI 1.60-3.01, P<.0001). For the frequency of use, people who used search engines "a great deal" have a 99.3% probability of selecting that, while people who reported using them "occasionally" only have a 37.5% probability of selecting search engines. For health literacy, one unit increase in health literacy is associated with a 119.8% increase in the predicted odds of selecting search engines. Slightly different from that for factual tasks, the selection of SNSs for exploratory tasks can be significantly predicted by not only health literacy (adjusted [OR] 0.76, 95% CI 0.63-0.92, P=0.0045), but also preference for information (adjusted [OR] 1.12, 95% CI 1.00-1.25, P=0.0468). One unite increase in health literacy is associated with a 24.4% decrease in the predicted odds of selecting SNSs. One unit increase in the preference for information is associated with a 12% increase in the predicted odds of selecting SNSs.

The selection of search engines for tasks seeking personal experiences can be significantly predicted by extraversion personality (adjusted [OR] 0.84, 95% CI 0.72-0.98, P=0.0216) and the frequency of use (adjusted [OR] 0.13, 95% CI 0.03-0.68, P<0.0131). This means that one unit increase in people's extraversion personality is associated with a 16.1% decrease in the predicted odds of selecting search engines, and that people who used search engine only occasionally is associated with an 86.9% decrease in the predicted odds of selecting search engines compared with people who used it very often.

5. DISCUSSION

The most consistent predictor of source selections across different types of task is the frequency of use. It predicted the selection of search engines for all three types of task and the selection of social Q&A sites for factual tasks. The result is not surprising as the frequency with which a behavior has been performed in the past is a good predictor of later action [1, 17]. For the same reason, however, why it was not a significant predictor for other source selection cases (e.g., the selection of social Q&A sites for personal experiences and the selection of SNSs for factual tasks) merit further investigation.

It is a unique contribution of the present study to reveal that health literacy is a significant predictor of several conditions of source selection. Specifically, people with higher health literacy were more likely to select search engines for factual and exploratory tasks and less likely to select SNSs and crowd-sourcing sites for factual tasks. It is possible that people with higher health literacy have better information search skills, and thus are more capable of and comfortable with searching and handling the abundant information that search engines return.

Preference for information is only significant in predicting the selection of SNSs for exploratory tasks. The result is not surprising as it is consistent with the defining characteristic of people with a high preference for information: they desire more information and are more engaged with information seeking in health crises. Driven by this impetus, as most respondents (74.1%) decided not to resort to SNSs for exploratory tasks, they still wanted to give this source a try.

The present study also found that extraversion personality negatively predicts the selection of search engines for personal experience tasks. A possible reason is that, extraverts are more likely than their counterparts to refer to social media, an alternative source for personal experiences [5]. However, this speculation is not supported by our results, in which extraversion did not predict the use of SNSs, Q&A sites, or online health communities. Thus, it is possible that extraverts are more likely to refer to other social media or interpersonal sources for personal experience information [9]. This merits further study.

6. CONCLUSION

Our preliminary results indicate that the most significant predictors of people's selection of online information sources for health information are how frequent a source is used by an individual and the individual's health literacy. Preference for information and personality have an impact on the selection of certain types of sources for certain types of task. Prior studies consistently reported that, demographic factors, like gender, health status, and income, are significant predictors of online health information seeking. However, we found that these factors do not predict users' selection of online health information sources. Due to the fact that our sample was not representative of the online health information seeker population in terms of age and education, we were not able to examine their relationships with source selections. Future studies should pursue a larger and more representative sample to further investigate the relationships between these demographic variables and the selection of online sources for health information.

7. REFERENCES

[1] I. Ajzen. Residual effects of past on later behavior: Habituation and reasoned action perspectives. *Personality and Social Psychology Review*, 6(2):107–122, 2002.

[2] N. L. Atkinson, S. L. Saperstein, and J. Pleis. Using the internet for health-related activities: findings from a national probability sample. *JMIR*, 11(1), 2009.

[3] G. D. Bodie and M. J. Dutta. Understanding health literacy for strategic health marketing: ehealth literacy, health disparities, and the digital divide. *Health Marketing Quarterly*, 25(1-2):175–203, 2008.

[4] A. Chevalier, A.-C. Maury, and N. Fouquereau. The influence of the search complexity and the familiarity with the website on the subjective appraisal of aesthetics, mental effort and usability. *Behaviour & Information Technology*, 33(2):117–132, 2014.

[5] T. Correa, A. W. Hinsley, and H. G. De Zuniga. Who interacts on the web?: The intersection of users' personality and social media use. *Computers in Human Behavior*, 26(2):247–253, 2010.

[6] D. Elsweiler and M. Harvey. Engaging and maintaining a sense of being informed: Understanding the tasks motivating twitter search. *JASIST*, 66(2):264–281, 2015.

[7] Y. Feng and W. Xie. Digital divide 2.0: The role of social networking sites in seeking health information online from a longitudinal perspective. *Journal of Health Communication*, 20(1):60–68, 2015.

[8] S. Folkman. *Stress, appraisal, and coping*. Springer Publishing Company LLC, 1984.

[9] V. P. Goby. Personality and online/offline choices: Mbti profiles and favored communication modes in a singapore study. *CyberPsychology & Behavior*, 9(1):5–13, 2006.

[10] J. P. Gopie, R. Timman, M. T. Hilhorst, S. O. Hofer, M. A. Mureau, and A. Tibben. Information-seeking behaviour and coping style of women opting for either implant or diep-flap breast reconstruction. *Journal of Plastic, Reconstructive & Aesthetic Surgery*, 64(9):1167–1173, 2011.

[11] S. D. Gosling, P. J. Rentfrow, and W. B. Swann. A very brief measure of the big-five personality domains. *Journal of Research in Personality*, 37(6):504–528, 2003.

[12] T. M. Hale, A. S. Pathipati, S. Zan, and K. Jethwani. Representation of health conditions on facebook: content analysis and evaluation of user engagement. *JMIR*, 16(8), 2014.

[13] J. D. Johnson, W. A. Donohue, C. K. Atkin, and S. Johnson. A comprehensive model of information seeking tests focusing on a technical organization. *Science Communication*, 16(3):274–303, 1995.

[14] D. S. Krantz, A. Baum, and M. v. Wideman. Assessment of preferences for self-treatment and information in health care. *Journal of Personality and Social Psychology*, 39(5):977, 1980.

[15] L. Lu and Y. C. Yuan. Shall I Google it or ask the competent villain down the hall? the moderating role of information need in information source selection. *JASIST*, 62(1):133–145, 2011.

[16] J. A. Nelson, J. Tchou, S. Domchek, S. S. Sonnad, J. M. Serletti, and L. C. Wu. Breast reconstruction in bilateral prophylactic mastectomy patients: factors that influence decision making. *Journal of Plastic, Reconstructive & Aesthetic Surgery*, 65(11):1481–1489, 2012.

[17] P. Norman and L. Smith. The theory of planned behaviour and exercise: An investigation into the role of prior behaviour, behavioural intentions and attitude variability. *European Journal of Social Psychology*, 25(4):403–415, 1995.

[18] P. Vakkari. Task-based information searching. *ARIST*, 37(1):413–464, 2003.

[19] B. D. Weiss, M. Z. Mays, W. Martz, K. M. Castro, D. A. DeWalt, M. P. Pignone, J. Mockbee, and F. A. Hale. Quick assessment of literacy in primary care: the newest vital sign. *The Annals of Family Medicine*, 3(6):514–522, 2005.

[20] M. L. Wilson, S. Ali, and M. F. Valstar. Finding information about mental health in microblogging platforms: a case study of depression. In *Proceedings of the 5th IIiX Symposium*, pages 8–17. ACM, 2014.

[21] Y. Zhang. The impact of task complexity on people's mental models of medlineplus. *Information Processing & Management*, 48(1):107–119, 2012.

[22] Y. Zhang. Toward a layered model of context for health information searching: An analysis of consumer-generated questions. *JASIST*, 64(6):1158–1172, 2013.

[23] Y. Zhang. Beyond quality and accessibility: Source selection in consumer health information searching. *JASIST*, 65(5):911–927, 2014.

Measuring Engagement with Online Forms

Paul Thomas
Microsoft*
pathom@microsoft.com

Heather O'Brien
University of British Columbia
h.obrien@ubc.ca

Tom Rowlands*
tom.rowlands@ieee.org

ABSTRACT

Online form-filling and transactions are extremely common, both for industry and government; and it is important to provide a satisfying user experience during these tasks if customers or citizens are to continue using online channels. However, reliable measures of experience in these cases are limited. Other areas of information interaction, e.g., online search, news, and shopping, are increasingly exploring and attempting to measure the concept of user engagement (UE). In this study, we ask whether UE is an appropriate outcome for the utilitarian activities of online form-filling and transactions.

We describe work in progress which measures UE using the User Engagement Scale (UES) with utilitarian tasks, and which looks for behaviours which correlate with the UES. Early results suggest that, first, the UES can be adapted to such situations; and second, that readily observable user behaviours including time on site, mouse movements, and keypresses correlate with UES sub-scales and can, to some extent, predict users' responses.

1. USER EXPERIENCE FOR FORMS

Online form-filling and transactions are ubiquitous in electronic commerce (shopping carts, delivery instructions, contact forms) and in government ("self-service" applications such as changing address records, filing reports, or applying for programmes and services).

If users have a poor experience with these tasks, in most cases there is an alternative. For commerce, the alternative is to go elsewhere, and a poor experience may mean a lost sale. For government, one alternative is to use a different channel—for example phone, letter, or drop-in centre—instead of an online service, with implications for speed, consistency, convenience, and cost [5]. Another alternative is simply not to engage, in which case citizens may either neglect a civic responsibility or miss out on an entitlement.

Measures that capture the nuances of transaction-based tasks and their outcomes are limited. In particular, it is infeasible to use volume of sales, completed forms, or other measures of success: a poor experience may still "succeed", but dissuade users from engaging in future. To inform the design of online services, we are interested in finding measure(s) which speak to *affect* rather than *mechanics*, and *experience* rather than *success*.

Two lines of work are of note in this regard. First, work on the "User Engagement Scale" (UES) [15] suggests it is possible to measure not just success but experience, and in particular user engagement, in a principled way. The scale, comprised of several dimensions (focussed attention, felt involvement, novelty, aesthetic appeal, perceived usability, and endurability), has been validated through extensive experimental work and used to measure many aspects of engagement with online services, including shopping [13] and news services [14]. The scale is, however, a large instrument—users are asked to respond to 31 items—which makes it impractical to use at volume. In addition, it relies on self-report which cannot always be obtained in large-scale transaction-based environments.

In another approach, user experience is measured through proxies of user behaviour: for example, through the position of clicks or the time on a task. This has been used a great deal in searching [e.g. 1, 9, 11] and browsing tasks [17]. The approach scales well, and places no burden on users—indeed, they need not even know that they are tracked. However, mapping these proxies to users' affective states is complex. For example, spending a long time to complete a task may be indicative of both engagement and frustration.

Recent work by Arapakis et al. [3] found a negative correlation between self-reported affect, focussed attention, and cursor movements, where negative emotions were most indicative. Further, Parra and Brusilovsky [16] investigated the relationship between aspects of user engagement and objective information retrieval metrics, such as precision and Mean Average Precision (MAP). They found that user engagement affected performance metrics depending on the order in which people interacted with the baseline and experimental system. This suggested that using the baseline system first helped familiarise participants to the system, improving their subjective experience and subsequently affecting their behaviours.

Our ongoing work seeks to marry subjective and behavioural approaches in the context of utilitarian web-based tasks, by asking two research questions:

1. Does the UES, which was designed for online tasks of a more open (and entertaining) nature, work to capture engagement in the more constrained setting of online transactions; particularly where the user's goal is unlikely to be itself "engaging"?

2. If so, are there behaviours—click patterns, dwell times, keyboard actions—which correlate with the UES and which can be used as proxies for it?

If the answer to the second question is "yes", then it will be possible to measure engagement in near real-time and at scale, on a live site, with every user. Past experience has shown this provides useful feedback for both large- and small-scale design decisions [17],

*This work was carried out at CSIRO.

and, with sufficiently accurate proxies, it may even be possible to intervene in real-time to, e.g., provide extra help.

In this short paper we discuss our early experimental work and first observations.

2. AN EXPERIMENT

Our experiment-in-progress assigns participants a series of tasks, across different websites. They are told to carry them out as best they can using their preferred techniques. They use an instrumented browser, which records every interaction with the web, and after each task they are asked a series of questions about the task and site they have just seen. We do not assign a time limit, nor restrict the sites or tools participants can use.

Software and hardware. The experiment uses the Firefox web browser, plus custom software to manage the experiment and record interactions. This software is available on request.

Each participant progresses through five tasks, the first of which is a warm-up task and discarded. For each remaining task, participants are given instructions and then started at an appropriate "start" page according to the task (for example, the product listing page at Amazon). They are encouraged to use more tabs, browsing, searching, the forward/backward buttons, or any other technique to complete the task. A Firefox extension overlays buttons to finish the task and to repeat the instructions. After finishing each task, participants are given a series of statements from the UES—for example, "I consider my experience a success".

The control software logs participants' progress through their tasks, and questionnaire responses. Additional logging of interaction with each web page is implemented with a custom Firefox extension.

Tasks. The assigned tasks are designed to cover a range of types, based on Broder's examples of "transactional" web tasks [4]— "shopping, finding various web-mediated services, downloading various type of file (images, songs, etc), accessing certain data-bases (e.g. Yellow Pages type data), finding servers (e.g. for gaming) etc". We also cover a range of difficulty, as estimated in advance; different complexity of form or other interactive elements; and different amounts of information presented to or required from participants.

"Purchase" tasks involve filling out a series of forms to purchase an item online. They included creating an account, filling in credit card details, etc. "Sign up" are relatively simple forms, signing up for a mailing list or event. "Post" tasks involve posting short text to an aggregating site. "Database" tasks require searching a database and examining the results, with a simple form but less well-defined criteria for success.

Each participant is assigned one each of the "purchase", "sign up", "post", and "database" types, and each task comes in several variants over several sites (for a total pool of 35 task variants). Tasks are presented in counterbalanced order.

Tasks are fixed, and limited to form-filling: for example, participants are directed to make a specified purchase rather than to shop for something they like, or to look for businesses at a specified location rather than where they live. This makes the data much simpler to interpret, as we do not need to separate the transaction from browsing or searching. This is also intended to mimic government sites—there is of course no deciding what type of tax to pay, or from whom to claim a benefit.

Data recorded. We are recording browser interactions (page loads, tab opens/closes/switches, key presses, mouse moves, mouse clicks and drags); screen capture; and audio and video of each participant. We also collect basic demographic information and ask whether the assigned tasks were understandable and representative.

All data collected will be made available, except audio and video since these are identifiable.

The User Engagement Scale. Earlier work [17] followed the practice of, for example, the UK Government [10] in using a single five-point item to measure satisfaction. This has the advantage of being quick and easy for respondents, but it is not well-validated and does not capture much information. We adopt a more nuanced approach by using the User Engagement Scale [15]. The full scale has 31 items, each recorded on a five-point Likert scale ranging from "strongly disagree" to "strongly agree". In this work we used a subset (see Appendix) that measured the following dimensions:

Felt involvement (items #8–10) reflects the "feeling of being drawn into and involved" in a task. It is believed that involvement is based on a person's needs and how well the interaction satisfies those needs; the user's perception of the importance, relevance, and significance of the encounter may influence felt involvement [15].

Novelty (#11–13) pertains to users' curiosity, or response to new information.

Endurability (#14–18) is the user's overall assessment of the experience, and includes whether or not the user would re-engage with the system in future or recommend it to others: it also covers the extent to which a transaction or site is successful, rewarding, or worthwhile. This is of particular interest in e-government applications, since this may be expected to drive continued use and even digital uptake.

Perceived usability (#24–31) describes the affective (e.g., frustration) and cognitive (mentally taxing) aspects of interacting with the system, including the user's sense of control over a site or transaction.

We did not include the focussed attention or aesthetic appeal sub-scales of the UES in this study, as they were considered less important in this context. Although aesthetic appeal has been shown to influence perceived usability [12] and willingness to engage with a system [15], we were most interested in exploring engagement with the assigned tasks as opposed to attracting participants to a particular resource. Focussed attention, derived from characteristics of Flow [7], is a state of complete absorption and a general lack of awareness of external stimuli. We did not feel confident engendering such a state in an experimental setting, nor did we feel it was necessary for evaluating the user experience in this context. Pragmatically, each participant completed the UES items four times, once per task, and the experiment required extensive searching and form filling. Our decision to use four of the six sub-scales reflected our desire to reduce participants' mental workload by keeping UES items on one page and with a legible font, and reduce some of the redundancy of completing the same questionnaire multiple times. We anticipated that fewer items would lead to better quality responses than administering the entire scale.

3. OBSERVATIONS ON THE UES

Six participants have completed our pilot. All are native English speakers, degree-educated, and familiar with web forms. Ages range from 21 to 64, and men and women are equally represented.

We had twenty-four responses to the UES sub-scales to draw upon. With this sample size, it was not possible to perform factor analysis to examine the dimensionality of the items we used.

UES sub-scale	Cases	Items	Cronbach's α	Mean (SD)	PUs	END	NO
Perceived usability (PUs)	23	8	.904	4.08 (0.78)	1		
Endurability (END)	24	5	.894	3.65 (0.88)	.617**	1	
Novelty (NO)	24	3	.746	3.06 (0.75)	.352	.504*	1
Felt involvement (FIN)	23	3	.472	3.11 (0.61)	.185	.254	.702**

Table 1: Reliability analysis and descriptive statistics for UES sub-scales. * p significant at .05, ** p significant at .01 (two-tailed test).

However, we did look at the internal consistency of the sub-scales before investigating the relationship between UES responses and performance measures.

First, we reverse coded some items (see Appendix) and examined the data for missing values. There were two instance of missing responses for one Perceived Usability (PUs) and one Felt Involvement (FIN) item; these missing items were recorded for two different participants (P2; P3) and for two different tasks (sign up; purchase).

We explored the reliability of the four sub-scales using Cronbach's α based on the item groupings suggested by O'Brien and Toms (Table 1). Based on DeVellis' guidelines [8], Cronbach's α values between 0.7 and 0.9 were considered optimal. The endurability (END), Novelty (NO), and Perceived Usability (PUs) sub-scales demonstrated good internal consistency; there may have been some redundancy with PUs, but removing items would not have substantially changed the α value. We retained all items, particularly as we were dealing with a small pilot sample.

The reliability of the Felt Involvement (FIN) sub-scale was poor (0.472). We examined the inter-item correlations of the FIN items and found that the item "I felt involved in this task" was uncorrelated with the other two items (0.033); removing this item increased Cronbach's α to 0.76. Alpha levels are affected by small numbers of items [6], so for the purposes of this exploratory analysis we retained all three items.

Based on the reliability analysis, we computed composite values for the sub-scales to use in the remainder of the analysis. All items within the sub-scale were added and divided by the total number of items; this was done to give equal weight to all items within each sub-scale and ease comparisons across the sub-scales. We then examined the means (standard deviations) and inter-scale correlations.

Means for the NO, END and FIN sub-scales were average for a five-point scale, while perceived usability was high. This may reflect inflation in participants' responses; on the other hand it may indicate few challenges with the functionality of the systems, and indicate that evaluating other aspects of users' experiences is feasible and useful. While PUs and END, NO and END, and NO and FIN were significantly correlated, there were poor correlations between PUs, NO and FIN, and END and FIN. Given the poor correlations observed when we examined the distinct NO and FIN sub-scales, we explored the reliability of a combined 6-item FIN and NO sub-scale (Cronbach's $\alpha = 0.816$) and its relationship to PUs ($r = 0.336$, $p = .094$) and END ($r = 0.426$, $p = .043$).

The high correlation between NO and FIN suggested that these two sub-scales may be tapping into the same variable in this study. The combined NOFIN had greater internal consistency than either of the NO or FIN sub-scales on their own, and was moderately correlated with PUs and END, though only the correlation with END was significant.

4. OBSERVATIONS ON BEHAVIOURS

The User Engagement Scale provides a useful tool for understanding, and quantifying, relevant aspects of user experience. The scale was, however, designed for controlled experiments, and is fairly complex and slow to complete; even in the final, abbreviated,

Sub-scale	Behaviour	Coef.	p
PUs	Time on task (s)	0.001	.12
	Sequence in session	-0.203	.15
END	Mouse distance (px)	1.4×10^{-5}	.03*
	Keypresses	9.4×10^{-4}	.17
NO	Time on task (s)	0.002	.05*
FIN	Keypresses	0.001	.03*
NOFIN	Keypresses	9.8×10^{-4}	.05*
	Mouse distance (px)	6.5×10^{-6}	.17

Table 2: Best built models for each sub-scale. * p significant at .05.

version there are 18 items and displayed on one entire screen, so the UES may not always be suitable for online experimentation.

Inspired by the success of implicit feedback in search evaluation, we ask: are there behaviours which we can observe, and which predict how people will respond to the UES? If there are, we can use these behaviours as proxies for the full scale (or items from it), which would allow us to infer something about engagement with transactions at scale, at close to real-time, and over the complete set of users. This in turn may allow targeted and timely feedback for designers, based on how people use their site "in the wild".

For each participant in our pilot, and each task/site, we have recorded a good deal of interaction information (Section 2). To answer the question above, we built linear models to predict participants' replies on each sub-scale as a response to keyboard and mouse activity (keypresses, backspaces, clicks, mouse moves, total mouse distance); browsing activity (pages viewed, tabs opened and closed, maximum tabs open at once, switches in focus amongst page elements); and time (elapsed time per task, task sequence in the run). Models were selected to minimise AIC [2], which combines accuracy with a penalty for each variable introduced.

Table 2 summarises the models built from our pilot data. For each sub-scale, a different set of observations provides the best fit: for example perceived usability is predicted by time and sequence, while endurability correlates with total mouse distance and keypresses. In general, we see that more interactions predicts greater satisfaction on the endurability, felt involvement, and combined novelty/felt involvement sub-scales; while time on task predicts greater novelty and usability. There is also evidence of an order effect for perceived usability (only), with later tasks recording lower scores, although this is controlled for in our design.

Note that while the coefficients are small, the range of each explanatory variable is large: for example, the first- to third-quartile range of mouse distances is 14,330 to 38,750 pixels which corresponds to 0.34 points (of 5) on the endurability sub-scale. There are similar effect sizes for other variables.

These are early results, but they give us some confidence that the answer to our second research question is "yes", and that automated analysis of user engagement is possible to some degree. We also note that the differences in Table 2 argue for using several sub-scales for engagement, rather than a single combined scale.

5. SUMMARY AND FURTHER WORK

There has been little attention, to date, on measuring the usability (or other aspects of experience) of online forms and other transactions in a way which scales well and which is theoretically grounded. The User Engagement Scale, which has been validated in other contexts, appears to work well in this setting with minor modifications. Further, several easily observable user behaviours—including time on task and mouse movement—correlate with each UES sub-scale and have some promise as a proxy for the full scale.

We emphasise that this is early work and, as well as gathering further data, there are several directions for future investigation. First, we intend further analyses of the UES data to validate it in this context; with more data, factor analysis techniques can be brought to bear and we hope to confirm (or otherwise) the dimensions examined above. Second, given the current instrumentation there are further signals which may serve to predict UES responses: for example, the number of times a user re-visits a form element or the number of times a user scrolls back up a page. Finally, we have not yet collected enough data to consider the effect of task type: it may be that different types of task can make use of different types of signal. If we can determine sufficiently precise predictors, it will be possible to analyse experience at scale and provide automated assistance for form and transaction design. It may also be possible to connect this analysis of transactions with existing work analysing search and browsing, to provide a fuller picture of user experience with web sites.

References

[1] E Agichtein, E Brill, and S Dumais. Improving web search ranking by incorporating user behaviour information. In *Proc. SIGIR*, pages 19–26, August 2006.

[2] H Akaike. A new look at the statistical model identification. *IEEE Trans. Automatic Control*, 19(6):716–723, 1974.

[3] I Arapakis, M Lalmas, and G Valkanas. Understanding within-content engagement through pattern analysis of mouse gestures. In *Proc. CIKM*, pages 1439–1448, 2014.

[4] A Broder. A taxonomy of web search. *SIGIR Forum*, 36(2), Fall 2002.

[5] Cabinet Office. Digital efficiency report, November 2012. Retrieved 21 August 2013 from http://publications.cabinetoffice.gov.uk/digital/efficiency/digital-efficiency-report.pdf.

[6] J M Cortina. What is coefficient alpha? An examination of theory and applications. *J Applied Psychology*, 28(1):98–104, 1993.

[7] M Csikszentmihalyi. *Flow: The Psychology of Optimal Experience*. Harper & Row, New York, 1990.

[8] R F DeVellis. *Scale development: Theory and applications*. Sage, Thousand Oaks, California, 2nd edition, 2003.

[9] H Feild, J Allan, and R Jones. Predicting searcher frustration. In *Proc. SIGIR*, pages 34–41, 2010.

[10] Government Digital Service. Government service design manual: User satisfaction, 2014. Retrieved 17 August 2014 from https://www.gov.uk/service-manual/measurement/user-satisfaction.html.

[11] T Joachims, L Granka, B Pan, H Hembrooke, F Radlinksi, and G Gay. Evaluating the accuracy of implicit feedback from clicks and query reformulations in web search. *ACM Trans. Info. Systems*, 25(2), April 2007.

[12] G Lindgaard, G Fernandes, C Dudek, and J Brown. Attention web designers: You have 50 milliseconds to make a good first impression! *Behaviour and Information Technology*, 25: 115–126, 2006.

[13] H L O'Brien. The influence of hedonic and utilitarian motivations on user engagement: the case of online shopping experiences. *Interacting with Computers*, 22(4):344–352, 2010.

[14] H L O'Brien and P Cairns. Generalizing the User Engagement Scale to online news websites. *Information Processing and Management*, 51(4):413–427, 2015.

[15] H L O'Brien and E G Toms. The development and evaluation of a survey to measure user engagement. *J American Society for Information Science and Technology*, 61(1):50–69, 2010.

[16] D Parra and P Brusilovsky. User-controllable personalization: A case study with set-fusion. *Int. J Human-Computer Studies*, 77:43–67, 2014.

[17] P Thomas. Using interaction data to explain difficulty navigating online. *ACM Transactions on the Web*, 8(4):24, 2014.

APPENDIX

Our study used the following subset of UES items:

Felt involvement:
8. I was really drawn in to my task.
9. I felt involved in this task.
10. This experience was fun.

Novelty:
11. I continued using this website out of curiosity.
12. The content of the website incited my curiosity.
13. I felt interested in my task.

Endurability:
14. Using this website was worthwhile.
15. I consider my experience a success.
16. This experience did not work out the way I had planned.[†]
17. My experience was rewarding.
18. I would recommend using this website to my friends and family.

Perceived usability:
24. I felt frustrated while visiting this website.[†]
25. I found this website confusing to use.[†]
26. I felt annoyed while visiting this website.[†]
27. I felt discouraged while visiting this website.[†]
28. Using this website was mentally taxing.[†]
29. This experience was demanding.[†]
30. I felt in control of my experience.
31. I could not do some of the things I needed to do on this website.[†]

Item numbering reflects the original [15]. Items marked † are reverse coded.

Exploring the Benefits of 2D Visualizations for Drum Samples Retrieval

Chloé Turquois
chloeturquois@live.fr

Martin Hermant
martin.hermant@upf.edu

Daniel Gómez
daniel.gomez@upf.edu

Sergi Jordà
sergi.jorda@upf.edu

Music Technology Group
Universitat Pompeu Fabra
Roc Boronat, 138
08018 Barcelona, Spain

ABSTRACT

This paper explores the potential benefits of using similarity-based two-dimensional classifications and their corresponding GUIs, for drum samples retrieval in a creativity-oriented context. Preliminary user studies with professional electronic music producers point up the frustration and laboriousness of finding suitable drum samples in the increasingly large libraries of sounds available, and suggest the need for alternative interfaces and approaches. To address this issue, two novel spatial visualizations (respectively organized by name and by timbre-similarity) are designed as potential alternatives to the traditional 1D list-based browsers. These visualizations are implemented and compared in a music creation task, in terms of both the exploration experience and the resulting production quality, within a system for drum kit configuration. Our study shows that spatial visualizations do improve the overall exploration experience, and reveals the potential of similarity-based arrangements for the support of creative processes.

Keywords

Music interaction, creativity, spatial visualization, user studies.

1. INTRODUCTION

The creation of music is an essential creative human activity and it can be seen as the most paradigmatic of the creative arts. In contemporary music production, machines constitute an integral part of this creativity. However, most current tools for digital music production still lack of support for creative exploration and inspiration. Music production professionals would like to work faster; creative musicians and producers envision free-flowing and inspiring tools that could boost their creativity by minimizing technical difficulties and personal limitations. Nowadays, one of the most well identified bottlenecks to creativity in digital music production is the difficulty of finding suitable sound samples. Samples are short sound files such as a drum hit, often arranged rhythmically and put together to form a track. Producers dispose of increasingly large libraries of samples (often several thousands) from numerous databases. The current interfaces, displaying the samples in long scroll lists of sometimes poorly indicative file

names, seem unadapted for browsing such large sound libraries. Interviews performed with 16 expert music producers [1] confirmed the tediousness of this type of interfaces and the need for more intuitive and inspiring modes of exploration. On the other hand, the current state of Music Information Retrieval (MIR) provides methods for automatically classifying sounds according to criteria, such as their pitch or timbre, which are potentially more meaningful than their file name.

We are interested in the potential of two-dimensional (2D) visualizations, and especially similarity-based 2D visualizations (using timbre classification tools), in replacing the traditional 1D list for the exploration of samples libraries. Therefore we examine the suitability of: a) using a 2D visualization for browsing drum samples, and b) using perceptual similarity algorithms for organizing this 2D visualization, so that two samples that sound similar are placed close to each other. In this paper, we present a comparative study using different visualizations of a drum samples library. The visualizations are used by participants in a creative task, where they have to choose a set of drum samples to compose a rhythmic track. We explore how these interfaces affect the overall exploration, user satisfaction and outcome quality. The rest of this document is structured as follows: Section 2 reviews some related work in the psychology and sound computing research communities, Section 3 presents the alternative spatial visualization we designed, which is compared within a study described in Section 4 and further discussed in Section 5, before concluding in Section 6.

2. BACKGROUND

2.1. Creativity and Flow

There is currently a growing interest in HCI research for designing tools that promote creativity and not only productivity [12]. Creativity, according to its more agreed definition, is the generation of something that is both original and valuable [13]. In psychology, the most recognized theories depict creativity as a combination of divergent, free-flowing processes, where the subject generates many solutions in a rather unconstrained manner, and of convergent, analytical processes, where she interprets, evaluates and refines these solutions[4][7]. To promote creativity, a system should therefore support both types of creative processes: unrestricted, divergent processes on the one hand, and convergent, critical processes on the other hand. On another hand, flow, an "almost autotelic, effortless, yet highly focused state of consciousness" [3], has been positively correlated with higher performance in creative activities [10]. It is thus important, when supporting creativity, to try and preserve the flow that the user might be experiencing. Indeed, flow is a very fragile state that is easily disrupted by tedious or unrelated tasks.

2.2. Timbre, MIR and Timbre Spaces

Timbre is usually described as the "color" of a sound, or all the qualities of a sound that are not its pitch, level, duration and location [8]. It is a multidimensional property that is related to the changes of amplitude and phase of the spectral components of the sound. Music Information Retrieval allows to extract many attributes from a sound to describe its timbre. These descriptors can be used to classify sounds by similarity. Although we cannot yet guarantee which dimensions are the most relevant for perceptual similarity in a given group of sounds, mapping perceptual similarity to spatial proximity, so that timbres that are similar are placed close to each other, is called a timbre-space [6].

To help handling the increasingly large amounts of multimedia content, researchers have developed several tools for browsing audio materials by similarity, using spatial representation and content-based information retrieval. The Snare-Drum Navigator [5] is a 2D timbre-space interface of snare drum sounds represented as colored rectangles. The efficiency of this interface was evaluated in a study where users had to find a given sample as fast as possible. They showed that users' performance improved faster when the samples were sorted by similarity than randomly. However, until now, user studies on such tools have focused mostly on efficiency, only involving non-creative tasks.

3. DRUMSPACE

We designed Drumspace as an alternative to the aforementioned scroll lists for browsing drum samples. Using 2D representation and Music Information Retrieval, Drumspace aims to improve the exploration and retrieval of samples, and in particular to better support the creative workflow in these activities.

3.1. Objectives

To support the creative workflow in the search of sounds, the interface should support the two "directions" of creative processes (convergent and divergent). Considering the divergent processes, the interface should allow for an unrestricted exploration and facilitate direct access to a diversity of materials. On the other hand, and with consideration to the convergent/critical side, we need to facilitate the evaluation of samples in context (fitness with the other drum sounds and the overall composition) and the reduction of the solution space. More generally, despite not being a musical instrument in itself, the system should be suited for a creative utilization. That is, the musicians should be able to use it for coming up with novel and relevant sounds or ideas. To support the state of flow, the system should require as little cognitive effort as possible, be easy to learn and to use. The number of features and commands should be limited to what is strictly necessary in order not to disrupt the flow or obstruct the user from her goal and her ongoing creation.

3.2. 2D representation of samples

The first advantage of a 2D representation over the list is to offer an instant overview of all the available samples. Unlike the linear exploration afforded by 1D lists, the exploration can be guided by other various strategies. Finally, scattering the samples on 2D takes advantage of the human ability to deal with spatial locations and relationships [11].

Current list browsers often display sample names ordered alphabetically. The correspondence between name and sound is mostly arbitrary and the large number of samples does surely not allow memorizing all these correspondences. Nor does it allow inferring where a particular sample could be located. Timbre, on the other side, is probably the most relevant quality for describing a

drum sound. If sound samples are arranged by timbre on a 2D plane, their proximity to each other will suggest their similarity, while their position on the plane will directly inform on some perceptual timbral qualities. This can guide the exploration such that if a user listens to a sample that happens to be very different from what she needs, she should go and explore another zone, and inversely, refining her choice progressively towards the sounds she likes. With time, she can memorize the overall spatial arrangement and develop expectations as to where she is most likely to find a certain type of sound.

4. COMPARATIVE STUDY

Can spatial visualization improve the exploration of sound libraries and support better creativity in music production? The goal of this comparative study is to explore the suitability and the convenience of a) using 2D interfaces for exploring sounds in a database, and more particularly of b) using timbre similarity algorithms for automatically clustering these sounds in 2D. The hypothesis is that these solutions will ease the process of finding suitable sounds, thus improving the user's experience and creative outcome.

4.1. Experiment prototype

To test this hypothesis, we integrated Drumspace into a browser application for the creation of drum kits. Users can browse a library of 1226 drum sounds and select 4 of them to be used together on a given rhythmic track. As shown in Figure 1, the interface is split into 4 panels, one for each sample family that we have selected as voices for the rhythmic tracks, namely: Kick, Snare, Open Hi-Hat and Closed Hi-Hat. Each panel contains all the samples of a family, which can be displayed in three different views, as later explained in *Visualizations*. The central red button allows playing and stopping the drum track, which consist of a predefined rhythm to which the selected samples are applied in real-time.

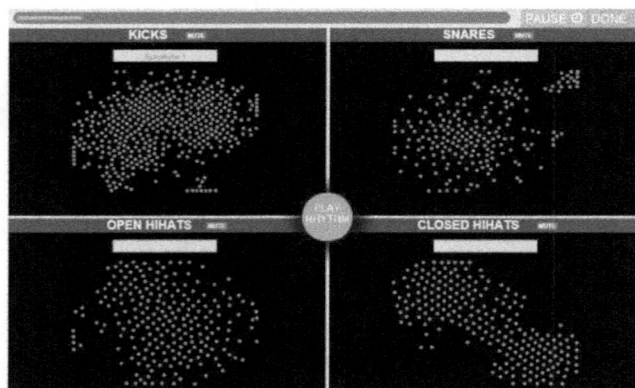

Figure 1. Interface for drum kit creation created for this study.

4.1.1. Interaction

Users interact with the application using a normal desktop mouse and a keyboard. Each sample is represented by a circle. The user can listen to any sample by just pointing the mouse over it. The user selects a sample (e.g. a *kick*) by clicking on its circle; the circle is highlighted in red and the sample becomes the current *kick* voice within the rhythm.

4.1.2. Visualizations

For the purpose of our comparative study we implemented three visualizations of the library, which differ in dimensionality and ordering: 1D list; alphabetical 2D; and similarity based 2D. As shown in Fig. 2a, the list view resembles as closely as possible the library browsers used in most DAWS: 1 dimension, alphabetical order, with the file names visible. The second view (Fig. 2b) differs from the list by its dimensionality (2 dimensions), but maintains the alphabetical order. Samples are arranged on lines based on the first letter of their names. Finally, the third view (Fig. 2c) differs from the list in both its dimensionality and in the spatial arrangements of samples: samples are scattered on the 2D plan according to their timbre similarity. This timbre similarity space was built using the open-source C++ library Essentia for audio analysis and audio-based MIR [2], based on the list of audio descriptors used in Timbre Toolbox [9], and a Student-t Stochastic Neighbor Embedding (tSNE) 2D dimension reduction [14].

4.2. Methods

The experiment was composed of two parts: Drum kit creation, in which participants used alternatively the three different views of the samples to compose drum sets for different given rhythmic patterns, and a Drum kit evaluation, in which listeners were asked to evaluate the quality of the loops created in the first phase.

4.2.1. Part I: Drum kit creation

20 participants took part in this first phase (18 musicians and 2 nonmusicians). The experiment was composed of 9 consecutive trials with a maximum duration of 3 minutes each, with each of the 3 views being used on 3 respective trials. In each trial, participants were given a rhythmic pattern with 4 very basic "default" sounds (kick, snare, open and closed hi-hat), playing on loop. Participants were asked to browse the drum samples and choosing one sample for each family (1 kick, 1 snare, 1 open hi-hat and 1 closed hi-hat) in order to replace the initial default sounds within the given rhythm. At the end of each trial, participants were asked to rate how satisfied they were with 1) the given rhythmic pattern, and 2) the drumkit they had created (i.e. the sounds they chose). The rating was made on a discrete 3-point Likert scale from 0 ("not at all") to 2 ("very satisfied"). Upon completing the 9 different patterns of the experiment, participants were also invited to comment briefly on the three different views in an open-interview format. They commented freely on their overall experience, and were finally asked which view they preferred to use and why.

4.2.2. Part II: Drum kit evaluation

In this test, the drum loops created by the participants in the first part were listened and evaluated by 24 listeners, both musicians (10 of them experienced in digital music production) and non-musicians. The evaluation was done remotely using an online application. Each evaluator was assigned a set of 21 rhythmic loops to evaluate (out of the 180 -- 9 patterns x 20 participants -- created in the first part). Each set comprised 7 different rhythmic patterns, and 3 different drumkit sound combinations per pattern, created by different creators using different views. The sets were presented in a randomized order, and evaluators were asked to base their rating on

any criteria that they found relevant, such as overall quality of the loop, fitness of the chosen samples to the rhythm, or originality.

4.3. Results

4.3.1. Part I

First, the number of listened samples per trial was significantly lower with the list view (M=46.9) than with either of the two 2D views (M=93.2 with the alphabetical 2D view, and M=101.2 with the similarity-based 2D view), $\chi2(2)$ =30.9, p<0.001 at the p<0.017 significance level.

For studying the alphabetic repartition of samples chosen, a score was assigned to each selected sample according to the alphabetic index of its name's first letter (e.g. "Beastie" gets 2 points, "Zyklotron" gets 26 points). There was a significant effect of the view on the alphabetic position of the chosen samples, F(2,38)=14.6, p<0.001. Scheffe post hoc analyses indicated that the List view score (M=29.5, SD=22.4) was significantly lower than the Alphabetical 2D view (M=43.7, SD=12.6) or the 2D-timbre view (M=47.4, SD=13.9), which did not differ from each other. Regarding *Result satisfaction*, a Friedman test of differences on repeated measures showed a close to significant effect, with participants being more satisfied with their creation when using the Alphabetical 2D view: $\chi2(2)$=5.9, p=0.052.

During the post-hoc interviews, 8 participants out of 20 declared preferring the 2D-timbre view, 8 preferred the 2D-alphabetical view, 3 preferred the list view, and 1 expressed no preference. Considering the dimensionality exclusively, chi-square goodness-of-fit showed a significant preference for 2D views over 1D List, $\chi2$ (2, N=20) = 19.9, p < 0.005.

4.3.2. Part II

We did not measure any significant difference between the scores of the drum kits created by the three views. To isolate the appreciation of the chosen sounds from that of the rhythm itself, we subtracted to each score the score given by the same evaluator to the same rhythm rendered with default sounds. Again the view used for creating the drum kits did not have any significant effect on their assessed quality, X(2)=2.155, p=0.34. Although we randomized the repartition and order of presentation of the kits, a much larger number of evaluators would probably be required to counterbalance the subjectivity of the appreciation of drum loops.

5. DISCUSSION

5.1. Improving the exploration with 2D

The results from the first part of our study support our first hypothesis that a 2D visualization provides a better experience than a traditional list interface and seems to improve the exploration. 2D visualizations increase the diversity of samples chosen. This can be

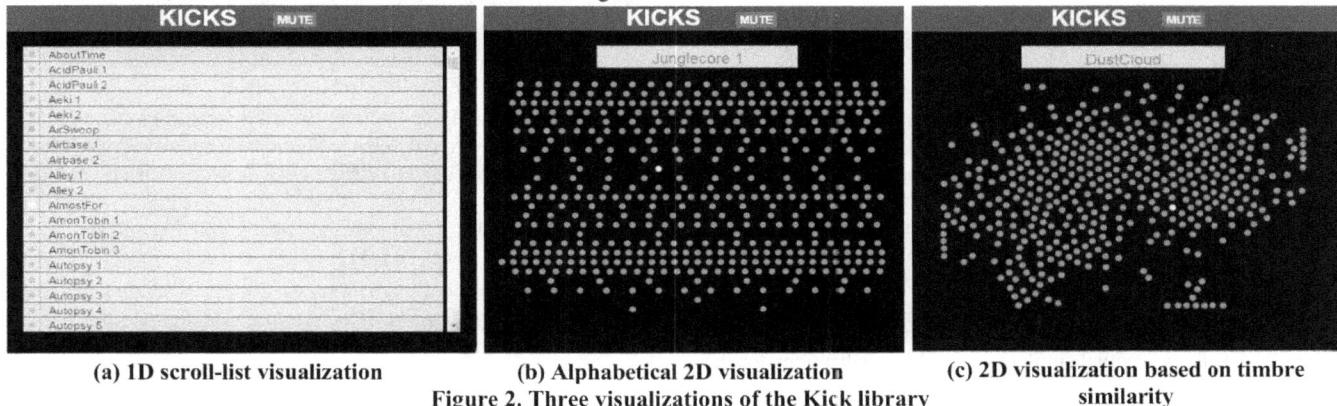

(a) 1D scroll-list visualization **(b) Alphabetical 2D visualization** **(c) 2D visualization based on timbre similarity**

Figure 2. Three visualizations of the Kick library

considered a direct benefit of the global "bird view" on the whole library: the user gets instant access to all the available samples. The follow-up interviews revealed that this encouraged a non-linear exploration rather than following the vertical distribution of the list. We also found that the 2D views let users listen to more samples over the same time span. The short distance between the samples facilitates their playback, providing the direct feedback necessary in the support of flow states, and seemingly improving the user experience (participants said it was "easier", "faster", "more pleasant", and "more fun"). This is further attested by the large preference reported by users for the 2D views over the list, and by the satisfaction ratings showing that participants tended to be more satisfied with their creation when using the 2D alphabetical view. Participants' feedback also highlighted the "experimental" aspect of the exploration on 2D interfaces. Many of them reported having discovered unexpected and inspiring sounds thanks to the non-linear and rapid browsing. For these reasons, we suggest that 2D visualizations, as they facilitate and broaden the exploration, provide an improvement in the support of flow states and, by favoring inspiration, of creativity. This however is a purely theoretical interpretation and calls to future experimentations that focus on these phenomena.

5.2.   Issues with the Timbre Space

Our results do not show any significant improvement brought by the arrangement by perceptual similarity. In the light of participants' feedback, it appears that the similarity-based arrangement was unexpectedly difficult to understand and to use efficiently. This visualization represents all samples identically and displays no axis or any indicator of the timbre similarity. It lacks transparency and does not allow the user to understand the organization of the sample space. Experimenting with more explicit representations would be necessary in order to design a more intuitive timbre space interface. For instance, the use of colors to indicate some timbral features might improve the understanding of the similarity clustering.

5.3.   Supporting Flow and Creativity

Participants who preferred the 2D-timbre view appreciated the freedom and "implicit" guidance provided by the similarity-based organization. They described their navigation as progressing from random exploration to "fine-tuning". This closely resembles the processes described in the theories on creativity (the divergent, unrestricted navigation, followed by examining and fine-tuning processes), suggesting that the 2D-timbre view is a good candidate for supporting the musicians' creative workflow.

Our results suggest that a 2D visualization of samples facilitates the exploration and improves the user experience. This suggests that spatial visualizations are beneficial for supporting the states of flow, where fluency, direct feedback and enjoyment are important factors. Therefore it would be highly relevant to design a more formal evaluation of how much this type of visualization sustains flow.

6. CONCLUSION

As an alternative to traditional list browsers we proposed a 2-dimensional visualization, where algorithms for audio-based music information retrieval allow displaying the samples in a timbre space according to their perceptual properties. Although some studies have already examined the potential of such visualizations for audio materials retrieval, they have rather been focused on efficiency and accuracy. Instead we considered the importance of the qualitative aspects in music creation: quality of the experience and quality of the outcomes. Our comparative study examined the qualitative benefits of using perceptual similarity and 2D visualizations for the exploration of samples libraries in a creative task. As predicted, users reported a strong preference for the 2D visualizations. Although we could not measure any effect on the quality of the drum loops created, 2D visualizations by facilitating the navigation and offering a broader overview, seem to improve the exploitation of the available sounds, and to promote discovery and inspiration. Contrary to our hypothesis, the arrangement by perceptual similarity did not appear more advantageous than an arbitrary arrangement by sample name. However, users' feedback on the experience suggests that perceptual similarity arrangement promotes a different, more musical exploration. It opens many perspectives for the design and the investigation of novel spatial visualizations and their potential for supporting flow and creative processes in music creation.

7. ACKNOWLEDGEMENTS

This research has been partially supported by the EU funded GiantSteps project (FP7-ICT-2013-10 Grant agreement 610591).

8. REFERENCES

[1] Andersen, K. et al. 2015. "Update on Qualitative and Quantitative Methodological Frameworks". Deliverable 2.3, GiantSteps FP7-610591. Retrieved from: http://assets.contentful.com/xrzr1u3na612/5lpsdiQKuQoOKE WwgmiQSK/04b084584af567aa04b696ee00365db7/GiantSte ps_D2.3_WP2_2015_30June_STEIM_v1.0.pdf.

[2] Bogdanov, D. et al. 2013. Essentia: an open-source library for sound and music analysis. *Proceedings of the 21st ACM international conference on Multimedia* (2013, October), 855-858.

[3] Csikszentmihalyi, M. 1997. Flow and the Psychology of Discovery and Invention. *HarperPerennial,New York*, 39.

[4] Finke, R. et al. 1992. *Creative cognition*. MIT Press.

[5] Fried, O. et al. 2014. AudioQuilt: 2D Arrangements of Audio Samples using Metric Learning and Kernelized Sorting.

[6] Grey, J. 1977. Multidimensional perceptual scaling of musical timbres. *The Journal of the Acoustical Society of America*. 61, 5 (1977), 1270.

[7] Guilford, J. 1967. Creativity: Yesterday, today and tomorrow. *The Journal of Creative Behavior*, *1*(1), 3-14.

[8] Krumhansl, Carol L. 1989. Why is musical timbre so hard to understand. *Structure and perception of electroacoustic sound and music*. 9: 43-53.

[9] Peeters, G. et al. 2011. The timbre toolbox: Extracting audio descriptors from musical signals. *The Journal of the Acoustical Society of America*, *130*(5), 2902-2916.

[10] Perry, S. 1999. *Writing in flow: Keys to enhanced creativity*. Writers Digest Books.

[11] Robertson, G. et al. 1998. Data Mountain: using spatial memory for document management. *Proceedings of the 11th annual ACM symposium on User interface software and technology* (1998), 153-162.

[12] Shneiderman, B. et al. 2006. Creativity support tools: Report from a US National Science Foundation sponsored workshop. *International Journal of Human-Computer Interaction*, *20*(2), 61-77.

[13] Stein, M. 1953. Creativity and culture. *The journal of psychology*, *36*(2), 311-322.

[14] Van der Maaten, L., & Hinton, G. 2008. Visualizing data using t-SNE. *Journal of Machine Learning Research 9*, (2008), 2579-2605.

Category Oriented Task Extraction

Manisha Verma
University College London
m.verma@cs.ucl.ac.uk

Emine Yilmaz
University College London
emine.yilmaz@ucl.ac.uk

ABSTRACT

With increasing amounts of digital content, users can accomplish complex tasks online, thus making task extraction from query logs an active area of research. Recently, some approaches have proposed entity based extraction of tasks, where they either use entities as features or construct task dictionaries that contain multiple tasks. While text based features do not exploit entities directly, task dictionaries do not provide concise or distinct representation of tasks. We overcome these shortcomings by extracting category oriented tasks by exploiting properties of an existing, publicly available category hierarchy. We evaluate quality of these tasks with implicit, explicit and application based evaluation. Empirical evaluation shows that category based task extraction results in more accurate and useful tasks.

Categories and Subject Descriptors

H.3.3 [**Information Search and Retrieval**]: Information Search and Retrieval

Keywords

search tasks, query log analysis, task discovery

1. INTRODUCTION

Information retrieval systems are indispensable today. Users interact with search engines for trivial things like reading news and for complex goals like planning their weddings online. While some information needs can be expressed concisely with a single query, relatively complex user goals require users to issue several queries to the search engine. While significant work exists [4, 6, 7, 9] to understand atomic information need from a single query, understanding user goals from multiple queries is relatively unexplored. Understanding search tasks spanning several queries (or sessions) is exacerbated when users try to accomplish several goals in parallel. It has been shown that approximately 75% of user

CHIIR '16, March 13-17, 2016, Carrboro, NC, USA
© 2016 ACM. ISBN 978-1-4503-3751-9/16/03. . . $15.00
DOI: http://dx.doi.org/10.1145/2854946

search sessions involve multi-tasking activity [9]. Thus, understanding and differentiating between different user goals is a crucial step in satisfying an information need.

Often, such goals are centered around some real world '*object*' or '*thing*'. It has been shown that several search queries consist of an object or thing. For instance, for '*planning a trip*', user queries may contain entities of type *location* (e.g., 'Mexico','India') or *company* (e.g., 'orbitz', 'tripadvisor'). Thus, entities in the query, surrounding non-entity terms and corresponding clicked documents provide an intuition about the task user is trying to accomplish. Also, different users can perform similar tasks with homogeneous entities. For example, two users trying to plan a trip to 'London' and 'Mexico' respectively will issue similar queries regarding 'ticket booking' or 'hotel booking'. Thus, tasks can be extracted by aggregating queries from different users that contain entities of same type[1]. Primary advantage of extracting entity specific tasks is that these tasks are user and session agnostic. Entity specific tasks do not rely on session demarcation (via time splitting) or number of users in the data, it results in tasks that exist globally.

Verma *et al.* [11] explore building task dictionaries by exploiting entities directly. However these dictionaries will contain terms from multiple tasks. The dictionary itself does not contain meaningful tasks and its terms need to be grouped further to form coherent tasks. Also, their work does not exploit the type hierarchy to prune tasks. In this work, we build upon [11] by exploring several techniques to group queries in these category dictionaries into tasks. We also use entity category hierarchy to prune and improve quality of extracted tasks. We use implicit and explicit means of evaluation to compare our approach with existing task extraction baselines. Experiments on manually tagged AOL[2] search log indicate that entity specific clustering achieves better accuracy and coverage on task extraction. We also evaluate the quality of extracted tasks with query term prediction. Given a session, we use task terms related to entities in the first query to predict terms of subsequent queries in the session. Experiments indicate that entity oriented tasks can predict query terms significantly better than existing task extraction baselines.

2. RELATED WORK

Recent work on task extraction [4, 6, 7, 9] from search logs focused on aggregating queries from a *single* or multi-

---

[1]Entity type, category or class refer to DBpedia ontology
[2]http://www.gregsadetsky.com/aol-data/

Figure 1: AOL queries tasks for child nodes of type: Organization

Company
 a. [addresses of dreamworks studios, location microsoft seattle, ashley furniture store get to]
 b. [aol contact phone, america online customer number, yellow pages whirlpool phone number]
 c. [apple stores, store that sells power battery]

Educational Institution
 a. [get into community college, georgia tech admission]
 b. [career technology center ny, valencia medical community college]
 c. [address cincinnati public library]

ple search sessions of a single user into different tasks. Primary goal is to segment a search session into disjoint sets of sequential queries, each set indicating different task. Tasks extracted from such approaches have to be clustered across users to get a global set of tasks (as shown in [10]). Some researchers have attempted to extract cross-session tasks [1, 7, 10, 12] from search log based on classification and clustering methods. Lucchese *et al.* In [10] cluster tasks across users via text-based features clustering to create a global representation. While we also use Wikipedia categories to calculate semantic features, we explore task extraction for entity-types present in DBPedia ontology.

Hua *et al.* [5], also use knowledge base entities to find task phrases. Their assumption is that a single query represents an atomic task. They do not exploit sessions or entity-type hierarchy to group related tasks. The works most related to ours is White *et al.* [2] and Verma *et al.* [11] respectively. While the former attempts to build a network of all possible tasks from search logs, the latter uses entities to build task dictionaries. Our work differs from [2] in that they rely on rules to extract task terms and phrases. Although, this results in high precision of extracted tasks, it severely affects the recall as these rules will have limited coverage. In [11], each category is represented by a dictionary of terms which in-turn will capture several tasks. These category dictionaries have to be clustered *further* to identify meaningful tasks. We build upon these dictionaries, not using terms but queries and group queries in every category to form meaningful tasks. They also do not leverage the type hierarchy to group queries into tasks, which is also a contribution of our work.

3. METHODOLOGY

Our objective is to identify tasks associated with entity categories present in a knowledge base. Search intents are usually associated with some entity, and similar entities in-tun can be grouped into broad classes. Thus, we can identify what type of user tasks are associated with these classes by mining search logs. We define tasks to be a coherent group of queries that elicit same action or intent with respect to an entity-type. For our work, a cluster of queries that capture entity specific intent is a task. Some examples of category oriented tasks are provided in Figure 1.

Given a hierarchy of N entity categories $\mathcal{H} = \bigcup_{i=0}^{N} C_i$, a query log $\mathcal{L} = \bigcup_{j=0}^{M} q_j$ with M queries, our objective is to group queries assigned to each category node C_i into coherent and disjoint sets of tasks i.e. $C_i = \bigcup_{k=1}^{N_{it}} T_{ik}$, where each task is a set of queries, i.e. $T_{ik} = \bigcup_{m=1}^{N_{ikq}} q_{ikm}$. Here, number of tasks in C_i is N_{it} and number of queries in task T_{ik} is given

by N_{ikq}. The process of task extraction be summarized in following steps:

1. **Entity Tagging and Query Aggregation** : First step is to identify all the entities in a query with an entity tagger. Queries are then aggregated as per their entity-type.

2. **Task Extraction** : Since a single user goal can be represented by several queries, we cluster queries in each category to extract distinct tasks. When a query is not assigned an appropriate task cluster at a category node, it is moved to most similar cluster on neighboring nodes. This follows from intuition that a query may not be as relevant to a task of particular category but could be more relevant to tasks in either its parent or children nodes.

3.1 Entity Tagging And Query Aggregation

We use Dexter [3] to link queries with entities. We rely on DBpedia[3] for their type information. For each query, Dexter returns the phrases in the query that map to an entity (entity mentions), the entity and its categories.

Since queries follow Zipfian distribution, constructing query clusters for each entity will yield too many entities with only handful of queries and entities that occur rarely in the logs will have too few queries. Aggregation of these queries over entity-types alleviates this problem. Post aggregation, each category node in hierarchy has several queries containing entities of that category. For example in Figure 1, queries mapped to type '*Company*' contain several entities like '*aol*' and '*America online*'.

3.2 Task Extraction

Final step is to cluster queries in each category into tasks. Several approaches exist in the literature that can be adapted to cluster short text. We propose an approach that exploits DBpedia type hierarchy to arrange queries into tasks. Firstly, we prune categories with very few queries or categories with high overlap with its neighbors via a merge factor min_{sp}. By varying min_{sp}, we control the depth of resultant hierarchy of categories. Secondly, we use parent-child relationship to re-assign queries with low clustering coefficients. This controls the percentage of outliers in tasks.

Centroid based clustering approaches need number of categories prior clustering. It is infeasible to set number of clusters for each category in the hierarchy. Hence, so as to tune minimum parameters per category, we adopt DPMeans[8] to cluster queries. DPMeans is a non-parametric variant of kmeans which does not require number of clusters but determines it from input data. Our approach iteratively groups queries in each category into tasks, while exploiting DBpedia category hierarchy to handle queries with low clustering coefficients.

A query can be represented with help of several attributes like ngrams, clicks etc. We use the following feature space to represent each query.

Text and Log based features.

Query unigrams (uni_i) and bigrams (bi_i) are used as features. A query may be issued by multiple users and several documents may be clicked for the same query. Since search

---

[3]version 3.9

Algorithm 1 Category specific task extraction
___
Input: Category hierarchy $\mathcal{H}$, Queries $\mathcal{L}$, min_{sp}, min_{sc}
Output: Category hierarchy $\mathcal{H}'$ with tasks
1: **for** $q_i, q_j \in \mathcal{L}$ **do**
2: $\quad sim[q_i][q_j] = \sum_k w_k cos(f_{ki}, f_{kj})$
3: **end for**
4: **for** category $C_i \in \mathcal{H}$ **do**
5: $\quad$ **for** parent $P_{ij} \in par(C_i)$ **do**
6: $\quad\quad$ **if** $\frac{|C_i \cap P_{ij}|}{|C_i \cup P_{ij}|} > min_{sp}$ **then**
7: $\quad\quad\quad$ merge(C_i, P_{ij})
8: $\quad\quad$ **end if**
9: $\quad$ **end for**
10: **end for**
11: **for** category $C_i \in \mathcal{H}$ **do**
12: $\quad C'_i = dpmeans(C_i, sim)$[8]
13: **end for**
14: **for** category $C'_i \in \mathcal{H}'$ **do**
15: $\quad$ **for** queries $q_{ij} \in \mathbf{C}'_{\mathbf{i}}$ **do**
16: $\quad\quad$ **if** $sc(q_{ij}) < min_{sc}$ **then**
17: $\quad\quad\quad$ merge with nearest cluster $\in \{par(C'_i) \cup child(C'_i)\}$
18: $\quad\quad$ **end if**
19: $\quad$ **end for**
20: **end for**
___

logs are usually divided in sessions, these queries could appear in multiple sessions as well. Thus, a query is represented by union of following vectors: Clicked URLs (url_i) vector, where each dimension is number of times a URL was clicked for the query. We represent number of times query was issued by different users as a vector ($user_i$) and number of times it appeared in a session by vector ($sess_i$).

Semantic features.

Since a query may contain entities and these entities may belong to some categories, both entity (ent_i) and category (cat_i) of a query can be used as features.

3.2.1 Grouping queries into Tasks

The algorithm used to cluster queries into tasks is shown in Algorithm 1. Algorithm takes category hierarchy $\mathcal{H}$, query log $\mathcal{L}$ and minimum thresholds (min_{sc} (minimum clustering coefficient) and min_{sp}) (merge factor) as input. The algorithm begins by calculating similarity between each pair of queries (Steps 1-3). We use linear combination (w_k) of cosine similarity (cos) between features (f_k) described above. For simplicity, we uniformly combine these similarities (i.e. $w_k = \frac{1}{7}$) to obtain final similarity between two queries.

There may be several categories that significantly overlap with other categories in the hierarchy. Such categories can be safely merged with highly similar parents ($par(C_i)$) for speed up. Steps 4-11 merge categories (C_i) with parents (P_{ij}) that exceed threshold min_{sp} of query overlap using $merge$ function. Pruned categories (C_i), with (sim) similarity matrix are clustered using $dpmeans$ function in Steps 12-14.

Some queries get mapped incorrectly to a category due to error in entity tagging and will have low clustering coefficient. We re-assign queries with clustering coefficient (sc) less than certain threshold (min_{sc}) to appropriate tasks from neighboring categories in Steps 15-21. For example in query

'garfield sheriff department', the entity 'garfield', if mapped to *cartoon* instead of the *county* 'garfield', would be an outlier in category 'comics', its parents as well its child nodes. Thus, such queries should either be re-assigned or removed. Finally, we obtain a hierarchy of categories (entity-types), each category node comprised of query clusters, each cluster representing a unique and distinct task.

4. EXPERIMENTAL SETUP

We use publicly available 2006 AOL to extract entity oriented tasks. For evaluation data, five annotators were asked to label 11976 queries from 500 users into tasks. Our objective was not to segment a session but to collect user and session agnostic task labels. Since manual grouping of large number of queries into tasks is difficult, we asked each annotator to label a query pair on either same or different task. This way we collected task labels for queries from different sessions and users. Two queries were defined to be on same task if user would issue them to accomplish similar tasks. For example, 'amazon buy clothes' and 'ebay buy shirts' would map to same task. In total, 24566 pairs were marked on same task. Inter-rator agreement (Fleiss kappa) was 0.67 which is substantial agreement.

4.1 Evaluation Metrics

Evaluation of approaches that group data points into clusters can be done in two ways – Internal and External evaluation. In internal evaluation, quality of clusters is summarized by average inter-cluster and intra-cluster distances. External evaluation can be used for labeled data. However, for tasks we can also employ application oriented evaluation which captures the utility of extracted tasks for a certain application. In this work, we report results for all these evaluation mechanisms.

4.1.1 External And Internal Evaluation

Commonly used evaluation metric for task extraction is pairwise precision p_{pair} and recall r_{pair} as defined in [12], where p_{pair} evaluates number of query pairs predicted in the same task; and r_{pair} evaluates how many pairs annotated in the same task are recovered by the algorithm. For internal evaluation, we report average inter-cluster and intra-cluster distance across categories on labeled data. For implicit and explicit evaluation we report metrics averaged over 20 runs on this data.

4.1.2 Term Prediction

In this work, we use term prediction to evaluate the quality of extracted tasks. Often, users issue several queries to accomplish a task. They may add or remove terms over multiple queries. This modification of terms is an indication of their importance to a particular task. Given the first query of session, if a system were to correctly detect its underlying task, it can also predict the terms that are likely to be added or removed from subsequent queries. Thus, tasks associated with entities in first query can be used to predict terms of future queries.

For each session, we use the first query to predict terms in subsequent queries of the session. We follow the approach proposed in [11] to predict terms. For each query, we use its terms to find most likely task cluster. Cosine similarity of task cluster vector with query term vector is used to rank clusters. We report the change in Precision@10 with

Figure 2: Precision & Recall with increasing #clusters (K-means) or merge factor (T-Clust) and connected-component threshold in (QCC)

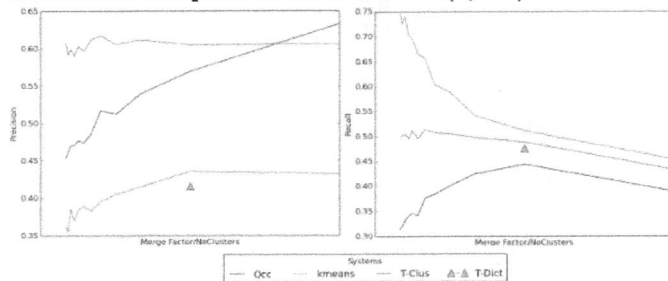

Figure 3: Precision vs #predicted terms

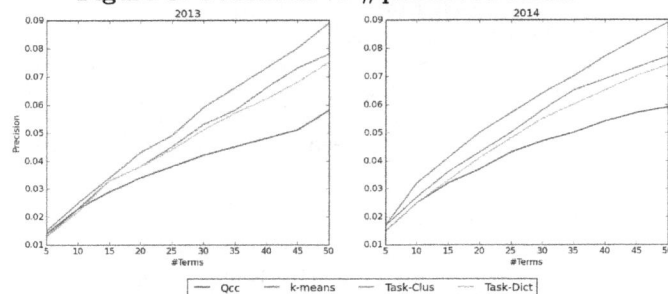

varying number of predicted terms. For term prediction, we use 2013-2014 Session Track Data[4] as used in [11]. We use 80% of sessions in session track data to build clusters and remaining 20% are used for term prediction.

4.2 Baselines

Several systems have been proposed to extract tasks. However **QCC** [9] is a popular means of extracting them from a search log. We also compare the proposed approach with our implementation of recent work (**T-Dict**) [11] which focuses on entity oriented task extraction. Since we employ clustering to group queries into tasks, we also compare with **Kmeans**. We use **T-Clust** to denote our approach. Parameter settings for each baseline is given below.

- **QCC:** We adopt a variant of QCC, as the proposed algorithm only divides one session into tasks. We build the graph using entire search log and extract its connected components. Queries grouped in a single component are considered to be on same task.

- **K-Means:** We run K-Means on the whole search log to construct clusters. Queries in a cluster are attributed to same task.

- **T-Dict:** Each category in this work [11] consists of a dictionary of terms. We use the same thresholds used in the paper for our implementation.

5. RESULTS

We use DBpedia category hierarchy for pruning tasks (Steps 4-9 and 14-20 in Algo 1). Variation in Precision and Recall

---

[4]http://trec.nist.gov/data/session.html

with increasing number of clusters (**K-Means**), or threshold for connected components (**QCC**) and merge factor (**T-Clust**) respectively is presented in Figure 2. Since, there is no parameter for variation, T-Dict has a single point in both graphs. While K-Means performs better in recall, T-Clust greatly improves precision. T-Clust is fairly stable as niether recall drastically drops nor precision radically increases. As we increase the number of clusters/merge factor/threshold, number of queries in each cluster reduces which in leads to a gradual drop in recall. The reverse also holds, as we increase the number of clusters/merge factor/threshold, precision increases. There is a drop in recall suggesting that queries when aggregated and clustered using entities yield higher quality tasks but relatively smaller number of tasks.

We also compare inter-cluster and intra-cluster distances. QCC, K-Means, T-Clust and T-Dict have 0.56, **0.57**, 0.43 and 0.13 intra-cluster distance respectively. The inter-cluster distances are 0.82, 0.84, **0.98** and 0.11 for QCC, K-Means, T-Clust and T-Dict respectively. Category oriented task extraction shows some discrimination between clusters. While inter-cluster distances are higher than other baselines, intra-cluster distance is low. For term prediction on session-track, T-Clust performs better than the rest of systems, and the gap increases as more number of terms are retrieved.

6. CONCLUSION

To understand user tasks better, we proposed an approach to extract tasks from search logs. We extend previous work by extracting tasks per entity-type using a popular entity category hierarchy. Manual evaluation on labeled data and application specific evaluation via term predictions indicates that entity and entity category information can be exploited to improve task extraction and can also be used to predict terms relevant to query's underlying task. In future we shall evaluate utility of category oriented tasks for retrieval and query auto-completion.

7. REFERENCES

[1] E. Agichtein, R. White, S. T. Dumais, and P. N. Bennett. Search, interrupted: Understanding and predicting search task continuation. In *SIGIR 2012*.

[2] A. H. Awadallah, R. W. White, P. Pantel, S. T. Dumais, and Y. Wang. Supporting complex search tasks. In *CIKM 2014*.

[3] D. Ceccarelli, C. Lucchese, S. Orlando, R. Perego, and S. Trani. Dexter: An open source framework for entity linking. ESAIR '13. ACM.

[4] D. Donato, F. Bonchi, T. Chi, and Y. Maarek. Do you want to take notes?: Identifying research missions in yahoo! search pad. WWW '10. ACM.

[5] W. Hua, Y. Song, H. Wang, and X. Zhou. Identifying users' topical tasks in web search. WSDM '13. ACM.

[6] M. Ji, J. Yan, S. Gu, J. Han, X. He, W. V. Zhang, and Z. Chen. Learning search tasks in queries and web pages via graph regularization. SIGIR '11. ACM.

[7] A. Kotov, P. N. Bennett, R. W. White, S. T. Dumais, and J. Teevan. Modeling and analysis of cross-session search tasks. SIGIR '11. ACM.

[8] B. Kulis and M. I. Jordan. Revisiting k-means: New algorithms via bayesian nonparametrics. In *ICML-12*, 2012.

[9] C. Lucchese, S. Orlando, R. Perego, F. Silvestri, and G. Tolomei. Identifying task-based sessions in search engine query logs. In *WSDM*. ACM, 2011.

[10] C. Lucchese, S. Orlando, R. Perego, F. Silvestri, and G. Tolomei. Discovering tasks from search engine query logs. *ACM Trans. Inf. Syst.*, 31(3), 2013.

[11] M. Verma and E. Yilmaz. Entity oriented task extraction from query logs. In *CIKM 2014*.

[12] H. Wang, C. M.-W. H. X. W. R. W. Song, Yang, and W. Chu. Learning to extract cross-session search tasks. WWW '13.

System And User Centered Evaluation Approaches in Interactive Information Retrieval (SAUCE 2016)

Heather L. O'Brien
iSchool
University of British Columbia
Vancouver, British Columbia
Canada
h.obrien@ubc.ca

Nicola Ferro
Department of Information
Engineering
University of Padua
Via G. Gradenigo 6/B,
35131 Padua, Italy
ferro@dei.unipd.it

Hideo Joho
Faculty of Library, Information and
Media Science, University of Tsukuba
1-2 Kasuga, Tsukuba, Japan
hideo@slis.tsukuba.ac.jp

Dirk Lewandowski
Department of Information
Hamburg University of Applied
Sciences, Hamburg, Germany
dirk.lewandowski@haw-hamburg.de

Paul Thomas
CSIRO
GPO Box 664
Canberra, AUSTRALIA
paul.thomas@csiro.au

Keith van Rijsbergen
School of Computing Science
University of Glasgow
Glasgow G12 8QQ
cornelis.vanrijsbergen@glasgow.ac.uk

ABSTRACT

The purpose of this workshop is to bring together academic and industry interactive information retrieval (IIR) researchers with an interest in evaluation methodologies. The workshop articulates contemporary challenges in the investigation of IIR and invites user- and system-oriented researchers to work collaboratively to address these challenges by combining user- and system-centered methodologies in meaningful ways.

General Terms

Measurement, Experimentation, Human Factors

Keywords

Information retrieval; evaluation; system-centered; user-centered

1. RATIONALE, SCOPE AND NOVELTY OF THE WORKSHOP

In 2013, the organizers of this proposed workshop met at the *Evaluation Methodologies in Information Retrieval Seminar* held at the Schloss-Dagstuhl in Germany [1]. This workshop was built around five themes: frameworks for evaluation; evaluating search within and across sessions; evaluation criteria; user modeling; and evaluation methods and metrics. These themes were explored through presentations by leading interactive information retrieval (IIR) researchers and within working groups.

Our working group focused on reliability and validity, cornerstones of effective evaluation. Our group, comprised of system- and user-oriented researchers, spent a great deal of time exploring these terms and their different meanings within our respective frames of reference. We realized that a lack of a shared understanding of these terms was problematic for the advancement of IIR research - particularly in terms of utilizing and accurately assessing the merits

CHIIR'16, March 13–17, 2016, Carrboro, North Carolina, USA
ACM ISBN: 978-1-4503-3751-9/16/03.
DOI: http://dx.doi.org/10.1145/2854946.2886106

of each other's work. This led us to explore possibilities for collaboration that would bridge the gap between user- and system-centred evaluation approaches.

Nowadays, IIR continues to increase in complexity: user tasks and needs are demanding; data and information systems are rapidly evolving and greatly heterogeneous; and the interaction between users and IR systems is more articulated. For example, consider Web search today: highly diversified results are returned from Web pages, news, social media, image and video search, products and more, and all are merged through adaptive strategies driven by current and previous user-systems interactions. As a result, experimental evaluation needs to appropriately model these evolving tasks, needs, data sources and user interactions. An additional challenge pertains to the anticipated outcome of IIR research and application. It is no longer sufficient to focus solely on precision, recall and satisfaction: successful IIR systems must engage, inform, and relate to users, taking into account single session and more long-term use and re-use.

To effectively support the development of next generation IIR systems, it is necessary to bridge system- and user-oriented evaluation methods. Both approaches have advantages and drawbacks: while system-centered methods ensure greater internal validity, they may fail to take into account user and contextual factors that influence IIR; user-oriented methods may better approximate behavior, affect and cognition, but provide less experimental control of independent variables.

The goal of this workshop is to unite system- and user-centered IIR researchers for the purposes of:

- Sharing different user-centered and system-centred research methods, measures, and tools to foster knowledge exchange;
- Exploring the addition of user-centered evaluation strategies to system-oriented studies, and vice versa; and
- Initiating collaborations between user- and system-oriented researchers to further IIR research.

2. DESCRIPTION OF TOPICS

2.1 SYSTEM-CENTERED EVALUATION

A great deal of progress has been made in information retrieval (IR) on the back of so-called "system-centered" evaluations; that is, evaluations which are either abstract from the user or task entirely, or which treat user characteristics as confounds to be controlled. This has enabled dedicated concentration on aspects of information retrieval algorithms and systems. System-oriented evaluation is founded on the Cranfield methodology [14], which makes use of experimental collections consisting of: sets of documents representing domains of interest; topics, which simulate and abstract actual user information needs; and ground-truth, i.e. the "correct" answers, where relevant documents for each topic are pre-determined. System outputs, in the form of ranked lists of documents in response to a topic, are then scored with respect to ground-truth using a breadth of performance measures [13].

The benefit of the system-oriented approach is the portability and reusability of test collections: it is possible to directly compare systems, or system variants, over exactly the same tasks and with all sources of variation carefully controlled. As such, there are clear advantages in terms of the number of data points available for analysis, the ability to compare findings across different systems, and experimental control when compared to more user-focused techniques. However, since the "user" – indeed the entire context – is represented in a test collection by only a query and set of relevance judgments, there is plenty of reason to be concerned about the external validity and generalizability of the results.

Recent work has taken offline, system-centered evaluation techniques and begun to address these issue, largely by building user behavior models which can be incorporated in system metrics [12]; widening the pools from which topics and judgments are drawn [14]; and considering slightly more variation and richness in the representation of users and their needs, e.g., [4] or [6]).

Online evaluation approaches are another example of the increased interest in approximating user behavior [3; 9]. These approaches infer preferences about what documents are relevant for a given topic directly from user interactions with ranked result lists by considering a click on a document as a proxy for document relevance. There are two main instantiations of this paradigm: A/B testing and interleaving. A/B testing compares two alternative implementations of a system by switching a random sample of system users either to version A or B, and then comparing the clicks in both systems to determine which is "best." An interleaving method presents users with a ranked result list that contains documents from two or more systems and estimates their preferences by interpreting interactions with the interleaved list, e.g. which documents of which system gather more clicks. Online evaluation approaches operate on the basis that more activity, i.e., mouse clicks, is an indication that one system outperforms the other, or is more preferred by users. Yet, there may be other explanations for increased user activity, some of which may not be positive for user outcomes, such as disorientation, uncertainty, or lack of focused attention on the task. Hence, we need user-centered methods, to construct the *why* around the *what* of user behavior.

2.2 USER-CENTRED EVALUATION

User-centered approaches focus on users' affective and cognitive experiences with IIR systems, and the behaviors they exhibit during use or as a result of interacting with information. Thus, the goal in user-centered evaluation is to understand users' motivations, cognitive involvement and processes, and emotional responses to systems and/or search tasks, and how this relates to system performance and other outcomes. In addition to more traditional IR metrics, such as relevance [16] and informativeness [17], emerging work is exploring complex subjective phenomenon, including user engagement [10], learning [5], and serendipity [11].

Interest in subjective user experience, search environments, and outcomes necessitates the inclusion of more social science methods

in IIR research [7], including self-reports. Kelly, Harper and Landau [8] deftly summarize and illustrate the challenges (e.g., inflation, demand effects, acquiescence) associated with self-reporting in their study comparing different modes of administering questionnaires during an IR experiment. Nonetheless, questionnaires and other self-report methods, such as focus groups, interviews, and verbal elicitation, are staples of IIR studies [7]. As such, we require self-report measures that are appropriately constructed and robustly tested to ensure they meaningfully contribute to IIR research. This is accomplished, in part, by a solid theoretical foundation upon which to base self-report measures, and also by establishing their validity in relation to objective measures.

There has been much promising work in this regard. For instance, Arapakis et al. [2] linked self-report measures with eye tracking metrics, mouse clicks, and behavioral performance patterns in online news reading. This work, and others of its kind, illustrates attempts to link subjective and objective measures to obtain a more holistic picture of IIR. If mouse clicks can be equated with gaze and self-report measures, there is potential to understand user behavior at a much larger scale, making it possible to evaluate the experience of millions of users in naturalistic search settings (i.e., the Web) [2]. If large- and small-scale methods can inform each other, then it will enhance the robustness and generalizability of both types of methodological approaches.

3. WORKSHOP

This workshop seeks to explore the benefits and drawbacks of user- and system-centered approaches in greater depth. We will acknowledge and discuss various challenges through keynotes, an expert panel, a world café style discussion session, and position papers. Examples of some of the themes to be addressed in the workshop include:

- Scale, with reference to the number of data points collected: What is lost and gained when we investigate IIR with tens, hundreds, or thousands of users (or systems, or tasks)? How might small- and large-scale approaches inform each other?
- The trade-off between internal and external validity, i.e., in the "wild" versus in the laboratory.
- Relevance has been a long-standing measure of interest in IIR. However, there are other valuable outcomes to be measured pertaining to system effectiveness, user experience, and greater societal and political engagement. How might we develop measurement practices to capture IIR beyond relevance and beyond the evaluation of the system itself?
- Temporality, or the ability to examine a single IIR session and repeated or longitudinal system use. Analytic data collection makes it possible to follow user interactions over time, e.g., repeat visits to a website, but user-centered longitudinal studies are less common but nonetheless vital.
- The use of subjective measures, which may be biased, and objective measures, e.g., behavior or physiology), which may require specialized equipment and knowledge to collect and interpret the data. How do we capture and make sense of both the inner world of users and their observed behaviors?
- The collection of measures during user-system interaction (formative or process-based) and post-interaction (summative). What factors of the search process determine search effectiveness [15]? To what degree are we attending validity and reliability of the measures themselves?

3.1 Workshop Outcomes

It is anticipated that the workshop will: increase awareness of evaluation issues from multiple perspectives; facilitate knowledge exchange and spark innovative ideas. A desired outcome of the workshop is increased uptake of user-centered approaches by systems researchers, and vice versa; collaboration between researchers who previously unknown to each other; and the design of new research studies that would begin addressing current evaluation challenges. The main findings of and the lessons learned in the workshop will be summarized in a report in a journal, such as SIGIR Forum, to trigger further research on the topic.

4. WORKSHOP ORGANIZERS

Heather O'Brien is Assistant Professor at the iSchool, University of British Columbia in Vancouver, Canada. Her research focuses on the measurement of subjective user experience, namely the concept of user engagement. She developed a self-report instrument, the User Engagement Scale (UES), and has been concentrating on its utility, reliability, and validity in various information environments.

Nicola Ferro is Associate Professor at the Department of Information Engineering of the University of Padua. His research interests include IR, its experimental evaluation, multilingual information access, and digital libraries. He is the coordinator of the CLEF evaluation initiative of more than 200 research groups world-wide. He is the Chair of ECIR 2016 and has been the coordinator of PROMISE (2010-2013)..

Hideo Joho is Associate Professor at the Research Center for Knowledge Communities, Faculty of Library, Information and Media Science, University of Tsukuba, Japan. His research interests include cognitive and affective interactions between search engines and users. He has also been involved in the development of several test collections e.g., GeoCLEF, NTCIR VisEx, NTCIR Temporalia, and NTCIR Lifelog and a Program Co-Chair of NTCIR-9, 10, and 11 (2010-14).

Dirk Lewandowski is Professor of Information Research and Information Retrieval at the Hamburg University of Applied Sciences, Germany. His research areas are Web Information Retrieval, user behavior in Web search and the impact of Web search on knowledge acquisition in society.

Paul Thomas is Senior Research Scientist at CSIRO, Australia. His research includes evaluation techniques for information retrieval systems, especially models of user behavior and how to build offline methods that predict user performance or preference.

Keith van Rijsbergen is Professor Emeritus in the School of Computing Science, University of Glasgow and Honorary Member of the Computer Laboratory, University of Cambridge. His research spans theoretical and experimental aspects of IR, including the specification and implementation of several theoretical models and the design of appropriate logics to model information flow.

5. ACKNOWLEDGMENTS

Our gratitude for the Schloss Dagstuhl *Evaluation Methodologies in Information Retrieval Seminar* where this conversation began.

6. REFERENCES

[1] Agosti, M., Fuhr, N., Toms, E.G. and Vakkari, P. 2013. Evaluation Methodologies in Information Retrieval (Dagstuhl Seminar 13441). *Dagstuhl Report.* 3, 10 (2013), 92-126.

[2] Arapakis, I. Lalmas, M., Cambazoglu, B. B., Marcos, M.-C. and Jose, J.M. 2014. User engagement in online news: Under the scope of sentiment, interest, affect, and gaze. *J. Assoc. Inform. Sci. Tech.* 65, 10 (March. 2014), 1988-2005.

[3] Chuklin, A., Markov, I. and de Rijke, M. 2015. *Click Models for Web Search.* Morgan & Claypool Publishers, USA.

[4] Dean-Hall, A., Clarke, C. L. A., Kamps, J., Thomas, P. and Voorhees, E. 2014. Overview of the TREC 2014 Contextual Suggestion Track. In *Proceedings of the Text Retrieval Conference.* National Institute of Standards and Technology.

[5] Freund, L., Gwizdka, J., Hansen, P., He, J., Kando, N. and Rieh, S Y. (2014). *Searching as Learning Workshop, Information Interaction in Context* (IIiX) *Conference* (Regensburg, Germany, August 30, 2014).

[6] Gurrin, C., Albatal, R., Joho, H, and Hopfgartner, F. 2015. Lifelog: Pilot Task of NTCIR-12.

[7] Kelly, D. 2009. Methods for evaluating interactive information retrieval systems with users. *Foundations and Trends in Information Retrieval.* 3(1-2), 1-224.

[8] Kelly, D., Harper, D.J. and Landau, B. 2008. Questionnaire mode effects in interactive information retrieval experiments. *Inform. Process. Manage.* 44, 1 (January. 2008), 122-141.

[9] Kohavi, R., Longbotham, R., Sommerfield, D. and Henne, R. M. (2009). Controlled experiments on the web: Survey and practical guide. *Data Mining and Knowledge Discovery*, 18(1): 140–181.

[10] Lalmas, M.. O'Brien, H. and Yom-Tov, E. 2014. *Measuring User Engagement.* Morgan & Claypool.

[11] McCay-Peet, L. and Toms, E. G. 2011. Measuring the dimensions of serendipity in digital environments. *Information Research: An International Electronic Journal* 16, 3 (September 2011): n3.

[12] Moffat, A., Thomas, P. and Scholer, F. (2013). Users versus models: What observation tells us about effectiveness metrics. In *Proceeding of the 22th International Conference on Information and Knowledge Management*, 659–668. ACM.

[13] Sakai, T. 2014. Metrics, Statistics, Tests. In Ferro, N., ed, *Bridging Between Information Retrieval and Databases PROMISE Winter School 2013, Revised Tutorial Lectures*, 116–163. Lecture Notes in Computer Science (LNCS) 8173, Springer, Heidelberg, Germany.

[14] Sanderson, M. 2010. Test Collection Based Evaluation of Information Retrieval Systems. *Foundations and Trends in Information Retrieval*, 4(4), 247–375.

[15] Scholer, F., Moffat, A. and Thomas, P. 2013. Choices in batch information retrieval evaluation. In *Proceedings of the Australasian Document Computing Symposium*, 74-81. Brisbane, Australia.

[16] Su, L.T. 1992. Evaluation measures for interactive information retrieval. *Inform. Process. Manage* 28,(4), 503-516.

[17] Tague-Sutcliffe, J. 1992. Measuring the informativeness of a retrieval process. In *Proceedings of the 15th annual International ACM SIGIR Conference on Research and Development in Information Retrieval* (Copenhagen, Denmark, June 21-24, 1992). ACM, New York, NY, 23-26.

SEADE Workshop Proposal
The Serendipity Factor: Evaluating the Affordances of Digital Environments

Lori McCay-Peet
School of Information Management
Dalhousie University
6100 University Avenue
Halifax, Nova Scotia, Canada
mccay@dal.ca

Elaine G. Toms
Information School
The University of Sheffield
Regent Court, 211 Portobello
Sheffield, UK
e.toms@sheffield.ac.uk

Anabel Quan-Haase
Faculty of Information and Media
Studies and Department of Sociology
The University of Western Ontario
1151 Richmond Street
London, Ontario, Canada
aquan@uwo.ca

ABSTRACT

For two decades, research has sought to understand serendipity and how it may be facilitated in digital environments such as information visualizations systems, search systems, and social media. The motivation to support serendipity comes from its association with positive outcomes that range from personal benefits to global rewards. To date, research has made significant headway in defining and mapping the process of serendipity and new tools are emerging to support it. Creative and robust heuristics and methods of evaluation, however, are required to help move the research forward, to ensure that new or enhanced features, functions, or tools are providing affordances as intended. Without sound approaches, we are blind as to what facilitates serendipity and proposed heuristics to aid practitioners are speculative. SEADE (pronounced 'seed') is a one-day workshop that will examine how we balance the tension between diversity and novelty in designing digital environments and subsequently how we evaluate the 'serendipitousness' of those environments. Since 2006, in its earlier iterations as IIiX and HCIR, CHIIR has served as a venue for the discussion of user-centred information interaction in context. CHIIR provides an ideal venue for bringing together researchers from diverse information and computer science communities and beyond working on the problem of providing support for serendipity in digital environments.

Keywords
Affordances, Evaluation, Serendipity.

1. INTRODUCTION

In a piece for *The World Post*, Zeynep Tufekci [1], from the University of North Carolina, called out the 'tech press' for missing the fact that Facebook [2] admitted that its algorithms form 'echo chambers.' That is, algorithms, particularly those that enable personalization of content, curated for the individual, have the effect of reducing the diversity of information to which users are exposed. The notion of the 'filter bubble' [3] is one of the

CHIIR'16, March 13–17, 2016, Carrboro, North Carolina, USA
ACM 978-1-4503-3751-9/16/03.
http://dx.doi.org/10.1145/2854946.2878739

prime motivations behind serendipity research – bursting the bubble through the thoughtful design of digital environments.

The meaning of the term serendipity has evolved from its inception in the 18th century [4] but for the purposes of this workshop, we define serendipity as an unexpected experience prompted by a user's valuable interaction with information in a digital environment. The concept of affordances, originated by psychologist James Gibson [5] provides a useful approach to not only exploring what design features may support serendipity, but how a digital environment may be evaluated in this respect. An affordance is understood as "a relational concept that marries the material features of the technology with the subjective goals and perceptions of its users, such that the same technology may provide different affordances to different users" [5]. Affordances are thus non-deterministic; that is, while a digital environment such as an information visualization may be designed with a specific use in mind (e.g., support for exploration), it may be perceived and used differently by different people. The concept of affordances makes room for individuals' perceptions of chance or luck often associated with serendipitous experiences. But how can digital environments designed to afford experiences be evaluated?

Methods for evaluation of serendipitous environments have generally been applied to meet the needs of a specific digital environment under development. Yamaba et al. [7] developed a folksonomy-based book recommendation method and asked users directly the degree to which they were interested in the book, if they knew the book well, and the validity of the recommendation and concluded that 12% of the recommended books were serendipitous. Piao and Whittle [8] tested a method for automatically extracting Twitter users' interests in order to suggest serendipitous connections using natural language processing. Twitter users were asked to manually check and rank items based on the metrics of 'interesting' and 'surprising'. Their experiment suggested that analyzing not only a user's tweets but the tweets of other users who share hashtags may be an effective way of identifying serendipitous items for users.

With the goal of developing a tool for measuring different types of digital environments (e.g., digital libraries, social media), McCay-Peet, Toms, and Kelloway [8] developed self-report scales designed to measure how frequently people perceive they experience serendipity in general, in digital environments, and in a specific digital environment as well as how well a specific digital environment facilitates serendipity. Findings indicated digital environments (e.g., social media, websites) that are trigger-rich, enable connections, and lead to the unexpected, increase the likelihood of serendipitous experiences. Hand-in hand with methods of evaluation are the identification of heuristics for the development of serendipitous digital environments. For example, based on prior research, Thudt et al. [10] developed a set of design goals for the promotion of serendipity through information visualizations such as enticing curiosity, playful exploration, multiple visual access points, and highlighting adjacencies.

The rationale for the SEADE workshop is to take advantage of the growing interest for the support for diversity, novelty, and serendipity in digital environments—the desire to burst the filter bubble. A key research challenge that has thus far been primarily tackled on a research project by research project basis is how to evaluate digital environments for their ability to afford serendipity. SEADE will provide a venue for researchers interested in the development of evaluation methods for digital environments that can span research projects in order to provide some consistency and allow for comparisons across digital environments. SEADE is novel in that it is the first workshop on serendipity to focus on evaluation.

2. TOPICS
We have identified a series of related topics which can be grouped into two major themes: evaluation and design. Based on participant submissions and discussion during the workshop, new themes and sub-topics may emerge.

Evaluating whether or how digital environments enable serendipity

1. Use of qualitative methods such as interviews and think-aloud to evaluate user perceptions
2. Quantitative evaluation methods such as controlled experiments and log file analyses to test designs
3. Identification of factors other than the environment (e.g., context, individual differences, strategies, emotions, attitudes) that influence serendipity that should be taken into consideration during evaluation

Designing elements and functions in digital environments so that serendipity is facilitated

4. Application of theories and models in the design (or evaluation) of affordances related to serendipity
5. Design of serendipitous digital environments (e.g., information visualization systems, recommender systems, digital libraries, search engines)

3. WORKSHOP ORGANIZERS
Lori McCay-Peet is an Assistant Professor in the School of Information Management at Dalhousie University in Halifax, Nova Scotia, Canada. Her research focuses on people's perceptions and uses of digital information environments such as social media and digital libraries, particularly in the context of knowledge work. As part of her PhD dissertation, she developed two serendipity self-report scales, one to measure perceptions of serendipity and the other to measure how well a digital information environment facilitates serendipitous experiences [9]. She has served on a number of organizing committees including GRAND (Graphics, Animation, and New Media Canadian Network of Centres of Excellence) Café 2013 in Halifax, SCORE (Serendipity, Chance, and the Opportunistic Discovery of Information Research) 2012 in Montreal, and the International Workshop on Encouraging Serendipity in Interactive Systems at

INTERACT 2011 in Lisbon.

Elaine Toms is Professor of Information Science, University of Sheffield, UK. Her research interests include improving search systems to support real-life work tasks (rather than bags of words), new approaches to evaluating search systems, understanding serendipity and how systems can deliver on serendipity, and the relationship between human curiosity and browsing. She has previously served on the organising and programme committees of many conferences and has organised multiple workshops including SCORE (Serendipity, Chance, and the Opportunistic Discovery of Information Research) in Montreal, and the International Workshop on Encouraging Serendipity in Interactive Systems at INTERACT 2011, Lisbon.

Anabel Quan-Haase is Associate Professor of Information and Media Studies and Sociology at the University of Western Ontario. Her research interests include digital scholarship, networked work, serendipity in work practices, serendipity in social media, and the design of discovery systems that promote serendipity. She is the author of "Technology and Society: Social Networks, Inequality and Power" (Oxford University Press, 2015) and co-editor of the Handbook of Social Media Research Methods (Sage, 2016). She is the past president of the Canadian Association for Information Science and current Council Member of the Communication, Information Technology, and Media Sociology section of the American Sociological Association. She has organized several conferences including the Canadian Association for Information Science Annual Meeting and has served on numerous programme committees.

4. PROGRAM COMMITTEE
A set of ten international researchers whose work addresses serendipity-related research problems constitutes the Program Committee.

Naresh Argawal, Simmons College (USA)

Jamshid Beheshti, McGill University (CAN)

Lennart Björneborn, University of Copenhagen (DNK)

Sanda Erdelez, University of Missouri (USA)

Jannica Heinström, Åbo Akademi University (FIN)

Christoph Lutz, University of St. Gallen (CHE)

Stephann Makri, City University London (GBR)

Kim Martin, University of Western Ontario (CAN)

Xu Sun, The University of Nottingham Ningbo China (TWN)

Simon Wakeling, University of Sheffield (GBR)

These scholars will serve as reviewers to evaluate proposals submitted to the workshop and where appropriate may also be asked to help facilitate components of the workshop. Furthermore, they will provide input to the development and implementation of content.

5. HIGHLIGHTS
Featured events of the 1-day workshop include:

Keynote presentation, "Is there anything serendipity research can learn from creativity research?" by John Gero, University of North Carolina at Charlotte and Krasnow Institute for Advanced

Study, George Mason University. His research interests include design science, design cognition, design computing, artificial intelligence, computer-aided design, and cognitive science.

Lightning talks in which the authors of selected two-page extended abstracts present five-minute versions of their papers with opportunity for discussion.

Show and tell event where authors of selected two-page extended abstracts do brief demonstrations of their projects or prototypes with opportunity for discussion.

An interactive session in which workshop participants break into groups to brainstorm how to evaluate the 'serendipitousness' of two or three different features or types of digital information environments (potentially drawn from the show and tell session) that may require different design and evaluation heuristics and methods. Groups will present their findings.

A conversation about next steps to articulate future plans (e.g., special issue in a journal, book, workshop).

In addition, just prior to and during the workshop we will be conducting a whirlwind Delphi study to identify essential and novel measures for assessing "serendipitousness." The results of the group effort will be discussed at the workshop to highlight pertinent measures.

6. PARTICIPANTS

We anticipate 20 to 30 participants from the information science and HCI community, a mix of researchers who study the phenomenon of serendipity and those who develop and evaluate digital environments to support it. Researchers from other research communities whose research interests align with that of the workshop may also attend. For example, digital humanities scholars' work focuses on how to make historical documents and archival resources available via information-rich digital information environments to a wide audience of users that includes experts and lay individuals.

7. PREVIOUS WORKSHOPS

SEADE is a natural progression from three prior workshops on the topic of serendipity.

IWODI (International Workshop for the Opportunistic Discovery of Information), organized by Sanda Erdelez, was held in 2010 at the University of Missouri. The workshop was the first of its kind and brought together international researchers who share a common interest in the technological support for serendipity. IWODI spurred a special on ODI in *Information Research* [11].

Encouraging Serendipity in Interactive Systems Workshop, Application of theory and models in the design or evaluation of digital environments organized by Stephann Makri, Elaine G. Toms, Lori McCay-Peet, and Ann Blandford, at INTERACT 2011 in Portugal provided a venue for researchers to identify key requirements and research challenges for designing and evaluating user-centred systems with the goal of facilitating serendipity.

SCORE (Serendipity, Chance, and the Opportunistic Discovery of Information Research), organized by Elaine Toms, Jamshid

Beheshti, Sanda Erdelez, Stephann Makri, and Lori McCay-Peet was held in Montreal in 2012 and built on the foundation established at the INTERACT and IWODI workshops and further lay the groundwork for future collaboration. It was at this workshop that evaluation was discussed as an area in which more work was needed.

8. REFERENCES

[1] Tufekci, Z. 2015, May 11. Facebook said its algorithms do help form echo chambers. And the tech press missed it. *The World Post*. Retrieved from http://www.huffingtonpost.com/zeynep-tufekci/facebook-algorithm-echo-chambers_b_7259916.html

[2] Bakshy, E., Messing, S. and Adamic, L.A. 2015. Exposure to ideologically diverse news and opinion on Facebook. *Science, 348*(6239), 1130-1132.

[3] Pariser, E 2011. The filter bubble: What the internet is hiding from you. London: Viking.

[4] Merton, R. K. and Barber, E. 2004. The travels and adventures of serendipity. Princeton, NJ: Princeton University Press.

[5] Gibson, J. J. 1986. The ecological approach to visual perception. Hillsdale, NJ: Lawrence Erlbaum.

[6] Ellison, N. B., Gibbs, J. L., and Weber, M. S. 2015. The use of enterprise social network sites for knowledge sharing in distributed organizations: The role of organizational affordances. *American Behavioral Scientist, 59*(1), 103–123.

[7] Yamaba, H., Tanoue, M., Takatsuka, K., Okazaki, N., and Tomita, S. 2013. On a Serendipity-oriented Recommender System based on Folksonomy and its Evaluation. *Procedia Computer Science, 22*, 276–284.

[8] Piao, S. and Whittle, J. 2011. A Feasibility Study on Extracting Twitter Users' Interests Using NLP Tools for Serendipitous Connections. In *2011 IEEE Third Int'l Conference on Privacy, Security, Risk and Trust and 2011 IEEE Third Int'l Conference on Social Computing* (pp. 910–915). Boston, MA: IEEE.

[9] McCay-Peet, L., Toms, E. G., and Kelloway, E. K. 2015. Examination of relationships among serendipity, the environment, and individual differences. *Information Processing and Management, 51*(4), 391–412.

[10] Thudt, A., Hinrichs, U., and Carpendale, S. 2012. The bohemian bookshelf: Supporting serendipitous book discoveries through information visualization. In *Proceedings of the 2012 ACM annual conference on Human Factors in Computing Systems - CHI '12* (pp. 1461–1470). New York, New York, USA: ACM Press. http://doi.org/10.1145/2207676.2208607

[11] Erdelez, S. and Makri, S. 2011. Introduction to the theme issue on opportunistic discovery of information. Information Research, 16(3), odiintro. Retrieved from http://InformationR.net/ir/16-3/odiintro.html

Nonlinear Composite Search Results

Horatiu Bota
2nd year PhD student
University of Glasgow
h.bota.1@research.gla.ac.uk

Supervised by Prof. Joemon Jose

ABSTRACT

Modern search engines aggregate information from a variety
of sources (e.g. images, videos) and return this information
to users, merged into a single results page. Various novel
interface elements have been added to the results page to
help users access diverse content, from interactive aggregated search blocks to contextual entity cards. These novel
elements merge various types of media into coherent objects
displayed on the results page. We define these elements
as *composite search results* and study methods to construct
them, as well as their effect on user search behaviour. Our
findings suggest that result composition can be an effective
search paradigm and that nonlinear composite results can
positively impact search behaviour in certain contexts.

Keywords: Novel interfaces; User behaviour; Web search

1. MOTIVATION

The past three decades have seen an explosion of information on the Web, in terms of both quantity and diversity
of content. Today, modern search engines aggregate information from a variety of heterogeneous sources (e.g. images,
videos, social media) and return this information to users,
merged into a single results page. To help users access diverse content, numerous nonlinear elements are integrated
into the search interface: adverts, related searches, aggregated results, various types of entity and definition cards,
knowledge carousels and others. Our research focuses on
user interaction with novel search interface components that
display the following properties:

- *Nonlinear* – these elements are presented as contextual components of the page, to one side of the organic
  Web results – as in the case of entity cards – or clearly
  delimited from the organic Web results through the
  use of visual borders.

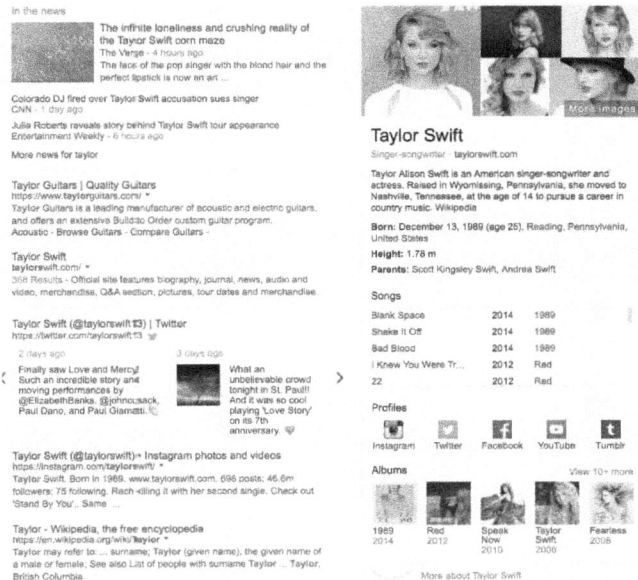

Figure 1: Google results page for query *"taylor"*

- *Composite* – these elements merge various types of
  media (e.g. images, videos, sound clips, maps) into a
  coherent object on the results page.

Figure 1 shows several examples of nonlinear composite
interface elements used by modern search engines, in particular the entity card displayed on the right of the organic
Web search results, and the social media carousel merged
into the organic Web results ranking.

Because of the development of novel interface elements,
the traditional *ten blue links* is no longer an accurate description for the modern search results page *(SERP)*. With
multiple heterogeneous components competing for users' attention and interaction, traditional models of search behaviour and engagement do not reliably reflect user experience
with modern SERPs. In addition, evaluating novel search
results pages is a considerable challenge. Whole page relevance has been proposed as a solution for evaluating nonlinear results pages, and it defines how well all of the elements
on the search interface and their corresponding attributes
respond to users' information needs [6]. However, to accurately evaluate search engine performance in the context of
nonlinear results, it is essential to understand searcher behaviour around these novel interface elements and our work
contributes a necessary first step in this direction.

With the immense popularity of mobile devices, more and more searchers are turning to their mobile devices for answers: mobile search is slowly becoming more popular than desktop search[1]. To overcome platform specific constraints, such as limited visual real-estate and constrained user interaction, search engines are using novel interface elements on mobile devices. This is intended to satisfy complex information needs directly on the results page and to generate what is know as *good abandonment* [12]. Given the ever-growing popularity of mobile search, and the increasing usage of novel interface elements on the mobile results page, it is of great practical importance to understand how searchers make use of composite results in mobile search – not only in terms of traditional user engagement, but also incorporating users' contextual signals (e.g. time of day, device size, user location) into understanding how these interface elements provide utility to searchers. Our work aims to analyse the usage of composite results on mobile devices and contributes a thorough understanding on the role contextual signals play in engagement with novel interface elements on the mobile results page.

2. RESEARCH QUESTIONS

Our work focuses on answering two major questions regarding nonlinear composite results: *(i)* How can these results be constructed and what information should they contain? *(ii)* How do users engage with these novel components of the results page? In broad terms, we aim to answer the following research questions:

1. **(RQ1)**: From the users' perspective, what information should be displayed within composite results? What roles do individual documents play in composite search results?

2. **(RQ2)**: How does the presence of nonlinear entity cards on a traditional search results page influence users' interaction with the organic Web results?

3. **(RQ3)**: How can composite results be evaluated? How can cross-component coherence and whole-page relevance be integrated into the evaluation of novel results pages, on both mobile and desktop?

3. METHODOLOGY

In our approach so far, we explored the problem from three different perspectives. Firstly, we designed and ran a laboratory-based study to understand how users generate composite results using documents from a variety of heterogeneous sources. Secondly, we designed and ran a crowdsourced experiment where we investigated the effects of entity cards on interaction with organic Web results in desktop search. Finally, we designed and evaluated, using traditional Cranfield-style metrics, several algorithms for constructing composite results from heterogeneous sources.

With regard to future work, we propose a number of experiments that focus on the utility of composite results in mobile search, as well as evaluation issues for composite results. Firstly, we want to understand how engagement with entity cards differs in mobile versus desktop search, given

[1]In certain cases, it has already become more popular than desktop search: http://adwords.blogspot.ro/2015/05/building-for-next-moment.html

the differences exhibited by entity cards between the two platforms (for example, mobile cards are displayed in-line, in a compact layout, whereas on desktop, they are placed besides search results). For this analysis, we will make use of mobile engagement metrics from a commercial search engine log that is available to us. Furthermore, we aim to find whether there is an interaction between engagement with entity cards and users' context: we want to find out whether entity cards are more useful in certain mobile contexts. This analysis will be valuable in informing intent prediction: in a given user context, should the card be displayed on the results page? What facet of an ambiguous query should the card focus on, given users' context? What contextual signals are most important in determining whether the card should be displayed or not (or what facet to be displayed in the card)? For this part of our study, we will conduct an eye-tracking study, in context, to better understand user behaviour, attention and satisfaction in a card-driven mobile search scenario. Finally, based on our analysis so far, we aim to develop a theoretical framework for the evaluation of composite results that takes into consideration result properties, as well as cross-component coherence and whole-page relevance.

4. PROGRESS

To address our first research question, we designed and ran a user study to analyse user-generated composite results. Our main objective was to determine how composite results are manually generated by searchers. In particular, our interest was to analyse composite results with respect to their topical focus, content and user-assessed characteristics (i.e. relevance, cohesion, diversity). Our findings show that, firstly, there is an agreement between users on the topical focus of composite results — namely that different users construct results which focus on similar aspects of a given topic. Secondly, we observe that composite results contain documents that play different roles. For instance, central documents (or pivots), are assessed by users as being more relevant than other document within the composite object, and reflect the result title, whereas ornament documents are less relevant but provide value to searchers through composition with pivots. Finally, our analysis suggests that no clear hierarchy of user-assessed object characteristics can be determined and that, although explicit relevance is crucial in search, composition of diverse results can generate additional value to users. Results are available in Bota et al. [8].

For our second research question, we explored the effects entity cards (*ECs*) have on user interaction with organic Web results. Entity cards are intended to enhance search experience in several ways: *(i)* they help searchers navigate diversified results, *(ii)* provide a summary of relevant content directly on the results page and *(iii)* support exploratory search by highlighting relevant entities associated with a given user query. We designed and ran a large-scale crowdsourced user study, with more than 700 unique searchers, in which we studied the effect of entity cards and their properties (relevance, cohesion and diversity) on search behaviour and perceived task workload. Our findings suggest that the presence of ECs has a strong effect on both the way users interact with search results and their perceived task workload. The results of our investigation indicate that ECs have significantly different effects in simple versus complex tasks. Furthermore, by manipulating EC properties (*content, co-*

herence and *diversity*), we uncovered different effects and interactions between card properties on measures of search behaviour and workload.

Finally, to partially address our last research question, we adapted an existing composite retrieval framework [1] to Web search. Due to the heterogeneous nature of the multi-vertical environment we explored, novel ways to model and estimate the various components of our proposed framework were developed. We applied our algorithms on a federated search test collection [15], which contained results from 108 search engines categorised into 11 different verticals. Our findings indicate that using traditional, Cranfield-style evaluation metrics, composite results can significantly improve performance over various current search paradigms, such as traditional "general web only" ranking, federated search ranking and aggregated search. Our results have implications for work in heterogeneous information access and diversity in IR, and an in-depth analysis of our findings is presented in Bota et al. [9].

5. FUTURE WORK

In terms of future work, many open questions remain. With regard to our first and second research questions, our work so far provides an extensive analysis of user behaviour in both a result composition scenario, and in an entity-card search scenario. However, because there is limited understanding of presentation strategies for composite results, we aim to investigate presentation optimisation strategies for result composition in Web search. Secondly, given that mobile devices have become ubiquitous, and that Web search is increasingly prevalent on mobile devices, we intend to investigate the role result composition can play in mobile Web search. In particular, our objective is to understand whether user context (e.g. time, location, device size) can predict and explain the utility of composite results, as reflected by user engagement metrics, in mobile Web search. Finally, understanding result composition requires the development of comprehensive evaluation metrics that take into account both the content and the presentation of composite objects, as well as whole-page relevance. More rigorous evaluation metrics, tailored to nonlinear search environments need to be developed in order to reliably investigate result composition performance. We aim to explore theoretical approaches to evaluation of composite results in future work.

6. CONCLUSION

As the Web has made available an enormous variety of textual and multimedia resources, people have started performing increasingly more complex search tasks, aimed at finding rich answers that require information extracted from various sources. To satisfy these complex information needs, modern search systems need to build solutions that aggregate information, taking into account users' intents and preferences. We argue that composition of results can provide users with a more structured approach to Web search. Our work so far suggests that returning composite results to users' search queries can not only provide a better search experience, in terms of traditional IR metrics, but can also positively impact user search behaviour and perceived task workload in certain contexts.

7. REFERENCES

[1] S. Amer-Yahia, F. Bonchi, C. Castillo, E. Feuerstein, I. Méndez-Díaz, and P. Zabala. Complexity and algorithms for composite retrieval. In *Proceedings of the 22nd international conference on World Wide Web companion*, pages 79–80. International World Wide Web Conferences Steering Committee, 2013.

[2] J. Arguello and R. Capra. The effect of aggregated search coherence on search behavior. ACM CIKM '12, pages 1293–1302

[3] J. Arguello and R. Capra. The effects of vertical rank and border on aggregated search coherence and search behavior. ACM CIKM '14, pages 539–548, 2014.

[4] J. Arguello, F. Diaz, J. Callan, and B. Carterette. A methodology for evaluating aggregated search results. In *ECIR*. 2011.

[5] J. Arguello, F. Diaz, and J.-F. Paiement. Vertical selection in the presence of unlabeled verticals. In *Proceedings of the 33rd International ACM SIGIR Conference on Research and Development in Information Retrieval*, SIGIR '10, pages 691–698, New York, NY, USA, 2010. ACM.

[6] P. Bailey, N. Craswell, R. W. White, L. Chen, A. Satyanarayana, and S. Tahaghoghi. Evaluating whole-page relevance. In *Proceedings of the 33rd International ACM SIGIR Conference on Research and Development in Information Retrieval*, SIGIR '10, pages 767–768, New York, NY, USA, 2010. ACM.

[7] R. Blanco, B. B. Cambazoglu, P. Mika, and N. Torzec. Entity recommendations in web search. In *The Semantic Web–ISWC 2013*, pages 33–48. Springer, 2013.

[8] H. Bota, K. Zhou, and J. Jose. Exploring composite retrieval from the users' perspective. In A. Hanbury, G. Kazai, A. Rauber, and N. Fuhr, editors, *Advances in Information Retrieval*, volume 9022 of *Lecture Notes in Computer Science*, pages 13–24. Springer International Publishing, 2015.

[9] H. Bota, K. Zhou, J. M. Jose, and M. Lalmas. Composite retrieval of heterogeneous web search. In *Proceedings of the 23rd International Conference on World Wide Web*, WWW '14, pages 119–130, New York, NY, USA, 2014. ACM.

[10] R. Capra, J. Arguello, and F. Scholer. Augmenting web search surrogates with images. ACM CIKM '13, pages 399–408, 2013.

[11] D. Lagun, C.-H. Hsieh, D. Webster, and V. Navalpakkam. Towards better measurement of attention and satisfaction in mobile search. In *ACM SIGIR '14*, pages 113–122.

[12] J. Li, S. Huffman, and A. Tokuda. Good abandonment in mobile and pc internet search. In *32nd Annual International ACM SIGIR Conference on Research and Development in Information Retrieval*, pages 43–50, 2 Penn Plaza, Suite 701, New York 10121-0701, 2009.

[13] V. Navalpakkam, L. Jentzsch, R. Sayres, S. Ravi, A. Ahmed, and A. Smola. Measurement and modeling of eye-mouse behavior in the presence of nonlinear page layouts. In *ACM WWW '13*, pages 953–964.

[14] V. Navalpakkam, R. Kumar, L. Li, and D. Sivakumar. Attention and selection in online choice tasks. *UMAP*, pages 200–211, 2012.

[15] D. Nguyen, T. Demeester, D. Trieschnigg, and D. Hiemstra. Federated search in the wild: the combined power of over a hundred search engines. In *Proceedings of the 21st ACM international conference on Information and knowledge management*, pages 1874–1878. ACM, 2012.

[16] M. Shokouhi and Q. Guo. From queries to cards: Re-ranking proactive card recommendations based on reactive search history. In *Proceedings of the ACM International Conference on Research and Development in Information Retrieval (SIGIR2015)*. ACM – Association for Computing Machinery, May 2015.

[17] S. Sushmita, H. Joho, M. Lalmas, and R. Villa. Factors affecting click-through behavior in aggregated search interfaces. In *ACM CIKM '10*, pages 519–528. ACM, 2010.

[18] C. Wang, Y. Liu, M. Zhang, S. Ma, M. Zheng, J. Qian, and K. Zhang. Incorporating vertical results into search click models. ACM SIGIR '13, pages 503–512.

Exploring the Role of Culture in Online Searching Behavior from Cultural Cognition Perspective.

Sara Chizari

3rd year PhD Candidate

University of South Carolina

Professor Samantha Hastings

chizari@email.sc.edu

ABSTRACT

The purpose of this study is to identify if cultural differences affect information-searching behavior of users on Google with the use of eye tracking and mouse tracking technologies. Even though cultural differences and individual cognitive style have been the main concerns of several information behavior studies in the last 10 years, there are only a limited number of studies that investigate cognitive differences between online information seekers from cultural cognitive perspective. The theoretical framework of this study is driven from Vygotsky and Nisbett's theory of cultural cognition. According to this theory, culture has a significant impact on how we organize our thoughts and our relationships, how we perceive the world, and how we decide to behave and act. In this study, I aim to investigate if the theory of cultural cognition is applicable to the users' online information searching behavior.

CCS Concepts

• **Information systems~Web searching and information discovery, Web search engines, Users and interactive retrieval, Search interfaces, Information extraction**
• **Human-centered computing~Human computer interaction (HCI), User studies, Laboratory experiments, Web-based interaction, Empirical studies in HCI**

Keywords

Eye-tracking; mouse-tracking; cultural cognition; cross-cultural; search behavior; human information interaction

1. MOTIVATION

Humans perceive and act in the context of culture. We live in cultural settings in which our perception, cognition, and action are being formed by value and belief systems and practices shared by our communities. According to findings of recent studies of cultural neuroscience, it is clear now that culture and social experience may influence our brain function [5]. Recent neuroimaging evidence [20] also shows cultural differences in attention (i.e. Easterners tend to be more relational and Westerners more focused). With that said, the use of psycho-cognitive tools (e.g. mouse tracking, eye tracking, fMRI, etc.) in cross-cultural studies of information behavior is still relatively new.

Also, several cognitive psychologist and anthropologists believe that people of different cultures tend to have different cognitive processing styles (e.g. [4, 6, 10, 16, 18, 19, 22, 23]). The results of Nisbett's studies on cognitive processing differences between Western and East Asian cultures demonstrate that Westerns tend to have more analytical cognitive style whereas East Asians tend to have more holistic or contextual cognitive style [23]. The cognitive differences between East Asians and Westerns have been the focus of several cultural cognitive studies since Nisbett introduced his theory of cultural cognition in 2001. However, there are only a limited number of studies that investigate cognitive differences between Eastern, Middle Eastern and Western online information searchers. In this study, the goal is to investigate the role of culture in online search behavior by means of eye tracking and mouse tracking technologies and through the lens of cultural cognition.

This area of research is becoming increasingly important as at present, some two and half billion people from all over the world are interacting with online information systems. Those two and half billion Internet users often have to use the same interface, drawing on their cognitive and evolutionarily shaped behaviors [2, 11].

2. RESEARCH QUESTIONS

The overarching research questions that are sought in this research are: Does culture play a role in information searching behavior of users? If yes, can we apply Nisbett's theory of cultural cognition to online information seeking?

To answer the above questions, the following sub-questions will be studied:

- How do users formulate their information need (top-down vs. bottom-up approach)?
- How often do they reformulate their search query?
- What type of information does user look at? (e.g. headlines, tags or descriptive information)
- How long does it take for users to decide where to click?
- How much time they spent on browsing? And how much time they spent on thinking/reading?
- What is the visual pattern of web navigation (holistic vs. analytic)?

3. METHODOLOGY

This research is an experimental study and is conducted in a usability lab in the University of South Carolina (USC). Participants are invited and selected from the Iranian, Chinese and American graduate student communities through an email invitation. Data are collected through three channels: questionnaire survey to gather demographic information;

TechSmith Morae application to record and manage the users' searching activities and mouse movements; and MyGaze eye-tracker to record the participants' eye movements and eye fixations. The users are asked to use Google as their search engine to perform a few information-searching tasks. For data analysis, a mixed method analysis will be employed. The analysis will include both qualitative (e.g. search query formulation and visual gaze pattern) and quantitative (e.g. ANOVA, activity counts and Mixed Effect Analysis) approaches to examine the collected data from different perspective.

4. PROGRESS MADE SO FAR

The basic steps toward conducting a research on human subjects (such as IRB approval, consent form, study invitation, funding planning and software/hardware purchase) have been taken by far. A pre-dissertation pilot study is conducted to test the feasibility of the proposed study, the recording technologies, and to find potential obstacles and limitations. For the test study, the participants (age 25-34) were invited and selected from three groups of graduate students at the USC: American, Chinese and Iranian (10 subjects per group). Each participant was provided with $10 incentives after the experiment. More than 90 percent of the Chinese and Iranian participants' TOEFL iBT score were over 95 (maximum 120). The experiments were conducted in English and in a usability laboratory at the USC. The research participants were asked to use Google as their search engine and Internet Explorer as their browser to perform four information-searching tasks without any time limitation.

The pilot study helped to identify the major limitations of this study. Also, it helped me to find a new direction in my study and achieve new hypothesis through the preliminary data analysis.

5. FUTURE PLAN

The lessons that were developed from the pilot study lead the future approaches. The main changes in research design include: changes in task scenarios and task types. Also, for triangulation purposes, the Extended CSA-WA test [1] will be employed to elicit cognitive differences between groups. More participants will be recruited and new statistical methods will be employed to investigate the relationships between culture and online searching behavior.

Upon completion of my dissertation, I intend to do the study in the users' mother language and compare the results with the dissertation findings. Also, I hope to find the chance to travel to different countries and do the study with users who have not been exposed to any languages/cultures other than their own.

6. REFERENCES

[1] Arguello, J., Wu, W. C., Kelly, D., & Edwards, A. 2012. Task complexity, vertical display and user interaction in aggregated search. In *Proceedings of the 35th international ACM SIGIR conference on Research and development in information retrieval* (pp. 435-444). ACM.

[2] Bates, M. J. 2010. Information Behavior *Encyclopedia of Library and Information Sciences* (Vol. 3, pp. 2381-2391). New York: CRC Press.

[3] Chau, P. Y. K., Cole, A. P. M., Massey, M. M.-W., & O'Keefe, R. M. 2002. Cultural Differences in the Online

Behavior of Consumers. *Communications of the ACM, 45*(10), 138-143.

[4] Chen, S. Y., & Macredie, R. D. 2002. Cognitive styles and hypermedia navigation: Development of a learning model. *Journal of the American society for information science and technology, 53*(1), 3-15.

[5] Chiao, J. Y., Cheon, B. K., Pornpattananangkul, N., Mrazek, A. J., & Blizinsky, K. D. 2013. Cultural neuroscience. *Advances in Culture and Psychology*, 4, 1.

[6] Chua, H. F., Boland, J. E., & Nisbet, R. E. 2005. Cultural variation in eye movements during scene perception. In *Proceedings of the National Academy of Sciences of the United States of America, 102*(35), 12629-12633.

[7] Dong, Y., & Lee, K. P. 2008. A cross-cultural comparative study of users' perceptions of a webpage: With a focus on the cognitive styles of Chinese, Koreans and Americans. *International Journal of Design, 2*(2), 19-30.

[8] Faiola, A., & Matei, S. A. 2005. Cultural cognitive style and web design: Beyond a behavioral inquiry into computer mediated communication. *Journal of Computer Mediated Communication, 11*(1), 375-394.

[9] Granka, L. A., Joachims, T., & Gay, G. 2004. Eye-tracking analysis of user behavior in WWW search. In *Proceedings of the 27th annual international ACM SIGIR conference on Research and development in information retrieval*.

[10] Han, S., Northoff, G., Vogeley, K., Wexler, B. E., Kitayama, S., & Varnum, M. E. 2013. A cultural neuroscience approach to the biosocial nature of the human brain. *Annual review of psychology, 64*, 335-359.

[11] Komlodi, A. 2005. Cultural Models of Hall and Hofstede. *Theories of information behavior* (pp. 108-112): Information Today, Inc.

[12] Komlodi, A., & Carlin, M. 2004. Identifying Cultural Variables in Information-Seeking. *AMCIS*

[13] Komlodi, A., & Hercegfi, K. 2010. Exploring Cultural Differences in Information Behavior Applying Psychophysiological Methods. Paper presented at *the CHI 2010*, Atlanta.

[14] Kralisch, A., & Berendt, B. 2004. *Cultural Determinants of Search Behaviour on Websites*.

[15] Marcos, M.-C., Garcia-Gavilanes, R., Bataineh, E., & Pasarin, L. 2013. Using Eye Tracking to Identify Cultural Differences in Information Seeking Behavior. Paper presented at *the CHI'13*, Paris, France.

[16] Kitayama, S., Duffy, S., Kawamura, T., & Larsen, J. T. 2003. Perceiving an object and its context in different cultures: A cultural look at new look. *Psychological Science, 14*(3), 201-206.

[17] Marcus, A. 2002. User-interface design, culture, and the future. In *Proceedings of the Working Conference on Advanced Visual Interfaces* (pp. 15-27). ACM.

[18] Marcus, A., & Gould, E. W. 2000. Cultural Dimensions and Global Web User-Interface Design. Paper presented at *the 6th Conference on Human Factors and the Web*.

[19] Masuda, T., & Nisbet, R. E. 2006. Culture and change blindness. *Cognitive Science, 30*(2), 381-399.

---

[1] Extended Cognitive Style Analysis - Wholistic Analytic Test

[20] Na, J., & Chan, M. Y. 2015. Culture, Cognition, and Intercultural Relations. In *Neuroscience in Intercultural Contexts* (pp. 49-71). Springer New York.

[21] Nisbett, R. E., & Masuda, T. 2003. Culture and point of view. *Proceedings of the National Academy of Sciences, 100*(19), 11163-11170.

[22] Nisbett, R. E., & Norenzayan, A. 2002. Culture and cognition. *Stevens' handbook of experimental psychology.*

[23] Nisbett, R. E., Peng, K., Choi, I., & Norenzayan, A. 2001. Culture and systems of thought: holistic versus analytic cognition. *Psychological review, 108*(2).

[24] Pan, B., Hembrooke, H. A., Gay, G. K., Granka, L. A., Feusner, M. K., & Newman, J. K. 2004. The determinants of web page viewing behavior: an eye-tracking study. Paper presented at *the 2004 symposium on Eye tracking research & applications.*

[25] Riding, R., & Rayner, S. 1998. *Cognitive styles and learning strategies: Understanding style differences in learning and behavior.* Routledge.

Investigating Information Search Behavior using Personal and Social Contextual Signals

Dongho Choi
School of Communication and Information
Rutgers, The State University of New Jersey
dongho.j.choi@rutgers.edu

ABSTRACT

People have their behavioral patterns, through which they determine how to use, seek and share information. Also, the patterns interact with a person's intrinsic and extrinsic characteristics such as values, attitudes, social and cognitive capitals, affecting behaviors in different contexts and situations. Meanwhile, the emerging trends of smartphones and wearable computing allow for the creation of a rich user behavioral profile. Such a behavioral (personal, social, mobile, and cognitive) profile goes beyond traditional browser-based context and allows one's personality type and social capital to become pivotal indicators of search behavior. Through the multi-modal data analysis, I want to identify the correlations between different signal types as observed in everyday life information seeking contexts and predict individuals' search behavior using personal and social contextual signals.

1. MOTIVATION

People search for information for shopping, doing hobbies, important news, and other personal interests in their daily lives. In his model of Everyday Life Information Seeking (ELIS), Savolainen [8] incorporates information seeking and the way in which people make sense of information around them. The model includes two substantial elements that form individual's everyday life information seeking behavior, *way of life* and *mastery of life*. The concept of 'way of life' was inspired by Bourdieu's idea of *habitus* [2], which can be understood as a socially and culturally determined system of thinking, perception, and evaluation of individuals. Based on this, 'way of life' describes internalized 'order of things,' and 'mastery of life' represents the actions, or activities, to 'keep things in order,' when the order of things being shaken and threatened. These two elements interact each other (re)forming individuals' information behavior pattern.

Considering the concept of *habitus*, can we say that people's behaviors are consistent across different contexts and situations? An individual has several intrinsic character-istics, such as general behavioral style and personality, as well as distinct social relationship and physical activities. Multiple studies have acknowledged the effect of individual personality, demographic descriptors, and personal context in human information behavior (e.g. [3]). However, most studies had to focus on traits that could be easily observed (e.g. gender, ethnicity) or elicited in a short time in laboratory settings. In effect, the human personal context was captured by observations made in short, unnatural settings, as recorded or reported by participants or the study conductor and had to contend with multiple challenges, including subjectivity in observation, recall/cognitive/socio-cognitive biases, and limited observation opportunities (e.g. [1, 4]).

In this sense, I am interested in exploring data captured by various types of sensors and/or devices to understand people's behavioral traits, leading to knowledge about information search behavior.

2. RESEARCH QUESTIONS

My research questions are as follows:

RQ1. To what extent, if any, do intrinsic characteristics, such as general behavioral style, personality, and social capital, relate to information seeking behavior?

RQ2. To what extent, if any, do personal and social contexts observable via mobile phones and wearable devices relate to information seeking behavior?

3. METHODOLOGY

In this section, I describe the methodology we have used in the on-going study. To observe and understand how everyday life behaviors are associated with their information seeking behavior, we have conducted a field study followed by a lab study with the same participants. The workflow of each session is described in Table 1.

3.1 Field study

Through a two-week field study, we collect data about participants' everyday lives and their intrinsic characteristics. During the field study, participants are asked to carry a wearble device, keep an app installed on their smartphones, and answer to three types of questionnaires.

3.1.1 Wearable Device

Each participant is given a wearable device, *Fitbit Charge*

Permission to make digital or hard copies of part or all of this work for personal or classroom use is granted without fee provided that copies are not made or distributed for profit or commercial advantage and that copies bear this notice and the full citation on the first page. Copyrights for third-party components of this work must be honored. For all other uses, contact the owner/author(s).

CHIIR '16 March 13-17, 2016, Carrboro, NC, USA

© 2016 Copyright held by the owner/author(s).

ACM ISBN 978-1-4503-3751-9/16/03.

DOI: http://dx.doi.org/10.1145/2854946.2854953

Table 1: Session Workflow.

Session	Procedure	Description
Field Session	Introduction	Introduce the study, install required apps and sync the wearable device with a dedicated app.
	Field task	Have participants keep using wearable devices in everyday lives and apps on the phone, collecting their individual and social context data.
	Survey	In the middle of the field session period, ask about their behavioral style, social capital, and information behavior.
Lab Session	Introduction	Introduce the lab session and information-seeking tasks the participants will be given.
	Lab task 1	Exploratory search task-1. Includes pre-survey and post-survey.
	Lab task 2	Exploratory search task-2. Includes pre-survey and post-survey.
	Wrap-up	Wrap-up study and (optional) interview.

HR^1. The device provides a way to collect data related with participants' personal and contextual (heavily focusing on physical activities) information, such as number of steps per day, working-out distance and time, heart rate, hours of sleep, and so on.

3.1.2 Mobile App

The participants are also be given an app for their smart phones (Android OS) that will records their mobility and social behavior data, such as how many people they are calling/texting and when, how many different locations they visited, which measured by the number of near cell towers and GPS data.

3.1.3 Survey

In the middle of the field study, we ask three kinds of survey to the participants, which include Miller Behavioral Style Scale [6], Williams Social Capital profiles [11], and Big Five Factors [5]. Through them, we examine each participant's information seeking style, social capital, and general personality.

3.2 Lab study

The participants are invited to a lab session after a month of field data collection to perform two exploratory searches, individual task and collaboration as pairs. In order to measure and evaluate the participants' information searching behaviors, the study adopted a subsets of evaluation measures suggested in [9] and [10]. A brief description of the framework is presented in Table 2.

4. PROGRESS MADE SO FAR

We have ran four batches of user study with 35 student participants in total during Spring and Summer semester in 2015. While we are working on the analysis with the whole 35 participants, the preliminary analysis with the first 25 participants (12 pairs in collaborative work) provides several results as follows.

4.1 Individual Search

Regarding data collected through mobile app, two features show correlation with some of search performance. The number of SMS has positive relationship with Unique Relevant Coverage, while Distinct Location also has positive relationship with Unique Coverage.

---

[1]https://www.fitbit.com/chargehr

The variable of Number of SMS shows the extent to which a person interacts with other individuals through mobile texts. Higher value of this variable means a person frequently sends and receives text messages to and from other people no matter who they are. In the meantime, higher value of Unique Relevant Coverage indicates that a person visited relatively much number of relevant Web pages during the search task. More specifically, when considering the term "unique," the person might have distinct and unique criteria for relevancy. When it comes to the exploratory search, the tendency also infers that an individual who sends/receives relatively higher number of messages per day tends to understand and learn the topic differently from others who does not.

One additional interesting finding is the positive relation between Unique Coverage and Distinct Location. The variable of Distinct Location measures that the total number of distinct locations during a day, captured by different cell tower IDs and/or GPS data. This information does not necessarily imply the intention of locational changes, whether for activities or commuting. No matter what the purposes of movement, the result indicate that a person who moves more tends to visit Web pages that have not visited by other participants. This brings us an interesting question: "Does geo-locational movement affect information exposure to an individual and affect again toward the way of thinking and understanding?"

4.2 Collaborative Search

Among the features extracted signals, we found relationship between the dissimilarity in the number of SMS counterparts and the synergy effect. This means that the more participants are different with regard to the social activities that are measured how many people they are keeping to talk with, the less synergy effect they have when working together. Though it is not significant enough, we can see the negative relationship between distinct users for SMS and the ratio of increased Coverage. However, if we selected sample with negative synergy effect, the relationship is much stronger and significant.

An another aspect of SMS usage, the number of SMS that an individual sends and receives per day, shows a relationship with the synergy effect on Relevant Coverage in collaboration ($N = 12, R^2 = .344, p = .045$). This implies that if members in a pair have substantial difference of the extent of using SMS, they tend to have less synergy effect regarding information relevancy.

Table 2: Variables used in Analysis

Data Source	Features	Description
Wearable Device	Steps	The average number of steps per day of a user during the field study
	Minutes of Sedentary	Average minutes of being sedentary per day recognized by the wearable device
	Minutes of Very Active	Average minutes of being very active per day recognized by the wearable device
	Minutes of Sleep	Average minutes of being asleep per day recognized by the wearable device
Mobile App	Total Call Time	Average minutes of total call time per day
	Number of Calls	Average number of call per day
	Number of SMS	Average number of SMS sent/received per day
	Distinct User (Call)	Average number of distinct caller/receiver per day
	Distinct User (SMS)	Average number of distinct sender/receiver for SMS usage per day
	Distinct Location	Average number of distinct location per day, captured by the app using the number of cell tower around and GPS data
Searching Task	Coverage	The total number of distinct Web documents visited by a participant
	Unique Coverage	The total number of Web documents visited only by one participant
	Relevant Coverage	The total number of distinct relevant Web documents visited by a participant
	Unique Relevant Coverage	The total number of distinct relevant Web documents visited only by one participant
	Distinct Queries	The number of distinct queries that were submitted to search engines by participant

Seeing the data, even with very limited number of samples, we came up with an interesting question: "Do the large differences in the values of the same feature from the collaborators matter? Or does the minimum value of each feature among the collaborators matter more for group synergy?" This question is inspired by the "Liebig's Law of Minimum [7]," which is originally a concept applied to plant or crop growth. The law refers the fact that increasing the amount of plentiful nutrients do not always cause the increasing plat growth and the yield. Likewise, we suspected even if one participant in a team has incredible potential in terms of productivity and efficiency in the task, the results might not be productive as expected, when the other one cannot support him/her very well.

4.3 Future Plan

Current methodology might have a couple of weaknesses. First, two-week of field study and the collected data through can have bias due to seasonal effect and accidental situations happened to the participants. Also, the participants can feel uncomfortable in the exploratory search setting with 30-minute limit, avoiding to explore information enough to achieve goal(s). I am expecting to capture much richer amount of data and want to explore the behaviors revealed in a longer-term study. One of the important and critical work to be done shortly is about the measures and evaluation framework for information search behavior. Though we employed several measures that describe the behavior, other schemes, even from other disciplines such as psychology may give us profound implications for the future work.

5. REFERENCES

[1] P. P. Biemer, R. M. Groves, L. E. Lyberg, N. A. Mathiowetz, and S. Sudman. *Measurement errors in surveys*, volume 173. John Wiley & Sons, 2011.

[2] P. Bourdieu. *Distinction: A Social Critique of the Judgement of Taste*. Harvard University Press, 1984.

[3] T. A. Burdick. Success and Diversity in Information Seeking: Gender and the Information Search Styles Model. *School Library Media Quarterly*, 25(1):19–26, 1996.

[4] N. Eagle and A. Pentland. Reality mining: sensing complex social systems. *Personal and ubiquitous computing*, 10(4):255–268, 2006.

[5] O. P. John and S. Srivastava. The Big Five trait taxonomy: History, measurement, and theoretical perspectives. *Handbook of personality: Theory and research*, 2(1999):102–138, 1999.

[6] S. M. Miller. Monitoring and blunting: validation of a questionnaire to assess styles of information seeking under threat. *Journal of personality and social psychology*, 52(2):345, 1987.

[7] E. P. Odum, H. T. Odum, and J. Andrews. *Fundamentals of ecology*, volume 3. Saunders Philadelphia, 1971.

[8] R. Savolainen. Everyday life information seeking: Approaching information seeking in the context of "way of life". *Library & Information Science Research*, 17(3):259–294, 1995.

[9] C. Shah. Evaluating collaborative information seeking - synthesis, suggestions, and structure. *Journal of Information Science*, 40(4):460–475, Apr. 2014.

[10] C. Shah, C. Hendahewa, and R. González-Ibáñez. Two's Company, But Three's No Crowd: Evaluating Exploratory Web Search for Individuals and Teams. *Journal of Information Science*, Sep, 2015.

[11] D. C. Williams. On and Off the 'Net: Scales for Social Capital in an Online Era. *Journal of Computer-Mediated Communication*, 11(2):593–628, 2006.

Building Realistic Simulations for Interactive Information Retrieval

David Maxwell
School of Computing Science
University of Glasgow
Glasgow, Scotland
d.maxwell.1@research.gla.ac.uk *

ABSTRACT

Simulation has been used within the field of *Information Retrieval (IR)* for many years to evaluate retrieval models and other aspects of the wider IR process. In recent years, there has been a renewed interest towards using simulation for *Interactive Information Retrieval (IIR)*, an area which focuses on the study of human interactions with IR systems. A variety of different interaction models (e.g. click models) associated with behavioural aspects of searchers have over time been developed and evaluated using simulation in order for us to better understand the complex processes involved. Despite these advances, such models are still relatively naïve, and further work is required to make simulations of searchers more realistic. To this end, this project seeks to build more realistic simulations, using a more *Complex Searcher Model (CSM)*. Within the CSM, each component and decision point can be varied and customised as required. The CSM can then be instantiated using components that are grounded from empirical evidence based upon actual real-world searcher behaviour and interaction data.

Categories and Subject Descriptors: H.3.3 [**Information Storage and Retrieval**]: Information Search and Retrieval:Search Process H.3.4 [**Information Storage and Retrieval**]:Systems and Software:Performance Evaluation

Keywords Simulation; User Modeling; Search Strategies; Search Behavior; Querying Strategies; Stopping Strategies; Evaluation

1. INTRODUCTION AND MOTIVATION

The *Information Retrieval (IR)* community has centred much of its recent research upon the so-called *Cranfield Paradigm*. The paradigm revolves around the idea of a test collection and associated relevance judgements for documents within said collection. This approach provides a standardised way in which one can evaluate their retrieval system against a given baseline. While the general concepts of the paradigm have remained in place since the 1960s, components have over the years evolved as the associated data and tasks have become ever more complex in nature [8]. Examples of use today include the *NIST*-sponsored *Text REtrieval Conference (TREC)* and other evaluation forums.

The Cranfield Paradigm today still largely remains the *de facto* means of IR evaluation. Despite this however, the approach possesses a simplistic means of examining the actions with which a real-world searcher undertakes. As such, several different scientific approaches have been developed to better understand the complex sequence of interactions taking place, and are readily used in the study of *Interactive Information Retrieval (IIR)* which deals specifically with the interactions between humans and search engines. As outlined by Keskustalo et al. [9], the approaches can be split into four distinct categories:

1. obtaining data from searchers in real-world situations (e.g. log data from a commercial search engine);

2. observing searchers perform simulated search tasks (e.g. a user study involving a search engine);

3. performing simulations in a lab environment (e.g. simulations of interaction, without real-world searchers); and

4. traditional lab-based research, sans real-world searchers.

Experimentation with real-world searchers undertaking either real or simulated search tasks is the preferred way to study IIR (approaches *1* and *2*). However, such experiments require a significant level of effort to organise and setup. They are also laborious to run, and are usually very costly - both for the researcher and subject involved [3]. Approach *4* can be argued as a simplistic form of *'TREC-style'* simulation, assuming a single query with a fixed number of documents examined in a linear fashion. This approach however is not interactive, and can be considered naïve.

This therefore leaves the simulation of real-world searchers, incorporating *interactive* components such as relevance feedback and other interaction components (approach *3*) as a means of exploring IIR. As the main focus of this project, simulation provides a rapid means of exploring the potential limits of real-world searcher interactions at a low cost. Current means of simulation are limited because they assume searchers act in a fixed way, or act stochastically by examining content with fixed probabilities. Research has shown that in reality, searchers tend to adapt their interactions based upon the quality of the presented ranked list [14].

---

*The author is currently a third year PhD student, supervised by Dr Leif Azzopardi (Leif.Azzopardi@glasgow.ac.uk) and Professor Roderick Murray-Smith (Roderick.Murray-Smith@glasgow.ac.uk).

CHIIR'16, March 13 - 17, 2016, Carrboro, NC, USA
Copyright is held by the owner/author(s).
ACM 978-1-4503-3751-9/16/03
http://dx.doi.org/10.1145/2854946.2854950

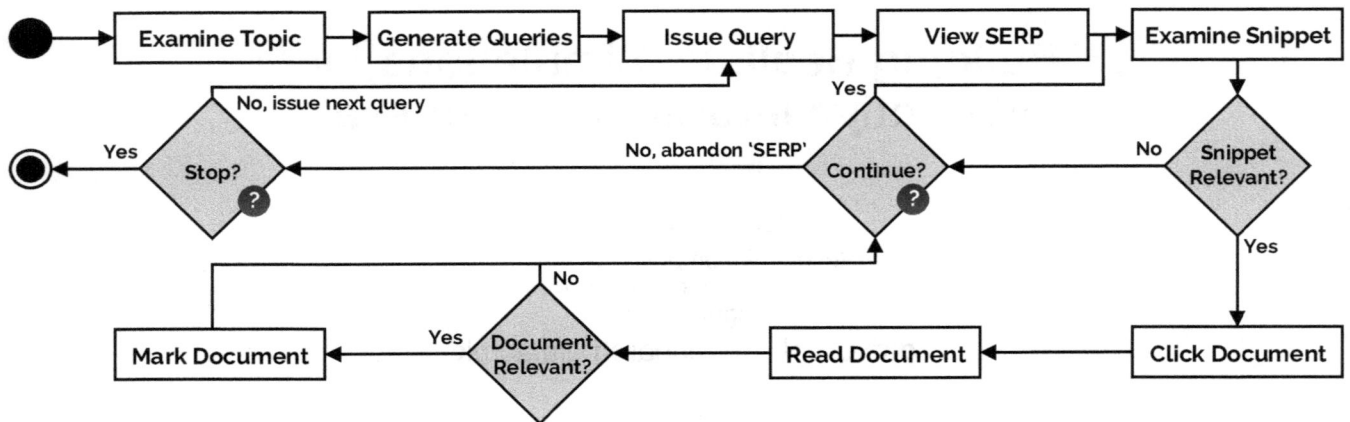

Figure 1: A flowchart of the current iteration of the CSM, complete with decision points (shown in grey) and tasks (shown in white) that a searcher undertakes within the wider search/IIR process. The model is adapted from Baskaya et al. [4] and Thomas et al. [16], with the figure itself adapted from Maxwell et al. [13].

Simulations of course would not be effective if the underlying models and assumptions do not adequately represent the actions that real-world searchers would be inclined to undertake [3]. While the IIR community has recently made advances in user modelling (e.g. [1, 2, 4, 16]), a significant amount of work is still required to make simulations of searchers more credible. To this end, this project aims to build more realistic simulations, starting with a *Complex Searcher Model (CSM)*, illustrated as a flowchart in Figure 1. Within the CSM, a complex search process is modelled, where each component (e.g. query generation) and decision point (e.g. deciding when to stop) can be varied and customised. We also instantiate the CSM with components grounded from empirical evidence based upon actual real-world searcher behaviour and interaction data, providing realism to the simulations.

2. RESEARCH QUESTIONS

The initial focus of this project will involve addressing the first three research questions, which revolve around improving querying and stopping components. The latter part of this project will then ensure the realism, flexibility and validity of the developed components as a whole.

RQ1 How can we create more realistic stopping components that reflect different types of searcher stopping behaviour?

Addressing this research question will require research to **RQ1.1** examine what factors specifically influence the stopping behaviours of searchers, and **RQ1.2** which operationalised stopping strategies best reflect the actual stopping behaviours of real-world searchers.

We also address the issue of query generation.

RQ2 How do we create more realistic querying components that reflect upon different types of searcher querying behaviour?

Specifically, we wish to examine **RQ2.1** what factors influence querying behaviours; **RQ2.2** how we can rank and select queries for issuing to the underlying search engine; and **RQ2.3** how we can revise the list of possible queries that can be issued as the simulated searcher 'learns' from examining snippets and documents. This final point is of

particular importance to building a realistic query generation component for the CSM, but will however require a modification of the CSM to allow for the updating of potential query terms. These findings, in combination with the findings related to stopping behaviour, leads to the following overarching question.

RQ3 What is the interplay between querying and stopping strategies, and other components of the CSM?

Of course, the CSM presented in Figure 1 contains a variety of different components that can be explored. While the time available for this project does not permit a thorough exploration of all, there are still some areas in which potential improvements in realism can be made.

RQ4 What other components of the CSM can be improved or refined to make the underlying model more realistic and flexible?

For example, based upon the data available at a given point, how can we **RQ4.1** assess the quality of a provided *Search Engine Results Page (SERP)* from first impressions? **RQ4.2** What features do searchers look for that give them confidence the SERP may contain useful information related to their information need?

Our final research question can neatly encapsulate all of the efforts towards the previous four questions, examining the realism of the simulations run with the CSM.

RQ5 With grounded CSM components, will the actions performed by simulated searcher be indistinguishable from those performed by actual searchers?

This question revolves around the concept of the so-called *Belkin test*. When provided with the interaction logs of both a real-world searcher and simulated searcher under similar conditions (e.g. time constraints), would one be able to differentiate between the two?

3. METHODOLOGY AND PROGRESS

This section details the work that has been undertaken thus far towards this project, highlighting the key accomplishments and findings towards addressing the overarching research questions provided in Section 2. The main approach taken for this project entails: *(i)* the collection of real-world searcher interaction log data through a controlled user study [11]; *(ii)* the design and implementation of an IIR simulator (Section 3.1); and *(iii)* the use of the simulator and searcher interaction log data to implement and evaluate new components for the CSM (Section 3.2).

3.1 SimIIR and the CSM

Underpinning the remainder of this project, we have developed an open-source searcher simulator framework called *SimIIR*, available at `http://git.io/vZ5mH`. SimIIR operationalises the CSM, as detailed in Figure 1, and is based upon two salient interaction models by Baskaya et al. [4] and Thomas et al. [16]. Experimental setups for publications utilising SimIIR are also available at `http://git.io/vOBLz`.

3.2 Modelling Stopping Behaviours

We then began an investigation into a series of different stopping strategies, a means to describe the point at which searchers decide to stop examining a provided SERP. The stopping strategies are encoded within the CSM as the two decision points, highlighted with question marks (*?*) as seen in Figure 1. Many studies examining the stopping behaviours of searchers have found searchers use their intuition when deciding when to stop, with the belief that what they find is 'good enough' [13]. Despite this, several researchers proposed a series of stopping rules and heuristics [5, 6, 7, 10].

We used some of these defined rules and heuristics and operationalised them, examining the effectiveness of each with a simulated analysis [12]. We used a fixed-depth baseline stopping strategy (e.g. $P@k$) and two implementations of the *frustration point/disgust* stopping rules [6, 10], one considering the total number of snippets judged non-relevant, with the other considering the number of snippets judged non-relevant *contiguously*. The simulations were conducted over the AQUAINT and WT2g collections using topics associated with each collection, with each stopping strategy trialled over a wide range of thresholds (e.g. stop after x snippets are judged non-relevant). Our findings from the study showed that our implementations of the frustration point/disgust rules resulted in higher levels of gain per second across a number of different querying strategies. This work was then taken further with the implementation of three additional, more sophisticated stopping rules [13]. We also compared simulated behaviours against that of our real-world searcher log data [11], finding that the same, adaptive stopping strategies yielded the closest approximations.

4. FUTURE WORK

As much of the work related to **RQ1** is complete, some aspects do still remain. For example, Smucker [15] identified different categories of searcher depending on their interaction characteristics (e.g. searchers who are fast at examining snippets, and likely to consider them relevant). By clustering searchers from our user study [11], we could determine what stopping strategies and associated threshold values best approximates searcher behaviours by cluster/group.

Secondly, with regards to **RQ2**, work is required to determine how to construct better queries based upon content examined by a simulated searcher as they progress through a search task. A detailed analysis on the factors that influence querying behaviour, coupled with a closer examination between the links of stopping and querying behaviours, should provide us with a means to address **RQ3**.

With so many different components of the CSM that can be addressed, we will then explore the phase of *initial SERP examination*, addressing **RQ4**. Understanding behaviours exhibited by searchers at this phase would allow us to significantly improve the realism of the CSM, as skipping poor SERPs would save the simulated searcher time and effort.

With these implemented components and observed improvements in real-world searcher approximations, we should then be able to provide an answer to **RQ5**, or at least specify which aspects still need improvement. A final important question that can be raised is whether the findings from these simulated studies will generalise across different searchers. As such, it may be beneficial to conduct a further user study for comparison against our simulations and examine if the results generalise across studies.

Acknowledgments: The author wishes to thank his primary supervisor, Dr Leif Azzopardi, for all the help, guidance, patience and friendship shown during his studies at *UoG*. *Thank you so much, Leif!* The author also thanks the two reviewers for their feedback, and Professor Kalervo Järvelin and Dr Heikki Keskustalo at the University of Tampere, Finland for their co-operation and participation in a STSM, funded by the MUMIA Cost Action (reference ECOST-STSM-IC1002-080914-049840). The author is also financially supported by the UK Government through the EPSRC, grant number 1367507.

References

[1] L. Azzopardi. The economics in interactive information retrieval. In *Proc. 34th ACM SIGIR*, pages 15–24, 2011.

[2] L. Azzopardi. Modelling interaction with economic models of search. In *Proc. 37th ACM SIGIR*, pages 3–12, 2014.

[3] L. Azzopardi, K. Järvelin, J. Kamps, and M.D. Smucker. Report on the sigir 2010 workshop on the simulation of interaction. *SIGIR Forum*, 44(2):35–47, 2011.

[4] F. Baskaya, H. Keskustalo, and K. Järvelin. Modeling behavioral factors in interactive information retrieval. In *Proc. 22nd ACM CIKM*, pages 2297–2302, 2013.

[5] G.J. Browne, M.G. Pitts, and J.C. Wetherbe. Stopping rule use during web-based search. In *Proc. HICSS-38*, page 271b, 2005.

[6] W.S. Cooper. On selecting a measure of retrieval effectiveness part ii. implementation of the philosophy. *J. of the American Soc. for Info. Sci.*, 24(6):413–424, 1973.

[7] W.S. Cooper. The paradoxical role of unexamined documents in the evaluation of retrieval effectiveness. *Info. Processing and Management*, 12(6):367 – 375, 1976.

[8] D. Harman. Is the cranfield paradigm outdated? In *Proceedings of SIGIR 2010*, pages 1–1, 2010.

[9] H. Keskustalo, K. Järvelin, and A. Pirkola. Evaluating the effectiveness of relevance feedback based on a user simulation model: Effects of a user scenario on cumulated gain value. *Information Retrieval*, 11(3):209–228, 2008.

[10] D.H. Kraft and T. Lee. Stopping rules and their effect on expected search length. *IPM*, 15(1):47 – 58, 1979.

[11] D. Maxwell and L. Azzopardi. Stuck in traffic: How temporal delays affect search behaviour. In *Proc. 5th IIiX*, pages 155–164, 2014.

[12] D. Maxwell, L. Azzopardi, K. Järvelin, and H. Keskustalo. An initial investigation into fixed and adaptive stopping strategies. In *Proc. 38th ACM SIGIR*, pages 903–906, 2015.

[13] D. Maxwell, L. Azzopardi, K. Järvelin, and H. Keskustalo. Searching and stopping: An analysis of stopping rules and strategies. In *Proc. 24th ACM CIKM*, pages 313–322, 2015.

[14] A. Moffat, P. Thomas, and F. Scholer. Users versus models: What observation tells us about effectiveness metrics. In *Proc. 22nd ACM CIKM*, pages 659–668, 2013.

[15] M.D. Smucker. An analysis of user strategies for examining and processing ranked lists of documents. In *Proc. of 5th HCIR*, 2011.

[16] P. Thomas, A. Moffat, P. Bailey, and F. Scholer. Modeling decision points in user search behavior. In *Proc. 5th IIiX*, pages 239–242, 2014.

Supporting Ideation by Integrating Exploratory Search, Browsing, and Curation

Yin Qu
Interface Ecology Lab
Department of Computer Science and Engineering
Texas A&M University
yin@ecologylab.net

ABSTRACT

This research integrates exploratory search, browsing, and curation in information-based ideation (IBI) environments, to support users finding, discovering, and combining web content. Information-based ideation refers to open-ended activities in which humans work to imagine, generate, and develop new problems and solutions. We use web semantics as a basis for summarizing and representing heterogeneous content from diverge sources involved in ideation tasks. To enable working with web semantics, we develop a novel type system that brings together data models, dynamic extraction, and presentation of semantic information. Based on the web semantics type system, we build interfaces that preserve contexts during exploratory browsing, and plan to build integrated interactive environments to address exploratory search, curation, and ideation. We will investigate how integrated environments affect people's practices with finding and combining information, and derive new principles for supporting exploratory search, browsing, curation, and ideation. Methods, techniques, and findings developed through this research have the potential to transform infrastructures and human experiences of the web.

Categories and Subject Descriptors

H.5.2 [**Information interfaces and presentation: user interfaces**]: Graphical user interfaces

1. MOTIVATION

To generate and develop new problems and solutions, people perform open-ended ideation tasks, such as planning a wedding or designing a course. These tasks require exploratory search for and browsing of diverse content. The present research develops a novel web semantics type system as the basis for representing diverse, contextual searches, results, and linked documents, to support exploration.

Prominent researchers have emphasized the importance of developing new methods for synthesizing different types of

CHIIR '16 March 13-17, 2016, Carrboro, NC, USA

© 2016 Copyright held by the owner/author(s).

ACM ISBN 978-1-4503-3751-9/16/03.

DOI: http://dx.doi.org/10.1145/2854946.2854948

information from different sources into unified representations, to help users focus on *meaning* in the context of tasks [23]. Kerne et al call this process of synthesis, *curation*, and show how curation is inherent in the performance of ideation tasks [10]. We apply the new semantic type system to generate consistent representations across exploratory search, browsing, and curation interfaces, integrated to form an ideation support environment.

Ideation tasks involve searching for new information. Found information can be used to remedy incomplete or inaccurate understandings [1], solve task-related problems, or stimulate the generation of new ideas [21, 9, 24, 10]. Search and browsing are important methods people use to find information on the web, both purposefully and serendipitously [13, 22]. Exploratory search extends search from a one-time query-document matching act to an iterative process, involving browsing, learning, and discovery [25, 12]. Prior work finds exploratory search useful for understanding collections and relationships [20, 27, 5, 28]. Exploratory browsing and search are intrinsic to the performance of sensemaking [19] and information-based ideation tasks [10, 18].

Interfaces supporting ideation need to address fundamental cognitive limitations. For instance, human working memory, which is essential to comprehension, learning, and ideation, only holds approximately 4 elements at a time [15, 4]. However, the number of elements that must be understood, reflected upon, and synthesized in the performance of contextualized ideation tasks is often larger. Typical browsers present information in separate tabs and windows, making it difficult to keep track of relationships among documents, or think about and combine information across documents. As the result, users may lose orientation during navigation, or digress from the task at hand [14, 6]. We need to discover interactive systems that help users maintain context during exploration, sensemaking, and ideation.

Curation is the creative process of gathering, assembling, annotating, and exhibiting found information elements [10]. It is valuable for curation environments to provide external representations to help users—who by nature possess limited working memory—think about and combine information encountered during search and browsing to form new ideas. Curation environments can promote synthesis by supporting iteratively gathering found objects, representing and interpreting objects and relationships, integrating thoughts and explanations as annotations, formulating solutions across objects, and presenting formulated solutions as holistic exhibits for reflection and communication. During synthesis, new information needs may emerge, leading

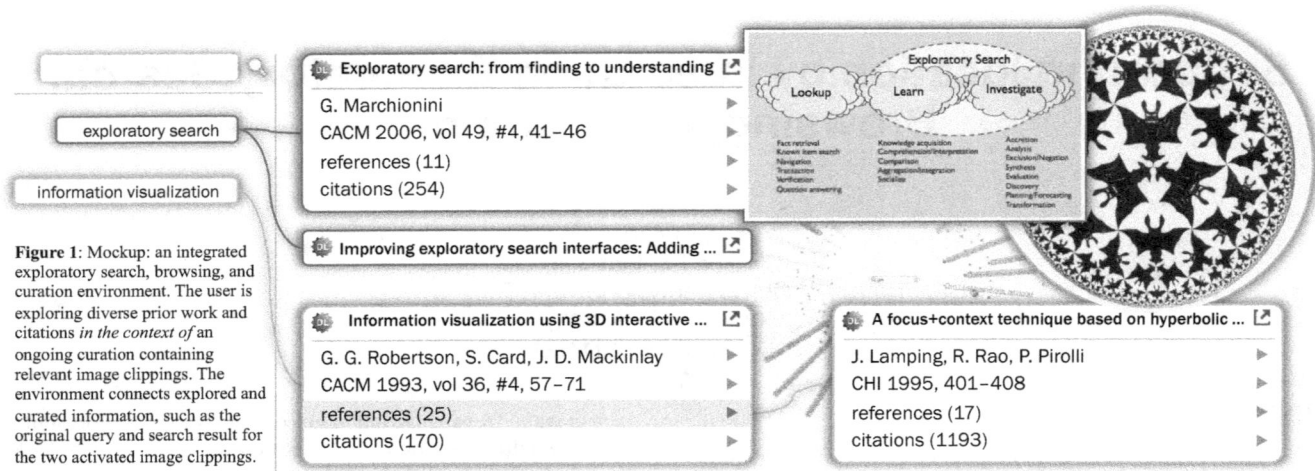

Figure 1: Mockup: an integrated exploratory search, browsing, and curation environment. The user is exploring diverse prior work and citations *in the context of* an ongoing curation containing relevant image clippings. The environment connects explored and curated information, such as the original query and search result for the two activated image clippings.

to further exploratory search and browsing [8, 16]. Thus, search, browsing, curation, and synthesis mutually motivate one another, and are inherent to information-based ideation.

However, despite this inherent relationship, prior tools separate exploratory search, browsing, and curation. This forces users to split attention, resulting in extraneous cognitive load [3, 26]. The motivation of this research is to investigate and develop methods for integrating and contextualizing exploratory search, browsing, and curation, to reduce cognitive load, and support synthesis for ideation.

2. RESEARCH QUESTIONS

This research investigates the following research questions:

1. How do people find, discover, and combine web information to form new ideas in practice?
2. How to integrate exploratory search, browsing, and curation in one environment? How to support a large and growing number of types, sources, and use cases?
3. How do an integrated environment and consistent representations affect users in exploratory search, browsing, curation, and ideation?
4. How to contextualize exploratory search and browsing with curation? How does seeing search results and linked documents in context of curated information affect cognition and experience?
5. What are implications for the design of future web interfaces?

3. METHODOLOGY

The present research investigates integration of exploratory search, browsing, and curation, using a novel web semantics type system as a basis. *Web semantics* involve significant attributes, descriptions, representations, and relationships of objects people find on the web. During exploratory search and browsing, web semantics can support derivation of summaries of search results and linked web pages, enabling users to see diverse significant information in a single context. Derived summaries can be brought into curation products, providing external representations for users to understand, combine, synthesize, and reflect on.

We use a web semantics type system as the basis for deriving document summaries [17]. With this method, we do not rely on websites to publish structured semantic information, such as RDF [11]. Instead, structured semantic information

is extracted from regular, semi-structured web pages, using code snippets called *wrappers*. To derive summaries, wrappers integrate data models, extraction rules, and presentation semantics, and can be reused through inheritance and polymorphism [2]. This research will extend extraction rule capabilities to support diverse semantic formats and schemes used on the web, including microdata, Facebook Open Graph, and Twitter Cards. Presentation semantics regulate how semantic information is presented to end users, ensuring visual consistency and usability. Types enable dynamic resolution of a web page to a semantic type at runtime, containing a contextually specific data model, extraction rules, and presentation semantics. Polymorphism enables the development of rich interfaces that operate on a base type to dynamically present detailed semantic information from heterogeneous web pages encountered at runtime.

This research involves the following activities:

1. Develop a web semantics type system that integrates data models, extraction, and presentation. The working hypothesis is that the new web semantics type system can be used as the basis for extracting and presenting usable summaries of webpages for many information types, sources, and use cases.
2. Use extracted summaries to build integrated exploratory search and browsing interfaces. The working hypothesis is that the integrated exploratory search and browsing interface will mitigate issues with typical browsers, such as disorientation and digression.
3. Use the new web semantics type system as the basis for integrating dynamic exploratory search and browsing interfaces into a curation environment (Figure 1). We hypothesize that the integrated environment will reduce the cognitive load of splitting attention, and promote synthesis and ideation.
4. Conduct laboratory and field studies to evaluate how the integrated environment affects people's exploratory search, browsing, curation, and ideation experiences.

4. CURRENT PROGRESS

We have developed a functional prototype of the web semantics type system, and built an example dynamic exploratory browsing interface using it. The example interface presents summaries from linked web pages in one space, starting from a particular source document, to facilitate navigation without leaving the current context. A preliminary study shows that the example interface helps users maintain orientation and focus on the task at hand during exploratory browsing [17]. We also used the type system to provide contextual information in a curation environment, which helps users understand, explore, and reflect on their curations [24].

5. FUTURE PLAN

We are working on a dynamic interface that integrates exploratory search and browsing, using the new web semantics type system to support deriving summaries for search results and linked pages. The interface presents summaries in a single context, to help users maintain orientation and focus. Queries, search results, and browsing history will be preserved across sessions, to support iterative exploratory search and browsing spanning an extended period of time. We plan to further integrate the exploratory search and browsing interface with a web-based curation environment (Figure 1) to enable seeing new information in the context of the task at hand, and so support synthesis and ideation.

We will evaluate the integrated environment's impact on people's exploration and ideation experiences through laboratory and field studies. For controlled laboratory studies, we will invite researchers to explore prior work, curate, and ideate, to form project ideas related to pre-selected topics. We will build on Kerne et al [10] and Jain et al's [7] ideation metrics, and develop practical methods for measuring exploratory search, browsing, curation, and ideation. We will collect qualitative data from subjects and corroborate with quantitative metrics, to gain a deeper understanding of their practices and experiences. We will distill implications for designing future exploratory search, browsing, curation, and ideation environments from study results.

6. REFERENCES

[1] N. Belkin. Anomalous states of knowledge as a basis for information retrieval. *Canadian Journal of Information and Library Science*, 5:133–143, 1980.

[2] G. Booch et al. *Object-Oriented Analysis and Design with Applications*. Pearson Education, 2007.

[3] P. Chandler and J. Sweller. Cognitive load theory and the format of instruction. *Cognition and Instruction*, 8(4):293–332, 1991.

[4] N. Cowan. The magical number 4 in short-term memory: a reconsideration of mental storage capacity. *The Behavioral and brain sciences*, 24(1):87–114, 2001.

[5] S. Dumais et al. Stuff i've seen: A system for personal information retrieval and re-use. In *Proc of ACM SIGIR*, pages 72–79, 2003.

[6] C. L. Foss. Detecting lost users: Empirical studies on browsing hypertext. Technical report, 1989.

[7] A. Jain et al. Evaluating TweetBubble with ideation metrics of exploratory browsing. In *Proc. of ACM Creativity and Cognition (C&C)*, pages 53–62, 2015.

[8] K. Jarvelin and P. Ingwersen. Information seeking research needs extension towards tasks and technology. *Information Research*, 10(1), 2004.

[9] A. Kerne et al. combinFormation: Mixed-initiative composition of image and text surrogates promotes information discovery. *ACM TOIS*, 27(1):1–45, 2008.

[10] A. Kerne et al. Using metrics of curation to evaluate

[11] O. Lassila and R. R. Swick. Resource description framework (RDF) model and syntax specification. 1999.

[12] G. Marchionini. Exploratory search: From finding to understanding. *Commun. ACM*, 49(4):41, 2006.

[13] G. Marchionini and B. Shneiderman. Finding facts vs. browsing knowledge in hypertext systems. *Computer*, 21(1):70–80, 1988.

[14] R. McAleese. Navigation and browsing in hypertext. In *Hypertext: Theory into practice*, pages 6–44. Intellect Books, Oxford, 1989.

[15] G. A. Miller. The magical number seven, plus or minus two: some limits on our capacity for processing information. *Psychological review*, 63(1):81–97, 1956.

[16] P. Pirolli and S. Card. The sensemaking process and leverage points for analyst technology as identified through cognitive task analysis. In *Proc. of International Conference on Intelligence Analysis*, volume 5, pages 2–4, 2005.

[17] Y. Qu et al. Metadata type system: integrate presentation, data models, and extraction to enable exploratory browsing interfaces. In *Proc. of ACM EICS*, pages 107–116, 2014.

[18] Y. Qu and G. W. Furnas. Sources of structure in sensemaking. In *Proc. of ACM CHI EA*, pages 1989–1992, 2005.

[19] D. M. Russell et al. The cost structure of sensemaking. In *Proc. of ACM CHI*, pages 269–276, 1993.

[20] m. c. scheraefel et al. mSpace: interaction design for user-determined, adaptable domain exploration in hypermedia. In *Proc. of AH*, 2003.

[21] J. J. Shah et al. Collaborative sketching (C-Sketch) – an idea generation technique for engineering design. *The Journal of Creative Behavior*, 35(3):168–198, 2001.

[22] J. Teevan et al. The perfect search engine is not enough: A study of orienteering behavior in directed search. In *Proc. of ACM CHI*, pages 415–422, 2004.

[23] J. J. Thomas and K. Cook. A visual analytics agenda. *Computer Graphics and Applications*, 26(1):10–13, 2006.

[24] A. M. Webb et al. Promoting reflection and interpretation in education: Curating rich bookmarks as information composition. In *Proc. of ACM Creativity & Cognition*, pages 53–62, 2013.

[25] R. W. White et al. Introduction to supporting exploratory search. *Commun. ACM*, 49(4):36–39, 2006.

[26] M. L. Wilson and m. schraefel. Improving exploratory search interfaces: Adding value or information overload? In *Proc. of 2nd Workshop on HCIIR*, pages 81–84, 2008.

[27] K.-P. Yee et al. Faceted metadata for image search and browsing. *Proc. of ACM CHI*, pages 401–408, 2003.

[28] J. Zhang and G. Marchionini. Evaluation and evolution of a browse and search interface: Relation Browser++. In *Proc. of National Conference on Digital Government Research*, pages 179–188. Digital Government Society of North America, 2005.

information-based ideation. *ACM TOCHI*, 21(3):14:1–14:48, 2014.

Improving Query Reformulation in Voice Search System

Ning Sa
Informatics Department, University at Albany, SUNY
BA 310 1400 Washington Ave.
Albany, NY 12222
nsa@albany.edu

ABSTRACT

During online search, users frequently modify the existing query to get better results. For voice search users, the system error is a second reason of query reformulation. In keyboard system, query reformulation usually involves partial modification which is not well supported by the current voice search systems. In this proposal, I aim to develop a set of voice commands which will improve the user experience in query reformulation during voice search. The study will include four phases. Firstly, a survey will be used to collect the user's perception of the current voice search system. Secondly, an experiment will be performed to find out how the users would like to communicate with the system. Thirdly, a set of voice commands will be developed based on the findings of the second phase. Finally, another experiment will be used to test the effects of the voice commands.

Keywords

Voice search; query reformulation; user study

1. MOTIVATION

The process of issuing a second query based on the previous queries and their corresponding results is referred to as query reformulation. It is found to be commonly used during online search and usually involves partial modification of the previous query. During voice search, system errors are reported to be frequent and also require to be fixed with query reformulation [9]. However, in current voice search systems, users do not have the option of partially modifying the existing query. Instead, they need to enter a complete query, which might cause cascading errors. Based on previous studies in Information Retrieval, I argue that query reformulation enabled by partial modification will improve user experience during voice search.

1.1 Query reformulation

In web search, users employ query reformulation to refine their search and to get better results. According to Kamvar and Baluja [11], in all the query pairs collected in the study, the second query is refined based on the previous query 58.6% of the time. Huang and Efthimiadis [6] listed 13 reformulation patterns in traditional text search. Rieh and Xie [14] categorized reformulation patterns into several facets and ranked the patterns by their frequency. The most commonly used reformulation strategies were found to be: adding, deleting, re-ordering, and substituting words. All these

operations could be easily performed by partially modifying the previous query with a keyboard.

1.2 Query reformulation in current voice search system

Studies on user behavior during voice search have been performed and published. Begany, Sa, and Yuan [1] and Yuan, Belkin, and Sa [16] compared the user search behavior and their perception of spoken search system vs. keyboard search system. Crestani and Du [3] compared the queries issued by typing and speaking on a virtual voice system. However in these studies, the users either could not reformulate a query or had to enter a complete query.

The voice search systems by the major search engines do not support query reformulation by partial modification, either. Jiang, Jeng, and He [8] focused on the reformulation caused by the system recognition errors when using Google voice search. Almost half of all the voice queries in the study were transcribed incorrectly by the system. To fix the recognition error in the previous query, instead of modifying the current query, the users would have to issue a second query, which might fail to fix the previous error and might also introduce new recognition errors. In their works, major categories of errors and the way the users tried to fix the errors were identified. Substitution, re-ordering, addition, removal, stressing, slowing down, spelling, and using different pronunciations were reported to be the strategies employed by the users. However, the errors may still exist after using the strategies.

1.3 Current error correction methods used in voice system

System errors are found not only in voice search systems, but also in various speech recognition applications. Error correction has been pointed out as one of the key components of successful voice application interface [10]. One popular way in error correction is multimodal input interface, where the users can switch the input method from speaking to other types freely [5]. According to Shokouhi [15], in all the mobile query reformulation samples, 13.3% was voice query followed by voice query while 2.9% was voice query followed by text query. However, based on an early study of Halverson et al. [4], the users will not switch input method until they achieve certain spiral depth, which refers to "the number of times a subject continues to re-dictate the same word, despite incorrect recognition" [13]. It can be deduced that when the users finally switch to typing from speaking, they simply give up voice input. It is also possible that the users perform voice search when it is not convenient to type. In this case, multimodal will not be a proper solution.

There exist some commercial software which helps with error correction in voice input by providing a set of commands and an interface [12]. However, the commands are used for fixation, not the overall reformulation which includs adding and deleting words.

Also the voice commands are sometimes taken as part of the speech input [4].

As stated above, be it to refine the search or to fix the system errors, it is important that the voice search systems are able to better facilitate the users in query reformulation. Instead of issuing a complete new query which may cause cascading errors or switching input method which is mainly due to desperation, I aim to find out voice commands which can support various partial query modifications and are natural to the users.

2. RESEARCH QUESTION

I want to find out the user perception about the current voice search systems, e.g. under what circumstances they would use voice search, on what topics they usually search, what are the limits of the current voice search system, etc. As a result, the first research question (RQ) is:

1. *How do users perceive current voice search systems?*

It is hypothesized that the recognition error and the reformulation method are two of the limitations of the voice search system. To better support query reformulation, I plan to develop a set of commands natural to the users because one rule in designing is to "accept human behavior the way it is, not the way we would wish it to be" [17]. My second RQ is:

2. *What are better ways of enabling users to conduct partial query modification in voice search?*

After developing the commands, I would like to confirm whether or not they can improve the user experience in using voice search so the third RQ is:

3. *How will our proposed partial query modification technique improve user experience during voice search?*

3. METHODOLOGY

To answer the three research questions, I'm proposing a 4-phase research project. Each of the four phases will be explained in detail below.

3.1 Phase I: Survey

The purpose of the survey is to answer the first research question. The survey contains several parts. Firstly the demographic information is collected. Then the users' search experience and their usage of electronic devices are asked. The major part of the survey is about the usage of voice system and voice search system. Questions cover the general usage of voice search, how the users perform voice search, and their perspective about voice search. The survey can be viewed from the following address: http://goo.gl/forms/6ZVR78wp8a

3.2 Phase II: Experiment I

The second RQ will be investigated by using an experiment, aiming at finding out the natural ways of query reformulation in voice search. Graduate students will be recruited from the university. The participants will perform 4 pre-defined tasks. The task topics will be decided based on the survey results.

3.2.1 Experimental design

At the beginning of the experiment, demographic information will be obtained from the participants. Then they will perform 4 search tasks, each of which will require more than 1 query. Google voice search will be used to enter a complete query. Then, a Wizard of Oz method will be employed to perform the partial query modification. The participants will be instructed to communicate

with the system in the way they like to change the queries. The only limitation will be that they cannot switch to typing. The google voice search interface can obtain real world voice system errors. The Wizard of Oz can reduce the cognitive load caused by the cascading errors. After the 4 tasks, there will be an interview asking the participants about their perceptions about the experiment.

Morae 3.3 (http://www.techsmith.com/morae.html) will be used to capture desktop activity and audio record all the conversation. A touch screen will be used to display the search results. The touch screen and the software are available in our human computer interaction lab directed by Dr. Yuan.

3.3 Phase III: Command Development

Content analysis will be performed on the Morae data of phase II. Though each participant "talks" with the system in his/her own way, it is hypothesized that certain patterns can be obtained. A set of voice commands will be developed based on the content analysis results. The commands should cover all kinds of query reformulations mentioned before.

3.4 Phase IV: Experiment II

A within-subject experiment will be performed to measure the usability of the voice commands developed in Phase III. During the experiment, graduate students recruited from our university will perform voice search over the tasks used in phase II on each of the two systems (a baseline system and an experimental system).

3.4.1 Experimental design

The participants will firstly fill in a questionnaire about their demographic information. Then they will perform 2 search tasks on each system. After each search task, a post-task questionnaire will ask the users about their degree of satisfaction with the search. Finally a post-experiment interview will collect the user's opinion about the two systems.

Figure 1. The initial query

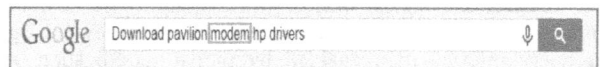

Figure 2. The second query after query reformulation

Google voice search will be used in both the experimental and the baseline system. In the baseline system, no modification will be made and each time the user has to speak the complete query. In the experimental system the user can perform partial query reformulation by using the commands developed in phase III. Figure 1 and figure 2 show an example of query reformulation. The initial query is displayed in figure 1. In the reformulated query in figure 2, "modem" is inserted to the initial query. In baseline system, the user will have to speak the complete string of "download pavilion modem hp dirvers" while in the experimental system, the user can insert the word "modem" by using voice command. In both systems, the users are encouraged to search with voice but they can switch to typing when they want to.

I aim at comparing the usability of the two systems. The user's perception, such as the degree of satisfaction about the search, which system they like better, which system is easier to use, and so on, will be collected from the post-task questionnaire and the content analysis of the post-experiment interview. The user's search behavior in the two systems will also be compared based on the variables such as the number of queries issued, the length of the query, the time used to enter the query, the time to complete the task, whether the users switch to tying or not, etc.

It is hypothesized that the user's search experience will be improved in the experimental system with the new modification feature than in the baseline system and the user's search behavior in the experimental system will be different from that of the baseline system.

4. PROGRESS MADE SO FAR

I'm currently collecting the survey data in phase I. The target number of complete results received is 150.

5. FUTURE PLAN

I plan to finish the survey data collection by end of October 2015. It will take about one month to analyze the survey results. By end of January 2016, the design of phase I experiment should be completed and the IRB approval should be obtained. The following month will be used to run pilot studies. The phase II experiment will be complete by the middle of April 2016. Phase III will be performed in May 2016. Phase IV experiment will be finished by August 2016. Then all the results will be analyzed and published.

6. REFERENCES

[1] Begany, G. M., Sa, N., and Yuan, X. 2015. Factors Affecting User Perception of a Spoken Language vs. Textual Search Interface: A Content Analysis. *Interacting with Computers, iwv029.*

[2] Burke M., Amento B., and Isenhour P. 2006. Error correction of voicemail transcripts in scanmail. In *Proceedings of the SIGCHI Conference on Human Factors in Computing Systems* (CHI '06). 339-348. DOI= http://doi.acm.org/10.1145/1124772.1124823

[3] Crestani, F., and Du, H. 2006. Written Versus Spoken Queries: A Qualitative and Quantitative Comparative Analysis. *J. Am. Soc. Inf. Sci. Technol., 57*(7), 881–890.

[4] Halverson C., Horn D., Karat C., and Karat J. 1999. The beauty of errors: patterns of error correction in desktop speech systems. *In Proceeding of the INTERACT 99.* 133-140

[5] Hoste, L., Dumas, B., and Signer, B. 2012. Speeg: a multimodal speech-and gesture-based text input solution. *In Proceedings of the InternationalWorking Conference on Advanced Visual Interfaces.* 156–163.

[6] Huang, J. and Efthimiadis, E. N. 2009. Analyzing and Evaluating Query Reformulation Strategies in Web Search Logs. In *Proceedings of the 18th ACM Conference on Information and Knowledge Management.* 77–86. New York, NY, USA: ACM.

[7] Huggins-Daines, D. and Rudnicky, A. 2008. Interactive asr error correction for touchscreen devices. *In Proceedings of the 46th Annual Meeting of the Association for Computational Linguistics on Human Language Technologies: Demo Session.* 17–19.

[8] Jeng, W., Jiang, J., and He, D. 2013. Users' perceived difficulties and corresponding reformulation strategies in voice search. *HCIR 2013.*

[9] Jiang, J., Jeng, W., and He, D. 2013. How Do Users Respond to Voice Input Errors?: Lexical and Phonetic Query Reformulation in Voice Search. In *Proceedings of the 36th International ACM SIGIR Conference on Research and Development in Information Retrieval* 143–152. New York, NY, USA: ACM.

[10] Kamm, C. 1995. User interfaces for voice applications. *Proc.National Academy of Sciences, 92*(22), 10031-10037.

[11] Kamvar, M., & Baluja, S. 2007. Deciphering Trends in Mobile Search. *Computer* 40, 8 (August 2007), 58-62. DOI= http://dx.doi.org/10.1109/MC.2007.270

[12] Nuance. Dragon naturally speaking. http://www.nuance.com/dragon/index.htm

[13] Oviatt, S. and van Gent, R. 1996. Error resolution during multimodal human-computer interaction. In *Proceedings of the Fourth International Conference on Spoken Language Processing*, University of Delaware and AI Dupont Institute, New York, 204-207

[14] Rieh, S. Y., and Xie, H. (Iris). 2006. Analysis of multiple query reformulations on the web: The interactive information retrieval context. *Information Processing & Management, 42*(3), 751–768.

[15] Shokouhi, M., Jones, R., Ozertem, U., Raghunathan, K., and Diaz, F. 2014. Mobile query reformulations. *In Proceedings of the 37th international ACM SIGIR conference on Research & development in information retrieval (SIGIR '14).* ACM, New York, NY, USA, 1011-1014. DOI= http://doi.acm.org/10.1145/2600428.2609497

[16] Yuan, X., Belkin, N., and Sa, N. 2013. Speak to Me: A wizard of Oz study on a language spoken interface. *HCIR 2013.*

[17] Norman, D. A. 2013. The Design of Everyday Things. New York, NY, USA: Basic Books, Inc

Information Retrieval Behaviors among EBM Practitioners when performing Evidence Based Medicine

Vinesha Selvarajah (1st Year PhD)
Supervised by: Anushia Inthiran, Nathorn Chaiyakunapruk, Lai Nai Ming
School of Information Technology, Monash University Malaysia,
Bandar Sunway, 47500 Subang Jaya, Selangor, Malaysia
vinesha.selvarajah@monash.edu

ABSTRACT

This paper reveals the preliminary analysis of how EBM practitioners retrieve EBM related information during their clinical rounds at a public teaching hospital in Malaysia. We focused on studying EBM practitioners' searching behaviors during EBM process. However, in this paper we only present analysis for query issuing pattern and result viewing behavior of the retrieval process. We collected our preliminary data using Morae's Key-Logging software that captures participants' information searching behavior. We recorded 30 preliminary search sessions via convenience sampling and analyzed our data using descriptive statistics. Our findings indicate that 90% of the search sessions successfully returned results that the participants searched for. Among the queries issued, 24.47% were ineffective queries. Result viewing behaviors revealed 56 online sources were clicked where 33.33% belonged to PubMed, Medscape and UpToDate. Our result shows higher average query length and the number of medical terms used in queries compared to previous studies. We also found that result viewing behavior using multiple tabs confuses the participants and are more likely to cause overlooking of online resources on some of the opened tabs. The outcome of our study leads to better initiatives on query issuing and result viewing strategies for EBM related searches to improve the EBM process among practitioners.

CCS Concepts

• Information systems→Information Retrieval

Keywords

Interactive Information Retrieval, Evidence Based Medicine, Practitioners, Search Behaviors, NICU, Malaysia

1. INTRODUCTION

Evidence-Based Medicine (EBM) is the practice of integrating medical evidences and clinical experiences in making medical decisions [9]. Several studies have revealed that a decade long of EBM related research and training in the medical field

CHIIR '16, March 13-17, 2016, Carrboro, NC, USA
ACM 978-1-4503-3751-9/16/03
DOI: http://dx.doi.org/10.1145/2854946.2854949

encouraged the practice of EBM among clinicians, physicians, nurses, medical students and all health officers within hospital settings [5; 6; 8]. These medical professionals integrate EBM into their clinical practice to solve problems faced during consultation especially when choosing best diagnostic and therapeutic procedures for patients. It is important to practice proper information retrieval skills when searching for information online so that the most relevant information is retrieved. Retrieving wrong or irrelevant information leads to making wrong medical decisions thus putting patients at risk.

Before the existence of Internet, sources of EBM evidences were limited to books, printed journals, and research papers. Ever since the Internet, medical professionals turned to online search engines such as Google.com and other medical domains such as UpToDate and Medscape when searching for health-related information [4]. The increasing dependency on digital devices such as computers, mobile phones and tablets further encouraged medical professionals to search for information online. Searching for information requires skills and experiences that are different from the traditional searching methods. Barriers faced when searching for EBM related information are lack of skills and knowledge to practice EBM, insufficient training, difficulty in searching and accessing resources, un-suitable appraisal techniques, and time constraints [14]. In developing countries, the difference in quality of study and trials among the EBM resources becomes a major challenge when choosing appropriate evidence for medical decision making locally since most evidences are derived from developed countries. Due to high quality threshold standards set for publication, many lower quality studies in developing countries are excluded [2]. Other issues includes limited access to literature database, lack of time to attend workshops, insufficient IT facility, poor internet resources, and the shortage of role models practicing [3]. Despite the all the self-perceived issues reported from past researches using self-administered questionnaires, the actual searching behavior of EBM practitioners when searching for online EBM related information have not been conducted in a developing country.

Therefore in this paper, we attempt to answer the following research questions: (i) what are the query issuing pattern and result viewing behavior of EBM practitioners when performing EBM? (ii) What are the sources used to perform EBM related search and why were they used? We conducted an exploratory study to analyze the searching behaviors of EBM practitioners when retrieving EBM related information. We collected 30 preliminary search sessions to observe what the preliminary results are showing us. The actual experiment is ongoing and will continue until theoretical saturation is achieved. This remainder of this paper is divided into 3 sections. We present our adopted methodology in Section 2, followed by our findings in Section 3 and the discussion of findings in Section 4. We then present our remaining work in Section 5, conclude our paper with our preliminary contributions and future works in Section 6.

2. METHODOLOGY

We conducted an exploratory study based on convenience sampling at the Neonatal Intensive Care Unit (NICU) of a public teaching hospital in Malaysia. We adopted user based study to study the searching behavior of EBM practitioners, Interactive Information Retrieval (IIR) [7] approach was applied. We used Morae Key-Logging software version 3.3.3 to record the search sessions. The software was installed on a HP Pavilion dm4 (model: ProBook 440 G1) laptop that is available at the NICU ward. The laptop runs on a 64-bit Window 7 Professional operating system, with a 2.40GHz Intel(R) Core™ i3-4000M processer, and Random Access Memory (RAM) of 4.00 Gigabyte (GB). The laptop is connected to the internet via the local network provider. We included semi structured interview to be collected before and after the search recordings. Data is collected when an EBM practitioner at the NICU ward finds the need to look for EBM related information online. The practitioner's consent to participate in this study is first obtained. The practitioners were then interviewed (pre-search interview) before searching for information to elicit information regarding purpose and factors contributing to search. The practitioners then proceed on searching for their information online via the laptop pre-installed with the recording software. Each search session is recorded from the beginning of search and stops when there is no more search activity for a particular search session, or when the practitioner decides to end the search. After the each session, the practitioners are interviewed again (post-search interview) to collect information on user experiences, feedback, and how the retrieved information is used in their medical decision making. The success of each search session was measured by the practitioners' self-perception. Search sessions are claimed to be successful when practitioners are able to find the answers they were looking for. Note taking and memos are recorded by the researcher to record any additional information to aid the analysis of the recordings later. The recordings are then analyzed using Morae Manager.

3. FINDINGS

We used descriptive statistical analysis to study the minimum value (Min), mean, median, standard deviation (SD), and the maximum value (Max) of our preliminary data. Overall, 27 out of the 30 search sessions were successful searches. We provide the result of the query issuing behavior from the searching process in Table 1. Majority of the search sessions have an average of 2 to 3 queries issued before achieving desired result. With the majority of successful search sessions, our analysis revealed that 24.47% out of total number of queries issued returned zero results. These queries are categorized as ineffective queries. We also found that there were 120 terms used in the issued queries and 75% of terms used were medical terms. At least 2 medical terms are found in an issued query. Table 2 shows the result viewing behavior from the search process. Our analysis revealed 56 different online sources accessed and viewed with an average viewing of 2 different sources per search session. The highest number of viewed sources equally belonged to PubMed (11.11%), UpToDate (11.11%) and Medscape (11.11%). Apart from the main sources, there were 11 out of 30 search referred sub links within a source to search for

information where 1 out of the 11 search session failed to produce desired outcomes. An exceptional search session reported to not have clicked any source or any links. As such, the data cannot be generalized. That particular session however had issued 1 query with a query length of 6 terms and found the answer on the search result page itself. The result viewing behavior also revealed that 50% of the search sessions recorded had opened more than one search tab to improve the result viewing process. However 13.33% of the search sessions that opened multiple tabs reported at least one of the tabs were opened without being viewed throughout the searching process.

4. DISCUSSION

The average number of query issued per search session showed similar pattern to previous researches indicating around 2.34 queries were issued per search session [12; 13]. However the average query length does not support previous study where in our case higher average query length was issued in the search sessions [13]. Query length differs with the purpose of search carried out. More sophisticated search may result in higher query length compared to simpler search. Similarly, the number of ineffective queries issued in our study is high. The recurrent of ineffective query in a search session lengthens the duration of the searches and affects the practitioners' time management. Search sessions during clinical round should be kept short as it conflicts with practitioners' patient consultation time.

Our findings indicate that a higher number of medical terms were used in the queries. This finding is supported by [13], a higher number of medical terms used in a query increase the probability of searching for desired information. However, our findings differed with [11] due to the differences in the search domains used. Our findings showed dissimilarities in average query length, issuance of ineffective queries and the number of medical terms used. There is a need to develop new query formulation strategy to increase the average query length, reduce the number of ineffective queries and increase the number of medical terms used in the queries.

Table 1. Query issuing behavior per search

Query Issuing Behaviors	Min	Mean	Median	SD	Max
Number of Queries	1	3.17	2.00	2.937	14
Ineffective Queries	0	0.93	0.00	1.437	5
Average Query Length	1	4.01	4.00	1.587	8
Number of Medical Terms	0	3.00	2.00	3.877	17

Table 2. Results viewing behavior per search

Result Viewing Behaviors	Min	Mean	Median	SD	Max
Number of sources viewed	0	3.00	2.00	2.449	11
Number of results clicked	0	3.50	2.00	3.256	14
Number of sub links clicked	0	1.27	0.00	2.778	13
Number of tabs opened	0	2.67	1.50	2.857	15

We found that the most visited sources are PubMed, UpToDate and Medscape. Previous researches indicates with UptoDate being the top referred source followed by PubMed [10]. However, our findings are supported by a recent research stating that when searching for medical information, the highest referral sources were UpToDate followed by Medscape and PubMed [1]. Apart from that, our study also revealed the drawbacks of having multiple tab opened when viewing results. Having multiple tabs opened confuses the user thus causing one or more tabs opened without viewing. Proper result viewing strategy should be established to educate practitioners on how to manage their results viewing behavior so that they are able to cover all important results in a shorter time. This would prevent the overlooking of retrieved results and important information.

5. REMAINING WORK

The project is further divided into several data collection methods including interview of the EBM practitioners (Pre-Post Search Interviews). The analysis of the interviews is still ongoing and we intend to use different methods of analysis on our data. Additionally, we intend include Focus Group Discussion (FGD) to our study to trigger discussion among EBM practitioners' on the barriers and challenges faced during the retrieval process.

6. CONCLUSIONS AND FUTURE WORK

This exploratory study analyses the query issuing and result viewing behaviors of EBM practitioner when performing EBM related search. We revealed issues related to ineffective queries and the ineffective usage of tab when viewing results. The outcome of our study provides design initiatives to query issuing and result viewing strategy to improve the retrieval process. The data from this study is only at its preliminary stage and analyzed only using descriptive statistical analysis. Future work in this study requires the completion of the remaining work described earlier and further analysis of the data using both qualitative and quantitative analysis method. A conceptual design framework to assist EBM practitioners in their EBM searching strategy will be implemented.

7. ACKNOWLEDGMENTS

The research study is funded by the Ministry of Education under the Fundamental Research Grant Scheme (FRGS) - FRGS/2/2013/ICT02/MUSM/03/1.

8. REFERENCES

[1] Boruff, J.T. and Storie, D., 2014. Mobile devices in medicine: a survey of how medical students, residents, and faculty use smartphones and other mobile devices to find information. *Journal of the Medical Library Association : JMLA 102*, 1 (02//received08//accepted), 22-30. DOI= http://dx.doi.org/10.3163/15365050.102.1.006.

[2] Chinnock, P., Siegfried, N., and Clarke, M., 2005. Is Evidence-Based Medicine Relevant to the Developing World? *PLoS Med 2*, 5, e107. DOI= http://dx.doi.org/10.1371/journal.pmed.0020107.

[3] Dans, A.L. and Dans, L.F., 2000. The need and means for evidence-based medicine in developing countries. *Evidence Based Medicine 5*, 4 (July 1, 2000), 100-101. DOI= http://dx.doi.org/10.1136/ebm.5.4.100.

[4] De Leo, G., Lerouge, C., Ceriani, C., and Niederman, F., 2006. Websites Most Frequently Used by Physician for Gathering Medical Information. *AMIA Annual Symposium Proceedings 2006*, 902-902.

[5] Dorsh, J.L., Aiyer, M.K., and Meyer, L.E., 2004. Impact of an evidence-based medicine curriculum on medical students' attitudes and skills. *Journal of the Medical Library Association 92*, 4 (10//received04//accepted), 397-406.

[6] Hersh, W R. and Hickam, D.H., 1998. How well do physicians use electronic information retrieval systems?: A framework for investigation and systematic review. *JAMA 280*, 15, 1347-1352. DOI= http://dx.doi.org/10.1001/jama.280.15.1347.

[7] Kelly, D. and Sugimoto, C.R., 2013. A systematic review of interactive information retrieval evaluation studies, 1967–2006. *Journal of the American Society for Information Science and Technology 64*, 4, 745-770. DOI= http://dx.doi.org/10.1002/asi.22799.

[8] Majid, S., Foo, S., Luyt, B., Zhang, X., Theng, Y.-L., Chang, Y.-K., and Mokhtar, I.A., 2011. Adopting evidence-based practice in clinical decision making: nurses' perceptions, knowledge, and barriers. *Journal of the Medical Library Association : JMLA 99*, 3 (11//received02//accepted), 229-236. DOI= http://dx.doi.org/10.3163/1536-5050.99.3.010.

[9] Sackett, D.L., 1997. Evidence-based medicine. *Seminars in Perinatology 21*, 1 (2//), 3-5. DOI= http://dx.doi.org/10.1016/S0146-0005(97)80013-4.

[10] Sayyah Ensan, L., Faghankhani, M., Javanbakht, A., Ahmadi, S.-F., and Baradaran, H.R., 2011. To compare PubMed Clinical Queries and UpToDate in teaching information mastery to clinical residents: a crossover randomized controlled trial. *PLoS one 6*, 8 (2011), e23487. DOI= http://dx.doi.org/10.1371/journal.pone.0023487.

[11] Yang, L., Mei, Q., Zheng, K., and Hanauer, D.A., 2011. Query Log Analysis of an Electronic Health Record Search Engine. *AMIA Annual Symposium Proceedings 2011*(10/22), 915-924.

[12] Zhang, J., Wolfram, D., Wang, P., Hong, Y., and Gillis, R., 2008. Visualization of health-subject analysis based on query term co-occurrences. *Journal of the American Society for Information Science and Technology 59*, 12, 1933-1947. DOI= http://dx.doi.org/10.1002/asi.20911.

[13] Zhang, Y., Wang, P., Heaton, A., and Winkler, H., 2012. Health information searching behavior in MedlinePlus and the impact of tasks. In *Proceedings of the Proceedings of the 2nd ACM SIGHIT International Health Informatics Symposium* (Miami, Florida, USA2012), ACM, 2110434, 641-650. DOI= http://dx.doi.org/10.1145/2110363.2110434.

[14] Zwolsman, S., Te Pas, E., Hooft, L., Waard, M.W.-D., and Van Dijk, N., 2012. Barriers to GPs' use of evidence-based medicine: a systematic review. *The British Journal of General Practice 62*, 600 (06/2509/06/received10/10/revised12/09/accepted), 511-e521.DOI= http://dx.doi.org/10.3399/bjgp12X652382

Spoken Conversational Search: Speech-only Interactive Information Retrieval

Johanne R. Trippas
1st year PhD student
School of Computer Science and Information Technology
RMIT University, Melbourne
Johanne.trippas@rmit.edu.au
Supervisors: L. Cavedon, M. Sanderson, D. Spina

ABSTRACT

This research investigates a new interface paradigm for interactive information retrieval (IIR) which forces us to shift away from the classic "ten blue links" search engine results page. Instead we investigate how to present search results through a conversation over a speech-only communication channel where no screen is available. Accessing information via speech is becoming increasingly pervasive and is already important for people with a visual impairment. However, presenting search results over a speech-only communication channel is challenging due to cognitive limitations and the transient nature of audio. Studies have indicated that the implementation of speech recognizers and screen readers must be carefully designed and cannot simply be added to an existing system. Therefore the aim of this research is to develop a new interaction framework for effective and efficient IIR over a speech-only channel: a *Spoken Conversational Search System* (SCSS) which provides a conversational approach to defining user information needs, presenting results and enabling search reformulations. In order to contribute to a more efficient and effective search experience when using a SCSS, we intend for a tighter integration between document search and conversational processes.

Keywords

Spoken Retrieval; Search Result Summarization; Conversational Search; Voice Search; Interactive Information Retrieval

1. MOTIVATION

Speech-based applications are becoming more prominent and are increasingly accepted among the wider population. Google documented in 2010 that 25% of queries on Android devices were submitted by voice[1]. Even though much research has been conducted into supporting search by voice input, only a few studies have focused on the presentation of information where no display is used [17]. Speech output is easily understood for factoid-style

---

[1] https://www.youtube.com/watch?v=DtMfdNeGXgM

CHIIR'16, March 13–17, 2016, Chapel Hill, North Carolina, USA.
© 2016 Copyright held by the owner/author(s).
ACM ISBN 978-1-4503-3751-9/16/03.
DOI: http://dx.doi.org/10.1145/2854946.2854952

queries (e.g, "Who is the president of the United States?") by systems such as Siri, Google Now or Cortana. However, when users seek answers to non-factoid style queries, the system falls back on displaying a result list on screen such as in a multimodal system [18]. Nevertheless, there are many different scenarios where a speech-only user interface is preferred, such as when operating machinery [6, 7]; when no screen or keyboard is available [24]; when users are on the move [16, 21]; or when using wearable devices [5].

More importantly, some user groups such as visually impaired users [17], people with dyslexia, or people with limited literacy skills are disadvantaged in accessing information on screen. Visually impaired users have been using screen reader software for many years, however this software is still often difficult and frustrating to use because the content is mainly expressed visually and is only accessible via a mouse.

Listening to search results over audio is very taxing for users since audio is a temporal medium and does not leave any traces to which to user can refer [14, 23]. Since speech is a linear medium, it is also challenging to present complex structures. Thus, it is difficult to convey large amounts of information via audio without overloading the user's short-term memory [14, 18, 21]. It has also been shown that word frequency and speech rate have an effect on short-term serial recall [11]. In particular, we seek a better understanding of how to present search results over audio while not overwhelming the users with information [21], nor leaving users uncertain as to whether what they have covered the information space [22]. However, we believe that conveying information through an interactive channel will alleviate some complexities which are associated with speech and will allow users to find information in an efficient and effective manner.

The proposed research will advance the knowledge base by:

- Developing new interaction models for IIR over a voice-only communication channel.

- Determining new methods for providing summary-based result-presentation for unstructured documents.

- Providing an understanding of which strategies and techniques for SCSS are best for users.

Thus, the proposed research will transform search over a voice-only communication channel by using an inherently interactive and conversational search experience.

2. RESEARCH QUESTIONS

The overall aim of the proposed research is to investigate a new framework and interaction model for efficient and effective information retrieval over a speech-only communication channel: a *Spo-*

ken Conversational Search System (SCSS) which provides a conversational approach to determining user information needs, presenting results and enabling search reformulation.

Researchers have defined the information-seeking process in many different ways [15]. Nevertheless, there are several distinct stages to a SCSS which follow the information-seeking behaviours: establishing the intent of a user's initial query; allowing the user to conversationally interact with search results; and interpreting query reformulations [17].

The proposed research seeks to answer the following research questions:

- Are there any existing **interaction models** which fit the SCSS?

- What are effective techniques to **present query results** using audio so users can efficiently locate items, determine their relevance, provide feedback, and refine their query?

- What are effective techniques to **structure the conversation** interaction to minimize cognitive load in order to support the user in the information seeking processes with search engines?

- Are there **differences** between visually impaired and sighted users in the interaction with a SCSS?

3. RESEARCH METHODOLOGY AND PROPOSED EXPERIMENTS

This section presents a brief overview of the results of experiments to date. It also discusses the research methodology and experiments for the proposed research.

3.1 Results so Far

A short paper was published at SIGIR 2015 with preliminary results of a study which analyzed the result description (information abstract on a Search Engine Result Page) for query results over a speech-only communication channel [20].

The impact of the search result summary length in speech-based web search was investigated and these results were also compared to a text baseline. A crowdsourcing platform was used as a data collection tool. The χ^2 goodness-of-fit test [13] was used to assess whether changing the result summary had an effect on user preference. Table 1 shows that users preferred full text summaries rather than their truncated counterpart. For example, 57% of the users would recommend full text summaries to a friend.

The data showed that while users preferred longer and more informative summaries for text presentation, for single-faceted queries users preferred shortened summaries for audio. For multi-faceted summaries for audio, user preferences were not as clear, suggesting that more sophisticated techniques are required to handle these complex queries.

The above experiment allowed us to gather information about user preferences and query judgements. However, as mentioned in Section 1, audio output can be a very taxing medium for users, so we propose to extend this experiment to capture workload related factors. Capturing the workload would allow us to better understand and design the presentation of search summary results over audio. One of the tools we plan to use is the NASA TASK Load Index (NASA-TLX) [10].

A work in progress paper was accepted and presented at the First International Workshop on Novel Web Search Interfaces and Systems (NWSearch'15) co-located with CIKM 2015. The paper discusses the future directions regarding a novel spoken interface targeted at search result presentation, query intent detection, and interaction patterns for audio search [19].

Table 1: Exit questionnaire results for preferences in the search engine result summaries.

Exit Question	Text		Audio	
	Summary	Truncated	Summary	Truncated
Recommend to a friend	572▲ (57%)	434 (43%)	529 (51%)	512 (49%)
Easier to find relevant result	548▲ (54%)	458 (46%)	514 (49%)	527 (51%)
Gave better result	576▲ (57%)	430 (43%)	539 (52%)	502 (48%)
More efficient to use	529 (53%)	477 (47%)	499 (48%)	542 (52%)

▲ indicates statistical significance with $p < .01$.

3.2 Research Methodology and Experiments

This research project aims to develop new interaction models for IIR over a speech-only communication channel. It has been suggested that investigating usability is necessary for interactive speech development and that one should not translate interactive speech theories literally into practice [4]. For this reason, the development of interaction models during my PhD will be an iterative process using mixed-methods. We will use an observational experiment to form our hypothesis which will then be tested in a Wizard of Oz experiment as explained in Section 3.2.2. In parallel we will analyze interaction logs as explained in Section 3.2.1.

The methodologies and experiments described in this section will be carried out for both visually impaired and sighted users to understand if there are any interaction differences between these two user groups.

3.2.1 Interaction Log Analysis

Interaction logs do not record the user's intention and motivation. Nevertheless, the interaction logs have the advantage that they capture the "real search process" of the user [12].

We have access to interaction logs from a speech-only interaction system which is used by people with visual impairments. The interaction logs are provided by an industry partner[2] who developed a system in which users can search for audio books, podcasts, or news. All the interactions are performed solely over speech.

For the first iteration of the interaction model of a speech-only interaction system, we are analyzing the interaction history with a focus on the linguistic history which records the surface language such as speech acts [4]. Our aim is to decode the user and system utterances to better understand the interaction control of the system. This first iteration of the interaction model will be made for frequent users and non-frequent users. We are also analyzing the logs to investigate data such as query length, query terms, session times, speed of speech, query categories, query reformulation, and GPS coordinates.

It has been suggested that voice system usage behaviour differs in unfamiliar environments. For example, users might change their behaviour because of privacy concerns or social appropriateness [2]. Thus, the GPS coordinates in the interaction logs might provide insight into how people behave when they are not in their home environment.

3.2.2 Observational and Wizard of Oz Experiments

We address a broader and less restrained way of speech than spoken dialogue systems which allows more complex information to

[2] http://www.realthing.com.au

be conveyed. Therefore it is important to understand and predict the interactions between the user and the system [1]. It is suggested that Wizard of Oz (WOZ) methodologies are relevant for iterative development and evaluation of interactive interfaces [4]. However, WOZ methodologies can only be considered if certain pre-conditions are met [9]. One of these pre-conditions will be challenging for our experiment, namely that it must be possible to simulate the future system. Thus, for the first iteration of user studies we will use an observational methodology to discover what kind of language models users expect to use and to hear from a SCSS and how a search might be conducted in a fully audio setting instead of a WOZ experiment.

In the initial observational experiment, one participant will be the SCSS and the other will be the user. This observational setup will have resemblances to collaborative search. The data from the observational experiment allows us to develop a new iteration of the interaction model for spoken conversation search as explained in Section 3.2.1. Hence, the observational experiment will model user interaction to understand their linguistic behaviour [8] and dialogue patterns [4].

WOZ experiments will be conducted once we develop a better understanding of the users' search behaviour and language model and are able to simulate the SCSS. In a WOZ experiment, the human is simulating the system (the wizard). The wizard simulates the spoken interaction with the user who thinks they are interacting with a real system. The WOZ experiments allow us to conduct performance evaluations while the system is being simulated. These simulations may include different restrictions on whether a automatic speech recognizer is used or a text-to-speech module is used. The following parameters can be collected during a WOZ: average utterances used per turn; average number of turns per for wizard and participants together; and vocabulary to inform the next iteration of the interaction model for speech.

When participants are involved in a user study, they will first answer a pre-test questionnaire to obtain user profile information. Then the empirical user test will be conducted to gain knowledge of how participants would interact with the application and to discover problems. The user study will be recorded to allow for data to be analyzed after the test. Once the user study is finished, the participants will complete a post-test questionnaire and a Likert-scale questionnaire [21] and the tester will conduct a semi-structured interview. These measures will evaluate user satisfaction, usefulness of the system and naturalness of the system specifically for the presentation of query results and the structure of the conversation. The analyzed information of the user study will lead to another iteration of an improved interaction model for speech. This allows us to understand how to structure the conversation interaction and how the query results should be presented.

3.2.3 New Interaction Models for Speech

The findings presented in our earlier work emphasize the importance of developing techniques that can both predict when a query needs to be refined and provide suggestions for refinement to a conversational interface [20]. We will develop an interaction model which uncovers the linguistic structure such as speech acts, references and discourse segments [4]. Demands placed on a user could lead to reduced performance and could translate into a slower response and increased errors [3].

To our knowledge, no existing interaction models fit the SCSS and hence we started identifying interactions in an existing log (explained in Section 3.2.1) to either adapt existing models with these findings or develop a new model.

4. REFERENCES

[1] J. F. Allen, D. K. Byron, M. Dzikovska, G. Ferguson, L. Galescu, and A. Stent. Toward conversational human-computer interaction. *AI magazine*, 22(4):27, 2001.

[2] S. Azenkot and N. B. Lee. Exploring the use of speech input by blind people on mobile devices. In *Proc. SIGACCESS*, 2013.

[3] C. Baber, B. Mellor, R. Graham, J. M. Noyes, and C. Tunley. Workload and the use of automatic speech recognition: The effects of time and resource demands. *Speech Communication*, 20(1):37–53, 1996.

[4] N. O. Bernsen, H. Dybkjær, and L. Dybkjær. *Designing interactive speech systems: From first ideas to user testing*. Springer, 1998.

[5] E. Chang, F. Seide, H. M. Meng, C. Zhuoran, S. Yu, and L. Yuk-Chi. A system for spoken query information retrieval on mobile devices. *Speech and Audio Processing, IEEE Transactions on*, 10(8):531–541, 2002.

[6] V. Demberg and A. Sayeed. Linguistic cognitive load: implications for automotive uis. In *Proc. of AutomotiveUI 2011*, 2011.

[7] V. Demberg, A. Winterboer, and J. D. Moore. A strategy for information presentation in spoken dialog systems. *Computational Linguistics*, 37(3):489–539, 2011.

[8] L. Dybkjær, N. O. Bernsen, and W. Minker. Evaluation and usability of multimodal spoken language dialogue systems. *Speech Communication*, 43(1):33–54, 2004.

[9] N. M. Fraser and G. Gilbert. Simulating speech systems. *Computer Speech Language*, 5(1):81 – 99, 1991.

[10] S. G. Hart and L. E. Staveland. Development of nasa-tlx (task load index): Results of empirical and theoretical research. *Advances in psychology*, 52:139–183, 1988.

[11] C. Hulme, S. Roodenrys, R. Schweickert, G. D. Brown, S. Martin, and G. Stuart. Word-frequency effects on short-term memory tasks: Evidence for a redintegration process in immediate serial recall. *Journal of Experimental Psychology: Learning, Memory, and Cognition*, 23(5):1217–1232, 1997.

[12] B. J. Jansen and A. Spink. How are we searching the World Wide Web? A comparison of nine search engine transaction logs. *Inf. Process. Manag.*, 42(1):248–263, 2006.

[13] D. Kelly. Methods for evaluating interactive information retrieval systems with users. *Foundations and Trends in Information Retrieval*, 3(1–2):1–224, 2009.

[14] J. Lai and N. Yankelovich. Speech interface design. In *Encyclopedia of Language & Linguistics (Second Edition)*, pages 764–770. Elsevier, 2006.

[15] G. Marchionini and R. White. Find what you need, understand what you find. *International Journal of Human-Computer Interaction*, 23 (3):205–237, 2007.

[16] L. J. Najjar, J. J. Ockerman, and J. C. Thompson. User interface design guidelines for speech recognition applications. In *Proc. of IEEE VRAIS '98*, 1998.

[17] N. G. Sahib, D. Al Thani, A. Tombros, and T. Stockman. Accessible information seeking. *Proc. of Digital Futures*, 12, 2012.

[18] J. Schalkwyk, D. Beeferman, F. Beaufays, B. Byrne, C. Chelba, M. Cohen, M. Kamvar, and B. Strope. "your word is my command": Google search by voice: A case study. In *Advances in Speech Recognition*, pages 61–90. Springer US, 2010.

[19] J. R. Trippas, D. Spina, M. Sanderson, and L. Cavedon. Results presentation methods for a spoken conversational search system. In *First International Workshop on Novel Web Search Interfaces and Systems (NWSearch'15)*, 2015.

[20] J. R. Trippas, D. Spina, M. Sanderson, and L. Cavedon. Towards Understanding the Impact of Length in Web Search Result Summaries over a Speech-only Communication Channel. In *Proc. of SIGIR'15*, pages 991–994, 2015.

[21] M. Turunen, J. Hakulinen, N. Rajput, and A. A. Nanavati. *Evaluation of Mobile and Pervasive Speech Applications*, pages 219–262. 2012.

[22] S. Varges, F. Weng, and H. Pon-Barry. Interactive question answering and constraint relaxation in spoken dialogue systems, 2006.

[23] N. Yankelovich and J. Lai. *Designing speech user interfaces*. 1998.

[24] N. Yankelovich, G.-A. Levow, and M. Marx. Designing speechacts: Issues in speech user interfaces. In *Proc. of the SIGCHI'95*, pages 369–376. 1995.

Understanding Users' Language Selection: Code-switching in Online Searches

Jieyu Wang
University of Maryland, Baltimore County
1000 Hilltop Circe
Baltimore, MD 21250
(+1)443-251-9098
wajieyu1@umbc.edu

Anita Komlodi
University of Maryland, Baltimore County
1000 Hilltop Circle
Baltimore, MD 21250
(+1)410-455-3212
komlodi@umbc.edu

ABSTRACT

Non-native English users search for information on websites that mostly present content in English. There has been increasing concern as to whether web users who speak non-native English languages can access information as effectively as native English users. Few studies have been done on how multi-lingual users search for information in two or more languages online, specifically how they switch languages in order to get satisfying search results. This research investigates the factors that impact native Chinese users' code-switching (Chinese-English) search behaviors when they seek information online and the challenges that users encounter. The methods of this research consist of two phases. In-context interviews will allow us to explore natural behaviors in the users' context in the first phase. Fifteen native Chinese participants will be recruited. A controlled eye-tracking study is planned for the second phase in order to examine different reading patterns of these bilingual web users and what web elements they focus on. Thirty native Chinese will be recruited in this phase. The research aims to explore when, how, and why users switch languages, and examine the role of languages that users select in online searches.

Keywords

Eye-tracking; code-switching; multi-lingual search

1. MOTIVATION

Since the Internet was introduced, the number of web users who search information on it have increased to 2.8 billion [8]. Among these Internet users 26.8% of them are native English users and 56.6% of the information on the web is in English [8]. However, as the Internet has been developing and web users who are speakers of other languages are increasing, the role of languages on the web is becoming important.

CHIIR'16, March 13–17, 2016, Carrboro, North Carolina, USA
ACM ISBN: 978-1-4503-3751-9/16/03.
DOI: http://dx.doi.org/10.1145/2854946.2854955

Recent studies have focused on different factors that influence non-native English users' web surfing, for example, language proficiency and culture, domain knowledge, other languages' web accessibility, language translation, and mixed-script information retrieval [4] [7] [9] [10] [12]. However, few researchers have studied how users with multi-lingual backgrounds search for information by switching their native languages and second languages in order to get more satisfying search results. Code-switching phenomena have been studied outside the online environment by social scientists for decades. A group of researchers have defined and analyzed code-switching in different social contexts [3] [6] [11] [16]. Only a few researchers have studied web users' code-switching behaviors in an online environment. For example, Wang and Joardan examined Facebook users' language selection behaviors [14]. They found that Facebook users switched languages due to the factors such as context, language proficiency, locality, and their audience. This paper investigates web users' code-switching behaviors when they seek information on the web.

This study focuses on users' code-switching between their native languages and their second language or foreign languages when they search for information online. The difference between a second language and a foreign language is that the second language is spoken in the immediate environment of the speaker while the foreign language is not spoken in that environment [13]. This study will recruit 30 participants whose native language is Chinese and second/foreign language is English to search information online by switching languages. The study aims to explore different factors that impact multi-lingual users' code-switching in online searches and the roles of the languages. The research will contribute to cross-cultural website design and applications which benefit the large number of non-native English web users.

2. RESEARCH QUESTIONS

Research questions for Phase 1:

1. When and why do users search for information using two or more   languages for the same search task?

2. How do users switch languages when they interact with information? What are users' code-switching patterns in online searches?

3. What language tools do they use?

4. What are the roles of the languages that users select when they search?

Research questions for Phase 2:

5. What are users' search tactics when selecting different languages?

5.1 How are eye-tracking patterns different in native and foreign language searches?

5.2 What are users' search patterns when they switch languages?

3. METHODOLOGY

3.1 Phase 1: Demographic Surveys and In-Context Interviews

The purpose of this Phase 1 study is to explore when, how, and why users switch different languages when they search online in order to satisfy their information needs. The environments that users search for information in and the tools that they use should be the same or similar to their daily settings. For example, college participants will be asked to search for information in libraries or labs in the way they usually do. Therefore, in this study fifteen participants will be recruited and first complete online demographic surveys on Survey Monkey. Then in-context interviews will be conducted. Data will first be collected by taking notes, pictures, and audio recordings and then later analyzed. Each participant will be paid $15.

3.1.0 Participants

This proposed study will recruit participants whose native language is Chinese and second/foreign language is English. Moreover, these participants should be chosen from a variety of disciplines.

The sample size of in-context interviews is expected to be around 15. However, when theoretical saturation is reached that any new information cannot be offered by participants, interviews should be stopped. Participants will be recruited by email or phone. Two pilot studies of the in-context interviews were' conducted in August, 2015.

3.1.1 Demographic Survey

Surveys are used to efficiently find out answers for specific questions from sample participants. The surveys in this study can offer the sample users' demographic and background information. Demographic surveys will be provided to the participants through Survey Monkey. Survey Monkey is an online survey website which offers free survey services to customers. In the surveys, participants will be required to report their language proficiency. Because multi-lingual users' domain knowledge and majors do affect their online information seeking behaviors [5] [9], participants' information about their majors and occupations which are closely related to their domain knowledge will be requested in the survey.

3.1.2 In-Context Interviews

In-context interviews will be conducted in this proposed work for the advantage of uncovering the natural process of users' information seeking, in which even users themselves are not aware of certain behaviors. Considering the fact that participants are likely to be university students, the interviews will be conducted in libraries or labs with participants on their own

computers so that participants could actually show to the interviewer how they seek information in their natural environment. Context related factors should be captured and analyzed when participants search for information. The interviews will last about two hours. Data will be collected by taking notes, pictures, and audio recordings of participants at work.

3.1.2 Data Analysis

The data from the surveys will first be collected online. When analyzing data, for the open-ended questions content analysis methods will be applied. For the multiple choices questions, especially questions related to gender, age, computer experiences, the data will be coded for descriptive statistics. Means and percentages in descriptive statistics will be applied to present the data.

The text content of interview transcripts will be analyzed following the Grounded Theory. In the open coding process new themes will be created. Then axial coding will organize these new themes and make connections among them. In order to refine the relationships of these themes, selective coding will be done. The connections of the themes will be refined in the selective coding process.

3.2 Phase 2: Lab-Controlled Eye-Tracking Study

The experiment will be conducted in a controlled lab environment. While this phase will not examine natural behavior, it will allow us to understand specific features of users' eye movements. These eye movement recordings would help us explore where on webpages searchers focus when searching in their native vs. a foreign language and how the reading patterns differ. Thirty participants whose native language is Chinese and second/foreign language is English are expected to be recruited by phone or email. The demographic survey design is the same as the survey study in the Phrase 1 experiments.

The participant will be asked to perform three information seeking tasks. Their interaction with information will be recorded in the eye-tracker. Factors such as their task performance time, errors, reading sequences, interested areas, and fixation lengths will be analyzed. In order to reduce bias the Latin-square rule will be applied.

The participants will be interviewed after their tasks. The study will conduct semi-structured interviews. A page of open-ended questions will be designed for the semi-structured interviews. The interviews will be about 40 minutes. The transcripts will be written after the interviews and stored. Each participant will be paid $15.

The data from the surveys and interviews will be analyzed in the same way as the previous study in Phase 1. The eye tracker data will be recorded in the Tobii computer. Read sequences, areas of interest, and fixation lengths will be analyzed in the Tobii computer.

4. PROGRESS

In the previous research I have studied participants' code-switching in a non-web environment (classroom), code-switching in an online environment (Facebook) [14], and the difficulties and challenges that non-native English web users encountered when they seek information online [15]. In our previous study we also explored the criteria that the participants applied to judge a website's credibility by analyzing the participants' questionnaires

[1] and the impact of user personality in websites credibility judgment [2]. These studies build a strong foundation for me to further study non-native English users' code-switching behaviors when they search online.

Currently the following chapters of the proposal have been written: introduction, literature review, research questions, previous data collection, and proposed method. The IRB application of this research was approved in August, 2015. Two pilot studies have been conducted in order to test the design of surveys and in-context interviews. The results showed that users whose native language is Chinese and second/foreign language is English do code-switching when they seek information online. They usually select different languages when they need translation, go online shopping, and seek medical information. The data collection in Phase 1 has been carrying out since September, 2015.

5. FUTURE PLAN
This proposal will be defended in spring 2016. The Phase 1 data collection will be likely completed in spring 2016. The Phase 2 data collection is expected to be completed in fall 2016. The dissertation is hopefully to be defended before May, 2017

REFERENCES
[1] Ahmad, R., Komlodi, A., Wang, J., and Hercegfi, K. 2010. The impact of user experience levels on web credibility judgments, In *Proceedings of the 73rd ASIS&T Annual Meeting on Navigating Streams in an Information Ecosystem* (Pittsburgh, Pennsylvania, October 22 – 27, 2010). American Society for Information Science, Silver Springs, MD, USA.

[2] Ahmad, R., Wang, J., Hercegfi, K., and Komlodi, A. 2011. Different people different styles: impact of personality in web sites credibility judgment. In *Human Interface and the Management of Information*, M. J. Smith & G. Salvendy ,Ed. Springer, New York, NY, 521-527.

[3] Auer, P. 1998. *Code-Switching in Conversation*. London: Routledge.

[4] Berendt, B. and Kralisch, A. 2009. A user-centric approach to identifying best deployment strategies for language tools: the impact of content and access language on Web user behavior and attitudes. *Inf. Retr.*, 12, 3, 380-399.

[5] Clough, P. and Eleta, I. 2010. Investigating language skills and field of knowledge on multilingual information access in digital libraries. *International Journal of Digital Library Systems,* 1, 1, 89- 103.

[6] Gumperz, J. 1982. Discourse Strategies. Cambridge, Cambridge University Press.

[7] Parth Gupta, Kalika Bali, Rafael E. Banchs, Monojit Choudhury, and Paolo Rosso. 2014. Query expansion for mixed-script information retrieval. In *Proceedings of the 37th international ACM SIGIR conference on Research & development in information retrieval* (SIGIR '14). ACM, New York, NY, USA, 677-686. DOI=http://dx.doi.org/10.1145/2600428.2609622

[8] Internet World Statistics. 2012. Top Ten Languages Used in the Web (Number of Internet Users by Language) Accessed April, 2012. http://www.internetworldstats.com/stats7.htm

[9] Kralisch, A., and Berendt, B. 2005. Language-sensitive search behaviour and the role of domain knowledge. *New Review of Hypermedia and Multimedia*, 11, 2, 221-246.

[10] Marlow, J., Clough, P., Recuero, J. C., and Artiles, J. 2008. Exploring the effects of language skills on multilingual web search. In C. Macdonald, I. Ounis, V. Plachouras, I. Ruthven, & R. W. White (Eds.), In *Proceedings of the IR research, 30th European conference on Advances in information retrieval* (Berlin, Heidelberg, 2008). Springer, New York, NY, 126-137.

[11] Myers-Scotton, C. 1993. *Social Motivations for Codeswitching: Evidence from Africa*. Oxford: Clarendon.

[12] Nzomo, P., Rubin, V. L., and Ajiferuke, I. 2012. Multi-lingual information access tools: user survey. In *Proceedings of the 2012 iConference* (Toronto, Canada, February 7 – 10, 2012). ACM, New York, NY, *530*-532. DOI=http://doi.acm.org/10.1145/2132176.2132276

[13] Ringbom, H. 1980. On the distinction between second language acquisition and foreign language learning. In *Proceedings of Nordic Conference on Applied Linguistics* (Hanasaari,Espoo, Finland, November 23-25, 1979).

[14] Wang, J., and Joardar, S. 2015. Cultural capital at work in Facebook users' selection of different languages. In *Cross-Cultural Design: Applications in Mobile Interaction, Education, Health,, Transport and Cultural Heritage*, P. L. P. Rau, Ed. Springer, New York, NY, 101-109.

[15] Wang, J , and Komlodi, A. 2016. Second language online searching: user behavior and challenges. In *Proceedings of the 7th International Conferece on Appllied Human Factors and Ergonomics* (Bay Lake, Florida, July 27 - 31, 2016). Springer, New York, NY.

[16] Woolard, K.A. 2004. Codeswitching. In *A Companion to Linguistic Anthropology,* A. Duranti, Ed. Oxford, Blackwell, 73-94.

Health Information Seeking Behavior among College Students: A Case in a Developing Country

Tesfahun Melese Yilma (1st year PhD Student)
Advised by: Anushia Inthiran and Daniel Reidpath
School of Information Technology, Monash University Malaysia
Bandar Sunway, 47500 Subang Jaya, Selangor, Malaysia
tesfahun.melese@monash.edu

ABSTRACT

Literature on Health Information Seeking Behavior (HISB) is available and well documented in developed countries. People in developed countries have also better understanding and awareness on online health information sources. However, the research coverage is very limited in developing countries, especially among college students. Previous studies showed higher risks of chronic diseases, stress, and risky sexual behavior among college students. Improving their HISB has the potential to reduce these risks. Our proposed research attempts to describe HISB and its associated factors in developing country with a specific focus on a college student population. Our study will attempt to create a better understanding of HISB in developing country thereby making it available for health promotional activities. It will also have potential contribution to suggest design strategies to improve health information retrieval systems.

CCS Concepts

• **Information systems→Users and interactive retrieval**
• **Applied Computing→Life and Medical Sciences→Consumer health.**

Keywords

Health; Information Seeking; Information Searching; Developing Countries; College Students; Malaysia

1. INTRODUCTION

HISB is defined as the ways by which individuals obtain information about health, illness, health promotion, and risks to health [7]. It influences an individual's judgments, beliefs, and attitudes as well as alternative methods of action against risk perceptions [7]. As a result, many countries pointed out HISB as a key element of health communication for health outcomes. Health Information searching behavior, on the other hand, can be operationalized as a subset of HISB focused on the interactions of users with an information retrieval system [15].

Literature on HISB focuses on the developed countries where many healthcare services are available. People in developed nations have demonstrated higher level of literacy and awareness

of online health information sources. Consequently, they are active health information seekers and have opportunities to make shared decisions with their physicians on health conditions and treatment options [2]. A very recent bibliometrics analysis on PubMed investigated publication trends of research on Internet HISB [8]. The study found that the major research contributions on HISB were from a small number of developed countries in North America, Europe, and Australia, suggesting pressing needs for more HISB researches particularly in developing countries. This study further identified students as a potential target group for Internet HISB research. At the same time, the group is often considered as a neglected target group when it comes to health promotions [6]. The group is also at risk of chronic diseases due to sedentary behavior [5] which increases the chance of getting a disease or a condition that may kill youths prematurely [3]. In order to prevent chronic diseases among young people, the World Health Organization recommended a strategy of ensuring that health information is widely available and easily understood [16]. Therefore, it is necessary to have a precise understanding of students' HISB and identify its associated factors, thereby making them available for use in health promotion campaigns.

In developing countries, where there is shortage of health literate human resources as well as infrastructures, both theoretical and empirical researches on HISB are lacking. Only limited studies have been done, mostly among specific patients and general population [10; 18]. These studies identified magnitude of HISB, as considerably low (e.g. 46% in Malaysia [10] and 59% in China [18]). Seeking for health information is also complex in developing countries for the following reasons: health systems are not sufficient enough to reach out the entire population [17], the people have difficulties in accessing and understanding information and technologies, and people often have limited online information searching skills [11].

On the other hand, there is a great increase in the number of websites and portals worldwide that give widespread access to various health information. There is also wide access to the Internet enabling developing countries to have their own health information portals (e.g., www.myhealth.gov.my in Malaysia and www.nhp.gov.in in India). At the same time, there is increased interest to use the Internet for health information due to the ease and prompt access [4]. These create massive opportunities for people to have the chance to keep their health [1]. Hence, investigating HISB in developing countries gains importance.

Given their socioeconomic differences from other more developed nations, it is important to study HISB in the context of developing countries. Such study could inform healthcare planning and policy making to improve health condition of the society in those countries. Our study will have also the potential to suggest design strategies to improve health information retrieval systems. Therefore, the purpose of this research study is to describe health information seeking and searching behaviors of college students in developing country. Specifically, our goal is to answer the following research questions:

1. What is the health information seeking behavior of college students in developing countries? In this case, the sources of health information used and the types of health information sought will be described.
2. What factors influence college students' health information seeking behavior in developing countries?
3. What behaviors do college students in developing country exhibit when searching for health information?
4. What challenges do college students in developing countries face while searching for health information?

2. THEORETICAL FRAMEWORK

We adopt the following four basic health information seeking models for our conceptual framework: 1) Wilson's 1999 nested model of information seeking and searching research areas [15], 2) Longo's 2010 expanded model of health information seeking behavior [9], 3) Health Belief Model (HBM) [12], and 4) Sutcliffe and Ennis's process model of information searching [13].

The Wilson's model is selected because it enables us to view information searching behavior as a subset of information seeking behavior research area. This allows us to look at information searching as a complex process embedded in information seeking behavior.

We choose the Longo's model as it takes into account the contextual and personal factors affecting HISB comprehensively. The model also includes health literacy and cross-cultural communication concerns of HISB. Further, it fills the gaps in the current HISB literature in developing countries considering that people in developing countries are not just active information seekers. They can also receive health information passively. The limitation of the Longo's model is that it doesn't consider psychological factors, such as perceived susceptibility to and severity of health problems and health self-efficacy, which are well described in the HBM. These factors in HBM are considered as driving forces behind health information seeking. Together with health information seeking, the factors are central to health-related perceptions and behavior for health outcome. Combining Longo's model and HBM enables us to have comprehensive conceptual framework that includes the factors contributing to and the barriers inhibiting information seeking behavior. The factors are shown in the outer rectangle boxes of Figure 1.

The fourth model used in our conceptual framework is the Sutcliffe and Ennis' process model of information searching. This model views information seeking as an interaction cycle consisting of identifying tasks, followed by formulating queries, viewing results, and if needed, reformulating queries. The process is repeated until a satisfactory result is found. The model will allow us to study and understand users' querying and result viewing behaviors while interacting with an information retrieval system. Profiling these behaviors could help to suggest strategies to design or improve health information retrieval systems.

3. RESEARCH METHODOLOGY

We will employ a quantitative and qualitative cross-sectional study design. A total sample size of 355 students will be recruited in a university setting in Malaysia. Convenience sampling technique will be used to select participants in each field of study after proportional allocation is made.

3.1 Data Collection Tools and Techniques

Our data collection tools will include questionnaire, interview, simulated situations, and key logging software. We will use the questionnaire to obtain information on HISB, socio-demographic, health related, behavioral, and psychological factors. The questionnaire will be adopted mainly from the 2014 US Health Information National Trends Survey [14]. Simulated situations and key logging software will be used to gather information on querying and result viewing behaviors. We will also conduct an interview to find out search challenges of participants.

3.2 Simulated Situation

We will provide each student with three simulated situations to perform three search tasks in a private room. To reflect real information needs, we will develop the simulated situations based on the health problems that young people in developing countries are commonly facing. All search tasks will be performed using MedlinePlus (www.medlineplus.gov/), which is a free medical website produced by the U.S. National Library of Medicine. Searching in MedlinePlus works only based on text matching so that actual search interaction of users, without being influenced by query suggestion can be observed.

3.3 Data Collection Procedure

Students will be approached through personal communications. After they agreed to participate in the study, an appointment will be made. Upon arrival, the students will receive a brief introduction about the study. Then, we will request them to review and sign an informed consent form. After consent, they will be requested to complete the survey tool. Following the survey, five minutes will be given to explore and familiarized with MedlinePlus. If participants are found already familiarized with this domain, they will be told to proceed with the search tasks. Three tasks in random order (to balance task order effect) will be given one at a time to the students. We will instruct the students to perform each task using only MedlinePlus. They will be also told to take as much time as they want to complete the tasks. After completing the tasks, we will ask the students to rate their satisfaction on search results. We will also interview them about their impression with the searching process and the MedlinePlus.

3.4 Data Analysis Procedure

We will use descriptive statistics to explain HISB and socio-demographic variables. Bivariate analysis will be carried out to identify potential predictors for multivariate analysis. Odds ratio with 95% confidence interval will be computed to determine the strength of association between HISB and its predictors. We will transcribe key logged data and interviews of the experiment for analysis. Transcribed data will be analyzed using NVivo version 10 software, a qualitative data analysis software. Coding themes will be developed based on search activities (querying and result viewing behaviors), challenges, and search outcomes. Pattern of query reformulations (specification, generalization, replacement, and parallel movement) will be analyzed.

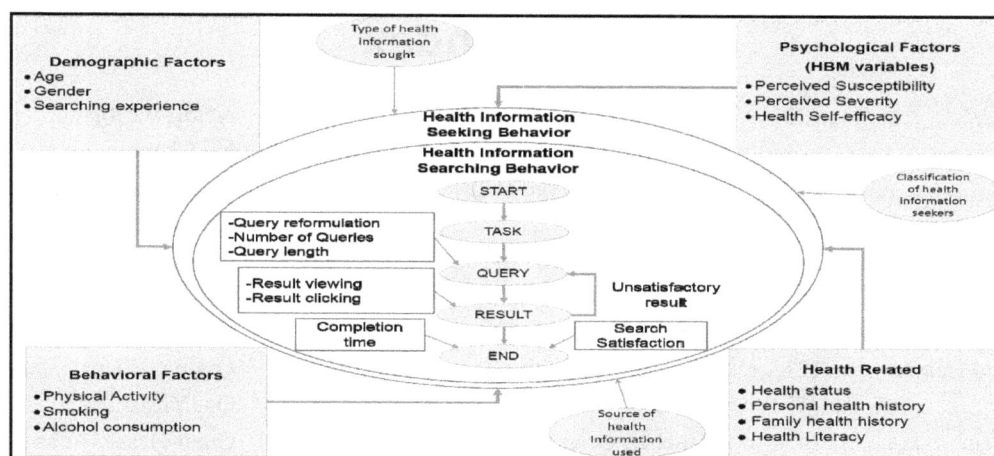

Figure 1: Conceptual Framework of Health Information Seeking Behavior

4. REFERENCES

[1] Allen, S., Geiger, B.F., Howard, V.J., Ivankova, N.V., Martin, M.Y., O'neal, M., and Safford, M.M., 2013. Development and validation of a survey instrument to assess health information-seeking behaviors among African American young professionals. In *Health Education/Promotion (Education)* University of Alabama at Birmingham, Birmingham, 303.

[2] Anker, A.E., Reinhart, A.M., and Feeley, T.H., 2011. Health information seeking: a review of measures and methods. *Patient Educ Couns 82*, 3 (Mar), 346-354. DOI= http://dx.doi.org/10.1016/j.pec.2010.12.008.

[3] Biswas, A., Oh, P.I., Faulkner, G.E., Bajaj, R.R., Silver, M.A., Mitchell, M.S., and Alter, D.A., 2015. Sedentary time and its association with risk for disease incidence, mortality, and hospitalization in adults: a systematic review and meta-analysis. *Ann Intern Med 162*, 2 (Jan 20), 123-132. DOI= http://dx.doi.org/10.7326/m14-1651.

[4] Cutilli, C.C., 2010. Seeking health information: what sources do your patients use? *Orthop Nurs 29*, 3 (May-Jun), 214-219. DOI= http://dx.doi.org/10.1097/NOR.0b013e3181db5471.

[5] Deliens, T., Deforche, B., De Bourdeaudhuij, I., and Clarys, P., 2015. Determinants of physical activity and sedentary behaviour in university students: a qualitative study using focus group discussions. *BMC Public Health 15*. DOI= http://dx.doi.org/10.1186/s12889-015-1553-4.

[6] Hunt, J. and Eisenberg, D., 2010. Mental Health Problems and Help-Seeking Behavior Among College Students. *J Adolescent Health 46*, 1 (1//), 3-10. DOI= http://dx.doi.org/10.1016/j.jadohealth.2009.08.008.

[7] Lambert, S.D. and Loiselle, C.G., 2007. Health information seeking behavior. *Qual Health Res 17*, 8 (Oct), 1006-1019. DOI= http://dx.doi.org/10.1177/1049732307305199.

[8] Li, F., Li, M., Guan, P., Ma, S., and Cui, L., 2015. Mapping publication trends and identifying hot spots of research on Internet health information seeking behavior: a quantitative and co-word biclustering analysis. *J Med Internet Res 17*, 3, e81. DOI= http://dx.doi.org/10.2196/jmir.3326.

[9] Longo, D.R., Schubert, S.L., Wright, B.A., Lemaster, J., Williams, C.D., and Clore, J.N., 2010. Health Information Seeking, Receipt, and Use in Diabetes Self-Management. *Annals of Family Medicine 8*, 4, 334-340. DOI= http://dx.doi.org/10.1370/afm.1115.

[10] Mohd-Nor, R., Chapun, T.E., and Wah, C.R.J., 2013. Malaysian rural community as consumer of health information and their use of ICT. *Malaysian Journal of Communication 29*, 1, 161-178.

[11] Raj, S., Sharma, V.L., Singh, A., and Goel, S., 2015. The health information seeking behaviour and needs of community health workers in Chandigarh in Northern India. *Health Info Libr J 32*, 2 (Jun), 143-149. DOI= http://dx.doi.org/10.1111/hir.12104.

[12] Rosenstock, I.M., 1974. Historical Origins of the Health Belief Model. *Health Educ Behav 2*, 4 (December 21, 1974), 328-335. DOI= http://dx.doi.org/10.1177/109019817400200403.

[13] Sutcliffe, A. and Ennis, M., 1998. Towards a cognitive theory of information retrieval. *Interact Comput 10*, 3, 321-351. DOI= http://dx.doi.org/10.1016/S0953-5438(98)00013-7.

[14] Us National Cancer Institute, 2014. Health Information National Trends Survey. In *Survey Instrument* National Cancer Institute, Louisville, USA.

[15] Wilson, T.D., 1999. Models in information behaviour research. *J Doc 55*, 3, 249-270. DOI= http://dx.doi.org/10.1108/EUM0000000007145.

[16] World Health Organization, 2003. *Report of a Joint WHO/FAO Expert Consultation: Diet Nutrition and the Prevention of Chronic Diseases.*

[17] World Health Organization, 2015. *World Health Statistics.*

[18] Yuli, Y., Su, Z., and Lijuan, X., 2012. Preventive health information seeking behavior among general population in China. In *Information Technology in Medicine and Education (ITME), 2012 International Symposium on*, 608-612. DOI= http://dx.doi.org/10.1109/ITiME.2012.6291380.

Author Index

www.ingramcontent.com/pod-product-compliance
Lightning Source LLC
Chambersburg PA
CBHW080702220326
41598CB00033B/5287